CLERGY OF

KILMORE, ELPHIN AND ARDAGH

CLERGY
of
KILMORE, ELPHIN
AND ARDAGH

BIOGRAPHICAL
SUCCESSION LISTS

compiled by
CANON J.B. LESLIE
and
revised, edited and updated by
CANON D.W.T. CROOKS

ULSTER HISTORICAL FOUNDATION

THE DIOCESAN COUNCIL
KILMORE, ELPHIN AND ARDAGH
2008

FRONT COVER ILLUSTRATION
The Arms of the Dioceses of Kilmore, Elphin and Ardagh

© Representative Church Body

Ulster Historical Foundation
www.ancestryireland.com

Kilkmore, Elphin and Ardagh Diocesan Council

ISBN: 978 1 903688 75 5

DESIGN
December Publications

PRINTED BY
Cromwell Press

CONTENTS

Foreword	xi
Introduction	xiii
Acknowledgements	xxi
Rev Canon J.B. Leslie: A Memoir	xxv
Rev Canon J.B. Leslie: A Personal Tribute	xxix
A Brief History of the Dioceses of Kilmore, Elphin and Ardagh	xxxv
List of Subscribers	xxxix
Abbreviations	xli
Bibliography and Sources	xlix
Parishes of Kilmore, Elphin and Ardagh with Lists of Clergy	1
Diocese of Kilmore	3
Diocese of Elphin	129
Diocese of Ardagh	231
Biographies of the Clergy	313

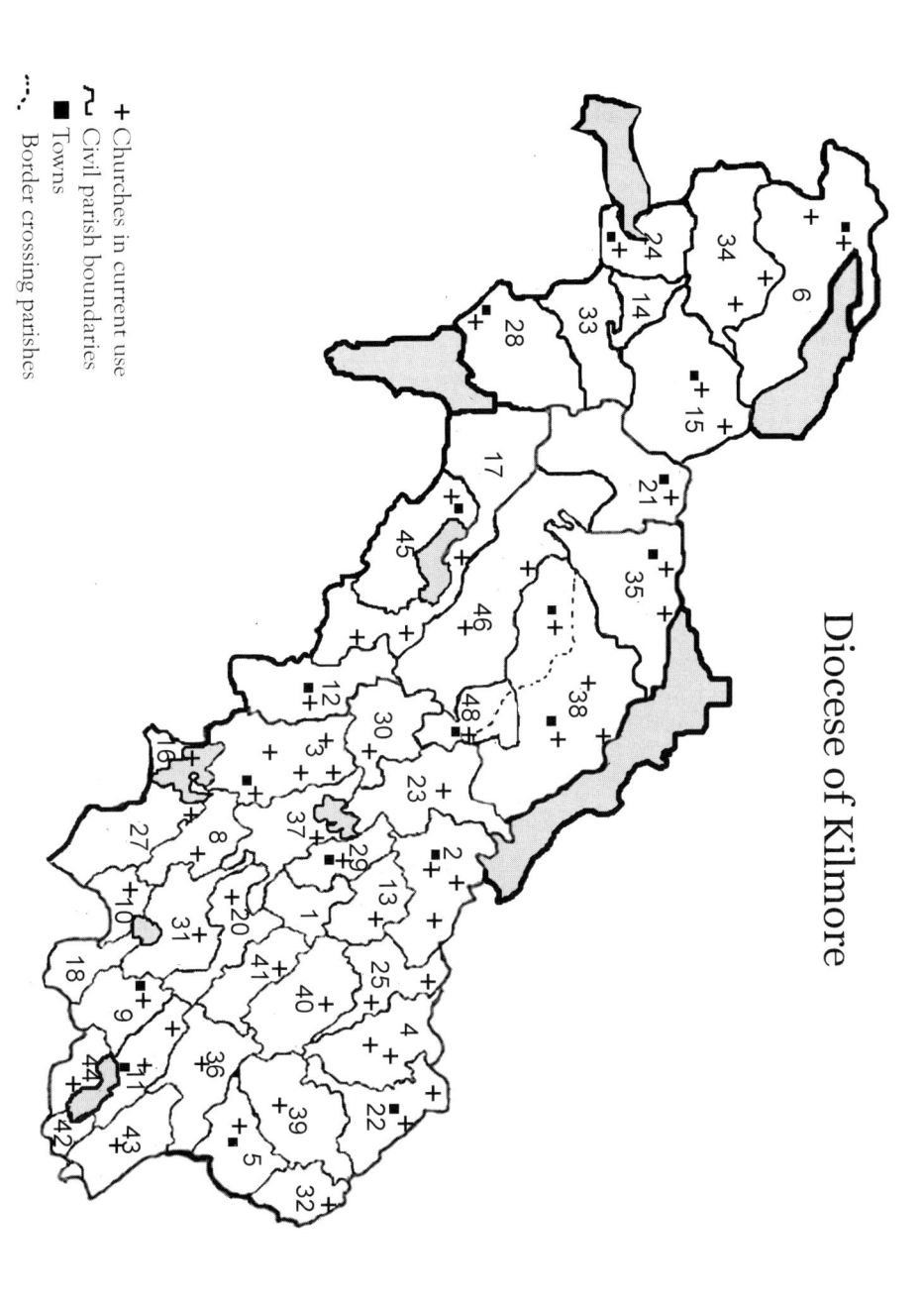

PARISHES OF KILMORE

1* Annagelliffe
2 Annagh [Belturbet]]
3 Arvagh [in Killeshandra civil parish]
4 Ashfield [in Killesherdoney Parish]
5 Bailieborough [Moybologue]
6* Ballaghmeehan [in Rossinver civil parish]
7U Ballineanthowal
8 Ballintemple
9 Ballyjamesduff [in Castlerahan civil parish]
10 Ballymachugh
11 Billis [in Lurgan civil parish]
12 Carrigallen
* Castlerahan — *see* Ballyjamesduff
13 Castleterra [Ballyhaise]
14* Clonlogher [in Cloonclare]
15 Cloonclare [Manorhamilton]
Cloverhill — *see* Annagh
16 Columbkille — *see* Ardagh list.
17 Corrawallen [in Drumreilly civil parish]
Crom chapel [*see* Kinawley]
18* Culbrydyn and Sendamar [Kilbride]
19U Cuylofflynd
20 Denn
Dernakesh chapel [in Drumgoon]
Derryheen [in Killeshandra parish — *see* Arvagh
Derrylane [in Killeshandra parish] — *see* Arvagh
* Disert Finchill [= Killdrumsherdan] — *see* Ashfield
21* Dowra Chapel [in Killinagh civil parish]
Drumaloor chapel — *see* Annagh
22 Drumgoon [Cootehill]
Druminiskill chapel [in Killesher]
23 Drumlane
24 Drumlease [Dromohaire]
Drumreilly — *see* Corrawallen
25 Drung
Enga = Annagh
26U Fignsaidin
Finner [Bundoran] — *see* Ballaghmeehan
27 Gowna [in Drumlummon civil parish]
28 Innismagrath [Drumkeeran]

29* Kedy [in Urney]
30 Kildallon
31 Kildrumferton [Kilnaleck][in Crosserlough]
32* Killan — *see* Shercock
33* Killargue
34 Killasnett [Glencar]
Killegar [in Killeshandra civil parish] — *see* Arvagh
Killeshandra — *see* Arvagh
35 Killesher [Florencecourt]
Killesherdoney — *see* Ashfield
Killinagh [Blacklion] — *see* Dowra
36 Killinkere
Killoughter [Redhills] — *see* Drung
37 Kilmore
Kiltyclogher [in Cloonclare civil parish, now Clogher]
38 Kinawley [Derrylin]
Kinawley chapel — *see* Swanlinbar
39 Knockbride
40 Larah [with Lavey]
41 Lavey [with Larah]
42* Loughan
Lurgan [Virginia] — *see* Billis
Lurganboy chapel — *see* Killasnett
* Moybologue — *see* Bailieborough
43 Mullagh
44 Munterconnaught
Newtowngore [in Drumreilly civil parish]
45 Oughteragh or Outragh [Ballinamore]
* Quivvy chapel — *see* Annagh
Rossinver [Kinlough]
Shercock — *see* Killan
46 Swanlinbar [In Templeport civil parish]
47U Teallacheach and Mageangady
Templeport — *see* Swanlinbar
48 Tomregan
Urney — *see* Kedy
49U Yniscayn

* church closed, sold, ruined, or no longer in existence
u = parish unidentified

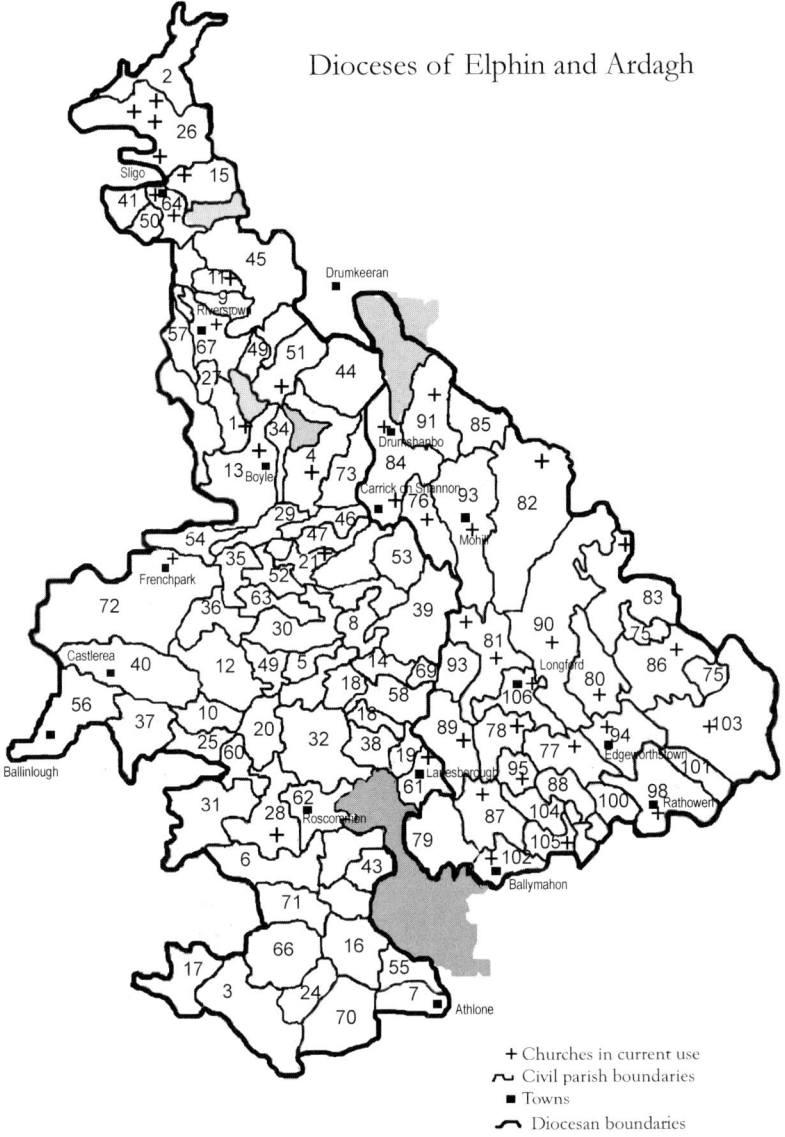

PARISHES OF ELPHIN

1. Aghanagh [Ballinafad]
2* Ahamplish
3* Ahascragh
4. Ardcarne
5* Ardclare [with Kilcooley]
6* Athleague [Mt Talbot]
7. Athlone [now Meath and Kildare]
8* Aughrim
9* Ballinakill
10* Ballintubber
11. Ballysumaghan and Kilross
12* Baslick
13. Boyle
14* Bumlin [Strokestown]
15. Calry
16* Camma
17* Castleblakeney *alias* Killasoolan
18* Clonfinlough
19* Clontuskert
20* Clonygormacan
21* Creeve
   Croghan — *see* Creeve
22U Culea
23U Derran
24* Disert
25* Drimtemple
26. Drumcliffe
27* Drumcollum
28. Dunamon
29* Eastersnow
30* Elphin
31* Fuerty and Kilbegnet
32U Ivernon
33* Kilbride
34* Kilbryan
35* Kilcola
* Kilcooley — *see* Ardclare
36* Kilcorkey
37* Kilcroan
38* Kilgeffin
39* Kilglass
40* Kilkeevan
41* Killaspicbrone
42U Killeiniregard
43* Killenvoy
44* Killeroran [or Kilronan]
45* Killery [Killenumery]
46* Killukin
47* Killumada
48U Killyngyn
* Killyon — *see* Killeroran
49* Kilmacallen
50* Kilmacoen
51. Kilmactranny
52* Kilmacumsy
53* Kilmore
54* Kilnamanagh
55* Kiltoom
56* Kiltullagh [Ballinlough]
   Knocknarea — *see* Sligo
57* Kyllmurchayn [also listed in Achonry]
58* Lisanuffy
   Lissadell and Munninane Chapels — *see* Drumcliffe
* Loughglynn [in Tibohine civil parish]
59U Minbrisg
* Ogulla — *see* Elphin)
60* Oran
61. Rathcline [Lanesborough]
62* Roscommon [Templeneilan]
   Rosses Point [in Drumcliffe civil parish]
63* Shankill
64. Sligo, St John's Cathedral
65U St. Bernanus de Manso
66* Taghboy
67. Taunagh [Riverstown]
* Teatby — *see* Taghboy
68U Terebrine
69* Termonbarry
70* Termoncaelyn
71* Tessaragh
72. Tibohine
73* Toomna
74U Tullagh

PARISHES OF ARDAGH

75* Abbeylara
76. Annaduff [Drumsna] = Annaduff East Chapel
77. Ardagh
   Aughavas [in Cloone]
   Aughrim — *see* Elphin list
   Ballymachugh — *see* Kilmore list
78. Ballymacormick
79* Cashel
80. Clonbroney [Ballinalea]
81. Clongish [Newtownforbes]
   Clooncumber [Bornacoola]
82* Cloone, & Lough Rynn Castle Chapel
83. Columbkille — *see* Kilmore list
   Drumlish Chapel — *see* Clongish
   Drumlummon — *see* Gowna in Kilmore list
   Drumreilly [*see* Kilmore list]
84. Drumshanbo [chapel in Kiltoghart]
* Farnaught [in Cloone] — *see* Cloone
85* Fenagh
   Gowna [incl Inishmore] — *see* Kilmore list
86. Granard
* Inismor — *see* Gowna in Kilmore list.
87. Kilcommick [Kenagh]
88* Kilglass, Co. Longford
89. Killashee
* Killenumery [Killery] — *see* Elphin list
* Killery [Killenumery] — *see* Elphin list
90. Killoe
* Killukin — *see* Elphin list
* Kilmore, Co. Roscommon — *see* Elphin list
* Kilronan — *see* Elphin list
   Kiltoghart [Carrick on Shannon] — *see* Drumshanbo
91. Kiltubrid Kilmactranny [Ballinafad] — *see* Elphin list.
92U Mogbrechi — *see* Streete
93. Mohill
94. Mostrim [Edgeworthstown]
95. Moydow
96U Munterangaile
97U Muntireolis
   Outragh or Oughteragh [Ballinamore] — *see* Kilmore list
98. Rathaspeck [Rathowen]
   Rathcline [St John, Lanesborough] — *see* Elphin list
100* Rathreagh and Aghery
101* Russagh
10+ Shrule [Ballymahon]
103. Streete
104* Taghsynod
105. Tashinny
106. Templemichael [Longford]
* Termonbarry — *see* Elphin list
* Toomna — *see* Elphin list

* church closed, sold, ruined, or no longer in existence
u = parish unidentified

FOREWORD

"Those who forget the past are condemned to repeat it" are the words of a Spanish philosopher. They are wise, timely, and relevant. There is a danger in our contemporary culture of believing that anything new must be true and anything old is no longer significant. What a contrast to the story of God's people which is a salvation story of God's dealings with His people throughout history in the past, in their lives in the present and in His purposes for the future.

This book is a reminder of the "cloud of witnesses" who served in the Dioceses of Kilmore Elphin and Ardagh in past centuries and of those who are serving today. We thank God for the faithful witness of their lives and witness and for the uniqueness of ordained ministry. In public and in private, at times of joy and in circumstances of great sorrow, in wartime and in peace, clergy respond to God's call, work out their vocation and seek to live lives worthy of their calling. This book gives us some information about each of them.

We also read of their families and how appropriate that is. Often in a parish the family of the clergyperson is the forgotten family and indeed sometimes the neglected family. Some of the great heroes of the faith are the spouses and children of clergy. We honour them.

I sincerely thank Canon David Crooks. His perseverance is legendary. His enthusiasm for this project is indescribable. His dedication and commitment to the completion of this book is awesome. It is not a cliché to say that without him this book would not be in your hands. Thank you to him and all who have enabled the idea of this book to become reality!

Enjoy this reservoir of factual details and remember the importance of the ministry of those who are called to being shepherds of God's people and feed His sheep.

+Ken Kilmore Elphin and Ardagh

Easter 2008

INTRODUCTION

Early Succession Lists

The production of lists of clergy originated early in the nineteenth century with the publication by Samuel Percy Lea of *The Present State of the Established Church, or Ecclesiastical Register of Ireland for the Year 1814*. This was followed in 1817 with the publication by J.C. Erck of the *Ecclesiastical Register of the Names of the Dignitaries and Parochial Clergy and of the Parishes and their Respective Patrons, etc*. Erck produced revisions of this work in 1818, 1820, 1825 and 1835. In 1843, J.M. Bourns published *The Irish Clergy List and Ecclesiastical Almanack*.

These early works were basically just lists of clergy with little biographical information. The first to produce succession lists of clergy with biographical and other details was Henry Cotton, Dean of Lismore, who published *Fasti Ecclesiae Hibernicae*, subtitled *The Succession of the Prelates and Members of the Cathedral Bodies of Ireland*. The first volume, which appeared in 1847, covered the Province of Munster. Subsequent volumes for Leinster, Ulster and Connaught were produced in 1848, 1849 and 1850 respectively. Cotton amended and corrected his work in later editions. In the *Fasti*, Cotton gives varying amounts of detail as regards academic qualifications and appointments of the bishops, deans, canons and other dignitaries of the Irish cathedrals from the fifth to the nineteenth centuries, along with some biographical information.

The first to produce diocesan succession lists was Rev William Maziere Brady, who published lists of clergy of Cork, Cloyne and Ross in 1863 and 1864. In 1903, Rev John Harding Cole produced *Church and Parish Records of the United Diocese of Cork, Cloyne and Ross*. Further work on the Diocese of Ross was done in 1936 by the Dean of Ross, Charles Webster.

Later Twentieth-Century Succession Lists

Following on from the work of Brady and Cole, a great deal of work on the production of succession lists of clergy was done in the middle period of the twentieth century. Archdeacon St John Drelincourt Seymour, who spent all of his ministry in the Dioceses of Cashel and Emly, produced the *The Succession of Parochial Clergy in the United Diocese of Cashel and Emly* in 1908. In 1920, the Rev. William Henry Rennison, Rector of Ardmore, published *Succession Lists of the Bishops, Cathedral and Parochial Clergy of the Dioceses of Waterford and Lismore*. However, in the main, these are lists of clergy, containing little biographical information.

Hugh Jackson Lawlor, Dean of St Patrick's Cathedral, Dublin, who had earlier attempted unsuccessfully to revise Cotton's *Fasti*, published in 1930 *The Fasti of St Patrick's, Dublin*. The Dean of Dromore, Henry B. Swanzy, had almost completed *Succession of the Diocese of Dromore* at the time of his tragic death in 1932.

James Blennerhassett Leslie, 1865–1952

The most prolific and arguably the greatest producer of biographical succession lists of clergy was Canon James Blennerhassett Leslie, Rector of Kilsaran Parish, Castlebellingham, County Louth, in the Diocese of Armagh, from 1899 to 1951. Leslie was a most careful and meticulous scholar who spent many hours over many years gathering and recording information from a huge variety of sources. Perhaps our greatest debt to him is the preservation for posterity of much that was to be lost in the devastating fire at the Four Courts Public Record Office in Dublin in 1922.

Canon Leslie's first published succession lists, *Armagh Clergy and Parishes*, appeared in 1911. The other volumes he published were *Clogher Clergy and Parishes* (1929), *Ossory Clergy and Parishes* (1933), *Ferns Clergy and Parishes* (1936), *Derry Clergy and Parishes* (1937), *Ardfert and Aghadoe Clergy and Parishes* (1940) and *Raphoe Clergy and Parishes* (1940). Leslie, with Dean Swanzy, published *Biographical Succession Lists of the Clergy of the Diocese of Down* in 1936, and in 1933 he published Swanzy's *Succession Lists of the Diocese of Dromore*. Leslie also produced a supplement to *Armagh Clergy and Parishes* in 1948.

For financial or other reasons Canon Leslie was not able to publish all his succession lists. Those that were not published are in manuscript in the Library of the Representative Church Body in Dublin. They are lists for the Dioceses of Ardagh, Connor, Dublin, Elphin, Glendalough, Kildare, Kilfenora, Clonfert and Kilmacduagh, Killala and Achonry, Killaloe, Kilmore, Leighlin, Limerick, Meath and Tuam, as well as Christ Church Cathedral, Dublin. There is also a biographical index to the clergy of the Church of Ireland.

In his works, Canon Leslie lists the archbishops/bishops, deans, archdeacons, prebendaries, canons and any other dignitaries. There follow in alphabetical order the parishes of the diocese in question, with biographical details of the clergy from as early as they can be traced to the time of writing. Leslie also includes short historical notes on each parish. For each entry Leslie gives the clergyman's name, parentage, date and place of birth, details of education and academic qualifications, date of ordination, details of appointments, preferments, marriage and children and date of death. Obviously, not all of this information is available for each entry. It must be noted that Leslie omitted many curates – it seems that he was most concerned with incumbents.

Recent Updating of Succession Lists

Miss Geraldine Fitzgerald, Librarian of the Representative Church Body Library in Dublin, amended and updated Canon Leslie's succession lists in the form of supplements. Her successor, Miss Geraldine Willis, continued this work and also amended the work of Cole and Rennison.

In recent times there has been a renewal of interest in this whole subject. In 1993 a sub-committee of the Down and Dromore and Connor Library Committee, of which the secretary was Mr Fred Rankin, updated and published Leslie's unpublished Connor succession lists with *Clergy of Connor from Patrician Times to the Present Day*. The committee followed this in 1996 with an updating of Swanzy's Dromore lists and Leslie's Down lists in a volume entitled *Clergy of Down and Dromore*. In 1999, Canon David Crooks and Canon Frederick Fawcett published *Clergy of Derry and Raphoe*, an update of Leslie's two volumes of lists of clergy of Derry and Raphoe. In 2000, Canon W.E.C. Fleming published *Armagh Clergy 1800–2000*, followed in 2001 by W.J.R. Wallace's update of Leslie's two unpublished volumes on Dublin and Glendalough. In 2006 Canon David Crooks and Dean Thomas Moore updated Leslie's 1929 *Clogher Clergy and Parishes*. In 2008, the Rev. Iain Knox published an update of the Rev. W.H. Rennison's Lists for Waterford and Lismore, and of Canon Leslie's *Ferns Clergy and Parishes*, and Canon David W.T. Crooks has updated and published Canon Leslies manuscripts for the Dioceses of Tuam, Killala and Achonry. With the exception of Canon Fleming's Armagh update, these works have been published by the Ulster Historical Foundation in Belfast.

The Kilmore, Elphin and Ardagh Lists
Canon Leslie produced biographical succession lists for the Diocese of Ardagh in 1932 and for the Diocese of Elphin in 1934. His lists for Kilmore are undated, but were produced at around the same time. None of these was published, and they are all preserved in typescript in the Library of the Representative Church Body.

In revising and updating the lists for each diocese Leslie published, the original volumes were reproduced along with a biographical list of the clergy since Leslie's time, arranged in alphabetical order rather than by parish. In this volume, as with the others so far that are updates of books Leslie did not publish, we begin by giving a list of the bishops, deans, archdeacons, prebends and canons of the Diocese of Kilmore. Then the parishes, in alphabetical order with the clergy who served in them who can be traced, are listed. There follow similar lists for Elphin and for Ardagh.

Many of the bishops since earliest times – i.e., the fifth to the fifteenth centuries – are known, but very few of the clergy are known until the end of the fourteenth century. The names of many of the late-medieval clergy are known, but there are large gaps, needless to say. Information from the turbulent Reformation period in the sixteenth century is scarce, so there are large gaps for that period. More clergy from the seventeenth century are known, but it cannot be possible to be sure that we have a complete list even from the eighteenth century onwards. All clergy who appear in the *Church of Ireland Directory*, which began in 1862, are included.

The next section of this update is a biographical succession of all the clergy of Kilmore, Elphin and Ardagh together in alphabetical order. In this volume, the information given is the date and place of birth, details of education and university prizes, date of ordination, details of appointments and preferments, parents and grandparents, date and place of marriage, details of wife or husband, children and their marriages and children, and date and place of death and burial. We also give any publications.

Needless to say, it would be impossible to obtain all this information for every clergyman and woman listed, but we have tried to supply as much as possible. In the production of a work of this magnitude it is impossible to guarantee complete accuracy, but every effort has been made to be as precise as possible.

In updating Canon Leslie's work we have endeavoured to be as faithful as possible to the original manuscripts. This means that we have included, for example, his Latin professional terms, such as *armiger* and *agricola*.

The reader should be aware of certain problems with the pre-Reformation medieval clergy. They were, of course, all Irish with Irish names, which could be confused. Therefore, there are entries for clergy of the period with similar names who could be the same person. Examples are Oferrall, Ofergail, O'Feargail, O'Sheridan and O'Syridean.

There were also early parishes that have long disappeared, such as Lisonuffy, Disert Finchill and Culloflynd. The modern reader may well be puzzled as to why clergy in the seventeenth and eighteenth centuries were able to hold several incumbencies in places that were far apart. Plurality of living was common in those days, when a rector looked after one parish and employed curates to look after the others.

Photographs and Historical Notes

The photographs of the churches of Kilmore, Elphin and Ardagh were all taken during the long hot summer days of July and August 2006. The priority was to obtain photographs of all the churches that are currently in use. Other churches, which are either falling into ruin or are already at an advanced state of ruin, are included. Some have been demolished or are too far gone to be worth including, but most of the churches that have been closed relatively recently are included. The excellent and tidy condition of the churches is a great credit to the people of the united dioceses, and to their faith.

The historical notes that accompany the lists of clergy at the beginning of this book are reproductions of Leslie's own notes, where he had such notes, hence their brevity and style. Notes for whichever parishes are included are very brief, mainly giving the date of building, if known, and any other relevant information that could be found. In the case of a few parishes, there are excellent parish histories, which were most helpful. It has to be admitted that it is not possible in every case to be absolutely certain about exact dates of amalgamations of parishes and closures of churches, even when these occurred relatively recently.

The Bibliography

Canon Leslie compiled an extensive bibliography for his *Armagh Clergy and Parishes* in 1911. There he lists printed books, manuscripts, newspapers, journals and all sorts of other sources. However, in the unpublished manuscripts for Kilmore, Elphin and Ardagh, he gives no such bibliography. He refers in abbreviated form to many publications, however. Some of these are in the Armagh bibliography and some are not. In the bibliography in this volume we have endeavoured to give as many as possible, but some were indecipherable. For this we beg the reader's understanding.

It would be impossible to pay sufficient tribute to the many people who over nearly two centuries have provided biographical succession lists of clergy. Head and shoulders above them all forever stands Canon James Blennerhassett Leslie. These men have provided researchers in particular, and the people of the Church of Ireland and many others beyond in general, with a treasure trove of most valuable information. This update of Canon Leslie's three volumes of Kilmore, Elphin and Ardagh is a humble offering to the people of those dioceses, and a small tribute to Canon Leslie.

ACKNOWLEDGEMENTS

The publication of the updates to Canon Leslie's succession lists has been ongoing now since 1993, when the lists for the Diocese of Connor were updated. As more and more of the original diocesan lists appear, those of us who are involved in this work wish to express our gratitude for the help we have received, based on the experience gained. In particular, mention is made of the expertise of the Very Rev Norman and Mrs Florence Barr, Canon George Little, Canon Ted Fleming, Canon Edgar Turner, Mr Fred Rankin and others who have been involved. I mention in particular the Rev Iain Knox, who has been working on updating the succession lists for Waterford, Lismore and Ferns. His knowledge of history has been of great help in ensuring accuracy of detail.

The reading of proofs before the publication of a work of this nature is an exacting and painstaking task. For this I am particularly indebted to Canon Ted Fleming. He went to immense trouble, putting his expertise and experience at my disposal, pointing out numerous errors and omissions. In this task, Canon Fleming was assisted by Canon George Little. Their work is acknowledged with sincere appreciation.

I wish to acknowledge the expert work of the publishers, the Ulster Historical Foundation in Belfast, and in particular Mr Fintan Mullan. They have produced another fine volume, which compares favourably with others that have appeared recently.

The staff of the Representative Church Body Library in Dublin were at all times most courteous and helpful. I acknowledge most gratefully the assistance of Dr Raymond Refaussé and his colleagues there. They made available photocopies of the Leslie's entire manuscripts for Kilmore, Elphin and Ardagh, as well as much other useful relevant material. I acknowledge the value of the work done by former librarians Miss Geraldine Fitzgerald and Miss Geraldine Willis, who kept Leslie's manuscripts up to date over the years.

Sincerest thanks are due to the Very Rev'd. Susan Patterson, Dean of Killala, who produced the maps of the Diocese of Kilmore and of the Dioceses of Elphin and Ardagh. They are a significant and valuable contribution to this book.

Above all, it is the local people in the Dioceses of Kilmore, Elphin and Ardagh who have been of greatest assistance, for without them a work like this could not be attempted, let alone completed. I especially acknowledge and thank the Bishop, the Rt Rev Ken Clarke. He has at all times been most gracious, charming and appreciative. I thank also the clergy who filled in the questionnaires, who provided vast amounts of useful information and who helped in all sorts of ways. As awareness increased that this update was being produced, numerous people with local interest and information became involved and gave me the kind of information that adds to a work like this and that deepens its interest. I am particularly grateful, amongst many others, to Dr Fergus O'Ferrall, who gave me his very interesting article on the early-nineteenth-century Protestant evangelical rector of Kilcommick, County Longford, the Rev George Brittaine.

A special tribute of gratitude must be paid to the Rev Canon Robin Richey. Canon Richey spent all but two of the 50 years of his ministry in Kilmore Diocese as Rector of Killinagh group of parishes. His knowledge of Kilmore Diocese and its parishes and history was unfathomable. His death in 2006 has deprived the Diocese and the Church of a fine scholar and pastor. His assistance in the production of this book was of inestimable value and we are most grateful.

The Rev Stanley Johnson, former Archdeacon of Elphin and Ardagh, and his wife, the Rev Shiela Johnson, both now near neighbours in Raphoe Diocese, were also of great help. As well as placing much local knowledge at my disposal, Shiela accompanied me on a tour to photograph some churches in remote places, which I would never have found on my own. I owe the same debt of gratitude to Mr Bill Turner, a retired commercial traveller who, like Sheila, knows the lanes, highways, byways and hedgerows of Counties Cavan, Leitrim, Longford, Sligo and Roscommon like the back of his hand. He too helped me to find the more inaccessible and remote churches and prevented me from becoming hopelessly lost. There were others, too, mainly local people – and I thank them for their friendliness and Christian hospitality.

I must also acknowledge the kindness of my wife, Anne, who entrusted me with her digital camera on these excursions. Both she and Canon Sam Barton, Rector of Fahan, and the Rev Mervyn Peoples, kept me right with the computer, and without their tolerance of my digital incompetence this work would not have been completed.

I wish to express most grateful thanks to those who gave grant aid for the production of this book. I acknowledge a generous grant from the General Synod Royalties Fund, and from the Firm of Kingspan in Cavan. Most of the cost of production was met using the means which Canon Leslie himself used, by obtaining subscriptions in advance, and the names of all who subscribed are recorded. For assuming responsibility for this, I thank Miss Maud Cunningham and Mrs Ann Smith of the Kilmore Diocesan Office in Cootehill. They were most helpful and co-operative in this and in numerous other ways.

DAVID W.T. CROOKS

THE REV CANON J.B. LESLIE
MA, D Lit, MRIA
1865–1952

A MEMOIR

JAMES BLENNERHASSETT LESLIE was born on 28 May 1865, the third son of James Leslie, farmer, of Clouncannon, Co Kerry, and Mary Anne Leslie (*née* Blennerhassett). Both J.B. Leslie's grandfathers were farmers: Thomas Leslie had farmed the 63 acres of Clouncannon before passing it on to James Leslie; and Mary Anne's father, Thomas Arthur Blennerhassett, one of the Ballyseedy Blennerhassetts, had a farm of 56 acres in the townland of Gortatlea. Clouncannon was in the townland of Kilclogherane, just west of Killarney.

J.B. Leslie was one of seven children; he had three brothers, Thomas, William and John Herbert, and three sisters, Jane, Susan and Mary. His mother seems to have destined her two eldest sons for a commercial life in Cahirciveen, while the two younger were to follow an academic line, perhaps in preparation for a clerical future. J.B. Leslie studied privately under a Mr MacGillacuddy and also attended Pococke School in Kilkenny. In 1885 he matriculated at the Royal University of Ireland and read Civil and Constitutional History, Political Economy and General Jurisprudence at Queen's College, Cork, graduating BA in 1888 and MA in 1889. In 1890 he entered the Divinity School in Trinity College Dublin, where he was awarded Bishop Forster's Prize (1st), Divinity Composition Prize, Ecclesiastical History Prize (2nd), Warren Prize and in 1891 1st of 1st class Divinity Testimonium. Much later, in 1908, he proceeded to the degree of MA *ad eundem* at Queen's College, Belfast and in 1931 was awarded D Lit there by virtue of his printed works.

His clerical career, described in part two of this memoir, lasted for more than 60 years. He died in 1952 and was buried with his wife in Kilsaran Churchyard.

The inscription on the tombstone reads:

In Loving Memory
Mary
Beloved wife of
Rev Canon James B. Leslie
Born 20 July 1861
Died 22 July 1949
also of the above
Rev Canon J.B. Leslie
Born 28 May 1865 Died 20 April 1952
Rector of this Parish 1899–1951
and of their daughters
Muriel
Born 31 May 1894 Died 18 Feb 1971
Kathleen
Born 9 Aug 1897 Died 4 Dec 1973

Inside the Church placed near the Communion Table a plaque reads:
In grateful memory of Canon James B. Leslie MA, D Lit, MRIA
Rector of this Parish 1900–1951
Erected by his parishioners and friends
The Good Shepherd Giveth His Life for the Sheep. St John 10 v 11

Most of Canon Leslie's near relatives are now dead, including his brother, John Henry Leslie, who became Dean of Lismore and Isabel Mary (Smith), the Dean's daughter, who, under the pen-name of Temple Lane, wrote many novels and poems. Another niece, Mrs Evelyn Talbot, lives at Doneraile and from her vivid memories of her uncle has supplied most of the material in this memoir that is not the work of Canon Love; Leslie's great-nephew, Mr Ronald F. Miller, still lives in the family home at Clouncannon. The Canon's memory is still cherished at Kilsaran, where flowers are regularly placed on his grave.

W. C. Kerr

THE REV CANON J.B. LESLIE
MA, D Lit, MRIA

A PERSONAL TRIBUTE
by The Rev Canon H. W. Love

CANON LESLIE BEGAN HIS MINISTRY in the Church of Ireland in 1891. In that year he was ordained Deacon for the Assistant Curacy of Christ Church, Belfast, and then moved to St Mark's, Portadown on the nomination of Augustine Fitzgerald (who later became Dean of Armagh).

In 1899 he was nominated to the Parish of Kilsaran (Castlebellingham), Co Louth, and in February 1900, on petition, the Court of the General Synod declared the nomination invalid, although Leslie had been already instituted. The invalidity was due to a technical fault in the omission of a summons to one of the Parochial Nominators. In 1900 he was again nominated and duly instituted. He remained in that parish until his retirement in 1951, moving to live in Glenageary, Co Dublin where he died in 1952.

In 1893 he married Mary, elder daughter of William Bulfin of Dublin, and had two daughters, Mary Muriel Elizabeth and Kathleen Margaret Bulfin.

In 1903 he published *The Mission of St Patrick; Was it from Rome?* (published by Tempest, Dundalk). In 1901 he began the publication of the *Irish Churchwarden's Handbook*, published by the Church of Ireland Printing Company. In 1908 he published a *History of Kilsaran*, printed by Tempest, Dundalk. He became the editor of the *Irish Clergy List* in 1910, also printed by Tempest. In 1911 he published a *History of the Parish of Portadown* and in the same year compiled the *Armagh Clergy and Parishes*. This was his *magnum opus*; he published a supplement in 1948.

From 1929 he continued his work with clerical biographies, publishing in that year the Clogher list; in 1933 he published the list for Ossory, in 1936 Ferns, in 1940 Raphoe and also Ardfert and Aghadoe.

He published jointly with Dean Swanzy the *Clerical List of the Diocese of Down* in 1936. In 1933 he edited Swanzy's *Biographical Succession List of Dromore*.

He also edited the *Irish Church Directory* 1928–40; the bishops of Ireland in *Handbook of British Chronology*, 1939; the catalogue of MSS in RCB Library; the Calendar of Deeds in St Patrick's Cathedral 1660–89 (in *Journal of RSAI*); an Old Dublin Vestry Book (in *Journal of RSAI*); *History of Kilternan* (Church of Ireland Printing Company). Canon Leslie would be the first to acknowledge the help he received from William Tempest, then a young printing apprentice from Rostrevor, who set up business on his own in Dundalk and founded the firm of Wm Tempest Ltd. His son Harry G. Tempest continued the cooperation with Canon Leslie. The Tempest connection is represented by Mrs O. Tempest, on the board of Dundalgan Press. Possibly the last work they did in this connection was the present writer's own *Records of the Archbishops of Armagh*.

Our first meeting with Canon Leslie was in 1931 at an ordination examination for Deacon's Orders, under Archbishop Charles Frederick D'Arcy, at which Canon Leslie was one of the examiners.

He was a heavily built and robust country parson who had spent years since the beginning of the century in the old Public Record Office in Dublin, where the records of the Disestablished Church of Ireland were the subject of his research. He was an exceedingly persistent and patient researcher, and the debt the Church of Ireland owes him is incalculable. As he worked there day after day for nearly a decade he little knew how vital his work would become – for in 1922, as a result of the political upheaval following on the Proclamation of Independence of Ireland, the old Public Record Office and the documents from which Leslie had worked were lost. Had it not been for his work we would today have almost no records of the clergy and parishes of the Church of Ireland.

He was a large-hearted man, generous to a fault, who reeked with the odour of tobacco smoke. He was rarely without his pipe and was usually clad in a rough tweed Norfolk jacket and cape. He was of a type utterly unknown to the Church of Ireland today, although his beard, short and black, was before the end of the century to become commonplace.

He never owned or drove a motor car. On arrival at Kilsaran he travelled around the parish on what would now be an antique velocipede – to the modern reader, a bicycle – which he never learned to mount in the usual fashion by first stepping on the pedal and propelling one's initial motion. Instead, he would run some yards with the bicycle and, at a suitable point, he would leap into the saddle (he was a heavy weight, be it noted) and wobble for quite a while before achieving equilibrium and pursuing his journey.

Throughout the years of his incumbency at Kilsaran he extended a warm welcome on every occasion to the present writer and other visitors. We remember, on being admitted to his study, having to pick our step carefully across a floor strewn with books and papers of every sort. Despite the methodical work produced by him he was not by nature a tidy man. The collection of information was in large measure due to his great curiosity and to his inveterate habit of indulging in clerical gossip. During his early years in Co Louth he was one of about 50 members of the clergy, licensed or beneficed, in the two Rural Deaneries of Creggan and Athirdee; almost all of the parishes could be conveniently reached from one or other of the stations or halts of the Great Northern Railway; there were minor halts between Drogheda and Dundalk, and Leslie and his brethren made great use of that means of locomotion.

There was during those years and until comparatively recently a thriving Louth Clerical Union, the members of which, gathering every month and spending a whole day in theological, biblical and ecclesiastical discussion, met in the various rectories throughout the County. The strange thing is that although he was a man of generous hospitality, Leslie never entertained his brother clergy in Kilsaran, Glebe; he may have thought it would be too great a burden for his wife, who would be obliged to negotiate long flights of stairs on that day. It was a very large mansion and Mary Anne Leslie rarely appeared to any guest.

When his turn came to entertain his brethren of the Louth Clerical Union he reserved the dining room and the reception room at the old Greenore Railway Hotel, a very fashionable place in those days, particularly for the golfing fraternity. The sumptuous repast provided by Canon Leslie in the summer session of the Union was an unforgettable experience; it was difficult to understand that the scholar who could spend many hours, indeed many days, poring through the ancient records and manuscripts of the Irish Church, could on occasion be as happy as a sandboy, with great sense of humour and vociferous laughter.

His manner in fellowship was deceptive, since his mind was always alert to pick up any new information that might be included in his clerical biographies. One of the last memories we have of him was at a meeting of the Union in Heynestown Rectory. When we were all sitting around a magnificent coal fire in the drawing room at coffee (and it was no substitute coffee!) awaiting the arrival of the oldest member, Abraham Lockett Ford, then Rector of Ardee, Leslie and the present writer were comfortably seated on the settee. On Ford's entry into the room, and walking across to the fireplace, he faced the assembled brethren; reaching to his breast pocket he announced, 'Gentlemen, I have a letter from the Primate' (nobody called him Archbishop in those days). Before Ford could set to reading the letter Leslie leaped from the settee, nearly throwing his neighbour out of it, and shouted with great joy, 'The new Archdeacon, the new Archdeacon!' There was no need to read the letter. Charles King

Irwin, former Archdeacon of Armagh, had been appointed Bishop of Limerick, Ardfert and Aghadoe, and Leslie had jumped to an accurate conclusion.

They were great days, and the standard of discussions and debates was maintained at a high level. Our historian is affectionately remembered by his parishioners in the Kilsaran Group as well as by his innumerable colleagues and friends throughout the County.

He was of course a prominent member of the County Louth Archaeological and Historical Society, in which he happily mixed in the fellowship of many Roman Catholic clergy and laity. Leslie was no Protestant bigot, but a hail-fellow-well-met to all and sundry; he was a man of great natural humility as well as of scholarly attainments. He became Vice-President of the Society in 1918.

Having retired from the active ministry in 1951 he went to live in Glenageary. His death there in 1952 removed from the Church of Ireland a most valuable historian, a delightful friend, and a truly faithful colleague.

HECTOR W. LOVE
28 February 1991

A BRIEF HISTORY OF THE DIOCESES OF KILMORE, ELPHIN AND ARDAGH

The Diocese of Kilmore
The Diocese of Kilmore, which comprises the modern county of Cavan, together with the northern section of County Leitrim from Lough Allen to the Atlantic seaboard and a small part of County Fermanagh, is practically coterminous with Breiffne, the patrimony of the Ui-Briuin, the mediaeval *Tirbriuinensis*. The region abounds in traces of ancient Neolithic inhabitants, Celtic tribes and early-Christian settlers.

St Patrick brought the Christian faith to Breifne. The influence of Christianity on the Ui-Briuin is evidenced by the large number of ecclesiastical foundations in the area from an early time. Amongst the early saints were St Feidhlimidh, founder of the Diocese, St Dallan and St Laighne of Killinagh.

St Fethlimidh is patron of the Diocese of Kilmore and is generally accepted as its first bishop. Born some time after AD 500, his parents Carill and Dedive came from Breifne and were descended from a ruling chieftain of the territory. There is an early tradition that St Fethlimidh founded a church at Kilmore, though there is no mention of this in the monastic annals.

The early Celtic Church was based mainly in monasteries, where the Abbot was head of the community. The modern dioceses of the Irish Church, including Kilmore, Elphin and Ardagh, were formed at the great Synods of Rathbreasail in 1111 and Kells-Mellifont in 1152. At Rathbreasail, the Kingdom of Breifne was included in the Diocese of Ardagh, but at Kells, in 1152, Kells in County Meath was designated the Episcopal See for part of Breifne, whilst the rest of the territory was left without a see.

There was a succession of bishops of Breifne or Tir Briuin from c 1100. The situation remained confused for some centuries, until eventually the present diocese gained much the same territory that it occupies today.

Monastic life continued alongside diocesan life after Rathbreasail. In the middle ages, Breifne possessed some important monasteries and other centres of learning and religion. These included Drumlane, the Premonstratensian priory on Trinity Island in Lough Oughter with its Hiberno-Romanesque doorway (now in Kilmore Cathedral), and the Franciscan establishment at Cavan.

At the time of the Reformation in the sixteenth century, the Irish Church regained its independence. In the seventeenth century, Kilmore produced one of the greatest figures in the history of the Church, Bishop William Bedell (1570–1642), Bishop of Kilmore from 1629 to 1642. An Englishman, Bedell was an eminent Irish scholar who believed that it was essential that the scriptures and liturgy of the Church should be available to the people in their native language, Irish. Thus, he set about translating the Bible into Irish and had translated the Old Testament before his death in 1642.

The Diocese of Elphin

According to tradition, Ono, son of Oengus, gave his house to St Patrick around AD 450. Patrick renamed it *Ail Fionn*, the clear or fair stream. There, he placed his disciple Assicus in charge as first bishop of Elphin. Assicus died c 470.

Assicus was reputed to be 'an admirable worker in precious metals, and in his capacity as a goldsmith, greatly adorned his cathedral church with articles of his handicraft'. He is supposed to have been succeeded by his nephew, Bite (Batheus), but this is conjecture. At any rate, there are no further records of the monastery at Elphin, nor of bishops until after the Synod of Rathbreasail established Elphin as a diocese for east Connaught. Today, the diocese comprises most of County Roscommon, the northern part of County Sligo and a small portion of east County Galway, as well as a small part of County Mayo.

The first thirteenth-century cathedral was destroyed and replaced by another, which was itself destroyed in the Rebellion of 1641. By 1757 it was in a ruinous condition. It was rebuilt, to form what was to be the last cathedral in the town of Elphin. In 1957 the Diocesan Synod decided to abandon Elphin Cathedral, following its destruction in a storm, and in 1961 the Church of St John the Baptist in Sligo was raised to cathedral status and became the cathedral for the Dioceses of Elphin and Ardagh with the dedication of St Mary the Virgin and St John the Baptist.

In 1685, Bishop John Hodson established Bishop Hodson's Grammar School. A famous son of the diocese was the playwright, novelist and poet Oliver Goldsmith (1728–1774), who was educated there. Charles Dodgson, Bishop of Elphin 1775–1795, was the grandfather of the Rev Charles Lutwidge Dodgson, better known as Lewis Carroll, author of *Alice in Wonderland*. The Rev Arthur Hyde, Rector of Tybohine from 1866 to 1905, was the father of the well-known Gaelic scholar and writer Dr Douglas Hyde (1860–1949), first President of Ireland (1937–1945). Another son of the diocese, William Butler Yeats (1865–1939), arguably Ireland's greatest poet, wrote much of his poetry around Sligo and is buried in Drumcliffe Churchyard.

The Diocese of Ardagh

Ardagh, *Ard Achaidh*, a high field, in County Longford, was the site of a monastery which St Patrick is supposed to have founded. Ardagh is forever associated with St Patrick's nephew, St Mel (died c 490), who, according to tradition, accompanied Patrick to Ireland.

At Rathbreasail, Ardagh and Ardcarne were selected as alternative sees for the diocese and Ardagh was chosen. At the Synod of Kells, when the enlarged Kingdom of Breifne was attached to Kells, the territory of Conmaicne became a diocese with its see at Ardagh. This diocese was placed in the Province of Armagh, but as Ui-Briuin Breifne and Conmaicne were of Connaught origin, the Archbishop of Tuam laid claim to Ardagh.

Successive popes decided in favour of Armagh and the dispute was eventually settled in 1326.

It cannot be established with certainty which of the two ruined churches at Ardagh was the cathedral. At any rate, various churches that were successively built and destroyed in the middle ages had cathedral status. In 1496, the cathedral that existed at the time was destroyed in feuding between the various branches of the O'Ferrall family – which, as one can see from the succession lists, provided numerous clergy and some bishops in Ardagh Diocese.

The Diocese of Ardagh was held by the bishops of Kilmore at various periods during the seventeenth century. Bishop Bedell, Bishop of Kilmore and Ardagh from 1629 to 1642, writing to the Archbishop of Canterbury, William Laud, said:

'I have been about my dioceses, and can set down out of knowledge and view what I shall relate: and shortly to speak much ill matter in a few words, it is very miserable.'

Ardagh ceased to have cathedral status after 1630; thereafter, the cathedral at Elphin served both dioceses.

In the Church of Ireland arrangement, the Sees of Ardagh and Kilmore were united in 1839. Elphin was united with Kilmore in 1841 to form the Dioceses of Kilmore, Elphin and Ardagh. In recent times there have been some minor alterations to boundaries.

LIST OF SUBSCRIBERS

RORY AND PEARL ANDERSON, Erris, Boyle, Co. Roscommon

ARMAGH PUBLIC LIBRARY, 43 Abbey Street, Armagh

ASHFIELD PARISH CHURCH, via Christine McAdam, Cootehill, Co. Cavan

MR. IVAN BLACK, Cavan

MR. RICHARD BRETT, St. Columba's College, Whitechurch, Dublin 16

REV. GEORGE W. BROWNE, Copy presented in his memory by Kildallon Group of Parishes

MRS. CYNTHIA BURNS, ASHFIELD, COOTEHILL, Co. Cavan

CAVAN COUNTY LIBRARY SERVICES, Farnham Street, Cavan

DR. JONATHAN CHERRY, Belfield, Dublin 14

MR. KEITH CLARKE, Ballyhaise, Co. Cavan

THE RIGHT REV'D. K. H. CLARKE, Bishop of Kilmore, Elphin and Ardagh, Carrickfern, Cavan (50 copies)

MR. A. COOKE, 25 Sydenham Crescent, Belfast

MR. ARCHIE CORNWALL, Swancurragh, Manorhamilton, Co. Leitrim

VEN. G.T.W. DAVISON, The Rectory, Cloghan, Derrylin, Co. Fermanagh

PEARL DEANE, Cordoagh, Cootehill, Co. Cavan

MR. WILLIAM DEANE, Cordoagh, Cootehill, Co. Cavan

DIOCESES OF DOWN AND DROMORE AND CONNOR, Church of Ireland House, Belfast

DUBLIN DIOCESAN OFFICE, via Mr. K. Dungan, Diocesan Office, Church House, Rathmines, Dublin 6. copies)

REV. CANON F.W. FAWCETT, Kilrea, Co. Londonderry

PROFESSOR DAVID FITZPATRICK, MRIA, Dept. of History, Trinity College, Dublin

REV. W.E.C. FLEMING, Richhill, Co. Armagh (2 copies)

EVA GIBSON, Eonish, Killeshandra, Co. Cavan

DAVID AND DOROTHY GILLESPIE, Mount Prospect House, Boyle, Co. Roscommon

ROSEMARY GREENLEE, Greystones, Co. Wicklow

REV. D. GRISCOME, The Rectory, Convoy, Co. Donegal

THE MOST REV'D. A.E.T. HARPER, 5 Beresford Row, Armagh

MR. WINSTON HEASLIP, Drumheckna, Co. Cavan

MRS. LOUISA HENLEY, Ballinlough, Co. Roscommon

JEAN HENRY, Virginia, Co. Cavan

MR. JOHN HEWITT, Cavan

REV. STANLEY JOHNSON AND REV. SHIELA JOHNSON, Ballymore Rectory, Port-na-Blagh, Dunfanaghy, Co. Donegal

MR. AND MRS GEORGE AND RUTH JOHNSTON, lisburn, Co. Antrim

MRS GLADYS JOHNSTON, Derrylane, Killeshandra, Co. Cavan

DR. JACK JOHNSTON, Ratory, Clogher, Co. Tyrone

MR. LESLIE VICTOR JOHNSTON (BALLINTEMPLE), Armagh

MR. WILLIAM KELLS, Belturbet, Co. Cavan

CANON ALBERT WM. KINGSTON, Ballymahon, Co. Longford

SADIE KINGSTON AND ROSEMARY KINGSTON, The Rectory, Carrickmacross, Co. Monaghan

REV. IAIN J.E. KNOX, Clonmel, Co. Tipperary

CANON MARK LIDWILL, The Rectory, Cavan

REV. CECIL LINDSAY AND THE REV. SANDRA LINDSAY, Clementstown House, Cootehill, Co. Cavan

REV. CANON G.N. AND MRS. LITTLE, Markethill, Co. Armagh

MR. MERVYN LLOYD, Farnaught, Mohill, Co. Leitrim

LONGFORD COUNTY LIBRARY SERVICES, Longford

DELL LUNDY, Blackrock, Co. Dublin

REV. CANON LIZ McELHINNEY, Dollingstown, Co. Armagh

VEN. W.A. MACOURT, 19 Abbey Court, Belfast

THE RT. REV'D. M.H.G. MAYES, The See House, North Circular Road, Limerick

REV'D. JOHN MERRICK, Dunfanaghy, Co. Donegal

MR. CHARLES MOLLAN, Blackrock, Co. Dublin

REV. ARLENE MOORE, Sheffield, Yorkshire

MR. MICHAEL O'DWYER, College Gardens, Kilkenny

DR. FERGUS O'FERRALL, Cabinteely, Dublin 18

MRS. OLIVE O'MALLEY, Richmond Hill, Ontario, Canada

THE REV'D. JOHN A. PICKERING, Portadown, Co. Armagh

REPRESENTATIVE CHURCH BODY LIBRARY, Braemor Park, Churchtown, Dublin 14

REV. W.J. RITCHIE, The Rectory, Tullow, Co. Carlow

MR. K.L. ROBERTS, Carrickaline, Co. Cork

MR. NOEL ROSS, Dundalk, Co. Louth

P AND B ROWAN, 92 Malone Road, Belfast (2 copies)

ELIZABETH SHARP-PAUL, Buningyong, Victoria, Australia

REV. CANON JIM SIDES, Edgeworthstown, Co. Longford

REV. NIALL J. SLOANE, Taney, Dundrum, Dublin

MR. BARRY SMITH, Winchester, Hants.

REV. RICHARD W. STAFFORD, Cavan

JANET STEPHENSON, Glenboy, Manorhamilton, Co. Leitrim

St. JOHN'S CATHEDRAL, SLIGO, via the Very Rev'd. Arfon Williams, The Deanery, Sligo

Dr. ALICIA St. LEGER, 36 Mary St. Cork

STOKES BOOKS, South Great George's Street, Dublin 2

WENDY SWAN, Monery, Crossdoney, Co. Cavan

MR. JOHN TAYLOR, Fannybrook, Riverstown, Co. Sligo

MR. ROBERT THOMPSON, KILLESHER PARISH, Florencecourt, Co. Fermanagh

MR. TREVOR THOMPSON, Bailieborough, Co. Cavan

REV. CANON W.R. TWADDELL, Portadown, Co. Armagh

MR. ALBERT WALKER, Knocknaveigh, Virginia, Co. Cavan

MR. AND MRS. AUBREY AND BRIGID WALKER, Brookhill House, Londonderry

DR. HUGH W.L. WEIR, Whitegate, Co. Clare

MR. DESMOND WEST, Convoy, Co. Donegal

MR. S.M. WILLIAMS, Reading, Berkshire

EDWARD AND PRIMROSE WILSON, Portadown, Co. Armagh

REV. JAMES L. WILSON, Loughgilly Rectory, Co. Armagh

ABBREVIATIONS

Note: See also bibliography for abbreviated references to sources.

A
A & A	Ardfert and Aghadoe Diocese
Abp	Archbishop
Acad	Academical, Academy
acc	according
ACC	Anglican Consultative Council
ACCS	Associate, Corporation of Certified Secretaries
ACG	Assistant Chaplain General
ACGI	Associate, City and Guilds of London Institute
Ach	Achonry Diocese
ACIS	Associate, Institute of Chartered Secretaries and Administrators
ACS	Additional Curates Society
ACT	Australian College of Theology
AD	Anno Domini, Year of our Lord
Adel	Adelaide Diocese
ad eund	*ad eundem* (to the same)
adm	admitted
AFM	*Annals of the Four Masters*
AH	*De Annatis Hiberniae*
A & I	Argyll and the Isles Diocese
AKC	Associate, King's College London
ALCM	Associate, London College of Music
Al Dub	*Alumni Dubliniensis*
All SS	All Saints
AMICE	Associate Member, Institution of Civil Engineers
Ann Loch Cé	*Annals of Loch Cé*
Ann Ult	*Annals of Ulster*
Anon	Anonymous
A & O	Aberdeen and Orkney Diocese
APCK	Association for the Promotion of Christian Knowledge
Archd	Archdeacon
Arch Soc	Archaeological Society
ARCS	Associate, Royal College of Science
Ard	Ardagh Diocese
Ardf	Ardfert Diocese
Arm	Armagh Diocese
ARSCM	Associate, Royal School of Church Music
Assoc	Association
Asst	Assistant
Aux	Auxiliary

B
b.	born
BA	Bachelor of Arts
Bach	Bachelor
Ban	Bangor Diocese
BAI	Bachelor of Engineering
BAO	Bachelor of Obstetrics
BAOR	British Army on the Rhine
bapt	baptised
Bapt	Baptist
Batt	Battalion
BBA	Bachelor of Business Administration
BC	Bishop's Curate, British Columbia
BCh	Bachelor of Surgery
BCL	Bachelor of Civil Law
BCMS	Bible Churchmen's Missionary Society
BComm	Bachelor of Commerce
Bd	Board
BD	Bachelor of Divinity
B & W	Bath and Wells Diocese
Beds	Bedfordshire
BEF	British Expeditionary Force
BEng	Bachelor of Engineering
Bibl	Biblical
Biol Sci	Biological Science
Birm	Birmingham Diocese
BL	Bachelor of Law, Barrister-at-Law
Blackb	Blackburn Diocese
BLG	Burke's Landed Gentry
BLGI	Burke's Landed Gentry of Ireland
BMus	Bachelor of Music
Bp(s)	Bishop(s)
Bpric	Bishopric
BRA	Belfast Royal Academy
Bradf	Bradford Diocese
Bris	Bristol Diocese
bro.	brother
BSc	Bachelor of Science
BSocAdmin	Bachelor of Social Administration
BSocSc	Bachelor of Social Science
BSSc	Bachelor of Social Science
Bt	Baronet
BTh	Bachelor of Theology
bur.	buried
BVM	Blessed Virgin Mary

C		CMJ	Church Mission to Jews
c.	circa	CMS	Church Mission(ary) Society
C	Curate, Curacy, Cure	Co, Cos	County, Counties
CA	Church Army, California	C of E	Chapel of Ease, Church of England
Cal Reg	Calendar of the Register of (see bibliography)	C of I	Church of Ireland
Camb	Cambridge	Col	Colonel
Cand Bach	Candidate Bachelor	Coll	College
Cant, Cantuar	Canterbury Diocese	coll	collated, collation
Cantab	Cambridge	Comp	Composition
Capt	Captain	Conn	Connor Diocese
Carl	Carlisle Diocese	consec	consecrated, consecration
Cash	Cashel Diocese	contrib.	contributor, contributed
Cath	Cathedral	Cov	Coventry Diocese
CB	Companion, Order of the Bath	CP and CR	Calendar of Irish Patent and Close Rolls
CBE	Commander, Order of the British Empire	CPL	Calendar of Papal Letters
		CPP	Calendar of Papal Petitions
CCCS	Commonwealth and Continental Church Society	CPR	Calendar of Papal Registers
		CPRE	Calendar of Patent Rolls of England
CCS	Colonial and Continental Society	CPRI	Calendar of Papal Rolls, Ireland
CDI	Calendar of Documents relating to Ireland	CSPI	Calendar of State Papers, Ireland
CE	Civil Engineer		
Cert	Certificate	D	
CertEd	Certificate of Education	d	deacon
CEZ Missy	Church of England Zenana Missionary	DACG	Deputy Assistant Chaplain General
CEZMA	Church of England Zenana Missionary Association	dau., daus.	daughter, daughters
		DBS	Diploma in Biblical Studies
CF	Chaplain to the Forces, Cotton's *Fasti*	DC	District of Columbia/District Curate
CF (EC)	Chaplain to the Forces (Emergency Commission)	DCL	Doctor of Civil Law
		DD	Doctor of Divinity
Ch	Chapter, Church	depr	deprivation, deprived
Chald	Chaldean	Dep Sec	Deputation Secretary
Chanc	Chancellor, Chancellorship	Dept	Department
Chapl	Chaplain	Dep TCD	Deposition of persons who suffered in the 1641 Rebellion in the Library of Trinity College, Dublin
ChB	Bachelor of Surgery		
Chelmsf	Chelmsford Diocese		
Ches	Chester Diocese		
Chich	Chichester Diocese	DI	District Inspector
Chmn	Chairman	Dio	Diocesan, Diocese
CI	Chief Inspector	Dio C	Diocesan Curate
C-in-c	Curate-in-charge	Dio Reg	Diocesan Registrar
C I Dir	Church of Ireland Directory	Dip	Diploma
CIG	*Church of Ireland Gazette*	DipEd	Diploma in Education
CITC	Church of Ireland Theological College	DipHE	Diploma in Higher Education
		DipHum	Diploma in Humanities
CIYC	Church of Ireland Youth Council	DipLit	Diploma in Literature
		DipTh, Dip Theol	Diploma in Theology
CIYMCA	Church of Ireland Young Men's Christian Association	Dir	Director, Directory
		disp	dispensed, dispensation
cl	class	Distr	District
Cler (V)	Clerical (Vicar)	Div	Divinity
Clk	Clerk	Div Prem	Divinity Premium
Clogh	Clogher Diocese	Div Test	Divinity Testimonium
Clonf	Clonfert Diocese	DL	Deputy Lieutenant

DLitt	Doctor of Letters		Society of Ireland
DNB	*Dictionary of National Biography*	FRHistSoc	Fellow, Royal Historical Society
do	*ditto*	FRIBA	Fellow, Royal Institute of British Architects
Dom Chapl	Domestic Chaplain		
DPH	Diploma in Public Health	FRS	Fellow, Royal Society
DPhil	Doctor of Philosophy	FRUI	Fellow, Royal University of Ireland
DPT/DPTh	Diploma in Pastoral Theology		
Dr	Doctor	FSA	Fellow, Society of Antiquaries
DR	Diocesan Register	FTCD	Fellow, Trinity College Dublin
Drom	Dromore Diocese	FTCL	Fellow, Trinity College of Music, London
dss	deaconess		
DSO	Companion, Distinguished Service Order	Fus	Fusiliers
DU	Dublin University	**G**	
Dub	Dublin Diocese	G	Group
DUFEM	Dublin University Far Eastern Mission	G & G	Glasgow and Galloway Diocese
		GCB	Grand Commander of the Bath
DUM	Dublin University Mission	Gen	General, gentleman
Dur	Durham Diocese	Geog	Geography
		Gk	Greek
E		Glend	Glendalough Diocese
Eccles	Ecclesiastical	Glouc	Gloucester Diocese
Econ	Economics	Gloucs	Gloucestershire
ECUSA	Episcopal Church of the United States of America	GNRI	Great Northern Railway, Ireland
Ed	educated, education	GOE	General Ordination Examination
ed	edited, editor		
EICS	East Indies Civil Service	Govt	Government
Elec Eng	Electrical Engineering	GPO	General Post Office
Elph	Elphin Diocese	Gram Sch	Grammar School
Eng	English	GSR	Great Southern Railway
Eng Lit	English Literature	Guildf	Guildford Diocese
ent	entered		
Est	Established, Establishment	**H**	
Eth	Ethics	Hants	Hampshire
Ex	Exeter Diocese	HBM	His/Her Britannic Majesty
Exam	Examination	HBS	Hibernian Bible Society
Exam Chapl	Examining Chaplain	HCF	Honorary Chaplain to the Forces
Exhib	Exhibition, Exhibitioner		
		HDipEd	Higher Diploma in Education
F		Heb	Hebrew
FC	Fellow Commoner	HEICS	Honourable East Indies Civil Service
F Eliz/Henry/Edward VI	Calendar of Fiants Henry VIII to Elizabeth I		
		Heref	Hereford, Hereford Diocese, Herefordshire
FF	First Fruits (Board of)		
Form	Formularies	Herts	Hertfordshire
FRAS	Fellow, Royal Astronomical Society	Hib	Hibernian
		Hist	History
FRCOG	Fellow, Royal College of Obstetricians and Gynaecologists	HM	His/Her Majesty('s)
		HML	His/Her Majesty's Lieutenant
		HMS	His/Her Majesty's Ship
		HNC	Higher National Certificate
FRCS	Fellow, Royal College of Physicians and Surgeons of England	Hon	Honorary, Honors, Honourable
		hon causa	*honoris causa* (as an honour)
		Hond	Honduras Diocese
FRCSI	Fellow, Royal College of Surgeons of Ireland	Hons	Honors
		Hosp	Hospital
		hse	house
FRGSI	Fellow, Royal Geographical	Hur	Huron Diocese

I

I	incumbent
I(s)	Island(s)
ib	*ibidem*
ICC	Irish Council of Churches
ICM	Irish Church Missions
Id	Ides
IEG	*Irish Ecclesiastical Gazette*
incl	including, include(s)
incorp	incorporated, incorporation
info	information
Insp	Inspector
Inst	Institute, Institution
inst	installed, installation
IOM	Isle of Man
IOW	Isle of Wight
ISPEPSI	Incorporated Society for Promoting English Protestant Schools in Ireland
ISPPSI	Incorporated Society for Promoting Protestant Schools in Ireland

J

jd	*jure dignitatis* (by right of distinction)
JP	Justice of the Peace
Jun	Junior
Jun Mod	Junior Moderatorship

K

KBE	Knight Commander, Order of the British Empire
KC	King's Counsel
KCB	Knight Commander, Order of the Bath
KCMG	Knight Commander, Order of St Michael and St George
Kild	Kildare Diocese
Kilf	Kilfenora Diocese
Kilm	Kilmore Diocese
Kilmac	Kilmacduagh Diocese
K Lett	King's Letters
Kt	Knight

L

Lancs	Lancashire
Langs	Languages
LDip	Diploma in Law
Ld Lt	Lord Lieutenant
LDS	Licentiate in Dental Surgery
Lect	Lecturer
Leic	Leicester Diocese
Leigh	Leighlin Diocese
Lic	license, licensed
Lich	Lichfield Diocese
Lic Pr	Licensed Preacher
Lic to Off	Licence to Officiate
Lim	Limerick Diocese
Linc	Lincoln Diocese
Lincs	Lincolnshire
Lism	Lismore Diocese
Lit	literary, literature
LittD	Doctor of Letters
Liv	Liverpool Diocese
LJS	London Jews' Society
LLAM	Licentiate, London Academy of Music and Dramatic Art
Lland	Llandaff Diocese
LLB	Bachelor of Laws
LLCM	Licentiate, London College of Music
LLD	Doctor of Laws
LM	*Liber Munerum*
LMus	Licentiate in Music
Log	Logic
Lon	London Diocese
Lr	Lower
LRCPI	Licentiate, Royal College of Physicians of Ireland
LRCSI	Licentiate, Royal College of Surgeons in Ireland
LRCVSI	Licentiate, Royal College of Veterinary Surgeons of Ireland
Lt	Lieutenant
LTCL	Licentiate, Trinity College of Music, London
LTh	Licentiate in Theology

M

m.	married
MA	Master of Arts
Manch	Manchester Diocese
Mass	Massachusetts
Maths	Mathematics
matric	matriculated, matriculation
MB	Bachelor of Medicine
MBE	Member, Order of the British Empire
MC	Military Cross
MD	Doctor of Medicine
MDiv	Master of Divinity
Med	Medical
MEd	Master of Education
Mem	Memorial
Ment & Mor Philos	Mental and Moral Philosophy
Ment & Mor Sci	Mental and Moral Science
Meth	Methodist
MICE	Member, Institution of Civil Engineers
Middx	Middlesex
Min	Minister, Ministry
Miss	Mission
Missy	Missionary
ML	Marriage Licence

MLitt	Master of Letters	P, p	priest
Mod	Moderator, Moderatorship, Modern	PA	Pennsylvania
		Par	Parish
Mod Lit	Modern Literature	Parl Ret	Parliamentary Return
Mon	Monmouth Diocese	Past Theol	Pastoral Theology
Mor Philos	Moral Philosophy	PC	Perpetual Curate
MP	Member of Parliament	Perm to Off	Permission to Officiate
MPSI	Member, Pharmaceutical Society of Ireland	Pet	Peterborough Diocese
		PhD	Doctor of Philosophy
M R & C	Moray, Ross and Caithness Diocese	Phil, Philos	Philosophy
		P-in-c	Priest-in-charge
MRAS	Member of the Royal Astronomical Society	Pol Econ	Political Economics
		Pol Sci	Political Science
MRCS	Member, Royal College of Surgeons	Portsm	Portsmouth Diocese
		poss	possibly
MRCSE	Member, Royal College of Surgeons of Edinburgh	POW	Prisoner of War
		Pk	Park
MRCVS	Member, Royal College of Veterinary Surgeons	Pr	Preacher
		PR	Patent Rolls
MRCVSI	Member, Royal College of Veterinary Surgeons of Ireland	Preb	Prebend, Prebendary
		Prec	Precentor
MRIA	Member, Royal Irish Academy	Prelim	Preliminary
MSc	Master of Science	Prem	Premium
MS(S)	Manuscript(s)	Prep	Preparatory
Mt	Mount, Mountain	pres	presented
MTh	Master of Theology	Pres	President
MU	Mothers' Union	Presby	Presbyterian
MVO	Member, Royal Victorian Order	Prin	Principal
		Pri(s)	Prize(s)
N		prob	probably
NB	New Brunswick	Prof	Professor
Newc	Newcastle Diocese	prov	provided, provision
NI	Northern Ireland	PTE	Premium Theological Examination
NJ	New Jersey		
nom	nominated	Publ Pr	Public Preacher
Nor	Norwich Diocese	P Will	Prerogative Will
NS	National School, Nova Scotia	publ	published
NSM	Non-Stipendiary Minister, Non-Stipendiary Ministry	**Q**	
		QC	Queen's Counsel
NSW	New South Wales	QCB	Queen's College Belfast
NT	New Testament	QUB	The Queen's University of Belfast
NUI	National University of Ireland		
NUU	New University of Ulster	QUI	Queen's University in Ireland
NW	North-West	qv	*quod vide* (which see)
NY	New York		
NZ	New Zealand	**R**	
		R	Rector, Rectory
O		RA	Royal Army, Royal Artillery
OBE	Officer, Order of the British Empire	RAChD	Royal Army Chaplains' Department
Off	Officer	RAF	Royal Air Force
ONC	Ordinary National Certificate	RAFVR	Royal Air Force Volunteer Reserve
Orat	Oratory		
ord	ordained, ordination	RAMC	Royal Army Medical Corps
Org Sec	Organising Secretary	Raph	Raphoe Diocese
Oss	Ossory Diocese	RASC	Royal Army Service Corps
OT	Old Testament	RBAI	Royal Belfast Academical Institution
OU	Open University		
Ox, Oxon	Oxford, Oxford Diocese	RC	Roman Catholic
P			

RCB	Representative Church Body	SCM	Student Christian Movement
RCPI	Royal College of Physicians, Ireland	Sec	Secretary
		Sel Pr	Select Preacher
RCSI	Royal College of Surgeons, Ireland	Sen	Senior
		Sen Mod	Senior Moderatorship
Rd	Road	Sen Soph	Senior Sophister
RD	Rural Dean	seq	sequestered, sequestrator, sequestration
RE	Royal Engineers		
Reg	Register, Registrar	SFTCD	Senior Fellow, Trinity College Dublin
Reg Prof	Regius Professor		
Regt	Regiment	SHAPE	Supreme Headquarters Allied Powers Europe
Rel	Religious		
Rep	Representative	Sheff	Sheffield Diocese
res	resignation, resigned	Siz	Sizar
Res	Residentiary	Soc	Social, Society
Resp	Respondency	sp	*sine prole* (without issue)
ret	retired	SPCK	Society for Promoting Christian Knowledge
Rev	Reverend		
RFC	Royal Flying Corps	SPG	Society for the Propagation of the Gospel
RGA	Royal Garrison Artillery		
ROI	Republic of Ireland	SR	Subscription Rolls
RIA	Royal Irish Academy/Royal Irish Artillery	SRN	State Registered Nurse
		SS	Saints, Sunday School
RIC	Royal Irish Constabulary	SSC	Special Service Clergyman
RIF	Royal Inniskilling Fusiliers, Royal Irish Fusiliers	St	Saint
		St A	St Alban's Diocese
Rip	Ripon Diocese	Staffs	Staffordshire
RIR	Royal Irish Rifles, Regiment	St As	St Asaph Diocese
RM	Resident Magistrate	St D	St David's Diocese
RMA	Royal Military Academy	St E	St Edmundsbury Diocese
RMS	Royal Mail Ship	STh	Scholar in Theology
RN	Royal Navy	Stn	Station
RNR	Royal Naval Reserve	Studs	Studies
RNVR	Royal Naval Volunteer Reserve	Sub	Subscription
Roch	Rochester Diocese	Suff Loy Lists	
RSA	Royal Society of Arts		Suffering Loyalists Lists
RSAI	Royal Society of Antiquaries of Ireland	Suppl	Supplemental
		Supt	Superintendent
RSV	Revised Standard Version	Svce	Service
RTC	Regional Technical College	SW	South-West
Rt Hon	Right Honourable	S'wark	Southwark Diocese
Rt Rev	Right Reverend	S'well	Southwell Diocese
RTS	Religious Tract Society	Syr	Syriac
RUC	Royal Ulster Constabulary		
RUI	Royal University of Ireland	T	
Rupld	Rupertsland Diocese	TCD	Trinity College Dublin
RV	Royal Visitation	TCert	Teacher's Certificate
		TCF	Temporary Chaplain to the Forces
S			
s.	son	TCL	Trinity College London
S	South	Tech	Technical, Technology
S & B	Swansea and Brecon Diocese	Temp-in-c	Temporarily-in-charge
S & M	Sodor and Man Diocese	Temps	Temporalities
SAMS	South American Missionary Society	Theo Exhib	Theological Exhibitioner
		Theol	Theological, Theology
Sarum	Salisbury Diocese	ThL	Theological Licentiate
SC	Senior Commoner	Th Trip	Theological Tripos
Sc, Sci	Science	Treas	Treasurer
Sch	Scholar, Scholarship, School	Trip	Tripos

TV	Team Vicar	*agricola*	farmer
U		*armiger*	armour bearer, Esquire
U	Union	*argentarius*	banker
UCC	University College Cork	*bibliopola*	bookseller
UCD	University College Dublin	*candelarius*	candlemaker
UCG	University College Galway	*caupo*	innkeeper
UJA	*Ulster Journal of Archaeology*	*causidicus*	advocate, barrister
Univ	University	*cervisarius*	alehouse keeper
unm.	unmarried	*clericus*	clergyman
Upr	Upper	*colonus*	farmer/colonist
USA	United States of America	*coactor*	rent collector
USPG	United Society for the Propagation of the Gospel	*dux*	captain, leader, military commander
UTV	Ulster Television	*dux militum*	military leader
UUJ	University of Ulster Jordanstown	*eques*	horseman, knight (Sir)
		faber aurarius	goldsmith
V		*faber ferrarius*	blacksmith
V	Vicar, Vicarage	*ingenuus*	of noble birth, honourable
vac	vacant, vacated	*jurisconsult*	lawyer
VB	Visitation Book	*jurisperitus*	barrister-at-law
V Chor	Vicar Choral	*linteo*	linen maker/merchant
Ven	Venerable	*ludimagister*	schoolmaster
V Gen	Vicar General	*mechanicus*	mechanic
VP	Vice Principal	*medicus*	doctor, physician
		mercator	merchant
W		*miles*	soldier
w	with	*militaris*	soldier
W	West	*militum doctor*	military doctor
WA	Washington	*nuper centurionis*	former military commander, officer
Wakef	Wakefield Diocese		
Warks	Warwickshire	*nuper miles*	former soldier
Waterf	Waterford Diocese	*opifex*	worker
Wilts	Wiltshire	*pharmacopola*	drug seller/chemist
Win	Winchester Diocese	*pragmaticus*	solicitor
Worc	Worcester Diocese	*protator*	tax collector
WWI	World War I	*publicanus*	tax collector
WWII	World War II	*sartor*	tailor
		telonarius	tax collector
Y		*tribunus militum*	colonel (originally commander of legions)
YOI	Young Offender Institution		
yr	younger	*vectigalis exactor*	tax collector
yst	youngest	*vestiarius*	tailor/clothes merchant

Latin Terms

BIBLIOGRAPHY AND SOURCES

Note: In biographical notes, references given by author's/editor's surname except where indicated below in square brackets.

PRINTED WORKS

Barnard, T.C. and W.G. Neely, W.G. (eds), *The Clergy of the Church of Ireland, 1000–2000: Messengers, Watchmen and Stewards* (Dublin, 2006).

Bourns, J.M., *The Irish Clergy List and Ecclesiastical Almanack* (Dublin, 1843).

Brady, W.M., *Clerical and Parochial Records of Cork, Cloyne and Ross* (2 vols, Dublin, 1863, 1864).

Burke's Landed Gentry [BLG].

Burke's Landed Gentry of Ireland [BLGI].

Burtchaell, G.D. and T.U. Sadleir (eds), *Alumni Dublinensis: Being a Register of Students and Graduates of Trinity College, Dublin* (Dublin, 1935) [Al Dub].

Church of Ireland Directory (1862–) [C I Dir].

Cole J.H., *Church and Parish Records of the United Dioceses of Cork, Cloyne and Ross* (Cork, 1903).

Cotton, H., *Fasti Ecclesiae Hibernicae: the Succession of the Prelates and Members of the Cathedral Bodies of Ireland* (I (Munster), 1st edition 1847, 2nd edition 1851; II (Leinster) 1848; III (Ulster) 1849; IV (Connaught and Consecrations) 1850; V (Illustrations, Corrections and Additions with General Indexes by John Ribton Garstin) 1860; Supplement continuing work –1870 (Disestablishment) by Charles P. Cotton, 1878).

Crockford's Clerical Directory.

Dictionary of National Biography [DNB].

Duncan, Thomas (ed.), *The 1608 Royal Schools* (Premier Print and Design, Aghalee, Co. Armagh, 2007).

Dunlop, R., *Ireland under the Commonwealth* (Manchester, 1913).

Erck, J.C., *The Irish Ecclesiastical Register* […] *Containing the Names of the Dignitaries and Parochial Clergy* […] *in the Province of Armagh* (Dublin and London, 1825).

Erck, J.C., *Ecclesiastical Register of the Names of the Dignitaries and Parochial Clergy and of the Parishes and their Respective Patrons, etc.* (Dublin, 1818, 1820, 1830).

Fleming, W.E.C., *Armagh Clergy 1800–2000* (Dundalk, 2001).

Forster, J., *The Life and Times of Oliver Goldsmith* (London, 1855).

Galloway, P., *The Cathedrals of Ireland* (Belfast, 1992).

Hutchinson, S., *Towers, Spires and Pinnacles: a History of the Cathedrals and Churches of the Church of Ireland* (Bray, 2003).

Irish Church Directory.

King, W., *The State of the Protestants of Ireland under the Government of King James II* [...] (Dublin, 1886).

Lawlor, H.J., *The Fasti of St Patrick's, Dublin* (Dublin, 1930).

Lea, S.P., *The Present State of the Established Church, or Ecclesiastical Register of Ireland for the Year 1814* (Dublin, 1814).

Leslie, J.B., *Succession Lists of the Clergy of Ardfert and Aghadoe, Armagh (with Supplement), Clogher, Derry, Down, Ferns, Ossory, Raphoe* (1911–48).

Leslie, J.B., *Clergy of Connor from Patrician Times to the Present Day* (W.N.C. Barr, ed., Belfast, 1993).

Leslie, J.B., *Clergy of Derry and Raphoe* (D.W.T. Crooks and F. Fawcett, eds, Belfast, 1999).

Leslie, J.B., *Clergy of Down and Dromore* (J.F. Rankin, ed., Belfast, 1996).

Leslie, J.B., *Clergy of Dublin and Glendalough* (Wallace, W.J.R., ed., Belfast, 2001).

Lodge, J., *Obits.*

Lodge, J., *The Peerage of Ireland* (Mervyn Archdall, ed., 7 vols, Dublin, 1789).

Mant, R., *History of the Church of Ireland* (2 vols, London, 1840).

Meissner, J.L.G., *History of the Church of Ireland* (W.A. Phillips, ed.), 1933.

O'Connell, P., *The Diocese of Kilmore: Its History and Antiquities* (Dublin, 1936).

Rennison, W.H., *Succession List of the Bishops, Cathedral and Parochial Clergy of the Dioceses of Waterford and Lismore* (Waterford, 1920).

Seymour, St J.D., *The Succession of Parochial Clergy in the United Diocese of Cashel and Emly* (Dublin, 1908).

Sirr, *A Memoir of the Honorable and Most Reverend Power Le Poer Trench, Last Archbishop of Tuam* (Dublin, 1845).

Swanzy, H.B., *Succession Lists of the Diocese of Dromore* (Belfast, 1933).

Theiner, *Vetera Monumenta Hibernorum et Scotorum, 1216–1547* (folio, Rome, 1864).

Ware, J., 'Bishops' in *Whole Works of Sir James Ware* (Dublin, 1739).*

Watt, J., *The Church in Medieval Ireland* (Dublin, 1972).

Webster, C.A., *The Diocese of Ross: Its Bishops, Clergy and Parishes* (Cork, 1936).

PARISH HISTORIES

Bradley, T., *Manorhamilton Parish Church: Glimpses of Our History, 1783–1983* (Cavan, 1983).

Combe, J.C., *St Fethlimidh's Cathedral, Kilmore: A Short History*.

Durand, S., *Drumcliffe: the Church of Ireland Parish in its North Sligo Setting* (Manorhamilton, 2002).

Gamble, W., *History of Killougher Parish Co. Cavan*.

Sloane, N.J., *A History of Lough Gowna Parish Church* (Loch Gowna, 2001).

UNPUBLISHED MANUSCRIPTS

Fitzgerald, G., Biographical Additions to Canon Leslie's Succession Lists for Kilmore, Elphin and Ardagh –1947.

Leslie, J.B., Succession Lists of the Clergy of Achonry, Ardagh, Connor, Elphin, Kildare, Killala, Killaloe, Kilmore, Leighlin, Limerick, Meath, Tuam (Representative Church Body Library, Dublin) [Leslie's MSS].

Willis, G., Supplements to Canon Leslie's Succession Lists for Ardfert and Aghadoe, Ardagh, Armagh, Clogher, Derry, Elphin, Ferns, Kilmore, Ossory and Raphoe; Supplements to Cole's Lists for Cork, Cloyne and Ross; Supplements to Rennison's Lists for Waterford and Lismore.

MANUSCRIPTS

British Museum Manuscripts [BM MSS].

Calendar of Carte Papers.

Commonwealth Papers (the principal authorities used for the period 1649–60. Particulars concerning them are to be found in the 13th Report of the Deputy Keeper (1881). They include: (1) names and salaries of the ministers of religion; (2) issues of money to same out of tithe, etc; (3) Crown rental of tithes, etc.)

Collections of Depositions of Persons who Suffered during the 1641 Rebellion (Library of Trinity College, Dublin).

Diocesan Registers 1700–, Containing Records of Institutions, Consecrations, Ordinations, etc [DR].

First Fruit Rolls and Transcripts, Containing a Yearly Return of the First Fruits Payable into the Exchequer since the Reformation by Bishops and Clergy. (Some rolls have been lost, but a transcript of them is in existence. Similar particulars are supplied also by Bishops' Returns and in some cases by Hanaper Rolls) [FF].

Hood, S., Abbreviations Used in the Clerical Succession Lists of the Church of Ireland.

Lodge MSS: Succession Lists of Armagh Clergy, Brought Up to Date by Bishop Reeves and Precentor Morgan, LLD.

Royal Visitations: Visitations of the Clergy Made for the Crown [RV].

Seymour, St J.D, Archdeacon of Cashel, Notes Relating to Commonwealth Ministers of the Gospel, Extracted from the Commonwealth Records in the Public Records Office (now destroyed) [Seymour's MSS].

Visitation Books, Containing Particulars of Returns Made by the Rural Deans at the Bishops' Visitations 1690–1870 [VB].

GOVERNMENT PUBLICATIONS, STATE PAPERS

Annals of Loch Cé [Ann Loch Cé].

Annals of Ulster (5 vols, Dublin) [Ann Ult].

Liber Munerum Publicorum Hiberniae (2 vols, folio) [LM].

Morrin, J., ed., *Calendar of the Patent and Close Rolls of Chancery in Ireland, 1514–1603, 1625–1633* (3 vols, Dublin, 1861–1863).

Patent Rolls of James I (folio, Dublin, n.d., unpublished) [PR].

Subscription Rolls [SR].

Parliamentary Returns (consisting of returns of various kinds made to the Irish Parliament) [Parl Ret].

Third Report of His Majesty's Commissioners on Ecclesiastical Revenue and Patronage in Ireland, 1836.

SERIAL PUBLICATIONS

Annual Reports of the Deputy Keeper, Public Records of Ireland, Dublin 1869–1910, including:

Calendar of Early Pipe Rolls.

Calendar of Fiants, Henry VIII–Elizabeth I [F Henry VIII; F Eliz I; F Ed VI].

Rolls Series:

Calendar of Documents Relating to Ireland/State Papers Relating to Ireland, 1509–1670 (24 vols, London, 1860–1912) [CDI].

Calendar of Papal Letters [CPL].

Calendar of Papal Petitions [CPP].

Calendar of Papal Registers [CPR].

Calendar of Patent Rolls of England [CPRE].

Calendar of Patent Rolls of Ireland [CPRI].

Calendar of State Papers, Ireland (various issues) [CSPI].

Calendar of the Carew Papers/Manuscripts Preserved in the Archiepiscopal Library at Lambeth, 1515–1524 (6 vols, London, 1867–73) [Carew MSS].

Calendar of the Register of George Cromer, Archbishop of Armagh 1522–39 [Cal Reg Cromer].

Calendar of the Register of George Dowdall, Archbishop of Armagh 1543–58 [Cal Reg Dowdall].

Calendar of the Register of John Mey, Archbishop of Armagh 1444–56 [Cal Reg Mey].

Calendar of the Register of John Prene, Archbishop of Armagh 1439–43 [Cal Reg Prene].

Calendar of the Register of John Swayne, Archbishop of Armagh 1418–39 [Cal Reg Swayne].

Calendar of the Register of Milo Sweetman, Archbishop of Armagh 1361–80 [Cal Reg Swet].

Calendar of the Register of Nicholas Fleming, Archbishop of Armagh 1404–16 [Cal Reg Flem].

Calendar of the Register of Octaviano [Cal Reg Octav].

GENERAL LITERATURE

Costello, A.M., *De Annatis Hiberniae: a Calendar of First Fruit Fees Levied on Papal Appointments to Benefices in Ireland, A.D. 1400 to 1535* (Dundalk, 1909) [AH].

King's Letters [K Lett].

O'Donovan, J. (ed.), *Annals of the Four Masters* (5 vols, 1848–51) [AFM].

Suffering Loyalists Lists [Suff Loy Lists].

NEWSPAPERS, PERIODICALS, JOURNALS AND OTHER ARTICLES

Church of Ireland Gazette [CIG].

Irish Ecclesiastical Gazette [IEG].

Journal of the Royal Society of Antiquaries of Ireland [JRSAI].

London Magazine.

The Scribe (Kilmore, Elphin and Ardagh Diocesan Magazine).

O'Ferrall, F., 'Rev George Brittaine (1788–1848): Rector of Kilcommick and Novelist'.

Refaussé, R., 'Church of Ireland Clerical Succession Lists and their Compilers'.

*This is the first of the two volumes of Walter Harris's edition of the *Whole Works of James Ware*, originally in Latin. Two editions were published, in 1739 and 1764, the latter being a mere reissue not brought up to date. Besides plates in the text, there are 18 full-page engravings chiefly of the cathedrals c 1739. The book has copious information about bishops only down to 1739.

PARISHES OF KILMORE, ELPHIN AND ARDAGH
WITH LISTS OF CLERGY

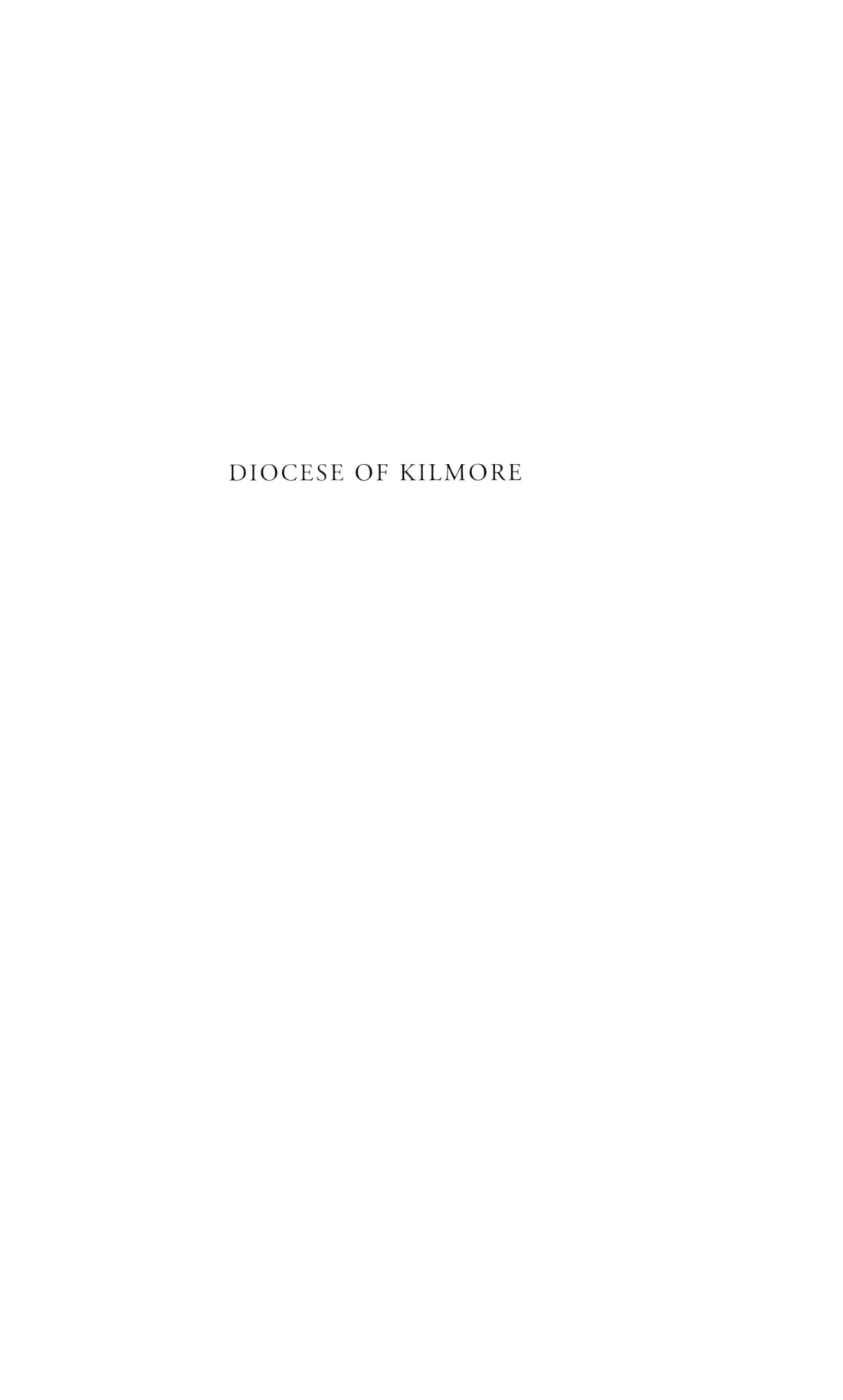

DIOCESE OF KILMORE

THE DIOCESE OF KILMORE

BISHOPS OF KILMORE

–1136	HUGH O'FINN
1136–1149	MURTOUGH O'MULMOCHERY
1149–1179	TUATHAL O'CONNAGHTY
1179–1231	FLANN O'CONNAGHTY
1231–c. 1250	CONGHALACH MACIDHNEOIL
1251–1285	SIMON O'ROURKE (O'RUAIRC)
1286–1307	MAURICE
1307–1314	MATTHEW MACGWENEY (MACDUIBHNE)
1314–1328	PATRICK O'CRIDAGAIN
1328–1355	CORNELIUS McCONAMA (McKINAWE)
1356–1369	RICHARD O'REILLY
1369–c. 1393	JOHN O'REILLY*
1389–1393	THOMAS DE RUSHOOK*

* John O'Reilly got into trouble with the authorities and Thomas de Rushook seems to have held the see alongside him. Leslie and O'Connell give varying dates for the 14th century bishops.

NICHOLAS MACBRADY+

+ These dates are given in O'Connell. Leslie has 1394 and his successors John and David O'Reilly in 1401 and 1409.

1401	JOHN O'REILLY (O'RAGYLICH)
1409	DAVID O'FARRELLY
1421–1444	DONATUS O'GOWAN
1444–1455	ANDREW MACBRADY
1455–1465	THADY MAGNWIN (? McGOWAN) (O'Connell)
–1464	FEARSITHE MACDUIBHNE (McGIVNEY) (not in O'Connell's list)
1465–1476	JOHN O'REILLY
1476	CORMAC MAGAURAN
1480–1511	THOMAS MACBRADY
1512–1529	DERMOT O'REILLY
1530–1550	EDMUND NUGENT — deposed 1540 (O'Connell)

The See remained vacant for over 30 years. Richard Brady who had been Roman bishop in 1584 and had intruded into the See was deprived of his usurped position by Sir John Perrott. Mant, *History of the Church of Ireland,* I, 130, quotes a letter of Sir John Perrott dated evidently about 1584 stating, "that of late there was a lewd friar come from Rome as a delegate of the Pope's who usurped (the See) dispensing abroad seditious bulls… that he (Sir John) had dispossessed him", and now recommended Sir John Garvey for the bishopric.

1584/85–90   JOHN GARVEY

The See was vacant and was in commission to Rev Edward Edgeworth, Prebend of Christ Church and St Patrick's Cathedral Dublin, 1589, but it appears that Miler Magrath, Archbishop of Cashel, was granted the See with Waterford by Patent, 19 December 1592, and he resigned it 22 February 1607 (C.P.R. James I, 106a). Query, is 1607 correct? On 15 July 1593, Archbishop Garvey recommended William Hughes, MA for it, (C.S.P.I. 1st series v. 127), and on 25 June 1596, Walter Chatfyld applied for it, (ib. 541).

1603/04–1612	ROBERT DRAPER
1612–1628/29	THOMAS MOIGNE
1629–1641/42	WILLIAM BEDELL
1643–1672	ROBERT MAXWELL
1672/73–1681	FRANCIS MARSH
1681/82–1693	WILLIAM SHERIDAN
1693–1698/99	WILLIAM SMYTH
1699–1713	EDWARD WETTENHALL
1714–1727	TIMOTHY GOODWIN
1727-1741	JOSIAH HORT
1757-1772	JOHN CRADOCK
1772-1774	DENISON CUMBERLAND
1775-1790	GEORGE LEWIS JONES
1790–1796	WILLIAM FOSTER
1796-1801	Hon CHARLES BRODRICK
1802–1841	GEORGE DE LA POER BERESFORD
1841–1854	JOHN LESLIE
1854–1862	MARCUS GERVAIS BERESFORD
1862–1870	HAMILTON VERSCHOYLE
1870	CHARLES LESLIE
1870–1874	THOMAS CARSON
1874–1884	JOHN RICHARD DARLEY
1884–1897	SAMUEL SHONE

1897–1915	ALFRED GEORGE ELLIOTT
1915–1930	WILLIAM RICHARD MOORE
1930–1939	ARTHUR WILLIAM BARTON
1939–1950	ALBERT EDWARD HUGHES
1950–1955	FREDERICK JULIAN MITCHELL
1956–1958	CHARLES JOHN TYNDALL
1959–1981	EDWARD FRANCIS BUTLER MOORE
1981–1993	WILLIAM GILBERT WILSON
1993–2000	MICHAEL HUGH GUNTON MAYES
2000–	KENNETH HERBERT CLARKE

Sees of Ardagh and Kilmore united 1839
Sees of Elphin and Kilmore united 1841 to form the United Dioceses of Kilmore, Elphin and Ardagh

CHAPTER OF KILMORE

DEANS OF KILMORE

–1325	THOMAS O'COINDERE (O'CONNERY)
1366	ADAM McTIERNAN
1369	——O'BARDAIN
1375	LUKE
1426	ANDREW
–1446	DONATUS O'GOWAN (O'GOBAND)
1446	LAURENCE O'FARRELLY
1446	THOMAS O'GOWAN (O'GOBAND, YGOBAND)
–1460	ANDREW O'SHERIDAN (O'SIRIDEAN)
1460	JOHN O'GOWAN (O'GOBAND)
1469	CORMAC O'SYRIDEAN
–1590	——JORDAN
–1619	THOMAS ROBINSON
1619–1627	JOHN HILL
1627–1637	NICHOLAS BERNARD
1637-1645	HENRY JONES
c. 1645–1661	LEWIS DOWNES
1661–c. 1664	JOHN WALWOOD
1664–1691	EDWARD DIXIE
1691–1700	ENOCH READER
1700	RICHARD READER

1700–1734   JEREMIAH WILLIAM MARSH
1734/35–1751   JOHN MADDEN
1751–1765   Hon HENRY MAXWELL
1765–1768   CHARLES AGAR
1768–1796   THOMAS WEBB
1796–1801   GEORGE DE LA POER BERESFORD
1801–1825   WILLIAM MAGENNIS
1825–1860   HENRY VESEY FITZGERALD
1860–1870   THOMAS CARSON
1870–1886   JOHN MAUNSELL MASSY BERESFORD
1886–1912   WILLIAM HENRY STONE
1913–1926   ISAAC COULTER
1926–1931   ALBERT EDWARD KING
1931–1955   WILLIAM JAMES ASKINS
1955–1965   FREDERICK WILLIAM GRANT
1965–1985   ROBERT CHRISTOPHER HOWARD TURKINGTON
1985–1989   HERBERT CASSIDY
1990–1996   JOHN CHARLES COMBE
1997-2004   DAVID SAMUEL GEORGE GODFREY
2005–   WALLACE RAYMOND FERGUSON

ARCHDEACONS OF KILMORE

–1296   MAOL-PETER O'DUIGENAN
–1343   JOHN McDUIBHNE
–1368 or 1369 MURRAY O'FARRELLY
–1409   THOMAS
1436   THOMAS O'SHERIDAN (O'SIRIDEAN)
1436   ANDREW MACBRADY
1444/45   EUGENE O'RAHILLY (O'RAGILLACH)
1474   THOMAS MACBRADY
–1538   PATRICK MACBRADY
1538   ANDREW MACBRADY
–1622   WILLIAM ANDREWES
1638–1661   THOMAS PRICE
1661–1662/63   ALEXANDER MARTIN
1663–1678   AMBROSE BARCROFT
1678–1684   ROBERT WILSON
1684–1690   ISAAC COLLYER
1691–1739/40   MATTHEW HANDCOCK
1740–1745   WETTENHALL SNEYD
1745–1767   JOSEPH STORY

1768–1770	ARTHUR MOORE
1770–1776	WILLIAM CRADOCK
1776–1816	JOHN CAULFIELD
1816–1866	Hon JAMES AGAR
1866–1878	JOHN CHARLES MARTIN
1878–1884	SAMUEL SHONE
1884–1899	WILLIAM CREEK
1899–1910	JAMES McCREIGHT JACKSON
1910–1923	JOSEPH MAYNE
1923–1932	MATTHEW JOHN PORTEUS
1932–1943	ERNEST ALFRED KILLINGLEY
1943–1965	HENRY WILLIAM SHIRE
1965–1971	JOHN RUTHERFORD ENNIS
1972–1987	GUY NEWELL CAVE
1987–1989	GEORGE CHARLES ALEXANDER MILLER
1989–2003	WILLIAM DEREK JOHNSTON
2003–	GEORGE THOMAS WILLIAM DAVISON

CANONS OF KILMORE
whose Prebends or parishes are unidentified

1442	JOHN O'MULMOCHERY
1450	DAVID O'TARPA
1453	PATRICK MACCONCAING (MACCONAI(Y)NG)
1453	ANDREW MACBRADY
1454	JOHN O'GOBAND
1455	TERENCE O'CARBRY
1455	JOHN MAGAMRAN
1455	FERGAL O'FERGUSSA
1456	DERMIT O'MITHYAN
1457	JOHN O'GOBAND
1457	MALACHY MACBRADY
1458	THOMAS O'SYREDAN
1458/59	CORNELIUS MACHLACHLAND O'RUAYRC
1459	CORNELIUS MACLACLAYND
1459	JOHN O'MULMOCHERY
1460	MAURICE OMALMOCHORY
1460	TERENCE ORAGYLLYG
1460	JOHN MACMAEMLARTAYN
c. 1461	GEOFFREY MACBRADY
1461	DONALD O'FLAYN
1461	MAGONIUS MEGUYBENE (?McGORNEY)

1461	JOHN O'GOBAND
1461	NEMEAS O'DROMA
1461	CORMAC O'SIRIDEAN (O'SHERIDAN, O'SYRIDEAN)
1461	ANDREW O'SIRIDEAN
1464	THOMAS O'SIRIDEAN
c. 1465	WILLIAM O'FERGUSA
1465	ENEAS O'DROMA
1466	JOHN McCULMARTAYN
c. 1488	ARTHUR MACCONRICH
c. 1495	THOMAS McBRIDE (MEGBRYD)
1502	ADAM OFFEGAYD
1530	LOUIS DROMA
1540	FELIM O'LINNOCHORE
1557	EUGENIUS O'GOBAN
1557	CORNELIUS O'CORVAN

Canons of Kilmore, or Prebendaries of Annagh, Drumlease and Triburnia in St Fethlimidh's Cathedral, Kilmore, first appear in the 1935 Church of Ireland Directory.

PREBENDARIES OF ANNAGH

1935–1942	WILLIAM McALISTER
1942–1944	JOHN HERBERT JACKSON
1944–1956	WILLIAM BRADFIELD
1956–1957	WILLIAM GAMBLE
1957–1964	JOHN JAMES JENNINGS
1965–1972	HENRY IRVINE KEYS ANDERSON
1972–1983	JOHN RICHARD WHEELOCK
1983–1985	CHARLES LUDWIG BIRBECK HILL MEISSNER
1985–1989	WILLIAM DEREK JOHNSTON
1989–2006	JAMES ROBERT SIDES

PREBENDARIES OF DRUMLEASE

1935–1941	WILLIAM ALCORN MacDOUGALL
1941–1949	FREDERICK WILLIAM GRANT
1949–1956	JOHN HENRY McBRIEN
1957–1965	ROBERT CHRISTOPHER HOWARD TURKINGTON
1965–1973	WILLIAM JOHN MITCHELL

1973–1977	ALEXANDER WOODSIDE SCOTT
1977–1987	GEORGE CECIL ALEXANDER MILLER
1987–1988	WILLIAM EDWARD RICHARD GARRETT
1988–1997	JOHN ROBERT THOMAS WATSON
1998–2002	ROBERT GORDON KEOGH
2002–2003	GEORGE THOMAS WILLIAM DAVISON
2003–2004	SUSAN MARGARET PATTERSON
2004-	vacant

PREBENDARIES OF TRIBURNIA

1935–1943	HENRY WILLIAM SHIRE
1943–1949	CHARLES EDWARD KEANE
1949–1959	SAMUEL CARTER ARMSTRONG
1959–1971	ROBERT ERNEST TRENIER
1971–1979	GEORGE GARNETT WARRINGTON
1979–1998	ROBERT SAMUEL PAYNE RICHEY
1998–	MARK ROBERT LIDWILL

At the Disestablishment of the Church of Ireland in 1870, each Diocesan Group was allocated a Prebend of the National Cathedral of St. Patrick in Dublin. The holder of the Prebend at the time usually held his Prebend until he retired or died, and then a clergyman in each Diocese was awarded a Prebend of St. Patrick's Cathedral. Kilmore, Elphin and Ardagh were allocated the Prebend of Mulhuddart, which became available upon the death of the Rev. Canon George Ayres in 1882.

PREBENDARIES OF MULHUDDART
in St. Patrick's Cathedral, Dublin

1882–1889	WILLIAM HENRY STONE
1889–1897	ALFRED GEORGE ELLIOTT
1898–1904	FRANCIS BURKE
1904–1921	ROBERT WALLACE BOYD
1922–1927	ALBERT EDWARD KING
1927–1944	WILLIAM FLANNERY
1944–1949	JOHN HERBERT JACKSON
1949–1955	FREDERICK WILLIAM GRANT
1955–1965	JOHN RUTHERFORD ENNIS
1965–1972	GUY NEWELL CAVE
1972–1979	HENRY IRVINE KEYS ANDERSON

1979–1982	GEORGE GARNETT WARRINGTON
1983–1994	THOMAS PATRICK SCARBOROUGH WOOD
1994–1998	ROBERT SAMUEL PAYNE RICHEY
1998–2001	IAN GALLAGHER
2001–2004	DAVID SAMUEL GEORGE GODFREY
2005–	JANET MARGARET CATTERALL

DIOCESAN CURATES OF KILMORE, ELPHIN AND ARDAGH

1906–1908	BERNARD FREDERICK GOOD
1908–1910	JAMES FERGUSON ANDERSON
1910–1912	JOHN ORR
1912	SAMUEL RICHARD MILLER
1913–1921	GEORGE INGHAM
1922–1925	ISAAC HILL MCCOMBE
1925–1928	ARTHUR REGINALD BURRISS
1928–1929	JOHN CRAWFORD TROTTER
1930–1931	WILLIAM GEORGE COLEMAN
1931–1932	WILLIAM KELLY
1932–1939	BENJAMIN NORTHRIDGE
1939–1940	JOHN CLAUDIUS WILLIAM BERESFORD
1940–1945	JOHN ALEXANDER MONTGOMERY
1946–1954	RICHARD ALBERT ROBINSON

THE DIOCESE OF KILMORE

PARISHES OF KILMORE

*denotes Mediaeval and long-obsolete parishes

Annagelliffe
Annagh
Arvagh
Ashfield

Bailieborough and Moybologue
Ballaghmeehan
Ballineanthowal*
Ballintemple
Ballyjamesduff
Ballymachugh
Billis

Carrigallen
Castlerahan
Castleterra
Clonlogher*
Cloonclare
Cloverhill
Columbkille
Corrawallen
Culbrydyn and Sendamar*
Cuylofflynd*

Denn
Derryheen
Derrylane
Disert Finchill*
Dowra
Drumaloor
Drumgoon, Dernakesh Chapel of Ease
Drumlane
Drumlease
Drumreilly
Drung

Enga*

Fignsaidin*
Finner

Gowna

Innismagrath

Kedy*
Kildallon
Kildrumferton
Killan (see Shercock)
Killargue
Killasnett, Lurganboy Chapel of Ease
Killegar
Killeshandra
Killesher, Druminiskill Chapel of Ease
Killesherdoney
Killinagh
Killinkere
Killoughter
Kilmore
Kiltyclogher
Kinawley, Crom District Chapel
Knockbride

Larah
Lavey
Loughan
Lurgan

Moybologue, see Bailieborough
Mullagh
Munterconnaught

Newtowngore

Oughteragh or Outragh

Quivvy

Rossinver

Shercock
Swanlinbar

Teallacheach and Mageangady*
Templeport
Tomregan

Urney

Yniscayn*

ANNAGELLIFFE

RECTORS
1407   Odo Macbradaich
1466   John McCulmartayn

RECTOR and VICAR
−1626   Robert Whiskens

VICAR
1637   William Bayley (Baylie)

NOTES
The parish seems to have been united to Urney from 1661. The church was closed about 1976.

Annagh, Belturbet, Co Cavan

ANNAGH

VICARS
1407	Nemeas O'Fahy (Offeagaid)
–1449	Patrick O'Higgegan
–1449/50	Patrick O'Bigeon
1449/50	Thomas Magrachan
1449/50	Adam O'Fahy (Ofegaich)
1470	Thomas O'Fahy (Offegayd)
1617	William Andrews
1635–1637	James Margetson
1637–1640	Godfrey Rhodes
1640–1661	John Hodson
1653	John Read (Commonwealth Minister)
1655	Eber Birch (Commonwealth Minister)
1661–1673	William Hodson
1673–1690	Robert Robinson
1690–1709	Robert Maxwell
1709–1747	John Richardson
1747–1765	Henry Maxwell
1765–1768	Charles Agar
1768–1796	Thomas Webb
1797–1798	Henry Wynne
1798–1811	Henry Maxwell
1811–1835	Richard Wynne
1835–1868	Andrew William McCreight
1868–1880	Thomas James Jackson
1880–1910	James McCreight Jackson
1910–1925	Bernard Frederick Good
1925–1929	Andrew William McvGarvey
1929–1932	Matthew John Porteus
1932–1944	James Poyntz
1944–1956	Edward Morgan Griffin

1956–1983	John Richard Wheelock	1891–1894	William Siers
1984–1999	William Derek Johnston	1894–1897	William Alcorn McDougall
1999–2003	vacant	1898–1901	Charles Arthur Rainsford
2003–2006	Eric Robert Glenn West	1901–1904	Arthur Reginald Burriss
2007–	Stephen Kenneth Clark	1904–1907	William Ashton Campion
		1907–1910	William Henry Porteus

CURATES

1641	Thomas Oge Brady	1911–1912	Thomas Hutchinson Martin
1661	William Hodson	1912–1914	Walter Bothwell
1673	David McQuaine	1915–1918	James John Lougheed
1745	Andrew Irvine	1919–1923	Edgar Parker Mills
–1754	John Smyth	1925–1926	James Wilson Wright
1754	Andrew Nixon	1927–1930	William John Mitchell
1774	John Gumley	1930–1932	Robert William Wolfe
–1780	Brinsley Nixon	1933–1934	W. Bolton Battersby
1797	Henry Woodward	1934–1937	Cecil Maurice Kerr
–1811	Norman Garstin	1937–1940	Robert Christopher Howard Turkington
1824	J. Hearn	1940–1942	Arthur Hugh Thompson
1830	William Hearn	1942–1944	Thomas James Bond
c. 1843	Henry Monk Winder	1987–1990	Mark Robert Lidwill
1846–1849	James Godley	1990–1993	Ian Gallagher
c. 1850	James Michael Henry Strangways	1993–1996	Peter Dawson Thornbury
1855–1858	William Wallace	1996–1998	Eileen Catherine O'Reilly
1858–1860	William Wallace		
1858–1865	George A. Johnson		
1860	Walter Vandeleur Dudgeon		
1860	Joseph Carson Moore		
1861–1865	Graham Craig		
1865–1869	James McCreight Jackson		

with Quivvy 1912–1986
with Drumaloor 1924–
with Cloverhill 1975–
with Drumgoon, Dernakesh, Ashfield and Killesherdoney 1987–1998
with Drumlane 1991–

NOTES

The Patron was St Mochonna of Earnaidhe. The Glebe house was purchased 1810. The church was very old, and was improved and enlarged in 1813 and 1828 with a loan from the Board of First Fruits.

Arvagh, Co Cavan

ARVAGH

PERPETUAL CURATES/RECTORS		
c. 1819	Richard Lyde	
1822	Andrew William McCreight	
1826–1827	Henry Dalton	
1835–1852	John Taylor	
1853–1871	Peter Henry Schoales	
1873–1874	Robert Leech	
1873–1881	William Noblett	
1881–1890	Thomas Samuel Chapman	
1890–1895	Edwin Barry Christie	
1895–1910	Thomas Vigogne Faussett	
1910–1916	William Henry Porteus	
1917–1920	James Williamson Camier	
1921–1941	William Alcorn McDougall	
1941–1953	John William Clements	
1954–1977	Alexander Woodside Scott	
1978–1981	David Brian Wilson	
1982–1997	John Robertson Thomas Watson	
1999–2002	James Christopher Healey	
2006–	George William Browne, P-in-c	

CURATES		
c. 1830	Edward Nangle	
1850–1852	Peter Henry Schoales	

with Carrigallen 1921–
with Gowna, transferred from Ardagh Diocese, 1959–
with Columbkille, transferred from Ardagh Diocese, 1977–

NOTES
Established as Perpetual Curacy out of Killeshandra Parish *c.* 1819. The Church was built in 1821, and cost £803 15s 4½d British.

Ashfield, Co Cavan

ASHFIELD, CO CAVAN

PERPETUAL CURATES/RECTORS
c. 1795–1808	Benjamin Adams
c. 1810–1824	Joseph Welsh (Walsh)
1825–1828	Robert Thomas Bell
1828–1848	John Harris
1849–1861	James Godley
1862–1865	Henry George John Clements
1866–1872	Lewis Richards
1873–1906	Richard Plummer
1906–1910	Edward George Burland
1910–1931	Thomas Vigigne Fausset
1932–1936	Frederick James Powell
1936–1940	Claud Edward Robert Sinclair C-in-c
1941–1956	Matthew Thomas Porteus
1956–1971	Robert Ernest Trenier
1971–1974	Robert Peel Beresford Mathews
1974–1980	John Alexander Pickering
1982–1985	Peter Tarleton
1987–1998	William Derek Johnston
1998–2000	Eileen Catherine O'Reilly BC
2000–	vacant

CURATE
1808–1810   Joseph Walsh
see also Annagh and Drumgoon

NSM
1996–1998   Eileen Catherine O'Reilly
2000–   Richard William Stafford

with Drumgoon and Dernakesh 1942–
with Killesherdoney 1972–
with Annagh, Drumaloor and Cloverhill 1987–1998

NOTES
Certain townlands of Killersherdiney Parish were erected into Perpetual Curacy of Ashfield on 21st May 1795. The church was built 1796–1800 and consecrated 'on a Sunday in July 1800'. A Perpetual Curacy was endowed 9 Oct 1860 and a Faculty was granted to improve the church on 24th April and 14th November 1861.

Bailieborough, Co Cavan

BAILIEBOROUGH

RECTORS and VICARS

1542	Patrick Magerrigan
1619–1631	George Creighton
1631–1640/41	Terence Comyne (Connell)
1640/41–*c.* 1661	Manus McAuley
1661–1663	Patrick Maxwell
1663–1669	Herbert Ferris
1669–1682	Patrick Maxwell
1682–1697	Andrew Charlton
1697–1745	William Brookes
1745–1752	Ralph Grattan
1752–1773	William Cosby
1773–1778	John Handcock
1778–1808	John Brougham
1808–1837	John Gumley
1837–1848	Charles Claudius Beresford
1848–1861	Frederick Fitzpatrick
1862–1868	Thomas James Jackson
1868–1878	Andrew Todd Gillmor
1878–1898	William Henry Hutchinson
1898–1900	Arthur John Pike

1900–1907	John Claudius Beresford
1907–1925	William Philip Lowe
1925–1928	William Thomas Stewart
1928–1931	Robert James Charters
1931–1936	Robert Warrington
1936–1947	John Rutherford Ennis
1947–1955	Robert Christopher Howard Turkington
1955–1960	Thomas James Bond
1960–1975	Allen James Nelson
1975–1988	William Edward Richard Garrett
1991–1995	Denis Francis Wann
1996–2000	Brian Robert Russell
2005–	Alan William Matchett

CURATES

1778	Richard Bull
1799	James Young
1807	Richard Marlay
1826–1847	Thomas Pentland
1849	Joseph King
1850	Frederick Fitzpatrick
1857–1858	Samuel Scott Frackleton
1861	Alfred George Elliott
1862–1869	Digby Samuel Cooke
1870–1871	James William Smith
1870–1873	Albert Charles Fowler
1873–1875	Frederick Fisher
1876–1877	John Wallace Taylor
1877–1879	James Porter

NSM

1993–1997	Alexandra Jane Lindsay
2000–2005	Alexandra Jane Lindsay
2006–	Tanya Joy Woods

with Mullagh 1960–
with Knockbride 1966–
with Shercock 1957– 1960 and 1972–

NOTES

The Meath end of the Parish containing the Church of Moybologue was transferred to Meath Diocese in 1873. The church was built about 1780. The Glebe house was built in 1811 and cost £1,425 4s 7½d. The St Luke window in Bailieborough Church was dedicated in 1964 and a new rectory was dedicated on 26th April 1964.

BALLAGHMEEHAN, CO LEITRIM

Note: Formed out of Rossinver Parish.

VICARS
1857–1873	Alexander Smullen
1873–1897	William Scott
1897–1902	John Richard Gahagan
1903–1926	Edward Flower

with Kiltyclogher 1873–1930
with Killasnett 1930–1962
with Cloonclare 1943–1962
closed *c.* 1962

BALLINEANTHOWAL

RECTOR
–1474   Thady Ofeghalit

Long-obsolete medieval parish.

Ballintemple, Co Cavan, St Patrick

BALLINTEMPLE

VICARS

–1393	Cristin O'Fearllania
–1393	John Macmulmartain
1407	Lazarianus O'Gowan (Ogaband)
–1421	Donatus O'Gowan (Ogaband)
1422	Gillibertus O'Gowan (Ogaband)
–1471	Cormac O'Sheridan (O'Syridean)
1618	John Patrick
1619–1627	John Hill
1627–1637	Nicholas Bernard
1637–1645	Henry Jones
1645–1661	Lewis Downes
1661–c. 1664	John Walwood
1664–1691	Edward Dixie
1691–1700	Daniel Neylan
1700	Richard Reader
1700–1734	Jeremiah William Marsh

1734/35–1751	John Madden
1751–1765	Hon Henry Maxwell
1765–1768	Charles Agar
1768–1796	Thomas Webb
1796–1801	George de la Poer Beresford
1801–1825	William Magenis
1825–1860	Henry Vesey Fitzgerald
1860–1870	Thomas Carson
1872–1875	James Caulfield Willcocks
1875–1900	Edward Potterton
1900–1906	Tooke Johnson Luscombe
1906–1910	William Thomas Stewart
1910–1920	Edward Henry Weir
1920–1930	Robert John Walker
1930–1934	John Bradley Hazley
1934–1947	William Bolton Battersby C-in-c
1947–1950	Henry William Shire C-in-c
1950–1955	William James Askins C-in-c
1955–1985	Robert Christopher Howard Turkington
1986–1989	Herbert Cassidy
1990–1996	John Charles Combe
1997–2004	David Samuel George Godfrey
2005–	Wallace Raymond Ferguson

CURATES

1739–c. 1769	William Sneyd
1769–c. 1777	Thomas Sneyd
1775–	Carncross Cullen
1778	Thomas Sneyd
1788–c. 1827	James Pollock
1831–1847	Stuart Smith
1848–1871	James Caulfield Willcocks

see also Kilmore

with Kilmore 1950–
with Kildallon, Newtowngore and Corawallen 1986–1992
with Killeshandra, Killegar and Derrylane 1992–1996

NOTES

With the exception of Enoch Reader, Dean of Kilmore 1691–1700, Deans were Incumbents from 1619 until Disestablishment 1870. Ballintemple Church was built 1821 with a loan from Board of First Fruits of £1,101 13s 10¼d. The font from Oldcastle Church, Co Meath and was given to Ballintemple 1962. A new organ dedicated 9 Jan 1977.

Ballyjamesduff, Co Cavan

BALLYJAMESDUFF

PERPETUAL CURATES/RECTORS
1831–1840	Christopher Eades
1840–1848	Samuel Henry Lewis
1849–1853	Thomas Watson Skelton
1853–1861	George MacDonnell
1861–1869	George Frederick Stoney
1872–1876	Nathaniel Sneyd Taylor
1876–1878	Alfred George Elliott C-in-c
1878–1901	Francis John Beere
1901–1917	William Flannery
1918–1921	Robert Cooke Birney
1923–1924	John Alexander Pollard C-in-c
1924–1926	Samuel Carter Armstrong

CURATES
1860	Herbert H. Franklin
1866–1868	Charles Dancer Campbell
1869–1870	James Appleyard
1892–1894	William Hamilton Lowry

with Castlerahan 1872–
with Billis 1927–1972 and 1988–1994 qv
with Munterconnaught 1961–1972
with Kildrumferton and Ballymachugh 1972–
with Lurgan 1988–1994

NOTES
Ballyjamesduff was formed as a Perpetual Curacy created 11 Oct 1831 out of parts of Parishes of Lurgan, Castlerahan, Kildrumferton and Denn.

Ballymachugh, Co Cavan, St Paul

BALLYMACHUGH

Transferred from Ardagh 1910.

RECTORS

1910–1912	Henry Bredin Crawford
1912–1922	Thomas Hutchinson Martin
1923–1931	Robert William Gibson C-in-c
1931–1934	William Alexander Russell C-in-c
1934–1943	William James Allcard C-in-c
1943–1945	Thomas Clements C-in-c
1945–1987	Guy Newell Cave C-in-c
1988–1992	Robert George Kingston
1994–1996	Robert Alan Chalmers
1997–2006	James Robert Sides

CURATES
see Kildrumferton
with Kildrumferton 1923–
with Ballyjamesduff 1972–
with Lurgan, Killinkere, Munterconnaught and Billis 1988–1994

Billis, Co Cavan, St Bartholomew

BILLIS

PERPETUAL CURATES/RECTORS

1844–1848	Brent Neville
1848–1896	Walter Cunningham Peyton
1897–1901	William Arthur Shaw
1901–1910	William McAlister
1910–1913	William Wallace
1913–1920	William Thomas Stewart
1920–1921	Vivian William Darling
1921–1933	Hugh Parker Woodhouse
1934–1943	William Alexander Russell
1943–1954	Henry Irvine Keys Anderson
1955–1957	George Charles Alexander Miller
1957–1959	John McCaughan Linnegan BC
1960–1965	Coslett William Charles Quin
1965–1967	Samuel Lindsay McQuoid BC
1968–1971	William Henry McAleese (McLees)
1973–1984	William Derek Johnston
1985–1992	Robert George Kingston
1994–1998	Warren David Nelson

1999–2003   William Derek Johnston
2004–   Craig William Leslie McCauley

CURATE
1894–1897   William Arthur Shaw

NSM
see Lurgan

with Ballyjamesduff and Castlerahan 1927–1972
with Munterconnaught 1961–
with Killinkere and Lurgan 1973–
with Loughan 1974–1975
with Lurgan 1974–
with Kildrumferton, Ballyjamesduff and Ballymachugh 1988–1994

NOTES
Billis Parish was formed as a Perpetual Curacy out of Killinkere, Lavey and Lurgan (Deed dated 27 Mar 1844). A Faculty was granted to enlarge the church on 30th June 1860, and another was granted to improve the church on 29th March 1865.

Carrigallen, Co Leitrim

CARRIGALLEN

RECTORS and VICARS

–1422	Maurice O'Flynn (Offloynd)
1622	John Evatt
1634–c. 1639	Robert Vaux
1639	Walter Fraser
1657	Denis Sheridan
1661–1663	Josias Hollington
1663/64–1698	William Conyngham
1698–1705	Arthur Harris
1705–1752	Peter Lombard
1752–1767	Joseph Story
1768–1769	George Knox
1769–1774	Henry Whyte
1774–1804	James Cottingham
1804–1809	Charles Cobbe Beresford
1809–1866	Hon James Agar

1866–1904	James Godley
1905–1906	Thomas Sutcliffe Humphreys C-in-c
1907–1911	Frederick William Woods C-in-c
1911–1916	John Blaney C-in-c
1916–1921	Edward Aubrey Forster

CURATES

1753	Manley Gore
1766–c. 1768	Arthur Richardson
1799	William Gore
1804	Joseph Borrowes
c. 1825/26	Robert Lloyd
1841–1843	John Meade Hobson
1843	Archibald St George
1847–1856	William James Slacke
1849–1866	Thomas Knott
1899–1902	Ernest Maxwell Carlyle Hughes

with Arvagh 1921–
with Gowna, transferred from Ardagh Diocese 1959
with Columbkille, transferred from Ardagh Diocese 1977

NOTES
Act 9, Queen Anne XII Section 9 ordered a new church to be built at Mogh and to be the Parish Church (LM VI 32). The church was built 1812 with a loan from Board of First Fruits and cost £1,384 12s 3¾d. A Chapel of Ease was built at the expense of John Godley Esq at Killigar. The Glebe was house built in 1819.

Castlerahan, Co Cavan

CASTLERAHAN

RECTORS and VICARS

? 1527	Thomas O'Gowyn
1622	Nicholas Smith
1628	George Creighton
c. 1663	possibly Herbert Ferris
1673–1692	John Aungier
1692–1700	William Hansard
1700–1737/38	Luke Sterling
1737/38–1740	Joseph Caddy
1740–c 1777	William Smith
1777–1781	John Caulfield
1781–1794	Joseph Story
1794–1797	George Cox
1797–1802	Henry Mahon
1802–1813	Henry Maxwell

1813–1860   Henry Vesey Fitzgerald
1860–1871   Andrew Hogg

CURATES
1774–1776   Albert Nesbitt
1774   Thomas Stephens
1774   Thomas Sneyd
1776   James Young
1799   Norman Garstin
1804   Cuthbert Fetherston
c. 1821–*c.* 26   Robert Bell
c. 1825–c 1830 E. Moore
1826–c 1858   James Armstrong
1860–1863   Thomas Biddall Swanzy
1863   Francis Henry Dopping
1864–1866   Orange Sterling Kellett
1866   Robert Gordon Cumming
1867–1868   Alfred Montgomery Walsh
1867–1869   Bedell Stanford
1869–1871   J. Franklin

with Ballyjamesduff 1872–
with Billis 1927–
with Munterconnaught 1961–

NOTES
The Rev William Smith was ordered to rebuild Castlerahan Church at the Triennial Visitation on 24th September 1742. A new church was built about 1775, and a Glebe house in 1918. A Faculty to erect a new church in a more convenient site was granted on 7th February 1862. The new church was consecrated on 3rd April 1864. It was in use for occasional services in 1959 and was closed in the 1970s.

Castleterra, Ballyhaise, Co Cavan

CASTLETERRA

RECTORS and VICARS

–1395	Nicholas Macbrady
1398	Cristinus Macbrady
1398	John Macbrady (Macbradaich)
–1420	Malachy Macbrady
1420	John Macbrady (Macbradaych)
1420–1428	John Magennis (Magangassa)
1428	Philip Macbrady (Magbradaych)
1436	Donatus Magennis (Magamgussa)
–1461	William Macmeol
–1461/62	John Macgmissa
1461/62	Geoffrey Macbrady
1615	Francis Parkes
1625	Thomas Groves
1625	Faithful Teate
1661–1662	Alexander Martin
1662–1663	David Straton
1663–1678	Ambrose Barcroft
1678–1684	Robert Wilson
1684–1690	Isaac Collyer
1690–1740	Matthew Handcock
1740	Wettenhall Sneyd
1740–41/43	Patrick Moore
174– –1774	James Cooksey
1774–1780	John Cooksey
1780–1808	John Brougham
1809–1821	Hon George Gore
1821–1834	Francis Fox
c. 1834–	
c. 1835	Andrew William McCreight
1835–1873	Arthur Knox
1873–1878	Thomas Gloster
1879–1882	Jonathan Christopher Head

1883–1885	John William Frederick Falkiner	1995–2002	Janet Margaret Catterall
1885–1899	William Doran Falkiner Wilkinson	2004–	Raymond Moore P-in-c

CURATES

1899–1901	Joseph Henry Chapman
1901–1907	Henry Paul
1907–1914	John Frederick William Hewitt
1914	Arthur Reginald Burriss
1915–1919	Donald McWatty Hamilton
1919–1921	Aylmer Richard Armstrong
1921–1927	Ernest Alfred Killingley
1927–1933	David Herbert Kelly C-in-c 1927–1931, R 1931–1933
1933–1936	John Rutherford Ennis
1936–1939	Robert William Wolfe
1940–1947	Robert Christopher Howard Turkington C-in-c
1948–1965	Henry William Shire, R Urney C-in-c
1965–1969	George Cecil Alexander Miller
1969–1983	James Gordon Benjamin Roycroft
1983–1993	vacant
1993–1995	George William Butler

1647	John Jones
1673	James Boner
1689	James Goulding (possibly Golden)
1799	Joseph Druitt
1840–c. 1861	Arthur Moneypenny
1861–1862	William Scott
1862–1863	Abraham Hutchinson
1863–1864	Richard Clarke
1864–1865	Richard Alfred Burnett
1866–1867	Matthew Cassan Browne
1867–1870	Alfred Montgomery Walshe
1869–1872	Richard Morris
1876–1877	Alfred Hamilton
1990–1993	George William Butler

AUXILIARY MINISTER

2006–	Roberta Moore

with Urney, Annagelliffe, Denn and Derryheen 1948–1969

with Drung 1958–1960 and 1970–
with Killesherdoney 1969–1972
with Larah and Lavey 1972–
with Killoughter 1975–

NOTES

The parish had aliases, viz Aghaleeduffe alias Ballyhayes alias Ballyhaise. The church was built in 1820 and the Glebe house in 1788. Brockhill Newburgh bequeathed £10 yearly for repairs of the church (PR Oct 1777).

CLONLOGHER

Long-obsolete medieval parish.

VICARS
–1428	Matthew Magglandchayd
1622	William Holliwell
1626	William Bolton
1632–1635	Henry Hathershall
1635	Cormack O'Hogley (possibly Hoghy)

with Cloonclare 1661–

Cloonclare, Manorhamilton, Co Leitrim

CLOONCLARE

VICARS

1401	Thomas O'Sheridan (O'Syridean)
–1412	Cornelius O'Ruairc
1412	William O'Michian
1428	Matthew Magglandchayd
–1441	Tatheus O'Mithian
–1455	Dermit O'Nuthian
1455	William O'Carnean
1456	Dermicius Omychan
1456	William O'Cunean
1622–1625	John Johnson
1625–1636	Matthew Moore
1637–1661	John Coningham
1661–1681	Robert Wasse (Commonwealth Minister 1657–)
1681–1686	Thomas Hardcastle
1686–1698	John Twigge
1698–1721	John Smith
1721–1743	Caulfield Cuffe
1743–1775	Thomas Cuffe

1775–1781	John Caulfield
1781–1792	Hugh Montgomery
1792–1807	Carncross Cullen
1807–1810	William Bushe
1810–1823	John Leahy
1823–1842	Abraham Hamilton
1842–1856	John Hamilton
1856–1868	John Hamilton
1868–1877	Richard Nash Standish
1878–1887	Robert Grierson
1887–1897	Isaac Coulter
1897–1924	Matthew John Porteus
1924–1928	Henry William Shire
1928–1941	Arthur Reginald Burriss
1942–1947	Desmond Charles O'Connell
1947–1971	John Rutherford Ennis
1972–1979	David Samuel George Godfrey
1979–1987	Philip John Knowles
1988–1990	Thomas Percival Robert Kenny
1991–	Christopher James Stevenson BC

Lurganboy Chapel Of Ease, Co Leitrim

CURATES

1738	Thomas Cuffe
–1766	William Fox
1769	John Clarke
1778	William Johnston
1783	Edward Hamilton
1793	Samuel Johnston
c. 1825	John Radcliff
c. 1827	Leo Robinson
1827	George D. Cooke
c. 1840	Richard Athill
1841	John Hamilton
–1843	George Thompson
1858–1868	Julius Strike Hearne
1885–1886	Thomas W. Moulsdale
1886–1887	William Henry Parker
1942–1944	Horace Launcelot Uprichard

NSM

2004–06	Noel Henry Likely Regan

with Clonlogher 1661–
with Kiltyclogher in 19th century
with Killasnett and Ballaghmeehan 1942–
with Drumlease 1972–
with Killenumery 1973–1975
with Lurganboy Chapel of Ease 1987–
with Rossinver and Finner 1992–
with Innismagrath 2002–

NOTES
Cloonclare, Manorhamilton, may have been pre-Reformation Cluainfairth or Cluayn Farcli. A Mandate was granted in 1401 to erect into a benefice certain townlands of Parish of Clachacail (identified by Editor of Papal Letters as Coolkill, now in 'Crosserlough Parish' but may be Cloonclare) and of the Parish of Maydmassa (which may be Killasnett). After the Plantation of 1609, land was granted in mid-Leitrim to Sir Francis Hamilton, who developed the settlement of Manorhamilton in 1621–. Though Hamilton became Presbyterian, the church in Manorhamilton was Church of Ireland. The church of 1637 was replaced by the present church in 1783. Lurganboy Chapel of Ease is a small corrugated iron building which dates from 1860.

Cloverhill, Co Cavan, St John

CLOVERHILL

PERPETUAL CURATES
1860–1861	Walter Vandeleur George Dudgeon
1861–1865	Graham Craig
1867–1873	Henry Ellis Ashe
1873–1877	William Alexander Reynell
1877–1879	Michael Neville Kearney
1879–1883	Henry Taylor
1884–1887	William Warnock Smith
1888–1907	William Philip Lowe
1907–1909	George Ernest Fry
1909–1915	Charles Arthur Rainsford
1915–1930	Frederick William Shorten

with Killoughter as Curacy-in-charge 1930–1974
with Annagh Group 1975–

NOTES

A pastoral district was assigned to St John's, Cloverhill Chapel of Ease out of the Parish of Annagh on 1st November 1860. The Deed of Endowment is dated 4th December 1860, the date of the consecration of Church. The Patron, Miss Saunderson, had endowed it in 1856. Centenary Service held 27 Dec 1956.

Columbkille, Aughnacliffe, Co Cavan, St Thomas

COLUMBKILLE

transferred from Ardagh Diocese to Kilmore Diocese 1977
with Arvagh Group 1977–

Corrawallen, Co Cavan

CORRAWALLEN

PERPETUAL or DISTRICT CURATES
1858–1862   Tobias Gumley Lapiere (La Pierre)
1862–1868   Robert Gumley
1868–1870   Charles Dancer Campbell
1870–   see Newtowngore

with Drumreilly –1959
with Kildallon 1959–
with Swanlinbar, Templeport and Tomregan 2007–

NOTES
A Perpetual Curacy in Drumreilly Parish was established in 1854. Corrawallen Church was erected, and a district was assigned to it on 16th March 1854. The parish was absorbed into Newtowngore in 1870.

CULBRYDYN and SENDAMAR

Long-obsolete medieval parish.

VICARS
–1398   Cristen MacBrady
1398   John MacBrady

RECTORS
1398   Nicholas MacBrady
1398   John MacBrady

NOTES
Cuil Brighdin, the country of the MacBradys, lay in vicinity of the parishes of Drung, Laragh and Castleterra. It was a benefice *sine cura*.

CUYLOFFLYND

Long-obsolete medieval parish.

VICARS
1459/60   Maurice O'Floyn
1459/60   John O'Mulmochory

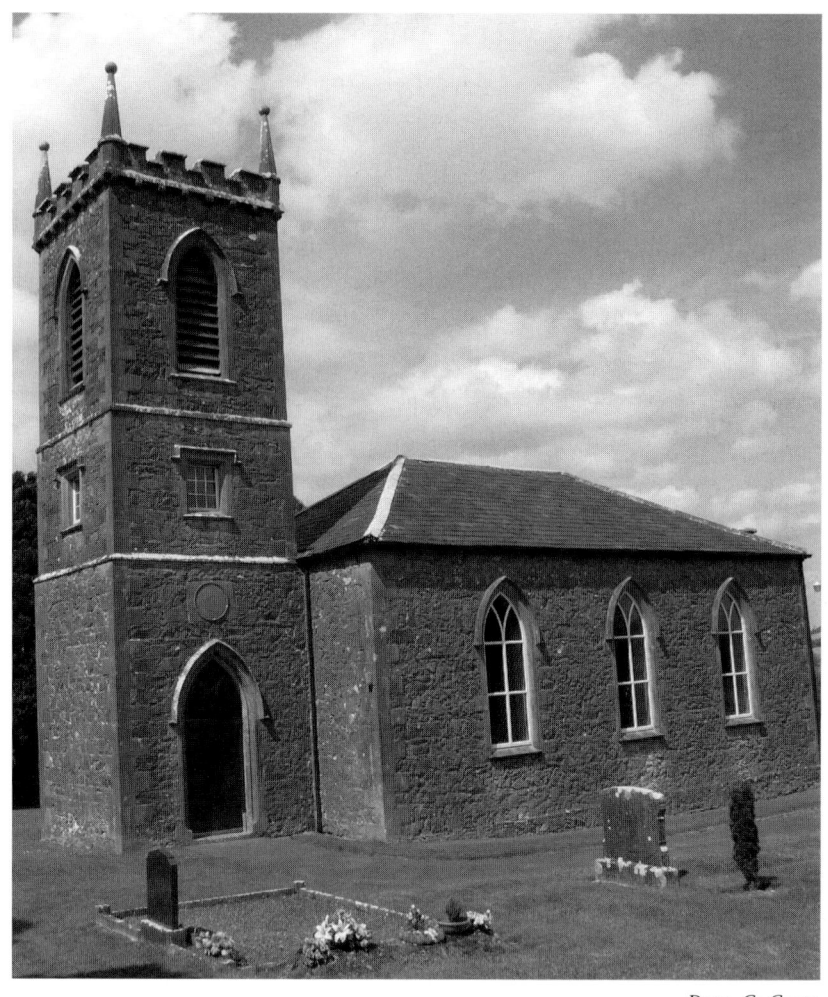

Denn, Co Cavan

DENN

VICARS

1622–1634	Robert Whiskens
1634/35–1637	William Bayly
1637–1640	Alexander Clogy
1640–c 1659	William Wallace
1659–1660/61	John Wallwood
1661–*c.* 1691	Edward Dixie
1691–1700	Daniel Neylan
1700	Richard Reader
1702–1709	Samuel Colby
1709–1726	John Bennett
1726–1740	John Charlton

1740–1776	Arthur Moore
1776–1780	William Fox
1780–1812	Albert Nesbitt
1812–1813	Josiah Erskine
1813–1835	Joseph Druitt
1835–1846	James Collins
1846–1854	Edmund Nugent
1854–1859	Henry Perceval
1859–1860	Henry O'Brien
1860–1877	Samuel Roberts
1877–1878	Dawson Massy
1879–1880	Richard Clarke
1880–1885	Hugh Alexander
1886–1903	Edward Flower
1903–1923	Joseph Mayne C-in-c

CURATES

–1777	Henry Dundas
1800	Hon George Gore
1806	William Grattan
1854	James S Paget
1856–1860	Edward Gabbett
1860–1863	Cornelius Carleton Boomer
1864–1865	John Edge
1865–1867	Edward Montague
1866	— Mussen
1866–1869	John Lyster
1870–1875	Lewis Oliver Bryson
1875–1877	John Gaggin

with Larah and Lavey 1903–1923
with Urney Group 1923–

NOTES

Denn Church was built in 1817, and the Glebe house in 1818. Denn District Chapel of Ease was licensed for marriages on 19th November 1866. The Earl of Westmeath was impropriator of tithes.

Derryheen, Co Cavan

DERRYHEEN

PERPETUAL CURATES
1834–1839	John William Finlay
1839–1842	William Ross Mahon
1842–1862	Thomas James Jackson
1862	George Johnston Schoales
1862–1874	James Moffatt
1876–1877	William Swayne Little
1877–1879	Charles Frederick Archer
1880–1885	Robert Mease
1888–1924	Frederick Staples Atkinson

CURATES
1870–1875	Henry Grattan Moore
1875–1876	Henry William Clarke
1879–1880	Robert Mease
1886–1888	Frederick Staples Atkinson

with Drumaloor –1924
with Urney Group 1924–

NOTES
A Perpetual Curacy was formed out of Kilmore, Drumlane, Castleterra and Annagelliffe Parishes. The deed of the church is dated 6th January 1833. The church was built in 1833/34. A chalice is inscribed 'Derryhean Church 1861' and was given by Garvary Parish to Trory Church, both in Clogher Diocese, 1961. The font came from Loughan Church in 1974.

Derrylane, Co Cavan

DERRYLANE

PERPETUAL CURATES/CURATES IN CHARGE
1831–1864	John Charles Martin (R Killeshandra)
1864–1868	John Whitelaw Schoales
1868–1872	Robert Gumley
1872–1875	Samuel R. Adams
1875–1890	John Johnstone Egan
1890–1902	Henry Gordon
1903–1904	Bernard Frederick Good
1904–1908	Andrew William McGarvey
1908–1911	Robert William Gibson
1911–1920	Frederick William Grant
1921–1925	John Henry MacBrien
1925–1930	Isaac Hill McCombe C-in-c
1930–1942	William John Mitchell
1942–1952	Arthur Hugh Thompson
1953–1955	Samuel James Bell
1955–1965	George Paul Sutcliffe Sythes

RECTORS
1967–1970	Thomas Robert Jennings
1971–1978	George Kingston
1979–1981	James Lewis Wilson
1982–1987	Hugh Gollan Jamieson
1992–1996	John Charles Combe
2000–2004	Graham Thomas Doyle

NSM
1996– 2000	Cecil Lindsay
2006–	Cecil Lindsay

CURATES
1843–1850	Peter Henry Schoales
c. 1847	Matthew Nesbitt Lauder
1852–c 1860	Alexander Nicholls
1860–1864	John Whitelaw Schoales

see also Kilmore
with Killeshandra and Killegar 1968–
with Kilmore and Ballintemple 1992–1996

NOTES
Derrylane Church was built as chapel of ease in Killeshandra Parish and consecrated in 1833. It cost £900 of which Lord Farnham gave £100 and the Board of First Fruits £800. A district was assigned to it as Perpetual Curacy, 25th July 1864.

DISERT FINCHILL

Long-obsolete medieval parish.

VICARS
1403	Cathal O'Kerbalay
1415	Prior of Fore/Sir Donat O'Gown
1424	David McBrady
–1427	David O'Mochan
1428	Philip McBrady
1444	Malachy O'Goband (O'Gowan)
1444	Edmund O'Syridean
–1446	Adam Yfegayd (O'Fary)
1446	John O'Goband (O'Gowan)
1449/50	Gilbert Magawadarh (possibly Maguire)
1491	James Macculmarthayn

RECTORS
–1410	David O'Farrelly
1410	Denis O'Goband
–1424	David McBrady
1426	Philip McBrady
1426	David O'Mochan
1433	Cormac Maconaynd

NOTES
Disert Fincheall can probably be identified with Killesherdoney. Dependency of Abbey of Fore, Co Westmeath.

DOWRA

PERPETUAL CURATES
1854–1860	Charles Lewis Morgan Jones
1860–1871	Stephen Radcliff
1872–1873	Joseph Potter
1873–1876	George Alexander Papendick Arbuthnot
1878–1881	Henry Francis White
1881–1884	William Newton Guinness
1886–1887	Edmund Maturin
1887–1888	Alexander Kenny
1888–1900	John Charles Martin

with Innismagrath 1900–1955 and 1961–1975
with Killinagh and Kiltyclogher 1955–
with Ballaghmeehan and Killargue 1972–
Church closed c 1975

NOTES

A Perpetual Curacy was established out of Innismagrath, Killargue, Killinagh and Drumreilly. The church was built by the Irish Society as a mission church about 1850, and was consecrated on 4th June 1873.

Drumaloor, Co Cavan, St Andrew

DRUMALOOR

PERPETUAL CURATE/CURATES-IN-CHARGE
1869–1892   James McCreight Jackson
1892–1903   Curacy-in-charge, prob with Derryheen
1903–1924   Frederick Staples Atkinson

CURATES
1870–1872   Charles Strong
1872–1903   James Clarke

with Derryheen 1903–1924
with Annagh Group 1924–

NOTES
St Andrew's, Drumaloor was formed as a parish in 1869 out of the endowment of the Rev Andrew McCreight. The church was opened for divine worship in January 1871, and consecrated on 4th June 1875. It was re-opened after extensive redecoration and refurnishing on 14th January 1958.

Drumgoon, Cootehill, Co Cavan, All Saints

DRUMGOON

RECTORS
1366	Nemeas McMulmartyn
1407	Luke Oqueogan
–1417	Philip Macgillayssa
1427/28	David O'Mochan
1432/33	Cormac Maconaind
–1453	Malachy MacBrady

–1453/54	Andrew MacBrady
1453/54	Patrick Macconaing (Macconayng)
1454/55	John Magueran
1454/55	John Macculmarthayn
1455	Andrew Macbrady
1501	Eugene Macbrady
1612	Hugh McCome (McComyn)
1625–1627	Faithful Teate
1627	James Moorhead
1629	Thomas Frasor
1633/34–c. 1660	William Aldrich
1657	Jonathan Edwards, Commonwealth Minister
1660	Alexander Martin
1661–c. 1681	William Aldrich
1681–1683	Michael Arnott
1683–1689	John Archdall
1689–1718	Michael Arnott
1718–1736	John Singleton
1736–1763	Peter Richardson
1763–1770	Francis Lucas
1770–1792	Edward St George

Dernakesh Chapel Of Ease, Co Cavan

1792–1815	Edward Lucas
1815–1826	James Hamilton
1826–1831	Robert Thompson
1832–c. 1850	Archibald Edward Douglas
1850–1866	John Richard Darley
1866–1870	Hugh Murray
1870–1904	Thomas Moore
1904–1931	William Ryland Rainsford Moore
1932–1935	William Kelly
1936–1937	John William Salter
1937–1940	Hugh Maurice Daunt
1941–1956	Matthew Thomas Porteus
1956–1971	Robert Ernest Trenier
1971–1974	Ronald Peel Beresford Mathews
1974–1980	John Alexander Pickering C-in-c
1982–1985	Peter Tarleton
1987–1999	William Derek Johnston
1999–2000	Eileen Catherine O'Reilly BC

CURATES

1729	Michael Lee
1760–1766	William Warren
1770	Colin Young
1799	George Forster
1813	Frederick Fitzpatrick
1819–1835	Henry Lefroy
1820	James Elliott
1821–1825	Robert Staveley (Stavelly)
1824–1829	George Kirkpatrick
1834	James Adams
1835	William Tomlinson
1835–1843	Philip Brabazon
1843	John Maxwell
	Alexander Nicholls
1844	John Maxwell Weir
1847–1851	Thomas Moore
1856–1860	Lewis Richards
1860–1862	Henry Hare
1861–1864	William Shaw Darley
1864–1866	William Robert Laurenson Kinahan
1866–1867	Thomas Kemmis
1866–1870	Thomas Moore
1866	Henry Thomas Symmons
1868–1872	Robert Armstrong
1872–1873	Joseph Morley Dennis, later Swifte-Dennis
1873–1875	John Healy
1875–1877	Thomas W. Fussell
1877–1878	Edward Fitzhardinge Campbell
1878–1880	Henry Wilson Swinburn Given

1880–1881	Edmund M. Rambaut
1881–1882	Alexander Duncan
1882–1885	George Alexander Montgomery
1885–1887	Meyrick Rainsford
1887–1889	Edwin Barrie Christie
1889–1892	Burton Trimnell Turney
1892–1893	Tooke Johnson Luscombe
1893–1895	William Francis Nunan
1895–1896	Samuel Patton Mitchell
1897–1900	John Claude Beresford
1900–1903	John Frederick William Hewitt
1904–1906	Henry Egerton
1907–1909	Humphrey Ellison
1942–1944	John Richard Wheelock
1945–1948	George Norton Dickson
1949–1952	Robert Lumley
1987–1990	Mark Robert Lidwill
1990–1993	Ian Gallagher
1993–1996	Peter Dawson Thornbury
1996–1998	Eileen Catherine O'Reilly

NSM
2000–   Richard William Stafford

with Ashfield 1942–
with Shercock 1966–1972
with Killesherdoney 1972–
with Annagh, Drumaloor and Cloverhill 1987–1998
with Drumlane 1991–1998

NOTES

Dedicated to St Patrick, the ancient name of Drumgoon was *Machaire an Iubair*, plain of the yew trees. Drumgoon is probably Druim Gamhan, the ridge of the calves. In 1766 there were 232 Protestant and 490 RC families in Drumgoon Parish. 'The Church at Cootehill to be the Parish Church' (9 Queen Anne XII Section 13; LM VI 32). 'Parish Church at Cootehill, date unknown. A Chapel of Ease built 1826', probably Dernakesh (Report of 1836), cost £3,223 1s 6½d British, including £369 4s 7½d donation from Bishop. Dernakesh was a Chapel of Ease in Drumgoon Parish, but never a Perpetual Curacy or separate parish. Dernakesh Church was presented with furniture by Knockcrockery Church, Roscommon. A new altar/Communion Table in Drumgoon Parish Church was dedicated on 7th April 1955. The vestry was built by voluntary labour and service of dedication was held on 15th August 1959. The Glebe house was built in 1831, and cost £2,360. The rectory was sold in 1967, and a new rectory was built adjoining the church on a site given by General Eric O'Gowan of Bellamont Castle. The name Cootehill derives from Thomas Coote (died 1671), Governor of Coleraine, who married Frances Hill of Hillsborough.

Drumlane, Co Cavan, St Columba

DRUMLANE

RECTORS (or COARBS)
1366	(Master) William O'Farrelly (Oferallaich)
–1401	Marianus O'Farrelly (Offarchellaych)
–1401	Nicholas O'Farrelly
–1401	William O'Farrely
–1401	Maurice O'Farrelly
1401	David O'Farrelly
1438	Marianus O'Farrelly
1438	Nicholas O'Farrelly

VICARS
–1401	William O'Farrelly
–1401	Maurice O'Farrelly
1401	David O'Farrelly
1612	Nathaniel Hollington
1625	Faithful Teate
1625	Thomas Groves
1634–1661	Thomas Price
1661–1662	Alexander Martin
1663–1665	James Spens
1665–1669	John Bird

1669–c. 1685	Robert Robinson	1948–1950	Ian William McDougall
1685–1740	Charles Rossell	1951–1955	David Murphy
1740–1767	Joseph Caddy	1957–1960	Hugh Maurice Daunt
1767–1773	Peter Lombard	1960–1968	Kenneth Edward Ruddock
1773	William Wade		
1773–1792	Richard Burgh	1968–1972	David Samuel George Godfrey
1792–1810	John Creery		
1810–1821	William Magennis	1973–1980	James Robert Sides
1821–1835	John Isaac Beresford	1983–1986	Cyril George Webb
1835–1836	Charles Claudius Beresford	1991–1999	William Derek Johnston
1837–1842	Guy Percival L'Estrange	2003–2006	Eric Robert Glenn West
1842–1874	George Beatty Moffatt	2007–	Stephen Kenneth Clark
1874–1907	Robert Leech		
1907–1908	Thomas Alexander Beckett C-in-c		

CURATES

1908–1910	Bernard Frederick Good
1767	George Knipe
1911–1920	William AlcornMcDougall
1773	John Gumley
c. 1792–1812	Josiah Erskine
1921–1924	Aylmer Richard Armstrong
–1817	William Montgomery
c. 1824–1830	Thomas Moffett
1925–1927	Frederick Barcroft Worrall
1824 and 1825	George Beatty Moffatt
1928–1932	Percy Harold Richardson C-in-c
1846–1851	Campbell Jamieson
1860–1862	James Moffatt
1932–1934	William John Chambers C-in-c
1862–1866	William Henry Stone
1867–1871	Claude Cregan
1935–1938	John Blaney C-in-c
1938–1941	Matthew Thomas Porteus C-in-c

see also Annagh

with Tomregan 1957–1990
with Annagh Group 1991–

1942–1944	Coslett William Charles Quin C-in-c
1945–1947	Henry Lloyd Phair C-in-c

NOTES

The Augustinian Priory of Drumlane was of great importance in Middle Ages. It was associated with St Mogue but may have been founded by St Columba. Extensive ruins, including a round tower, remain. The Prior of Drumlane stated that the Bishop had restored to the Priory, the Vicarage of Drumlane, which used to be served by them in ancient times, but to which the Bishop had collated a number of secular priests 13th August 1409 (CPL VI 159). A Papal Indulgence for 3 years and 3 quarantines were granted to penitents that gave alms for repair of the Parish Church of St Medocius of Drumlane 7 Dec 1436 (CPL VIII 589). The church was built in 1821. The Glebe house, said to have cost £1,384 12s 3¾d British, was built in 1824. Licence to perform divine service in Killavilly Church in Drumlane Parish was granted on 24th October 1865. The church was renovated in 1965. A stained glass window from Monivea Church in Co. Galway and other gifts were blessed on 22nd June 1965.

Drumlease, Dromahaire, Co Leitrim

DRUMLEASE

VICARS

–1448	Andrew O'Cregan (Ycridagan)
c. 1448	Malachy Otirburyn
1450	Donatus O'Cregan (Ycridagan)
1479	John O'Molmochere
1505	Bartholomew Imitia (Omyan)
–1612	John Bostock
–1622	William Andrews
1633	John Johnson
1661–1674	John Layng
1675–1678	Robert Wilson
1678–1681	John King
1681–1684	Ralph Rule
1684–1686	James Echlin
1686–1699	Robert Whitelaw
1699–1737	William Hansard
1737–1774	Charles Dodd
1774–1808	Roger Dodd
1808–1811	Crinus Irwin
1811–1824	Nicholas Herbert
1824–1834	Hon James Butler
1834–1860	William Willoughby Wynne
1860–1873	Henry Perceval
1873–1878	Joseph Potter
1878–1897	Alfred George Elliott
1897–1926	Isaac Coulter
1927–1932	Ernest Alfred Killingley

1932–1947	Thomas William Coursey
1948–1959	Samuel Carter Armstrong
1959–1962	Frederick Rudolph Mitchell
1962–1967	Henry Lawton
1967–1971	William Edward Richard Garrett
1972–1979	David Samuel George Godfrey
1979–1987	Philip John Knowles
1988–1990	Thomas Percival Robert Kenny
1991–	Christopher James Stevenson BC

CURATES

1763–1766	Roger Dodd
1817	William Walsh
1826	William Walker
1835–1836	Henry Purdon Disney
1838–1847	James O'Connor
1843	John Hudson
1850–1868	Richard Nash Standish
1868–1873	Frederick George McNally
1870–1872	Thomas Richard Conway
1887–1890	Edward Daniel Crowe
1890–1897	John Richard Gahagan
1897	Bedell Stanford
1897–1900	William Walter Peyton
1900–1903	Edward William McFarland
1903–1908	Frederick William Woods
1908–1913	Leopold Andrew Pakenham Walsh Hunter
1913–1916	Richard Ferguson
1917–1923	James Edmund Bennett Ashton
1923–1924	William Arthur Ernest Foley
1924–1925	George Kirwan Birmingham

with Killargue late 1890s
with Killargue *c.* 1905–1926
with Killenumery and Killargue 1955–1972
with Cloonclare, Killasnett and Lurganboy and Killenumery 1972–
with Rossinver and Finner 1992–
with Inismagrath 1955–1961 and 2002–

NOTES

Drumlease is a Patrician foundation — the ancient name was *Druim Daro*, ridge of the oaks. The name Drumlease, *Druim Lias*, derives from huts or sheds Patrick built as residences for his followers. It became an important ecclesiastical centre with a Franciscan friary. The church was built in 1816 and cost £1,044 British. The Glebe house was built in 1833, and cost £1,387 6s 1¾d. A Faculty to improve Drumlease Church was granted on 29th August 1865, and a site for a new place of worship in the parish was granted on 12th January 1867. Mr Lane Fox endowed the parish with £650 in 1902, and also Killenumery with £650, Killargue with £200 and Manorhamilton with £100 to replace an annual subscription. The oak reading desk from St Patrick's Church, Greystones was transferred to Drumlease in 1960. Renovations and improvements were carried out between 1972 and 1979 and there was a service of dedication on 10th June 1979.

Drumreilly, Co Leitrim

DRUMREILLY

VICARS
–1401	Robert McNeill
1401	Gelasius Omulmorthairge
–1414	Fergus Omaylmochoir
1414	John Omaylmochoir
–1453	Bernard Offoind
1453	John Omulmochory

RECTORS
c. 1400	Matthew Micgillasmaid
–1401	Robert McNeill
1401	Gelasius Omolmochory
1409/10	Luke Orodochan
1414	Gelasius O'Mulmochory
1422	Maurice Offloynd (O'Flynn)
–1445/46	Gelucius Ycridigen
1445/46	Maurice O'Molmocory
1478	John Omulomochory

RECTORS and VICARS
1622	John Evatt
–1634	Robert Vaux (possibly Wasse)

1634	Bernard Reynolds
1634	Edward Stanhope
1636–c. 1647	John Cresswell
1661	Ambrose Barcroft
1663	Josias Hollington
1669–1723	James Maxwell
1723–1734/35	Peter Lombard
1734/35–1767	Peter Lombard Jun
1767–1778	George Knox
1778–1794	Richard Swanne
1794–1810	Joseph Story
1810–1835	William Bushe
1835–1847	William Waller (possibly Walker)
1857–1874	Thomas Pentland
1874–1877	John James Ferguson Guthrie
1877–1879	Richard Charles Clarke
1879–1881	Joseph Chapman
1881–1888	William Hautenville Rambaut
1889–1893	William Wolfe Wagner
1893–1894	William Morgan O'Connell
1895–1900	William Francis Nunan
1900–1906	William Walter Peyton
1906–1908	Robert William Gibson
1908–1915	Robert Doherty
1916–1920	Robert John Walker
1921–1930	Samuel Francis Hazlett
1930–1934	John Owen Evans
1935–1941	George Holmes Gibson Bolton C-in-c, R
1936–	
1941–1944	Robert John Doonan
1945–1951	Cecil Harold Bruce Browne
1951–1956	William Gladstone Russell
1956–1959	vacant

CURATES
1785	Rowland Beattie
1840–1848	Thomas Knott
1852	James Topham
1874	John James Ferguson Guthrie
1870–1874	George Thomas

with Templeport 1661–1835
with Newtowngore and Corrawallen 1923–1959
transferred to Ardagh Diocese 1959

NOTES
Drumreilly is *Druim an Bhealaigh*, the ridge of the eastern road. The Patron was St Everan. The church is said to have been built by the Gore family.

Drung, Co Cavan

DRUNG

VICARS

1396	Gilbert Macbrady
1396	Augustine Macbrady (MacBradaicgh)
1409–1421	Nemeas O'Fegrath (O'Feargayth)
1421	Adam O'Feargayth (O'Feogaygh)
1426	Andrew Macbrady
–1430	Adam O'Segaich
1430/31	Cornelius Macconayng (Cormac McConaing)
–1495	Thomas McBride (Megbryd)
1495	Patrick Macconayd
–1594	David McConyn
1594	Thomas Brady
1622	Robert Taylor
1625/26–c. 1634	Faithful Teate
1635	Hugh Swiney (McSwiney)
1635–1645	Faithful Teate
1645–1661	Denis Sheridan
1661	John Turbridge
1662–1682	William Sheridan
1682–1691	Robert Lloyd
1691–1700	Michael Arnott
1700–1721	Peter Peacy (Peze de Gallineer)
1721–1740	Oliver King
1740–1766	Daniel Hearn
1767–1827	Thomas Cradock
1828–1854	Marcus Gervais Beresford

1855–1870	Charles Leslie
1870–1908	Ralph James Hope
1908–1925	Andrew William McGarvey
1925–1957	John Henry McBrien
1958–1960	Henry William Shire
1960–1967	Thomas George Corrigan
1967–1983	James Gordon Benjamin Roycroft
1983–1993	vacant
1993–1995	George William Butler
1995–2002	Janet Margaret Catterall

NSM
2004–	Raymond Moore P-in-c
2006	Roberta Moore

CURATES
–1634	Richard Parsons
1673	James Colden
1745	William Warren
1761–c. 1766	John Wardlaw
1775–c. 1778	Henry Dundas
1799	George Forster
1808–1811	Caesar Otway
1811	John Richardson
c. 1824	James Faris
1826	Francis Faris
1829	Henry James Erskine
c. 1835	Thomas Alfred Lyons
1844–1845	Thomas Fetherston
1850–1868	Joseph King
1860–1870	Ralph James Hope
1869–1872	William Henry Cotter
1899–1902	Herbert Maziere Halahan
1902–1905	Humphrey Ellison
1990–1993	George William Butler

with Larah 1396–1855
with Urney, Annagelliffe, Denn, Derryheen and Castleterra 1958–1960
with Killesherdoney 1960–1972
with Castleterra 1970–
with Larah and Lavey 1972–
with Killoughter 1974–

NOTES

The Gaelic name *Drong* means a crowd or an assembly. According to legend, St Patrick observed a large gathering of people, preached to them and made many converts. During the Rebellion, a Roman Catholic priest named Turlagh O'Gowan alias Smith demanded the key of the Church of Larah and got it. Drung Church was built 1728. A new site for Church of Drung was granted on 3rd May 1833. This was probably Lara New Church, built in 1832 (Report of 1836). Tombstone inscriptions on the old church include an elaborate one to the Clement family in Latin. A new school opened on 4th November 1970.

ENGA

Long-obsolete medieval parish.

VICARS
-1470 William Megwol
-1474 Odo Offegay

NOTES
Enga was another name for Annagh.

FIGNSAIDIN

Long-obsolete medieval parish.

VICAR
c. 1415 Thomas —

Finner, Bundoran, Co Donegal, Christ Church

FINNER

RECTORS
1951–1982	George Garnett Warrington
1985–1986	Charles Ralph Temp-in-c
1992–	Christopher James Stevenson

transferred from Clogher Diocese 1974
with Rossinver 1974–
with Cloonclare Group 1992–
with Innismagrath 2002–

Gowna

GOWNA

transferred from Ardagh Diocese to Kilmore Diocese 1959
with Arvagh and Carrigallen 1959–
with Columbkille transferred from Ardagh Diocese 1977

Innismagrath, Drumkeeran, Co Leitrim

INNISMAGRATH

VICARS

1530	anonymous
	(unjust claim made by Eugenius McBrady)
1619	Thomas Sarcott
1622–1625	John Johnson
1625–1636	Matthew Moore
1636–c. 1661	Thomas Jones
1661–c. 1685	Robert Ross
1700–1704	William Brookes
1704–1719	Philip Brady
1719–1726	John Bennet
1726–1740	William Handcock
1740–1745	John Richardson
1745–1768	George Knox
1768–1771	Michael Lee

1771–1792	William Lee
1792–1796	Richard Burgh
1796–1806	Nesbitt Seely
1806–1810	John Leahey
1810–1815	William Johnston
1815–1817	James Spencer Knox
1817–1830	John Russell Knox
1831–1859	Charles Lyons Montgomery
1859–1873	John Radcliff
1873–1889	Alexander Smullen
1890–1893	Edward Daniel Crowe C-in-c
1893–1897	Matthew John Porteus C-in-c
1897–1911	William Alcorn McDougall C-in-c –1901
1911–1916	Paul Quigley
1917	Edward Furlong
1917–1923	Alan Armstrong
1924–1931	John James Jennings
1932–1934	John Collen Robb
1934–1935	William Lee Mather Giff C-in-c
1935–1955	George Paul Sutcliffe Sythes C-in-c
1955–1959	Samuel Carter Armstrong
1959–1961	Frederick Rudolph Mitchell
1961–1998	Robert Payne Samuel Richey
2002–	Christopher James Stevenson

NSM

1998–2001	Beatrice Anne Pitt

CURATES

–1766	Roger Dodd
1799	William Walker
1803	Thomas Sandford
1855–1862	William Edward James
1860	Adam Gordon Farquhar
1862–1866	Charles Dancer Campbell
1870–1872	William Henry Nassau Brennan

with Dowra 1900–1955 and 1961–c. 1975
with Drumlease, Killenumery and Killargue 1955–1961
with Killinagh and Kiltyclogher 1960–2002
with Killargue 1972–1997
with Cloonclare, Killasnett, Lurganboy, Drumlease, Rossinver and Finner 2002–

NOTES

The Glebe house was built 1815 and cost £1,200 British. The church was built 1829 and cost £1,115 14s 6½d British. 'The Vicar receives all the tithes and pays the Bishop £20 per annum' (Report of 1836). The value of the Vicarage was £16 in 1634.

KEDY, KEADUE

Long-obsolete medieval parish.

RECTORS, VICARS

1407	Thomas O'Syridean
1407	John O'Syridean
1423	John O'Siredean
1426–1436	Andrew McBrady
1427	Patrick O'Farrelly (Ofaercheallaich)
1427	Patrick O'Siredean, (O'Sheridan)
1436–1443	Thady O'Goband
1443	Cormac McConaing (Cornelius Macconayng)
–1475	John Machiarnan
1475	Bernard O'Farrelly
–1484	John Maelmactain
1484	Malachy Macalerickem
–1594	Philip Brady
1594	John Fitzjohns

with Kilmore 1619–

NOTES
Benefice in Parish of Urney.

Kildallon, Co Cavan

KILDALLON

VICARS

1618–c. 1656	Martin Baxter
1656–c. 1661	William Gillice
1661–1668	James Layng
1668–1678	John Layng
1678–1684	Ralph Rule
1684–c. 1691	Aylott Sams or Sands
1691–1704	Philip Brady
1704–1736	William Brooke or Brookes
1736–1745	John Richardson
1745–1768	George Knox
1768–1803	William Warren
1803–1810	Edward Story
1810	Richard Brooke
1810–1821	William Meara
1821–1825	William Magenis
1825–1828	Marcus Gervais de la Poer Beresford
1828–1873	Francis Saunderson
1874–1899	William Creek
1899–1931	Albert Edward King
1931–1964	John James Jennings

PARISHES OF KILMORE WITH LISTS OF CLERGY

1964–1971	Charles Ludwig Birbeck Hill Meissner BC
1964–1965	William Edward Richard Garrett
1976–1982	Albert William Kingston
1985–1989	Herbert Cassidy
1990–1992	John Charles Combe
1992–1997	Stanley Johnson
2000–2004	Susan Margaret Patterson
2007–	Samuel Godfrey Wilson

NSM

1988–1990	Cecil Lindsay
1997–2000	Alexandra Jane Lindsay
2002–2007	George William Browne

CURATES

1661	Josias Hollington
1673	John Fortune
1766	Francis Saunderson
1774–1789	John Faris
1790	Nicholas Wade
1792–c. 1830	Thomas Hyde Villiers
1828	Nathaniel Sneyd
1831	John Taylor
1835	James Vincent Rodney
1844–1852	Walter Irvine
1852–1857	Matthew Nesbitt Lauder
1860–1874	William Creek
1863–1864	William Alexander Reynell
1864–1865	Samuel Carleton Kenah
1893–1895	Robert John Mitchell
1895–1900	John Thomas Webster

with Newtowngore and Corrawallen 1959–
with Kilmore and Ballintemple 1986–1992
with Swanlinbar, Templeport and Tomregan 2007–

NOTES

Kildallon Church was founded by St Dallan Forgaill (died c. 598), a cousin of St Mogue. In 1766, there were 106 Protestant and 197 RC families, one priest and one friar. The church was built in 1816. A Faculty to improve it was granted on 13th December 1864. A new graveyard at Kildallon consecrated on 7th August 1966. A new rectory at Ardlougher was blessed on 8th August 1966.

St Patrick, Kildrumferton, Kilnaleck, Co. Cavan

KILDRUMFERTON
alias CROSSERLOUGH or CLOYGNES

RECTORS

−1529	Thomas O'Bogan (Ybogan)
1529	Malachy O'Golan (O'Goban)
1529	Cognoscius O'Gowan (Ocawanna)
−1540	John MacBrady
1622	Nicholas Smith
1630	Nicholas Bernard
1636/37	Edward Dunsterville
1637–1645	Henry Jones
1647	Lewis Downes

1658	Patrick Maxwell
1661	John Walwood
1667–1691	Edward Dixie
1691–1700	Daniel Neylan
1700	Richard Reader
1701–1730	Francis Schuldham
1730–1740	Patrick Moore
1740–1752	John Charlton
1752–1772	Ralph Grattan
1772–1773	James Cottingham
1773–1783	William Wade
1783–1801	John William Dudley Ryves
1801–1807	Henry Woodward
1807–1846	Thomas Skelton
1846–1856	William Edward Hearn
1856–1871	Henry James Erskine
1872–1878	William James Slacke
1878–1879	Charles Elliott
1879–1885	Thomas Lindsay
1885–1906	James Crichton
1906–1911	Thomas Sutcliffe Humphreys
1911–1931	Robert William Gibson
1931–1934	William Alexander Russell C-in-c
1934–1943	William James Allcard C-in-c
1943–1945	Thomas Clements C-in-c
1945–1987	Guy Newell Cave C-in-c –1976
1988–1992	Robert George Kingston
1994–1996	Robert Alan Chalmers
1997–2006	James Robert Sides

CURATES

1631	John Smith
1752	Robert Moore
1761–1766	William Wade
1799	Robert Saunderson
1828–*c.* 1846	George Hindes
1840	Henry Collins
c. 1844	Orange Sterling Kellett
1853–1856	Campbell Jamieson
1856–1871	James Clarke
1883–1884	Robert Bradshaw

with Ballymachugh 1923–
with Ballyjamesduff 1972–
with Lurgan, Killinkere, Munterconnaught and Billis 1988–1994

NOTES

Kildrumferton Church was built in 1812 and consecrated in 1816. The Deed of a gift of land is dated 21st July 1816. An extension was restored and renovated in 1972.

KILLAN

Note: see Shercock.

Killargue, Co Leitrim

KILLARGUE

VICARS

1441	Florence Otreabair
–1622	William Holliwell
1626–1632	William Bolton
1632–1634	Archibald Campbell
1634–c 1661	Henry Hathersall
1661–1673	John Lang (Layng)
1673–c. 1675	Robert Wasse
1675–1678	Robert Wilson
1678–1681	John King
1681–1684	Ralph Rule
1684–1686	James Echlin
1686–1699	Robert Whitelaw
1699–1737	William Hansard
1737–1774	Charles Dodd
1774–1777	Arthur Moore
1777–1780	Albert Nesbitt
1780–1796	Nesbitt Seeley
1796–1808	John Gumley
1808–1810	William Johnston
1810–1828	John Stephens
1828–1831	Charles Lyons Montgomery

1831–1846	William Edward Hearn
1846–1858	George Hindes
1858–1859	John Radcliff
1859–1860	Henry Perceval
1861–1868	William Moore Wilkins
1868–1878	John Hamilton
1878–1879	Edward Bell
1880	Digby William Duane Digby
1881–1885	John Magill
1885–c. 1905	vacant
c. 1905–1926	Isaac Coulter
1926–1932	John William Clements C-in-c
1933–1946	Thomas William Wills
1947–1949	Edward Frederick Forrest
1951–1953	Alan Armstrong
1955–1959	Samuel Carter Armstrong
1959–1962	Frederick Rudolph Mitchell
1962–1967	Henry Lawton
1969–1971	William Edward Richard Garrett
1972–1998	Robert Samuel Payne Richey

CURATES

1671/79	Alexander Robinson
1766	Roger Dodd
1792	William Walker
1860	Thomas Jameson
	William McWilliams
1870–1873	Thomas Hirst

see also Drumlease

with Drumlease c. 1905–1926 and 1955–1972
with Killenumery 1926–1972
with Innismagrath 1955–1961
with Killinagh, Kiltyclogher, Ballaghmeehan, Innismagrath and Dowra 1972–1998
Church closed 1998

NOTES

During rebuilding of Killargue Church in 1830–32, divine service was performed in houses for which rent of £3 6s 8d appears in accounts, and also Killargue Chapel £1 13s 4d (Report of 1836).

Killasnett, Glencar, Co Leitrim

KILLASNETT

VICARS

–1412	John McEgan (Macaedagan)
1412	Cornelius O'Ruairc
1441	Cornelius McLoughlin Sen
1449–1451	Cornelius McLoughlin Jun
1451	Donald O'Mithian
1624	James Medcalf (Metcalf)
1626	Felix Crane
1661–1681	Robert Wasse
1681–1856	see Cloonclare
1856–1875	John Hudson
1875–1877	Dawson Massy
1878–1890	Joseph Mayne
1890–1905	Joseph Russell Little
1905–1914	Arthur Reginald Burriss
1914–1915	George Robinson Nixon
1915–1921	John Henry MacBrien
1922–1927	Richard Ferguson
1929–1942	Francis Jennings Patterson
1942–1947	Desmond Charles O'Connell
1947–1971	John Rutherford Ennis
1972–1979	David Samuel George Godfrey
1979–1987	Philip John Knowles
1988–1990	Thomas Percival Robert Kenny
1991–	Christopher James Stevenson

CURATES

c. 1839	John Hudson
1861–1871	Julius Henry Griffith
1870–1872	William Benjamin Greer
1873–1875	William Swayne Little
1881–1883	William Knox

see also Cloonclare

with Ballaghmeehan 1930–1962
with Cloonclare Group 1942–

NOTES

Glencar (Glenlough) Chapel of Ease was built in 1821. Lurganboy Chapel of Ease in Killasnett Parish was consecrated on 5th December 1862. Land for Lurganboy Church and graveyard was given by Hon J. Wynne.

Killegar, Co Leitrim

KILLEGAR

DISTRICT and PERPETUAL CURATES
1827–1860	Henry O'Brien
1860–1871	George Henry Martin
1871–1873	Hill Wilson
1874–1877	Michael Fleming Carey C-in-c
1879–1886	George Seymour Clarke C-in-c
1887–1892	John Henry Prescott Gosselin, C 1887–89
1892–1893	Richard Charles Berkeley Gray
1893–1904	Alexander Duncan
1904–1905	Patrick Percival O'Sullivan C-in-c
1905–1906	Richard D'Olier Martin
1907–1908	Richard William Talbot
1908–1911	David Montgomery Taylor C-in-c

with Killeshandra as Curacy-in-charge 1911–
with Derrylane 1968–

Killeshandra, Co Cavan

KILLESHANDRA

VICARS

–1398	Augustine Mackiernan
1398	John Mackiernan
–1411	Nemeas MacKernan (Magthigernayn)
1411	Nicholas O'Farrelly (Ofarchealleych)
–1412	John Macaedagan (McEgan) (possibly Killasnett)
1427	Edmund McKernan (McGuynugan)
before 1430	John O'Sheridan (O'Syredan)
before 1430	Nicholas O'Farrelly
c. 1430	Edmund McKernan (Machyernan)
c. 1430	Cornelius Micamagister
1436	Thady Macfflaind (MacFlynn)
1467	John O'Murcha
1470	John O'Gowan (O'Goband)

PARISHES OF KILMORE WITH LISTS OF CLERGY

1470	Odo McCiernan
1614–1618	vacant
–1622	Adam Watson
1631–1633	Henry Jones
1633	Adam Watson
1651–c. 1661	James Layng (Lang)
1661–	possibly William Aldrich
1673/74–1678	John Layng
1678	Robert Hassard
1682	William Cunningham
1692–1705	Anthony Iveson
1705–1729	Hugh Skellern
1729–1764	William Henry
1764–1787	William Martin
1787–1831	William Hales
1831–1878	John Charles Martin
1878–1882	John Charles Martin
1882–1906	Henry Francis John Martin
1906–1929	Richard D'Olier Martin
1929–1932	James Richard Brady
1932–1943	Ernest Alfred Killingley
1943–1955	William Alexander Russell
1956–1966	William Edward Drury
1967–1970	Thomas Robert Jennings
1971–1978	George Kingston
1979–1981	James Lewis Wilson
1982–1987	Hugh Gollan Jamieson
1992–1996	John Charles Combe
2000–2003	Graham Thomas Doyle

NSM

1996–2000	Cecil Lindsay
2006–	Cecil Lindsay

CURATES

1729	Richard Knight
1753–1761	William Brooke
1763	William Luther
1768	John Beatty
1777	William Anderson
1802	Irwine Whitty
1803	John Egan
1804	Thomas Wade
1824–1826	Charles Moore Echlin
1825/26	James Hales
c. 1830	Thomas Alfred Lyons
1838	William Bourke
1843	Dawson Massy

1844–1847	James Vincent Rodney
1848–1856	Christopher Adamson
1852–1855	William Wallace
–1853	William Stevenson
1855–1878	John Charles Martin
1859–1863	Henry Francis John Martin
1861–1864	John Whitelaw Schoales
1863–1864	Henry William Gayer
1864–1878	Edward Montgomery Moore
1878–1882	Henry Francis John Martin
1879–1882	Arthur Neville Halpin
1882–1884	Frederick William Bamford
1883–1888	John Charles Martin
1890–1893	Robert John Mitchell
1894–1895	Arthur Henry Mant Martin
1898–1902	John George Frederick Holmes
1903–1905	Richard D'Olier Martin
1911–1913	Richard Graeme Fenton Singleton
1913–1919	Charles Henry Preston Lyndon
1921–1925	Frederick Barcroft Worrall
1925–1929	Francis Jennings Patterson

see also Kilmore

Geraldine Fitzgerald adds Rev Joseph Denham (died 21 Oct 1834), who may have been Presbyterian, and Rev William Sweeny of Killeshandra, who may have been Curate: no date given.

with Killegar 1911–
with Derrylane 1968–
with Kilmore and Ballintemple 1992–1996

NOTES
Killeshandra Church probably built before the Reformation. Addition was made to it c. 1746. TCD purchased the advowson in 1763. The church was re-opened after renovation and redecoration in December 1969. A new rectory was blessed on 30th June 1974, and a new school was opened on 11th July 1978.

Killesher, Florencecourt, Co Fermanagh, St John

KILLESHER

VICARS
1488   Arthur Macconrich
1626–1634   James Slacke
1634–1683   Denis Sheridan (O'Sheridan, O'Syredan, O'Suraden)

1683–1731	William Greene
1731–1740	William Henry
1740–1781	Dive Downes
1781–1797	John Caulfield
1797–1804	William Montgomery Cole
1805–1850	Charles Cobbe Beresford
1851–1855	CharlesLeslie
1855–1879	Josiah Crampton
1879–1886	Campbell Jamieson
1886–1888	William Richey Bailey
1888–1908	William Knox
1908–1910	John Oliver
1910–1913	James Ferguson Anderson
1914–1925	John Frederick William Hewitt
1925–1949	John Herbert Jackson
1949–1954	Alfred Stanley O'Connor
1954–1979	Henry Irvine Keys Anderson
1980–1997	James Robert Sides
1998–2001	George Pitt
2001–2006	Gordon Mark Stewart Watson
2007-	Ivan John Ruiters

NSM

2002–2006	Tanya Joy Woods

CURATES

1730	Barlow Scott
1765	Nesbitt Seely
1808	John Cole
1817–1825	William Grattan
1826	Charles Moore Echlin
–1844	Thomas Jebb
1845–1846	James Godley
1846–1853	William Sheppard
1853	Thomas Gloster
1854–1855	Edward Samuel Woods
1856–1879	Campbell Jamieson
1870–1876	William Watson King Ormsby
1879–1881	Matthew Banks Hogg
1881–1883	Francis William Montgomerie Caulfield
1883–1887	William Knox
1887–1889	Meyrick Rainsford
1890–1892	Herbert James Northridge
1892–1894	Herbert Samuel Goff
1894–1898	George Agmondisham Vesey
1898–1900	Alfred Ernest Leigh Stuart
1901–1904	William Popham Hosford
1905–1907	William Bradfield
1907–1908	Henry William Shire

1912–1915	John James Jennings
1919–1920	Charles Henry Preston Lyndon

with Killinagh 2002–

NOTES

Cill Laisir, Church of St Laisir (died *c.* 405), was descended from Niall of the Nine Hostages. Druminiskill Church was *c.* 1760 and enlarged in 1819. Land was granted on 13 September 1860 for the erection of a new church in Druminiskill townland. Druminiskill Chapel of Ease was licensed on 19th April 1862 and consecrated on 2nd June 1863. A stained glass window was given to Killesher Church by Earl of Enniskillen in memory of his sister, Lady Kathleen Mary Villiers, and was dedicated on 18th May 1958. The church was accidentally burned down on 18th September 1979, and has been rebuilt.

Druminiskill Chapel Of Ease, Co Fermanagh

Killesherdoney (Killersherdiney), Co Cavan, St Mark

KILLESHERDONEY

RECTORS

–1626	Nicholas Smith
1628–c 1638	Laurence Robinson
–1660	Alexander Martin
1661–c. 1681	William Aldrich
1681–1691	Aylott Sams (Sands)
1691–1710	James Colden
1710–1740	Wettenhall Sneyd
1740–1754	Charles Rossell
1754–1767	Joseph Story
1768–1793	William Cradock
1793–1808	John William Keatinge
1808–1811	John Brougham
1811–1859	Crinus Irwin
1860–1877	Hon Henry O'Brien
1877–1892	Francis Alexander Sanders
1892–1895	Thomas Torrens
1896–1900	Michael Hamilton Gibson Willis

1900–1903	John Charles Martin (Tertius)
1903–1907	John Frederick William Hewitt
1907–1915	Donald McWatty Hamilton
1915–1949	Charles Edward Keane
1950–1956	Matthew Thomas Porteus, R Drumgoon, C-in-c
1956–1957	Francis Jennings Patterson, R Larah and Lavey, C-in-c
1957–1960	George Cecil Alexander Miller
1960–1967	Thomas George Corrigan
1967–1972	James Gordon Benjamin Roycroft
1972–1974	Ronald Peel Beresford Mathews
1974–1980	John Alexander Pickering C-in-c
1982–1985	Peter Tarleton
1987–1998	William Derek Johnston
1999–2000	Eileen Catherine O'Reilly BC

NSM

2000–	Richard William Stafford

CURATES

1754–c 1768	Michael Lee
1802	Skelton Gresson
1811	Richard H. Robinson
1813	Frederick Fitzpatrick
1813–c. 1825	Samuel Adams
1825–c. 1835	Henry Lefroy
1836–1860	Samuel Roberts
1857–1860	Joseph Carson Moore
1860	William Wallace
1868	Philip John Moran
1895–1896	Michael Hamilton Gibson Willis
1996–1998	Eileen Catherine O'Reilly
see also Annagh	

with Drumgoon 1950–1956 and 1972–
with Larah and Lavey 1956–1957
with Knockbride 1957–1960
with Drung 1960–1972
with Castleterra 1969–1972
with Ashfield 1972–
with Annagh 1987–1998
with Drumlane 1991–1998

NOTES

Ashfield Chapel of Ease was formed out of Killesherdoney Parish in 1794–1795 (LM V 173). Killesherdoney Church was built 1795. Accounts of 1831 include 'contingent expenses for the Roman Catholic Chapel', £7 10s.

Killinagh, Blacklion, Co Cavan

KILLINAGH

VICARS

1430	Rory Magauran (Magamrughay)
1613	John Patrick
1626/7–1636	Thomas Jones
1636–c. 1661	Matthew Moore
1661–1663	Ambrose Barcroft
1663–1669	Josias Hollington
1669/70–1686	James Maxwell
1686–c. 1704	James Lowry (Lawry)
1704–1712	John Forster
1712–1728	John Lowry (Lawry)
1728–1739/40	Henry Brooke
c. 1740–1764	Peter Lombard
1764–1776	James Crawford
1776–1822	John Clarke
1822–1823	Charles Lyons Montgomery
1823–1836	Thomas La Nauze
1836–1845	Edmund Nugent
1845–1848	Charles Moore Echlin
1848–1852	Gibson Black
1852/57–	William Moore Wilkins
c. 1857–c. 1861	Henry Gibson (possibly V)

1861–1875   John Johnstone Egan
1875–1879   Matthew Nesbitt Thompson
1879–1883   Francis Edward Clarke
1883–1885   George McMurray
1885–1915   Hugh Alexander
1915–1917   Charles Arthur Rainsford
1917–1925   Edward Furlong
1926–1939   Henry Fyers Crampton C-in-c
1940–1944   William George Coleman
1944–1950   Coslett William Charles Quin
1950–1998   Robert Samuel Payne Richey
1998–2001   Beatrice Anne Pitt C-in-c
2001–2006   Gordon Mark Stewart Watson
2007-   Ivan John Ruiters

NSM
2002–2006   Tanya Joy Woods

CURATES
1712   John Fletcher
1845–1847   Gorges Irvine
–1860   G.L. Jones
1861   John Johnstone Egan

with Kiltyclogher 1930–2002
with Dowra 1955–c. 1975
with Innismagrath 1960–2002
with Killargue 1972–1998
with Killesher 2002–

NOTES
Killinagh Church was built in 1797, and the Glebe house in 1827. Rectorial tithes were claimed by the Saunders family in right of an Abbey 1836 'but none was paid for the last 30 years' (Report of 1836).

Killinkere, Co Cavan

KILLINKERE

Note: *See also* Mullagh.

RECTOR
1407   Donald Oquaroghan (possibly O'Corrigan)

VICARS
1527	Thomas O'Gowyn
1618/19	John Patrick
1619	John O'Gowan
1629–1631	Edward Dunsterfield (Dunsterville)
1631–	Daniel Crane (Crean)
c. 1658	Patrick Maxwell, Commonwealth Minister
1661–1682	Patrick Maxwell
1682–1697	Andrew Charlton
1697–1745	William Brookes
1745–1760	Joseph Story
1760–1798	Dawson Crowe
1798–1817	Arnold Cosby
1817–1821	William Meara
1821–1827	Spencer Meara
1827–1828	Ambrose Power
1835–1845	Alexander Warham Durdin
1828–1845	Henry Frederick Williams
1845–1855	Henry Monck Winder
1856–1866	John Taylor
1866–1874	Decimus William Preston

1875–1889	Samuel Adams Robinson
1890–1894	Joseph Mayne
1894–1908	Charles Robert Cooney
1908–1909	Thomas Alexander Beckett C-in-c
1910–1942	William McAlister
1942–1973	William John Mitchell
1973–1984	William Derek Johnston
1985–1992	Robert George Kingston
1994–1998	Warren David Nelson
1999–2003	William Derek Johnston
2004–	Craig William Leslie McCauley

NSM

2003–2004	Cecil Lindsay

CURATES

1742	Anthony Sheridan
1754	John Handcock
1756	John Wardlaw
1761	John Hynes
1789	James Young
1802–1810	Edward Mahaffy
1819–	Charles Atkinson Caffry
1828	Matthew Fox
1835–1845	Alexander Warham Durdin
1840	Brent Neville
1852–1856	Digby Samuel Cooke
1856	Nathaniel Sneyd Taylor
1857–1861	William Scott
1865–1866	Thomas Kemmis
1871–1872	John Evans Preston
1876–1877	James William Smith
1878–1885	James Crichton
1885–1887	John Wills Evans
1887–1894	John Jennings
1895–1901	William Flannery
1901–1904	Herbert Maxwell Carlyle Hughes
1904–1907	William Alexander Roe
1988–1991	David Williams
1991–1994	Robert Alan Chalmers

with Mullagh –1960
with Lurgan and Loughan 1961–
with Billis and Munterconnaught 1973–
with Kildrumferton, Ballyjamesduff and Ballymachugh 1988–1994

NOTES

A Faculty to improve Killinkere Church was granted on 29th August 1865. The Glebe house was built in 1815 at cost of £1,823 1s 6½d and was condemned in 1837. Mullagh was a Chapel of Ease in the parish, which was grouped with Bailieborough and with Moybologue in 1960. The rectory was sold for £18,000 in 1975 to be used as community centre.

Killoughter, Redhills, Co Cavan

KILLOUGHTER

PERPETUAL CURATES and INCUMBENTS

1815–1837	James Gumley
1837–1857	William Ashe
1857–1870	John Maunsell Massy
1870–1879	Thomas George Johnson Phillips
1879–1880	Matthew Nesbitt Thompson
1880–1882	Charles Launcelot Handcock
1883–1884	Charles William O'Hara Mease
1884–1887	Frederick William Bamford
1887–1894	Arthur John Pike
1894–1914	William Christopher Hanbury
1914–1957	William Gamble
1958–1962	Hugh Henry Morrow
1962–1964	William Desmond Henderson
1965–1973	Robert Ferguson Meally
1974–1983	James Gordon Benjamin Roycroft
1993–1995	George William Butler
1995–2002	Janet Margaret Catterall

NSM

2004–	Raymond Moore
2006–	Roberta Moore

CURATES

1867–1870	Philip John Moran
1990–1993	George William Butler

with St John, Cloverhill as Curacy-in-charge 1930–1974
with Drung Larah, Lavey and Castleterra 1974–

NOTES
Redhills district was separated from Annagh Parish, Belturbet, and established as a Perpetual Curacy in 1813. Killoughter Church was built in 1814, and cost £1,107 13s 10¼d.

Kilmore, Co Cavan, Cathedral Church Of St Fethlimidh

KILMORE

dedicated also to St Michael
Bedell Memorial Church

VICARS
1366	Nemeas McMulmarayn
–1398	Nicholas Macronynd
1398	Nicholas O'Sheridan (O'Siridean)
1398	Cormac Macronynd
1411	Patrick O'Sheridan (O'Siredean)
–1415	Nimeas
1427	Patrick O'Farrelly (Ofaercheallaich)
1436	Thady Magnwin
1446	Thomas O'Gowan (Ygoband)
1471	Cormac O'Syridean

RECTOR
1461/62	Cormac O'Sheridan (O'Syridean)

Note: The Deans of Kilmore seem to have held Vicarage of Kilmore 1619–1870. Some before 1618 may also have held the Rectory or Vicarage of Kilmore.

VICARS/RECTORS/DEANS
1619–c. 1627	John Hill
1627–1637	Nicholas Bernard
1637–1645	Henry Jones

c. 1645–1661	Lewis Downes
1661–c 1664	John Walwood
1664–c 1691	Edward Dixie
1691–1700	Enoch Reader
1700	Richard Reader
1700–1734	Jeremiah William Marsh
1734/35–1751	John Madden
1751–1765	Hon Henry Maxwell
1765–1768	Charles Agar
1768–1796	Thomas Webb
1796–1801	George de la Poer Beresford
1801–1825	William Magenis
1825–1860	Henry Vesey Fitzgerald
1860–1870	Thomas Carson
1872–1906	William Henry Stone
1906–1955	William James Askins
1955–1985	Robert Christopher Howard Turkington
1985–1989	Herbert Cassidy
1990–1996	John Charles Combe
1997–2004	David Samuel George Godfrey
2005–	Wallace Raymond Ferguson

CURATES

1728	Bernard Northcote
1745–c. 1754	Fowke Moore
1756	Henry Maxwell
1766	James Creighton
1767	Thomas Cradock
1769	George Knox
1770–c. 1774	William Fox
1776–1777	Albert Nesbitt
1811–1823	Thomas La Nauze
1828	John Radcliff
–1847	George MacDonnell
1848–1871	James C. Willcocks
1853–1860	Ralph James Hope
1859–1866	Thomas Bourchier
1860–1862	William Percy Robinson
1862–1864	Richard Henry Donovan
1865–1871	Thomas William Carson
1866–1867	Walter Riddall
1866–1872	William Henry Stone
1873–1874	Robert Leech
1874–1877	Thomas Benjamin Willson
1878–1879	Edward Fitzhardinge Campbell
1879–1880	Charles Richard Williams
1880–1895	Thomas Vigigne Fausset
1895–1901	William McAlister
1902–1906	William James Askins

1907–1908	William Bradfield
1908–1911	Samuel Randal Sproule Colquhoun
1911–1913	William Frederick Crosthwait
1913–1915	John Anthony Lombe Atthill
1952–1954	Eric Simon Wallace
1986–1989	Nigel John Wesley Sherwood
1989–1992	Stanley Johnson
1992–1995	Lester Desmond Donald Scott

NSM
1998–1990	Cecil Lindsay

with Ballintemple 1950–
with Kildallon, Newtowngore and Corrawallen 1986–1992

NOTES

In early times, the See of Kilmore known as *Triburnia*. Few remains of the medieval church at Kilmore can still be seen. The building adjacent, now in use as Parish Hall, is the older cathedral of Bishop Bedell's time. Kilmore Cathedral was consecrated on 17th July 1860 as a memorial to Bishop Bedell. It incorporates a Hiberno-Romanesque doorway from the ancient abbey nearby. A stained glass window depicting the Good Shepherd by Miss O'Brien of Dublin was given by Miss F. Askins in memory of her parents and dedicated 14th July 1957. Other gifts were dedicated 9th November 1958. The bell from Elphin Cathedral was placed in the Cathedral and dedicated on 3rd March 1963. A brass bowl for the font, which was given in memory of Archbishop Barton, was also dedicated. The three-light window depicting Love, Joy and Courage, designed by Miss O'Brien, was given by Lord and Lady Farnham in 1944. Dean Askins's memorial window depicting Christ blessing the children, designed by Miss O'Brien, was given by Orange lodges in 1961. A new school for Kilmore and Ballintemple was opened on 18th April 1975.

The old Cathedral, Kilmore, Co. Cavan

Kiltyclogher, Co Leitrim

KILTYCLOGHER

PERPETUAL CURATE
1862–1897   William Scott, R 1873–

RECTORS
1897–1902   John Richard Gahagan
1903–1926   Edward Flower
1927–1930   R Cloonclare in charge
1930–1939   Henry Fyers Crampton C-in-c
1940–1944   William George Coleman
1944–1950   Coslett William Charles Quin
1950–1998   Robert Samuel Payne Richey
1998–2001   Beatrice Anne Pitt
2001–2002   Gordon Mark Stewart Watson

CURATE
1891–1893   William Wilkes Dungan

with Ballaghmeeghan 1873–1930
with Killinagh 1930–2002
transferred to Clogher Diocese 2002

NOTES
A district was constituted out of Boho, Devenish and Cleenish Parishes in Clogher Diocese, and Rossinver and Cloonclare in Kilmore. The church was in the Parish of Cloonclare. The site was granted on 31st March 1865. Kiltyclogher was constituted a new parish or Perpetual Curacy on 21st January 1865. The church was licensed on 8th March 1867 and consecrated on 24th July that year.

Kinawley, Derrylin, Co Fermanagh

KINAWLEY, CROM and DRUMANY Chapel of Ease

VICARS

–1426	Lucas McGranrugan
–1444	Patrick O'Droma
1444	Matthew O'Droma
1622–1634	James Slacke
1634	William Bedell
c. 1656–c. 1676	George Creighton
1676–1690	John Lowry (Lawry)
c. 1690–1712	John Forster
1712–1728	John Lowry (Lawry)
1728–1739	Henry Brooke
1740–1774	William Sneyd
1774–1808	Dixie Blundell
1808–1810	John William Keatinge
1810–1822	James Langrishe
1822–1870	John James Fox
1870–1882	John Maunsell Massy Beresford
1882–1905	Jonathan Christopher Head
1905–1920	John McKnight
1920–1965	Frederick William Grant
1965–1971	Matthew James Frederick Lynn
1971–1985	Charles Ludwig Birbeck Hill Meissner
1985–1995	vacant
1995–	George Thomas William Davison

Crom, Co Fermanagh, Holy Trinity

CURATES

1741	John Ingham
1766	William Nickson
1766	William Fox
1770	James Creighton
1773	John Cooksey
1774	Thomas Stephens
1783	James Gumley
1799	John Jebb
1825	William Grattan
1830	Charles Kendal Bushe
c. 1836	Carleton Cathcart
1840–1850	Orange Sterling Kellett
–1843	Osbert Denton Toosey
1843–1853	Archibald Crawford
1846–1848	Richard Augustus Hall
1850–1862	Charles Maxwell Fox
1860	John J. Egan
1863–1877	Harloe Knott Elwood
1872–1878	Francis John Beere
1879–1881	Charles Frederick Archer
1879–1881	Edward Flower
1881–1882	William Gore Burroughs
1882–1883	John Wybrants Johnston
1883–1884	James Edward Revington-Jones
1884–1887	Henry Gordon

Drumany Chapel of Ease near Co. Fermanagh, Christ Church

1887–1888	John McKnight
1889–1890	Herbert James Northridge
1890–1893	Matthew John Porteus
1893–1894	James Leonard Poe
1894–1895	William Flannery
1895–1898	Bernard Frederick Good
1898–1900	James Jackson Griffin
1900–1901	John Alfred Kennedy Anderson
1901–1902	Samuel McKee Shannon Stuart
1902–1905	Thomas Sutcliffe Humphreys
1905–1909	Arthur Haire
1909–1914	William Gamble
1915–1916	John Hilton Spratt
1916–1922	Samuel Francis Hazlett
1922–1925	James Wilson Wright
1932–1935	George Paul Sutcliffe Sythes
1927–1930	Herbert John McKane
1935–1937	Hugh Hastings Richard Mayes
1937–1942	George Garnett Warrington
1942–1944	Isaac Reburn Sloane

DISTRICT CURATES OF HOLY TRINITY

1853–1873	John Thomas Ringwood
1874–1882	Frederick William Rogan
1883–1910	John Haughton Steele

NOTES

A Vestry book dates from 1775. Kinawley Church was built in 1825 and enlarged in 1861. Holy Trinity District Chapel, Crom, in Kinawley Parish, seems to have been joined to Kinawley as a Curacy-in-charge *c.* 1910. Drumany Chapel of Ease was opened on 28th December 1883. Derrylin Church reopened after extensive repairs in 1958.

Knockbride, Co Cavan

KNOCKBRIDE

RECTORS and VICARS

–1622	Robert Taylour
1625	Alexander Comyn (Commyn, Cummin)
c. 1630	Alexander McWhiddy
1660	William Gillis (Gillice)
c. 1661–c. 1682	Patrick Maxwell
1682–1708	Andrew Charlton
1708–1726	Arthur Charlton
1726–1728	Henry Brooke
1728–1739	John Lawry (Lowry)
1739–c. 1774	Barlow Scott
1774–1775	John Caulfield
1775–1802	Thomas Sneyd
1802	John Paul
1802–1813	Daniel Palmer
1813–1819	Josiah Erskine
1819–1828	Francis Saunderson
1828–1835	George de la Poer Beresford
1835–1840	James Lowry Dickson
1842–1852	Guy Percival L'Estrange
1852–1866	Thomas Biggs Popham

1866–1872	Henry Hugh O'Neill
1873–1877	William Verner
1877–1881	William Swayne Little
1881–1887	Isaac Coulter
1887–1888	Ambrose Conway
1888–1889	Henry Drought Sheppard
1889–1917	George Mortimer Anderson
1917–1944	William Flannery
1944–1956	Robert Ernest Trenier
1957–1965	George Charles Alexander Miller
1966–1975	Allen James Nelson C-in-c
1975–1988	William Edward Richard Garrett
1991–1995	Denis Francis Wann
1996–2000	Brian Robert Russell
2005–	Alan William Matchett

NSM

1993–1997	Alexandra Jane Lindsay
2000–2003	Alexandra Jane Lindsay
2006–	Tanya Joy Woods

CURATES

1730	Thomas How
1736	Arthur Moore
1754	John Beatty
1761 and 1766–	William Lee
1773	James Cooksey
1788	Allen Noble Adams
c. 1825	Patrick Smith
1842–1845	Joseph North
1850–1864	Orange Sterling Kellett
1862–1865	William John Wesley Webb (Everitt)
1870–1873	William Verner

with Killesherdoney 1957–1960
with Shercock or Killan 1933–1957 and 1960–
with Bailieborough or Moybologue and Mullagh 1966–

NOTES

Knockbride Church, which dates from 1825, was reopened after decoration and alteration. Gifts, including the font, were given by Dr William Gamble and dedicated on 12th October 1958
Knockbride Rectory was sold to Mr D. Corrie in 1971.

Larah, near Stradone, Co Cavan

LARAH

VICARS
1396–1855   with Drung
1856–1888   Thomas Jebb

CURATES
c. 1835   Thomas Alfred Lyons
–1856   Thomas Jameson
1893–1894   George Charles O'Keeffe
see also Lavey

with Lavey 1888–
with Denn 1903–1923
with Drung and Castleterra 1972–
with Killoughter 1974–

Lavey, near Stradone, Co Cavan

LAVEY

VICARS

1620–c. 1661	Thomas Brady (Bradye)
1661–1662	John Turbridge
1662–1682	William Sheridan
1682–1704	John Chetwood
1704	Rowland Singleton (presented but not instituted)
1704–1721	Alexander Douglas
1721–1733	James Cottingham
1733–1736	John Richardson
1736–1745	William Brookes
1745–1752	Ralph Grattan
1752–c. 1777	Fowke(s) Moore
1778–1793	John Handcock
1793–1840	Thomas Sneyd
1840–1861	James Lowry Dickson
1861–1866	James Godley
1866	Henry Hugh O'Neill
1866–1886	Arthur Moneypenny
1888–1894	William Christopher Hanbury

1894–1923	Joseph Mayne
1924–1929	Matthew John Porteus
1930–1932	Samuel Francis Hazlett
1932–1941	John William Clements
1942–1972	Francis Jennings Patterson
1972–1983	James Gordon Benjamin Roycroft
1983–1993	vacant
1993–1995	George William Butler
1995–2002	Janet Margaret Catterall

CURATES

1754	Anthony Sheridan
1756–1778	John Handcock
1782	James (or Joseph) Waters
1803–c. 1829	Andrew Tracey
1836	Wiley Gerard
1838	John McDermott
1845–1847	James McKee
1847–1848	Walter Conyngham Peyton
1854–1866	Denis Knox
1882–1886	William Harris Winter
1887–1889	Thomas Pearson
1889–1890	Gerald Nenon O'Grada Bere
1891–1893	Alexander Duncan
1893–1894	George Charles O'Keeffe
1894–1896	George Viviliers Jourdan
1896–1898	William James Mayne
1898–1900	Gilbert Kemmis
1900–1906	Austin Sweetnam
1906–1910	William Wallace
1910–1913	John Achilles Rogers
1913–1915	Henry Foxton Beaumont
1916–1922	Richard Ferguson
1990–1993	George William Butler

NSM

2004–	Raymond Moore
2006–	Roberta Moore

with Larah 1888–
with Denn 1903–1923
with Drung and Castleterra 1972–
with Killoughter 1974–

NOTES

Leamhaidh, a place abounding in elm trees, is associated with St Derlugha, virgin. There were five Protestant families in Lavey Parish in 1766, viz. Alexander Burrowes, James Maguire, Thomas McDowell, Patrick Maguire and James Usher, and 254 RC families; Joseph Reilly was RC priest.

LOUGHAN

with Lurgan –1974
with Munterconnaught –1961
with Killinkere 1961–

NOTES
Loughan Church was deconsecrated on 15th November 1974. The font was given to Derryheen Church.

Lurgan, Virginia, Co Cavan

LURGAN

VICARS

1527	Charles Oclerian
c. 1609	anonymous I
1619–c 1658	George Creighton
1658–1661	Patrick Maxwell
1661–c. 1667	Eber Birch
1667–1692	John Aungier
1692–1700	William Hansard
1700–1737/38	Luke Sterling
1737/38–1762	Edward Sterling
1763–1769	William Cradock
1769–1812	William Sneyd
1812–1845	John Rowley
1845–1861	Henry Hunt

1861–1870	Frederick Fitzpatrick
1870–1909	Denis Knox
1909–1925	Henry Minchin Lloyd
1925–1956	William Bradfield
1956–1961	Edward Morgan Griffin
1961–1973	William John Mitchell
1973–1984	William Derek Johnston
1985–1992	Robert George Kingston
1994–1998	Warren David Nelson
1999–2003	William Derek Johnston
2004–	Craig William Leslie McCauley

NSM

2003–2004	Cecil Lindsay

CURATES

1817–1824	Robert Sergeant (Sargent)
1825–c. 1830	Joseph Stephens
1829–1847	Henry Gibson
1830	Decimus William Preston
1829–1847	Henry Gibson
1848–1851	Samuel Martin
1854	Thomas Bourchier
1856–1862	Digby Samuel Cooke
1861–1868	Alfred George Elliott
1890–1891	Henry Rogers Somerville Bury
1891–1895	Charles Edward Hardy
1895–1898	William Coates Harvey
1898–1900	Alfred Ernest Killingley
1900–1907	George Ernest Fry
1988–1991	David Williams
1991–1994	Robert Alan Chalmers

with Munterconnaught –1845, 1925–1961 and 1974–
with Loughan 1974–
with Killinkere 1961–
with Billis 1974–
with Kildrumferton, Ballyjamesduff and Ballymachugh 1988–1994

NOTES

Pynnar's Survey says, 'Captain Culme holds 1,000 acres as undertaker. He is to build a town called Virginia, for which he is allowed 250 acres. Upon this he hath built eight timber houses, and put into them English tenants, of which town there is a Minister which keepeth school and is a very good preacher' 1609. 18 Church of Ireland families, 17 Dissenting families and 569 RC families, = 164 Protestant and 2,003 Roman Catholic souls, and 3 Roman Catholic priests in Lurgan and Munterconnaught 1766. Lurgan Church was built in 1821 and accidentally burned in 1830. Accounts of the General Vestry for 3 years –1832 include, '£50 for repairs to RC Chapel'.

MOYBOLOGUE

with Bailieborough –1873

NOTES
In 1873, Moybologue part of Bailieborough Parish, which was in Co Meath, separated.

Mullagh, Co Cavan

MULLAGH
alias MULLOGH, alias KILMOKAIR, alias BALLYCLAN PHILLIP, alias TEMPLECALLY, alias TUILLIE

DISTRICT CURATES
c. 1811–1820	Edward Mahaffy
1814–1817	Arnold Cosby
1819–1856	Charles Atkinson Caffry
1856–1872	Nathaniel Sneyd Taylor
1872–1874	John Evans Preston

with Bailieborough 1960–

NOTES
From early times, Mullagh was a place of historical importance, dedicated to St Cillian (died c. 689), apostle and martyr of Franconia, Germany. There was a District Curacy in Killinkere Parish c. 1814–. The church was built in 1819, and a Perpetual Curacy was established in 1832. It was absorbed again into Killinkere in 1872. The font from Enniscoffey Church in Meath Diocese was transferred to Mullagh Church in 1958.

Munterconnaught, Co Cavan

MUNTERCONNAUGHT

RECTORS and VICARS
For Rectors –1845 see Lurgan
1845–1866 Henry Hugh O'Neill
1866–1870 Denis Knox
1871–1876 Alfred George Elliott
1877–1889 Joseph King
1889–1899 Albert Edward King
1900–1908 John Thomas Webster
1908–1956 William Bradfield
1956–1961 Edward Morgan Griffin
1961–1965 Coslett William Charles Quin
1965–1967 Samuel Lindsay McQuoid
1968–1971 William Henry McAleese (McLees)
1973–1984 William Derek Johnston
1985–1992 Robert George Kingston
1994–1998 Warren David Nelson
1999–2003 William Derek Johnston
2004–   Craig William Leslie McCauley

CURATES
see also Lurgan
1838–1839 Theophilus Fitzhardinge Campbell
–1845   Henry Hugh O'Neill

with Lurgan –1845, 1925–61 and 1974–
with Loughan –1961
with Billis 1961–
with Killinkere 1973–
with Ballyjamesduff and Castlerahan 1961–1972
with Kildrumferton, Ballyjamesduff and Ballymachugh 1988–1994

Newtowngore, Co Cavan

NEWTOWNGORE

Note: Formed out of Carrigallen.

PERPETUAL CURATES and RECTORS

1856–1872	William James Slacke, PC –1870
1872–1879	Claude Cregan, C-in-c –1874
1879–1883	Samuel Atkinson Adams
1883–1894	Charles Robert Cooney
1894–1923	William Siers
1923–1930	Samuel Francis Hazlett
1930–1934	John Owen Evans
1935–1941	George Holmes Gibson Bolton, C-in-c –1936
1941–1944	Robert John Doonan
1945–1951	Cecil Harold Bruce Browne
1951–1956	William Russell
1959–1964	John James Jennings
1964–1971	Charles Ludwig Birbeck Hill Meissner, BC 1964–1965
1972–1975	William Edward Richard Garrett
1976–1982	Albert William Kingston
1985–1989	Herbert Cassidy
1990–1992	John Charles Combe
1992–1997	Stanley Johnson
2000–2004	Susan Margaret Patterson
2007–	Samuel Godfrey Wilson

CURATES and NSM
see Kildallon

with Corrawallen 1870–
with Drumreilly 1923–1959
with Kildallon 1959–
with Kilmore and Ballintemple 1986–1992
with Swanlinbar, Corrawallen and Newtowngore 2007–

Oughteragh (or Outragh), Ballinamore, Co Leitrim

OUGHTERAGH

VICARS

–1414	Simon O'Maylmochoir
1414	John O'Maylmochoir
1422	Maurice Offloynd
1453	Fergus alias Offoind
1453	John O'Mulmochory
1461	Nemeas O'Droma
1474	John O'Mulmochere
1474	Gerald Orodachayn
1622	John Evatt
1634	William Hammond
1635	Valentine Gonnys
1638	Samuel Sotheby (Southby)
1641	David Murdoe
1661	Josias Hollington
1673–1698	William Conyngham (Cunningham)
1698–1705	Arthur Harris
1705/06	John Jones
1709	James Monroe
1716–1743	Dominick Bulteel
1743–1745	Joseph Story
1745–1757	Nicholas Wade

1757–1771	Manley Gore
1771–1794	John Wardlaw
1794–1803	Edward Story
1803–1806	John Beresford Hill
1806–c. 1835	Francis Percy
1836–1842	Thomas La Nauze
1842–1846	Alexander Hudson
1846–1852	Richard Samuel Clifford
1852–1866	Daniel Oliver Etough
1866–1874	John Knox Barklie
1874–1880	George McClenaghan
1880–1897	Richard Charles Clarke
1897–1902	Hamlet McClenaghan
1902–1906	Ernest Alfred Killingley
1906–1949	Austin Sweetnam

CURATES

1773	Francis Kiernan
1799	Francis Percy
1834	Gilbert Percy
1843	James Dillon MacDonogh
1843–1846	James Michael Henry Strangways
1872	John Beaufort Berkeley Barter

transferred to Ardagh Diocese 1910

NOTES
The Glebe house was built in 1816 and cost £1,089 7s 1d British. The church was built in 1787.

QUIVVY

PERPETUAL CURATES
1856–1873	Thomas Gloster
1873–1877	Frederick George McNally
1877–1880	Digby William Duane Digby
1880–1882	Thomas Cloudsdale C-in-c
1882–1894	Richard Augustus Hall

CURATE
1853–1856	Thomas Gloster

with St John, Cloverhill as Curacy-in-charge 1894–
with Annagh 1912–1986
closed *c.* 1986

NOTES

Quivvy Chapel of Ease was endowed on 15th July 1856. The Patron, Lord Lanesborough, built and endowed the church at his own expense. The organ was given by Professor and Mrs Greene and dedicated on 29th July 1979.

Rossinver, Kinlough, Co Leitrim

ROSSINVER

VICARS

–1441	Tatheus Ofyrgussa
1441	John Omithian
1505	Bartholomew Imitia (Omyan)
1530	Bernard Macchago
1532	Bartholomew Offirgissa
1618	George Creighton
1619–c. 1622	William Roycroft
1622	James Metcalf (Medcalf)
1626–c. 1634	Felix Crane
1636	Thomas Roberts
1661–c. 1681/2	Robert Wass (Wasse)
1681/82–1685	Thomas Hardcastle
1685–1698	John Twigge
1698–1721	John Smith
1721–1724	Thomas Abercromby
1724–1739	Caulfield Cuffe
1739–c. 1775	Francis Cuffe
1775–c. 1782	James Duncan
1782–1793	Thomas Sneyd
1793–1815	Francis Saunderson
1816–1835	James Lowry Dickson
1835–1846	Edward Hales
1846–1851	Archibald St George
1851–1856	Decimus William Preston

1856–1872	William Ashe
1872–1894	Richard Tate
1894–1902	John McKnight
1902–1909	John Richard Gahagan
1909–1921	Ernest Alfred Killingley
1922–1945	Thomas Hutchinson Martin C-in-c
1946–1982	George Garnett Warrington
1985–1986	Charles Ralph Temp-in-c
1992–	Christopher James Stevenson

CURATES

–1685	— Andrews
1728	Arthur Moore
1749	John Major
1776	Guy Henry Luther
1780	Thomas Inglis
1786	James Pollock
1796	Robert Saunderson
1808	John Williamson
–1844	John Johnstone Egan
1845–1849	James Smith Franks
1870–1872	Richard Tate

with Finner 1974–
with Cloonclare Group 1992–
with Innismagrath 2002–

NOTES
Rossinver Church, capable of accommodationg 450 people, was built at expense of the Parish, but when or at what cost is unknown.

Rossinver, Kinlough, Co. Leitrim

Shercock, Formerly Killan, Co Cavan

SHERCOCK

VICARS

–1571	William Cusack
–1621/22	Alexander Commyn
–1622	Robert Taylor
1660–1662	William Gillis (Gillice)
1661/62–1682	Patrick Maxwell
1682–1708	Andrew Charlton
1708–1726	Arthur Charlton
1726–1733	Daniel Hearn
1733	William Hansard
1733–1746	James Cottingham
1746–1754	Joseph Story
1754–1772	Ralph Grattan
1772–1790	William Pigott
1790–1792	Carncross Cullen
1792–1815	Hugh Montgomery
1815–1848	Frederick Fitzpatrick
1848–1870	John Harris
1871–1874	Stephen Radcliff
1875–1889	James Caulfield Willcocks
1889–1890	Meyrick Rainsford

1890–1892	Richard Hunsley Taylor
1892–1904	Burton Trimnell Turney
1904–1933	Thomas William Wills
1933–1944	William Flannery
1944–1956	Robert Ernest Trenier
1957–1960	Thomas James Bond
1960–1965	George Charles Alexander Miller
1965–1971	Robert Ernest Trenier, R Drumgoon, C-in-c
1972–1975	Allen James Nelson
1975–1988	William Edward Richard Garrett
1991–1995	Denis Francis Wann
1996–2000	Brian Robert Russell
2005–	Alan William Matchett

NSM

1993–1997	Alexandra Jane Lindsay
2000–2003	Alexandra Jane Lindsay
2006–	Tanya Joy Woods

CURATES

1754	William Cosby
1782	Arnold Cosby
1799	Allen Noble Adams
1857	Cornelius Carleton Boomer
1863–1869	Samuel Henry Lewis
1863	George Blake Concannon
1887–1888	Ambrose Going Adams

with Knockbride 1933–1957 and 1960–
with Bailieborough 1957–1960 and 1972–
with Mullagh 1972–

NOTES

Shercock Church was consecrated in July 1800. A Faculty to improve it is dated 6th March and 18th October 1862. A new primary school was opened on 7th March 1961. The old school was then about 126 years old.

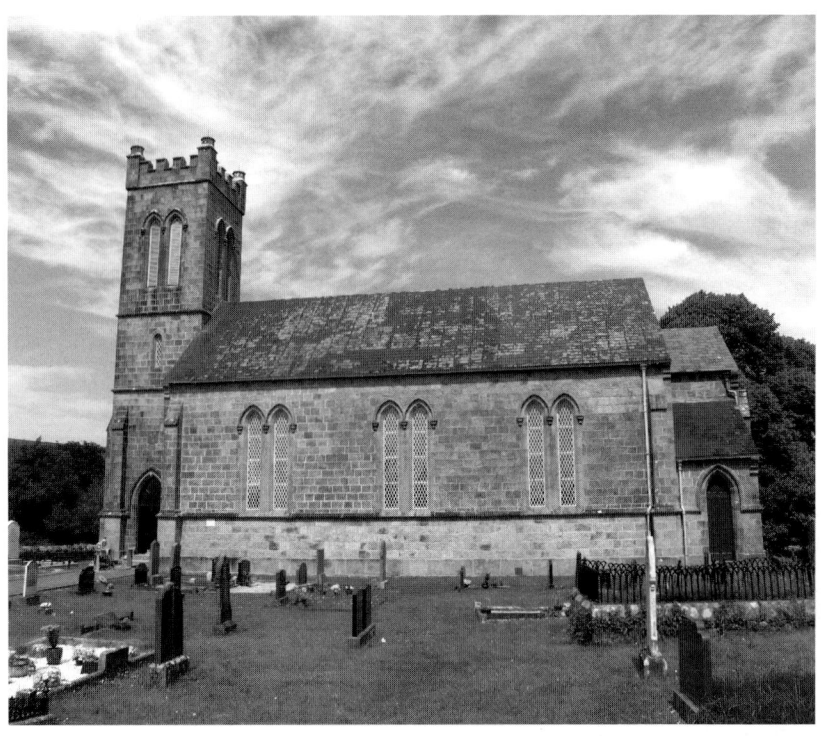

Swanlinbar, Co Cavan, St Augustine

SWANLINBAR

PERPETUAL CURATES/BISHOP'S CURATES etc

1846–1860	John Johnstone Egan
1860–1876	Matthew Nesbitt Lawder
1877–1880	Thomas Walton Fussell
1880–1888	William Christopher Hanbury
1888–1894	John McKnight
1895–1905	Thomas Torrens
1906–1909	Ernest Alfred Killingley
1910–1913	William Thomas Stewart
1913–1924	Henry William Shire
1924–1925	John Warren
1925–1927	Charles Frederick Hazlitt Carroll
1928–1929	Thomas Percival Rose C-in-c
1929–1932	James Poyntz C-in-c
1932–1939	George Alexander Milligan
1939–1944	Robert Ernest Trenier
1944–1950	Robert John Doonan
1951–1956	John Richard Wheelock
1957–1962	Robert Cecil Armstrong
1963–1965	Derek Cecil Dunwoody C-in-c
1965–1969	George Kingston

1970–1973	William Derek Johnston
1973–1982	John Robertson Thomas Watson
1990–2002	Robert Gordon Keogh
2007–	Samuel Godfrey Wilson

CURATES

1803	Skelton Gresson
? 1807–1844	William Grattan (see bibliography)
1857–1860	Matthew Nesbitt Lauder
1870–1874	William Christopher Hanbury
1875–1877	William Joseph Frazer Whelan
2004–2007	Samuel Godfrey Wilson

with Templeport 1951–
with Tomregan 1990–
with Kildallon, Corawallen and Newtowngore 2007–

NOTES
The Church (possibly at Callowhill) was built in 1766 (Report of 1836). Swanlinbar was a chapel of ease in Kinawley Parish in 1836, and was erected as a Parochial District and Perpetual Curacy on 24th January 1863. Swanlinbar Church was consecrated on 19th June 1849. St Paul's Chapel of Ease, Kinawley (not same as Kinawley, Florencecourt) was consecrated on 5th February 1932.

Kinawley Chapel Of Ease, Co Fermanagh, St Paul

TEALLACHEACH and MAGEANGADY
Long-obsolete medieval parish.

VICARS
1412	Augustine MacBrady
1430	Ronaldus Magamrughan
1430	Cormac Magamrughan
1470	Odo Ofergail

NOTES
This area of Co Leitrim, east of Lough Allen, was inhabited by the sept.in the Parish of Drumreilly.

Templeport, Co Cavan, St Peter

TEMPLEPORT

VICARS

−1414	Andrew Macgamragan
1414	Magonius Macamragan
1419	Nemeas Magyum
1425	Rory Maghamrugan
1453	Nemeas O'Droma
1455	Cristinus Magamrugan
1455–1461	Rory Magramrugan
1461	Cormac Magabraim
−1471	possibly Bernard O'Farrelly
1471	Nellanus Macghamrugan
1619	John Patrick
1626/27	Thomas Groves (or Jones)
1632	Murtagh King

1638	possibly William Bayley
1661–1663	Ambrose Barcroft
1663–1669	Josias Hollington
1669–1723	James Maxwell
1723–1734	Peter Lombard
1734/35–1767	Peter Lombard
1767–1778	George Knox
1778–1794	Richard Swanne
1794–1810	Joseph Story
1810–1835	William Bushe
1835–1842	George de la Poer Beresford
1842–1852	Thomas La Nauze
1852–1856	John Taylor
1856–1860	Frederick Fitzpatrick
1860–1866	John Richard Brougham
1866–1877	Francis Alexander Sanders
1878–1907	Joseph Rawlins
1907–1916	William Alexander Roe
1916–1920	William Willans
1920–1925	James Williamson Camier
1926–1929	James Richard Brady
1930–1948	Samuel Carter Armstrong

CURATES

1745	William Brooke
1753	Veitch Betty (Beattie)
1785	Rowland Betty (Beattie)
1802–c 1830	Joseph Story Noble
1825	James Collins
1832	John Joseph Spear
1840	Thomas Knott
1855–1856	Nathaniel Sneyd Taylor
1856	Thomas Jameson
1860–1865	Christopher Eades
1870–1874	George D. McGhee
1875–1876	Samuel Devinney

with Swanlinbar 1951–
with Tomregan 1990–
with Kildallon, Corrawallen and Newtowngore 2007–

NOTES

St. Mogue (Moaedhog), a native of Breiffne, was born in the Parish of Templeport *c.* 555. The Glebe house was built in 1775 and enlarged in 1824. The church was built in 1815 and cost £1,384 12s.

Tomregan, Ballyconnell, Co Cavan

TOMREGAN

VICARS

–1411	Macrobius O'Blaichsich
1411	John O'Sheridan (O'Syridean)
–1453	Thomas O'Calman
1453	Nemeas Odroma

RECTORS and VICARS

1626	Martin Baxter
1661–1662	Alexander Martin
1663–1665	James Spens
1665–1669	John Bird
1669–1685	Robert Robinson
1685–1740	Charles Rossell
1740–1754	George Leslie
1754	unknown
1758–1767	Walter Lindsay
1767–1773	Peter Lombard
1773–1783	William Cosby
1783–1794	William Wade
1794–1801	John Wardlaw
1801–1818	Richard Brooke

1818–1835	Joseph Story
1835–1843	Henry Lefroy
1843–*c*. 1850	John Frith
1850–1856	Henry James Erskine
1856–1866	Decimus William Preston
1866	James Godley
1866–1897	Orange Sterling Kellett
1898–1900	Thomas Ernest Rudd
1900–1902	Charles Sinclair
1902–1909	Henry Gordon
1909–1916	Mervyn Warren Rogers
1916–1925	John Herbert Jackson
1925–1930	George Kirwan Birmingham
1930–1940	Alfred Birch C-in-c
1940–1960	Hugh Maurice Daunt
1960–1968	Kenneth Edward Ruddock
1968–1972	David Samuel George Godfrey
1973–1980	James Robert Sides
1983–1986	Cyril George Webb
1990–2002	Robert Gordon Keogh
2004–2007	Samuel Godfrey Wilson

CURATES

1756	Thomas Sneyd
1769	Francis Saunderson
1808	Newcomen Whiteley
1829	Robert Delap
1831	Thomas Carson
1840	Richard Smith
1841–1843	John Meade Hobson
1889–1891	George Cottingham Griffith
1891–1892	Osborne Chesnutt
1893–1896	Robert Forsyth
2007–	Samuel Godfrey Wilson

with Drumlane 1957–1990
with Swanlinbar and Templeport 1990–
with Kildallon, Corrawallen and Newtowngore 2007–

NOTES

Tomregan is ancient *Tuaim Drecuin*, Drecon's burial mound. Drecon was a pagan who lived in pre-Christian times. In Christian times, Tomregan became a great seat of learning, with 3 schools of Law, Classics and Humanities. A change was made in the parish by Order in Council dated 17th June 1734, when portions of Drumlane and Kinawley was incorporated. The church was built *c*. 1756 at the expense of Colonel Montgomery and enlarged in 1820 at a cost of £923, and further enlarged *c*. 1835. There is fine interior plasterwork. The Tomregan Stone is a relic of a mediaeval church, associated with St Bricin, a 7th-century saint reputed to be a surgeon. In 1766, there were 88 Protestant and 152 RC families. A new school was opened on 16th January 1967. The church was damaged in a storm in 1976.

Urney, Cavan, Co Cavan

URNEY

RECTORS
–1466	Thomas O'Siridean
1466	John Macculmarchyn (Macculmartayn)

VICARS
–1401	John Maccomaid
–1401	Denis O'Syredan
–1401	Donald alias Denis O'Mulbridy
1401	Thomas O'Syridean
–1425	Macrobius O'Farrelly (Ofarcheallach)
–1425	Thomas O'Gowan (O'Gobann)
1425	Matthew O'Gowan (O'Gobann)
–1431	Patrick O'Farrelly (O'Fairecalliach)
1436–1455	Thady Magnwin (possibly = McGowan)
1455	Nemeas O'Dromo
1457	John Macculmarchyn (Macculmartayn)
–1501	Nicholas McBrady
1620–1638	Laurence Robinson
1638–1639	William Bayley
1639–1640/41	John Floyd
1641	Alexander Clogy
1657/58	David Nairne
1659–c. 1665	John Walwood

1665–1678	Ambrose Barcroft
1678–1684	Robert Wilson
1684–1690/91	Isaac Collyer
1690/91–1740	Matthew Handcock
1740–1745	Wettenhall Sneyd
1745–1746	Joseph Story
1746–1804	James Cottingham
1804–1805	Richard Bagwell
1805–1835	Richard Wynne
1835–1838	Joseph Story
1838–1854	Thomas Carson
1854–1860	Andrew Hogg
1860–1866	Hugh Murray
1866–1884	Samuel Shone
1884–1886	Frederick John Hamilton
1886–1888	Arthur Robinson Barton
1889–1904	William Cornelius McCausland
1904–1928	Edward Daniel Crowe
1928–1965	Henry William Shire
1965–1989	George Charles Alexander Miller
1990–	Mark Robert Lidwill

NSM

1996–1997	Shiela Johnson
1999–2000	Richard William Stafford

CURATES

1766	Lewis Kerr
1803–1805	Joseph Druitt
1817–1825	George Spaight
1826	James Collins
1828	Samuel Roberts
1836–1840	William Henry Krause
1838	Decimus William Preston
1843–1857	William Moore Wilkins
1851–1860	William Henry Stone
1860	George Henry Martin
1860–1871	Joseph Carson Moore
1860–1875	William Henry Hutchinson
1870–1871	William Prior Moore
1875–1879	John Thomas Archer
1879–1880	Charles Launcelot Handcock
1880–1883	George MacMurray
1884	Frederick John Hamilton
1884–1886	Robert Smyly Greer Hamilton
1887–1889	Kivas Collingwood Brunskill
1888	Charles William O'Hara Mease
1889–1891	Richard Fitzthomas Fleming
1891–1895	Thomas Ernest Rudd

1895–1898	Charles Benjamin Dowse
1898–1900	William Tarrant Browne
1899–1902	George Alexander Bayly
1900–1902	Ernest Alfred Killingley
1902–1903	Joseph Henry Howard Scott
1903–1904	Horace George Warren
1903–1904	Henry Egerton
1904–1907	David George Allman
1907–1911	Reginald Percy Rowan
1911–1914	Alfred Victor Smyth
1915–1918	John Alexander Pollard
1918–1921	Frederick Barcroft Worrall
1921–1924	Samuel Carter Armstrong
1924–1928	James McCann
1929–1932	George Alexander Milligan
1932–1935	George Holmes Gibson Bolton
1935–1936	Samuel Wallace Baker
1936–1938	Sidney Robert Colstan Watts
1938–1939	Robert Ernest Trenier
1939–1941	Robert John Doonan
1942–1945	William Wynne Slack
1945–1949	Alfred Stanley O'Connor
1949–1951	Henry Lawrence Young
1952–1954	Cecil Moffatt Wilson
1955–1958	George Henry Marsden
1958–1960	Thomas George Corrigan

with Annagelliffe *c.* 1661–
with Denn 1923–
with Derryheen 1924–
with Castleterra 1948–1969

NOTES

Urney may derive from *Earnaidhe*, a pre-Christian tribe, though as with the Parish of Urney in Co. Tyrone, the name means 'oratory'. The ancient church, situated on banks of the Erne, was a dependency of the Abbey of Fore. Urney Parish Church in Cavan Town was opened for worship on Sunday 12th November 1815. The building, by the architect John Bowden, is situated on a site donated by Lord Farnham and cost £4,963 1s. The east window is of German design. The Farnham memorial monuments are on the south wall of the chancel.

YNISCAYN
Long-obsolete medieval parish.

VICARS
c. 1415   Thomas —
1454   Patrick McGillakgogi

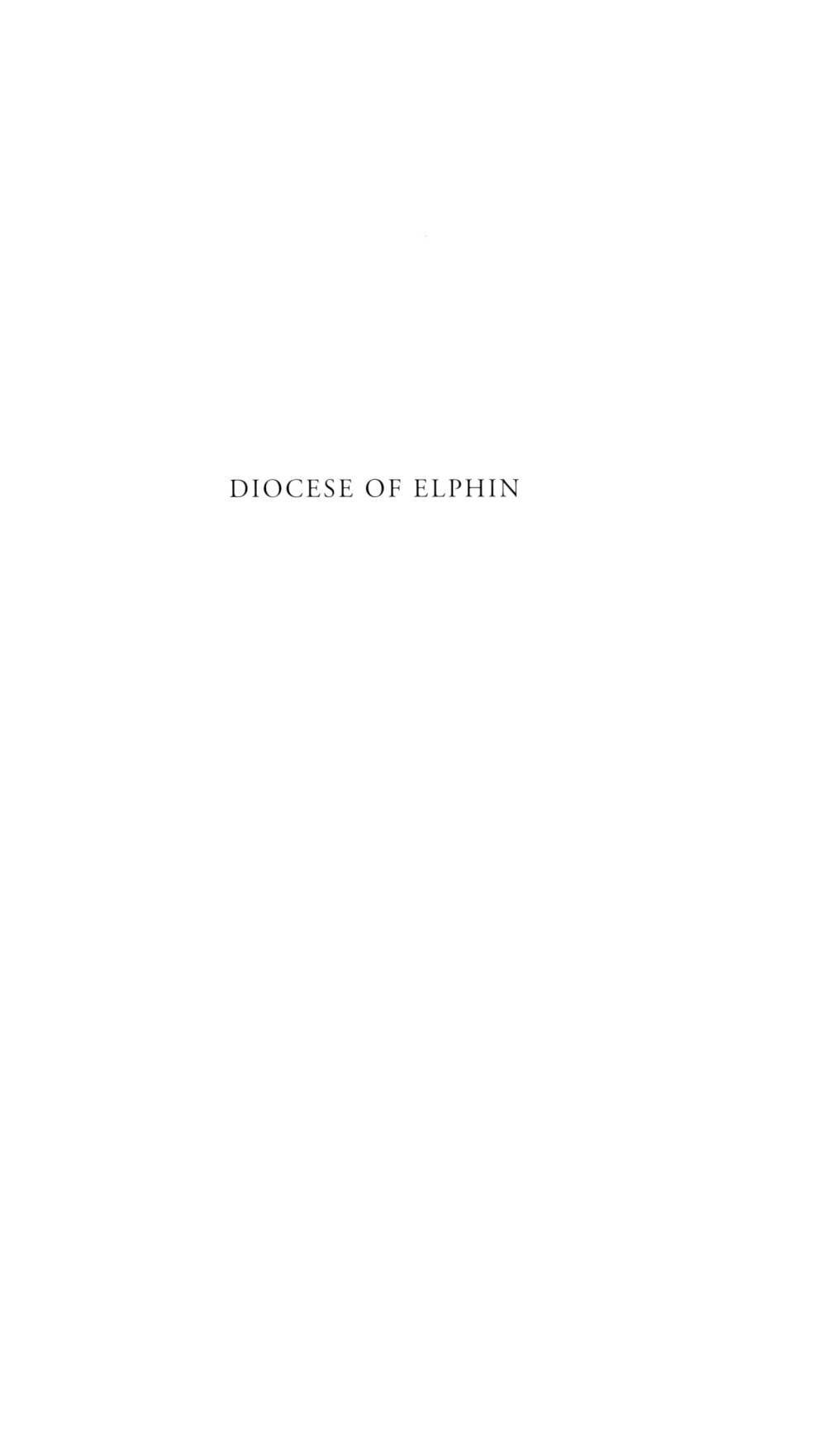

DIOCESE OF ELPHIN

DIOCESE OF ELPHIN

BISHOPS OF ELPHIN

c. 435	ASSICUS
–1136/37	DONALD O'DUFFY
–1152	MAELISA O'CONACHTAIN
–1181	THOMAS O'CONNOR
–1195	FLORENCE McRIAGAN O'MULRONEY
–1206	ALAN O'CONOR
–1229	DIONYSIUS O'MORE
1231	DONATUS (or DONOGH) O'CONOR
1245	JOHN O'HUGROIN
1246	CORNELIUS RUFUS (or CONOR ROE) said to have succeeded
1247	THOMAS O'CONNOR
1260	MILO O'CONNOR
1262	THOMAS McDERMOTT
1266	MAURICE O'CONNOR
1285/86	GELASIUS O'CONNOR
1296	MALACHI McBRIEN
1303	DONAT (or DONOUGH) O'FLANAGAN
1308	CHARLES O'CONOR
1310	MALACHY McHUGH
1312/13	LAURENCE O'LAGHTNAN
1326	JOHN DE ROSCOMMON (or JOHN O'FINNAGHTY)
–1357	CHARLES
1356/57	GREGORY O'MEGHAN
1372	THOMAS BARRETT
1405	JOHN O'GRADA
1412	THOMAS COLBY
1418	ROBERT FOSTEN
c. 1421	THOMAS COLBY
?1423	JOHN O'GRADA again?
1429	LAURENCE O'BOLAND (or O'BEOLLAYN)
1430	MAGONIUS
?*c.* 1430	WILLIAM O'HEDIAN

1449	CORNELIUS O'MULALLY (or O'MELAGHLIN)
1458	NICHOLAS O'FLANNAGAN
1499	GEORGE BRANN (or de BRANA)
1525	JOHN MAX
1539	GABRIEL de SANCTO SERIO
1539	WILLIAM MAGINN
1544/45	CONAL O'SHIEL
1552–1580	ROLAND de BURGO
1580–1584	THOMAS CHESTER
1584–1611	JOHN LYNCH
1611–1638/39	EDWARD KING
1639–165	HENRY TILSON
1660/61–1667	JOHN PARKER
1667–1685/86	JOHN HODSON
1691–1720	SIMON DIGBY
1720–1724	HENRY DOWNES
1724–1729	THEOPHILUS BOLTON
1729–1740	ROBERT HOWARD
1740–1762	EDWARD SYNGE
1762–1772	WILLIAM GORE
1772–1775	JEMMETT BROWNE
1775–1795	CHARLES DODGSON
1795–1810	JOHN LAW
1810–1819	Hon. POWER TRENCH
1819–1854	JOHN LESLIE

Under an Act of Parliament of 1834, on the death of the Bishop of Kilmore, George de la Poer Beresford in 1841, the See of Elphin was joined with that of Kilmore and Ardagh, and Dr. Leslie became Bishop of the United Dioceses. For Bishops of the Union, see Kilmore.

CHAPTER OF ELPHIN

DEANS OF ELPHIN

–1240	GILLA UA NAOMH O'DREAIN
–1258	GILCHRIST O'CORMACAIN
1271	SIMON MAGRATH
–1309/10	SOLOMON
c. 1310	DONALD O'MURDI

1311-1349	PATRICK O'TARPI
1350	NICHOLAS O'FLANAGAN
1383	MALACHY OCHYNERIGE (O'HENRY)
1390	GILBERT MACHABRICHYN
1390	THADY O'KEALL
1405	MALACHI O'FLANAGAN
1405	FINBARBUS O'MUEALINNAIN
1409	DONALD MacDONNCHID (McDONOGH)
1411	ODO MacDIARMADA
–1425	CORNELIUS MacDONCHENY
–1447	FERGALLUS O'BRUACHAN
–1447	THOMAS O'FFLANAGAN
1447	LEWIS O'FFLANAGAN
1465	MALACHY O'MOCHAN
–1487	THOMAS O'HEIDIGAN
c. 1583	? OWEN O'CONOGHER
1591	THOMAS BURKE
1603	EDWARD KING
1606	ERILL (or HILARY) O'HIGGIN
1613/14	JOHN EVATT
1634–1642	RICHARD JONES
1642–1648	JOSEPH WARE
c. 1648–1660	EDWARD SYNGE
1661–1663	CLEMENT PAYNAM (or PAMAN)
1663–1666	DANIEL NEYLAN (NEILAN)
1666–1683	THOMAS CROFTON
1683–1700	ANTHONY COPE
1700–1722/23	EDWARD GOLDSMITH
1722/23–1739	PETER MAHON
1739–1757	CHRISTOPHER LLOYD
1757–1768	JAMES DICKSON
1768–1778	ROBERT BLIGH
1778–1794	JOHN BARRY
1794–1796	FRANCIS BROWNE
1797–1848	JOHN FRENCH
1848–1894	WILLIAM WARBURTON
1894	FRANCIS BURKE
1894-1912	ALEXANDER MAJOR KEARNEY

Deanery vacant to 1929 — united to Ardagh 1929

DEANS OF ELPHIN AND ARDAGH

1929–1933	WILLIAM WOLFE WAGNER
1933–1944	JOHN ROCHE ARDILL
1944–1949	JOHN CLAUDIUS BEREDFORD
1949–1953	THOMAS SUTCLIFFE HUMPHREYS
1953–1963	JAMES WILSON
1963–1966	GEORGE HOLMES GIBSON BOLTON
1967–1983	CECIL CHARLES WYNDHAM BROWNE
1983–1991	HUGH STERLING MORTIMER
1992–1999	STUART IRWIN McGEE
1999-2004	DAVID GRISCOME
2004–	ARFON WILLIAMS

PRECENTORS OF ELPHIN

In early times, the Precentors were known as Provosts, as below.

–1260	A Provost unnamed appears
–1436	RAYGNOYD YCHERNAY
1436	DONATUS YMURAYN
c. 1436	BERNARD O'FFLANAGAN
1436	WILLIAM OFFLANAGAN
c. 1437	THADY MACDIARMADA
1441	RORY O'MOCHAN
1447	CHARLES OCONCHUBYR (O'CONNOR)
1460	DONALD O'MYNACHAYN
1460	RORY McMANUS O'CONNOR
–1461	MUIRGEAS WILLIAM O'FLANAGAN
–1466/67	ODO O'MOCHAN
1466/67	DERMIT O'FLANAGAN
1591	NICHOLAS O'CELLY
1594	DONATUS O'HORAN
1603	RICHARD PENTONY
1615	FLORENCE KELLY
1616	CONNOR (or CORNELIUS) TULLIE
1633	JAMES CROXTON
1635	JOSEPH WARE
–1646	WALTER REYLY
1666	HENRY DODWELL
1674	SAMUEL HAWKES
1674–1682	EDWARD HAWKES

1682–1703	JONATHAN LAW
1703–1720/21	WILLIAM BRERETON
	?
1723-1741	GEORGE MANBY
1742-1743	NICHOLAS SYNGE
1745-1752	PHILIP SMYTHE
1752-1785	WILLIAM FRENCH
1785-1789	STEPHEN RADCLIFFE
1797-1835	RICHARD WYNNE
	The Precentorship was suspended by the Privy Council
1838–	THOMAS CRAWFORD
c. 1838–1847	The Precentorship was suspended until it was restored by the Privy Council on 17 April 1847.
1848	HENRY IRWIN
1848–1876	FREDERICK HAMILTON
1876–1885	JAMES GULLY
1888–1892	WILLIAM HENRY PARKER
1892–1904	FRANCIS EDWARD CLARKE
	The Dignitary lapsed in 1904

TREASURERS OF ELPHIN

1245	GILBERT
	No further Treasurers recorded. Ware (p. 629) says that there was a Treasurer unnamed in 1260.

ARCHDEACONS OF ELPHIN

1232	CLARUS MAIOLIN O'MULCONRY
1241	JOHN O'HUGROIN
–1255	THOMAS MACDERMOTT
–1265	MAOLBRIDE O'GROGAN
–1287	FLORENCE O'GIBELLAIN
1309	WALTER RENAGH
–1362	OIRECHTAGH MACBRENNAN
–1402	MURTOGH O'FLANAGAN
1403	MAGONIUS O'TAIC
1403	AUGUSTINE MACBRADAIC(G)H (MACBRADY)
–1427	ODO MACDIARMADA
c. 1440	CORNELIUS YCONEL (O'CONNELL)
–1443	MAGONIUS O'MOCHAN

1444	THADY MACGEAREACTAYD
1478	EUGENE O'BIRN
–1591	THADEUS MCKORGLESSE
1615	JOHN FOSTER
1616/17	ERASMUS MATTHEWS
1661/62	WILLIAM PORTMAN
1665	JAMES WILSON
1668/69	VINCENT CAVE
1669/70–1683	ANTONY COPE
1683–1700	JOHN BROWN
1700–1722	PETER MAHON
1722/23–1743	LOUIS HAMILTON
1743–c. 1747	ARTHUR MAHON
1747–1756	EDWARD MUNNS?
1756–1761	HENRY CUNNINGHAM
1761–1769	JOHN McLOUGHLIN
1769–1781	JOHN WARDLAW
1782–1798	EPHRAIM MONSELL
1798–1809	OLIVER CARY
1809–1823	WILLIAM DIGBY
1823–1845	JOHN ORSON OLDFIELD
1845–1847	LEWIS HENRY STREAN
1848–1878	HENRY IRWIN
1879	HENRY JOHNSTON
1880-1904	ALEXANDER MAJOR KEARNEY
1904–1910	FRANCIS EDWARD CLARKE
1910–1929	WILLIAM WOLFE WAGNER

Archdeaconries of Ardagh and Elphin united 1929

ARCHDEACONS OF ELPHIN AND ARDAGH

1929–1940	HENRY JOHN JOHNSON (Archdeacon of Ardagh from 1921)
1940–1945	RICHARD GEORGE STANHOPE GREGG
1945–1951	JOHN ARMSTRONG
1951–1956	CHARLES JOHN TYNDALL
1956–1966	CECIL MAURICE KERR
1966–1978	ARTHUR HUGH THOMPSON
1978–1991	THOMAS JAMES BOND
1991–1996	ROBERT STEWART JACKSON
1997–2001	STANLEY JOHNSON
2002–2007	ANDREW JAMES FORSTER

PREBENDARIES OF ELPHIN

The following was the order of precedence:
1. Kilgoghlin
2. Ballintubber
3. Terebrine
4. Kilmacallen
5. Kilcoole (or Kilcooley)
6. Tibohine alias Artough
7. Oran
8. Termonbarry
   Canon Leslie places them in alphabetical order in his List. There was a Prebendary of Killukin, which first appears in 1931 in the Church of Ireland Directory, and which was held by the Archdeacon of Elphin and Ardagh until it lapsed in 2001.

PREBENDARIES OF BALLINTUBBER

1625–1628	ROBERT MAWE
1628/29–1662	HENRY SHARPE
1662–1683	JAMES HAMILTON
1683–1716	SAMUEL HODSON
1716–1734	ROBERT BREDIN
1734–1740	WILLIAM HARRISON
1743–1761	NATHANIEL BARTON
1761–1777	HENRY CUNNINGHAM
1777–1809	WILLIAM SANDFORD
1809–1813	JAMES WHITELAW
1813–1844	WILLIAM BLUNDELL
1845–1860	JOHN ORSON OLDFIELD
1860–1876	GEORGE GRIFFITH
1876–1889	WILLIAM CORNELIUS McCAUSLAND
1890–1910	EDWARD LEATHLEY SHEA
	Prebendary lapsed 1910

PREBENDARIES OF KILCOOLE (or KILCOOLEY)

1615	HUGH BREHAN
1619	HUGH STANLEY
1627	WILLIAM ROYCROFT

1661–1667	THOMAS CROFTON
1667/68–1709	EDWARD NICHOLSON
1709/10–1729	JOHN BULLINGBROKE
1729–1743	MICHAEL GRIFFIN
1743–1767	OLIVER CARY
1767–1809	WILLIAM DIGBY
1809–1846	OLIVER CARY
1847–1866	JOHN MULOCK MAGUIRE
c. 1867	ROBERT GORDON CUMMING
1867–1878	JOHN ACHESON
1878–1929	EDWARD IRWIN
1930–1932	WILLIAM FRANCIS NUNAN
1932–1940	FRANCIS SADLEIR STONEY
1940–1945	ISAAC MAYNE
1945–1953	RICHARD FERGUSON
1953–1964	ALFRED BIRCH
1965–1966	ARTHUR HUGH THOMPSON
1966–1981	WILLIAM THOMPSON HOWARD SLATOR
1981–1984	JOHN ARTHUR KNOWLES
1984–1985	RICHARD ALBERT ROBINSON
	THOMAS GEORGE HUDSON
	Prebendary lapsed 1998

PREBENDARIES OF KILGOGHLIN

1455/56	MAURUS MACINFIRMANAIG
–1463	CRISTINUS MACHIDIAN
–1463	ODO O'FLANAGAN
–1463	CHARLES MACHEDIAN
1473	TOMULTHEUS O'MULMICHAEL
–1475	MALACHY O'FLANAGAN
1475	THOMAS O'HEDIAN
1615	RUDOLPH O'DONOVAN
1627	JOHN KING
1666–1707	THOMAS ECCLESTON
1707–1731	GEORGE DIGBY
1731–1752	WILLIAM FRENCH
1752–1777	JAMES BLAIR
1777–1783	JOHN McLAUGHLIN
1783–1785	STEPHEN RADCLIFFE
1785–1806	GABRIEL STOKES
1806-1826	JOHN BRINKLEY

1827–1870	GEORGE EDWARD VENABLES VERNON
1870-1878	JOSEPH MORTON
1878–1881	MICHAEL NEVILLE KEARNEY
1882–1892	MARTIN BRADSHAW
1892–1898	WILLIAM HENRY PARKER
1899–1917	GEORGE McCLENAGHAN
	The Prebendary was allowed to lapse until 1931
	Since 1931, held by the Bishop

PREBENDARIES OF KILLUKIN

1931–2001	The Archdeacon of Elphin and Ardagh

PREBENDARIES OF KILMACALLEN

Prebendaries of Kilmacallen to Disestablishment were Rectors of Taunagh

1615	in hands of a layman, Sir John King
1634–1661	MILES SUMNER
1661–1668	ROBERT BROWNE
1668–c. 1684	EDMUND ROWLATT
c. 1684–?1705	HENRY YEADON (or HEYDON)
?1705–1750	THOMAS WALLS
1750–1755	JAMES BLAIR
1755–1760	RICHARD DOGHERTY
1760–1799	ROBERT CURTIS
1799–1840	THOMAS HACKETT
1841–1853	ROBERT CADGE
1853–1872	GRAHAM PHILIP CROZIER
1872–1876	Prebendary vacant
1876–1878	GEORGE ALEXANDER PAPENDICK ARBUTHNOT
1878–1879	JOHN BLACK
1880–1886	NEVILLE KEARNEY
1886–1934	JAMES ALLAN FRENCH
1934	MORGAN WILLIAM GARNIER HAMMICK
1934–1937	ROBERT JOHN MITCHELL
1938–1944	FRANCIS JAMES McCORMICK
1944–1950	AUSTIN SWEETNAM
1950–1958	CHARLES GORDON METCALFE
1961–1967	CECIL CHARLES WYNDHAM BROWNE
1967–1978	THOMAS JAMES BOND
1978–1980	JOHN ALEXANDER MONTGOMERY

1980–1981	BASIL GORDON YOUNG McGLAUGHLIN
1981–1987	JOHN MAURICE GLOVER SIRR
1987–1996	CHARLES LUDWIG BIRBECK HILL MEISSNER
1997–2001	IAN GALLAGHER
	Prebendary lapsed 2001

PREBENDARIES OF ORAN

1615	A layman, Henry Molloy held the tithes of the Prebend
1635/36–1668	JOHN WILKINSON
1668/69–1696	COOTE ORMSBY
1696–1730	JOHN FONTANIER
1730–1758	THOMAS CONTARINE
1758–c. 1794	JOHN HICKES
1794–1795	LUKE MAHON
1795–1805	JOHN CROMIE
1805–1807	THOMAS RADCLIFFE
1807–1825	WILLIAM CUNNINGHAM
1825–1831	JOHN HENRY GOULDSBURY
1832–1851	JOHN MULLOY
1851–1853	RICHARD HUGH LOW
1853–1880	JAMES HUNT
1880–1883	THOMAS FRANCIS EASTWOOD
1883–1901	FREDERICK FLOOD
1902–1933	JOHN ROCHE ARDILL
1933–1938	CHARLES SINCLAIR
1938–1944	JOHN CLAUDIUS BERESFORD
1944–1945	JOHN ARMSTRONG
1945–1953	EDWARD FURLONG
1953–1966	WILLIAM JAMES ALLCARD
1967–1984	THOMAS PATRICK SCARBOROUGH WOOD
1984–1991	IVAN RICHARD BIGGS
1991–2001	Prebendary vacant
2001-2004	JOHN MERRICK

PREBENDARIES OF TEREBRINE (or TIRBRIEN)

–1441	CHARLES MacDONNANY
1441	RORY OMOCHAN (YMOCHAN)
1447	EUGENE O'BEYRUN
–1482	CARBRICUS O'BORIND

1615	WILLIAM ROYCROFT
1616–1636	NICHOLAS COXHEAD
1636–1640	ROBERT KING
1640–c. 1660	ARTHUR WARE
1660/61–1674	SAMUEL HAWKES
1674–c. 1682	JOHN STEEVENS
1682–1683	SAMUEL HODSON
1683–1704	ANDREW PATTERSON
1704–c. 1722	JOSEPH GRAVES
?1752–1760	GEORGE ANTROBUS
1761–1767	WILLIAM PHIBBS
1767–1769	JOHN WARDLAW
1769–1777	JOHN McLAUGHLIN
1777–1801	ANTHONY WELDON
1801–1813	ROBERT HAWKSHAW
1813–1856	SAMUEL ADAMS
1857–1859	HUGH JOHN FLYNN
1859–1860	GEORGE GRIFFITH
1861–1871	ANDREW ROBINSON
1871–1876	Prebendary vacant
1876	FREDERICK FOSTER
1876–1894	FRANCIS BURKE
1895–1899	FLETCHER SHERIDAN LeFANU
1900–1936	ROBERT IRVINE FORD
1936–1939	WILLIAM ANDREW STEWART BLAINE
1940–1947	WILLIAM POPHAM HOSFORD
1947–1983	WILLIAM WYNNE SLACK
1983–1987	ERBERTO MAHON NEILL
1987–1991	Prebendary vacant
1991–1995	WILLIAM EDWARD RICHARD GARRETT
1995–	ALBERT WILLIAM KINGSTON

PREBENDARIES OF TERMONBARRY

c. 1405	MAURICE O'FLANAGAN
1409	JOHN MACCOLICH
–1461	WILLIAM O'FARRELL (O'FFEARGAYLL)
1461	DONALD MASCALY
–1466	ISAAC O'MULLALY
1615	Prebendary held by a layman, Robert Nugent
1619	DANIEL O'FARRELL
1627	MICHAEL SMYTH

1636	WILLIAM NEWMAN
1639	HENRY CRISPE
1661	ARCHIBALD CARR
1671	JAMES HONAN
1678–1720	JOHN KEOGH
1720–1730	EDWARD MUNNS
1730–1731	WILLIAM FRENCH
1731–1743	GEORGE BLACKBURNE
1743–1774	THOMAS PALMER
1774–1775	WESLEY BOND
1775–1816	JOHN CLIFFE
1816–1841	EDWARD BULLINGBROKE AYRES
1841–1866	FRANCIS IRWIN
1866-1872	JOHN STEWART GUMLEY
1872–1880	Prebendary vacant
1880–1909	WILLIAM BOURKE WRIGHT
	Prebendary lapsed 1909

PREBENDARIES OF TIBOHINE *alias* ARTOUGH

1615	FLORENCE KELLY or perhaps NELLY
1628	GILBERT SEABROOKE
1637	WILLIAM DOMVILL — probably Prebendary of Tibohine, not Vicar
1641	JOHN WALLIS — probably Prebendary of Tibohine, not Vicar
1662–*c.* 1698	EDWARD HAWKES
1698–1703	WILLIAM BRERETON
1703–*c.* 1724	JONATHAN LAW
1724/25–1731	GEORGE COPE
1731–1761	WESTENRA CRUMPE
1761–1770	NATHANIEL BARTON
1771–1785	WILLIAM FRENCH
1785–1819	JOHN HENRY GOULDSBURY
1819–1863	WILLIAM FRENCH
1863–1866	HENRY JOHNSTON
1867-1905	ARTHUR HYDE
	The Prebendary lapsed until the amalgamation of Elphin with Ardagh in 1929
1930–1943	HENRY JUSTICE
1943–1949	THOMAS SUTCLIFFE HUMPHREYS
1949–1953	JAMES WILSON

1953–1955	CECIL MAURICE KERR
1956–1963	GEORGE HOLMES GIBSON BOLTON
1963–1966	WILLIAM ALEXANDER RUSSELL
1966–1978	JAMES MANSEL EGERTON MAGUIRE
1978–1988	DOUGLAS WRIXON GRAHAM
1988–1992	ROBERT FLEMING HAYMAN
	Prebendary vacant 1992–2004
2004-2007	MARY ELIZABETH ELLEN McELHINNEY

ANCIENT PREBENDS

For other ancient Prebends which lapsed in the 17th century, see the Parishes of Baslick, Drumcliffe, Kilbegnet and Killukin.

CANONS
whose Prebends are unknown

1310	MALACHY McHUGH (McAEDHA)
1313	LAURENCE O'LACHLNAN
1326	JOHN O'FINASA (O'FINNAGHTY)
1327	MAURICE O'GIBELLAIN
1343	DONAGH CLERACH O'MULBRENAN
c. 1353	GREGORY
1383	JOHN O'MOCHAN
1398	MALACHY O'KEALLAICH
1400	THOMAS McMURTAGH (McMURHEARTAIGH)
1401	FINBARDUS O'MAILANNA
1404	MARIANUS O'FLANAGAN
1404	ODO MACDOIMCAIDNABARG
1404	PAUL O'SOMOCHAN
1407	DERMIT McGILLARUAID (MACHGILLAMORGH
1410	THADY O'KELLAID
1411	JOHN MACCOLICH (MACOLY)
1413	THADY McDIARMADA
1413	ECGILBERTUS MACHABRECHIM
1413	CRISTIN MACHABRECHIM
1413	NICHOLAS O'HEDIAN
1414	NICHOLAS O'KAELLY
1414	THADY MACDIARMADA
1414	MAURICE MACKEDYGAYN (McGEOGHEGAN)
c. 1420	MAURICE MACQUEDIAN (possibly same as above)

1426	LAURENCE O'BEOLLAYN (O'HEOLLAYN)
1426	MAURICE O'CONNOR (O'CONCUBAIR)
1427	DONALD O'MOCHAHAN
1427	NEHEMEAH (NEMEAS) O'BEOLAN (O'BEOLAYN)
1427	THOMOTHEUS (THADY) McDIARMADA
1428	CHARLES O'GARA
1428	DERMIT O'MOCHAN
1428	BERNARD O'HEADRA
1428	REGINALD ODUBUNRA
1428	LEWIS MACHRANAN
1428	CORMAC O'HEADRA
1429	JOHN McGILLACIARAN
1430	CORMAC McDONAGH (MacDONNCHDID)
1430/31	DERMIT MAGAEDAGAN
1432	ODO O'FLANAGAN
1433	CORNELIUS MacGRIABHED (McGRIFFITH)
1440	DONALD McDONAGH (MacDOMCHAID)
1443	CORNELIUS O'SYYNYN
1443	MANUS O'FUORORI (O'FFUORCHAID)
1444	DERMIT MAGEAGAN
1444	MAGONIUS McDONAGH (MacDONNCHIAD)
1445/46	CHRISTINUS McEOGHEGAN (MacDEDIAN)
1445/46	DONALD MacKYLRUYD (MacGILLARUAYD)
1446	CHARLES O'FLANAGAN
1446	DONALD O'CONNOR (O'CONCHUBUYR)
1447	DERMIT O'HARA
1447	CORMAC O'CHUINN (?O'QUINN)
1448	NEMEAS O'RUOGRI
1450	CORMAC O'MOCHAN
1450	CRISTIN MacCRIAN
1453	JOHN O'THONAIR (O'TONOR or O'CONOR)
1453	EUGENE O'CONEIL
1454	CHARLES MacGILLANAGUSSAN
1454	THOMAS OAHARTAGAN (OHACTAGAN)
1455/56	CHARLES MAGOREACTAYD
1455/56	THOMAS O'HACCYAN
1456	CORNELIUS O'KAHALAN
1456	DONALD McGEOGHEGAN (MacDAEGAYN)
1456	DERMIT O'FLANNAGAN
1456	EUGENE O'BERNYN
1456	SEANCHANUS O'STINGYN
1460	MALACHY O'MOCHAN
1460	JOHN OFFAYND (O'FLOYND)

1460	JOHN O'HAIGADAN
1461	WILLIAM O'FLANAGAN
1461	DONALD O'CONAIR
1462	CRISTINUS O'HEDIAN
1463	CORMAC O'HEDIAN
1463	FERGALLUS O'BRUCAN
1465	DONALD MacGILLARUAY
1465	FELEMY MacDUBGALLY
1465	ODO MacDOMCAYRDUAN
1466	ISAAC O'MULLALYD
1488	CHARLES McGEOGHEGAN
1501	PETER O'SCINGYN
1501	CHARLES O'FALLEVY
1511	CORNELIUS O'LEYNAN (O'FLAHERTY)
1532	BERNARD O'CONOR
1532	EUGENE O'CONNEGEAN
1540	JOHN HOVEDEN

PARISHES OF ELPHIN

*denotes Mediaeval and long-obsolete parishes

Aghanagh
Ahamplish
Ahascragh
Ardcarne
Ardclare
Athleague
Athlone, St Peter
Aughrim

Ballinakill*
Ballintubber
Ballysumaghan and Kilross
Baslick
Boyle
Bumlin

Calry
Camma*
Castleblakeney *alias* Killasoolan
Clonfinlough
Clontuskert
Clonygormacan*
Creeve
Croghan
Culea*

Derran*
Disert*
Drintemple*
Drumcliffe
Drumcollum*
Dunamon

Eastersnow
Elphin

Fuerty and Kilbegnet

Ivernon*

Kilbride
Kilbryan
Kilcola*
Kilcooley*
Kilcorkey*
Kilcroan*
Kilgeffin*
Kilglass

Kilkeevan
Killaspicbrone*
Killeiniregard*
Killenvoy
Killeroran or Kilronan
Killery
Killukin
Killumada*
Killyngyn* (? Killyon)
Killyon or Killeroran
Kilmacallen
Kilmacoen*
Kilmactranny
Kilmacumsy*
Kilmore
Kilnamanagh*
Kiltoom
Kiltullagh
Knocknarea
Kyllmurchayn*

Lisanuffy*
Lissadell and Munninane Chapel of Ease
Loughglynn

Minbrisg*

Ogulla*
Oran

Rathcline
Roscommon
Rosses Point

Shankill*
Sligo, St John's Cathedral
St. Bernanus de Manso*

Taghboy*
Taunagh
Teatby*
Terebrine*
Termonbarry*
Termoncaelyn*
Tessaragh*
Tibohine*
Toomna
Tullagh*

Aghanagh, Ballinafad, Co Sligo

AGHANAGH

VICARS
see Kilmactranny 1666 and Boyle, with which it was united
with other parishes which subsequently joined Boyle
with Roscommon Group 1997–2000
with Boyle, Taunagh, Croghan, Ardcarne, Tybohine, Ballysumaghan and Kilmactranny 2003–

NOTES
A schoolhouse was licensed for public worship in 1844. The church was consecrated on 28th September 1855, and replaced an old building situated on the shores of Lough Arrow.

Ahamplish, Grange, Co Sligo

AHAMPLISH

VICARS
1615	Charles O'Connor
1635–1640	William Newport
1640	William Young (Yonge)
1641–1674	Robert Browne
1674–c. 1723	James Reed
1723–1750	Eubule Ormsby
1750–1769	Andrew Knox
1769–1770	George Hicks
1770–1773	William Wade
1771–1774	Andrew Nixon
1774–1776	Matthew Browne
1776–1841	Charles West
1841–1881	John Evelyn Greene
1881–1886	James Todd
1886–1918	John Harpur McCormick
1918–1931	William Francis Nunan
1931–1937	John Allen
1937–1963	James Wilson
1963–1969	Samuel Derek Hamilton
1969–c. 1976	John Maurice Glover Sirr

CURATES
1730	Edward Munns
1874–1877	Isaac Coulter
1877–1881	John Magill
1881	James Todd

with Drumcliffe and Rosses 1918–
with Lissadell 1959–
Church closed c. 1976

NOTES
Ahamplish Church built 1813.

AHASCRAGH, St Catherine

VICARS
c. 143–	Maurice Yfynduayn
c. 1430	Malachy O'Fallyn
1430	Malachy O'Cormic
1432	William O'Falluyn
1442	Thady McGeraghty (MacGereachtayd)
1449	Thomas MacBrysson
1449	Cornelius O'Callaghan (O'Cathalain)
1573	Edward Browne
1615	Roger O'Sally
1628	Gilbert Seabrooke
1635	John Browne
1666	Henry Dodwell
1674–1685	Leonard Hodson
1685	Stephen Handcock
1685–1729	Fielding Shaw
1730	William Glass

RECTORS
1620	Henry Dodwell
1674–1701	Alexander Murray
1701	Stephen Handcock
1701–1717	Francis Knapp (Knappagh)
1717–1718	Jonathan Smedley
1718–c. 1729	John Thewles
1730–	William Digby
1777–1799	Jonathan Cope
1799–1829	Peter Browne
1829–1845	Henry Hunt
1845–1880	Peter Browne

transferred to Clonfert Diocese after Disestablishment 1870.

CURATES
1725	William Glass
1786	Armstrong Kelly
1800	Daniel Powell
1863–1865	Robert Gilbert Eccles
1865–1869	Robert Holmes Orr

NOTES

'The Church was built 40 years ago; was kept in repair for many years at the expense of Mr. Mahon of Castlegar living in said parish' (PR 1777). 'The Church was built [possibly rebuilt] 1810–14, cost £923 odd', of which £92 was gift of the Board of First Fruits (Report of 1837). The church was handsomely rebuilt in modern times.

Ardcarne, Co Roscommon

ARDCARNE

RECTORS
–1411	Dermit O'Duffy (Oduthaid)
	Thady McDermott (MacDiarmada)
1639	Andrew Frere

VICARS
1427	Philip MacBrechim
1427	Odo McDermott (Macdiarmada)
1428	Philip Macabrechim
1440	Magonius Mickechin
–1446	Patrick O'Stingen
1446	Cornelius McDermott (Macdiarmada)
1460	Ronaldus O'Colla
1460	Fergal O'Gormly
1590	Teige O'Coan
1590	Hugh O'Coan
1615	John Evett
1618	Erasmus Matthews
1639	Andrew Frere
1665	James Wilson
1668/69	Vincent Cave
1669/70	Anthony Cope
1700–1722	Edward Goldsmith

RECTORS and VICARS

1710–1722	George Manby
1723–1743	Lewis Hamilton
1743–1752	William French
c. 1752–	Thomas Figsbee
1776–1784	—
c. 1784–	John Orr
1797–1825	John Henry Gouldsbury
1825–1846	John Orson Oldfield
1846–1860	George Griffith
1861–1871	Andrew Robinson
1872–1876	Frederick Foster
1876–1904	Francis Burke
1904–1909	Horace George Warren
1911–1944	Francis James McCormick
1946–1949	Thomas Norman Bateman C-in-c
1949–1953	Edward Furlong C-in-c
1953–1954	vacant
1956–1978	Arthur Hugh Thompson
1978–1980	George Kingston
1981–1987	Erberto Mahon Neill
1988–1995	William Edward Richard Garrett
1995–	vacant
1997–2001	Shiela Johnson Aux Min
2001–2004	Noel Henry Likely Regan Aux Min
2004–	Kenneth Arthur Lambart Barrett

CURATES

1806	John French
c. 1810	Charles Seymour
1843–1845	Arthur Hyde
1900–1902	Henry Acheson
1902	Patrick Percival O'Sullivan

with Croaghan 1949–1955
with Boyle Group 1956–
with Roscommon Group 1997–2000

ARDCLARE, Co Roscommon, St George

Note: Probably with Prebendary of Kilcooley –1846.

RECTOR

1846–1878	Richard Cowen

with Elphin 1904–
with Bumlin 1934–
possibly Church closed 1878

Athleague, Co Roscommon

ATHLEAGUE / MOUNT TALBOT

VICARS

–14–	Thomas Yriana
–14–	David Ykahan
–1441	Dermit Maggillaruayd
1441	John Macaedagain
–1461	Charles MacGillaruaig
1461	Bernard O'Kelly (Occallaig)
1466	William O'Kelly (Oceallaygh)
1616	Thomas Gawin (Gwin)
1622	Nicholas Steere
1625	Robert Mawe (Wawe)
1629–*c.* 1662	Gilbert Seabrooke
1662–1683	James Hamilton
1683–1716	Samuel Hodson
1716–1734	Robert Bredin
1734–c 1780	John Hickes
c. 1780–1785	Stephen Radcliff
1785–1809	Thomas Crawford
1809–1837	James Crawford
1837–1847	Thomas Crawford
1847–1861	Andrew Robinson
1861–1870	Fitzmaurice Hunt
1871–1909	William Bourke Wright
1909–1919	John Richard Gahagan

Mount Talbot, Co Roscommon

1919–1922	Leopold Andrew Pakenham Walsh Hunter C-in-c
1924–1928	John Harpur McCormick
1929–1931	Richard Hans de Brabant Cooke
1931–1936	Frederick Charles Hill C-in-c
1936–1941	George Kirwan Birmingham C-in-c
1942–1953	Thomas Sutcliffe Humphreys
1954–1966	James Mansel Egerton Maguire
1966–1975	Douglas Wrixon Graham

with Killyon and Castleblakeney 1924–1931
with Killeroran 1931–1940
with St Peter, Athlone 1940–1941
with Roscommom Group 1941–1975
Church closed *c.* 1975

NOTES

The two churches of Athleague and Mount Talbot are very old. The first stone of new church at Athleague laid on 18th August 1841.

ATHLONE, St John

VICARS
1682/83–1688	George Thewles
1688–1694	Joseph Stoughton
1694	Edward Hawkes

ATHLONE, St Mary

VICAR
1683–1723	Edward Waller

ATHLONE, St Peter

VICAR
1615   John Ankers

PERPETUAL CURATES/RECTORS
1802–1837   Annesley Strean
1837–1860   Hugh Murray
1860–1880   James Gully
1880–1910   George McClenaghan
1910–1913   Gordon John Walsh
1913–1925   James Ferguson Anderson
1926–1930   William Cecil de Pauley
1930–1941   George Kirwan Birmingham

CURATES
–1766   William Digby
–1827   Samuel Hodson
c. 1828   Edward Powell
1832   John William Fairbrother Drought
1835   James Janns
1848   Robert Lauder
1851–1852   Thomas Preston Ball
1854–1856   John Maurice Gillington
1856–1860   William Henry Hutchinson
1860   Henry Johnston
1864   Richard Allen White
1866–1867   Charles Knox Strong
1867–1879   Robert Foster
1979–1880   Henry Brownrigg Hewson
1887–1888   George William Baile

with Kiltoom 1926–
transferred to Meath Diocese 1941

NOTES
The church was built in 1804. The new church was consecrated on 22nd June 1841.

AUGHRIM, Co Galway

For Rectors, see Prebendaries of Terebrine of which this Rectory was the corps.

VICARS		CURATES	
–1412	Patrick O'Dulgumach	–1806	Michael Griffin
	John O'Brynd	1817–c. 1826	John Lloyd
–1447	Malachy O'Thanayn	1843–1846	Joseph Morton
–1447	John McDiarmada	1848–1849	Richard Nash
1447	Eugene O'Beyrun		Standish
1615	John Evett	1851	Michael Bell Cox
–1640	Richard Wolly	1857–1860	James Sutcliffe Paget
1640	Nicholas Coxhead	1882–1885	Edward Arthur or
1681/82	Andrew Paterson		Rose Power, C
1704	Robert Jones		Killukin
1705	Michael Griffin		
1743	George Blackburne	with Kilmore	
1788–1811	John Barton	with Killukin	
1811–1820	Michael Griffin		
1820–1835	William Smith		
1835–1847	John Lloyd		
1848–1878	Henry Irwin		

NOTES

The church was demolished in late 19th century.

BALLINAKILL

Long-obsolete medieval parish.

with Ballysumaghan 1444 and 1666–1866
part of corps of Prebendaries of Oran
united with Dunamon 1710

BALLINTUBBER

VICARS
–c. 1410	Eugene O'Floenn
–1413	Thomoltheus O'Maybreynand
1413–c. 1440	Maurice McGeoghegan
	(Mackedygayn or Maguedan)
–1445	Finnardus O'Fyachney
	(O'Fyachreay or O'Fychnaid)
1446	Dermit O'Flannagan
1615	Florence Nelly
–1673	Matthew Moore
1673	John Ferris, appointed sequestrator
1673	Samuel Hindes
1674	Edward Nicholson

RECTORS
see Prebendaries of Ballintubber

CURATES
see Baslick

Ballysumaghan, Co Sligo

BALLYSUMAGHAN

VICARS

–1440	Muricius O'Somochan
–1440	Donald O'Somochan (Yhoomochan)
1440	Donatus O'Somochan
1615	Thomas King
1622	Nicholas Steere
1666	Edward Rowlatt
c. 1684	—
c. 1696–1716	Tobias Caulfield
1716–1718	John Thewles
1718–1729	Edward Munns
1729–	John Holmes
–1766	William French
1797–1801	Thomas Hacket
1801–1802	Hugh Johnston
1802–1840	Thomas Hacket
1841–1861	Edmund Allen Lucas
1861–1866	Arthur Moneypenny

1867–1874	Thomas Knott
1875–1885	Martin Bradshaw
1886–1894	Thomas W. Moulsdale, C (possibly in-c)
1886–1887	
1895–1900	Charles Sinclair
1900–1931	James Leonard Poe
1931–1946	Robert William Gibson C-in-c
1946–1949	Thomas Patrick Scarborough Wood C-in-c
1950–1955	Walter Cyril Spence
1955–1956	Robert Desmond Holtby C-in-c
1956–1959	William Russell C-in-c
1960–1985	Richard Albert Robinson
1987–1990	Robert Gordon Keogh
1992–1994	Stuart Irwin McGee
1995–1999	Arthur Minion
1999–2004	Noel Henry Likely Regan Aux Min
2004–	Kenneth Arthur Lambart Barrett

RECTORS

–1439	Paul O'Somochan (Ysomochan)
1444	Malachy Macgillacearan
1615	Henry Malby

NSM

1999–2004	Noel Henry Likely Regan

with Killery 1912–1990
with Killenumery 1956–1960
with Taunagh and Kilmactranny 1960–
with Sligo Cathedral Group, Knocknarea and Rosses Point, Taunagh and Kilmactranny 1992–1994
with Boyle Group, Taunagh, Aghanagh, Croghan, Ardcarne, Tybohine, and Kilmactranny 2003–

BASLICK

RECTORS or PREBENDARIES
–1402	Maurice (Murtogh) O'Flannagan
1402	Odo Macormaic
1404	Marianus O'Flanagan
1432	Charles O'Fflanagan
1623	Robert Mawe
1637/38	William Freeman

VICARS
–1413	Henry Stondun
	Maurice Mackedygyan
1552	Bernard O'Conegan
1623	Robert Mawe
1627/28	William Newcomen
1635–1640	Conell (Cornelius) Tully
1640	Robert Conway
–1673	Matthew Moore
1673	Samuel Hindes

CURATES
probably several including
1732	Mordaunt Hamilton

probably with Ballintubber *c.* 1552–

Boyle, Co Roscommon

BOYLE

VICARS	
1615	John Evatt
1633	Erasmus Matthews
1653	William Portman
1683	John Brown
c. 1689–1698	Henry Yeadon (Heydon)
1701	John Holmes
1718–1729	Edward Munns
–1766	William French
–1782	Alexander Gouldsbury
1785–1797	Thomas Hackett Jun
1797–1840	Thomas Hackett
1842–1866	John Mulock Maguire
1866–1879	Henry Johnston
1880–1883	Thomas Francis Eastwood
1883–1910	Francis Edward Clarke
1910–1933	William Wolfe Wagner
1933–1938	Edward Furlong
1938–1952	William Thompson Howard Slator
1952–1978	Arthur Hugh Thompson
1978–1980	George Kingston
1981–1987	Erberto Mahon Neill
1988–1995	William Edward Richard Garrett

1996–1997	Robert Alan Chalmers C-in-c
1997–2001	Shiela Johnson C-in-c
2004–	Kenneth Arthur Lambart Barrett

CURATES

1732	Robert Phipps
1785	John Henry Gouldsbury
1790	William Smyth
1802	Samuel Davis
1824	John McCrea
1827	Thomas Gregg
1843–1847	Edward Morse
1846–1861	Fitzmaurice Hunt
1854–1856	Christopher Adamson
1856–1860	William Baker Fry
1860	Zachary Barry
1861	James Edward Butler
1863–1866	John Davis
1866	Edgeworth Conolly Wheler
1867	Robert Gordon Cumming
1868–1881	Henry Fry
1881–1882	James William Ford
1883	Edward Alexander Cooke
1884	James Edward Cullen
1884–1886	Francis Travers Cockle
1887–1890	James Carey
1890–1894	Richard Booth Bryan
1894–1908	Thomas Irwin
1908–1912	Thomas Gordon Sharpe
1913–1915	John Henry McBrien

NSM

1999– 2004	Noel Henry Likely Regan

with Aghanagh from early times
with Aghanagh and Ardcarne 1956–; Croaghan added 1983
with Kilbryan 1956–1996
with Roscommon Group 1997–2000
with Taunagh, Ballysumaghan and Kilmactranny 2004–

NOTES

'The church having been ruinous some ages and distant above an Irish mile from the Town of Boyle and very inconvenient to ye Parishioners to resort to for Divine Worship, or for building a new church there, and Edward, Lord Kingston, having conveyed to William, Bishop of Elphin, (Patron) for ever an acre and 21 perches of ground in Boyle for building a new church and for a church yard, ye site was removed thither by Order in Council' 17th May 1765. The church was consecrated on 20th July 1772. The schoolhouse at Aghana was licensed for public worship in April 1844, and the burial ground was consecrated on 8th May 1875. A new rectory was provided in 1960.

Bumlin, Strokestown, Co Roscommon, St John The Baptist

BUMLIN

For Rectors to Disestablishment, see Prebendaries of Kilgoghlin.

VICARS
1615	John Foster
1634/35	John Nairn
–1640	Richard Peck (Pyke)
1640	William Yonge
–1672	Archibald Carr

1674	James Honan
1678–1720	John Keogh
1730	William Harrison
1741	William Wemyss
1745	Richard Garrett
1769	—
c. 1790	Maurice Mahon
1811–1847	Edward Mahon
1847–1878	Joseph Morton
1878–1881	Michael Neville Kearney
1882–1888	Alfred Hackett
1888–1934	James Allen French
1934–1939	William Andrew Stewart Blaine C-in-c
1940–1945	Isaac Mayne
1945–1982	William Wynne Slack

CURATES

1805–1812	Arthur Mahon
1823	William Hewson
1830	Walter Gibbs
1835–1846	Richard Cowen

with Elphin and Ardclare 1934–
Kilgeffin and Kilglass added
Croaghan, Creeve, Eastersnow and Tybohine added 1956

NOTES

"Church being ruinous and inconveniently situated ordered to be removed to more convenient site — parcel of land on lands of Lisrayne near centre of Parish adjoining town of Strokestown containing 1 acre conveyed by Thomas Mahon of Strokestown to Bishop and successors for erecting new church 8 Mar 1754." The present church was built in 1820, and opened and dedicated on 27th August. The last service was held on 26th June 1977. The church was closed and deconsecrated on 6th March 1981. The building, in the village of Strokestown, Co Roscommon, opened as a heritage centre 1982.

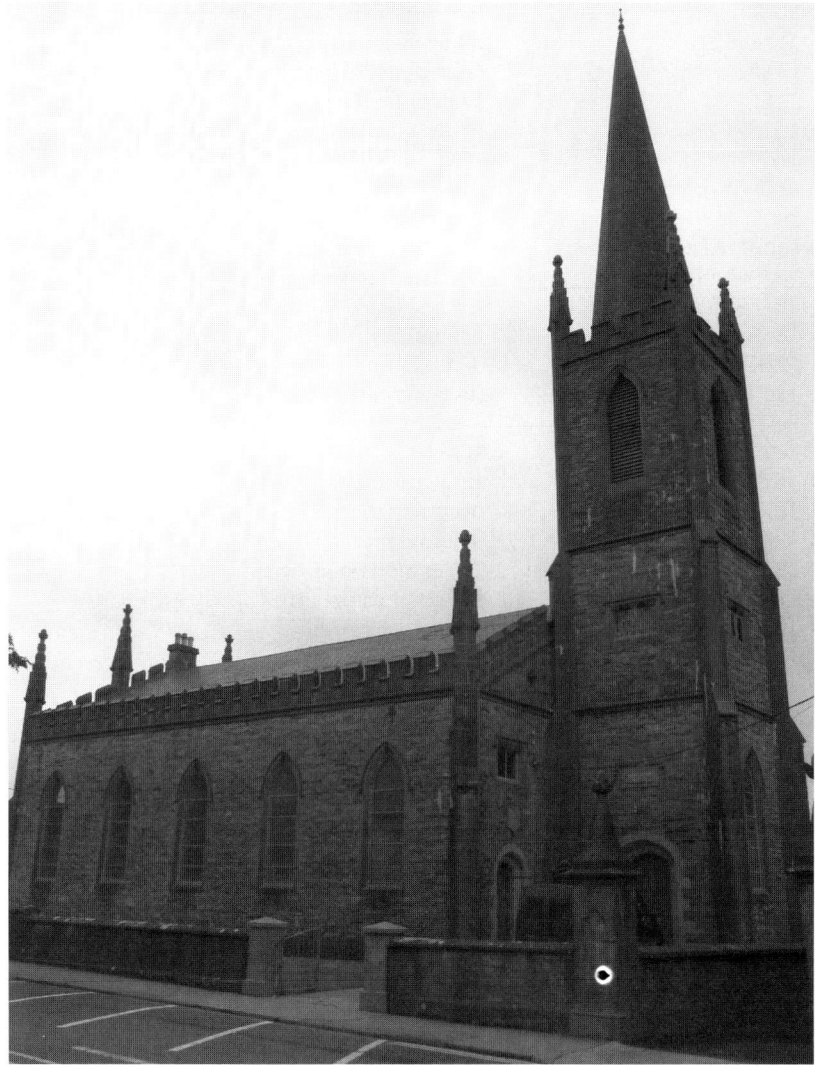

Calry, Sligo, Co Sligo

CALRY

RECTORS
–1409	Maccraith Maabreicheannin, V Cuilleada (possibly = Calry)
1409	John Obeachnachan
1428	Maurice O'Conor (O'Concubayr)
1440	Thady Macdonagh (Macdonchayd)

VICARS
c. 1450   Thomas O'Hactigan (Yhactigan)
–1456   Cornelius O'Heactagan
1456   Dermit O'Hactigan
1622   William Roycroft
1640   Henry Prickett
united with St John, Sligo *c.* 1660

PERPETUAL CURATES
1823–1840   William Armstrong
1840–1856   Andrew Todd Gillmor
1856–1866   Samuel Shone
1866–1867   Thomas C. Moore
1867–1871   John Dowden

RECTORS
1872–1875   Robert McWalter
1876–1877   Matthew Magill
1877–1886   Thomas Heany
1887–1890   James Fleetwood Berry
1890–1899   Llewelyn Paul Tahan Ledoux
1899–1944   John Roche Ardill
1945–1956   Charles John Tyndall
1956–1994   Thomas Patrick Scarborough Wood
1995   Caroline Walling BC
1995–1999   David Griscome, BC 1995–1997
2001–2007   Mary Elizabeth Ellen McElhinney

NSM
1993–2004   John Merrick

CURATES
1867–1869   Thomas Simpson Jones
1870–1872   Robert Young Lynn
1893–1898   Thomas Johnston Bayly
1898–1900   Joseph Samuel Wylie
1900–1903   Leonard Leader Cooper
1904–1907   Charles John Algernon Harris
1909–1913   John Fitzgerald Kellett
1913–1915   Hugh Bourchier Eaton

NOTES
The Glebe house was built in 1822. Calry Church in Sligo town, was built in 1824 and cost £5,246 15s 3d.

CAMMA
Long-obsolete medieval parish.

1615 John Hathersall

V with Kiltoom 1636–

Castleblakeney, Co. Galway

CASTLEBLAKENEY alias KILLASOOLAN

VICARS
c. 1423	Malachy O'Dubigan
1425	Donatus O'Geruayn
1430	Thady O'Kelly (O'Kellaig)
1435	Dermit O'Dubagayn
1459–1461	Nicholas O'Lachnayn
1573	Edward Browne
1615	Hugh O'Greaghan

RECTORS
1620	Henry Dodwell
1661	Henry Dodwell Jun
1664	Henry Dodwell
1674	Alexander Murray
1674	Richard Horne

RECTORS and VICARS
1698	Joseph Graves
1701–1717	Francis Knapp

1717–c. 1730	Jonathan Smedley
1730–c. 1743	William Glass
1743/44–	William Tisdall
–1754	Francis Ormsby
1754–c. 1765	Samuel Pullein
1765–1780	Alexander Seton
1780–1823	Alexander Gunning
1823–1828	Daniel Lucas
1828–1857	Charles Milley Doyle
1857–1859	John Mulloy
1859–1865	William Jeffcott
1865–1871	George Knox
1873–1891	James Hunt
1891–1908	William Noblett, also R Killyon
1908–1918	Robert Miller
1918–1928	John Harpur McCormick
1929–1931	Richard Hans de Brabant Cooke
1931–1936	Frederick Charles Hill
1936–1941	George Kirwan Birmingham, R Athlone, C-in-c
1941–1953	Thomas Sutcliffe Humphreys
1954–1966	James Mansel Egerton Maguire
1966–1975	Douglas Wrixon Graham, R Roscommon Group –1988

CURATES

1711	Robert Bredin
1732	Thomas Abbott
1832	Robert Cadge
1842	Richard Hugh Low
1850	John Stewart Gumley
c. 1859	John French
1869	John O'Rorke
1874	Francis Carr

with Killyon 1894–1931
with Athleague and Mount Talbot 1924–1975
with Killeroran 1931–1975
with Roscommon, Dunamon and Killenvoy added 1941–1975
with Rathcline transferred from Ardagh 1965–1975
possibly Church closed 1975

NOTES

Record of consent of parishioners and Vestry of Killasoolan to building of new parish church on lands of Cappavarrigy alias Coughter near town of Castleblakeney, being 2 acres given by Robert Blakeney Esq. Robert Bredin, Curate, Robert Blakeney and George Petty, Church Wardens signed (Tuam DR). 7 Queen Anne XII Section 20 enacted that this church when built and consecrated to be called Parish Church of Castleblakeney alias Killasoolan 1711.

CLONFINLOUGH

VICARS

–1401	Reginald Odubunra (Idubanra)
1401	Eneas Orachtagan
1401	Matthew Orachtagan
–1428	Reginald Odubunra
1428	Lewis Machranan
1674	James Honan
1678	John Keogh
1731	Oliver Cary
1742	Francis Bosquet
1797	James Little
1832–c. 1852	Thomas Gordon Caulfield

NOTES

No Vicar's name appears in records of 1678–1731, but was probably held with the Vicarage of Clontuskert later. The Rectory was corps of the Prebendary of Kilgoghlin in 19th century. No church or glebe — Incumbent non-resident.

CLONTUSKERT

VICARS

1664	James Honan
1674	George Thewles
1688	Joseph Stoughton
1698–1731	George Digby

with Clonfinlough 1731–

CLONYGORMACAN

Long-obsolete medieval parish.
See Kilmactranny.

CLOONAFF alias CLONCRAFF or CLONCREEF

Long-obsolete medieval parish.

VICARS
-1411   Charles O'Berind
-1412   John O'Macny

CREEVE

VICARS
1674	James Honan
1674	John Keogh
1737–1747	Arthur Mahon
1771	John Wardlaw
1798–1846	Oliver Cary
1846–1847	Joseph Morton
1847–1848	Henry Irwin
1848–1879	Frederick Hamilton

CURATES
1766	John Byrne
1869–1870	William Henry Frazer

with Croghan 1870
Church closed

Croghan, Co Roscommon, Holy Trinity

CROGHAN

PERPETUAL CURATES

1856–1861	possibly Frederick Augustus Potterton
c. 1859	possibly George Frederick Stoney
1861	Daniel Leahy
1862–1863	Andrew Tyrrell Labatt
1863–1866	Charles Knox Strong
1867–1869	Benjamin Irwin

RECTORS

1871–1879	Frederick Hamilton
1879–1886	Neville Kearney
1887–1898	William Henry Parker
1898–1902	George Frederick Courtenay
1902–1938	Charles Sinclair
1938–1953	Edward Furlong
1956–1982	William Wynne Slack
1984–1987	Erberto Mahon Neill
1988–1995	William Edward Richard Garrett
1996–1997	Robert Alan Chalmers
1997–2001	Shiela Johnson C-in-c
2004–	Kenneth Arthur Lambart Barrett

NSM
1999–2004　　　　　　　　　Noel Henry Likely Regan

with Creeve 1870–
with Eastersnow 1879–
with Tibohine 1924–1960
with Ardcarne 1949–1955
with Elphin Group 1955–1962
with Bumlin and Ardclare 1963–1983
with Boyle, Aghanagh, Kilbryan and Ardcarne 1983–
with Rathcline and Kiltullagh 1996–2000
with Roscommon Group 1997–2000
Taunagh, Tybohine, Ballysumaghan and Kilmactranny added 2003

NOTES
Croghan established as a Chapel of Ease in Killukin Parish *c.* 1856. The church was built in 1862 on a site granted by Guy Lloyd of Croghan House and consecrated on Easter Thursday 22nd April 1862 by Bishop Marcus Gervais Beresford.

CULEA

Long-obsolete medieval parish.

VICARS
1615	Hugh Drehin
1620	Hugh McBrehone
1639	Robert Prickett
1640	Henry Prickett

DERRAN

Long-obsolete medieval parish.

VICAR
1634   Henry Compton

DISERT

Long-obsolete medieval parish.
See Tessaragh.

DRIMTEMPLE

Long-obsolete medieval parish.
See Oran.

VICARS
1615   Thomas Gawyne
1633   Miles Somner

Drumcliffe, Co Sligo, St Columba

DRUMCLIFFE

PREBENDARIES and RECTORS
−1414	Cornelius O'Coneil
1414	Charles O'Gara
−1428	Thomas O'Tarpa
1428	Dermit Magaedagan
1583	Owen O'Conogher
1622	William Roycroft
1661	possibly Robert Browne (see Cotton)

VICARS
−1402	John O'Connel
1403	Dermit Macherleginn
1403	Cornelius O'Connel

–1425	Dermit O'Coneil
1425	Nemeas O'Beollayn
1446/47	William O'Beollan
1455	Eugene O'Coneil
1611	Thomas Pilley
1615	Hugo Hohy
1619	William Rycroft
1661–1673	Robert Browne
1674–c 1723	James Reed
1723–1730	Eubule Ormsby
1730–1756	Edward Munns
1758–1760	Richard Dogherty
1760–1766	Robert Curtis
1767–1783	Michael Obins
1783–1785	Thomas Cowper
1785–c. 1796	Stephen Radcliff
1797–c. 1811	Richard Wynne
1811–1846	John Yeats
1847–1871	Thomas Crawford
1871–1877	Julius Henry Griffith
1877–1879	John James Ferguson Guthrie
1879–1889	James Alan French
1889–1899	John Roche Ardill
1899–1931	William Francis Nunan
1931–1937	John Allen
1937–1963	James Wilson
1963–1969	Samuel Derek Hamilton
1969–1987	James Maurice Glover Sirr
1988–1992	Robert Fleming Hayman
1993–2001	Ian Gallagher
2002–2007	Andrew James Forster
2008–	Barry Ian Linton

CURATES

1804	Edward Bullingbroke Ayres
1823	Charles Dunne
1827	George Vaughan Hart
1832–1841	Edward Lloyd Elwood
1842–1854	Francis Hassard
1858–1866	John Langford Finnerty
1867–1869	Robert Edward Briscoe

with Rosses Point 1902–1960
with Ahamplish 1918–c. 1976
with Lissadell 1959–

NOTES

Drumcliffe Church was built in 1809 and cost £738 9s 2¾d. The poet William Butler Yeats (1865–1939) is buried in Drumcliffe Churchyard.

DRUMCOLLUM

Note: In Boyle Union.
Long-obsolete medieval parish.

VICARS
1615   Hugh Brehon
1620–1640   see Kilmacallan

Dunamon, Co Roscommon

DUNAMON

VICARS

–1421	Nellanus Ymochayn
–1421	Cornelius O'Somochan
–1421	Dermit O'Somochan
1425	Odo O'Somochan
1441	see Fuerty
1456	see Kilbegnet
1615	Thomas Gawine (Gwin)
1622	Nicholas Steere
1635	William Hollywell
–1641	William Domville
1641	Tempest Illingworth
1662–1683	James Hamilton

1683–1716	Samuel Hodson
1716–1734	Robert Bredin
1734–c 1741	Thomas Contarine
c. 1741–1780	John Hickes
1780–1794	Stephen Radcliff
1794–1795	Luke Mahon
1795–1805	John Cromie
1805–1807	Thomas Radcliff
1807–c. 1825	William Conyngham
1825–1831	John Henry Gouldsbury
1831–1865	George Knox
1866–1880	Francis Irwin
1880–1881	Henry W.S. Given
1881–1902	Joseph Chapman
1902–1914	Henry Sutton Varian Daly
1914–1917	James Williamson Camier
1917–1926	Richard Wolfe Landey
1926–1953	Thomas Sutcliffe Humphreys
1954–1966	James Mansel Egerton Maguire
1966–1988	Douglas Wrixon Graham
1988–1992	Douglas Wrixon Graham Temp-in-c
1992–1996	Robert Stewart Jackson Temp-in-c
1996–1997	Robert Alan Chalmers BC
1997–2001	Shiela Johnson BC
2001–	vacant

NSM

1991–1996	Cecil Lindsay
2005–	Jane Alexandra Lindsay

CURATES

–1718	T. Gordone
1786	Luke Mahon
1826	George Knox
c. 1830	Gustavus Warner

with Fuerty at various times
with Roscommon Group 1917–

NOTES

Dunamon, Kilbegnet, Ballynakill and Kileroane were united in one parish with the name of Dunamon 1710 by 9 Queen Anne XII Section 19 (LM VI 32).

Eastersnow, Co Roscommon

EASTERSNOW

VICARS
1615	Edward Crofton
1634/35	Edward Burt
1683–1700	Anthony Cope
1700–1722	Edward Goldsmith
1737–1747	Arthur Mahon
–1766	Patrick Kerr
1790–1798	Oliver Cary
1798–1812	Thomas Lloyd
1812–*c.* 1820	Arthur Mahon
1820–1837	Thomas Crawford
1837–1840	Charles Coote Mulloy
1840–1845	Lewis Henry Strean
1845–1879	Frederick Hamilton

CURATES
1851	John Acheson
1851–1852	John Howlin Monsarrat
c. 1853	George Gillington
1854–1858	Thomas Phibbs

with Kilcola in early times
with Croghan 1879–
Church closed early, possibly before 1900
with Elphin 1955–

NOTES
The Glebe house was built in 1823. The church, which was very old and of unknown date, has been closed for many years.

Elphin Cathedral, Co Roscommon, St Mary

ELPHIN

RECTORS
For Rectors –1895, see Deans
1895–1929   Edward Irwin
1929–1939   William Andrew Stewart Blaine
1940–1945   Isaac Mayne
1945–1958   William Wynne Slack

VICARS
1402   Ynarus Odubginnach
1615   John Foster

CURATES
1734   Samuel Griffin
–1806–*c.* 1830   William Smith
1842–1846   Henry Irwin
1847–1848   Joseph Morton
1848–1851   Thomas Flynn

1851–1853	Francis John Beere
1853–1862	Hugh John Flynn
1862–1865	John Fitzharris Cousins
1865–1872	John Acheson
1872–1876	Stephen Moxley
1876–1895	Edward Irwin

with Kilgeffin and Kilglass
with Ardclare 1904–
with Bumlin 1934–
with Croghan, Creeve, Eastersnow and Tibohine 1955–

NOTES

The town of Elphin grew around a church founded by St Patrick *c.* 440. Legend says that a clear stream at the place where it was erected, emerged from the earth at night from under big rock (*ail*). The stream was called fair (*fionn*), hence the name *Ail Fionn*, Elphin. Present ruins mark site of the Cathedral of Elphin dating from *c.* 1240. The medieval cathedral was partly destroyed in 1641, and was re-built in.and again in 1823. The tower was built in 1757. The apse was added in 1872. Oliver Goldsmith received his early education at Elphin Diocesan School. Elphin Cathedral was severely damaged in a storm on 4th February 1957. It was deconsecrated on 17th November 1958 and St John's Church, Sligo became the Cathedral of the Diocese of Elphin. The Bishops' Chair and stalls were transferred in January 1960 to St. Patrick's Cathedral, Trim, and the bell was donated to Kilmore Cathedral. The Cathedral was demolished in 1964, and the present remains and site were restored by the local GAA Club in 1982.

FUERTY and KILBEGNET

PREBENDARIES etc
1421	Dermit Macgillaruaid
1442	Thady Magereachayd
–1456	Charles O'Conor (Yconchubur)
–1456	Milerus de Burgo
1456	Patrick O'Stingen
–1475	John McGillaroyd
–1475	Dermit O'Flanagan
1475	Charles O'Fallayn
1482	Manus O'Scurra
1615	Henry Malby
1623	Robert Mawe
1633	Richard Thorpe

VICARS
1464/65	Donald MacGyllaruayd
1615	Thady O'Rourck (O'Roark)
1615	Henry Dodwell
1622–1837	with Athleague
1837	John Flanagan
1854–1856	Francis Hassard
1856–1865	John Stewart Gumley

CURATE
1804	William French

united to Dunamon 1865
Church closed

IVERNON

Long-obsolete medieval parish.

VICARS
1635/36	Edward Burt
1718	William Digby
1731–1741	George Manby
1742	Richard Garrett
1745	James Henthorn

KILBRIDE

Long-obsolete medieval parish.

PREBENDARIES
–1434	Nicholas Maccochaidykellaid
1434	Odo O'Martayn
1450	Charles Magoreacchy

VICARS
1615	Christopher Delahyd
1634/40	Henry Compton

NOTES
Vicarage seems to have gone with Roscommon after 1640.

Kilbryan, Co Roscommon

KILBRYAN

Long-obsolete medieval parish.

VICARS
1633	Joseph Kempe
–1640	Henry Sharpe
1640	Arthur Ware
1698	John Brown
1743	Robert Phibbs (Phipps)
–1766	Patrick Kerr
1790–1798	Oliver Cary
1798–1812	Thomas Lloyd
1812–1813	Arthur Mahon
1813–1825	Charles Seymour
1825–	John Orson Oldfield
1845–1852	Arthur Hyde
1852–1860	George William Dalton
1860–*c.* 1862	William Parrett (possibly Garrett)
1862–1866	Daniel Leahy
1866–1883	John Davis

CURATES
1857–1858	George Alexander Johnson
1858–	possibly Hutchinson Henry Holmes
1859	Thomas George Johnston Phillips

with Kilmactranny 1883–
Church closed *c.* 1996

KILCOLA

Probably Culdea (Coola) or Cuilleada (Coola), though Culdea may be Calry, and Cuilleada is identified with Ballynakill (CPL IX 446).
Long-obsolete medieval parish.

VICARS
–1409	Maccdraith Maabreachannin	–1449	Charles O'Conor (Ochonchabuyr)
1409	John O'Beachnachan	1615	Thomas Parkington
1425	Nellanus O'Mochayn	–1640	John Wright
1428	Fergallus O'Congalan	1640	Joseph Kempe
–1430	Paul O'Somochan	1674	James Honan
1430	Malachy MacGillaciaran	1678–1720	John Keogh
		1737–1747	Arthur Mahon
–1449	Cormac O'Hedyan		

with Eastersnow

KILCOOLEY

VICARS
–1412	Reginald O'Dimura	–1640	Nicholas Coxhead
1412	Donatus MacBraein	1640	William Holywell
1615	Hugh Brehon	1640/41	William Domvill (possibly Daniel)
1627	William Roycroft	1846	Richard Cowen

NOTES
The parish probably went with Killukin after 1641, and certainly from 1698–. They appear as part of the corps of the Precentor –1846.

KILCORKEY

VICARS

1433/34	Thomas Yhaccagan
–1469	Cornelius O'Hehactigan
–1469	William O'Fflannagan
1469	Magonius Ochactagan
1615	Florence Nelly
1635–1640	Cornelius (Conor) Tully (Tullie)
–1640	Matthew Newbold
1640	William Yonge
? 1641	Robert Browne
1674	Samuel Hawkes
1681/82–1722	Jonathan Law
1723–1741	William Caulfield
1741–1742	James Blair
1742	Oliver Cary
1766–1770	Nathaniel Barton
1785–1797	Thomas Hackett Jun
1797–1799	Thomas Hackett
1799–1820	William Smith
c. 1823–c 1845	John Orson Oldfield
1845–1871	Harloe Fleming

KILCROAN

See also Prebendaries of Oran.
Long-obsolete medieval parish.

VICARS

c. 1463	Thomas O'Counihan (O'Cuynkeannayn)
–1464/65	Malachy Oconceanaynd
1464/65	Cornelius Macaedagayn
1615	Henry Dodwell
1622	Nicholas Steere

united to Dunamon

KILGEFFIN

VICARS

1634/35	Edward Loveless
1664–1674	James Honan
1674	George Thewles
1688–1694	Joseph Stoughton
1698–1731	George Digby
c. 1740–1777	Alexander Gunning
1793	—
1797–1802	Thomas Hackett
1802–1838	Oliver Cary
1838	William Henry Beeche
1849–1852	Charles Broderick Swayne
1853–1856	William Shepherd
1856–1861	Francis John Armstrong Beere
1861–1874	George McDonnell

CURATES

1822	Lewis Hawkes
c. 1825	John Armstrong

with Bumlin Union 1874–closure well before 1900

NOTES

By Order in Council, 9 May 1764, 'the church being ruinous and very ill-suited to resort to, a new church to be built on ground (1 acre) in lands of Canoward given by Lady Frances Caningsby'. New church built 1824, cost £830 15s 4½d.

KILGLASS

VICARS

–1401	Finbardus O'Mailumayn
–1407	Alan Mescallagi
1407	Florence O'Maelymnayn
1411	John Maceolich
1454	Thomolteus Macbryan
–1455	Dermit Maconcagaid
1634/35	John Nairn
1640	Robert Cole
1674	James Honan
1678	John Keogh
1729–1730	Edward Munns
1730–1740	William Harrison
1741	Samuel Griffin
–1766	Lewis Hawkes
–1806	John Cromie
1809	Henry Mansergh
1822–1871	Thomas Lloyd

CURATES

1730	William Wemyss
1786	George Sweeny
1794	Hon Maurice Mahon
1825	John Armstrong

NOTES

The parish was amalgamated with Elphin in 1871. The church seems to have closed at this time.

Kilkeevan, Castlerea, Co. Roscommon, Holy Trinity

KILKEEVAN, CASTLEREA,
Co Roscommon, Holy Trinity

VICARS		
–1590	Hugh O'Connegane	
1615	Florence Nelly	
–1640	Henry Sharpe	
1640	Arthur Ware	
1674	Edward Nicholson	
1688–1694	Joseph Stoughton	
1694–1698	Ralph Bunbury	
1709/10–1728	John Bullingbrooke	
1729–1743	Michael Griffin	
1743–1761	Nathaniel Barton	
1761–1777	Henry Cunningham	
1777–1809	William Sandford	
1809–1813	James Whitelaw	
1813–1844	William Blundell	
1845–1860	John Orson Oldfield	
1860–1876	George Griffith	
1876–1889	William Cornelius McCausland	
1889–1935	Robert Irvine Ford	
1936–1940	Frederick James Powell	
1940–1949	Cormac MacArt Lloyd	

1952–1955	Thomas James Bond	1867–1875	Charles Knox Strong
1955–1958	Alfred James Murray BC	1875–1876	John Robert Porte
		1877–1878	Henry Francis White
1959–1966	John Alexander Montgomery	1878–1880	James Black
		1880–1882	Richard William Murphy
1967–1975	Robert Desmond Holtby	1882–1884	Joseph Henry Miles
		1884–1886	William Henry Parker
1977–1988	Douglas Wrixon Graham	1886–1889	William Wolfe Wagner
1988–1991	Douglas Wrixon Graham Temp-in-c	1890–1891	Thomas Ernest Rudd
		1891–1893	George Graham Glenn
1991–1996	Robert Stewart Jackson Temp-in-c	1894–1895	Charles Dowse
1996–1997	Robert Alan Chalmers BC	1895–1896	Henry Gordon Waller Scott
		1897–1900	Henry Acheson
NSM		1900–1901	Edward Aubrey Forster
1997–2001	Shiela Johnson	1901–1903	John Arthur Duff
CURATES		1903–1906	George Robert Montgomery
1729	Oliver Cary		
1732	Mordaunt Hamilton	1906–1908	Robert Miller
1784–1786	John Barton	1909–1911	William Henry Nassau Ruddock
1788–1813	Thomas Young		
1827	Francis Irwin	1911–1913	Thomas Vesian Wallace
1838–1845	John Lindsay Chute		
1849	John Wills Browne	1913–1914	James Robert Hanna Craig
1853	William Augustus Dawson		
		1914–1916	Geoffrey Moffatt Wilson
1853–1863	William Baker Fry		
1854	John Irving		
1865	Frederick Foster		

with Tibohine 1906–1924 and 1960–
with Loughglynn 1907–1962
with Oran 1920–1962
with Kiltullagh 1952–1997
with Roscommon Group 1978–

NOTES

9 Queen Anne XII Section 1 enacted that Parish Church of Kilkeevan in town of Castlereagh be parish church of Union of Kilkeevan, Baslick and Ballintubber, to be called Parish of Kilkeevan. The brass lectern from Castlerea was transferred to the new Church of the Holy Name, Jordanstown, Belfast in 1956. A new rectory was blessed on 25th July 1961. The church closed on 28th December 1997.

KILLASOOLAN
See Castleblakeney.

KILLASPICBRONE
Long-obsolete medieval parish.

VICARS
–1404	Cristinus Macgillabugi
1404	Dermit Maginbun
–1408	More O'Gilligan
1408	Phillip Macgillabugi
–1423	Thady O'Coneyl
1423	Cornelius O'Channichy
1427	Donatus O'Bedlayn
1615	William Roycroft
1635–1640	William Newport
1640	Edward Bust (possibly Rust)
1668–1695	Coote Ormsby

NOTES
The parish seems to have gone with Sligo since.

KILLEINIREGARD
Long-obsolete medieval parish.

VICARS
–1454	Thomas O'Hachtagan the Elder
1454	Thomas O'Hachtagan the Younger

KILLENVOY

VICARS

–1639	John Waddinge
1639	John Nyrne (Nairn)
1674–c. 1718	Leonard Hodson
1718	William Digby
1742	possibly Richard Garrett
1766–c 1789	John Vance
1788–1811	Michael Griffin
1811–1827	Owen Gallagher
1828–1829	Henry Hunt
1829–1845	Peter Browne
1845–1855	William Sandes Ashe
1856–1868	Andrew Todd Gillmor
1868–1877	Joseph King
1878–1908	Edward Leathley Shea
1908–1911	Thomas Irwin
1911–1953	Thomas Sutcliffe Humphreys
1954–1959	James Mansel Egerton Maguire

CURATES

1688	Joseph Stoughton
1798	James Magrath

with Kiltoom 1911–1926
with Roscommon Group 1926–1959

NOTES

The church was closed, and on 3rd December 1959, the Diocesan Council recommended that Killenvoy Church should be demolished.

KILLERORAN or KILRONAN

See also Killyon. Not to be confused with Kilronan in Ardagh Diocese.

VICARS

c. 1420	Maurice Macquedian
–1445	Finnardus O'Fyachreay (O'Fyachney)
1615	Roger O'Sally
1628	Gilbert Seabrooke
1666–1673	Henry Dodwell
1674–1698	Richard Horne
1698–1743	Joseph Graves
1743–c. 1754	William Tisdall

with Killyon 1799–

NOTES

Killeroran and Killyon seem to be interchangeable.

KILLERY

transferred to Elphin Diocese from Ardagh 1923
with Ballysumaghan 1923–1990 qv
with Taunagh 1963–
possibly Church closed 1990

Killukin, Co Roscommon

KILLUKIN

RECTORS
1615	Maurice Griffiths
1635–1640	William Newport

VICARS
–1410	Patrick MacMurerchaid
–1443	Donald Mackheagayn
–1443	Tiernanus Miccagayn
1443	William Ytuchaid
1453	Eugene O'Conuaayn
1453/54	Magonius Macabard
–1463	Cormac O'Hadyian
–1463	Luke Igumur
–1463	Fergallus O'Bruchan
–1463	John Mechaig
1463	Fergallus O'Bruchan
1590	Nicholas O'Colly
1615	Ralph O'Dumvy
1635–1640	William Hallowell
1640/41	William Domvill (possibly Daniel)
1665–1698	Edward Hawkes

1698–1700	William Brereton
1700–1703	Peter Mahon
1703–1722	Jonathan Law
1723–1725	Louis Hamilton
1725–c. 1741	William Caulfield
1741–1742	James Blair
1742–1743	Oliver Cary
1743–c. 1767	Arthur Mahon
1767–1809	William Digby
1809–1846	Oliver Cary

RECTORS and VICARS

1845–1847	Lewis Henry Strean
1848–1878	Henry Irwin

CURATES

1728	Edward Poole
1796–1799	William Smith
1822–1823	Matthew James Shaw
1838–1840	Lewis Henry Strean
1848–1850	Thomas Kirkwood Little
c. 1850	William C Murphy
1856	James S. Paget
1859	Frederick Stoney
1878–1880	George McMurray
1880–1882	William Henry Morrison
1882–1885	Edward Rose Arthur Power

joined to Kilmore c. 1884
transferred to Ardagh Diocese 1959
Church closed c. 1962

NOTES
Croghan Chapel of Ease was established in Killukin Parish c. 1856. The Church was built in 1862.

KILLUMADA
Long-obsolete medieval parish.

VICARS
1615   John Johnson
1664   Henry Dodwell

KILLYNGYN (possibly KILLYON)
Long-obsolete medieval parish.

VICAR
1615   Thady O'Roark (O'Rourck)

KILLYON (or KILLION or later KILLERORAN)

VICARS

–1460	Magonius MacHaband
1460	John O'Tuohy (O'Tuhaid)
1615	Hugh O'Greaghan
–1650	Henry Dodwell
1661–1664	Henry Dodwell
1674–1685	Leonard Hodson
1685	Stephen Handcock
1685–1701	Fielding Shaw
1701–1717	Francis Knappagh (Knapp)
1718–1730	John Thewles
1730–c. 1743	William Glass
1799–1811	Owen Gallagher
1811–1824	John Barton
1824–1832	Erasmus Borrowes
1832	Michael Smyth
1832–1834	Denis Kelly
1835–1841	Francis Irwin
1841–1866	James Janns
1866–1879	John Nesbitt Thompson
1881–1908	William Noblett
1908–1918	Robert Miller
1918–1928	John Harpur McCormick
1929–1931	Richard Hans de Brabant Cooke
1931–1936	Frederick Charles Hill C-in-c
1936–1942	George Kirwan Birmingham, R St Peter, Athlone, C-in-c
1942–1953	Thomas Sutcliffe Humphreys
1954–1966	James Mansel Egerton Maguire
1966–1988	Douglas Wrixon Graham

CURATES

–1848	Trevor Fox
1850	John Stewart Gumley
1852–1855	John Allman Burke
1856–1857	James Laurence Cotter
1857	John W. Wheeller
1860–1864	Robert Holmes Orr
1879–1881	Thomas Kemmis

with Kilronan 1799–
with Castleblakeney 1894–
with Athleague and Mount Talbot 1924–
with Roscommon Group 1942–
Church closed c. 1975

NOTES

The Parish name is given as Killyon in Church of Ireland Directory –1931 and as Killeroran thereafter. Killeroran and Kilronan seem to have been the same place in early times.

KILMACALLEN

For Rectors *see* Prebends.

VICARS
1409	Maccraith Macabreicheamin
c. 1449	John Machabruhim
c. 1449	Cornelius Machabruichim
c. 1450	Dermit Machabruym
1452	Cornelius MacHabriuchim
–1454	Dermit MacCabrihim
–1457	Cornelius Maccabrechim
1457	Cornelius Maccabrehim
1473	Cornelius Macybreym
1473–1480	Cornelius Macmurayn
1480	Matthew O'Callanan
1583	Eugene O'Conogher
1607/08	Miler Magrath
1620	Hugh McBrehone
–1640	Master Reynolds
1640–1641	Robert Browne
1641	Walter Reyly

CURATE
1804	John Maxwell
1820–*c.* 1830	John Maxwell

NOTES
The Vicarage seems to have gone with Taunagh since 1641.

KILMACOEN

Long-obsolete medieval parish.

VICARS
1404	Cristinus O'Conor (Ichonair)
1404	Imarus O'Conar (Ymarus Yconayr)
–1417	vacant
1417	Dermit McGillaruair
1418	Cornelius (alias Corc) O'Chonayr
–1441	Dermit McGyllaruayd (possibly same as below)
1441	Donald McGyllaruayd
c. 1441–c. 1455	William Oryagam
–1456	Patrick O'Sungyn (O'Stingen)
1456	John O'Tonor (possibly = O'Conor)
1464/65	John Ycouir (Yconir = O'Conor)
1635/36	Edward Burt

NOTES
The Vicarage went with St John, Sligo after 1668 and probably before then.

Kilmactranny, Co Sligo

KILMACTRANNY

VICARS

c. 1236	Magrath MacMailin
1615	Edward Crofton
1634/35	Samuel Hawkes
1665–1668	James Wilson
1668–1669	Vincent Cave
1669/70–1700	Anthony Cope
1700–1722	Edward Goldsmith
1722/23–	John Holmes
1741–1742	James Blair
1742–1743	Oliver Cary
1743–1801	hiatus in succession list; prob held with Boyle
1801–1817	Thomas Hacket

1817–1823	George Brittaine
1823–1829	Matthew James Shaw
1830–1841	John Maxwell
1841–1852	Edward Lloyd Elwood
1852–1867	Arthur Hyde
1867–1884	Daniel Leahy
1884–1893	Richard Wolfe Landey
1893–1910	William Wolfe Wagner
1910–1914	John Thomas Webster
	Charles John Algernon Harris
1918–1922	vacant
1922–1927	Andrew Graham C-in-c
1927–1930	William George Coleman C-in-c
1931–1937	Henry Angus Victor Kennedy
1937–1946	James Nelson McCullough
1947–1950	William Bolton Battersby
1951–1954	John Alexander Montgomery C-in-c
1954–1985	Richard Albert Robinson
1987–1990	Robert Gordon Keogh
1992–1994	Stuart Irwin McGee
1995–1999	Arthur Minion

NSM

1999–2004	Noel Henry Likely Regan

CURATES

c. 1815	William Radcliffe Smith
1869–1877	John Lyster
1878–1879	William Johnson Wallace

transferred to Ardagh Diocese and with Kilronan 1924
also with Drumshambo and Kiltubrid 1951
transferred back to Elphin and with Taunagh 1951–
with Ballysumaghan 1960–
with Sligo Group 1992–1994
with Boyle Group 2003–

NOTES
The Glebe house was built in 1816. The church was also built in 1816 and cost £738 9s 2 ¾d.

KILMACUMSY

Long-obsolete medieval parish.

RECTORS
1455	Milerus de Burgo
1455	William Oregayn
1615	John Foster
1683	Jonathan Law
1731–1742	Oliver Cary
1742–1743	Nathaniel Barton
1743–	Oliver Cary
1809–1846	Oliver Cary
1846–1848	see Creeve

Kilmore, Co Roscommon

KILMORE

RECTORS and VICARS
–1681/82	Samuel Hawkes
–1681/82	James Hog
1720–1723	Oliver King
1723–c. 1770	George Blackburne
1773	William Thompson
1821–1838	Robert Jones
1838–1884	Robert King
1885–1887	Lewis Walter Algeo
1887–1890	Alfred Mitchell
1891–92/98	James Carey

1898–1903	Thomas Johnston Bayly
1903–1908	Leonard Leader Cooper
1908–1916	Edward Aubrey Forster
1917–1958	Charles Gordon Metcalfe
1959–1966	William Alexander Russell
1966–1981	William Thompson Howard Slator
1982–1991	Ivan Richard Biggs

CURATES

c. 1710	Thomas Contarine
1821	Thomas Lloyd
–1840	— Nesbitt
1843–1845	William Bourke
c. 1852	James J. Newbold

with Killukin c. 1884–
with Annaduff in Ardagh Diocese 1933–
also with Aughrim 1944–
also with Termonbarry 1955–1959
transferred to Ardagh 1959
also with Kiltoghart and Toomna 1959–1996
also with Drumshambo, Toomna and Kilronan 1962–1996
Church closed 1996

KILNAMANAGH

VICARS
c. 1440	Maurice Maguedan
–1445	Finnardus O'Fychnaid (O'Fyachney or O'Fyachreay)
–1446	Morianus O'Flanagan
1446	Charles O'Flanagan
–1447	John Magillaruayd
1447	Patrick O'Stingen
1615	John Evett
1683–1700	John Brown
1721	William Caulfield
1731	William Trench
1743	Robert Phibbs (Phipps)
1744	Henry Cunningham
1765	Mark Anthony Tisdall
1793–1828	Stephen Lyster
1828–1841	Charles Smith (Smyth)

CURATE
1729	Edward Poole

united with Boyle after 1841

KILTOOM

RECTORS
–1431	Dermit O'Murigi
c. 1431	Thomas O'Cearnan
1433	Maurice O'Synnan

VICARS
1615	John Hathersall
1636/37	William Newman
1688	Joseph Stoughton
1718	William Digby
–1777–1822	Thomas Young
1822–1828	Henry Hunt
1828–1853	John Armstrong
1853–1860	Richard Hugh Low
1861–1872	James Fitzgerald
1872	Thomas Richard Rice
1873–1874	Edward George Campbell
1874–1910	Isaac Mitchell
1911–1926	Thomas Sutcliffe Humphreys
1926–1930	William Cecil de Pauley
1930–1941	George Kirwan Birmingham

CURATE
1873–1874	John Ussher

with Killenvoy 1911–1926
with St Peter, Athlone 1926–
transferred with Athlone to Meath Diocese 1941

NOTES

Kiltoom and Camma united forever by 9 Queen Anne XII Section 18 and called Parish of Camma; 'the Church to be built in same convenient place in the lands of Millton Pass to be ye parish Church: Luke Dillon, Edmund and John Kelly or their heirs, first conveying a sufficient site'. The church was deconsecrated on 17th May 1963.

Kiltullagh, Ballinlough, Co Roscommon

KILTULLAGH

Transferred from Diocese of Tuam to Diocese of Elphin 1952.

with Kilkeevan 1952–1997
also with Roscommon Group 1978–

Knocknarea, Co Sligo, St Ann

KNOCKNAREA

Perpetual Curacy in St John, Sligo –1867

PERPETUAL CURATES

1843–1860	James Gully
1861–1864	John Westropp Chambers
1864–1867	Charles Hans Hamilton

RECTORS

1867–1877	William Alexander Day
1877–1881	Isaac Coulter
1881–1884	Frederick John Hamilton
1884–1892	John Galbraith
1893–1916	Richard Wolfe Landey
1916–1927	Frederick William Ernest Wagner
1927–1929	Charles Arthur Rainsford
1930–1932	William Cecil de Pauley
1933–1947	William Popham Hosford
1947–1983	Cecil Charles Wyndham Browne
1983–1991	Hugh Sterling Mortimer
1992–1999	Stuart Irwin McGee
1999–2004	David Griscome
2004–	Arfon Williams

with St John, Sligo 1927–

KYLLMURCHAYN

Killruane in CPL. In Achonry Diocese according to Achonry succession lists.
Long-obsolete medieval parish.

VICARS
–1405   Morianus Macrechlain
1405   Donatus O'Mynachan
1409   Cormac O'Callanan

LISANUFFY

Long-obsolete medieval parish.

RECTORS
–1410   Matthew Orechtagain
1410   Matthew O'Mulymuan

Lissadell, Co Sligo

LISSADELL and MUNNINANE

PERPETUAL CURATES
1842–1859	William Jeffcott
1859–1876	Capel Wolseley
1876–1885	Thomas Cosgrave
1885–1900	Frederick Sheridan Le Fanu

RECTORS
1900–1907	William Dudley Saul Fletcher
1907–1912	Thomas Arnold Harvey
1912–1943	Samuel Richard Miller
1943–1946	Cecil Herbert Smyth
1946–1948	Dermot Nicholas Bowers
1950–1959	Arthur Cotter
1959–1963	James Wilson
1963–1969	Samuel Derek Hamilton
1969–1987	James Maurice Glover Sirr
1988–1992	Robert Fleming Hayman
1993–2001	Ian Gallagher
2002–2007	Andrew James Forster
2008–	Barry Ian Linton

CURATES
1880–1881	John Crampton Triphook
1881–1884	Frederick William Austin

with Ahamplish and Drumcliffe 1959–
with Rosses 1959–1960

NOTES
The Church of Lissadell was built and endowed by Sir Robert Gore Booth and consecrated on 6th June 1841. The Chapel of ease at Munninane consecrated on 4th June 1896.

Munninane Chapel of Ease, Co Sligo, St Kevin

LOUGHGLYNN, Co Roscommon

Long-obsolete medieval parish.

PERPETUAL CURATES
1819–1822	William Baker Stoney
1822–1824	Thomas Lloyd
1824–1871	Harloe Fleming
1871–1881	Richard Fitzjames Fleming

CURATE
1870	Richard Fitzjames Fleming

with Kilkeevan 1907–1962

NOTES
Loughglynn Church was consecrated on 17th October 1819. The parish became part of Tibohine from which it was originally taken in 1871. The church was demolished in 1965.

MOUNT TALBOT, Co Roscommon

Long-obsolete medieval parish.
See Athleague.

OGULLA

Long-obsolete medieval parish.

VICARS
–1411	Lewis O'Flannagan
1411	Donald O'Fiachna
1414	Matthias O'Fiachna
1445/46	Malachy Ifihacgna
1457	Cornelius O'Syachna
1457	Dermit Macilend
1457	Malachy O'Syachna
–1477	Cormac O'Hedian
1481	Donald Offyacaynagy

NOTES
Seems to have gone with Elphin after 1481.

Oran, Co Galway

ORAN

For Rectors, *see* Prebends of Oran.

VICARS
c. 1430	Dermit McGillaruayd
–1433	Donald O'Deallayd
1433/34	Matthew O'Clabayd (Yclabayd)
1441	Maurice O'Clabaid (Iclabaid)
1444	Cornelius Oclabayd

1450	John O'Chonyr
1454	Cornelius Oclabaid
1454	Maurice Oclabaid alias Omeanachan
1456	Cornelius O'Stingyn
1622	Nicholas Steere
1634	Henry Compton
–1640	William Burle (or possibly Buirly)
1640	Walter Reyley
1641	Thomas Rookby
1673	Samuel Hindes
1674	Edward Nicholson
1729	Thomas Contarine

CURATES

1823	Percival Weldon
1829	George Knox
1854–1856	John Stewart Gumley

with Kilkeevan, Tibohine and Loughglynn 1920–1962
Church closed *c.* 1962

From 1730, the Vicarages of Oran and Drimtemple were united with the Prebendary of Oran until Disestablishment in 1870.

Rathcline, Lanesborough, Co Longford, St John

RATHCLINE

transferred to Elphin from Ardagh 1965 (see also entry in Ardagh section) with Roscommon Group

NOTES

There was a church in this area in the 5th century. In the 15th century, it was under control of Canons Regular of St Augustine of Saints' Island in Lough Ree. The Manor and lands of Rathcline were granted to Sir George Lane of Tulsk, Co Roscommon in the 1660s. The village of Beal Atha Liag was renamed Lanesborough. Sir George became 1st Viscount Lanesborough. Lane rebuilt the parish church. After the Battle of the Boyne, there was a battle in Lanesborough between troops of King James and troops of King William which resulted in damage to the church in 1691. Repairs were carried out in 1740. The present church was built in 1861.

Roscommon, Co Roscommon

ROSCOMMON

Note: Anciently known as Templeneilan.

VICARS

1615	Thomas Gawine
1627	Thomas Hallowell
1640	William Burley
1665	Edward Hawkes
1698–1731	George Digby
1731–1741	George Manby
1742–1777	James Blair
1777–1791	unknown
1797–1805	Thomas Radcliffe
1805–1845	Thomas Blakeney
1845–1863	John Lindsay Chute
1863–1875	Matthew Nesbitt Thompson
1876–1878	George Alexander Papendick Arbuthnot
1878–1882	George Frederick Courtenay
1882–1885	Richard Clarke
1885–1892	Martin Bradshaw
1892–1916	Keogh Kempston
1916–1926	Richard Wolfe Landey

1926–1953	Thomas Sutcliffe Humphreys
1954–1966	James Mansel Egerton Maguire
1966–1988	Douglas Wrixon Graham
1988–1992	Douglas Wrixon Graham Temp-in-c
1992–1996	Robert Stewart Jackson Temp-in-c
1996–1997	Robert Alan Chalmers BC

NSM
1991–1996	Cecil Lindsay
1997–2001	Sheila Johnson
2006–	Alexandra Jane Lindsay

CURATES
1730	Edward Poole
c. 1774	possibly Samuel Willams
1784	Alexander Seton
1797	Thomas Blakeney
–1844	Edward Day
1846–1861	James Fitzgerald
1858	George Alexander Johnson
1861–1863	Matthew Nesbitt Thompson
1870–1876	Thomas Richard Rice
1876–1877	Richard Charles Clarke
1941–1943	Eric Herbert Despard
1944–1947	George Christopher Curry
1948–1950	Walter Cyril Spence

with Dunamon 1917–
with Killenvoy 1926–1959
with Castleblakeney, Athleague and Mount Talbot 1941–1975
with Killyon or Killeroran 1942–
with Rathcline 1965–
with Kilkeevan, Kiltullagh and Tybohine 1978–
with Boyle, Aghanagh, Ardcarne and Croaghan 1997–2000

NOTES
Date of church unknown.

Rosses Point, Co Sligo

ROSSES POINT

RECTORS
1869–1901   Frederick Flood

parish first appears in Church of Ireland Directory 1869
with Drumcliffe 1902–1960
with Sligo 1960–

SHANKILL

Long-obsolete medieval parish.

VICARS
1615–1616   John Foster
1639   Robert Prickett
1640   Henry Prickett

NOTES
For 1683–, *see* Kilmacumsy.

Cathedral Church of St. Mary the Virgin and St. John the Baptist, Sligo

SLIGO

RECTORS
1427	Bernard O'Flanagan (Yfflanagan)
1428	Bernard McConcayd
1430	Cormac MacDonnchad
1430	Bernard O'Coneil
1444	Magonius MacDonnchad
1583	Eugene O'Conogher
1608/09	Miler Magrath
1637–1640	John King
1640	Cleremont (Clement) Panham

VICARS
1419	Thomas O'Cuathalan
1419–1427	Abbot of Boyle in possession
1427	Marianus O'Kyanan
1615	William Roycroft
1635	William Newport
1640/41	Robert Browne
1654	Marmaduke Clapham
1665–1660	John Wilkinson
1661	Cleremont (Clement) Panham
1669–1695	Coote Ormsby
1696–1730	John Fontanier
1730–1770	Eubule Ormsby

1771–1775	Manley Gore
1775–1820	Wensley Bond
1820–1844	Charles Hamilton
1844–1876	Edward Day
1876–1912	Alexander Major Kearney
1912–1917	John Orr
1917–1929	Charles Arthur Rainsford
1930–1932	William Cecil de Pauley
1933–1947	William Popham Hosford
1947–1983	Cecil Charles Wyndham Browne
1983–1991	Hugh Sterling Mortimer
1992–1999	Stuart Irwin McGee
1999–2004	David Griscome
2004–	Arfon Williams

CURATES

1700	Edward Nicholson
1728	James Blair
1761	John Palmer
1771	James Armstrong
1801	Edward Coates
1802–1823	William Chambers Armstrong
1819	Henry Hunt
–1823	William Armstrong
1824	Erasmus Burrowes (Borrowes)
1825	Graham Philip Crozier
1828	Hugh Hamilton
1830	Hugh Murray
1835–1840	John Evelyn Greene
1840–1847	Andrew Robinson
1841	George Montgomery
1842	Knox Homan
1844	William Lauder
1846–1856	Samuel Shone
1856	Oliver Josef Tibeaudo
1857–1864	Morgan Woodward Jellett
1864–1867	John Dowden
1866–1867	William Alexander Day
1868–1876	Alexander Major Kearney
1870–1872	Michael Neville Kearney
1877–1879	James Alan French
1880–1881	Frederick John Hamilton
1881–1882	John Crampton Triphook
1882–1886	Henry Mills
1886–1891	Charles Wesley Darling
1891–1892	Henry Morrell Armstrong
1892–1895	Richard Arthur McClean
1895–1896	John Alfred Thompson
1896–1901	James John Hall
1901–1906	George Cathcart Phair
1906–1909	John Allen

1909–1911	Paul Quigley
1911–1912	George Thomas Berry
1912–1915	Albert Robinson Fowler
1927–1930	Alan Darnley Huston Stewart
1931–1933	Ivan Ridley Kirkpatrick
1933–1936	Robert Lionel Stuart
1936–1939	Worrall Reginald Leadbeater
1939–1944	John Ernest Leeman
1944–1947	Thomas James Bond
1947–1949	Frederick William Rodgers
1949–1953	Herbert James Stuart
1953–1956	Richard Henry Bertram
1959–1961	James Irwin Armstrong

with Knocknarea 1927–
with Rosses Point 1960–
with Taunagh, Kilmactranny and Ballysumaghan 1992–1994

NOTES

The Rectory seems to have gone with the Vicarage after 1640. The oldest church on site dates from the 13th century. In 1741, William Phipps gave £625 to build a church in the Union of Sligo. The architect was Cassels, also architect of Leinster House and the Dining Hall of Trinity College, Dublin. The church was remodelled in 1812 with addition of battlements and tower. The seat or cathedral for the Dioceses of Elphin and Ardagh was removed from Elphin by a Bill passed by General Synod 1958 to St John's Church, Sligo, to be known as the Cathedral Church of St Mary the Virgin and St John the Baptist. St John's constituted as the Cathedral for Elphin and Ardagh at a service on 25 Oct 1961, at which the Bishop was enthroned and the throne and Canons' stalls were dedicated. The organ was completely rebuilt in memory of Mr Mark Franklin, Organist for many years, and dedicated on 16th September 1973. The Rectory was sold in 1958, and a new one was built in 1959/60 and blessed on 15th January 1960.

Cathedral Church of St. Mary the Virgin and St. John the Baptist, Sligo

St BERNANUS de MANSO

Long-obsolete medieval parish.
Unidentified; perhaps Kilmacallen.

VICARS
–1401	Dermit O'Hamlyd
1401	Finbardus O'Mailumayn (O'Mailanna, O'Muealinnain)

TAGHBOY

Long-obsolete medieval parish.
Possibly Teatby.

VICARS
–*c.* 1427	Angelus O'Molan
–1427	Roger O'Mochlan
–1463	Magonius McGeraghty (Magoyrectan)
1463	William O'Ffallunin
–1472	Rory O'Mothain
–1472	Magon Magorricachdaig
1472	Cornelius O'Doigelian
–1480	Cornelius O'Doelan
–1480	Charles O'Fallayn
–1641	William Domevill
1641	John Wallis

NOTES
Entries under Tibohine 1640 may be Taghboy 1666– as in Tessaragh.

Taunagh, Riverstown, Co Sligo

TAUNAGH

Rectors of Taunagh until Disestablishment in 1870 were Prebendaries of Kilmacallen.

VICARS

c. 1333/34	John de Cotgrave
c. 1429	Matthew Maccaclerid
c. 1429	Odo Maccaclerid
1444	Imarus Macaclerid
1465	Cornelius Machaclery
–1615	Thomas Parkington
1615	Erasmus Matthew
1620	Hugh McBrehowne
1640–1641	Robert Browne
1641	Walter Reyly
1665–1668	James Wilson
1668	Vincent Cave
c. 1683	John Brown
–1716	Tobias Caulfield
1716–1718	John Thewles
1718–1729	Edward Munns

1729	Adam Caulfield
1732	John Holmes
1743	Arthur Mahon
1744/45	Robert Phipps
1760–1766	Robert Curtis
–1766	William Phibbs
1785–1790	Thomas Cowper
1790	Francis Drake Kenney
1795–1801	James Armstrong
1801–1840	Thomas Hacket
1841–1853	Robert Cadge
1853–1871	Graham Philip Crozier
1873–1875	William Henry Pilcher
1875–1878	Robert Grierson
1878–1879	John Black
1879–1886	William Johnson Wallace
1886–1895	William Harris Winter
1895–1909	Francis Travers Cockle
1909–1931	John Allen
1932–1949	William Hugh Ingolsby de Massy
1951–1954	John Alexander Montgomery
1954–1985	Richard Albert Robinson
1987–1990	Robert Gordon Keogh
1992–1994	Stuart Irwin McGee
1995–1999	Arthur Minion
2004–	Kenneth Arthur Lambart Barrett

NSM

1999–2004	Noel Henry Likely Regan

CURATES

1766	Thomas Figsbee
1790	Hugh Johnston
1804	John Maxwell
c. 1826	John Lloyd
1870–1872	Alexander Brock Spaight

anciently with Drumcollum
with Kilmactranny 1951–
with Ballysumaghan 1960–
with Killery 1963–
with Sligo Cathedral Group 1992–1994
with Boyle Group 2003–

TEATBY

Possibly Taghboy, qv.

TEREBRINE

Long-obsolete medieval parish.

VICARS
1635 — Nicholas Coxhead
c. 1636–1640 — Richard Woolley
1640 — Nicholas Coxhead

TERMONBARRY, Co Longford

Long-obsolete medieval parish.

RECTORS of CLUONCORPE or CLUAINCASPE
(identified by CPL with Termonbarry)
–1397 — Donald Mascalaid
1397 — Maurice Mascalaid
1397/98 — Donald Mascalaid
–1460 — John O'Mochan
1460 — William O'Ffergayl

VICARS
–1397 — Patrick Mascalaid
1397 — Donald Mascalaid
–1411 — Alan Mascalaid
1411 — Donald Offini
1615 — Florence Kelly

CURATES
1730 — William Wemyss
1831 — William Burkitt Moorehead

NOTES
The Glebe house was built in 1813 and cost £553 16s 11d. The church is now closed.

TERMONCAELYN

Long-obsolete medieval parish.
Possibly = Kilmacallen.

VICARS
1404	William Machgillaychny
1404	Marianus O'Flanagan
c. 1440	Ymanus O'Reachmayl
1443	Charles O'Flannigan

TESSARAGH

VICARS
1463	William O'Ffalunin
1615	Henry Dodwell
1633	Richard Thorpe
1666–1671	Thomas Eccleston
1671/72–1685	Leonard Hodson
1685	Stephen Handcock
1685–1718	Fielding Shaw
1718	William Digby
1783	William McLaughlin
1811–1834	Henry Marcus Crofton
1817	John Maxwell
1834	Charles Dunn
1839–1841	Robert Cadge
1841–1873	William McClelland

CURATE
1730	Lewis Hawkes

NOTES

The parish was united after 1873 with Athleague. The church was built in 1766 at a cost of £415 7s 8½d, and is now closed. The site of the church for Tessaragh, Taughboy, Disert and Rahara was changed to the townland of Charingly, 1 acre given by William Talbot; old church in ruins (8 George III).

Tibohine, Frenchpark, Co Roscommon

TIBOHINE

VICARS

–1406	Thomas McMorrissy (Macimurgyssa)
1407	Maurice McGillichairaich
1615	John Evett
1637	William Domvill
–1640	Erasmus Matthews
1640	Thomas Rookby
1641	John Wallis
1819–1863	William French
1863–1866	Henry Johnston
1866–1905	Arthur Hyde
1906–1924	Robert Irvine Ford
1924–1938	Charles Sinclair
1938–1953	Edward Furlong
1955–1959	William Wynne Slack
1959–1966	John Alexander Montgomery
1967–1975	Robert Desmond Holtby
1978–1988	Douglas Wrixon Graham
1988–1991	Douglas Wrixon Graham Temp-in-c

1991–1996	Robert Stewart Jackson Temp-in-c
1996–1997	Robert Alan Chalmers

NSM

1997–2000	Shiela Johnson
2001–2004	Noel Henry Likely Regan

CURATES

1785	Thomas Lloyd
1843–1853	Arthur Hyde
1857–1863	Charles Knox Strong

with Loughglynn
with Kilkeevan 1906–1924 and 1960–
with Croghan 1924–1960
with Elphin Group 1955–1960
with Roscommon Group 1978–2000
with Boyle Group 1997–

NOTES

The Vicarage seems to have been held by Prebendaries of Tibohine from 1662–. The ancient Parish Church of Tibohine alias Artough, being decayed, ruinous and inconvenient, ordered to be removed to more convenient piece of ground granted by Arthur French of French Park, Esq., to Edward, Bishop of Elphin, Patron, and successors, for building new church and enclosing churchyard by Act of Council 14 Feb 1742. Dr Douglas Hyde, 1st President of Ireland, grew up in Tibohine where his father, Rev Arthur Hyde, was Rector.

Toomna, Co Roscommon

TOOMNA

RECTORS
–1411	Bernard O'Duffy (Oduthaid)
1411	Thady Macdiarmada

VICARS
–1423	Donald Ocuiryth
–1423	Thomas Ycolla
1423	Reginald Othomathaych
1427	Thomas MacDiarmada
c. 1615	Thomas Parkington
c. 1633	John Wright
1665–1668	James Wilson
1668–1669	Vincent Cave
1669–1700	Anthony Cope
1798–1846	Oliver Cary
1846–1848	John Strean
1848–1861	Brent Neville
1861–1872	Francis John Beere
1872–1882	Charles Ellis

1882–1885	William Swayne Little
1886–1896	Theophilus Patrick Landey
1896–1906	Robert John Mitchell
1906–1923	William Walter Peyton
1923–31	vacant (served by R Kiltoghart)
1931–1953	William Alexander Potter

CURATES

1724	Michael Neligan
1766	John Byrne
1840–1845	Frederick Hamilton
1845–1846	John Strean
1852–1860	William Baker Fry
1853–1856	Francis John Beere
1858–1859	Thomas George Johnston Phillips
1859	Thomas Phibbs

NOTES

The Vicarage was held with the Archdeaconry to 1809. The parish was transferred to Ardagh Diocese and united with Kiltoghart in 1954.

TULLAGH

Long-obsolete medieval parish.
In Kilcorkey Parish.

VICARS

1410	Matthew O'Mulymanan
1417	Maurice O'Connor

DIOCESE OF ARDAGH

THE DIOCESE OF ARDAGH

BISHOPS OF ARDAGH

454	MEL
c. 670	ERARD
–874	FAELGHUS
–1048	CELE
–1152	McGRATH O'MORAN
–1171	CHRISTIAN O'HOEY
–1187	—O'TIRLENAN
–1189	—O'HISLENAN
–1216	ANNADH O'MURRAY
1217	ROBERT
c. 1224	M.
c. 1225	MACRATH MACSHERRY (MACSEIRIGH)
c. 1225	JOSEPH McTEICHEDHAIN (or McEOIGH)
1233	JOCELIN or GIOLL ISSA O'TORNEY
1238	BRENDAN McTEICHEDHAN (or McEOIGH or MAGODAIG)
1255	MILO DE DUNSTABLE
1289/90	MATTHEW O'HOEY

There seems to have been a contest as to Matthew's successor. According to Ware, Alexander was appointed his successor, but in C.P.L. II, 238, we are told that "David, Chancellor of Armagh" was elected on Matthew's death by the Chapter, and refused the See, (C.P.L II, 238. The Pope appointed.

1323	ROBERT
1324	JOHN McEOIGH or McKEOGH
–1344	OWEN O'FERRALL
1369	WILLIAM McCORMACK

After William's death, three persons claimed to have been elected by the Chapter, viz.
CHARLES O'FERRALL
RICHARD O'FERRALL and

1373	JOHN AUBREY

?Charles was consecrated: A.F.M. 373 at his death speak of him as Bishop. Ann. Hib. I 184 is incorrect in saying that

	John was set over the See on the demise of O'Ferrall. John Aubrey is called John O'Freac (or O'Frayn) in the Ann. Loch Ce
1395	GILBERT (alias Comedinus) MACBRADY Henry Nony, a Dominican was prov. in error 29 April 1392 to the See on the death of Charles (sic) (A.E. I 184). The See was not then vacant. He was Friar Preacher and was consecrated lately 10 April 1400. (C.P.L V 331).
1400	ADAM LEYNS
1418/19	CORNELIUS O'FERRALL
1425	RICHARD O'FERRALL
1444	CORMAC MAGAURAN In 1467, Pope Paul II provided Donatus or Donough O'Ferrall to the See " vacant by the death of the last bishop" (A.H. I 145). This was evidently a mistake, for in 1469 John was provided to the See.
1469	JOHN
1479	WILLIAM O'FERRALL
1517	RORY O'MALONE In 1540, the Pope seems to have provided Patrick McMahon of the Order of St. Francis to the See (Cal. L & P.E. VIII, xvi, 1327), but he does not seem to have got possession at that time,
1541	RICHARD O'FERRALL
1553	PATRICK McMAHON from 1572, the See seems to have remained vacant for some years. John Garvey, Dean of Christ Church was recommended for it Oct. 1, 1572, (see C.S.P.I., 1st Series, i. 484, 495, 511), and Queen Elizabeth directs "Mr Barry" (=Mr Garvey) to be appointed to it 6 Nov, 1572 (C.P.R.I., i. 551), but there were faults in the warrant", Lord Deputy to Burleigh, 23 Nov. 1573, (C.P.S.I., 1st Series I, 529). He was made Bishop of Kilmore. Sir Henry Sidney recommended Sir John Pettit for the See "vacant by the death of Patrick McMahon", 13 June 1576, (ib. II 94). The latter phrase seems to imply that the deposition of McMahon by the Pope was ignored. Loftus applied on behalf of the Bp.of Kilmacduagh, to whom custody of the temporalities had been given between 29 May 1578 and Oct. 1579, by Lord Justice Drury, and the Sees were united 10 June 1580, (ib. II. 227).
1583	LYSACH O'FERRALL
1604–33	See held with Kilmore

1603/04	ROBERT DRAPER
1612-1629	THOMAS MOIGNE
1629-1633	WILLIAM BEDELL
1633-1654	JOHN RICHARDSON
	See held with Kilmore qv.
1661-1672	ROBERT MAXWELL
1673-1681	FRANCIS MARSH
1682-1692	WILLIAM SHERIDAN
1692	ULYSSES BURGH
	See held with Kilmore
1693-1699	WILLIAM SMYTH
1699-1713	EDWARD WETTENHALL
1715-1727	TIMOTHY GOODWYN
1727-1741	JOSIAH HORT
1741-1751	JOSEPH STORY
	See held with Tuam
1752-1775	JOHN RYDER
1775-1782	JEMMET BROWNE
1782-1794	Hon. JOSEPH DEAN BOURKE
1794-1819	Hon. WILLIAM BERESFORD
1819-1839	Hon. POWER LE POER TRENCH
1839	See united with Kilmore qv.and with Elphin 1841

THE CHAPTER OF ARDAGH

DEANS

c. 1245	THADY
–1249	MAURICE (ib.)
–1369	'UA BARDA(I)N
–1373	RICHARD O'FERRAL (or O'FARRELL
–1407	SIR CHARLES
c. 1410	DONATUS
–1412	CORNELIUS O'FARRELL (O'FERGAIL)
1418	JOHN M.GILLAVANEM
1422	RICHARD O'FARRELL (OFFERGAYL)
1422/23	RICHARD O'FARRELL
–1431	JOHN McGILLEVANEM
1431	GERALD O'FARRELL (OFFERGAYL)
1460	JOHN

1468/69	THOMAS MACMUIRCHEARTAIGH
1475	FANTICCIUS O'FARRELL (YFERGAIL)
1485	CORNELIUS O'FARRELL (YFERGAIL)
1512	PATRICK McGRAIDIN
–1522	DONATUS O'FARRELL (OFFREUILL)
1522	WILLIAM O'FARRELL (OFFREUILL)
1531	SIR GERALD WAYLSHE
–1551	JOHN O'FARRELL (O'FERGAIL)
–1552	RICHARD WAKEFIELDE
1552	JOHN BOWERMAN
1563	WILLIAM BRADY
–1571	SHANE O'FERRALL
–1595	PATRICK O'FARRELL
1595	ROBERT RICHARDSON
1606	LEWIS JONES
1625	HENRY JONES
1637	NICHOLAS BERNARD
1661-1701	JOHN KERR
1702/03-1718	JOHN BARTON
1719-1720	CHARLES COBBE
1720/21-1722	JOSIAH HORT
1722-1726	ROBERT HOWARD
1726/27-1749	LEWIS SAURIN
1749-1757	GEORGE SANDFORD
1757-1769	THOMAS WHITE
1769-1785	WILLIAM FRENCH
1785-1789	LILLY BUTLER
1790-1800	CHARLES MONGAN (WARBURTON)
1801-1813	Hon. RICHARD BOURKE (not 1800)
1814-1829	RICHARD GRAVES
1829-1854	RICHARD MURRAY
1854-1860	HUGH USHER TIGHE
1860-1880	AUGUSTUS WILLIAM WEST
1880-1896	ALEXANDER ORME
1896	SAMUEL EVANS HOOPS
1896-1912	FREDERICK AUGUSTUS POTTERTON
1913-1930	THOMAS REILLY

The Deanery remained vacant from the death of Dean Reilly until 1929, when it was joined with the Deanery of Elphin qv.

ARCHDEACONS

1217	An Archdeacon unnamed appears
1227	JOSEPH McKEOGH (MAGODAIG)
1255–1259	CHRISTIAN
1324	JOHN McKEOGH (McEOIGH)
1343	OWEN O'FARRELL
1346	HENRY McMURTAGH (MACMURQUIRTID)
c. 1400	WILLIAM O'FARRELL (YFERGAIL)
1407	MAURICE McGILLAVANEAM
1411	CABRICIUS O'FARRELL (O'FERGAIL)
1425	MAGONIUS
c. 1428	JOHN O'MOYLE
1443	WALTER O'FARRELL
1530/31	NICHOLAS NUGENT
1619	MAURICE O'MULCONRY
1619	EDWARD HATTON
1633	WILLIAM WATSON
1661-1681	JOHN AYTON
1681-1683	JOSEPH DUNBAR
1683-c1696	ANDREW CHARLTON
1705-1749	THOMAS TAYLOR
1749-1762	ROBERT HORT
1763-1778	JOHN OLIVER
1778-1790	CHAMBRE CORKER
1790-1804	ROBERT BEATTY
1805-1821	ROBERT BEATTY Junr
1821-1839	CHARLES LE POER TRENCH
1839-1854	MARCUS GERVAIS BERESFORD
1854-1866	JOHN CHARLES MARTIN
1866-1874	JOHN RICHARD DARLEY
1874-1875	THOMAS WEBB GREENE
1875-1883	ROBERT JAMES CARD
1883-1891	FITZMAURICE HUNT
1891-1896	FREDERICK AUGUSTUS POTTERTON
1896-1915	WILLIAM RICHARD MOORE
1916-1921	ROBERT WALLACE BOYD
1921-1940	HENRY JOHN JOHNSON

Archdeaconries of Elphin and Ardagh united 1929 — see Elphin

CANONS

1290	MATTHEW O'HOEY (O'HEOTHY)
1353	ARTHURIUS
1353	ANDREW PANTALEONIS
−1369	WILLIAM McCORMACK
1373	SIR JOHN OFFYNE
1395	MAURICE McGILLAVANEM
1397	DENIS O'MOLBRIDE
1397	FLORENCE McMURTAGH
1400	THOMAS McMURTAGH
1423	ANDREW McGILLARUAYTH
1427	CABRICIUS O'FERRALL (OFERGALL)
1428	PAUL MACCHEAN
1438	RAYMOND MACAGARRTAGH
1443	PAUL O'SULECKAN
1447/48	THOMAS O,SIRIDEAN
1451	JOHN O'FLYN
1451	CORNELIUS O'FERRALL
1454	EUGENE McMURTAGH
1458	JOHN O'GOBHAN
1461	WALTER O'FERRALL (OFERGAIL)
1461	THADY McGRANAILL
1461	CHARLES O'FLANIT
1461	MARIANUS McGOLBORTH
1461	DONAT O'FERRALL (OFERGAIL)
1461/62	CORMAC or CORNELIUS MAGAURAN
1461/62	EUGENE ORODOCHAN
1461/62	CORMAC MACGRANAILL
1465/66	EUGENE MACCONTAGRY
1465	JOHN O'FERRALL (OFERGAIL)
1467	DONAT O'FERRALL
1529	DONALD McGRANAILL
1540	LUCIUS O'FERRALL

PARISHES OF ARDAGH

*denotes Mediaeval and long-obsolete parishes

Abbeylara
Annaduff, Drumsna = Annaduff East
Chapel of Ease
Ardagh
Aughavas
Aughrim

Ballymachugh
Ballymacormick

Cashel
Clonbroney
Clongish, Drumlish Chapel of Ease
Clooncumber
Cloone, Lough Rynn Castle Chapel
Columbkille

Drumlummon
Drumreilly
Drumshambo

Farnaught
Fenagh

Gowna
Granard

Inismor*

Kilcommick
Kilglass
Killashee
Killenumery

Killery
Killoe
Killukin
Kilmore
Kilronan
Kiltoghart
Kiltubrid
Kilmactranny

Mogbrechi *(unidentified mediaeval parish, = Street?)
Mohill
Mostrim
Moydow
Munterangaile *
Muntireolis *

Outragh or Oughteragh

Rathaspeck
Rathcline
Rathreagh and Aghery
Russagh

Shrule (Ballymahon)
Streete

Taghsynod*
Tashinny
Templemichael
Termonbarry
Toomna

ABBEYLARA, Co Longford

VICARS/RECTORS

1622–1647	Ferrall McCall
	— Lindsey
1661	Herbert Ferris
1670	Henry Bird
1685/86	Robert Ramsay
1698	Charles Barclay
1701	Robert Harrison
c. 1751	Christopher Harrison
1768	—
1797–1807	Alexander Montgomery
1807	Robert Gouldsbury
1829	Nicholas Gosselin
1832–1865	John Shea
1865–1867	George Little Horneck
1868–1871	Archibald Nicholls
1872–1878	John Keane
1878–1881	James Tresham Cooke
1881–1885	Francis de Burgh Sidley
1886	George Mortimer Anderson
1886–1909	William Devenish
1909–20	Woodley Joseph Lindsay
1922–1925	Arthur Reginald Burriss
1925–1933	Edward Furlong
1934–1937	Hugh Maurice Daunt
1938–1940	Charles Richard Ryall C-in-c
1941–1962	Cecil Maurice Kerr

CURATES

1780	Thomas Lloyd
c. 1826	John Shea
1840	Robert Walsh
1843–1865	George Little Horneck

with Drumlummon 1900–1962
with Granard 1922–1962
with Mostrim 1941–1962
with Gowna –1959
possibly closed 1962

NOTES

Lord Westmeath was the impropriator of the Rectory from 1622. In 1836 there was no glebe house but the Vicar resided in a very old condemned thatched house on the glebe. Abbeylara Church was licensed on 23rd July 1839 (DR). Lt Col Arthur Lewis granted a site for a licensed house of worship and a schoolhouse in the townland of Tubber on 1st July 1861 (DR). List of names of 16 Protestant families here given in Parish Returns 1766; 252 RC families.

Annaduff, Drumsna, Co Leitrim, St Ann

ANNADUFF

VICARS and RECTORS

–1412	Mineas Mecran
–1412	Andrew Maccilruaig
–1477/78	Dermit Macanknaid
–1477/78	Magonius Makahkaid
1477/78	Maurice Macandyan
1615	Florence Nellye
–1622	Nathaniel Hollington
1634	John Wilkinson
1661	George Blackburne
1668/69	Robert Ross
? 1693	Robert Whitelaw
1714	John Winder
1714/15	Oliver King
1721	Daniel Hern
1726	John Bennett
1740	Elias Handcock
–1766	James Janns
1777–1811	Thomas Mahon
1811	—
1813	Thomas Smyth
1831–1838	John Gustavus Handcock
1838–1864	George Shaw

1864–1878	Theodore Octavius Moore
1879–1885	William Welwood
1886–1887	Digby Duane William Digby
1887–1890	Joseph Russell Little
1890–1927	Thomas Fahy
1928–1932	Charles Gordon Metcalfe C-in-c
1932–1949	John Claudius Beresford
1949–1955	Thomas Norman Bateman
1955–1966	William Alexander Russell
1966–1981	William Thompson Howard Slator
1982–1991	Ivan Richard Biggs
1991–1996	vacant
1996–2001	Ivan Richard Biggs in charge
2003–	Forrest William Atkins

CURATES

–1830	Charles Kean
–1838	George Shaw
1838	Lowry McClintock
1840–1848	Francis Kane
1852–1864	James John Newbold

with Kiltoghart 1932–1954 and 2000–
with Mohill, Cloone, Lough Rynn and Aughavas 1959–1962
with Kilronan and Toomna 1962–1996
with Drumshambo 1963–
with Mohill, Farnaught, Aughavas, Kiltubride, Oughteragh and Drumreilly 2000–

NOTES
The church was built in 1820 and cost £1,476 18s 5½d. Annaduff East Chapel of Ease was built at expense of Francis Nisbett of Derrycarn. The Parish appears as Annaduff to 1932, then as Annaduff West 1932–1959. Annaduff West appears separate from Annaduff 1959–1962. Annaduff East and West in Elphin Diocese 1954–59. Annaduff East appears separate from Annaduff 1963–1976.

ANNADUFF EAST
Chapel of Ease, DROMOD, St Ann

with Mohill, Farnaught and Aughavas 1963–1976

ANNADUFF (WEST)
In Elphin 1954–1959.

with Kiltoghart, Toomna, Kilmore, Aughrim, Killukin and Termonbarry 1959–1962
(Termonbarry with Templemichael 1960–)

Ardagh, Co Longford, St Patrick

ARDAGH

For Rectors to 1880, see Deans of Ardagh.

VICAR
-1443   Walter Offergayl

RECTORS
1880–1891	Francis Thornton Gregg
1891–1907	Henry John Johnson
1908–1934	Morgan William Garnier Hamick
1934–1938	Henry Tertius Hutchings
1938–1939	Reginald George Darley

1939–1941	Cecil Maurice Kerr
1941–1943	Edward Joseph McKew
1943–1966	William James Allcard
1967–1980	John Alexander Montgomery
1980–1981	James Pickering
1982–	Albert William Kingston BC

CURATES

1615	George Flawne
1622	Thomas Mayes
c. 1830	Richard Thomas Hearn
? –1833	Alexander Stewart
1841–1844	James Johnston Rowley
1856–1857	Henry Johnston
1861–1864	William Kirk Hobart
1880–1882	Richard H. Graves
1882–1884	Richard Wolfe Landey
1885–1887	Thomas Dowzer
1887–1889	Henry John Johnson
1889–1890	Matthew John Porteus

with Moydow 1920–1932 and 1955–
with Kilglass 1932–1965
with Tashinny and Shrule 1965
with Kilcommick and Cashel 1971–

NOTES

The church was built in 1809 and cost £1,383, of which £100 was a gift from the Board of First Fruits. The Glebe house dates from 1809 (1812 according to Lewis). A new cemetery consecrated May 1806. A new rectory was blessed on 12th April 1964.

Aughavas, Co Leitrim

AUGHAVAS

with Cloone and Lough Rynn 1944–1962
with Mohill 1954–
with Annaduff 1955–1962 and 2000–
with Annaduff East 1962–1976
with Farnaught 1962–
with Oughteragh, Kiltubride and Drumreilly 1981–
with Drumshambo, Annaduff and Kiltoghart 2000–

AUGHRIM

Transferred from Elphin 1959.

with Kiltoghart, Toomna, Kilmore, Annaduff West, Killukin and Termonbarry 1959–1962
(Termonbarry with Templemichael 1960–)

BALLYMACHUGH, Co Cavan

RECTORS
1838–1867	Henry Cottingham
1870–1878	Robert Beatty
1878–1908	John Keane
1908–1910	John Thomas Webster

CURATES
1809–c. 1829	Richard Goslin
1841–1844	William Pennefather
1844–1848	James Watson Skelton
1856–1860	Benjamin Christmas Fawcett
1860–1867	Robert Beatty

NOTES

The Rectory was transferred to Kilmore 1910. Rectory impropriate. The Vicarage was held with Granard 1766–1838. The church was built in 1800 and cost £500 Irish (£461 10s 9¼d), a gift of the Board of First Fruits. Hon Richard Maxwell got a faculty dated 7th March 1860 for a pew in the Church lately occupied by Abel Holmes, 'the 4th pew on the west side of the north transept, opposite the pulpit, as long as he continues a resident in said parish but no longer' (DR).

Ballymacormack, Co Longford

BALLYMACORMACK

VICARS
–1550	Richard McCarmyke
1550	Eugene McCarmyke
1616	George Griffin
1640	Thomas Trafford
? 1641	
–1647	Jeremy Flawne
1662	Joseph Dunbar

PARISHES OF ARDAGH WITH LISTS OF CLERGY

1673	James Sterling
1693–1813	with Templemichael
1693	Benjamin Span
1718/19	Essex Edgeworth
1737	Robert Hort
? 1749–1753	Robert Edgeworth
	Arthur Gardiner (possibly R or C)
1756–1791	John Ryder
1791–1795	Thomas Lewis O'Beirne
1795–1813	Hon Richard Bourke
1813–1838	Henry Maxwell, Lord Farnham
1839–1842	Alexander Hudson
1842–1866	Francis Thornton Gregg
1866–1875	Gilbert Percy
1875–1878	Arthur Patrick Hanlon
1879–1882	Henry Johnston
1882–1900	Thomas Reilly
1900–1922	William Pollard
1924	Frederick Staples Atkinson
1925–1930	Walter Bothwell
1931–1932	Walter Long Fenton
1932–1950	Richard Ferguson
1950–1953	Jervis Uprichard
1955–1967	Robert William Wolfe C-in-c
1967–1970	John Luttrell Haworth BC
1971–1991	Thomas James Bond
1991–1996	Robert Stewart Jackson
1997–2001	Stanley Johnson
2002–	David Arnold Catterall

CURATES

1844–1846	Thomas Kirkwood Little
1870–1871	Abraham Smyth King
1872–1874	William Chapman
1874–1875	Andrew Lyons Joynt
1877–1881	James Tresham Cooke
1879–1882	William McEndoo
1882–1883	John Crawford Irwin

with Killashee 1871
with Kilcommick 1965–1971
with Templemichael, Clongish, Termonbarry and Clooncumber 1971–

NOTES
The Vicarage was held with Templemichael. In 1807 report, the Parish is said to have been 'united to Templemichael 100 years and upwards'. The church was built in 1827 and cost £900 Irish.

CASHEL, Co Longford, St Catherine

VICARS

1622	Sir Patrick Barnewall intruded
1624	William Gregory
1663	James Spencer
1671	James Milus
1680	Robert Ramsay
1685	Arthur Forbes
1727–1740	Eliah Handcock
1740–1780	Richard Knight
1780–1813	Robert Moffett
1813–1838	Richard Hartley Sinclair
1838	Robert Blundell
1838–1853	Charles Richard Harrison
1853–1856	Thomas Webb Green
1856–1869	Samuel Evans Hoops
1869–1875	Richard Conolly
1875–1891	Thomas William Ireland
1891–1900	William Pollard
1900–1906	John Browne
1906–1937	Robert John Mitchell
1937–1939	Alan Leigh Stuart C-in-c
1939–1955	Robert William Wolfe
1955–1959	William Daniel Norman

CURATES

1835–1837/38	Lowry McClintock
1878–1882	Thomas Reilly
1884–1885	Lewis Algeo
1888–1891	Arthur Wellesley Chapman
1891	Andrew John Tilson

with Rathcline 1882
with Kilcommick 1955–1959
closed *c.* 1959

NOTES

The Glebe house was built in 1819 and cost £738 9s 3d, half a gift of the Board of First Fruits. The church was built in 1816 and closed *c.* 1959.

Clonbroney, Ballinalea, Co Longford, St John

CLONBRONEY

VICARS

–1397	Denis O'Dunchun
–1440	Maurice Magillaneani
c. 1440	Eugene Macgillaneany
1440	Thomas Macmurcheartayd
–1444	Matthew Oforgail
1611	Fergall (or Farrell) McCashell (or McCahell)
1661	Herbert Ferris
1670	Henry Bird
1685	Robert Ramsay
c. 1700	Thomas Pollard
1722–1724	Aegidius Firmin
1724–1730	Patrick Moore
1730/31	James Brabazon
1731/32–1750	Moses Lloyd
c. 1750	—

1801–1821	John Booker
1821–1846	George Crawford
1846–1864	Theodore Octavius Moore
1864–1872	James John Newbold
1872–1889	Frederick Potterton
1889–1907	Charles Browne
1908–1940	Henry John Johnson
1940–1945	Alfred Birch
1945–1950	James Mansel Egerton Maguire
1950–1952	David George Alexander Clarke
1952–1966	William Thompson Howard Slator
1966–1971	Ronald Peel Beresford Mathews
1977–1978	James Mansel Egerton Maguire
1978–1982	Robert Henderson
1983–1997	Thomas George Hudson
2002–	Janet Margaret Catterall

CURATES

1826	Richard Quintus St George
–1827	Edward Hoare
1827	George Shaw
–1836	Travers Jones
1840	C. Robinson
1841–1846	Theodore Octavius Moore
1869–1870	Essex Edgeworth
1870–1871	Fitzwilliam Henry West
1900–1901	Charles Stanley Stewart
1901–1903	E. Aubrey Forster
1903–1904	Paul William Nassau Shirley

with Killoe 1901–
with Columbkille 1955–1976
with Mostrim, Granard, Rathaspeck, Streete and Kilglass 1978–

NOTES

The church was built in 1836 and cost £1,015 7s 8¼d. It was enlarged in 1832 and cost £300, of which Lady Rosse gave £200, Colonel Palliser £20 and the Incumbent £10 (Report of 1836). The Glebe house was built in 1827 and cost £829 8s 5d, of which £369 4s 7d was a gift of the Board of First Fruits. Vestry levies of 1832 include £1 8s 8d 'Rent of Churchyard'. The old hall and schoolhouse were converted into a community centre for Clonbroney Group of Parishes 1969–70.

Clongish, Newtownforbes, Co Longford, St Paul

CLONGISH
DRUMLISH Chapel of Ease, Co Leitrim

Drumlish appears in Directories between 1900 and 1932.

CLOONCUMBER Chapel of Ease

VICARS

−1397	Nicholas Machian
−1412	Cornelius O'Ffergail
−1424	Maurice Ymaelmothlaid
1424	Cornelius Offergail
1541	Henry O'Sullivan
−1615	John Aston
1616	George Griffin
1640	George Bunbury
1662	Joseph Dunbar

Clooncumber Church, Co. Leitrim

1673	James Sterling
1693–	possibly with Templemichael
1698	Benjamin Spann
1711	Samuel Spann

RECTORS and VICARS

? 1761	Dudley Charles Ryder
1795–1822	Edward Berwick
1822–1846	George Crawford
1846–1866	William Digby
1866–1873	John Hugh Johnston Powell
1873–1905	George Richard Peyton
1906–1938	John Browne
1938–1943	George Edwin Camier
1944–1951	John Richard Wheelock
1951–1952	William McQuade
1953–1956	Samuel John Leighton
1960–1991	Thomas James Bond
1991–1996	Robert Stewart Jackson
1997–2001	Stanley Johnson
2001–	David Arnold Catterall

CURATES

c. 1777	Samuel Little
1798	George Crawford
1826	Alexander Hudson
1828	Hamilton Verschoyle
c. 1838	Arthur John Wade
1841–1845	Robert James Card
1845	Thomas Ferguson Creery
1846	J. Shepherd
1846	George Beatty Moore
1853	William Cathcart Murphy
1847–1869	Richard Conolly
1858–1869	John Archer
1863–1864	Richard Tate
1869–1870	R.P. Homan
1870–1876	Francis James Costello
1872	P O'Malley
1872–1873	George Richard Peyton
1877–1879	Charles Robert Cooney
1879–1880	Ralph William Doyle
1881–1883	James Stanley Monck
1883–1885	Charles Browne
1885–1887	Andrew Cooper
1887–1893	George Henry Clark
1893–1897	Francis John Armstrong Beere
1897–1898	John George Smith
1898–1899	Arthur Thomas Webb
1899–1902	Samuel Frederick Kellett
1902–1903	Frederick William O'Connell
1903–1905	Victor Frederick Lindsay
1905–1906	Samuel Frederick Kellett

with Clooncumber 1933–
with Templemichael 1959–
with Termonbarry 1960–c. 1977
with Killashee and Ballymacormack 1971–

NOTES

The Mother church (Newtownforbes) was rebuilt c. 1820 and cost of £1,384 12s 3¾d. Chapel of Ease at Drumlish built 1828, cost £950. The Glebe house was built in 1809 and cost £1,107 13s 10¼d. The Parish appears as Clongish and Clongish Killoe in the 1862 Church of Ireland Directory.

Cloone, Co Leitrim, St James

CLOONE and LOUGH RYNN

RECTORS

–1406	Nicholas Macheydan
1406	Gelasius Macheydan
1406	Andrew Macheydan
1407	Sir Gelasius
–1417	Nicholas Mickethean
–1417	Rory Mickethean

PARISHES OF ARDAGH WITH LISTS OF CLERGY

VICARS

–1405	Magonius Yanfyn
–1405	Andrew Maccheydan
–1416	John Mackeythan
1425	Nehemiah Meckehan
–1428	John Macchean
1428	Paul Macchean
1615	Florence Nellye
1622	George Griffin
1634	John Wilkinson

RECTORS

1668/69	Robert Ross
? 1693	Robert Whitelaw
? 1714–1737	William Whitelaw
1737/38–c 1767	Luke Sterling
c. 1767–1815	Dudley Charles Ryder
1816–1830	Hon William Beresford
1830–1854	William Le Poer Trench
1854–1860	Thomas Carson
1860–1877	Frederick Fitzpatrick
1877–1880	Michael Fleming Carey
1881–1885	James Tresham Cooke
1885–1888	Thomas Edward Guard Condell
1888–1910	Louis Cloak
1910–1917	Andrew Graham
1917–1926	Henry Fyers Crampton
1927–1932	Richard Ferguson
1933–1945	Richard George Stanhope Gregg
1946–1952	Rupert Gustavus Musgrave Harris
1954–1962	George Holmes Gibson Bolton

CURATES

1407	Sir Trenotus
1807	Patrick Jaffrey (or Gaffrey)
1832	Andrew Hogg
1840	E. Hoops
1843–1845	John Crofton
1843	Alexander Smullen
1844	John Thomas Warren
1846	Richard Connolly
1851	James Moffatt
1852–1863	Harloe Knott Elwood
1855–1858	Robert Rogers
1861	Roland Savage Morewood
1862–1873	Alexander Nicholls
1864–1867	Samuel Adams
1868–1870	John Hales Sweet
1871–1874	Michael Fleming Carey

Lough Rynn Castle nr Mohill, Co. Leitrim

1874–1875	Arthur Gough Gubbins
1876–1877	Thomas Toovey Hedges
1881–1883	Edward Alexander Cooke

LOUGH RYNN CASTLE CHAPEL

CHAPLAIN

1885–1933	Joseph Robert Garven Digges

with Drumshambo 1886
with Aughavas 1944–1962
with Mohill 1954–1962
possibly Church closed 1962

NOTES

The church was built in 1821 and cost £1,384 12s 3¾d. The Glebe house was condemned in 1836, and a new Glebe house was built in 1843. The church closed *c.* 1972. The bell was given to Cleenish Church, Diocese of Clogher in 1966.

COLUMBKILLE, Co Longford, St Thomas

RECTOR
−1410 Florence

VICARS
with Granard −1838
1838–1853 Thomas Webb Green
1853–1864 William Noble
1863–1869 Samuel Henry Lewis
1869–1894 Francis Henry Dopping
vacant −1903 when joined to Gowna
1903–1917 George Guthridge Wadsworth
1917–1922 Andrew Graham
1922–1925 William Thomas Stewart
1925–1926 Percy Harold Richardson
1926–1930 Samuel Carter Armstrong
1930–1937 James Wilson C-in-c
1937–1939 Cecil Maurice Kerr
1939–1943 Henry Irvine Keys Anderson
1944–1945 William John McKenna
1946–1952 Robert Desmond Holtby
1952–1966 William Thompson Howard Slator
1966–1971 Ronald Peel Beresford Matthews

CURATES
1784 James Adams Ker
1863–1869 Francis Henry Dopping

with Gowna 1903–1952
with Clonbroney and Killoe 1955–1977
with Arvagh, Carrigallen and Gowna in Kilmore Diocese 1977–

NOTES
Church consecrated 15 Oct 1829.

DRUMLUMMON

VICARS

–1626/27	John Richardson
1674/75	John Hodson
with Granard 1807 and probably before, and –1838	
1838–1870	Matthew Webb

CURATES

1784	James Adams Ker
c. 1788	John Beatty
1788	William Brooke
c. 1826	William Elliott
1845–1868	Thomas William Ireland
1868–1870	Abraham Smyth King
1870–1872	Philip John Moran

joined to Ballymachugh 1872
with Abbeylara 1886–1962
with Granard and Mostrim 1944–1977
with Gowna 1952–1959
closed c. 1977

NOTES
Ballymackilenny or Scrabby Church in Drumlummon Parish was licensed for divine service in October 1840. Clonlohan Schoolhouse was licensed for divine service on 16th July 1842 (DR).

Drumreilly, Co Leitrim

DRUMREILLY

transferred from Kilmore 1959
with Oughteragh 1959–
with Fenagh 1959–1976
with Kiltubrid 1962–
with Mohill, Farnaught and Aughavas 1981–
with Drumshambo, Kiltoghart and Annaduff 2000–

Drumshambo, Co Leitrim, St John

DRUMSHAMBO

CURATES-IN-CHARGE and RECTORS
1886	Thomas Edward Guard Condell
1887–1889	Henry West C-in-c
1891–1893	William Morgan O'Connell C-in-c
1894–1903	George Guthridge Wadsworth C-in-c
1903–1905	Frederick William O'Connell C-in-c
1905–1914	Richard Hemphill C-in-c

1914–1920	Hugh Parker Woodhouse C-in-c 1914–16, R
1916–20	
1921–1923	Richard Bertram Blackwell Smyth
1924–1945	Andrew Graham
1945–1950	John Alexander Montgomery
1951–1952	Alan Leigh Stuart
1953–1955	George Harold Kidd
1956–1962	Robert Desmond Holtby BC
1962–1966	William Alexander Russell
1966–1981	William Thompson Howard Slator
1982–1991	Ivan Richard Biggs
1991–1996	vacant
1996–2001	Ivan Richard Biggs in charge
2003–	Forrest William Atkins

CURATES
1861–1869	James Topham
1865–1866	Richard Tate
1870–1872	Charles Ellis
1873	George Alexander Papendick Arbuthnot
1873–1875	Robert Grierson
1875–1876	Thomas Heron Aldwell
1876–1878	John Black
1878–1879	Charles Richard Williams
1879–1881	Alexander McKinney
1881–1883	Eyre Stratford Dallton
1883–1885	William Jordan
1889–1891	John Robert Gumley

NSM
2002–	Cecil Lindsay

with Kiltoghart 1828–1885 and 1962–
with Cloone 1886
with Kiltubrid 1930–1962
with Kilmactranny (transferred back to Elphin 1951) 1951
with Kilronan 1951–1996
with Kilmore and Toomna 1962–1996
with Annaduff 1963–
with Mohill, Farnaught, Aughavas, Oughteragh and Drumreilly 2000–

NOTES
Drumshambo Chapel of Ease was built in 1828 with a loan of £1,800 (Report of 1836). It was in the Parish of Kiltoghart.

Farnaught, Co Leitrim

FARNAUGHT

with Annaduff East 1962–1976
with Mohill and Aughavas 1962–
with Oughteragh, Kilbride and Drumreilly 1981–
with Drumshambo, Kiltoghart and Annaduff 2000–

Fenagh, Co Leitrim, St Catherine

FENAGH

VICARS

–1615	Florence Nellye
1622	John Price
1635	George Gonne (or Guinne)
1673	Richard Blackburne
1680–c. 1700	John King
1700–c. 1740	William Hansard
1740–1766	Daniel Hearn (possibly there 1732/33)
c. 1767–c. 1815	Dudley Charles Ryder
1816–1842	Hon George de la Poer Beresford
1843–1869	Hon George de la Poer Beresford Jun
1869–1882	Francis Kane
1882–1896	Samuel Evans Hoops
1897–1922	William Welwood
1922–1949	Austin Sweetnam
1949–1950	Thomas Patrick Scarborough Wood

1950–1953	Richard Ferguson
1953–1960	Jervis Uprichard
1962–1965	Robert Desmond Holtby
1965–1966	Frederick William Frank Davis C-in-c
1966–1967	Cecil Harold Bruce Browne
1967–1971	John Alexander Pickering C-in-c 1967–68
1971–1976	Basil Gordon Young McGlaughlin

CURATES

1787	Francis Percy
1796	Patrick Jaffrey
c. 1825	John Moore
1836–1837	Henry Garrett
1837	— Fallon
1843	Alexander Nicholls
1857–1862	Thomas H. Roe
1862–1865	Oliver Josef Tibeaudo
1865–1869	Richard Tate
1880–1881	R. Allen Smyth
1881–1883	George Henry Tessier La Nauze

with Oughteragh 1922–
with Drumreilly 1959–
with Kiltubride 1962–
last appearance in Church of Ireland Directory 1976: possibly closed

NOTES

The church was built in 1787 and cost £360 British. The Glebe house was built in 1827 and cost £1,330 British of which £100 was a gift of the Board of First Fruits.

Gowna or Loch Gowna, Co Cavan

GOWNA

RECTORS

1626/27	John Richardson
1674/75	John Hodson
1761–1805	William Brooke
1805–1811	John de la Poer Beresford
1811–1837	Christopher Robinson
1838–1870	Matthew Webb
1871–1872	Robert Beatty
1872–1877	Philip John Moran C-in-c 1872–1875, R
1875–1877	
1877–1879	Thomas Lindsay
1879–1880	Samuel Slinn Skeen
1880–1902	Thomas Taylor
1903–1917	George Guthridge Wadsworth
1917–1922	Andrew Graham
1922–1925	William Thomas Stewart C-in-c
1925–1926	Percy Harold Richardson

1926–1930	Samuel Carter Armstrong
1930–1937	James Wilson
1937–1939	Cecil Maurice Kerr C-in-c
1939–1943	Henry Irvine Keys Anderson C-in-c
1944–1945	William John McKenna C-in-c
1946–1952	Robert Desmond Holtby C-in-c
1952–1959	Cecil Maurice Kerr

CURATES

1791–1803	Kilner Davison
1803–1816	Newcomen Whitelaw
1816–1826	James Adams Ker
1826–1845	William Elliot
1845–1868	Thomas Ireland
1868–1870	Abraham Smyth King
1872–1874	Philip John Moran

in Ardagh –1959
with Columbkille 1903–1952
with Granard, Mostrim, Abbeylara and Drumlummon 1952–1959
with Arvagh, Carrigallen and Gowna in Kilmore Diocese 1959–

NOTES

St Columba founded a monastery in Loch Gowna *c.* 550, under Augustinian Canons in the Middle Ages. The present building was licensed for worship in October 1840 and cost £730. 4s. 0d. Gowna was a chapel of ease in Drumlummon Parish. It was transferred to Kilmore Diocese and united with Arvagh 1 Jan 1959.

Granard, Co Longford, St Patrick

GRANARD

VICARS

1369	Sir John Offyne
1389	Nemeas O'Sculaghan
–1438	Matthew Ycam
–1438	William Yfergail
–1438	Matthew McAeda
1438	Eugene Macmurcheartayd
–1441	William Ofergail
1441	Maurice Macgillarnean
–1455	Eugene McMuircertaig
1455/56	William Cilleg
1536–1539	Richard Wacfield (or Wakefield)
1552	John Drover (or Derver)
1556/57	Robert Nugent
1610	John Richardson
–1630	William Smith
1661/62–1664	William Baylie
1665–1702	John Ker
1702–1737	Essex Edgeworth
1737–1741	Samuel Span
1741–1761	Michael Neligan

1761–c. 1805	William Brooke
1805–1811	John de la Poer Beresford
1811–1837	Christopher Robinson
1838–1863	William Tomlinson
1863–1875	Thomas Webb Green
1876–1885	Frederick Foster
1885–1914	Francis de Burgh Sidley
1914–1925	Arthur Reginald Burriss
1925–1933	Edward Furlong
1933–1934	Isaac Mayne
1934–1937	Hugh Maurice Daunt
1938–1940	Charles Richard Ryall
1941–1966	Cecil Maurice Kerr
1966–1978	James Mansel Egerton Maguire
1978–1982	Robert Henderson
1983–1997	Thomas George Hudson
2002–	Janet Margaret Catterall

CURATES

1615	William Griffith
1622	William Smith
1622	John Smith
1753	William Hughes
1762	John Beatty
1762	Archibald (or Alexander) Armstrong
1787	Thomas Beatty
1791–1803	Kilner Davison
1803–1816	Newcomen Whitelaw
1816	Henry Liscar (or Lesac) Webb
c. 1826	— Thompson
1826–1845	William Elliot
1830	Christopher Robinson Jun
1846	Alexander Smullen
1856	Matthew Nesbitt Thompson
1861	Francis Henry Dopping

with Abbeylara 1922–1962
with Mostrim 1941–
with Drumlummon 1944–1976
with Gowna 1952–1959
with Clonbroney, Killoe, Rathaspeck, Streete and Kilglass 1977–

NOTES

Granard had a great abbey in early times. The date of the church is unknown. The Glebe house was built in 1835 and cost £1,015 7s 8d British. Gowna held with Granard 1952–58. The church was restored and reopened on 24th October 1965.

INISMOR alias LOCHAGANA

Small parish on island in Loch Gowna.
Long-obsolete medieval parish.

–1457	Eugenius McMurtagh (Macmurcertheid)
–1457	William O'Farrell (Offerguyll)
1458	Henry O'Sullivan O'Sulechan)

Kilcommick, Kenagh, Co Longford, St George

KILCOMMICK

VICARS
1411	Bernard Macmurchercaid
–1412	Andrew Maccilruaig
1479	Wilhelmus Offergail
1479	Bernard Offergail
–1480	John McGillewyd
–1480	Dermit O'Flanagan
1480	Charles O'Fallayn
1615	John Aston
1623–1654	Nathaniel Hollington
–1649	James Cahill intruded
c. 1661	Robert Fullerton
? 1684	— Knox
1691	John Wilson
1717/18	William Wilson

17–	Henry Palmer
? 1776	}
1780–1784	} William Elliott
1805–1821	Robert Beatty
–1807	Edward Beatty
1823–1848	George Brittaine
1848–1866	Thomas Henry
1866–1867	Francis Thornton Gregg
1867–1883	Robert James Card
1883–1885	Henry Ruthe Wilson
1886–1897	William Welwood
1897–1917	Paul Kemp Lyon
1917–1951	John Armstrong
1951–1965	William Daniel Norman C-in-c 1951–1956, R
1956–1965	
1965–1967	Robert William Wolfe
1967–1970	John Luttrell Haworth
1970–1980	John Alexander Montgomery
1980–1981	James Pickering
1982–	Albert William Kingston BC

CURATES

c. 1778–1784	James Smith
1787	James Gordon
1817	Prince Crawford
c. 1826	William Grave
1827–1832	Benjamin Cronin
1840–1847	Thomas Henry
1863–1867	George Galbraith

with Moydow 1912–1955 and 1971–
with Cashel and Rathcline 1955–1965
with Killashee and Ballymacormack 1965–1971
with Ardagh and Cashel, Tashinny and Shrule 1971–

NOTES

The Glebe house was built in 1827 and cost £784 12s 3¾d. 'Old Church very inconveniently circumstanced and built about a century ago. New one just erected on new site by the Dowager Countess of Rosse at cost of £2,500 British' (Report of 1836). Kilcommick Church was built in 1832 near Kenagh during the incumbency of Rev George Brittaine, a noted Protestant evangelical preacher and writer, and dedicated to St George.

KILGLASS, Co Roscommon, St Ann

VICARS/RECTORS

–1396	Marianus Ocongalom
1396	Donatus Offergail
1407	Maurice Macgillananaeim
–1411	Thomas Macmurkertaid
1411	Thomas Maccega
1411	Nicholas O'Branagan
–1465	William O'Branagayn
1465	Eugene Maccontagry (Macconkagry)
1479	Thady O'Farrell
1615	Kedaghe O'Farrell
1634	George Bunbury
1662	Joseph Dunbar
1683/85	Edward Sympson
? 1697	—
1732	Maurice Neligan, V
1732/33	Thomas White, R
1754	—
c. 1780–1802	Christopher Browne
? 1802–1806	George de la Poer Beresford
1806–1812	Henry Bate Dudley
1813–1842	Robert Fetherston Jessop
1843–1870	Charles Robinson
1870–1875	John Wilson Stenson
1876–1884	Thomas William Cusack Russell
1885–1887	Charles Browne
1887–1891	William Pollard
1891–1892	Andrew John Tilson
1892–1894	Ambrose George Townshend
1895–1922	William Lea
1922–1927	Richard Hemphill
1927–1929	Frederick Staples Atkinson
1929–1932	Francis Sadleir Stoney
1932–1934	Morgan William Garnier Hammick
1934–1938	Henry Tertius Hutchings
1939–1941	Cecil Maurice Kerr
1941–1943	Edward Joseph McKew
1943–1966	William James Allcard
1966/67–1969	George Frederick Morrow
1969–1976	John Arthur Knowles BC
1978–1982	Robert Henderson
1983–1997	Thomas George Hudson

CURATES

1809	Thomas Brown
1838–1847	John Wilkinson
1851–1852	Maurice Neligan
1852–1863	George Galbraith
1863–1867	Robert Thomas Bevan
1867–1869	Thomas B. Wills
1869–1870	Fitzwilliam Henry West

with Mostrim 1922–1929 and 1977–1997
with Ardagh 1932–1965
with Moydow 1955–1966
with Rathaspeck and Streete 1965–1997
with Granard, Clonbroney and Killoe 1978–1997

NOTES

Kilglass, Aharagh and Rathrea were united by Order in Council dated 6th May 1737 (LM V 126). The church was built in 1815 and cost £989 6s 3d British; faculty for alteration dated 13th May 1867 (DR). The Glebe house was built in 1815 and cost £923 1s 6½d British (Report of 1836). The church was closed c. 1997.

Killashee, Co Longford, St Paul

KILLASHEE

VICARS

–1411	Celestine Yfergail
1411	Carbricus Offergail
1422	Richard Yfergail
–1427	Richard Yfergail
1427	Carbricus Offergail
1432	Roricus Macmurcheartaich
1479	Thomas Findd
1510	John Yfergal
–1549	John O'Feroll
1549	John Northaghe
–1622	George Flawne
–1647	Jeremy Flawne
1662	Joseph Dunbar
1683	Andrew Charlton
1697–1749	Thomas Taylor
1749–1767	Fletcher Piers
c. 1767–1768	—
? 1800–1813	Sir James Hutchinson

1813–1823	Henry William Cobbe
1823–1846	William Digby
1846–1856	Alexander Hudson
1856–1871	Hugh Crawford
1871–1875	Gilbert Percy
1875–1878	Alexander Patrick Hanlon
1879–1882	Henry Johnston
1882–1900	Thomas Reilly
1900–1922	William Pollard
1924–1925	Frederick Staples Atkinson
1925–1930	Walter Bothwell
1931–1932	Walter Long Fenton
1932–1950	Richard Ferguson
1950–1953	Jervis Uprichard
1955–1967	Robert William Wolfe
1967–1970	John Luttrell Haworth C-in-c
1971–1991	Thomas James Bond
1991–1996	Robert Stewart Jackson
1997–2001	Stanley Johnson
2002–	David Arnold Catterall

CURATES

1766	Thomas Jessope
1785	James Ferrall
1839–1843	John Hugh Johnston Powell
1846	Thomas John Price
1846–1850	James Michael Henry Strangways
1850–1853	Henry Faussett
1853	W. Dowdsley
1854–1855	James Alexander Crozier
1855–1857	Robert Thomas Bevan
1874–1875	Andrew Lyons Joynt
1875–1876	A.J. Burnett
1876–1877	Thomas Reilly
1878–1879	Francis Edward Clarke
1879–1882	William McEndoo
1880–1883	John Crawford Irwin

with Ballymacormack 1871
with Kilcommick 1965–1971
with Templemichael, Clongish, Termonbarry and Clooncumber 1971–

NOTES
Church old. Glebe house built 1786, cost £511 7s 8d.

KILLENUMERY

VICARS

–1426	Thomas Macmoclaid
1426	Mauricius Ocrebair
1427	Matthew Macmoglay
1435	Roger Ohuban
–1468	Rory O'Gurtan
–1469	Bernard Macmoglay
1475	Cormac Machymogley
1615	Eugene McGillahilge
1622–1660	John Johnson
1661	John Layng
1674	Alexander Robinson
1697	George Forbes
1701–1721	John Parkes
1721–1724	Patrick Moore
1724–1727	John Rastall
1727–1774	Charles Dodd
c. 1774–1791	Oliver Dodd
1791–c. 1817	Charles Robinson
1817–1860	Michael Boland
1861–1885	Edmund Allen Lucas
1885–1887	William Hamilton
1887–1920	Francis Lewis Riggs

CURATES

c. 1827	Michael Hobart Seymour
1856–1861	Julius Henry Griffith
1870–1872	John W. Costello
1870–1885	Martin Bradshaw

with Killery 1876–1920
transferred to Kilmore 1920

NOTES

The church was built in 1822 and cost £923 1s 6½d. The Glebe house was built in 1812 and cost £723 9s 3d of which £323 1s 6½d was a gift of the Board of First Fruits.

KILLERY

RECTORS
–1381/82	John Eylward
–1382	Thomas Omoltorka claimed Parish but was annulled
1381/82	William Fitzsimond Lawles

VICARS
–1421	Enias Macnoglaidh
–1421	Charles MacNaglaid
–1421	Thady O'Mulaid
1421	Florence Matannoglaych
1431/32	Florence Macnoglaidh
1622–1835	with Killenumery
1835–1838	William Newton Guinness
1861–1874	William Moore
1876–1884	Edmund Allen Lucas
1885–1886	William Hamilton
1887–1920	Francis Lewis Riggs

CURATES
–1798–*c.* 1826	Isaac Dodd
1870–1875	Martin Bradshaw

with Killenumery 1876–1920
transferred to Elphin 1923

NOTES
Church built in 1715 by a private individual.

Killoe, Co Longford, St Catherine

KILLOE

VICARS

–1408	Sir Donat O'Farrell
1487	Eugene Yconalcha
1541	Denis O'Ferrall
1615	Edward Hatton
1635	George Bunbury
1661	Maurice O'Mulconry
1662–1673	James Sterling
1673–1874	with Templemichael
1870–1875	William Henry Hodges
1875–1876	Digby William Duane Digby
1876–1879	John Gaggin
1879–1880	Arthur George Hetherington Long
1880–1881	Ralph William Doyle
1881–1883	William Malcolm Foley
1883–1886	Eyre Stratford D'Alton
1886–1888	Francis Thomas Caldwell
1888–1890	George Henry Christie
1890–1900	Charles Edward Keane
1901–	*see* Clonbroney

CURATES

1828	John le Poer Trench
1878–1879	Thomas Taylor

with Clonbroney 1901–
with Columbkille 1955–1976
with Mostrim, Granard, Rathaspeck, Streete and Kilglass 1977–

NOTES
Church built 1824.

Killukin, Co Roscommon

KILLUKIN

transferred from Elphin 1959
with Kiltoghart, Toomna, Kilmore, Annaduff West, Aughrim and
Termonbarry 1959–1962
(Termonbarry with Templemichael 1960–)
closed *c.* 1962

Kilmactranny, Co Sligo

KILMACTRANNY

transferred from Elphin 1924, and with Elphin again 1951
with Kilronan 1924–1951
with Drumshambo and Kiltubrid 1951
see also Elphin list

Kilmore, Co Roscommon

KILMORE

transferred from Elphin 1959
with Kiltoghart, Toomna, Annaduff West, Aughrim, Killukin and Termonbarry 1959–1962
(Termonbarry with Templemichael 1960–)
with Drumshambo, Annaduff and Kilronan 1962–1996
closed *c.* 1996

Kilronan, Co Roscommon, St Thomas

KILRONAN

VICARS

1398	Andrew Macrylruiag
–1428	George Oduigeannan
–c. 1428	Cornelius Oduigrannan
–c. 1428	Philip O'Dorchan
1428	Philip Macabrechim
–1443	Gregory Iduibgenan
1443	Thomas Macdiannada
1443	Tatheus McGillamane
1559	Dionysius Moore
1619	Thomas Sarcott
–1622	Ellice Griffin
c. 1640	Robert Heigh
1661	Robert Ross
1674	Alexander Robinson
1715–1740	John Lloyd
1740–1752	Thomas Fysbie
1752–	John Mailly
17–	Joseph Bennett
1791–1829	John Little

1829–1834	Charles Seymour
1834–1875	Edward Charles Eager
1875–c. 1889	Richard Connolly
1893–1896	Theophilus Patrick Landey
1896–1921	Robert Wallace Boyd
1922–1927	Andrew Graham C-in-c
1927–1930	William George Coleman C-in-c
1931–1937	Henry Angus Victor Kennedy
1937–1946	James Nelson McCullough
1947–1950	William Bolton Battersby
1951–1996	with Drumshambo etc

CURATE

1893–1896	Theophilus F. Landey

with Kilmactranny (transferred from Elphin 1924 and back to Elphin 1951) 1924–1951
with Drumshambo 1951–1996
with Kiltubrid 1951–1962
with Kiltoghart, Annaduff, Kilronan, Toomna and Kilmore 1962–1996
closed c. 1996

NOTES

The Glebe house was built in 1815 and cost £672, of which £369 was a gift of the Board of First Fruits. The present church was built in 1780 and rebuilt c. 1894. Carolan the Bard is buried here. The organ was transferred from Kilronan Castle. A silver cross was placed in the church 1966. Closed about 1996.

Kiltoghart, Carrick-On-Shannon, Co Leitrim, St George

KILTOGHART

VICARS
c. 1440	Andrew Miccabruoig
–1442	John Magellahuly
1442	Ffergalus Magellahuly
1447/48	John Magillachuli
1447/48	Charles Oflaynd
1460	John Offaynd
–1461	John Ylamud
–1461	John Magellasulig
1461	Fergallus Magellakuly

RECTORS

–1470	Cornelius Offergayl
1470	Tatheus Macgillasulid

VICARS

1477/78	Cornelius McKanayll
1481	Cornelius Magranayll
–1506	John Magillhasulich
1506	Nemeas Magehadgayn
–1615	Eugene Magillasuly
1622	John Evat
1634	William Hamon
1634	Edward Stanhope
1635	James Stevenson
1661	George Blackburne
1673	Richard Blackburne
1680	John King
1700	William Hansard

RECTORS and VICARS

c. 1732–1740	Daniel Hearn
1740–c 1790	John Bennett
1790–	John Chetwood
1807–1814	John Chetwood – possibly same as above
1814–1836	Thomas Jones
1836–1869	William Alexander Percy
1869–1886	Samuel Henry Lewis
1886–1907	William Richard Moore
1907–1949	John Claudius Beresford
1949–1955	Thomas Norman Bateman
1955–1966	William Alexander Russell
1966–1981	William Thompson Howard Slator
1982–1991	Ivan Richard Biggs
1996–2001	Ivan Richard Biggs in charge
2003–	Forrest William Atkins

CURATES

1743	Joseph Bennett
1781	Joseph Bennett
1798	Isaac Dodd
c. 1826	William Percy
1836–1846	Richard Samuel Clifford
	Henry Garrett
1837	William Noble
1847	William Cunningham Peyton
1853	Milnard Crooke
1855	John Michael Heffernan
1855–1869	James Topham

1856	Joseph Carson Moore
1858	Christopher Halahan
1861–1862	Oliver Josef Tibeaudo
1863–1867	Gilbert Percy
1867–1868	Thomas Kemmis
1868–1869	Alfred George Elliott
1870–1872	Charles Ellis
1870–1872	Joseph Potter
1873–1875	Robert Grierson
1875–1876	Thomas Heron Aldwell
1875	John Black
1878–1879	Charles R. Williams
1879–1881	Alexander McKinney
1881–1883	Eyre Stratford Dalton
1883–1885	William Jordan

NSM

2002–	Cecil Lindsay

with Drumshambo Chapel of Ease 1828–1885 and 1962–
with Annaduff West = Annaduff 1932–1954 and 1959–1962
with Toomna and Kilmore 1959– 1996
with Termonbarry 1959–1960
with Annaduff 1962–
with Kilronan 1962–1996
with Annaduff West, Aughrim and Killukin 1959–1962
with Mohill, Farnaught, Aughavas, Oughteragh, Drumreilly and Kiltubride 2000

NOTES

In 1436 an indulgence of 3 years' and 3 quarantines' penance granted to penitents and 100 days' to those who visited and gave alms for repair of Church of Gillthacurt, Ardagh (CPL VIII 524). In 1698 'the Church of Kiltohorke, Co Leitrim shall be built at the parish charge in Carrick Drumruiskeon, land set apart by Sir George St George to be henceforth the Parish Church' (Act 10 William III c VI section 9; LM VI 27). The mother church at Carrick-on-Shannon was built in 1829 and cost £2,500 of which £529 was raised by the sale of materials and the old church and assessment. The church was restored 1910–1914. The Glebe house was built in 1818 and cost £1,384 12s 3¾d, of which £92 6s 1¼d was a gift of the Board of First Fruits. The old rectory was sold in 1886 and a new rectory was built in 1890–91 and occupied for first time on 20th October 1891. The organ was restored in 1977. Major renovations were carried out in 2005–06.

Kiltubride, Co Leitrim, St Brigid

KILTUBRIDE

RECTOR
1470 — Tatheus Macgillasulid

VICARS
–1410	Sir Bernard O'Colla
1410	Dermot McIncebruoyd
1413	Firgall Machilruays
1425	John Machgillaciaran
1434	Macsifius O'Drinan
c. 1460	Andrew McCowlog
–1615	Florence Nellye
1622	John Price
1635	George Gonne (or Gunn)
1661	George Blackburne
1673	Richard Blackburne
1680	John King
1700–c. 1732	William Hansard

c. 1732–1740	Daniel Hearn
1740–1763	John Lloyd
c. 1766–	Heywood Jenkins
17– –1823	Thomas Kennedy
1823–1868	George Dallas Mansfield
1869–1882	Samuel Evans Hoops
1883–1884	Charles Henry Bewick C-in-c
1885–1915	Thomas Frederick Browne C-in-c
1915–1928	Robert Doherty
1928–1945	Andrew Graham
1945–1951	John Alexander Montgomery C-in-c
1951–1953	Alan Leigh Stuart
1953–1955	George Harold Kidd
1956–1965	Robert Desmond Holtby BC
1965–1966	Frederick William Frank Davis C-in-c
1966–1967	Cecil Harold Bruce Browne
1967–1971	John Alexander Pickering
1971–1981	Basil Gordon Young McGlaughlin
1981–1984	John Arthur Knowles
1985–1996	Charles Ludwig Birbeck Hill Meissner
1997–2000	Jeremiah Thomas Paul Twomey
2003–	Forrest William Atkins

CURATES

c. 1763	Arthur Henderson
c. 1826	Andrew Crawford
1856–1861	Robert James Wallace
1861–1865	Frederick Benjamin White
1866–1868	William Robert Lawrenson Kinahan
1872–1876	Thomas Lindsay

NSM

2000–2003	Cecil Lindsay

with Drumshambo 1930–1962
with Kilronan 1951–1962
with Kilmactranny (transferred back to Elphin 1951) 1951
with Fenagh 1962–1976
with Oughteragh, and Drumreilly 1962–
with Mohill, Farnaught and Aughavas 1981–
with Drumshambo, Kiltoghart and Annaduff 2000

NOTES

The church was built in 1785. 'Evening service in some hamlet in the parish as many of the parishioners are living at a distance' (Report of 1836). The Glebe house was built c. 1815 and cost £1,114 6s 2d, of which £230 15s 4¾d was a gift of the Board of First Fruits.

MOGBRECHI (possibly = STREETE)

Long-obsolete medieval parish.
Unidentified parish.

VICAR
1397   Stephen

Mohill, Co Leitrim, St Mary

MOHILL

VICARS

1615	vacant
1622	John Neile
1663/64–1698	William Cunningham (Conyngham)
1698	John Smith
1699–1721	Peter Peacy alias Gallineer
? 1721–1724	Langle Ross (possibly Randall Rose)
1724–1756	Aegidius Firmins
1756–1791	John Ryder
1791–1795	Thomas Lewis O'Beirne
1795–1801	Hon Richard Bourke
1801–c. 1806	Charles Mongan Warburton
c. 1807–1816	George de la Poer Beresford
1816–1870	Arthur Hyde
1870–1891	Fitzmaurice Hunt
1891–1916	Henry Justice
1916–1921	Thomas Johnston Bayly
1921–1932	George Ingham
1932–1941	David Herbert Kelly
1941–1966	George Holmes Gibson Bolton
1967–1973	Thomas Oswald Sturdy
1976–1984	John Arthur Knowles BC
1985–1996	Charles Ludwig Birbeck Hill Meissner
1997–2000	Jeremiah Thomas Paul Twomey
2000–2001	Ivan Richard Biggs in charge
2003–	Forrest William Atkins

NSM

2000–2003	Cecil Lindsay

CURATES

–1698	James Hog
c. 1779	Thomas Jones
c. 1826–1847	Morgan Crofton
1837	William Jeffcott
1839–1856	Samuel Evans Hoops
1857–1861	Benjamin Dugdale Hastings McAdam
1861–1870	Thomas George Johnston Phillips
1862–1864	Samuel Adams
1864–1868	Alexander Major Kearney
1868–1870	Augustus Charles Edward Hill
1871–1873	Henry Robert Lopdell
1873–1874	Matthew Campbell
1874–1878	Thomas White Manning
1874–1875	Horace Thomas Edward Townsend
1875	Alfred Mitchell
1875–1876	Samuel Hyde
1876–1879	Samuel Atkinson Adams
1877–1879	William Welwood
1879–1883	Charles Robert Cooney
1883–1884	Joseph Robert Garven Digges
1885–1887	Alfred Mitchell
1888–1890	William Henry Giles
1890–1891	William Forster
1891–1895	William Goldsmith Squires
1895–1897	John Browne
1897–1899	Thomas Sandes Gibbings
1899–1901	Frederick William Baron Jobson
1900–1910	Robert Burke
1910–1913	Frank William Bonynge
1913–1916	Charles Gordon Metcalfe
1917–1921	George Hamilton
1922–1925	Henry Scott Burd
1965–1966	Frederick William Frank Davis

with Termonbarry 1900–1954
with Cloone, Lough Rynn Castle Chapel, Annaduff 1954–1962
with Aughavas 1954–
with Annaduff East (= Annaduff) 1962–1976
with Farnaught 1962–
with Oughteragh, Kiltubride and Drumreilly 1981–
with Drumshambo, Kiltoghart and Annaduff 2000–

NOTES

There was a monastery at Mohill before the Reformation. Church old; enlarged in 1815. The Rectorial tithes (one third of whole) belonged to the Crofton family. Another third belonged to the Bishop c. 1622 and probably went with Vicarial thirds subsequently. The Glebe house was built in 1823 and cost £1,569 4s 7½d. The Parochial Hall in memory of Archdeacon Hunt was built in 1893. The 'Good Shepherd' window was designed by A.E. Child at Tower of Glass in 1937. The church clock was restored with the help of subscriptions from all denominations in Mohill, and was dedicated jointly by the Bishop of Kilmore and the RC Bishop of Ardagh on 16th May 1971.

Mostrim, Edgeworthstown, Co Longford, St John

MOSTRIM

RECTOR
1410   Nemeas Offergail

VICARS
1539   John O'Farrell
1615   Edward Hatton
1619   Morris O'Mulconry
1634   Edward Singe
1635   George Bunbury
1636   James Nangle
1663   John Kerr
1670   John Kerr
1702   John Brisbin or Brisbane
1705   Richard Vaughan

1732–1737/38	Joseph Caddy
1737/8–c. 1750	Robert Edgeworth
c. 1750–c. 1778	Hutchinson Hamilton
c. 1778–c. 1784	John Bork
c. 1784–	possibly Roger Boyce
1801–1840	George Keating
1840–1843	Charles Robinson
1843–1863	John Hugh Johnston Powell
1864–1868	William Noble
1868–1874	George Little Horneck
1874–1875	Edward George Campbell
1875–1882	William Henry Lynn
1882–1885	William Hamilton
1885–1886	Robert Young Lynn
1886–1888	George Mortimer Anderson
1889–1891	Henry John Johnson
1891–1897	Paul Kemp Lyon
1897–1899	John Browne
1900–1913	Charles Edward Keane
1914–1927	Richard Hemphill
1927–1931	Frederick Staples Atkinson
1931–1932	William Francis Nunan
1932–1936	Robert William Wolfe C-in-c
1936–1939	Robert Warrington C-in-c
1941–1966	Cecil Maurice Kerr
1966–1978	James Mansel Egerton Maguire
1978–1982	Robert Henderson
1983–1997	Thomas George Hudson
2002–	Janet Margaret Catterall

CURATES

1615	George Flawne
1747	Patrick Hughes

with Kilglass 1922–1929 and 1977–1997
with Abbeylara 1941–1962
with Granard 1941–
with Drumlummon 1944–1977
with Gowna 1952–1959
with Clonbroney, Killoe, Rathaspeck, Streete and Kilglass 1978–

NOTES

The church, which is old, was enlarged in 1816 and cost £552 13s 10¼d. The Glebe house was built in 1732 and was subsequently enlarged. The organ was given in memory of Archdeacon C.M. Kerr, and dedicated on 24th September 1967.

Moydow, Co Longford

MOYDOW

VICARS

–1412	Donatus Micgillaclain
1412	John Offergail
–1615	Keadagh McConnell O'Ferrall
1624	James Fathy (possibly Futhy)
1635	John Price
1658	Jeremy Flawne
1661	Jeremy Flawne
1662	Joseph Dunbar
1683	Edward Sympson
1732	Maurice Neligan
17– –1770	Daniel Sandford
c. 1770–c. 1793	Robert Beatty
1793–1821	Robert Beatty Jun
1823–1868	William Chambers Armstrong
1868–1896	Alexander Orme
1897–1912	Edward Briscoe
1912–1917	Paul Kemp Lyon
1917–1951	John Armstrong
1951–1955	William Daniel Norman
1955–1966	William James Allcard
1967–1980	John Alexander Montgomery
1980–1981	James Pickering
1982–	Albert William Kingston BC

CURATES

1823–1825	Richard Henry D'Olier
1855–1863	Robert Thomas Bevan
1863–1867	Alexander Orme

with Kilcommick 1912–1955 and 1971–
with Ardagh 1920–1932 and 1955–
with Kilglass 1955–1966
with Tashinny and Shrule 1965–

NOTES

The church was built in 1765, and repaired and rstored after a fire in 1831. The Glebe house was built in 1830 and cost £840 of which £800 was a gift of the Board of First Fruits. The church closed in 1987.

MUNTERANGAILE

Long-obsolete medieval parish.

RECTORS
1430	Gerald Ofergail
–1444/45	Thomas Macmurcertaych
1465/66	Eugene Mayconkagry

MUNTIREOLIS

Long-obsolete medieval parish.

RECTORS
1397	Nicholas Machian
1397	John Offergayl
1412	John Offergail
1433	Donald Mcgranaill
–1444	John O'Feargail
–1444/45	Paul Macechan
1444/45	Cornelius Ofeargail
1458	Robert Macgranayll
1460	Malachy Machwkuarg or Machwlruayg (MacGilroy)
–146–	Donatus O'Feargayl
–1463	Robert Macgranail
–1463	Rory Macgranail
1463	Donald O'Feargayl
1469	Eugene Macchonkagri
1470	Tatheus Macgillasulid
1475	Donald O'Farrell
1481	Cornelius Macgravayll
1489	Maurice Macgranayll
1610/11	Henry Reinold
1615	Eugene McGillasulye
1618/19	Nathaniel Hollington
1682	Anthony Cope

Oughteragh or Outragh, Ballinamore, Co Leitrim

OUGHTERAGH

RECTORS
1906–1949	Austin Sweetnam
1950–1953	Richard Ferguson
1953–1960	Jervis Uprichard
1962–1965	Robert Desmond Holtby
1965–1966	Frederick William Frank Davis C-in-c
1966–1967	Cecil Harold Bruce Browne
1967–1971	John Alexander Pickering
1971–1981	Basil Gordon Young McGlaughlin
1981–1984	John Arthur Knowles
1985–1996	Charles Ludwig Birbeck Hill Meissner
1997–2000	Jeremiah Thomas Paul Twomey
2003–	Forrest William Atkins

transferred from Kilmore 1910
with Fenagh 1922–1976
with Drumreilly 1959–
with Kiltubride 1962–
with Mohill, Farnaught and Aughavas 1981–
with Drumshambo, Kiltoghart and Annaduff 2000–

Rathaspeck, Co Westmeath, St Thomas

RATHASPECK

Impropriate Curacy.

VICARS and IMPROPRIATE CURATES
1615	Leonard Helagh
1622–1661	vacant
1661	Herbert Ferris
1670	Henry Bird
1685/86	Robert Ramsay
1698–1701	Charles Barclay
1742–1768	Fletcher Piers
1768–18–	no entry
1807–c 1816	Patrick Sweeny
1816–1818	Michael Boland
1818–1843	Henry Lesac Webb
1843–1855	Alexander Orme
1855–1858	Thomas Francis Bushe
1858–1861	Hilkiah Bedford Hall
1862–1873	Henry William Stewart

1873–1899	Herbert Schomberg St George
1900–1920	Thomas Reilly
1920–1939	Woodley Joseph Lindsay
1940–1949	Frederick James Powell
1950–1956	Thomas Patrick Scarborough Wood
1958–1964	Edward Frederick Forrest
1964–1969	George Frederick Morrow
1969–1976	John Arthur Knowles
1978–1982	Robert Henderson
1983–1997	Thomas George Hudson
2002–	Janet Margaret Catterall

CURATE

1870–1871	Edward M. Stewart

with Russagh 1855–
with Streete 1932–
with Kilglass 1965–1997
with Mostrim, Granard, Clonbroney and Killoe 1978–

NOTES

The church was built in 1814 and cost £738 9s 2¾d. The Glebe house was built in 1817 and cost £461 10s 8¼d. A new school was opened at Rathowen on 1st February 1962.

Rathcline, Lanesborough, Co Longford, St John

RATHCLINE

VICARS

1396	Luke Magruani
–1406	Richard Ferrall (Fergail)
1406	Charles Macarmayc
1615	'Church possessed by a Papist Curate'
1622	Cure; Sir Patrick Barnewall intruded (RV)
1624	William Gregory
1663	James Spencer
1671	James Milus
1680/81	Robert Ramsay
1685/86	Arthur Forbes
1727–1740	Eliah Handcock
1740–1780	Richard Knight
1780–1813	Robert Moffett
1813–1834	James Ferrall (or Farrell)
1834–1838	Robert Blundell
1875	Richard Thomas Hearn
1839–1868	Thomas Frederick Miller Wilson
1868–1891	Thomas William Ireland
1891–1900	William Pollard
1900–1906	John Browne

1906–1937	Robert John Mitchell
1937–1939	Alan Leigh Stuart C-in-c
1939–1955	Robert William Wolfe C-in-c
1955–1965	William Daniel Norman
1965–	see Elphin list

CURATES

–1670	James Gordon
1766	Arthur Gardner
c. 1780	James Moffett
1809	James Ferrall
1878–1882	Thomas Reilly, C Cashel
1888–1891	Arthur Wellesley Chapman

transferred to Elphin Diocese 1965
with Cashel 1882
with Kilcommick 1955–1965
In Elphin Diocese 1965–

NOTES

The church was built by the Lanesborough family in 1678. There was no Glebe house in 1837.

RATHREAGH and AGHERY

VICARS

–1397	Paul Omuledi
1397	Thomas Maceda
1397	Donatus Ofeargail
1615	V of Rathreagh and Aghery held as impropriations by Mr Patrick Foxe
1616	John Robinson
1629	Nedellus O'Kinge
1633	William Watson
1662	Joseph Dunbar
1685	David Prosser
1737	joined to Kilglass

RUSSAGH

VICARS

1411	Nicholas O'Branagan
–1487	Eugene Yconalcha (O'Connolly)
1492	Eugene Yconalborha (possibly same as above)
–1622	John Robinson
1661–1698	with Rathaspeck
c. 1701–1807	with Abbeylara
1807–1829	Robert Gouldsbury
1829–1837	Joseph Forde Leathley
1837–1848	James Lyster
1848–1855	Francis Kane

with Rathaspeck 1855–

NOTES
In 1836 no Glebe house and no Church. Service in private house.

Shrule, Ballymahon, Co Longford, St Catherine

SHRULE

VICARS
1520	a Clerk was coll V by the Primate
1615	served by RC C seq; J. Aston seq
1634	William Hamond
1638	Edward Gublin
1640	Bartimeus Heardman
1673	John or Robert Fullerton
1674	Robert Fullerton

1691	John Wilson
1717/18–1735	Edward Hughes
1717/18	John Blashford, also coll R and V
1735–1754	Thomas Hughes
1754–1769	Guy Stone
1769–c. 1800	Samuel Auchmuty
1800	Arthur Rolleston
1800–1806	John Leahy
1806–1844	Francis Maguire
1844–1855	Hugh Crawford
1855–1869	Francis Kane
1869–1881	James Topham
1881–1882	Thomas David Parke
1882–1885	Robert Young Lynn
1886–1891	Simon Carter Armstrong
1891–1932	Purefoy Poe
1932–1940	Francis Sadleir Stoney
1940–1945	Cyril Crowden Ellison
1946–1964	Alfred Birch
1965–1966	William James Allcard
1967–1980	John Alexander Montgomery
1980–1981	James Pickering
1982–	Albert William Kingston

CURATES

	William Robinson
1731–1735	Thomas Hughes
1731–1738	William Campbell
1755–1760	William Bredin
1755–1765	Robert Beatty
1769	Henry King
1791–1807	Samuel Auchmuty
1800	Arthur Rolleston
	James Moffett
	A. Smullan
1854–1858	William Disney Roe

with Tashinny 1932–
with Ardagh 1965–
with Moydow 1966–
with Kilcommick 1971–

NOTES

Order in Council to remove Shrule Church to Ballymahon 8 Jul 1793 (Armagh DR); similar one 19 May 1794 (LM V 124). In 1819, The church was enlarged and improved at a cost of £1,141 with loan of £700 from the Board of First Fruits and a donation of £441 from Captain Schuldam. The church was built at Ballymahon and enlarged in 1824 at a cost of £1,052 6s 1¾d. The Glebe house was built in 1813 and cost £719 15s 4½d, more than half of it a gift.

Streete, Co Westmeath

STREETE

VICARS

–1397	John Ofergail
1397	Florence Macmircheartaid
–1431	Fergallus Macmurkartaich
1431	John Maigilladgon
1431	Gerald Offergail
–1492	Theobald de la Mayr
1550	Walter Roone
–1594	William O'Donohue
1594	Fergall McCahill
1615	held by 'a most ignorant priest'
1616	John Aston
1661	Herbert Ferris
1670	Joseph Dunbar
1683	Eugene Reilly
1698	Charles Barclay
c. 1701–1752	Robert Harrison
c. 1755–c 1780	Frederick Grier
c. 1780–1795	Richard Butler
1796–c 1816	James Webster
1817–1848	William Boles
1848–1855	Francis Kane
1855–1867	Edward Fawcett
1867–1900	Robert Thomas Bevan
1900–1907	Francis John Armstrong Beere
1908–1910	Andrew Graham
1910–1931	Walter Long Fenton

1932–1939	Woodley Joseph Lindsay
1940–1949	Frederick James Powell
1950–1956	Thomas Patrick Scarborough Wood
1958–1964	Edward Frederick Forrest
1964–1969	George Frederick Morrow
1969–1976	John Arthur Knowles
1978–1982	Robert Henderson
1983–1997	Thomas George Hudson
2002–	Janet Margaret Catterall

CURATES

	John Murphy
1811	Richard Hartley Sinclair
c. 1819	Edward Synge
1829–1837	Joseph Forde Leathley
1837–1848	James Lyster
1860–1861	Thomas George Johnston Phillips
1864–1865	George Fortescue Reade
1866–1867	Thomas Phibbs
1897–1900	Francis John Armstrong Beere

with Rathaspeck and Russagh 1932–
with Kilglass 1965–1997
with Mostrim, Granard, Clonbroney and Killoe 1978–

NOTES

The church in 1615 was thatched with straw. It was old in 1836. Columber Schoolhouse was licensed for divine service on 11th February 1861 (DR). An addition to the graveyard, given by John Wilson, JP, of Daramona, was consecrated on 20th November 1899. The Glebe house was built in 1812. The bell from Streete Church was sent to a church in Australia in 1961. A new organ was dedicated on 4th October 1962.

Streete, Co. Westmeath

TAGHSYNOD

VICARS
1684	John Moore
1691	John Wilson
1732–1754	Maurice Neligan

with Moydow

Tashinny, Co Longford

TASHINNY

Tashinny and Taghsynod have often been confused. They were adjacent parishes and some of the entries below may be under the wrong parish.

RECTORS
–1406	Thomas Macmurc(acc)n
–1406	Charles Macarmayc

VICARS
–1397	Charles Offeargail
1397	Patrick Maghaga
–1427	Richard Yfergail
–1427	Carbricius Yfergail
–1468	Garald Offergail
–1615	Kedagh O'Farrell
–1622	Kedagh McConnell Fferrall
1661	Robert Fullerton
1691	John Wilson
1717/18	William Wilson

1720	Daniel Hearn
1721	David Bosquet
17–	Josias Hort (— Knox acc to Lyster)
1807–1812	Sir James Hutchinson
? 1812	Hon David Curry (Lyster, Memorials 266)
? 1812–	Hon J.G. Handcock (Lyster, Memorials 266)
1815–1819	Robert Moffett
1819–1823	David Richardson Curry
1823–1831	John Gustavus Handcock
1831–1834	Richard Quintus St George
1834–1848	Nicholas Gosselin
1848–1854	James Lyster
1855–1856	Hugh Crawford
1856–1863	Thomas Webb Green
1863–1866	John Hugh Johnston Powell
1866–1867	Robert James Card
1868–1890	William Noble
1890–1940	Francis Sadleir Stoney
1940–1945	Cyril Crowden Ellison
1946–1964	Alfred Birch
1965–1966	William James Allcard
1967–1980	John Alexander Montgomery
1980–1981	James Pickering
1982–	Albert William Kingston

CURATES

1780–1820	Robert Moffett
c. 1808	Robert Lockwood
c. 1811	Frederick Holmes
1817	Peter Lewis Langley
c. 1843–1845	Essex Edgeworth
1846–1848	Thomas Kirkwood Little
Samuel Martin	
1870–1871	Hill Wilson
1889–1890	Francis Sadleir Stoney

with Shrule 1932–
with Ardagh and Moydow 1965–

NOTES

In Memorials 1899, pages 264–72, there is much about the Parish from Dean Lyster's notes; also inscriptions on tablets, illustration of Gore (Annaly) tomb, inscriptions on Church plate. The Glebe house was built in 1825 and cost £923, of which £230 was a gift of the Board of First Fruits.

Templemichael, Longford, Co Longford, St John

TEMPLEMICHAEL

VICARS

–1412	John Yreachdagan
–1412	Andrew Maccilruaig
1425	Nehemiah (Nemias) Meckehan
1434	Nehemiah (Nemias) Meckehan
1443	Walter O'Farrell (Offergayl)
–1615	George Flawne
–1647	Jeremy Flawne
1660	James Sterling
1693	—
1710–1718	Benjamin Span
1718/19–1737	Essex Edgeworth
1737–c 1749	Robert Hort
c. 1749–1753	Robert Edgeworth
c. 1753–1756	Arthur Gardner (possibly C)
1756–1791	John Ryder
1791–1795	Thomas Lewis O'Beirne

1795–1813	Hon Richard Bourke	1866–1872	Frederick Foster
1813–1838	Henry Maxwell	1872–1873	Thomas Clarke
1839–1866	John le Poer Trench	1872–1873	W. Ormsby
1866–1874	John Richard Darley	1872–1874	William Henry Hodges
1874–1889	Henry Matthew West	1874	Michael Neville Kearney
1889–1907	Frederick Augustus Potterton	1875–1876	William Swayne Little
1907–1915	William Richard Moore	1877–1879	Richard Arthur English
1916–1943	Henry Justice	1879–1881	Henry Rennison
1943–1946	George Edwin Camier	1882–1885	William Richard Moore
1946–1960	Arthur Maurice Broughton Mills	1885–1886	Henry Justice
1960–1991	Thomas James Bond	1888–1889	Fergus William Greer
1991–1996	Robert Stewart Jackson	1890–1896	Robert Wallace Boyd
1997–2000	Stanley Johnson	1896–1903	John Alfred Thompson
2002–	David Arnold Catterall	1903–1905	John Francis Little
		1906–1907	George Alexander Bayly

CURATES

–1756	Francis Warren	1907–1912	Josiah Francis Shearman
c. 1761–c. 1766	Arthur Gardner	1912–1915	Robert Cecil Sylvester Devenish
c. 1780	Robert Johnston	1918–1920	James William Maver
1797	Daniel Viridett	1921–1927	William George Coleman
1817–c. 1830	Charles Henry Minchin	1932–1935	William James Ewart
–1827	R. Flood	1935–1938	Robert Cecil Armstrong
–1827	H.B. Macartney	1938–1943	Charles Benjamin Pigott Roberts
–1839	Alexander Hudson		
1839–1856	William Moore		
1839	Hugh Crawford		
1846–1866	A. Martin		
1844–1866	Robert James Card		
1855–1862	Matthew Nisbett Thompson		
1861–1872	Frederick Augustus Potterton		
1866–1867	John Bowles Daly		

with Clongish 1959–
with Termonbarry 1960–c. 1977
with Clooncumber, Killashee and Ballymacormack 1971–

NOTES

The church was built in 1812 and cost £3,221 10s 10d. It was dedicated to St Catherine (Brandon also gives present dedication, St John). The Glebe house was built before 1760. In 1763, £1,388 was expended on the glebe house, and £300 and £600 in 1799. In his Will 1743 (proved 1744) Clement Nevill of Dollardstown, Co Kildare left £100 to the poor of Templemichael and £100 to the poor of Athy. A new rectory was built in 1961/62, and blessed on 29th July 1962. The parish appears as Templemichael and Templemichael Killoe in the 1862 Church of Ireland Directory.

TERMONBARRY, Co Longford

with Mohill 1900–1954
with Kilmore in Elphin Diocese 1954–59
with Kiltoghart, Toomna, Kilmore, Annaduff West, Aughrim and Killukin 1959–1960
with Templemichael and Clongish 1960–*c.* 1977
with Clooncumber, Killashee and Ballymacormack 1971–*c.* 1977
Church closed *c.* 1977

Toomna, Co Roscommon

TOOMNA

in Elphin Diocese –1954
with Kiltoghart 1954–1996
with Annaduff West, Aughrim, Killukin and Termonbarry 1959–1962
in Kilmore Diocese 1959–1996
(Termonbarry with Templemichael 1960–*c.* 1977)
with Drumshambo, Annaduff and Kilronan 1962–1996
closed *c.* 1996

BIOGRAPHIES OF CLERGY

ABERCROMBY, THOMAS –1724

C Cleenish (Clogh) 1687; C Derrybrusk and Killany (Clogh) 1692; C Derryvullan (Clogh) 1693–1703; V Rossinver (Kilm) 1721–24

Died 1724

ABBOTT, THOMAS –1762

lic C Killeshan & Kilronan *alias* St Paul's Castleblakeney (Elph) 12 Jul 1732; R Moylough (Tuam) –1762

Died Jan 1762

ACHESON, HENRY 1866–1947

b. 1866; TCD BA 1895 Div Test 1897 MA 1900

d 1897 (Armagh for Kilmore) p 1900 (Kilmore); C Kilkeevan (Elph) 1897–1900; C Ardcarne (Elph) 1900–02; R Tubbercurry (Ach) 1902–09; R Dunlavin (Glend) 1909–37

m. 14 Jan 1903 Maud Elizabeth only **dau.** of James Parker Mills of Kilbrogan Hill Bandon Co Cork. Issue incl 1. Hazel Mabel; 2 Trish H

Died 8 Feb 1947

ACHESON, JOHN 1824/25–1899

b. 1824 or 1825 Co Roscommon; ent TCD 1 Jul 1844 aged 19 BA 1850

d 1851 p; C Eastersnow (Elph) 1851; C Myshall (Leigh) 1863; C Elphin and Ogulla 1865–*c.* 69; C Donacavey (Clogh) 1869–70; Preb of Kilcooley (Elph) 1867–78; res

s. of James, *agricola*.

Died 28 May 1899 aged 75

ADAMS, ALLEN NOBLE 1765–1805

b. 1765 Co Cavan; ed by Rev Mr Meares; ent TCD 3 Jul 1781 BA 1787

d 15 Jun 1788 (Kilmore) p 15 Sep 1793 (Kilmore); C Knockbride (Kilm) 1788; C Killan, now Shercock (Kilm) 1799

2nd **s.** of Richard, *armiger* of Shercock Co Cavan, JP, High Sheriff Cavan 1783 and Monaghan 1785

m. Jun 1791 Isabella (**died** 20 Jun 1852 aged 84 **bur.** Mt Nugent) **dau.** of John Battersby of Lakefield Co Meath. Issue 1. Richard **m.** and had issue; 2. John, Rear-Admiral RN **m.** twice and had issue; 3. Stuart (**died** 1820 **unm.**); 4. Allen Noble (**died** 1817) **b.** 1800; 5. Cosby **m.** and had issue a **dau.**; 6. Rev James, C Drumgoon (Kilm) qv; 3 **daus.**

Died Mar 1805 **bur.** Knockbride

ADAMS, AMBROSE GOING 1850/51–1888

b. 1850 or 1851; JP

d 1887; C Shercock (Kilm) 1887–88

Died 11 Jan 1888 aged 37

ADAMS, BENJAMIN 1755/56–1840

b. 1755 or 1756; Univ of Glasgow matric 1772

R Killinick (Ferns) 1779–1810; PC Ashfield (Kilm) *c.* 1795–1808

5th **s.** of Allen of Corneary Hse Co Cavan

m. 14 Apr 1777 Elizabeth (**died** 28 Feb 1833 aged 77) **dau.** of John Clarke then of Castleknock Co Dublin, **s.** of Dr Samuel Clarke, R St James' London. Issue sons 1. William Allen (**died** young); 2. John, JP Co Cavan; 3. Rev Samuel, Dean of Cashel; 4. Charles James, Lt RN, JP Co Cavan; 6 **daus.**

Died 10 or 18 Jun 1840 aged 84

ADAMS, JAMES 1804–1889

b. 22 Nov 1804 Cavan; ent TCD 7 Jul 1823 BA 1832

d 1833 (Dromore) p 25 Oct 1834 (Kilmore); C Seagoe (Drom) 1833; C Drumgoon (Kilm) 1834; C Carne (Ferns) 1843; R Kilbride Castlecor (Meath) 1845–85

6th **s.** of Rev Allen Noble, C Killan (Kilm) qv by Isabella **dau.** of John Battersby of Lakefield Co Meath

m. (1) 24 Dec 1835 Elizabeth (**died** 7 Jun 1839 aged 25) **dau.** of James Denham of Forwood Pk Co Fermanagh. Issue 1. Allen Cosby (**died** 12 Jan 1860 unm), Lt RN; 2. Elizabeth Emilia **m.** 28 Apr 1864 Monkstown Ch Edward Roper of Kingstown Co Dublin

m. (2) 14 Apr 1841 Frances Maria **dau.** of Rev Richard Bevan, R Carne (Ferns). Issue 1. Rev Richard **b.** 23 Jan 1844 C St Stephen S Lambeth (S'wark); 2. Mary Louisa; 3. Frances Augusta

Died Easter Sunday 21 Apr 1889 at Kingstown (Dun Laoghaire) aged 84

ADAMS, SAMUEL 1788–1856

b. 17 Feb 1788 Co Cavan; ed by Dr Burrowes; ent TCD 23 Dec 1803 BA 1808 MA 1829; was JP for Co Cavan and Co Monaghan

d 18 Sep 1808 (Limerick) p 14 Mar 1813 (Kilmore); C Killesherdoney (Kilm) 1813–*c.* 25; Preb of Terebrine (Elph) 1813–56; Dean of Cashel 1829–56

3rd **s.** and heir of Rev Benjamin, PC Ashfield (Kilm) qv (**s.** of Allen) by Elizabeth **dau.** of John Clarke

m. 4 Jan 1809 Frances (**died** 28 Nov 1869) 6th **dau.** of John Hervey of Killiane Castle Co Wexford. Issue 1. Benjamin William, **died** young; 2. John Hervey of Northlands Co Cavan, High Sheriff of Monaghan; 3. Charles Stewart, JP of Ashfield Co Meath; 4. Rev Benjamin William (*secundus*) **b.** 1827 Co Cavan (**died** 26 June 1886) TCD BA 1850 MA 1853 BD 1863 DD 1865 d. 1851 (Killaloe) p

1851 (Cork) C St Mary Shandon (Cork) 1851–54 R Cloghran 1854–76 (w C Santry 1870–76) (Dub) R Santry (Dub) 1876–86 **m.** (1) 14 Dec 1854 Georgina Roberts (**died** 16 May 1863) **dau.** of John Drew Atkin and had issue (i) Samuel Arthur (**died** 10 Mar 1869) **b.** 10 Sep 1857 (ii) Georgina Roberts (iii) Frances Hervey; **m.** (2) 11 Aug 1864 Louisa Jane (**died** 9 Jan 1930) **dau.** of William O'Brien Adams, MD of Kingstown and had issue (i) William Augustus **b.** 27 May 1865 (ii) Herbert Algernon **b.** 3 Jan 1872 (iii) Constance Louisa; Dean Samuel Adams also had 3 **daus.**

Died 7 or 8 Dec 1856 **bur.** Knockbride

ADAMS (later ADAMS ROBINSON), SAMUEL 1837/38–

b. 1837 or 1838 Shercock Co Cavan; ent TCD 25 Jun 1858 aged 20 BA 1861 Div Test 1862 MA 1879

d 20 Jul 1862 (Down) p 11 Oct 1863 (Kilmore); C Mohill (Ard) 1862–64; C Cloone (Ard) 1864–68; C Drumcliffe (Elph) 1868–72; R Derrylane (Kilm) 1872–75; R Killinkere (Kilm) 1875–89; ret

s. of James, MD; he took the additional name of Robinson

m. Jane Morrison (**died** 14 Jun 1920 at Drutamon Hse Bailieboro). Issue incl 1. a **dau. b.** 10 Nov 1870; 2. Anne Catherine (**died** 12 Dec 1893 Belfast); 3. his 3rd **dau.** Jane (**died** 22 Aug 1882 at Skerries Co Dublin aged 7)

Last entry in C I Dir 1899

ADAMS, SAMUEL ATKINSON

TCD BA 1877 Div Test (2) 1878

d 1876 p1877 (Kilmore); C Mohill (Ard) 1876–79; I Newtowngore & Corrawallen (Kilm) 1879–83; C Dalton-in-Furness (Carl) 1883–93; Org Sec SPG for Archdeaconry of Furness 1892–97; V Rampside and Chapl Barrow U (Carl) 1893–1916

ADAMSON, CHRISTOPHER 1820/21–1856

b. 1820 or 1821 Dublin; ed by Mr Sterling; ent TCD 2 Jul 1839 aged 18 BA & Div Test 1847

C Killeshandra (Kilm) 1848–56; ?C Boyle (Elph) 1854

Died 1856

†AGAR, CHARLES 1736–1809

b. 22 Dec 1736 Gowran Co Kilkenny; ed Westminster Sch; matric at Christ Ch Coll Oxford 31 May 1755 BA 1755 MA 1762 DCL 1765

Chapl to the Lord Lt 1763–65; R & V Ballymagarvey and Skryne (Meath) 1763–65; Dean of Kilmore & R Annagh Kilmore and Ballintemple (Kilm) 1765–68; Bp of Cloyne 1768–79; Abp of Cashel 1779–1801; Abp of Dublin and Bp of Glendalough 1801–09

3rd **s.** of Henry, MP of Gowran by Anne **dau.** of Dr Welbore Ellis, Bp of Meath 1732–34; Privy Counsellor of Ireland; created Baron Somerton 1795; Viscount

Somerton 1800; Earl of Normanton 1806

m. 22 Nov 1776 St Mary's Dublin Jane (**died** 1826) eldest **dau.** of William Benson of Co Down. Issue 1. Welbore Ellis **b.** 12 Nov 1778 ed Westminster Sch matric Christ Ch Coll Oxford 6 Jun 1798 BA succeeded his father as 2nd Earl in 1809 **m.** and had issue; 2. George Charles (**died** 24 Jan 1856 unm) **b.** 1 Aug 1780 ed Westminster Sch matric Christ Ch Coll Oxford 18 Jun 1800 BA 1804 MA 1807 FRS; 3. Rev James, Archd of Kilmore qv; 4. Frances Anne (**died** 1839) **m.** Thomas Ralph, 2nd Viscount Hawarden

Died 14 Jul 1809

AGAR, Hon. JAMES 1781–1866

b. 10 Jul 1781; ed Westminster Sch; matric Christ Ch Coll Oxford 15 May 1801 BA 1805 MA 1808

Preb of Timothan in St Patrick's Cath Dublin 1805–09; C St Nicholas Within (Dub) 1805–09; pres in error to Preb of St Michan in Christ Ch Cath Dublin 1809; V Timolin (Glend) 1809; V Carrigallen (Kilm) 1809–66; R & V Holywood (Glend) 1814–66; Archd of Kilmore 1816–66

3rd **s.** of Most Rev Charles, Dean of Kilmore and Abp of Dublin qv (**s.** of Henry) by Jane

m. 7 Jul 1829 Louisa (**died** 15 Mar 1885) yst **dau.** of Samuel Thompson of Greenmount Co Antrim

Died 6 Sep 1866 at Donnishall Co Wexford **bur.** Christ Ch Cath Dublin

ALDRICH, WILLIAM

ord d & p by James (Heygate) Bp of Kilfenora 25 Mar 1633/34; R Drumgoon (Kilm) 1633/34–60; R Drumgoon (w Killesherdoney to *c.* 1673) (Kilm) 1661–*c.* 1681; according to VB, he was coll again R Drumgoon 24 Jul 1643; was Commonwealth Minister at Clones (Clogh) 1654–59, at first at £50, subsequently increased to £80

m. Frances. Issue incl 1. Frances; 2. Hannah; 3. Elizabeth

Will proved 1682

ALDWELL, THOMAS HERON

d 1875 (Kilmore) p 1876; C Drumshambo and Kiltoghart (Ard) 1875–76; R Dowra (Kilm) 1876–78; R Castlerickard (Meath) 1878–86; R Ardnurcher U (Meath) 1886–88; R Kilcleagh (Meath) 1888–1904; ret to live in England

ALEXANDER, HUGH 1847/48–1915

b. 1847 or 1848; TCD BA 1868 Div Test 1869

d 1869 (Armagh) p 18 Dec 1870 (Down for Armagh); C Galloon (Clogh) 1869–72; C Sallaghy (Clogh) 1872–73; R Derrybrusk (Clogh) 1873–80; V Denn (Kilm) 1880–85; R Killinagh (Kilm) 1885–1915

m. Louisa Harriett (**died** 24 Jan 1920 Warrenpoint Co Down **bur.** Killinagh)

Died 19 Feb 1915 at Blacklion Co Cavan aged 67

ALGEO, LEWIS WALTER 1859/60–1903

b. 1859 or 1860; TCD BA 1881 Div Test 1885

d 20 May 1883 (Down for Armagh) p 1885 (Kilmore); C Charlestown (Arm) 1883–84; C Cashel (Ard) 1884–85; R Kilmore (Elph) 1885–87; R Holy Trinity Barking Road Essex (St A) 1887–88; R Ardara (Raph) 1889–1903

only **s.** of Lewis, JP of Glenboy Manorhamilton Co Leitrim

m. 10 Jul 1883 Florence Harriet (**died** 17 Jul 1927 at Glenboy aged 65) **dau.** of Archibald Collum, Solicitor of Enniskillen. Issue incl 1. eldest **dau.** Ethel Mary **m.** 5 Nov 1925 Robert Mecredy of Manorhamilton (**s.** of Robert Mecredy of Ballyshannon Co Donegal); 2. Nora Eileen **m.** 31 Dec 1914 Eustace, MB only **s.** of Rev Ashleigh Thorp MA, R Annaghmore (Arm) 1895–1906

Died 23 May 1903 aged 43

ALLCARD, WILLIAM JAMES –1973

TCD Silver Medal Ment & Mor Sci Jun Mod BA 1911 St Aidan's Coll Birkenhead 1911 MA 1925;

d 1913 p 1915 (Chester); C St George Stockport (Ches) 1913–15; C Tadley (Win) 1916–21; C Stokesley and Seamer-in-Cleveland (York) 1921–28; V Bilsdale Midcable (York) 1928–35; C-in-c Kildrumferton w Ballymachugh (Kilm) 1934–43; I Ardagh and Kilglass (w Moydow from 1955 and w Tashinny and Shrule from 1965) (Ard) 1943–66; Dom Chapl to Bp 1951–59; Preb of Oran (Elph) 1953–66; ret

m. Mabel

Died 1973

ALLEN, JOHN 1875/76–1937

b. 1875 or 1876; TCD BA 1902 Carson Bibl Pri Downes Pri (2) Heb Pri Abp King Pri 1904 Bibl Gk Pri Eccles Hist Pri (1) Chaldean and Syriac Pri 1905 Div Test (1) 1905 MA & BD Theol Exhib (1) 1906 LLB & LLD 1915

d 1906 p 1907 (Kilmore); C St John Sligo (Elph) 1906–09; R Taunagh (Elph) 1909–31; R Drumcliffe (Elph) 1931–37

m. Alice (**died** 28 Jun 1965 Larkhill Sligo)

Died 25 Jan 1937 aged 61

ALLMAN, DAVID GEORGE 1878–1960

b. 1 Oct 1878; TCD BA (Sen Mod) & Wray Pri 1900 Abp King's Pri 1901 Eccl Hist Pri 1902 Div Test 1903 MA 1909

d 1903 (Kilmore for Armagh) p 1904 (Dublin for Armagh); C Drumcree (Arm) 1903–04; C Urney and Annagelliffe (Kilm) 1904–07; C St George Dublin (Dub) 1907–09; C St James Dublin & Chapl Dr Steevens' Hosp (Dub) 1909–14; R Louth and Killincoole (Arm) 1915–21; R Kildress (Arm) 1921–30; R Brantry and Derrygortreavy (Arm) 1930–37; R Donaghpatrick and Kilshine (Meath) 1937–53; RD of Skryne (Meath) 1944–53; ret

s. of Samuel, Sen Insp of National Schools (**s.** of William) by Annie Eliza **dau.** of

George Nicol
Died 26 Oct 1960 **unm.** Dublin

ANDERSON, GEORGE MORTIMER   –1917
TCD BA 1878

d 1881 p 1882 (Tuam); C Ballinrobe (Tuam) 1881; C Tuam Cath and Chapl Tuam Workhouse (Tuam) 1881–83; C St Luke Liverpool (Liv) 1883–84; I Ardoyne (Leigh) 1885; R Abbeylara w Drumlummon (Ard) 1885–86; R Mostrim (Ard) 1886–89; R Knockbride (Kilm) 1889–1917

m. Issue incl Kathleen **m.** 23 Jul 1925 John Bennett of Sligo Gram Sch

Died 29 Jul 1917

ANDERSON, HENRY IRVINE KEYS 1909–1985

b. 1909 Fintona Co Tyrone; ed Omagh Academy; TCD BA 1933 Div Test 1934 MA 1940

d 1934 (Armagh for Down) p 1935 (Down); C Carrickfergus (Conn) 1934–39; C-in-c Gowna w Columbkill (Ard) 1939–43; R Billis w C-in-c Ballyjamesduff and Castlerahan (Kilm) 1943–54; R Killesher (Kilm) 1954–79; Preb of Annagh in Kilmore Cath 1965–72; Dio Reg Kilmore 1965–69; Preb of Mulhuddart in St Patrick's Cath Dublin 1972–79; RD of Drumlease 1972–79; ret

s. of Irvine Arthur by Margaret Elizabeth

m. 14 Dec 1938 Dorothy Margaret (**died** 14 Apr 1982) **dau.** of John Seeds Garrett of Burnfield Monkstown Co Antrim. Issue 1. Hilary Mary Elizabeth **b.** 10 Jan 1943; 2. Catherine

Died 1985

ANDERSON, JAMES FERGUSON 1874–1951

b. 11 Mar 1874 Belfast; RUI BA 1899; TCD Warren Pri & Div Test (1) 1901

d 22 Nov 1901 p 21 Dec 1902 (Cork); C Marmullane (Cork) 1901–04; C St Andrew (Dub) 1904–08; Dio C Kilmore Elphin and Ardagh 1908–10; R Killesher (Kilm) 1910–13; R St Peter Athlone (Elph) 1913–25; Chapl St Mark Alexandria Egypt (w All SS from 1926) 1925–47; C-in-c Termonfeckin and Beaulieu (Arm) 1948–51

s. of Hamilton of Belfast (3rd **s.** of Arthur of Saintfield Co Down) by Sophia Maria 2nd **dau.** of H **m.** Coleman of Philadelphia USA

m. 10 May 1910 Clones Par Ch Co Monaghan Frances Muriel (**died** 21 Jan 1959 Dublin) **dau.** of Henry Swayne of Clones Co Monaghan. Issue 1. Muriel Hilda **b.** 26 Aug 1911 **m.** 18 Jul 1936 St Mark's Ch Alexandria Robert Massy Tweedy of Carrickmines Dublin; 2. Henry A R **b.** 25 May 1914 at Athlone; 3. Dorothy Elizabeth **b.** 27 Aug 1916 at Athlone; 4. Leila **m.** (1) Flying Officer G Woodroffe; **m.** (2) Rev G E Hope

Died 12 May 1951 at Termonfeckin Rectory **bur.** Deans Grange Dublin

ANDERSON, JOHN –1982

ed Dundalk Gram Sch; Mountjoy Sch Dublin; TCD

d 1928 p 1930; Lic to Off Dios Kilmore Elphin and Ardagh 1928–82; Headmaster Royal Sch Cavan 1929–70; Dom Chapl to Bp of Kilmore 1954–82

m. (1) Martha

m. (2) … Issue 1. Cyril; 2. Bill; Douglas who succeeded him as Headmaster **m.** Hazel

Died 1982

ANDERSON, JOHN ALFRED KENNEDY

C Kinawley (Kilm) 1900–01; last entry in C I Dir 1902

ANDERSON, WILLIAM –c. 1805

poss William Anderson who ent TCD 11 Nov 1761 ed by Mr Harwood, no degrees recorded; but this William Anderson is MA in S.R.

C Killeshandra (Kilm) 1777–c. 1805

Will prov as C Killeshandra 1805

ANDREW

"Dean of Drumleachan" (may not = Kilmore) (Kilm) 1426, is named with Thomas, Archdeacon (Cal. Reg. Swayne, 1.)

ANDREWS, …

C Rossinver (Kilm) to 1685

ANDREWES, WILLIAM

MA

Archd of Kilmore to 1622; was V Annagh (Kilm) 1617 and was probably Archd of Kilmore from that date. As Archd of Kilmore and V Annagh he got a grant of a glebe Jan 1626/27 (Morrin III. 186); also V Drumlease (Kilm) in 1622; "a preacher"

ANKERS, JOHN

V St Peter Athlone (Elph) 1615

ANTROBUS, GEORGE 1724–1760

b. 1724; ent TCD 6 Jan 1740/41 BA 1745 MA 1748 Leslie has him Preb of Terebrine (Elph) 1722–60, and his predecessor resigned before then, but 1752 would be a more likely date; C St Michan in Christ Church Cath Dublin 1750; 4th Canon of Kildare 1751–60

s. of Rev John DD (**died** 28 Apr 1761) Preb of St Michan Dublin 1736–61 by his 2nd wife Rebecca (**died** 10 Jun 1748)

Died 1760 **bur.** 3 Aug St Peter Dublin

APPLEYARD, JAMES
TCD BA 1868
d 1869 p 29 Sep 1869 (Kilmore); C Ballyjamesduff (Kilm) 1869–70

ARBUTHNOT, GEORGE ALEXANDER PAPENDICK
d 1873 (Derry) p 1873 (Kilmore); C Drumshambo 1873; R Dowra (Kilm) 1873–76; R Roscommon (Elph) 1876–78; Preb of Kilmacallen (Elph) 1876–78; C St Andrew (Dub) 1878–82; C All Souls Marylebone (Lon) 1882–86; C Tunbridge (Cant) 1887–90; R Littledean (Glouc) 1891–1902; last entry in Crockford 1903

ARCHDALL, JOHN *c.* 1651–1689
b. *c.* 1651 Lusk Co Dublin; ed by Mr Tennison; ent TCD 7 Mar 1667/68 aged 16 Sch 1668 BA 1671 MA 1675

V Donabate and Lusk (Dub) 1678–89; R Dromdane *alias* Dromgoone *alias* Dromdeene = Drumgoon (Kilm) 1683–89

> only **s.** of Ven John, V Donabate and Lusk (Dub) 1661–74, Archd of Killala and Archd of Achonry (**s.** of John of Norsam Hall Norfolk) by Miss Donnellan of Croaghan Co Roscommon
>
> **m.** Elizabeth (M.L. 1 Apr 1679) **dau.** of John Bernard of Dromin Co Louth. Issue 1. William **m.** and had issue Rev Mervyn the Historian; 2…; 3. Bernard, Burgess of New Ross Co Wexford 1722–36
>
> **Died** 1689

ARCHER, CHARLES FREDERICK 1852–1920
b. 1852 Dun Laoghaire Co Dublin; ed The Royal Sch Dungannon; TCD BA and Div Test 1876

d 1876 (Down for Armagh) p 1877 (Armagh); C Armaghbreague (Arm) 1876–77; C Derryheen (Kilm) 1877–79; C Kinawley (Kilm) 1879–81; R Mullaglass (Arm) 1881–85; R Acton (Arm) 1885–95; R Moy (Arm) 1895–1917; ret

> **s.** of Rev Arthur Ellis, BA, R Aghadoe (A & A) (**s.** of Charles Palmer, Alderman of Dublin 1823) by Margaret eldest **dau.** of John Samuels of Dun Laoghaire
>
> **m.** 28 Apr 1886 Richhill Par Ch Co Armagh Eliza Jane (**died** 27 Dec 1933 aged 80) eldest **dau.** of Lt Col T Richardson Griffiths of Richhill. Issue 1. Ethel Margaret Du Plat **b.** 19 Aug 1888 **m.** 7 Apr 1920 at Yarnton Oxfordshire Rev Leonard Hodgson, Fellow Magdalen Coll Ox and Canon of Christ Ch Cath Oxford 1938–58 Regius Prof of Divinity Christ Ch Coll Ox 1944–58; 2. Eleanor Lucinda Du Plat **b.** 7 Jun 1890; 3. Helen Mary Du Plat **b.** 25 Dec 1891; 4. Muriel Emily Du Plat **b.** 26 May 1892; 5. Eva Geraldine Du Plat **b.** 20 Jun 1896
>
> **Died** 20 Oct 1920 Whitehead Co Antrim

ARCHER, JOHN 1827/28–1905
TCD BA 1853 Div Test (1) 1854

d 1856 p 1857 Dublin); C Clongish (Ard) 1858–72; R St Mary Drogheda w Culpe U (Meath) 1872–1905

Died 13 Mar 1905 aged 77

ARCHER, JOHN THOMAS

TCD BA 1873 Div Test 1875

d 1875; C Urney (Kilm) 1875–79; C Bray (Dub) 1879–80

s. of Rev Arthur Ellis, V Donard (Dub) 1861–72 (**s.** of Charles, Alderman of Dublin) by Margaret **dau.** of John Samuels; **bro.** of Rev Charles Frederick, R Moy (Arm)

ARDILL, JOHN ROCHE 1860–1947

b. 1860 Co Tipperary; ent TCD 24 Jan 1881 aged 20 BA (Resp) 1884 Div Test 1885 LLB & LLD 1892

d 1884 (Meath) p 1885 (Dublin for Meath); C St Mary Athlone (Meath) 1884–86; C Derryvullen N (Clogh) 1886–87; C St Andrew (Dub) 1887–89; R Drumcliffe (Elph) 1889–99; R Calry (Elph) 1899–1944; Preb of Oran (Elph) 1902–33; Dean of Elphin 1933–44; ret

s. of James, landowner

m. and had issue 1. Harry Roche **m.** 16 Oct 1915 in Ontario Morna 2nd **dau.** of Frederick W Clements of Bala Ontario; 2. William Theobald Morrison **m.** Ethel **dau.** of P A Hamilton Reid of Glenageary Co Dublin; 3. George Hubert (**died** 9 Apr 1961 Dublin) of Mabel Lodge Rosses Point Co Sligo; 4. Constance Isabel (**died** 14 Aug 1963) TCD BA 1914 **m.** 14 Apr 1928 St John Paddington Archibald H Shepherd–Smith of Colwall Malvern

Died 19 Jan 1947

PUBLICATIONS
Forgotten Facts of Irish History, 1905
The Closing of the Irish Parliament, 1907
St. Patrick, A.D. 180, 1931
The Date of St. Patrick, 1932

ARMSTRONG, ALAN 1880–1968

b. 24 Aug 1880 Manorhamilton Co Leitrim; ed Rathmines Sch Dublin; TCD Div Test 1905 BA 1906

d 1905 p 1906 (Cork); C Castletown Berehaven (Cork) 1905–08; C Templemore (Cash) 1908–09; C St Mary Magdalene Peckham London (S'wark) 1909–10; C Fanlobbus (Cork) 1910–11; C Kilmacabea (Ross) 1912–15; C Cloughjordan (Killaloe) 1915–16; C Santry U (Dub) 1916–17; R Dowra and Innismagrath (Kilm) 1917–23; in ECUSA 1923–28; C-in-c Ballycommon and Killaderry (Kild) 1928–29; C Sallaghy (Clogh) 1929–32; R Drumkeeran (Clogh) 1932–33; C-in-c Kilcluney (Arm) 1933–34; R Dry Drayton, Hardwicke and Childerley (Ely) 1934–51; R Killargue and Killenumery (Kilm) 1951–53; ret eldest **s.** of Rev Chancellor Simon Carter, R Shrule (Ard) qv (**s.** of Alan) by Eliza (Cosie) **dau.** of John Martin of Dublin; **bro.** of Rev Samuel Carter, R Drumlease (Kilm) qv and of Rev John, R Kilcommick (Ard) qv and of Rev Aylmer Richard, R Drumlane (Kilm) qv

m. 16 Oct 1917 St George's Ch Dublin Olive Marie (**died** 22 May 1970) **dau.** of Rev Richard Herbert Neill, R Headford (Tuam). Issue 1. Carter; 2. Charles; 3. Theodore; 4. Violet

Died 22 Dec 1968

ARMSTRONG, ARCHIBALD (or ALEXANDER) 1733/34–

perhaps Archibald Armstrong **b.** 1733 or 1734 Sligo; ed by Mr Kerr; ent TCD as Sizar 26 May 1752 aged 18 Sch 1754 BA 1756

lic C Granard (Ard) 19 May 1762

s. of John, *agricola*

ARMSTRONG, AYLMER RICHARD –1965

TCD BA 1912

d 1912 p 1913 (Limerick); C Aghnavallen w Kilnaughton (A & A) 1912–15; C-in-c New Quay w Rathbourney (Killaloe) 1915; served in RASC & RGA 1915–19; R Castleterra (Kilm) 1919–21; R Drumlane (Kilm) 1921–24; R Kenmare w Templenoe and Kilgarvan (A & A) 1924–59; Treas of Limerick Cath 1952–59; ret

s. of Canon Simon Carter, R Shrule (Ard) qv (**s.** of Alan); **bro.** of Rev Alan, R Killargue (Kilm) qv and of Rev Samuel Carter, R Drumlease (Kilm) qv and of Ven John, Archd of Elphin qv

m. 25 Oct 1919 Norah Alice yst **dau.** of William Wright Belton of Luton Beds

Died Dec 1965

ARMSTRONG, HENRY MORRELL

TCD BA 1888 MA 1893

d 1891 (Kilmore) p 1892 (Dublin); C St John Sligo (Elph) 1891–92; C St Kevin (Dub) 1893–96; R Christ Ch Sheepville Millarville Calgary Alberta 1902

ARMSTRONG, JAMES –*c.* 1801

ed by Rev Dr Dunkin; ent TCD as Siz 1759 Sch 1762 BA 1763

C Sligo (Elph) 1771; R Taunagh (Elph) 1795–1801

m. Margaret (**died** Jan 1838 aged 95 at Moydow Glebe). Issue incl Rev William Chambers, R Moydow (Ard) qv

Died *c.* 1801; Will proved 1801

ARMSTRONG, JAMES 1793–1878

b. 1793 Dublin; ed by Mr Falloon; ent TCD 3 Sep 1810 aged 17 BA 1815

d 1819 p; C Castlerahan (Kilm) from 1826; still there in 1843 and in 1858; he was said at his death to have been "for 35 years Minister of Castlerahan"

s. of Samuel, *Miles*

Died 26 Nov 1878 Sandymount Dublin aged 84

ARMSTRONG, JAMES IRWIN 1925–1994

b. 25 Mar 1925 Dromahair Co Leitrim; ed St Aidan's Coll Birkenhead

d 5 Jul 1959 (Kilmore) p 10 Jul 1960 (Kilmore); C St John Sligo (Elph) 1959–61; R Stradbally U (Leigh) 1961–65; R Badoney U (Derry) 1965–75; R Camus-juxta-Bann (Derry) 1975–85; R Drumragh w Mountfield (Derry) 1985–89; Canon of Derry 1986–89; ret

s. of John of Cleen Dromahair by Margaret Ann (*née* Irwin) of Ballysadare Co Sligo

m. 21 Jan 1964 Christ Ch Leeson Pk Dublin Elizabeth Mabel **dau.** of Edward George Dwyer of Ballickmoyler Co Laois and Frances Sophia (*née* Bradley) of Castlecomer Co Kilkenny and **sister** of Rev Thomas Bradley, R Kilnehue U (Ferns). Issue 1. Jennifer Ruth **b.** 26 Apr 1965 **m.** 21 May 1993 Robert McKay of Ballymena Co Antrim; 2. Heather Elizabeth Margaret **b.** 1 Aug 1967; 3. John Edward **b.** 10 Jun 1970

Died 3 Oct 1994

ARMSTRONG, JOHN 1801–1853

b. 1801 Co Roscommon; ed by Rev Mr Keane; ent TCD as FC 5 Apr 1819 aged 18 BA *c.* 1825; Univ of Camb MA

lic C Kilgeffin (Elph) 1825; V Kiltoom and Camma (Elph) 1825–53

s. of Capt Francis, Roscommon Regt of Militia by Rebecca **dau.** of Major Francis Waldron, 75th Regt and Sarah **dau.** of Capt Thomas Mainwaring

m. 8 Jul 1825 Clifton Ch Catherine (**died** 1873 Dublin) yst **dau.** of John Yeaden Lloyd of Lissadorn Co Roscommon and Catherine **dau.** of Rev Henry Crofton, Chanc of Ardfert. Issue sons 1. Francis (**died** 1887) **b.** 1834 **m.** and had issue; 2. John (**died** 1915) **b.** 1835 Capt NZ Volunteers **m.** Emma Mace and had issue; 3. Rev William (**died** 2 Sep 1887) **b.** 1836 Co Roscommon TCD BA & Div Test 1858 d 1859 p 1860 C Kildollagh (Conn) 1861–63 C Kilconriola (Conn) 1863–64 PC Newtowncrommelin (Conn) 1864–67 R Scarva (Drom) 1867–72 C Kilconriola (Conn) 1882–86 C Ballymacarrett (Down) 1886–87 **m.** 2 May 1862 Ellen Sophia **dau.** of Charles O'Hara, JP and had issue (i) Rev George Innes (ii) Charles Arthur (iii) John (iv) William Crofton (v) Francis James (vi) Henry Owen (vii) Catherine Anne (viii) Dorothea Elizabeth (ix) Ellen Frances; **daus.** 1. Katherine; 2. Rebecca Frances; 3. Ellen; 4. Marian **died** *c.* 1912 Dublin; 5. Louisa (**died** 6 Sept 1914 Dublin)

Died 5 May 1853 aged 51 **bur.** with his widow at Boyle

ARMSTRONG, JOHN 1884–1951

b. 11 Aug 1884 Dublin; TCD BA 1907

d 1907 p 1908 (Cork); C Kilbrogan (Cloyne) 1907–14; I Clonfert (Clonf) 1914–17; R Kilcommick and Moydow (Ard) 1917–51; Preb of Oran in Elphin Cath 1944–45; Archd of Elphin and Ardagh 1945–51

> **s.** of Rev Simon Carter, R Shrule (Ard) qv (**s.** of Alan) by Eliza **dau.** of John Martin of Dublin; **bro.** of Rev Alan, R Killargue (Kilm) qv and of Rev Samuel Carter, R Drumlease (Kilm) qv and of Rev Aylmer Richard, R Castleterra (Kilm) qv
>
> **m.** 6 Jan 1921 Carrickmines Ch Dublin Elizabeth Barrett (**died** 28 Mar 1957) of Dunmore Co Galway. Issue 1. John Carter **b.** 31 Dec 1921 **m.** 29 Aug 1968 St John's Ch Dun Laoghaire Kathleen Dunbar (**died** Dec 1994) and had issue (i) Elizabeth **b.** 27 Oct 1969 (ii) John **b.** 26 Dec 1970 (iii) …**b.** 14 May 1976
>
> **Died** 20 May 1951

ARMSTRONG, RICHARD 1887–1965

b. 6 Oct 1887; TCD BA 1912

d 1912 p 1913 (Limerick); C Kilnaughtin U (A & A) 1912–15; C-in-c New Quay (Killaloe) 1915; CF 1915–19; R Castletarra (Kilm) 1919–21; R Drumlease (Kilm) 1921–24; R Kenmare U (A & A) 1924–59; Preb of Kilpeacon in Limerick Cath 1945–52; Treasurer 1952–59

> **s.** of Rev Simon Carter qv below (**s.** of Alan) by Eliza **dau.** of John Martin of Dublin; **bro.** of Rev Alan, R Innismagrath (Kilm) qv and of Rev Samuel Carter and Rev John
>
> **m.** 28 Oct 1919 Norah Alice (**died** 13 Oct 1986) yr **dau.** of William Wright Belton of Luton Beds. Issue 1. Bernard Aylmer **b.** 19 Jul 1921 **died** 30 Jul 1986; 2. Simon Richard **b.** 30 May 1926 **died** 9 Apr 1996
>
> **Died** Dec 1965

ARMSTRONG, ROBERT 1841/42–1902

b. 1841 or 1842; TCD BA 1867 Div Test (2) 1868 MA 1870 BD & DD 1889

d 17 Sep 1868 (Armagh for Kilmore) p 20 Dec 1869 (Kilmore); C Drumgoon (Kilm) 1868–72; R Cloydagh and Bilbo (Leigh) 1872–76; R Stradbally U (Leigh) 1876–1902; Chanc of Leighlin 1896–1902

> **s.** of Robert of Clinkeenham Co Monaghan
>
> **m.** Charlotte (**died** 26 June 1917 at Rathmines Dublin). Issue 1. an eldest **s.** who died in W Australia; 2 **daus.** incl 1. Jennie m…Castro and lived in Tuscon Arizona
>
> **Died** 15 Aug 1902 aged 60 **bur.** Stradbally

ARMSTRONG, ROBERT CECIL –1967

b. Dublin; ed the High Sch Dublin; TCD BA & Div Test 1934 MA 1937

d 1935 p 1936; C Templemichael (Ard) 1935–38; C Mariners' Ch Kingstown (Dun Laoghaire) (Dub) 1938–40; R Narraghmore w Fontstown (Glend) 1940–50; RD

Omurthy (Glend) 1945–50; R Thurles (Cash) 1950–57; R Swanlinbar w Templeport (Kilm) 1957–62; R Shrawley (Worc) 1962–67

> **s.** of Joseph of Morehampton Rd Dublin
>
> **m.** 1940 Dorothy Mina Evanson **dau.** of Hamilton E Oswald of Dun Laoghaire. Issue 1. Elizabeth; 2. Rosaleen; 3. Richard; 4. Sylvia
>
> **Died** 22 Feb 1967

ARMSTRONG, SAMUEL CARTER 1883–1961

b. 13 Mar 1883; TCD BA 1912

d 1911 p 1912 (Cork); C Abbeystrewery (Ross) 1911–13; C-in-c Kilmurry (Killaloe) 1914–16; C Cloughjordan w Modreeny (Killaloe) 1916–20; C Urney (Kilm) 1921–24; C-in-c Ballyjamesduff w Castlerahan (Kilm) 1924–26; C-in-c Gowna and Columbkille (Ard) 1926–30; R Templeport (Kilm) 1930–48; RD Templeport 1943–48 and 1951–52; R Drumlease (w Killenumery, Killargue and Innismagrath from 1955) (Kilm) 1948–59; Preb of Triburnia in Kilmore Cath 1949–59; ret

> **s.** of Rev Canon Simon Carter, R Shrule (Ard) qv (**s.** of Alan) by Eliza **dau.** of John Martin; **bro.** of Rev Alan, R Killargue (Kilm) qv and of Ven John, Archd of Elphin and Ardagh qv and of Rev Aylmer Richard, R Drumlane (Kilm) qv
>
> **Died unm.** 1 Aug 1961

ARMSTRONG, SIMON CARTER 1856–1942

b. 26 Aug 1856; ed at Private Sch Blackrock Co Dublin; Bournemouth Prep Coll; Rathmines Sch Dublin; TCD BA & Div Test 1885

d 1885 (Cashel) p 1886 (Kilmore); C Drumcannon (Waterf) 1885–86; I Shrule (Ard) 1886–91; I Tubbercurry (Ach) 1891–92; C Portadown (Arm) 1892–94; I Templederry (Killaloe) 1894–1911; I Kilrush (Killaloe) 1911–23; Chanc of Killaloe 1917–23; C-in-c Finglas (Dub) 1923–28; ret

> **s.** of Alan of Lakeview Manorhamilton Co Leitrim
>
> **m.** 2 Apr 1878 St Peter's Ch Dublin Eliza (Cosie) (**died** 7 Sep 1942) **dau.** of John Martin, Solicitor of Dublin. Issue 1. Eliza Violet (**died** Mar 1978) **b.** 1 Mar 1879 Deaconess CEZMA; 2. Rev Alan, R Innismagrath (Kilm) qv; 3. Aileen Jane (**died** 21 Feb 1958 Bray) **b.** 20 Nov 1881, Deaconess in DUFEM.; 4. Rev Samuel Carter, R Drumlease (Kilm) qv; 5. Rev John, Archd of Elphin and Ardagh qv; 6. Carter **b.** 23 Jun 1886 MRCVS; **died** 1 Jan 1930; 7. Rev Aylmer Richard, R Drumlane (Kilm) qv; 8. George **b.** Jun 1889 **died** 4 Dec 1902; 9. James Septimus (**died** 14 Apr 1936 in Tanganyika) **b.** 5 Oct 1891 TCD BA MB 1924 served in Great War MC **m.** 21 Jun 1928 Agatha Mary **dau.** of Dr Hough, Bp of Woolwich; 10. Charles Martin **b.** 15 May 1893 Portadown; killed in action 1917 **bur.** Ancre Cemetery France; 11. Henrietta (Hetty) **b.** 4 Dec 1894 (**died** 13 Jan 1978) TCD MB 1924 **m.** Matthew H Armstrong (**died** 10 Mar 1996) of Tempo Co Fermanagh; 12. a son stillborn 20 Sep 1896; 13. William **b.** 28 Feb 1898 **died** 24 May 1915; 14 Ruth Rose (**died** 30 Jul 1942) **b.** 25 Dec 1899 TCD MB 1927 **m.** 1 Jun 1932 Rev James Henry Alcock; 15. Mary (**died** 30 Jul 1942) **m.** 22 Nov 1939 Rev A C Kennedy and had issue a **dau.**

Died 31 Jul 1942

PUBLICATIONS

The Cooneyites or Dippers, a plain refutation of their errors

ARMSTRONG, WILLIAM 1780/81–1840*

b. 1780 or 1781 Co Sligo; ed by Mr Armstrong; ent TCD 9 Nov 1797 aged 16 BA (not recorded in Al Dub); perhaps W A who was MA 1829; may be different from W A below

C Sligo (Elph) to 1823; PC Calry (Elph) 1823–40

he was poss **s.** of Rev James, V Taunagh (Elph)

m. Aug 1827 Cassandra (**died** 5 Feb 1851 Dublin) yst **dau.** of John Young of Castlerea and had issue incl 1. his eldest **s.** John (**died** 19 May 1850 Blackrock Dublin); 2. Rev William Bettesworth (**died** 13 Oct 1900 Caledon aged 70) TCD BA 1852 Div Test (1) 1853 MA 1872 d 1853 p 1855 (Armagh) C Aghalurcher (Clogh) 1853–55 PC Caledon (Arm) 1855–1900 Preb of Yagoe in St Patrick's Cath Dublin 1886–1900 **m.** Isabella Jane (**died** 1 Sep 1902) 2nd **dau.** of Henry Leslie Prentice, DL; 3. Simon Robert (**died** 5 Oct 1867); 4. Robert Young **b.** Sligo ent TCD 13 Oct 1856 aged 17

Died 29 Mar 1840 Calry, Sligo; monument in Enniskillen Cath gives his age as 48; monument in Calry Church gives his age as 46

ARMSTRONG, WILLIAM CHAMBERS 1780/81–1871*

b. 1780 or 1781 Co Sligo; ed by Mr Armstrong; ent TCD 9 Nov 1797 BA aged 16

d 20 Apr 1802 p 15 Sep 1805; C St John Sligo 1802–23; R & V Moydow & Teighsinod 1823–68; ret

s. of Rev James, R Taunagh (Elph) qv

his wife **died** 18 Apr 1868 aged 77. Issue 1. Margaret (**died** 17 Jul 1895 at Clifton) **m.** Rev Richard Parkinson, V Northants Herts; 2. Williamena Mary (**died** 9 Nov 1911) **m.** Rev Alexander Orme, Dean of Ardagh qv; 3. Capt J Welling who was killed at the Battle of Belmont Missouri USA in Dec 1861

Died 25 Jan 1871 at Moydow aged 91

* William Armstrong and William Chambers Armstrong are clearly two different people whose details of birth and education have become confused in Canon Leslie's MSS

ARNOTT, MICHAEL –1718

R Drumgoon (Kilm) 1681–83; had been pres by the Crown 20 May 1681 (L.M. V. 117), but the Lucas family on *Quare Impedit* recovered the Advowson in 1683; R Drumgoon again 1689–1718; R Drung and Larah (Kilm) 1691–1700

Died 1718

ARTHURIUS

Canon of Ardagh 1353 (Theiner 357)

ASHE, HENRY ELLIS 1836/37–1873

b. 1836 or 1837 Co Tyrone; ent TCD 2 Nov 1855 aged 18 BA & Div Test 1861

PC St John's Cloverhill (Kilm) 1867–73

prob Henry Ashe **s.** of Rev Isaac, R Kildress (Arm)– see Canon Fleming *Armagh Clergy 1800–2000* pp544–545

Died 12 Mar 1873 aged 36

ASHE, WILLIAM 1803–1884

b. 1803 Derry; ed by his father; ent TCD 3 Jul 1820 aged 17 BA 1825

d 1827 (Derry) p; C Ematris (Clogh) to 1837; PC Killoughter (Kilm) 1837–57; R Rossinver 1856–72

s. of Rev Isaac

m. Jane (**died** 15 Jun 1878) and had issue incl his yst **dau.** Bessie **m.** Rev Richard Tate, R Rossinver (Kilm) qv, and had issue Margaret Elizabeth

Died 1884 **bur.** Killoughter

ASHE, WILLIAM SANDES 1792/93–?1855

b. 1792 or 1793 Co Limerick; ed by his father; ent TCD 5 Feb 1810 aged 17 BA 1814

V Killenvoy (Elph) 1845–55

s. of Rev William, Preb of Croagh (Lim)

? **Died** 1855

ASHTON, JAMES EDWARD BENNETT   –1978

TCD BA 1917 MA 1940

d 1917 p 1919 (Kilmore); C Drumlease (Kilm) 1917–23; C-in-c Kilmacshalgan (Killala) 1923–28; R Killala w Dunfeeny and Ballysakeery 1928–68; RD of Straid 1944–61; Dean of Killala 1946–68; ret

eldest **s.** of Rev James

m. 1 Apr 1932 Jessie Sydney (**died** 1 Apr 1974) yst **dau.** of S J Gilmour of Dromahair Co Leitrim

Died 19 Feb 1978 **bur.** Drumlease

ASKINS, WILLIAM JAMES *c.* 1879–1955

b *c.* 1879; TCD BA 1901 MA 1906

d 1902 p 1903 (Kilmore); C Kilmore (Kilm) 1902–06; R Kilmore (w C-in-c Ballintemple from 1950) (Kilm) 1906–55; Dean of Kilmore 1931–55

3rd **s.** of Canon William James, R Dunany and Dunleer (Arm) 1872–95 (**s.** of John of Dublin) by Jane **dau.** of Ven Francis King, DD, Archd of Dromore

m. (1) 10 Jun 1902 St Mary's Ch Donnybrook Dublin Annie (**died** 24 Jul 1904) **dau.** of Rev Jackson Smyth, DD, Minister 1st Armagh Presby Ch and ex–Moderator of the General Assembly. Issue Annie (**died** 18 Mar 1905 aged 8 months)

m. (2) 14 Aug 1907 St Mary's Ch Staines Surrey Caroline Elizabeth (**died** 21 Nov 1941) **dau.** of Charles F Leake of Hale Hse Staines. Issue 1. Ruth (**died** 3 Jun 1931 aged 22); 2. Frances (**died** unm 1984); 3. Charles (**died** 19 Feb 1924 aged 11)

Died 28 Feb 1955

†ASSICUS –470

is said to have been made Bp of Elphin by St Patrick. He was a celebrated artist in metals. He **died** at Rathcunge in Tirconnell (Co. Donegal). Meissner *History of the Church of Ireland* I. 125, thinks that he was succeeded by Bite, but this is only a conjecture. No other Bishop is known for several centuries

Died 470, Feast Day 27 April

ASTON, JOHN

BA

V Clongish (Ard) to 1615; sequestrator Shrule (Ard) 1615 whilst incumbency occupied by RC Curate; V Kilcommick (Ard) 1615–c23, a preacher non–resident, church ruinous 1622; V Street (Ard) 1616, and in 1622 not resident, church not well repaired (R.V.)

ATHILL, RICHARD

poss C Cloonclare (Kilm) *c.* 1840

ATKINS, FORREST WILLIAM 1959–

b. 28 Feb 1959 Barnet Herts; ed Mount Grace Comprehensive Sch; Christ Ch Coll Camb BA 1981 MA 1985; Ridley Hall Camb 1983; Univ of London BD 1984

d 1986 p 1987; C Normanton (Derby) 1986–90; P-in-c Stratford St John and Christ Ch w Forest Gate St James (Chelmsf) 1990–97; Asst Chapl Dubai and Sharjah w N Emirates (Dio Cyprus and the Gulf) 1997–2003; I Mohill Farnaught Aughavas Oughteragh Drumreilly Kiltubride Drumshambo Kiltoghart and Annaduff (Ard) 2003–

s. of Forest William of Plymouth (**s.** of Aaron of Kingstown Dublin and Elizabeth (*née* Driscoll)) by Margaret Clifford **dau.** of Very Rev Austin Fulton, Moderator of the Presbyterian Ch in Ireland 1961 and Flora (née Porter)

m. at Sialkot Punjab India Jamila Emanuel **dau.** of Rev Emanuel Sardar Khokar, Presbyter-in-charge Central Ch Lahore by Alvenus

ATKINSON, FREDERICK STAPLES 1860/61–1945

b. 1860 or 1861; TCD BA 1885 Div Test 1887 MA 1888

d 1886 p 1887 (Kilmore); C Derryheen (Kilm) 1886–88; R Derryheen (Kilm) 1888–1924 (w C & C-in-c St Andrew Drumaloor (Kilm) 1903–24); (was C-in-c Derryheen (Kilm) 1903–14); R Killashee and Ballymacormick (Ard) 1924–25; Gen Lic Dio Clogher 1925–26; C-in-c Mostrim (Ard) 1927–31; ret

s. of Charles of Greenhall Armagh

m. Elizabeth Anne (**died** 28 Dec 1954 at Dun Laoghaire **bur.** Enniskerry) yr **dau.** of Capt Robert Fury of Dargan Collooney Co Sligo 3rd Royal Lancs Regt

Died 5 Oct 1945 aged 84

ATTHILL, JOHN ANTHONY LOMBE

Ridley Hall Camb 1909; Selwyn Coll Camb BA 1912 MA 1916; Edinburgh Theol Coll 1913

d 1913 (Kilmore) p 1915 (Canterbury); C Kilmore (Kilm) 1913–15; C Lydd (Cant) 1915–16; C Christ Ch Chorley Wood (St A) 1916–18; R St Andrew Fortrose (w C Cromarty Miss) (M R & C) 1918–20; P-in-c Dufftown (A & O) 1920–21; P-in-c St Mary Bocas del Toro Panama (Dio Hond) 1921–22; Dio Supernumerary Aberdeen & Orkney 1923–26; R Fochabers (M R & C) 1926–28; C St Thomas Durban (Dio Natal) 1928–29; Perm to Off Dio Brechin from 1929 Perm to Off Dio A & O 1930–34; Perm to Off Dio Edinburgh from 1934; last entry in Crockford 1938

†AUBREY, JOHN

Friar Preacher of Trim. (Cal. Reg. Swet. 244). Aubrey seems to have got possession of the See of Ardagh in 1373 and was prov. by the Pope on 29 Apr 1374 (Theiner, 351). He is called John O'Freac or O'Frayn in the Ann. Loch Ce; Ann. Hib. I. 184 is incorrect in saying that John Aubrey was set over the See of Ardagh on the demise of Charles O'Ferrall qv

AUCHMUTY, SAMUEL 1738/39–

b. 1738 or 1739 Co Longford; ed by Rev Mr Gouldsbury; ent TCD 7 Dec 1757 aged 18 BA 1762 MA 1766

R Shrule (Ard) 1769–c. 1800

> **s.** of Samuel of Brianstown by Mary **dau.** of John King who was grandson of Rt Rev Edward King, Bp of Elphin qv;
>
> **m.** his cousin Susannah Maria **dau.** of Francis Savage by Elizabeth **dau.** of Dean James Auchmuty. Issue 1. Rev Samuel qv; 2. Robert Forbes; 3. Elizabeth Maria; 4. Sarah Caroline; 5. Helen Forbes

AUCHMUTY, SAMUEL 1767/68–

b. 1767 or 1768 Co Longford; ed by Mr Meares; ent TCD 3 Jun 1786 aged 18 BA 1791

C Shrule (Ard) 1791–1807

> **s.** of Rev Samuel qv above (**s.** of Samuel and Mary (née King)) by Susannah Maria **dau.** of Francis Savage
>
> **m.** (1) Sarah King of St Mary's Dublin (ML 11 Jul 1794)
>
> **m.** (2) Margaret Christina Lyons (ML 1806). Issue incl Rev Samuel Forbes (**died** 15 Apr 1871) Brasenose Coll Ox MA, R Broad Blunsdon Wilts 1864–71 **m.** and had issue Rev Arthur Compton Ox MA, V Lucton (Heref) 1883

AUNGIER, JOHN
coll V Lurgan & Munterconnaught (Kilm) 15 Oct 1667 and again coll 12 Dec 1673 with Castlerahan (Kilm); held to 1692

AUSTIN, FREDERICK WILLIAM 1858–1935
b. 12 Jun 1858; ed The High School Dublin; Grammar School Galway; TCD BA 1900 MA 1904

d 1881 (Kilmore) p 14 Jun 1884 (Ossory); C Lissadell (Elph) 1881–84; C Castlecomer (Oss) 1884–85; R Creggan (Arm) 1885–90; R Drumcree (Arm) 1890–1900; R St Barnabas Belfast (Conn) 1900–04; R St Columba Knock (Down) 1904–30; Preb of St Andrew in Down Cath 1920–30; ret

> **s.** of Rev William Duncan (**died** 22 Jun 1901 at Kingstown aged 67), R Castlecomer (Oss) 1880–1901; **bro.** of Rev George Herbert (**died** 8 Apr 1912 aged 46), R Ballymena (Conn) 1900–12
>
> **m.** 1886 Florence Louisa **dau.** of Rev William Anthony Voss, V Allonby (Carl)
>
> **Died** s.p. 30 Oct 1935

AYRES, EDWARD BOLINGBROKE 1770–1841
b. 1770 Dublin; ed by Mr Mercer; ent TCD 23 Jan 1790 BA 1794

C Drumcliffe (Elph) 1804; C Castlemacadam (Glend) 1804; V Ballymore Eustace (Glend) 1811–16; Preb of Termonbarry (Elph) 1816–41

> **s.** of William, merchant
>
> **m.** 10 Apr 1817 Elphin Cathedral Anne eldest **dau.** of Rev Luke Mahon, Preb of Oran (Elph) qv and had issue incl Rev George **b.** 1813 (**died** 1 Dec 1881 Blessington Co Wicklow) St John's Coll Camb BA 1849 MA 1852 d 1851 p 1852 (Ely) C Layham (St E — then Ely) 1852–56; V Kilbride (Glend) 1857–72 Preb of Mulhuddart in St Patrick's Cath Dublin 1869–81 **m.** Apr 1861 Florence Anne **dau.** of John H Owen of Belmont Co Laois and had issue (i) a son **b.** 13 Sep 1866; (ii) a son **b.** 14 Mar 1870; (iii) a son **b.** 16 Feb 1872; (iv) a **dau.** m Sir Thomas Myles
>
> **Died** 1841

AYTON, JOHN –1683
Episcopally ordained 1655; Appointed Commonwealth minister at Tynan (Arm) 5 Jan 1656/56, appointment to date from 25 Sep last; Preb of Tynan (Arm) 1656/57–61; Archd of Ardagh 1661–1681; certain charges were made against him in 1679. He either resigned or was deposed in 1681

> was **m.** and had a son James ent TCD 19 May 1682 aged 16
>
> **Died** 1683

BAGWELL, RICHARD 1777–1825
b. 1777 Co Cork; ed by Mr Carey; ent TCD 5 Aug 1793 aged 15 BA 1797; he seems to have become an MP two years later as he sat in the Irish Parliament in 1799 as MP for Cashel

V Urney and Annagelliffe (Kilm) 1804–05; Dean of Kilmacduagh 1804; Prec of Cashel 1805–25; Dean of Clogher 1805–25

2nd **s.** of John, MP for Co Tipperary, of Marlfield Clonmel

m. 1808 Margaret **dau.** of Edward Croker of Ballynagarde. Issue **sons** 1. John **b.** 3 Apr 1811, JP DL, High Sheriff for Co Tipperary 1834, MP for Clonmel 1857–74 **m.** 21 Jun 1838 Hon. Frances Eliza Prittie, **sister** of Henry, 3rd Lord Dunalley and had issue Richard the Historian; 2. Edward **b.** 21 Aug 1819, Capt 3rd Dragoon Guards, Lt. Col Tipperary Militia, JP DL, High Sheriff for Co Tipperary 1856 **m.** twice and had issue; **daus.** 1. Margaret **m.** Joseph Gore of Derrymore Co Clare; 2. Mary **m.** George Gough of Woodstown Co Tipperary; 3. Jane **m.** 13 Nov 1841 Benjamin B Freud

Died 25 Dec 1825 **bur.** Clogher Cathedral

BAILE, GEORGE WILLIAM 1866–1918

b. 1866; ed by his father; TCD BA (Resp) and LLB 1886

d 1887 (Kilmore) p 1888 (Dublin); C St Peter Athlone (Meath — then Elph) 1887–88; C St Werburgh (Dub) 1888–92; Dep Sec S S Soc for Ireland and Gen Lic Dios Dublin Glendalough and Kildare 1892–93; Head Master Kilkenny Coll (Oss) 1893–1902; C St Saviour Tollington Pk London (Lon) 1902–03; Chapl Consulate Pernambuco 1903–17; CF with BEF 1917–18

s. of Robert, Head Master Ranelagh Sch Athlone Co Westmeath

m. (1) Jane McQuade. Issue 1. Robert Carlyle; 2. George Frederick Cecil; 3. Cyril James; 4. Olive **b.** 1893; 5. Eileen Mary **b.** 1897; 6. Enid; 7. Jane Elizabeth **b.** 1900

m. (2) 1916 Mathilda Emily Hatton of Folkestone. Issue Rosemary Patricia

Died 27 Jan 1918 on active service; **bur.** Etaples Military Cemetery France

BAILEY, WILLIAM RICHEY 1817–1888

b. 3 Feb 1817 Co Fermanagh; TCD BA (Resp) & Div Test (2) 1847 MA 1850 BD & DD 1865

d 1847 p 1848; C Aghalurcher (Clogh) 1847; PC Lisnaskea (Clogh) 1852–64; R & V Monaghan (Clogh) 1864–74; R & V Clogher (Clogh) 1874–85; Preb of Kilskeery (Clogh) 1874; R Killesher (Kilm) 1886–88. He was a skilled musician, mechanic and architect, and he restored with his own hands the stairway of Clogher Cathedral. (Leslie *Clogher Clergy and Parishes* p 69).

s. of Rev Robert, Methodist Minister

Died 28 Sep 1888

BAKER, SAMUEL WALLACE 1909–*c.* 1975

b. 7 Nov 1909; ed Royal Sch Dungannon; Royal Sch Armagh; TCD BA & Div Test 1932

d 18 Dec 1932 p 17 Dec 1933; C All SS Clooney Londonderry (Derry) 1932–35; C Urney Annagelliffe Denn and Derryheen (Kilm) 1935–36; R Murragh w Killowen (Cork) 1936–49; CF 1949–59; HCF 1959; R Ash-cum-Ridley (Roch) 1959–68; V St

John the Evangelist Bromley (Roch) 1968–

    eldest **s.** of Rev Samuel Hutchinson, R Brantry (Arm) (**s.** of Samuel and Eliza Alice (*née* Good)) by Susan Frances Dawson **dau.** of Rev John Wallace Taylor, R Errigle Truagh (Clogh) and Maria (*née* Dawson)

    m. 24 Apr 1935 Magheraculmoney Par Ch Co Fermanagh Margaret Millicent only **dau.** of J A Aiken of Kesh Co Fermanagh. Issue 1. Pamela Margaret Frances; 2. Edgar Wallace; twins 3. Elizabeth Anne and 4. Richard Acheson

    Died *c.* 1975

BALL, THOMAS PRESTON 1825–1913

b. 1825 Co Wicklow; ed by Mr Flynn; ent TCD 11 Oct 1844 aged 19 BA & Div Test 1850 MA 1857

d 25 Jul 1850 (Kilmore) p 1852 (Tuam); C St Peter Athlone (Elph) 1851–52; C Omey Clifden (Tuam) 1852–53; C Kinvarra 1853–54; C St Jude Liverpool (Liv) 1854–55; C Sefton (Liv) 1855–62; PC St John Liscard (Ches) 1862–79; I Trinity Ch Dublin (Dub) 1879–84; V Dundry (B & W) 1884–87; Gen Lic Dublin 1889

    s. of Rev John, C Delgany (Glend) 1827–30

    m. Henrietta Walsh (ML 1852)

    Died 25 Oct 1913 aged 88 at Northbrook Rd Dublin

PUBLICATION

    Two Ancient Institutions, The Sabbath and Marriage, Church of Ireland Printing Co. Dublin

BAMFORD, FREDERICK WILLIAM

ed St Bee's Coll Durham

d 1882 p 1883 (Kilmore); C Killeshandra (Kilm) 1882–84; R Killoughter (Kilm) 1884–87; Army Chapl in India 1889–92; Jhelum, Lahore 1887–88 and 1889–92; C Delgany (Glend) 1892–94; R Donabate (Dub) 1894–99; res

    m. 7 Oct 1884 Agatha Mant eldest **dau.** of R H Clifford, Bengal Civil Service of Greenville Co Cavan. Issue incl 1. Percival Clifford, Indian Police **m.** 20 Nov 1919 at Calcutta Geraldine Beatrice **dau.** of Hon. F C French; 2. yst **s.** Wilfrid Clifford, CE, Nigerian Govt Service **m.** 30 Apr 1924 at Kells Co Meath Evelyn Maud **dau.** of Capt G L and Mrs H **m.** Bomford of Kells

    Last entry in C I Dir 1901

BARCLAY, CHARLES

V Streete Russagh and Abbeylara (Ard) 1698–*c.* 1701, coll 1 Jul 1698 (FF)

BARCROFT, AMBROSE

d; p 22 Dec 1639 (Ferns); was Commonwealth Minister at Birr from 25 Jun 1657; previously schoolmaster in Athlone Precinct; V Templeport Drumreilly & Killinagh (Kilm) 1661–63; R Castleterra (Kilm) 1663–78; Archd of Kilmore 1663–78; V Urney

& Annageliffe (Kilm) 1665–78

   2nd **s.** of Ambrose of Foulridge Hall Lancashire

BARKLIE, JOHN KNOX 1837–1917

b. 1837 Londonderry; ed Portora Royal Sch Enniskillen; ent TCD 2 Jul 1856 aged 19 BA 1861 Div Test 1862

d 1862 p 1863 (Derry); C Tamlaghtfinlagan (Derry) 1862–65; DC Whitehouse (Conn) 1865; R Oughteragh (Kilm) 1866–74; R Moira (Drom) 1874–98 C Geraldine, Canterbury NZ (Dio Christchurch) 1898–1910

   s. of George of Portrush Co Antrim

   m. 18 Feb 1864 Holy Trinity Westminster Lizzie only **dau.** of Alfred Smythe of Pimlico London by Caroline Georgina

   Died 10 Mar 1917 in New Zealand aged 79

BARNEWALL, SIR PATRICK

intruded into the vacant parish of Cashel (Ard) and detained 2 parts of the tithes being Mensal belonging to the Bishop 1622 (R.V.)

BARRETT, KENNETH ARTHUR LAMBART 1960–

b. 17 Mar 1960 Dublin; ed Campbell Coll Belfast; TCD BTh 1997

d 1997 p 1998 (Down); C Seagoe (Drom) 1997–2000; R Booterstown and Mount Merrion (Dub) 2000–04; R Boyle Taunagh Aghanagh Croghan Ardcarne Tybohine Ballysumaghan and Kilmactranny (Elph) 2004–

   s. of Basil Reginald Lambart of Dundrum Dublin (**s.** of Rex and Edna of Dublin) by Patricia Ann **dau.** of Ted and Gladys Mayne of Groomsport Co Down

   m. 5 Sep 1987 Dun Laoghaire Methodist Ch Brigid Jane **dau.** of Roy and Rosalie Parker of Dublin. Issue twins 1. Charles Robert Lambart **b.** 8 Jun 1993; 2. Nathan Basil Lambart **b.** 8 Jun 1993; 3. Lucy Rachel **b.** 11 Aug 2000

†BARRETT, THOMAS –1404

Archdeacon of Annaghdown, was consecrated for the See of Elphin in 1372. In 1383 the Antipope suspended him for supporting the Pope (Urban VI), but he seems to have held possession, and to have been a man of high reputation as Bishop till his death in 1404 at Derry. The A.F.M. state that he was buried in Errew of Lough Conn, in the parish of Crossmolina

   Died 1404

BARRY, JOHN 1726/27–1794

b. 1726 or 1727 Cork; ent TCD 17 Jan 1742 aged 15 BA 1747 MA 1750 DD 1777

d; p 1753 (Cork); V Killaconenagh (Ross) 1753–56; V Durrus U (Cork) 1756–68; Preb of Kilmaclenine (Cloyne) and Preb of Desertmore (Cork) 1768–94; Dean of Elphin 1778–94 yr s. of Sir Edward, MD Bt by Jane **dau.** of Anthony Dopping, Bp of Ossory 1741–43

m. (1) May 1771 Sarah **dau.** of John Bateman of Oak Park Tralee Co Kerry

m. (2) (ML 11 Aug 1781) Susan Swan (**died** 2 Feb 1825 aged 82). Issue Edward, Bt

Died Jan 1794

BARRY, ZACHARY 1827/28–

b. 1827 or 1828 Co Cork; ent TCD 4 Nov 1844 aged 16 BA 1849 LLB & LLD 1868

d 1850 p 1851 (Chester); C St Mary Edgehill (Liv) 1850–52; Colonial Chapl for Western Australia 1852–53; acc to *Crockford* 1883, he was I St John Fremantle (Perth) 1853–62; acc to Leslie, he was C Boyle (Elph) 1860; Org Sec ICM in Ireland 1862–65; I St Jude Randwick (Sydney) 1865–68; I Paddington (Sydney) 1868–after 1883

s. of David, MD by Mary Peacock **dau.** of Ven Zachary Cooke–Collis

m. Elizabeth Struan Robertson of Abbeyview Boyle and had issue incl 1. Zachary Collis who **m.** and had issue Ruth **m**... Wansey; 2. a **s. b.** 2 Mar 1863; 3. Edmund William (**died** 8 Jul 1865)

BARTER, JOHN BEAUFORT BERKELEY

Chichester Theol Coll 1865; MRIA 1880; FRGSI

d 1865 (Rochester) p 1869 (Ely); C Stevenage (St A) 1865–66; C Burwell (Ely) 1868–69; C Swaffham-Bulbeck (Ely) 1870–71; C Aghaderg (Drom) 1874–75; C Drumbanagher (Arm) 1875–76; C Timolin (Glend) 1876–77; C Moira (Drom) 1877–78; C Kilmore (Arm) 1878–80; C Cappoquin (Lism) 1880–81; C Kilbolane (Cloyne) 1881; Asst Chapl to Seamen Cobh (Cloyne) 1882–85; C Inishmacsaint (Clogh) 1885–86; Chapl at Turin 1886– still there in 1897

BARTON, ARTHUR ROBINSON 1848–1900

b. 1848 Dublin; ed privately; TCD BA 1869 Div Test (2) 1870 MA 1872 BD & DD 1886

d 1870 (Meath) p 1872 (Dublin); C Drumcree (Meath) 1870–71; C Coolock (Dub) 1871–79; R St Paul's Dublin (Dub) 1879–86; R Urney (Kilm) 1886–88; R Enniscorthy (Ferns) 1889–95; R Zion Rathgar (Dub) 1895–1900

s. of James and Ellen (*née* Page) of Clontarf Dublin

m. (1) 9 Jan 1873 at Whitechurch Anne **dau.** of William Armstrong Hayes of Edmonston Park Co Dublin. Issue **sons** 1. Samuel Page, Medical Missy at Bannu, India; 2. Most Rev Arthur William, Bp of Kilmore and Abp of Dublin qv; **daus.** 1. Emily Gertrude, CEZ Missy at Sukkur, India; 2. Edith Eileen **b.** 18 Jul 1875 **m.** Rev Herbert Whitehead, Missy in Uganda; 3. Kathleen Elizabeth, Missy in Uganda

m. (2) 23 Apr 1883 St Paul's Ch Harriet Elizabeth widow of P S Nelson. Issue 1. Harold Stewart **b.** 1 Aug 1896; 2. Elsie H **m. b.** 13 Jan 1900

Died 13 Jan 1900

PUBLICATION

Infant Baptism, a pamphlet, *c.* 1887

†BARTON, ARTHUR WILLIAM 1881–1962

b. 1 Jun 1881 Dublin; ed St Columba's Coll Dublin; TCD Carson Bibl Pri BA (Resp) 1903 BD 1906 DD (j.d.) 1930

d 1904 p 1905 (Down) Bp 1930; C St George (Dub) 1904–05; C Howth (Dub) 1905–07; C-in-c Howth (Dub) 1907–11; Head of TCD Mission Belfast (Conn) 1912–14; R Dundela (Down) 1914–25; Treasurer of Down 1923–25; Prec of Down 1925–27; R Bangor (Down) 1925–30; Archd of Down 1927–30; elected Bp of Kilmore Elphin and Ardagh by the United Synods 4 Apr 1930; consec 1 May 1930 St Patrick's Cath Armagh; enthroned in St Fethlimidh's Cath Kilmore 29 May 1930; enthroned in Elphin Cath 3 Jun 1930; Bp of Kilmore Elphin and Ardagh 1930–39; elected Archbishop of Dublin, Bp of Kildare and Glendalough and Primate of Ireland by Synod 7 Feb 1939; Abp of Dublin and Primate of Ireland and Bp of Kildare and Glendalough 1939–56; Preb of Cualan in St Patrick's Cath Dublin 1939–56; ret

> **s.** of Rev Arthur, R Urney (Kilm) 1886–88 qv (**s.** of James and Ellen (*née* Page) of Clontarf Dublin) by his 1st wife Anne **dau.** of William Armstrong Hayes of Co Dublin

> **m.** 21 Apr 1914 Zoe Margaret Victoria (**died** 27 Sep 1968) **dau.** of Henry Alexander Cosgrave of Dublin. Issue 1. Diana Mary (**died** 7 Apr 2000) **m.** (1) Rev Canon Richard Randall Hartford (**died** 7 Aug 1962) DD, Regius Prof of Divinity TCD 1957–62 **m.** (2) James McFarlan; 2. Barbara **m.** Jul 1950 Maxwell Alexander Lane and had issue; 3. Arthur Henry, Pay–Lt RN **m.** 17 Dec 1940 Marjorie **dau.** of ES Lumsden, RSA Edinburgh

> **Died** 22 Sep 1962 **bur.** at Kilmore

PUBLICATIONS
Further Instructed Talks to a Confirmation Class
An Archbishop Looks Back and other Sermons, ed by Rev. JRH Royds, 1966

BARTON, JOHN 1652/53–1718

b. 1652 or 1653 Poulton Lancs; ed by Mr Moore; ent TCD 3 Aug 1669 aged 16 Sch 1672 BA 1674 Fellow 1677 MA 1677 BD 1686 DD 1692 LLD 1694 Vice Provost and Prof of Laws 1693

V Slane and Paynestown and V Danestown (Meath) 1694–1718; R Baldungan (Dub) 1694–1702; R Eirke (Oss) 1695–1718; pres to the Deanery of Ardagh 21 Mar 1702/3 and inst. 29 Sep 1703 (F.F.); Leslie's *Ossory Clergy and Parishes* has him Dean of Ardagh 1695–1718; R Kentstown (Meath) 1702–18

> **s.** of Richard

> **m.** 4 Mar 1701 Eleanor **dau.** of Henry Jenny, Preb of Mullabrack and had several children including 1. Rev James **b.** at Paynestown ed by Mr Sheridan ent TCD 27 Feb 1720/21 aged 18 Sch 1723 BA 1725 MA 1728 Preb of Lattin (Emly) 1746–65 **died** 22 Mar 1765; 2. Rev Richard **b.** at Paynestown ed by Mr Sheridan ent TCD 9 Feb 1721/22 aged 15 Sch 1724 BA 1726 MA 1731 C Shankill Lurgan (Drom) and author of several works on Natural Philosophy; 3. Rev Nathaniel **b.** *c.* 1711 Sch 1729 BA 1731 d Leighlin 1738 Preb of Ballintubber 1741–61 Preb of Tibohine 1761–70 **died** 1770; He also had Benjamin, Henry and Eleanor.

> **Died** Jun 1718

BARTON, JOHN –1824

evidently J B ed by Dr Norris at Drogheda; ent TCD 1 Nov 1766 Sch 1769 BA 1772

C Kilkeevan (Elph) 1784–86; V Aughrim (Elph) 1788–1811; V Killyon and Kilronan (Elph) 1811–24

BARTON, NATHANIEL 1710/11–1770

b. 1710 or 1711 Co Meath; ed by Mr Sheridan at Dublin; ent TCD 18 Jan 1726/27 aged 16 Sch 1729 BA 1731

d 13 Aug 1738 (Leighlin); p; R Shankill and Kilmacumsy (Elph) 1742–43; V Kilkeevan and Preb of Ballintubber (Elph) 1743–61; Preb of Tibohine (Elph) 1761–70; V Kilcorkey (Elph) 1766–70

>s. of Very Rev John, Dean of Ardagh qv (s. of Edward) by Eleanor **dau.** of Henry Jenny; **bro.** of Rev James and Rev Richard

>m. Bridget **dau.** of Owen Young of Castlerea Co Roscommon by Bridget **dau.** of Very James Wilson, Dean of Tuam

>**Died** 1770 **bur.** Castlerea

BATEMAN, THOMAS NORMAN 1900–1974

b. 19 Jan 1900 Dublin; ed Diocesan Sch Dublin; The King's Hosp Dublin; TCD BA (Resp) 1932

d 1932 p 1933 (Ossory); C Kilnamanagh (Ferns) 1932–34; C-in-c Templeshambo (Ferns) 1934–35; I Mulrankin (Ferns) 1935–38; C-in-c Crosspatrick w Kilcommon (Ferns) 1938–42; Asst Chapl Miss to Seamen Belfast 1942–43; Chapl Miss to Seamen Swansea 1943–46; C-in-c Ardcarne and Kilbryan (Elph) 1946–49; I Kiltoghart w Annaduff (Ard) 1949–55; RD of Edgeworthstown 1953–55; V St Philip Dewsbury (Wakef) 1955–58; V Landrake w St Erny (Truro) 1958–70; Perm to Off Dio Wakefield 1971–74

>eldest s. of Arthur William of Dublin

>m. 24 Jul 1922 Mabel Craig 3rd **dau.** of James George Potter of Dublin. Issue Derek Arthur b. 26 Jan 1925 and killed on active service in RN in WWII

>**Died** 20 Jun 1974 **bur.** Thornes Wakefield

BATTERSBY, WILLIAM BOLTON 1899–1953

b. 1899; TCD BA 1933 MA 1937

d 1933 p 1934 (Kilmore); C Annagh (Kilm) 1933–34; C–in c Ballintemple (Kilm) 1934–47; R Kilronan and Kilmactranny (Ard) 1947–50

>s. of Rev Francis Hoffmann, R Kilcock (Kild) 1896–1924 by Elizabeth Bolton (**died** 31 Dec 1915) **dau.** of William Wallace Hartford of Blackrock Dublin; **bro.** of Rev John Alexander, R Christ Ch Hemel Hempstead (St A)

>m. 5 Feb 1929 Rathmines Dublin Eva Barry (**died** 10 Jan 1965 Hastings) elder **dau.** of Rev Adolph Paul Weinberger, C St Matthias (Dub) 1897–99. Issue 1. Lilac Brigid b. 27 Dec 1933; 2. Daphne Rachel m. 22 Dec 1958 at Hove Bryan Christopher elder s. of Ernest MacD Foster of Uckfield Sussex

Died 27 Apr 1953 Dublin

BAXTER, MARTIN

d 31 May 1618 p 1 Nov 1618 (Kilm); V Kildallon (Kilm) 1618–*c.* 56. The R & V Tomregan (Kilm) were united to Kildallon by the Bishop 20 Oct 1626 and Baxter was coll R & V Tomregan 1 Nov 1626. He got a grant of a glebe here 25 Jan 1626/27; in Tomregan in 1634 and poss to 1661

BAYLEY (BAYLIE), WILLIAM

inst V Annagelliffe (Kilm) 1637; also inst V Templeport (Kilm) 21 Aug 1637; again inst V 6 Jun 1638 and 25 Jun; V Denn (Kilm) 1634–37; poss V Urney (Kilm) 1638–39; may be same as Bp William Baylie qv In Harcourt's *Remonstrance*, "Dr. Bayly of Cavan", is said to have fled to England in 1641

†BAYLIE, WILLIAM –1664

pres to R Granard (Ard) 15 Feb 1661/62 (LM V 114), Bp of Clonfert, 1644–64; vacated the V by his death in 1664 (FF)

Died 1664

BAYLY, GEORGE ALEXANDER –1949

TCD BA & Div Test 1899 MA 1903

d 1899 p 1900 (Kilmore); C Urney w Annagalliffe (Kilm) 1899–1902; C Sandford (Dub) 1902–03; C St Matthew Hammersmith (Lon) 1903–04; C St Paul Cliftonville Margate (Cant) 1904–06; C Templemichael (Ard) 1906–07; C Kilnamanagh (Ferns) 1907–08; R Glascarrig (Ferns) 1908–15; R Clonmore (Leigh) 1915–17; V Woodmancote (Win) 1917–27; V Kingsley w Oakhanger (Win) 1927–30; Chapl Poor Law Inst Winchester from 1931; Chapl RAF 1933–39; Officiating at RN Air Station Worthy Down from 1939

m. Susannah Sophia (**died** 1 Nov 1963)

Died 5 Aug 1949 Winchester

BAYLY, THOMAS JOHNSTON 1870–1946

b. 26 Jan 1870; ed Rathmines Sch Dublin; TCD BA 1893 MA 1907

d 1893 p 1894; C Calry (Elph) 1893–98; I Kilmore (Elphin) 1898–1903; C St Peter Drogheda (Arm) 1903–08; I Termonmaguirke (Arm) 1908–16; R Mohill (Ard) 1916–21; R Theberton (w C-in-c Bruisyard 1928–35 and w Dunwich 1933–35) (St E) 1922–35; R Stanningfield and Bradfield Combust (St E) 1935–

s. of Thomas Lonsdale Alexander of Terenure Dublin

m. 30 Jun 1908 St Peter's Ch Drogheda Caroline Annette Kinnear (Carrie) 3rd dau. of Alexander Milne Provincial Bank Hse Drogheda

Died 8 May 1946

BEATTY, EDWARD 1760/61–

is probably E B **b.** in Cavan; **b.** 1760 or 1761 Co Cavan; ed by Mr Beatty; ent TCD 6 Apr 1778 aged 17 BA 1782

d 13 Jul 1783 (Ossory) R & V Kilcommick 1807 and 1814; held also Moydow?

probably E B **s.** of Robert, Farmer

BEATTY, JOHN 1726/27–c. 1809

b. 1726 or 1727 Co Cavan; ed by Mr Hughes; ent TCD as Sizar 11 Jun 1744 aged 17 Sch 1747 BA 1749; he was a schoolfellow of Oliver Goldsmith at Edgeworthstown, and afterwards shared rooms with him at No 35 TCD (Forster's *Life of Goldsmith*)

Lic C Knockbride (Kilm) 29 Apr 1754; C Granard (Ard) 1762; C Killeshandra (Kilm) 2 Jul 1768; V Garvaghy (Drom) 1777–93; res.

s. of Edward of Dingens Co Cavan, Capt Cavan Militia

m. (1) 23 Aug 1760 in Killeshandra Par Ch Abigail **dau.** of Matthew Young of Lahard Co Cavan by Frances **dau.** of William Nesbitt of Dromalee Co Cavan, High Sheriff Co Cavan 1704; she was buried at Killeshandra 22 Nov 1767. Issue **sons** 1. Rev Thomas qv below; 2. John MD of Molesworth St Dublin, **m.** and had issue incl Rev John, R Donaghcloney (Drom); **daus.** 1. Frances **m.** Rev Arnold Cosby MA, R Killinkere Co Cavan; 2. Catherine who **died** in childhood Mar 1771

m. (2) Eleanor widow of Robert Beatty of Springtown Co Longford and **dau.** of ——Thompson

Died *c.* 1809

BEATTY, JOHN

a John Beatty was ordained priest 22 June 1788 (SR); probably C Drumlummon (Ard); signed Parl Ret 1766

BEATTY, ROBERT 1725–1804

b. 1725 Newry; ent TCD 19 Mar 1739/40 Sch 1742 BA 1744 MA 1747

C Shrule (Ard) 1755–65; R Muckno (Clogh) 1768–93; R Moydow (Ard) *c.* 1770 to at least 1777 and poss 1793; V Gen Ardagh 1776–1804; Archd of Ardagh 1790–1804

s. of William

m. Jan 1769 Ellen **dau.** of Theobald Butler of Priestown Co Meath and Waterville Co Kerry by Mary **dau.** of Sir Nathaniel Whitwell of Dublin. Issue 1. Ven Robert jun qv below; 2. James, Barrister at Law; 3. Ellen

Died 26 Dec 1804 aged 79

BEATTY, ROBERT 1773/74–1821

b. 1773 or 1774 Co Longford; ent TCD 7 Jul 1790 aged 16 BA 1795 MA 1799

R Moydow (Ard) 1793–1821; he appears R & V Teighsinod or of Tashinny (Ard) in report of 1807 and Lea 1814, and evidently held it with Moydow. From Tuam S.R. it appears that he was inst R & V Taghsinod & Moydow & Kilcommick (Ard) 25 Feb

1805; Archd of Ardagh 1805–21

    s. of Ven Robert qv above

    m. (ML 6 May 1809) Elizabeth Beatty of the Parish of St Andrew Dublin and **sister** of Sir William Beatty. Issue Eliza m. 11 Oct 1830 Clontarf Par Ch Dublin William Carlile Henderson QC

    Died 4 Sep 1821 at Moydow

BEATTY, ROBERT

inst R & V Kilcommick (Ard) 25 Feb 1805

probably same as Robert Beatty, Archd of Ardagh qv above

BEATTY, ROBERT 1832/33–1921

b. 1832 or 1833; TCD BA & Div Test 1856 MA 1877

d 1857 p 1858; C Ballymachugh (Ard) 1860–70; R Ballymachugh (Ard) 1870–78; poss same as Robert Beatty C Gowna 1871–72; R Kilnaughtin (A & A) 1878–1916; R Kilfergus (Lim) 1891–1916; Treas of Ardfert 1903–05; Chanc of Ardfert 1905–11; Dean of Ardfert 1911–16

    s. of William, Capt Clare Militia, formerly Cornet 8th Hussars

    Died 7 Feb 1921 aged 88

BEATTY, THOMAS 1761/62–1841

b. 1761 or 1762 Co Longford; ed by his father; ent TCD 6 Jul 1779 aged 17 BA 1785

d 21 Aug 1785 (Drom) p 4 Jun 1786 (Drom); C Granard (Ard) 1787–*c*. 91; V Gen of Drom 1 May 1789; V Garvaghy (Drom) 1793–1813; JP Co Down in 1797; V Tullylish (Drom) 1813–29; R Moira (Drom) 1829–36

    s. of Rev John, V Garvaghy (Drom) qv above (s. of Edward) by Abigail dau. of Matthew Young of Lahard Co Cavan

    m. 14 May 1797 his first cousin Letitia (**died** 30 Aug 1833) dau. of Capt Robert Armstrong, 50th Foot of Hackwood Co Cavan by Dorothy dau. of Matthew Young of Lahard Co Cavan

    Died 28 Sep 1841 in his 80th year without issue

BEAUMONT, HENRY FOXTON 1890–1962

b. 1890; ed St Andrew's Coll Dublin; TCD & Div Test (1) 1913 MA 1927

d 1913 p 1914 (Kilmore); C Larah & Lavey (Kilm) 1913–15; TCF 1915–19; C St John Monkstown (Dub) 1919–20; Asst Master Plymouth Coll and SSC Dio Exeter (Ex) 1920–25; C Buckland Monachorum (Ex) 1925–27; V Stoke Gabriel (Ex) 1927–62; Chapl RN 1942–45

    s. of William of Ballinrobe

    m. 14 Jun 1917 Eileen dau. of James Frederick Knowles of Birkdale Lancs. Issue 1. Elizabeth Knowles b. 29 Dec 1919; 2. Bruce Gabriel Mayne b. 28 Apr 1927

    Died 12 Aug 1962

BECKETT, THOMAS ALEXANDER 1873/74–1925

b. 1873 or 1874; TCD BA 1900 MA 1903

d 1901 p 1902 (St. Alban's); C St John's Stratford (St A) 1901–04; C Drumcliffe Ennis (Killaloe) 1904–07; C-in-c Drumlane (Kilm) 1907–08; C-in-c Killinkere (Kilm) 1908–09; R Tubbercurry (Ach) 1910–25

> **m.** Elizabeth (Lily) (**died** 26 Feb 1968 Dublin **bur.** Dean's Grange) and had issue incl 1. Thomas **m.** 18 Oct 1941 Gladys **dau.** of Mr Audley of Woodley England; 2. Lolo **m.** Michael **s.** of Michael Hunter of Worplesden
>
> **Died** 23 Jan 1925 aged 51

†BEDELL, WILLIAM 1571–1642

b. 1571 at Black Notley Essex; bapt 14 Jan 1572; ed at Braintree Essex; adm Pensioner Emmanuel Coll Camb 1 Nov 1584 Sch 1585 BA 1589 MA 1592 Fellow 1593 BD 1599

d; ord p 10 Jan 1597 at Colchester Bp 1629; served at St Mary Bury St Edmunds (now St E) 1602–07; served as Chapl to Sir Henry Wotton, British Ambassador at Venice 1607–10; R Horningsheath Suffolk (then Nor) 1616–27; 5th Provost of TCD 1627–29; appointed Bp of Kilmore (w Ardagh to 1633) by Patent 20 May 1629 and was consec at St Peter's Drogheda 13 Sep 1629; Bp of Kilmore (w Ardagh to 1633) 1629–43.

> 2nd **s.** of John (**died** 1600), yeoman by Elizabeth (*née* Aliston or Elliston) (**died** 1624)
>
> **m.** 29 Jan 1612 Leah L'Estrange or Bowles (**died** 26 Mar 1638) **b.** *c.* 1581 widow of Robert Mawe (**died** 1609). Issue 1. William **b.** 14 Feb 1613 qv; 2. Grace **b.** 29 May 1614 **m.** Alexander Clogie; 3. John **b.** 9 Aug 1616; 4. Ambrose **b.** 21 Mar 1618
>
> **Died** 7 Feb 1642 **bur.** Kilmore
>
> Bishop Bedell was a noted scholar and linguist. He learned Irish in order to translate the Bible into Irish, in the hope that the Irish people might be encouraged to conform to the Church of Ireland in the turbulent period following the Reformation. He died at the hands of rebels shortly after being released from Clough Oughter Castle where he had been imprisoned in freezing conditions in the winter of 1642. He was widely respected by many on all sides, nevertheless, for his gentle and gracious manner

PUBLICATIONS

Il libro delle preghiere publiche ed administrazione de sacramenti…secundo l'uso della chiesa Anglicana, Italian translation of the Prayer Book and other pious works, published posthumously, London 1685

Petri Suavis Polani historiae Concilii Tridentini, a translation into Latin of Part of Paolo Sarpi's history of the Council of Trent, 1620

The Copies of Certaine Letters which have passed between Spaine and England in matter of Religion, concerning the generall motives to the Roman obedience betweene J. Wadesworth, a late member of the holy Inquisition in Siuill, and W. Bedell a minister of the Gospell of Iesus

Christ in Suffolk, W. Stansby for W. Barrett and R. Milbourne, 1624

The Free School of Warre, or a treatise, whether it be lawfull to beare armes for the seruice of a Prince that is of a diuers religion, a translation of a book by Paolo Sarpi, John Bill, London, 1625

Interdicti Venetia Historia, de motu Italiae sub initia Pontificatus Pauli V Commentaries…Recens ex Italico converses, Cambridge, 1626

An Examination of Certaine Motives to Recusansie, 1628

Aibigtir I Theaguisg Cheudtosugheadh an Chriostaidhe (The A.B.C., or, The Institution of a Christian, A Catechism with parallel English and Irish texts, Company of Stationers, Dublin, 1631

Irenicum, in quo casus conscientiae praecipui de viis quaerendae &

Constituendae inter Ecclesius evangelicas religiosae pacis breviter

Proponuntur & decidujntur, 1654

*Leabhuir na Seintiomna …*The Books of the Old Testament translated into Irish by the care and diligence of Doctor William Bedel, late Bishop of Kilmore, London, 1685

Of the Efficiency of Grace Psalms in Irish, Hanna & Neale, London, 1912

A Letter to Mr. James Waddesworth in reply to several letters from him upon the principal points of controversy between Papists and Protestants;

to which is added the Prospectus of the Christian Institute, and an

address which was delivered at its formation, London, Howell &

Stewart, 1827

Some Original Letters of Bishop Bedell, concerning the steps taken toward a reformation of religion at Venice, upon occasion of the quarrel between that State and Pope Paul V, Ed. Edward Hudson, Dublin, George Faulkner, 1742

A protestant memorial: or, the shepherd's tale of the Powder–Plot. A poem in Spenser's style; published from an original MS, J. Roberts, London,

1713

An da chead leabhar do Mhaoise, Genesis agus Exodus, ar na ttaruing… chum Gaoilge tre churam, G & J Grierson & M. Keene, Dublin, 1827

The judgement of the late Archbishop of Armagh and Primate of Ireland. Of Babylon (Rev. 18.4) being the present See of Rome. (With a sermon of Bishop Bedell's upon the same words). Of laying on of hands (Heb. 6.2). to be an ordained ministry. Of the old form of words in ordination. Of a set form of prayer. Published and enlarged by Nicholas Bernard D.D. and preacher to the Honourable Society of Gray's Inn, London. Unto which is added a character of Bishop Bedell and an answer to Mr. Pierce's fifth letter concerning the late primate, 1659.

The Life and Death of Desiderius Erasmus To the Right Honourable the Lords Justices and Council. The humble Remonstrance of the Gentry, and Commonality, of the County of Cavan, &c.

BEDELL, WILLIAM

coll V Kinawley (Kilm) 6 Jun 1634 and 5 Aug 1635; same as the Bishop above?

MA of Oxford or Cambridge

d 5 Jun 1634 p; coll V Kinawley (Kilm) 6 Jun 1634 and 5 Aug 1635; R Rattlesden Suffolk 1645-70; Preb of Inniscattery and R Kilrush (Killaloe) 1672-74; V Kilballyhone Moyberta and Kilmichill (Killaloe); Preb of Tulloh (Killaloe) 1672-88

eldest s. of Rt Rev William, Bp of Kilmore, qv.

m. and had issue 1. Ambrose of Cavan; 2. William b. at Rattlesden ent TCD 26 May 1662 aged 17 Sch 1663; 3. Isabella m. 1668 Major Daniel French of Belturbet Co Cavan; 4. a dau. m. Rev J Laury.

BEECHE, WILLIAM HENRY

BA

coll V Kilgeffin (Elph) 29 Nov 1838; may have been there to 1849

BEERE, FRANCIS JOHN 1825–1912

b. 1825 Dublin; ed by Mr Flynn; ent TCD 6 Nov 1843 aged 18 BA & Div Test 1848

d 1851 p 1852 (Kilmore); C Elphin (Elph) 1851–53; C Toomna (Elph) 1853–56; V Kilgeffin (Elph) 1856–61; V Toomna (Elph) 1861–72; C Kinawley (Kilm) 1872–78; R Ballyjamesduff w Castlerahan (Kilm) 1878–1901; ret

s. of George, *pragmaticus*

m. Eleanor Martha (died 4 May 1900) dau. of Rev Thomas Flynn of Elphin, qv Issue incl his eldest son Francis William (died 10 Feb 1924 London); his yst dau. Minnie (died 24 Nov 1943)

Died 3 Sep 1912 Virginia Co Cavan aged 86

BEERE, FRANCIS JOHN ARMSTRONG 1869/70–1932

b. 1869 or 1870; TCD BA 1894 MA 1898

d 1893 p 1894; C Clongish (Ard) 1893–97; C Streete (Ard) 1897–1900; R Streete (Ard) 1900–07; R Forgney (Meath) 1907–13; R Kilbixy (Meath) 1913–24; R Kells (Meath) 1924–32

3rd s. of Nenon Francis of Abercorn Hse Dublin

m. 24 Oct 1898 Lucie Maude (died 2 Apr 1956) only dau. of Very Rev Frederick Potterton, Dean of Ardagh qv Issue 1. Thekla Jane TCD BA (Sen Mod) LLB; 2. Jocelyn Ruth m. 30 Sep 1930 Dr Hubert elder s. of George H Lowry, Sheriff of Meath

Died 12 May 1932 aged 62

BELL, EDWARD 1823/24–c. 1881

b. 1823 or 1824 Co Cork; ed at Ennis Coll; ent TCD 6 Nov 1843 aged 19 BA 1848 MA 1857 d 1849 p; C Durrus (Cork) 1849–54; C Kinneigh (Cork) 1855–60; C Killough (Down) 1860–62; C Dundalk (Arm) 1862–67; PS Sixmilecross *alias* Cooley (Arm) 1867–71; C New Ross (Ferns) 1871–73; R Killermogh (Leigh, then Oss) 1873–78; prob same as Edward Bell R Killargue (Kilm) 1878–79

    s. of Thomas, solicitor

    m. (1) 3 Jan 1860 St Peter's Ch Cork Mary Anne Gibben. Issue 1. a **dau.** b 5 Jan 1862 Killough Co Down; 2. Edith **b.** 6 Aug 1863 Dundonald Belfast

    m. (2) 12 May 1870 St Mark's Ch Portadown Anne Chamney (**died** 13 Dec 1876 at Killermogh aged 50) yst **dau.** of Mr E Atkinson

    Died *c.* 1881

BELL, ROBERT THOMAS 1790/91–1828

b. 1790 or 1791 Co Cavan; ent TCD as FC 1 Feb 1808 aged 17 BA 1813

C Castlerahan (Kilm) *c.* 1821–25; PC Ashfield (Kilm) 1825–28

    s. of Andrew, *armiger*

    m. (ML 1827) Elizabeth Jane widow of Moutray Erskine of Cavan **dau.** of Thomas Wilson, MA of Cavan

    Died 6 Jan 1828 at Ashfield Glebe **bur.** Kilmore

BELL, SAMUEL JAMES

Univ of Saskatchewan BA 1945; Emmanuel Coll Saskatchewan LTh with distinction 1945

d 1936 (Saskatchewan for Athabasca) p 1937 (Athabasca); Missy at Hines Creek 1936–41; V Manville Alberta (Dio Saskatchewan)1941–46; V Wetaskiwin Alberta (Dio Edmonton) 1946–48; Missy at Fort Simpson NW Territories (Dio Mackenzie River) 1948–53; BC Derrylane (Kilm) 1953–55; R Hanover Ontario (Dio Huron) 1955–57; R Timmins (Dio Moosonee) 1957–58; Dean of Moosonee 1957–61; Exam Chapl to Bp of Moosonee 1960–61; Missy at Hay River NW Territories (Dio Mackenzie River) 1961–63; I Walter Falls (Dio Huron) 1963–66; R Kirkton Ontario (Dio Huron) 1966–69; R Chesley Ontario (Dio Huron) 1969–75; P-in-c Wheatley Ontario (Dio Huron) 1976–78; R St Patrick Mt Pleasant Tobago (Dio Trinidad) 1981–*c.* 83

BENNETT, JOHN 1681/82–

b. 1681 or 1682 Cavan; ed at Westminster Sch; ent TCD 20 May 1701 aged 19 Sch 1703 BA 1705

V Denn (Kilm) 1709–26, holding also by faculty V Innismagrath (Kilm) 1719–26; R & V Annaduff (Ard) 1726–40, coll 4 (or 14) Mar 1726 (F.F.)

    prob John Bennet (or Bennett) **s.** of George

    m. and had issue incl Rev Joseph, R Kilronan (Ard) qv

BENNETT, JOHN

coll V of Kiltoghart (Ard) 1740–c90; coll 27 Oct 1740

BENNETT, JOSEPH 1710/11–

b. 1710 or 1711 nr Cootehill Co Cavan; ed by Rev Maurice Neligan, Longford; ent TCD 3 Jun 1729 aged 18 BA 1739

V Kilronan (Ard) 17–

    s. of Rev John, V Annaduff (Ard) qv

    m. and had issue incl Joseph **b.** Co Leitrim ed by Mr Kenny ent TCD 1 Jul 1776 aged 17 BA 1781

BENNETT, JOSEPH

C Kiltoghart (Ard) lic 17 Jun 1743 (S.R.)

BENNETT, JOSEPH

C Kiltoghart (Ard) lic 1 May 1781 (S.R.)

BERE, GERALD NENON O'GRADA

d 1889; C Larah & Lavey (Kilm) 1889–90

BERESFORD, CHARLES CALUDIUS 1810–1848

b. 14 Dec 1810; ed Royal Sch Armagh; ent TCD as SC 3 Nov 1828 BA 1832 Div Test 1833

d 10 Aug 1834 (Down) p 3 May 1835 (Kilmore); V Drumlane (Kilm) 1835–37; R Bailieborough and Moybologue (Kilm) 1837–48

    3rd **s.** of Rev Carles Cobbe, R Killesher (Kilm) qv (**s.** of Rt Hon John and Anne Constantia) by Amelia **dau.** of Sir William Montgomery, Bt; **bro.** of Rev John Isaac, R Drumlane (Kilm) qv

    m. 8 Aug 1838 Anna Maria only **dau.** of Rev Frederick Fitzpatrick, MA, R Lurgan (Kilm) qv Issue **sons** 1. Charles Cobbe; 2. Frederick John Isaac; **daus.** 1. Edwina Katherine (**died** 11 Mar 1926 aged 83); 2. Amelia Mary Selina (also **died** 11 Mar 1926 aged 78)

    Died 29 Aug 1848

BERESFORD, CHARLES COBBE 1770–1850

b. 2 Oct 1770 Co Dublin; ed privately; ent TCD 16 Jan 1787 BA 1790 MA 1807

Preb of Timothan in St Patrick's Cath Dublin 1798–1805; Chanc of Christ Ch Cath Dublin 1802–09; R Carrigallen (Kilm) 1804–09; R Killesher (Kilm) 1805–50; R Termonmaguirke (Arm) 1809–50

    4th **s.** of Rt Hon John, Barrister-at-Law (**s.** of Sir Marcus, 1st Earl of Tyrone) by Anne Constantia (**died** 26 Oct 1770) **dau.** of Gen Count de Ligondes; **bro.** of Rt Rev George, Bp of Kilmore qv, and nephew of Henry, Marquess of Waterford; nephew of Most Rev William, Abp of Tuam qv

    m. 22 Nov 1795 Amelia (**died** 14 Mar 1839 **bur.** Termonmaguirke) **dau.** of Sir William Montgomery, Bt of Magbiehill, Peebles. Issue 1. Rev John Isaac, R

Drumlane (Kilm) qv; 2. George John **b.** 21 Jul 1807, Col in RA **m.** and had issue; 3. Rev Charles Claudius, R Bailieborough or Moybologue (Kilm) qv

Died 13 Dec 1850 **bur.** Termonmaguirke

BERESFORD, Hon. GEORGE de la POER 1775–1842

b. 1775; ent TCD 28 Dec 1791 aged 16 LLB & LLD 1797; Emmanuel Coll Camb

d 25 Jun 1797 p 1 May 1798 (Dublin); Preb of Faldown and R Killererin (Tuam) 1798–1816; R Kilglass (Ard) *c.* 1802–06; V Mohill (Ard) *c.* 1807–16; V Fenagh (Ard) 1816–42; V Chor Cork 1816–26; Provost of Tuam 1816–42

    2nd **s.** of Most Rev William, 1st Lord Decies, Abp of Tuam qv below and **bro.** of Rev John and Rev William qv

    m. May 1798 Susan 3rd **dau.** of Hamilton Gorges of Kilbrew. Issue 1. Rev William; 2. Lt Gen Marcus; 3. Rev George Hamilton qv below; 4. John Gorges; 5. Capt Henry; 2 **daus.**, 1. Elizabeth Anne **m.** Myles O'Reilly; 2. Susan **m.** (1) Matthew O'Reilly; **m.** (2) 2 Jun 1842 Gerald S Fitzgerald

    Died 10 Aug 1842 at Bundoran Co Donegal aged 67

†BERESFORD, GEORGE de la POER 1765–1841

b. 19 Jul 1765 Dublin; ed by Dr Stokes; ent TCD as SC 30 Oct 1782 aged 17 BA 1786 DD by Diploma 1802

Preb of Seskenan (Waterf) 1789–1801; R & V Donoughmore (Oss) 1790–97; Treas of Ossory 1792–97; Prec of Waterford 1793–1801; Dean of Kilmore and V Kilmore & Ballintemple (Kilm) 1796–1801; Bp of Clonfert 1801–02; consec at St Thomas' Ch Dublin 1 Feb 1801; Bp of Kilmore (w Ardagh from 1839) 1802–41

    s. of Rt Hon John (**s.** of Sir Marcus and Catherine) by Anne Constantia **dau.** of Gen Count de Ligondes; **bro.** of Rev Charles Cobbe, R Carrigallen (Kilm) qv; nephew of Most Rev William, Abp of Tuam qv below,

    m. (ML 26 Mar 1794) Frances (**died** 19 May 1843 at Ballyhaise Rectory) **dau.** of Gervais Parker Bushe of Kilfane. Issue **sons** 1. John, Colonial Sec of St Vincent **m.** and had issue; 2. Marcus Gervais DD, Bp of Kilmore and Abp of Armagh qv; 3. Rev George de la Poer, C Kildallon (Kilm) qv; **daus.** 1. Charlotte Mary (**died** 1851) **m.** (1) 2 May 1812 Frederick L Savile (**died** 1827) **m.** (2) 20 Jul 1839 Robert Henry Southwell; 2. Frances (**died** 17 Nov 1833) **m.** Hon Rev Francis Howard

    Died 15 or 16 Oct 1841 **bur.** Kilmore

Bishop Beresford built the Palace at Kilmore

BERESFORD, Hon. GEORGE HAMILTON de la POER –1869

b. in Cork; ed by Mr Caldwell; ent TCD 5 Apr 1819 BA 1824

d 1825 p 1826 (Cloyne); R & V Monanimy (Cloyne) 1826–28; R Knockbride (Kilm) 1828–35; R Templeport (Kilm) 1835–42; R Fenagh (Ard) 1843–69

    3rd **s.** of Hon George qv above by Susan (*née* Gorges)

    m. (1) Nov 1829 Elizabeth **dau.** of Matthew Nisbet of Derrycarn Co Leitrim and had issue

m. (2) 8 Mar 1853 Marian Sarah widow of Rev John Delap and **dau.** of Robert Saunderson

One of his **daus. m.** Capt Antoine Sloet Butler yr **s.** of Sir Thomas, RM, and by her (his 1st wife) had a **s.** G B Butler, RM

Died 2 Mar 1869 at Fenagh Rectory

BERESFORD, JOHN de la POER 1773–1855

b. 20 Jan 1773

d 1803 (Cloyne) p 1803; R & V Burrishoole Kilmina and Achill (Tuam) 1803–09; inst V Maghery Granard & Gowna (Ard) 25 Feb 1805; R Gowna & Granard 1805–11; did he succeed Robert Beatty who was same day inst to Kilcommick and Moydow (Ard)? R Aherne and Ballymore (Cloyne) 1806–55; Preb of Kilrossanty (Lism) 1812–55

s. of Most Rev William, 1st Baron Decies, Abp of Tuam 1795–1819 (3rd **s.** of Marcus, Earl of Tyrone) by Elizabeth **dau.** of John FitzGibbon; succeeded his father as 2nd Baron Decies in Sep 1819; **bro.** of Rev George, Provost of Tuam; **bro.** of Rev William, Preb of Laccagh (Tuam)

m. 26 Jul 1810 Charlotte Philadelphia only **dau.** of Robert Horsley of Bolam Hse Northumberland and assumed the name of Horsley–Beresford. Issue 1. William Robert John, 3rd Lord Decies; **daus.** 1. Georgina Catherine **m.** (1) William Watson **m.** (2) Henry Edward Brown; 2. Louisa Elizabeth **m.** Hon. Ernest Bruce **s.** of the 1st Marquess of Salisbury; 3. Caroline Agnes **m.** 1836 the Duke of Montrose

Died 1 Mar 1855

BERESFORD, JOHN CLAUDIUS 1871/72–1949

b. 1871 or 1872; TCD BA 1896 Div Test 1898 MA 1898

d 1897 (Armagh for Kilmore) p 1898 (Kilmore); C Drumgoon (Kilm) 1897–1900; R Bailieborough (Kilm) 1900–07; R Kiltoghart (w C-in-c Toomna in Dio Elphin 1923–31 & w Annaduff W from 1932) (Ard) 1907–49; Chapl to Leitrim Co Infirmary 1907–49; Chapl to Seamens' Miss to port of Carrick-on-Shannon 1912–49; TCF 1918; RD Fenagh 1921–49; Chapl Actors' U 1929–49; Chapl Leitrim Co Home 1937–49; Preb of Oran (Elph) 1938–44; Dean of Elphin and Ardagh 1944–49

s. of Major–General Beresford of Portrush Co Antrim; Dean Beresford was grandson of Rev. William Smyly, R Aghanloo (Derry) who married a **dau.** of the Lord Mayor, whose son took the name of Beresford

m. Frances Alice (**died** 15 Jan 1968 Greystones Co Wicklow) and had issue incl 1. elder or eldest **s.** Vyvyan (**died** 13 Jan 1956 at Perth Western Australia aged 45); 2. his yr **s.** Rev John Claudius William, Dio C Kilmore Elphin and Ardagh qv; 3. a **dau.**

Died 5 Jul 1949 aged 77

BERESFORD, JOHN CLAUDIUS WILLIAM 1911–*c.* 1990

b. 1911; TCD BA 1935 MA 1950; MC 1945

d 1936 p 1937 (Oss); C Rathdowney (Oss) 1936–39; Dio C Kilmore Elphin and

Ardagh 1939–40; CF (EC) 1940–46; I Loughrea w Tynagh and Killinane (Clonf) 1946–50; R Carbury (Kild) 1950–54; R Naas U (Kild) 1954–86; Treas and Canon of St Brigid's Cath Kildare (Kild) 1961–64; Chanc of Kildare 1964–72; Prec of Kildare 1972–76 Archd of Kildare 1976–79; Prec of Kildare 1979–86; ret

    s. of Very Rev John Claudius, Dean of Elphin and Ardagh qv (**s.** of Major–General Beresford)

    m. 1941 Jean Graham Hastings 3rd **dau.** of Rev J Little, Presby Minister

    Died *c.* 1990 Last entry in C I Dir 1990

BERESFORD, JOHN ISAAC 1796–1857

b. 13 Oct 1796 Dublin; ed by Dr Dowdall; Royal Sch Dungannon; ent TCD 2 Jan 1815 BA 1818 MA 1821

V Drumlane (Kilm) 1821–35; Preb of Moyne (Oss) 1821–23; R Donoughmore (Oss) 1823–47

    s. of Rev Charles Cobbe, R Killesher (Kilm) qv (**s.** of Rt Hon John and Anne Constantia) by Amelia **dau.** of Sir William Montgomery, Bt; **bro.** of Rev Charles Claudius, R Moybologue (Kilm) qv

    m. 13 Jun 1824 Sophia (**died** 27 Nov 1858) **dau.** of Robert White of Aghavoe Co Laois. Issue 1. Emily Sarah **m.** 6 May 1851 Very Rev John Maunsell Massy Beresford, Dean of Kilmore qv; 2. George Robert **b.** 18 Oct 1830 (**died** 6 Apr 1871 unm) of Machie Hill NB, Capt 88th Foot; 3. Harriet Selina **m.** 1856 William Allan Woodrop of Dalmarnoch NB

    Died 9 Feb 1857

BERESFORD, JOHN MAUNSELL MASSY 1823–1886

b. 26 Sep 1823; ed by Mr Hartshorn; ent TCD as SC 2 Jul 1841 BA 1846 MA 1849; assumed the additional name of Beresford in 1871 on succeeding to the estate of Macbie Hall in Scotland

d 1848 p 1850 (Cork); PC Killoughter (Kilm) 1856–70; R Kinawley (Kilm) 1870–82; Dean of Kilmore 1870–86

    3rd **s.** of Hon John Massy (**s.** of Hugh, 2nd Baron Massy)

    m. 6 May 1851 Emily Sarah (**died** 28 Jul 1893 London aged 65) **dau.** of Rev John Isaac Beresford, R Drumlane (Kilm) qv Issue incl **sons** 1. John George Beresford, JP (**died** Jul 1923) **b.** 1856; 2. a **s. b.** 1857; 3. a **s. b.** 11 Mar 1864; **daus.** 1. Anna Sophia; 2. Emily Louisa Maria

    Died 22 Oct 1886 at Macbie Hall

†BERESFORD, MARCUS GERVAIS de la POER 1801–1885

b. 14 Feb 1801 at the Custom House Dublin; ed at Richmond Yorks; Trinity Coll Camb BA 1820 MA 1827 (*ad eund*) TCD 1832) DD 1844

d 9 May 1824 p 20 Mar 1825 (Kilmore) Bp 1854; I Kildallon (Kilm) 1825–28; V Drung and Larah (Kilm) and VGen Kilmore 1828–54; Archd of Ardagh 1839–54; appointed Bp of Kilmore Elphin and Ardagh by Letters Patent and consec at Armagh

Cath 24 Sep 1854; enthroned in Cavan 8 Oct 1854; enthroned in Elphin Cath 20 Oct 1854; Bp of Kilmore Elphin and Ardagh 1854–62; Abp of Armagh and Bp of Clogher and Primate and Metropolitan of All Ireland 1862–85; Prelate of the Most Illustrious Order of St Patrick and Lord Almoner to Queen Victoria

> 2nd **s.** of Rt Rev George de la Poer DD Bp of Kilmore and Ardagh 1802–41 qv (**s.** of John, Commissioner of Revenue in Ireland) by Frances **dau.** of Gervais Parker Bushe of Kilfane Co Kilkenny, MP for Kilkenny

> **m.** (1) 25 Oct 1824 Mary (**died** 31 Dec 1845) **dau.** of Col Henry Peisley L'Estrange of Moystown Co Laois and widow of Richard Edward Digby of Geashill Co Laois. Issue (1) George de la Poer **b.** 22 Apr 1831 of Auburn Co Cavan, DL JP High Sheriff 1867 MP for Armagh City 1875–85 **m.** 24 Apr 1860 Mary Annabella **dau.** of Rev William Vernon Harcourt of Nuneham Berks, nephew of 2nd Lord Vernon; he died 3 Aug 1906; 2. Henry Marcus **b.** 2 Mar 1835 Major in 9th Foot Regt **m.** 10 Apr 1861 Julia Ellen **dau.** of Rev Frances Richard Maunsell R Castleisland (A & A); he died 5 Feb 1895 leaving issue; 3. Charlotte Henrietta **m.** 16 Aug 1853 Henry Beilby William Milner, MA (**died** 7 Jun 1876) of Kirkstall Grange, Leeds; she died 15 Sep 1884 leaving issue; 4. Mary Emily **m.** 16 Aug 1853 Col Thomas Heywood DL of Hatley St George Worcestershire **sister** of Mary Sumner founder of MU and had issue (i) Henry de la Poer Beresford **b.** 23 Jan 1855 **m.** 15 Jun 1882 Minnie Florence Newton (ii) Constance Mary **m.** 7 Dec 1882 Alfred J Butler DLitt, Fellow of Brasenose Coll Oxford (iii) Emily Frances **died unm.** 12 Sep 1919

> **m.** (2) 6 Jun 1850 Elizabeth (**died** 1 Jul 1870) widow of Robert George Bomford of Rahenstown Co Meath and only **dau.** of James Trail Kennedy of Annadale Co Down

> **Died** 26 Dec 1885 at the Palace, Armagh **bur.** Armagh Cathedral

> Note: Archbishop Beresford was Primate at the time of the Disestablishment of the Church of Ireland in 1870, a time of turbulence and uncertainty, and his guidance and leadership of the Church then are generally acknowledged to have enabled it to set up sound administrative structures, and to face the future with confidence

†BERESFORD, Hon. WILLIAM 1743–1819

b. 16 Apr 1743; ed by Dr Hewetson at Kilkenny Coll which he entered 24 Jun 1751; ent TCD as FC 18 Dec 1759 BA 1763 MA 1766 DD 1780

Preb of Rathmichael in St Patrick's Cath Dublin and V Bray (Dub) 1764–68; R Bray (Dub) 1765–68; R Termonmaguirke (Arm) 1767–80; R Urney (Derry) 1768–80; consec Bp of Dromore 8 Apr 1780 in the Chapel Royal Dublin; Bp of Dromore 1780–82; Bp of Ossory 1782–95; enthroned 7 Jul 1782; Abp of Tuam and Bp of Ardagh 1795–1819; created Baron Decies 21 Dec 1812

> 3rd **s.** of Marcus, 1st Earl of Tyrone by Lady Catherine Poer **dau.** and heir of James 3rd Earl of Tyrone of the former creation and **bro.** of George, 1st Marquess of Waterford; uncle of Rt Rev George de la Poer, Bp of Kilmore qv

> **m.** 12 Jun 1763 Elizabeth 2nd **dau.** of John FitzGibbon of Mountshannon Co Clare and **sister** of John, Earl of Clare, Lord Chancellor of Ireland. Issue 1. Rev John de la Poer, Preb of Killrossanty (Lism) 1812–65 who succeeded him as Baron Decies; 2. Rev George de la Poer qv; 3. Rev William qv; 5 **daus.**; 1. Catherine Eleanor **m.** Rev William Armstrong of Mealiffe; 2. Araminta Anne **m.** Very Rev A

J Preston, Dean of Limerick; 3. Harriet **m.** Thomas B H Sewell; 4. Frances **m.** Col Thomas Burrowes of Dangan Castle; 5. Louisa **m.** (1) Thomas Hope of Surrey; **m.** (2) Viscount Beresford

Died 8 Sep 1819 Tuam **bur.** Clonegam Co Waterford

BERESFORD, Hon WILLIAM 1780–1830

b. 20 Nov 1780 Dublin; ent TCD 14 Jun 1798 MA 1809; matric Worcester Coll Oxford 19 May 1800 BA 1802

Preb of Lacca (Tuam) 1808–30; Preb of Tullaghorton (Lism) 1809–30; V Ch Tuam 1812–30; R Cloone (Ard) 1816–30

s. of Hon. William, Abp of Tuam qv above (**s.** of Marcus) by Elizabeth (*née* FitzGibbon); **bro.** of Rev John and Rev George qv above

m. Jul 1804 Anna (**died** Sep 1836) **dau.** of Charles, Earl of Tankerville. Issue 1. William; 2. Alicia **m.** Horace Hammond

Died 27 Jun 1830

BERNARD, NICHOLAS –1665

DD FTCD 1633/34

d & p 24 Dec 1636; Chapl to Abp Ussher; V Kilronasartan = Kildrumferton (Kilm) 1630; Dean of Kilmore and V Kilmore & Ballintemple (Kilm) 1627–37; R St Peter Drogheda (Arm) 1634–37; Dean of Ardagh; pres. Jun 22, 1637; appointed Preb of Dromara (Down) 3 Jul 1637

Died 1665

PUBLICATIONS

Life of Primate Ussher, re–published London 1856
The Whole Proceedings of the Siege of Drogheda, 4to 1642

BERRY, GEORGE THOMAS 1887–1969

b. 1887; TCD BA 1910 Div Test (2) 1911 MA 1913

d 1911 p 1912 (Kilm); C St John Sligo 1911–12; C Delvin w Killalon (Meath) 1912–15; R Clonard (Meath) 1915–24; C-in-c Clonfadforan w Castletown (Meath) 1924–26; R Mullingar (Meath) 1926–58; Preb of Tipper in St Patrick's Cath Dublin 1952–58; Canon of Meath 1955–58; ret

yst **s.** of S S Berry of Enniskean Co Cork

m. 29 Dec 1914 Grangegorman Ch Dublin Edith Jane (**died** 22 Nov 1976 **bur.** Drogheda) yr **dau.** of J Watt of Crossakiel. Issue Dermot George, BA BAI **m.** 10 Jan 1945 Adeline **dau.** of E S Doble of Knebworth Hants

Died 5 Feb 1969

BERRY, JAMES FLEETWOOD 1857–1925

b. 1857; TCD BA 1879 Div Test (2) 1881 MA 1883 BD 1889

d 1881 p 1882 (Dublin); C Christ Ch Kingstown (Dun Laoghaire) (Dub) 1881–83;

Dio C Meath 1883–84; C St Matthias (Dub) 1884–87; R Calry (Elph) 1887–90; R St Nicholas Galway 1890–1925; Chapl Galway Workhouse, Prison and Hosp; Dean of Residence UCG 1890–1925; Exam Chapl to Bp of Tuam 1913–25; Acting CF; Canon of Balla in Tuam Cath 1916–23; Chapl to Lord Lt 1919; Archd of Tuam 1923–25

s. of Ven Edward Fleetwood, Archd of Meath

m. Mary E (died 25 Jan 1956 at Salt Hill Galway) dau. of Vice Chancellor Abraham Chatterton of Clyde Rd Dublin. Issue Edward Fleetwood, Wiltshire Regt and Gurkha Rifles (died 17 or 18 Mar 1916 in Great War aged 27).

Died 2 Jul 1925

PUBLICATION

The Story of St Nicholas' Collegiate Church, Galway, 1912

BERTRAM, RICHARD HENRY 1927–

b. 25 Jun 1927 Virginia Co Cavan; ed Cavan Royal Sch; TCD BA & Div Test 1950 MA 1964

d 29 Sep 1953 p 29 Sep 1954; C St John Sligo 1953–56; C Booterstown and Carysfort (Dub) 1956–57; R Stranorlar Meenglass and Kilteevogue (Raph) 1958–65; R St Catherine and St James (Dub) 1965–73; R Irishtown (w Donnybrook from 1974) (Dub) 1973–2002; Canon of Christ Ch Cath Dublin 1986–2002; ret

s. of Joseph Frederick of Virginia and Mary (*née* Byers) of Virginia

m. 10 Jun 1958 Greystones Co Wicklow Doreen Florence dau. of Alexander Robert Thompson of Greystones and Florence (*née* Edwards). Issue 1. Frederick Dudley Alexander b. 4 Nov 1959 m. Dec 1993 Charmaine Digue and resident in Australia; 2. Hilary Lynne b. 4 May 1966

BERWICK, EDWARD 1753/54–1820

b. 1753 or 1754 Co Down; ed by Mr Dubourdieu; ent TCD as Sizar 12 Jun 1770 aged 16 Sch 1773 BA 1774

d 1776 (Down) p 1784 (Killaloe); V Tullylish (Drom) 1787–95; R & V Clongish (Ard) 1795–1820; V Leixlip (Glend) 1795–1820; Dom Chapl to the Earl of Moira

s. of Duke

m. (1) (ML 7 Jan 1791) Anne Bermingham (died 24 Jul 1800) of Monkstown Co Dublin and had issue at least two sons 1. George b. 1799 and 2. Walter b. 1800, Judge of the Bankruptcy Court of Ireland 1859–68; both ent TCD 3 Jul 1815

m. (2) (ML 11 Dec 1802) Rebecca dau. of Pooley Shuldham of Ballymulvey Co Longford. Issue 1. Edward b. 1804, President of Queen's Coll Galway; 2. John b. 1810

Died 3 Jun 1820

PUBLICATIONS

Classical and Theological works including *Lives of Marcus Valerius, Messala Corvinus and Titus Pompinius* 1821
Editor of *The Rawdon Papers*

Rev Edward Berwick gained a reputation for his literary work and there is a life of him in DNB

BETTY (BEATTIE), ROWLAND

ent TCD 8 Jul 1765 BA not recorded

d p 1 May 1773 (Kilmore); C Derryvullan (Clogh) 1773; C Templeport 1785; R Rathbeggan (Meath) 1805–11; was C at Lowtherstown

 prob **s.** of Rev Veitch, C Templeport (Kilm) qv

 Will prov 1811

BETTY (BEATTIE), VEITCH

MA

d May 1750 p 31 Dec 1752; lic C Templeport (Kilm) 13 Nov 1753; again lic 29 Jun 1761 and 10 Jul 1762

 would appear to be a grandson of Adam Betty of Ardcarney Co Fermanagh and afterwards of Aughnecuag Co Cavan who **m.** (ML 14 Oct 1708) Jane widow of — Thornton and **dau.** of —Veitch, and Will dated 16 Mar 1725 proved in Diocese of Kilmore 3 May 1726, having had two **sons** Veitch and John and two **daus.** Mary and Margaret

 Rev Veitch Betty of Lakefield Co Cavan mentions in his Will, proved 12 Jul 1796, 5 children, **sons** 1. Rev Rowland, C Templeport (Kilm) qv; 2. William, TCD LLD; **daus.** 1. Jane **m.** Richard Simpson of Jamestown Co Leitrim; 2. Susanna; 3. Anne

BEVAN, ROBERT THOMAS 1814/15–1908

b. 1814 or 1815 TCD BA & Div Test 1855 MA 1862

d & p1855 (Kilmore); C Killashee (Ard) 1855–57; C Moydow (Ard) 1857–63; C Kilglass (Ard) 1863–67; V Streete (Ard) 1867–1900; ret

 Died 29 Nov 1908 aged 93

BEWICK, CHARLES HENRY *c.* 1851–1943

b. *c.* 1851 Co Dublin

d 1883 (Kilmore) p 1883 (Down for Kilmore); C Kiltubrid (Ard) 1883–84; I Armaghbreague (Arm) 1884–1940; ret

 Died unm 1 Jun 1943 at Armaghbreague Rectory **bur.** Lisnadill Co Armagh

BIGGS, IVAN RICHARD 1922–2001

b. 1922; Edgehill Theol Coll Belfast 1949; was a Methodist Minister before ordination in C of I

d 24 Feb 1973 p 1 Jul 1973; BC Killea (Waterf) 1973–82; R Kiltoghart w Drumshambo Annaduff Kilmore Toomna and Kilronan (Ard) 1982–91; in charge Drumshambo Kiltoghart and Annaduff (w Mohill Farnaught Aughavas Oughteragh Drumreilly Kiltubride from 2000) (Ard) 1996–2001; Preb of Oran (Elph) 1984–91;

Dio Sec Elphin and Ardagh 1987–91; ret

    Died 7 Nov 2001 at Castlebaldwin

BIRCH, ALFRED 1880/81–1973

b. 1880 or 1881; ed St John's Coll Manitoba

d 1913 p 1915 (Rupld); C McGregor (Dio Brandon) 1913–15; I Griswold (Dio Brandon) 1915–20; R Emerson (Dio Rupld) 1920–21; I Gladstone (Dio Brandon) 1922–24; R Elgin, Manitoba (Dio Brandon) 1924–30; RD of Souris 1926–29; I Tomregan (Kilm) 1930–40; R Clonbroney w Killoe (Ard) 1940–45; R Tashinny and Shrule (Ard) 1946–64; RD of Newtownforbes 1951–53; Preb of Kilcooley (Elph) 1953–64; ret

    m. Ellen Elizabeth (**died** 5 Apr 1960 Tashinny Rectory). Issue incl **daus.** 1. Maud Henson **m.** 29 Dec 1952 Rev Robert Desmond Holtby, R Ballingarry (Killaloe) & R Kilkeevan (Elph) qv and had issue 2 **sons** incl Robert (**died** 11 Jan 1958) and a **dau. b.** 7 Jun 1954; 2. Bettie Alfreda **m.** 21 Apr 1965 Tashinny Par Ch James Jones of Tashinny Co Longford

    Died 2 Jun 1973 Edgeworthstown aged 92 **bur.** Carrickedmond

BIRCH, EBER

Commonwealth Minister at Belturbet in Annagh Parish (Kilm) 21 Jul 1655 during the incumbency of John Hodson qv; coll to Lurgan and Munterconnaught (Kilm) 24 Apr 1661

BIRD, HENRY

d; p 7 Oct 1663 (VB 1673); V Abbeylara (Ard) and Imp C Rathaspeck (Ard) 1670–84; coll 3 June (FF) or 15 July by Primate (F.F.) with Clonbroney (Ard); again coll R & V with V Clonbroney Russagh & Rathaspeck (Ard) 7 April 1674 (F.F.) He signed the address to James II as V 18 Mar 1684

BIRD, JOHN c. 1622–

b. *c.* 1622 Dublin; ed by Mr Cockman, Dublin; ent TCD 17 Mar 1640/41 aged 18

V Drumlane and Tomregan (Kilm) 1665–69; PC St Nicholas Without Dublin (Dub) 1669; V Donard and Donaghmore and R & V Hollywood (Dub) 1672–74

    prob John Bird eldest **s.** of Ralph

BIRMINGHAM, GEORGE KIRWAN 1883–1941

b. 30 Apr 1883 Dublin; ed Rathmines Sch; St Andrew's Coll Dublin; TCD BA 1907 Div Test 1911 MA 1914

d 1909 p 1911 (Down); C Ballymoney (Conn) 1909–12; C St John Monkstown (Dub) 1913–14; C Wexford (Ferns) 1914–17; C Clonmore (Ferns) 1917–22; I Mothel (Oss) 1922–24; I Drumlease (Kilm) 1924–25; I Tomregan (Kilm) 1925–30; I St Peter Athlone and Kiltoom (w C-in-c Castleblakeney Killyon or Killeroran Athleague and Mount Talbot 1936–41) (Elph) 1930–41 yst **s.** of John and Mrs B B of Dublin

m. 1914 Ruth Violet **dau.** of Archibald Leech & Mrs Ormsby–Scott. Issue 1. George; 2. Arthur Michael; 3. Ethel Maeve

Died 22 Jan 1941

BIRNEY, ROBERT COOKE 1879/80–1921

b. 1879 or 1880; TCD BA 1909 Div Test & LLB 1910

d 1911 (Armagh for Down) p 1912; C St Michael Belfast (Conn) 1911–15; C Carrickfergus (Conn) 1915–18; R Ballyjamesduff and Castlerahan (Kilm) 1918–21

yst **s.** of William of Clontarf Dublin

Died 14 Dec 1921 aged 41

BLACK, GIBSON 1801–1887

b. 1801 Dublin; W.J.R. Wallace in *Clergy of Dublin and Glendalough* has him **b.** 1799; ed by Mr Fea; ent TCD 6 Oct 1817 aged 16 BA 1822

d 1826 p 25 Jul 1827 (Kilmore); Asst Chapl Bethesda Dublin (Dub) 1835; C St George Dublin (Dub) 1839–48; V Killinagh (Kilm) 1848–52; PC Inch and Kilgorman (Glend) 1852–87

s. of John, banker

m. Mary Rebecca (**died** 21 Mar 1886) and had issue incl 1. Rev John (**died** 7 May 1883 Dublin) **b.** 1829 Co Cavan TCD BA 1852 d 1852 (Cork) p 1854 (Meath for Dublin) C Inch (Glend) 1852 Chapl Mountjoy Prison Dublin 1854 C St Mary Dublin (Dub) 1859–83 **m.** 8 Jul 1862 Anna Maria **dau.** of Francis McDonogh, MP and had issue a **son b.** 2 Jul 1863; 2. George Garrett, RIC **m.** 8 Jan 1861 Jane Rebecca **dau.** of Dr Abraham Cronyn of Callan Co Kilkenny; 3. Sarah Anne Dunlop **m.** 8 Oct 1874 Rev Francis Wingfield King, R Charlemont (Arm) 1874–75; 4. Victoria Rhoda; 5. William Bushe (**died** 29 Dec 1861 at Inch aged 20); 6. Mary Louisa (**died** 3 Mar 1932) **m.** 12 Jul 1870 Rev Thomas Richard Setford Collins, BD and had issue incl (i) Most Rev Thomas Gibson George, Bp of Meath 1926–27 (ii) Canon Charles Stuart, R Dalkey (Dub) 1914–55 (iii) John Rupert (iv) Mary Isabel **m.** Rev George Foster, R Kircubbin (Down) 1905–18 (v) Annie Ruth

Died 15 Jul 1887 aged 85 at Inch Rectory

BLACK, JAMES

TCD BA 1877

d 1878 p 1879 (Kilmore); C Kilkeevan (Elph) 1878–80; Chapl RN 1880; served in HMS *Ruby* in India 1881–83; *Tenedos* N America 1883–86; *Raleigh* Cape Stn 1886–88; *Impregnable* Devonport 1888–89; *Royal Adelaide* Devonport 1889; RN Barracks Devonport and Examiner in Nautical Astronomy to RN Greenwich 1889–93; HMS *Ramillies* Mediterranean 1893–

BLACK, JOHN
TCD BA 1878 MA 1883

d 1876 p 1877 (Kilm); C Drumshambo (Ard) 1876–78; R Taunagh (Elph) and Preb of Kilmacallen in Elphin Cath 1878–79; Chapl Eccles Est Trivandrum and Bangalore India 1880–82 and 1887–88; Vepery 1880–90 and 1892–94; St George's Cath Madras 1883–87; Ootacamund 1890–92; Bangalore 1892–94; Vepery 1894–95; furlough 1895–97; last entry in Crockford 1897

BLACKBURNE, GEORGE
V Annaduff w V Kiltoghart and Kiltubrid (Ard) 1661–*c.* 68, coll 9 May 1661 (F.F.)

BLACKBURNE, GEORGE
R & V Kilmore (Elph) 1723–; Preb of Termonbarry (Elph) 1731–43; V Aughrim (Elph) 1743–88
   Will dated 1770, proved 1797

BLACKBURNE, RICHARD
d, p (Kildare); V Fenagh and Kiltoghart (Ard) 1673–*c.* 80; coll 21 Jul 1673 (F.F.)

BLACKWELL–SMYTH, RICHARD BERTRAM 1891–1969
b. 2 May 1891 Dublin; ed St. Andrew's Coll Dublin; Trent Coll Derbys; TCD BA 1915 MA 1918

d 2 Feb 1915 p 21 Dec 1916 (Derry); C Drumragh Omagh (Derry) 1915–17; C St James (Dub) 1917–19; C Portadown (Arm) 1919–21; C-in-c Drumshambo (Ard) 1921–23; R Clogherney (Arm) 1923–28; R Donaghmore (Arm) 1928–60; R Kilsaran (Arm) 1960–67; Preb of Tynan in St Patrick's Cath Armagh 1961–67; ret
   s. of George Traffic Manager GSR and Rebecca Jane (*née* Blackwell)
   m. 27 Apr 1921 at Drumragh Par Ch Omagh Olive Marion (**died** 5 Apr 1985 in Cornwall **bur.** Armagh) **dau.** of William Arthur Scott, District Superintendent GNRI. Issue 1. Herbert Brian **b.** 21 May 1922 ed Campbell Coll Belfast **m.** 9 Jan 1953 at Castlecaulfield Doreen Marguerite **dau.** of Samuel Davison of Millisle Co Down and had issue (i) Michael Anthony **b.** 31 May 1956 (ii) Patrick Richard **b.** 20 Nov 1958 (iii) Jacqueline **b.** 31 Jan 1961; 2. Helen Hamill **b.** 15 Aug 1924 **m.** (1) at Castlecaulfield 12 Jun 1946 John Lyndon **s.** of William John McBride DI RUC of Bangor and have issue Mary Rosaleen **b.** 17 Jun 1947; **m.** (2) 10 Sep 1956 Lt Commdr Arthur Pringle RN; 3. Rev Charles Peter Bernard **b.** 9 Jul 1942 ed Campbell Coll Belfast TCD BA 1964 MA 1971 MB BCh BAO 1973 Gen Theol Seminary New York 1965 MDiv d 1965 (Montana) p 1966 (Down) C Bangor Abbey (Down) 1965–67 C Christ Ch Leeson Park Dublin 1967–69 P-in-c Carbury (Kild) 1973–75 Hon C St Stephen in Brannel (Truro) 1987–91 Perm to Off Dio Truro 1991– **m.** (1) 11 Sep 1965 St Peter's Ch Peekshill NY Kathleen Mildred eldest **dau.** of Howard G Nippert of Peekshill and have issue (i) Katie Marie **b.** 21 Apr 1967 (ii) Claire **b.** 25 Jun 1969 (iii) Bertram Russell Scott **b.** 20 Jun 1971 **m.** (2) 24 Jun 1976 St Mary's Ch Truro Helen widow of John Herdman

who **died** 26 Oct 1971

Died 29 Jan 1969 **bur.** Armagh

BLAINE, WILLIAM ANDREW STEWART 1887/88–1939

b. 1887 or 1888; Univ of London BSc 1911 AKC (Sc) 1912; was Science Master at Tech Sch Coleraine

d 1922 p 1923 (Down); Gen Lic Down 1922–29; R Elphin and Ardclare (w Bumlin from 1934) (Elph) & Head Master Bp Hodson's Sch Elphin 1929–39; Preb of Terebrine (Elph) 1936–39

Died 20 Oct 1939 aged 51

BLAIR, JAMES 1705/06–1777

b. 1705 or 1706 Sligo; ed by his father; ent TCD as Siz 14 Jun 1723 aged 17 BA 1727

d 4 Aug 1728 p 7 Sep 1729; C St John Sligo (Elph) 1728; V Kilmactranny Killukin Kilcooley Kilcorkey & Cormagormacan (Elph) 1741–42; V Roscommon Kilbride & Kilteevan (Elph) 1742–77; Preb of Kilmacallen (Elph) 1750–55; Preb of Kilgoghlin (Elph) 1752–77

probably **s.** of Andrew, *ludimagister*

Died 1777

BLAKENEY, THOMAS   –1845

C Roscommon (Elph) 1797; R Roscommon (Elph) 1805–45

was probably of the Castleblakeney Family

m. Aug 1801 Alice **dau.** of Abp Newcome. Issue incl **sons** 1. Charles William ent TCD 3 Jan 1820 aged 17, became a member of the Irish Bar 1836 and afterwards a Judge of the High Court in Queensland; 2. Thomas ent TCD 7 Jul 1823 aged 19 BA 1827; 3. Robert ent TCD 3 Jul 1826 aged 18 BA 1836 Irish Bar 1836; **daus.** 1. Anne **m.** (1) John Nugent; **m.** (2) 17 Aug 1837 Rev William Trocke; 2. Catherine **m.** 1841 John **s.** of Lt Col William Battersby of Bobsville

Died 17 Jan 1845

BLANEY, JOHN 1871/72–1938

b. 1871 or 1872 Moneymore Co Derry; ed at Moneymore; ent TCD 25 Jan 1897 aged 25 BA & Div Test 1901 MA 1904

d 1901 p 1903 (Manchester); C St Luke Preston (Manch) 1901–03; C St James Barrow-in-Furness (Carl) 1903–04; C Christ Ch Pennington (Manch) 1904–05; C Lr Moville (Raph — then Derry) 1905–07; C St Michael Buslingthorpe Leeds (Rip) 1907–09; C Kilnaughton (A & A) 1909–11; C-in-c Carrigallen (Kilm) 1911–16; R Newtownhamilton (Arm) 1916–21; C-in-c Kilcluney (Arm) 1921–32; R Clonaslee (Kild) 1932–35; C-in-c Drumlane (Kilm) 1935–38

s. of Thomas, merchant, of Moneymore

m. Evelyn Maddison. Issue Kathleen Marguerite **b.** 24 Apr 1913 TCD BA 1935

Died 17 Oct 1938

BLASHFORD, JOHN

coll R & V Abbeyshrule (Ard) 12 Mar 1717/18 (F.F.)

BLIGH, ROBERT 1702/03–1778

b. 1702 or 1703 Athboy; matric Christ Ch Coll Oxford 21 Jun 1721 aged 18 BA 1725; TCD MA 1728

Preb and V Timoleague (Ross) 1735–78; R & V Kilsillagh (Ross) 1736–78; R Kilmalooa (Ross) 1746–78; Dean of Elphin 1768–78

    3rd **s.** of Thomas MP for Co Meath and **bro.** of the 1st Earl of Darnley

    m. (1) 7 Jul 1742 Catherine Elliott widow of Charles Boyle of Co Cork

    m. (2) 24 Mar 1757 Frances Winthrop. Issue 1. Thomas Cherbourg **m.** his cousin Lady Theodosia **dau.** of the 3rd Earl of Darnley; 2. Robert matric Christ Ch Coll Oxford 30 Jun 1786 aged 17 and **died unm.**; 3. Frances Theodosia **m.** Robert 3rd Earl of Roden; 4. Catherine Maria **m.** 1793 at Brittas Hugh Howard 3rd **s.** of 1st Viscount Wicklow

    Died Apr 1778

BLUNDELL, DIXIE 1726–1808

b. 1726 Dublin; ed by Dr Burnet; ent TCD 26 Mar 1742 aged 15 Sch 1744 BA 1746 MA 1749 BD & DD 1765; incorp at Oxford 1756; Stearne Lect at St Werburgh's Dublin 1774

d 1751 (Dublin) p; C Kells (Meath) 1752; C St Ann Dublin (Dub) 1754; City Chapl Dublin 1756–1800; R Kilskyre (Meath) 1765–69; R St Paul Dublin (Dub) 1769–75; Preb of Kilquane (Clonf) and Prec of Kilmacduagh 1771–82; V Gen & Reg Dios Killaloe & Kilfenora *c.* 1772; V Kinawley (Kilm) 1774–1808; Preb of St Michael's in Christ Church Cath Dublin (Dub) 1775–82; Preb of St John's in Christ Church Cath Dublin (Dub) 1782–87; 3rd Canon of Kildare 1782–87; Dean of Kildare 1787–1808; Preb of St Michan's in Christ Church Cath Dublin (Dub) 1787–89; R St Mary's Dublin (Dub) 1789–1808

    s. of Ralph, merchant

    m. 15 Jul 1760 Elizabeth **dau.** of Alderman William Ogle of Drogheda. Issue incl **sons** 1. Rev William, Preb of Ballintubber (Elph) qv; 2. Rev Ralph (**died** Jan 1801) **b.** Dublin ent TCD 4 Oct 1779 aged 16 BA 1784 R Aghalurcher (Clogh) 1787–88 V Balscadden (Dub) 1787–1801; **daus.** 1. Jane (**died** 22 Jan 1837 aged 73) **m.** Richard Carden of Fishmoyne Co Tipperary; 2. a **dau.** m Feb 1788 Stearne Tighe; 3. yst **dau.** Hannah (**died** 27 Mar 1842 Clontarf Dublin)

    Died 2 Nov 1808 aged 82 **bur.** St Michan's Ch Dublin

BLUNDELL, ROBERT 1805/06–1887

b. 1805 or 1806 Co Roscommon; ed by his father; ent TCD 4 Nov 1822 aged 16 BA 1827 MA 1833

d & p 1830 (Tuam); C Claremorris (?Kilcolman (Tuam)) 1830–31; Leslie also has him C Kilcommon, Hollymount (Tuam) 1830–35; C Aglish = Castlebar (Tuam) 1831–

33; R Rathcline (Ard) 1834–38; R Cashel (Ard) 1838; V Kiltullagh (Tuam) 1838–67; R Headford (Tuam) 1867–87

> **s.** of Rev William, Preb of Ballintubber qv
>
> **m.** Juliet (**died** 1 Mar 1895 in her 87th year at Skerries Co Dublin)
>
> **Died** 29 Jun 1887 aged 81

BLUNDELL, WILLIAM 1766–1844

b. 1766 Dublin; ed by Dr Buck; ent TCD 3 Nov 1783 BA 1788 DD (*hon causa*) 1813

C St Michan (Dub) 1789; C St Mary (Dub) 1790; City Chapel Dublin 1800; V Balscadden (Dub) 1801–44; V Kilkeevan and Preb of Ballintubber (Elph) 1813–44

> **s.** of Dixie (1726–1808), R Kinawley (Kilm) qv (**s.** of Ralph) by Elizabeth **dau.** of Alderman William Ogle of Drogheda; **bro.** of Rev Ralph, V Balscadden (Dub) 1787–1801
>
> **m.** 7 Oct 1794 St Mary Dublin Gertrude King. Isue 1. Dixie **b.** 1801 Dublin ent TCD 5 Aug 1816 aged 15 BA 1821; 2. Rev Robert, V Cashel (Ard) qv; 3. Elizabeth (**died** 21 May 1859 at Ruskey Glebe) **m.** Rev F Irwin
>
> **Died** 7 Sep 1844 in Dublin

BOLAND, MICHAEL 1784/85–1860

b. 1784 or 1785 Co Galway; ent TCD 1 Jul 1805 aged 20 BA 1811

PC Rathaspeck (Ard) 1816–18; R Killenumery (w Killery to 1835) (Ard) 1817–1860

> **s.** of Anthony, *Linteo*
>
> **m.** Anne and had issue 1. Samuel ed at Lucan School ent TCD 3 Jul 1843 aged 16; 2. Edward **b.** Co Leitrim ent TCD 9 Nov 1846 aged 17
>
> **Died** 3 Aug 1860 at Clada Glebe Co Leitrim

BOLES, WILLIAM   –1855

held a curacy in Cork Diocese; I Streete (Ard) 1817–48 (Erck has from 1823); was non–resident in Streete but kept a curate and had a licence for non–residence 2 Sep 1842 (D.R.)

> yst **s.** of John of Springfield Co Cork by Anne only **dau.** of Thomas Garde of Dunsfort Co Cork
>
> **Died** 19 Jan 1855 s.p

BOLTON, GEORGE HOLMES GIBSON 1904/05–1966

b. 1904 or 1905; TCD BA & Div Test 1930 MA 1935

d 1930 p 1931 (Dublin); C St James Dublin (Dub) 1930–32; C Urney Denn and Derryheen (Kilm) 1932–35; C-in-c Newtowngore w Corrawallen and Drumreilly (Kilm) 1935–36; R 1936–41; R Mohill (w Termonbarry to 1954 and w Cloone and Chapl Lough Rynn 1954–62 and w Annaduff from 1959) (Ard) 1941–66; Dom Chapl to Bp 1951–66; Dio Reg Elphin and Ardagh 1953–56; Preb of Tibohine (Elph) 1956–63; RD of Newtownforbes 1960–66; Dean of Elphin and Ardagh 1963–66

s. of Rev George (1872–1934) C-in-c Castlemacadam (Glend) 1922–34

m. (1) Kathleen (died 21 Nov 1957). Issue incl 1. Margaret m. 23 Feb 1957 Mohill Par Ch Roger H s. of late Mr & Mrs J T Lewis of Kidderminster; 2. Dorothy Gibson m. 6 Sep 1955 Mohill Par Ch Robert David s. of Mr & Mrs R F Pittman of Station Hse Tuam Co Galway; 3. John Gibson; 4. George Gibson died 2 Feb 1965 in Glasgow.

m. (2) Dorothy…

Died 26 Dec 1966 aged 61 bur. at Farnaught

†BOLTON, THEOPHILUS 1677/78–1744

b. 1677 or 1678 Co Mayo; TCD Sch 1695 BA 1698 MA 1701 BD & DD 1716

d 1702 (Dublin) p 26 Sep 1703 Bp 1722; C St Kevin Dublin (Dub) 1706; Preb of Monmohenock in St Patrick's Cath Dublin 1707; Preb of Stagonil in St Patrick's Cath 1707–14; PC St Nicholas' Without Dublin (Dub) 1713–16; Chanc of St Patrick's Cath & R St Werburgh Dublin (Dub) 1714–22; V Finglas (Dub) 1720–23; V Gen Dublin 1721–22; Prec of Christ Ch Cath Dublin 1722–23; Bp of Clonfert 1722–24; Bp of Elphin 1724–29; translated to Cashel 6 Jan 1729 and enthroned 5 Jun 1729; Abp of Cashel 1729–1744

Died 31 Jan 1744 aged 66 bur. St Werburgh's Dublin

PUBLICATION

A Sermon preached before the Irish House of Commons, on the Anniversary of the Irish Rebellion, 23rd October 1721, 4to Dublin, 1721

Dr. Bolton endeavoured to restore the ancient Cathedral on the Rock of Cashel. He bequeathed his library of several thousand volumes, now the Bolton Library at Cashel

BOLTON, WILLIAM

poss William Bolton who was ord d & p by Bp of Petertborough 1602; Treas of Ross 1614–31; R & V Creagh (Ross) 1614–38; V Clonlogher and Killargue (Kilm) 1626–c. 32; Preb of Desertmore (Cork) 1630–38; Dean of Ross 1634–38

BOND, THOMAS JAMES 1918–2006

b. 1918; BA & Div Test 1941 MA 1968

d 1942 p 1943 (Kilmore); C Annagh w Drumaloor and Cloverhill (Kilm) 1942–44; C St John Sligo (Elph) 1944–47; I Kilgobbin (A & A) 1947–49; I Bourney w Dunkerrin (Killaloe) 1949–52; I Kilkeevin w Kiltullagh (Elph) 1952–55; R Bailieborough (w Shercock from 1957) (Kilm) 1955–60; R Templemichael Clongish and Clooncumber (w Killashee and Ballymacormack from 1971) (Ard) 1960–91; Preb of Kilmacallen (Elph) 1967–78; Archd of Elphin and Ardagh 1978–91; ret

m. 27 Aug 1947 Zion Ch Rathgar Dublin Rosemary South. Issue 1 Geoffrey b. 14 Sep 1953 TCD BA Business Studs 1976; 2. Shirley Rosemary Elizabeth bapt 4 Aug 1957 m. 22 Sep 1978 St John's Ch Longford Rev George William Butler, R Drung G 1993–95 qv; 3. Daphne Patricia b. 12 Mar 1960; 4. Heather Matilda Anne b. 5 May 1963

Died 4 Aug 2006

BOND, WENSLEY 1742–1820

b. 1742 Co Longford; ed by Rev Mr Hynes; ent TCD 17 May 1758 aged 16 Sch 1761 BA 1763 MA 1766; incorp MA Magdalen Coll Oxford 17 Dec 1772 aged 30

Dean of Ross 1773–1813; Preb of Termonbarry (Elph) 1774–75; R St John Sligo 1775–1820; Treas of Ferns and R Ballycanew Mullomoling Leskinfere Clough and Kilturk (Ferns) 1776–1820;

> 2nd **s.** of Rev James, Presby Min of Corboy Co Longford by Catherine **dau.** of Rev Dr Wensley of Co Donegal
>
> **m.** 1778 (M L 10 Aug) Rebecca **dau.** of William Forward of Fermoy Co Cork. Issue 2 **sons**, 1. Rev James Forward (**died** 17 Jul 1830 Co Wicklow) ent TCD 24 Nov 1806 aged 21 BA 1810 d 24 Aug 1810; p; C Leskinfere (Ferns) probably from 1810 Dean of Ross 1813–30 R Dunurlin (A & A) 1817–30 **m.** (1) Sarah Hester (**died** 1816) **dau.** of John Croker of Waterford and had issue a **son** died young; **m.** (2) 21 May 1825 Christiana Margaretta **dau.** of Rev Lorenzo Hely Hutchinson and had issue two children; 2. Richard Wensley (**died** 3 Oct 1860) TCD BA 1818; **daus.**, 1. Christina **m.** Thomas Golfin Young of Enniskerry Co Wicklow; 2. Rebecca **m.** Rev William Jennings of Tralee Co Kerry; 3. Catherine **m.** George Tyrrell; 4. Louisa
>
> **Died** 1820

BONER, JAMES

appears C Castleterra (Kilm) 1673

BONYNGE, FRANK WILLIAM

QUB BA (2 cl Hon) 1907 MA 1913; TCD Div Test (2) 1910 Eccles Hist Pri Helen Blake Sch in National Hist Elrington Pri

d 1910 p 1911 (Kilmore); C Mohill w Termonbarry (Ard) 1910–13; Lic Pr Dios Dublin and Kildare 1913–14; C Moyliscar w Enniscoffey and Castlelost (Meath) 1914–17; R Rathconnell (Meath) 1917–21

BOOKER, JOHN 1755/56–

b. 1755 or 1756 Dublin; ed at Eton Coll by Dr Foster; ent TCD 8 Jul 1773 aged 17 BA 1778

V Clonbroney (Ard) 1801–*c.* 21; is V Clonbroney (Ard) 1807 and 1814

> **s.** of Francis, merchant

BOOMER, CORNELIUS CARLETON 1821/22–1879

b. 1821 or 1822 Belfast; ent TCD 1 Jul 1844 aged 22 BA 1853

d 1854 p; C Killan, now Shercock (Kilm) 1857; C Denn (Kilm) 1860–63; C Killinchy (Down) 1864–75

> **s.** of John
>
> **Died** 13 Oct 1879 Holywood Co Down

BORK, JOHN

Signs Sub. Rolls as V Mostrim (Ard) between 1778 and 1784. Perhaps John Burgh, V of Naas (Kild) 1750–52

BORROWES (BURROWES), JOSEPH 1774/75–1840

b. 1774 or 1775 Dublin; ed by Mr Dowling; ent TCD 5 Jul 1791 aged 16 BA 1796

C Carrigallen (Kilm) 1804–*c.* 25; V Emlaghfad (Ach) 1807–21; Minor Canon St Patrick's Cath Dublin 1822–37

   s. of Sir Kildare Dixon, 6th Bt by his 2nd wife

   m. Anne Trench (or poss Mary) (**died** 20 Mar 1854 **bur.** Carrickbrennan Co Dublin) sister of Lord Ashtown. Issue Mary **m.** Hartstonge Robinson

   Died 31 Jan 1840

BOSQUET, DAVID

V Tashinny and Abbeyshrule (Ard) from 1721, coll 2 Nov

BOSQUET, FRANCIS 1707/08–

b. 1707 or 1708 Lisburn Co Antrim; ed by Mr Clark at Lisburn; ent TCD as Siz 8 Jun 1726 aged 18 Sch 1728 BA 1730

V Clonfinlough Clontuskert and Kilgeffin 1742–.

   s. of Francis, MD

BOSTOCK, JOHN

perhaps the John Bostock who matriculated at Cambridge as Sizar from Pembroke College, Easter 1585, BA about 1589–90

d 20 Dec 1589 (London) p 29 Mar 1591; V Southill, Bedfordshire 1598–1610; V Drumlease (Kilm) to 1612

BOTHWELL, WALTER 1886–1964

b. 7 Mar 1886 Articlave Coleraine; TCD Abp King and Bp Forster Pris 1911 Warren Pri & Div Test & BA (1) 1912 BD 1923

d 26 Sep 1912 p 12 Nov 1913 (Kilm); C Annagh w Quivvy (Kilm) 1912–14; C Kilnamanagh (Ferns) 1914–18; R Fethard Templetown Hook and Tintern (Ferns) 1918–25; R Killashee and Ballymacormack (Ard) 1925–30; I Drumcar (w Dunany from 1940) (Arm) 1930–60; Exam Chapl to Abp of Armagh 1945–60; Preb of Ballymore in Armagh Cath 1951–60; RD of Dundalk 1952–56

   s. of David, Schoolmaster of Articlave by Georgina (*née* Hawke)

   m. 17 Nov 1914 Alice Maud **dau.** of the late Thomas Noble, Bank of Ireland Wexford (eldest **s.** of Sinnamon Noble of Moy) by Katherine **dau.** of Rev William Radcliffe, Preb and I of Donaghmore (Glend). Issue Rev David George **b.** 30 Jun 1916 Monamolin Rectory Gorey Co Wexford (**died** 24 Jun 1988) TCD BA 1939 Div Test 1941 d 1941 p 1942 (Down) C St Mary Newry and Donaghmore (Drom)

1941–45 C St Mark Portadown (Arm) 1945–47 I Donaghendry and Ballyclog (Arm) 1947–83 **m.** St Aidan's Ch Kilmore Co Armagh 12 Nov 1946 Lilian **dau.** of Edward Ruddock of Kilmore (**died** 12 Aug 1996) and had issue a **dau.** Bronagh Caroline **b.** 1954 **m.** 1985 Michael Liddicoat; 2. Edith Maud **b.** 28 Dec 1917; 3. Irene Caroline Radcliffe **b.** 18 Feb 1919 New Ross Co Wexford **m.** 19 Aug 1950 Drumcar Par Ch Co Armagh Charles John Robinson of Blackrock Co Dublin and have issue Anne and Trevor; 4. Mary Ruth **m.** Dr Tony Beattie of Broadstairs Kent; 5. Catherine **b.** 1 Nov 1920 Fethard Co Wexford

Died 16 Nov 1964

PUBLICATIONS
Several articles and reviews for the *Church of Ireland Gazette*

BOURCHIER, THOMAS

C Lurgan (Kilm) in 1854; C Kilmore (Kilm) 1859–66

†BOURKE, Hon. JOSEPH DEAN 1735/36–1794

b. 1735 or 1736 Co Kildare; ed by Mr Davis; ent TCD 8 Jun 1751 aged 15 BA not recorded MA 1758 DD 1773

was Preb of Loughgall (Arm) 1760–69; Dean of Killaloe 1768–72; R Kilskyre (Meath) 1769–72; Dean of Dromore 1772; consec Bp of Ferns and Leighlin in St Thomas' Ch Dublin 11 Oct 1772; Bp of Ferns and Leighlin 1772–82; Abp of Tuam and Bp of Ardagh 1782–94; succeeded to the Earldom of Mayo as 3rd Earl on the death of his elder **bro.** John 20 Apr 1792

2nd **s.** of 1st Earl of Mayo

m. 1760 (ML 4 Jun) Elizabeth (**died** 13 Mar 1807) **dau.** of Sir Richard Meade and **sister** of the 1st Earl of Clanwilliam. Issue 4 **sons**; 1. John 4th Earl of Mayo DCL (Oxon) GCB **died** 1849; 2. Richard qv below; 3. Hon. Joseph **b.** 24 Dec 1771 (**died** 3 May 1843 Co Dublin); TCD BA 1791 MA 1795 d 27 Oct 1793 p 8 Dec 1793 (Tuam) R Drumconrath (Meath) 1795; R Athenry (Tuam) 1795–1812; Dean of Ossory 1795–1843; V Offerlane (Oss) 1797–1835; Chanc of Waterford 1812–43; **m.** 23 Apr 1799 Maria eld **dau.** of Sackville Gardiner of Dublin and had issue (i) Joseph Dean bapt 13 Apr 1800 (ii) Rev Sackville Gardiner, R Hatherop Glouc who **m.** 1839 Georgina eldest **dau.** of the 4th Earl of Bessborough; (iii) Rev John William, R Offerlane (Oss); 2 **daus.** (i) Elizabeth Charlotte bapt 5 Oct 1802 **died unm.** 15 Jul 1858; (ii) Henrietta Margaret bapt 2 Feb 1804; 4 Hon. George Theobald **b.** 15 Apr 1776 **died** 22 Dec 1847 TCD BA 1796 MA 1811 LLB & LLD 1827 d 17 Apr 1797 (Oss) V Clonard (Meath) 1799–1815 V Ballinafagh (Kild) 1811–19 R Kilmacow (Oss) 1815–47 Preb of Clashmore (Lism) 1817–19 V Ardfinnan (Lism) 1819–47 Preb of Seskinan (Lism) 1819–20 Preb of Kilgobinet (Lism) 1820–27 Prec of Lismore 1827–47 **m.** 1808 Augusta Georgiana (**died** 15 Jan 1847 aged 85) 2nd **dau.** of Thomas Webster of Lisanrurk and had issue (i) Richard **b.** 1811 **died** 21 May 1856 **m.** Gertrude; (ii) Rev John **b.** 15 Aug 1812 V Kilmeaden (Lism) 1837–91 **m.** 8 Feb 1842 Louisa Maria (**died** 14 Nov 1870); he died 15 Mar 1891; (iii) Lt Col Thomas Joseph Deane **b.** 7 Mar 1815 **m.** and had issue; Archbishop Bourke also had 8 **daus.** 1. Catherine; 2. Mary **m.** 19 Feb 1789 Edward Southwell, Lord de Clifford; 3. Elizabeth; 4. Mary Anne **m.** Mar 1806

Thomas Sotheby, Rear Admiral; 5. Charlotte (**died** 15 Jun 1806) **m.** 1794 William Browne of Browne's Hill Co Carlow; 6. Harriet d. 5 Oct 1781; 7. Louisa; 8. Theodosia Eleanor **m.** Feb 1807 Capt Hale eldest **s.** of Blagden Hale of Aldersley Glouc

Died 17 Aug 1794 at Kilbeggan Co Meath **bur.** Naas

Archbishop Bourke gave the great bell to Tuam Cathedral in 1793

†BOURKE, Hon RICHARD 1767–1832

b. 22 Apr 1767; matric Christ Ch Coll Oxford 12 Jan 1784 Christ Ch Coll Oxford BA 1787 MA 1790 DD by diploma 1813

d 21 Dec 1790 p 10 Apr 1791 Bp 1813; Preb of Killabegs (Tuam) 1791–1813; R and Preb of Crossboyne and Mayo (Tuam) 1791; R Athenry to 1795; R Templemichael (w Mohill (Ard) to 1801) 1795–1813; Prec of St Patrick's Cath Dublin and R Lusk (Dub) 1798–1800; pres to the Deanery of Ardagh 15 Dec 1800 (L.M. V. 170) and inst 29 Jan 1801 (F.F.); Dean of Ardagh 1801–13; Bp of Waterford and Lismore 1813–32

2nd **s.** of Most Rev and Hon Joseph Dean Bourke, Abp of Tuam and 3rd Earl of Mayo by Elizabeth **dau.** of Sir Richard Meade; **bro.** of Hon Joseph, V Offerlane (Oss) and Dean of Ossory 1797–1843

m. 20 Mar 1795 Frances (**died** 1827) 2nd **dau.** of Most Rev Robert Fowler Abp of Dublin 1779–1801. Issue a **s.** Robert who succeeded as 5th Earl of Mayo and three **daus.** 1. Mildred **b.** 18 Dec 1795 **m.** Robert Uniacke of Co Waterford; 2. Frances **b.** 15 Dec 1799 **m.** William Henry Carter of Co Kildare; 3. Catherine **b.** 19 Jul 1804 **m.** Rev Henry Prittie Perry, R Newcastle (Lim)

Died 15 Dec 1832 **bur.** Kill Dublin

BOURKE, WILLIAM 1805/06–

b. 1805 or 1806 Co Mayo; ed by Mr Traynor; ent TCD 16 Oct 1826 aged 20 BA 1832

d 1833 ? p 6 Jan 1837 (Limerick); C Killeshandra (Kilm) 1838; C Kilmore (Elph) 1843–45; C Killanin (Tuam) 1858; R Lackan (Tuam) 1872–80

probably William Bourke s. of Palmer, *armiger*

? **m.** (1) (ML 1850) Harriett Sarah West

? **m.** (2) Catherine (**died** Aug 1859 at Castlekirke Rectory). Issue incl eldest **son** Capt William Henry, Queen's Royal Tower Hamlets Militia **m.** 12 Jun 1877 Sarah Louisa **dau.** of James J Young

BOWERMAN, JOHN

nom. Dean of Ardagh 29 Apr 1552, pres. May 5 (L.M., and F. Edward VI, 990; C.P.R.I., I. 282)

BOWERS, DERMOT NICHOLAS 1913–?

b. 1913; TCD BA and BCom 1936 MA 1963

d and p 1941 (Clogher); C Monaghan (Clogh) 1941–42; Chapl RAF 1942–46; R

Lissadell (Elph) 1946–48; Asst Sec CCCS (Irish Aux) 1948–53; Hon Clerical V Christ Ch Cath Dublin 1952; R Baltinglass (Leigh) 1953–57; R Enniscorthy (Ferns) 1957–66; Preb of Kilrane and Taghmon (Ferns) 1963–66; V Christ Ch Cath Bangkok Thailand with Vientiane Laos 1966–72; V St Thomas Apostle Douglas IOM (S & M) 1972–79; Canon of Peel Cath (S & M) 1978–79; Canon Emer 1980–*c.* 87; C Bramley (Sheff) 1981; last entry in Crockford 1987/88

> **m.** 12 Apr 1943 Monica Monkman. Issue 1. Terence; 2. Kevin John **m.** Sheelagh Ismay and had issue (i) Andrew (ii) Jane (iii) Kirsty Sheelagh **b.** 1976; 3. Valerie Monica **m.** 1 Jul 1972 at St Chrysostom's Ch Manchester Stuart A Coldwell; 4. Frances Elizabeth bapt 1 Aug 1954

BOYCE, ROGER

Clk of Edgeworthstown appears in Suff. Loy. Lists of 1798; perhaps was V Mostrim (Ard)

BOYD, ROBERT WALLACE   –1921

RUI Queen's Coll BA (1cl) Hons Biol Sci & 1 cl Exhib 1884

d 28 Jun 1887 p 20 Dec 1888 (Oss); C Maryborough, Portlaoise (Leigh) 1887–89; C Templemichael (Ard) 1890–96; Dio Reg Ardagh 1891; V Kilronan (Ard) 1896–1921; Preb of Mulhuddart in St Patrick's Cath Dublin 1904–21; Archd of Ardagh 1916–21

> **Died** 10 Nov 1921 **bur.** Mt Jerome

PUBLICATION
> Compiled *Companion to the Prayer Book*

BRABAZON, JAMES 1692–*c.* 1734

b. 3 Jan 1692

V Clonbroney (Ard) 1730–31 coll 8 Jun 1730 (SR); FF has 1731; V Carberry and Kilrenny (Kild) 1731–*c*34

> **s.** of John of Castlecarberry
>
> **Died** *c.* 1734, Will proved 1734

BRABAZON, PHILIP 1804–1843

b. 1804 Co Meath; ent TCD 3 Jun 1822 aged 17 BA 1827

C Drumgoon (Kilm) 1835–43

> **s.** of Rev George, V Peynestown (Meath) 1822–51 (**died** 30 Mar 1851) (**s.** of Anthony) by Honora (**died** 3 Jan 1860) **dau.** of Rev Robert Heyland, R Coleraine (Conn) 1769–1802
>
> **Died** 19 Jul 1843 aged 39

BRADFIELD, WILLIAM   –1956

TCD BA 1904 Div Test 1905 MA 1907

d 1905 p 1906 (Kilmore); C Killesher (Kilm) 1905–07; C Kilmore (Kilm) 1907–08;

R Munterconnaught (w Loughan from 1923 and w Lurgan from 1925) (Kilm) 1908–56; Preb of Annagh (Kilm) 1944–56

> m. Alicia Jane (died 7 Dec 1977). Issue incl 1. elder son Claud Wilfred Patrick (died 18 Feb 1967) MD Derbyshire Royal Infirmary m. Enid; 2. eldest dau. Eva Sylvia Mary (died 9 Sep 1957 Farnborough Kent) TCD BA 1932 m. John Hyslop; 3. Alice m. Robert B Griffin s. of Canon James Jackson Griffin, C Kinawley (Kilm) qv; 4. Denise m. 29 Jan 1949 at Chichester Charles Hampden s. of Theodore
> Died 6 Jan 1956

BRADSHAW, MARTIN   –1892

TCD BA (Resp) Div Test (1) & Ch Form Pri 1871 MA 1875

d 1870 p 1871 (Kilmore); C Killery and Killenumery (Ard) 1870–75; R Ballysumaghan (Elph) 1875–85; Preb of Kilgoghlin (Elph) 1882–92; R Roscommon (Elph) 1885–92

> m. 4 Jun 1878 Janie dau. of William R Tredennick of Fort William Co Donegal
> Died 9 Sep 1892

BRADSHAW, ROBERT 1854/55–1935

b. 1854 or 1855; TCD BA 1878 MA 1883

d 1883 p 1884 (Kilmore); C Kildrumferton (Kilm) 1883–84; C Tuam (Tuam) 1884–85; R Killinane (w Kilconickney from 1907) (Kilmacd) 1885–1933; Canon of Kinvarra and Preb of Kilteskill (Kilmacd) 1918–20; Dean of Clonfert and Kilmacduagh 1920–33; ret

> m. and had issue incl Irene (died 27 Apr 1973 Dublin bur. Templemore)
> Died 11 Jan 1935 aged 80

BRADY, JAMES RICHARD   –1971

TCD BA 1917 MA 1932

d 1918 p 1919 (Down); C Dundonald (Down) 1918–21; C Ballymacarrett (Down) 1921–24; C Christ Ch Belfast (Conn) 1924–26; R Templeport (Kilm) 1926–29; R Killeshandra (Kilm) 1929–32; R St Andrew Belfast (Conn) 1932–51; C-in-c Culfeightrin (Conn) 1951–59; ret

m.; his wife died at Culfeightrin Rectory 1954

Died 25 Sep 1971

BRADY, PHILIP

V Kedy (Kilm) to 1594, is deposed

BRADY, PHILIP

was an Irish poet; was an R C priest; was a clk in Kilmore Dio when he signed address to King James II 1683/84; V Kildallon (Kilm) 1691–1704; R Innismagrath (Kilm) 1704–19

> m. Mary Broderick of Cavan (ML 12 Nov 1682)

BRADY, THOMAS
is pres to V Drung (Kilm) 10 Aug 1594

BRADY(E)
d & p (Kildare) 14 Sep 1618; coll V Lavey (Kilm) 12 Dec 1620 (R.V. 1634); is still V 1634; got a grant of a glebe here 25 Jan 1626/27 (Morrin III.188); "a minister of country birth" (R.V. 1622); prob same as Thomas Oge below

BRADY, THOMAS OGE
Minister of the Parish of Belturbet = Annagh (Kilm) in 1641, an Irish RC who turned. Perhaps he was "the Irish Curate who rends the services in the Irish tongue and got £10 per annum" (R.V. 1622)

BRADY, WILLIAM
V Kilberry (Meath); pres to the Deanery of Ardagh 10 Sep 1563 (L.M. V. 100)

†BRANN (or de BRANA), GEORGE   –1530
Bp of Dromore 1483–99, was prov to the See of Elphin 18 Apr 1499. He was an Athenian, and lived to 1530, under which year the A.F.M. state that, "the Greek Bishop of Elphin died". However, he was possibly succeeded in 1525 by John Max qv

    Died 1530

BREDIN, ROBERT 1682/83–1741
b. 1682 or 1683 Newtownbutler; ed by Dr Walker at Drogheda; ent TCD 24 May 1701 ager 18 Sch 1703 BA 1705

Preb of Ballintubber (Elph) 1716–34; V Athleague Dunamon and Fuerty (Elph) 1716–34, and poss to 1741.

    s. of Thomas
    Died 1741; Will prov 1741

BREDIN, ROBERT
C Castleblakeney (Elph) 1711; prob same as above

BREDIN, WILLIAM 1710/11–*c*. 1770
b. 1710 or 1711 Cloncallows Co Longford; ed by Rev Mr Neligan, Longford; ent TCD 3 Jun 1729 aged 18 BA 1733

C Shrule 1755–60

    s. of Christopher, *colonus*
    Died *c*. 1770– Prerogative Will proved 1770

BREHAN, HUGH JOHN
appears Preb of Kilcooley (Elph) 1615

BREHON, HUGH
V Drumcollum (Elph) 1615; prob same as above; also prob same as Hugh Brehon V Kilcooley (Elph) 1615

BRENNAN, WILLIAM HENRY NASSAU 1846/47–1935
b. 1846 or 1847; ed Mountjoy Sch Dublin; TCD BA 1875 MA 1896

d 1870 (Kilmore) p 1876 (Chester); C Innismagrath (Kilm) 1870–72; C St James Haydock (Liv) 1872–79; C St Nicholas Liverpool (Liv) 1879–81; Chapl ACIS Allahabad 1881–85; Chapl St Anne Indore India 1885–94; R Killea (Raph) 1894–98; R Culmore (Derry) 1898–1916; ret; Lic to Off Dio Guildford from 1916; Lic to Off Dio Winchester from 1920

   Died 17 Mar 1935 aged 88

BRERETON, WILLIAM 1663/64–1720
b. 1663 or 1664 Queen's Co (Laois); ed by Mr Rylands; ent TCD 24 May 1682 aged 18 BA 1686 MA 1692

d 2 May 1686 (Lim) p 29 Sep 168– (Lim); Preb of Killeedy (Lim) 1686–1720; Preb of Tibohine (Elph) 1698–1703; V Killukin (Elph) 1698–1700; Precentor of Elphin and V Kilmacumsy Shankill and Kilbeckey, coll 25 Mar 1703 (F.F.) 1703–20; V Abbeyfeale (A & A) 1710–20; V Chor Limerick (Lim) 1717–20

   s. of Francis

   m. and had issue incl Simons **b.** at Boyle ed at Limerick by Mr Cashin ent TCD 28 May 1716 Sch 1718

   Died 1720

†BRINKLEY, JOHN 1762/63–1835
b. 1762 or 1763; ed Caius Coll Cambridge; became Senior Wrangler; MA 1791; TCD (*ad eund* Camb) MA 1792 DD 1806; was appointed Prof of Astronomy 1790; Astronomer Royal for Ireland — he created much stir in the scientific world by his discoveries; FRS 1803; Pres RIA 1822–26; Copley Medal Royal Soc 1824; Pres Royal Astronomical Soc 1830–33

R Derrybrusk (Clogh) 1806–09; Preb of Kilgoghlin & V Bumlin (Elph) 1806–26; Archd of Clogher 1808–26; V Laracor (Meath) 1808–09; was coll to R Clones (Clogh) 20 Oct 1810, but on a *quare impedit*, his collation was annulled — the Crown, not the Bishop having the right to present

consec Bp of Cloyne in TCD Chapel 3 Oct 1826; Bp of Cloyne 1826–35

   s. of John Toler of Woodbridge Suffolk

   m. Esther **dau.** of Matthew Welsh. Issue 1. Rev John **b.** Co Dublin (**died** 14 Feb 1847 **bur.** Cloyne) ent TCD 2 Nov 1807 aged 14 BA 1812 MA 1815 d 1817 p

1818 (Clogher) C Clontibret (Clogh) 1817–27 Preb of Glanworth (Cloyne) 1828–47 **m.** (ML 1824) Anna **dau.** of Rev Walter Stephens of Dublin and had issue (i) John, 9th Lancers **died unm.** in India; (ii) Walter Stephens, 4th Hussars **m.** and had issue; (iii) Sarah who **died unm.**; 2. Matthew **b.** 1794 Dublin TCD BA 1816 MA 1832, Lay V Chor in Cloyne; 3. Sarah **m.** Robert J Graves, MD

Died 14 Sep 1835 Dublin aged 72 **bur.** in the vaults of TCD Chapel

PUBLICATION
Elements of Astronomy, 1808

BRISBIN (or BRISBANE), JOHN

V Mostrim (Ard) 1702–05; coll 6 May 1702 (F.F.)

BRISCOE, EDWARD 1854/55–1935

b. 1854 or 1855

d 15 Jun 1879 p 22 May 1880 (Ossory); C Inistioge (Oss) 1879; C Kilmanagh (Oss) 1879–80; C Kilpatrick (Ferns) 1880–83; C Cloydagh (Leigh) 1883–96; Dio C Leighlin 1897; R Moydow 1897–1912; ret

m. 3 Jun 1880 Mary Anne **dau.** of Matthew Sutcliffe of Broomhill Ballingarry Co Tipperary. Issue a **son** C W E Briscoe who was a brilliant journalist

Died 8 Aug 1935 aged 80

BRISCOE, ROBERT EDWARD 1844–1901

b. 1844; ed Wesleyan Sch; TCD BA 1866 MA 1872

d 1867 p 1868 (Kilmore); C Drumcliffe (Elph) 1867–69; C Dorrha (Killaloe) 1869–74; C St Andrew Belfast (Conn) 1874–80; C Billy (Conn) 1880–82; C Ballinderry (Conn) 1882–85; C Drumgath (Drom) 1885–95; R Drumnakilly (Arm) 1895–1901

s. of Abraham of Rathmines Dublin

m. (1) 23 Mar 1886 Ballinderry Co Antrim Margaret Elizabeth (**died** 25 Jul 1890 aged 44) **dau.** of William John Turtle

m. (2) 2 Jun 1891 Loughgall Par Ch Co Armagh Susan **dau.** of Samuel Corrigan of Loughgall

Died 17 Aug 1901 **bur.** St Patrick's Cath Churchyard Dublin

BRITTAINE, GEORGE 1788–1848

b. 1788; ent TCD 6 Sep 1804 aged 16 and–a–half years BA 1809; C St Nicholas Without (Dub) 1811; C Bray (Dub) 1811; C Muckno (Clogh) 1811–17; V Kilmactranny (Elph) 1817–23; R & V Kilcommick (Ard) 1823–48

s. of Rev Patrick, C St James Dublin (Dub) 1789–1804 (**s.** of Thomas)

m. 1816 Anna Maria **dau.** of Col Henry Monck Mason. Issue Georgina Charlotte **m.** as his first wife (ML Dublin 1845) Rev Thomas Henry, C Kilcommick (Ard), qv, and had issue George bapt 22 Sep 1846 — she died in childbirth

George Brittaine was a noted Protestant evangelical preacher and writer of his time.

See article by Dr. Fergus O'Ferrall, to whom I am much indebted

Died 28 Mar 1848

PUBLICATIONS

A Visitation Sermon preached in Elphin Cathedral 19 Aug 1819 on Jeremiah Ch 13 v 2, Dublin 8vo 1819, quoted in Sirr's Life of last Archbishop of Tuam with account of connection with Archbishop Trench

Brittane also published eight novels

Recollections of Hyacinth O'Gara, Richard Moore Tims, Dublin 1828
The Confessions of Honor Delany, Richard Moore Tims, Dublin 1829
Irish Priests and English Landlords, Richard Moore Tims, Dublin 1830
Irishmen and Irishwomen 1830, 3rd Ed 1831
Mothers and Sons, Richard Moore Tims, Dublin 1833
Johnny Derrivan's Travels, Richard Moore Tims, Dublin 1833
Nurse McVourneen's Story, Richard Moore Timms, Dublin 1833
The Election, 1840
Contributor to *Dublin University Magazine*

†BRODERICK, Hon CHARLES 1761–1822

b. 3 May 1761; Clare Coll Camb MA 1782 DD 1795

d 24 Aug 1787 p 9 Dec 1787 (Cloyne) Bp 22 Mar 1789; R & V Dingindonovan and Preb of Killenemer (Cloyne) 1789–89; Preb of Donoghmore (Cloyne) 1789; Treas of Cloyne 1789–95; consec Bp of Clonfert in the Castle Chapel Dublin 22 Mar 1789; Bp of Clonfert 1789–96; Bp of Kilmore 1796–1801; enthroned 29 Jan 1796; Abp of Cashel 1801–1822

4th **s.** of George, 3rd Viscount Midleton

m. (ML 6 Dec 1786) Mary (**died** 28 Mar 1799) **b.** 11 Jun 1767 2nd **dau.** of Richard Woodward, Bp of Cloyne 1781–94. Issue **sons** 1. Charles, 6th Viscount Midleton; 2. Rev George (**died unm.** 2 May 1861) **b.** 23 Apr 1797 matric Oriel Coll Oxford 14 Mar 1815 BA 1819 MA 1822 Preb of Killardry (Cash) R Titsey Surrey 1842–61; 3. Rev William John, 7th Viscount Midleton matric Balliol Coll Oxford 21 Jun 1816 aged 17 BA 1820 MA 1823 Dean of Exeter 1863 and Chapl in Ordinary to Queen Victoria; **daus.** 1. Mary Susan **m.** 1809 at Cashel the Earl of Bandon; 2. Albinia **m.** Sir James A Maude, RN CB; 3. Louisa **m.** James Scott; 4. Frances **m.** Henry D Tolly, CB

Died 6 May 1822 **bur.** Midleton C o Cork

BROOKE, HENRY 1681/82–1739

b. 1681 or 1682 Co Cavan; ed by Mr Bren of Cavan; ent TCD 4 Apr 1698 aged 16 Sch 1701 BA 1702 MA 1705 LLD 1718

R & V Knockbride (Kilm) 1726–28; R Killinagh & Kinawley (Kilm) 1728–39

3rd **s.** of William of Dromavana, *pharmacopola* (**s.** of Rev John D)

m. Thomasina **dau.** of Rev Thomas Tucker of Moynalty. Issue 1. Henry, Governor of Madras; 2. Honor (Norah) **m.** her cousin Robert Brooke

Died Mar 1739

BROOKE, RICHARD 1760/61–1818

b. 1760 or 1761 Longford; ed by Mr Kerr; ent TCD 1 May 1775 aged 14 BA 1780

d 1780 p 1783 (Kilmore); V Tomregan (Kilm) 1801–18; V Kildallon (Kilm) for 11 days only, 7th–18th Sep 1810, and coll again V Tomregan 18 Sep 1810

> s. of Rev William, V Granard (Ard) (s. of Alexander) by Elizabeth **dau.** of Matthew Young
>
> **Died** 5 Mar 1818

BROOKE, WILLIAM 1720–1811

b. 1720 Co Cavan; ed by Dr Sheridan; ent TCD 25 May 1737 aged 16 Sch 1740 BA 1742 MA 1744

d and p 1745 (Kilmore); C Templeport & Drumreilly (Kilm) 1745; C Killeshandra (Kilm) 1753; V Granard and Gowna (Ard) 1761–1805

> s. of Alexander, Pharmacist
>
> m. 27 Sep 1755 at Cavan Elizabeth **dau.** of Matthew Young of Lahard Co Cavan. Issue **sons** 1. Rev Richard, V Tomregan (Kilm) qv; 2. Rev Edward (acc to Leslie was a son, but may have been a grandson) — Leslie has him as Prec of Dromore but Swanzy does not mention him; 3. William ent TCD 5 Oct 1784 aged 16; **daus.** 1. Honor **m.** Eyles Irwin; 2. Elizabeth **bur.** 26 Feb 1768 Killeshandra
>
> **Died** 1811

BROOKE, WILLIAM

probably C Drumlummon (Ard) *c.* 1788; signed Parl Ret 1766

BROOKES, WILLIAM 1667/68–1745

b. 1667 or 1668 Cavan;; ed by Mr Brook, Cavan; ent TCD 13 May 1685 Sch 1687 BA 1689 MA 1694

R Bailieborough and Moybologue and V Killinkere (Kilm) 1697–1745; V Innismagrath (Kilm) 1700–04; V Kildallon (Kilm) 1704–36; V Lavey (Kilm) 1736–45; was ordered by the Primate to reside in the parish within 6 months, 24 Sep 1742

> evidently William Brookes **s.** of William, *pharmacopola* of Cavan
>
> m. 1704 Lettice **dau.** of Dr Simon Digby, Bp of Elphin, qv Issue (in *Al. Dubl.*, evidently the eldest), 1. Digby **b.** Cavan ed by Mr Brooke of Cavan ent TCD 23 Sep 1714 BA 1719 MA 1722; also, in B.L.G., 2. Henry of Rantavan ent TCD 7 Feb 1720/21 aged 17 Barrister-at-Law and an author; **m.** Catherine Meares and had 22 children; 3. Robert **m.** his cousin Norah **dau.** of Rev Henry Brooke, R Killinagh and Kinawley (Kilm) qv and had issue; 4. Letitia **m.** (1) Charles Luther; **m.** (2) Dublin (ML 1748) John ?Farmer of Cavan (4th **s.** of John by Alice) and had issue (i) John (ii) Thomas (iii) Robert (iv) Abraham (v) William (vi) Alice (vii) Elizabeth
>
> In *Brookiana*, London 1804, an account of his son Henry Brooke, the author, there is the following reference to William Brooke; "Mr Brooke's father was descended of an ancient family of that name in the County of Fermanagh. He was originally intended for the army, but as he grew up, his father discovered that his inclination

and studies pointed to the Church. He was accordingly educated at Trinity College Dublin, and ordained by Dr Wetenhall, Bishop of Kilmore, who was so highly pleased with his unaffected piety and literary acquirements, that he gave him the livings of Killinkere and Moybologue, about £200 a year, a large income in those days."

Died 10th Nov 1745 aged 77

BROUGHAM, JOHN 1748/49–1811

b. 1748 or 1749; Fellow King's Coll Camb BA 1771 MA 1775 DD

R Bailieborough and Moybologue (Kilm) 1778–1808; R Castleterra (Kilm) 1780–1808; R Killersherdiney (Kilm) 1808–11

yr **s.** of Henry of Brougham Westmoreland; uncle of Henry, 1st Lord Brougham and Vaux

m. 17 Oct 1785 Sarah **dau.** of James Scanlan by Anne Babington. Issue Rev Henry, V Tallow (Lism) **m.** and had issue incl Very Rev Henry, Dean of Lismore 1884–1913

Died 22 May 1811 aged 62 **bur.** Castleterra

BROUGHAM, JOHN RICHARD 1829–1913

b. 4 Aug 1829 Tallow Co Waterford; TCD BA & Div Test (1) 1852 MA 1865

d 29 Aug 1852 (Cork) p 21 Aug 1853 (Meath for Derry); C Cappagh (Derry) 1852–53; V Killea and Rathmoylon (Lism) 1854–56; R Raymunterdoney (Raph) 1856–60; R Templeport (Kilm) 1860–66; V Timolin (Kild) 1866–79; Canon of Christ Ch Cath Dublin (Dub) 1876–79; V Clonagoose (Leigh) 1880–81; V Barrow Gurney (B & W) 1881–83; R Corkbeg (Cloyne) 1883–86; R Castlehaven (Ross) 1886–90; Preb of Timoleague (Cork) 1886–89; Preb of Glanore (Cloyne) 1889–1913; R St Edmund's Cork (Cork) 1890–91; R Monkstown Cork (Cork) 1891–1903

s. of Rev Henry, V Tallow (Lism); **bro.** of Henry, Dean of Lismore

m. 12 Jul 1855 Frances Maria (**died** 5 Jul 1917 at Passage West Cork aged 86) **dau.** of Richard Rothwell of Rockfield Co Meath. Issue Rev Richard Henry Vaux TCD BA & Div Test (2) 1894 MA 1905 d 1894 p 1895 (Winchester) C St Paul Southampton (Win) 1894–96 C Mallow (Cloyne) 1896–1902 R Rathbarry (Ross) 1902–06 R Castle Magner G (Cloyne) 1906–14 R Marmullane (Cork) 1914–19 TCF 1917–19 Chapl Miss to Seamen at Marseilles 1919–22 Chapl Miss to Seamen and C Runcorn (Ches) 1922–24 Chapl Miss to Seamen Adelaide 1924–30 Temp Chapl Hong Kong 1930 Kobe 1930–31 Asst Chapl Port of London and Chapl Seamen's Hosp Greenwich (S'wark) from 1931

Died 27 Aug 1913 at Glenbeigh Cork aged 84

PUBLICATION

A Sermon on Baptismal Regeneration

BROWN, JOHN 1624/25–1700

b. 1624 or 1625 at Villa Baleinaschulloge; ed by Mr Ryan, Dublin; ent TCD as Siz 22 Apr 1641 aged 16 Sch (MA in DR)

V Chor St Patrick's Cath Dublin 1682; V Taunagh *c.* 1683; V Killukin Boyle Kilnamanagh Aghanagh Toomna and Kilbrine = Kilbryan (Elph) and Archd of Elphin 1683–1700; R Tullyallen (Arm) and Dowth and Truby (Meath) and V Kilmessan (Meath) 1693–1700; coll V Kilbrine = Kilbryan (Elph) 23 Oct 1698

>**m.** Margery Donellan who survived him and lived many years at Drogheda after 1714
>
>**Died** 1700

BROWNE, CECIL CHARLES WYNDHAM 1916–1991

b. 3 May 1916 Dublin; ed High Sch Dublin; TCD BA 1939 Div Test (1) 1940 BD 1944

d 1940 p 1941 (Armagh); C Portadown 1940–42; C St Ann (Dub) 1942–47; R St John Sligo and Knocknarea (w Rosses Point from 1960) 1947–83; RD of N Elphin 1953–83; Preb of Kilmacallen (Elph) 1961–67; Exam Chapl to Bp of Kilmore 1961–83; Dean of Elphin and Ardagh 1967–83; ret

>**s.** of John Naylor of Cliftonville Rd Dublin by Augusta (*née* Blackmore) of Ennis Co Clare
>
>**m.** 27 Sep 1946 St Peter's Ch Belfast Muriel Joan **dau.** of Thomas and Eva Brownell of Castle Ave Belfast. Issue 1. Philip **b.** 7 May 1949; 2. Heather **b.** 17 Jun 1952; 3. Peter Thomas **b.** 9 Dec 1958 (**died** 18 May 1978 in a bicycle accident in Dublin)
>
>**Died** 24 Oct 1991

BROWNE, CECIL HAROLD BRUCE 1909–1987

b. 5 Jul 1909; TCD BA & Div Test 1936 MA 1963

d 1936 (Limerick for Armagh) p 1937 (Derry for Armagh); C St Mark Armagh (Arm) 1936–38; C St Nicholas Galway (Tuam) 1938–39; R Knappagh U (Tuam) 1939–45; R Newtowngore Corrawallen and Drumreilly (Kilm) 1945–51; R Collon and Tullyallen (Arm) 1951–64; R Aghabog Newbliss and Killeevan (Clogh) 1964–66; R Oughteragh Fenagh Kiltubride and Drumreilly (Ard) 1966–67; R Ematris Rockcorry and Aghabog (Clogh) 1967–79; ret

>**s.** of Andrew, Engineer of Dunmurry Co Antrim
>
>**m.** (1) 1938 Dublin Charlotte Victoria Cox of Athy Co Kildare (**died** 29 Mar 1968 **bur.** Derriaghy)
>
>**m.** (2) 14 Oct 1972 Jean (*née* Abbott), widow of Robert Patterson of Ballybay Co Monaghan
>
>**Died** 11 Dec 1987 **bur.** Derriaghy

BROWNE, CHARLES 1857/58–1931

b. 1857 or 1858; TCD BA 1890 MA 1893 LLB & LLD 1894

d 1883 p 1884 (Kilmore); C Clongish (Ard) 1883–85; R Kilglass (Ard) 1885–87; R Bicester (Ox) 1887–89; R Clonbroney (w Killoe from 1901) (Ard) 1889–1907; R Butcombe Bristol (B & W) 1908–14; V Yatton (Heref) 1914–16; V Chew Magna (B & W) 1916–31

m. 13 Oct 1885 Amice 3rd **dau.** of Thomas Gee of Hanley Castle Worcs
Died 17 Jul 1931 aged 73

BROWNE, CHRISTOPHER 1755/56–1802

b. 1755 or 1756 Cork; ed by Mr Browne; ent TCD 1 Feb 1773 aged 17 BA 1777 d; he could not have been ordained priest before 1780; R & V Kilglass Rathrea and Aharagh (Ard) *c.* 1780–84; may have been there to 1802.

s. of Ven Edward, Archd of Ross

Died unm 1802

BROWNE, EDWARD

had a dispensation to hold the livings of Killasoolan = Castleblakeney and Ahascragh (Elph) with the Deanery of Tuam 1573

BROWNE, FRANCIS 1758–1796

b. 1758 Dublin; ed by Mr Ball; ent TCD 8 Jul 1773 aged 15 BA 1778 LLB 1781 LLD 1794

C St Andrew (Dub) 1779; Chapl to the Lord Lt 1782; C St Michan (Dub) 1784–87; R & V Dunmore (Tuam) 1787–96; Archd of Kilmacduagh 1791–96; Dean of Elphin 1794–96

s. of Rev William, V St Andrew (Dub) 1757–84 by his first wife Frances **dau.** of Ven Francis Hutchinson, Archd of Down 1733–68; **bro.** of Rev William, C Belfast 1817

m. (ML 4 Mar 1791) Anna Marie eldest **dau.** of James Noble of Glassdrummond Co Fermanagh. Issue incl 1. Catherine Elizabeth **b.** 1793 (**died** 29 Dec 1874 at Craigs Co Antrim) **m.** 17 Mar 1829 Rev George Kirkpatrick, C Drumgoon (Kilm) qv; 2. Frances **m.** 1816 St Peter's Ch Dublin Hon. Thomas A Stewart

Died Nov or Dec 1796

BROWNE, GEORGE WILLIAM 1942–2007

b. 11 Oct 1942; ed Cavan Royal Sch Corgar Ballinamore Co Leitrim; CITC 1999; St John's Coll Nottingham Cert Theol

d 2002 (Kilmore) p 2003; NSM Kildallon Newtowngore and Corrawallen 2002–2005; P-in-c Arvagh Carrigallen Gowna & Columbkille (Kilm) 2005–2007

eldest **s.** of Samuel and Susan

m. Pearl

Died 8 Dec 2007

†BROWNE, JEMMET 1702–1782

b. 18 Aug 1702 Cork; ent TCD 6 Apr 1718 as James Browne BA 1723 MA d; p 29 Dec 1723 Bp 1743; Treas of Ross 1723–33; V Desertserges (Cork) 1723–24;

V Chor Cork 1724; Prec of Cork 1724–32; R & V Little Island (Cork) 1732–43; Dean of Ross 1733–48; Preb of Killaspugmullane and R & V Rincurran and Taxas (Cork) 1742–43; Bp of Killaloe 1743–45; Bp of Cork 1745–72; Bp of Elphin 1772–75; Abp of Tuam and Bp of Ardagh 1775–82

 s. of Edward, Mayor of Cork 1714 (a relative of Bp Peter Browne of Cork 1710–35) by Judith Jemmett

 m. (1) 11 Nov 1723 Alice **dau.** of Thomas Waterhouse. Issue including 1. Rev Edward, Archd of Ross; 2. Rev Thomas, Prec of Cork; 3. Elizabeth **m.** Rev Charles Corker

 m. (2) 21 Oct 1773 St Ann Dublin Jane widow of Capt Barry

 Died 15 Jun 1782 **bur.** 17 Jun Cork Cathedral

PUBLICATIONS
Letter from a Clergyman, 1749
Philadelphians 1749
Letter, 1750

BROWNE, JOHN
V Ahascragh (Elph) 1635–*c.* 66

BROWNE, JOHN 1862–1954

b. 1862; TCD BA (Sen Mod Eth and Log) 1894 Div Test (1) 1895 BD 1900

d 1895 p 1896 (Kilm); C Mohill (Ard) 1895–97; V Mostrim (Ard) 1897–1900; R Cashel (Ard) 1900–06; R Clongish (Ard) 1906–38; Preb of Kilmacallan in Elphin Cath 1937–38; ret

 m. Sarah Anne (**died** 5 Apr 1926) and had issue incl Florence Muriel **m.** Rev Woodley Joseph Lindsay, R Abbeylara (Ard) qv

 Died 21 Dec 1954 aged 92

BROWNE, JOHN WILLS 1820/21–

b. 1820 or 1821 Co Clare; ed by Mr King; ent TCD 16 Oct 1840 aged 19 BA 1845 MA 1854

d 21 Dec 1845 (Elphin) p 1846 (Kilmore); C Kilkeevan (Elph) 1849–; V Trent Vale (Lich) 1854–c96

 s. of John, Inspector

BROWNE, MATTHEW 1735–1788

b. 1735 Co Monaghan; ed by Mr Folds; ent TCD 27 May 1755 aged 20 Sch 1757 BA 1759 MA 1762

d; p 1761 (Limerick); C St Andrew (Dub) 1761; V Ahamplish (Elph) 1774–76; V St James (Dub) 1776–84; V St Catherine (Dub) 1784–88

 s. of William, *colonus*

 m. (ML 4 Mar 1762) Jane Overend of St Andrew's Parish Dublin. Issue incl 1.

Joshua ent TCD 7 Jul 1781 aged 16; 2. Rev Chatworth (**died** 1858) ent TCD 4 Jun 1788 aged 15 BA 1793 MA 1809 d 15 Mar 1795 p 24 Aug 1795 C St Patrick Kilkenny (Oss) 1795–99 V Rathcore (Meath) 1799–1802 V Mayne (Meath) 1802–09 V Rathgraffe (Meath) 1802–47 V Killaloan (Lism) 1814–47 acted as C Kilsheelan 1845; **m.** (ML 21 Sep 1797) Frances Lodge of Kilkenny

Died Mar 1788

BROWNE, MATTHEW CASSAN 1813/14–1871

b. 1813 or 1814 Wexford; ent TCD 6 Jul 1829 aged 15 BA 1837 MA 1859

d 9 Aug 1863 p 24 Jul 1864 (Down); C Knockbreda (Down) 1863; C Ballymoney (Conn) 1864–65; C Castleterra (Kilm) 1866–67. In an action for libel against him when he was C Castleterra, by Rev John McErlane, RC priest, for writing that he had administered the last rites to an unconscious person, he was mulcted in £20 damages and costs having withdrawn the allegation.

s. of Very Rev Peter, R Ahascragh (Elph) & Dean of Ferns qv, by Alicia Dorcas Howse; **bro.** of Rev Peter, R Ahascragh (Elph) qv

m. Josephine (**died** 8 May 1909 aged 81) **dau.** of William and Thomasina Eleanor (*née* Reed) Swan

Died 22 Mar 1871 aged 57

BROWNE, PETER 1765/66–1842

b. 1765 or 1766 Co Mayo; ed by Dr Norris at Drogheda; ent TCD 3 Nov 1783 aged 17 Sch 1786 BA 1788 MA 1791; JP for Co Wexford 1794

d; p 8 Jul 1792; Dean of Ferns 1794–1802; R Ahascragh (Elph) 1799–1829

s. of Peter

m. (M L 1802) Alicia Dorcas Howse. Issue **sons** 1. Rev Peter, R Ahascragh (Elph) qv; 2. John **b.** Co Galway ent TCD 6 Nov 1820 aged 15; 3. Otway **b.** Co Galway ent TCD 3 Jul 1826 aged 17; 4. Rev Matthew Cassan, C Castleterra (Kilim) qv; **daus.** 1. Catherine **m.** 10 Nov 1841 Michael Bingham Kelly of Cloncannon Co Galway; 2. Elizabeth **m.** 16 Nov 1841 Richard Carey MD of Weston Newtownbarry

Died 21 Jul 1842 Gorey Co Wexford

BROWNE, PETER 1802/03–

b. 1802 or 1803 Co Wexford; ed by his father; ent TCD 3 Jul 1820 aged 17 BA 1825 MA 1832

d 1826 p 1827 (Cloyne); PC Kilnehue (Ferns) 1828–9; V Killenvoy (Elph) 1829–45; R & V Ahascragh (Elph, transferred to Clonfert 1870) 1845–80

s. of Rev Peter, R Ahascragh (Elph) qv (**s.** of Peter) by Alicia Dorcas Howse; **bro.** of Rev Matthew Cassan, C Castleterra (Kilm) qv

m. (1) (M L 1834) Mary Clifford. Issue incl his 3rd **son** John Otway **died** 2 Aug 1875 aged 33

m. (2) 27 Aug 1842 Annie widow of Rev H G Webbe, R Ballinakill (Leigh).

BROWNE, ROBERT

MA

V St John Sligo (Elph) 1640–41; V Taunagh (Elph) 1640–41; V Ahamplish and poss also Kilcorkey (Elph) 1641–74; was Commonwealth Minister at Strabane (Derry) at £40 & subsequently at Elphin at £60 1656–60; V Drumcliffe (Elph) 1661–73; poss also R Drumcliffe (Elph) 1661; Archd of Killala 1661–68; is named as one of the Prebendaries of Elphin, probably Kilmacallen of which he was Vicar with Drumcollum 1640–41

BROWNE, THOMAS

lic C Kilglass (Ard) 7 Sep 1809 (S.R.)

BROWNE, THOMAS FREDERICK   1845/46–1919

b. 1845 or 1846; TCD BA 1884 MA 1896

d 1885 p 1886 (Kilmore); C-in-c Kiltubrid (Ard) 1885–1915

   m. Nannie Isabella (*née* Miller); Issue Rev Charles Henry **b.** 10 Jul 1872 Mountmellick Co Laois TCD BA 1893 MA 1902 d 1903 (Norwich) p 1907 (Lucknow) C St Lawrence Ipswich (St E) 1903–05 Chapl Naini Tal 1905–08 Prin & Chapl Lawrence Military Sch Murree 1908–09 Perambur 1910–26 C-in-c Ardclinis (Conn) 1926–40 **m.** 4 Oct 1922 St Mary Woodford Essex Kathleen Maude Vera **dau.** of Rev Robert Andrew Phenix, R Kilwaughter and Cairncastle (Conn) 1882–1901; he died 22 Jun 1940; 2. a yr **dau.** Maude Isobel **died** 4 Aug 1968 Colchester Essex

   Died 31 Jan 1919 Cork aged 73 **bur.** at Kiltubrid

BROWNE, WILLIAM TARRANT   1864/65–1939

b. 1864 or 1865; TCD BA (Resp) 1895 Downes Div Pri 1895 and 1896 Div Test (1) 1896 BD 1909

d 1896 p 1897; C St Mary Belfast (Conn) 1896–98; C Urney (Kilm) 1898–1900; C St Stephen Belfast (Conn) 1900–02; R Stoneyford (Conn) 1902–08; R Killyleagh (Down) 1908–29; Dio C Down Dromore and Connor 1929–34; ret

   s. of James of Clones Co Monaghan by Elizabeth **dau.** of Joshua Tarrant Hoskins

   m. 6 Jun 1905 St Mary's Par Ch Belfast Mary Scott (**died** 24 May 1932) **dau.** of Benjamin Whitsett of Rosslea Co Fermanagh

   Died 25 Nov 1939 aged 74

BRUNSKILL, KIVAS COLLINGWOOD   1864–1922

b. 2 Mar 1864; ed Rathmines Sch Dublin; TCD BA 1885 Div Test 1886 MA 1890

d 1887 (Clogher for Kilmore) p 1888 (Kilmore); C Urney and Annagelliffe (Kilm) 1887–89; C St Mark Armagh (Arm) 1889–91; R Termonmaguirke (Arm) 1891–1907; R Donaghendry (Arm) 1907–13; R Ballymascanlan (Arm) 1913–18; ret

   eldest **s.** of Thomas Richard, Banker of Rathmines Dublin (**s.** of William of Portlaoise) by Anna Jane **dau.** of Commander Kivas Tully, RN

m. 20 Jun 1906 Mary Alice (**died** 29 Jun 1911) **dau.** of Rev Lewis Richards, DD, R Drumglass (Arm) and Charlotte Georgina, 3rd **dau.** of the Hon. Rev John Charles Maude, R Enniskillen (Clogh). Issue Kivas Ralph Louis **b.** 28 Jun 1907 ed Portora Royal Sch Enniskillen **m.** 5 Jun 1937 Ethel Vera Image of Wisbech Cambs and had issue Ralph Richard Redmond **b.** 21 Feb 1940

Died 9 Mar 1922

BRYAN, RICHARD BOOTH 1868–1947

b. 21 Nov 1868 Arklow Co Wicklow; TCD BA 1889 Div Test 1890 MA 1894 MD MCh BAO 1907

d 1890 p 1892 (Kilm); C Boyle (Elph) 1890–94; C St James (Dub) 1894–1908; Missy with CMS at Salt, Syria 1908–11; R Killadeas (Clogh) 1911–19; served as Capt with RAMC 1916–25; was until 1928 Civil Surgeon to British troops at Newry; C-in-c Ballysakeery (Killala) 1925–28; R Kilmacshalgan (Killala) 1928–38; R Tallow w Kilwatermoy (Lism) 1938–47

s. of Rev Thomas (**died** 12 Jan 1915), R Clonmore (Leigh) 1882–1915

m. 19 Feb 1908 Ethel Maureen **dau.** of Thomas Love of Alberta Canada. Issue 1. Rev Charles Rigney **b.** 1910 TCD BA 1947 MA 1950 Univ of Leeds MA 1960 d 1937 p 1938 C St Hilda w St Peter Middlesbrough (York) 1937–39 C Helmsley (York) 1939–40 CF (EC) 1940–46 V Alne w Aldwark (York) 1945–47 Clerical Sec Christian Evangelism Soc in Northern Province 1950–58 V St Nathaniel Sheffield (Sheff) 1965–77 ret 1978; 2. Oliver Richard; 3. Pamela Rosemary Elizabeth; 4. Beryl Hilary; 5. Rosalind Veronica

Died 23 Jan 1947

PUBLICATION
The Early History of Cerebro–spinal Meningitis and the Modern Treatment of same

BRYSON, LEWIS OLIVER 1822/23–1891

b. 1822 or 1823 Co Armagh; ed by Mr McKee; ent TCD 25 Apr 1851 BA 1859; was a Teacher prior to ordination

d 1870 p 1871; C Denn (Kilm) 1870–75; C Drumglass (Arm) 1875–76; R Derrygortreavy (Arm) 1876–91

s. of Oliver, Farmer

m. 13 Feb 1851 at the Scots Church Dublin Eliza **dau.** of Thomas Moffett, Teacher of Swords Co Dublin. Issue incl Charles

Died 27 Aug 1891 at Derrygortreavy Co Tyrone aged 68

BULL, RICHARD

ed by Mr Buck; ent TCD as SC 11 Jun 1763 BA 1778

d 1778 p 1 Aug 1779 (Kilmore); lic C Bailieborough & Moybologue 7 Oct 1778

BULLINGBROKE, JOHN 1666/67–c. 1728

b. 1666 or 1667 Galway; ed by Mr Shaw; ent TCD 1 Jun 1685 aged 18 BA 1689

V Kilkeevan and Preb of Kilcooley (Elph) 1709/10–28

    s. of John, MD of Galway

    m. and had issue incl 1. Edward b. c. 1711 LLD 1744; 2. William b. c. 1715 MA 1740

    Died c. 1728; Will prov 1729

BULTEEL, DOMINICK 1669/70–1743

b. 1669 or 1670 Co Kerry; ed by Mr Shaw at Galway; ent TCD 29 Apr 1685 aged 15 Sch 1687 BA 1689

C Cleenish (Clogh) 1692–1712; R Derrybrusk (Clogh) 1714–21; R Oughteragh (Kilm) 1716–43

    s. of John

    m. Magdalene **dau.** of Henry Gwyllym and **grand–dau.** of Capt Thomas Gwyllym, High Sheriff Co Cavan 1669. Issue 1. Brockhill (**died** 1735); 2. John; 3. Catherine; prob 4. Sandford (**died** 1745) of Ballinamore Co Leitrim

    Died 1743

BUNBURY, GEORGE

V Kilglass (Ard) 1634–62; V Clongish (Ard) 1640–62

BUNBURY, GEORGE

inst V Mostrim (Ard) 16 Nov 1635; resigned for Killoe (Ard); V Killoe (Ard) 1635–62; inst 19 Apr 1635; — probably same as above

BUNBURY, RALPH 1659–1698

b. 1659 Redcastle Co Donegal; ed by Mr Matthew Spring; ent TCD 9 Jul 1675 Sch 1677 BA 1680 MA 1683; signed Address from the Clergy of Dublin to James II in 1675

C St John the Evangelist (Dub) 1684–94; R Baldongan (Dub) 1690–92; Prec of Kildare 1692–95; R & V Kilkerrin and V Annaghdown and Kilscobe (Tuam) 1694–98; R Kilkeevan (Elph) 1694–98

    s. of Rev John, Preb of Moville (Derry) 1662–72 (s. of John)

    m. and had issue incl Rev John (**died** 1765) b. Galway ent TCD 22 May 1711 aged 16 BA 1715 ord p 5 Mar 1723/24 lic C Mallow (Cloyne) 26 Sep 1732 V Aglish (Ardf) 1728–65 V Carrigamleary and Rahan (Cork) 1743–65

    Died 1698

BURD, HENRY SCOTT 1891/92–1945

b. 1891 or 1892; TCD BA (Resp) 1917 MA

d 1918 p 1921 (Kilmore); C Rathaspeck (Ard) 1918–20; C Killesher (Kilm) 1920–22; C Mohill w Termonbarry (Ard) 1922–26; Dio C Killaloe 1926–31; R Borrisokane w Ardcroney and Aghlishclohane (Killaloe) 1931–45; Preb of Lockeen in Killaloe Cath 1943–45

Died 27 Jun 1945 aged 53

BURGH, RICHARD   –1796

prob Richard Burgh ed by Dr Norris; ent TCD 1 Feb 1768 BA 1772

V Drumlane (Kilm) 1773–92; V Innismagrath (Kilm) 1792–96

Died 1796

†BURGH, ULYSSES   –1692

TCD Sch and BA 1660

Preb of St Munchin's, Limerick 1667–92; Dean of Emly 1685–92; Bp of Ardagh upon the separation of the See from Kilmore on the deprivation of Bp Sheridan by K. Lett 7 April and Letters Patent. Mandate for consecration dated 8 Sep 1692 (D.R. Dub) Consec in Christ Ch Dublin 11 Sep 1692 by the Abp of Dublin assisted by Abp of Cashel and Bps of Kildare and Killala.

s. of Richard of Dromkeen Co Limerick

m. Mary **dau.** of William Kingsmill of Ballibeg Co Cork. Issue 1. Rev Richard of Dromkeen (**died** Jul 1739) TCD BA 1685 DD d p 10 May 1685 Prec of Emly 1685–1739 Preb of Kilbragh (Cashel) R Fethard and Kilbragh (Lism) 1691–1739 R Cullen 1691–1736 was married and had issue; 2. William of Bert, ancestor of Lord Downes; 3. Thomas of Oldtown, MP for Naas, Surveyor General of Ireland; 4. Charles; 5. John of Troy Hse Monmouthshire; he also had **daus.** Dorothea **m.** Thomas Smyth who became Bp of Limerick in 1695, and Margaret **m.** Ven John Shepherd, Archd of Aghadoe 1704–05

Died end of 1692, Castleforbes

BURKE, FRANCIS 1832/33–1904

b. 1832 or 1833 Co Cork; ent TCD 15 Jan 1858 BA 1861 Heb Pri and Div Test (1) 1862 MA 1880

d 1862 p 1863 (Tuam); C Killaraght (Ach) 1862–76; R Ardcarne (Elph) 1876–1904; Preb of Terebrine (Elph) 1876–1894; Dean of Elphin 1894–1904; Preb of Mulhuddart in St Patrick's Cath Dublin 1898–1904

s. of Richard

m. (1) Mary (**died** 12 Apr 1896 at the Abbey, Boyle). Issue incl his eldest **dau.** Marion Jane **m.** 29 Apr 1895 Richard Stephen **s.** of Richard N G Stafford.

m. (2) 21 May 1900 Harriet (**died** 23 Jun 1900) eldest **dau.** of Rev Thomas Jameson, V Finglas (Dub) 1858–73

m. (3) 17 Sep 1902 Bessie Georgina (**died** 17 Jun 1944 at Drung Rectory) eldest **dau.** of Rev Frederick Hamilton, R Easternsnow (Elph)

Died 19 Feb 1904 aged 71

PUBLICATION
Lough Ce and its Annals, North Roscommon and the Diocese of Elphin in time of old. Hodges, Dublin 1895

BURKE, JOHN ALLMAN

TCD BA 1852

d 1852 (Tuam) p 1853 (Meath for Kilmore); C Killyon (Elph) 1852–55; C Oola 1855–56; Head Master St Philip's Gram Sch Sydney NSW 1856–58; C Hunter's Hill (Dio Sydney) 1858; C Carcoar (Dio Bathurst)1858–67; Gen Lic Dio Sydney from 1867; still there 1909

BURKE, ROBERT –1910

TCD BA 1899 Div Test 1900

d 1900 p 1902 (Kilmore); C Mohill (Ard) 1900–10

> **Died** 4 or 5 Jul 1910 **bur.** 7 Jul 1910 Seaforde

BURKE, THOMAS –1603

V Ballynakill (Clonf) 1551; Archd of Clonfert 1591; Dean of Elphin 1591–1603 (MS TCD E. 3. 14)

> **Died** 1603

BURLAND, EDWARD GEORGE 1872–1946

b. 15 Jun 1872; ed Rathmines Sch; TCD BA 1894 Div Test (2) 1895 MA 1900

d 1895 p 1896 (Down); C St Aidan Belfast (Conn) 1895–98; C St Thomas (Dub) 1898–1906; R Ashfield (Kilm) 1906–10; R St Thomas (Dub) 1910–20; C Blidworth (S'well) 1920–24; C Christ Ch Croydon (S'wark) 1924–28; C Christ Ch Mountsorrel (Leic) from 1928

> **s.** of John Whitmore of Carnew Co Wexford
>
> **m.** Sarah Ann (**died** 18 Nov 1958). Issue 1. John Whitmore **m.** 11 Jul 1931 Margaret Irene **dau.** of Rev Hugh Boscawen of Bristol; 2. Kathleen Constance **m.** 28 Apr 1934 Gerald Harry **s.** of Rev Henry Edwards of Leicester
>
> **Died** 12 Sep 1946

BURLEY (? BUIRLY), WILLIAM *c.* 1603

b. c 1603; Malvern Coll Ox BA 1624

V Bruhenny & Inchinabacky (Cloyne) 1625–30; R Schull (Cork) 1630–40; Preb of Tipper 1630–69; V Cahir (Lism) 1630–38; Dean of Clonmacnoise 1634–40; Dean of Emly 1640–66; V Roscommon (Elph) 1640–; res the V Oran (Elph) 1640.

> **s.** of George of Easterton Wilts

BURNETT, A. J

d 1855 p; C Killashee (Ard) 1875–76 (C I Dir)

BURNETT, RICHARD ALFRED *c.* 1841–1920

b. *c.* 1841; TCD BA 1862 Div Test (2) 1863 MA 1865

d 1864 p 1865 (Kilmore); C Castleterra (Kilm) 1864–65; C Killeban (Leigh) 1865–74; C Graigue (Leigh) 1874–79; R Graigue w St Mullin's U (Leigh) 1879–1920; Canon of Ullard (Leigh) 1907–20

s. of Robert, MD of Tullow

Died 14 Feb 1920

BURRISS, ARTHUR REGINALD   –1941

TCD BA & Div Test 1900

d 1901 p 1902 (Kilm); C Annagh (Kilm) 1901–04; C Killoughey (Meath) 1904–05; R Killasnett (Kilm) 1905–14; R Castleterra (Kilm) 1914; R Granard (w Abbeylara from 1922) (Ard) 1914–25; Dio C Kilmore 1925–28; R Cloonclare (Kilm) 1928–41

s. of Arthur of Cloughjordan Co Tipperary

m. (1) Lily Emmeline (**died** 23 Sep 1920 at Granard Rectory) **dau.** of R A Rutherford of Manorhamilton

m. (2) Harriet Isabella Marris (**died** 5 Apr 1971) **dau.** of John Marris Roberts, BAI AMICE **m.** (2) 28 Apr 1943 Rev Wesley Daly, Archd of Killaloe

Died 10 Dec 1941

BURROUGHS, WILLIAM GORE

TCD BA 1886

d 1881 (Dublin) p 8 Jul 1882 (Ossory); C Kinawley (Kilm) 1881–82; C Rathdowney (Oss) 1882–83; C Mullinacuff (Leigh) 1883–84; V Kilbeacon and Listerlin (Oss) 1884–87; C St Jude Southsea (Portsm — then Win) 1888–90; Chapl Eccles Est at Toungoo Burma 1890–93; Fort Dufferin Mandalay Burma 1893; Dagshai 1893–95; Fort Dufferin 1895–96; Port Blair 1896–99; Furlough 1900–01 & 1903–04; Chapl Christ Ch Cantonments 1901–03 & 1906–07; Dagshai 1904–05; Shwebo 1905–08

prob **s.** of Rev William Gore, R Kilbeacon (Oss) (**s.** of Ephraim) by Margaret Jephson

BURROWES (BORROWES), ERASMUS DIXON 1799–1866

b. 21 Sep 1799 Queen's Co (Laois); ed Royal Sch Armagh under Dr Carpendale; ent TCD as FC 4 Nov 1816 no degrees recorded. On the death of his brother in 1834, he succeeded as 8th Baronet

d 1823 (Kilmore) p 1 Aug 1824 (Cloyne); C Ardmore (Drom) *c.* 1824; C Ballyphilip (Down) *c.* 1823; C St John Sligo 1824; V Killyon and Kilronan (Elph) 1824–32; C Ballymaglassan (Meath) *c.* 1827; R Ballyroan (Leigh) 1832–62. The Lord Lt who appointed him to Ballyronan, Lord Angelsea, was his first cousin. He resigned it in

1862 having procured it for his curate, Matthew Young

yr **s.** of Sir Erasmus Dixon, Bt by Henrietta de Robillard **dau.** of the Very Rev Arthur Champagne, Dean of Clonmacnoise

m. 7 Mar 1825 St George Dublin Harriet 4th **dau.** of Henry Hamilton of Ballymacoll Co Meath. Issue 1. Erasmus, 9th Bt; 2. Walter; 3. Joseph; 2 daus

Died 27 May 1866 at Laragh Portarlington

BURT, EDWARD

pres V Eastersnow (Elph) 13 Feb 1634/35 (P.R. Lodge); pres to V Kilmacoen and Ivernon (Elph) 13 Feb 1635/36 (L.M. V. III)

BURY, HENRY ROGERS SOMERVILLE

BA 1888

d 1890; C Lurgan (Kilm) 1890–91

BUSHE, CHARLES KENDAL 1805/06–1872

b. 1805 or 1806 Tipperary; ed by Mr Clarke; ent TCD 7 Jul 1823 aged 17 BA 1828 MA 1831 BD & DD 1870

d *c.* 1830 p 25 Mar 1834 (Limerick); C Kinawley (Kilm) 1830; C Gowran (Leigh) 1838; C Tascoffin (Oss) 1845; Preb of Tascoffin (Oss) 1845–58; V Mothel (Oss) 1858–65; Preb of Mayne (Oss) 1861–65; R & V New Ross (Ferns) 1865–72

s. of Robert

m. 17 Oct 1838 at Templepatrick Ann Hamilton (**died** 22 Mar 1875) yst **dau.** of Lt Col Graham. Issue incl 1. an elder **dau.** Anne Hamilton (**died** 28 Apr 1868); 2. Mildred (**died** 28 Sep 1923)

Died 8 Aug 1872 aged 66 **bur.** Kilfane

BUSHE, THOMAS FRANCIS   –1858

TCD BA 1854

d 1855 p; V Russagh and Imp C Rathaspeck (Ard) 1855–58

m. Apr 1856 Elizabeth Jackson of Blackrock Co Dublin **dau.** of Thomas Greer of Tullylagan. Issue incl Brigadier Gen Thomas F, JP (**died** 1 Feb 1951)

m. Bessie **dau.** of Thomas Auchinleck of Crevenagh Co Tyrone

Died 19 May 1858 at Folkestone

BUSHE, WILLIAM 1777–1844

b. 1777 Co Kilkenny; ed by Dr Pack; ent TCD 3 Nov 1794 aged 17 Sch 1797 BA 1799 MA 1810

d 21 Dec 1799 p; C Stradbally (Lism) 1799; Treas of Waterford 1800–07; Preb of Modeligo (Lism) 1800–44; R St George Dublin (Dub) 1805–44; R Cloonclare (Kilm) 1807–10; R Templeport and Drumreilly (Kilm) 1810–35

2nd s. of Gervais Parker, *armiger* of Kilfane

m. (1) Letitia (**died** 1819 at Clifton) **dau.** of Frederick Geale. Issue 1. Isabella Charlotte (**died** 26 Dec 1874 Bray Co Wicklow) **m.** Henry Monck–Mason, Barrister-at-Law; 2. Letitia

m. (2) (ML 1825) Elizabeth Dawson. Issue William Jackson **b.** Co Cavan ed Portora Royal Sch Enniskillen ent TCD 6 Nov 1843 aged 17

Died 23 Feb 1844 Dublin **bur.** St George's Cemetery

PUBLICATION

Sermon on St. Matthew xxii v29, being an introductory Lecture on Romish Doctrines, preached in St. George's Church, Dublin 5 Nov 1823, 8vo Dublin, Tims 1824, 28pp

BUST (? RUST), EDWARD

coll V Killaspicbrone (Elph) 9 Jul 1640

BUTLER, GEORGE WILLIAM 1952–

b. 27 Jul 1952 Dunamon Streete Co Westmeath; ed Wilson's Hosp Sch Multyfarnham Co Westmeath; CITC Dip Theol 1990

d Jun 1990 p Jun 1991; C Drung Castleterra Killoughter Laragh and Lavey (Kilm) 1990–93; R Drung G (Kilm) 1993–95; R Castlemacadam w Ballinaclash and Aughrim G (Glend) 1995–; Canon of Christ Ch Cath Dublin 2003–

s. of William Harold and Elizabeth Gladys (*née* Connolly) of Co Westmeath

m. 22 Sep 1978 St John's Ch Longford Shirley Rosemary **dau.** of Ven Thomas James Bond, Archd of Elphin and Ardagh qv and Rosemary (*née* South). Issue 1. Richard George William **b.** 9 Dec 1980; 2. Andrew Thomas **b.** 12 Jun 1983

BUTLER, Hon. JAMES 1791–1834

b. 26 Apr 1791 Kilkenny; ed by Mr Lawlor; ent TCD as SC 7 Jul 1810 BA 1813 MA 1817

C Gowran (Leigh) 1815; C Knockgraffan (Cash) 1816–24; V Drumlease (Kilm) 1824–34; Dom Chapl to Earl of Carrick

s. of Henry Thomas, Earl of Carrick

Died unm 11 Aug 1834

BUTLER, JAMES EDWARD

b. Rathkeale Co Limerick; TCD BA 1861

d & p 1861 (Kilmore); C Boyle (Elph) 1861; in charge of ? Loch Fields Mission, Walworth 1864–66; C St Mark Whitechapel *c.* 1870

s. of Thomas, farmer

BUTLER, LILLY

b. at Bletchingley, Surrey; admitted Sizar Clare Coll Camb 20 Dec 1749; BA 1754 MA 1757

d 1754 p 1755 on Letters Dimissory from Canterbury; PC Wooton Underwood, Bucks 1756–82; V Battersea, Surrey 1757–58; V Witham, Essex; Chapl to the Duke of Buckingham, Ld. Lt of Ireland; pres to the Deanery of Ardagh 19 Mar 1785 and installed Apr 5 1785; res in 1789 for R Loughgilly (Arm); R & V Creagh (Ross) 1782–89

> probably **s.** of Lilly, DD, R St Ann London 1716–36
>
> Brady ii, 562 says that he was MA TCD 1782 (this is not mentioned in Al. Dub.), and that he **m.** Anne **dau.** of Rev Jacob Houblon R Moreton, Essex

BUTLER, RICHARD 1757/58–1841

b. 1757 or 1758 Co Meath; ed by Mr Kerr; ent TCD 10 Jul 1773 aged 15 BA 1778 BD & DD 1800

C Muckno (Clogh) 1781; V Streete (Ard) *c.* 1781–95; R Burnchurch (Oss) 1795–1841; he resided at Burnchurch till 1830 when he was obliged to leave in consequence of the Tithe War; Preb of Mayne in Kilkenny Cath 1795–1819; V Trim (Meath) 1818–19; while in Street, he appointed a curate and went to Edinburgh to study Medicine and duly qualified as a doctor, came home and practised among his parishioners *gratis*

> eldest **s.** of James of Priestown Co Meath (of the Dunboyne Butlers) by Dorothy **dau.** of Sir Richard Steele, Bt.
>
> **m.** 1792 Martha 2nd **dau.** of Richard Rothwell of Burford Co Meath. Issue 1. Rev James **b.** 1793 TCD BA 1814 C Burnchurch (Oss) 1818 and 1825 subsequently British Chapl at Homburg, ? R Navan (Meath) 1859–75 **m.** Elizabeth (ML 1818) eld **dau.** of Thomas Rothwell of Rockfield Kells Co Meath and had issue (i) Richard (**died** 1851) **b.** Kilkenny 1822; (ii) Thomas JP of Priestown; (iii) James **m.** 7 Jun 1864 Mary Elizabeth **dau.** of Tottenham Ally of Hill of Ward Co Meath, and 5 **daus.**; 2. Rev Richard **b.** 14 Oct 1794, V Trim and Dean of Clonmacnoise, a celebrated Antiquary and author, **m.** and **died** s.p. 17 Jul 1862; 3. Thomas Lewis, Capt 79th Highlanders **died** 1848; 4. Whitwell **m.** and had issue; 5. Rev Edward **b.** Kilkenny 1800 or 1801 (**died** 23 Feb 1877 at Llangoed Castle Brecknockshire) BA 1824 **m.** (1) 1830 Henrietta (**died** 1832) **dau.** of Henry Skryne of Warleigh Somerset and had issue a **son** Bagot who **died** young; **m.** (2) 1835 Anne Elizabeth (**died** 1845) **dau.** of William Woodville and had issue Theobald William **b.** 1838; **m.** (3) 1847 Trinity Ch Marylebone Blanche **dau.** of Philip Perring of Devonshire Place London and had issue a **son** Edward; **m.** (4) 18 Jun 1868 Mary Elizabeth eldest **dau.** of Richard Rothwell of Rockfield Kells and had issue Dorothea; 6. John **m.** and had issue; 7. Maria (**died** 12 Jan 1866 at Cheltenham)
>
> **Died** 27 May 1841

BYRNE, JOHN

appears C Creeve (Elph) 1766; appears C Toomna (Elph) 1766

CADDY, JOSEPH 1693/94–c. 1767

b. 1693 or 1694 Ravenglass Cumberland; ed at Ravenglass by Mr Barrow; ent TCD as Siz 7 Jun 1712 aged 18 BA 1716 MA 1719

V Mostrim (Ard) 1732–38; R & V Castlerahan (Kilm) 1738–40; V Drumlane (Kilm) 1740–c67

    s. of William

    Died *c.* 1767– Will proved 1767

Towards the end of his life, the following advertisment appeared in *Faulkner's Dublin Journal,* 24–27 June 1766; "Whereas the Rev. Joseph Caddy of Tunnyarachill in the County of Cavan, after a short Indisposition was, in the Month of February last, struck with a Palsy or Paralytic Disorder, which hath ever since deprived him of the Use of his Limbs and Speech; and the said Joseph Caddy having no Family, other than Servants about him, soon afterwards became a Prey to certain designing Persons, who, under Colour of a distant Relationship, made Use of Means to get at and possess themselves of all the said Joseph Caddy's ready Money, Bills, Bonds, Mortgages, and other Securities for Money, then locked up in his Desk and Escritoires, to the Amount of 4,000 l. and upwards; together with a Will duly made by him in favour of John Lyndon, Jane his Wife, Patrick Sheridan, Elizabeth his Wife, and others, the said Joseph's nearest relations, who were always the immediate Objects of his Contemplation. Now this is to caution every Person, as well the tenants of the said Joseph Caddy as all others, who are indebted to him in any Sum or Sums of Money, not to pay the same, or any Part thereof, to any Person or Persons whatsoever, until a fit Guardian of the Person and Fortune of the said Joseph Caddy shall be duly appointed, for which and other purposes, a Bill will be preferred, and an application forthwith made to the High Court of Chancery, on behalf of the said John Lyndon, Jane his Wife, Patrick Sheridan, Elizabeth his Wife, and others. Dated this 27th Day of June 1766. John Lyndon, Jane Lyndon, Patrick Sheridan, Elizabeth Sheridan"

In the paper of 8–12 July following, John Caddy, grand–nephew of the said Joseph, published a long counter–advertisement, dated 5 July 1766. He says he lived and was educated in the said Joseph's house and family since his childhood, and when about nine months ago he married his present wife Esther Connell, Joseph made a settlement on him of a considerable part of his fortune. He also before his illness made a Will, then in John's keeping, making John his executor and trustee, and leaving him 100 l besides the settled funds. Only 150 l was in it bequeathed to the Lyndons and Sheridans. The monies stolen were taken by the servants, and "the said Lyndon entertained one of the said servants at his House for several Days after they had so taken away the said Securities and Will"

CADGE, ROBERT 1804/05–1854

b. 1804 or 1805 Dublin; ent TCD 5 Nov 1821 aged 16 BA 1828 MA 1832

Lic C Killasoolan = Castleblakeney (Elph) 1832; V Tessaragh (Elph) 1839–41; Preb of Kilmacallen and R & V Taunagh (Elph) 1841–53; V Rathconnell (Meath) 1853–54

    s. of William, *vectigalis exactor*

    Died 1854

CAFFRY, CHARLES ATKINSON 1779/80–1856

b. 1779 or 1780 Dublin; ed by Mr White; ent TCD 1 Jun 1795 aged 15 BA 1801 MA 1832

d 1802 p 1804 (Kilmore); DC Mullogh as part of Killinkere (Kilm) 1819–56; C Killinkere (Kilm) 1819; there in 1821

    s. of Bernard, *pragmaticus*

    m. and had issue incl 1. Fitzherbert **b.** Co Cavan ed by Mr Hawkesworth ent TCD 16 Oct 1835 aged 16 BA 1841; 2. John Rowley ent TCD 1 Nov 1841 aged 18; 3. Jane (**died** 20 Jul 1902)

    Died 23 May 1856 at Mullogh Glebe aged 76

CAHILL, JAMES

a Roman Catholic, intruded into the V Kilcommick (Ard) before 1649

CALDWELL, FRANCIS THOMAS 1846/47–1925

b. 1846 or 1847; TCD BA 1882 MA 1892

d 20 May 1883 p 8 Jun 1884 (Down); C Knockbreda Belfast (Down) 1883–86; R Killoe (Ard) 1886–88; R Almoritia (Meath) 1888–98; R Leney w Stonehall (Meath) 1898–1913; R Delvin (Meath) 1913–23; ret

    m. 17 Jul 1883 at Ballyburley Ch Jennie (**died** 16 Feb 1923) eldest **dau.** of Rev William K Kempston, R Ballyburley (Kild)

    Died at Whitehill Ballinamallard Co Fermanagh 17 Mar 1925 aged 78 **bur.** Deans Grange Dublin

CAMIER, GEORGE EDWIN –1946

TCD BA & Div Test 1935

d 1935 p 1936 (Dublin); C St Thomas Dublin (Dub) 1935–38; R Clongish and Clooncumber (Ard) 1938–43; R Templemichael (Ard) 1943–46

    s. of John L of Skibbereen Co Cork

    m. 19 Oct 1938 Helen Elizabeth **dau.** of Edward Byrne of Ailesbury Rd Dublin. Issue 1. Joyce Avril Frances; 2. Graham

    Died 7 Mar 1946

CAMIER, JAMES WILLIAMSON –1949

TCD BA 1906 Div Test 1907 BD 1922

d 1907 p 1908 (Ossory); C Killaban (Leigh) 1907–09; C Aghold (Leigh) 1909–13; C Ballymackey (Killaloe) 1913–14; C-in-c Dunamon (Elph) 1914–17; R Arvagh (Kilm) 1917–20; R Templeport (Kilm) 1920–25; R Tallow (Lism) 1925–35; R Donohill (Cash) 1935–40; R Kilvemnon U (Lism) 1940–49

    m. (1) Ellen Phoebe (**died** 21 Aug 1931)

    m. (2) Alberta (**died** 10 Jan 1968 Cork) elder **dau.** of J Davie of Ardamine Gorey Co Wexford.

Issue (by which wife?) incl 1. Ernest TCD MSc **m.** Mabel Elizabeth eldest **dau.** of Johnson Meares; 2. Eileen Mary (**died** Apr 1959) TCD BA **m.** 14 Sep 1942 John Basil Bryan of Gurteen Mullinahone Co Tipperary

Died 24 Nov 1949

CAMPBELL, ARCHIBALD

d 16 April 1632 (Killaloe) p 23 Apr 1632 (Kilmore); V Killargue (Kilm) 1632–34

CAMPBELL, CHARLES DANCER 1835/36–1883

b. 1835 or 1836 Co Monaghan; also known as Charles Dillon Campbell; ent TCD 13 Oct 1854 aged 18 BA 1859 MA 1865

d 1861 p; C Creggan (Arm) 1861–62; C Inismagrath (Kilm) 1862–66; C Ballyjamesduff (Kilm) 1866–68; PC Corrawallen (Kilm) 1868–70; C Kilmore (Meath) 1870; C Rathfarnham (Dub) 1871–73; went to England

s. of Rev Canon Adderley Willcocks, Preb of Tullycorbet (Clogh) (**s.** of Burrowes of Dublin) by Jemima Matilda, 2nd **dau.** of Sir Amyrald Dancer, Bt

m. 6 Jul 1861 St Peter's Ch Dublin Anna Selina **dau.** of Alexander Reid of Dublin. Issue incl 1. a **dau.** b 12 May 1862; 2. a **dau.** b 26 Feb 1863

Died 1883 at the Vicarage, Redesham Suffolk

CAMPBELL, EDWARD FITZHARDINGE 1850–1932

b. 1850 Belfast; ed The Royal Sch Dungannon; TCD BA & Div Test 1877 MA 1881

d 1877 p 1878 (Kilm); C Drumgoon (Kilm) 1877–78; C Kilmore (Kilm) 1878–79; R Ballyeglish (Arm) 1879–86; R Killyman (Arm) 1886–1921; RD Dungannon (Arm) 1917–21; ret

only **s.** of Very Rev Theophilus Fitzhardinge, DD, C Munterconnaught (Kilm) qv

m. 28 Jun 1876 Lydia yst **dau.** of Robert Morris, solicitor of Lurgan Co Armagh. Issue 1. Jane (**died unm.** 1959) **b.** 1878; 2. Rev Edward Fitzhardinge (**died** 13 Dec 1957) **b.** 17 Jan 1880 TCD BA & Div Test 1903 MA 1932 d 1903 p 1904 C St Mary Dublin (Dub) 1903–04 C St Comghall Bangor (Down) 1904–06 CF 1906–32 DACG 1917 ACG 1927 V Glen Magna and Stretton Magna (Leic) 1932–52 **m.** 1917 Edith Mary **dau.** of Edward Dunk of Gravesend Kent and had issue (i) Monica (ii) Patricia; 3. Isabel Caroline Berkeley (**died** 1968) **b.** 1 Aug 1881 **m.** 1 Feb 1910 Charles de Burgh, Lt RN and had issue (i) Lydia Anne **b.** 1923 (ii) Coralie Isabel **b.** 16 Sep 1924 **m.** 8 Sep 1950 Sir Robert Kinahan, JP DL Lord Mayor of Belfast 1959–61 and had issue; 4. Robert Morris, CBE (**died** 1949) **b.** 5 Jul 1883 **m.** 14 Nov 1907 Louise Eleanor **dau.** of Alexander Henry; 5. Geoffrey Alexander (**died** 1965) DSO **b.** 6 Sep 1884 m *c.* 1923 Elizabeth Anderson and had issue (i) Nigel (ii) Sandra; 6. George Richard Colin (**died** 10 Oct 1918 with his wife and **dau.** on RMS *Leinster* when torpedoed by a German submarine in Dublin Bay) **b.** 9 Oct 1886 Lt Commander RN **m.** 1912 Eileen Hester Louise **dau.** of Lt Col John H Knox–Browne and had issue Eileen Elizabeth; 7. Rev Theophilus Francis (**died** 13 Nov 1956) **b.** 19 Sep 1888 TCD BA 1911 Div Test 1912 MA 1916 d 1912 p 1913 C Willowfield Belfast (Down) 1912–15 C Dundalk (Arm)

1915–21 C-in-c Sixmilecross (Arm) 1921–24 R Dundalk (Arm) 1924–34 R Derrynoose and Middletown (Arm) 1934–53 Dio Sec Armagh 1934–50 Preb of Ballymore (Arm) 1947 Prec of Armagh Cath 1947–53 **m.** 18 Oct 1921 Dundalk Par Ch Constance Elsie Maria (**died** 3 Jun 1974) 2nd **dau.** of Sinclair Dickson Smith Chatterton, RIC and had issue Morris Edward Dickson **b.** 21 May 1925

Died 26 Apr 1932

CAMPBELL, EDWARD GEORGE 1810/11–1896

b. 1810 or 1811 Co Dublin; ed by Mr Little; ent TCD 6 Jul 1829 aged 18 BA 1834 MA 1848

d (with 51 others) 12 May 1836 at Limerick p 6 Jan 1836; C Clontibret (Clogh) 1836–37; Asst Chapl Steeven's Hosp Dublin 1843; Asst Chapl Hibernian Marine Sch, Phoenix Park Dublin 1845–55 as stated in his *Letters Testimonial* 1855; R Kilderry (Oss) 1855–73; V Kiltoom (Elph) 1873–74; R Mostrim (Ard) 1874–75; R Clonaslee (Kild) 1875–80; R & V Killaderry (Kild) 1880–88; C Carogh (Kild) 1888–94; ret

s. of Archibald *agricola*

m. and had issue an only child Edward G A **died** 24 May 1875

Died 8 Oct 1896

CAMPBELL, MATTHEW –1882

TCD MA 1871

d 21 Dec 1872 (Down) p; C Mohill (Ard) 1873–74

Died 2 Mar 1882 in Surrey

CAMPBELL, THEOPHILUS FITZHARDINGE 1811–1894

b. 1811 Co Dublin; ed by Mr Huddart; ent TCD 20 Oct 1828 aged 17 BA & Div Test 1838 MA 1849 BD & DD 1879

d 1838 (Kildare) p 1839 (Dublin for Kilmore); C Munterconnaught (Kilm) 1838–39; R Tunstall (Lich) 1839–43; PC Trinity Ch Belfast (Conn) 1843–65; R Finvoy (Conn) 1865–69; R Shankill Lurgan (Drom) 1869–94; Exam Chapl to Bp 1886; Chapl Lurgan Workhouse; Archd of Dromore 1886–87; Dean of Dromore 1887–94

s. of Alexander, Solicitor of Dublin by Julia Henrietta (*née* Berkeley) widow of Edward Elsmere

m. 12 May 1843 Seapatrick Ch Banbridge Co Down Isabella (**died** 12 Dec 1891 at the Rectory Lurgan) yst **dau.** of William Hayes of Banbridge Co Down. Issue 1. Margaret Julia (**died** 8 Feb 1875); 2. Caroline Isabella **m.** 9 Jun 1876 Adam West Watson and had issue Rt Rev Campbell West Watson, Bp of Christchurch NZ; 3. Henrietta Louisa (**died** 13 Apr 1859); 4. Rev Edward Fitzhardinge, C Kilmore (Kilm) qv

Died 23 Apr 1894 at the Rectory Lurgan aged 82

PUBLICATIONS
Annihilation and Universalism Examined
Studies in Biblical and Ecclesiastical Subjects, ed by his son, Elliott Stock 8vo 1895

CAMPBELL, WILLIAM 1677/78–*c.* 1738

b. 1677 or 1678 Limerick; ed by Mr Cashin; ent TCD 24 Dec 1696 aged 18 BA 1701 MA 1704

C Shrule (Ard) 1731–38

> **s.** of William
>
> **Died** *c.* 1738– Will dated 28 Dec 1738, proved 30 May 1739

CAMPION, WILLIAM ASHTON 1879–1953

b. 1879 Dublin; ed The High Sch Dublin; TCD BA & Div Test 1903 MA 1920

d 1904 p 1905 (Kilmore); C Annagh (Kilm) 1904–07; C Naas (Kild) 1907–16; R Ballycommon (Kild) 1916–23; R Narraghmore (Kild) 1923–35; C-in-c Holmpatrick (Dub) 1935–51; Canon of Christ Ch Cath Dublin 1950–51; ret

> **s.** of John Alfred and Mary of Dublin
>
> **m.** 24 Jun 1919 Mary Alice Wilhelmina (**died** 11 May 1980) **dau.** of Thomas Potterton of Carbury Co Kildare. Issue 1. Alan Hubert; 2. Margery Isa TCD MA 1942 **m.** REA; 3. Mary Ashton
>
> **Died** 27 Apr 1953 Glenageary Dublin

CARD, ROBERT JAMES 1816/17–1883

b. 1816 or 1817 Dublin; ed by Mr Turpin; ent TCD 3 Nov 1834 aged 17 BA 1839 MA 1842

d 1840 p; C Clongish (Ard) 1841–45; C Templemichael (Ard) 1844–66; R Tashinny & Abbeyshrule (Ard) 1866–67; R & V Kilcommick (Ard) 1867–83; Archd of Ardagh 1875–83

> **s.** of Francis James, Solicitor TCD BA 1791 (**s.** of Ralph, merchant of Dublin)
>
> **Died** 7 Mar 1883 at Kilcommick Rectory

CAREY, JAMES

TCD Div Test 1889 BA 1890

d 1887 (Kilmore) p 1890 (Clogher for Kilmore); C Boyle (Elph) 1887–90; R Kilmore (Elph) 1891–98

> **s.** of Michael Richard, Officer in HM Probate Court; **bro.** of Rev Thomas, I Caledon (Arm) 1905–32 and C-in-c Termonfeckin (Arm) 1932–41
>
> **m...** (**died** 21 Dec 1958 Dublin aged 93) and had issue 1. James **m.** 22 Oct 1924 Muriel Mabel elder **dau.** of J G Firth of Glasgow and had issue Very Rev James Maurice George Carey (**died** 20 Apr 2001) **b.** 1926 Dean of Cork 1971–92; 2 Amy Lucinda Armstrong **m.** 21 Jul 1917 George Henry Dane Gibson of Dublin. Last entry in C of I D and Crockford 1898, though C I Dir gives his death at Killarvillen 3 May 1892

CAREY, MICHAEL FLEMING

d 1871 p; C Cloone (Ard) 1871–74; C-in-c Killegar (Kilm) 1874–77; R Cloone (Ard) 1877–80

CARR, ARCHIBALD –*c.* 1674

MA

d 28 Apr 1628 p 14 Sep 1630; R & V Dromore (Clogh) 1630–35; R & V Aghavea (Clogh) 1638/39–47; probably same as A C, Preb of Termonbarry (Elph) 1661–71; V Bumlin (Elph) to 1672

   Died *c.* 1674

CARR, FRANCIS *c.* 1824–

b. *c.* 1824; TCD BA 1858 Div Test 1859

d 1860 p; C Castleblakeney (Elph) 1874 in Leslie MSS but not in C I Dir; a Francis Carr, d 1860 was R Ballymacward (Clonf) at this time

   s. of Andrew **b.** Kilkenny; in the Army

CARROLL, CHARLES FREDERICK HEZLET –1962

TCD BA & Div Test (2) 1915

d 1916 p 1917 (Cork); C Garrycloyne (Cork) 1916–19; C Layde & Cushendun (Conn) 1919–20; C Donaghcloney (Drom) 1920–24; C St Donard Belfast (Down) 1924–25; R Swanlinbar (Kilm) 1925–27; C Hove (Chich) 1927–29; Perm to Off at Ellacombe (Ex) 1929–30; C St Michael E Teignmouth (Ex) 1930–34; V Binham and Cockthorpe (Nor) 1934–62

   s. of Rev Robert Hezlet Meade, R Teampol–na–mBocht (Cork) by Christina Louise **dau.** of Rev James Frederick Newell, R Kilbehenny (Emly)

   Died May 1962

†**CARSON,** THOMAS 1805–1874

b. 27 Aug 1805; ed by Mr Coghlan at Glanmire Grammar School, Cork; ent TCD 15 Oct 1821 BA 1826 LLB & LLD 1832

d 1831 p 16 Oct 1831 Bp 1870; C Tomregan (Kilm) 1831; V Urney and Annageliffe (Kilm) 1838–54; R Cloone (Ard) and V Gen Kilmore 1854–60; Dean of Kilmore and V Kilmore & Ballintemple (Kilm) 1860–70; consec at Armagh Cath Bp of Kilmore Elphin and Ardagh 2 Oct 1870; Bishop of Kilmore Elphin and Ardagh 1870–74

   eldest **s.** of Rev Thomas, R Kilmahon and Clonmult (Cloyne) by Elizabeth eldest **dau.** of Christopher Waggett of Cork; **bro.** of Rev Joseph, FTCD

   m. 29 Sep 1833 Eleanor Anne eldest **dau.** of Robert Burton of Dublin. Issue **sons** 1. Rev Thomas William, C Kilmore (Kilm) qv; 2. Joseph John Henry **m.** Maria Alicia **dau.** of Henry G Johnston and had issue; 3. Rev Robert Burton (**died** 19 Jun 1899 London) **b.** 18 Sep 1845 TCD Sch 1866 BA (Sen Mod Classics) 1869; incorp at St Edmund's Hall Oxford 1869 MA 1872 d 12 Jun 1870 (Down) p 1870

(Kilmore for Dublin) C Kilternan (Dub) 1870–78 C Tullow (Dub) 1878–80 C St John Torquay (Ex) 1880–85 Chapl Hotel des Baines, Aigle Switzerland 1885–88 V Haynes (St A) 1888–94 Chapl at Aigle 1894–97 **m.** 3 Nov 1870 Elizabeth eldest **dau.** of Rev William Allen Fisher R Kilmoe (Cork) and had issue (i) Thomas Allen **b.** 9 Sep 1871 (ii) William Robert **b.** 2 Aug 1874 (iii) Rev Robert Burton Coleridge; 4. Rev Henry Watters (**died** 1 Sep 1895 at Lucerne Switzerland) **b.** 12 Jul 1847 TCD Sch 1869 BA 1871 Div Test (1) 1872 Theo Exhib (1) 1873 MA 1875 BD 1878 d 1870 p 1872 C Woods Chapel (Arm) 1870–72 R Ballyclog (Arm) 1872–74 Asst Lect in Divinity TCD 1884–89 C Rathmichael (Dub) 1889–90 V Santry (Dub) 1890–95 **m.** 26 Jun 1872 Isabel Jane (**died** 25 Jan 1921) 3rd **dau.** of Hon Henry Martley, Judge of the Landed Estates Court, Dublin; **daus.** 1. Eleanor Isabella; 2. Elizabeth (**died unm.** 27 May 1865); 3. Isabella Deborah **m.** 25 Oct 1871 Herbert Baldwin Colthurst BA Asst Master Royal Sch Armagh and had issue incl Rev Joseph Riversdale, R Calary (Glend); 4. Harriet Anna Mary (**died** unm 4 Oct 1874)

Died 7 Jul 1874 at Portrush Co Antrim **bur.** Ballywillan

CARSON, THOMAS WILLIAM 1834–1895

b. 20 Dec 1834 Dublin; ed by Dr Graham; ent TCD 15 Oct 1852 Sch 1854 BA 1857 MA 1860 Div Test (1) 1864

d 1864 p 1866; C Jonesboro (Arm) 1864–65; C Kilmore (Kilm) 1865–70; Chapl to his father, Bp of Kilmore Elphin and Ardagh 1870–74; subsequently lived in Dublin

eldest **s.** of Rt Rev Thomas, Bp of Kilmore qv (**s.** of Rev Thomas) by Eleanor Anne **dau.** of Robert Burton; **bro.** of Rev Robert Burton; **bro.** of Rev Henry Watters

Died s.p. 23 Nov 1895

CARY, OLIVER 1704/05–1777

b. 1704 or 1705 Carrick; ed by Mr Manby at Carrick; ent TCD 4 Jul 1720 aged 15 Sch 1722 BA 1724 MA 1740

d 26 Jun 1726 p 17 Sep 1729 (Ardagh); C Kilkeevan (Elph) 1729; R Shankill Kilmacumsy Clonfinlogh Clontuskert & Kilgeffin (Elph) 1731–42; V Shankill Kilmacumsy Kilcorkey Killukin Kilmactranny Kilcooley and Clomnagarmacan (Elph) 1743–; Preb of Kilcooley (Elph) 1743–67; V Enniscorthy (Ferns) 1758–77; R Rossdroit (Ferns) 1758–67; Prec of Ferns 1767–77; R & V Templeshanbo (Ferns) 1767–77

s. of Charles

m. 10 Feb 1749/50 St Peter Dublin Frances (**died** 26 Jan 1804 aged 90 at Monalty) **dau.** of Col William Southwell. Issue incl 1. Rev Edward (**died** about 1 Oct 1798) **b.** 1753 or 1754 Co Roscommon TCD BA 1776 R & V Newtownbarry (Ferns) 1778–98 **m.** Mary (**died** 17 Jun 1780) **dau.** of Sir Edward Loftus, Bt; 2. Harriet (**died** 5 Apr 1808 aged 53 at Monalty) **m.** Norman Steele of Monalty

Died 1777

CARY, OLIVER 1761/62–1846

b. 1761 or 1762 Co Roscommon; ed by Mr Kenny; ent TCD 3 Jul 1777 BA 1781 MA 1810

d 15 Dec 1782 p 18 Jul 1784 (Ardagh); R Croghan (Elph) 1790–97; R Eastersnow Kilcola & Kilbrine = Kilbryan (Elph) 1790–98; Archd of Elphin 1798–1809; V Toomna and Creeve (Elph) 1798–1846; R Kilgeffin (Elph) 1802–38; R Killukin and Kilmacumsy and Preb of Kilcooley (Elph) 1809–46

> **s.** of William, farmer
>
> **m.** Catherine Tomlinson (ML 31 May 1797) of St Peter's Dublin; commanded a Troop for the defence of Elphin district in 1798
>
> **Died** 24 May 1846 in England aged 84

CASSIDY, HERBERT 1935–

b. 25 Jul 1935 Cork; ed Cork Gram Sch; TCD Carson, Kyle, Downes & Cox Comp Pris BA 1957 Div Test (1) 1958 MA 1965; OU Course Cert

d 29 Jun 1958 p 25 Jul 1959 (Connor); C Holy Trinity Belfast (Conn) 1958–60; C Christ Ch Londondery (Derry) 1960–62; R Aghavilly and Derrynoose (Arm) 1962–65; Hon V Chor Armagh Cath 1963–85; C St Columba Portadown (Arm) 1965–67; R St Columba Portadown (Arm) 1967–85; Dean of Kilmore and R Kilmore Ballintemple Kildallon Newtowngore and Corrawallen (Kilm) 1985–89; Dean of Armagh and Keeper of the Public Library Armagh 1989–2006; Hon Sec Gen Synod 1990–2006; Exam Chapl to Abp of Armagh 1993–2006; ret

> **s.** of Herbert (**s.** of Robert and Frances (*née* Patterson)) by Frederica Jane **dau.** of George and Isabella (*née* Farrar) Somerville of Cork
>
> **m.** 4 Apr 1961 St Patrick's Cath Armagh Elizabeth Ann **dau.** of Rev Henry Francis Osborne Egerton, R Derryloran (Arm) 1939–41 and Rebecca. Issue 1. Nicola Jane **b.** 1 Feb 1962 **m.** 28 Dec 1990 St Patrick's Cath Armagh John Mervyn **s.** of Mervyn and Iris Heatley of Portadown and have issue (i) Emma Rebecca **b.** 27 May 1992 (ii) James Patrick **b.** 14 Oct 1993 (iii) Catherine Naimh **b.** 2 Jul 1996 (iv) Maeve Hannah **b.** 13 Jun 1998; 2. Ian Richard **b.** 31 May 1964 **m.** Victoria Norton; 3. Joanne Patricia **b.** 4 Mar 1968 **m.** 30 Dec 1992 St Patrick's Cath Armagh David Johnston and have issue (i) Daire George **b.** 17 Nov 1994 (ii) Anna Catherine **b.** 31 Jan 1996

PUBLICATIONS
Teaching Topics, 1983
It Moves all the Same, 1985

CATHCART, CARLETON 1802/03–

b. 1802 or 1803 Co Fermanagh; ed by Mr Ewing; ent TCD 3 Jul 1826 aged 23 BA 1831

was C Kinawley (Kilm) *c.* 1836

> **s.** of Alexander

CATTERALL, DAVID ARNOLD 1953–

b. 1953; Univ of London BSc 1974 ARCS 1974; Cranmer Hall Durham Dip Theol 1978

d 1978 p 1979; C Swinton St Peter (Manch) 1978–81; C Wythenshawe St Martin (Manch) 1981–83; C Heaton Norris Christ w All SS (Manch) 1983–88; R Fanlobbus U (Cork) 1988–95; Canon of Cork and Ross 1993–95; Warden Church's Ministry of Healing in Ireland 1995–2002; R Templemichael Clongish Clooncumber Killashee and Ballymacormack (Ard) 2002–

m. Rev Janet Margaret qv

CATTERALL, JANET MARGARET 1953–

b. 1953; Univ of Wales Bangor BA 1974; Cranmer Hall Durham Dip Theol 1977

dss 1981 d 1987 p 1990; C Wythenshawe St Martin (Manch) 1981–83; C Heaton Norris Christ w All SS (Manch) 1983–88; C Bandon U (Cork) 1988–89; Dio Youth Adviser (Cork) 1989–94; Dio Youth Chapl (Cork) 1994–95; I Drung Castleterra Larah Lavey and Killoughter (Kilm) 1995–02; C-in-c Mostrim Granard Clonbroney Killoe Rathaspesk and Streete (Ard) 2002–; Preb of Mulhuddart in St Patrick's Cath Dublin 2005–

m. Rev David Arnold Catterall qv

CAULFIELD, ADAM 1695/96-1772

b. 1695 or 1696 Co Sligo; ed by Dr Drury, Dublin; ent TCD 17 Apr 1712 aged 16 BA 1716 MA 1726

ordained p 21 Jun 1726 (Ardagh); prob same as Adam Caulfield who was coll V Taunagh (Elph) 24 Nov 1729; C Dunboyne (Meath) 1733; prob succeeded his father as Preb and V Ballisodare (Ach) in 1736 — was there in 1742 — there to 1772

s. of Rev Tobias (**s.** of Capt Thomas)

m. (ML 17 Dec 1729) Eleanor Palmer of St Bride's Ch Dublin.

Died Jun 1772 bur St Mary's Dublin

CAULFIELD, FRANCIS WILLIAM MONTGOMERIE 1856–1924

b. 1856; TCD BA 1880 MA 1884

d 1881 p 1883 (Kilmore); C Killesher (Kilm) 1881–83; C Newry (Drom) 1883–85; C Lyncombe (B & W) 1885–88; Dio C Clogher 16 Feb– 27 Apr 1889; R Charlestown (Arm) 1889–99; Chapl CCS 1899–1902; C St John Bapt Southend (Chelmsf — then St A) 1902–05; C St Dunstan East Acton (Lon) 1906–07; C St John Isleworth (Lon) 1907–11; C Morval (Truro) 1912–13; C St Paul Wokingham (Ox) 1916–18; subsequently living in Quainton, Aylesbury

3rd **s.** of Lt. Col William Montgomerie of Dublin by Dora Jane **dau.** of William French of Clonyquin Co Roscommon

Died 4 Dec 1924 Plymouth

CAULFIELD, JOHN 1737/38–1816

b. 1737 or 1738; ed Westminster Sch; matric Christ Ch Coll Oxford 8 Jun 1757 aged 19 DD

R Knockbride (Kilm) 1774–75; R Cloonclare Clonlogher and Killasnett (Kilm) 1775–81; Archd of Kilmore 1776–1816; R Castlerahan (Kilm) 1777–81; R Killesher (Kilm) 1781–97; Preb of Devenish (Clogh) 1797–1816; R Derryloran (Arm) 1797–1816

2nd **s.** of Col William of Raheenduff Queen's Co (Laois) and Inverness, Lt-Governor of Fort George (grandson of William 5th Baron and 2nd Viscount Charlemont by Catherine **dau.** of Ven John Moore, Archd of Cloyne

m. (1) Euphemia Gordon (**bur.** 23 Jun 1808) of Kenmure Dumfriesshire. Issue 1. Lt.Col William, Roscommon Militia **m.** Lucy Saunderson of Clover Hill Co Cavan and had issue 3 **sons** and 4 **daus.** incl John **b.** 2 Jan 1792 **m.** 17 May 1824 Anne Lovell Bury; 2. Thomas Gordon, RN (**died** 23 Jun 1821) **b.** 1768 **m.** 1802 Theodosia **dau.** of W Talbot of Mt Talbot Co Roscommon and had issue (i) Rev William (**died** 28 Oct 1867) **b.** 2 Dec 1813, R Molahiffe (A & A) **m.** 9 Jul 1840 Ellen (**died** 1890) and had issue; 3. John; 4. George; 5. Alexander; 6. Robert, Capt RN; 7. Major–Gen James (**died** 4 Nov 1852) **b.** 30 Jan 1782, MP for Abingdon **m.** (i) 14 Dec 1814 Letitia (**died** Aug 1826) **dau.** of Lt Gen Hugh Stafford and had issue 4 sons; **m.** (ii) Annie Rachel Blake and had issue 3 sons; 8. a **dau.** (**bur.** 30 Dec 1821 aged 49 at Derryloran) **b.** *c.* 1772 **m.** Capt Gordon of Scotland

m. (2) 1808 Maria Farellow

Died 2 Mar 1816 aged 78 **bur.** Derryloran Cookstown Co Tyrone

CAULFIELD, THOMAS GORDON 1801–1875

b. 1801 Co Westmeath; ed by Mr Needham; ent TCD 3 Nov 1817 aged 16 BA 1821

C Bonowen (Meath) 1823–26; V Clonfinlough and Clontuskert (Elph) 1832–*c.* 52; R Stackallen (Meath) 1852–54; R Ballyloughloe (Meath) 1859–75

3rd **s.** of Lt William of Bonowen

m. Elizabeth (**died** 28 Dec 1885 at Rathmines Dublin aged 81) **dau.** of John Pratt Winter of Augher

Died 8 Nov 1875 aged 74

CAULFIELD, TOBIAS 1670/71–1735/36

b. 1670 or 1671 Co Galway; ed by Dr Hinton at Kilkenny Coll; ent TCD 13 Jul 1690 aged 19 BA 1694

V Ballysumaghan (Elph) *c.* 1696–1716; res V Taunagh (Elph) 1716; Preb of Ballysadare (Ach) 1696–1735; Proctor in Convocation 1704; Preb of Clondehorkey (Raph) 1716–35; V Gen of Achonry 1724; Archd of Killala 1725–35

7th **s.** of Capt Thomas of Donamon

Died 1735/36

CAULFIELD, WILLIAM (GEORGE)

V Kilnamanagh (Elph) 1721–; V Kilcorkey (Elph) 1723–41; v Killukin (Elph) 1725–*c.* 41

CAVE, GUY NEWELL 1919–

b. 4 Feb 1919 Killoughey Rectory Tullamore Co Offaly; ed Rossall Sch Fleetwood Lancs; TCD BA & Div Test 1941 MA 1958

d 22 Feb 1942 p 23 Mar 1943; C Knockbreda (Down) 1942–45; C-in-c Kildrumferton and Ballymachugh (w Ballyjamesduff from 1972) (Kilm) 1945–87; RD Ballymachugh 1956–63; Dio Sec Kilmore 1960–72; Preb of Mulhuddart in St Patrick's Cath Dublin 1965–72; Archd of Kilmore 1972–87; Exam Chapl to Bp of Kilmore 1972–87; ret

s. of Rev Arthur Meagher, R Moyliscar (Meath) (**s.** of William of Cork) by Eve Eleanor **dau.** of Ven John Healy, R Kildrumferton (Kilm) qv and Mary; **bro.** of Very Rev Stephen Arthur, Dean of Raphoe 1967–72

m. 4 Jul 1945 Swords Co Dublin Freda Disney (Holly) **dau.** of Frederick F and Margaret (née Hopkins) Elvery of Swords Co Dublin. Issue 1. Heather Margaret **b.** 9 Sep 1947 **m.** 1972 John Ransom of London and have issue (i) Kerry (ii) Gilly (iii) Gavan; 2. Mary Elizabeth **b.** 31 Dec 1949 **m.** 1977 Christopher Furlong and have issue (i) Greg (ii) Scott

CAVE, VINCENT 1639/40–1669

b. 1639 or 1640 at Simonstone Lancs; ed at Hoddesdon Sch Herts and at London; ent Caius Coll Camb 20 Aug 1658 aged 18 Sch 1658–63 LLB 1664; incorp at Oxford 1664 Fellow 1665

was R Ardcarne Kilmactranny Killukin and Toomna (Elph) 1668–69; Archd of Elphin 1668–69; coll V Taunagh (Elph) 18 Feb 1668

s. of Henry

Died 1669

†CELE –1048

Bp of Ardagh to 1048 (A.F.M.)

Died 1048

CHALMERS, ROBERT ALAN 1966–2003

b. 1966; LLCM; QUB LLB 1988; TCD Isaac, Corkey, Gk, Purser Shortt Lit Pris, Moncrieff Cox Sermon Pri BTh 1991

d 1991 p 1992; C Lurgan Kildrumferton Ballyjamesduff Ballymachugh Killinkere Munterconnaught & Billis (Kilm) 1991–94; Dio Reg Kilmore Elphin and Ardagh 1992–94; R Kildrumferton Ballymachugh and Ballyjamesduff 1994–96; BC Boyle Aghanagh Ardcarne Croghan Dunamon Rathcline Kilkeevan Kiltullagh and Tybohine (Elph) 1996–97

Died 11 Dec 2003

CHAMBERS, JOHN WESTROPP 1833–1901

b. 29 Jun 1833 Co Tyrone; ed Dungannon Royal Sch by Mr Ringwood; ent TCD 4 Nov 1853 aged 20 Classical Sch 1856 BA 1858 Div Test (2) 1859 LLB & LLD 1875

d 1859 p 1859 (Derry); C Killaghtee (Raph) 1859; C Ballinascreen (Derry) 1860; PC Knocknarea (Elph) 1861–64; Sen Classical Master Royal Sch Dungannon 1864; Head Master Drogheda Gram Sch 1868; Head Master Kingstown Sch 1871; R Glascarrig (Ferns) 1878–1900; Preb of Whitechurch (Ferns) 1897–1901; ret

    s. of Richard, solicitor

    Died 21 Apr 1901 Kingstown (Dun Laoghaire) aged 67

CHAMBERS, WILLIAM JOHN   –1949

d 1925 (Chelmsford for Exeter) p 1928 (Down); C Charles Plymouth (Ex) 1925; C St Mathew Belfast (Conn) 1927–32; C-in-c Drumlane (Kilm) 1932–34; C St Matthew Belfast (Conn) 1934–36; C-in-c Glenavy (Conn) 1936–37; R Glenavy (Conn) 1937–49

    m. and had issue 1. Kathleen; 2. Doris; 3. Frederick

    Died Aug 1949

CHAPMAN, ARTHUR WELLESLEY

Camb Theol Coll Harvard Univ BD 1880

d 1881 (Huron) p 1882 (Massachusetts); R St James Amesbury Mass 1882–84; C-in-c Hampstead (Lon) 1885–87; C Cashel and Rathcline (Ard) 1888–91; C St Michael (Lim) 1891–92; Org and Dep Sec for Irish Soc for England and Scotland and Lic to Off Dio Liverpool 1898–99; Chapl at Villierstown (Lism) 1899–02; still living in 1909

CHAPMAN, JOSEPH

d 1877 p 1878 (Kilm); C Killasnett (Kilm) 1877–79; R Drumreilly (Ard — then Kilm) 1879–81; V Dunamon and Fuerty (Elph) 1881–1902; C-in-c St Paul Yelverton (Ex) 1902–03; C Lydford (Ex) 1903–06; V Bolventor & Temple (Truro) 1906–11

    m. 1 Feb 1883 Catherine Ogilvy **dau.** of Rev Philip Cartlyon, V Wisbech St Mary's (Ely)

CHAPMAN, JOSEPH HENRY 1836/37–1924

b. 1836 or 1837; ed St Bee's Coll Durham 1875

d 1877 p 1878 (Durham); C Byker (Dur) 1877–80; V Dromara (Drom) 1880–99; R Castleterra (Kilm) 1899–1901; R Killermogh (Oss) 1901–09

    s. of William of Malone Belfast

    m. (1) Anne Allen. Issue two children John and Anne deceased

    m. (2) Jane Crawford. Issue 1. Henry; 2. Eleanor Isabella; 3. Jeannie Crawford **m.** 3 Feb 1909 Rev John Durie Cowen BA, R Kilnaboy (Killaloe)

    Died 3 Nov 1924 aged 87

CHAPMAN, THOMAS SAMUEL 1854/55–1912

b. 1854 or 1855

d 1878 p 1880; C Kilmoremoy (Killala) 1878–80; C Omey (Tuam) 1880–81; R Arvagh (Kilm) 1881–90; R Kilrush (Ferns) 1890–1906; ret

m. 7 Apr 1880 Ardnaree Ch Mary Anne widow of Major Warren, Capt 13th Regt and N Mayo Regt of Militia

Died 18 Feb 1912 at Dun Laoghaire (Kingstown) aged 57

CHAPMAN, WILLIAM 1820/21–1899

b. 1820 or 1821

d 1872; C Ballymacormick (Ard) 1872–74; C Maguiresbridge (Clogh) 1874–80

Died 27 Mar 1899 aged 78

†CHARLES

Bp of Elphin to 1357; deposed.

CHARLES

Sir Charles...Dean of Ardagh to 15 April 1407 (Cal. Reg. Flem. No.57)

CHARLTON, ANDREW   –1724

d 9 Nov 1673; V Killinkere (Kilm) 1682–1697; R & V Killashee (Ard) and Archd of Ardagh 1683–96; He was coll Archd of Ardagh 3 Aug 1683, but seems to have resigned it upon his appointment to Chancellorship of Armagh 1696; Chanc of Ardagh 1685; Chanc of Connor 1692–96; V Baileborough (Kilm) 1682–1697; V Killan (Shercock) and Knockbride (Kilm) held by faculty with the Chancellorship 1696–1724 (Leslie *Armagh Clergy and Parishes*); Chanc of Armagh 1696–1724. He was Proctor for the clergy of Kilmore Diocese at the Convocation of 1704 (C.F. III and V)

In the Kilmore MSS, he is V Killan and Knockbride (Kilm) with R Kilmore (Arm) 1682–1708 and V Killinkere (Kilm) 1682–97, and was succeeded in Killan and Knockbride by Rev Arthur qv, prob his son in 1708

3rd s. of John of Aghabane Co Cavan

Died 1724

PUBLICATION

A Sermon preached before the House of Commons at St. Andrew's Church, Dublin, 4to 1704

CHARLTON, ARTHUR   –1726

he was either

(1) s. of Rev Andrew, qv, b. at Mullagh; ed by Mr Harvey, Lisburn; ent TCD 13 Jun 1700 aged 15 Sch 1702 BA 1704 MA 1707, or

(2) bro. of Rev Andrew, qv, and 4th s. of John of Aghabane Co Cavan; ent TCD 4 Feb

1682/83 aged 18 BA 1687

V Killan (Shercock) and V Knockbride *alias* Knockloyd *alias* Kilcama (Kilm) 1708–26; if (1), he was Chapl to the Duchess of Ormonde

Died 1726

CHARLTON, JOHN 1679–1752

b. 1679 near Longford; ed by Mr Harvey, Lisburn; ent TCD 11 May 1698 aged 18 BA 1701

V Denn (Kilm) 1726–40; V Kildrumferton (Kilm) 1740–52

s. of William of Aughabane Co Cavan

Died 1752

CHARTERS, ROBERT JAMES 1897–1975

b. 16 May 1897 Shankill Co Dublin; ed High Sch Dublin; TCD BA 1921 Div Test 1922 MA 1924; served in Great War as Lt Irish Rifles 1915–19 and was POW in 1918 in Germany

d 1922 p 1923; C Ballymoney (Conn) 1922–24; C St James Ashted Birmingham (Birm) 1924–25; C Carlow U (Leigh) 1925–27; C Oldcastle U (Meath) 1927–28; R Bailieborough (Kilm) 1928–31; R Drumconrath U (Meath) 1931–33; R Kilcleagh (Meath) 1933–44; R Dunboyne U (Meath) 1944–45; R St Mary Drogheda (Meath) 1945–64; Dio Reg Meath 1952–58; RD Skryne (Meath) 1954–58; Canon of Meath 1955–58; Dean of Clonmacnoise 1958–61; Archd of Meath and Exam Chapl to Bp of Meath 1961–64; ret

s. of John of Shankill Co Dublin and Sarah

m. 5 Sep 1923 at Carrickfergus Anne Matthews (**died** 15 Jul 1974) of Carrickfergus Co Antrim. Issue 1. John Charles (killed 29 Mar 1957 aged 32 at Nairobi) TCD MA **m.** Denise and had issue a dau; 2. Robert Gordon; 3. Mary Elizabeth **m.** 7 Jun 1949 Herbert James Walker MB LLB and had issue a **dau.** b 25 Feb 1955

Died 29 Sep 1975 Wexford

CHESNUTT, OSBORNE 1837/38–1908

b. 1837 or 1838 Co Sligo; ed Kildare Place Sch Dublin; ent TCD 1 Nov 1873 aged 35 BA 1877 Div Test 1878 MA 1880

d 1877 p 1878; C Kiltinanlea (Killaloe) 1877–78; C Stow–Bardolph and Wimbotsham (Ely) 1878–79; R Milford (Raph) 1879–80; C Derg (Derry) 1880–81; C Kenmare (A & A) 1882–84; Chapl to Bp of Victoria, Hong Kong and CF, Hong Kong 1884–87; C Belleek (Arm) 1888–90; C Tomregan (Kilm) 1891–92; C Ballinderry (Arm) 1893; R Ballyclog (Arm) 1894–1908

s. of William, coastguard by Susan (**died** 30 May 1902 aged 98)

Died 8 Sep 1908 **bur.** Donaghendry churchyard Stewartstown Co Tyrone

†CHESTER, THOMAS –1584

b. in London

Bp of Elphin 1580–84

> s. of Sir William, Lord Mayor of London
>
> Died June 1584 at Killiathan

CHETWOOD, JOHN 1652/53–1704

b. 1652 or 1653; ent TCD 10 May 1670 aged 17 BA 1674 MA 1677

V Lavey (Kilm) 1682–1704; R Ardbraccan Liscartan and Ratane (Meath) 1681–1704

> 2nd s. of Valentine of Trinity Coll Oxford; bro. of Knightley, Dean of Gloucester
>
> m. and had issue an only son Knightley, a friend and correspondent of Swift, who was of Woodbrook, Queen's Co. (Laois) m. 29 Aug 1700 St Michan's Ch Dublin Hester Booking and had issue Knightley ent TCD 24 Nov 1725 aged 17
>
> Died 1704 bur. St Kevin's Ch Dublin

CHETWOOD, JOHN

R & V Kiltoghart (Ard) 1790–

CHETWOOD, JOHN –1814

R & V Kiltoghart (Ard) before 1807–1814; most probably same as JC above; living on his benefice in Cork.

> m. Elizabeth Hamilton and had issue
>
> Died 13 Apr 1814

CHRISTIAN

Archd of Ardagh 1255–59 (MS. F. I. 18)

CHRISTIE, EDWIN BARRY 1859–1921

b. 1859 Rathmines Dublin; ed Rathmines Sch; TCD Div Test 1886 Candidate Bachelor 1887

d 1887 p 1888 (Kilmore); C Drumgoon (Kilm) 1887–89; C Enniscorthy (Ferns) 1889–90; R Arvagh (Kilm) 1890–95; R Middletown (Arm) 1895–1921

> 2nd s. of Sanderson (s. of James) of Rathgar Dublin by Charlotte Phoebe dau. of Frederick Mann of Dublin
>
> m. 29 May 1888 at the Moravian Ch Belfast Julia Pasche yr dau. of Rev Joseph Carey of Kilwarlin Hillsborough Co Down. Issue 1. Reginald Barry b. 1890 m. 4 May 1929 at Melbourne Dora elder dau. of Rev Andrew Asboe of Belfast; 2. Cedric Pasche (died 16 Dec 1915 in France in Great War) b. 24 Apr 1892 Comber Co Down Temp 2nd Lt King's Liverpool Regt; 3. Robert Francis Sanderson (killed in Great War 15 Oct 1917) b. 9 Jun 1897 2nd Lt RFC
>
> Died 3 Oct 1921 Rathgar Dublin bur. Mt Jerome Dublin

CHRISTIE, GEORGE HENRY –1934

TCD & Div Test 1884

d 1884 p 1885 (Down); C Layde (Conn) 1884–88; R Killoe (Ard) 1888–90; C St Paul Hulme Manchester (Manch) 1890–92; C St Mary Birmingham (Birm) 1892–94; C Holy Trinity West Bromwich (Lich) 1895–99; C St Matthias Plymouth (Ex) 1899–1901; C Wicklow (Glend) 1902–04; I Calary (Glend) 1904–11; Lic Pr Dio Dublin 1911–22; Chapl Female Orphan Hse 1922–23; C-in-c Finglas 1923; Lic Pr Bangor (Down) 1923

Died 18 Jan 1934 at 24 Southsea Ave Southbourne Hants

CHUTE, JOHN LINDSAY 1800/01–1871

b. 1800 or 1801 Co Kerry; ed by Mr Slattery; ent TCD 6 Jan 1817 aged 16 BA 1823

d 10 Oct 1824 p 18 Dec 1825 (Limerick); C Kilkeevan (Elph) 1838–45; R Roscommon (Elph) 1845–63; PC and R Dingle U (A & A) 1864–71

s. of Arthur by Frances **dau.** of John Lindsay

m. 24 Apr 1832 Jane Lucinda (**died** 9 Oct 1855 Drumcondra Dublin) **dau.** of William Dobbs Burleigh of St Stephen's Green Dublin. Issue incl 1. Capt P Chute (**died** 1858 in India), 84th Regt; 2. Arthur (**died** 31 Dec 1899 aged 63 at Castlecoote); 3. William Burleigh **b.** Co Roscommon ent TCD 1 Jul 1856 aged 18; 4. Rev John (**died** 10 Jan 1913) **b.** Co Roscommon ent TCD 1 Jul 1859 aged 17 Sch 1862 BA (Resp) 1864 Div Test (1) 1866 MA 1867 V St Jude Hunslet Leeds (Ripon); 5. his 2nd **dau.** Frances Wills **m.** 2 Jul 1861 William John McLoughlin of Castlecoote Co Roscommon; 6. his yst **dau.** Ruth (**died** 26 Jan 1923 at Clevedon)

Died 3 or 6 Jan 1871

CLAPHAM, MARMADUKE

is Commonwealth Minister of St John's Sligo from 5 Sep 1654

CLARK, GEORGE HENRY

TCD BA 1885

d 1887 (Kilm) p; C Clongish (Ard) 1887–93

m. Emily Florence (**died** 15 Jan 1940 Rathgar Dublin)

CLARK, STEPHEN KENNETH 1952–

b. 1952; Univ of Bristol BEd 1974; Wycliffe Hall Ox 1980

d 1983 p 1984; C Pitsea (Chelmsf) 1983–86; Chapl Scargill Hse 1986–89; R Elmley Castle w Bricklehampton and Combertons (Worc) 1989–96; Chapl Burrswood Christian Centre (Roch) 1996–2001; Chapl Team Leader Burrswood Christian Centre 2001–07; R Annagh Drumaloor Cloverhill and Drumlane (Kilm) 2007–

CLARKE, DAVID GEORGE ALEXANDER 1923–2004

b. 11 Mar 1923 Belfast; ed Methodist Coll Belfast; TCD Sch 1945 Abp King Forster Hebrew Downes Weir & Ryan Pris BA 1947 MA 1951 BD 1955 PhD 1957

d 1948 (Down) p 1949 (Clogher); C Dromore (Drom) 1948–49; C-in-c Drum (Clogh) 1949–50; R Clonbroney and Killoe (Ard) 1950–52; R Clogher (Clogh) 1952–54; C Abbeystrewry (Ross) 1955–57; R Usworth (Dur) 1957–61; R Kilrossanty G (Lism) 1961–74; RD Dungarvan 1965–67; Preb of Newcastle in St Patrick's Cath Dublin 1965–89; Prec of Waterford and Lismore 1967–73; Dean and R Cashel (Cashel) 1973–83; R Ballymascanlon and Creggan U (Arm) 1983–89; ret

s. of Robert and Eileen (*née* Whitford) of Belfast

m. 20 Jun 1949 Dromore Cath Dorothy Eileen **dau.** of William and Dorcas (*née* Crookshanks) Dickson of Dromore Co Down. Issue 1. Hilary Ann **b.** 6 Dec 1950 **m.** (1) 26 Mar 1973 St Mary's Ch Dungarvan Co Waterford Anthony Hynes of Athlone and had issue (i) Jonathan (ii) Peter (iiii) Karen **m.** 2 Jul 1994 London Jeffrey Good of Aherla Bandon Co Cork 2. Jeremy Dickson **b.** 9 Aug 1952 **m.** 27 May 1994 St Patrick's Cath Dublin Sally Ann Fanagan of Dublin; 3. Jennifer Eileen **b.** 7 Jan 1955 d 2003 p 2004 Aux Min Waterford Cath G (Waterf) 2003– **m.** 9 Jul 1977 Cashel Cath Noel Crowley of Stradbally Co Waterford and have issue (i) Charles (ii) Robert (iii) Thomas and (iv) Ruth

Died 10 Jul 2004

PUBLICATION
Life After Death

CLARKE, FRANCIS EDWARD 1847/48–1910

b. 1847 or 1848; TCD BA 1867 MB 1868 MA 1872 MD 1873 LLB & LLD 1877; MRIA 1876 MRCSE

d 1878 p 1879 (Kilmore); C Killashee (Ard) 1878–79; R Killinagh (Kilm) 1879–83; R Boyle (Elph) 1883–1910; Precentor of Elphin 1892–1904; Archd of Elphin 1904–10

s. of Francis, MB, FRCS

m. and had issue a son who died 4 Nov 1950; his 2nd **s.** James Flexman died 20 Nov 1918 at Mill Hse Newtownbarry; his eldest **dau.** Blanche Marie Rebecca (**died** 6 Dec 1936 Drogheda) **m.** 3 Nov 1896 Rev Francis Travers Cockle, MA, R Taunagh (Elph) qv and had issue incl Kenneth **b.** 1901; a **dau.** Daphne Florence Isabel (**died** 14 Mar 1922) **m.** Henry Grattan Griffin, Manager National Bank, Edgeworthstown; a twin **dau.** Marion Violet (**died** 13 Apr 1972 Greystones Co Wicklow) **m.** Charles E Johnstone, Bank of Ireland and had issue (i) Alan (ii) Irene (iii) Michael (iv) Fred (v) Daphne

Died 9 Mar 1910 aged 62 **bur.** Boyle, where three windows in the church commemorate him

CLARKE, GEORGE SEYMOUR 1831/32–

b. 1831 or 1832 Co Antrim; ed by Mr O'Connor; ent TCD 1 Jul 1850 aged 18 BA & Div Test 1855 d 1857 (Cashel) p 1858 Waterford); C Clashmore (Lism) 1857–60; C Keady (Arm) 1860–64; C Magheracloone (Clogh) 1866–73; C St Luke Holliscroft Sheffield (Sheff — then York) 1874–76; DC Killegar (Kilm) 1879–86

CLARKE, JAMES 1830/31–1903

b. 1830 or 1831; TCD BA & Div Test (2) 1856 MA 1861

d 1856 p 1857 (Kilmore); C Kildrumferton (Kilm) 1856–71; C St Andrew Drumaloor (Kilm) 1872–1903

Died 20 Apr 1903 aged 72

CLARKE, JOHN

d p 1769 (Kilm); C Cloonclare (Kilm) 1769; V Killinagh (Kilm) 1776–1822

†CLARKE, KENNETH HERBERT 1949–

b. 23 May 1949 Belfast; ed Sullivan Upper Sch Holywood; TCD Downes Written Comp Pri BA (Phil) 1971 Div Test 1972

d 1972 p 1973 Bp 2001; C Magheralin (Drom) 1972–75; C Dundonald (Down) 1975–78; SAMS Missy Valdivia Chile 1979–81; Archd of La Region de los Lagos Chile 1981; R Crinken (Dub) 1982–86; R St Patrick Coleraine (Conn) 1986–2001; Steering Group member of Evangelical Contribution on Northern Ireland 1988–; Chmn SAMS Ireland 1993–; Preb of Kilroot (Conn) 1996–98; Archd of Dalriada in Dio Conn 1998–2001; elected Bp of Kilmore Elphin and Ardagh by Electoral College 13 Nov 2000; consec in St Patrick's Cath Armagh 25 Jan 2001; enthroned in St Fethlimidh's Cath Kilmore 18 Feb 2001; enthroned in Cath of St Mary the Virgin and St John the Baptist Sligo 25 Feb 2001; Bp of Kilmore Elphin and Ardagh 2001–

> **m.** 26 Jun 1971 Glanmire Cork Helen (**sister** of Rt Rev. Kenneth Raymond Good, Bp of Derry and Raphoe 2002–) **dau.** of Rev Canon William Raymond Good, R Carrigrohane (Cork) 1973–82 by Jean. Issue 1. Alison Ann **b.** 2 May 1973; 2. Tanya Mai **b.** 21 Mar 1974; 3. Lynda Jean **b.** 18 May 1976; 4. Nicola Jayne **b.** 26 Jul 1978

> PUBLICATION
> *Called to Minister? A consideration of Vocation to the Ordained Ministry,* 1990

CLARKE, RICHARD 1838/39–

b. 1838 or 1839; ent TCD 2 Jul 1856 aged 17 BA 1861 Div Test (2) 1862

d 11 Oct 1863 p; C Castleterra (Kilm) 1863–64; C Kilmoremoy (Killala) 1864–65; PC Dunseverick (Conn) 1866–72; R Ballyburley (Kild) 1872–80; V Roscommon (Elph) 1882–85; went to Australia

> **s.** of Rev Richard, Preb of Geashill (Kild)

> **m.** 1 Oct 1868 at Portrush Par Ch Helen **dau.** of John Stott

CLARKE, RICHARD CHARLES 1841/42–1900

b. 1841 or 1842

d 1876 p 1878; C Roscommon (Elph) 1876–77; R Drumreilly (Kilm) 1877–79; R Denn (Kilm)1879–80; R Oughteragh (Kilm) 1880–97

    m... (**died** 15 Apr 1951 Dublin). Issue Rev Richard, Missy in India

    Died 12 Nov 1900 aged 58

CLARKE, THOMAS

d 1872 p; C Templemichael (Ard) 1872–73 (C I Dir)

CLARKE, WILLIAM HENRY

TCD BA (Resp) 1864 Div Test (2) 1866

d 1866 (London) p 1875 (Kilmore); C St Matthew Mary–le–Bow (Lon) 1866–67; C Derryheen (Kilm) 1875–76; living in Liverpool 1883

CLEMENTS, HENRY GEORGE JOHN 1829–1913

b. 3 Nov 1829; ed Rugby Sch; Christ Ch Coll Ox matric 19 Oct 1848 BA 1852 MA 1856; was President of Sidmouth Cricket Club in Devon for nearly 50 years

d 1854 p 1856 (Exeter); C Sidmouth (Ex) 1854–60; C St Mark Torquay (Ex) 1861–62; PC Ashfield (Kilm) 1862–65; V Sidmouth (Ex) 1865–1913

    2nd **s.** of Col John Marcus of Ashfield Lodge, MP for Co Leitrim

    m. (1) 31 Oct 1855 his cousin Selina **dau.** of Lt Col Henry J Clements

    m. (2) Catherine Frances **dau.** of Godfrey Wentworth of Wakefield

    Died 12 Sep 1913

CLEMENTS, JOHN WILLIAM 1879–1957

b. 25 Jul 1879 Markethill Co Armagh; QUB BA 1915

d 1916 p 1917 (Down); C Coleraine (Conn) 1916–18; C Glenavy (Conn) 1918–26; C-in-c Killargue and Killenumery (Kilm) 1926–32; R Laragh and Lavey (Kilm) 1932–41; R Arvagh and Carrigallen (Kilm) 1941–53; ret

    s. of Thomas Waugh by Caroline (*née* Bain)

    m. 11 Jun 1911 Margaret Douglas Norwood (**died** 31 Jan 1946) of Belfast. Issue 1. Dorothy Caroline (**bur.** 13 Sep 1952 Kensington Cemetery London); 2. Edith; 3. Rev Thomas, C-in-c Kildrumferton (Kilm) qv; 4. Sarah Kathleen

    Died 1957

CLEMENTS, THOMAS 1916–1983

b. 13 Mar 1916 Belfast; ed Portora Royal Sch Enniskillen; TCD BA 1938 Div Test 1939 BD 1954

d 1939 (Tuam for Down) p 1940 (Down); C St Donard Belfast (Down) 1939–41; St Anne's Cath Miss Distr Belfast (Conn) 1941–43; C-in-c Kildrumferton and

Ballymachugh (Kilm) 1943–45; C-in-c Mullaghdun (Clogh) 1945–48; R Finner (Kilm — then Clogh) 1948–50; R Enniskillen (w Trory to 1954) (Clogh) 1950–82; Preb of Donacavey (Clogh) 1957–59; RD Enniskillen 1957–82; Chanc of Clogh 1959–60; Prec of Clogher 1960–67; Dean of Clogher 1967–82; ret

> **s.** of Rev John William, R Arvagh and Carrigallen (Kilm) qv (**s.** of Thomas Waugh) by Margaret Douglas (*née* Norwood) of Belfast
>
> **m.** 30 Sep 1941 St Donard's Par Ch Belfast Elizabeth Lyons **dau.** of James and Ann Houston. Issue 1. Raymond Houston **b.** 2 May 1944 **m.** Heather Patricia Ferguson of Cookstown Co Tyrone; 2. Margaret Elizabeth **b.** 9 Oct 1946 **m.** William McBride; 3. Thomas Adrian **b.** 13 Dec 1949 **m.** Patricia Coleman
>
> **Died** 20 Sep 1983

PUBLICATIONS

In the Name of God, collection of sermons and addresses, 1970

But I'd rather be a Pelagian, 1979

CLIFFE, JOHN 1736–1816

b. 1736 New Ross Co Wexford; ent Kilkenny Coll 7 Aug 1746; ent TCD 8 Jan 1755/56 BA 1760 MA 1774

C Carrigrohane (Cork) 1771; C Killaspugmullane (Cloyne) 1772; V Ballyfeard (Cork) 1772–1816; Preb of Termonbarry (Elph) 1775–1816

> **s.** of William of New Ross by Elinor Vigors
>
> **m.** (1) 9 Apr 1771 Belinda (*died* 8 Aug 1772 aged 27) **dau.** of Thomas Glendove of Dublin. Issue Belinda (*died* 7 Dec 1772 aged 4 months)
>
> **m.** (2) (ML Dublin May 1776) Sarah **dau.** and co–heir of Richard Wilson of Dublin. Issue 1. John (drowned 1817) TCD BA 1811; 2. Sarah **m.** H L Tottenham; 3. Anne **m.** Rev Thomas Mercer Vigors
>
> **Died** 4 or 14 Feb 1816 **bur.** New Ross

CLIFFORD, RICHARD SAMUEL 1799/1800–

b. 1799 or 1800 Co Leitrim; ed by Mr Kane; ent TCD 6 Nov 1815 aged 15 BA 1823 MA 1832

d 1825 p; C Kiltoghart (Ard) 1836–46; V Oughteragh (Kilm) 1846–52; V Teynham (Cant) 1852–60; PC St Mary's Spitalfields (Lon) 1855– was there in 1865

> **s.** of Samuel (*died* 1815)
>
> **m.** 24 Feb 1840 Harriet Young eldest **dau.** of Capt Cox, JP of Carrick-on-Shannon

CLOAK, LOUIS

d 1879 (California) p 1881 (Wisconsin); R Lancaster Wisconsin 1880–82; R Mohegan New York 1882; C St Patrick Walsall Staffs (Lich) 1882–83; C St Andrew Bordesley (Birm) 1883–85; C Monaghan (Clogh) 1885–88; R Cloone (Ard) 1888–1910; living in Sutton Surrey 1927; Last entry in Crockford 1928

> **m.** and had a **dau.** Amy E

CLOGY, ALEXANDER 1614–

b. 1614 Scotland; ed at Dublin

Chapl to Bp Bedell; V Denn (Kilm) 1637–40; V Urney (Kilm) 1641; persecuted by the rebels; was Army Chapl in England 1643; R Wigmore (Heref) 1647–98

PUBLICATION
Memoir of Bishop Bedell, 1675

CLOUDSDALE, THOMAS

St. Aidan's Coll Birkenhead 1876

d 15 Jun 1878 p 14 Jun 1879 (Ossory); C Wexford (Ferns) 1878–80; PC Quivvy (Kilm) 1880–82; Chapl to Earl of Lanesborough 1880–82; C Geashill (Kild) 1882–86; C Bilton (Ripon) 1886–88; C Linthwaite (Wakef) 1889–91; C Irnham (Linc) 1892–95; C Moston (Manch) 1895–97; C Wormegay w Tottenhill (Nor) 1897–1903

COATES, EDWARD 1761–1833

b. 1761 Co Roscommon; ed by Mr Prendergast; ent TCD 7 Nov 1775 aged 14 BA 1781

C St John Sligo (Elph) 1801; may be same as C Charlestown (Arm) 1806–07; C Kilbroney (Drom) 1808; C Clonduff (Drom) 1820

s. of James

there was a Prerogative Marriage Licence dated 26 Jun 1788 between the Rev Edward Coates of Castlepollard Co Westmeath and Delia Hemmings of St Thomas's Dublin

Died 11 Nov 1833 aged 71

†COBBE, CHARLES 1685/86–1765

b. 1687 Winchester; ed Winchester; Trinity Coll Oxford, matric 12 Nov 1705 aged 16 BA 1709 MA 1712 DD by diploma 9 Jul 1744; TCD BD & DD *ad eundum* 1736

Chapl to Charles, Duke of Bolton, Ld Lt of Ireland and R Skryne and Ballymagarvey (Meath) 1713–19; Dean of Ardagh 1719–20; consec Bp 14 Aug 1720 St Patrick's Cath Dublin; Bp of Killala and Achonry 1720–26; enthroned 8 May 1727; Bp of Dromore 1726–31; Bp of Kildare and Dean of Christ Ch Cath Dublin 1731–43; Abp of Dublin 1743–65

s. of Thomas, Governor of the Isle of Man (**s.** of Richard, MP for Hampshire 1656) by Veriana **dau.** of James Chaloner, MP

m. Dorothea widow of Sir John Rawdon, Bt. of Moira Co Down, **dau.** of Rt Hon Sir Edward Levinge, Bt., Speaker of the Irish House of Commons, and Lord Chief Justice of the Court of Common Pleas in Ireland. Issue Thomas, MP of Newbridge Co Kildare

Died 14 Apr 1765 **bur.** Donabate Co Dublin

COBBE, HENRY WILLIAM 1784/85–1823

b. 1784 or 1785; matric Trinity Coll Oxford 31 Oct 1803 aged 18 BA 1807 MA 1810

Preb of Kilmainmore (Tuam) 1811–13; V Killashee (Ard) 1813–23

    3rd **s.** of Charles, MP of Newbridge Co Dublin by Anne Power Trench **sister** of William, 1st Earl of Clancarty

    Died 1823

COCKLE, FRANCES TRAVERS 1859–1931

b. 1859; TCD BA 1883 MA & Div Test 1887; was two years in TCD School of Engineering before Ordination. He was a Freeman of Dublin in right of his grandfather

d 1884 p 1885 (Kilmore); C Boyle (Elph) 1884–86; C Tuam (Tuam) 1887–89; C Holy Trinity Cork (Cork) 1889–95; R Taunagh (Elph) 1895–1909; R Kilconduff U (Ach) 1909–26; C-in-c Aasleagh (Tuam) 1926–31

    4th **s.** of George John, merchant of Dublin by Jane **dau.** of Bernard Shaw

    m. 3 Nov 1896 Blanche Marie Rebecca (**died** 6 Dec 1936 at Drogheda) eldest **dau.** of Ven Francis Edward Clarke, Archd of Elphin qv Issue incl 1. Kenneth Bernard (**died** 1 Jan 1939 near Brighton) **b.** 1901; 2. his eldest **dau.** Beryl Frances Emily **b.** 1899 **m.** 10 Dec 1924 George Ernest **s.** of William Moore of Lisnaskea Co Fermanagh; she was a well–known archaeologist; 3. Violet Daphne Shaw **m.** May 1941 Alan **s.** of TM Caskell of Balbriggan Co Dublin; 4. Sophia Gertrude **m.** 26 Apr 1941 Arthur Raymond **s.** of R Bristowe of Cramer Kent

    Died 25 May 1931 aged 71

COLBY, SAMUEL 1667/68–

b. 1667 or 1668 Yorkshire; ed by Mr Torway, Dublin; ent TCD 8 Oct 1685 aged 17; St John's Coll Camb as Siz 8 Oct 1689

C St Michan (Dub) 1698–1705; V Denn (Kilm) 1702–09; went to Jamaica as the first Missionary of SPG; there in 1710

    s. of John, Schoolmaster in Dublin

†COLBY, THOMAS

a Carmelite Friar of Norwich, seems to have been prov to the See of Elphin vacant by the death of Thomas Barrett, April 1412 (C.P.L. VI. 240), and as Bp elect of Elphin was granted a faculty for consecration on 7 Apr 1412 (ib 310). The Pope translated him to Waterford in 1414, but he did not get possession of that See, as John Geese, Bp of Waterford was in possession and was confirmed in that See by Henry VI in 1422. However, he seems to have got possession again, as his death as "Bishop of Elphin" is recorded in the Patent Rolls of 20 Henry VI. (1423)

COLDEN, JAMES   –1710

MA (not in TCD Lists)

d 23 Apr 1668 p 1669; C Carrickmacross (Clogh) 1669; C Magheracloone and

Donaghmoine (Clogh) 1669; C Drung and Larah (Kilm) 1673; R Killesherdoney (Kilm) *c.* 1691–1710

Died 1710

COLE, JOHN

d; ord p 11 Dec 1808; lic C Killesher (Kilm) 12 Nov 1808

COLE, ROBERT
MA

coll V Kilglass (Elph) 31 Mar 1640

COLE, Hon. WILLIAM MONTGOMERY 1773–1804

b. 14 Oct 1773; ent TCD 4 Jul 1790 BA 1794 MA 1804

d 1 Mar 1795 (Ossory) p 1795 (Kilmore); R Derryloran (Arm) 1796–97; V Killesher (Kilm) 1797–1804; Dean of Waterford 1804

3rd **s.** William Willoughby, created 1st Earl of Enniskillen 18 Aug 1789 by Anne **dau.** of Galbraith Lowry Corry of Caledon Co Tyrone and **sister** of the 1st Earl of Belmore

Died 2 Sep 1804 unm at Florencecourt **bur.** there

COLEMAN, WILLIAM GEORGE 1890–1958

b. 1890; TCD BA 1918 MA & Div Test 1921

d 1921 p 1922 (Kilmore); C Templemichael (Ard) 1921–27; C-in-c Kilronan and Kilmactranny (Ard) 1927–30; Dio C Kilmore Elphin and Ardagh 1930–31; C-in-c Cooneen and Mullaghfad (Clogh) 1931–40; R Killinagh & Kiltyclogher (Kilm) 1940–44; R Clogh (Clogh) 1944–58

s. of James of Baillieborough Co Cavan

m. 23 Sep 1931 Derrylane Par Ch Lily Margretta (**died** 12 Feb 1976) **dau.** of Andrew Gardiner of Ferndale Hse Killeshandra Co Cavan. Issue Hazel **m.** Stanley Bell in New Zealand, and Edna **m...** Stewart.

Died 30 Jan 1958

COLLINS, HENRY 1802/03–

b. 1802 or 1803 Dublin; ent TCD 18 Oct 1819 aged 16 BA 1840

d 29 Sep 1840 (Limerick) p; lic C Kildrumferton (Kilm) 16 Dec 1840

prob Henry Collins **s.** of John

COLLINS, JAMES 1800/01–1868

b. 1800 or 1801 Co Louth; ent TCD 5 Feb 1821 aged 20 BA 1825 MA 1832 BD & DD 1842

C Drumreilly & Templeport (Kilm) 1825; lic C Urney (Kilm) 19 Nov 1826; V Denn

(Kilm) 1835–46; Dean of Killala 1846–68; Chapl to Lord Heytesbury, Lord Lt of Ireland

    s. of Francis, merchant

    m. 26 Mar 1828 Elizabeth (**died** 5 Aug 1879 Dublin) **dau.** of Rev Josiah Erskine, R Knockbride (Kilm) qv Issue **sons** 1. Robert Erskine (**died** 1840); 2. James Francis **m.** 6 Jul 1859 at Monkstown Anna Maria **dau.** of Rev William Prior Moore; 3. Lt. Col. Josiah Erskine; 4. William Erskine (**died** 3 Mar 1862 aged 19); 5. John Henry; 5 **daus.**

    Died 19 Jun 1868 aged 67 **bur.** with his widow in Killala Cathedral

PUBLICATIONS

    The Nature and Attributes of the Church, 8vo, Dublin, 1834

    Lectures on the Principal Features of the United Church of England and Ireland, 8vo, Dublin, 1838

    Pastoral Tracts, etc, addressed to his parishioners, 1842

    A Voice from the Cathedral, Letters to the Parishioners of Killala, 1845

    The Gorham Case and the Doctrine which it concerns considered, 1850

    A Visitation Sermon, preached at Killala September 1854, 8vo Dublin 1855

COLLYER. ISAAC 1651/52–1720

b. 1651 or 1652 London; ed by Mr Price; ent TCD as Siz 3 Jan 1667/68 aged 15 BA 1671 Sch 1672 MA 1675; Head Master Armagh Royal Sch 1674–84

Archd of Kilmore & V Urney and R Castleterra (Kilm) 1684–90; R Clonleigh (Derry– now Raph) 1690–1701; R Donaghmore (Derry– now Raph) 1701–20

    s. of Isaac

    m. Margaret **dau.** of Walter Dawson of Armagh, ancestor of the Earls of Dartrey. Issue **s.** Thomas of Mount Collier Belfast **b.** Lifford Co Donegal ed by Mr Campbell at Raphoe ent TCD 13 Mar 1709/10 aged 16 BA 1714 **m.** 1721 Barbara Duff (**died** 18 Apr 1788 aged 84); **daus.** 1. Elizabeth **m.** after 1720 R Nicholson **s.** of William, Abp of Cashel 1727; 2. Mary **m.** after 1720 Rev Patrick Hamilton, R Killyleagh (Down) 1729–49 and had issue (i) Hugh bapt 7 Mar 1715/16 (ii) Robert bapt 8 Dec 1717 (iii) John bapt 27 May 1721 (iv) Rev James (**died** 18 Nov 1796) bapt 9 Jul 1722, R Rathmullan (Down) (v) Margaret bapt 16 May 1723 (vi) Isaac bapt 27 Oct 1724 (vii) Letitia bapt 21 Sep 1725 **bur.** 30 Dec 1725 (viii) Mary Angelica bapt 18 Aug 1726 **bur.** 31 Jul 1729 (ix) Sophia bapt 25 Apr 1728 **bur.** 13 Aug 1729 (x) Thomas bapt 5 Jun 1729 **bur.** 9 Dec 1729 (xi) Somerset Butler bapt 20 Aug 1730 **bur.** 21 Jan 1746/47 (xii) John bapt 9 Sep 1731 (xiii) Jane bapt 1 Jan 1732/33; 3. Sidney **m.** Rev John Graham of Hockley and had issue (i) Arthur (ii) Isaac

    Died Apr 1720

COLQUHOUN, SAMUEL RANDAL SPROULE 1883/84–1961

b. 1883 or 1884; TCD BA 1906 Div Test 1908

d 1908 p 1909; C Kilmore (Kilm) 1908–11; Dio C Derry 1911–16; C Fahan Lr (Raph

— then Derry) 1916–17; R Convoy (Raph) 1917–26; R Donaghpatrick U (Meath) 1926–30; V St John Sandymount Dublin (Dub) 1930–60; ret

> s. of Very Rev William, Archd of Derry 1897–1914 (s. of Samuel, MA of Strabane Co Tyrone) by Maria **dau.** of John Cashel of Randalstown Co Antrim
>
> **m.** 31 Dec 1912 Annie Marian 4th **dau.** of David R Babington of Londonderry
>
> **Died** 8 or 9 Jul 1961 aged 77

COMBE, JOHN CHARLES 1933–

b. 27 Jan 1933 Limerick; ed Avoca Sch Dublin; TCD Carson Bibl Pri Eccles Hist (1) & Past Theol Pris BA 1953 Div Test (1) 1954 MA 1956 BD 1957 MLitt 1965; QUB PhD 1970; Fitzwilliam Hse Camb

d 22 Jul 1956 p 16 Jun 1957 (Cork); C St Luke and St Anne Shandon (Cork) 1956–58; C Ballynafeigh (Down) 1958–61; R St James Crinken (Dub) 1961–66; Hon Clerical V Christ Ch Cath Dublin 1964–66; Sec Dublin Council of Churches 1965–66; C St Bartholomew Belfast (Conn) 1966–70; R St Barnabas Belfast (Conn) 1970–74; R St Mark Portadown 1974–84; R St Mark Armagh w Aghavilly (Arm) 1984–90; Preb of Tynan (Arm) 1985–86; Preb of Loughgall (Arm) 1986–88; Preb of Mullabrack (Arm) 1988–90; Dean of Kilmore 1990–96; R Kilmore and Ballintemple (w Kildallon Newtowngore and Corrawallen to 1992 and w Killeshandra Killegar and Derrylane 1992–96) (Kilm) 1990–96; Sec Irish Coll of Preachers 1993–96; ret

> **s.** of Frederick William Charles of Dublin (s. of John Charles and Margaret (*née* Sloane) of Lurgan Co Armagh) by Edna Mabel **dau.** of Robert Edmund and Mabel (*née* Boyd) Moreland of Cork
>
> **m.** 14 Oct 1961 St Jude's Par Ch Ballynafeigh Belfast June Olivia **dau.** of Thomas William and Margaret Eleanor (*née* Maguire) Woods of Belfast. Issue 1. Frederick William Charles **b.** 28 Sep 1962 **m.** 2 May 1991 Christ Ch Cath Dublin Aideen **dau.** of Edward and Alice O'Byrne of Aughrim Co Wicklow and have issue (i) Caitlin Alice **b.** 8 May 1994 (ii) Patrick Edward Charles **b.** 9 Mar 1996; 2. Jonathan Woods **b.** 11 Jul 1964 **m.** 6 Sep 1991 Church of the Holy Saviour Tynemouth Priory Caroline **dau.** of Ian and Karen Davis of Tynemouth and have issue (i) Rebecca Grace **b.** 6 Jun 1994 (ii) Eleanor Olivia **b.** 25 Feb 1996; 3. Timothy Edmund **b.** 22 Feb 1966 **m.** 15 Aug 1996 Shankill Par Ch Lurgan Suzanne **dau.** of Brian and Eleanor Odgers of Lurgan; 4. Stephen Christopher **b.** 25 Feb 1968 **m.** 9 July 1994 Melanie **dau.** of John and Nina Neale of Chertsey Surrey; 5. Margaret Edna **b.** 26 Jun 1974 **m.** Gordon Macleod of Airdrie N Lanarkshire

PUBLICATIONS

> *Treasures Old and New,* Reflections on the Church Canticles, 1979
>
> *Even Unto Bethlehem,* Reflections on the Nine Christmas Lessons, 1980
>
> *These and They,* Reflections on the Church's Saints' Days, 1982
>
> *St. Fethlimidh's Cathedral, Kilmore– A Short History,* 1993
>
> Contributor to C of I Journal, *Search*

COMMYN (COMYN, CUMMIN), ALEXANDER

MA

d ord p 20 Jul 1623 by Thomas (Moigne) Bp of Kilmore; adm to Curacy of Killan, now Shercock and Knockbride (Kilm) 21 Feb 1621/22; coll V Killan and Knockbride (Kilm) (? A 2nd time) 21 Jan 1625/26; got a grant of a glebe for Killan 25 Jan 1626/27 (Morrin, III, 187)

COMPTON, HENRY

pres to V Kilbride & Derran = Oran (Elph) 19 May 1634; (L.M. V. 110)

COMYNE (CONNELL), TERENCE –1640/41

Terence *alias* Terlagh O'Conelly was adm d & p by Miler McGrath, Abp of Cashel 18 Jun 1615 (R.V. 1634); R & V Bailieborough (Kilm) 1631–40/41

> Died 31 Jan 1640/41

CONCANNON, GEORGE BLAKE 1823/24–

b. 1823 or 1824 Co Galway; ent TCD 1 Oct 1840 aged 16 BA 1845 Div Test (2) 1846 LLB & LLD 1881

d 1847 p 19 Mar 1848 (Kilmore for Clonfert); C Clonfert (Clonf) 1847; R Dromod and Prior (A & A) 1855–70; lic C Killan, now Shercock (Kilm) 5 Jan 1863; Chapl to Earl of Gainsborough 1865–70; C St Katherine Buxton (Derby — then S'well) 1873–74; Dep Sec Irish Soc; C St Paul Buxton (Derby — then S'well) and Chapl to Lord Valentia 1881

6th s. of Edmund John

> **m.** 8 Dec 1849 Georgina Henrietta 2nd **dau.** of Capt Hugh Pollock, RN of Castle Wilder Co Longford. Issue 1. William Augustus; 2. a **dau.**

CONDELL, THOMAS EDWARD GUARD 1857/58–1937

b. 1857 or 1858; ed Univ of Durham St Bee's Coll BA 1887

d 1884 p 1885 (Manchester); C Ashton under Lyne (Manch) 1884–85; R Cloone (w Drumshambo 1886) (Ard) 1885–88; R Donadea (Kild) 1888–91; C St Alkmund Derby 1891–93; R Monamolin (Ferns) 1893–95; C Kilnamanagh (Ferns) 1895–98; R Ballycarney (Ferns) 1898–1901; R Kilscoran (w Killinick from 1922) (Ferns) 1901–35

> **m.** and had issue including Thomas, MRCVS Kilkenny; a **dau.** Lalla **m.** Rev Charles Angus Cutts Purkis BA, R Aghour (Oss), and another **dau.**
> Died 26 Nov 1937 aged 79

CONINGHAM, JOHN

adm V Cloonclare (Kilm) 2 Aug 1637

CONNOLLY, RICHARD 1815/16–*c.* 1890

b. 1815 or 1816 Co Leitrim; ed by Mr Bradshaw; ent TCD 5 Jul 1832 aged 16 BA 1837 MA & Div Test 1842

C Wicklow (Glend) 1840–43; C Cloone (Ard) 1843–47; C Clongish Killoe (Ard) 1847–69; R Cashel (Ard) 1869–75; R Kilronan (Ard) 1875–*c.* 89

s. of Richard, merchant

m. 26 Mar 1846 at Newtownforbes Ch Eliza 2nd **dau.** of the late George West of Drumbore Co Leitrim. Last entry in C I Dir 1889

Died *c.* 1890

CONTARINE, THOMAS 1682/83–1758

b. 1682 or 1683 Chester; ed by Mr Maxwell at Wrexham; ent TCD as Siz 2 Oct 1701 aged 18 Sch 1705 BA 1706

is said to have been R Kilmore (Elph) but was perhaps C Kilmore *c.* 1710; coll V Oran and Drimtemple 3 Sep 1729; Preb of Oran (Elph) 1730–58; poss V Dunamon (Elph) 1734–41

s. of Austin "colonus"; was descended from a well–known Venetian family. His grandfather, a monk, eloped with a nun and married her. She died of smallpox in France. He then went to London and on the way to Ireland, he met at Chester a Miss Chaloner, a relative of Dr Chaloner, Provost of TCD whom he married. He conformed and is said to have received a benefice in Elphin, but there is no record of this.

m. Jane (**died** 12 Jun 1744 in her 63rd year) **sister** of Rev Charles Goldsmith and aunt of the poet Oliver Goldsmith and had issue Jane (**died** 1790 Dublin) **m.** James Lawder of Kilmore who was murdered in 1779. He is said to have been the clergyman "passing rich on £40 a year", mentioned in the *Deserted Village*, and was "a man of talent and great goodness of heart"

Died 1758

CONWAY, AMBROSE 1847/48–1902

b. 1847 or 1848; TCD BA 1878

d 21 Dec 1878 p 20 Dec 1879 (Ossory); C Wexford (Ferns) 1878–81; R Kilnehue (Ferns) 1881–87; R Knockbride (Kilm) 1887–88; R Leskinfere (Ferns) 1888–1901

m. Isabella (**died** 27 Apr 1921 Rathmines Dublin). Issue 1. Harriet Alicia (**died** 29 Sep 1896) bapt 22 Sep 1881; 2. Maude Elizabeth bapt 27 Feb 1883; 3. Blanche Anna Constance **b.** 11 Nov 1883; 4. Albert **b.** 5 Apr 1885; 5. George Walker **b.** 31 Aug 1886; 6. Arthur **b.** 18 Aug 1888

Died 23 Feb 1902 aged 54

CONWAY, ROBERT

MA FTCD 1631–36

V Baslick (Elph) 1640–

CONWAY, THOMAS RICHARD 1835/36–1910

b. 1835 or 1836

d 1870 (Down) p 1871 (Kilmore); C Drumlease (Kilm) 1870–72; R Drummully (Clogh) 1872–1910

m. and had issue incl Capt J Hobson M, RAMC DSO m. and had issue

Died 29 Jul1910 aged 74

CONYNGHAM (CUNNINGHAM), WILLIAM   –c. 1698

d; p 17 Jul 1663; coll V Carrigallen (Kilm) w Mohill (Ard) 11 Feb 1663/64; again coll R & V Carrigallen (Kilm) and Mohill (Ard) w Oughteragh (Kilm) 21 Jul 1673; was probably in charge from 1663; seems to have held Mohill, Carrigallen and Oughteragh to 1698

m. Margaret *alias* French and had issue incl 1. Henry; 2. Hugh; 3. John

Died *c.* 1698

CONYNGHAM, WILLIAM

V Dunamon, Kilcrosne and Ballynakill (Elph) 1807–*c.* 25

COOKE, DIGBY SAMUEL 1827/28–1914

b. 1827 or 1828 King's Co (Offaly); ed by Mr Earle; ent TCD 1 Jul 1846 aged 18 Heb Pri 1850 & 1851 BA & Div Test (2) 1851

d 1852 (Down for Kilmore) p 1853 (Kilmore); C Killinkere (Kilm) 1852–56; C Lurgan (Kilm) 1856–62; C Bailieborough and Moybologue (Kilm) 1862–69; C Ballinaclash (Glend) 1869–72; R Narraghmore (Kild) 1873–1905

yst s. of Rev Digby; bro. of Rev John, C Geashill (Kild) 1848–51

m. 14 Jan 1862 Virginia Ch Mary Louisa 2nd dau. of Rev Charles Sheridan Young, C St Paul Dublin (Dub) 1840–47. Issue 1 & 2 twin sons b. 3 Aug 1863; 3. Digby William (died 8 Feb 1866 aged 2½); 4. Caroline Louisa; 5. Mary Frances; 6. Letitia Digby

Died 22 Feb 1914 aged 86

COOKE, EDWARD ALEXANDER

TCD 1878; Hobart Coll NY Hon MA 1892; FSA (Scotland) 1884

d 1881 p 1882 (Kilmore); C Cloone (Ard) 1881–83; C Boyle (Elph) 1883; C St Patrick Brighton (Chich) 1883; C Kilrossanty (Lism) 1883–85; V Kilnasoolagh (Killaloe) 1885–87; C Tamworth (Lich) 1887–88; V Attleborough Warks (Cov) 1888–92; V Reddal Hill (Worc) 1893–1907; V St Paul Brentford (Lon) 1907–21; V Christ Ch Brockham Green (S'wark) 1921–*c.* 29; Last entry in Crockford 1931

yr s. of Anthony by Elizabeth Salmon Hendrick and bro. of James Tresham qv

PUBLICATIONS

Diocesan History of Killaloe 1886

Life and Work of St. Columba 1888

COOKE, GEORGE D 1802/03–1836

b. 1802 or 1803 St. Kitts; ed by Mr Lyons; ent TCD 4 Jan 1819 Sch 1822 BA 1824

C Cloonclare (Kilm) 1827

    s. of John, *colonus*

    m. a **dau.** of Thomas Clarke

    Died 5 or 25 Oct 1836 aged 33 **bur.** Taney Dublin

COOKE, JAMES TRESHAM 1853–1891

b. 1853

d 1877 p 1878 (Kilmore); C Ballymacormack 1877–81; R Cloone (Ard) 1881–85; R Kilmanaheen (Kilf) 1885–91

    s. of Anthony by Elizabeth Salmon Hendrick and **bro.** of Rev Edward Alexander qv

    m. 1875 Dora Jane **dau.** of JE Mannix. Issue **sons** 1. Tristram Edward; 2. John Anthony, 2nd Lt RIF **m.** 20 Feb 1917 Frances Mary eldest **dau.** of William McGusty of Skeries Co Dublin; 3. Rev Hans de Brabant; 4. Shirley Victor; **daus.** 1. Maude Ann Elizabeth **m.** George A Deverell and had issue Ann; 2. Dora Amy (**died** 1 Mar 1925) **m.** 16 Jul 1918 Robert Fergus Smith

    Died 11 Apr 1891 Dublin aged 37

COOKE, RICHARD HANS de BRABANT *c.* 1887–1950

b *c.* 1887; TCD BA Hons Mod Hist 1904 MA & Div Test 1909

d 1910 (Down for Armagh) p 1911 (Armagh); C St Mark Portadown 1910–14; CF 1914–29; R Killyon Castleblakney & Athleague (Elph) 1929–31; R Loughrea and Tynagh (Clonf) 1931–40; Preb of Kilquane (Clonf) & RD of Loughrea 1938-40; R Nenagh and Monsea (w Ballymackey and Kilruane from 1950) (Killaloe) 1940-50; Preb of Rath (Killaloe) 1943-45 (delete Canon of Killaloe); Treas of Killaloe 1945–48; RD of Ikerrin (Killaloe) 1945–46; Archd of Killaloe 1948–50

    4th s. of Rev James Tresham LLD of Ennistymon Co Clare

    m. Aileen Warren

    Died 5 Dec 1950

COOKSEY, JAMES 1709/10–

b. 1709 or 1710 Kilkenny; ed Kilkenny Coll by Mr Lewis; ent TCD 16 Jun 1726 aged 16 BA 1730

R & V Castleterra (Kilm) *c.* 1741–74

    s. of John, *armiger*

    m. (settlements 6 Mar 1743/44) Susanna **sister** of George Moore. Issue 1. Rev John, R Castleterra (Kilm) qv; 2. Rev James, C Knockbride (Kilm) qv; 3. Martha **m.** (settlements 3 Nov 1777) George Mee of Butler's Bridge Co Cavan; 4. Frances **m.** as his 1st wife Robert Thomas 2nd **s.** of Rev Daniel Hearn, R Drung and Larah (Kilm) qv by his 2nd wife Anne (*née* Dowley) and had issue

COOKSEY, JAMES

ed by Mr Carr; ent TCD 1 Feb 1768 BA 1772

d 29 Jun 1772 p 1 May 1773 (Kilm); C Knockbride (Kilm) 1773

s. of Rev James, R Castleterra (Kilm) qv (s. of John); **bro.** of Rev John, R Castleterra (Kilm) qv

COOKSEY, JOHN

ed by Mr Cottingham at Cavan; ent TCD 1 Nov 1763 Sch 1766 BA 1768

d 1770 p 1771 (Kilm); C Kinawley (Kilm) 1773; R Castleterra (Kilm) 1774–80

s. of Rev James, R Castleterra (Kilm) qv (s. of John); **bro.** of Rev James, C Knockbride (Kilm) qv

m. (ML 5 Apr 1780) Deborah 2nd **dau.** of Rev Samuel Madden, R Kells (Oss) 1785–1800 and Cassandra **dau.** of Michael Travers; she survived him and afterwards **m.** Rev Robert Hawkshaw

Died or resigned 1780

COONEY, CHARLES ROBERT –1924

TCD BA 1874; RUI BA 1884

d 1877 p 1878 (Kilmore); C Clongish (Ard) 1877–80; C Mohill (Ard) 1880–83; R Newtowngore & Corrawallen (Kilm) 1883–94; R Killenkere w Mullagh U (Kilm) 1894–1908

s. of Rev Charles, C-in-c Poulthomas (Killala); **bro.** of Rev Stewart Emerson, C-in-c St John Belfast (Conn) 1893–1907

m. 16 Jul 1879 Sarah eldest **dau.** of William R Lemon. Issue incl his 1. eldest **dau.** Margaret Jane Lamont (**died** 16 Nov 1929); 2. a **dau. m...** Ellison

Died 2 Nov 1924 at his daughter's residence in Liverpool

COOPER, ANDREW   –1950

TCD BA 1884 MA 1888

d 1885 p 1886 (Kilmore); C Clongish (Ard) 1885–87; C Moyliscar (Meath) 1887–90; R Ballymore (Meath) 1890–1926; ret

m. Arabella and had issue incl **sons** 1. Rev Marcus Humphrey (**died** 5 Jun 1966) **b.** 10 Apr 1901 TCD BA & Div Test 1929 MA 1934 d 1929 p 1930 C Rathdowney (Oss) 1929–31 R Timahoe (Leigh) 1931–34 R Kells (Oss) 1934–36 R Rathmolyon (Meath) 1936–40 R Athlone U (Meath) 1940–58 R Rathmolyon 1958–c. 66 **m.** 7 Jan 1930 Sarah Caroline elder **dau.** of William Corrigan MPSI of Celbridge Co Kildare and had issue a **s.** Rev Cecil William Marcus **b.** 1932 R Drumbeg (Down) 1982–2000 and a **dau.** Isobel Hazel **m.** 3 Aug 1953 Very Rev Thomas Andrew Noble Bredin, Dean of Clonmacnois 1979–89; 2. Henry; **daus.** incl 1. Winifred Louise **m.** 2 Aug 1922 William George Lowe of Beechmount Moate; 2. Julia Beryl **m.** 8 Aug 1930 Eric William **s.** of Harris Martyn of Sunnyside Co Longford; 3. Evelyn Florence; 4. Arabella Roberta **m...** Stewart

Died 31 Jul 1950

COOPER, LEONARD LEADER 1869/70–1936

b. 1869 or 1870; TCD Div Test 1893; Univ of Durham BA 1899 MA 1905

d 1900 p 1901 (Kilmore); C Calry (Elph) 1900–03; R Kilmore w Aughrim & Killukin (Elph) 1903–08; C Gosforth (Newc) 1908–10; Chapl of High Ashurst, Headley (Win) 1910–13; V Appleby (Linc) 1913–20; Chapl Lugano Switzerland 1924–32; R Drinagh (Cork) 1934–36

    s. of Rev Francis, V Cahir (Lism) 1872

    Died 12 Jan 1936 aged 66

COPE, ANTHONY 1647/48–1705

There were two of the same name living at this time who are much confused.

b. 1647 or 1648; ent TCD 20 Jan 1665 aged 17; his degrees are not recorded, but he was LLD

d; ordained p 1669 at Elphin; R Ardcarne Toomna and Kilmactranny (Elph) 1669/70–1700; Archd of Elphin & R Killukin (Elph) 1669–83; Preb and V Killaraght (Ach) 1673-c. 84; pres by Crown R Muntireolis (Ard); Preb of Killaraght (Killala) 1673–; pres by the Crown R Muntireolis (Ard) 15 Feb 1682 (L.M. V. 118), coll 25 Feb (F.F.); Dean of Elphin & V Easternsnow (Elph) 1683–1700 pres 28 Aug and installed 11 Sep 1683 (L.M. V. 118, F.F.); Prec of Armagh 1693–1705; exchanged this Deanery for Preb of Rasharkin (Conn) 1700–05

    s. of Walter of Drumilly Co Armagh

    m. Elizabeth **dau.** and heiress of Henry Cope of Loughgall Co Armagh by Maria **dau.** of Robert Barclay, Dean of Clogher. Issue 1. Robert **b.** 1678/79, MP for Lisburn 1711 and for Co Armagh 1713–14 and 1727–53 **m.** and had issue a **s.** Anthony who was Dean of Armagh 1753–63; 2. Henry **b.** at Boyle ed by Mr Walls, Dublin ent TCD 24 Dec 1701 aged 17 MD 1717 Reg Prof of Physic 1738; 3. Anthony **b.** 1684/85; 4. Bartholomew **b.** 1686/87 TCD BA 1708 MA 1711; 5. Rev Barclay (**died** 1757) TCD MB & MD 1718 R Drumglass and Tullaniskin (Arm) 1720–23 Preb of Loughgall in Armagh Cath 1724–41 Preb of Ballymore in Armagh Cath 1741–57; 6. Rev George, Preb of Tibohine (Elph) 1724–31 qv

    Died 1705 **bur.** St Peter's Dublin

    NOTE: Leslie in *Armagh Clergy and Parishes* 1911 has him R Dunbin 1690–1700 and R & V Dromiskin (Arm) 1692–1709, and Preb of Killaraght (Ach) 1673–79 and that he died in 1709 and was **bur.** in St Catherine's Church, Dublin. This seems to be a contemporary but different Anthony Cope, and it is possible that some of the sons above may have been his

COPE, GEORGE 1696/97–1758

b. 1696 or 1697 Boyle Co Roscommon; ed by Mr Clarke at Lisburn; ent TCD 19 Feb 1714/15 aged 18 Sch 1717 BA 1719 MA 1722

Preb of Tibohine (Elph) 1724–31; R Killyman (Arm) 1731–37; R & V Drumcree (Arm) 1737–58

    s. of Very Rev Anthony, Dean of Elphin qv (**s.** of Walter) by Elizabeth **dau.** of Henry Cope; **bro.** of Rev Barclay

    Died 30 May 1758

COPE, JONATHAN 1726/27–1799

b. 1726 or 1727 Dublin; ed by Mr Perry; ent TCD 8 Jan 1742/43 aged 15– no degree recorded

d; p 21 Apr 1751 (Ossory); R Ahascragh (Elph) *c.* 1777–99

> **s.** of Henry
>
> **Died** 1799

CORKER, CHAMBRE –1790

ed by Mr Wood; ent TCD 12 Nov 1759 BA 1765 MA 1769

d 1765 p 1766 (Cork); Dom Chapl to Bp of Cork 1766; Preb of Cahirlag and R Rathcooney (Cloyne) 1767–90; R & V Insula Parvae 1769–90; Archd of Ardagh 1778–90

> **s.** of Thomas of Cork by Alice Neville
>
> **m.** Elizabeth **dau.** of Abp Jemmett Browne Abp of Tuam 1775–82 and had issue incl 1. Elizabeth **m.** Rev Philip Trench; 2. Katherine **m.** Rev Horatio Townsend
>
> **Died** 1790

CORRIGAN, THOMAS GEORGE 1928–

b. 20 Nov 1928 Rathvilly Co Carlow; ed The King's Hosp Dublin; TCD DBS 1956; Greenwich Univ Sch of Theol BTh 1991

d 29 Jun 1958 p 14 Jun 1959; C Urney and C-in-c Drung (Kilm) 1958–60; R Drung and Killesherdoney (Kilm) 1960–67; R St Michael Belfast (Conn) 1967–70; R Kingscourt w Drumconrath Syddan and Moybologue (Meath) 1970–96; Archd of Meath 1981–96; Dio Reg Meath 1987–90; ret 1996

> **s.** of Robert of Rathvilly (**s.** of Thomas and Bessie) by Margaret Elizabeth **dau.** of Thomas and Margaret Foley of Wicklow
>
> **m.** (1) 4 Jul 1953 St Kevin's Ch Dublin Elizabeth Charlotte (**died** 1967) **dau.** of Henry Thomas and Charlotte (*née* Deane) Maude of Dublin. Issue 1. Margaret (Madge) Charlotte **b.** 1 Apr 1954 **m.** Kingscourt Par Ch 18 May 1974 Trevor Cruikshank; 2. Stephen George **b.** 23 Feb 1957 **m.** Gladys Pico; 3. Faith Maude **b.** 14 Jan 1966 **m.** Gareth Evans
>
> **m.** (2) 9 May 1998 Archbishop of Dublin's Private Chapel Mary (May) Gilmore (*née* Clarke) of Bailieborough Co Cavan.

COSBY, ARNOLD 1759/60–1817

b. 1759 or 1760 Co Cavan; ed by Mr Beatty; ent TCD 4 May 1778 aged 18 BA 1782 MA 1812

d 1782 p 1783; C Killan, now Shercock (Kilm) 1782; V Killinkere (w DC Mullagh in Killinkere Par 1814–17) (Kilm) 1798–1817; V Stradbally (Leigh) 1813–17

> eldest **s.** of Thomas, "armiger" of Beeks Court Co Fermanagh, High Sheriff Co Cavan 1765 by Catherine **dau.** of Capt William Stopford, 1st Horse and **bro.** of 1st Earl of Courtown

m. Frances **dau.** of Rev John Beatty, V Moira (Drom) 1777–93 by his 1st wife Abigail (**bur.** 22 Nov 1767 at Killeshandra) **dau.** of Matthew Young of Lahard Co Cavan and Frances **dau.** of William Nesbitt of Dromalee Co Cavan. Issue incl 1. Edward **b.** Cavan ent TCD 7 Nov 1814 aged 17; 2. Sophia **m.** 1 Aug 1810 Rev Edward Mahaffy, C Killinkere (Kilm) qv and had issue incl 2nd **s.** Edward **m.** 17 Aug 1848 Susan Frances and a **dau.** Mary A **m.** 12 Oct 1847 James L Bailey

Died 19 Jan 1817 "at 8 oclock in the fournoon" (Par Reg)

COSBY, WILLIAM

appears C Killan, now Shercock (Kilm) 1754

COSBY, WILLIAM 1707/08–1783

b. 1707 or 1708 Kevate Co Cavan; ed by Mr Elwood, Dublin; ent TCD 19 Oct 1726 aged 18 BA 1731 MA 1734; JP for Co Cavan 1761

R Bailieborough and Moybologue (Kilm) 1752–73; R Tomregan (Kilm) 1773–83

yr **s.** Edward of Skeen Co Cavan, High Sheriff Co Cavan 1701 and 1711 by his 2nd wife Catherine **dau.** of George Stewart of Strabane Co Tyrone

Died 1783

COSGRAVE, THOMAS 1823/24–1890

b. 1823 or 1824 Dublin; ent TCD 23 Nov 1847 aged 23 BA & Div Test 1852

d 29 Sep 1852 (Down) p 29 Sep 1853 (Down); C Ballynure (Conn) 1852–56; C Shankill (Drom) 1856–60; PC Lambeg (Conn) 1860–72; R Odogh (Oss) 1873–76; PC Lissadell (Elph) 1876–85; in Canada 1885–88; R Shercock (Kilm) 1888–90

s. of William, *pragmaticus* (solicitor) by Lucretia **dau.** of Rev Thomas Baker, V Naul (Dub)

m. 26 Sep 1866 at Booterstown Ch Dublin Theodosia Mary 2nd **dau.** of Rt Rev Charles Caulfield, DD, Bp of Nassau by Grace Anne **dau.** of Sir Richard Bligh St George, Bt. Issue 1. William Nassau **b.** 2 Jul 1867; 2. Grace St George **b.** 30 Jul 1868 (**died** 1890); 3. Charles St George **b.** 1870 (**died** 1886 in Canada); 4. Thomas **b.** Nov 1871 (**died** May 1929 Dublin)

Died 16 May 1890

COSTELLO, FRANCIS JAMES 1841/42–1919

b. 1841 or 1842

d 1870 p 1871 (Killaloe); C Clongish (Ard) 1870–76; C O'Brien's Bridge (Killaloe) 1876; R O'Brien's Bridge 1876–81; R Tulloh (Killaloe) 1881; R Kilgarvan (A & A) 1882–83; R Ballymackey (Killaloe) 1883–1918

s. of John, Barrister-at-Law

m. 22 Feb 1877 Matilda **dau.** of John Lopdell JP of Raheen Park Athenry Co Galway and Waterloo Rd Dublin

Died 4 Dec 1919 aged 77 at Raheny Cottage, Cloughjordan Co Tipperary **bur.** Ballymackey

COSTELLO, JOHN WALTER 1831/32–

b. 1831 or 1832 Gort Co Galway; ed at Ventry College Sch; ent TCD 3 Dec 1858 aged 26 Bedell Sch 1862

d 1869 p 1870; C Killenumery (Ard) 1870–72; R Kilmactigue (Ach) 1873–81; R Straid (Ach) 1881–96

s. of John, barrister-at-law

m. Georgina (**died** 17 Dec 1913 at Clontarf Dublin aged 80). Issue incl 1. John Edmund **m.** 17 Jun 1943 Alice Julia 2nd **dau.** of C F Bailey of Bath; 2. Elizabeth (**died** 24 May 1944)

COTTER, ARTHUR 1879/80–1961

b. 1879 or 1880

d 1923 p 1924 (Los Angeles); Chapl at Chantilly 1936–40; Chapl at Embassy Ch Paris 1940–44; Control Commission for Germany 1945–47; Chapl of Rio Tinto Mines Huelva Spain 1947–49; Perm to Off Dio Chichester 1949–50; R Lissadell (Elph) 1950–59; ret

Died 23 May 1961 Dublin

COTTER, JAMES LAURENCE 1824–

b. 14 Aug 1824; ent TCD 1 Jul 1840 BA 1845 MB 1847 MD 1876; Univ of London MRCS 1847

d 1854 (Peterborough) p 9 Sep 1855 (Kilmore); C Castor (Pet) 1854–55; C Killyon (Elph) 1856–57; C St Peter (Dub) 1857; C Greetland (Wakef) 1857–59; C St Stephen (Liv) 1859–61; PC Lydiate (Liv) 1861–70; PC St Paul (Liv) 1870–78; R Burmarsh (Cant) 1882

2nd **s.** of Rev Joseph Rogerson, Preb of Donoughmore (Cloyne)

m. (1) Mary **dau.** of Rev Robert Gaggin, R Clonmult (Cloyne)

m. (2) 3 Sep 1856 Mary Beatrice **dau.** of William Bromilow of Haresfinch Hse Lancs and had issue

COTTER, WILLIAM HENRY 1843/44–1931

b. 1843 or 1844; TCD BA 1869 MA 1872 LLB & LLD 1875

d 1869 (Kilmore) p 1869 (Tuam for Kilmore); C Drung (Kilm) 1869–72; C Buttevant (Cloyne) 1874–77; R Buttevant (w Charleville from 1924) 1877–1927; RD of Bothon (Cloyne) 1909–27

Died 17 Feb 1931 aged 87

COTTINGHAM, HENRY 1793/94–1870

b. 1793 or 1794 Dublin; ed by Dr Burrowes; ent TCD 4 Jul 1810 aged 16 BA 1814 MA 1827

d 1817 p 181–; R Ballymachugh (Ard) 1838–70; the parish was sequestered in 1867 to Rev Robert Beatty qv as curate's salary had not been paid

3rd **s.** of James Henry (**s.** of Rev James, R Urney (Kilm) qv)

m. (1) 15 Oct 1819 Mary Catherine (**died** 25 Mar 1849 at Portsmouth) **dau.** of Jason Hassard of Garden Hill Co Fermanagh

m. (2) (ML 1853) Mary Margaret Freeman

Died 15 Oct 1870 at Niagara Canada

COTTINGHAM, JAMES 1676/77–1753

b. 1676 or 1677 Dublin; ed by Mr Shorting, Dublin; ent TCD 7 Dec 1694 aged 17 BA 1699 MA 1702

V Lavey (Kilm) 1721–33; V Killan, now Shercock (Kilm) 1733–46

s. of James, goldsmith

m. and had issue 1. Rev James, DD, V Urney (Kilm) qv; 2. William ent TCD 27 Jun 1732 aged 18

Died in Dublin **bur.** 11 Nov 1753 St. Werburgh's Dublin

COTTINGHAM, JAMES 1723/24–1804

b. 1723 or 1724 Co Cavan; ed by Mr Clerk; ent TCD 23 Nov 1740 aged 16 Sch 1743 BA 1745 DD1776

d 5 Jan 1745/46 p 12 Jan 1746; V Urney and Annagelliffe (Kilm) 1746–1804; Head Master Royal Sch Cavan 1761–; V Kildrumferton (Kilm) 1772–73; V Carrigallen (Kilm) 1774–1804; V Gen Kilmore 1777–1804

s. of Rev James, V Killan (Kilm) qv (**s.** of James)

m. 20 Apr 1754 Rose (bur 21 May 1813 aged 84) **dau.** of Capt Charles Wardlaw. Issue James Henry **b.** Cavan ent TCD 6 Nov 1779 aged 17 Irish Bar 1789 **m.** and had issue Rev James, R Ballymachugh (Ard) qv

Died 26 Mar 1804 **bur.** Cavan

COULTER, ISAAC 1854/55–1934

b. 1854 or 1855; TCD BA 1877 MA 1880 BD & DD 1891

d 1874 p 1875 (Kilmore); C Ahamplish (Elph) 1874–77; R Knocknarea (Elph) 1877–81; R Knockbride (Kilm) 1881–87; R Cloonclare (Kilm) 1887–97; V Drumlease (w Killargue from *c.* 1905) (Kilm) 1897–1926; Dean of Kilmore 1913–26; ret

s. of John of Dundalk by Margaret (*née* Shaw) of Skreen Co Sligo; **bro.** of Ven William Coulter, Archd of Wilts

m. Fanny (**died** 9 Jul 1952). Issue **sons** 1. John (**died** 15 Mar 1923) **b.** 1 Apr 1889 ed Royal Sch Cavan and TCD; 2. Charles (**died** 24 May 1922 aged 20); 3. Ernest Alfred; **daus.** 1. Hilda Florence **m.** 19 Feb 1930 John Buchanan, MD **s.** of John Burgess of Athlone; 2. Ida G **m.** 27 Apr 1922 John Owens of Ballymena Co Antrim; 3. Fanny May (**died** 5 Dec 1972); 4. Gladys (**died** 9 Mar 1975 Cheltenham); 5. Dorothy (**died** 29 Jul 1977) **m.** Vere Huston of Dublin

Died 23 May 1934 aged 79

COURSEY, THOMAS WILLIAM 1879/80–1949

b. 1879 or 1880; ed Pococke Sch Kilkenny; TCD BA (Resp) 1910

d 1916 p 1917 (Clogher); C Enniskillen (Clogh) 1916–18; C-in-c Maguiresbridge (Clogh) 1918–21; C-in-c Currin (Clogh) 1921–23; R Derryvullen N (Clogh) 1923–32; R Drumlease (Kilm) 1932–47

s. of Cornelius of Enniscorthy Co Wexford

m. and had issue 1. Maud Frances **m.** 18 Sep 1944 Simon E P **s.** of William Armstrong of Springville Dromahair Co Leitrim; 2. James E who served in RUC and was Campaign Dir for C of I Christian Stewardship

Died 23 Mar 1949 at Dromahair Co Leitrim aged 69

COURTENAY, GEORGE FREDERICK 1834/35–1924

b. 1834 or 1835 Co Dublin; ed by Rev Robert Hogg; ent TCD 15 Oct 1850 aged 15 BA & Div Test 1860 MA 1886

d 1862 p 1863 (Down); C Kilbroney (Drom) 1862–64; C Aghaderg (Drom) 1864–66; C St James (Dub) 1866–67; PC Cloughjordan (Killaloe) 1867–73; R Quin (Killaloe) 1873–78; R Roscommon (Elph) 1878–82; V Broomfield Somerset (B & W) 1882–84; V Burrington (Heref) 1884–91; V Temple Bruer (Linc) 1891–95; V St Peter Birmingham (Birm — then Worc) 1895–98; R Croghan (Elph) 1898–1902; ret

s. of Robert, lawyer

Died 26 Aug 1924 aged 89

COUSINS, JOHN FITZHARRIS 1827/28–1893

b. 1827 or 1828; TCD BA & Div Test 1858

d 27 Nov 1859 (Down) p 21 Dec 1860; C Templepatrick (Conn) 1859; C Bangor (Down) 1860–62; C Elphin (Elph) and Deputy Dio Reg 1862–65; C Downpatrick (Down) 1867–78

eldest **s.** of Rev John, Preb of Ballycahane (Lim)

Died 29 Mar 1893 aged 65 Downpatrick

COWEN, RICHARD 1802/03–

b. 1802 or 1803 Normandy; ed by Mr Keane; ent TCD 19 Jun 1821 aged 18 BA 1830

d 3 Jan 1835 (Elphin) p; C Bumlin (Elph) 1835–46; R Ardclare w Kilcooley and Clomagamacan (Elph) 1846–78; last entry in C I Dir 1878

s. of Thomas C Miles

acc to Canon Leslie's MSS **died** 9 Nov 1886 aged 90

COWPER, THOMAS –1790

V Drumcliffe (Elph) 1783–85; V Taunagh (Elph) 1785–90

Died 1790

COX, GEORGE 1764/65–1799

b. 1764 or 1765; matric New Coll Ox 20 Feb 1782 aged 17 BA 1786 MA 1789 R & V Castlerahan (Kilm) 1794–97; R St Martin's *alias* Carfax (Ox)

perhaps **s.** of Charles of Holywell Oxford

Died 1799

COX, MICHAEL BELL 1825/26–1897

b. 1825 or 1826 in England; ed by Mr Sargent; ent TCD 11 Oct 1844 aged 18 BA & Div Test 1849 MA 1874

d 26 May 1850 (Ossory for Kildare) p 5 Jun 1851 (Kilmore for Elphin); C Aughrim (Elph) 1851–c56; R Glenties (Raph) 1856–97; Archd of Raphoe 1880–97; appointed Dean of Raphoe 1897 but died before he was installed

s. of Charles, merchant

Died 13 Aug 1897

COXHEAD, NICHOLAS

adm Preb Terebrine (Elph) 3 Oct 1616 (F.F.); pres again to Preb 16 Dec 1635 (L.M. V, III); seems to have resigned 1636; R Terebrine (Elph) 1635; coll again R Terebrine (Elph) 27 May 1640; V Kilcooley (Elph) to 1640; V Aughrim & Cloncreffe (Elph) 1640–*c.* 1681/82

†CRADOCK, JOHN 1708–1778

b. 25 Feb 1708 Wolverhampton; ed Trentham Sch Staffs; St John's Coll Camb BA 1728 MA 1732 Fellow 1732–56 BD 1740 DD 1749; TCD DD *ad eund* 1759

d 1731 (Lincoln) p 1737 (Rochester) R Thornhaugh Northants (Pet) 1741; R Dry Drayton Cambridge (Ely) 1753–55; R Layham (Chich) 1754–56; R St Paul Covent Garden (Lon) 1755–58; Chapl to the Duke of Bedford, Lord Lt 1757; appointed Bp of Kilmore by Patent dated 15 Nov 1757 and consec 4 Dec 1757 St Michan's Dublin; Bp of Kilmore 1757–72; Abp of Dublin and Bp of Glendalough 1772–78

s. of Rev William (**died** 1734), R Donnington (Lich) by Anne

m. 28 Aug 1758 St Michan's Ch Mary widow of Richard St George of Kilrush and **dau.** of William Blaydwin of Boston Lincs by whom she had issue Richard St George **b.** 1752 or 1753. Issue John Francis (**died** Jul 1839) **b.** 12 Aug 1762, Governor of Cape of Good Hope became Baron Howden **m.** and had issue incl John Hobart (**died** s.p. 1857), 2nd Baron Howden

Died 21 Dec 1778 at St Sepulchre's Palace Dublin

PUBLICATIONS

A Sermon on 1 Cor I, vv 23–24, on the Insufficiency of the Principal Objections to Christianity, Cambridge 1739

A Sermon on 1 Peter II v 16, preached on 30 Jan 1752, London 1752

A Sermon on Jeremiah VI v 8, preached on the Fast, London 1756

CRADOCK, THOMAS 1743–1827

b. 3 Jan 1743 Wolverhampton; ed at Shrewsbury Sch by Mr Newling; adm pensioner at St John's Coll Camb 28 Jun 1760 aged 17 LLB 1766; TCD MA *ad eund* Camb 1776

d 7 Dec 1766 (Dublin) p 21 Dec 1766 (Limerick); lic C Kilmore (Kilm) 3 Apr 1767; R Drung and Larah 1767–1827; Preb of Rathmichael in St Patrick's Cath Dublin 1774–76; Preb of St Audoen in St Patrick's Cath Dublin 1776–1827; Keeper of Marsh's Library, Dublin 1776–1815

> **s.** of Rev Thomas (1710–57), Preb of Wolverhampton; **bro.** of Rev William, V Lurgan (Kilm) qv; nephew of Rt Rev John Cradock, Bp of Kilmore qv
>
> **m.** Susanne Russell (**died** 18 Apr 1815 aged 67). Issue 1. Rev Thomas Russell (**died** 9 Mar 1853) **b.** 1770 Co Cavan TCD BA 1792 MA 1816 d 1794 (Kilmore) p C St Audoen (Dub) 1796–1805 V Chor St Patrick's Cath Dublin 1798–1817 Asst Librarian Marsh's Library Dublin 1803–15 C St Audoen (Dub) 1811–17 Keeper Marsh's Library Dublin 1815 PC St Nicholas Within (Dub) 1817–53 **m.** (M. L. 9 Mar 1804) Mary Bury (**died** 4 Sep 1841) and had issue (i) Rev Thomas Russell William, C St Nicholas Within (Dub) 1843 (ii) Susannah (iii) Mary (iv) James Verschoyle (v) John (vi) Charles Bury (vii) Elizabeth (viii) Rev Frederick Keating **b.** 1824 R St John Belize British Honduras 1858–60 ; 2. Francis; 3. Richard; 4. Frederica; 5. Maria
>
> **Died** 14 Nov 1827 **bur.** in the family vault in St Patrick's Cath Dublin

CRADOCK, WILLIAM 1740–1793

b. 1740 Wolverhampton Staffs; ed Shrewabury Sch; St John's Coll Camb Sch 1760 MA; TCD BA 1768 MA

d 19 Dec 1762 p 10 Apr 1763 (Kilmore); R & V Lurgan & Munterconnaught (Kilm) 1763–68; V Killesherdoney (Kilm) 1768–93; Archd of Kilmore 1770–76; Keeper of Marsh's Library Dublin 1773–76; Preb of St Audoen in Christ Ch Cath Dublin 1774–75; Dean of St Patrick's Cath Dublin 1775–93

> elder **s.** of Rev Thomas, Preb of Wolverhampton (Lich); **bro.** of Rev Thomas, V Drung and Larah (Kilm) qv; nephew of Rt Rev John, Bp of Kilmore qv
>
> **m.** Martha Newburgh (**died** 13 Dec 1804 without issue by either husband aged 73) **dau.** of Col Henry Cary of Co Derry and widow of Thomas Newburgh of Ballyhaise Co Cavan
>
> **Died** 1 Sep 1793 Edinburgh **bur.** Greyfriars Churchyard Edinburgh

CRAIG, GRAHAM 1830/31–1904

b. 1830 or 1831 Co Down; ed by Dr Boyle; ent TCD 4 Dec 1852 aged 21 BA & Div Test (1) 1857 MA 1863

d 1857 (Durham for Meath) p 1858 (Meath); C Athboy (Meath) 1857–60; C Christ Ch Belfast (Conn) 1860–61; C St John Cloverhill in Annagh Par (Kilm) 1861–65; C Kildalkey (Meath) 1865–69; R Tullamore w Lynally (Meath) 1869–1902; C Tullamore 1903–04; Chapl to Prison and Workhouse Tullamore (Meath) 1869–1902; Dio Reg Meath 1882–1902; RD of Ardnurcher (Meath) 1889–1902; Chapl to Bp of Meath

1893–1904; Archd of Meath 1898–1900; Dean of Clonmacnoise 1900–04; Acting CF

>s. of Stewart

>m. 18 Aug 1863 Catherine Helen dau. of Rev Robert Noble, R Athboy (Meath). Issue 1. Very Rev Robert Stewart (died 8 Oct 1929 aged 65) TCD BA 1887 Div Test (2) 1888 MA 1894 d 1887 p 1888 (Meath) C Tullamore w Lynally (Meath) 1887–1902 R Tullamore w Lynally (Meath) 1902–29, Dean of Clonmacnoise 1923–29 m. Emily Cecilia dau. of Henry and Frances Augusta Fetherstonhaugh and had issue Rev Graham Fetherstonhaugh (died 24 Apr 1988) b. 15 Feb 1906 R Drumbo (Down) 1966–70; 2. Very Rev Herbert Newcombe (died 22 Jul 1938) TCD BA & Div Test (2) 1891 MA 1898 d 1891 p 1892 (Cork) C Ballymodan (Cork) 1891–95 C Holy Trinity Weymouth (Sarum) 1895–1902 Dio Insp of Schools Sarum 1898–1902 C Tullamore w Lynally (Meath) 1902–05 Hon Cler V Christ Ch Cath Dublin 1905 C St Bartholomew (Dub) 1905–09 R Newtownmountkennedy (Glend) 1909–13 R Clane (w Donadea from 1924) (Kild) 1913–28 Canon of Kildare 1918–20 Prec of Kildare 1920–28 Dean of Kildare and R Kildare w Lackagh (Kild) 1928–38 m. and had issue incl (i) Rev Richard Newcombe, V Alfreton (Derby) (ii) Eleanor Stewart (iii) Mary Waller; 3. Vice Admiral Arthur (died Feb 1943) RN, who took the name of Craig–Muller; 4. Henry (died of smallpox 11 Jan 1896 at Pozanoli Italy aged 30

>Died 8 Oct 1904 aged 73

CRAIG, JAMES ROBERT HANNA 1877/78–1953

b. 1877 or 1878; TCD BA 1913 MA 1916

d 1913 (Kilmore) p 1914 (Limerick); C Kilkeevan (Elph) 1913–14; C Tralee (A & A) 1914–17; R Dromtariffe w Drishane (A & A) 1917–26; R Drinagh (Cork) 1926–28; R Kilkeedy (Lim) 1928–55

>m. Eva Grace (died 21 May 1958 bur. Mt Jerome Dublin) and had issue incl 1. his eldest s. James Samuel Wauchope (died 22 May 1926 at Drinagh Rectory aged 9); 2. his eldest dau. Margaret Hugh m. Richard Desmond Hodgins, MRCVSI

>Died 24 Jan 1953 aged 75 bur. Mt Jerome

CRAMPTON, HENRY FYERS 1868–1940

b. 8 Feb 1868 Aughrim Rectory Ballinasloe Co Galway; ed Eastbourne Coll; TCD BA 1893 Div Test 1894

d 1894 p 1895 (Ossory); C Newtownbarry (Ferns) 1894–1900; C Moyliscar (Meath) 1900–04; R Rathconnell (Meath) 1904–09; C St Stephen Belfast (Conn) 1909–11; R Crossduff (Clogh) 1911–17; R Cloone (Ard) 1917–26; C-in-c Killinagh (w Kiltyclogher from 1930) (Kilm) 1926–39; ret

>s. of Very Rev John Fiennes Twistleton, Provost of Kilmacduagh 1885–88

>m. 1908 Margaret (died 10 Jan 1951) widow of John Crawford of Lisnaskea Co Fermanagh. Issue Margaret Winifred Charlotte

>Died 23 Nov 1940

CRAMPTON, JOSIAH 1809–1883

b. 18 May 1809 Dublin; ed Eton Coll; ent TCD as SC 1 Nov 1824 BA 1829 MA 1832

PC Malahide (Dub) 1834–38; R Raheny (Dub) 1838–55; R Killesher (Kilm) 1855–79; R Great Sutton (St A) 1879–83

2nd **s.** of Sir Philip, Bt, President RCSI by Selina (*née* Cannon)

m. (1) Jul 1833 Elizabeth Dorothea (**died** 10 Jan 1873 at Florencecourt) **dau.** of Rev Josiah Crampton, R Stradbally (Killaloe) 1803–42. Issie 1. Elizabeth Anna **b.** 17 Apr 1842; 2. Charlotte Twistleton **b.** 1 Jun 1845; 3. Georgina Emma Elizabeth **b.** 6 Feb 1850; 4. Pamela Adelaide Alice **b.** 22 May 1851 **m.** 13 Oct 1881 Rev Andrew Noble Bredin, jun; 5. Eugenie Elizabeth Philippa **b.** 22 May 1853; 6. Dorothea Henrietta Waller **m.** 13 Sep 1860 William Gore, JP of Ennismore Hall Enniskillen; 7. Selina Catherine; 8. Eugenie Elizabeth

m. (2) 4 Jan 1879 Margaret Florence Julia **dau.** of Rev Andrew Noble Bredin, sen, R Taney (Dub) 1851–57; she survived him and **m.** Rev Lewis Williams, R Llanwnda (St D)

Died 8 Mar 1883 at Great Sutton Essex aged 73

PUBLICATIONS

The Cottager's Family Prayers, 1846

A Few of the Excuses made by Professing Christians for their Neglect of the

Lord's Supper briefly stated and answered, 1847

Astronomical Essays, Dublin 1851

The Lunar World; its Survey, Dublin, Herbert 1853

A Night Watch or a short account of the Occultation of Mars by the Moon, London 1854

The Great Solar Eclipse of March 15th, 1858, Dublin, Herbert 1858

CRANE (CREAN), DANIEL

R Donagh (Raph — then Derry) 1630–31; V Killinkere (Kilm) 1631; is V there in 1634

CRANE, FELIX

ord p by William (Redman) Bp of Norwich 1 Jan 1600

coll V Rossinver and Killasnett (Kilm) 22 Jun 1626; is V in 1634

CRAWFORD, ANDREW

Perhaps this was "Mr. C.", "the aged minister who had long officiated as Curate" Kiltubrid (Ard) *c.* 1826 when Rev George Dallas Mansfield, qv became Rector, who was retired with a pension equal to his full salary, half paid by the Abp of Tuam, half by the Rector. He died soon after. (Sirr's *Memoir of the Last Archbishop of Tuam* p 256)

CRAWFORD, ARCHIBALD 1814/15–

b. 1814 or 1815 Co Antrim; ed by Mr Boyle; ent TCD 17 Oct 1834 aged 19 BA & Div Test 1842 MA 1856

d & p 1843 (Killaloe); C Kinawley (Kilm) 1843–53; C Thomastown (Kild) 1853–54; C Loughgall (Arm) 1854–58; R Christ Ch Castlemaine (Dio Melbourne) 1859–84; Archd of Melbourne 1869–84; Canon of St John's (Melbourne) 1871

    s. of Arthur, merchant

    m. Elizabeth… Issue incl Archibald **b.** 23 Mar 1854 at Loughgall Co Armagh

CRAWFORD, GEORGE 1775/76–1846

b. 1775 or 1776 Co Longford; ed by Mr Keating; ent TCD 5 Nov 1792 aged 16 BA 1797 MA 1822 LLB & LLD 1828 DD

d 27 Aug 1797 (Down) p; C Clongish (Ard) 1798–1821; V Clonbroney (Ard) 1821–46; R Clongish (Ard) 1822–c46; V Gen of Ardagh

    s. of Samuel

    m. 1798 Mary **dau.** of Francis West of Cloone. Issue **sons** 1. George John TCD LLD; 2. Rev Francis **b.** 1812/13 (**died** 18 Oct 1881) ent TCD 1829 aged 16 Sch 1832 BA 1834 LLB & LLD 1872 d 1843 p 17 Dec 1843 C Newtownhamilton (Arm) 1843–44 C Loughgall (Arm) 1844–50 PC Portadown (Arm) 1850–59 R Derryloran (Arm) 1859–79 R Milton Bryant (Ely) 1879–81 **m.** 17 Jul 1851 Agnes Jane **dau.** of Marcus Synnott of Ballymoyer and had issue (i) Mary Edith **b.** 4 Nov 1853 at Portadown (ii) Marcus Synnott **b.** 25 Apr 1855; 3. Samuel BA 1831; 4. William ent TCD 1817 aged 17; **daus.** 1. Marie St Maurice **m.** 1 Feb 1825 Rev Lewis Potter, R Dromard (Killala) 1838–50 and had issue (i) Samuel Reginald ent TCD 16 Oct 1845 aged 18 BA 1850 MB 1856 **m.** 5 May 1859 Ducabella Jane eldest **dau.** of Charles Maitland of Bradninch Devon (ii) Rev Francis Lewis **b.** 1829 or 1830 Co Galway ent TCD 18 Oct 1846 aged 16 BA 1851 MA 1856 V Cullompton (Ex); 2. Selina Frances **m.** Capt Nicholas Gosselin 46th Regt and had issue incl Sir Nicholas; 3. H Madeleine **m.** 17 Aug 1830 Rev Arthur Palmer C Carbury (Kild) and later Archd of Toronto

    Died 1846

CRAWFORD, HENRY BREDIN 1875/76–1916

b. 1875 or 1876; TCD BA 1897 MA & Div Test (2) 1902

d 1903 p 1904 (Killaloe); C Creagh (Clonf) 1903–07; C Kilfenora w Lisdoonvarna (Kilf) 1907–08; R Kilfenora w Lisdoonvarna (Kilf) 1908–09; R Ballymachugh (Kilm) 1910–12; R Kilmanaheen and Lahinch (Kilf) 1912–; Chapl Ennistymon U (Killaloe) 1912–16

    Died 26 Jan 1916 aged 40

CRAWFORD, HUGH 1807–1871

b. 1807 Donegal; ent TCD 1 Nov 1824 aged 17 BA 1829

d 24 Mar 1830 p; C Templemichael (Ard) 1839; V Shrule (Ard) 1844–55; R Tashinny

(Ard) 1855–56; R & V Killashee (Ard) 1856–71
>   eldest **s.** of Major–General Robert C Miles
>   **m.** 20 Jan 1837 in Longford Ch Jemima yst **dau.** of James Hunt of Dublin
>   **Died** 6 Jan 1871 at Templeton Glebe in his 64th year

CRAWFORD, JAMES   –1779

V Killinagh (Kilm) 1764–76; prob same as John Crawford, R Templecrone (Raph) 1775–79
>   John Crawford, R Templecrone **m.** 25 Aug 1761 at Monaghan a **sister** of Rev Thomas Wilson, FTCD. Issue John **b.** Co Leitrim ent TCD 23 May 1780 aged 17 BA 1784
>   **Died** 1779

CRAWFORD, JAMES 1785/86–

b. 1785 or 1786 Co Galway; ed by Mr Smith at Elphin; ent TCD as Siz 15 Oct 1803 aged 17 BA 1808 MA 1832

V Athleague (Elph) 1809–37; V Fuerty & Kilbegnet 1809–26
>   **s.** of Rev Thomas qv
>   **m.** and had issue Thomas William (**died** Aug 1841 aged 15 at Athleague Glebe)

CRAWFORD, PRINCE 1795–

b. 1795 Dublin; ed by Mr Higgins; TCD BA 1815 MA 1832

C Kilcommick (Ard) 1817; C Donnybrook (Dub) 1821–24
>   **s.** of Prince
>   **m.** and had issue including Prince Irwin **b.** 1821

CRAWFORD, THOMAS

ed by Mr Kenny at Elphin; ent TCD as Siz 16 Jun 1767 Sch 1769 BA 1772

d 1773 (Kilmore) p; V Athleague Fuerty & Kilbegnet (Elph) 1785–1809
>   **m.** and had issue a **s.** Rev James qv

CRAWFORD, THOMAS 1787/88–1871

b. 1787 or 1788 London; ed by Mr O'Beirne; ent TCD 5 Nov 1804 aged 16 BA 1810

d 3 May 1818 (Dromore) p 19 Jul 1818 (Down); C Aghaderg (Drom) 1819; R Eastersnow and Kilcola 1820–37; R Croghan (Elph) 1820–47; V Athleague & Kilbegnet, Fuerty being separated (Elph) 1837–47; was elected to the office of Precentor of Elphin by the Dean and Chapter in1838, but no entry appears in D.R. On 17 Apr 1847, the Privy Council removed the suspension, but severed the revenues from the office. R Drumcliffe (Elph) 1847–71
>   prob **s.** of Thomas (**s.** of Adair, MD)

m. Anne Armstrong (ML 1822)
Died 3 Jul 1871

CREEK, WILLIAM 1836/37–1899

b. 1836 or 1837 Newry; ent TCD 2 Jul 1855 aged 18 BA & Div Test 1860 MA 1862 BD & DD 1884

d 1860 p 1861; C Kildallon (Kilm) 1860–74; R Kildallon (Kilm) 1874–99; Archd of Kilmore 1884–99

s. of James

m. 22 Sep 1863 Kildallon Par Ch Emilia 2nd **dau.** of the late Capt R Clifford, JP of Carn Cottage Co Cavan. Issue Isabella Ogle (**died** 30 Dec 1930 Coleraine) **m.** 18 Sep 1888 Lowry Cliffe Loftus Tottenham, DI RIC, 2nd **s.** of Henry

Died 14 Sep 1899 aged 62

CREERY, JOHN –1810

ed Univ of Edinburgh

d p May 1773; C Ballymore (Arm) *c.* 1783–89; PC Acton (Arm) 1789–93; V Ballybay (Clogh) 1798–1810; held also V Drumlane (Kilm) 1798–1810

m. and had issue incl **sons** 1. Rev Leslie (**died** 16 Jan 1849 aged 66) **b.** Co Armagh ent TCD 4 Nov 1799 aged 16 BA 1804 MA 1818 C Ballymore (Arm) 1808–17 Preb of Dunsfort (Down) 1817–18 V Kilmore (Down) 1819–31 Chanc of Connor and R Ramoan (Conn) 1831–34 R Billy (Conn) & Archd of Connor 1834–49 **m.** 3 May 1808 Isabella (**died** 17 Mar 1877 aged 94) **dau.** of Moses Moreland of Tandragee by Margaret **dau.** of Andrew McCreight and had issue (i) John **b.** 23 Sep 1809 (**died** 14 Feb 1837) (ii) Rev Andrew **b.** 14 Nov 1810 TCD BA 1833 d 1834 p C Ramoan (Conn) 1834–41 PC Dunseverick (Conn) 1841–61 R Kilmore (Down) 1871–89 **m.** (1) 1843 Mary **dau.** of James Stewart Moore **m.** (2) 9 Aug 1852 Alice **dau.** of John Tate and had issue 6 **sons** and 3 **daus.** (iii) Charles Albert **b.** 1 May 1812 **m.** Anna (iv) Henriette de Salis **b.** 11 Jan 1814 **m.** 4 Sep 1840 Charles Scudamore (v) Leslie Edward **b.** 28 Jul 1815 **m.** Eliza McCreight (vi) William Frederick Carter **b.** 20 Jan 1817 (**died** in W Australia 1841) (vii) James Moreland **b.** 6 Oct 1818 **m.** Louisa **dau.** of William Stewart (viii) Maria Christina **b.** 6 Oct 1818 **m.** 16 Apr 1836 Charles George Stewart (ix) Leslie **b.** 27 Mar 1820 (**died** 22 Jan 1867) (x) Henry Leslie **b.** 9 Jun 1822 (**died** 1829) (xii) Isabella **b.** 23 Aug 1824 **m.** Samuel Mercer (xii) Margaretta **b.** 9 Sep 1826 **m.** 1846 Alexander Tate (xiii) Alice **b.** 17 Jun 1828 **m.** 12 Feb 1847 William Ford Hutchinson; 2; John; **daus.** 1. Ann; 2. Elizabeth; 3. Isabella

Died 2 Aug 1810

CREERY, THOMAS FERGUSON 1821–1856

b. 1821 Co Armagh; ent TCD 13 Oct 1837 aged 16 BA 1843

d 1845 p 1846 (Down); C Clongish (Ard) 1845–46; C Ballymoney (Conn) 1846–53; I St John's Episcopal Chapel, Forres (M R & C) *c.* 1853–56

s. of John of Orange Hill Co Armagh by Judith **dau.** of James Moreland of Tullyhue

m. 1 Oct 1845 All SS Maidstone Kent, Lucy **dau.** of William Scudamore of Maidstone

Died 17 Jan 1856 in Edinburgh aged 34

CREGAN (CRIGAN), CLAUDE 1833/34–

b. 1833 or 1834 Dublin; ed by Dr Flynn; ent TCD 4 Nov 1853 aged 19 BA (not given in TCD Catalogue)

d 1867 p; C Drumlane (Kilm) 1867–71; C-in-c Corawallen and Newtowngore (Kilm) 1872–74 and R 1874–79

s. of Rev Martin

CREIGHTON, GEORGE

adm V Rossinver (Kilm) 1 Feb 1618; V Rush

CREIGHTON, GEORGE

d 9 Jan 1619/20 p 20 Jul 1623; admitted "Curate" Lurgan (Kilm) 4 Nov 1619 with Castlerahan and Munterconnaught; coll again 3 Oct 1628; there in 1641; R & V Lurgan were impropriate 1622; was Commonwealth Minister Kinawley (Kilm) *c.* 1650 settled on the tithes of Kinawley and Killasser at a salary of £60, but in 1660 had got no more than £9.15.0 from the tithes. He is to get balance to make up £60 for his pains in the ministry; seems to have been also minister at Drumlane, Seymour's *Commonwealth MSS*. He was coll to the parish of Kinawley 24 Apr 1661, appeared by his Proctor John Creighton at Triennial Visitation 1673; was again coll V or *Pariochiani* 13 April 1674. He was probably George Creighton who was R Bailieborough and Moybologue (Kilm) 1619–31 and V Lurgan 1619 and there in 1641 and the rebels did not meddle with him, and R Castlerahan in 1628. Given the time span, there may have been two clergy called George Crieghton

CREIGHTON, JAMES

ed by Mr Cottingham; ent TCD as Siz 2 Jul 1760 BA 1764

d & p 1765 (Kilmore); C Kilmore (Kilm) 1766; C Kinawley (Kilm) 1770– still there in 1777

m. 1778 Alice **dau.** of Rev John Ingham, C Kinawley (Kilm) qv

CRESSWELL, JOHN

is V Drumreilly (Kilm) in 1636; was still V in 1647 and resident at Newry (Carte Papers xxi. 346)

CRICHTON, JAMES   –1915

d 1878 p 1879 (Kilmore); C Killinkere (Kilm) 1878–85; V Kildrumferton (Kilm) 1885–1906; ret

m. and had issue incl 1. Edith (**died** 9 Apr 1932 Belfast) **m.** Rev Henry Gordon; 2. Ven Walter Richard (**died** 29 Apr 1942) TCD BA 1907 MA 1911 d 1907 p 1908 C Seagoe (Drom) 1907–11 C Hillsborough (Down) 1911–14 Sec LJS for Province of Armagh 1914–17 Chapl at Bangalore 1917–19 and 1924 Cannanore w Calicut 1919–20 Ootacamund 1920–22 Secunderabad 1922–23 Furlough 1923–24 & 1928 St George's Cath Madras 1924–25 St Mary's Fort St George 1925–26 Wellington 1926–28 officiating Archd of Madras 1929–31 Commisssioner-in-charge Madras 1930 Archd of Madras from 1931

Died 16 Apr 1915

CRISPE, HENRY

Preb and V Termonbarry (Elph) 1639–; The Deposition of his wife Ruth in 1643 says that he was murdered by the rebels and that she lost £500 by the rebellion. There were two of the name Graduates of Cambridge, one BA 1626/27, the other BA 1629 ord d & p 1629

CROFTON, EDWARD

is V Eastersnow (Elph) in 1615 (R.V.); V Kilmactranny (Elph) 1615 (R.V.)

CROFTON, HENRY MARCUS 1783/84–

b. 1783 or 1784 Co Roscommon; ed by Mr Eaton; ent TCD 9 Jun 1802 aged 18 BA 1805

d 22 Jan 1806 (Ardagh) p; coll V Taghboy Disert and Lissonuffy (Elph) 20 Aug 1811; R Tessaragh (Elph) 1811–34

    s. of Edward, Bt

CROFTON, JOHN 1812/13–1868

b. 1812 or 1813 Co Leitrim; ed by Mr Hawksworth; ent TCD 5 Jul 1830 aged 17 BA 1835

d 1837 p; C Cloone (Ard) 1843–45; C Kilkenny West (Meath) 1853–57; R Portloman (Meath) 1857–68

    3rd **s.** of Duke, JP DL by Alicia **m.** 18 Aug 1808 **dau.** of William Jones

    m. 1 Jul 1843 Anne Newcomen **dau.** of Berry Norris of Mohill Co Leitrim. Issue 1. Duke Fraser (**died** in infancy); 2. William Jones TCD MB Capt AMS; 3. Dorcas Alice; 4. Elizabeth Anna **m.** Berry Norris of USA; 5. Helen Augusta; 6. Henrietta Dorothea

    Died Dec 1868

CROFTON, MORGAN

C Mohill (Ard) *c.* 1826–47

CROFTON, THOMAS –1683

TCD Sch 1638 (MA in Cotton)

d Sep 1641 (Elphin) p Mar 1641/42 (Dublin); Preb of Kilcooley in Elphin Cath 1661–67; Preb of Mulhuddart in St Patrick's Cath Dublin 1661–83; Dean of Elphin 1666–83, inst 10 Jul 1666 (F.F.)

3rd **s.** of John of Lisdorn Co Roscommon

m. Catherine **dau.** of Rev Edward Hawkes. Issue Catherine **m.** Robert Goldsmith of Balloughtra; their grandson was the Poet Oliver Goldsmith; 2. Thomas

Died 1683

CROMIE, JOHN 1755/56–

b. 1755 or 1756 London; ed by Dr Norris; ent TCD 2 Nov 1773 aged 17 BA 1778

Preb of Oran & V Dunamon (Elph) 1795–1805; V Straid (Ach) in 1806; V Kilglass (Elph) 1806–09; V Ballinrobe (Tuam) *c.* 1809–23

s. of William

m. (1) Hon Emily Juliana Browne (ML 1795) of Castlelost Co Meath.

m. (2) Ellen (**died** 1840 Torquay) only **dau.** of Henry Palmer of Dublin

had issue by one of his wives 1. Rev William **b.** Co Mayo ent TCD 5 May 1817 aged 16 BA 1821 C Kilruane (Killaloe) 1822; 2. St George **b.** 1803 Co Mayo ent TCD 5 Jun 1820

†CRONIN, BENJAMIN –1871

C Kilcommick (Ard) 1827–32; became 1st Bp of Huron, Canada; Bp of Huron 1857–71

Died 1871

CROOKE, MILWARD

C Kiltoghart (Ard) 1853–55, lic 25 Jun 1853

CF 1855; stationed in Birr Co Offaly in 1858

m. 2 May 1860 Emily **dau.** of Thomas Hackett. Issue a **s**, **b.** 2 Jul 1865 at Templemore

CROSTHWAIT, WILLIAM FREDERICK –1930

TCD BA 1912 MA 1916

d 1911 p 1913 (Kilmore); C Kilmore (Kilm) 1911–13; C Booterstown (Dub) 1913–16; CF 1916–30

s. of John of Clonskeagh Dublin

m. 26 Sep 1917 Gwendolyne Harriette (**died** 15 Dec 1969) **dau.** of Frank Gethin of Greystones Co Wicklow. Issue Daphne

Died 27 Dec 1930 Hong Kong

CROWE, DAWSON 1716/17–1798

b. 1716 or 1717 Dublin; ed by Dr Elwood, Dublin; ent TCD 16 Jun 1732 aged 15 Sch 1734 BA 1736 MA 1739

Preb of Whitechurch (Ferns) 1759–60; R Killinkere (Kilm) 1760–98; R Kilshine (Meath) 1771–90; JP for Co Cavan 21 Apr 1766

s. of William

m. Frisweed **dau.** of Rev John Ball, V Charlestown (Arm). Issue 1. a **dau. m**... Noble and had issue (i) William (ii) Rachel (iii) Elizabeth **m.** Rev William Garde; 2. Henrietta **m.** Michael Tisdall of Charlesfort Co Meath; 3. Sarah (**died** 1811) **m.** 8 Feb 1785 at St Bride's Dublin Rev William Slicer Hamilton, V Julianstown (Meath)

Died *c.* 10 Feb 1798

CROWE, EDWARD DANIEL 1864–1928

b. 25 Sep 1864 Bray Co Wicklow; ed Aravon Sch Bray; TCD BA 1884 Div Test & MA 1888

d 1887 p 1888 (Kilmore); C Drumlease (Kilm) 1887–90; C-in-c Innismagrath (Kilm) 1890–93; C Armagh (Arm) 1893–95; C Ballyeglish (Arm) 1895–97; R Camlough (Arm) 1897–1900; R Drumcree (Arm) 1900–04; R Urney (Kilm) 1904–28; Exam Chapl to Bp of Kilmore 1907–17

s. of Edward, builder of Bray by Jane (*née* Roberts)

m. 1893 Sarah Florence **dau.** of William Crowe of Hereford. Issue 1. Kathleen Florence **b.** 1895; 2. Eileen Frances **b.** 1897; 3. Edward Ernest **b.** 1898 **m.** 24 Sep 1924 Laura Southwell 2nd **dau.** of John Crowe of Weston–super–Mare; 4. Noreen Isobel **m.** 7 Mar 1940 George H Tarr of Harton Cross Somerset

Died 11 Jan 1928

CROXTON, JAMES 1606–

b. 10 Mar 1606; ed Merchant Taylors' Sch; matric at Oxford from St John's Coll 17 Jan 1622/23 BA 1626 MA 1630

He was an Englishman, sent to Ireland by Abp Laud as Chapl to Lord Mountnorris;

Precentor of Elphin 1633; was admitted R of the College of 4 Chapels of the Church of Gowran (Oss) 28 Jul 1636 (F.F.); V Gowran (Oss) 1637–55; coll by the Abp of Dublin as "Preb of Killaigie and Coulstuffe" (Ferns) 1639; he seems to have resigned in a few months; V Ballyellin (Ferns) 1641

s. of William of London

CROZIER, GRAHAM PHILIP 1801–1872

b. 1801 Dublin; ed by Dr Miller at Armagh Royal Sch; ent TCD 4 Jan 1819 aged 17 BA 1823

d 29 Apr 1824 (Dromore) p 2 Oct 1825 (Elphin); Lic C St John Sligo 1825; C Seapatrick (Drom) 1828; V Monasteroris (Kild) 1830–42; V Rathconnell (Meath) 1842–53; R Taunagh (Elph) 1853–71; Preb of Kilmacallen (Elph) 1853–71

s. of George, Lawyer of Banbridge Co Down

m. Anne (**died** 8 Dec 1870 at Riverstown Rectory Co Sligo) **dau.** of Roger Robinson, JP of Cloombarry Co Sligo. Issue incl 1. Francis d **unm.**; 2. his only **dau.** Katie Jane **m.** 5 Oct 1859 W Christian Horsfall, eldest **s.** of W Horsfall of Calverley House Leeds Yorkshire

Died 27 Oct 1872 aged 71 at Blackrock

CROZIER, JAMES ALEXANDER 1822–

b. 1822 Co Antrim; ed by Mr Flynn; TCD BA 1843 Div Test 1844 MA 1845

d 1844 (Llandaff) p 1845 (Dublin); C Rathdrum (Glend) 1846–47; I Kilkenny West (Meath) 1847–54; almost certainly same as James Alexander Crozier who was C Killashee (Ard) Jul 1854–Jan 1855 whilst awaiting his call-up to HM Forces; CF in Crimea 1855–56; Corfu 1856–; Chapl Household Cavalry 1871–80; V Weston (Ches) 1880–84; R Mundesley (Nor) 1884–86; R Coston Milton Mowbray (Leic, then Pet) 1889–1902

s. of William, Examiner in the Exchequer

CRUMPE, WESTENRA 1687/88–1761

b. 1687 or 1688 Birr Co Offaly; ed by Mr Harvey at Dungannon; ent TCD 12 May 1705 aged 17 BA 1709 MA 1712

was Chapl to Brig Gen Jacob Orr's Troop in 1717; Preb of Tibohine (Elph) 1731–61

s. of Rev Richard, DD

m. (1) Susan Sherigley of Swords Co Dublin (ML 4 Sep 1714)

m. (2) Martha Campbell (Will proved 1755) who is mentioned in the Will of Rev William Campbell of Shrule which was proved in 1739

Died 1761

CUFFE, CAULFIELD *c.* 1685–*c.* 1760

b *c.* 1685 Galway; ed by Mr Price, Galway; ent TCD as Siz 25 Mar 1703/04 aged 18 Sch 1707 BA 1708

C Kiltullagh (Tuam) 1710; V Cloonclare Clonlogher and Killasnett (w Rossinver 1724–39) (Kilm) 1721–43; R Inismacsaint (Clogh) 1739–60

s. of Thomas

m. and had issue incl 1. Rev Thomas, V Cloonclare (Kilm) qv; 2. Rev Francis, V Rossinver (Kilm) qv;

Died *c.* 1760; Will proved 1760

CUFFE, FRANCIS 1714/15–

b. 1714 or 1715 Co Roscommon; ed by Dr Blayer, Sligo; ent TCD 3 May 1731 aged 16; R Rossinver (Kilm) 1739–c75. C Inishmacsaint (Clogh) 1747–57

s. of Rev Caulfield, V Cloonclare (Kilm) qv (s. of Thomas); **bro.** of Rev Thomas, V Cloonclare (Kilm) qv

CUFFE, THOMAS 1713/14–1775

b. 1713 or 1714 Co Roscommon; ed by Mr Blayr, Sligo; ent TCD 2 May 1731 aged 17 BA 1735

C Cloonclare (Kilm) 1738; V Cloonclare Clonlogher and Killasnett (Kilm) 1743–75

s. of Rev Caulfield, V Cloonclare (Kilm) qv (s. of Thomas); **bro.** of Rev Francis, V Rossinver (Kilm) qv

Died 1775

CULLEN, CARNCROSS 1753/54–1807

b. 1753 or 1754 Co Leitrim; ed by Mr F D Kenny; ent TCD as SC 2 Nov 1770 aged 16 BA 1774

d 1774 p; C Ballintemple (Kilm) 1775–c. 88; R & V Killan, now Shercock (Kilm) 1791–92; V Cloonclare U (Kilm) 1792–1807

eldest s. of Patrick, "armiger" of Skreeney Co Leitrim, High Sheriff 1782 by Isabella dau. of Carncross Nesbitt of Aughmore Rosshire

m. c 1783 Ellen (or Elizabeth) dau. of James Soden of Grange Co Sligo. Issue sons 1. Carncross of Glenada m. and had issue; 2. John James, JP of Skreeney m. and had issue; 3. Henry Francis m; 3 daus.

Died 1807

CULLEN, JAMES EDWARD 1852/53–1912

b. 1852 or 1853; TCD BA 1880 MA 1886

d 1875 p 1876 (Cork); C Ballymodan (Cork) 1875–77; R Ballyboys (Meath) 1877–78; Dio Insp Schools for Meath 1878–79; R Clonmacnoise 1880–81– 1881–84 in Crockford — not in C I Dir; C Rathvilly (Leigh) 1881; C Boyle (Elph) 1884, in Leslie's MSS, but not in C I Dir or Crockford; R St John Westport NZ (Dio Nelson) 1884–94; R Drishane (Cork) 1895–96; R Ballyheige (A & A) 1896–1912

m. and had issue Maria Geraldine m. 8 Jan 1916 Capt Alexander Norman Crawford, FRCSI RAMC s. of Rev William of Dublin

Died 11 Feb 1912 whilst robing for a morning service aged 59

†CUMBERLAND, DENISON –1774

ed Westminster Sch; Trinity Coll Camb MA 1728

Preb of Stow Longa (Linc); R Stanwick (Pet) 1757; V Fulham (Lon) 1757–63; Chapl to Lord Lt 1760; Preb of Reculverland (Lon) 1761–63; consec Bp of Clonfert 19 Jun 1763; Bp of Clonfert 1763–72; translated to Kilmore by Patent 6 Mar 1772; enthroned 22 Apr 1772; Bp of Kilmore 1772–74

2nd s. of Ven Richard, Archd of Northumberland (only s. of Rt Rev Richard, Bp of Peterborough 1691–1718)

m. Joanna 2nd dau. of Dr Richard Bentley. Issue Richard (**died** 7 May 1811 aged 80 bur. Westminster Abbey) m. Elizabeth Ridge

Died Nov 1774 Dublin bur. Kilmore Cathedral

CUMMING, ROBERT GORDON
TCD BA 1865 MA 1866

d 1866 (Armagh) p 1868 (Kilmore); C Castlerahan (Kilm) 1866; C Boyle (Elph) 1867; C Elphin (Elph) 1868; R Drumconrath (Meath) 1870–72; held curacies in England 1873–84; C-in-c Mumby Chapel (Linc) 1884

> **m.** Georgina Emma Gordon (**died** 9 Feb 1873 at Preston). Issue incl 1. eldest **dau.** Maria Georgina **m.** 24 Jul 1873 Theophilus Thompson, JP of Fort Lodge Co Cavan; 2. Fanny Henrietta (**died** 15 Feb 1870 Dublin aged 14)

CUNNINGHAM, HENRY 1706/07–1777

b. 1706 or 1707 Limerick; ed by his father at Limerick; ent TCD 7 Jul 1725 aged 18 Sch 1728 BA 1729 BD & DD 1762

Archd of Elphin 1756–61; (Cotton has 1750/51 which Leslie thinks is a misreading of the Roll); V Kilkeevan and Preb of Ballintubber 1761–77

> poss **s.** of James
> **Died** Jul 1777 aged 70 **bur.** St Thomas Dublin

CUNNINGHAM, WILLIAM

V Killeshandra (Kilm) 1682–c. 92; pres by the Saunderson Family

> **m.** Penelope Saunderson; she "received a pension of £100 compensation for their great losses occasioned by the siege of Londonderry" in 1694/95; both she and her husband were natives of Scotland

CUNNINGHAM, WILLIAM 1779/80–1824

b. 1779 or 1780 Londonderry; ed by Mr Knox Foyle Coll Londonderry; ent TCD 2 Mar 1797 aged 17 Sch 1800 BA 1801

Preb of Oran (Elph) 1807–24

> **s.** of Dickson, merchant
> **Died** 17 Jul 1824 aged 44 **bur.** Londonderry

CURRY, Hon. DAVID RICHARDSON 1785/86–1823

b. 1785 or 1786 Londonderry; ed by Mr Knox Foyle Coll Londonderry; ent TCD 1 Apr 1805 BA 1809

was, according to Dean Lyster's notes in *Memorials,* 1899, p 266, V Tashinny (Ard) *c.* 1812–15, though see also Robert Moffett below; in Leslie's unpublished MSS he is R & V Tashinny & Abbeyshrule (Ard) 1819–23

> **s.** of Joseph, "mercator" of Derry by Anne **dau.** of David Richardson of Drum Co Tyrone, High Sheriff for Tyrone 1743
> **m.** 22 Aug 1821 Derry Cathedral Maria only **dau.** of Alexander Lecky of Milton Lodge
> **Died** of apoplexy 7 Oct 1823 in his 38th year at Prospect near Ballymahon Co Longford

CURRY, GEORGE CHRISTOPHER 1914–2006

b. 22 May 1914 Clontibret Co Monaghan; ed The King's Hospital Dublin; TCD BA Mod (2) Ment & Mor Sci 1942 MA 1955

d 8 Oct 1944 p 4 Nov 1945; C Roscommon G (Elph) 1944–47; C Camus–juxta–Mourne (Derry) 1947–57; R Edenderry (w Clanabogan from 1964) (Derry) 1957–86; Chapl Tyrone and Fermanagh Hosp; RD Omagh 1976–86; Canon of Derry 1976–86; ret

    s. of William Robert of Clontibret (s. of Joseph and Jane (*née* McComb)) by Isabella Brooke dau. of James Wilson and Isabel (*née* Donaldson) of Co Fermanagh

    m. 10 Jun 1957 Crom Ch Charlotte dau. of John and Ann Jane Phair of Derrylin Co Fermanagh. Issue 1. Susan Charlotte (died 19 Oct 1984) b. 16 Nov 1961; 2. Noreen Anne b. 10 Dec 1963

Died 9 Oct 2006

CURTIS, ROBERT 1728/29–1799

b. 1728 or 1729 Co Tipperary; ent TCD 3 Nov 1746 aged 17 BA 1750 MA 1753

V Drumcliffe and Taunagh (Elph) 1760–66; Preb of Kilmacallen (Elph) 1760–99

    s. of Rev Robert, Preb of Tomgraney (Killaloe)

    m. and had issue a s. Robert b. Tipperary ent TCD 11 Sep 1779 aged 17

Died Aug 1799

CUSACK, WILLIAM

"V of the Kyllan, dio of Kilmore" = Killan, now Shercock (Kilm); reserves £20 tithes, 13 Feb 1571.

D'ALTON, EYRE STRATFORD

TCD Sch & BA 1878 MA 1882

d 1881 p; C Drumshambo and Kiltoghart (Ard) 1881–83; R Killoe (Ard) 1883–86.

DALTON, GEORGE WILLIAM 1824/25–

b. 1824 or 1825 Malta; ent TCD 4 Jul 1842 aged 17 BA 1847 MA 1859 BD & DD 1877; as a young man in Dublin he was known as *Boanerges*, so great was his gift of speech

d 1849 (Oxford) p 1851 (Down); C Bicester (Ox) 1849–51; C Skerry (Conn) 1851–52; V Kilbryan (Elph) 1852–60; Asst Chapl Baggotrath (Dub) 1860–62; Missy Holy Land 1862–63; V St Paul Wolverhampton (Lich) 1863–67; PC St Paul Glenageary (Dub) 1867–89; R Todwick (Sheff) 1891–93; Lic Pr Dio London 1893; Exeter 1898; Worcester 1901; Chichester 1904

    s. of George Edward (died 1825), MD, Medical Missy to the Jews at Jerusalem by Jane dau. of Rev H Braddell of Co Wexford and widow of J Nicholson, BL

    m. (1) 9 Nov 1849 Mary Cordelia (died 9 Apr 1851) dau. of Poole Henn. Issue George Edward b. 1 Jan 1851 died 19 Jan 1852

m. (2) 22 Jun 1852 Rathfarnham Ch Dublin Elizabeth Emily **dau.** of Capt Robert Smith of Rathgar Dublin. Issue George Edward Robert **b.** 1855 **died** 4 Jan 1927 at Portsmouth aged 71

PUBLICATIONS
Notes on Neology, 1861
Prophetic Synopsis, 1863
Russia's Future, 1879

DALTON, HENRY *c.* 1805

b. *c.* 1805 Dublin; ed privately; ent TCD 14 Oct 1822 BA 1827 MA 1845; *ad eund* Ox

d 1826 p 1827; PC Arvagh (Kilm) 1826–27; Chapl to Earl of Leinster; PC Frithelstock (Ex) 1856–60

s. of George Forster, solicitor

PUBLICATIONS
Our Dangers
Lectures on the First and Second Advent
Brief Remarks on the Irish National Education Plan
Body, Mind and Spirit

DALY, HENRY SUTTON VARIAN 1872/73–1931

b. 1872 or 1873; TCD BA 1893 Div Test (2) 1897 MA 1900

d 1896 (Dublin for Killaloe) p 1897 (Killaloe); C Kilmacduagh (Kilmacd) 1896–97; C Creagh (Clonf) 1897–1900; C Tuam (Tuam) 1900–02; R Dunamon and Fuerty (Elph) 1902–14; R Kilfenora and Lisdoonvarna (w Rathbourney from 1926) (Killaloe & Kilf) 1914–31; Canon of Lockeen in Killaloe Cath 1925–31

s. of Ven Henry Varian, Archd of Clonfert 1881–1925

m. 3 Jun 1902 Clara Irene (**died** 3 Dec 1944) **dau.** of Rev John McLulich, R Tuam (Tuam) 1898–1902. Issue incl his eldest **dau.** Mary Evelena **m.** 24 Mar 1934 Richard Theodore **s.** of Lord Justice R R Cherry

Died 15 May 1931 aged 58 **bur.** Kilmacduagh

DALY, JOHN BOWLES

d 1866 p; C Templemichael (Ard) 1866–67

may be same as John Bowles Daly who was **b.** 1839 or 1840 Cheshire ent TCD 4 May 1857 aged 17 BA 1866 LLB and LLD 1872 d 1867 p 1868 C Derryloran (Arm) 1867–68; C Kilbarron (Raph) 1868–69; C Monkstown (Cork) 1869; C St Peter Clerkenwell (Lon) 1869–; C St Peter Safron Hill (Lon) 1883–84

s. of Robert, Officer in HM Service.

†DARLEY, JOHN RICHARD 1799–1884

b. Nov 1799 Cavan; ed Royal Sch Dungannon; ent TCD 11 Jun 1816 Sch 1819 BA 1820 MA 1827 BD & DD 1875 d 1826 p 1827 Bp 1874; Master Dundalk Gram Sch 1826–31; Head Master Royal Sch Dungannon 1831–50; R Drumgoon (Kilm) 1850–66; R Templemichael (Ard) and Archd of Ardagh 1866–74; elected Bp of Kilmore Elphin and Ardagh by the United Synods 23 Sep 1874; consec in St Patrick's Cath Armagh 25 Oct 1874; Bp of Kilmore, Elphin and Ardagh 1874–84

>3rd **s.** of Richard, brewer of Fairfield Co Monaghan by Elizabeth **dau.** of B Brunker of Rockcorry Co Monaghan
>
>**m.** (1) 18 Nov 1826 Anne (**died** 1 Jul 1850 Dungannon) **dau.** of Alderman Darley
>
>**m.** (2) 1851 Nanette (**died** 14 Apr 1900 aged 75) eldest **dau.** of the 3rd Lord Plunket by Charlotte **dau.** of Hon Charles Kendal Bushe, Chief Justice
>
>**Died** 20 Jan 1884

PUBLICATIONS
Ministerial Faithfulness and Wisdom, An Ordination Sermon, McGlashan, Dublin 1851
The Grecian Drama, A Treatise on the Dramatic Literature of the Greeks

DARLEY, REGINALD GEORGE   –1969

Linc Coll Oxford BA 1921 MA 1925; Wells Theol Coll 1923; Asst Master City of Oxford Sch 1922–29

d 1929 p 1930 (Oxford); C Highfield (Ox) 1929–32; Succ St Patrick's Cath Dublin 1932; Head Master Christ's Sch and Minor Canon and Prec Chester Cath 1932–33; I Rathmolyon w Laracor (Meath) and Treas V St Patrick's Cath Dublin 1933–36; Chapl and Lect St Mark's Coll Chelsea 1936–37; PC Braywood (Ox) 1938–39 (in Crockford); R Ardagh and Kilglass (Ard) 1938–39 (in C I Dir); V Forest Hill w Shotover (Ox) 1939–41; R Corkbeg (Cloyne) 1941–44; R Hacketstown w Clonmore U (Leigh) 1945–47; Asst Master Woodbridge Sch 1947–54; Lic to Off Dio St E 1949–54; C Christ Ch Leeson Pk (Dub) 1959–60; Lic to Off Dio Dublin 1960–69

>**Died** 2 Feb 1969

DARLEY, WILLIAM SHAW   1838–1908

b. 1838 Dublin; ed by Dr Stacpoole; TCD Sch 1859 BA (Jun Mod Hist & Eng Lit) 1860 Bibl Gk Pri & Div Test (2) 1861 MA 1878

d 1861 (Cork) p 1862 (Down for Kilmore); C Drumgoon (Kilm) 1861–64; PC Straffan (Dub) 1864–76; Insp Board of Rel Ed Down and Connor and Dromore 1876–1908

>**s.** of Henry F, solicitor
>
>**m.** 21 May 1862 Monkstown Ch Dublin Frances **dau.** of George Digges La Touche. Issue a **dau.** b 5 Oct 1865
>
>**Died** 17 Apr 1908

PUBLICATION
Duty of the Church of Ireland in Relation to Religious Education, 1887

DARLING, CHARLES WESLEY –1948

TCD BA & Div Test (1) 1885 Ch Formularies Pri & Warren Pri 1886 MA 1891

d 1886 p 1887 (Kilmore); C St John Sligo (Elph) 1886–91; C St Ann (Dub) 1891; SPG & TCD Missy at Hazaribagh India 1891–95; Chapl ACS at Asanol 1895; Chapl Eccles Est India at Dum Dum 1895; Jun Chapl St Paul's Cath Calcutta 1896; Howrah 1897–99; Ranikhet 1899–1902; Nagpur 1902–03; C Christ Ch Kingstown (Dub) 1903–04; Chapl at Saugor India 1904–07; Jubbulpur 1907–15; Furlough 1911 and 1915; Canon of Nagpur 1914–17; C Ringwood (w in charge Harbridge) (Win) 1915–26; V Ellingham (Win) 1915–38

    s. of Richard of Port of Spain

    m. 1895 Hester Barklie of the DUM Chota Nagpur

    Died 8 Dec 1948 Belfast

DARLING, VIVIAN WILLIAM 1885/86–1965

b. 1885 or 1886; TCD Brooke Exhib Abp King's Pri 1913 BA (1) & Div Test (1) 1914 BD 1926

d 1914 p 1915 (Cork); C Kilbrogan (Cork — now Cloyne) w Killowen (Cork) 1914–20; TCF 1917–20; R Billis (Kilm) 1920–21; C St Luke Cork (Cork) 1921–22; R St John Cork (Cork) 1922–25; R Youghal (Cloyne) 1925–34; Org Sec CCCS Dios Cork Cloyne and Ross 1928–35; R St Nicholas Cork (Cork) 1934–50; Preb of Tymothan in St Patrick's Cath Dublin 1936–64; R Abbeystrewery U w Tullagh, Clear I and Castlehaven (Ross) 1950–62; Treas of St Fin Barre's Cath Cork 1954–59; Chanc of Cork 1959–60; Prec of Cork 1960–64; R Macroom U (Cloyne) 1962–65; Archd of Cloyne and Preb of Liscleary (Cork) 1964–65

    m. Honor Frances Garde **dau.** of Rt Rev William Edward Flewett Bp of Cork Cloyne and Ross and Alice (*née* Garde). Issue incl Rt Rev Edward Flewett **b.** 24 Jul 1933 Cork TCD BA (Resp) 1955 Div Test 1956 MA 1958 d 8 Jul 1956 p 21 Sep 1957 Bp 30 Nov 1985 C St Luke Belfast (Conn) 1956–59 C Orangefield Belfast (Down) 1959–62 C-in-c Carnalea (Down) 1962–72 R St John Malone Belfast (Conn) 1972–85 Bp Limerick Killaloe Ardfert & Aghadoe 1985–2000 **m.** 2 Aug 1958 Edith Elizabeth Patricia **dau.** of Very Rev Alfred Weller Mussen Stanley Mann, Dean of Down 1964–68 by Alice Graham **dau.** of John and Elizabeth Saulters and have issue (i) David Edward **b.** 9 Feb 1960 (ii) Colin Patrick **b.** 20 Aug 1961 (iii) Philip John **b.** 21 Nov 1963 (iv) Alison Patricia **b.** 28 Sep 1966 (v) Linda Vivienne **b.** 8 Mar 1968

    Died 31 Jan 1965 aged 79

DAUNT, HUGH MAURICE 1893–1961

b. 14 Feb 1893

TCD BA (Sen Mod Log & Eth) 1916

d 1917 p 1918 (Down); C Willowfield Belfast (Down) 1917–20; not in C I Dir 1920–34; R Granard w Abbeylara and Drumlummon (Ard) 1934–37; R Drumgoon (Kilm) 1937–40; R Tomregan (w Drumlane from 1957) (Kilm) 1940–60; ret

    s. of Rev Edward Stephen Townsend (1846–1928) (**s.** of Achilles JP and Mary (*née*

Heard) of Tracton Abbey Kinsale Co Cork, R Greystones (Glend) 1876–1922) by Sarah Gertrude **dau.** of Rev Robert William Whelan, Canon of St Patrick's Cath Dublin; **bro.** of Rev William Percy

m. 1932 Anna Janetta (**died** 11 Jan 1973 at Drogheda) **dau.** of Rev W J Keane, California USA

Died 17 Nov 1961 **bur.** Greystones Co Wicklow

DAVIS, FREDERICK WILLIAM FRANK 1896–

b. 1896; TCD

d 21 Mar 1965 p 20 Mar 1966 (Kilmore); C Mohill G and C Oughteragh, Fenagh, Kiltubride and Drumreilly (Ard) 1965–66; C St Matthias Canning Town (Chelmsf) 1966–68; Perm to Off Dio Chelmsford 1968–75 and in Dio Winchester 1975–80 and in Dio Ox from 1980

a native of Guernsey

DAVIS, JOHN 1810/11–1883

b. 1810 or 1811 Queen's Co (Laois); ed by Mr Bell; ent TCD as Siz 4 Jun 1828 aged 17 Sch 1832 BA 1836

C Boyle (Elph) 1863–66; R Kilbryan (Elph) 1866–83

s. of Jones, *publicanus*

Died 1883 **bur.** Kilbryan Churchyard

DAVIS, SAMUEL 1771/72–

b. 1771 or 1772 Co Dublin; ed by Dr Adamson; ent TCD as Siz 28 May 1793 aged 21 BA 1797

V Boyle (Elph) 1802–c24

s. of Samuel, merchant

DAVISON, GEORGE THOMAS WILLIAM 1965–

b. 5 Apr 1965 Belfast; ed Methodist Coll Belfast; Belfast Coll of Technology; Univ of St Andrews BD 1988; Oak Hill Theol Coll 1990; CITC BTh 1992

d 14 Jun 1992 p 23 Jun 1993; C St Mark Portadown (Arm) 1992–95; R Kinawley w Drumany and Crom (Kilm) 1995–; Dio Dir of Ordinands 1997–; Preb of Drumlease (Kilm) 2002–03; Archd of Kilmore 2003–

s. of George Dennis of Belfast (**s.** of William John and Elizabeth (*née* Lowry)) by Norah Margaret **dau.** of Thomas and Emily (*née* Carberry) Getgood of Belfast

m. 24 Aug 1990 Knockbreda Par Ch Belfast Nadine Phyllis **dau.** of Edward Stanley and Edith Phyllis (*née* Bryson) Rolston of Belfast. Issue 1. Erin Clare **b.** 24 Mar 1994; 2. James Edward Lowry **b.** 17 Feb 1997

DAVISON, KILNER

lic C Scrabby in Granard Parish (Ard) 23 Jan 1791; C there w Gowna 1791–1803

DAWSON, WILLIAM AUGUSTUS 1826/27–1857

b. 1826 or 1827 Co Dublin; ent TCD 1 Jul 1844 aged 17 BA 1849

C Kilkeevan (Elph) 1853–

yst **s.** of Henry of Drummartin Castle Dundrum

Died 15 Jul 1857 Dublin

DAY, EDWARD 1802/03–1886

b. 1802 or 1803 Co Kerry; ed by Dr Burrowes; ent TCD 18 Oct 1819 aged 16 BA 1824 MA 1865

d 1826 p; C Roscommon (Elph)–1844; R & V Sligo (Elph) 1844–76

s. of Rev Edward

m. (1) Anne Holmes (**died** 9 Mar 1877) and by her had issue 4 **sons** incl his eldest **s.** Edward J, JP (**died** 21 Aug 1877 at Enniskillen); Rev William **m.** Isabella Hill; a **dau.** Harriet **m.** as his 3rd wife Rev William Newton Guinness, R Killery (Ard) 1835–38 qv and had issue; Elizabeth **m.** T Ridley; his 3rd **dau.** Frances Anne **m.** 13 Nov 1857 Charles Prendergast Hackett, Civil Magistrate of Melbourne Australia; Lucy **m.** E Smith

m. (2) 19 Mar 1878 Elizabeth (**died** 25 Oct 1894) **dau.** of Abraham Martin of Cleveragh Co Sligo

Died 23 Jul 1886 **bur.** St John's Churchyard Sligo

DAY, WILLIAM ALEXANDER 1839/40–1920

b. 1839/40; TCD BA 1872

d 1866 p 1868 (Kilmore); C St John Sligo 1866–67; R Knocknarea (Elph) 1867–77; R Castlekirke (Tuam) 1877–81; R Kilcoleman U (Tuam) 1881–1910; ret

m. 3 Dec 1873 at Castlebar Isabella Adine (**died** 30 Nov 1945 aged 95 at Heacham Norfolk) only **dau.** of Richard T Hill of New Zealand and niece of Rev William Townsend of Castlerea. Issue incl 1. his eldest **s.** Edward William (**died** 16 Feb 1901 Claremorris Co Mayo); 2. a **s. b.** 9 Oct 1875; 3. Isabella Margaret (**died** 9 Nov 1881 aged 10 weeks)

Died 29 Nov 1920 aged 80 at Heacham

de BURGO, MILERUS

R Clonchumosig = Kilmacumsy (Elph) to 1455; Preb of Fuerty and Kilbegnet (Elph) to 1456; became an Augustinian Canon

†de BURGO, ROLAND   –1580

Bp of Clonfert, was also appointed Bp of Elphin 1 Apr 1552, the King having united the Sees at the request of the Bishop on 23 Nov 1551 (Morrin I, 284). He took the Oath of Supremacy and held his See against the Pope. Wolfe, the Papal Legate admitted this, and the latest RC Historian, Ronan, gives full corroboration of the fact. Yet it is curious that the Four Masters, describing his death in June 1580 say, "The loss of this good man was the cause of great lamentation in his own country". Brady was discreetly silent about him, but quoted this to imply that the Four Masters thought him to have died a Roman Catholic

Died June 1580

DE COTGRAVE, JOHN
V Taunagh (Elph) *c.* 1333/34 (C.P. & C.R. 8 Edward III p38)

†DE DUNSTABLE, MILO −1288 or 1289
elected Bp of Ardagh 1255. He is Bp of Ardagh Jan 13, 1255/56 and granted the temporalities and allowed time to go to England to take the Oath of fealty (C.D.I. ii. 486), and was confirmed by the King on May 20 (C.D.I. ii. 501)

Died 28 Oct 1288 or 1289 (Ann. Loch Ce; Ann. Ult)

DE GALLINEER, PETER PEZE
see **PEACY**, PETER PEZE DE GALLINEER

DELAHYD, CHRISTOPHER
V Kilbride (Elph) 1615

DE LA MAYR, THEOBALD
R Multyfarnham Co Westmeath is prov to V Streete (Ard) because previous incumbent, Gerald Offergail was not ordained priest 3 Mar 1492 (A.H. I. 170)

DELAP, ROBERT 1801–1885
b. 1 Apr 1801; ent TCD as SC 30 May 1820 BA 1824; Irish Bar 1825

d 1829 p; C Tomregan (Kilm) 1829; PC Monellan (Raph) 1830–85

  s. of Samuel Francis of Monellan Co Donegal by Susanne (*née* Bennett)

  m. 16 Nov 1835 Isabella **dau.** of Sir James Galbraith. Issue 1. James Bogle; 2. Sarah Dorothea

Died 28 Jul 1885 at Monellan

DE MASSY, WILLIAM HUGH INGOLSBY 1892/93–1952
b. 1892 or 1893; TCD BA 1915 Div Test 1919

d 1916 p 1918 (Limerick); BC Kilkeedy (Lim) 1916–19; Dio C Limerick 1919–22; C and V Chor Limerick Cath (Lim) 1922–23; R Kilcornan (Lim) 1923–32; R Taunagh (Elph) 1932–49; R Castlemacadam (Glend) 1949–52

  m. Ethel (**died** 7 Aug 1961) and had issue incl Avril

Died 13 Jul 1952 aged 54

DENNIS (later SWIFTE–DENNIS), JOSEPH MORLEY –1909
RCSI MD

d 1872 p 1873 (Kilmore); C Drumgoon (Kilm) 1872–73; R Ardnurcher (Meath) 1873–75; R Odoghe (Oss) 1875–77; R Mothel (Oss) 1877–79; R Ballinaclough (Killaloe) 1879–91; R Edermine w Ballyhuskard U (Ferns) 1891–1904

> eldest **s.** of Rev George Morley, R Enniscoffy (Meath); took the name of Swifte–Dennis
>
> **m.** 18 Jun 1856 Alicia Mary 2nd **dau.** of John Devereux Byrne of Leighlinbridge Co Carlow. Issue 1. Morley Saunders Meade (**died** 1934), Capt 5th Batt, 18 RIR, Major RASC; 2. Harloven Devereux Aldborough **died unm.**), Lt 5th RIR; 2 **daus.**
>
> **Died** 1909

†De PAULEY, WILLIAM CECIL 1893–1968

b. 28 Jun 1893 Portrush Co Antrim; ed Coleraine Acad Inst; TCD BA (Sen Mod Ment and Mor Philos) 1914 Gold Medal, Moderatorship Pri Bp Forster's Pri 1915 Downes Premium Essay 1915 & 1916 Div Test 1916 BD 1917 MA 1921 DD 1926

d 1 Jul 1917 p 1918 (Ossory) Bp 1958; C Enniscorthy (Ferns) 1917–19; C Booterstown (Dub) 1919–20; Canon St John's Cath Winnipeg Canada 1920–26; Treas 1923–26; Prof St John's Coll Manitoba 1920–26; Exam Chapl to Abp of Rupld 1924–26; R St Peter Athlone w Kiltoom (Elph) 1926–30; R St John Sligo w Knocknarea 1930–32; Exam Chapl to Bp of Kilmore 1932; Prof of Systematic Theol and Asst Chapl at Trinity Coll Toronto 1932–39; Sel Pr TCD 1926 1930 & 1940; R St Matthias Dublin (Dub) 1939–45; Chapl to Actors' Ch Union 1940–45; Asst Lect Divinity Sch TCD 1942–52; Exam Chapl to Abp of Dublin 1944–56; R Tullow (Dub) 1945–50; Canon and Preb of Tassagard in St Patrick's Cath Dublin 1945–50; Dean of St Patrick's Cath Dublin 1950–58

elected Bp of Cashel Emly Waterford and Lismore by the House of Bishops 18 Jun 1958; consec 29 Sep 1958 in St Patrick's Cath Dublin; enthroned St John the Baptist and St Patrick's Rock Cashel 8 Oct 1958; enthroned in St Carthage's Cath Lismore 9 Oct 1958; enthroned in Christ Ch Cath Waterford 10 Oct 1958; Bp of Cashel Emly Waterford and Lismore 1958–68

> **s.** of William
>
> **m.** Winifred (**died** 11 Mar 1947) **dau.** of Ven Henry John Johnson, Archd of Ardagh qv Issue John Cecil Yeats
>
> **Died** 1968

PUBLICATIONS
> *Punishment, Human and Divine,* London 1925
> *Beccaria and Punishment,* International Journal of Ethics 1925
> *The Divine in Man,* Cambridge 1931
> *The Candle of the Lord: Studies in the Cambridge Platonists,* London 1937
> *A Study in Christian Perfection,* Hermathena, May and November 1957
> *Temptation,* Dublin 1962
> *Richard Baxter Surveyed,* Church Quarterly Review, January 1963

†DE ROSCOMMON (O'FINNAGHTY, O'FINASA), JOHN –1354

a Canon of Elphin, was then elected Bp of Elphin by the Chapter, confirmed by the King and consecrated by the Abp of Tuam, 1326. His temporalities were restored on 1 Mar 1326/27 (C.P. and C.R. p 37). He was still Bp in 1353 (C.P.L. III. 382)

died 1354 and **bur.** in his Cathedral

†DE RUSHOOK, THOMAS –1393

In 1352, he was prior of the Black Friars of Hereford. Richard II made him his Confessor in 1377 and presented him to the Archdeaconry of Asaph in 1382. He became Bp of Llandaff in 1383, consec 3 May 1383; trans to Chichester 1385. In a dispute between the King and Parliament *c.* 1385, the Lords temporal found him guilty of treason, and banished him to Cork, or within two leagues of it. The Pope then translated him to Kilmore in 1389, and on account of the poverty of the See, he was granted an exchequer pension of £40 a year, 10 Mar 1389/90. This pension was paid to him up to 25 Jan 1392/93. He died in England about that time and was buried in the Church of Seal in Kent (A.H. I. 255, C.P.R.E. Richard II IV 228, 239). De Rushook occupied the See of Kilmore during the episcopate of John O'Reilly, qv, who had been deposed, but still seems to have held on to 1393

Died 1393

†DE SANCTO SERIO, GABRIEL

Bp of Elphin 1539; was translated to Ferns by the Pope and became the 1st RC Bp of Ferns in 1539

DESPARD, ERIC HERBERT 1917–

b. 1917; ed Villiers Sch Limerick; TCD BA Mod (Hist & Pol Sci) 1940 Elrington Pri & Div Test (2) 1941 MA & BD 1948

d 1941 p 1942 (Kilmore); C Roscommon (Elph) 1941–43; C St Peter (Dub) 1943–50; R Blessington U (Glend) 1951–65; Hon Cler V Christ Ch Cath Dublin 1952; RD of Rathdrum 1963–77; R Lucan and Leixlip (Glend) 1965–92; Canon of Christ Ch Cath Dublin 1973–87; RD of Ballymore 1977–85; RD of Omurthy 1986–92; Preb of St John's in Christ Ch Cath Dublin 1987–89; Preb of St Michael's Christ Ch Cath Dublin 1990–92

s. of Robert William and Minnie (*née* Garnett) of Limerick

DEVENISH, ROBERT CECIL SYLVESTER 1888/89–1973

b. 1888 or 1889; TCD BA & Div Test 1911 MA 1934; was a Hockey International

d 1912 p 1913 (Kilmore); C Templemichael (Ard) 1912–15; TCF 1915–19; Chapl (Eccles Est) St James' Delhi 1919–20; Peshawar 1920–24; Waziristan Field Force 1921–22; furlough 1923, 1927, 1930, 1933–34 and 1938; Risalpur 1923–24; Kohat 1924–27; Nowshera 1927–30; Quetta 1930–33; Lahore 1933–40; Bp's Commisary 1934 and 1937; Archd of Lahore 1934–40; R St Paul Esquimalt BC Canada 1941–46; Chapl Upr Chine Sch Shanklin I O W 1946–51; Perm to Off Dios Winchester and Portsmouth 1947–51; C St Mary Abbots Kensington (Lon) 1951–59; Lic to Off Dio

Guildford from 1959; Perm to Off Dio Exeter from 1963

> yst **s.** of Very Rev Robert Jones Sylvester, Dean of Cashel 1913–16 by Rosamond Kate only **dau.** of Rev W J Price, LLD of Waterford
>
> **m.** Lily
>
> **Died** 23 Aug 1973 at Torquay aged 84

DEVENISH, WILLIAM 1839/40–1913

b. 1839 or 1840 Co Roscommon; ed privately; ent TCD 14 Oct 1856 aged 16 BA 1861 Div Test (2) 1864

d 1864 p 1865 (Arm); C Kilskeery (Clogh) 1864–69; C Ballyclog (Arm) 1869–72; C Drumcree (Arm) 1872–77; C All SS Vauxhall (Liv) 1877–85; C Holy Trinity St Helen's (Liv) 1885–86; V of Abbeylara and Drumlummon (Ard) 1886–1909; ret

> **s.** of John, JP of Mount Pleasant Co Roscommon and **bro.** of Rev Robert Jones Sylvester Devenish C St Patrick Waterford
>
> **Died** 8 Jan 1913 unm at Cypress Ave Belfast having suffered from paralysis for some years

DEVINNEY, SAMUEL

TCD BA 1881 MA 1888 LLB & LLD 1895

d 1875 p 1876 (Kilmore); C Templeport (Kilm) 1875–76; C Clones (Clogh) 1876–80; R Lack (Clogh) 1880–82; C St James West Bromwich (Lich) 1883–88; C St Catherine Wigan (Liv) 1888–91; C St Martin-in-the-Fields Liverpool (Liv) 1891–99; C St Philip Liverpool (Liv) 1900–05; C Holy Trinity Toxteth Pk (Liv) 1905–07; C St John Bapt Earlstown 1907–12; C St Ambrose Liverpool (Liv) 1912–17; Lic Pr Dio Liverpool from 1918

> **m.** 24 May 1877 Anna **dau.** of Francis Finlay of Corville Hse Co Cavan

DICKSON, GEORGE NORTON 1921–1989

b. 1921; TCD BA (2) Mod 1943

d 1945 p 1946; C Drumgoon w Dernakesh and Ashfield (Kilm) 1945–48; C Woodhouse Huddersfield (Wakef) 1948–49; C-in-c Glencolumbcille (Raph) 1949–50; R Rathcormac (Cloyne) 1950–55; R Glascarrig (Ferns) 1955–71; R Liskinfere Ballycanew and Monamolin (Ferns) 1972–89

> **m.** and had issue incl his 2nd **dau.** Miriam **m.** 1 Jan 1972 at Glascarrig Ch Nigel yr **s.** of Mr and Mrs W L Bannon of Mountnugent; **sons** 1. Robert; 2. Walter
>
> **Died** 15 Mar 1989

DICKSON, JAMES   –1787

TCD BA 1732

d 22 Dec 1734 p 21 Dec 1735 (Dromore); C Donaghmore (Drom) 1735; C Garvaghy (Drom) 1742–43; C Magherally (Drom) 1746; Dean of Elphin 1757–68; Dean of Down 1768–87

s. of John of Rathfriland Co Down

m. (1) (ML 19 Sep 1741) Hannah Houston (**died** March 1784 at Newry). Issue 1. William **b.** 5 Feb 1744 (**died** 19 Sep 1804) ed Eton Coll; Hartford Coll Ox BA 1767 MA 1770 DD 1784 Bp of Down and Connor 1783–1804 **m.** 6 Jun 1773 St Ann's Ch Dublin Henrietta (**died** 21 Mar 1816 at Brighton) **dau.** of Rev Jeremiah Symes of Ballybeg Co Wicklow and had issue sons (i) Lt Gen Sir Jeremiah KCB; (ii) Rev William Henry **b.** c 1778 (**died** 1850), Preb of Rasharkin (Conn) 1804–50; (iii) Rev Stephen **b.** c 1780 (**died** 1849) Preb of Cairncastle (Conn); (iv) Robert (**died** 16 Dec 1800 at Cootehill Co Cavan); **daus.** (i) Jane (**died** 30 Nov 1850 Edinburgh); (ii) Caroline Elizabeth **m.** 20 Apr 1830 at Berne Switzerland Charles Thomas Bourke, Lt 48th Regt; (iii) Louisa Sarah; 2. John (**died** 6 May 1814 aged 72) TCD BA 1772 MA 1775 Archd of Down 1790–1814 **m.** (1) Eleanor **dau.** of Richard Symes of Ballyarthur Co Wicklow and had issue Eleanor; **m.** (2) 16 Jan 1773 Down Par Ch Anne (**died** 29 Jul 1804 aged 51) elder **dau.** of William Moore of Killinchy Co Down and had issue **sons** (i) John TCD BA 1796; (ii) James drowned in Strangford Lough Oct 1798; (iii) William **b.** 12 Jan 1778 (**died** 5 Jun 1805) at Hillsborough Co Down Lt Bengal Army; (iv) Arthur Hill, Lt Col 64th Foot 1830; **daus.** (i) Jane **b.** 1776 **m.** 16 Jan 1804 John Douglas; (ii) Anne **m.** Dec 1798 William Cunninghame Cunningham–Graham of Perthshire; (iii) Henrietta (**died** 10 Jul 1814) **m.** 12 Oct 1813 Major Francis Hartwell; 3. Mary **m.** 20 Dec 1771 at Downpatrick Rev Edward Trotter LLD, Preb of St Andrew's in Down Cath and had issue sons (i) Edward Southwell **b.** 3 Nov 1773 (**died** 31 Mar 1836); (ii) John Bernard **b.** 1774 (**died** 1 or 5 Oct 1818); (iii) William Ruthven Major 83rd Foot killed at Buenos Aires 5 Jul 1807; **daus.** (i) Frances **b.** 1772 died in infancy Nov 1772; (ii) Mary Anne **b.** 20 Oct 1777 (**died** 1842) 4. Margaret **m.** Jan 1785 at Kilmeagan John Holmes, Lt 66th Regt afterwards Lt 12th Dragoons (see Leslie's Down Lists and Swanzy's Dromore Lists for more detail)

m. (2) 5 May 1785 Letitia (**died** 17 Jan 1814 at Philipstown Co Louth in her 89th year) widow of Ven George Howse, Archd of Dromore 1742–70 and **dau.** of Rev John Wynne DD, R Drumgooland (Drom) 1742–48

Died 8 Apr 1787 during a service in Banbridge Church Co Down

DICKSON, JAMES LOWRY 1782/83–1861

b. 1782 or 1783 Co Leitrim; ed by Dr Carpendale; ent TCD 8 Oct 1800 aged 17 BA 1805 MA 1816

V Donard and C Crehelp (Glend) 1814–35; V Rossinver (Kilm) 1816–35; R Knockbride (Kilm) 1835–40; V Lavey (Kilm) 1840–61

2nd **s.** of Thomas of Woodville Co Leitrim by Hester **dau.** of Rev James Lowry

m. Mary **dau.** of Daniel Eccles of Co Tyrone

Died 25 Mar 1861 aged 78

DIGBY, DIGBY DUANE WILLIAM
TCD LLD

d 1872 p 1873; C Bingley (Bradf — then Ripon) 1872–73; C Holywood (Glend) 1875; R Killoe (Ard) 1875–76; PC Quivvy (Kilm) 1877–80; R Killargue (Kilm) 1880;

R Ballinafagh U (Kild) 1880–81; Chapl to Lord Borthwick 1885–86; R Annaduff (Ard) 1886–87

DIGBY, GEORGE 1667/68–*c.* 1731

b. 1667 or 1668 Dublin; ed by Mr Cusack, Dublin; ent TCD 4 Oct 1686 aged 18 BA 1691

V Roscommon Kilmeen Kilbride Kilgeffin Kilteevan and Clontuskert (Elph) 1698–1731; Preb of Kilgoghlin (Elph) 1707–31

s. of Thomas

m. and had issue incl 1. Thomas **b.** Co Roscommon ent TCD 14 May 1714 aged 16 BA 1718; 2. Richard **b.** Roscommon ent TCD 11 Nov 1718 aged 17

Died *c.* 1731

†DIGBY, SIMON 1644/45–1720

b. 1644 or 1645 Kilminchy Queen's Co (Laois); ed by Mr Hill at Dublin; ent TCD 14 May 1661 aged 16 BA 1664 LLD 1680; Oxford MA 1676

R & V Dunshaughlin (Meath) 1669–71; Preb of Geashill in St Brigid's Cath Kildare 1670–71; Preb of Kilgobinet in Lismore Cath 1670–98; Dean of Kildare 1678–79; consec Bp of Limerick 23 May 1678/79 in Christ Church Cath Dublin; Bp of Limerick 1679–91; Bp of Elphin 1691–1720

eldest **s.** of Essex, Bp of Dromore (**s.** of Sir Robert of Coleshill Warwickshire and Lady Lettice FitzGerald) by his first wife Thomasine **dau.** of Sir William Gilbert of Kilminchy

m. Elizabeth (**died** 15 Apr 1720 at Tessaragh (Mt Talbot)) **dau.** of Warner Westenra of Dublin and by her had nine sons and eight **daus.** incl the following; **sons** 1. Simon **b.** at Castlerea Co Roscommon ed by Mr Blair, Dunamon ent TCD 22 Jun 1700 aged 19 BA 1703; 2. John of Landenstoun Co Kildare, MP for Kildare 1731 ed by Mr Graves ent TCD 24 May 1707 aged 16 BA 1710; **m.** and had issue incl Very Rev William Preb of Kilcooley (Elph) qv; 3. Rev William, R Ahascragh (Elph) qv; 4. Gilbert **b.** at Mt Talbot ed by Mr Griffin at Elphin ent TCD 13 Jan 1718 aged 19; 5. Benjamin **b.** at Mt Talbot ed by Mr Griffin at Elphin ent TCD 14 Jan 1718 aged 17 BA 1722 who became Preb of Geashill in Kildare Cath **m.** Mary **dau.** of Lewis Jones and had issue; **daus.** 1. Mary **m.** 1722 Edward Bertles of Ardmagragh, High Sheriff of Co Westmeath 1703; 2. Abigail **m.** 1721 Rev Joseph Grave; 3. Lettice **m.** Rev William Brookes, R Kildallon (Kilm) qv; 4. Elizabeth 2nd wife of Very Rev Jeremiah William Marsh, Dean of Kilmore qv

Archbishop King, writing to William Wake, Archbishop of Canterbury on 12 April 1720, gives a quaint reason for Simon Digby's elevation to the Episcopal Bench, "He was a great master in painting in little water colours, and by that, greatly recommended himself to men in power, and ladies; and so was early made a bishop" Mant ii, 366, Swanzy *Succession Lists of the Diocese of Dromore* p 7

Died 7 Apr 1720 acc to Cotton; 17 Apr 1720 acc to Foster's *Peerage* **bur.** Tessaragh

DIGBY, WILLIAM 1693/94–

b. 1693 or 1694 Moate Co Roscommon; ed by Mr Griffin at Elphin ent; TCD 7 Jun 1712 aged 18 BA 1716 MA 1719

R Ahascragh (Elph) 1730–

> 3rd **s.** of Rt Rev Simon, Bp of Elphin qv (**s.** of Essex, Bp of Dromore) by Elizabeth **dau.** of Warner Westenra of Dublin

DIGBY, WILLIAM

coll V Taghboy Disert Lisonuffy Camma Killenvoy Raharrow Ivernon Kiltoom and Tessaragh (Elph) 12 May 1718; prob same as above

DIGBY, WILLIAM

C St Peter Athlone to 1766; same as below?

DIGBY, WILLIAM 1730–1812

b. June 1730; ed by Mr Perry; ent TCD 23 Jan 1746/47 BA 1751 MA 1754

Dean of Clonfert 1766–1812; V Killukin (Elph) and Preb of Kilcooley (Elph) 1767–1809; Preb of Geashill (Kild) 1769–1812

> 4th **s.** of John of Landestoun Co Kildare (**s.** of Rt Rev Simon, Bp of Elphin qv and Elizabeth)
>
> **m.** (1) 4 Jun 1760 Mary Anne **dau.** of Edward Bertles of Ardnagrath Co Westmeath
>
> **m.** (2) Mary (**died** 1790) **dau.** of Rev Benjamin Digby. Issue incl 1. William, Archd of Elphin qv; 2. Simon; 3. Benjamin; 4. Robert, and several other children
>
> **m.** (3) 1792 Elizabeth (*née* Wood) widow of Mr Cooper. Issue incl Kenelm Henry **b.** 1797
>
> **Died** June 1812 Dublin

PUBLICATIONS

> *21 Lectures in Divinity,* 8vo Dublin 1787
> *Essays on Religious Education,* Dublin 1788
> A Letter on Dr Geddes' Translation of the Bible in *Antholog. Hiberniae* II. 261

DIGBY, WILLIAM 1784–1866

b. 1783 King's Co (Offaly); ed by Rev John Moore; ent TCD 7 Oct 1799 aged 15 BA 1804 MA 1820

d; p 1809 (Elphin); R & V Killukin (then Elph) 1809–23; Archd of Elphin 1809–23; R Killashee (Ard) 1823–46; R & V of that part of Killoe called Clongish Killoe (Ard) 1846–66

> eldest **s.** of Very Rev William, Dean of Clonfert by his 2nd wife Mary **dau.** of Rev Benjamin Digby
>
> **Died** 1866

PUBLICATIONS

> A Sermon on the All–Sufficiency of Scripture

Statistical Account of Killukin Parish in Mason's Parochial Survey
A Reply to Dr Milner's "End of Religion" Controversy, 8vo 1824
Courts Explication Historique des Sceaux et des Trompetes de l'Acopalypse, Toulouse

DIGGES, JOSEPH ROBERT GARVEN 1861/62–1933

b. 1861 or 1862; TCD BA (Resp) 1882 MA 1895

d 1883 (Kilmore) p 1885 (Dublin for Down); C Mohill (Ard) 1883–84; C St George Belfast (Conn) 1884–85; Private Chapl to H J B Clements at Lough Rynn Castle in Cloone Parish (Ard) 1885–1933

m. 6 Aug 1885 St George's Belfast Edith Helena Louisa (**died** 16 Apr 1926) **dau.** of Henry Alexander Bate, Solicitor of Dublin. Issue 1. Ethel Elizabeth Alice **m.** Rev Hugh Eaton later Dean of Kildare; 2. a son

Died 6 Aug 1933 aged 71

PUBLICATIONS

Fighting Industries and Financing Emigration in Ireland
Irish Bee Guide 1904, 8th ed 1936
The practical Bee Guide 1910
Cure of Inebriety
Ed *Irish Bee Journal*
Ed *Beekeepers Gazette*

DISNEY, HENRY PURDON 1806/07–1854

b. 1806 or 1807 Dublin; ed by Mr Craig; ent TCD 1 Jul 1822 aged 15 BA 1828 MA 1832

C Drumlease (Kilm) 1835–36; C Tynan (Arm) 1836–40; PC Kildarton (Arm) 1840–47; PC Killochonnigan (Meath) 1847–53; C Newtownhamilton (Arm) 1854

6th **s.** of Thomas (**died** 9 Jan 1851 aged 84) of Rocklodge Co Meath; **bro.** of Rev Ogle, R Richhill (Arm) and **bro.** of Rev Thomas, R Killyman (Arm)

Died 11 Jul 1854 **unm.** of typhus fever

DIXIE, EDWARD

V Urney (Kilm) 1661–65; V Denn (Kilm) 1661–91 — may have held Denn to 1700, though more likely held by Daniel Neylan qv; V Kilmore and Ballintemple (Kilm) 1664–91; Dean of Kilmore 1664–91; V Kildrumferton (Kilm) 1667–91. As Dean, he signed an address to James II, 18 Mar 1684/85, and was attainted as Dean in 1689

m. and had issue a **s.** Wolstan **b.** Co Cavan ent TCD 13 May 1682 aged 15 BA 1686

DODD, CHARLES 1695/96–1775

b. 1695 or 1696; ed by Mr Griffin, Elphin; ent TCD 26 May 1714 aged 18 Sch 1716 BA 1718 MA 1721

V Killenumery and Killery (Ard) 1727–74, and possibly 1774; also V Drumlease and Killargue (Kilm) 1737–74

s. of John of Carne Co Sligo (s. of Charles of Cnockbawn Co Sligo) by Elizabeth dau. of Capt John s. of Edward King, Bp of Elphin qv

m. Helen (died 12 Jul 1777 aged 80 bur. Drumlease) dau. of Ven Roger Ford, Archd of Derry. Issue 1. John (died *c.* 1782 s.p. TCD BA m. Sarah Bradburn; 2. Josiah who was killed at the Battle of Minden in 1759; 3. Judith (died 1790) m. Harloe Phibbs; 4. Margaret (died 1807) m. 1775 Kerr Anthony of Dublin; 5. Elizabeth m. Feb 1770 John Johnston of Tully Co Louth; 6. Rev Roger, R Drumlease (Kilm) qv; 7. Rev Oliver, R Killenumery (Ard) qv

Died 1775 bur. St Ann's Dublin

DODD, ISAAC

C Killery (Ard) before 1798; still there *c.* 1826; C Kiltoghert (Ard) 1798, lic 23 Jan

s. of Rev Oliver qv (s. of Rev Charles qv)

DODD, OLIVER   −1799

R Killenumery and Killery (Ard) *c.* 1774–*c.* 91. He and Rev Isaac Dodd (?Curate) appear as of Kingsfort, Killery 1798

s. of Rev Charles qv

m. Elizabeth (died 1807) dau. of John Knox of Sligo issue 1. Charles; 2. Rev Isaac qv; 3. Thomas; 4. Capt. Roger was m

Died Sep 1799

DODD, ROGER   1730–1808

b. 18 Jun 1730 Co Longford; ed by Dr Ford; ent TCD 28 Mar 1749/50 Sch 1752 BA 1754 MD

C Inishmacsaint (Clogh) 1757–61; C Drumlease (Kilm) 1763–66; C Killargue and Inismagrath (Kilm) 1766; V Drumlease (Kilm) 1774–1808

s. of Rev Charles, R Drumlease (Kilm) qv by Helen dau. of Ven Roger Ford

m. (1) Sarah King (died s.p.)

m. (2) 28 Mar 1792 Margaret dau. of Matthew Phibbs. Issue Charles Roger of London

Died 8 Oct 1808 bur. Drumlease

†DODGSON, CHARLES   −1795

an Englishman; St John's Coll Camb BA 1746 MA 1758; TCD DD; *ad eund* Cantab 1763. FRS 1762

He was tutor in the family of the Duke of Northumberland, and kept a school for some years in Stanwix, Cumberland, and was for some time R of Kirby Wyche, Dio of Ripon. He seems to have owed his promotion to the Duke of Northumberland, whose chaplain he was

Bp of Ossory 1765–75; consec 11 Aug 1765 in St Werburgh's Ch Dublin; enthroned 22 Aug 1765; Bp of Elphin 1775–95

m. Frances Radcliffe. Issue 1. Elizabeth; 2. Anne; 3. Charles, Capt 4th Dragoons **m.** Mar 1799 Lucy **dau.** of James Hume; he was killed in King's Co (Offaly) 16 Dec 1803; 4. Thomas; 5. Percy. Bp Dodgson was grandfather of Rev Charles Lutwidge Dodgson, better known as Lewis Carroll, author of *Alice in Wonderland*.

Died in Dublin 21 Jan 1795 (acc to Cotton), 6 Feb 1795 (acc to *Gentleman's Magazine*), 7 Mar 1795 (acc to Reeves). Leslie thinks that Reeves is correct

PUBLICATIONS

A Sermon on Proverbs iii, 27 for Middlesex Hospital, 4to. London 1761

A Sermon on Isaiah lviii, 6–8 for Incorporated Society, 4to. Dublin 1768

DODWELL, HENRY

V Kilbegnet (Elph) 1615; V Kilcroan (Elph) 1615; V Tessaragh 1615; prob same as below

DODWELL, HENRY

pres by the Crown to R Ahascragh & Killasoolan = Castleblakeney (Elph) 30 Sep 1620 (L.M. V. 105); a Henry Dodwell, prob same, was V Killyon (Elph) and **died** 1650

DODWELL, HENRY   –1674

BA *c.* 1634 MA 1636 DD 1664

d Sep 1634 (Tuam) p 12 Jan 1636 (Elphin); he fled from Ireland during the rebellion of 1641; adm R Hemley, Suffolk 3 Nov 1643; R Newbourne, Suffolk 20 Nov 1645; came back to Ireland as Commonwealth Minister of Killucan (Meath) 1658 ("on the tithes £120"); V Killyon (Elph) 1661–64; V Killumada (Elph) 1664; gets a faculty to hold V Killean = Killyon and Killasoolan = Castleblakeney (Elph) 4 Jul 1664 and is confirmed in the same 6 Jul (L.M. 114); pres by the Crown to V Ahascragh (Elph) 25 Apr 1661 (L.M. V. 113), and inst 3 Apr 1666; Dean of Killala 1664–74; R Rathfarnham (Dub) 1666–; V Kilronan or Killeroran (Elph) 1666–73; Precentor of Elphin 1668

3rd **s.** of Rev Henry, prob same as above (**died** 1650), V Killyon (Elph), who got grants of land in Sligo and Roscommon between 1632 and 1641

m. 2 Mar 1647/48 Mary Huish of Newbourne

Died 1674

DOGHERTY, RICHARD   1708/09–1760

b. 1708 or 1709 Co Cork; ed by Mr Lloyd, Dublin; ent TCD 25 Aug 1724 aged 15 BA 1729

Preb of Kilmacallen (Elph) 1755–60; V Drumcliffe (Elph) 1758–60

s. of Letham, *Dux*

Died 1760

DOHERTY, ROBERT 1856/57–1946

b. near Lurgan Co Armagh; TCD BA 1893 MA 1911

d 1903 p 1905 (Durham); C Rainton (Dur) 1903–06; C Offerlane (Oss) 1906–07; C Lurgan (Kilm) 1907–08; R Drumreilly (Ard) 1908–15; R Kiltubrid (Ard) 1916–30; ret

    s. of Robert of Tusvene Lurgan

    Died 28 Dec 1946 aged 89

D'OLIER, RICHARD HENRY 1795/96–

b. 1795 or 1796 Dublin; ed by Mr White; ent TCD 5 Oct 1812 aged 16 BA 1817 MA 1821

C Moydow (Ard) 1823–25; V Ballymore Eustace (Glend) 1825–32

    s. of Isaac

DOMVILL (DOMEVILL or perhaps DANIEL), WILLIAM

probably V & Preb of Tibohine (Elph) 1637; res V Taghboy (Elph) 1641; res the V Dunamon (Elph) 1641; coll V Killukin (Elph) 22 Mar 1640/41; also V Kilcooley (Elph) 1640/41

†DONATUS

Dean of Ardagh *c.* 1410; was a Bp (C.P.L. VII. 230)

DONOVAN, RICHARD HENRY 1839/40–1887

b. 1839 or 1840 Cork; ed by Mr O'Callaghan; ent TCD 15 Jan 1858 aged 18 BA 1862

d 1862 p; C Kilmore (Kilm) 1862–64; Chapl RN

    s. of Rev Charles, R Ballinadee (Cork) by Alicia **dau.** of Richard Sullivan of Ardcahan Cork.

    m. Miss Creaghe. Issue 1. Rev Richard Henry, Chapl RN; 2. Charles Creaghe, Capt RA; 3. William, engineer; 4. Stephen John, Lt

    Died 1887

DOONAN, ROBERT JOHN 1913–1993

b. 1913; TCD BA & Div Test 1936

d 1937 p 1938 (Clogher); C Carrickmacross (Clogh) 1937–38; C Magheraculmoney (Clogh) 1938–39; C Urney (Kilm) 1939–41; R Newtowngore Corrawallen and Drumreilly (Kilm) 1941–44; R Swanlinbar (Kilm) 1944–50; R Garvary (Clogh) 1950–53; R Magheraculmoney (w Muckross and Templecarne from 1970 and Drumkeeran from 1972) (Clogh) 1953–78; RD of Kesh 1957–78; Canon and Exam Chapl to Bp of Clogher 1968–78; ret

    m. Marian Ferguson of Clones Co Monaghan. Issue 1. Dorita, a teacher who was

killed on voluntary service in Nigeria 19 Dec 1971 aged 23; 2. William Kenneth
Died 5 Apr 1993

DOPPING, FRANCIS HENRY *c.* 1838–1907
TCD BA & Div Test 1861 MA 1877

d 1861 (Kilmore) p 1862 (Down); C Granard (Ard) 1861–63; C Castlerahan (Kilm) 1863; C Columbkille (Ard) 1863–69; V Columbkille (Ard) 1869–94

only **s.** of Henry of Ernehead by Frances **dau.** of Robert Jessop of Mt Jessop Co Longford

m. 28 Oct 1890 Mary Florence (**died** Nov 1894) 2nd **dau.** of Edward Hudson of Trentham Leopardstown Co Dublin by Emily Eleanor **dau.** of the Rev William Grattan of Sylvan Park Co Meath. Issue 1. Henrietta Annie Dorothy **m.** 16 Sep 1912 St John's Ch Monkstown Co Dublin Rev Charles Latham (**died** 8 Jan 1919) MA, R Kilmeague (Kild) **s.** of Ven James King Latham, DD, Archd of Ferns; 2. Emily Frances Veda

Died 14 May 1907

DOUGLAS, ALEXANDER   –1721
V Lavey (Kilm) 1704–21

Died 1721 before 17 Jul

DOUGLAS, EDWARD ARCHIBALD   1777/78–
b. 1777 or 1778 Dublin; ed by Mr Barry; ent TCD 7 Oct 1793 aged 15 BA 1798 MA 1809

R Drumgoon (Kilm) 1832–c50; R Ardfinnan (Lism) 1807; was pres to the Deanery of Ardfert 1808 but did not get possession; V Carnalway (Kild) 1809–32; V Cloncurry U (Kild) 1811–32; was residing in Blackrock Dublin in 1850

s. of Archibald, *militum doctor*

†DOWDEN, JOHN 1840–1910
b. 29 Jun 1840 Cork; TCD BA (Sen Mod Eth & Log) 1861 Eccl Hist Pri 1861 Div Test (1) 1864 MA 1867 BD 1874 DD 1876; Univ of Edinburgh Hon LLD; founded the Scottish Historical Soc 1886

d 17 Jul 1864 p 11 Jun 1865 (Kilmore) Bp 1886; C St John Sligo (Elph) 1864–67; PC Calry (Elph) 1867–71; Chapl to Lord Lt 1870–74; Asst C St Stephen (Dub) 1871–74; Pantonian Prof of Theol and Bell Lecturer in Education Glenalmond Theol Coll Perthshire 1874–80; Prin Scottish Episcopal Theol Coll Edinburgh 1880–86*; Canon of St Mary's Cath Edinburgh 1880–86; Donnellan Lect TCD 1885–86; Bp of Edinburgh 1886–1910

s. of John Wheeler

m. 1864…and had issue incl Alice

Died 30 Jan 1910

PUBLICATIONS
> *The Saints in the Calendar and the Irish Synod,* a Sermon, Dublin 1873
> *The Knowledge of God a Spiritual Knowledge,* Dublin
> *Reasons for Gratitude and Incentives to Duty in the Scottish Episcopal Church,* Edinburgh 1879
> *The Beauty of Nature, A Revelation of God,* Edinburgh
> *Historical Account of the Scottish Communion Office,* 1884
> *Annotated Scottish Communion Office,* 1884
> *Questianculae Liturgicae,* Edinburgh 1886
> *The Celtic Church in Scotland,* 1894
> *The Workmanship of the Prayer Book,* 1899
> *Further Studies in the Prayer Book,* 1900
> *The Mediaeval Church in Scotland,* 1910
> Contributor to the *Contemporary Review*

* The Scottish Episcopal Theological College moved from Glenalmond to Coates Hall in Edinburgh in 1880 after a fire at Glenalmond. Glenalmond continues to this day as one of the Scottish Episcopal Church's great public schools

DOWDSLEY, W

d Meath for Ardagh 1853; C Killashee (Ard) 1853

DOWNES, DIVE 1690/91–1781

b. 1690 or 1691 Dublin; ed by Dr Jones, Dublin; ent TCD 10 May 1706 aged 15 BA 1710

R Athlumney 1715–33; V Oldcastle and Kilbride Castlecor (Meath) 1723–56; R Killesher (Kilm) 1740–81

> **s.** of Lewis

> **m.** and had issue incl Dive **b.** Co Meath ed by Mr Thompson ent TCD 12 May 1747 aged 17 BA 1751 MA 1754; he may have been Rev Dive who **m.** 20 Feb 1760 Ann Ligoe in St Mary's Dublin (if he was not his father)

> **Died** Feb 1781 Summerhill Dublin

†DOWNES, HENRY 1666/67–1734

b. 1666 or 1667; matric New Coll Oxford 30 Aug 1686 aged 19 BA 1690 MA 1693/94

V Brington Northants (Pet) 1699; R Sywell (Pet) 1707; R Alderton Northants (Pet) 1710; Chapl to King George I and to King George II

consec Bp of Killala 12 May 1717; Bp of Killala 1717–20; Bp of Elphin 1720–24; Bp of Meath 1724–1727; Bp of Derry 1727–1734

> **s.** of Robert of Leighton Buzzard

> **m.** Elizabeth **dau.** of Thomas Wilson, Dean of Carlisle. Issue incl 1. Rev Robert **b.** 1705 or 1706 (**died** 30 Jun 1763 Dublin) matric Pembroke Coll Oxford 15 Jul 1722 aged 16 Merton Coll BA 1724 MA 1726/27; TCD BD and DD 1740 R Desertmartin (Derry) 1728–40 R Camus–juxta–Mourne (Derry) 1729–34 Dean

of Derry 1740–44 Bp of Ferns 1744–52 Bp of Down 1752–53 Bp of Raphoe 1753–63 **m.** 7 Aug 1729 Mrs Jane Blackall and had issue incl a **s.** Andrew and a **dau.** Jane **m.** 10 Apr 1756 Rev Cary Hamilton and a **dau.** Henrietta (**died** 6 Oct 1802) **m.** Ven Arthur Mahon Archd of Elphin qv; 2. Rev Philip **b.** 1706 or 1707 (**died** Jan 1746) TCD BA 1726 MA 1729 R Leckpatrick (Derry) 1730–31 R Fahan (Derry — now Raph) 1731–46; 3. Thomas matric New College Oxford 21 Apr 1719 aged 18 BA 1722/23 MA 1726/27; 4. Charles matric New Coll Oxford 15 Jul 1718 aged 18; 5. George; he also had several **daus.** His **dau.** Mary **m.** 1725 Rev George Alcock

Died 14 Jan 1734 **bur.** St Mary's Dublin

PUBLICATION
A Volume of Sermons, London, 1708

DOWNES, LEWIS 1606/07–1664

b. 1606 or 1607; matric at Oxford from Magdalen Hall 31 Oct 1623 aged 16 BA 1626/27 MA 1629 BD 1639

V Belfast (Conn) 1642–c45; Dean of Kilmore and V Kilmore & Ballintemple (Kilm) 1645–c61; appears as "Deane of Kilmore " residing in Dublin 1647 (Carte Papers xxi. 346); prob V Kildrumferton (Kilm) 1647– record not extant; R Thornby, Notts (Pet) 1648. He was again pres to the Deanery and V of Kilmore 10 Aug 1660

only **s.** of Dive of East Haddon

m. and had issue 1. Dive (**died** 3 Nov 1709) **b.** 24 Oct 1653 Thornby ed at Lisburn by Mr Haslam TCD BA 1671 MA & FTCD 1675 BD 1686 DD 1692 Bp of Cork 1699–1709; 2. Samuel, Freeman of Belfast 10 Jan 1664 Town Clerk of Belfast 1667; 3. Elizabeth (**bur.** 12 Apr 1656) **b.** 25 Jul 1650 at Thornby; 4. Lewis **b.** 2 Oct 1665 **m.** Elizabeth Scott

is deceased in Aug 1664

DOWSE, CHARLES BENJAMIN 1870–1948

b. 1870 Co Laois; ed the King's Hospital Dublin; the High Sch Dublin; TCD BA 1893 Div Test 1894 MA 1898

d 1894 p 1895 (Kilmore); C Kilkeevan (Elph) 1894–95; C Urney (Kilm) 1895–98; R Kiltegan (Leigh) 1898–1907; R Clonenagh (Leigh) 1907–10; R St John Monkstown (Dub) 1910–45; Canon Christ Ch Cath Dublin 1935–44; Preb St John's Christ Ch Cath Dublin 1944–45; ret

s. of Richard Henry and Mary (née Halahan) of Killeen Co Laois

m. 12 Oct 1898 Edith Helen (**died** 13 Nov 1938) **dau.** of Dr Mark Moore of Cavan. Issue 1. Rev Richard Henry (**died** 13 Sep 1983) **b.** 1900 Kiltegan TCD BA 1923 MA 1934 d 1926 p 1927 (Down) C Bangor (Down) 1926–29 C St Ann (Dub) 1929–34 R St Peter and St Audoen (Dub) 1934–75 Preb of St Audoen in St Patrick's Cath Dublin 1962–73 Precentor of St Patrick's Cath 1973–75 **m.** Constance **dau.** of Robert Christie of Dun Laoghaire and had issue (i) Peter Richard Charles (ii) Victor Henry Brooke **b.** 15 Nov 1939; 2. Katherine Mary; 3. Eva Dolier

Died 30 Apr 1948

DOWZER, THOMAS 1858–1922

b. 1858; ed in Dublin; ent TCD 24 Jan 1878 aged 20 BA 1884 MA 1894

d 1885 p 1886 (Kilmore); C Ardagh (Ard) 1885–87; C St George Belfast (Conn) 1887–91; R Skerry w Rathcavan (Conn) 1891–1922

    s. of Thomas, merchant

    m. Miss Redfern **dau.** of Peter, MD FRCS FRUI Prof of Anatomy and Physiology Queen's Coll Belfast and had issue

    Died 3 Aug 1922 aged 63

DOYLE, CHARLES MILLEY 1775/76–

b. 1775 or 1776 Co Cork; ed by Mr Carey; ent TCD 5 Mar 1792 aged 16 BA 1795

d 29 Jun 1796 (Ossory) p 1 Apr 1798 (Ossory); V Chor Ossory 1797–1806; Chapl to the troops at Kilkenny 1800; V Kilmocar (Oss) 1803–06; V Kilsallaghan (Dub) 1806–28; V Castleblakeney (Elph) 1828–57

    s. of Rev Nicholas Milley, Preb of Cashel (3rd s. of Charles of Bramblestown Co Kilkenny) by a **dau.** of Rev Rev John Milley (s. of Rev Nicholas Milley, Preb of Ullard)

    m. (ML 1805) Harriet Elizabeth Doyle and had issue incl 1. John b. Kilkenny ent TCD 6 Nov 1820 aged 14; 2. Nicholas b. Dublin ent TCD 6 Nov 1820 aged 13

DOYLE, GRAHAM THOMAS 1948–

b. 1948; St Barnabas' Coll Adelaide ThL 1972 ThSchol 1977; ACT ThL 1973; Worcester Coll Ox BA 1985 MA 1990

d 1973 p 1974; C Leeton NSW (Dio Riverina) 1973–76; C Broken Hill (Dio Riverina) 1976–77; C St David's Cath Hobart (Dio Tasmania) 1977–79; P-in-c Latrobe (Dio Tasmania) 1979–80; R Latrobe (Tasmania) 1980–83; Perm to Off Dio Oxford 1983–85; C Cobbold Rd St Saviour w St Mary (Lon) 1986; P-in-c St Oswald Chapel Green Bradford (Bradf) 1986–91; Chapl Belgrade w Zagreb (Dio Europe) 1991–93; Chapl Belgrade (Dio Europe) 1993–97; Taiwan 1997–2000; R Killeshandra Killegar and Derrylane (Kilm) 2000–03; R Athlone Meath) 2003–

DOYLE, RALPH WILLIAM

Queen's Coll Camb BA 1901 MA 1919

d 1879 p 1880 (Kilmore); C Clongish (Ard) 1879–80; V Killoe (Ard) 1880–81; Chapl CCS 1882–85; Chapl Bologna 1882; Florence 1882; Aix–les–Bains 1883; Genoa 1884–85; C All SS Paddington Middx (Lon) 1885–86; C Rondebosch Cape Colony 1886–87; R Wynberg Cape Colony 1887–94; Acting CF 1887–94; C Gerrard's Cross (Ox) 1894–95; C Kentisbeare (Ex) 1896–98; C Holy Trinity Camb (Ely) 1898–1901; Chapl at Biarritz 1901–06; Lic Pr Dio London 1907–19; Dio S'wark 1910–19; Dio Bristol 1912–19; Prin Hatfield Hse Sch 1912–14; active service with British Red Cross 1914–16; C Bacton (Nor) 1916–17 & CF 1916–17; C Wembley (Lon) 1918–19; SSC Dio London 1920–25; R Greenstead (Chelmsf) 1925–35; Last entry in Crockford.1937

†DRAPER, ROBERT –1612

R Trim (Meath) was made Bp of Kilmore and Ardagh with R Trim *in commendam* by Letters Patent, March 1603/04. In the King's letter, it says that he owes his promotion on account of his knowledge of the district and people and of the Irish tongue. Bp of Kilmore and Ardagh 1603/04–1612

was married

Died Aug 1612

DREHIN, HUGH

V Culea (Elph) 1615

DROMA, LOUIS

is a Canon of Kilmore 1530 (Reg. Cromer)

DROUGHT, JOHN WILLIAM FAIRBROTHER 1809–1891

b. 20 Sep 1809; ent TCD 2 Jul 1827 BA 1832

d 30 Nov 1832 (Elph) p; C St Peter Athlone 1832–35

eldest **s.** of George Meares John, JP of Glencarrig Co Wicklow

m. (1) 15 Mar 1837 Anna Maria (**died** 28 May 1867) **dau.** of Richard Reynell of Killyon Co Westmeath. Issue 1. George William Fairbrother, Capt King's Co Rifles; 2. Richard Reynell **m.** 26 Jun 1869 at Rathconnell Ch Isabella E A Nugent; 3. John Thomas Acton; 4. Eliza Harriet (**died** 1874)

m. (2) 10 Nov 1869 Caroline (**died** 9 May 1899) **dau.** of Rev Theobald Butler of Co Tipperary

Died 23 Feb 1891

DROVER (or DERVER), JOHN

clk; pres to the V Granard (Ard) 5 May 1552 (F. Edward VI. 991), also F.F. 1553

DRUITT, JOSEPH 1774/75–1835

b. 1774 or 1775 Dublin; ed by Mr Fenton; ent TCD 21 May 1790 aged 15 BA 1796 MA 1809

d p 1799; C Castleterra (Kilm) 1799; C Urney (Kilm) 1803–05; V Denn (Kilm) 1813–35; Preb of Tipperkevin in St Patrick's Cath Dublin 1817–20

s. of Edward, merchant

m. (1) 1802 Esther Johnston. Issue incl 1. John **b.** Cavan ed by Mr Stokes ent TCD 15 Oct 1821 aged 16; 2. Charles **b.** Co Cavan ed by Mr Hearn ent TCD 3 Jul 1826 aged 16; 3. Rev Joseph (**died** 25 Oct 1869) **b.** Cavan ed Royal Sch Cavan ent TCD 1 Jan 1829 aged 16 BA 1834 V Colpe (Meath) **m.** (1) when "of Kilmeague" 28 Sep 1838 in Balrothery Ch Mary only **dau.** of Rev Francis Baker of Corduff Hse Co Dublin **m.** (2) 4 Mar 1845 Jane Anne eldest **dau.** of Charles Thorp of Dublin; 4. Judith; 5. 2nd **dau.** Jane **m.** 14 Sep 1837 at Lusk Rev Thomas

Bowman of Dean Lancs; 6. his yst **dau.** Esther **m.** 28 Sep 1836 at Lusk Charles Halpin of Cavan

m. (2) 21 Mar 1822 Bridget (**died** 1835 Dublin) **dau.** of Rev William Garrett of Ballymote and widow of Peter Tyndall of Dublin

Died 15 Sep 1835 **bur.** Ballyhaise

DRURY, WILLIAM EDWARD −1974

a native of Bournemouth; Exeter Coll Ox BA (2cl Mod Hist) 1909 MA 1912; Bp's Hostel Farnham 1910

d 1910 (Winchester) p 1911 (Winchester); C Cranleigh (Guildf — then Win) 1910–15; TCF 1915–19; Hon CF 1920; C St Michael Aldershot (Guildf — then Win) 1920–24; R Spetisbury w Charlton Marshall (Sarum) 1924–43; V Wilton w Netherhampton (Sarum) 1943–56; R Killeshandra and Killegar (Kilm) 1956–66; ret

s. of William Vallancey by his 3rd wife

m. Nora

PUBLICATION
Camp Follower, Dublin 1968

DUDGEON, WALTER VANDELEUR GEORGE −1879

TCD BA 1852 Div Test (1) 1854 MA 1855

d 1854 p; Preb of Donadea (Kild) 1856–60; PC St John's Cloverhill (Kilm) 1860–61; C Skerry and Racavan (Conn) 1861–69; Chapl Castlewellan (Drom) 1869–71; R Castlewellan (Drom) 1871–78

yst **s.** of James of Dublin

m. 14 May 1861 St Peter's Par Ch Dublin Mary 2nd **dau.** of Walter Ringwood of Dublin. Issue 1. James **b.** 9 Feb 1862; 2. William Richard **b.** 11 Feb 1863; 3. Walter Vandeleur George **b.** 12 May 1864 **bur.** 4 Jun 1864; 4. Edward Alexander **b.** 1 May 1865; 5. Christopher **b.** 12 Jul 1866; 6. Henry (**died** 28 Sep 1867 aged 5 months)

Died 16 Dec 1879 London

DUDLEY, HENRY BATE 1745–1824

b. 1745 at Fenny Compton, Worcs; ed Queen's Coll Camb; was a well-known journalist and Court favourite; created a Baronet 1812

C Hendon (York) 1773; subsequently R Farmbridge, Essex; C Bradwell-juxta-Mare, Essex *c.* 1780; Chanc of Ferns 1805–12; was he same as R Kilglass (Ard) 1806–12?; R Willingham (Ely) 1812–; Preb of Ely

His father's name was Bate, but he took the additional name of Dudley

Died 1824

PUBLICATIONS
Editor of a newspaper *The Morning Post* 1775–80
Editor of a newspaper *The Morning Herald* from 1780

Editor of *The English Chronicle*
Editor of *The Courier de la Europe*
Author of several popular dramas including *The Flitch of Bacon*
A Short Address to the Primate: Recommending a Commutation of Tythes 8vo London, 3rd ed 1808

DUFF, JOHN ARTHUR –1947

TCD BA 1900 Div Test 1901

d 1901 p 1903 (Kilmore); C Kilkeevan (Elph) 1901–03; C Horncastle (Linc) 1903–04; C Dunganstown (Glend) 1904–05; C St Peter Birkenhead (Liv) 1905–10; C Northenden (Manch) 1910–12; C St Mary Athlone (Meath) 1912–13; R Forgney (Meath) 1913–15; C St Clement Chorlton–cum–Hardy (Manch) 1915–18; C Ashton–under–Lyne (Manch) 1918–19; Prin Higher Tranmere Coll Birkenhead 1922–24; Perm to Off Ledsham w Fairburn (York) 1925–26; C Newhall (Derby) 1926–27; C Woolton w C-in-c Hunts Cross (Liv) 1927–28; C Talke (Lich) 1928–29; R Ashby Parva (Leic) 1929–33; Perm to Off Dios Liverpool and Chester 1933–47

Died 18 Dec 1947 at West Kirby Cheshire

DUKE, WILLIAM –1838

C Ballisodare (Ach) 1817; poss C St John Sligo (Elph) *c.* 1830.

m. Mary. Issue incl eldest Lucinda J **m.** 3 Dec 1834 as his first wife Rev Samuel Simpson, R Derrynoose (Arm) 1860–80 and had issue (i) Thomas (ii) Alexander Duke (**died** 7 Nov 1874) **b.** 13 Nov 1842 (iii) Robert (**died** 2 Mar 1908) **b.** 1843 **m.** 29 Jan 1879 Harriette May (iv) Rev Samuel (**died** 16 Feb 1925) **b.** 1846 **m.** 17 May 1883 Augusta Laura **dau.** of David Fielding Jones

Died 5 Jan 1838

DUNBAR, JOSEPH

MA (of Glasgow?)

ordained d & p by John Leslie Bp of Raphoe; V Ballymacormack and Clongish (Ard) 1662–73, Apr 5, faculty to hold both 3 Nov 166– (VB 1673); V Kilglass, Moydow, Rareagh and Killashee (Ard) 1662–81 or 1683; V Streete (Ard) 1670–83, coll and inst 23 Jul 1670; Archd of Ardagh 1681–82/83

DUNCAN, ALEXANDER

TCD 1877

d 1878 p 1879 (Killaloe); C Kilnahy w Kilkeedy (Lim) 1878–81 (in Crockford but not in C I Dir); in C I Dir, A Duncan is C Kilnaboy (Killaloe) 1878–79 and Alexander Duncan is C Creagh (Clonf) 1879–81; C Drumgoon (Kilm) 1881–82; Gen Lic Dublin 1889–91; C Larah and Lavey (Kilm) 1891–93; R Killegar (Kilm) 1893–1904; Last entry in C I Dir 1906

DUNCAN, JAMES

ed by Rev. Mr McMullan; ent TCD as SC 16 Nov1759 BA 1763

d ord p 17 Dec 1775; V Rossinver (Kilm) 1775–*c*. 82

DUNDAS, HENRY –1813

prob b. Co Fermanagh; ed Portora Royal Sch Enniskillen by Dr Dunkin; ent TCD 9 Jul 1766 BA 1771

C Drung (Kilm) 1775– still there 1778; C Denn (Kilm)–1777; V Corcomohide (Lim) 1794–1813; V Mullingar (Meath) 1800–13

m. 11 May 1771 St Ann's Ch Dublin Arabella widow of William Henry Nassau Stephens of Stephensfort Co Cavan and dau. of William George Dowley, 3rd s. of Rev Daniel Hearn, R Drung (Kilm) qv; Issue incl 1. Ann Charlotte (died 12 Dec 1866); 2. Henry (died June 1795 aged 16 Bloomfield Co Cavan)

Died Apr 1813

DUNGAN, WILLIAM WILKES 1866–1937

b. 1866; TCD BA 1889 Div Test 1890 MA 1892

d 1891 p 1892 (Kilmore); C Kiltyclogher (Kilm) 1891–93; C St Mark Victoria Docks (St A) 1893–95; C St Bennett Stepney (Lon) 1895–1902; C St James Crinken Bray (Dub) 1902–04; C St Mark Dublin (Dub) 1904–05; C Old Molyneux Ch Dublin (Dub) 1905–08; Minor Canon St Patrick's Cath Dublin 1907–13; I Molyneux Ch Dublin (Dub) 1908–14; Treasurer's V St Patrick's Cath Dublin 1913–14; Cler V Christ Ch Cath Dublin 1914–37; Stearne Lecturer St Werburgh's Dublin 1923; Wallace Divinity Lecturer TCD 1924–37

s. of William, draper of Rathmines Dublin by Hannah dau. of Rev Wiliam Hawes Cooper, Dissenting Minister

m. (1) Miss Dapen

m. (2) Julia Ellen Tucker (died 9 Jun 1954). Issue 1. Bertha Marie Cooper b. 7 Sep 1910; 2. Frederick William b. 4 Jul 1913; 3. Rev Victor Samuel (died 3 Sep 1994) b. 19 Jan 1917 Dublin TCD BA (Resp) 1939 Div Test (1) 1941 BD 1943 d 1942 p 1943 (Connor) C Derriaghy (Conn) 1942–45 R Killanne and Templeudigan (Ferns) 1945–48 R Kilnamanagh U (Ferns) 1948–49 C Zion Rathgar (Dub) 1949–53 Hon Cler V Christ Ch Cath Dublin 1951 R Dunganstown U (Glend) 1953–59 R Christ Ch Leeson Pk Dublin (Dub) 1959–71 R Killiney (Dub) 1971–83 Hon Cler V and Canon of Christ Ch Cath Dublin 1982–84 m. 7 Jun 1944 Milltown Par Ch Dublin Iris Susannah dau. of Richard and Susannah Roberts of Wexford and had issue (i) Rev Hilary Anne b. 17 Jan 1946 C Armagh (Arm) 2000–03 R Maryborough (Leigh from 2003 (ii) David Brian b. 20 Feb 1948 (iii) Norman Stewart b. 9 Mar 1950 (iv) Graham Nicholas b. 9 Dec 1961; 4. Rev Eric Noel b. 26 Nov 1923 TCD BA 1948 MA 1953 d 1948 p 1949 (Dublin); C Crumlin and St Werburgh's Dublin (Dub) 1948–55 Hon Cler V Christ Ch Cath Dublin 1953 C St Peter Pietermaritzburg (Dio Natal) 1955–60 C Enniscorthy (Ferns) 1961–62 R Tormentine New Brunswick (Dio Fredericton) 1962–63 R Moncton (Fredericton) 1963–70 R Advent Montreal (Dio Montreal) 1970–92 m. 9 Jul 1957 Milltown Par Ch Dublin Helen Margaret dau. of Very Rev Alfred Forbes, Dean of

Ferns 1936–49 and had issue (i) Michael James **b.** 16 Jun 1963 (ii) Robert Cowper **b.** 12 May 1966 (iii) Siobhan **b.** 21 Jul 1970

Died 11 Sep 1937

DUNN, CHARLES 1797/98–

b. 1797 or 1798 Co Leitrim; ed by Mr Kean; ent TCD 15 Jun 1813 aged 15 BA 1817 MA 1820 BD 1850

V Tessaragh (Elph) 1834–*c.* 39; PC St Peter Walsall (Lich) 1846

    s. of John

    m. 16 Jun 1836 at Newtownlimavady Co Derry Elizabeth yst **dau.** of Robert Conn

DUNNE, CHARLES

C Drumcliffe (Elph) 1823; poss same as above

DUNSTERFIELD (DUNSTERVILLE), EDWARD

TCD Sch 1621 BA 1625

V Killinkere (Kilm) 1629–31; Archd of Kilmacduagh 1630–37; pres V Kildrumferton (Kilm) 3 Jan 1636/37 but does not seem to have been installed; Preb of Whitechurch (Ferns) 1637–38; Chapl to Lord Chancellor

    perhaps Hugh Dunsterville, Archd of Cloyne 1661–65 was his son

DUNWOODY, DEREK CECIL 1934–

b. 1934; TCD Dip Bibl Studs 1963

d 30 Jun 1963 (Kilmore) p 29 Jun 1964 (Kilmore); C-in-c Swanlinbar and Templeport (Kilm) 1963–65; Bp's V St Canice's Cath Kilkenny and C Kilkenny (Oss) 1965–67; Dio Reg Dios Ossory Ferns & Leighlin 1965–67; C St Lambert (Montreal) 1967–70; I Thorndale Pierrefonds (Montreal) 1970–71; C Gt Grimsby (in charge of St Mark) 1972; I Hodgson–Peguis (Rupld) 1972–74; I St Mary Magdalene Winnipeg (Rupld) from 1974

    m. Heather Costelloe and had issue

DURDIN, ALEXANDER WARHAM 1810/11–

b. 1810 or 1811 Co Cork; ent TCD 6 Nov 1826 aged 15 BA 1831 MA 1865

d 1835 p 1836; C Killinkere (Kilm) 1835–45; became PC St George Colegate (Nor) 1852

    s. of Robert A, JP of Cranemore Hse Carlow

    m. 7 Oct 1847 Lydia only child of Robert Pitcher of King's Lynn Norfolk

EADES, CHRISTOPHER 1802/03–

b. 1802 or 1803 Wexford; ed by Mr Newland; ent TCD 5 Jul 1821 aged 18 BA 1829 MA 1832 d 1828 p; lic PC Ballyjamesduff (Kilm) Jul 1831; he appears to have been lic C = DC Ballyjamesduff 10 Nov 1828 and lic PC 29 Mar 1835 (a 2nd time); seems to have resigned in 1840 and gone to England; C Templeport (Kilm) 1860–65; poss same as W C Eades qv below

    s. of William George, merchant

    m. and had issue Rev William Christopher, qv

EADES, WILLIAM CHRISTOPHER 1835–1918

b. 1835 Co Longford; ed Royal Sch Armagh; TCD Sch 1855 BA 1858 Div Test (2) 1865 MA 1868

d & p

Head Master, Dio Sch Sligo 1857–c. 70

    s. of Rev Christopher, qv

    Died 24 Nov 1918 Kingstown

EAGAR, EDWARD CHARLES 1807/08–1875

b. 1807 or 1808 Co Mayo; ed by Mr Lavelle; ent TCD 24 May 1826 aged 18 BA 1831

V Kilronan (Ard) 1834–75

    s. of Henry Thomas, *Publicanus* (Tax Collector) of Kerry and Ballina by his 2nd wife Susanna **dau.** of Rev Charles Seymour, R Kilronan (Ard) 1829–34 qv above

    m. Elizabeth **dau.** of John Noble of Co Fermanagh

    Died 28 Oct 1875

EASTWOOD, THOMAS FRANCIS 1824/25–1893

b. 1824 or 1825

d 1870 p 1871 by Bp Colenso of Natal; C Ballyculter (Down) 1879–80; R Boyle and Preb of Oran (Elph) 1880–83; R Knocktopher (Oss) 1883–92; res.

    m. and had issue incl his 2nd **dau.** Emily Maud **m.** 24 Mar 1885 at Greytown Natal Charles R, eldest **s.** of J R Saunders

    Died 9 Jan 1893 Pietermaritzburg aged 68

EATON, HUGH BOURCHIER 1887/88–1972

b. 1887 or 1888; TCD BA & Div Test 1913 MA 1929

d 1913 p 1914 (Kilmore); C Calry (Elph) 1913–15; C Tuam (Tuam) 1915–18; R Easkey (Killala) 1918–30; R Kilcullen w Carnalway (Kild) 1930–52; Dom Chapl to Abp of Dublin 1940–45; Canon of Kildare 1942–52; Chanc of St Brigid's Cath Kildare 1944–52; R Kildare w Lackagh (Kild) and Dean of Kildare 1952–63; ret

    m. Ethel Elizabeth Alice Digges (**died** 22 Oct 1962)

    Died 28 Apr 1972 **bur.** Kilcullen aged 84

ECCLES, ROBERT GILBERT 1825–1880

b. 1825; ed Royal Sch Dungannon; ent TCD 3 Jul 1843 BA 1848

d 1850 p; C Aughaval (Tuam) 1850–53; C Maguiresbridge (Clogh) 1853–63; C Ahascragh (Elph) 1863–65; C Clabby (Clogh) 1865–66; C-in-c Ballybay (Clogh) 1866–67; R and Preb of Kilbrogan (Cork) 1867–80

> yst **s.** of John Dickson, DL of Ecclesville Co Tyrone by Jemima **dau.** of Major Thomas Dickson, MP
>
> **m.** 24 Aug 1853 Ann Elizabeth eldest **dau.** of Lt Col Robert Lowry Dickson, 15 Bengal National Infantry of Hollybrook Lisnaskea Co Fermanagh. Issue 1. Alicia Dora (**died** 1921) **m.** Rev L R Fleury; 2. Jemima Hester **m.** Rev J D E Newcombe; 3. John Dickson; 4. Anna Florence (**died** 1909) **m.** Rev G G Greene; 5. Rev Canon Robert Lowry Dickson (**died** 9 Jan 1924) TCD BA 1884 Div Test 1886 MA 1918 d 1884 p 1885 (Killaloe) C Lickmolassy (Clonf) 1884–86 C Blessington (Glend) 1886–87 C Birr (Killaloe) 1887–91 R Loughrea w Tynagh (Clonf) 1891–1920 Canon of Kilquane (Clonf) and Canon of Kilchreest (Kilmacduagh) 1909–20 ret; 6. Charles Reginald (**died** 1912) **m.** Florence **dau.** of Frederick Cosgrave of Kilsallaghan; 7. Frances Harriette (**died** 1918); 8. Maud Ada; 9. Evelyn Blanche (**died** 1908); 10. Hester Catherine; 11. Constance Gertrude Isabel; 12. Rev Lionel Gilbert Frank St. John TCD BA (Resp) 1909 Div Test (1) 1910 d 1909 p 1910 (Clogher) C Tyholland (Clogh) 1909–10 C Tydavnet (Clogh) 1910–16 R Aghadrumsee (Clogh) 1916–18 R Clonmacnois w Tissaran (Meath) 1918–48 **m.** Muriel Beatrice Talbot (**died** 4 May 1971) **dau.** of Ven David Charles Abbott, Archd of Clogher 1906–17 and had issue (i) Ethel Frances (ii) Joan Elizabeth (iii) Leonie Muriel; 13. Ethel Violet
>
> **Died** 16 Feb 1880

ECCLESTON. THOMAS   –1707

MA

V Taghboy Disert Tessaragh & Lissonuffy (Elph) 1666–71; Preb of Kilgoghlin (Elph) 1666–1707; Preb & V Kilmeen *alias* Kilvine (Tuam) 1671–1707. V Chor Tuam 1678.

> **Died** 1707

ECHLIN, CHARLES MOORE 1794/95–1848

b. 1794 or 1795 Dublin; ent TCD 2 Nov 1812 aged 17 BA 1817 MA 1832

C Killeshandra (Kilm) 1824; C Killesher (Kilm) 1826; R Killinagh (Kilm) 1845–48

> eldest **s.** of Daniel Moore, *pragmaticus*, of Fitzwilliam Sq Dublin
>
> **m.** Sydney (**died** 17 May 1860 at Newcastle Lodge). Issue incl yst **s.** Charles Henry (drowned 15 Sep 1870 while boating on Lough Erne)
>
> **Died** 4 Jun 1848 Dublin

ECHLIN, JAMES 1663/64–1704

b. 1663 or 1664 Co Down; ed by Mr Harvey; ent TCD 10 May 1680 aged 16 Sch 1682 BA 1684

V Drumlease and Killargue (Kilm) 1684–86; coll V Castlemore (Ach) 5 Jun 1686; V Dunfeeny and Lackan (Killala) 1686-97; I Dunfeeny (Killala) 1686–1703; R Loughgilly (Arm) 1703–04

s. of Robert

m. (ML 26 Jan 1683) when living in Portaferry Co Down Hannah Champney

Died 1704

EDGE, JOHN 1818–

b. 1818 Arklow Co Wicklow; ed by Mr Hutchins; TCD BA 1843

d 1850 p 1852; C Ballynure (Leigh) 1861–64; C Denn (Kilm) 1864–65; PC Calary (Glend) 1866–95

s. of Isaiah

m. and had issue incl E H Edge

EDGEWORTH, ESSEX 1678/79–1737

b. 1678 or 1679 Co Longford; ed by Mr Shaw; ent TCD 21 Sep 1695 aged 16 BA 1700 MA 1703

d 170– p 12 Aug 1702 at Naas; V Granard (Ard) 1702–37; V Templemichael (Ard) 1718/19–37; V Gen and Chanc of Ardagh in 1729 when Boulter recommended him for a Bishopric; Chapl to Lord Lieutenant 1731; gave an acre of land for use of a Schoolmaster 5 Feb 1733/34 (L.M. V. 126).

s. of Sir John *Eques*, by his 2nd wife Anne

Died 4 Jun 1737 (Lodge Obits.)

EDGEWORTH, ESSEX

C Tashinny (Ard) *c.* 1843–45

EDGEWORTH, ESSEX

C Clonbroney (Ard) 1869–70

EDGEWORTH, ROBERT –1753

b. Co Longford; ent TCD 20 Aug 1731 BA 1735 MA 1739

V Mostrim (Ard) 1737/38–*c.* 1750; coll 27 June 1737/38 (F.F. & S.R.); R Templemichael (Ard) *c.* 1749–53

s. of Rev Essex (same as above?)

m. 1739 Martha dau. of Christopher Ussher. Issue incl Essex, Robert, Ussher, Henry; his yst dau. (died 26 Jan 1845 in London) m. Leonard McNally

Died Oct 1753

EDWARDS, JONATHAN
DD

Commonwealth Minister at Drumgoon (Kilm) from 29 Sep 1657 at £120 (Seymour's *Commonwealth MSS*, p 211)

EGAN, JOHN

there were two of this name, one of whom was ord p 1803 (Kilmore); C Killeshandra 1803; no 2 is more likely.

(1) **b.** 1777 or 1778 Dublin; ed by Mr Keller; ent TCD as Siz 5 Jun 1792 aged 14 Sch 1795 BA 1797

   s. of Sylvester, *pharmacopola*

(2) **b.** 1766 or 1767 Co Tipperary; ed by Mr Buckley; ent TCD as Siz 20 May 1788 aged 21 Sch 1790 BA 1792 MA 1796

Minor Canon Cork; Preb of Kilbrittan (Cork) 1850–55

   s. of Owen, *agricola*

   Died 17 June 1855

EGAN, JOHN JOHNSTONE 1815/16–c. 1890

b. 1815 or 1816 Co Sligo; ed by Mr O'Connor; ent TCD 14 Dec 1836 aged 20 BA & Div Test 1841

d 1841 p 1842; C Rossinver (Kilm) 1844; PC Swanlinbar (Kilm) 1846–60; prob same as John J Egan who appears C Kinawley 1860 in V.B; C Killinagh (Kilm) May– Jun 1861; R Killinagh (Kilm) 1861–75; PC Derrylane (Kilm) 1875–90; Last entry in C I Dir 1890

   s. of James

   m. 17 Sep 1850 Aughnamullan Par Ch Co Monaghan Isabella Maria (**died** 15 Jun 1880 at Derrylane) yst **dau.** of Rev James Morell of Ballybay Co Monaghan. Issue incl his eldest **s.** James Morell (**died** 24 Apr 1876)

EGERTON, HENRY 1874–1948

b. 2 Jun 1874 Liskilly; ed C of I Training Coll Dublin; TCD BA 1901 Div Test (1) 1903; was a School Teacher before Ordination

d 1903 p 1904 (Kilmore); C Urney and Annagelliffe (Kilm) 1903–04; C Drumgoon (Kilm) 1904–06; C Ballymore (Arm) 1906–08; C Donaghmore Upr (Arm) 1908–09; R Donaghmore Upr (w Pomeroy from 1929) (Arm) 1909–48

   s. of James, farmer of Liskilly Rosslea Co Fermanagh by Jane (née Johnston); uncle of Rev Henry Egerton, R Lissan (Arm) 1936–51

   Died 15 Jul 1948 at Lissan Rectory unm **bur.** Donaghmore Upr Churchyard

†ELLIOTT, ALFRED GEORGE 1828–1915

b. 29 Mar 1828 Cork; ed by Mr Foley; ent TCD 1 May 1854 BA & Div Test (2) 1858 MA 1879 BD & DD 1890 d 1858 p 1859 Bp 1897; C Aghnameadle (Killaloe) 1858-60; C Bailieborough and Moybologue (Kilm) 1860–61; C Lurgan (Kilm) 1861–68; C Kiltoghart (Ard) 1868–69; C Shercock (Kilm) 1870–71; R Munterconnaught (Kilm) 1871–76; R Castlerahan & PC Ballyjamesduff (Kilm) 1876–78; R Drumlease (Kilm) 1878–97; Preb of Mulhuddart in St Patrick's Cath Dublin 1889–97; elected Bp of Kilmore Elphin and Ardagh by United Synods 2 Sep 1897; consec in St Patrick's Cath Dublin 17 Oct 1897; enthroned in the Cathedral of St Mary the Virgin Elphin 16 Nov 1897; enthroned in St Fethlimidh's Cathedral Kilmore; Bp of Kilmore Elphin and Ardagh 1897–1915

s. of William, shopkeeper

Died 28 Sep 1915 at the See House Kilmore aged 87

ELLIOTT, CHARLES

BA

d 1870 p; R Kildrumferton (Kilm) 1878–79

ELLIOTT, JAMES 1792/93–1873

b. 1792 or 1793 Co Tipperary; ed by Mr Lyon; ent TCD 7 Nov 1808 aged 15 BA 1815 MA 1832

d 11 Oct 1818 (Cloyne) p 20 May 1821 (Cork); C Knocktopher (Oss) 1818; C Drumgoon (Kilm) 1820; C Castlecomer (Oss) 1826; PC Crumlin (Dub) 1831–65

2nd s. of John of Clonmel Co Tipperary (s. of Richard of Rathculbin Co Kilkenny) by Mary dau. of Rev William Ellis and niece of Dr Thomas Ellis sometime Clerk of the House of Commons in Ireland

m. (1) (ML 1821) Jane Potterton

m. (2) c. 1826 Charlotte (died 26 Nov 1874 aged 74) dau. of Capt Robert 3rd s. of Ven Henry Cary, Archd of Killala c. 1826. Issue 1. John Chetwood (died 1831 aged 4); 2. Harriet (died aged 8); 3. James (died 1832 aged 2); 4. Mary Isabella (died 1857 aged 26); 5. Charlotte H C (died 7 Nov 1862 aged 28); 6. Anne Harriet m. 15 Feb 1859 Capt George Cary, 77th Regt

Died 23 Nov 1873 at Laurel Lodge, Roundtown bur. Crumlin

ELLIOTT, WILLIAM

may have been R & V Kilcommick (Ard) in 1776; was there 1780–84; a William Elliott was V Trim (Meath) 1780–1813– see Meath Lists

ELLIOTT, WILLIAM

C Ballymacleery in Parish of Drumlummon w Gowna (Ard) 1826–45

ELLIS, CHARLES

C Drumshambo (Ard) 1870–72; R Toomna (Elph) 1872–82

m. 11 Oct 1871 St George's Par Ch Dublin Bessie eldest dau. of the late Francis Nesbitt Cullen of Corry Co Leitrim. Issue incl 1. his eldest s. Edward Charles (died

8 Jul 1930); 2. his eldest **dau.** Marie Louise (**died** 3 Mar 1954 at Warrenpoint Co Down) **m.** William Charles Burlington; 3. Josephine **m.** 8 Sep 1913 William J F Starkie of Cork

ELLISON, CYRIL CROWDEN 1913–

TCD Sizar BA 1935 Div Test (1) 1936 MA 1940

d 1936 p 1937 (Birmingham); C St Thomas Birmingham (Birm) 1936–38; C Newcastle–under–Lyme (Lich) 1938–40; R Tashinny w Shrule (Ard) 1940–45; R Kilcleagh U (Meath) (w C-in-c Ferbane (Clonf) 1952–54) 1945–54; R Navan U (Meath) 1954–69; Dio Reg Meath 1958–77; Canon of Meath 1966–69; ret; living in Cornwall in 1989; Last entry in C I Dir 1989

ELLISON, HUMPHREY

TCD BA 1901

d 1902 p 1903 (Kilmore); C Drung (Kilm) 1902–05; C Haddlesey (York) 1905–07; C Drumgoon (Kilm) 1907–09; C St Clement Bristol (Bris) 1909–10; Gen Lic Dio Dublin 1910–20; R Chasetown Walsall (Lich) 1920–25; last entry in Crockford 1925

ELWOOD, EDWARD LLOYD 1808/09–

b. 1808 or 1809 Roscommon; ent TCD 20 Oct 1825 aged 16 BA 1829

d; p 6 Nov 1831 (Kilmore); C Drumcliffe (Elph) 1832–41; V Kilmactranny (Elph) 1841–52; vacated parish by death or resignation

    s. of Rev James, Preb of Killaraght (Ach) 1820–36 (**s.** of Edward); **bro.** of Rev Harloe Knott, qv

    m. (1) 15 Sep 1836 Ellen **dau.** of Rev John Yeats, V Drumcliffe qv

    m. (2) 20 Jan 1840 Eleanor **dau.** of John Hone of Dublin

ELWOOD, HARLOE KNOTT 1817/18–

b. 1817 or 1818 Co Roscommon; ed by Mr Quill; ent TCD 6 Nov 1837 aged 19 BA 1842

d 1844 p 1845 (Kilmore); C Cloone (Ard) 1852–63; C Kinawley (Kilm) 1863–77; commuted and compounded at Disestablishment for £1,121

    s. of Rev James, Preb of Killaraght (Ach) 1820–36 (**s.** of Edward); **bro.** of Rev Edward Lloyd, qv

ENERY, WILLIAM 1704/05–1764

b. 1704 or 1705 Co Cavan; ed at Carrickmacross; ent TCD 17 Apr 1722 aged 15 BA 1726 MA 1729 BD & DD 1753

V Killeshandra (Kilm) 1729–64

    2nd **s.** of John of Bawnboy, JP Co Cavan

    m. 1732 Dorothy (**died** 30 May 1776 Dublin) 2nd **dau.** of Rev John Dennis, DD, R Cleenish (Clogh) 1714–45 by Margaret. Issue 1. Frances **m.** 1753 Rev Robert

Pringle; 2. Dorothy **m.** 1769 Rev Samuel Morrow; 3. Mary **m.** 19 Jun 1775 Henry Dixon of Kilkea Co Kildare; 4. Alicia **m.** 1776 William Higginbotham of Co Kildare

Died 24 Feb 1764 Dublin

ENGLISH, RICHARD ARTHUR

TCD BA 1876 Div Test (2) 1877 MA 1880

d 1877 p 1878 (Dublin); C Templemichael (Ard) 1877–79; Canon Residentiary Christ Ch Cath Dublin 1879–82; C St Peter Liverpool (Liv) 1883–85

ENNIS, JOHN RUTHERFORD 1902–1975

b. 1902; TCD BA 1925 Bibl Gk Abp King's & Bp Forster's Pris Div Test (1) 1926 MA 1958

d 1926 p 1927 (Limerick); C St Mary's Cath Limerick (Lim) 1926–28; C Rathfarnham (Dub) 1928–33; Hon V Chor Christ Ch Cath Dublin 1928–33; R Castleterra (Kilm) 1933–36; R Bailieborough (Kilm) 1936–47; R Cloonclare and Killasnett (Kilm) 1947–71; Preb of Mulhuddart in St Patrick's Cath Dublin 1955–65; Archd of Kilmore 1965–71; ret

m. Jean Simpson (**died** 14 Feb 1990). Issue 1. Arnold; 2. Joan Margaret; 3. Sybil

Died 30 Nov 1975

†ERARD

Bp of Ardagh *c.* 670

Died at Ratisbon

ERSKINE, HENRY JAMES 1803/04–1877

b. 1803 or 1804 Co Monaghan; ed by Mr Henderson; ent TCD 4 Dec 1821 aged 17 BA 1827 MA 1832

d 1828 p 1829 (Kilmore); C Drung (Kilm) 1829; R Tomregan (Kilm) 1850–56; R Kildrumferton (Kilm) 1856–71

2nd **s.** of Rev Josiah, R Knockbride (Kilm) qv (**s.** of Robert) by Marianne **dau.** of Henry Swanzy

m. 23 Sep 1857 at Balrothery Co Dublin Anne (**died** 1 Aug 1917 London aged 83) **dau.** of James Elliott. Issue Dora Maxwell **m.** 1886. Issue incl Jane **m.** 29 Apr 1835 Peter Quinn of Newry

Died 24 Mar 1877 Newry

ERSKINE, JOSIAH 1766/67–1819

b. 1766 or 1767 Cavan; ed by Mr Meares; ent TCD 3 Nov 1783 aged 16 BA 1789

d p 19 Feb 1792 (Kilmore); C Drumlane (Kilm) *c.* 1792–1812; V Denn (Kilm) 1812–13; R Knockbride (Kilm) 1813–19 eldest **s.** of Robert, Merchant by Elizabeth **dau.** of Josiah Parr of Cavan

m. 1799 Marianne **dau.** of Henry Swanzy of Avelragh Co Monaghan by Anne (**died** 5 Jul 1852 Newry) **dau.** of Rev Andrew Nixon of Nixon Lodge Co Cavan. Issue **sons** 1. Robert of Cavan (**died unm.** 31 May 1883 aged 82), JP, High Sheriff Co Cavan 1872, Lt Royal African Colonial Corps; 2. Rev Henry James, V Kildrumferton (Kilm) qv; 3. Archibald (**died** 7 Nov 1881), MD of Newry **m.** and had issue; 4. John Swanzy (**died unm.**); 5. James Francis (**died** 2 Feb 1908 aged 93) of Newry, JP **m.** and had issue; **daus.** 1. Anne (**died** 12 Feb 1885 aged 84) **m.** 17 Jan 1825 her cousin Thomas Biddall Swanzy of Newry and had issue; 2. Elizabeth (**died** 5 Aug 1879) **m.** 26 Mar 1828 Very Rev James Collins, DD, Dean of Killala and had issue; 3. Araminta (**died** Nov 1821 aged 15); 4. Sarah Jane (**died** 5 Jan 1889) **m.** 29 Apr 1835 Peter Quinn of Drumbanagher Co Armagh, JP MP for Newry 1859–65 and had issue incl Florence (**died** 6 Nov 1934) **m.** Rev Thomas Benjamin Willson, C Kilmore (Kilm) qv

Died 1 Feb 1819

ETOUGH, DANIEL OLIVER 1818/19–

b. 1818 or 1819; matric Lincoln Coll Ox 3 May 1838 aged 19

V Teynham (Cant) to 1852; V Oughteragh (Kilm) 1852–66

2nd **s.** of Richard, DD of Croxton Leics

EVANS, JOHN OWEN

St. David's Coll Lampeter BA 1892; St. Michael's Divinity Sch Cardiff 1893

d 1895 (Falkland Is) p 1900 (Bombay); C St John Baptist Buenos Aires (Dio Argentina) 1895–97; Harbour Chapl Bombay 1899–1902; Chapl AClS at Bhusaval India (Dio Bombay) 1902; Tundla India (Dio Lucknow) 1919–29; Perm to Off at Abingdon (Ox) 1929; R Drumreilly Newtowngore and Corrawallen (Kilm) 1930–34; C-in-c Kilnaboy and Killeedy (Killaloe) 1934–36; R Kilmacduagh & Ardrahan (Kilmacd) 1936–38

EVANS, JOHN WILLS

TCD BA 1882 Div Test (2) 1883 MA 1885

d 1883 p 1884 (Cork); C Fanlobbus (Cork) 1883–85; C Killinkere and Mullagh (Kilm) 1885–87

EVAT, JOHN

V Kiltoghart (Ard) 1622, is resident; church ruinous (R.V.)

EVATT, JOHN

appears R & V Carrigallen with Drumreilly and Oughteragh (Kilm) 1622; poss same as above

EVATT (EVETT), JOHN –1634

MA

most probably same as John Evat above; Dean of Elphin 1613/14–34; R Ardcarne (Elph) 1615–18

    m. (1)…

    m. (2) Blanche (**died** *c.* 1658) **dau.** of Edmund Mervyn. Issue (by which marriage?) Bridget **m.** Gregory Philpot

    Died in Easter week 1634 **bur.** Kiltoghart

EVERITT, WILLIAM JOHN WESLEY
see **WEBB, WILLIAM JOHN WESLEY**

EVETT, JOHN

V Aughrim (Elph) 1615; V Kilnamanagh (Elph) 1615; R Artough *alias* Tibohine (Elph) 1615; may be same as above; prob same as John Evett, R Boyle (Elph) 1615

EWART, WILLIAM JAMES 1892/93–1969

b. 1892 or 1893; ed Edgehill Theol Coll Belfast 1919

d 1932 p 1933 (Kilmore); C Templemichael (Ard) 1932–35; C-in-c Easkey (Killala) 1935–42; R Kilmoremoy (w Castleconnor from 1943 and Straid from 1952) (Killala) 1942–65; Dio Sec Dios Killala and Achonry 1944–61; Preb of Ardagh and Killanly in Killala Cath 1946–65; RD of Emlaghfad 1949–61; R Easkey w Kilglass (Killala) 1965–69; Archd of Killala and Achonry 1965–69

    m. Harriet (**died** 8 Apr 1968 at Easkey Co Sligo). Issue 1. Joan **m.** 29 Oct 1964 St Columb's Cath Londonderry Joseph eldest **s.** of T G Mills of Malvern Hse Co Armagh; 2. Monica

    Died 24 Mar 1969 aged 76

EYLWARD, JOHN

Parson of Killery, Ardagh, exchanged with William Fitzsimond Lawles 1381/82, qv; Archd of Cashel 1391

†FAELGHUS

Bp of Ardagh to 874

FAHY, THOMAS 1859/60–1927

b. 1859 or 1860 Co Mayo; TCD BA 1886 Div Test 1888

d 1887 p 1888; C Ballymodan (Cork) 1887–88; I Kilglass (Killala) 1889–90; V Annaduff (Ard) 1890–1927

    s. of Patrick

    m. Lilian Susan (**died** 17 Dec 1944)

    Died 15 Jan 1927 aged 67

FALKINER, WILLIAM FREDERICK 1847/48–1914

b. 1847 or 1848; TCD BA 1870 MA 1883 MRIA

d 1875 (Kilmore) p 1876 (Tuam); C Monivea (Tuam) 1876–77; C Holy Trinity Limerick (Lim) 1877–79; R Ballymackey (Killaloe) 1879–83; R Castleterra (Kilm) 1883–85; R Kilmessan (Meath) 1885–92; R Killucan U (Meath) 1892–1911; ret; he was a well-known collector through whose hands various antiquarian objects reached different museums. He contributed papers to RIA and RSAI and was an accomplished draughtsman and a skilled metal worker with a special interest in Irish craftsmanship

only **s.** of Rev Richard, R Kilmaine (Tuam) 1873–77 and Isabella **dau.** of Nathaniel Wright of Co Monaghan

m. Aimee Mary McCready (**died** 26 Mar 1920 Rathgar Dublin **bur.** Mt Jerome Dublin)

Died s.p. 7 Jun 1914 Whitehead Co Antrim aged 66 **bur.** Mt Jerome

FARIS, FRANCIS 1798–1852

b. 1798 Dublin; ed by Mr Fea; ent TCD 3 Jul 1815 aged 17 BA 1820 MA 1832

C Drung (Kilm) 1825/26; V Donard (Glend) 1836–52

s. of Thomas, *pragmaticus*

m. 3 Jun 1837 Martha (**died** 5 Dec 1879 aged 70) 4th **dau.** of William Heightington of Donard Hse Co Wicklow, High Sheriff Co Wicklow 1803. Issue 1. Thomas (**died** 1 Oct 1889 aged 42), Surgeon-Major; 2. his 2nd **dau.** Mary **m.** 1 Sep 1859 Frederick Archer **s.** of Thomas William Barlow, late solicitor to the War Dept Ireland

Died 11 May 1852 at Donard aged 53

FARIS, JAMES

C Drung (Kilmore) *c.* 1824; may be same as Francis Faris qv

FARIS, JOHN 1754/55–1789

b. 1754 or 1755 Co Cavan; ed by Mr Beatty; ent TCD 1 Feb 1770 aged 15 BA 1774

C Kildallon (Kilm) 1774–89

s. of George

Died Aug 1789

FARQUHAR, ADAM GORDON 1835–

b. 1835 Banff; TCD BA 1860

d Jun 1860 p; C Innismagrath (Kilm) 1860; C Straid (Ach) 1866; C Ballinacourty (Tuam) 1864–65; C Crossmolina (Killala) 1866–69

s. of Robert, Coast Guard Service

FATHY (?FUTHY), JAMES

pres to V Moydow and Deffin (? = Annaduff) (Ard) 22 Jun 1624 (L.M. V. 106)

FAUSSETT, HENRY 1817/18–1885

b. 1817 or 1818 Sligo; ed by Mr Jamieson; ent TCD 2 May 1836 aged 18 BA 1843

d 18 Dec 1842 p 2 Jun 1844 (Ossory); C Thomastown (Oss) 1842–; prob same as H F, C Killashee (Ard) 1850–53; C Kilbarron (Raph) 1856; PC Drumclamph (Derry) 1862–66; R Edenderry (Derry) 1872–85

yst **s.** of Richard, MD of Ballina Co Mayo

m. 7 Jan 1875 at St Peter's Ch Drogheda the hymn writer and poetess Alessie **dau.** of Rev William Bond, R Ballee (Down)

Died Trinity Sunday 31 May 1855 at Edenderry Rectory nr Omagh

FAUSSET, THOMAS VIGOGNE 1857/58–1936

b. 1857 or 1858; TCD BA & Div Test (2) 1881

d 1880 p 1881 (Kilmore); C Kilmore (Kilm) 1880–95; R Arvagh (Kilm) 1895–1910; R Ashfield (Kilm) 1910–31; ret

6th **s.** of Robert, County Inspector RIC by Jane Elizabeth **dau.** of Herbert John Clifford, Lt RN

m. Sarah Augusta **dau.** of Robert William Spence. Issue Thomas Vigogne Robert Spence **b.** 1908

Died 12 Jul 1936 aged 78

FAWCETT, BENJAMIN CHRISTMAS (or CHARLES) 1829/30–1904

b. 1829 or 1830 Roscrea Co Tipperary; ed Kingstown Sch; ent TCD 11 Oct 1844 BA 1850 Div Test (1) 1852

d 1852 p 1853 (Cashel); C Clonea Ballylennon and Stradbally (Lism) 1853–54; PC Cappoquin (Lism) 1854–56; C Ballymachugh (Ard) 1856–60; C Ballymodan (Cork) 1860–71; C Carrigaline (Cork) 1872–76; C Queenstown Cobh (Cloyne) 1876–79; R Kilbrogan (Cork) 1880–1904

s. of Isaac, merchant

m. 1854 Dublin Matilda Eleanor Hewitt. Issue 1. Frances Jane **died** at Bandon 9 Jan 1941; 2. a **dau.** b 2 Sep 1871

Died 16 May 1904 aged 74

FAWCETT, EDWARD 1817/18–1880

b. 1817 or 1818 Dublin; ed by Mr McCaul; ent TCD 16 Oct 1835 aged 17 BA 1849

d 1851 (Cork) p; R Streete (Ard) 1855–67

s. of James *pragmaticus*

Died 13 Nov 1880 at Greenwich

FENTON, WALTER LONG 1871–1932

b. 1871 Wicklow; TCD BA & Div Test 1895 MA 1899

d 1896 p 1897 (Ossory); C Fiddown (Oss) 1896–1900; C Raphoe (Raph) 1900–02; Dio C Clogher 1902–03; R Barr (Clogh) 1903–07; Dio C Clogher 1907–10; R Streete (Ard) 1910–31; C-in-c Killashee and Ballymacormack (Ard) 1931–32

s. of Samuel, JP Co Wicklow and bro. of Rev Samuel (1865–1948) R Ballyscullion (Derry) 1894–1909

m. 10 Nov 1912 Elizabeth Therese 2nd dau. of Rev Robert Oswald, R Drumballyroney (Drom) by Elizabeth Therese dau. of Ada Greenslead of Londonderry. Issue 1. Walter Oswald b. 1915; 2. Alsager Fitzgerald b. 1918

Died 4 Mar 1932

FERGUSON, RICHARD –1954

TCD BA 1912 MA 1915

d 1913 p 1915 (Kilmore); C Drumlease (Kilm) 1913–16; C Lara & Lavey (Kilm) 1916–22; R Killasnett (Kilm) 1922–27; C-in-c Cloone (Ard) 1927–32; Preb of Kilcooley in Elphin Cath 1945–53; C-in-c Killashee and Ballymacormack (Ard) 1932–50; R Oughteragh and Fenagh (Ard) 1950–53; ret

m. 5 Oct 1927 Ethel Mary Daly and had issue a s.

Died 1 Oct 1954 at Royal Victoria Hosp Belfast bur. Clones

FERGUSON, WALLACE RAYMOND 1947–

b. 7 Sep 1947 Belfast; ed Methodist Coll Belfast; Stranmillis Training Coll Belfast Cert Ed; Queen's Coll Birmingham BTh 1976; CITC BTh; LTCL

d 1978 p 1979 (Down); C Shankill Lurgan (Drom) 1978–80; C Newtownards and Movilla Abbey (Down) 1980–84; R Mullabrack and Kilcluney (Arm) 1984–2000; Hon V Chor Armagh Cath 1986–2005; Chapl to Armagh retired clergy 1992–2005; R Carnteel (Arm) 2000–05; R Kilmore and Ballintemple (Kilm) and Dean of Kilmore 2005–

s. of Henry of Dunmurry Belfast and Margaret Elizabeth dau. of John James and Teresa Armstrong of Roslea Co Fermanagh

m. 14 Jul 1973 Knock Methodist Ch Belfast Rosemary (deceased) dau. of George and Sybil (née Thompson) Megahey of Belfast. Issue 1. Marina Louise b. 29 Jan 1975 ed Stranmillis Training Coll m. 21 Dec 1998 Mullabrack Par Ch William Andrew s. of Richard Andrew Elliott of Newtownbutler Co Armagh; 2. Peter Armstrong b. 21 Sep 1978 m. 19 Jul 2002 Amy McConnell; 3. David b. 23 Feb 1980; 4. Mark Richard b. 6 Jun 1981 m. 24 Jul 2002 Delia Serb; 5. Susan b. 26 Apr 1987

FERRALL or FARRELL, JAMES 1758/59–1834

b. 1758 or 1759 Tipperary; ed by Mr Burke; ent TCD (as Farrell) 3 May 1779 aged 20; Sch 1781 BA 1783

d 24 June 1785– ordained by the Bp of Dromore in the Castle Chapel Dublin; p; lic

C Killashee (Ard) 1 Sep 1785; lic C Rathcline (Ard) 7 Sep 1809 (S.R.); V Rathcline (Ard) 1813–34

s. of John, merchant.

m. and had issue **daus**. Maria, Annabella and Lucinda, and a **s**. James, Dean of Adelaide

Died 14 Oct 1834 at Lanesborough Co Longford

The executor of his Will was Rev Maurice Farrell of Lanesborough who may have been a son

PUBLICATION

A Survey of the Parish of Rathcline for Mason's *Parochial Survey*, vol II

FERRALL or FERGAIL, RICHARD

V Rathclayn = Rathcline (Ard) to 1406

FERRIS, HERBERT

V Abbeylara Clonbroney Strade = Streete Russagh and Rathasbegg = Rathaspeck (Ard) 1661, coll May 8 (F.F.); is Sequestrator of "Rahone & Denn" = Castlerahan (Kilm) *c.* 1663, but perhaps George Creighton, qv still held the parish; Bailieborough Parish (Kilm) was sequestered to him in Nov 1663 during the incumbency of Patrick Maxwell qv

FERRIS, JOHN

R & V Kiltullagh (Tuam) was appointed sequestrator of Ballintubber U (Elph) 6 May 1673 following deposition of Matthew Moore qv

FETHERSTON (FETHERSTONHAUGH), CUTHBERT 1782–1847

b. 1782 Co Westmeath; ed by Mr Henry Porter; ent TCD as SC 1 Oct 1798 aged 16 and a half BA 1802 MA 1825

C Castlerahan (Kilm) 1804; V Durrow (Meath) 1816–23; R Nenagh (Killaloe) –1830; R Hacketstown (Leigh) 1830–47

s. of Cuthbert Fetherston

m. and had issue incl 1. Frances **m.** 11 or 13 May 1845 William Fetherston, JP of Grouse Lodge Co Westmeath; 2. his yst **dau**. Emma Caroline **m.** 7 Sep 1842 Joseph Barker, Solicitor of Dublin

Died 17 Feb 1847

FETHERSTON, THOMAS

appears C Drung (Kilm) 1844

m. Adeline (**died** 21 Oct 1830 aged 26 **bur**. at St Peter's Ferns Co Wexford) **dau**. of Lt Col Godley

†FETHLIMIDH (FELIM)

born shortly after 500; founder of Kilmore Diocese *c.* 560, commonly accepted as first Bp. His parents, Carill and Dediva, belonged to the territory of Breiffne

Feast Day 9 August

FIGSBEE (FYSBIE), THOMAS 1698/99–*c.* 1776

b. 1698 or 1699 Carlingford Co Louth; ed by Mr Blackhall in Dublin; ent TCD as Siz 11 Jun 1718 aged 19 BA 1722

V Kilronan (Ard) 1740–*c.* 1752; coll 27 Oct 1740 (F.F.); R Ardcarne (Elph) *c.* 1752–76; C Taunagh (Elph) 1766

s. of Francis, *faber ferrarius*

m. and had issue incl Thomas ed by Mr Hawkey in Dublin ent TCD 27 May 1755 aged 26 Sch 1759 BA 1760

Died *c.* 1776

FINDD, THOMAS

V Kilfulan (Killashee?) (Ard) 17 Aug 1479 (A.H. I. 166)

FINLAY, JOHN WILLIAM 1805–1879

b. 4 Jul 1805 Derry; ed by Dr Burney; matric Trinity Coll Ox 18 Oct 1824; ent TCD as SC 7 Feb 1825 BA 1829 MA 1832

PC Derryheen (Kilm) 1834–39; poss same as John William Finlay, C Rathfarnham (Dub) 1842

eldest **s.** of Col Thomas of Corkagh

m. (1) 4 Jun 1837 Henrietta Isabella (**died** 2 Mar 1847) **dau.** of Major Henry Cole of Twickenham London. Issue 1. Elizabeth Owen **m.** Richard John Ussher of Cappagh Co Waterford; 2. Henrietta Ellen; 3. Selina Frances (**died** 1860); 4. Olivia Anne; 5. Henry Thomas **b.** 15 Feb 1847 JP Co Dublin, late 6th Royals Regt

m. (2) 13 Feb 1849 Caroline Elizabeth **dau.** of Charles Hamilton of Hanwood and widow of Trevor Stannus

Died 8 Dec 1879 at Kingstown (Dun Laoghaire) Co Dublin aged 74 **bur.** Clondalkin Co Dublin

FINNERTY, JOHN LANGFORD 1811/12–1873

b. 1811 or 1812 Co Kerry; ed by Mr McElligott; ent TCD 5 Jun 1833 aged 21 BA 1838

C Killallon (Meath) 1846; C Magheraculmoney (Clogh) from 1850; was there in 1856; C Drumcliffe (Elph) 1858–66

s. of Daniel

Died 12 Mar 1873 Dublin

FIRMIN, AEGIDIUS –1756

V Clonbroney (Ard) 1722–24, coll 3 Sep 1722 (F.F.); V Mohill (Ard) 1724–56; Chanc of Emly 1729–56

This name appears in two entries in F.F., but in another entry the name is Peter Lombard

Died 14 Apr 1756

FISHER, FREDERICK

TCD BA 1872 Abp King's Div Pri (1) 1873 Div Test (1) & Theo Exhib (1) 1874; St John's Coll Camb BA (2cl Theol Trip) 1878 MA 1881

d 1873 p 1875 (Kilmore); C Bailieborough (Kilm) 1873–75; C St Michael Limerick and V Chor and Hon Canon of Limerick (Lim) 1875–76; C Gt St Andrews Cambridge (Ely) 1876–78; C Mortlake (Roch) 1879–82; C St George Camberwell (Roch) 1882–85; Asst Dio Insp Dio Rochester 1885–87; C Newington (Roch) 1887–1901; V Kingsey (Ox) 1901–c. 20; Last entry in Crockford 1920

FITZGERALD, HENRY VESEY, 1788–1860

b. 28 Jul 1788 Dublin; ent TCD as SC 1 Oct 1802 BA 1806 MA 1811 LLB & LLD 1814

R Castlerahan (Kilm) 1813–60; Dean of Emly 1818–25; Dean of Kilmore and V Kilmore & Ballintemple (Kilm) 1825–60

> 3rd **s.** of James, Prime Sergeant MP PC (who was dismissed from office for opposing the Union and refused a Peerage) by Catherine **dau.** of Henry Vesey, Warden of Galway; she was created Baroness Fitzgerald and Vesey 27 Jun 1826; Dean Fitzgerald succeeded his elder **bro.** as 2nd Baron Fitzgerald and Vesey 1843
>
> **m.** 7 Sep 1825 Elizabeth (**died** 1834) **dau.** of Standish O'Grady of Elton. Issue 1. Matilda **m.** 23 Apr 1857 Rev Beauchamp W Stannus; 2. Letitia; 3. Elizabeth (**died** 3 Nov 1856 Paris); 4. Geraldine Catherine **m.** 15 Oct 1856 Walter Trevor **s.** of Dean Stannus; 5. Mary Georgina (**died** 7 Apr 191– aged 79, Will dated 11 Jan 1912)
>
> **Died** 30 Mar 1860 Danesfort Co Cavan **bur.** St Ann's Dublin– title became extinct

FITZGERALD, JAMES 1818/19–

b. 1818 or 1819 Drogheda; ed by Mr Frazer; ent TCD 12 Oct 1838 aged 19 BA 1843

d 21 Dec 1844 (Ossory) p; C Roscommon (Elph) 1846–61; V Kiltoom and Camma (Elph) 1861–72

> **s.** of John, school master
>
> **m.** and had issue incl his yr **s.** Lt Col J S Fitzgerald (**died** 7 Apr 1927)

FITZJOHNS, JOHN

pres to V Kedy (Kilm) on deposition of Philip Brady, qv 2 Jul 1594 (L.M. V. 101)

FITZPATRICK, FREDERICK 1790–1870

b. 1790 Co Dublin; ent TCD 2 Nov 1807 aged 17 BA 1812 MA 1832

d 29 Nov 1812 p 19 Dec 1813; lic C Killersherdoney (Kilm) 5 Jul 1813; lic C Drumgoon (Kilm) 1 Dec 1813; V Killan, now Shercock (Kilm) 1815–48; V Bailieborough and Moybologue (Kilm) 1848–61; R Lurgan (Kilm) 1861–70

> s. of Rev Joseph
>
> m. and had issue 1. Rev Frederick, R Templeport (Kilm) qv; 2. Anna Maria m. Rev Charles Claudius Beresford, R Bailieborough or Moybologue (Kilm) qv
>
> **Died** 23 Jul 1870 aged 79

FITZPATRICK, FREDERICK 1819/20–1898

b. 1819 or 1820

C Bailieborough & Moybologue (Kilm) 1850–; R Templeport (Kilm) 1856–60; R Cloone (Ard) 1860–77

> only s. of Rev Frederick, R Lurgan (Kilm) qv (s. of Rev Joseph)
>
> m. 10 Aug 1853 Olivia elder dau. of the 2nd Marquis of Headfort. Issue 1. Robert Persse m. 14 Jan 1885 Caroline Rebecca yst dau. of Very Rev Arthur Moore, Dean of Achonry; 2. Mary Adelaide Virginia Thomasina Eupatria m. 25 Oct 1878 St Patrick's Cath Dublin William Cornwallis West; 3. Edwina m. (1) 10 Jul 1878 John Monck Brooke; m. (2) 11 May 1892 Capt Guy Windham, 16th Lancs Regt and had issue Percy
>
> **Died** 5 Feb 1898 at Warren Hall Broughton Derbyshire aged 78

FLANAGAN, JOHN 1778/79–

b. 1778 or 1779; ed by Mr Shields; ent TCD 6 Nov 1809 aged 30 BA 1815 MA 1818 V Fuerty (Elph) 1837–c. 54

> s. of John *agricola*

FLANNERY, WILLIAM 1869/70–1948

b. 1869 or 1870; TCD BA 1894 BD 1910

d 1894 p 1895 (Kilmore); C Kinawley (Kilm) 1894–95; C Killinkere (Kilm) 1895–1901; R Ballyjamesduff w Castlerahan (Kilm) 1901–17; RD of Knockbride 1911–32; R Knockbride (w Shercock from 1933) 1917–44; Preb of Mulhuddart in St Patrick's Cath Dublin 1927–44; Exam Chapl to Bp of Kilmore 1932–44

> s. of Thomas of Shanbollard Co Galway
>
> m. Martha Elizabeth (Elsie) (**died** 16 Aug 1978 at Booterstown Dublin **bur.** Knockbride) and had issue incl 1. eldest s. Horace Thomas (**died** 24 Oct 1932 aged 36 at Lake Tanganyika) MB, Rhodesian Medical Services, late of Lancaster Regt; 2. Thomas (**died** 6 May 1963 Dublin); 3; Herbert; **daus.** 1. Winifred Alice (**died** 17 Dec 1967 Chertsey); 2. Eileen Maureen; 3. Zoe; 4. Patricia
>
> **Died** 28 Feb 1948 aged 78

FLAWNE, GEORGE

C Ardagh (Ard) 1615; C Mostrim (Ard) 1615 (R.V.); V Killashee (Ard) to 1622; serves the Cure, Church repaired; 2 timber houses built by the new incumbent (R.V.); V Templemichael (Ard) before 1615– still there in 1622; value of V 20 nobles; church and chancel in good condition (R.V.); church well repaired; a sufficient glebe house and office houses built by the new incumbent (R.V.)

FLAWNE, JEREMY –c. 1662

lately pres by the Lord Lt to the V Killisee Templemichael and Ballymacormick (Ard) (Carte Papers XXI.346) to 1647; Commonwealth Minister Moydow (Ard) on the tithes (Seymour's Commonwealth MSS) 1658; he was also Commonwealth Minister at £100 at Killashee and Templemichael (Ard) 1658 and on 11 June 1660, says that, "before the Rebellion, he was V Killashee and Templemichael (Ard) where he faithfully discharged the duty till disturbed by the rebels and that he officiated in said Vicarages and adjacent places for four years past and as income is small, he is granted also the livings of Moydow and Taghsynod" (Seymour's *Commonwealth MSS*); res Killashee etc 9 May 1661 for V Moydow and Templemichael (Ard) (FF). (Leslie's unpublished Lists has James Sterling V Templemichael (Ard) etc from 1660),

> **m.** and had a **dau.** Martha wife of Rev Henry Bunn who was imprisoned by the rebels in 1641, afterwards of Swords in 1654 (Hickson I. 345)
>
> Died *c.* 1662– will proved 1662
>
> NOTE: in the Commonwealth period in the 1650s, clergy often held several incumbencies together, and alternated between being Vicars and Commonwealth Ministers, which explains the somewhat confusing movements of Jeremy Flawne and others. It also accounts for two clergy claiming and occupying the same incumbency at the same time. These were confusing and troubled times

FLEMING, HARLOE 1798/99–1871

b. 1798 or 1799 Sligo; ed by Mr Smith; ent TCD 4 Nov 1816 aged 17 BA 1821

d 1822 p; V Loughglynn (w Kilcorkey from 1845) (Elph) 1824–71

> **s.** of William
>
> **m.** and had issue incl 1. Rev Thomas Henry (**died** 4 Apr 1905) **b.** 1832 Co Roscommon ent TCD 10 Oct 1853 aged 21 BA & Div Test 1858 MA 1880 d 1858 p 1859 C Renvyle (Tuam) 1858–64 PC Moyrus (Tuam) 1864–71 R Ballinakill (Tuam) 1871–92 Preb of Faldown (Tuam) 1879–1905 R Omey (Tuam) 1892–1905 **m.** 8 Jun 1859 Harriette eldest **dau.** of Henry Hildebrand of Charleville Hse Co Mayo and had issue incl a **s. b.** 12 June 1860 a **s. b.** 11 Mar 1863 and **daus.** (i) Eleanor Grace **m.** 15 Sep 1888 SQW Penrose eldest **s.** of Rev Samuel Penrose, C Rincurran (Cork) (ii) Cordelia Millicent **m.** 23 Jun 1888 Richard W only **s.** of Thomas Smith (iii) Lillie **m.** 17 Apr 1919 Frank Ellis–Parker (iv) Harriette Maud (**died** 15 Apr 1957) **m.** as his 2nd wife Rt Rev James O'Sullivan Bp of Tuam; 2. Rev Henry Acton, R Kilcommon Erris (Killala) 1872–74 R Kilmoremoy (Killala) 1874–79 **m.** 26 Sep 1866 Julia **dau.** of J J Stoney, MD; 3. Rev Harloe Robert, V Corhampton (Portsm — then Win) 1874; 4. Cordelia Anne **m.** 13 Aug 1857 Rev Nicholas Magrath, C Galtrim (Meath)
>
> Died 27 Mar 1871 at Loughglynn Glebe House

FLEMING, RICHARD FITZJAMES

d 1870 p 1871; C Loughglynn (Elph) 1870; R Loughglynn (Elph) 1871–81; R Moyrus Beauchamp (Tuam) 1881–87; went to live in Devonshire England

FLEMING, RICHARD FITZTHOMAS

TCD BA (Suppl Sen Mod Hist & Pol Sci) 1888 MA 1892

d 1888 (Kilmore for Tuam) p 1890 (Kilmore); C Galway (Tuam) 1888–89; C Urney (Kilm) 1889–91; C St Ann Dublin (Dub) 1891–92; C St Marychurch (Ex) 1892–96; C St Matthias Plymouth (Ex) 1897–98; C Stoke Damerel & Chapl S Devon Hosp (Ex) 1898–1901; V Langley (Nor) 1901–15; R Chedgrave (Nor) 1901–30; R Siseland (Nor) 1914–30; TCF 1916–18; V Dorney (Ox) 1930–42; ret

FLETCHER, JOHN *c.* 1688–?1758

b. *c.* 1688 Whitehaven; ed by Dr Jones, Dublin; ent TCD 23 Mar 1705/06 aged 17 BA 1710

C Killinagh (Kilm) 1712; may be same as John Fletcher Master of King St Sch Dublin who died 14 May 1758

   s. of Rev John

   m. (ML 9 Jul 1717) Mary ffrench of Belturbet. Rev William Fletcher, R Ballymoney (Conn) who was born *c.* 1701 is unlikely to have been his son — see *Clergy of Connor* p 331

   ?Died 14 May 1758

FLETCHER, WILLIAM DUDLEY SAUL 1862–1948

b. 1862; TCD Primate's Heb Pri (1) 1883, 1884 & 1885 Wall Bibl Sch 1886 BA and Div Test (1) 1887 Chald & Syr Pri 1889 Elrington Theol Pri 1889 BD 1890

d 1887 p 1888 (Dublin); C St Bartholomew (Dub) 1887–88; C Ballywillan (Conn) 1889; C Camus–juxta–Bann (Derry) 1889–92; C Magheralin (Drom) 1892–95; C Bray (Dub) 1895–1900; R Lissadell (Elph) and Chapl to Sir JAR Gore Booth, Bt 1900–07; R Killymard (Raph) Sept–Oct 1907; R Coolbanagher (Kild) 1907–27; RD of Lea 1922–27; R Leighlin and Wells (Leigh) 1927–46; Treas of Leighlin 1930–35; Canon of Killamery in St Canice's Cath Kilkenny (Oss) 1933–46; Prec of Leighlin 1935–46; ret

   s. of Rev James Saul, DD, R St Barnabas (Dub) 1872–99 (s. of William); **bro.** of Rev Victor James and of Rev Lionel and of Rev Arthur Henry

   m. 12 Jan 1899 Holy Trinity Ch Killiney Dublin Agnes Elizabeth eldest **dau.** of Richard Altamont Smyth of Lauragh Co Laois and Frances Anne Jane **dau.** of Sir Alan E Bellingham Bt of Castlebellingham Co Louth. Issue 1. Clayton (**died** 7 Feb 1920 at Sherborne Sch aged 18); 2. Alan Henry Saul TCD LLB, Indian Civil Service **m.** 6 Nov 1928 Beatrice Ida Maude **dau.** of Dr and Mrs Robert Reid of Whiteabbey Co Antrim

   Died 7 Apr 1948 Dublin

PUBLICATIONS
Rome and Marriage, 1911
Rome and Marriage, Warning, 1936

FLOOD, FREDERICK 1826–1901

b. 1826 Dublin; ed by Dr Smith; ent TCD 2 Jul 1839 aged 13 BA 1848

d 1848 p 1849 (Down); C Killinchy (Down) 1848–57; V Kilmood (Down) 1851–69; R Rosses (Elph) 1869–1901; Preb of Oran (Elph) 1883–1901

s. of Christopher, *pharmacopola*

m. 28 May 1856 Knockbreda, Anna Sarah (**died** 14 May 1889 Dublin) **dau.** of Nicholas Delacherois Crommelin, JP DL of Carrowdore Castle Co Down by Hon Elizabeth de Moleyne **dau.** of William, 2nd Lord Ventry

Died 19 Nov 1901 aged 74

FLOOD, R

C Templemichael (Ard) to 1827

FLORENCE

is R of Kylmor (in parish of Columkille) (Ard) 10 Aug 1410 (Cal. Reg. Flem, 129)

FLOWER, EDWARD 1846/47–1926

b. 1846 or 1847; TCD BA 1880

d 1879 p 1880 (Kilmore); C Kinawley (Kilm) 1879–81; C Kilcornan (Lim) 1881–86; V Denn (Kilm) 1886–1903; R Ballaghmeehan and Kiltyclogher (Kilm) 1903–26

m. and had issue incl his 2nd **s.** John James, BA BAI, Lt 1st Battalion Lancashire Fus

Died 20 Sep 1926 at Ballaghmeehan Rectory aged 79

FLOYD, JOHN

adm V Urney (Kilm) 4 Jun 1639; resigned 10 Jan 1640

FLYNN, HUGH JOHN 1829/30–*c.* 1917

b. 1829 or 1830 Dublin; ed by Mr Flynn; ent TCD 1 Jul 1845 aged 15 BA 1851 Div Test (1) 1853 MA 1857 BD & DD 1871

d 1853 (Kilmore) p 1854 (Meath); C Elphin (Elph) 1853–62; Head Master Elphin Diocesan Sch; Preb of Terebrine (Elph) 1857–59; V Clara (Meath) 1862–72; C St Mary Somerstown 1872; Chapl W London District Sch Ashford Middx 1872–99; Lic Pr Dio Truro 1906–

s. of Rev Thomas, qv

Died *c.* 1917

FLYNN, THOMAS 1787/88–

b. 1787 or1788 Co Down; ed by Mr O'Beirne; ent TCD 4 Jun 1810 aged 22 Sch 1812 MA 1818

C Elphin (Elph) 1848–51; he had probably been a schoolmaster for most of his working life

    s. of Daniel, schoolmaster

    m. and had issue incl 1. Gregory Thomas **b.** *c.* 1822; 2. Rev Hugh John, qv

FOLEY, WILLIAM ARTHUR ERNEST

TCD BA 1911 Div Test 1913 MA

d 1911 p 1912 (Limerick); Dio C Limerick 1911–13; C St Michael Limerick (Lim) 1914–16; R Bruff & Tullybrackey (Lim) 1916–20; C St Anne Birkenhead (Ches) 1920–22; C-in-c Nurney & Clonmulsh (Leigh) 1922–23; C Drumlease & Killargue (Kilm) 1923–24; C-in-c Timahoe (Leigh) 1924–27; Dep Sec HBS 1928–30; R Kiltennel (Leigh) 1930–33

    s. of Ven William Malcolm, R Killoe (Ard) qv by his 2nd wife Josephine Maude

    m. Eleanor Twigg. Issue incl William Arthur **b.** 1923

FOLEY, WILLIAM MALCOLM *c.* 1854–1944

b. c 1854; ed privately; TCD Bp Forster's Pri (2) 1876 Bibl Gk Pri (2) 1877 BA (Sen Mod Eth & Log) 1877 Div Test (1) 1877 Theo Exhib (2) 1878 BD 1880; Donnellan Lect TCD 1892–93

d 1877 p 1878 (Tuam); C Easkey (Killala) 1877–78; C Tuam (Tuam) 1878–81; R Killoe (Ard) 1881–83; Dep Sec Irish Soc 1883–85; R Askeaton (Lim) 1885–96; R Dunfeeny (Killala) 1896–1907; Preb of Ardagh (Killala) 1904–07; R Tralee (A & A) and Exam Chapl to Bp of Limerick 1907–22; Chapl to Tralee Prison 1907–17; Preb of Effin (Lim) 1907–20; Chanc of Ardfert 1911–15; Preb of Monmohenock in St Patrick's Cath Dublin 1911–30; Archd of Ardfert 1915–22; C-in-c Louth and Killincoole (Arm) 1922–24; R Drumcar (Arm) 1924–30; ret

    s. of Rev Peter, R Dunfeeny (Killala) (**s.** of Malachy)

    m. (1) 27 Aug 1879 Liss Ch Co Offaly Elizabeth Pauline (**b.** 1853) elder **dau.** of Thomas Hackett of Castletown Park Ballycumber Co Offaly. She died leaving issue Thomas William Winspeare TCD BA (Jun Mod) Lt Leinster Regt killed at the Somme Jul 1916

    m. (2) 12 Jun 1884 St Andrew's Ch Dublin Josephine Maude yst **dau.** of John S Clarke of Portumna Co Galway. Issue 1. Gerald Robert Edward TCD 1st Maths Sch BA (Sen Mod) OBE; served as DI & CI RIC and was Major in RI Regt in Palestine and Western Front in Great War; 2. Rev William Arthur Ernest, C-in-c Drumlease and Killargue (Kilm) qv; 3. Rev Hubert Francis St Patrick TCD MA d 1912 p 1913 (Limerick) C-in-c Ballingarry (Lim) 1912–14; C Mallow (Cloyne) 1914–17; C St Matthias (Dub) 1917–18; Sen Chapl RN 1918–46; 4. Ernest George; 5. Albert Maurice TCD BA (Mod) BAI; Lt RI Regt; **daus.** 1. Elizabeth Mary Josephine, TCD BA (Mod) **m.** Dr Apperly; 2. Irene Lucy Noel **m.** JW Lane; 3. Gladys Eva Winspeare **m.** James **s.** of Rev James Quarry Day, R Loughcrew

(Meath)

Died 19 Oct 1944

PUBLICATIONS
Christ in the World, Donnellan Lectures, 1893
The Song of Songs 1904
Contributed to Hasting's *Dictionary of Religion and Ethics* 1908 and 1915
Editor *Church of Ireland Gazette* 1931–1934

FONTANIER, JOHN   –1730

was a Huguenot refugee

appears Preb of Oran (Elph) in 1722 but was probably appointed 1696; Preb of Oran to 1730; R St John Sligo 1696–1730

m. Aline

Died 1730

FORBES, ARTHUR   1656/57–1727

b. 1656 or 1657

V Clonkeen (Arm) and V Drumconrath (Meath) 1661–79; V Cashel and Rathcline (Ard) 1685–1727

> **m.** and had issue a **s.** Rev Arthur (**died** 1737) V Drumconrath (Meath) 1699–1737.

Died 23 Aug 1727 aged 70

In Rathcline Churchyard, outside the village of Newtownforbes, a stone over his grave is inscribed, "here lyes the body of Anne Forbes Auchmouty with her three children, Nov 23, 1696, and also the body of the Revd. Arthur Forbes aged 70, and Vicar of this Parish for forty years who departed this life 23rd of August 1727".

NOTE: In Leslie's *Armagh Clergy and Parishes,* 1911, p 242–243, Arthur Forbes (son of above), was residing in Drogheda to 1724, and was probably C St Peter's Drogheda (Arm) from 1713. The Parish Register contains entries of the baptism of his children as follows: Armitage, 30 Jun 1713; George 6 Dec 1714; Ann 20 Oct 1717; Priscilla 7 Dec 1718; Mary 14 Jan 1719; Catherine 28 Jan 1720; Frances 26 Dec 1724

FORBES, GEORGE

coll V Killery and Killenumery (Ard) 9 Apr 1697 (F.F.)

FORD, JAMES WILLIAM   1850/51–1904

b. 1850 or 1851

d 1881 (Kilmore) p 1884 (Tuam); C Boyle (Elph) 1881–82; C Castleconnor (Tuam) 1882–84; R Skreen (Killala) 1884–90; R Athenry (Tuam) 1890–1904

> **m.** Charlotte Maude eldest **dau.** of Richard McClintock of Cabra Dublin; she **m.** (2) 17 Oct 1917 Thomas Henry eldest **s.** of Rev Thomas Pennefather, R Kiltennel

(Leigh)

Died 1904 aged 53

FORD, ROBERT IRVINE –1944

b. Co Fermanagh; TCD BA 1882 Div Test (1) 1885 BD 1890

d 1879 p 1881 (Tuam); C Castleconnor (Killala) 1879–82; C Booterstown (Dub) 1882; V Ballysakeery (Killala) 1882–85; R Christ Ch Moorside (Manch) 1885–87; C St Stephen Belfast (Conn) 1887–88; Supt ICM Belfast 1889; R Kilkeevan (w Tibohine and Loughglynn 1906–24) (Elph) 1889–1936; Preb of Terebrine (Elph) 1900–36; ret

s. of Robert of Coolbuck Hse Lisbellaw Co Fermanagh

m. (1) …Morrow and had issue 1 **s.** and 3 **daus.** incl Dorothea Georgina Sarah

m. (2) Dora Frances Elizabeth **dau.** of Robert G Maunsell of Spa Hill Limerick and had issue 2 **sons** and 2 **daus.** incl 1. Rev Arthur Theodore Irvine **b.** 8 Jun 1896 (**died** 7 Jun 1965) TCD Sch 1917 BA & Div Test 1921 MA 1927 C Taney (Dub) 1921–24 C St Cuthbert Darlington (Dur) 1924–27 Asst P St Mary and All Angels Runcorn (Ches) 1927–30 Org Sec CMS Birmingham 1930–34 Org Sec CMS NI 1934–38 R Ballymacarrett (Down) 1938–51 R St Mary Newry (Drom) 1951–65 Chanc of Dromore 1962–63 Archd of Dromore and Canon of St Anne's Cath Belfast 1963–64 Dean of Dromore and Treas of St Anne's Cath Belfast 1964–65 **m.** 1 Jun 1927 Ada S **m.** Brooks of Northumberland and had issue Beryl Irvine **m.** Dec 1951 at Newry John Adams Anderson of Holywood Co Down; 2. Ian George Lionel MB FRCS.

His **dau.** Frances Lilian (**died** 27 Sep 1957 Shropshire) **m.** Dr G S Stritch and his **dau.** Mabel E G of Rostrevor Co Down (**died** 3 Jan 1973 **bur.** Clonallon Warrenpoint) were born to one of these marriages. One **dau. m.** Major G H Noblett

Died 20 May 1944 Lisbellaw

FORREST, EDWARD FREDERICK 1902–1973

b. 28 Feb 1902 Dublin; ed St Patrick's Cath Gram Sch Dublin; Mountjoy Sch Dublin; TCD BA 1932 Div Test 1933

d 24 Jun 1933 p 1 Jul 1934 (Limerick); C Tralee and Dio C Ardfert (A & A) 1933–36; R Carnew (Ferns) 1936–39; R Kilnamanagh (Ferns) 1939–45; R Inch (Glend) 1945–46; R Drumcliffe (Elph) 1946–47; R Killargue and Killenumery (Kilm) 1947–49; BC Rathconnell (Meath) 1949–51; R Killucan (Meath) 1951–58; R Rathaspeck and Streete (Ard) 1958–64; R Julianstown (Meath) 1964–72; Canon of Meath 1971–72; ret

s. of Andrew and Margaret of Dublin

m. 19 Aug 1939 Hollyfort Ch Co Wexford Olive Edith Walker. Issue 1. Andrew (**died** 1991) **b.** 1940 **m.** and had issue three children; 2. Edith **b.** 1942 **m.** …Nutt and has issue three children; 3. Robert **b.** 1942 **m.** and has issue three children; 4. Very Rev Leslie David Arthur **b.** 5 Feb 1946 d 1970 p 1971 C Conwall U w Gartan (Raph) 1970–73 R Tullyaughnish G (Raph) 1973–80 R St Nicholas Galway 1980–95 Canon of Tuam 1986–91 Provost of Tuam 1991–95 Preb of Tassagard in St

Patrick's Cath Dublin 1991–R and Dean of Ferns 1995–; **m.** 4 Sep 1969 Avril **dau.** of John and Hannah Copeland of Enniscorthy and have issue (i) Fiona Margaret Ruth **b.** 30 May 1972 (ii) Nichola Sheila Marion **b.** 24 Dec 1974 (iii) Gillian Lesley Claire **b.** 24 Jan 1977; 5. Hazel **b.** and **died** 1947; 6. Kenneth **b.** 1948 **m.** and has issue three children; 7. June **b.** 1953 **m.** …Wilkinson and have issue one child; 8. Hugh **b.** 1955 **m.** and has issue one child

Died 20 Feb 1973

FORSTER, ANDREW JAMES 1967–

b. 14 Jun 1967 Belfast; ed Sullivan Upper Sch Holywood Co Down; QUB BA (Hons) 1989; CITC BTh 1992;

d 1992 p 1993; C Willowfield (Down) 1992–95; Dean of Residence QUB 1995–2002; C of I Adv Downtown Radio Newtownards 1996–2002; R Drumcliffe w Lissadell and Munninane (Elph) 2002–; Archd of Elphin and Ardagh 2002–07; R Drumglass (Arm) 2007–

    s. of Thomas Victor Hetherington of Holywood (**s.** of Cecil and Jane) by Joan Eileen **dau.** of Roger and Alexandra Botley of London

    m. 28 Aug 1991 Knockbreda Par Ch Belfast Heather Michelle **dau.** of Charles and Vida Finch of Belfast. Issue 1. Hannah Niamh **b.** 11 Jul 1996; 2. Patrick Charles **b.** 13 May 1998; 3. Megan Rose **b.** 15 Mar 1999

FORSTER, EDWARD AUBREY 1871/72–1961

also appears as **AUBREY–FORSTER** in C I Dir

b. 1871 or 1872; TCD BA 1896

d 1900 p 1901 (Kilmore); C Kilkeevin (Elph) 1900–01; C Clonbroney and Killoe (Ard) 1901–03; C Clane (Kild) 1904–05; C Kilmeague (Kild) 1905–06; C Drung (Kilm) 1906–08; R Kilmore U (Elph) 1908–16; R Carrigallen (Kilm) 1916–21; ret Temp-in-c Drummully (Clogh) 1932–42

    m. Caroline Mabel (**died** 19 Jul 1944) **dau.** of Theophilus Lucas Clements of Rathkenny

    Died 23 Feb 1961 aged 89 **bur.** Drung

FORSTER, GEORGE 1770–1833

b. 1770 or 1771; Trinity Coll Ox matric 21 Feb 1787 aged 16; ent TCD 26 Jun 1787 aged 17 BA 1791 MA 1809

d 1794 p 1795 (Kilmore); C Drumgoon (Kilm) 1799–c. 1813; poss also C Drung and Larah (Kilm) 1799; C Thurles (Cash) 1813–33

    5th **s.** of Nicholas of Corderry, *armiger*

    m. (1) Louisa **dau.** of Theophilus Clements of Rakenny Co Cavan; no issue

    m. (2) Mary **dau.** of Rev Marmaduke Cramer, DD. Issue George Marmaduke

    Died 1833

FORSTER, JOHN

V Kinawley *c.* 1690–1712; R Killinagh (Kilm) *c.* 1704–12

FORSTER, WILLIAM 1863–1934

b. 1863; TCD BA 1889

d 1890 (Kilmore) p 1892 (Cashel); C Mohill (Ard) 1890–91; C Clonegam (Lism) 1891–94; R Ballymacward (Clonf) 1894–1920; ret; living in Guernsey from 1920

Died 31 Dec 1934

FORSYTH, ROBERT

TCD BA 1883 Div Test 1884 MA 1886

d 1884 p 1886 (Killaloe); C Creagh (Clonf) 1884–88; Dio C and Inspector of Schools, Dio Ossory 1888–93; C Tomregan (Kilm) 1893–96; V Waitara NZ (Dio Auckland) 1896–98; V Plumstead Cape of Good Hope (Dio Cape Town) 1919–22; went to live in Carlisle

FORTUNE, JOHN 1645/46–

b. 1645 or 1646 Lisnaskea Co Fermanagh; ed by Mr Fortune; ent TCD as Siz 10 Nov 1666 aged 20 Sch 1667

C Kildallon (Kilm) 1673; V Cannaway (Cork) 1683–90; C Dromdaleague U (Cork) 1684; V Kinneigh (Cork) 1690–91; V Fanlobbus (Cork) 1692–94; V Glenbarrahan 1695–1705; C Kilmacabea U (Ross) 1700

s. of George

†FOSTEN, ROBERT

a Franciscan, dispensed as son of a priest, was prov to the See of Elphin, with a faculty for his consecration on 14 Mar 1418 (C.P.L. VII. 18). It is not known if he got possession

FOSTER, FREDERICK 1840–1904

b. 19 Feb 1840 Clifden Co Galway; ed at Ballinasloe; TCD BA (Resp) 1863 Div Test 1864 MA 1877

d 1864 (Tuam) p 1866 (Kilmore); C Kilkeevin (Elph) 1865–66; C Templemichael (Ard) 1866–72; R Ardcarne (Elph) 1872–76; Preb of Terebrine (Elph) 1876; R Granard (Ard) 1876–85; R Ballymacelligott (A & A) 1885–1904

s. of Rev Mark, R Killedan (Ach)

m. 22 Oct 1867 Kate Letitia (**died** 14 Jul 1920 at 89 Moyne Rd Dublin aged 79) eldest **dau.** of Joshua Holt of Dublin. Issue including 1. Frederick Henry (**died** 14 Feb 1934 at Miami Florida) 2. Kathleen Mary **m.** 16 Apr 1895 John Frederick Mathers; 3. Lydia Wolseley

Died 29 Jan 1904

FOSTER, JOHN

perhaps same as J F matric Siz Queen's Coll Camb 1576, of Cambridgeshire BA 1580/81 MA from Peterhouse 1584

d; p 20 Sep 1587 (Lincoln); R Dembley (Linc) 1588–1614; R S Kelsey 1589–1600; V Hotoft 1600; V Wigtoft (Linc) 1602–04; Archd of Elphin & V Bumlin Kilmacumsy Kiltrustan Shankill & St Mary's Elphin (Elph) 1615–16

FOSTER, ROBERT

TCD BA 1865 Div Test (2) 1866

d 1867 p 1868 (Kilmore); C St Peter Athlone (Elph) 1867–79; C Downpatrick (Down) 1879–80; Chapl Royal Hib Military Sch Phoenix Park Dublin 1880–1902, V Upavon (Sarum) 1902–06; Last entry in Crockford 1906

m. Sarah (**died** 9 Mar 1912 aged 67 at Hangleton)

†FOSTER, WILLIAM 1744–1797

b. 1744; ed by Mr Norris at Drogheda; TCD BA 1765 MA 1767 DD 1789; was admitted to the Middle Temple 27 Apr 1765

V Trim and Rathcore (Meath) 1776–80; R & V Ardbraccan (Meath) 1770–80; R Urney (Derry) 1780–89; R Louth (Arm) 1781–89; Chapl to Irish House of Commons; consec Bp of Cork and Ross in St Peter's Ch Dublin 14 Jun 1789; Bp of Cork and Ross 1789–90; Bp of Kilmore 1790–96; Bp of Clogher 1796–97

2nd **s.** of Anthony, Chief Baron of the Exchequer, Ireland; **bro.** of Lord Oriel, last Speaker of the Irish House of Commons

m. Catherine Letitia (**died** 23 Nov 1814 aged 57 **bur.** Dunleer Co Louth) **dau.** of Rev Henry Leslie DD, Preb of Ballymore (Arm) 1759–1803. Issue **sons** 1. John Leslie TCD LLB 1810 MP for Dublin University Judge of CP; 2. Rev William Henry (**died** 14 Dec 1861 aged 66), R Loughgilly (Arm) 1842–61 **m.** Catherine **dau.** of James Hamilton of Brown Hall Co Donegal and had issue (i) William John **b.** 1831 died 1909 Judge of the Supreme Court NSW; (ii) Arthur Hamilton, JP, St Ernan's Co Donegal; **daus.** 1. Catherine **m.** William Drummond Delap and had issue Robert Foster; 2. Anne **m.** Jonas Stawell and had issue Sir William Foster, Chief Justice Supreme Court Victoria; 3. Henrietta **m.** Jerome, Count de Salis; 4. Elizabeth **m.** Rev James M'Creight, R Keady (Arm); 5. Letitia **m.** John Henry North, KC MP for Dublin University

Died Nov 1797

FOWLER, ALBERT CHARLES c. 1847–1931

b. c. 1847; Univ of Durham BD 1897

d 1870 p 1871 (Kilmore); C Bailieborough and Moybologue (Kilm) 1870–73; C Christ Ch Liverpool (Liv) 1873–74; C Holy Trinity Leicester (Leic — then Pet) 1874–75; R Newtownhamilton (Arm) 1875–79; R Killeavy (Arm) 1879–81; Chapl Miss to Seamen for River Liffey (Dub) 1881–99

s. of James, Scripture Reader of Dun Laoghaire Co Dublin

m. (1) 1 Jan 1867 Monkstown Par Ch Dublin Mary Jane (**died** 19 Mar 1868) **dau.** of George Chrystal of Dun Laoghaire. Issue Mary Jane (**died** 15 Mar 1868)

m. (2) 1 Sep 1874 St Peter's Ch Dublin Charlotte Elizabeth (**died** 4 Feb 1947) **dau.** of Rev Thomas Robinson, DD, R Kilmainhamwood (Meath). Issue 1. Rev James Robinson (**died** Sep 1952) **b.** 18 Jun 1875 Newtownhamilton Rectory Co Armagh TCD BA 1899 MA 1920 d 1901 p 1902 C St Mark Marylebone (Lon) 1901–03 C Christ Ch St Marylebone (Lon) 1904–07 teaching in Mauritius 1908–28 C Quatre Bornes w Reduit (Dio Mauritius) 1928–31 Lic to Off Dio Bloemfontein 1931–48 and Dio Cape Town 1948–52; 2. Rev Albert Robinson, C St John Sligo (Elph) qv; 3. Robert **b.** 4 Oct 1880 at Killeavy

Died 5 Feb 1931

FOWLER, ALBERT ROBINSON 1877–1956

b. 17 Jan 1877 Bailieborough Co Cavan; ed Rathmines Sch Dublin; TCD Wall Bibl Sch & BA 1907 Downes Pri & MA 1911 Div Test 1912

d 1912 p 1914 (Kilmore); C St John Sligo (Elph) 1912–15; C St Stephen (Dub) 1915–16; TCF 1916–21; Hon CF 1921; C River w Guston and Temple Ewell (Cant) 1925–27; Perm to Off at St Marylebone (Lon) 1927–31; Perm to Off Frimley (Guildf) 1931–32; C St Jude Blackburn (Blackb) 1932–33; R Heveningham (St E) 1937–49

s. of Rev Albert Charles, C Bailieborough 1870–73 qv (**s.** of James) by his 2nd wife Charlotte Elizabeth; **bro.** of Rev James, in Mauritius from 1908

Died 18 Aug 1956 Worlington Suffolk

FOX, CHARLES MAXWELL 1827/28–

b. 1827 or 1828 Co Fermanagh; ed by Dr Graham; ent TCD 1 Jul 1844 aged 16 BA & Div Test 1850

C Kinawley (Kilm) 1850–62

s. of Rev John James, R Kinawley (Kilm) qv (**s.** of Richard) by Harriet Louisa **dau.** of Rev Charles Cobbe Beresford

m. Wilhelmina Banks and had issue

FOX, FRANCIS 1788–1834

b. 1788; Univ Coll Ox matric 20 Jun 1807 aged 18 BA 1811; TCD MA 1816

d 1812 p 1813; R Raheny (Dub) 1814–21; R Castleterra (Kilm) 1821–34

eldest **s.** of Richard of Dublin and Foxhall Co Longford, *armiger*, by Anne **dau.** of 1st Earl of Farnham; nephew of Lord Farnham

m. 1813 Frances **dau.** of Rev Jemmett Browne, DD of Riverstown Co Cork by Frances **dau.** of Arthur Blennerhassett of Ballyseedy. Issue 1. Richard Maxwell of Foxhall; 2. John James Barry; 3. Jemmett George; 5 daus

Died 2 Sep 1834 aged 46

FOX, JOHN JAMES 1792–1870

b. 30 May 1792; ed by Mr Craig; ent TCD as SC 2 Nov 1807 BA 1811 MA 1821

d 1815 p; V Kinawley (Kilm) 1822–70

>4th **s.** of Richard of Fox Hall Co Longford by Lady Anne Maxwell **dau.** of Barry, Earl of Farnham
>
>**m.** 15 Feb 1825 Harriet Louisa **dau.** of Rev Charles Cobbe Beresford. Issue **sons** 1. Willoughby George **b.** 1827 **m.** and had issue; 2. Rev Charles Maxwell, C Kinawley qv; 3. Henry John; 4. Francis Robert (**died** 12 Apr 1864 Bangalore) Lt 14 Madras Light Infantry; 5. Frederick; 6. Barry John George; **daus.** 1. Emily Grace (**died** 13 Oct 1885 Dublin) **m.** John Edward Thompson, JP of Co Longford; 2. Charlotte Sylvia; 3. Harriet Elizabeth **m.** 29 Dec 1869 at Granard Ch Francis Hercules Knox of Co Sligo
>
>**Died** 16 Mar 1870

FOX, MATTHEW 1803/04–1843

b. 1803 or 1804 Co Meath; ed by Mr Hamilton; ent TCD 15 Oct 1821 aged 17 BA 1826 MA 1834

C Killinkere (Kilm) 1828; was "of Moyallen, Co Down" when appointed C Clonard (Meath) 1836; V Galtrim (Meath) 1838–43

>prob Matthew Maine Fox eldest **s.** of James of Foxbrook Co Meath
>
>**m.** Ellen Armstrong (**died** 1845) of Kilclare King's Co (Offaly). Issue only **s.** James George Hubert of Kilcourney **m.** 14 Nov 1865 at Rathconrath Co Meath Elizabeth Amelia Lilian yst **dau.** of Rev J Brabazon Grant, R Rathconrath (Meath)
>
>in Miss Willis' MS, there is a note that Rev Matthew Maine Fox **m.** (?1) St Mary's Dublin 6 Sep 1832 Hannah eldest **dau.** of William Boyce of Moyally Co Down
>
>**Died** 1843

FOX, TREVOR 1823/24–1848

b. 1823 or 1824

C Killyon (Elph) to 1848

>**Died** 28 Feb 1848 aged 24

FOX, WILLIAM 1741/42–1780

b. 1741 or 1742 Co Leitrim; ed by Rev Mr Hynes; ent TCD as Siz 23 May 1758 aged 16 Sch 1760 BA 1762 LLB 1769

C Kinawley and Cloonclare (Kilm)–1766; C Kilmore (Kilm) 1770–c. 74; joint V Gen Kilmore with Ven Arthur Moore qv 1772; V Denn (Kilm) 1776–80

>**s.** of Michael
>
>**m.** Oct 1768 Elizabeth Sophia **dau.** of Ven Arthur Moore, Archd of Kilmore qv Issue **sons** 1 Frances bapt 15 Jul 1769 at Denn; 2. Mary bapt 25 May 1770 at Denn; 3. George Moore bapt 3 Feb 1774 at Kilmore; 4. William of Summerhill Dublin, Attorney at Law bapt 21 Apr 1775 at Denn **m.** (ML 15 Mar 1803) Martha

only child of John Young of Corlismore Co Cavan; 5. Arthur Johnston bapt 21 Jul 1776 at Denn; 6. Michael bapt 25 Jun 1778 at Denn; 7. Peter bapt 15 May 1779 at Denn

Died 1780

FRACKLETON, SAMUEL SCOTT 1830–1911

b. 23 Jun 1830 Co Down; TCD BA & Div Test (2) 1856 MA 1858

d 30 Nov 1856 (Down) p 30 Sep 1857 (Kilm); C Bailieborough (Kilm) 1857–58; C All SS Liverpool (Liv) 1858–59; R Magherahamlet (Drom) 1859–81; R Tamlaght O'Crilly Lr (Derry) 1881–1911

s. of John of Clarendon Place Belfast

m. (1) 5 Nov 1860 Holywood Co Down Mary (**died** 5 Jul 1865) **dau.** of J M'Cutcheon of Holywood

m. (2) 30 Aug 1870 Magherahamlet Ch Elizabeth Baxter (**died** 24 Aug 1914 aged 91) yst **dau.** of James Boyde of Moybrick Dromara Co Down

Died 29 Jul 1911

FRANKLIN, HERBERT H –1875

BA

C Ballyjamesduff (Kilm) 1860; Chapl RN in 1865

Died 10 Aug 1875

FRANKLIN, J

C Castlerahan (Kilm) 1869–71 (C I Dir); may be confused with H H Franklin qv

FRANKS, JAMES SMYTH 1805/06–

b. 1805 or 1806 Cork; ed by Mr Coghlan; ent TCD 18 Oct 1824 aged 18 BA 1832

d 21 Dec 1844 (Ossory for Kilmore) p; C Rossinver (Kilm) 1845–49; C St Thomas Dublin (Dub) 1849–52; C Kilconnell (Clonf) 1852–57; C Clonelty (Lim) 1858–59; C Newtownards (Down) 1860–62; C Donaghady (Derry) 1862–63; C Drakestown (Meath) 1863; C Crossmolina (Killala) 1864; C Donacavey (Clogh) 1866–68; C Seagoe (Drom) 1868; C Kildress (Arm) 1868–69; C Drakestown (Meath) 1873–74

s. of Charles, solicitor (**s.** of Henry of Moorestown Co Limerick) by Elizabeth (*née* Atkins)

FRASER, WALTER

adm V Carrigallen (Kilm) 29 Mar 1639; is V in 1647 and residing in Dublin (Carte Papers, xxi. 346)

FRASOR, THOMAS

adm R Drumgoon (Kilm) 23 Jan 1629

FRAZER, WILLIAM HENRY –1906

TCD BA 1868 MA 1871 BD & DD 1889

d 1869 (Tuam) p 12 Jun 1870 (Down); C Croaghan and Creeve (Elph) 1869–70; C Kilkenny (Oss) 1870–74; Chapl Mt Jerome Cemetery (Dub) 1874–76; C St Jude Gray's Inn Road (Lon) 1877–79; Asst Chapl at St Petersburg Russia 1879–80; Chapl at Seville 1882–84; C East Brent (B & W) 1887–88; Chapl at Ostend 1889–91; Acting CF 1899–1901; served with troops in S Africa

Died Jan 1906

FREEMAN, WILLIAM

pres to the Preb = R of Baslick (Elph) by the Crown 27 Feb 1637/38

FRENCH, JAMES ALLAN   1850/51–1935

b. 1850 or 1851

d 1875 p 1876 (Kilmore); C Killasnett (Kilm) 1875–77; C St John Sligo (Elph) 1877–79; R Drumcliffe (Elph) 1879–88; Preb of Kilmacallen (Elph) 1886–1934; R Bumlin w Strokestown and Kilglass (Elph) 1888–1934; ret

s. of John, Commissioner of Dacca

m. Anna Penrose of Cork (**died** 15 Aug 1921). Issue 1. Elsie May (**died** 8 Jan 1963 Cheltenham aged 69) TCD BA (Hons Hist 1915); 2. Edith de Vere (**died** 22 Feb 1957) **m.** 25 Jul 1912 William Boxwell, MD; 3. Dorothy (**died** 24 Jan 1945 Stockport); 4. Marjorie (**died** 22 Nov 1944 Belfast) **m.** J A Glen

Died 9 Apr 1935 aged 84

FRENCH, JOHN   1769/70–1848

b. 1769 or 1770 Co Roscommon; ed by Mr French; ent TCD 7 Nov 1787 BA 1790 Dean of Elphin 1797–1848; R Athy (Glend) 1812–48

2nd **s.** of Arthur of French Park Co Roscommon

m. Emily **dau.** of Richard Magennis of Waringstown Co Down. Issue Rev John, C Castleblakeney (Elph) qv

Died 14 Feb 1848 aged 78

FRENCH, JOHN

C Ardcarne (Elph) in 1806

FRENCH, JOHN   1815/16–1890

b. 1815 or 1816 **b.** Co Roscommon ent TCD 6 Jul 1829 BA 1833

C Achill (Tuam) in 1844; C Kilmore Erris (Killala) *c.* 1843; C Castleblakeney (Elph) *c.* 1859

s. of Very Rev John, Dean of Elphin, qv (**s.** of Arthur) by Emily

Died 29 Jul 1890 aged 74

FRENCH, WILLIAM
V Ballysumaghan (Elph) to 1766; same as below?

FRENCH, WILLIAM 1707–1785
b. 1707 Frenchpark Co Roscommon: ed by Mr Jackson at Mt Temple; ent TCD 26 Sep 1723 aged 16 BA 1728 MA 1731

Preb of Termonbarry (Elph) 1730–31; Preb of Kilgoghlin (Elph) 1731–52; VGen Elphin 1741; R Ardcarne (Elph) 1743–*c.* 52; prob same as W F, R Boyle (Elph) to 1766; Prec Elphin 1752–85; pres to the Deanery of Ardagh 20 Oct 1769 (L.M. V. 169) and inst. 8 Nov 1769 (F.F.) Dean of Ardagh 1769–85; Preb of Tibohine (Elph) 1771–85

yst **s.** of Col John

m. Arabella Frances (ML 22 Jan 1732) **dau.** of Very Rev Jeremy Marsh, Dean of Kilmore qv Issue 1. Robert James MD **b.** 28 Mar 1796 **m.** Anne **dau.** of Richard Wolfe (he **died** 2 Mar 1853); 2. Rev William, R Tibohine (Elph) qv; 3. Richard; 4. Anne **m.** 1776 Major Holt Waring; 5 Frances **m.** 9 Dec 1763 Brockhill Newburgh JP of Ballyhaise Co Cavan; 6. Arabella; 7. Harriet **m.** 5 Mar 1821 Matthew Brinkley 2nd **s.** of Rt Rev John Brinkley, Bp of Cloyne.

Died 16 Jan 1785 aged 77 **bur.** St Michan's Ch Dublin

FRENCH, WILLIAM
d 14 Mar 1803 p 24 Aug 1804; C Fuerty (Elph) 1804; prob same as below

FRENCH, WILLIAM   –1863
MA in Cotton?

V & Preb of Tibohine (Elph) 1819–63

2nd **s.** of Very Rev William, Dean of Ardagh qv by Arabella Frances

Died 5 Feb 1863 **unm.**

FRERE, ANDREW
is pres by the Crown to the R of Ardcarne (Elph) 2 Jul 1639. (L.M. V. 113); was prob also V

FRITH, JOHN 1787/88–?1850
b. 1787 or 1788 Co Fermanagh; ed by Dr Burrowes; ent TCD 4 Nov 1805 aged 17 BA 1812

C Carnew (Ferns) 1816–37; Preb of Tecolme (Leigh) 1837–43; R Tomregan (Kilm) 1843–c50

s. of James, *ingenuus*

m. 1823 Letitia Purdon. Issue incl 1. James **b.** Co Wicklow ed Cavan Sch ent TCD 3 Jul 1843 aged 17 BA 1848; 2. elder **dau.** Anne (**died** 24 May 1894 Enniskillen)

? **Died** 1850

FRY, GEORGE ERNEST 1876/77–1939

b. 1876 or 1877; TCD BA 1899 Div Test 1900 MA 1902

d 1900 p 1901 (Kilmore); C Lurgan (Kilm) 1900–07; R St John's Cloverhill (Kilm) 1907–09; R Slane (Meath) 1909–27; R Julianstown (Meath) 1927–39

Died 24 Sep 1939 **unm.** aged 62

FRY, HENRY 1820–

b. 1820 Co Roscommon; TCD BA 1842 Div Test 1843

d 1843 p; C Achonry (Ach) 1843–44; C Castlecarberry (Kild) 1845–54; C Boyle (Elph) 1868–81

    s. of Henry, gentleman

FRY, WILLIAM BAKER 1824–1913

b. 1824 King's Co (Offaly); ent TCD 7 Dec 1846 aged 22 BA & Div Test 1852 MA 1866

d 1852 (Cork) p 1853 (Meath); C Toomna (Elph) 1852–60; C Boyle (Elph) 1856–60 (in Leslie's MSS but not Crockford); C Kilkeevan (Elph) 1853–63 (C I Dir); C St Bartholomew London (Lon) 1864–67; C Edge Hill (Liv) 1867–69; V Turnditch (Derby — then S'well) 1870–73; R Templederry (Killaloe) 1873–79; R Rathdowney (Oss) 1879–1903; ret

    s. of William, R Kilruane (Killaloe) **s.** of Henry of Co Roscommon

    m. 20 Oct 1863 Holy Innocents' Ch Liverpool Elizabeth Mary yst **dau.** of Golding Bird. Issue incl 1. Canon William Robert (**died** May 1949) **b.** 8 Aug 1867 Liverpool TCD BA & Div Test 1890 MA 1908 d 1890 p 1891 (Ossory) C Maryborough (Leigh) 1890–92 C Rathdowney (Oss) 1892–96 R Horetown (Ferns) 1896–99 R Toombe (Ferns) 1899–1901 R Newtownbarry (Ferns) 1901–40 Preb of Kilrane and Taghmon (Ferns) 1914–30 Treas of Ferns 1930–34 Prec of Ferns 1934–40 **m.** 10 Jan 1894 Clontarf Par Ch Dublin Dorothea Gordon eldest **dau.** of William A Hunter of Clontarf; 2. Rev Golding Maddison (**died** 20 Oct 1937) **b.** 22 Dec 1869 TCD (1cl Mod Hist) 1887 BA 1892 Div Test 1893 MA 1914 d 30 May 1896 (Ossory) p 10 Jun 1897 (Dublin for Ossory) C Rathdowney (Oss) 1896–1903 R Ballycarney (Ferns) 1903–09 R Bannow w Duncormick (Ferns) 1909–29 C-in-c Preban w Moyne (Ferns) 1929–31 R Ballymackey (Killaloe) 1931– 37 **m.** 20 Jan 1904 Hannah Hilda Cochrane

Died 12 Dec 1913 aged 89

FULLERTON, ROBERT or possibly JOHN

d; p 1636 (V.B. 1673)

coll V Tassinine = Tashinny and Kildacommick = Kilcommick (Ard) 1661 (F.F.), and in 1674 was coll R & V Toghsenny, Kildecamoge and V Shrewer & Abbeyshrule (Ard) (F.F.)

MS reads "J...hes" ? Johannes but may be "Robertus"

FULLERTON, ROBERT

coll V Shrower = Shrule & Abbeyshrule (Ard) 6 Jun 1674; (same as above or perhaps his son?)

FURLONG, EDWARD –1953

TCD BA & Div Test 1909

d 1909 p 1910 (Oss); C Carlow (Leigh) 1909–13; C-in-c Eglish (Meath) 1913–17; R Innismagrath (Kilm) 1917; R Killinagh (Kilm) 1917–25; R Granard and Abbeylara (Ard) 1925–33; R Boyle (Elph) 1933–38; R Croghan and Tibohine (w C-in-c Ardcarne 1949–53) (Elph) 1938–53; Preb of Oran (Elph) 1945–53

> **m.** Margaret Grundy (**died** 13 Aug 1971 **bur.** at Boyle Co Roscommon). Issue 1. Dr H Furlong of Athlone; 2. Godfrey B, MA
>
> **Died** 29 Jul 1953

FUSSELL, THOMAS WALTON

St Bee's Coll Durham 1868

d 1869 (York) p 1870 (Dublin); C St Hilda Middlesborough (York) 1869–71; Sen C St Philip Sheffield (Sheff — then York) 1871–74; C Gt Berkhamsted (St A) 1875; C Drumgoon (Kilm) 1875–77; R Swanlinbar (Kilm) 1877–80; Chapl in Plymouth Waters 1881–84; Chapl Royal Albert Hosp Devonport (Ex) 1884

> **m.** 1871 a **dau.** of Col William Mauleverer. Issue William M

GABBETT, EDWARD 1831–1912

b. 14 Jan 1831 Dublin; ed by Mr Flynn; ent TCD 14 Jan 1848 BA 1852 MA 1855 Div Test 1856; ent Lincoln's Inn 1851

d 1856 p 1858; C Denn (Kilm) 1856–60; C Collon (Arm) 1861–63; C Kilmore and Grange O'Neiland *alias* Diamond (Arm) 1863–67; PC Diamond (Arm)1867–69; V Bruree (Lim) 1869–72; R Croom (Lim) 1872–1912; Treas of Limerick 1883–91; Chanc of Limerick 1891–1904; Archd of Limerick 1904–12

> 4th **s.** of Joseph, Barrister-at-Law of Dublin by Mary (née Litton)
>
> **m.** 28 Apr 1864 Grange Par Ch Co Armagh Ellen Frances **dau.** of Rev Cecil Smyly, BA, R Grange (Arm). Issue 1. Edward **m.** a **dau.** of Lt Col Richard J Knox of Ballytobin Co Kilkenny; 2. Michael **b.** 22 Aug 1872
>
> **Died** 16 Apr 1912

GAGGIN, JOHN RICHARD 1820–1894

b. 1820 Co Cork; ed by Mr Hodgens; TCD BA 1841

d & p 1875 (Kilmore); C Denn (Kilm) 1875–77; R Killoe (Ard) 1876–79; R Rathronan and Newchapel (Lism) 1881–94

> **s.** of Rev Richard, R Clonmult (Cloyne) by Catherine Foulke
>
> **Died** 14 Dec 1894

GAHAGAN, JOHN RICHARD 1855/56–1919

b. 1855 or 1856; RUI BA 1888; TCD Div Test (2) 1890

d 1890 p 1891 (Kilmore); C Drumlease (Kilm) 1890–97; R Kiltyclogher and Ballaghmeehan (Kilm) 1897–1902; R Rossinver (Kilm) 1902–09; R Athleague (Elph) 1909–19

    elder **s.** of John R (**died** 13 Oct 1911), Solicitor of Dublin

    m. 12 Jun 1918 Rathfarnham Par Ch Dublin Catherine R **dau.** of George Doherty. Issue incl **s.** James Henry

    Died Aug 1919 aged 63

GALBRAITH, GEORGE 1829–1911

b. 1829; ed Portora Royal Sch Enniskillen; ent TCD 6 Nov 1845 aged 16 BA and Div Test (1) 1850 MA 1864

d 1852 (Tuam) p 1854 (Kilmore); C Kilglass (Ard) 1852–63; C Kilcommick (Ard) 1863–67; R Cumber Lr (Derry) 1867–83; R Drumachose and Aghanloo, Limavady (Derry) 1883–1904; Canon of Derry 1891–1901; Dean of Derry 1901–04

    4th **s.** of Samuel, JP of Clanabogan Omagh Co Tyrone

    m. 4 Aug 1874 Florence Acheson yst **dau.** of Acheson Lyle, HML, The Oaks Londonderry. Issue 1. Major Samuel Harold Lyle **m.** 18 Aug 1915 Helen Mary **dau.** of Rev Canon W Graham Murphy DD of Grange Armagh; 2. Col James Ponsonby, RE; 3. Eleanor **m.** Rev Thomas Walter Benson, R Clanabogan (Derry) 1903–32

    Died 3 Oct 1911

GALBRAITH, JOHN 1820–1892

b. 8 Dec 1820 Co Roscommon; ent TCD 1 Jul 1837 BA 1842

d 1843 p 1844 (Waterford); C Ballintemple (Cash) 1843; C Lynally (Meath) 1845; C Kanturk (Cloyne) 1847; PC Kanturk (Cloyne) 1852–67; R Clonmeen (Cloyne) 1869–79; C Mallow (Cloyne) 1879–82; C St Catherine (Dub) 1882–84; R Knocknarea (Elph) 1884–92

    s. of Capt William, RIA

    m. Mary 2nd **dau.** of Thomas Connell of Cork and had issue

    Died 23 Dec 1892

GALLAGHER, IAN 1954–

b. 1954; TCD BTh 1990

d 1990 p 1991; C Annagh w Drumgoon and Ashfield (Kilm) 1990–93; R Drumcliffe w Lisadell and Munninane (Elph) 1993–2001; Preb of Kilmacallen (Elph) 1997–2001; Dio Sec Elphin and Ardagh 1997–2001; Preb of Mulhuddart in St Patrick's Cath Dublin 1998–2001; R Stillorgan and Blackrock (Dub) 2001–.

    m. 1977 Hilary **dau.** of Edgar and Isobel Johnston. Issue 1. Brian **b.** 1982; 2. James **b.** 1984

GALLAGHER, OWEN 1749/50–1827

b. 1749 or 1750 Co Leitrim; ed by Mr Kenny; ent TCD 9 Jul 1770 Sch 1773 BA 1775

R Castleblakeney Killyon and Kilronan (Elph) 1799–1811; R Kilmaine and Killenvoy (Elph) 1811–27

> **s.** of Matthew
>
> **m.** Catherine (**died** 23 Oct 1843 aged 86 Dublin) and had issue incl Matthew **b.** Co Roscommon ent TCD 20 May 1814 aged 14 BA 1821
>
> **Died** 9 Nov 1827 aged 77 **bur.** Kilmaine Churchyard

GAMBLE, WILLIAM –1959

TCD BA 1908 Div Test (1) 1909 MA 1911 LLB 1921 LLD 1925

d 1909 p 1910 (Kilmore); C Kinawley (Kilm) 1909–14; R Killoughter (w St John Cloverhill from 1931) (Kilm) 1914–57; Preb of Annagh (Kilm) 1956–57; ret

> **Died** 24 May 1959 at Clones Co Monaghan

PUBLICATIONS
> *Irish Antiquities and Archaeology*
> *Irish Poets*
> *William Bedell*
> *Irish Lakes*
> *History of Killoughter Parish*
> *Clonmacnoise*

GARDNER, ARTHUR 1706/07–

b. 1706 or 1707 Tulsk Co Roscommon; ed by Mr Neligan, Longford; ent TCD 8 Jun 1726 aged 19 BA 1730 MA 1743

d; p 1 Sep 1739; C Rathcline (Ard) 1766; he signs Parl Ret 1766 as C Templemichael (Ard); he was surrogate to John Ryder, R Templemichael (Ard) and V Gen of Ardagh 25 Jun 1761

> **s.** of Gilbert

GARRETT, HENRY 1813–1838

b. 1813 Co Sligo; ed at Carlow Sch; TCD BA 1834

C Fenagh (Ard) 1836–37; C Drumshambo (Ard) Mar–Oct 1837; C Carlow (Leigh) 1837–38

> **s.** of Rev John
>
> **Died** of fever Jul 1838

GARRETT, RICHARD 1706/07–69

b. 1706 or 1707 Athlone; ed by Mr Thewles at Athlone; ent TCD 1 Jun 1727 aged 20 Sch 1729 BA 1731

d ord p 3 Sep 1739; lic C Cong Roslee and Ballincholla (Tuam) 17 May 1739 @ £25 a year; C Killererin and Knockmoy (Tuam) 3 Dec 1739; V Kilmean Ivernon & Porterin (Elph) 1742; perhaps also held Killenvoy (Elph) from 1742; appears V Bumlin Kiltrustan & Lisonuffy (Elph) 1745–69

s. of Richard, tax collector

Died Feb 1769

GARRETT, WILLIAM EDWARD RICHARD 1929–1995

b. 1929

d 17 Dec 1967 (Kilm) p 1968; C Drumlease Killenumery and Killargue (Kilm) 1967–69 and R 1969–71; R Kildallon w Newtowngore and Corrawallen (Kilm) 1972–75; R Bailieborough w Knockbride Shercock and Mullagh 1975–88; Preb of Drumlease (Kilm) 1987–88; R Boyle Aghanagh Kilbryan Ardcarne & Croghan (Elph) 1988–95; Preb of Terebrine (Elphin and Ardagh) 1991–95

only s. of W B Garrett of Blackrock

m. 1 Sep 1961 St Ann's Par Ch Dublin Oonagh eldest dau. of Rev Canon Ernest George Daunt, R St Ann (Dub) 1953–62 and Elizabeth Emma (née McBride). Issue 1. Jonathan; 2. Simon; 3. Timothy Patrick b. 18 Mar 1967

Died 30 Mar 1995

GARSTIN, NORMAN   –1830

ent TCD 3 Nov 1790 BA 1795 MA 1832

d 1795 p 22 Dec 1799 (Kilm); lic C Castlerahan (Kilm) 31 Oct 1799; is C Annagh (Kilm) at the induction of Rev Richard Wynne, R Annagh qv 1811; Preb of Kilpeacon (Lim) 1814–22; res for colonial Chaplaincy in Ceylon

s. of Anthony (died 1782) JP of Braganstown Co Louth

m. Elizabeth sister of Major Boyd, 4th Dragoons. Issue 1. Rev Norman, DD, Colonial Chapl; 2. Anthony, Chapl HEICS; 3. William, Col 83rd Regt m. dau. of Rev Matthew Moore, Caherconlish (Lim); 4. Christopher; 7 daus.

Died 1830

†GARVEY, JOHN 1527–1595

b. 1527 Kilkenny; Univ of Oxford BA

Dean of Ferns 1558–59; Archd of Meath 1559–95; Preb of Tipperkevin in St Patrick's Cath Dublin 1561–85; Dean of Christ Ch Cath Dublin 1565–95; Chapl to the Earl of Sussex 1567; Privy Counsellor 1576; was raised to the See of Kilmore by Letters Patent 27 Jan 1584/85, and Queen's Letter for his consecration was issued on 20 Jan (Morrin ii. 91). He was allowed his Archdeaconry of Meath and Deanery of Christ Church Dublin *in commendam*. Bp of Kilmore 1585–89; He is named on a Commission 7 Feb 1588 (ib. ii. 145), and was translated to the Primacy in 1590. Abp of Armagh 1590–95.

s. of John of Morrisk Co Mayo

m. Rose, widow of Thomas Ussher and sister of Abp Ussher. Issue incl 1. William who was granted lands at Clontibret Co Monaghan 29 dec 1592; 2. Anthony ent

Univ of Oxford 11 Jan 1593/94 aged 18; 3. Christopher

Died 2 Mar 1595 Dublin **bur.** Christ Church Cath Dublin

PUBLICATION

The Conversion of Philip Curwen, a Franciscan Friar, to the Reformation of the Protestant Religion, 1589; published by Robert Ware 1681 — may be a forgery by Ware!

GAWIN (GAWINE, GAWYNE, GWIN), THOMAS

MA

V Drimtemple (Elph) & V Roscommon (Elph) 1615; is V Athleague (Elph) 1616

GAYER, HENRY WILLIAM 1835–1905

b. 1835 Dublin; ed by Mr Hartshorne; TCD BA (Jun Mod Hist & Eng Lit) 1858 Div Test 1859

d 1859 p 1860 (Meath for Dublin); C Rathdrum (Glend) 1859–63; C Killeshandra (Kilm) 1863–64; C St Bride Liverpool (Liv) 1864–65; C Cucklington (B & W) 1865–67; C Marston Magna (B & W) 1867–70; C Frodsham (Ches) 1870–73; V Ballynaclash (Glend) 1873–79; R Coolock (Dub) 1879–83; R Newcastle (Glend) 1883–1901; Canon of Christ Ch Cath Dublin 1894–1901; ret

s. of Arthur Edward, QC of Salerno Co Dublin

m. 19 Jun 1865 Walton-on-the-Hill Lancs Charlotte Adelaide **dau.** of Francis R Fetherston-Haugh

Died 8 Feb 1905

PUBLICATION

Strengthened with Power through His Spirit (Eph. 3 v 16), Marshall Bros, London

GELASIUS, Sir…

R Regles, parish Ch of Cluain (Cloone) (Ard) on appointment 1407 (Cal Reg Flem No 57); was deprived without due trial and as Andrew McQuickan had obtained it surreptitiously from the Pope, the Primate restored Gelasius

GERARD, WILEY

lic C Lavey (Kilm) 22 Dec 1836

GIBBINGS, THOMAS SANDES

TCD Sch 1891 BA (Sen Mod Classics) 1892 BD 1900

d 1897 p 1898; C Mohill (Ard) 1897–99; C Wicklow (Glend) 1899–1901; C Tralee (A & A) 1901–05; R Lismalin (Cash) 1905–07; last entry in C I Dir 1907

GIBBS, WALTER 1805/06

b. 1805 or 1806 Dublin; ed by Mr Leney; ent TCD 18 Oct 1824 aged 18 BA 1829 MA 1833

V Bumlin (Elph) 1830–c. 35

? Walter Carmichael, s. of George, Lawyer

GIBSON, HENRY 1789/90–1857

b. 1789 or 1790 Waterford; ed by Mr White; ent TCD 2 Jan 1815 aged 25 BA 1818 MA 1832

C Kentstown (Meath) 1826; C Lurgan and Munterconnaught (Kilm) 1829–47; may have been V Killinagh (Kilm) 1857–c61

s. of John, architect

m. and had issue Lydia (**died** 22 Mar 1880 Pembroke Rd Dublin)

Died 22 Sep 1857

GIBSON, ROBERT WILLIAM 1866/67–1946

b. 1866 or 1867; RUI BA 1898; TCD BA 1903

d 1902 p 1903 (Manchester); C St James Heywood (Manch) 1902–06; R Drumreilly (Kilm) 1906–08; R Derrylane (Kilm) 1908–11; R Kildrumferton (w C-in-c Ballymachugh from 1923) (Kilm) 1911–31; C–in c Ballysumaghan & Killery 1931–46

m. Mary Jane (née Boyce) and had issue incl 1. Eileen **m**... Taylor; 2. Rev George Francis (**died** 16 Apr 1978) **b.** 12 Jun 1898 Dublin TCD BA & Div Test 1928 MA 1931 d 1928 (Down for Armagh) p 1929 (Armagh) C Dundalk (Arm) 1928–31 C Wexford (Ferns) 1931–33 I Ballyfin (Leigh) 1933–35 I Fertagh (Oss) 1935–38 I Lickmolassy & Ballynakill (Clonf) 1938–42 I Killaloan U (Lism) 1942–55 I Clonmel U (Lism) 1955–60 Canon and Treas of Waterford Cath & Preb of Rossduff (Waterf) 1956–60 I Clonfad U (Meath) 1960–67 ret; **m.** 17 Jan 1930 Elizabeth Susan (**died** 16 Jul 1992) **dau.** of John Henry Robinson MA of Dublin and had issue (i) Dorothy Mary **b.** 29 Mar 1933 (ii) Enid Frances **b.** 29 Jun 1937

Died 12 Jun 1946 aged 79 **bur.** Mt Jerome Dublin

GIFF, WILLIAM LEE MATHER 1900–1986

b. 1900; QUB BSc 1925 MSc 1927; London Coll of Divinity 1925

d 1927 p 1928 (Southwark); C St Thomas Telford Pk Streatham (S'wark) 1927–29; CMS Missy Dio Upr Nile Uganda 1929–34; C-in-c Dowra and Innismagrath (Kilm) 1934–35; R Ballysodare U (Ach) 1935–47; Exam Chapl to Bp of Tuam 1946–48; Supt ICM & Chapl Mission Ch Townsend St Dublin (Dub) 1947–51; BC Rathmolyon w Laracor (Meath) 1951–52; R Clara (Meath) 1952–65; Exam Chapl to Bp of Meath 1957–69; Canon of Meath 1958–69; Preb of Tassagard in St Patrick's Cath Dublin 1959–69; RD of Ardnurcher and Clonmacnoise 1960–64; Archd of Meath 1964–69; R Killucan (Meath) 1965–69; ret

m. Agnes Hoy. Issue 1. Peter John Alan; 2. Gladys May **m.** 4 Dec 1954 Clara Par Ch Co Offaly Rev John Ormsby Rolston, Archd of Connor 1988–96 and had issue David **b.** 21 Feb 1961 **m.** 20 Apr 1985 Vernice McCarthy of Belfast

Died 11 May 1986

GILBERT

is Treasurer of Elphin at the election of John O'Hugroin as Bp of Elphin in 1245 (C.P.L. I. 218)

GILES, WILLIAM HENRY 1854/55–1925

TCD BA 1888

d 1888 (Clogher for Kilmore) p 1889 (Kilmore); C Mohill (Ard) 1888–90; C Fahan Upr (Raph — then Derry) 1890–91; R Ballyscullion (Derry) 1891–94; R Killowen (Derry) 1894–1923; ret

> Died 4 Jun 1925 aged 70

GILLICE (GILLIS), WILLIAM

MA

is Commonwealth Minister at Kildallon (Kilm) from 29 Sep 1656 at £60; is suspected of "scandal & insufficiency", 11 Apr 1659 (Seymour's MSS pp 15, 94, 167); is still Minister 1660 (ib. 122); seems to have been on the tithes of Killan and Knockbride (Kilm) in 1660; was V Killan (Kilm) 1661–62 but did not exhibit his title; was appointed to Enniskeen and Ardagh (Meath) 1660 (ib. 167)

GILLINGTON, GEORGE 1824–1899

b. 1824 Dublin; ent TCD 6 Nov 1843 aged 19 BA & Div Test 1850

d 1852 p 1853; C Easternsnow (Elph) *c.* 1853; prob same as George Gillington C Larne (Conn) 1855–; C Carrickfergus (Conn) 1857–62; C Ballymena (Conn) 1862–64; C Ramoan (Conn) 1864–77; C-in-c Ramoan (Conn) 1877–79; C Urney (Derry) 1880–83; Chapl Villierstown (Lism) 1887–99

> **s.** of George
>
> **m.** 25 Jan 1860 St Mary Dublin Mabel F Sharman (**died** 21 Jun 1861 aged 40) 2nd **dau.** of Hill Wilson of Carrickfergus
>
> Died 21 Dec 1899 aged 75

GILLINGTON, JOHN MAURICE 1827/28–

b. 1827 or 1828 Dublin; ed by Dr Wall; ent TCD 6 Nov 1845 aged 17 BA 1851 MA 1857

d 1851 (Meath) p 1852 (Cork for Meath); C Clara (Meath) 1851–53; C St Peter Athlone (Elph) 1854–56; C Neston (Ches) 1856–60; C Audlem (Ches) 1860–65; C Neston (Ches) 1865–67; Chapl Brookwood Asylum Surrey 1867–84; C Arreton IOW (Portsm) 1888–89; last entry in Crockford 1897.

> **s.** of George, *opifex*.

GILLMOR, ANDREW TODD 1806–1878

b. 1806 Co Sligo; ed by Mr Armstrong; ent TCD 6 Dec 1824 aged 18 BA 1829 LLB & LLD 1842 d 1831 p; PC Gartree (Conn) 1838–40; PC Calry (Elph) 1840–56; V Killenvoy (Elph) 1856–68; R & V Bailieborough and Moybologue (Kilm) 1868–78

s. of Gowan, JP of Ballyglass Co Sligo

m. 3 Jun 1843 St Mark Dublin Mary Jemima **dau.** of John Franklin of Madeira. Issue 1. Rev Gowan (**died** Oct 1928), Archd of Algoma Canada **m.** (1) 8 Jun 1871 Catherine Elizabeth **dau.** of Robert S Young of Clonsingle Co Tipperary; **m.** (2) 5 Jan 1891 at North Bay Ontario Mary **dau.** of Col Gregory, Commanding 2nd Cavalry Regt St Catherine's Ontario; 2. Rev William George (**died** 7 Apr 1913), V Dunmore East (Waterf); 3. Henry James (**died** 3 Feb 1918 at Perry Ohio); 4. Andrew Hercules (**died** 7 Jan 1941) TCD BA 1887 MA 1895 d 1892 p 1893 C Mountmellick (Kild) 1892–99 C St Anne Sheffield (Sheff — then York) 1899–1901 C Garrycloyne (Cork) 1901–02 C St Gregory w St Peter Sudbury (St E) 1902–03 C St Stephen Shepherd's Bush (Lon) 1903–04 C Wicklow (Glend) 1905–06 C Dunganstown w Redcross (Glend) 1906–09 R Begbroke (Ox) from 1909; 5. Caroline Margaret (**died** 1 Jan 1941)

Died 2 Apr 1878 aged 71 at Bailieborough Rectory

GIVEN, HENRY WILSON SWINBURN 1848–1925

b. 10 Oct 1848; ed Royal Gram Sch Lancaster; St Aidan's Coll Birkenhead 1878;

d 1878 p 1879 (Kilmore); C Drumgoon (Kilm) 1878–80; R Dunamon (Elph) 1880–81; R Clogh (Clogh) 1881–84; R Killeevan (Clogh) 1884–89; R Ematris (w Rockcorry from 1904) (Clogh) 1889–1924; Preb of Devenish (Clogh) 1911–20; Prec of Clogher 1920–24; ret

s. of Andrew of Limavady Co Derry

m. Annie Geraldine **dau.** of Rev Thomas Moore MA, R Drumgoon (Kilm) qv Issue 3 **sons** incl Rev Marcus Henry BA, R Enniskeen (Meath) and 2 **daus.**

Died 17 Oct 1925 at Sandycove Hse, Dublin

GLASS, WILLIAM 1698/99–

b. 1698 or 1699 Athlone; ed by Mr Thewles at Athlone; ent TCD 13 Nov 1717 aged 18 BA 1722

d 18 Apr 1725 p 26 Jun 1726; C Ahascragh (Elph) 1725; was either V or C St Peter Athlone (Meath) 1726–; V Ahascragh Castleblakeney & Killyon (Elph) 1730–c43

s. of Richard, *colonus*

m. (ML 24 Feb 1726) Margaret Thewles, probably a **dau.** of Rev George Thewles (**died** 1690) FTCD of Athlone

GLENN, GEORGE GRAHAM 1837/38–1926

b 1837 or 1838; TCD BA (Resp) 1890 MA 1903

d 1891 p 1893 (Kilmore); C Kilkeevan w Oran (Elph) 1891–93; R Turlough (Tuam) 1893–94; R Skreen (Killala) 1894–1926

s. of George (**died** at Maybole New Brunswick)

m. (1) 19 Apr 1894 Susan (**died** 24 Jun 1899) **dau.** of H Goodfellow of

Morehampton Rd Dublin

m. (2) Frances (**died** 17 Dec 1941 at Sandymount Dublin)

Died 28 Aug 1926 at Skreen Rectory aged 88

GLOSTER, THOMAS 1824/25–1895

b. 1824 or 1825 Limerick; ed by Mr Huddart; ent TCD 3 Nov 1845 aged 20 BA 1849 Div Test 1851 MA 1856

d 1852 p 1853 (Kilmore); C Killesher (Kilm) 1853; C Quivvy (Kilm) 1853–56; PC Quivvy (Kilm) 1856–72; R Castleterra (Kilm) 1873–78; res.

> **s.** of Edward, *pragmaticus*
>
> **m.** and had issue incl 1. his eldest **s.** Capt Edward, 1st E Yorks Regt **m.** 11 Feb 1895 Elinor Marion Hawkesworth, eldest **dau.** of Capt T J Smyth, DL of Ballynegall; 2. Capt Gerald Meade, 1st Devonshire Regt **m.** 16 Sep 1896 Wilhelmina Ormonde only **dau.** of Charles Brown, DI Gen, Punjab Police
>
> **Died** 13 Mar 1895 Dublin aged 70

GODFREY, DAVID SAMUEL GEORGE 1935–

b. 17 Jun 1935 Dublin; ed St Patrick's Cath Gram Sch Dublin, CITC GOE

d 25 Sep 1966 p 21 Sep 1967; C Christ Ch Londonderry (Derry) 1966–68; R Tomregan and Drumlane (Kilm) 1968–72; R Cloonclare Killasnett Drumlease and Kilenumery (Kilm) 1972–79; R Templebreedy Tracton and Nohoval (Cork) 1979–85; R Bray (Dub) 1985–97; Moderator of Inter–Church Affairs Board ICC 1992–2000; Can of Christ Ch Cath Dublin 1995–97; Dean of Kilmore & R Kilmore & Ballintemple (Kilm) 1997–2004; Preb of Mulhuddart in St Patrick's Cath Dublin 2001–04; ret

> **s.** of George of Belfast (**s.** of George and Elizabeth of Belfast) by Dorcas Evelyn **dau.** of Samuel and Rhoda Stedmond of Dublin
>
> **m.** 5 Sep 1966 St Paul's Ch Glenageary Dublin Heather Rosina Patricia **dau.** of Francis Keating and Marjorie Rosina (née Vaughan) of London. Issue 1. Karen **b.** 16 Aug 1969 **m.** 6 May 1995 Sean Thomas Lawlor of Belfast; 2. Fiona Heather **b.** 12 Jan 1971; 3. Philip David **b.** 13 Jul 1973

PUBLICATION

Signs of the Church of Ireland in Bray

GODLEY, JAMES 1821–1910

b. 1821 Co Leitrim; ed Winchester Sch; ent TCD 18 Dec 1839 aged 18; Trinity Coll Oxford matric 7 Jun 1841 aged 20 Exhib; Exeter Coll BA (2) Lit Humanities 1844 MA 1847

d 18 May 1845 p 21 Dec 1845 (Kilmore); C Killesher (Kilm)1845–46; C Annagh (Kilm) 1846–49; R Ashfield (Kilm) 1849–61; R Lavey (Kilm) 1861–66; R Tomregan (Kilm) 1866; R Carrigallen (Kilm) 1866–1904

> 2nd **s.** of John of Killegar Co Leitrim
>
> **m.** 24 Feb 1852 Eliza Frances **dau.** of Peter La Touche of Bellevue Co Wicklow.

Issue **sons** 1. Alfred Denis (**died** 27 Jun 1925) **b.** 22 Jan 1856 Balliol Coll Oxford matric 20 Oct 1874 aged 18 Sch 1874–78 Exhib BA 1879 MA 1882; Fellow and Tutor Magdalen Coll Oxford 1883 Sen Dean of Arts 1885 Public Orator to the Univ of Oxford 1910; 2. Col F C, MVO late commanding the Notts and Derby Regt; 3. John Cornwallis Corpus Christi Coll Oxford matric 21 Oct 1880 aged 19 Sch 1880–85 BA 1885 Dir of Ed in the Punjab; 4. Charlotte Maud (**died** 31 Mar 1946)

Died 30 Apr 1910 aged 88

GOFF, HERBERT SAMUEL

TCD BA 1892

d 1892 (Armagh for Kilmore) p; C Killesher (Kilm) 1892–94; C St Mark Dublin (Dub) 1894–96; C Christ Ch Leeson Pk Dublin (Dub) 1896

GOLDSMITH, EDWARD 1660/61–1722

b. 1660 or 1661; ent TCD 15 Jun 1677 aged 16 Sch 1680 BA 1681 MA 1684 DD 1699

d 11 Mar 1682/83 (Kildare) p 17 May 1684 (Kildare); C St Catherine (Dub) 1689–91; Preb of Rasharkin (Conn) 1692–1700; V Ballymena (Conn) 1693; R Magheragall (Conn) 1694–1700; V Ardcarne and Eastersnow and Kilmactranny (Elph) 1700–22; Dean of Elphin 1700–22

> **s.** of George of Moycastell Co Westmeath by Hester
>
> **m.** Elizabeth (**bur.** 6 Nov 1698 at Lisburn Cathedral) and had issue incl Very Rev Isaac, Dean of Cloyne
>
> **Died** 1722

GONNE (GUINNE, GUNN), GEORGE c. 1622–

b. c. 1622

pres to V Fenagh (Ard) 4 Nov 1635 (LM V 111), inst 13 Nov (FF), with Kiltubride (Ard); still there 1647, though living at Swords Co Dublin (Carte Papers xxi. 346); I Athboy (Meath) 1641.

> **m.** Martha of Swords Co Dublin. He and his wife took refuge in Longford Castle from the rebels but left it when the siege began

GONNYS, VALENTINE

coll V Oughteragh (Kilm) 11 Jan 1635

GOOD, BERNARD FREDERICK 1867/68–1925

b. 1867 or 1868; TCD BA 1895

d 1895 (Kilmore) p 1896 (Clogher for Kilmore); C Kinawley (Kilm) 1895–98; C Layde (Conn) 1898–1903; R Derrylane (Kilm) 1903–04; Dio C Kilmore 1906–08; R Drumlane (Kilm) 1908–10; R Annagh (Kilm) 1910–25

> **Died** 5 Jan 1925 aged 57

†GOODWYN, TIMOTHY –1729

ent Univ of Leyden 22 Nov 1691; Univ of Utrecht DD 9 May 1692; created MA Oxford from St Edmund's Hall 22 Jan 1696/97; incorp at Camb 1697; Lambeth DD 1 Oct 1714

R Rushook (Worc) 1701; Chapl to Bp of Oxford & Archd of Oxford 1707; R Heythrop (Ox) 1710–14; consec Bp of Kilmore 16 Jan 1714 at Dunboyne Ch Co Meath; enthroned 15 Feb 1714; Bp of Kilmore 1714–27; Abp of Cashel 1727–29

> **m.** Annie Maria (**bur.** 23 Dec 1729). Issue incl 1. Charles (**bur.** 6 Oct 1715); 2. Edmond bapt 17 Jun 1722 (poss same as Edward **bur.** 12 Nov 1725); 3. Charlotte bapt 18 Aug 1715 **bur.** 7 Jul 1742; 4. George bapt 8 Jun 1717; 5. John **b.** Worcester ent TCD 12 May 1727 aged 16 BA 1730 MA 1733
>
> **Died** 13 Dec 1729 Dublin **bur.** St Michan's Dublin

PUBLICATIONS
> *A Sermon*, preached before the Lords Justices, 4to, Dublin 1716
> *A Thanksgiving Sermon on Psalm 98 v 1*, 4to, Dublin 1716
> *A Charity Sermon* on Hebrews 13 v16, 4to, Dublin 1724
> *Life of Bishop Stillingfleet*

GORDON, HENRY 1857/58–1926

b. 1857 or 1858; QUB BA (2cl Hons) Classics 1881 BA 1882

d 1884 p 1885 (Kilmore); C Kinawley (Kilm) 1884–87; C Holy Trinity Belfast (Conn) 1887–90; R Derrylane (Kilm) 1890–1902; R Tomregan (Kilm) 1902–09; C St Mary Belfast (Conn) 1909–14; C-in-c Mariners' Ch Belfast (Conn) 1918–22

> **m.** Edith (**died** 9 Apr 1932 Belfast) **dau.** of Rev James Crichton, R Kildrumferton (Kilm) qv
>
> **Died** 26 Jun 1926 aged 68

GORDON, JAMES –1725

MA; d 27 Apr 1670 (Clogher) p 12 Jul 1671 (Kilmore and Ardagh); C Rathcline (Ard) 1670–71; V Eglistoun Islandedin, R & V Turlough Breaghivy Kildocomog 1671/72–1718; V Kilvine (Tuam) *c*. 1707–18; Preb of Faldown (Tuam) 1673–81; Preb of Balla (Tuam) 1681–1725; R Burriscarra (Tuam) *c*. 1708–25; V Castlebar *alias* Eglish and R Drumraney (Tuam) 1712–25

> **Died** 1725

GORDON, JAMES

lic C Kilcommick (Ard) 22 Jun 1787 (S.R.)

GORDONE, T

signs the Roll for C Dunamon (Elph) to 1718

GORE, Hon. GEORGE 1774–1844

b. 1774; ent TCD as SC 6 Jan 1790 aged 15 BA 1796 MA 1812

C Denn (Kilm) 1800; R Castleterra (Kilm) 1809–21; R Ardnageehy (Cloyne) 1814–17; Dean of Killala 1817–44; R Raheny (Dub) 1821–27; R Kilconduff (Ach) 1827–44

7th **s.** of the 2nd Earl of Arran by his 2nd wife

m. (1) Anne Burrowes (**died** 1819). Issue 1. Sophia Louisa **m.** James E P Turbett; 2. Frances **m.** 12 Dec 1834 John Sankey; 3. Louisa **m.** May 1839 William John Waldron of Balla Lodge Co Mayo

m. (2) 3 Feb 1820 Sophia (**died** Dec 1821) **dau.** of Sir George Ribton, Bt. Issue 1. Ven John Ribton (**died** 10 Nov 1894 at Dromard Rectory aged 74), **b.** 3 Nov 1820 TCD MA 1855 Archd of Achonry **m.** 1844 Frances Brabazon **dau.** of J D Ellard and had issue; 2. Robert **m.** 1852 Elizabeth **dau.** of Major Gore Edwards and had issue; 3. Anne **m.** Nov 1857 Arthur Frederick Lloyd

m. (3) 1823 Maria (**died** 23 Feb 1856) widow of Thomas Bunbury Isaac of Holywood Hse

Died 27 Aug 1844

GORE, MANLEY 1729/30–

b. 1729 or 1730 Kilkenny; ed by Mr Triddle; ent TCD 21 Nov 1747 aged 17 Sch 1751 BA 1752 MA 1759

d 31 Dec 1752 (Kilmore) p; C Carrigallen 1753; C Oughteragh (Kilm) 1757–c. 71; V "St. John's between the two bridges" = St John's Sligo (Elph) & V Kilmacoen Killaspicbrone & Calry (Elph) 1771–c75

s. of William

†GORE, WILLIAM   –1784

b. Fermoyle Co Tipperary; ent TCD 15 Apr 1729 BA 1733 MA 1743; DD (?of Oxford)

C Borris (Cashel) 1733; R Thurles (Cashel) 1734; Dean of Cashel 1736–58; R Cleenish (Clogh) 1747–58; Bp of Clonfert 1758–62; Bp of Elphin 1762–72; Bp of Limerick 1772–84

eldest **s.** of William, Dean of Clogher 1716–24 (**s.** of Sir William, Bt) by Honora **dau.** of Henry Prittie of Dunalley

m. (1) Mary (**died** 10 Jan 1765 s.p.) eldest **dau.** of Chidley Coote of Cootehill and widow of Guy Moore of Abbey Co Tipperary

m. (2) Mary (**died** 25 Mar 1822) **dau.** of Rev William French of Oakpark Co Roscommon, Dean of Ardagh qv, and had issue a **s.** Col William, MP for Carrick-on-Shannon and 3 **daus.**

Died 25 Feb 1784 at Bray Co Wicklow **bur.** St Mary's Ch Dublin

GORE, WILLIAM

There were two of this name, one of whom, almost certainly the former, was C Carrigallen (Kilm) 1799–1804:

(1) **b.** 1767 or 1768 Drogheda; ed by Mr Meares; ent TCD 19 Nov 1787 aged 19

s. of Lt John, 12th Dragoons by Sarah **dau.** of Thomas Henry of Bawnboy (M.L. 1767)

m. and had issue Robert Johnston

(2) **b.** 1771 or 1772 Co Sligo; ent TCD 2 Mar 1789 aged 17 BA 1793

s. of Arthur

GOSSELIN, JOHN HENRY PRESCOTT 1855/56–1930

b. 1855 or 1856; TCD Div Test 1888 BA 1889 MA 1906

d 1887 p 1888 (Kilmore); C Killegar (Kilm) 1887–89; DC Killegar (Kilm) 1889–92; C-in-c Kilnamanagh (Ferns) 1892–95; C Kilnamanagh (Ferns) 1895–97; R Muff (Derry) 1897–1915

only **s.** of Commander William H, RN of Newcastle Co Down

m. 27 Jun 1894 Annie J, **dau.** of William Astle Ryan of Cahore Gorey Co Wexford. Issue 1. Bertrand Nicholas (**died** 17 Feb 1913 at Muff Co Donegal aged 16); **daus.** incl 2. Cicely (**died** 1976 **bur.** Portarlington) **b.** 1898

Died 22 Sep 1930 aged 74 **bur.** Portarlington

GOSSELIN (GOSLIN), NICHOLAS 1778/79–1848

b. in 1778 or 1779 Queen's Co (Laois); ed by Mr Baggs; ent TCD 20 Jan 1795 aged 16 BA 1800

d 25 Mar 1801 (Ossory) p 24 Aug 1802 (Ossory); C Inchicologhan (Oss) 1804; C Ballymachugh (Ard) 1809 and *c.* 1826; V Abbeylara (Ard) 1829–32; C Granard (Ard) w R & V Ballinrobe (Tuam) 1834 (held it only for a few days); V Tashinny (Ard) 1834–48

s. of Nicholas

m. (1) Anne 2nd **dau.** of Matthew Fox of Foxbrook Co Meath **b.** 1790/91 and had issue 1. Elizabeth **b.** 1805/06; 2. Anne Alicia **b.** 1806/07 **m.** 11 Jan 1824 Thomas Elliott of Johnstown Co Carlow; 3. Sydney **b.** 1809/10 **m.** 22 Dec 1830 Henry Courtney 4. Ellen **b.** 1810/11; 5. Jane Margaret **b.** 1819/20 **m.** Tashinny Par Ch 4 Aug 1841 Thomas James Rawson MD of Carlow

m. (2) 19 Jan 1842 at Lurgan Church Helen eldest **dau.** of Alexander Cuppage of Lurgan

Died 30 Jul 1848: another authority has his death 15 Jul 1848

GOULDING (?GOLDEN), JAMES

"of Ballyhaise Clk" was attainted in 1689; prob C Castleterra (Kilm) 1689

GOULDSBURY, ALEXANDER –1782

DD

is said to have been "Pastor" at Boyle (Elph) –1782

a Rev Alexander Gouldsbury ent TCD 3 Jul 1769 but did not graduate; ent Univ of Galway 1771 MA 1772

    a Miss Gouldsbury of Boyle **m.** Apr 1777 William Grogan of Grange Co Roscommon

    Died 10 Nov 1782 Boyle

GOULDSBURY, JOHN HENRY 1745/46–1831

b. 1745 or 1746; ent TCD 1 Nov 1762 Sch 1765 BA 1767

C Boyle (Elph) 1785–90; Preb of Tibohine (Elph) 1785–1819; R Ardcarne (Elph) 1797–1825; V Chor Cork 1814–31; Preb of Oran and V Dunamon Kileroane Ballynakill and Drimtemple (Elph) 1825–31;

    s. of Rev Francis, R Leney (Meath) by Catherine Hamilton of Moydow

    m. Thomasina yst **dau.** of John Meares of Mearescroft

    Died 30 Aug 1831 aged 85 Boyle

GOULDSBURY, ROBERT –1829

V Abbeylara and Russagh (Ard) 1807–29

    m. and had issue a **dau.** m Richardson Turkington whose yst **dau.** Mary Sophia **m.** 17 Apr 1843 John King BA Principal of St Alban's Seminary Longford. He also had a 2nd **s.** Francis who **died** 7 Oct 1847 at Caldra Lodge Longford

    Died 21 Feb 1829

GRAHAM, ANDREW 1872/73–1947

b. 1872 or 1873; RUI BA 1900

d 1902 p 1904 (Bristol); C Christ Ch Barton Hill (Bris) 1902–04; C St Bartholomew Montpelier Bristol (Bris) 1904–05; C St Clement Bristol (Bris) 1906–08; R Streete (Ard) 1908–10; R Cloone (Ard) 1910–17; R Gowna w Columbkille (Ard) 1917–22; C-in-c Kilronan w Kilmactranny (Ard) 1922–27; R Drumshambo (w Kiltubride from 1928) (Ard) 1924–45; ret

    m. and had issue Rev Douglas Wrixon, R Roscommon (Elph) qv below

    Died 1947 aged 74

GRAHAM, DOUGLAS WRIXON 1913–2004

b. 1913; TCD BA 1939 Div Test 1940

d 1941 p 1943; C Donaghcloney (Drom) 1941–43; Crockford 2004/05 has him C Taney (Dub) 1942–43, though this is not in 1943 C I Dir, where his name is given without appointment; C New Ross (Ferns) 1943–50; R Killegney U (Ferns) 1950–66; R Roscommon G (Elph) 1966–88; Preb of Tibohine (Elph) 1978–88; ret; Temp-in-c Roscommon G 1988–91

    s. of Rev Andrew, R Drumshambo (Ard) qv

    Died 1 Apr 2004 aged 91

GRANT, FREDERICK WILLIAM –1970

RUI BA 1901; TCD Abp King's Pri (2) 1904 Div Test (1) 1905

d 1905 p 1906 (Down); C Kilkeel (Drom) 1905–11; R Derrylane (Kilm) 1911–20; R Kinawley (Kilm) 1920–65; RD of Manorhamilton 1925–32; RD N Kilmore 1932–41; Dio Reg Kilm Elph and Ard 1932–65; Preb of Drumlease (Kilm) 1941–49; RD of Kinawley 1949–55; Preb of Mulhuddart in St Patrick's Cath Dublin 1949–55; Dean of Kilmore 1955–65; Dom Chapl to Bp 1955–65; ret

s. of James of Hillsborough Co Down

m. Phoebe (**died** 17 June 1965 Enniskillen) **dau.** of Robert Warren McKnight of Arva Co Cavan

Died 16 Dec 1970 **bur.** Derrylin

GRATTAN, RALPH 1709/10–1772

b. 1709 or 1710 Mountcharles Co Donegal; ed by Mr Grattan, Enniskillen; ent TCD 3 Apr 1727 aged 17 BA 173– BD & DD 1747; was admitted a Freeman of the Borough of Cavan in 1756

Chapl The King's Hosp (Bluecoats Sch Dublin) 1732–54; C Powerscourt (Glend) 1744; R Bailieborough and Moybologue and Lavey (Kilm) 1745–52; V Kildrumferton (w Killan, now Shercock from 1754) (Kilm) 1752–72

s. of Rev William, FTCD, R Cappagh (Derry) (**s.** of Rev Patrick, R Cappagh (Derry)) by Sophia **dau.** of Sir William Gore, Bt; cousin of Henry Grattan, the celebrated Irish patriot

m. 4 Apr 1762 Abigail (**died** 1809 aged 80) widow of Charles Sadleir of Castletown Co Tipperary and **dau.** of Rev Joseph Grave, R Geashill (Kild)

Died 1772

GRATTAN, WILLIAM 1770/71–1844

b. 1770 or 1771 Co Meath; ed by Mr Austin; ent TCD 22 Oct 1788 aged 17 BA 1796

C Denn (Kilm) 1806; C Killesher (Kilm) 1817–25; C Kinawley (Kilm) 1825; acc to monument in Swanlinbar Ch, was C Swanlinbar for 37 years

s. of William, High Sheriff Co Meath 1778 (**s.** of Charles, FTCD)

m. 21 Jun 1808 at Killeshandra Anne Selina (**died** 9 Mar 1870 at Royal Sch Cavan) **dau.** of Humphrey Nixon of Nixon Lodge. Issue **sons** 1. William **died** young; 2. Copeland Humphrey **m.** Sophia Biggs and had issue; **daus.** 1. Maryanne **m.** 20 Feb 1844 Rev Orange Sterling Kellett, R Tomregan (Kilm) qv 2. Eliza Emily (**died** 22 Sep 1849) **m.** Richard Sadleir of Melbourne; 3. Anne **m.** Rev William Prior Moore; 4. Arabella (**died** 25 Aug 1849 Dublin)

Died 18 Mar 1844

GRAVE, WILLIAM 1782/83–*c.* 1839

b. 1782 or 1783 King's Co (Offaly); ent TCD 5 Feb 1810 aged 27 BA 1818

C Kilcommick (Ard) *c.* 1826

s. of William

Died *c.* 1839; his will proved 9 Feb 1839

GRAVES (or GRAVE), JOSEPH 1674/75–*c.* 1743

b. 1674 or 1675 Drogheda; ed by Mr Spotswood; ent TCD as Siz 7 Oct 1691 aged 16 Sch 1695 BA 1696

V Killasoolan & Kilronan or Killeroran (Elph) 1698–1743; R Killasoolan = Castleblakeney (Elph) 1698–1743; Preb of Terebrine (Elph) 1704–before 1722

s. of John *candelarius*

m. and had issue 1. Simon b. King's Co (Offaly) ent TCD 11 Feb 1737 aged 16; 2. Joseph b. Co Offaly ent TCD 18 Nov 1742 aged 17 BA 1747/48

Died *c.* 1743

GRAVES, RICHARD 1763/64–1829

FTCD 1786 Regius Prof Div 1814

Preb of St Michael's Dublin 1801–23; Dean of Ardagh 1814–29; pres to the Deanery 1 Mar 1814 (L.M. V 170) and inst 11 Mar (F.F.)

s. of Rev James R Kilfinnan (Lim) by Jane dau. of Rev Thomas Ryder R Mitchelstown (Cloyne)

m. Eliza Mary (died 22 Mar 1827) dau. of Rev James Drought DD, Regius Prof of Div TCD. Issue Rev Richard Hastings

Died 31 Mar 1829 aged 65 bur. Donnybrook Dublin

Dean Graves was a well known author. Cotton III, 190–1 gives a list of 17 of his published works which have been issued in a collected edition by his s., Rev Richard Hastings Graves

GRAVES, RICHARD H 1855/56–1882

b. 1855 or 1856;

d 1880; C Ardagh (Ard) 1880–82

Died 25 May 1882 aged 26 at Ardagh

GRAY, RICHARD CHARLES BERKELEY

Univ Coll Durham 1885; St Aidan's Coll Birkenhead 1886

d 1887 p 21 Dec 1888 (Ossory); C Tullow (Leigh) 1887–91; C Christ Church Londonderry (Derry) 1891–92; DC Killegar (Kilm) 1892–93; C Whitechurch Canonicorum (Sarum) 1893–96; V Hermitage and R Hilfield (Sarum) 1896–

2nd s. of Pope Gray of Blackrock Cork (s. of Rev Donald Davies of Cork)

m. 20 Oct 1891 at Baggotrath Ch Mary Cecile Elizabeth only dau. of William Elwood of Carlisle

GREENE, JOHN EVELYN 1806/07–

b. 1806 or 1807 Co Louth; ed by Mr Needham; ent TCD 7 Nov 1825 aged 18 BA 1830

d 1834 p; C St John Sligo (Elph) 1835–40; V Ahamplish (Elph) 1841–81

evidently John **s.** of James, *medicus*

m. 1841 Anne eldest **dau.** of Alexander Gibbons of Aberdeen

Last entry in C I Dir 1881

GREENE, THOMAS WEBB 1805/06–1875

b. 1805 or 1806 Cork; ed by Mr Cotter; ent TCD 5 Apr 1830 aged 24 BA 1834

d 1834 p 15 Apr 1835 (Cloyne); C Tallow (Lism) 1834; V Columbkille (Ard) 1838–53; V Cashel (Ard) 1853–56; R Tashinny and Abbeyshrule (Ard) 1856–63; V Granard (Ard) 1863–75; Archd of Ardagh 1874–75

s. of Roger, *telonarius* (tax collector), Port Surveyor of Youghal and Mayor 1799 by Jane **dau.** of Thomas Carleton Webb of Castlemartyr Co Cork

m. 24 Oct 1838 Ellinor Maria (**died** 19 Feb 1898 at Vancouver in her 90th year) only **dau.** of Rev William Gwynne of Castleknock Co Dublin. Issue 1. William John **b.** 1846 **died** 1873; 2. Roger Henry Carleton (**died** at Vancouver Canada 8 Nov 1924) **m.** and had issue an only **dau.** Aileen May **m.** at Christ Ch Vancouver 5 Oct 1916 Augustus N **s.** of John Cowdry; there were also three **daus.** incl the yst Eleanor Frances **died** 23 Jul 1933

Died 22 Nov 1875 at Granard Rectory aged 69

GREENE, WILLIAM –1731

MA

R Killesher (Kilm) 1683–1731; was pres by the Crown Prec of Clogher 1695, but there is no record of his institution. He signed the Address to James II 18 Mar 1683/84 and was attainted in 1689

s. of Marmaduke of Drumnisklin Co Fermanagh

m. a **sister** of Col Brockhill Newburgh of Ballyhaise Co Cavan

Died 1731

GREER, FERGUS WILLIAM 1863–1930

b. 1863; Univ Coll Durham BA 1887 MA 1898

d 1888 (Clogher for Kilmore) p 1889 (Kilmore); C Templemichael (Ard) 1888–89; C Zion Rathgar (Dub) 1890–94; I St Catherine (Dub) 1894–1909; I St George's U (Dub) 1909–25; Canon of Christ Ch Cath Dublin 1924–30; I Holy Trinity Killiney (Dub) 1925–30

m. and had issue 1. Fergus Ussher Morriss **m.** Durban Ruby Hutchinson **dau.** of Charles Thompson of Northenden Cheshire; 2. Roderick Denis, Capt 7th Gurkha Rifles **m.** 7 Jan 1920 Eileen Mary eldest **dau.** of RS Hopking of Dublin; 3. Kenneth McGregor MB **m.** 28 Apr 1932 Florence Christine 2nd **dau.** of Vincent Dearden of Leicester; and 4. (twins) Brigadier Eric Roberts ed St Columba's Coll Dublin; 5. Ursula Margaret Jane Elizabeth m. 18 Jul 1928 John Dermot Alexander only s. of Claude Malcolmson DL of Dublin

Died 11 Dec 1930

GREER, WILLIAM BENJAMIN –1919

TCD Sch 1868 BA (Sen Mod Classics) 1869 Vice–Chancellor's Pri (1) 1871 Div Test (2) 1872 MA 1873; member of Senate; Univ of Durham MA (*ad eund*) 1873

d 1870 p 1872 (Kilmore); C Killasnett and Lurganboy (Kilm) 1870–72; C St Peter Drogheda (Arm) 1872–73; C St Paul Alnwick (Newc) 1873; C Stokesay (Heref) 1874; C Hardingham (Nor) 1875–77; C Ashill (Nor) 1877–82; Minor Canon Liverpool 1881–85; Minor Canon of Limerick 1881–85; C St Mark Dalston (Lon) 1885–89; C St Dionis Fulham (Lon) 1889–91; C Woldingham (Roch) from 1891; there in 1913

Died 24 May 1919

GREGG, FRANCIS THORNTON 1804–1890

b. 1804 Longford; ed by Mr Wright; ent TCD 15 Oct 1821 BA 1826 MA 1832 BD 1853 DD 1857

d 4 Nov 1827 p 182–; R & V Ballymacormick (Ard) 1842–67; R Kilcommick (Ard) 1866–67; R Ardagh (Ard) 1880–90

s. of Thornton

m. Sep 1832 Henrietta **dau.** of Andrew Johnston of Dalkey Co Dublin and **sister** of Rev Richard Johnston of Kilmore. Issue incl 1. Rev Thomas Huband of Portland Weymouth Dorset **m.** 28 Apr 1864 Caroline yst **dau.** of Richard Garratt of Monkstown Co Dublin; 2. Andrew Thoms who received Poer Trench Scholarship TCD 1862; 3. Huband George of Oldtown Co Longford **m.** 5 Aug 1885 Violet Josephine **dau.** of Frederick Pilkington; 4. Thornton Francis **died** aged 5 years in 1841

Died 24 Jul 1890 aged 85

GREGG, RICHARD GEORGE STANHOPE 1883–1945

b. 9 Dec 1883 Southsea; ed Fermoy Coll Co Cork; TCD MB BCh and BAO 1907 MA 1927 BD and Div Test (1) 1929; was Lt Col in RAMC before ordination

d 1928 (Meath for Armagh) p 1929 (Armagh); C Derryloran (Arm) 1928–32; I Shinrone U (Killaloe) 1932–33; R Cloone and Chapl Lough Rynn (Ard) 1933–45; Archd of Elphin and Ardagh 1940–45; Dom Chapl to Bp 1940–45

s. of Col William, Leicestershire Regt and Susan May (née Atkins)

m. 21 Oct 1913 Violet Lesley Gordon **dau.** of Sinclair Sutherland of Dublin. Issue 1. John Arthur, Capt RA; 2. May Doran **m.** FH Ross MA; 3. Sheila Atkins

Died 26 May 1945

GREGG, THOMAS 1795–1846

b. 1795 Dublin; ed by Mr Kean; TCD (Siz) 1813 Sch 1816 BA 1818 MA 1821

C Boyle (Elph) 1827; C Delgany (Glend) 1834–45; C St Catherine (Dub) 1839–46; Chapl Richmond Prison (Bridewell) Dublin –1846

    s. of Thornton

    m. and had issue Elizabeth (**died** Dec 1848 aged 16)

    Died 22 Apr 1846 **bur.** Ardagh

†GREGORY

Provost of Killala was prov in error to the See of Down and was consec in 1353, but did not gain possession and was replaced as Provost and also Preb of Achonry and Elphin, 2 Jun 1354 (C.P.L. III. 482, 540)

GREGORY, WILLIAM

V Cashel and Rathcline (Ard) 1624–c. 1663, pres 22 Apr 1624 (L.M. V. 106)

GRESSON, SKELTON 1779/80–1853

b. 1779 or 1780 Co Cavan; ed by Mr Miller; ent TCD 6 Nov 1797 aged 17 BA 1802 MA 1832

d 24 May 1802 p 1803; C Killesherdoney (Kilm) 1802; C Swanlinbar (Kilm) 1803; V Clara (Meath) 1810–53

    s. of William

    Died Feb 1853

GRIER, FREDERICK 1708/09–

b. 1708 or 1709 Granard Co Longford; ed by Rev Maurice Neligan, Longford; ent TCD as Siz 4 Jun 1729 aged 20 Sch 1731 BA 1733; ent Univ of Glasgow 1734

V Streete (Ard) c. 1755/56–c. 1800.

    s. of Gerard, *colonus*

GRIERSON, ROBERT –c. 1923

TCD 1870

d 1873 p 1874 (Kilmore); C Drumshambo and Kiltoghart (Ard) 1873–75; R Taunagh (Elph) 1875–78; R Cloonclare (Kilm) 1878–87; res

    m. 31 Aug 1875 Maria Evans (**died** 19 May 1918) 2nd **dau.** of Very Rev Samuel Evans Hoops, Dean of Ardagh qv Issue 11 children incl Myra Constance (**died** 5 Nov 1954); his yst **dau.** Claire **m**… Fraser

    Died c. 1923

PUBLICATIONS
    Ballygowna
    The Invasion of Cromleigh

On the Waves of the World
a number of short stories

GRIFFIN, EDWARD MORGAN 1887–1962
b. 5 Apr 1887; ed Campbell Coll Belfast;TCD BA & Div Test 1911 MA 1940

d 1911 p 1912 (Derry); C All SS Clooney Londonderry (Derry) 1911–13; C Castleknock (Dub) 1913–18; TCF 1915–16 & 1918–19 & 1920; C Castleknock w Mulhuddart (Dub) 1919–22; C Ematris & Rockcorry (Clogh) 1922–24; C-in-c Augher (Clogh) 1924–26; C-in-c Aghavilly (Arm) 1926–32; R Ballinderry w Tamlaght (Arm) 1932–39; R Omey U (Tuam) 1939–44; R Annagh Quivvy and Drumaloor (Kilm) 1944–56; R Lurgan Munterconnaught and Loughan (Kilm) 1956–61; ret

    s. of Rev Edward, R St Barnabas (Dub) 1899–1918 by Elizabeth Anne **dau.** of Robert Saunderson, MD; **bro.** of Rev Robert Saunderson, C-in-c Hollywood (Glend) 1940–52

    m. 11 Jun 1923 Adelaide Victoria Walker (**died** 1973 **bur.** Dean's Grange Dublin) **dau.** of George and Adelaide Powell of Chapelizod Dublin. Issue 1. Victoria Elizabeth Joyce **b.** 31 Jan 1925 **m.** 1950 All SS Blackrock Dublin Edgar Llewellan Broadstock and had issue (i) Malcolm (ii) Lynne **m.** John Hill; 2. Georgina Yvonne **b.** 1930 **m.** at St Martin in the Fields London Brendan Dunne of Dublin and had issue (i) Karen (ii) Coral; 3. Desmond **b.** 13 Apr 1934 **m.** Karen and had issue (i) Karmode (ii) Danny; 4. Godfrey Winston **m.** Pam Horton of Dublin and had issue (i) Nicola (ii) Emma (iii) Connor

    Died 1 Oct 1962 **bur.** Dean's Grange Dublin

GRIFFIN, ELLICE
is V Kilronan (Ard), resident to 1622. "Church ruinous. A poore Irish (glebe) house". (R.V.)

GRIFFIN, GEORGE
MA

adm V of Ballymacormack and Clongish (Ard) 25 Sep 1616 (FF); is V in 1622, "a preacher" resident in Ballymacormick; again pres by Crown to V of Ballymacormack and Clongish (Ard) 12 Dec 1634 (L.M. V. 111)

GRIFFIN, GEORGE
V Cloone (Ard) 1622; church ruinous; most probably same as above

GRIFFIN, JAMES JACKSON 1873/74–1955
b. 1873 or 1874; TCD BA 1896 Div Test 1897

d 1898 p 1899 (Kilmore); C Kinawley (Kilm) 1898–1900; C Roscrea (Killaloe) 1900–02; R Lorrha (Killaloe) 1902–11; R Clontuskert w Kiltormer (Clonf) 1911–19; TCF 1916–19; R Drumcliffe w Clare Abbey and Kildysart (Killaloe) 1919–46; Canon of Killaloe 1923–46; Treas of Killaloe 1936–38; Chanc of Killaloe 1938–41; Preb of

Tipperkevin in St Patrick's Cath Dublin 1941–46; R Glengariffe (Ross) 1946–51; ret

 s. of Rev Edward Morgan of Dublin

m. (1) Evelyn (**died** 13 Dec 1942) and had issue incl 1. **sons** Robert (**died** 11 Sep 1947) TCD BAI **m.** Alice **dau.** of Rev William Bradfield, R Lurgan (Kilm) qv; 2. Cecil Baxwell, RAF **m.** 18 May 1945 at Witney Enid Mary 3rd **dau.** of Frank Lea of Witney; 3. Frank **m.** 1955 in Nigeria; 4.Gerald Baxwell **m.** 24 Aug 1945 Evelyn only **dau.** of Frederick Browett of Tramore Co Waterford and had issue a **dau.**; 5. Lt Col Charles (**died** 15 Jun 1963 Bristol) **b.** 1907 ed Portora Royal Sch Enniskillen Univ of Camb served with Corps of Royal Engineers **m.** Anne; **daus.** 1. Muriel **m.** 1942 Frederick, BA **s.** of George Langstaffe of Ripon Yorks; 2. Primrose **m.** 21 Jun 1940 at Ennis William Hugh Pakenham **s.** of Rev Canon G Browne, R Horetown (Ferns); 3. Marguerite Violet **m.** Rev Canon Britain Lougheed

m. (2) Margaret Jackson (died 16 Nov 1973 Dublin) **bur.** Ennis.

 Died 21 Nov 1955 Dublin **bur.** Ennis

GRIFFIN, MICHAEL 1674/75–c. 1756

b. 1674 or 1675 Dublin; ed by Mr John Spotswoode; ent TCD as Siz 1 Apr 1690 aged 15 BA 1695 MA 1698

Preb of Kilcooley (Elph) 1729–43; either he or his son Michael was V Kilkeevan (Elph) 1729–43; he was also Diocesan School Master

 s. of Richard, *sartor* of Dublin

 m. and had issue Rev Michael

 Died or res 1743 — may have **died** in 1756, the year in which his Will was proved

GRIFFIN, MICHAEL

V Aughrim (Elph) 1705–c. 43; coll 2 May 1705; prob same as above

GRIFFIN, MICHAEL

ed by Rev Mr Buck; ent TCD as Siz 3 Jun 1760 BA 1764

V Killenvoy Kilmean St John's Ivernon Porterin and Raharrow (Elph) 1788–1811; V Aughrim (Elph) 1811–20

 m. and issue incl Rev Michael, C Aughrim (Elph) qv

GRIFFIN, MICHAEL 1782/83–

b. 1782 or 1783 Co Roscommon; ed by Mr Smith; ent TCD 10 Jun 1800 aged 17

C Aughrim (Elph) to 1806

 s. of Rev Michael, V Killenvoy (Elph) qv

GRIFFIN, SAMUEL 1708/09–

b. 1708 or 1709 Elphin; ed by his father; ent TCD 29 Sep 1725 aged 16 BA 1730

d 18 Oct 1730 (Kilmore) p; lic C Elphin and Ogulla (Elph) 17 Aug 1734; V Kilglass

(Elph) 1741–.

s. of Rev Michael

GRIFFITH, GEORGE 1802/03–1876

b. 1802 or 1803 Dublin; ent TCD 1 Jul 1822 aged 19 BA 1827 MA 1832

R Ardcarne (Elph) 1846–60; Preb of Terebrine (Elph) 1859–60; V Kilkeevan and Preb of Ballintubber (Elph) 1860–76

s. of Richard

m. 1830 Ballyshannon Par Ch Co Donegal Frances widow of Robert Crawford and **dau.** of James Forbes of Danby Co Donegal. Issue incl 1. George **m.** 3 Aug 1863 Lucy Juliana yst **dau.** of James Courtenay Cottingham

Died 19 Sep 1876 Castlerea Co Roscommon

GRIFFITH, GEORGE COTTINGHAM

TCD BA 1886 Div Test 1888

d 1889 p; C Tomregan (Kilm) 1889–91

GRIFFITH, JULIUS HENRY 1826/27–1907

b. 1826 or 1827; TCD BA & Div Test (2) 1851 MA 1877 BD & DD 1891

d 1856 (Meath) p 1857 (Kilmore); C Killenumery (Ard) 1856–61; C Lurganboy C of E in Killasnett Parish (Kilm) 1861–71; R Drumcliffe (Elph) 1871–77; C St Michael (Lim) 1877–83; R St Patrick w Killeedy 1883; R Drumcliffe (Ennis) w Kilmaley and Clare Abbey (Killaloe) 1884–1907; Chapl to Lord Lt 1889

s. of Rev James, Preb of Dysart (Lim)

m. Elizabeth (**died** 8 Jun 1919 aged 81 at Borrisokane Rectory). Issue incl Dr Alexander **m.** and had issue a **s.** (**died** 26 Sep 1953)

Died 27 Apr 1907 aged 80 **bur.** Ennis Co Clare

GRIFFITH, WILLIAM

is C Granard (Ard) in 1615 (R.V.)

GRIFFITHS, MAURICE

R & Preb Killukin (Elph) in 1615

GRISCOME, DAVID 1947–

b. 10 Oct 1947 Upper Heath London; ed Horsenden Sec Mod Sch; Oak Hill Theol Coll London BA in Theol and Past Studs 1988; CITC 1989; was Church Army Capt before ordination; Chmn Raphoe Dio Youth Council 1984–86; Derry Dio Board of Youth Min 1989; member of Northern regional body of CIYC 1989–92

d 29 Jun 1989 p 24 Jun 1990; C Glendermott (Derry) 1988–91; R Clondehorkey Mevagh and Glenalla 1991–95; C-in-c Calry (Elph) 1995–99; R St John Sligo Cath

Rosses Point and Knocknarea and Dean of Elphin and Ardagh 1999–2004; res; R Convoy Monellan and Donaghmore (Raph) 2006–

    s. of William Ernest of Wembley Middlesex by Kathleen Doris (**died** 2006) (née Morrell) of Wembley

GROVES, THOMAS

R & V Castleterra (Kilm) 1625; V Drumlane (Kilm) 1625; he got a grant of a glebe on 25 Jan 1625/26; he was also V Templeport & Killinagh 1626; given as Jones in another record

GUBBINS, ARTHUR GOUGH

TCD BA 1875 MA 1891

d 1874 (Cork for Kilmore); p 1875; C Cloone (Ard) 1874–75; C Ballyboy (Meath) 1875–77; C-in-c Castletown/Vastina (Meath) 1877–79; C Blessington (Glend) 1879–80; C Prestbury (Ches) 1882–90; C Kilpeacon U (Lim) 1890–92; C Fair Oak (Win) 1892–

GUBLIN, EDWARD

V Shrewer = Shrule (Ard) 1638 (F.F.)

GUINNESS, WILLIAM NEWTON 1809/10–1894

b. 1809 or 1810 Dublin; ed by Mr Feinagle; ent TCD 26 Nov 1826 aged 16 BA 1831 MA 1835; *ad eund* Univ of Melbourne 1857

d 25 Mar 1834 (Limerick) p 1835 (Kilmore); R Killery (Ard) 1835–38; Preb and V Ballysadare (Ach) 1838–57; I Christ Ch Yarra (Dio Melbourne) 1857–80; R Dowra (Kilm) 1881–84; V Ballysadare (Ach) 1884–92

    only **s.** of William Lunell, merchant by Susanna Newton

    m. (1) 31 Mar 1835 Harriet **dau.** of Rear Admiral Hon. William le Poer Trench 3rd **s.** of William, 1st Earl of Clancarty. Issue 1. William Trench (**died** unm 8 Feb 1918 aged 81); 2. Zara (**died** 18 Apr 1883 Auckland NZ) **m.** Thomas Mahon Minchin

    m. (2) Aug 1844 Elizabeth Dora (**died** s.p. June 1845) **dau.** of Alexander Perceval of Temple Hse Co Sligo

    m. (3) Harriet **dau.** of Rev Edward Day, R Sligo (Elph) qv Issue several children incl 1. Henry William Newton, Capt 18th Regt; 2. Major Ernest Whitney (**died** 11 Jan 1933); 3. Lt Col Charles Davis, RA

    Died 5 Apr 1894 Dublin

GULLY, JAMES 1814/15–

b. 1814 or 1815 Kent; ed by Mr Flynn; ent TCD 4 Nov 1833 aged 18 BA 1839 MA 1857

d 1841 p; PC Knocknarea a district in St John's Sligo (Elph) 1843–60; R St Peter Athlone (Elph) 1860–80; Prec of Elphin 1876–85

s. of Phillip

m. 29 Apr 1863 Celbridge Co Kildare Penelope widow of Rev Archibald St George

GUMLEY, JAMES 1759/60–1837

b. 1759 or 1760 or 1761 Cavan; ed by Mr Beatty; ent TCD 3 Nov 1777 aged 16 BA 1782

d 16 Nov 1783 p 17 Sep 1786 (Kilmore); C Kinawley (Kilm) 1783; PC Killoughter (Kilm) 1814–37

    s. of John

    Died 20 Feb 1837 aged 77

GUMLEY, JOHN 1750/51–1837

b. 1750 or 1751; ed by Mr Kerr at Cavan; ent TCD 1 Nov 1767 BA 1772 MA 1811

d 29 Jun 1772 p 1 May 1773 (Kilm); C Drumlane and Outeragh (Kilm) 1773; C Annagh (Kilm) 1774–77 or later; V Killargue (Kilm) 1796–1808; R Bailieborough and Moybologue (Kilm) 1808–37

    m. and had issue incl John **b.** Cavan ent TCD 4 Jul 1810 aged 16 BA 1815 LLB & LLD 1831 Irish Bar 1820 **m.** Mary and had issue (i) Rev John Stewart BA 1844, R Fuerty (Elph) qv (ii) Thomas ent TCD 1843 (iii) Rev William, R Martock (B & W) (iv) R Robert, V Derrylane (Kilm) qv (v) Charles

    Died 22 Jun 1837 aged 86

GUMLEY, JOHN ROBERT

TCD Div Test (1) 1889

d 1889 p 1890 (Kilmore); C Munterconnaught (Kilm) 1889; C Drumshambo (Ard) 1889; C Clones (Clogh) 1889–92; R Killadeas (Clogh) 1892–1911; Continental Chapl CCCS 1912–14; C Caterham (S'wark) 1916–19; Perm to Off Dio Truro 1920–24; Special Service Clergyman Dio York 1924–30; V Askham Bryan (York) 1930–38

    s. of Rev Robert, V Derrylane (Kilm) qv (s. of John) by Florence **dau.** of Rev Thomas Pentland, R Drumreilly (Kilm) qv; **bro.** of Rev Francis Albert, PC Gateforth and Hambleton (York) 1915–37; **bro.** of Rev Edmund Maurice, R Clanabogan (Derry) 1933–40

GUMLEY, JOHN STEWART 1821/22–1880

b. 1821 or 1822 Cavan; ed by Mr Holywell; ent TCD 12 Oct 1839 aged 17 BA 1844

C Castleblakeney and Killyon (Elph) 1850–; C Oran (Elph) 1854–56; V Fuerty (Elph) 1856–65; Preb of Termonbarry 1866–72

    eldest s. of John of Dublin (s. of John, R Moybologue (Kilm) qv) by Florence **dau.** of Thomas Sadleir of Castletown Co Tipperary; **bro.** of Rev Robert, V Derrylane (Kilm) qv; **bro.** of Rev William, R Martock (B & W)

    m. Catherine (**died** 4 Jan 1877 at Cloughjordan Rectory. Issue incl his eldest s. John Stewart of Kemanaghanka Java **m.** 5 May 1880 at Cherleville Ch Isabella

Katherine 2nd **dau.** of Henry Harrison of Castle Harrison, Charleville
Died 21 Sep 1880

GUMLEY, ROBERT –1892

TCD & Div Test 1860

d 1860 p 1861; C Inver (Conn) 1860–62; PC Corrawallen (Kilm) 1862–68; V Derrylane (Kilm) 1868–72; V Drumsnatt (Clogh) 1872–80; R Killadeas (Clogh) 1880–92

s. of John of Dublin (**s.** of Rev John, R Moybologue (Kilm) qv); **bro.** of Rev John Stewart, V Fuerty (Elph) qv; **bro.** of Rev William, R Martock (B & W)

m. Florence **dau.** of Rev Thomas Pentland, R Drumreilly (Kilm) qv Issue 1. Rev John Robert, C Drumshambo (Ard) qv; 2. Rev Francis Albert TCD BA 1894 d 1895 p 1898 C Maryborough (Leigh) 1895–97 C Castlecomer (Oss) 1897–1901 C Newcastle (Drom) 1901–07 C St Mary Halifax (Wakef) 1907–08 C St Hilda Middlesborough (York) 1908–14 PC Gateforth w Hambleton (York) 1915–37; 3. Rev Edmund Maurice (**died** 6 Feb 1940) **b.** 14 Oct 1875 Co Monaghan TCD BA 1898 Div Test (2) BD 1919 d 1900 p 1901 C Castlejordan (Meath) 1900–01 C Carrickfergus (Conn) 1901–02 C St Mary Belfast (Conn) 1902–04 C Holy Trinity Marylebone (Lon) 1904–05 C St Matthew Canonbury (Lon) 1905–10 Dep Sec ICM for Ireland 1910–12 C St Mary Magdalene Belfast (Conn) 1912–15 R Dunaghy U (Conn) 1915–21 R Ballintoy (Conn) 1921–33 C-in-c Clanabogan (Derry) 1933–40 **m.** Kathleen Emma Mary **dau.** of Ven Francis James Hurst, Archd of Clogher; 4. Oonagh Norah **m.** 1927 St Paul's Ch Cape Town Rev F de Burgh Sidley **s.** of Rev Henry de Burgh Sidley, R Forgney (Meath); 5. Charles Henry, MD of Cincinnati Ohio

Died 8 Jan 1892

GUNNING, ALEXANDER 1710/11–*c.* 1793

b. 1710 or 1711 Dublin; ed there by Mr Johnston; ent TCD 13 Jul 1729 aged 18 BA 1734 MA 1739

V Kilgeffin (Elph) *c.* 1740–77

s. of Alexander, merchant

m. and had issue 1. Rev Alexander, R & V Castleblakeney (Elph) qv, 2. Rev George **b.** Roscommon ed by Mr Young ent TCD 26 Oct 1778 aged 15 BA 1783 C Coleraine (Conn) 1789

Died *c.* 1793; Will proved in 1793

GUNNING, ALEXANDER 1754/55–

b. 1754 or 1755 Roscommon; ent TCD 23 Sep 1774 aged 19 BA 1779

R & V Castleblakeney (Elph) 1780–1823

s. of Rev Alexander, R Kilgeffin (Elph) qv (**s.** of Alexander)

m. and had issue 1. Rev William Hodson (**died** 22 Apr 1880) **b.** Roscommon ent TCD 1 Jun 1812 aged 17 who was a Clk in Canada; 2. Mary **m.** 1809 Samuel Abbot

GUTHRIE, JOHN JAMES FERGUSON

d 1874 p 1874 (Kilmore); C Drumreilly (Kilm) 1874; V Drumreilly (Kilm) 1874–77; R Drumcliffe (Elph) 1877–79; Chapl Thames Mission London 1880

HACKETT, ALFRED   –1889

TCD BA 1874 Div Test 1876

d 11877 p 1878 (Cashel); C Tallow (Lism) 1877–82; V Bumlin (Elph) 1882–88; res

eldest **s.** of Rev Peter (**died** 6 Mar 1891), V Aghamacart (Oss) 1883–91; **bro.** of Rev Frederick John (**died** 19 Jan 1930 aged 68), R Kildollagh (Conn); **bro.** of Rev Rev William Montague (**died** 5 Oct 1903), R St Mary Hoxton (Lon); **bro.** of Rev Ernest Augustus (**died** 12 Jan 1929), R Kilgobbin (A & A)

Died 7 Jan 1889 Dublin

HACKETT, THOMAS

V Asselin *alias* Boyle w Kilcorkey 1785–97; there may be some confusion between these two Thomas Hacketts

HACKETT, THOMAS   1763–1840

b. 1763 Galway; ed by Rev Mr Hackett; ent TCD 5 Jun 1780 aged 16 BA 1784 MA 1817

Sacrist of Clonfert 1794–1802; V Ballysumaghan (Elph) 1797–1801 & 1802–40; V Kilcorkey & Kilgeffin (Elph) 1797–1802; V Boyle (Elph) 1797–1840; Preb of Kilmacallen (Elph) 1799–1840; V Taunagh Kilmacallen Drumcollum Aghana Killcredan and Shancoe (Elph) 1801–40; V Kilmactranny (Elph) 1801–17; Archd of Clonfert 1802–04; Preb of Killaspicmoylan (Clonf) 1804–12

s. of Rev Thomas

m. and had issue incl his 3rd **dau.** Anne **m.** 23 Feb 1840 Richard Bourke of Dublin

Died 1 Sep 1840 aged 77 **bur.** Boyle

HAIRE, ARTHUR   –1960

TCD BA & Div Test 1903 MA 1915

d 1903 (Southwell) p 1905 (Meath for Kilmore); C Somercotes (Derby — then S'well) 1903–05; C Kinawley (Kilm) 1905–09; C East Hoathly (Chich) 1909–13; V Laughton (Chich) 1913–26; TCF 1916–17; Hon CF; V Framfield (Chich) 1926–48; Perm to Off Dio Chichester from 1948

s. of Rev William John, Preb of Kilmovee (Ach) 1910-17

Died 10 Oct 1960

HALAHAN, CHRISTOPHER *c.* 1834–1921

b. *c.* 1834 Dublin; TCD BA 1855 Div Test 1857

d 1858 p 1859 (Kilmore); C Drumshambo and Kiltoghart (Ard) 1858–60; C Carnew

(Ferns) 1860–69; C Knockbreda (Down) 1869–71; resigned after Disestablishment and took his annuity; C Trory (Clogh) 1873–74; R Rossorry (Clogh) 1874–1906; R Donaghmoine (Clogh) 1906–20; ret

s. of Samuel

m. Elizabeth Catherine Dobbin (**died** 2 Mar 1925 aged 91). Issue 1. Jane Fleming bapt 9 Feb 1862 **died unm.** 20 Mar 1928 **bur.** Dean's Grange Dublin; 2. George Augustus Frederick bapt 31 May 1863 ed Portora Royal Sch Enniskillen; 3. Samuel Handy ed Portora Royal Sch TCD MB **m.** and had issue a **s.** Reeves **died** Jul 1915; 4. Christopher bapt 12 Feb 1867; 5. Elizabeth Catherine Dobbin **b.** 29 May 1868

Died 2 April 1921 Glenageary Dublin

HALAHAN, HERBERT MAZIERE –1919

TCD BA 1898 Div Test 1899 MA 1906

d 1899 p 1901 (Kilmore); C Drung (Kilm) 1899–1902; C Berehaven (Ross) 1902–07; resided in Castletown Berehaven to 1919.

Died 22 Jun 1919

HALES, EDWARD   1795/96–1846

b. 1795 or 1796 Dublin; ent TCD 6 Jul 1812 aged 16 BA 1818

V Rossinver (Kilm) 1835–46

s. of Rev William, V Killeshandra (Kilm) qv (s. of Rev Samuel) by Mary **dau.** of Rev Irwine Whitty, R Killeshandra (Kilm) qv

m. 6 Jan 1830 Anne eldest **dau.** of James Denham of Fairwood Park Co Fermanagh. Issue incl 1. Mary **m.** Thomas E Crooke; 2. yst **s.** Edward (**died** 3 Nov 1858 aged 22), Lt 19th Regt

Died Jun 1846

HALES, JAMES

C Killeshandra 1825/26

HALES, WILLIAM   1747–1831

b. 8 Apr 1747; ed by Mr Foley; ent TCD 1 Nov 1764 Sch 1767 FTCD 1768 BA 1769 MA 1772 BD 1779 DD 1784; TCD Prof of Hebrew and Oriental Languages 1782. He was a distinguished scholar and writer.

V Killeshandra (Kilm) 1787–1831; pres by TCD Chanc of Emly *c.* 1812–31

s. of Rev Samuel, DD, Preb of Kilbrittain (Cork)

m. 21 Jul 1791 at Providence Co Carlow Mary (or Mai) (**died** 12 Apr 1828 aged 69) **dau.** of Rev Irwine Whitty, C Killeshandra qv Issue incl **sons** 1. William; 2. Rev Edward, R Rossinver (Kilm) qv; **daus.** incl 1. eldest **dau.** Mary **m.** 11 Feb 1826 Col Pepper of Ballygarth; 2. Elizabeth **m.** 18 Oct 1825 Rev Edward Pepper of Barragh Co Carlow

Died 30 Jan 1831 aged 83

PUBLICATIONS
Sonorum doctrina rationalis et experimentalis, 1778
De motibus planetarum dissertatio, 1782
Analysis aequationum, 1788
The Inspector, or, Select Literary Intelligence for the Vulgar, 1799
Irish Pursuits of Literature, 1799
Methodism Inspected, 1803–05
A New Analysis of Chronology, 3 vols, 1809–12
Letters on the Tenets of the Romish Hierarchy, 1813

HALL, HILKIAH BEDFORD
Univ Coll Durham BA 1845 MA 1848 BCL 1859
d 1848 p 1849 (Durham); C Long Benton 1848; C Lesbury (Newc) in 1851; C Darlington (Dur) 1852; V Russagh (Ard) and PC Rathaspeck (Ard) 1858–61, coll 20 Oct 1858; afterwards Lecturer, Halifax Par Ch (Wakef) 1861

m. Issue incl a son **b.** at Rathowen Glebe 19 Sep 1859
PUBLICATIONS
A Companion to the Authorised Version N.T. 1856
Sodom, A Sermon 1860
A New Translation of the Epistle to the Colossians
Epiphany Lectures
Advent Lectures, etc

HALL, JAMES JOHN 1854/55–1901
b. 1854 or 1855; TCD BA 1896 Div Test 1898 MA 1899
d 1896 (Dublin for Kilmore) p 1898 (Kilmore); C St John Sligo 1896–1901
Died 26 Nov 1901 aged 46
PUBLICATION
Editor *Irish Church Directory,* 1897, 1898

HALL, RICHARD AUGUSTUS 1823–1895
b. 5 Sep 1823 Monaghan; ed privately; ent TCD 12 Oct 1839 BA & Div Test 1844 MA 1857
d 1846 p 1848; C Kinawley (Kilm) 1846–48; C Kilkeel (Drom — then in Exempt Jurisdiction of Newry and Mourne) 1849–51; PC Derrygortreavy (Arm) 1852–65; emigrated to found a colony in the Bay of Islands, NZ; R Howick (Dio Auckland) 1868–82; R Omeath (Arm) 1882–83; PC Quivvy (Kilm) 1883–94

s. of Richard Perry of Tully Hse Monaghan; **bro.** of Rev Alexander Lindsay, PC Armaghbreague (Arm)

m. 11 Dec 1849 Mary eld **dau.** of Thomas Gibson Henry, JP of Kilkeel Co Down. Issue 1. James Campbell **b.** 23 Oct 1851 TCD BA BCh MB 1878 **m.** 9 Feb 1880 Sarah Frances **dau.** of John Harrison Massue Wilson of Roscrea Co Tipperary by Sarah **dau.** of James Willington, DL; 2. Thomas **b.** 23 Feb 1853 **m.** Edith Whitelaw and had issue; 3. John Alexander Lindsay (**died** 1937) **b.** 5 Dec 1855 **m.** Harriette eldest **dau.** of Edward Mayne Tabuteau and had issue incl (i) Alice Mary (ii) Henrietta **m.** Reginald Lindesay (iii) Ethel Jane (**died** 1933) (iv) Edith (**died** 1917) (v) Norah **m.** Harold Peacocke of Papatoetoe NZ (vi) Aileen (vii) Winifred **m.** Beresford Hart of Timaru NZ (viii) Kathleen Grace (ix) Lilian **m.** Ralph Storey of Hamilton NZ (x) Gertrude Zilla (xi) Frances **m.** Arthur Sargent of Wellington NZ and had issue a dau; 4. Richard Augustus **b.** 1 Oct 1858 **m.** Sophia eldest **dau.** of John II Burnside of Auckland NZ and had issue incl Richard John Burnside **b.** 11 Oct 1894 **m.** Elizabeth Lumsden; 5. Charles Wiliam (**died** 1917) **b.** 28 Jan 1864 Capt Royal Irish Fusiliers

Died 5 Nov 1895

HALLOWELL, WILLIAM –*c.* 1640

TCD BA 1618 MA 1621

coll V Templenylan *alias* Roscommon (Elph) 10 May 1627; again pres by the Crown 12 Sep 1635; V Killukin (Elph) 1635–40

Died *c.* 1640

HALPIN, ARTHUR NEVILLE

TCD BA 1879 MA 1883

d 1879 p 1880; C Killeshandra (Kilm) 1879–82; C Birr (Killaloe) 1882–84; C Christ Ch Eccleston Lancs (Manch) 1884–86; C Newcastle–under–Lyme (Lich) 1886–90; Chapl Reading U (Ox) 1890– still there 1921

HAMILTON, ABRAHAM 1773–1861

b. 1773 Co Donegal; ed by Dr Norris, Drogheda; ent TCD as FC 9 Nov 1789 aged 16 BA 1794 MA 1810

V Donegal (Raph) 1796–1823; R Clonmany (Raph — then Derry) 1801–15; V Kinneigh (Cork) 1815–47; V Cloonclare (Kilm) 1823–42

s. of John of Ballintra Co Donegal by Isabella (née Stewart)

Died 16 Dec 1861 Dublin

HAMILTON, ALFRED –1932

TCD BA 1875

C Castleterra (Kilm) 1876–77

Died Oct 1932 Dublin

HAMILTON, CHARLES 1773–1840

b. 1773 Co Down; ed by Mr Cromie; ent TCD 19 Nov 1788 aged 15 BA 1793; JP Co Down

d 28 Sep 1794 (Drom) p 25 Apr 1795 (Down); V Tullylish (Drom) 1795–1813; V Gen Dromore 9 Dec 1813; V Garvaghy (Drom) 1813–28; V Killaney (Down) 1817–20; R & V St John Sligo (Elph) 1820–44;

s. of Hugh

m. (1) St Mary's Par Ch Newry Jane (died Jun 1828). Issue incl dau. 1. Margaret (died 24 Sep 1825 at Tullylish Vicarage aged 16); at least two sons 1. Rev Hugh Samuel (died s.p. 1 Jul 1858 at Bagnol–les–Bains France) b. Co Down ent TCD 2 Nov 1818 aged 15 BA 1823 MA 1829 R Garvaghy (Drom) in succession to his Father 1828–58 m. 13 Oct 1836 Trim Par Ch Co Meath Amelia Anne yst dau. of Joseph Fox of Doolistown Co Meath; 2. his yst s. Charles T, Lt 39th Regt and North Down Rifles m. 6 Oct 1847 at Clonallon Ch Warrenpoint Co Down Harriet Eleanor yst dau. of William Edward Reilly of Tamnaharrie Co Down, MP for Hillsborough and High Sheriff Co Down 1815 by Harriet dau. of Robert Hamilton of Strabane

m. (2) 11 Jun 1829 at Warrenpoint Sarah Anne (died 5 Mar 1839 bur. St Patrick's Ch Newry) eldest dau. of William Wallace of Newry

m. (3) Dec 1841 Booterstown Par Ch Dublin Eliza dau. of Dr Henry

Died 10 Apr 1844 at Sligo Rectory

HAMILTON, CHARLES HANS 1836–

b. 1836 Lancashire; TCD BA & Div Test (2) 1860

d Apr 1861 p 22 Dec 1861 (Derry); C Tullyaughnish (Raph) 1862; PC Knocknarea (Elph) 1864–67; C Campsall (York) 1868–77; R Horne (Roch) 1877–89; V Holybourne (Win) 1889–still there 1909, gone 1913

s. of Rev Charles James, PC St John Birkenhead (Ches)

HAMILTON, DONALD McWATTY

TCD BA 1896 Div Test 1898 MA 1899

d 1899 (Dublin for Tuam) p 1900 (Kilmore for Tuam); C Galway (Tuam) 1899–1903; C Castleknock U (Dub) 1903–07; R Killesherdoney (Kilm) 1907–15; R Castleterra (Kilm) 1915–19; Prec's V Kilkenny Cath (Oss) 1919–20; Perm to Off Dio Dublin 1920–23; P-in-c Glen Sutton Montreal (Dio Montreal) 1923–24; R St Paul Southampton Port Elgin (Dio Montreal) 1924–28; C St Andrew Bishop Auckland (Dur) 1928–31; R Timperley (Ches) 1931–

m. (1) Jessie Helen (died 28 Aug 1903) dau. of Canon T B Robertson, R St Munchin's Limerick (Lim)

m. (2) Maud dau. of Capt George Reynell Gresson, 27th Inniskilling Fus, Drogheda. Issue Donald William

HAMILTON, EDWARD 1755/56–

b. 1755 or 1756 Co Tyrone; ed by Mr Noble; ent TCD 1 Feb 1773 aged 17 BA 1777

d p 16 Nov 1783; C Cloonclare (Kilm) 1783; prob same as Edward Hamilton who became R Killaderry U (Kild) 1815

s. of John

m. Isabella yst dau. of William Nixon of Mullaghduff Co Fermanagh

HAMILTON, FREDERICK 1802/03–1892

b. 1802 or 1803 Sligo; ent TCD 5 Nov 1821 BA 1826 MA 1832

d 1828 p; C Toomna (Elph) 1840–45; V Eastersnow and Kilcola (Elph) 1845–79; R Creeve (w Croghan from 1871) (Elph) 1848–79; Precentor of Elphin 1848–76

s. of William *vectigalis exactor*

m. and had issue incl 1. William, MD (**died** 26 Feb 1924 at the Abbey, Boyle); 2. Rev Frederick John, R Knocknarea (Elph) qv; 3. eldest **dau.** Bessie Georgina **m.** 17 Sep 1902 Very Rev Francis Burke, Dean of Elphin qv

Died 9 Mar 1892 aged 89

HAMILTON, FREDERICK JOHN 1855–1932

b. 17 Mar 1855 Eastersnow Rectory; TCD (1st place at entrance) BA (Resp) and Wall Bibl Sch 1877 Heb Pri (1) Chald & Syr Pri & Div Test (1) 1878 BD 1887 DD 1893; Univ of London BD 1906

d 1878 (Tuam p 1879 (Ossory); C Gorey (Ferns) 1878–80; C St John Sligo 1880–81; R Knocknarea (Elph) 1881–84; C Urney (Kilm) 1884; R Urney (Kilm) 1884–86; Asst at St Thomas Finsbury Park (Lon) 1886–87; C Christ Ch Barnet (Lon) 1887–91; PC Rams' Episcopal Ch Homerton (Lon) 1891–1907

s. of Rev Frederick, V Eastersnow (Elph) qv (**s.** of William)

Died 21 Jun 1932

PUBLICATIONS

The Best Book of All and how it came to us
Editor of *The English Churchman* 1911–1929
Translation into Latin of the Syriac *Ecclesiastical History* of Zacharias Rhetor

HAMILTON, GEORGE –1967

TCD BA 1915 Div Test (2) 1916 MA 1920; QUB MB BCh BAO 1927

d 1917 p 1918 (Kilmore); C Mohill (Ard) 1917–21; res and went to QUB.

Died 1967

HAMILTON, HUGH

C St John Sligo (Elph) 1828

HAMILTON, HUTCHINSON 1725/26–1779

b. 1725 or 1726 Dublin; ed by Mr Piggott; ent TCD 7 Apr 1743 aged 17 BA 1747 MA 1750 LLB & LLD 1773

V Mostrim (Ard) *c.* 1750–1779

s. of Very Rev John, Dean of Dromore 1724–29 (**s.** of Rev James, R Knockbreda and Dundonald (Down) and Elinor Wauchope) by Frances only **dau.** of Rt Rev Frances Hutchinson Bp of Down and Connor

m. (settlements dated 17 Dec 1751) Catherine (**died** Jun 1805 Merrion Sq Dublin) eldest **dau.** of Most Rev John Ryder, Abp of Tuam and Kilmore qv

Died 1779

HAMILTON, JAMES

d 29 Sep 1630 (Durham); R Dundonald and Holywood (Down) from 1636; Treas of Dromore 1660–61; perhaps V Athleague Kilbegnet Balynakilly Kilcroan & Dunamon (Elph) 1662–83; Preb of Ballintubber (Elph) 1662–83

    s. of Rev Patrick, Minister of Enderwick in E Lothian; yst **bro.** of James 1st Viscount Clandeboye; see also Swanzy's *Succession Lists of the Diocese of Dromore*, pp 61–62

HAMILTON, JAMES 1768/69–1844

b. 1768 or 1769 Co Monaghan; ed by Mr Abraham Shackleton; ent TCD 13 Nov 1786 aged 17 BA 1791

R Drumgoon (Kilm) 1815–26; R Ardingley (Chich) 1826–44

    5th **s.** of Sir James of Cornacassa Monaghan, High Sheriff 1786

    m. Margaret widow of Col Samuel Black, HEICS and **dau.** of Major Jerome Noble 28th Regt

    Died 1844

HAMILTON, JOHN 1814/15–

b. 1814 or 1815; ed by Mr Wall; ent TCD 17 Oct 1834 aged 19 BA 1839

d 1841 p; C Cloonclare (Kilm) 1841; R Cloonclare (Kilm) from 1842; he or another John Hamilton was R Cloonclare and Clonlogher (Kilm) 1856–68; V Killargue (Kilm) 1868–78

    prob John Hamilton **s.** of James

HAMILTON, LOUIS 1686/87–1743

b. 1686 or 1687 Enniskillen; ed by Mr Dennis at Enniskillen Sch; ent TCD 21 Apr 1703 aged 16, degres not recorded, BA in D.R

R Killukin (Ard) 1722–25; R & V Ardcarne (Elph) 1723–43; Archd of Elphin 1723–43

    s. of Gustavus, *tribunus militum* (Colonel), Governor of Enniskillen by his 2nd wife Margaret **dau.** of Edward Cooper

    m. Mary Cooper

    Died 1743

HAMILTON, MORDAUNT 1704/05–

b. 1704 or 1705 Bangor Co Down; ed by Mr Clarke, Lisburn; ent TCD 5 Jun 1722 aged 17 Sch 1724 BA 1726 MA 1729

d 20 Sep 1730 (Dublin) p; lic C Kilkeevan Baslick and Ballintubber 12 Jul 1732; C Donaghmore (Drom) 1758

    s. of Rev Robert, V Bangor (Down) 1720–

HAMILTON, ROBERT SMYLY GREER *c.* 1857–1928

b. *c.* 1857; TCD BA 1883 Div Test 1884 MA 1893

d 1884 p 1885 (Kilmore); C Urney (Kilm) 1884–86; R Sixmilecross (Arm) 1886–96; R Derryloran (Arm) 1896–1905; R Dundalk (Arm) 1905–24; Preb of Ballymore (Arm) 1913–24; Dean of Armagh and Keeper of Armagh Public Library 1924–28

s. of Rev Robert, R Drumcre (Arm) 1870–79 (**s.** of Robert of Omagh Co Tyrone) by Emily eldest **dau.** of Thomas Kinley of Dungannon Co Tyrone; **bro.** of Rev Leigh Richmond, C Sixmilecross (Arm)

m. 2 Dec 1919 Constance Helen (**died** 10 Jun 1936) yst **dau.** of Frederick and Marian (née Hannay) Kinahan of Belfast

Died 23 Oct 1928 S.P. Belfast **bur.** Armagh Cathedral

HAMILTON, SAMUEL DEREK 1934–2005

b. 29 Jul 1934 Stoneyford Co Antrim; ed RBAI; Tyndale Hall Bristol 1954 Univ of Bristol BA (2cl Theol) 1958

d 1959 p 1960; C St Catherine (Dub) 1959–61; C Booterstown (Dub) 1961–63; R Drumcliffe Lissadell and Ahamplish (Elph) 1963–69; V Cahir (Lism) 1969–76; C Willowfield Belfast (Down) 1976–79; C-in-c Sallaghy (Clogh) 1979–83; ret

s. of Samuel Henry and Winifred Maud (née Armstrong) of Stoneyford

m. 8 Sep 1962 at Booterstown Angela **dau.** of Maurice and Ellen Stein of Ashford Kent. Issue 1. Catherine Jill **b.** 9 Apr 1965; 2. Susan Grace **b.** 25 Apr 1966; 3. Deborah Jane **b.** 10 Oct 1968; 4. Duncan Samuel **b.** 26 Nov 1974

Died Dec 2005

HAMILTON, WILLIAM

d 1879 p 1880 (Tuam); C Headford (Tuam) 1879–81; I Turlough (Tuam) 1881–82; V Mostrim (Ard) 1882–85; R Killery and Killenumery (Ard) 1885–87;

m. and had issue incl Sarah Millicent **m.** Oct 1938 Campbell Hemsworth Gardner of Groomsport Co Down

HAMMICK, MORGAN WILLIAM GARNIER 1866–1934

b. 1866; TCD Primate's Heb Pri 1889 BA 1890 Div Test (2) 1891 MA 1896 BD 1898

d 1890 p 1891 (Dublin); C Santry (Dub) 1890–96; Canon Res Christ Ch Cath Dublin 1896–1908; R Ardagh and Moydow (w Kilglass from 1932) (Ard) 1908–34; Preb of Kilmacallen (Elph) 1934

Died 26 Sep 1934 aged 68

HAMON, WILLIAM

V Kiltoghart (Ard) May to Jun 1634; inst 10 May (F.F.)

HAMOND, WILLIAM

pres to V Oughteragh (Kilm) and V Shrewer = Shrule (Ard) with Clause of union 20 Nov 1634 (L.M. V. 111)

HANBURY, WILLIAM CHRISTOPHER 1847–1930

b. 27 May 1847 Co Meath; TCD BA 1868 MA & BD 1891

d 1870 (Armagh) p 1871 (Kilmore); C Swanlinbar (Kilm) 1870–74; C-in-c Derryvullan (Clogh) 1874–75; R Derryvullan (Clogh) 1875–80; R Swanlinbar (Kilm) 1880–88; R Larah and Lavey (Kilm) 1888–94; PC Killoughter (Kilm) 1894–1914; ret

    s. of Christopher of Coolderry Co Meath by Susan

    m. 26 Jan 1881 Sophia Kate Hamilton 3rd **dau.** of Robert Barrett of Donnycarney Co Dublin

    Died 26 Feb 1930

HANDCOCK, CHARLES LAUNCELOT

TCD BA & Div Test (1) 1879

d 1879 p 1880 (Kilmore); C Urney (Kilm) 1879–80; PC Killoughter (Kilm) 1880–82; went to Australia; C Braidwood NSW (Goulburn) 1884

HANDCOCK, ELIAH

b. in Dublin; ed by Rev Hugh Quigg, Dublin; ent TCD 16 Feb 1727/28 BA 1732 MA 1736

V Innismagrath (Kilm) 1726–40; V Cashel & Rathcline (Ard) 1727–40; R Annaduff (Ard) 1740–*c.* 66; cited for not appearing and paying procurations for Annaduff Sep 1742 (Arm DR); was living in Meath in 1754; R Clonfadforan (Meath) 1768–71; C Athlone (Meath) 1768; Master of Endowed Sch Athlone

    s. of Ven Matthew, Archd of Kilmore qv (**s.** of William) by Elizabeth **dau.** of Sir Elias Best; **bro.** of Rev John, R Lavey (Kilm) qv

    was **m.** and had issue Thomas BA 1775 MA 1810

HANDCOCK, JOHN *c.* 1708–1793

b. *c.* 1708 Dublin; ed by Mr Sheridan, Dublin; ent TCD 27 Mar 1725/26 aged 17 BA 1730

C Lavey (Kilm) 1756–78; R & V Bailieborough & Moybologue (Kilm) 1773–78; R Lavey (Kilm) 1778–93

    s. of Ven Matthew, Archd of Kilmore qv (**s.** of William) by Elizabeth **dau.** of Sir Elias Best; **bro.** of Rev Eliah, R Annaduff (Ard) qv

    Died 1793

HANDCOCK, JOHN GUSTAVUS 1798/99–1838

b. 1798 or 1799 Co Roscommon; ed by Dr Burrowes; ent TCD 1 Nov 1813 BA 1818

d; p 26 Apr 1822 (Kildare); PC Benown (Meath) 1822–23; R Tashinny and

Abbeyshrule (Ard) 1823–31; R Annaduff (Ard) 1831–38

    4th **s.** of Richard 2nd Baron Castlemaine

    m. 13 Nov 1827 Frances Flood **dau.** of John Harward Jessop of Doory Hall Co Longford. Issue 3 **s.** and 3 **daus.**

    Died 2 Mar 1838 aged 39

HANDCOCK, MATTHEW 1658–1740

b. 1658 Co Meath; ed by Dr Wettenhall; ent TCD 4 Dec 1674 aged 16 BA 1678 MA 1682

V Urney and R Castleterra (Kilm) and Archd of Kilmore 1690–1740

    5th **s.** of William, MP of Twyford Athlone by Abigail **dau.** of Rev Thomas Stanley; **bro.** of Rev Stephen qv

    m. Jun 1693 Elizabeth **dau.** of Sir Elias Best. Issue incl 1. William **b.** Dublin ent TCD 28 Mar 1715/16 aged 18 BA 1720 LLB 1726; 2. Abigail bapt 9 Aug 1701; 3. Rev Elias, R Annaduff (Ard) qv; 4. Rev John, R Lavey (Kilm) qv

    Died 1740 **bur.** 21 Jan 1740 old churchyard of St Patrick's Dublin

HANDCOCK, STEPHEN 1657–1719

b. 3 Sep 1657; ed by Mr Wetenhall, Dublin; ent TCD 4 Dec 1674 BA 1678; adm Caius Coll Camb 9 May 1679 Sch 1679–81 Fellow 1681–83

V Ahascragh Killyon Tesseragh Taghboy Disert & Lisnuffy (Elph) 1685; Dean of Clonmacnois 1689–97; R Ahern (Cork) 1693–1719; Dean of Kilmacduagh 1700–19; was admitted R Ahascragh (Elph) 20 Dec 1701

    3rd **s.** of William, MP of Twyford Athlone (ancestor of the Earls of Castlemaine) by Abigail **dau.** of Rev Thomas Stanley; **bro.** of Rev Matthew qv

    m. 26 Oct 1688 Margaret (**died** 1721) **dau.** of Augustus Thomas Warner and widow of Francis Evatt of Kilgriffe. Issue incl a 2nd **s.** Gustavus, TCD BA 1730 Recorder and MP for Athlone **m.** and had issue; a **dau.** Margaret **m.** Rev Peter Wybrants

    Died 1719 Dublin

HANLON, ALEXANDER PATRICK, THE O'HANLON 1814–1898

b. 1814 Co Clare; was originally a Roman Catholic; ed by Dr King; ent TCD 5 Nov 1839 aged 25 BA 1844 Div Test 1846 LLB & LLD 1865

d 1846 (Killaloe for Ardfert) p 1847; C Murhir* (A & A) 1846–48; C Kingscourt (Enniskeen) (Meath) 1848–49; PC Altedesert (Arm) 1849–51; R Iniscaltra (Killaloe) 1851–71; C Tallow (Lism) 1872–75; R Killashee and Ballymacormack (Ard) 1875–78; Deputy Sec Irish Soc 1879

    s. of Patrick, Farmer

    m. Miss Parker

    Died 10 Dec 1898 at Ballyhalmet Hse Tallow Co Waterford aged 84

    * The Parish of Murhir near Tarbert in north Kerry had clergy until the mid 15th

Century. After the Reformation it seems to have been absorbed into the Parish of Aghavallin

HANSARD, WILLIAM

coll R & V Fenagh Kiltoghart and Kiltubrid (Ard) 18 Nov 1700 (FF) ? resigned 1732; R Castlerahan and V Lurgan and Munterconnaught (Kilm) 1692–1700; V Drumlease and Killargue (Kilm) 1699–1737; V Killan, now Shercock 1733

HARDCASTLE, THOMAS 1655–1701

b. 1655 Yorkshire; ed Ripon Sch; Christ's Coll Camb BA 1674 MA 1678

d p 1677 (London); V Cloonclare Clonlogher & Killasnett (Kilm) 1681–86; V Rossinver (Kilm) 1681/82–85; V Donoughmore and Donard (Glend) 1685–88; R & V Hollywood (Glend) 1685–88; Preb of Dunlavin in St Patrick's Cath Dublin 1686–91; V Castledermot Kilkea and Kinneigh (Glend) 1688–1701; Preb of Kilmactalway in St Patrick's Cath Dublin 1691–1701

s. of William of Laverton Yorks

Died 1701

HARDY, CHARLES EDWARD   –1957

TCD BA 1891 Div Test 1892 MA 1904

d 1891 (Down for Kilmore) p 1892 (Armagh for Kilmore); C Lurgan (Kilm) 1891–95; C Kells (Meath) 1895–98; R Almoritia w Rathconrath (Meath) 1898–1902; R Slane (Meath) 1902–09; R Welford w Wickham (Ox) 1909–1957

Died 5 Jun 1957

HARE, HENRY 1835–1911

b. 1835 Co Laois; TCD BA 1857 Div Test (2) 1859

d 1859 p 1860; C Drumgoon (Kilm) 1860–62; C Carbury (Kild) 1862–67; PC Girley (Meath) 1867–81; C Forgney (Meath) 1882; C Moira (Drom) 1883; C Baydon (Sarum) 1884–85; C-in-c Belleek and Slavin (Clogh) 1885; R Cleenish (Clogh) 1885–1904; ret

s. of Rev George, Chapl Royal Hosp Kilmainham Dublin

m. Helen (**died** 6 Mar 1924 Dublin). Issue incl 1. George (killed at Jerusalem 27 Dec 1917); 2. Edward Henry, 2nd Lt (killed in Afghanistan 23 Jul 1919)

Died 3 Jan 1911

HARRIS, ARTHUR c. 1670–1712

b. c. 1670 in the Parish of St. Bee's (Carl); ed by Mr Jackson of St. Bee's; ent TCD 26 Mar 1687/88 aged 17 BA 1692 MA 1695

V Carrigallen and Outragh or Oughteragh (Kilm) 1698–1705; Treas of Connor 1705–10; R Newtownards (Down) 1708–10; Chanc of Connor 1710–12

s. of Robert of Belturbet Co Cavan

m. Margaret. Issue 1. Mary; 2. Charity; 3. Elizabeth; 4. Jane. He was perhaps the person described in Burke's *Landed Gentry of Ireland*, 1912 article *Smyth of Mount Henry* as "Anthony Harris, DD", who married Margaret **dau.** of James Smyth of Lisnagarvey Co. Antrim and **sister** of Edward Smyth, Bishop of Down and Connor 1699–1720

Died 25 Nov 1712 Lambeg Co Antrim

HARRIS, CHARLES JOHN ALGERNON   1878–1944

b. 7 Nov 1878; ed Rathmines Sch; TCD BA & Div Test 1904

d 1904 p 1906 (Kilmore); C Calry (Elph) 1904–07; C Wexford (Ferns) 1907–14; R Kilmactranny (Elph) 1914–18; R Emlaghfad (Ach) 1918–29; R Kilmoremoy (Killala) 1930–41; ret

    s. of Rev Canon Samuel Musgrave (1846–1914) R Rathmines (Dub) 1883–1914 (**s.** of Joseph) by Nannie **dau.** of William Heron of Dublin; **bro.** of Rev Samuel Brent Neville (1874–1936), SPG Missy at Dharbad; **bro.** of Rev Ernest Musgrave, R Groomsport (Down) 1913–38

    m. Mary Ellen and had issue incl 1. Sheila Margaret Annette **b.** 14 Apr 1910 Wexford; 2. Rev Rupert Gustavus Musgrave, R Cloone (Ard) qv

    Died 11 Jan 1944

HARRIS, JOHN   1802–1882

b. 1802 Wicklow; ed by Mr Williams; ent TCD 6 Nov 1820 aged 17 BA 1825 MA 1832; Cantab BA by incorp 1825

PC Ashfield (Kilm) 1828–48; R Killan (Kilm) 1848–*c.* 70; res at Disestablishment; seems to have lived in Kent in the 1860s; got two years leave of absence 31 Dec 1865; was holding a curacy in Kent in 1883

    s. of Michael, *pragmaticus*

    m. 23 Mar 1836 Maria Belissa yst **dau.** of Chief Justice Charles K Bushe

    Died 24 Oct 1883 at St Valery, Hastings aged 81

HARRIS, RUPERT GUSTAVUS MUSGRAVE   1913–1990

b. 1913; TCD BA 1936 Div Test 1937 MA 1956

d 1937 p 1938; C Shankill Lurgan (Drom) 1937–41; CF (CE) 1941–46; R Cloone and Chapl Lough Rynn (Ard) 1946–52; R Castlebar (Tuam) 1952–56; R Galway (Tuam) 1956–80; Dom Chapl to Bp of Tuam 1957–80; Preb of Balla and Faldown and Provost of Tuam 1960–70; Archd of Tuam 1970–80; Chapl Univ Coll Galway; ret 1980

    s. of Rev Charles John Algernon, R Kilmactranny (Elph) 1914–18 qv (**s.** of Rev Canon Samuel Musgrave and Nannie **dau.** of William Heron of Dublin) by Mary Ellen

    m. and had issue a **s.** David and a **dau.** Sheelagh

    Died 16 Apr 1990

HARRISON, CHARLES RICHARD 1800/01–1853

b. 1800 or 1801 Galway; ent TCD 5 Jul 1819 aged 18 BA 1824 MA 1832

PC Monivea (Tuam) 1830–38; R Cashel (Ard) 1838–53

> **s.** of Thomas
>
> **m.** 12 April 1839 Newbury Ch Marianne yst **dau.** of Richard Pilkington, Capt 81st Regt; his eldest **dau.** Catherine Augusta **died** 9 May 1920 at 13 Beechwood Ave Ranelagh Dublin
>
> **Died** April 1853

HARRISON, CHRISTOPHER 1709/10–1768

b. 1709 or 1710; ed by his father; ent TCD 28 Jun 1732 aged 22 Sch 1734 BA 1736

V Abbeylara (Ard) *c.* 1751.

> **s.** of Rev Robert, qv; **bro.** of Rev William qv
>
> **Died** 1768

HARRISON, ROBERT –*c.* 1751

V Streete Abbeylara and Russagh (Ard) 1701–51

> **m.** and had issue 1. Robert **b.** at Streete 1700/01 ent TCD 23 Jan 1718/19 aged 18 Sch 1721 BA 1723; matric Christ Ch Oxford 21 Oct 1723 BA 23 Mar 1723/24; 2. Rev William qv; 3. Rev Christopher qv
>
> **Died** *c.* 1751, will prov 1752

HARRISON, WILLIAM 1701/02–1740

b. 1701 or 1702; ent TCD 18 Apr 1719 aged 17 Sch 1721 BA 1723 MA 1726

V Bumlin Kiltrustan Lisonuffy and Kilglass (Elph) 1730–40; Preb of Ballintubber 1734–40

> **s.** of Rev Robert, V Streete (Ard) qv; **bro.** of Rev Christopher qv
>
> **Died** Nov 1740; he was drowned in crossing a deep ford at Bumlin

HART, GEORGE VAUGHAN 1799/1800–1836

b. 1799 or 1800 Limerick; ed by Dr Stewart; ent TCD 3 Feb 1817 aged 17 BA 1821 MA 1832

d 1822 (Rochester) p; served a curacy near Blackheath 1822–25; C Mevagh (Raph) 1826; C Drumcliffe (Elph) 1827; C Aglish (Tuam) 1829–36

> **s.** of Rev George Vaughan Ledwich, R Castlebar (Tuam) 1818–38 (**s.** of John) by Maria Murray **dau.** of Very Rev John Hume, Dean of Derry
>
> **m.** Oct 1828 Miss Patterson of Drumcliffe. Issue six children
>
> **Died** of fever 18 Nov 1836 at Castlebar Co Mayo

†HARVEY, THOMAS ARNOLD 1878–1966

b. 7 Apr 1878; ed St Oswald's Coll, Ellesmere Salop; TCD Sch 1899 BA 1900 BD & Div Test (1) and Theo Exhib (1) 1903 Elrington Theol Special Pri 1907 DD (j.d.) 1935

d 1903 p 1904 Bp 1935; C St Stephen (Dub) 1903–07; Minor Canon St Patrick's Cath Dublin 1904–07; R Lissadell (Elph) 1907–12; R Ballywillan (Conn) 1912–16; R Booterstown (Dub) 1916–33; RD of St Mark (Dub) 1926–33; Prof of Past Theol Univ of Dublin 1929–34; Preb of Dunlavin and Canon of St Patrick's Cath Dublin 1930–33; Dean of St Patrick's Cath Dublin 1933–35; elected Bishop of Cashel Emly Waterford and Lismore by United Synods 25 Jan 1935; consec in St Patrick's Cath Dublin 25th Mar 1935; enthroned in Waterford Cath 4th Apr 1935; enthroned in Cashel Cath 12th Apr 1935; enthroned in Lismore Cath 25th Apr 1935; Bishop of Cashel Emly Waterford and Lismore 1935–58; ret

> **s.** of Rev Alfred Thomas (1843–1898) (**s.** of George), R Athboy (Meath) 1885–98 and Ida Susette (**died** 10 Mar 1943)
>
> **m.** 26 Apr 1911 Isabel Kathleen **dau.** of Rev Francis Robert and Theodosia Agatha (née Martin) Burrowes, Ancaster Hse Bexhill-on-Sea Sussex. Issue 1. Rev Clement Arnold TCD BA BAI 1949 Div Test 1954 d 1954 p 1955 C Ballywillan (Conn) 1954–57 C Finaghy (Conn) 1957–62 Min-in-Ch Conventional District Corby (Pet) 1962–68 became RC **m.** 21 Oct 1959 St Polycarp Finaghy Belfast Margaret Lee of Belfast and had issue (i) Timothy Arnold **b.** 10 Jun 1961; 2. Philip **m.** 24 Feb 1943 Patricia Edith **dau.** of WF Watt of Dunmore Co Waterford; 3. Very Rev Brian **b.** 14 Apr 1916 TCD BA (1) 1938 BD 1941 d 1940 p 1941 C St George (Dub) 1940–45 Sec (Ireland) SCM and Dean of Residences QUB 1945–48 TCD Miss to Chota Nagpur 1948–51 and 1955–63 Head of Miss 1951–55 Archd of Hazaribagh 1960–63 Exam Chapl to Bp of Connor 1963–70 R Kilkenny and Dean of Ossory 1970–91 Preb of Ullard in Leighlin Cath 1970–91 ret **m.** 19 Oct 1955 Mary Honor **dau.** of David Gillman and Amelia Emily Frances (née Wood) Scott of Bandon Co Cork and had issue (i) Rev Patrick Arnold **b.** 20 May 1958 R Abbeyleix (Leigh) 1991 (ii) Christopher Gillman **b.** 20 Feb 1960 (iii) Nicholas Martin **b.** 27 Nov 1961; 4. Ione Frances **m.** 11 Sep 1935 Maurice **s.** of Rev Frederick Dobbin, R Donaghpatrick (Meath); 5. Susette **m.** 25 Apr 1942 Lt John Howard Keesey, RAMC
>
> **Died** 25 Dec 1966 **bur.** St Patrick's Cathedral Graveyard Dublin

HARVEY, WILLIAM COATES 1871/72–1959

b. 1871 or 1872; TCD BA 1894 MA 1897 Div Test 1898 LLB & LLD 1907

d 1895 p 1896 (Kilmore); C Lurgan (Kilm) 1895–98; C St Mary Drogheda (Meath) 1898–1901; C Paynestown (Meath) 1901–02; R Paynestown and Stackallen (w Slane from 1933) (Meath) 1902–59; RD of Duleek (Meath) 1928–59; Dio Reg Meath 1936–45; Exam Chapl to Bp of Meath 1940–59; Dean of Clonmacnoise 1945–59

> **s.** of James of Belfast; **bro.** of Canon James Gerald, R Gartan (Raph) 1919–57
>
> **m.** 1902 Eveline Norcott (**died** 21 Jan 1948) 2nd **dau.** of William Adams, JP of Drumalta Hse Cootehill Co Cavan. Issue 1. Rev Norman William Brabazon Gifford (**died** 12 Nov 1929) **b.** 1903 Univ of Oxford Merton Coll MA d 1928

(Dublin) C Taney (Dub) 1928–29; 2. Arabel Eveline Chatterton **m.** 1938 Harold Archibald (**died** 28 Dec 1968) **s.** of Capt H Kenneth and Lady Diana Allison (née Montgomerie) and had issue (i) Diana **m.** 11 Apr 1977 in London Kenneth Kennedy (ii) Camilla

Died 4 Apr 1959 aged 87

HASSARD, FRANCIS 1802/03–1856

b. 1802 or 1803; TCD BA

C Drumcliffe (Elph) 1842–54; V Fuerty (Elph) 1854–56

s. of Jason

Died 25 Aug 1856 Dublin aged 53

HASSARD, ROBERT

b. Co Fermanagh; ent TCD 6 Jul 1671; ed by Mr Dunbar

V Killeshandra (Kilm) 1678–c82

s. of William; **bro.** of Capt Jason of Skea, High Sheriff Co Fermanagh 1695

HATHERSALL, HENRY

d 23 Sep 1632 p 6 Oct 1633 (Kilmore); V Clonlogher (Kilm) 1632–35. He seems to have held this V up till the Commonwealth period when he was appointed Commonwealth Minister at Dromahair Co Leitrim, being "of an unblameable conversation and with a savory frame of spirit" at £100 from 26 Dec 1657 (Seymour's *Commonwealth MSS*). A charge of "scandal" by company keeping seems to have been brought against him in 1659, but he was cleared of it

HATHERSALL, JOHN

is V Camma and Kiltoom (Elph) in 1615 (R.V.)

HATTON, EDWARD –1632

V Mostrim and "Killea" ?= Killoe (Ard) 1615–c. 1634; Archd of Ardagh 1619; still there in 1628; Chanc of Clogher pres by the Crown 12 July 1617; Preb of Tyholland in Clogher Diocese and R Monaghan (Clogh) from 1622. In 1629 he was named by the Crown as 5th Prebend but in 1630 and 1631 as 1st Prebend (Morrin iii, 464, 544, 615). He got a grant of a glebe in Galloon Parish (Clogh) 29 Feb 1631/32. In the *State of Dio of Meath*, 1622, he is V Clonarney and Castletowndelvin, and is described as an "MA and a preacher of good life and conversation and resideth sometimes in his vicarage at Castletowndelvin and sometimes at another living of his in the Diocese of Clogher".

m. Anne and had issue Martha **m.** Rev James Slacke, R Killesher (Kilm) qv

Died 1 Oct 1632

HAWKES, EDWARD 1638/39–

his name is Bankes in Tuam D.R.; prob E H **b.** 1638 or 1639 Burton-on-Trent; ed by Mr Hall at Newark Sch; adm Siz Christ's Coll Camb 21 Apr 1655 aged 16 matric 1655 BA 1656 MA 1660

Preb of Tibohine & V Templemoylan (Elph) 1662–*c.* 98; V Killukn (Elph) 1665–98; V Roscommon & Kilmenan (Elph) 1665–*c.* 98; Provost of Elphin 1674–82– but see Samuel Hawkes below; V St John Athlone Kilbride Kilgeffin Killeevan & Clontuskart (Elph) 1694

yst **s.** of Rev Samuel

m. and had issue 1. Charles **m.** Margaret Kirkpatrick; 2. John **m.** Catherine, aunt of Oliver Goldsmith; 3. Lewis of Ballinafad Co Roscommon **m.** Catherine; 4. Catherine **m.** Rev Thomas Crofton, later Dean of Elphin qv

HAWKES, LEWIS 1704/05–

b. 1704 or 1705 Co Roscommon; ed by Mr Contarine; ent TCD 20 Sep 1723 aged 18 BA 1728

d 9 Aug 1730 p 13 Aug 1732; C Tessaragh (Elph) 1730; R Kilglass (Elph) to 1766

s. of John

HAWKES, LEWIS 1795/96–

b. 1795 or 1796 Roscommon; ed by Mr Jelly; ent TCD 1 Jul 1811 aged 15 BA 1817

lic C Kilgeffin and Ardclare (Elph) 25 Jun 1822 — still there in 1830

s. of Charles

HAWKES, SAMUEL

prob father of Edward above; Preb of Terebrine (Elph) 1661–74; Provost = Precentor of Elphin and V Kilcorkey, inst 10 Apr 1674 (F.F).

HAWKES, SAMUEL

R Kilmore (Elph) before 1681/82 is deceased

HAWKSHAW, ROBERT 1749/50–1813

b. 1749 or 1750; ed by Mr Cottingham; ent TCD 8 Jul 1765 Sch 1769 BA 1770 MA

d 1771 (Kilmore) p; Preb of Droghta (Clonf) 1777–84; Preb of Islandeddy (Kilmacduagh) 1777–1813; Preb of Fenore (Clonf) 1784–1813; Preb of Aghold (Leigh) 1784–85; Preb of Taghmon and R Ballycormick and C Ballymitty (Ferns) 1785–1813; V Gen Clonfert 1790; Preb of Terebrine (Elph) 1801–13

s. of Rev John, R Monaghan (Clogh) and **bro.** of Rev Samuel (**died** 4 Mar 1806) Preb of Tyholland (Clogh) 1792–1806 **m.** 1788 Cassandra (**died** 12 Apr 1799) **dau.** of Rev Samuel Madden

m. (M.L. 24 Oct 1785) Deborah (**died** 1827) **dau.** of Rev Samuel Madden of Kells and widow of Rev John Cooksey. Issue Samuel **b.** Wexford ent TCD 4 Nov 1811 aged 17 BA 1816 probably = Rev Samuel Madden Hawkshaw

Died on or about 31 Jan 1813 aged 63 **bur.** Taghmon Co Wexford

HAWORTH, JOHN LUTTRELL 1928–2004

b. 1928; ed Wilson's Hosp Multyfarnham Co Westmeath; was in business in Cork before ordination; CITC GOE 1967

d 25 Jun 1967 (Kilm) p 23 Jun 1968 (Kilm); BC Kilcommick and Ballymacormack (w Killashee from 1969) (Ard) 1967–70; C Ballymacelligott (A & A) 1970–71; TV Tralee G (A & A) 1971–72; I Kinneigh w Ballymoney (Cork) 1972–76; I Kilmoremoy (Killala) and Straid (Ach) 1976–78; BC Kilcoran U (Lim) 1978–80; I Aughrim (Clonf) 1980–83; Preb of Inniscattery (Killaloe) 1982-83; I Monasterevan w Nurney and Rathdaire (Kild) 1983–87; I Kiltegan w Hacketstown, Clonmore & Moyne (Leigh) 1987–92; I Fermoy U (Cloyne) 1992–96; ret

m. Rose Treacy of Cork. Issue 2 **sons** and a **dau.**

Died 2 Jun 2004

HAYMAN, ROBERT FLEMING 1931–

b. 11 Dec 1931 Kittanning PA USA; ed The Western High Sch Washington DC; Princeton Univ BA 1953; Gen Theol Sem NY MDiv 1956

d 1956 p 1956; Asst Priest St George's Ch Rumson (Dio New Jersey) 1956–58; R St John's Ch Kirkland WA (Dio Olympia) 1958–77; Archd of Olympia 1977–83; R St Luke's Ch San Francisco CA (Dio California) 1983–87; R Drumcliffe w Lissadell and Munninane (Elph) 1988–92; Preb of Tibohine (Elph) 1988–92; ret Living in Seattle USA from 1992

s. of Firman of Salisbury MDand Catherine (née Fleming) of Kittanning PA

m. 8 Sep 1962 Sarah **dau.** of James and Anne (née Cassedy) Pritchard. Issue 1. Robert Fleming **b.** 16 Sep 1964 **m.** Sherry Wartnow; 2. Victoria **b.** 26 Nov 1965 **m.** James Ross Sutton

HAZLETT, SAMUEL FRANCIS 1892/93–1932

b. 1892 or 1893; TCD BA & Div Test 1916 MA 1924

d 1916 p 1917 (Kilmore); C Kinawley (Kilm) 1916–21; R Drumreilly (w Newtowngore and Corrawallen from 1923) (Kilm) 1921–30; R Larah and Lavey (Kilm) 1930–32

yst **s.** of James of Monaghan

m. Elizabeth (**died** Jan 1946). Issue Frances Mary (Maisie), SRN **m.** 6 Sep 1954 St Peter's Ch Belfast Dr Alexander Jamison only **s.** of Mr & Mrs J McC Woods of Bangor Co Down

Died 31 May 1932 aged 39

HAZLEY, JOHN BRADLEY –1934

TCD BA 1924 MA & Div Test 1927

d 1927 p 1928 (Dublin); C Portarlington (Kild) 1927–30; C-in-c Ballintemple (Kilm) 1930–34

Died 3 Jun 1934

HEAD, JONATHAN CHRISTOPHER 1826–1916

b. 1826 Co Tipperary; ent TCD 14 Oct 1842 aged 16 BA 1848 Div Test (2) 1853

d & p 1854 (Killaloe); C O'Brien's Bridge (Killaloe) 1854–56; V Terryglass (Killaloe) 1856–72; V Ballinaclough (Killaloe) 1872–79; R Castleterra (Kilm) 1879–82; R Kinawley (Kilm) 1882–1905; ret

yst **s.** of Very Rev John, Dean of Killaloe

m. 14 Jul 1864 Anne Jane (**died** 24 Nov 1921 Kingstown) eldest **dau.** of Col Henry Shakespear, Commandant Nagpur Irregular Forces India. Issue incl Edward, 38th Regt

Died 31 Dec 1916 aged 90

HEALEY, JAMES CHRISTOPHER 1944–

b. 7 Aug 1944 Straffan Co Kildare; Lincoln Theol Coll 1984–86

d 1986 p 1987 (Lincoln); C Boultham (Linc) 1986–90; TV Gt Grimsby St Mary and St James (Linc) 1990–91; R Narraghmore Timolin and Castledermot (Glend) 1991–93; R New Ross G (Ferns) 1993–97; Dean of Lismore & R Lismore G (Lism) 1997–99; Chanc Cashel Cath Canon of Ossory and Prec of Waterford 1997–99; R Arvagh Carrigallen Gowna and Columbkille (Kilm) 1999–2002; P-in-c Winthorpe and Langford w Holme (S'well) 2002–2003; R Coddington and Winthorpe and Langford w Holme (S'well) 2003–

s. of William and Florence Dorothea (née Stewart) Elliott

m. 17 Oct 1964 Jennifer Elaine Medley of Isle of Wight. Issue 1. William; 2. Patricia

HEALY, JOHN 1850–1942

b. 1850; TCD BA 1875 LLB & LLD 1879; Sel Pr Univ of Dublin 1898

d 1873 (Down for Kilmore) p 1874 (Kilm); C Drumgoon (Kilm) 1873–75; R Killesherdoney (Kilm) 1875–77; C Holy Trinity Dublin (Dub) 1877–79; C Ballyboy (Meath) 1879–85; R Ratoath U (Meath) 1886–87; R Kells and Chapl of Workhouse (Meath) 1887–1917; no further incumbencies; Preb of Tipper in St Patrick's Cath Dublin 1898–1935; Dio Reg Meath 1904–14; Chapl to Lord Lt 1906–21; Archd of Meath & Exam Chapl to Bp of Meath 1914–28; Treas of St Patrick's Cath Dublin 1935–42

s. of George, printer of Dublin

m. St John the Evangelist's Ch Blindley Heath Surrey, Mary **dau.** of Frederick Thornton, MD. Issue 1. John Robert; 2. Rev Theodore Lelievre **b.** 1 Oct 1878 (**died** 23 Feb 1944) TCD BA 1902 MA 1910 d 1903 p 1904 C St Luke Belfast (Conn) 1903–04 C Christ Ch Londonderry (Derry) 1904–06 Dio C Derry and Raphoe 1906–12 R Ardstraw (Derry) 1912–36; 3. Iris **m.** Ven William Frederick

Alment, Archd of Meath 1936–40; 4. Eve Eleanor **m.** Rev Arthur Meagher Cave, R Moyliscar (Meath) 1925–43; 5. Olive **m.** Rev Marcus Henry Moore Given, R Athlone (Meath) 1927–40

Died 8 Mar 1942

PUBLICATIONS
The Ancient Irish Church, RTS, 1895
The 39 Articles with Explanations and Scripture Proofs
Art Teaching of the Ancient Irish Church, 1896
St. Patrick, 1897
The Vikings in Ireland
History of the Diocese of Meath, 2 vols, 1908

HEANY, THOMAS

TCD BA 1869 Div Test 1870 MA 1873

d 1869 (Down) p 1870 (Ossory); C Clontibret (Clogh) 1869–70; C Enniscorthy (Ferns) 1870–73; C St James (Dub) 1873–74; C Trinity Ch (Dub) 1874–77; R Calry (Elph) 1877–86; Chapl at Calais 1887; C Christ Ch Guildford (Guildf — then Win) 1888; V St Stephen Hull (York) 1889–1918; Last entry in Crockford 1918.

m. and had issue incl his yst **dau.** Sarah Louisa (**died** 18 Aug 1877 Dublin)

HEARDMAN, BARTIMEUS

V Shrule (Ard) 1640–*c.* 1673; inst V Shrower = Shrule inst 9 Feb 1640 (F.F.);

In Carte Papers xxi. 346, he is called "Martin Headsman V. of Shrower" and is residing in Dublin

HEARN, DANIEL   –1766

TCD BA 1713 MA 1718

may be same as Daniel Hearn coll V Tashinny and Abbeyshrule (Ard) 7 Oct 1720; R & V Annaduff (Ard) 1721–26; R Killan, now Shercock (Kilm) 1726–33; (he probably res. Killan on getting Fenagh etc.); Prec Cashel 1727; Archd of Cashel 1728–66; Preb Doon (Emly) 1729–66, R & V Kiltoghart and Kiltubride (Ard) *c.* 1732–40; held Fenagh (Ard) with them but he evidently was still R of Fenagh as in Sep 1742, he as R & V Fenagh is admonished to name a Parish Clk. & Schoolmaster (Arm DR). He signs Parl Ret 1766 as R Fenagh, held also Drung and Larah (Kilmore) 1740–66,

m. (1) Anne (M.L. 17 Aug 1728) **dau.** of ——Maxwell of Tynan Co Armagh

m. (2) (M.L. 24 May 1732) Anne of St Peter's Dublin **dau.** of Marcus Dowley of Dublin by Abigail Wolfenden. Issue 1. Mark Anthony **b.** Dublin ent TCD 4 Mar 1751/52 aged 17 BA 1756 **m.** Frideswede Jane **dau.** of John Lyster of Rocksavage and had issue four **daus.**; 2. Robert Thomas of Co Fermanagh, Lt of Dragoons **m.** (1) Frances **dau.** of Rev James Cooksey, R & V Castleterra (Kilm) qv and had issue; **m.** (2) Juliet Frances **dau.** of Major Michael Fleming of Roodstown Co Sligo and had issue Rev William Edward Hearn, V Kildrumferton (Kilm) qv; 3. William George Dowley **b.** Dublin ent TCD as SC 13 Jul 1769 aged 18 **m.** Jane **dau.** of Richard Phepoe of Dublin and had issue 7 **sons** and 6 **daus.** incl (i) Anna Maria

m. 28 Feb 1756 St Peter's Dublin Godfrey Taylor of Noan Co Tipperary (ii) Arabella **m.** (1) 22 May 1765 St Peter's Dublin William Henry Nassau Stephens of Ballinacargy Co Cavan **m.** (2) 11 May 1771 St Ann's Ch Dublin Rev Henry Dundas, R Mullingar (Meath) (iii) Charlotte **m.** Apr 1766 Edward Reilly (**died** 16 May 1801) of Cullentra Co Cavan. There is a pedigree of his descendants in Ulster Office

Died 1766 **bur.** Nov 1766 St Ann's Ch Dublin

HEARN, J

C Annagh (Kilm) 1824

HEARN, JULIUS STRIKE 1830/31–1868

b. 1830 or 1831 Co Cavan; ed by Dr Graham; ent TCD 1 Jul 1846 aged 15 BA 1851 d 1852 p; C Cloonclare (Kilm) 1858–68

2nd **s.** of Rev William Edward, R Kildrumferton qv (**s.** of Robert Thomas) by Henrietta Alicia **dau.** of Lewis Decimus Reynolds

m. 27 Dec 1858 Elizabeth **dau.** of Rev Charles Lyons Montgomery, R Innismagrath (Kilm) qv

Died 10 or 11 Aug 1868

HEARN, RICHARD THOMAS 1782/83–1838

b. 1782 or 1783 Co Fermanagh; ed by Dr Murray; ent TCD 3 Jul 1797 BA 1802 MA 1832

C Ardagh (Ard) *c.* 1830; inst V Rathcline (Ard) 1838; was Registrar of Dio Ardagh

s. of George

m. Anne. Issue incl 2nd **dau.** Jane **m.** 5 Jun 1840 Marcus L 3rd **s.** of Marcus L Crofton of Liscormucke Co Longford; a **dau.** Anne **m.** 7 Jun 1845 William Young only **s.** of Capt William S Buxton, 60th Regt; a **dau.** Charlotte **m.** (1) Robert Thomas Blackburne (**died** 19 May 1850) eldest **s.** of Rev William Edward Hearn, V Kildrumferton (Kilm) qv; **m.** (2) 25 Jul 1851 St Mary's Ch Dublin Edward Allen Counters **s.** of Anthony Blackburne of Parsonstown Hse Co Meath; his 4th **dau.** Arabella **m.** 8 Sep 1843 St George's Ch Dublin Francis Rankin of Annesbrook Co Dublin; a **dau.** Maria **m.** Jul 1857 Finglas Ch Dublin James Daniel **s.** of Rev William Edward Hearn qv; his yst **s.** Richard Thomas **m.** 15 Sep 1843 Isabella eldest **dau.** of R A Neely of Grange

Died Dec 1838 in his 56th year

HEARN, WILLIAM EDWARD 1785–1856

b. 1785 Anglesey; ed by Mr Quead; ent TCD 1 Dec 1800 aged 15 Sch 1805 BA 1807 MA 1826

C Annagh (Kilm) 1830 V Killargue (Kilm) 1831–46; V Kildrumferton (Kilm) 1846–56

s. of Robert Thomas of Co Fermanagh, Lt 14th Dragoons (s. of Rev Daniel, V Drung (Kilm) qv by his 2nd wife Juliet Frances **dau.** of Major Michael Fleming of Roodstown Co Sligo

m. 22 Dec 1824 Henrietta Alicia only child of Lewis Decimus Reynolds of Kinsale Co Cork. Issue **sons** 1. Robert Thomas Blackburne (**died** 19 May 1850) **b.** Co Cavan ent TCD 22 Oct 1832 aged 17 BA 1837 **m.** Charlotte **dau.** of Rev Richard Thomas Hearn, R Rathcline (Ard) qv; 2. Rev Julius Strike, C Cloonclare (Kilm) qv; 3. Hon William Edward (**died** 23 Apr 1888) **b.** 21 Apr 1826 Belturbet Co Cavan ed Portora Royal Sch Enniskillen TCD LLD; QC Prof of Greek at Queen's Coll Galway; elected prof of Mod Hist and Mod Lit Log and Pol Econ in the Univ of Melbourne 1854; became Dean of the Faculty of Law in Melbourne Univ 1874 Chanc of Melbourne Univ 1886 Member of the Legislative Council of Victoria 1873 and Leader do. 1883 **m.** (1) 14 Dec 1848 St Paul's Ch Dublin Rosalie **dau.** of the Rev William Joseph Henry Le Fanu, V St Paul's (Dub) **m.** (2) 1878 Isabel **dau.** of Major W G St. Clair; 4. James Daniel **m.** Jul 1857 Finglas Ch Dublin Maria **dau.** of Rev Richard Thomas Hearn, R Rathcline (Ard) qv; 5. George Marcus MD of Woodville Co Cavan **m.** 4 Feb 1862 Derrylane Ch Elizabeth Mary Constance widow of Rev Christopher Adamson and **dau.** of Ven J C Martin DD; 2 **daus.** incl 1. Henrietta Frances (**died** 15 May 1856 aged 24)

Died 10 May 1856 aged 69

HEDGES, THOMAS TOOVEY

ed Lichfield Coll 1871

d 1873 (Lichfield) p 1876 (Kilmore); C Ockbrook (Derby — then S'well) 1873–74; C Ridding (Derby — then S'well) 1874–76; C Cloone (Ard) 1876–77; V Alfriston Sussex (Chich) 1877–82; R Pilham (w Springthorpe from 1895) (Linc) 1882–1909; Chapl Gainsborough Union 1885–92; Lic Pr Dio Chich 1926–27; Last entry in Crockford 1932

HEFFERNAN, JOHN MICHAEL 1794–

b. 1794 Limerick; ed by Mr O'Brien; TCD BA 1816 MA 1832

C Fethard (Lism, then Cash) in 1830; C Newport (Cash) in 1844; lic C Kiltoghart (Ard) 25 May 1855 (D.R.).

s. of William

HEIGH, ROBERT

inst V Kilronan (Ard) 5 Jul *c.* 1640 (F.F.)

HELAGH, LEONARD

BA

V Rathaspeck (Ard) 1615–*c.* 22; church in good state (R.V.)

HEMPHILL, RICHARD 1847–1928

b. 1847 Dublin; ed Harrick's Sch Dublin; TCD BA 1870 Div Test (1) 1872 MA 1894

d 1870 p 1873 (Cork); C Rathcormac (Cloyne) 1870–74; C Wellington (Lich) 1874–76; C Carysfort (Dub) 1876–78; Chapl at Pau and Versailles France 1879–80; C Old Buckenham 1880–82; C St Luke Barton Hill Brixton (S'wark) 1882–85; R Belleek (Clogh) 1886–87; C Donoughmore (Glend) 1887–92; C Kilternan (Dub) 1892–94; R Ballycanew (Ferns) 1894–99; Dio C Leighlin 1899–1902; C Haddlesey (York) 1902–05; C-in-c Drumshambo (Ard) 1905–14; R Mostrim (Ard) 1914–27; ret

> **s.** of Rev Richard, C Castlecomer (Oss) to 1840 Chapl N Strand (Dub) 1840–85 **died** 15 Aug 1885 (**s.** of Samuel, MD of Clonmel Co Tipperary) by Averina Purdon (**died** 23 Sep 1919) **dau.** of John Sherlock of Ballyheen Co Cork
>
> **Died** 26 Sep 1928

HENDERSON, ARTHUR

ent TCD 14 Jun 1759 Sch 1762 BA 1763

C Kiltubrid (Ard) *c.* 1763

> was **m.** and had issue Arthur **b.** Co Leitrim ent TCD 1792 aged 17

HENDERSON, ROBERT 1943–

b. 26 Mar 1943 Belfast; ed Graymount "Open Fields" Sch; Belfast Coll of Technology HNC Business Studs; TCD GOE 1966; UUJ Dipl in Guidance and Counselling 1987; Univ of Wales Dip Applied Theol; Lambeth STh 1994

d 1969 p 1970 (Arm); C Drumglass (Arm) 1969–72; Asst Chapl Miss to Seamen Belfast 1972–77; Chapl Miss to Seamen Mombasa Kenya 1977–78; R Mostrim Granard Clonbroney Killoe Rathaspeck Streete and Kilglass (Ard) 1978–82; R St Matthew Belfast (Conn) 1982–92; RD of Mid Belfast 1990–93; R Kilroot and Templecorran (Conn) 1992–98; ret

> **s.** of George Williams, RN (HMS *Caroline*) of Belfast (**s.** of John and Elizabeth Rachel of Glasslough Co Monaghan) by Agnes **dau.** of James and Agnes McCormack of Moy Co Armagh
>
> **m.** 28 Jul 1964 St Paul's Ch Belfast Elizabeth, NSM 1999 **dau.** of William John and Eleanor McGookin of Belfast. Issue 1. Michael Robert **b.** 5 Feb 1967 **m.** Janet Louise…of Northamptonshire and have issue Abby Louise; 2. Gillian Heather **b.** 24 Feb 1970 **m.** Bruce Douglas MacLean of Glasgow and have issue (i) Aidan (ii) Hannah

HENDERSON, WILLIAM DESMOND 1927–2006

b. 1927; TCD BA & Div Test 1956 MA 1964

d 1956 p 1957 (Armagh); C Derryloran (Arm) 1956–59; C Conwall U w Gartan (Raph) 1959–62; R Killoughter and Cloverhill (Kilm) 1962–64; R Kilrush (Killaloe) 1964–66; R Achonry, Tubbercurry and Kilmactigue (Ach) 1966-75; res.

> **s.** of Edward William of Newtowngore Co Leitrim (**s.** of Edward and Jane of Ballyconnell Co Cavan) by Agnes Gertrude **dau.** of James McGaffin and Agnes

(née McClean) of Newry; **bro.** of Canon Edward, R Stranorlar (Raph) 1985–93

m. Aug 1962 St Augustine Londonderry Audrey Valentine (**died** 7 Oct 2005) **dau.** of R Clarke.of Fahan Co Donegal

Died 21 Sep 2006

HENRY, THOMAS 1809/10–1866

b. 1809 or 1810 Co Westmeath; ed by Mr Waters; ent TCD 6 Nov 1826 aged 16 BA 1831 MA 1862

lic C Kilcommick (Ard) 22 Jun 1840, nom 23 Jan 1839; C Kilcommick (Ard) 1840–47; R Kilcommick (Ard) 1848–66

> **s.** of Laurence, *armiger*
>
> **m.** (1) (ML Dublin 1845) Georgianna Charlotte only **dau.** of Rev George Brittaine, R Kilcommick (Ard), qv and had issue George bapt 22 Sep 1846; she died in childbirth
>
> **m.** (2) (ML Dublin 1854) Rebecca Jane Bickerstaff; issue a **dau.** (**died** 1933)
>
> **Died** 4 Oct 1866 at Clonmaskill, the residence of his **bro.**

HENRY, WILLIAM   –1768

TCD MA 1748 DD 1750

R Killesher (Kilm) 1731–40; R Urney (Derry) 1740–68; Dean of Killaloe 1761–68

> was perhaps "Rev Mr Henry" who **m.** 14 Apr 1738 a **dau.** of Marcus Dowling, Esq
>
> **Died** Feb 1768 **bur.** St Ann's Dublin

PUBLICATIONS

Topographical Description of the Parish of Killesher, 1739 (in Armagh Library)
Letter to Walter Harris with Topographical Notices of Places in Co. Antrim
Hints towards Topographical Description of Cos. Sligo and Donegal
Upper Lough Erne, ed by Sir Charles S King, Bt. 1892

HENTHORN, JAMES 1706–

b. 1706 Co Meath; ed at Oldcastle Co Meath; TCD BA 1728

inst V Ivernon (Elph) 9 Jul 1745 (F.F.)

> **s.** of Isaac, farmer

HERBERT, NICHOLAS 1778/79–1871

b. 1778 or 1779 Co Tipperary; ed by Mr Clarke; ent TCD 3 Nov 1794 aged 15 BA 1801 MA 1811

d 1803 p 1804 (Kilm); C Knockgraffan (Cash) 1803–05; C Kilsheelan and Carrick-on-Suir (Waterf) 1805–11; Preb of Dysart and Kilmoleran (Lism) 1810–71; R Drumlease (Kilm) 1811–24; R Knockgraffan (Cash) 1824–63

> 3rd **s.** of Rev Nicholas, R Knockgraffan (Cash) 1762–97 (2nd **s.** of Edward, MP

of Muckross); **bro.** of Rev John Otway, R Knockgraffan (Cash) 1801–03

Died 22 Oct 1871 New Inn Co Tipperary aged 92

HEWITT, JOHN FREDERICK WILLIAM   –1957

TCD BA 1895 MA 1914

d 1897 p 1898 (Chester); C St Anne Birkenhead (Ches) 1897–1900; C Drumgoon (Kilm) 1900–03; R Killesherdoney (Kilm) 1903–07; R Castleterra (Kilm) 1907–14; R Killesher (Kilm) 1914–25

Died 12 Feb 1957

HEWSON, HENRY BROWNRIGG 1856–1936

b. 9 May 1856; ed Rathmines Sch; TCD BA 1880 MA 1883

d 1879 p 1880 (Kilmore); C Athlone (Elph) and acting CF 1879–80; C Holy Trinity and St Lawrence (Lim) 1880–84; R Drakestown (Meath) 1884–85; R Clonaslee (Kild) 1885–1926; CF 1902–04; ret

s. of Falkiner Minchin of Pembroke Rd Dublin

m. and had issue incl 1. a **s.** Major Frank Lloyd **m.** 15 Jun 1915 at St Martin's Salisbury Dorothy only **dau.** of Arthur Whitehead; 2. only **dau.** Eileen **m.** 2 Dec 1916 Bombay Cath Capt Bertram E Hickson, 27th Light Cavalry, Indian Army

Died 11 May 1936

HEWSON, WILLIAM 1785/86–

perhaps W H **b.** 1785 or 1786 Ballina Co Mayo; ed by Mr Logue; ent TCD as Siz 4 Jun 1806 aged 20

V Bumlin (Elph) 1823–c30.

s. of Henry

HICKES, GEORGE 1737/38–

b. 1737 or 1738 Co Roscommon; ed by Mr Gunning at Elphin; ent TCD 15 Jun 1756 aged 18 Sch 1758 BA 1760

V Ahamplish (Elph) 1769–70

perhaps **s.** of John, V Fuerty (Elph) qv

m. Jane **dau.** of Richard Hickes

Will proved 25 Jan 1775

HICKES, JOHN 1699/1700–*c.* 1780

b. 1699 or 1700 near Elphin; ed by Mr Griffin at Elphin; ent TCD 3 Jul 1718 aged 18 Sch 1725 BA 1726

signed Parliamentary Return of 1766 for Athleague Fuerty and Dunamon & Kilbegnet (Elph); V there 1734–*c.* 1780

probably **s.** of John (**s.** of Richard)

Died *c.* 1780– Will proved 1780

HICKES, JOHN 1722–1793

b. 1722 Co Roscommon; ed by Dr Griffin; ent TCD 2 Apr 1739 Sch 1741 BA 1743 MA 1747

Preb of Oran (Elph) 1758–93; was VGen Elphin in 1783

eldest **s.** of Richard by Catherine

Died 1 Sep 1793

HILL, AUGUSTUS CHARLES EEDWARD 1839–

b. 1839 Kent; BA 1861

C Mohill (Ard) 1868–70

s. of Lord George

HILL, FREDERICK CHARLES 1892/93–1970

b. 1892 or 1893; TCD Div Test and Bibl Gk Pri 1920 BA (Supp Sen Mod Oriental Langs) 1924 MA 1930

d 1925 p 1926 (Chester); C Northenden (Ches) 1925–27; Perm to Off St Paul Tranmere (Ches) 1927–28; C Southowram 1928–31; C-in-c Killeroran = Killyon Castleblakeney & Athleague (Elph) 1931–36; R Kilshannig (Cloyne) 1936–56; R Castlemagner U & Kanturk U (Cloyne) 1956–70

only **s.** of C A Hill of Belfast

m. 5 Aug 1931 Edith **dau.** of Canon Thomas Stewart Watson, R Carrickmacross (Clogh) 1914–37

Died 11 Dec 1970 aged 77

PUBLICATION

Contributor to *Hermathena*

HILL, JOHN

TCD BA

was pres to Deanery and V Kilmore and to V Ballintemple and R Kedy (Kilm) 30 Apr 1619 (L.M. V. 104); was resident at Togher in Kilmore Parish 1622, "value merely titulary"

m. Anna (**died** 29 May 1634) **dau.** of Capt Street and widow of Lt Ashley. Issue 1. John; 2. Jane

HILL, JOHN BERESFORD 1765–1806

b. 16 Dec 1765 or 1766 Londonderry; ed by Mr Blackhall; ent TCD 1 Jul 1782 BA 1787 MA 1801

R Langfield Lr (Derry) 1796–1805; Preb of Clonmethan (Dub) 1801–03; V Oughteragh (Kilm) 1803–06; Preb of Moville (Derry) 1806

s. of Sir Hugh Bt.

m. 7 Apr 1803 Letitia (**died** Oct 1855), who survived him and **m.** (2) Capt Steele,

23rd Regt, 2nd **dau.** of Dominick McCausland of Daisy Hill Co Derry. Issue incl 1. George who succeeded his grandfather as 3rd Bt; 2. Rowley John, Capt in the Army **m.** and had issue a **dau.** Mary (**died** 13 Jun 1879) **m.** 6 Oct 1829 Rev John 2nd **s.** of David Potts of Roscommon

Died 4 Dec 1806

HILTON–SPRATT, JOHN   –1958
TCD BA 1911 MA 1917

d 1912 p 1913; C St Barnabas Belfast (Conn) 1912–14; C Kinawley (Kilm) 1915–16; TCF 1916–20; Hon CF 1920; C St Anne's Cath Belfast (Conn) 1920–24; C St Martin's U (Cant) 1924–27; V Chilham (Cant) 1927–46; RD of Westbridge 1932–44; R Charlton Musgrave (B & W) and Chapl Wincanton Public Assistance Institution 1946–54

Died 19 Feb 1958

HINDES, GEORGE 1799–1858
b. 1799 Dublin; ed by Mr Craig; ent TCD 3 Nov 1817 aged 17 BA 1825 MA 1832 C Kildrumferton (Kilm) 1828–*c.* 44; V Killargue (Kilm) 1846–58

s. of Walter, *pragmaticus*

m. 1828 Frances Louisa Griffith (**died** 24 Oct 189– at Hastings aged 81)

Died 9 Jun 1858 aged 59

HINDES, SAMUEL
perhaps same as S H matric Siz from King's Coll Camb 1627 BA 1628/29; (? Merton Coll Ox BD 1636)

R Standish Lancs 1640; V Richmond Surrey 1653–55; V Banstead 1658–60; V Ballintubber Kilkeevin Oran Clonmagarmacan Baslick and Drimtemple (Elph) 1673, coll 9 Aug by Abp of Tuam

HIRST, THOMAS 1841/42–1918
b. 1841 or 1842; TCD BA 1870

d 1870 (Down for Kilmore); C Killargue (Kilm) 1870–73

bro-in-law of Rev R Leech, R Drumlane (Kilm) qv

Died 27 Nov 1918 aged 76

HOARE, EDWARD
C Clonbroney (Ard) to 1827; C Mostrim (Ard) 1827–; C Shrule (Ard)

HOBART, WILLIAM KIRK 1832–1902
b. 1832; TCD Sch 1852 BA (Resp) 1860 Div Test (1) 1861 LLB & LLD 1872

d 22 Dec 1861 (Kilmore) p 1862 (Down); C Ardagh (Ard) 1861–64; C Ballycushlane

(A & A) 1864–65; C Castleisland (A & A) 1865–66; C Templeshanbo (Ferns) 1867–76; C Aghadowey (Derry) 1877–79; Dio C Derry and Raphoe 1884–93 incl C Kilteevogue (Raph) 1887; R Killany (Clogh) 1893–1902

Died 24 Aug 1902

PUBLICATION

The Medical Language of St Luke 8vo Dublin 1882

HOBSON, JOHN MEADE 1814/15–1891

b. 1814 or 1815 Limerick; ed by Mr Darley at Royal Sch Dungannon; ent TCD 4 Jul 1831 aged 16 BA 1841 MA 1879

d 1841 (Kildare for Kilmore) p 1842 (Down for Kilmore); C Tomregan and Carrigallen (Kilm) 1841–43; C Carnew (Ferns) 1843–44; C Ferns (Ferns) 1844–46; C Kilnehue (Ferns) 1846–55; Preb of Blackrath w R St Mary Kilkenny (Oss) 1855–64; R Maryborough (Leigh) 1864–74; R Adamstown (Ferns) 1874–84; Preb of Whitechurch (Ferns) 1879–84

> s. of Rev Richard Jones, Preb of Connor by Bridget **dau.** of Bolton Waller, DL of Castletown Co Limerick
>
> **m.** (ML 1846) Matilda Catherine **dau.** of Edward Peed, Solicitor of Cork and **sister** of Canon James Peed, R Wexford (Ferns) Issue **sons** 1. Rev Richard Meade (**died unm.** 30 Jun 1880) TCD BA 1872 C Wareham (Sarum); 2. Ven Edward Waller (**died** 17 Apr 1924 aged 72 Armagh) **b.** 5 Dec 1851 Gorey Co Wexford ed Royal Sch Dungannon TCD Sch 1874 BA 1875 Div Test 1876 MA 1888 d 1876 p 1877 C Mariners' Ch Dun Laoghaire (Dub) 1876–78 C St Mark Portadown (Arm) 1878–81 R Moy (Arm) 1881–95 R Derryloran (Arm) 1895–96 R St Mark Portadown (Arm) 1896–1915 Prcb of Loughgall (Arm) 1904–08 Treas of Armagh Cath 1908–10 Chanc of Armagh 1910–13 Prec of Armagh 1913–14 Archd of Armagh and Keeper of the Public Library 1915–24 **m.** 11 Jun 1891 St Clement's Ch Bournemouth Frances Maria (**died** 3 Nov 1924 Co Carlow) **dau.** of Robert Westley Hall–Dare of Newtownbarry Hse Co Wexford; **daus.** 1. Mabella Olivia **m.** 18 Jul 1861 Edward Neill Banks of Belfast and had issue a **s.** and several **daus.** incl (i) Angel **m.** Rev Frederick Dobbin, MA, R Donaghpatrick (Meath) (ii) Alice Maude **m.** Very Rev John Percy Phair (**died** 28 Dec 1967), Dean of Ossory 1923–40 and Bp of Ossory Ferns and Leighlin 1940–62; 2. Elizabeth Annie **m.** 10 Aug 1892 David A Maxwell of Belfast and had issue; 3. Bridget Emily (**died** 4 Oct 1919 **bur.** Mt Jerome Dublin) **m.** as his 2nd wife Rev Benjamin Banks (**died** 12 Sep 1934), MA, Chanc of Connor 1914–29 and had issue (i) Charles Aemilius **b.** 13 Oct 1887 **m.** Edna **dau.** of Wingfield S Bonham of New York (ii) Frances Stephanie Nevill (**died** 21 Mar 1928) **b.** 22 Jul 1889 **m.** 12 Sep 1912 Hugh Craig Houston (iii) Lois Dorothea Wentworth **m.** 14 Oct 1925 Rev Harold Cecil Marshall (**died** 3 Jul 1987), P-in-c Culfeightrin (Conn) 1964–69
>
> **Died** 5 Dec 1891 Rathgar Dublin aged 76

HODGES, WILLIAM HENRY 1845/46–1927

b. 1845 or 1846 Clontarf Dublin; ed New Brighton Liverpool

d 1873 p 1874 (Kilmore); C Templemichael and Killoe (Ard) 1873–74; R Killoe (Ard)

1874; R Killaban (Leigh) 1874–77; C St Silas Lozells (Birm) 1877–79; R Killaban (Leigh) 1879–80; I Timahoe (Leigh) 1880–87; C Fethard (Ferns) 1887–89; C St Andrew Dublin (Dub) 1889–91; I Donadea (Kild) 1891–96; ret

> **m.** Charlotte Elizabeth Edge of Carlow. Issue **sons** 1. Thomas Richard **b.** 4 Sep 1875 Kingstown (Dun Laoghaire Co Dublin) **m.** 10 Apr 1917 Norah Margaret only **dau.** of Rev Chancellor Senior of Kilkenny; 2. William Henry **b.** 7 Jun 1878 Birmingham; 3. Elliott **b.** *c.* 1882 Timahoe; 4. George Henry Bertram **b.** 8 Jul 1885 Kilkenny **m.** 17 Sep 1920 Margery yst **dau.** of H A Hocknell of Blackburn; 5. Rt. Rev Evelyn Charles (**died** 18 Mar 1980) **b.** 5 Aug 1887 Co Carlow TCD Jun and Sen Exhib BA (Sen Mod Ment and Mor Philos) 1910 Div Test (2) 1911 MA 1913 BD 1923 HDip Ed 1920 DD (jure dign) d 1911 p 1912 Bp 1943 C Drumcondra (Dub) 1911–14 C Rathmines (Dub) 1914–17 Org Sec and Inspector Board of Rel Ed Dublin 1917–24 I Rathmines (Dub) 1924–27 Prin C of I Training Coll Kildare Pl 1928–42 Preb of Rathmichael in St Patrick's Cath Dublin 1934–43 Bp of Limerick Ardfert and Aghadoe 1943–60 ret P-in-c St Andrew Dublin 1965–71; **m.** 27 Dec 1927 Violet Blanche (**died** 1966) 3rd **dau.** of George Hill Crawford of Rathmines and had issue (i) Desmond William Hill **b.** 25 Sep 1928; (ii) Deirdre Elizabeth Jane **b.** 29 Mar 1933; **daus.** 1. Mary Kathleen **m.** Samuel George Forsyth; 2. Muriel Mary **m.** Thomas Wright; 3. Florence Ethelwyn **m.** 6 Apr 1920 Francis Russell 2nd **s.** of Campbell Ruttledge
>
> **Died** 4 Feb 1927 at Rathmines Rectory Dublin aged 81

†HODSON, JOHN   1608/09–1686

b. 1608 or 1609

V St Catherine (Dub) 1638–40; V Annagh (Kilm) 1640–61; Chapl to Dublin Castle 1641; Dean of Clogher and V Donagh and Errigal Truagh (Clogh) 1661–67; V St Peter Drogheda and R Louth and Beaulieu (Arm) 1661–67; Bp of Elphin 1667–1686; consec in St Nicholas' Galway 8 Sep 1667; pres to R Drumlummon (Ard) Co Roscommon (this one?) 17 Jan 1674/75 (L.M. V. 117); in Belturbet (Annagh), "he was a great sufferer by the rebellion and was necessitated for many years to absent himself in England and is not returned", 14 Aug 1660

> **bro.** of Rev Leonard, V Ahascragh (Elph) qv; he was ancestor of the Hodsons, Baronets of Hollybrook Co Wicklow.
>
> **m.** (1?) Abigail **dau.** of Robert Madden of Donore Co Meath by Joyce **dau.** of Edward Bassett of Yorkshire,
>
> **m.** (2) Elizabeth and had issue incl 1. William, R Annagh (Kilm) qv; 2. John; 3. Daniel; 4. a **dau.** who **m.** 23 Feb 1668 Henry Townley of Townley Hall Drogheda
>
> **Died** 18 Feb 1686 aged 77 **bur.** Elphin Cathedral
>
> Bishop Hodson in 1685 by deed, vested certain lands in Trustees, half rent of which was to go to maintain a Grammar School at Elphin, and the other half towards maintaining the Cathedral in repair

HODSON, LEONARD   –1685

V Tessaragh or Mount Talbot (Elph) 1671–85; V Ahascragh & Killyon (Elph) 1674–85; V Killenvoy (Elph) 1674–*c.* 1718.

bro. of Bp John qv
m. and had issue Rev Samuel qv
Died 1685

HODSON, SAMUEL 1646/47–1716

b. 1646 or 1647 at Walton; ent TCD 27 Jan 1666/67 aged 19 BA 1671

V Garvagh and Magherally (Drom) 1679–84; Preb of Terebrine (Elph) 1682–83; Preb of Ballintubber (Elph) 1683–1716; V Athleague Fuerty & Kilbegnet Kilcroan & Dunamon (Elph) 1683–1716; V Delvin and Killelagh (Meath) 1685–1709

s. of Rev Leonard qv

m. and had issue Leonard **b.** Dromore Co Down ed by Mr Cugh at Strokestown ent TCD 19 Feb 1696/97 aged 17 BA 1701 MA 1704 V Delvin (Meath) 1709–29; **m.** (ML 6 Sep 1712) Alice **dau.** of Thomas West of Corleagh Co Longford

Died 1716

HODSON, SAMUEL 1755/56–1827

b. 1755 or 1756; was JP for Co Roscommon

C St Peter Athlone and Chapl Athlone Garrison to 1827

Died 26 May 1827 at Hudson's Bay Co Roscommon aged 71

HODSON, WILLIAM

TCD Sch BA (Leslie has 1640, but this is hardly possible if his father was **b.** in 1608/09)

C Annagh (Kilm) 1661; R Annagh (Kilm) 1661–73

elder **s.** of Rt Rev John, Bp of Elphin qv by his 2nd wife Elizabeth

m. Elizabeth Pearce of Woburn. Issue incl 1. William **m.** Mary L'Estrange; 2. Susanna **m.** Robert L'Estrange

HOG, JAMES

R & V Kilmore (Elph) 1681/82–; pres 3 Mar 1681/82 by John Doherty, the Patron and inst 24 Mar

HOG, JAMES

C Mohill (Ard) to 1698

HOGAN, FREDERICK WILLIAM 1844/45–1921

b. 1844 or 1845; ed Royal Sch Armagh; TCD BA 1867 MA 1881

d 1869 p 1870; C Tamlaghtfinlagan (Derry) 1869–70; C Killowen (Derry) 1870–73; Chapl of Boyd Ch Ballycastle (Conn) 1873–74; Chapl to Earl of Erne and DC Holy Trinity Kilawley (Kilm) 1874–82; V All SS Eglantine (Conn) 1882–1915; was a well-known musician, and composed the hymn tunes *Magherafelt, Paradise* and *Sympathy*

s. of Rev James, R Magherafelt (Arm) 1861–78 (**s.** of William, Lawyer) by Sophia Margaret (née Ferrier); **bro.** of Rev Alexander Ferrier, C Llanfihangel Crucorney (Llandaff) 1864–72; **bro.** of Rev Henry, Prec of Christ Ch Cath Dublin 1895–1923; **bro.** of Rev James William, C Ballyculter (Down) 1879–86

m. 9 Sep 1873 Ellen 2nd **dau.** of Henry Kyle, JP DL of Laurel Hill Coleraine, High Sheriff 1868. Issue **sons** 1. James Clement **b.** 9 May 1876 TCD BA; 2. Henry Luke Kyle; 3. Wilfred Lawrence; 4. Rev William Kyle Patrick **b.** 10 Jul 1888 ed Campbell Coll Belfast TCD MA 1915 TCF in Great War Master in Dean Close Sch Cheltenham Gloucs 1920–23 V Horsford (Nor) **m.** 6 Oct 1932 Kathleen **dau.** of William Henry Foster Verschoyle of Dublin; **daus.** 1. Elizabeth Mary; 2. Sophia Margaret (**died** 1948) **m.** Lt Col Charles Marshall Ainslie, DSO RASC; 3. Annie Evangeline; 4. Frances Georgina Janet **m.** 23 Jun 1915 Maurice George **s.** of Rev Marcus Truman, V Arnold (S'well)

Died 1 Dec 1921 Bournemouth aged 76 **bur.** Hillsborough Co Down

HOGG, ANDREW 1807/08–1871

b. 1807 or 1808 Co Roscommon; ed by Mr Kaine; ent TCD 2 Jan 1826 aged 18 BA 1830 LLB & LLD 1858

d 1831 p; C Cloone (Ard) 1832; still there 1843; V Urney and Annagelliffe (Kilm) 1854–60; R Castlerahan (Kilm) 1860–71

He was instrumental in building two chapels of ease in Cloone Parish. He lived in the Glebe house. The out offices were maliciously burnt on 27 Nov 1836 and he was fired at, but escaped unhurt.

s. of James

m. 25 Oct 1856 Caroline yst **dau.** of James Bushe of Bray Co Wicklow. Issue incl his elder **dau.** Caroline **m.** 30 Apr 1890 Holy Trinity Ch Rathmines William Bull, Asst Surveyor–General GPO

(BLGI 1958 ed says that Alicia Mary **dau.** of D Crofton **m.** in 1855 Rev Andrew Hogg– could have been a first marriage)

Died 4 Jul 1871 at Castlerahan Rectory aged 63

HOGG, MATTHEW BANKS 1855/56–1931

b. 1855 or 1856; ent TCD 20 Nov 1874 aged 18 BA 1878 MA 1896 Div Test (1) 1897

d 1879 p 1880 (Kilmore); C Killesher (Kilm) 1879–81; C Ballymoyer & Clare (Arm) 1881–82; R Keady (Arm) 1882–1931; Chapl to Lord Lt 1895–98; Preb of Ballymore (Arm) 1924–31

s. of Matthew, merchant of Londonderry

m. 11 Apr 1882 Mary Violet (**died** 22 Jul 1931) **dau.** of Rev Campbell Jamieson, R Killesher (Kilm) qv Issue 1. Ethel Mary Violet **b.** 9 Apr 1883 **m.** 26 Jun 1913 Cyril Reeve yst **s.** of George Hicks, MRCSE of Hertfordshire; 2. Evelyn Frances Marguerite **b.** 20 Mar 1884; 3. Lt Col Rev William Matthew Banks **b.** 6 Feb 1888 TCD BA 1910 Div Test 1912 d 1911 p 1912 (Cashel) C Cahir & Derrygrath (Lism) CF 1914–41 V Newport IOW (Win) 1938–48 Hon Canon of Portsmouth

1942–48 Chapl Caymannas and Innswood Sugar Estates Jamaica 1957–58 Perm to Off Dio Chichester 1959–64 Dio Murray 1965; 4. Arthur Campbell (twin **bro.** of William Matthew) (**died** 17 Apr 1911) **b.** 6 Feb 1888.

Died 9 Sep 1931

PUBLICATION
A Short History of Keady, its Church and People, Ulster Gazette, Armagh, 1928

HOHY, HUGO
is V Drumcliffe (Elph) 1615

HOLLINGTON, JOSIAS *c.* 1627–
b. *c.* 627 Co Longford; ed at Longford; ent TCD 20 Jan 1642/43 aged 15
C Kildallon (Kilm) 1661; V Carrigallen w Outrath = Outragh or Oughteragh (Kilm) 1661–63; V Killinagh and Templeport (Kilm) 1663–69; V Thurles (Cash) 1668–74; Treas of Cashel 1669–70; VGen of Cashel

eldest **s.** of Rev Nathaniel, R Muntireolis (Ard) qv

m. and had issue Rev Josias **b.** Cashel ed by Mr Cammell at Cashel ent TCD 21 May 1686 aged 19 V Chor Cashel

HOLLINGTON, NATHANIEL   –1654
no doubt same as Nathaniel Hollington who was adm Siz Emmanuel Coll Camb 7 Sep 1602

V Drumlane (Kilm) 1612; appears V there 1617/18 and 1619 and 1622; R Muntereolis (Ard) 1619–54 pres 31 Jan 1619 (L.M. V 104); V Annaduff (Ard) to 1622; pres to V Kilcommick (Ard) 19 Dec 1623 (LM V 106); V Kilcommick 1623–54; in Dublin 1647 (Carte Papers xxi, 346); "a preacher"

was **m.** and had a son Josias, R Templeport (Kilm) qv

Died 1654

HOLLIWELL, WILLIAM
V Clonlocher and Killargue (Kilm) 1622

HOLMES, FREDERICK   –1860
formerly of Co Down
d 1811 (Kilmore) p; C Tashinny (Ard) 1811

Died 16 Apr 1860

HOLMES, HUTCHINSON HENRY 1812–
b. 1812 Co Down; ed by Dr O'Beirne; ent TCD 20 Oct 1831 aged 19 BA 1836 MA 1839
d, p 1841 (Down); C Kilbryan (Elph) 1858; C Aghaderg (Drom) 1859–60

s. of Rev William Anthony, V Holywood (Down)

m. 13 Apr 1852 St Thomas Dublin Margarette **dau.** of Thomas Burne, Royal Veteran Batt

HOLMES, JOHN 1653/54–

b. 1653 or 1654 Co Limerick; ed by Mr Burgess, Charleville; ent TCD 5 Nov 1673 aged 19– no degrees recorded

V Boyle (Elph) 1701–at least 1732 w V Kilmactranny (Elph) 1722– there in 1732; V Ballysumaghan Killery & Boyle (w Taunagh from 1732) (Elph) 1729–

perhaps was J H **s.** of Thomas

HOLMES, JOHN GEORGE FREDERICK –1952

TCD BA 1897 Div Test 1898 MA 1903

d 1898 p 1899 (Kilmore); C Killeshandra (Kilm) 1898–1902; C St Michael Shrewsbury (Lich) 1902–06; V St Michael Shrewsbury (Lich) 1906–17; Chapl HM Prison Shrewsbury 1913–17; V Stanton-on-Hine Heath (Lich) 1917–31; R Water Newton (Ely) 1931–36; R Hartford (Ely) 1936–47; Perm to Off Dio Cant from 1947

m. and had issue incl Elizabeth (**died** 16 Sep 1934 aged 7)

Died 9 Jul 1952 Hythe Kent

HOLTBY, ROBERT DESMOND 1910/11–1975

b. 1910 or 1911; TCD BA Div Test (2) 1939

d 1940 p 1941 (Clogher); C Drumsnatt w Kilmore and Tydavnet (Clogh) 1940–46; C-in-c Gowna w Columbkille (Ard) 1946–52; R Ballingarry w Loughkeen (Killaloe) 1952–55; BC Ballysumaghan w Killery (Elph) 1955–56; BC Drumshambo Kiltubride and Kilronan (Ard) 1956–62; BC Oughteragh Fenagh Kiltubride and Drumreilly (Ard) 1962–65; Dio C Elphin and Ardagh 1965–67; R Kilkeevan Kiltullagh and Tibohine (Elph) 1967–75

m. 29 Dec 1952 Maud Henson **dau.** of Rev Alfred Birch, R Tashinny (Ard) qv Issue two **sons** one of whom Robert **died** at Drumshambo Rectory 11 Jan 1958 in infancy, and a **dau.** b 7 Jun 1954

Died 26 May 1975 aged 64 Galway **bur.** Castlerea Co Roscommon

HOLYWELL, WILLIAM –1640

coll V Kilcooley (Elph) 26 May 1640

Died 1640

HOMAN, KNOX 1817/18–1908

b. 1817 or 1818 Sligo; ed by Mr Quill; ent TCD 4 Jul 1836 aged 18 BA 1841

d 1842 p 18 Dec 1842; C St John Sligo (Elph) 1842; PC Fermoyle (Derry) and C Dunboe (Derry) 1843–67; R Termonamongan (Derry) 1867–68; R Balteagh (Derry) 1868–96

s. of Francis

Died Feb 1908

HONAN, JAMES

b. Co Clare; ed at Dublin; ent TCD 7 Mar 1656/57 – no degree recorded

d; p 1671; R & V Kilgeffin Killerin and Clontuskert (Elph) 1664–74; Preb of Termonbarry (Elph) 1671–*c.* 78; R & V Kiltrustan Kilglass Bumlin Creeve Kilcola Congoghlin and Clonfinlough (Elph) 1674, coll 27 Apr (F.F.).

s. of Daniel

HOOPS, E

C Cloone (Ard) 1840; may be same as S E Hoops below

HOOPS, SAMUEL EVANS 1815–1896

b. 1815 Co Tipperary; ed by Mr Riordan; ent TCD 1 Jul 1833 aged 17 BA 1838 MA 1865 BD & DD 1875

d 1839 (Down) p 21 Dec 1840 (Elphin); C Mohill (Ard) 1839–56; V Cashel (Ard) 1856–69; V Kiltubrid (Ard) 1869–82; R Fenagh (Ard) 1882–96; Dean of Ardagh Nov–Dec 1896

s. of Robert

m. (1) Jemima Maria Mostyn (M.L. 1846) and had issue. His eldest **dau.** Meta **died** in Dublin 7 Apr 1876; his 2nd **dau.** Maria Evans (**died** 19 May 1918) **m.** Rev Robert Grierson R Cloonclare (Kilm) qv; his **s.** Robert **m.** in St Stephen Dublin 28 Apr 1881 Bertha yst **dau.** of John Robinson of Tallaght Dublin

m. (2) 6 Oct 1864 Leckhampton Par Ch Cheltenham Margaret yst **dau.** of John Engledue, RN of Portsmouth

Died 16 Dec 1896 aged 81 **bur.** Fenagh

HOPE, RALPH JAMES 1829/30–1908

b. 1829 or 1830; TCD BA & Div Test (2) 1851 MA 1865

d 7 Aug 1853 (Kilmore) p 5 Feb 1854 (Kilmore); C Kilmore (Kilm) 1853–60; C Drung (Kilm) 1860–70; V Drung (Kilm) 1870–1908

3rd s. of Ralph James, JP of Urelands Co Wicklow

m. 4 Apr 1878 St George's Ch Dublin Margaret Ismania Thomasina 2nd **dau.** of the late William Overend, Barrister-at-Law of 9 Upr Rutland St Dublin. Issue 1. Louisa Georgina **died** 2 Mar 1883 in infancy

Died 28 Feb 1908 aged 78

HORNE, RICHARD 1630/31–

b. 1630 or 1631 Almondbury Yorks; ed there by Mr George Ferrand; prob R H admitted aged 18 Sidney Coll Camb 25 Apr 1649 BA 1652/53

PC Stowe–by–Chartley (Lich) in 1655 & ? V Cosby (Leic — then Lich) 1659; V Killasoolan = Castleblakeney and Kilronan or Killeroran (Elph) 1674–poss 1698.

    s. of Francis

HORNECK, GEORGE LITTLE 1813/14–

b. 1813 or 1814 Wexford; ed by Mr Whitney; ent TCD 7 Nov 1831 aged 17 BA 1842

d 1841 p 1843 (Kilmore); C Drumtullagh (Conn) 1844; C Abbeylara (Ard) 1843–65; V Abbeylara (Ard) 1865–68; R Mostrim (Ard) 1868–74; living in Edgeworthstown, seemingly without appointment to 1880, though in Leslie's *Ossory Clergy and Parishes*, but not in C I Dir, he is C Kilfane (Oss) 1877–80; R Killinick (Ferns) 1880–1892; last entry in C I Dir 1892.

    s. of Philip; **bro.** of Rev Thomas Little Horneck, R Macollop (Lism)

    his widow **died** 26 Jan 1920. Issue Gertrude **m.** Rev William Foster Legge, R Ratoath (Meath)

†HORT, JOSIAH *c.* 1674–1751

b. *c.* 1674 Marshfield Gloucestershire; ed at a Gram Sch in Bristol and at an academy in London for Dissenting Ministers, where he had as a schoolfellow the celebrated Isaac Watts; adm Sizar Clare Coll Camb 28 Apr 1704; obtained no degree. "A report was current that he formerly was a Presbyterian Minister at Soham in Cambridgeshire" (Cole's MSS)

d 1705 (Nor) p 25 Sep 1705 (Ely); Bp 1721/22; R Wicken (Ely) 1705–06; R Wendover Bucks (Ox) 1706; came to Ireland as Dom Chapl to Marquess of Wharton 1709; pres to R Kilskyre (Meath) by the Crown in 1709 but his title was disputed by the Bp of Meath and a *quare impedit* was brought, and the verdict in favour of the Crown given. On an appeal to the British House of Lords, judgment after some years was given in 1717 for the Crown. Meanwhile he held R Haversham Bucks (Ox), but took possession of Kilskyre 1717–20; Dean of Cloyne 1718–20; R Louth (Arm) 1719–21; V Tashinny (Ard) *c.* 1721; Dean of Ardagh 1720/21; pres to the Deanery 17 June 1720/21 (L.M. V. 123), inst 27 Jul 1720/21 (F.F.); Appointed Bp of Ferns and Leighlin by Letters Patent 10 Feb 1721/22 but the Abp of Dublin refused to consecrate him as he was wrongly described in the Patent as "B.D." He however gave a Commission to do so to the Bp of Meath who consecrated him in Castleknock Church 26 Feb 1721/22; Bp of Ferns 1721–27; Bp of Kilmore and Ardagh 1727–41; translated to Tuam 27 Jan 1741; Abp of Tuam 1741–51

    s. of John of Marshfield Glouc

    m. 1725 (ML 18 Feb) Elizabeth (**died** 25 Jan 1745/46) **dau.** of Col William FitzMaurice of Gallane Co Kerry and **sister** of Thomas 1st Earl of Kerry. Issue 1. Josiah George **b.** 1732 **m.** 14 Jun 1766 Jane Maria **dau.** of John Hawkes of Pontenive Co Longford; **died** 1786; 2. John, Consul General at Lisbon, created a Baronet in 1781 **m.** and had issue; He also had 4 **daus.** 1. Anne; 2. Elizabeth **m.** Sir James Caldwell of Castle Caldwell; 3. Frances **m.** John Parker afterwards Lord Boringdon; 4. Mary **m.** John Cramer of Bellaville

    Died 14 Dec 1751 **bur.** old St George's Ch Dublin

PUBLICATIONS
A Charge, *Instructions to the Clergy of the Diocese of Tuam,* 1742, reprinted as *The Clergyman's Instructor,* Oxford University
A Sermon preached for the Incorporated Society, 23 March 1745
A Pamphlet *Private Devotions for Morning and Evening,* Grierson, Dublin 1728

HORT, ROBERT   1708/09–

matric at Brasenose Coll Oxford 18 Nov 1725 aged 16 BA 1729; TCD MA 1743 LLD *h.c.* 1754

R Templemichael (Ard) 1737–49?; Archd of Ardagh 1749–62; res in 1762 for preferment in England

s. of John of Calne Wilts; was probably a relative of Abp Josiah Hort qv above

HOSFORD, WILLIAM POPHAM   –1947

TCD BA & Div Test 1899

d 1901 p 1902 (Kilmore); C Killesher (Kilm) 1901–04; C Byfleet (Guildf) 1905–06; Chapl to Miss to Seamen at Barry and Penarth Wales 1906–20; Miss to Seamen Deal and the Downs Kent 1920–26; Supt Miss to Seamen Ireland 1926–47; SPCK Chapl for Port of Belfast 1927–33; R St John Sligo w Knocknarea (Elph) 1933–47; Preb of Terebrine (Elph) 1940–47

m. Anna Victoria (**died** 22 Oct 1963 Dublin **bur.** Sligo). Issue incl 1. a s. Rev William **b.** 29 Oct 1916 Barry Glamorgan (**died** s.p. 1 Feb 1986 TCD BA & Div Test 1939 MA 1948 OBE d 1939 p 1940 (Armagh) C Derryloran (Arm) 1939–42 C St Luke Belfast (Conn) 1942–44 Chapl Miss to Seamen S Shields and Lic to Off Dio Durham 1944–45 Chapl St Mary Rotterdam and Chapl Miss to Seamen Rotterdam 1945–70 V St George Brighton (Chich) 1970–77 Chapl Miss to Seamen Dublin 1977–81 ret **m.** June 1964 London Dorothy (**died** 1987) widow of Rev Charles Strong, MBE Chapl Miss to Seamen; 2. his eldest **dau.** Evelyn **died** 29 Jan 1955 **bur.** Castleknock Co Dublin; 3. Catherine; 4. another dau

Died 22 Apr 1947

†HOVEDEN, JOHN

was Canon of Elphin when appointed Bp of Cork by the Pope 1540

HOW, THOMAS

lic C Knockbride (Kilm) 9 Sep 1730

†HOWARD, ROBERT   1683–1740

b. 24 Sep 1683 Dublin; ed by Mr Jones, Dublin; ent TCD 13 Apr 1697 BA 1701 Fellow 1703–22 MA 1703 BD & DD 1716; Abp King's Lecturer in Divinity 1719

Preb of Maynooth 1711–23; V St Ann (Dub) 1717–21; R St Bride (Dub) 1718–22; Dean of Ardagh 1722–26; pres to the Deanery 27 Apr 1722 (L.M. V. 123) and inst 23 May 1722 (F.F.); Chanc of St Patrick's Cath Dublin 1723–26; Prec of Christ Ch

Cath Dublin 1723–26; V Finglas and R St Werburgh (Dub) 1723–26; Bp of Killala 1726–29; Bp of Elphin 1729–40; enthroned 26 Jun 1729

> 2nd **s.** of Ralph, MD Reg Prof of Physics TCD (**died** 1710) (**s.** of John and Dorothea **dau.** of Robert Hassels)
>
> **m.** Patience (**died** Jun 1764 **bur.** St Bride's Ch Dublin) **dau.** and heiress of Godfrey Boleyne of Fennor Co Meath. Issue 1. Rt Hon Ralph, 1st Viscount Wicklow MP for Co Wicklow, member of the Privy Council for Ireland and Baron Clonmore of Clonmore Castle Co Carlow **m.** 11 Aug 1755 Alicia, Countess of Wicklow, **dau.** of William Forward of Newtowncunningham Co Donegal and had issue (i) Robert 2nd Earl of Wicklow; (ii) William 3rd Earl of Wicklow (**died** 27 Sep 1818) **m.** Eleanor (**died** 2 Apr 1807 aged 38) **dau.** of Hon Francis Caulfield; 2. Robert of Castle Howard; 3. Hugh (**died** 1799) TCD BA 1752 LLD h.c. 1775 Irish Bar 1758 MP for St Johnstown and Athboy. He also had two **daus.**, the 2nd of whom, Catherine, **m.** John 2nd Baron and 1st Earl of Erne
>
> **Died** 3 Apr 1740

PUBLICATIONS
A Thanksgiving Sermon, Dublin 1722
A Sermon preached in Christ Church, Dublin before the Incorporated Society For promoting English Protestant Schools in Ireland, Dublin 1738

HUDSON, ALEXANDER 1790–1856

b. 1790 in Dublin; ed by Mr Lynne; ent TCD 4 Nov 1804 aged 14 and a half years BA 1809 MA 1813

C Clongish (Ard) 1826 then went to England; C Templemichael (Ard) to 1839; R & V Ballymacormick (Ard) 1839–42; V Oughteragh (Ard) 1842–46; R & V Killashee (Ard) 1846–56

> 2nd **s.** of Richard of Dublin by Catherine **dau.** of Alexander Nixon of Nixon Hall Co Fermanagh
>
> **m.** 9 May 1827 St Mary's Dublin Harriett Susan (**died** 13 Aug 1859 at Killashee) 3rd **dau.** of James Hunt of Sackville St Dublin
>
> **Died** s.p. 2 Oct 1856 at Mount Haig Kingstown (Dun Laoghaire)

HUDSON, JOHN 1808/09–1885

poss same as John Hudson **s.** of John, architect, **b.** 1808 or 1809 Sligo (obit states that he was born in London); ent TCD 3 Jan 1825 aged 16 BA 1829

d 1839 p; C Killasnett *c.* 1839–; C Drumlease (Kilm) 1843–; V Killasnett (Kilm) 1856–75; "laboured here for 41 years first as Curate…"

> **Died** 31 Dec 1885 at Mountshannon Hse **unm.**

HUDSON, THOMAS GEORGE 1932–2007

b. 26 Jul 1932 Bandon Co Cork; ed Cookstown High Sch; Royal Sch Armagh; TCD BA 1954 Div Test 1955 MA

d 3 Jul 1955 p 23 Dec 1956; C St Matthew Belfast (Conn) 1955–58; C Christ Ch

Belfast (Conn) 1958–60; C Carlow (Leigh) 1960–61; R Hacketstown U (Leigh) 1961–68; R Kinneigh U (Cork) 1968–72; R Monasterevan (Kild) 1972–83; R Mostrim Granard Clonbroney Killoe Rathaspeck Streete and Kilglass (Ard) 1983–97; Preb of Kilcooley (Elph and Ard) 1986–97; ret

s. of Charles Richard Garde of Dungarvan Co Waterford (s. of Charles Frederick of Dungarvan and Louise (née Hunt)) by Clementina Gladys (née Braddell) (**died** 28 Jan 1963) of Fermoy Co Cork

m. 26 Aug 1961 Monkstown Ch Hilda Olivia **dau.** of Thomas L and Margaret Carson Castlebar Co Mayo. Issue 1. Peter Thomas Braddell **b.** Aug 1962 **m.** and has issue two children; 2. Charles Richard Garde **b.** 11 Apr 1964

Died 1 Jun 2007

†HUGHES, ALBERT EDWARD 1878–1954

b. 13 Feb 1878; RUI BA 1902; TCD Div Test 1907 BA 1908 MA 1911 DD *(j.d.)* 1939

d 1907 p 1908 (Dublin) Bp 1939; C Drumcondra and N Strand (Dub) 1907–11; Dio Insp Rel Ed Dublin 1909–17; C Rathfarnham (Dub) 1911–17; R Rathfarnham (Dub) 1917–21; Chapl to the Lord Lt 1920–21; R Mariners' Ch Kingstown (Dub) 1921–23; R Christ Ch Leeson Pk (Dub) 1923–39; Canon of Christ Ch Cath Dublin 1929; Preb of Dunlavin in St Patrick's Cath Dublin 1933–39; Select Preacher Univ of Dublin 1927, 1931, 1939; Clerical Hon Sec General Synod 1934–39; consec Bp of Kilmore Elphin and Ardagh 25 Apr 1939 in St Patrick's Cath Armagh; Bp of Kilmore Elphin and Ardagh 1939–50; appointed Bp–elect of Armagh by the House of Bishops 13 Dec 1938; ret

m. 20 Apr 1911 Margaret Hall (**died** 21 Feb 1955) **dau.** of John Baker of Croydon. Issue 1. Bryan Watson; 2. John Derrick Watson; 3. Hazel Watson **m.** 1946 Capt Henry Francis Reade Morris, Royal Marines

Died 11 May 1954

HUGHES, EDWARD 1670/71–

b. 1670 or 1671 Dublin; ed by Mr Wilson; ent TCD as Siz 18 May 1689 aged 18 BA 1693 MA 1696

V Shrewell = Shrule (Ard) 1717/18–35, coll 7 Feb 1717/18 (F.F.)

s. of Roderick

m.… Issue incl Rev Thomas qv below

HUGHES, HERBERT MAXWELL CARLYLE –1946

TCD BA 1898 Div Test 1899 MA 1902

d 1899 p 1901 (Kilmore); C Carrigallen (Kilm) 1899–1901; C Killinkere & Mullagh (Kilm) 1901–04; R Kilmainhamwood (Meath) 1904–12; R Newtownfertullagh (Meath) 1912–45

s. of Rev Samuel Carlyle, DD, R St Werburgh's (Dub) 1887–1908 (s. of Joseph and Sarah of Eglish Co Armagh) by Rachel Mary (**died** 31 Mar 1935) **dau.** of Thomas

R Givens of Streamhill Co Tipperary; **bro.** of Rev Thomas Robert, R Dunaghy (Conn) 1921–47; his **sister** Mona Mary **m.** Godfrey James Wilson, C St Werburgh's (Dub) 1901–06

m. 30 Apr 1901 Eirene Gwendolyn **dau.** of Charles Stuart Adams, JP Co Cavan

Died 4 Dec 1946

HUGHES, PATRICK

lic C Mostrim (Ard) lic 2 Jun 1747 (S.R.)

HUGHES, THOMAS 1706/07–1754

b. 1706 or 1707 Co Longford; ed by Mr Neligan, Longford; ent TCD 13 Apr 1725 aged 18 BA 1729

C Shrule (Ard) 1731–35; V Shrule (Ard) 1735–54

> **s.** of Rev Edward qv above (**s.** of Roderick)
>
> **Died** 3 Sep 1754

HUGHES, WILLIAM

lic C Granard (Ard) 30 May 1753 (S.R.)

HUMPHREYS, THOMAS SUTCLIFFE 1873–1957

b. 1873; TCD BA 1897 Div Test 1902

d 1902 p 1903 (Kilmore); C Kinawley (Kilm) 1902–05; R Carrigallen (Kilm) 1905–06; R Kildrumferton (Kilm) 1906–11; R Killenvoy (Elph) (w Kiltoom to 1926) (w Roscommon G from 1926) (Elph) 1911–53; Preb of Tibohine in Elphin Cath 1943–49; Dean of Elphin and Ardagh 1949–53; ret

> **m.** Frances **dau.** of Thomas Fitzgerald of Kinnaule Co Tipperary. Issue 1. Dorothy Beatrice (**died** 25 Jun 1976) **m.** 1937 Stanley **s.** of Robert Pettigrew of Sligo; 2. Rev Benjamin Thomas **b.** 13 May 1913 Co Roscommon (**died** 1986) TCD BA & Div Test 1935 MA 1942 d 1935 p 1936 (Derry) C Baronscourt w Drumclamph (Derry) 1935–38 C Drumachose and Carrick (Derry) 1938–40 C-in-c Dunfanaghy (Raph) 1940–48 and I Dunfanaghy 1948–53 R Muff and Culmore (Derry) 1953–77 Canon of Derry 1971–77 **m.** 17 Feb 1943 St Matthias Dublin Frances Joyce **dau.** of Canon E Staunton, R Tramore (Waterf) and had issue (i) Elizabeth Frances **m.** 22 Jul 1967 Culmore Par Ch Londonderry William David eldest **s.** of Cecil McCandless of Culmore Point Londonderry (ii) Dorothy Joyce (iii) John D'Arcy **b.** Jun 1949
>
> **Died** 4 Dec 1957 aged 84

HUNT, FITZMAURICE 1820/21–1891

b. 1820 or 1821; TCD BA & Div Test (1) 1844 MA 1857

d (Kilmore) 19 Sep 1846 p 1847 (Kilmore); C Boyle (Elph) 1846–61; I Athleague & Kilbegnet (Elph) 1861–70; R Mohill (Ard) 1870–91; Archd of Ardagh 1883–91

2nd s. of Rev John of High Park Co Tipperary

m. Nov 1860 Frances (**died** 31 Mar 1914 at Sidcup Kent aged 90) **dau.** of Rev Arthur Hyde, R Mohill (Ard) qv below

Died 21 Apr 1891 aged 70

HUNT, HENRY 1791/92–1861

b. 1791 or 1792 Dublin; ed by Mr Dowdall; ent TCD 3 Sep 1810 aged 18 BA 1815 MA 1818

d 23 Dec 1815 (Dromore) p; C Seapatrick (Drom) 1815; C Dromore (Drom) 1816; C St John Sligo 1819; V Ballinafagh (Kild) 1819–27; V Rathconnell (Meath) 1819–20; PC Taney (Dub) 1820–21; V Kiltoom and Camma (Elph) 1822–28; Minor Canon St Patrick's Cath Dublin 1827–61; V Killenvoy (Elph) 1828–29; R Ahascragh (Elph) 1829–45; V Gen Elphin; R Lurgan (Kilm) 1845–61

s. of James, *Pharmacopola*, State Apothecary of Upr Sackville St Dublin

m. 12 Mar 1823 Rose Ann 3rd **dau.** of William Robert Adair of Mt Vernon Co Antrim. Issue incl his eldest **s.** Canon James, Preb of Oran (Elph) qv, and his 2nd **dau.** Mary Harriet **died** 5 Mar 1879 Montreux Switzerland

Died 23 May 1861 Donnybrook Dublin aged 69

HUNT, JAMES 1824/25–1894

b. 1824 or 1825 Co Roscommon; ed by Dr Moore; ent TCD 4 Nov 1844 aged 19 BA 1849

d 1851 p 1852 (Kilmore); C Oran (Elph) 1852–; Preb of Oran (Elph) 1853–80; R Oran 1856–69; C Castleblakeney (Elph) 1869–73; R Castleblakeney (Elph) 1873–94

s. of Rev Henry, V Gen of Elphin qv (s. of James) by Rose Ann Adair

m. 4 Jan 1879 St Michael Chester Sq London Eleanor Margaret yst **dau.** of T B Adair, DL of Loughanmore Co Antrim

Died 4 May 1894 Loughanmore

HUNTER, LEOPOLD ANDREW PAKENHAM WALSH 1881–1956

b. 1881 Enniskillen Co Fermanagh; ed Royal Sch Dungannon; TCD BA 1904 Div Test 1908 MA 1913 LLB 1927

d 1908 (Down for Kilmore) p 1909 (Kilmore); C Drumlease (Kilm) 1908–13; C New Ross (Ferns) 1913–19; C-in-c Athleague (Elph) 1919–22; R Balbriggan (Dub) 1922–37; R Castleknock (Dub) 1937–51; ret

s. of Dr Christopher of Belnaleck Hse Enniskillen

m. Sep 1922 Anne Mary Perceval (**died** 4 Aug 1935) **dau.** of Commander O'Rorke of Rowlands Castle Hants England

Died 9 Jul 1956 Dublin

HUTCHINGS, HENRY TERTIUS 1884–1949

b. 7 May 1884 Braidwood NSW; ed Drogheda Gram Sch; Theo Associate King's Coll

London 1911; Wells Theol Coll 1911

d 1911 (Oxford) p 1912 (Armagh); Chapl and Asst Master Imperial Service Coll Windsor 1911–12; C Heynestown (Arm) 1912–14; C Dundalk (Arm) 1914–15; I Heynestown (Arm) 1915–18; I Ballymascanlan (Arm) 1918–20; Chapl of Alberdi, Rosario (South American Mission) 1920–24; Flores and West Province (Argentina) 1924–29; SPG Missy Devoto and Hurlingham Buenos Aires 1929–31; I Keady (Arm) 1931–34; I Ardagh and Kilglass (Ard) 1934–38; I Donabate (Dub) 1938–43; I Malahide Portmarnock and St Dolough (Dub) 1943–49

> s. of Rev Edgar FitzHenry MA I Heynestown 1907–15 (born *c.* 1852 **died** 17 Feb 1915) (**s.** of Rev Henry MA (1818–99) I Kilcluney (Arm) and Charlotte (née Wall)) by Adeline Beatrice (**died** 1 Oct 1919) yst **dau.** of Rev Tresham Gregg DD, I St Nicholas Within the Walls Dublin and Sarah (*née* Pearson)
>
> **m.** 20 Jun 1920 Irvena Millicent (**died** 10 Oct 1977) **dau.** of William and Margaret (née Hart) Sansom of Blackrock Dundalk Co Louth. Issue 1. Edgar FitzHenry **b.** 10 Sep 1921 at Rosario de Sante Argentina **m.** 1944 Betty **dau.** of EH Richards of Ferndown Dorset; he **died** 20 Jul 1955; 2. Reginald Fourseth **b.** 2 Feb 1923 Rosario de Sante TCD MB FRCOG **m.** 1944 Monica Cynthia **dau.** of Sir G Boon, St Kitts West Indies; 3. Adeline Beatrice Irvena **b.** 3 Apr 1925 **m.** Clement Anthony Blower of Craven Arms Salop; 4. Henry Quartus **b.** 4 Sep 1927 TCD MB FRCS; Col RAMC **m.** 17 Nov 1962 Hannelore Vera **dau.** of Erich and Vera Kieselowsky of Allenstein East Prussia
>
> **Died** 8 Apr 1949 Malahide Co Dublin

HUTCHINSON, ABRAHAM

d 1862 p; C Castleterra (Kilm) 1862–63.

HUTCHINSON, Sir JAMES 1732/33–1812

b. 1732 or 1733 Co Antrim; ed by Mr Hawkey; ent TCD 11 Jul 1748 aged 15 Sch 1751 BA 1753 MA 1757; became 2nd Bt., succeeded his **bro.** Francis in 1807

Preb of Ardagh (Killala) 1760–66; Archd of Achonry 1760–1812; Preb of Killanly (Killala) 1766–1800; R & V Killashee *c.* 1800–12; also held Tashinny 1807–12

> 2nd **s.** of Samuel, Bp of Killala
>
> **m.** 1772 Elizabeth **dau.** of Charles Tottenham MP
>
> **Died** s.p. 1812

HUTCHINSON, WILLIAM HENRY 1830/31–1898

b. 1830 or 1831 Dublin; TCD BA & Div Test 1856 MA LLB & LLD 1874

d 1856 p 1857 (Kilmore); C St Peter Athlone (Elph) 1856–60; C Urney (Kilmore) 1860–75; C Kilmore (Kilm) 1875–78; R Bailieborough (Kilm) 1878–98; Dio Reg

> **s.** of John, gentleman
>
> **Died** 19 Sep 1898 aged 67 **bur.** Bailieborough

HYDE, ARTHUR 1788/89–1870

b. 1788 or 1789

Prec of Ross & V Mohill (Ard) 1816–70

eldest **s.** of Rev Arthur, Prec of Ross and V Killarney (A & A) (**s.** of Rev Arthur, V Culdaff) (Raph — then Derry)

m. 22 Oct 1817 Frances (**died** 20 Oct 1874) **dau.** of Sir Hugh Crofton Bt. of Mohill. Issue incl Rev Arthur, Preb of Tibohine qv below and 4 **daus.** incl 1. Ann **m.** 1859 John Kane JP DL of The Castle Mohill; 2. Barbara **m.** 5 Oct 1864 Mohill, Livesey Frank L Maberley; 3. Frances (**died** 31 Mar 1914 Sidcup Kent aged 90) **m.** Nov 1860 Ven Fitzmaurice Hunt Archd of Ardagh qv above; 4...

Died Aug 1870 in his 82nd year

HYDE, ARTHUR

C Tibohine (Elph) 1843–53; same as below?

HYDE, ARTHUR 1819–1905

b. 1819; ed by Mr Lowton; ent TCD 29 Nov 1835 aged 16 BA 1839 Div Test (2) 1840

d 1843 p 1844 (Kilmore); C Ardcarne (Elph) 1843–45; V Kilbryan (Elph) 1845–52; R Kilmactranny (Elph) 1852–67; R & V Tibohine (Elph) 1866–1905; Preb of Tibohine (Elph) 1867–1905

s. of Rev Arthur, Prec of Ross & V Mohill qv (eldest **s.** of Rev Arthur, Prec Ross and V Killarney (A & A) by Frances **dau.** of Sir Hugh Crofton Bt.

m. 23 Oct 1852 Elizabeth **dau.** of Ven John Orson Oldfield, Archd of Elphin qv Issue 1. Arthur **b.** 1853 (**died** 17 May 1879); 2. John Oldfield **b.** 1854 (**died** 1896); 3.Douglas **b.** 1860 (**died** 12 Jul 1949) TCD LLD LittD, the well-known Gaelic scholar and writer, First President of Ireland 1937–45 **m.** 10 Oct 1893 St Nicholas Blundellsands, Lucia Constantia (**died** 1939) **dau.** of Charles Kurtz of Betys y Coed Wales and of Austrian extraction; 4 Annette (**died** 11 Jan 1952) **m.** 4 Dec 1902 John Kane **s.** of John of the Castle Mohill Co Leitrim

Died 29 Aug 1905 aged 85

PUBLICATION

A Sermon, *The Duty of Forbearance among Protestant Communions,* Preached at Boyle 5 May 1850, Dublin, Oldham, 24pp

HYDE, SAMUEL 1840/41–1911

b. 1840 or 1841 Co Armagh; ed at Loughgall Co Armagh; TCD BA 1873 MA 1887

d 1874 p 1875 (Down); C Annaclone (Drom) 1874–75; C Mohill (Ard) 1875–76; R Aghancon (Killaloe) 1876–84; R Borrisokane U (Killaloe) 1884–99; Preb of Clondegad in Killaloe Cath 1896–1911; V Kilrush (Killaloe) 1899–1911

s. of Stewart

m. 1 Feb 1886 at Killodiernan Par Ch Jane Emily (**died** 16 Feb 1936 at Bangor Co Down) **dau.** of Thomas R Grey of Greyfort Borrisokane Co Tipperary

Died 17 Aug 1911 aged 65

HYNES, JOHN

b. Dublin; ed by Mr Hynes, Longford; ent TCD as Siz 27 May 1755 BA 1759 d; ord p 4 Sep 1763; C Inishmacsaint (Clogh) 1760–69; may be same as John Hynes who was C Killinkere (Kilm) 1761–

    s. of Timothy, *bibliopola*

IDUIBGENAN, GREGORY –*c.* 1443

vacated V Kilronan (Ard) by death *c.* 1443. May be same as George Oduigeannan qv

    Died *c.* 1443

IFIHACGNA, MALACHY

is coll to V Ogila = Ogulla (Elph) vacant per res of Matthias O'Fiachna qv to William Bp of Elphin 7 Feb 1445/46 (C.P.L. IX. 506)

IGUMUR, LUKE –1463

V Killukin (Elph) to 1463

    Died 1463

ILLINGWORTH, TEMPEST

V Dunamon (Elph) 1641–*c.* 62; Leslie's *Armagh Clergy and Parishes* has a Tempest Illingworth Preb of Donoughmore in St Patrick's Cath Dublin 1662–63; V Clonoe and prob also Arboe (Arm) 1663–66; R Drumcree (Arm) 1666; Dean of Emly 1666–69; see also *Clergy of Dublin and Glendalough.*

IMITIA (OMYAN), BARTHOLOMEW

of the Hospital of Balac is prov to the V Rossinver (Kilm) and the V Drumlease *alias* Plebs Dartry (Kilm) to be united to the Hospital, 3 Aug 1505 (A.H. I. 240–241)

INGHAM, GEORGE –1941

TCD BA 1908 Div Test 1909 MA 1913

d 1909 p 1910 (Down); C Shankill Lurgan (Drom) 1909–12; C Enniskillen (Clogh) 1912–13; Dio C Kilmore Elphin and Ardagh 1913–21; R Mohill (Ard) 1921–32; ret

    s. of Humphrey Thomas of Ballyfin Co Laois by Annie **dau.** of George Smith of Clarina Co Limerick

    Died 16 Jun 1941

INGHAM, JOHN 1699/1700–

b. 1699 or 1700 Belturbet Co Cavan; ed by Mr Brogan, Belturbet; ent TCD 6 Apr 1717 aged 17 BA 1721

C Kinawley (Kilm) 1741

eldest s. of Joseph of Drumcoran, Drumlane Parish

m. Mary dau. of John Veitch of Gartinardress Co Cavan. Issue incl 1. his yst s. David Univ of Glasgow matric 1769 MA 1771; 2. Alice m. 1778 Rev James Creighton, C Kinawley (Kilm) qv

INGLIS, THOMAS 1754/55–

b. 1754 or 1755 Co Donegal; ed by Dr Norris; ent TCD 3 Apr 1769 aged 14 BA 1775

C Castlemacadam (Glend) 1776–80; C Rossinver (Kilm) 1780; was C Wicklow (Glend) in 1783

s. of Rev Richard, R Kilcar (Raph); nephew of Rt Rev Charles Inglis, first colonial Bp of Nova Scotia 1787–1816

m. 1776 Anne dau. of Rev John Major, C Rossinver (Kilm) qv Issue 1. John; 2, Richard; 3. Charles; 4. Edward; 5. Elizabeth; 6. Catherine; 7. Alicia

IRELAND, THOMAS WILLIAM 1819/20–1891

b. 1819 or 1820 Co Leitrim; ed by Rev Charles Cain; TCD BA & Div Test 1844

d 1845 p; in Dio Ardagh from 1845; C Ballymacleery in Drumlummon Parish (Ard) 1845–68; R Rathcline (w Cashel from 1875) (Ard) 1868–91

s. of Cosby William, gentleman

m. Elizabeth (died 29 Jul 1889)

Died 21 May 1891 aged 71

IRVINE, ANDREW

Latin School Master of Belturbet (Kilm) in 1745

IRVINE, GORGES 1818/19–1895

b. 1818 or 1819 Irvinestown Co Fermanagh; ed Portora Royal Sch Enniskillen; ent TCD 6 Nov 1837 aged 18 BA Div Test LLB & LLD 1842

d & p 1845 (Kilmore); C Killinagh (Kilm) 1845–47; C Derryvullen (Clogh) 1847–63; R Muckno (Clogh) 1863–95

s. of Gorges of Castle Irvine Irvinestown

Died 18 Apr 1895 unm.

IRVINE, WALTER 1805/06–

b. 1805 or 1806 Co Tyrone; ed by Mr Reid; ent TCD 16 Jan 1836 aged 30 BA 1840 MA 1855

d 1840 p 1841; C Rosenallis (Kild) 184–; C Kildallon (Kilm) 1844; PC All SS Newcastle-on-Tyne (Newc) 1853– there 1874

IRVING, JOHN

Univ of Oxford BA 1820 MA 1856

d 1820 p 1820 (Llandaff); poss C Kilkeevan (Elph) from 1854 (Vestry Book); PC Stainmore (Cork) 1857

IRWIN, BENJAMIN 1842/43–1920

b. 1842 or 1843 Boyle; ed Ballinasloe Sch; ent TCD 22 Jun 1860 aged 17 Bedell Pri 1860 Bedell Sch 1861 BA 1864 Heb Pri 1864 and 1865 Div Test 1865

d 1865 (Armagh) p 1867 (Kilmore); C Trim (Meath) 1865–67; PC Croghan (Elph) 1867–69; C Omey (Tuam) 1869–70; V Errislannon (Tuam) 1870–86; R Kilconnell (Clonf) 1886–92; R Ballinakill w Renvyle (Tuam) 1892–1920.

s. of Ven Henry (**s.** of Harlow), Archd of Elphin qv

m. 6 Mar 1871 Drumbeg Ch Emily Burton (**died** 3 Feb 1928 at Moyard Co Galway aged 83) eldest **dau.** of Rev George Thomas Payne, R Drumbeg (Down) 1864–88 by his 1st wife Emily Burton (**died** 3 Mar 1854 aged 19). Issue incl 1. Henry George Hinde (drowned 17 Sep 1888 in Galway Bay aged 16); 2. Alfred William Adamson (**died** 25 Oct 1970 aged 95 at Clifden Co Galway) FRCSI Major RAMC OBE **m.** 6 Nov 1903 at St Lucia Muriel Garnet only **dau.** of Commander F Thimm, RD RNR and Katherine **dau.** of Joseph Spaworth of London; **daus.** 1. Mary Emily (**died** 18 Jun 1945) **m.** 18 Apr 1917 Noel Mever Rust, Sub Lt RNVR; 2. Alice Maud Lily (**died** 13 Aug 1931 Portsmouth); 3. Millicent Hazel (**died** 12 Sep 1951 Dublin) **m.** 12 Sep 1945 Nicholas Fletcher **s.** of Francis Henry Gifford; 4. Emily Jane (**died** 15 Dec 1947 Dublin)

Died 13 Sep 1920 at Ballynakill Rectory

IRWIN, CRINUS 1771–1859

b. 1771; Trinity Coll Camb BA 1794 MA; TCD MA 1807

d 1794 p 1795 (Waterford for Dublin); C St Ann Dublin (Dub) 1795; V Chor St Patrick's Cath Dublin 1797; V St Mark Dublin (Dub) 1799–1822; Preb of Tassagard in St Patrick's Cath Dublin 1799–1859; V Glasnevin (Dub) 1805–09; V Drumlease (Kilm) 1808–11; V Killesherdoney (Kilm) 1811–59; Archd of Ossory 1822–59; V Gen Ferns 1840–59

yr **s.** of Lewis Francis of Collooney Co Sligo by Elizabeth (née Harrison)

m. (ML 1807) Emily eldest **dau.** of Justice Chamberlaine, King's Bench. Issue sons 1. Rev John Lewis (**died** 5 Feb 1892) matric Christ Ch Coll Ox 14 Dec 1826 aged 18 BA 1830 d 19 Jun 1831 (Ossory) p 1832 V Chor Ossory and C St Patrick (Oss) 1832–35 C Thomastown (Oss) 1835 Archdeacon's V Chor St Patrick's Cath Dublin 1835–92 Preb of Blackrath (Oss) 1835 R Thomastown (Oss) 1835–69; 2. Lewis Chamberlain (**died** 12 Jun 1865), Capt 21st Regt; 4 **daus.** incl 1. Margaret (**died** 5 Dec 1883 Dublin) **m.** 13 Sep 1841 Tankerville William Chamberlaine; 2. a **dau.** who **died** 20 Mar 1857 Monkstown Dublin

Died 17 Dec 1859 at the Glebe Kilfane

IRWIN, EDWARD –1929

TCD BA (Jun Mod Ment & Mor Philos) 1880

d 1876 p 1877 (Kilmore); C Elphin 1876–95; Preb of Kilcooley (Elph) 1878–1929;

R Elphin 1895–1929; Headmaster of Elphin Gram Sch

> m. Marion (**died** 19 Sep 1891). Issue **sons** 1. Edward Thomas; 2. Joseph George; 3. Arthur Frederick; 4. Rev Percival Doherty (**died** Dec 1954 at Lyme Regis) TCD BA 1908 MA 1911 d 1907 (Tuam) p 1910 (Limerick) C Kilmoremoy (Killala) 1907–10 C Tralee (Ardf) and Dio C Ardfert and Aghadoe 1910–11 C Carlow (Leigh) 1911–12 C Killaban (Leigh) 1912–15 TCF 1915–18 Hon CF 1918 Org Sec Dios York and Sheffield 1918–19 R Killaban (Leigh) 1919–26 R Rathvilly (Leigh) 1926–30 R St Devereux w Wormbridge (Heref) 1930–32 R Byton and PC Kinsham (Heref) 1932–38 V N Stoke w Mongewell and Ipsden (Ox) 1938– m. Mabel; 5. Charles Henry; 6. Herbert Quintus, Lt 1st Connaught Rangers, killed in action in Great War 26 Apr 1915; **daus.** 1. Mary E, **m.** Mr Brown; 2. Florence Marion; 3. Eveline Mabel **m.** 29 Jul 1925 Rev Cyril Croome Roach

Died 5 Jan 1929 **bur.** Elphin

IRWIN, FRANCIS 1799/1800–

b. 1799 or 1800 Co Leitrim; ed by Mr Kean; ent TCD 1 Jun 1818 aged 18 BA 1824 MA 1832

d 1827; p; C Kilkeevin (Elph) 1827–; R Kilronan or Killyon 1835–41; Preb of Termonbarry (Elph) 1841–66; R Dunamon (Elph) 1866–80

> **s.** of John, *agricola*

> **m.** Elizabeth (**died** 21 May 1859) **dau.** of Rev William Blundell, DD of Castlerea Co Roscommon

IRWIN, HENRY 1811–1882

b. 16 Feb 1811; ed by Mr Whitley; ent TCD 27 Jul 1828 BA 1841 MA & BD 1852; before ordination was Asst Sec RTS in Dublin 1834–42;

d May 1842 (Elphin) p; C Elphin 1842–46; C Trinity Ch Dublin 1846–47; V Creeve Kilmacumsy and Shankill (Elph) and Prec of Elphin 1847–48; R & V Killukin (Elph) and also V Cloonaff Aughrim U and Killimood (Elph) 1848–78; Archd of Elphin 1848–78; ret; got leave of absence and was Principal of Malta Protestant Coll 1852–53

> **s.** of Harlow, *miles*, of Seafield Co Sligo (**s.** of John of Co Roscommon) by Mary eldest **dau.** of Samuel Bulteel, Collector of Customs, Sligo

> **m.** 31 Dec 1839 Frances Elizabeth (**died** 8 Mar 1910) **dau.** of Benjamin Hinde of Tarbert Co Kerry. Issue **sons** 1. Rev Benjamin, C Croghan (Elph) qv 2. Sir Alfred Macdonald Bulteel; 3. Henry Irwin, Indian Govt **m.** 24 Aug 1871 Rathcore Par Ch Henrieta Helen **dau.** of Rev Robert Irwin, R Rathcore (Meath); his eldest **dau.** Frances Elizabeth **died** 13 Apr 1864 at Killukin aged 16

Died 18 Nov 1882 at Errislannan Rectory

IRWIN, JOHN CRAWFORD 1857–1927

b. 1857; TCD BA & Div Test 1879 MA 1884 BD 1890

d 1880 p 1881 (Kilmore); C Killashee and Ballymacormack (Ard) 1880–83; C

Ballymodan (Cork) 1883–84; C St Thomas' (Dub) 1884–86; I Coolock (Dub) 1887–89; I St James' (Dub) 1889–1923; Chapl S Dublin Union; Catechist Mercer's Sch, Castleknock Dublin; ret

> m. Elizabeth Florence (**died** 25 Jan 1952) **dau.** of Oliver Barkey of Baynefield Co Meath. Issue incl Rev Oliver Arthur, VP St John's Coll Durham 1934–43
>
> **Died** 20 Dec 1927

IRWIN, THOMAS

TCD BA 1887 Div Test 1890

d 1890 p 21 Dec 1893; C Kenmare (A & A) 1890–94; C Boyle (Elph) 1894–1908; R Killenvoy (Elph) 1908–11; res; last entry in C I Dir 1923– death not recorded

IVESON, ANTHONY 1651/52–*c.* 1705

b. 1651 or 1652; from Black Bank Yorks

Univ Coll Ox matric 5 May 1668 aged 16 BA 1672 MA 1675; V Rothwell Yorks (Rip) 1682–; V Killeshandra (Kilm) 1692–1705

> m. Elizabeth
>
> **Died** *c.* 1705; Will prov 1705

JACKSON, JAMES McCREIGHT 1841–1912

b. 1841 Co Down; ent TCD 2 Nov 1860 aged 19 BA (Resp) 1864 Div Test (2) 1865 MA 1867

d 1865 (Cork) p 1866 (Kilmore); C Annagh (Kilm) 1865–69; PC St Andrew Drumaloor 1869–92 and prob to 1903; R Annagh (Kilm) 1880–1910; Archd of Kilmore 1899–1910; res.

> **s.** of Rev Thomas James (**s.** of James), R Annagh (Kilm) 1868–80 qv by Jane; **bro.** of Rev Edwin Sandys, V Great Sankey Warrington (Liv)
>
> m. 30 Apr 1873 Mary Jane (**died** 28 Mar 1914 at Bray Co Wicklow) yst **dau.** of Rev W H Nason, R Rathcormac (Cloyne)
>
> **Died** 14 Mar 1912 aged 70

JACKSON, JOHN HERBERT 1885–1949

b. 1885; TCD BA & Div Test (2) 1909 BD 1923

d 1909 p 1910 (Dublin); C St Thomas (Dub) 1909–12; C All SS Southport (Liv) 1912; C All SS Mullingar (Meath) 1912–13; C St Andrew (Dub) 1913–16; R Tomregan (Kilm) 1916–25; R Killesher (Kilm) 1925–49; Exam Chapl to Bp of Kilmore 1934–49; Preb of Annagh (Kilm) 1942–44; Preb of Mulhuddart id St Patrick's Cath Dublin 1944–49

> 2nd **s.** of John of Portadown Co Armagh
>
> m. 6 Jan 1920 Templeport, Dora Grace (**died** 13 Dec 1969 at Oxted Surrey aged 78) yst **dau.** of W Middleton of Dereham Norfolk. Issue 1. John Walter, TCD MB FRCS; 2. Monica Annette TCD MB 1945 **m.** C W Roberts, BAI
>
> **Died** 1 Apr 1949

JACKSON, ROBERT STEWART 1929–2001

b. 1929; TCD BA 1953 Div Test 1954 MA 1956; ALCM 1956

d 11 Jul 1954 (Down) p 26 Jun 1955; C Aghalee (Drom) 1954–57; R Derrybrusk (Clogh) 1957–61; R Magheracross (Clogh) 1961–68; R Lisnaskea (Clogh) 1968–91; Preb of Devenish in Clogher Cath 1979–85; Preb of Donaghmore in St Patrick's Cath Dublin 1985–91; R Templemichael Clongish Clooncumber Killashee and Ballymacormack (Ard) 1991–96; Archd of Elphin and Ardagh and Preb of Killukin 1991–96; Temp-in-c Roscommon G 1991–96; ret

eldest **s.** of Samuel Russell and Margaret Isobel (née Stewart) of Belfast

m. 14 Jul 1955 2nd Castlederg Presby Ch JF (Pearl) 2nd **dau.** of Mr & Mrs JB Sloane. Issue 1. Rt Rev Michael Geoffrey St Aubyn **b.** 24 May 1956 Lurgan TCD BA (1 cl Mod) Classics 1979 MA 1982 BA (1 cl) Theol and Rel Studs 1981 MA 1985 PhD (Cantab) 1986 MA DPhil by incorporation (Oxon) 1989 d 1986 p 1987 Bp 2002 C Zion Rathgar (Dub) 1986–89 Chapl Christ Ch Coll Oxford 1989–97 R St Fin Barre's U Cork and Dean of Cork 1997–2002 Bp of Clogher 2002–; **m.** 2 May 1987 Derryvullen S Par Ch Co Fermanagh Inez Elizabeth **dau.** of Cecil Daryl and Olive (née Armstrong) Cooke of Enniskillen and have issue Camilla Elizabeth St Aubyn **b.** 21 Mar 1990; 2. Claire Oonagh **b.** 1962 **m.** Rev Michael Andrew James Burrows **b.** 25 Jul 1961 **s.** of Rev Canon Walter Joseph Mayes Burrows **b.** 1908 (**died** 3 Jan 1990) I Taney (Dub) 1959–83 and Edna Mary (**died** 26 Apr 1996); C Douglas U (Cork) 1987–91 Dean of Residence TCD 1991–94 R Bandon U (Cork) 1994–2002 Dean of Cork in succession to Bp Jackson 2002–06 Bp of Cashel Waterford Lismore Ossory Ferns and Leighlin 2006 consec 3 Jul 2006

Died 26 Jan 2001 **bur.** Longford

JACKSON, THOMAS JAMES 1815–1881

b. 1815 Dublin; ed by Mr McCaul; ent TCD 1 Jul 1833 aged 17 BA 1838

d 1838 p; PC Derryheen (Kilm) 1842–62; V Bailieborough and Moybologue (Kilm) 1862–68; R & V Annagh (Kilm) 1868–80

s. of James, merchant

m. Jane (**died** 28 Jun 1870 at Belturbet Rectory). Issue incl 1. Rev. James McCreight, R Annagh (Kilm) qv; 2. Charles (**died** 2 Jun 1894 aged 48) MD, for 22 years Medical Officer of Ballyhaise district; 3. yst **s.** Rev Edwin Sandys (**died** 17 Sep 1911 at Youghal Co Cork aged 60) TCD BA & Div Test 1873 MA 1876 d 1874 p 1875 (Ches) C Sutton Lancs 1874–77 C Farnworth (Liv) 1877–80 V Great Sankey (Liv) 1880–1902

Died 16 Sep 1881 aged 66

JAFFREY (or GAFFRY), PATRICK

appears C Fenagh (Ard) 1796 (L.M. V. 233); Lic 25 Oct 1797 and again 7 Sep 1809 (SR); C Cloone (Ard) 1807; still there 1828 (LM V 233)

JAMES, WILLIAM EDWARD 1829–

b. 1829; TCD BA & Div Test (2) 1854 MA 1861

C Innismagrath (Kilm) 1855–62

> **s.** of Humphrey, solicitor

JAMIESON, CAMPBELL 1823/24–1891

b. 1823 or 1824 Cavan; ed by Mr Little; ent TCD 12 Oct 1839 aged 15 BA 1844 MA 1865

d 1846 (Killaloe) p 1847 (Tuam); C Drumlane (Kilm) 1846–51; C Templeport (Kilm) 1851–53; C Kildrumferton (Kilm) 1853–56; C Killesher (Kilm) 1856–79; R Killesher (Kilm) 1879–86

> **s.** of James *argentarius*; prob **bro.** of Rev Thomas, qv
>
> **m.** Margaret Frances Fleming (**died** 24 Jan 1891 Belfast). Issue incl Mary Violet (**died** 22 Jul 1931) **m.** Rev Matthew Banks Hogg, C Killesher (Kilm) qv
>
> **Died** 11 Jun 1891 at Holywood

JAMIESON, HUGH GOLLAN 1920–

b. 18 May 1920 Prestwick Scotland; ed Avoca Sch Blackrock Dublin; TCD BA & Div Test 1949

d 1949 p 1950; C Holy Trinity and St John Limerick (Lim) 1949–51; R Ballinaclough U (Killaloe) 1951–53; Sec BCMS Ireland 1953–56; R Murragh U (Cork) 1956–60; R Birkin w Haddlesey (York) 1960–63; R Derralossary and Calary (Glend) 1963–69; R Mothel G (Oss) 1969–76; R Badoney U (Derry) 1976–78; R Donagh U (Clogher) 1978–82; R Killeshandra Killegar and Derrylane (Kilm) 1982–87; ret

> **s.** of Archibald of Kilmarnock Ayrshire by Dora Eva **dau.** of William Holmes of Hayes Co Meath and Elizabeth (née Kellett) of Virginia Co Cavan
>
> **m.** 31 Jan 1950 Greystones Co Wicklow Irene Sheila **dau.** of Grattan Thomas Evans of Greystones and Annabella Jeanette (née McCoubrie) of Dublin. Issue 1. Douglas Brian **b.** 26 Jun 1952; 2. Victor Hugh **b.** 24 Mar 1955 **m.** 6 Sep 1986 Ann Seward of Rye, E Sussex

JAMIESON, THOMAS 1824/25

b. 1824 or 1825 Co Cavan; ed by Mr Rowe; ent TCD 9 Nov 1840 aged 15 BA 1846 MA 1870

d 1849; C Larah (Kilm) to 1856; C Templeport (Kilm) 1849–60; appointed C Killargue (Kilm) 28 Jun 1860; Chapl Ballisodare Chapel of Ease (Ach) 1860–86

> **s.** of James *argentarius*; prob **bro.** of Rev Campbell, qv

JANNS, JAMES 1723/24–

b. 1723 or 1724 Co Clare; ed by his father; ent TCD 26 May 1741 aged 17 Sch 1744 BA 1745 MA 1748

R Annaduff (Ard) to 1766

s. of Rev Richard

m. Feb 1767 Miss Carry of Carrick-on-Shannon Co Leitrim and had issue; (In Faulkner's Dublin Journal of 14 Mar 1767, this marriage is denied)

JANNS, JAMES 1811/12–1866

b. 1811 or 1812 Co Roscommon; ed at Galway Sch; ent TCD 6 Jul 1829 aged 17 BA 1834

C St Peter Athlone (Elph) 1835; R Killyon and Kilronan (Elph) 1841–66

s. of Richard *nuper miles*

m. and had issue incl Elouisa (**died** 7 Jul 1852 Newcastle Co Down **bur.** Annalong)

Died 15 Apr 1866 Rotherham Yorks

†JEBB, JOHN 1775–1833

b. 27 Feb 1775 Drogheda; ed by Mr Marshall; ent TCD 8 Jul 1791 Sch 1794 BA 1796 MA 1801 DD not recorded; FRS

d 24 Feb 1799 (Clonfert) p 22 Dec 1799 (Kilmore); C Kinawley (Kilm) 1799; R Kilteynan (Cash) 1805–10; R Abington (Lim) 1810–22; Archd of Emly 1821–23; consec 12 Jan 1823 Bp of Limerick in Cashel Cath; Bp of Limerick 1823–34

2nd s. of John, Alderman of Drogheda by Alicia Forster; the Jebbs claim to be descended John de Wilt who came to Ireland in the time of Charles II

He was all his life studious, and his piety and learning gave him a great influence on the thought of his day, and by his writings, he laid the foundations for the "Oxford Movement", though he would have been repelled by the extreme excesses to which that Movement advanced. He was never married, and for some years previous to his death, he suffered from paralysis to his right side. He died at East Hill near Wandsworth, Surrey on Dec 9, 1833, and was buried in St. Paul's Churchyard, Clapham. In the Church is a mural tablet to his memory with an inscription by his brother, Judge Jebb. In the Great N. Chapel in Limerick Cathedral, there was erected in recent years a monument to him, with a statue by Bailie, and bearing an inscription, "To the memory of John Jebb, Bishop of Limerick, this Monumental Statue is raised by friends of Religion and Literature in Ireland, England and America in commemoration of benefits conferred by his life and writings upon the Universal Church of Christ. Nat. Sep. 27, 1775. Obit. Dec. 9, 1833". (Leslie's Limerick MSS p 20)

Died 9 Dec 1833

PUBLICATIONS
from list published by Rev. B.H. Blacker, I.E.G. 1876

An Attempt to prove that the Nature and Attributes of the Deity cannot be Sufficiently demonstrated by Human Nature to render Revelation unnecessary; privately printed, Dublin 1799, 8vo

He had been awarded the 1st prize for a composition on this subject, on the Foundation of the Rev. Dr. Downes in Trinity Term 1797

A Speech on the Characters and Deaths of the Rev. John William Reid and John Sargint, Esq., delivered from the chair of the Historical Society of the University of Dublin, 12th Oct. 1798, 2nd Ed. Dublin 1800, 8vo

A Sermon preached before the Lord Lieutenant & the Members of the Association for Discountenancing Vice &c., 27th January 1803, in St Peter's Church, Dublin; with Notes & Illustrations, Dublin 1803, 8vo

A Sermon preached in St. Werburgh's Church, Dublin, 23rd March 1806 at an Ordination held by the Bishop of Kildare, Dublin, 1806, 8vo.

A Letter to a Young Clergyman of the Diocese of Cashel on Fashionable Amusements, privately printed, 1808

Sermons on Subjects chiefly Practical, with Illustrative notes and an appendix Relating to the Character of the Church of England, &c., London, 1815; 2nd Ed 1816, 3rd Ed 1824, 4th Ed 1832, 8vo

A Sermon preached at the Opening of the Chapel of the Female Orphan House, Dublin, Dublin 1818, 8vo

An Essay on Sacred Literature, reviewing and applying the Principles laid down by Bishop Lowth to the Illustration of the New Testament, London, 1820, 2nd Ed 1828, 3rd Ed 1831, 8vo

A Sermon preached on behalf of the Female Orphan House, Dublin, London, 1822, 8vo

A Sermon preached in the Cathedral Church of Cashel, 26th September 1822 at the Primary Visitation of Richard, Archbishop of Cashel, privately printed, Dublin, 1822, 8vo

"To those who love and venerate the memory of Archbishop Brodrick, this impression of a Discourse, humbly descriptive of his character and virtues, is presented and inscribed"

A Charge to the Clergy of the Diocese of Limerick at his Primary Visitation, 19th June 1823, Dublin, 1823

A Sermon preached in the Cathedral Church of Limerick, 29th October 1823 at The Funeral of the Rev. W.D. Hoare, A.M., Vicar–General to the Diocese, privately printed, Dublin, 1823

A Speech delivered in the House of Peers, 10th June 1824 on the Irish Tithe Composition Amendment Bill, London, 1824, 8vo

A Letter to the Rev. Charles R. Elrington, D.D. on the authority given by the Church of England to the Books of Homilies, Dublin, 1826, 8vo

Practical Theology; comprising Discourses on the Liturgy, &c. Critical and other Tracts; and a Speech delivered in the House of Peers, 1824, London 1830, 2nd Ed 1837, 2 vols, 8vo

Pastoral Instructions on the Character and Principles of the Church of England, selected from his former publications, London 1831, 2nd Ed 1844

Heavenly Conversation: A Sermon, privately printed, 1834, 8vo

A Sermon on I Thess. 5:17, printed in *Original Family Sermons*

Edited Dr Townson's *Practical Discourses* with a Biographical Memoir, London 1828, 2nd Ed London 1830, 3rd Ed 1834, 8vo

Edited *Piety without Asceticism,* or *The Protestant Kempis,* selected from the Writings of Scougal, Charles How and Cudworth, London 1830, 8vo

Reprinted in the *Protestant Episcopal Press,* New York, 1833

Edited *The Remains of William Phelan, D.D. with a Biographical Memoir,* London, 1832, 2 vols, 8vo

There was likewise a private impression of the Memoir, London, 1832

Edited *Bishop Burnet's Lives and Characters, with an Introduction and Notes,* London, 1833, 2nd Ed 1833

Remains of Alexander Knox, Esq, Vols I & II, London 1834, 2nd Ed 1836, Vols III & IV, 1837; 3rd Ed 1844, 4 vols, 8vo

Bishop Jebb's friend, Rev Charles Forster, BD, produced *The Life of John Jebb, D.D., F.R.S., Bishop of Limerick, Ardfert and Aghadoe, with a Selection from his Letters,* 3rd Ed 1851, and he edited *Thirty Years Correspondence with Alexander Knox, Esq, M.R.I.A.,* 2nd Ed. London, 1836, 2 vols. Bishop Jebb left his Library to his nephew, Canon John Jebb, Prebendary of Cashel

JEBB, THOMAS 1810–1888

b. 26 Dec 1810 Dublin; ed Oswestry Sch; ent TCD 5 Nov 1827 BA 1831

d 1834 p 1835 (Kilmore); C Killesher (Kilm) to 1844; Chapl to Earl of Enniskillen; R Larah (Kilm) 1856–88

4th **s.** of Hon. Richard, Justice King's Bench

m. 13 Nov 1847 Monkstown Par Ch Catherine Letitia **dau.** of Rev James McCreight, R Keady (Arm) 1835 and Elizabeth 4th **dau.** of Rt Rev William Foster DD, Bp of Clogher. Issue incl a **dau.** b 22 Dec 1861

Died 7 Jul 1888 aged 77

JEFFCOTT, WILLIAM 1811/12–1865

b. 1811 or 1812 Co Kerry; ed by Mr Kenna; ent TCD 19 Oct 1829 aged 17 BA 1834

C Mohill (Ard) 1837–; R Lissadell (Elph) 1842–59; R Castleblakeney (Elph) 1859–65

s. of Thomas, *caupo*

Died 17 Sep 1865 at Castleblayney Co Monaghan

JELLETT, MORGAN WOODWARD 1832–1896

b. 1832 Co Tyrone; ed by Dr Darley; TCD BA (Resp) and Div Test (2) 1857 MA 1867 LLB & LLD 1871

d 1857 (Killaloe) p 1858 (Kilmore); C St John Sligo (Elph) 1857–64; C St Peter (Dub) 1864–83; R St Peter (Dub) 1883–96; Canon of Christ Ch Cath Dublin 1880–93; Preb of St John's in Christ Ch Cath Dublin 1893–94; Preb of St Michan's in Christ Ch Cath Dublin 1894–96

s. of Morgan

m. 31 Jul 1861 St Peter's Par Ch Dublin Rebecca Low **dau.** of Nicholas Wade Monsarratt of Co Dublin.Issue 1…; 2. Nichola Margaret; 3. Adelaide Morgan; 4. Isabella Woodward.

Died 2 Jan 1896

PUBLICATIONS
The Compensation and Commutation Clauses considered, Dublin 1869
The Church and the Curates, 2nd ed, Dublin 1872
Edited *The Journal of the General Synod*
Contributed papers on the Church of Ireland to *The Church of England Yearbook* 1883–1886

JENKINS, HEYWOOD 1709/10–*c.* 1776

b. 1709 or 1710 Strabane Co Tyrone; ed by Dr Ballentine Strabane; ent TCD 8 Apr 1727 aged 17 BA 1732

C Drumachose Limavady (Derry) 1749; R Kiltubrid (Ard) *c.* 1766–

s. of Rev David, DD (**died** 19 Dec 1729), R Camus-juxta-Mourne, Strabane (Derry) 1703–28 by Mary

Died *c.* 1776– P Will proved 1776

JENNINGS, JOHN 1864/65–1931

b. 1864 or 1865; ed at Drimnagh Co Cork; ent TCD 19 Jun 1882 aged 17 BA 1886 Div Test 1887 BD 1892

d 1887 p 1888 (Kilmore); C Killinkere (Kilm) 1887–94; C St Mark Armagh 1894–96; Dio C and Inspector Armagh 1896–1900; R Forkhill (Arm) 1900–20; ret

s. of Edward, farmer of Co Cork

Died unm. 21 Jun 1931 Bandon Co Cork

JENNINGS, JOHN JAMES 1885–1972

b. 1885 Clifferna Straden Co Cavan; TCD BA 1911 Div Test (2) 1912

d 1912 p 1913 (Kilmore); C Killesher (Kilm) 1912–15; C All SS Clooney (Derry) 1915–18; C Bradley (Lich) 1918–19; C Kilnamanagh (Ferns) 1919–24; R Innishmagrath (Kilm) 1924–31; R Kildallon (w Newtowngore and Corrawallen from 1959) (Kilm) 1931–64; RD of Kinawley 1956–64; Preb of Annagh (Kilm) 1957–64; ret

s. of J Francis, farmer of Clifferna by Elizabeth **dau.** of R Patterson of Clifferna

m. 16 May 1916 Anna **dau.** of William Hill of Co Kerry. Issue 1. Theodora Elizabeth (Doreen) TCD BA 1939 MA (Mod) **m.** 19 Feb 1944 Rev Coslett William Charles Quin, R Billis and Ballyjamesduff (Kilm) qv and had issue; 2. Aubrey Francis Hill (**died** 12 Nov 1973 at Duesseldorf) TCD MA (Mod) **m.** Claire Glaser of Duesseldorf Germany; 3. Kathleen Violet (**died** 1985) **m.** 29 Dec 1958 Kildallon Par Ch Rev James Robert Lord Musgrave, R St Stephen Belfast (Conn) 1954–64 and had issue Stephen James **b.** 13 Mar 1960; 4. Ethel Gertrude TCD BA

1949 MB DPH **m.** Jan 1969 at Holy Trinity Ch Banbridge Ernest D, FRIBA only s. of the late Mr and Mrs Gilbert Taylor of Carlisle; 5. Marshall **m.** Maureen Howell of Birmingham; 6. Rev Thomas Robert, R Killeshandra (Kilm) qv; 7. Stanley; 8. Sheila Joyce BA 1952

Died 11 Jun 1972

JENNINGS, THOMAS ROBERT 1924–

b. 5 Sep 1924 Corry Rectory Drumkeeran Co Leitrim; ed Sligo Gram Sch; Mountjoy Sch Dublin; TCD Eccles Hist Pri and President's Pri, Coll Theol Soc BA & Div Test 1948 MA 1951

d 24 Jun 1948 p 26 Jun 1949; C Drumragh (Derry) 1948–51; RAChD 1951–67 serving in Korean War; with Parachute Regt in Hong Kong, Canal Zone, Suez, Berlin, Guyana, Germany, England and N Ireland; R Killeshandra Killegar and Derrylane (Kilm) 1967–70; R Newcastle w Newtownmountkennedy and Calary (Glend) 1970–92; Canon of Christ Ch Cath Dublin 1988–92; ret; founder member and Director Co Wicklow Assoc Mentally Handicapped Children and Manager and Director, Sunbeam Hse Adult Services 1971–92; Chmn Archbishop's Commission on Care of the Elderly 1987–92; Hon Life Member National Assoc Mentally Handicapped of Ireland

s. of Canon John James, R Kildallon (Kilm) qv (s. of J Francis Elizabeth (née Patterson) of Kildrumferton Co Cavan) and Anna **dau.** of William Hill of Ballymacelligott Co Kerry

m. 11 Feb 1956 St Michael's Ch Aldershot Hants Jean Margaret **dau.** of Charles William Jefford and Ethel (née Mainwaring) of Aldershot. Issue 1. Kerry Anna Jefford **b.** 27 Nov 1956 **m.** 2 Sep 1988 Malcolm Vanston Rumney; 2. Rosaleen Janet Jefford **b.** 7 Dec 1957 **m.** 1 Sep 1984 Edward Higgins; 3. Clodagh Mary Jefford **b.** 27 Jan 1961; 4. Catriona Pauline Jefford **b.** 12 Sep 1962; 5. Robert John Jefford **b.** 16 Sep 1964 **m.** 26 May 1988 Irene Foley

PUBLICATIONS

History of Calary Parish, 1984
History of St. Matthew's, Newtownmountkennedy, 1986
Glimpses of an Ancient Parish, History of Newcastle Parish Co Wicklow, 1989
The discovery of a horizontal water mill at Newcastle, AD 744
Kilcoole Co Wicklow: History, Folklore and Historical Walks, 1998

JESSOP, ROBERT FETHERSTON 1785–1842

b. 1785; matric St John's Coll Oxford 30 Jan 1804 BA 1808; TCD MA 1832; at Lincoln's Inn 1806

C St Nicholas Within (Dub) 1812–13; R & V Kilglass (Ard) 1813–42

2nd **s.** of John of Doory Hall Co Longford by Mary Anne Fetherston

m 1811 Catherine (**died** 10 Jul 1858 at Marlfield Cabinteely Dublin) 2nd **dau.** of Sir Thomas Fetherston. Issue **sons** 1. Robert **died** in childhood; 2. John Harward of Marlfield Cabinteely **died unm.** 18 Oct 1888 London; 3. a boy who died in infancy; **daus.** 1. Catherine **died unm.** 30 Apr 1889; 2. Elizabeth **died unm.** 8 Oct 1880 bur. Lucerne Switzerland

Died 1842

JESSOPE, THOMAS 1741/42–1825

b. 1741 or 1742; ed by Mr Haynes; matric TCD 2 May 1758 BA 1762 MA 1768 LLB 1777

C Killashee (Ard) 1766

2nd **s.** of Thomas of Mount Jessop Co Longford

m. 6 May 1772 St Ann's Ch Dublin Frances elder **dau.** of John Gaspard Battier of Dublin

Died 24 Apr 1825 **bur.** Moydow

JOBSON, FREDERICK WILLIAM BARON

Hatfield Coll Durham LTh 1897 BA 1898

d 1899 p 1900 (Kilmore); C Mohill (Ard) 1899–1901; C St David Birmingham (Birm) 1901–02; C Inishmacsaint w Slavin (Clogh) 1903–04; C St Mary Wakefield Yorks (Wakef) 1905–07; C St Cuthbert York (York) 1907–10; C Heapey Lancs (Blackb — then Manch) 1910–11; C SS Matthew & Mark Chadderton (Manch) 1911–18; C Lr Hulton 1919–22; C Failsworth (Manch) 1922–23; C Chapel–en–le–Frith (Derby — then S'well) 1923–26; V Braughing (St A) 1926–28; Perm to Off Dio London 1930–31; Perm to Off Dio S'wark 1931–39 and 1944–49; living in Hastings Sussex in 1961; last entry in Crockford 1961/62

†JOHN

Bp of Clonmacnoise is Dean of Ardagh 1460–c68 (Cal. Reg. Swayne)

†JOHN   –c. 1479

His name appears to have been John O'Farrell. Cormac Magauran had resigned the See of Ardagh to the hands of Pope Paul II who had prov. Donatus, but Donatus died before his bulls were perfected. The Pope then prov. John, a Canon of Ardagh, 28 July 1469 (A.H. I. 185; C.P.L. XII. 680 faculty for consecration July 29). John however appears as "Bp. elect" in 1462 (C.P.R.E., Ed. IV. I. 273; Theiner 447)

He is dead in 1479

JOHNSON, GEORGE ALEXANDER   –1913

TCD BA & Div Test 1857 MA 1882

d 1857 p 1858 (Kilm); C Kilbryan (Elph) 1857–58; C Roscommon (Elph) 1858; C Annagh (Kilm) 1858–65; C Otley (Ripon) 1865–66; C Gt Horton (Bradf) 1866–67; C Rushall 1867–71; C Ayton (York) 1871–74; C E Claydon (Ox) 1874–79; Ireland Lect at Keynsham 1879–81; V Corston w Rodbourne (Bris — then Glouc & Bris) 1881–97; V Dale Head (Ripon) 1897–1905; R Wyham w Cadeby (Linc) 1905–13

m. 1874 the elder **dau.** of Mr Neate of Marden Grange Wilts; she **died** 1912

Died May 1913

JOHNSON, HENRY JOHN 1861/62–1940

b. 1861 or 1862; TCD BA 1887 BD 1902

d 1887 p 1889 (Kilmore); C Ardagh (Ard) 1887–89; I Mostrim (Ard) 1889–91; I Ardagh (Ard) 1891–1908; I Clonbroney & Killoe (Ard) 1908–40; Archd of Ardagh 1921–40; Archd of Elphin & Ardagh 1929–40; Preb of Killukin in Elphin Cath 1930–40

m. (1) 1890 Eveline Grace Geraldine (**died** 17 Dec 1924) yst **dau.** of John Yeats, County Surveyor, Kildare. Issue 1. Arthur Joseph **died** 1 May 1932; 2. Richard Henry Ardagh BA **m.** 29 Nov 1930 Beatrice Juanita eldest **dau.** of Lt Comr Arthur E H Barry, RNR of Thames Ditton; 3. Marjorie Violet **m.** 4 April 1918 Smythe Alison elder **s.** of Dr W H Griffiths; 4.Maud **m.** 27 Apr 1927 James A Acheson; 5. Winifred (**died** 11 Mar 1947) **m.** Rt Rev Dr William Cecil de Pauley, Bp of Cashel qv

m. (2) Dora (**died** 28 April 1953 at Gorey Co Wexford **bur.** Clonbroney)

Died 21 Mar 1940 aged 78

JOHNSON, JOHN

V Killumada (Elph) 1615

JOHNSON, JOHN

?FTCD

a preacher is V Killenumery (Ard) 1622; pres (again?) 18 Nov 1629; V Killenumery and Killery (Ard) 1622–60 (L.M. V. 108); V Innismagrath (Kilm) 1622–25; V Cloonclare (Kilm) 1622–25; perhaps same as John Johnson, who appears as V Drumlease (Kilm) from 1633; appears V Drumlease in witness to a Will of Robert Morgan 31 May 1637; V Athenry (Tuam) 1639

JOHNSON, SHIELA 1943–

b. 7 Jul 1943 Aughnacloy Co Tyrone; ed Dungannon High Sch

d 1996 p 1997 (Aux Min); C Urney Denn and Derryheen (Kilm) 1996–97; C-in-c Roscommon Donamon Rathcline and Kiltullagh (w Kilkeevan 1997) (w Boyle Aghanagh Ardcarne Croghan and Tybohine to 2000) 1997–2001; BC Clondevaddock (Raph) 2001–

dau. of Herbert of Aughnacloy and Catherine Lucinda of Glaslough Co Monaghan (née Byers) Rowe

m. 1966 St James' Ch Aughnacloy Rev Stanley qv

JOHNSON, STANLEY 1942–

b. 14 Aug 1942 Belfast; ed Coleraine Acad Inst; QUB BSc Chemistry 1963; TCD BTh 1989

d 11 Jun 1989 p 17 Jun 1990; C Kilmore and Kildallon (Kilm) 1989–1992; R Kildallon Newtowngore and Corrawallen (Kilm) 1992–97; R Templemichael Clongish Clooncumber Killashee and Ballymacormack (Ard) 1997–2001; Archd of Elphin and

Ardagh 1997–2001; R Clondehorkey and Cashel w Mevagh (Raph) 2001–

s. of Edgar Stanley of Liverpool (s. of William and Mabel (née Windsor) by Margaret Campbell dau. of Joseph and Isabella (née Campbell) Walker of Keady Co Armagh

m. 5 Feb 1966 St James' Ch Aughnacloy Co Tyrone Rev Shiela qv dau. of Herbert and Lucinda (née Byers) Rowe. Issue 1. Timothy b. 11 Nov 1966; 2. Melanie b. 19 Jun 1968 m. 2 Aug 2000 Rosses Point Par Ch Co Sligo Werner Schaeffer of Dingolfing Germany; 3. Wendy b. 9 Dec 1972 m. 19 Jan 1995 Kildallon Par Ch Derrick Power of Waterford

JOHNSTON, HENRY 1821–1882

b. 1821 Co Leitrim; ed by Dr Miller; ent TCD 9 Nov 1840 BA 1846

C Ardagh (Ard) 1856–57; C St Peter Athlone (Meath) 1860; and Preb of Tibohine (Elph) 1863–66; R Boyle (Elph) 1866–79; R Killashee and Ballymacormack (Ard) 1879–82; Archd of Elphin 1879–80

s. of Robert, *jurisconsult*, of Kinlough Hse Co Leitrim

m. and had issue; his eldest s. Robert St George died 12 Jun 1938 at 13 Angelsea Rd Dublin; his dau. Jane Sophia (died 9 Jan 1932 in London) m. Rev John Francis Webb

Died 8 Oct 1882 aged 61

JOHNSTON, HUGH 1757/58–

b. 1757 or 1758 Co Fermanagh; ed by Dr Lamy; ent TCD 2 Jun 1777 aged 19 BA 1781

C Taunagh (Elph) 1790; V Ballysumaghan Kilross & Ballinakill 1801–02

s. of James

JOHNSTON, JOHN WYBRANTS *c.* 1855–1913

b. *c.* 1855; St Bees Coll Durham 1877; Univ Coll Durham 1892

d 1879 p 1880 (Durham); C Horton (Newc) 1879–82; C Kinawley (Kilm) 1882–83; Chapl at Corfu 1883–86; R Termonmaguirke (Arm) 1886–90; R Ballyboy (Killaloe — then Meath) 1890–1904; R Kilcleagh (Meath) 1904–13

2nd s. of Robert of Cashel Co Donegal

m. (1) 7 Jun 1883 Dromore Par Ch Co Tyrone Catherine Selina (died 1 Dec 1908) dau. of Rev Charles Maginnis, MA, R Dromore (Clogh). Issue Edward Norman, Lt 11th Lancers m. 1 Jun 1915 Madeline 2nd dau. of Arthur Mather of Cheltenham; 2. a s. stillborn 2 May 1889

m. (2) 11 Jan 1910 St James' Ch Dublin Sarah Elizabeth dau. of Frederick Sharpe of Dublin

Died 11 Jun 1913 Laytown Co Meath

JOHNSTON, ROBERT
C Templemichael (Ard) *c.* 1780

JOHNSTON, SAMUEL 1757/58–
b. 1757 or 1758 Co Leitrim; ed by Mr Beaty; ent TCD as Siz 27 May 1777 aged 19 BA 1781

C Cloonclare (Kilm) 1793

    s. of Joseph, *agricola*

    m. and had issue incl his yst **dau.** Margaret **m.** 22 Mar 1841 G F Mowlds of Larkfield Co Dublin

JOHNSTON, WILLIAM –1815
MA

C Cloonclare (Kilm) 1778; Preb of Tascoffin (Oss) 1806–09; poss C Killan, now Shercock (Kilm) 1808–10; V Killargue (Kilm) 1808–10; V Innismagrath (Kilm) 1810–15

    Died 2 Jun 1815

JOHNSTON, WILLIAM DEREK 1940–
b. 13 Sep 1940 Belturbet Co Cavan; ed Royal Sch Cavan; Collegiate Sch Monaghan; TCD GOE 1968

d 24 Jun 1968 p Jun 1969; C Templemore (Derry) 1968–70; R Swanlinbar and Templeport (Kilm) 1970–73; R Billis Killinkere Lurgan and Munterconnaught (Kilm) 1973–84; R Annagh Quivvy Drumaloor and Cloverhill (w Drumgoon Dernakesh Killesherdoney and Ashfield 1987–98) (w Drumlane from 1991) 1984–99; Preb of Annagh (Kilm) 1985–89; R Billis Killinkere Lurgan and Munterconnaught (Kilm) 1999–2003; Archd of Kilmore 1989–2003; ret

    s. of William of Emy Vale Co Monaghan (s. of Robert) by Maureen McKeown dau. of Sam Stewart of Emy Vale Co Monaghan

    m. 18 Sep 1968 Oldcastle Co Meath Sheena **dau.** of David and Anna Morton of Oldcastle. Issue 1. Gail Maureen **b.** 19 Aug 1969 **m.** 21 Jul 1995 Mark Peard; 2. David Morton **b.** 28 Sep 1970 **m.** 28 Sep 2004 Ann Marie Barrett; 3. Meriel Ann **b.** 4 May 1973 **m.** 11 Oct 2001 Christian Schmelter; 4. Emma Joy **b.** 8 May 1980

JONES, CHARLES LEWIS MORGAN 1821/22–1897
b. 1821 or 1822 Limerick; ed by Mr Darley; ent TCD 16 Oct 1840 aged 18 BA & Div Test (2) 1851

d 1851 p 1852 (Cork); C Aghadoe (A & A) 1852–54; PC Dowra (Kilm) 1854–60; may be C L Jones who appears C Killinagh (Kilm) in VB 1860; C Donaghmore (Raph — then Derry) 1860–64; PC Kilteevogue (Raph) 1866–79; C Glenealy (Glend) 1879–81 (not in C I Dir); R Preban and Moyne (Ferns) 1881–96

    s. of Rev Samuel, Preb of Ardcanny (Lim)

    m. Elizabeth and had issue his elder **dau.** Lucy Anne Headly **m.** 1 Sep 1885 James

McGillicuddy Mecredy, MA eldest **s.** of Thomas Tighe of Dalkey Co Dublin

Died 23 Jan 1897

†JONES, GEORGE LEWIS 1722/23–1804

b. 1722 or 1723; bapt St Giles Cripplegate London 12 Sep 1725; ed Eton Coll; Fellow of King's Coll Camb BA 1746 MA 1750 DD 1772; TCD DD *ad eund* 1773; Privy Counsellor 1793

d 29 Nov 1747 (Peterborough) p 20 Dec 1747; R Winkfield (Sarum); R Limpsfield (S'wark) 1757–75; R Tatsfield (S'wark) 1757–66; V Kenninghall (Nor) 1770; Chapl to Lord Harcourt, Lord Lt of Ireland; consec Bp of Kilmore 22 Jan 1775; Bp of Kilmore 1775–90; Dean of Christ Ch Cath Dublin 1790–1804; Bp of Kildare 1790–1804

    s. of Theophilus

    Died 9 Mar 1804 in London aged 81 **bur.** St George's Chapel Windsor

PUBLICATION

    A Poem, *Alpha and Omega*

†JONES, HENRY 1605–1681

b. 1605; TCD Sch 1616 BA 1621 MA & FTCD 1624 Vice Chancellor 1646

Dean of Ardagh 1625–37; Preb of Dromara (Drom) 1630–37; V Bellashandra = Killeshandra (Kilm) 1631–33; V Kildrumferton Ballintemple and Dean & V of Kilmore 1637–45; Archd of Killaloe *in commendam* 1638–61; consec Bp of Clogher in Christ Ch Cath Dublin 9 Nov 1645; Bp of Clogher 1645–61; Bp of Meath 1661–81

    eldest **s.** of Lewis, Bp of Killaloe by Mabel sister of Abp Ussher

    m. (1) Jane **dau.** of Sir Hugh Collum, MP

    m. (2) 31 Dec 1646 St Werburgh's Dublin Mary (**died** 5 May 1672) **dau.** of Sir Henry Piers of Tristernagh. Issue several children

    Died 5 Jan 1681 in Dublin **bur.** St Andrew's Ch

PUBLICATIONS

    The Cavan Remonstrance, 4to, London 1642

    A Remonstrance concerning the Church and the Kingdom of Ireland, 4to, London 1642

    St. Patrick's Purgatory, 4to, London 1647

    Sermons, published 1667, 1676, 1679

    See also Leslie, *Clogher Clergy and Parishes,* pp 11,12.

JONES, JAMES EDWARD

see **REVINGTON–JONES,** JAMES EDWARD

C Kinawley (Kilm) 1883–84 etc

JONES, JOHN

appears C Castlecarragh = Castleterra (Kilm), residing in Dublin 1647

JONES, JOHN

coll V Oughteragh (Kilm) 3 Apr evidently 1706; may have been John Jones Prec of Kildare 1695–1715

†JONES, LEWIS 1543–1646

b. 1543; a native of Dollymoch in Wales; Fellow of All Souls Oxford BA 1568

It is probable that he was V Ardee (Arm) before 1607, as we find a Lewis Jones of Atherdee obtaining a Chancery Decree in 1602 against M Barnewall, granting him a lease for 31 years of 2 parts of the manor of Atherdee (Leslie, *Armagh Clergy and Parishes*, 1911, p 98); R Dunbin 1602–22; Dean of Ardagh 1606; R Beaulieu 1606–18; Dean of Emly 1608–33; Preb of Kilbragh (Cashel) 1608–24; R Peppardstown and Crompstown 1608–34; R Templemore 1608; R Cooleagh 1609–33; consec Bp 12 Apr 1633; Bp of Killaloe 1633–46, being known as the "Vivacious Bishop"

> He **m.** when about 60 years old, Mabel **sister** of Primate James Ussher and had several children, including Henry, Bishop of Meath 1661–82 and Ambrose, Bishop of Kildare 1667–79
>
> **Died** 2 Nov 1646 **bur.** St Werburgh's Ch Dublin
>
> NOTE: Bishop Jones is said to have died in his 104th year (Leslie *Armagh Clergy and Parishes* p 98), though this may be a mistake, for Primate James Ussher whose sister he married, recommending him for the See of Cashel in 1629, says that he was then 69 years old; if so, he was born *c.* 1560 and died aged about 86. However, his birth in 1543 and his dying in his 104th year seems more probable if his sons were bishops in the 1660s, which they could not have been if he was born *c.* 1560, and married aged about 60!

JONES, RICHARD –1642

Cotton gives his Christian name as Nicholas; perhaps same as Richard Jones Jesus Coll Camb BA 1606/07 MA 1610

d 25 Sep 1608 (Peterborough) p 28 Dec 1608; Preb of Swords in St Patrick's Cath Dublin 1615–42; Dean of Waterford 1624–34; Dean of Elphin 1634–42

> **Died** 1642

JONES, ROBERT

V Aughrim (Elph) 1704–05

JONES, ROBERT 1794/95–1838

b. 1794 or 1795 Sligo; ed by Dr Carpendale; ent TCD 6 Mar 1815 aged 20 BA 1818 R Kilmore (Elph) 1821–38

> **s.** of Charles
>
> **Died** 20 Jul 1838 of apoplexy

JONES, THOMAS

ord d & p by Robert (Echlin), Bp of Down 6 Aug 1626; V Killinagh (Kilm)–1626/27; V Killinagh again 1632–36; V Innismagrath (Kilm) 1636–*c.* 61

JONES, THOMAS 1751/52–1836

b. 1751 or 1752; ent TCD 9 Jul 1772 BA 1777 MA 1809

C Mohill (Ard) *c.* 1779; V Moyglare (Meath) 1802–14; R & V Kiltoghart (Ard) 1814–36

> **s.** of Bolton of Dromard Co Leitrim by Elizabeth **dau.** of Hugh Crofton MP of Mohill Co Leitrim
>
> **m.** (ML 27 Sep 1781) Elizabeth of Leixlip Co Kildare **dau.** of John Arabin of Dublin.
>
> **Died** 29 Aug 1836 at Dromard aged 84

JONES, THOMAS SIMPSON

d 1867 p 186– (Kilmore); C Calry 1867–69; C Mullingar (Meath) 1870–72; went to England; poss same as T S Jones C Wellington (B & W) 1872–73; C All SS Ryde (Win) 1873–77; C All S Stoke Newington (Lon) 1877–79; C All SS Poplar (Lon) 1879–85

JONES, TRAVERS 1802–

b. 1802 Co Westmeath; TCD BA 1823 MA 1832

C Athlone (Meath) before 1832; C Aughaval (Tuam) *c.* 1826–32; C Clonbroney (Ard) 1832–36; R Creagh Ballinasloe (Clonf) 1836–45

> **s.** of William, gentleman

JORDAN, ———

Dean of Kilmore to 1590

> **m.** and had issue a son, "Cornelius Jordan son of the Dean from *Ecclesia Magna* (Kilmore) is pardoned, 29 Sep 1590 (F. Elizabeth I , 5466)

JORDAN, WILLIAM

QUI Galway BA Hons (3) 1881 MA (3) 1882; MRAS 1893

d 1883 p 1885 (Kilmore); C Drumshambo and Kiltoghart (Ard) 1883–85; C Holy Trinity Cork (Cork) 1885–88; C St Andrew Summer Hill NSW Australia 1889–90; I Jejedzerick NSW 1890–93; Minister of Moreland (Melb) 1894–1903; P-in-c W Farleigh 1909–10; P-in-c Grosmont (York) 1910–11; C Monks Kirby (Worc) 1912–16; C St Peter Worcester (Worc) 1917–18; C Otterington N (York) 1918–19; C St Michael du Valle Guernsey (Win) 1921–22; living in Surrey in 1926.

JOURDAN, GEORGE VIVILIERS 1867–1955

b. Apr 1867; TCD BA 1893 Div Test 1895 BD 1909 DD 1914 LittD (*stip cond*) 1935; FRHist Soc 1915; MRSAI 1933; MRIA 1934

d 1894 p 1895 (Kilmore); C Larah & Lavey (Kilm) 1894–96; C Mullingar (Meath) 1896–1900; C St Paul Cork (Cork) 1900–02; C Midleton (Cloyne) 1902–06; R Rathbarry w Ardfield (Ross) 1906–15; R St Mary Shandon (Cork) and Chapl Cork District Asylum 1915–40; Chapl Cork N Infirmary 1926–40; Preb of Clonmethan in St Patrick's Cath Dublin 1931–44; Exam Chapl to Bp of Cork 1933–38; Beresford Prof of Eccles Hist TCD 1933–55; C-in-c Dunboyne w Moyglare & Raddanstown (Meath) 1940–44; R Dunboyne Kilcock Maynoth & Moyglare (Meath) 1942–44; ret

yst **s.** of John (eldest **s.** of John, Major of Artillery of the first French Empire) and Sarah of Dublin; of Huguenot descent

Died 8 Dec 1955

PUBLICATIONS
The Movement towards Catholic Reformation in the Early Sixteenth Century, 1914
The Stress of Change, 1931
The Reformation in Ireland in the XVI Century, 1932
Contributor to *The History of the Church of Ireland*, 1933
The XVI Century Reformation, in St. Patrick's Cathedral Commemoration Booklets
Contributor to *Church Quarterly Review, Hermathena, Irish Church Quarterly* and other publications

JOYNT, ANDREW LYONS

d 1870 (Tuam) p 1874 (Kilmore); C Castlemore (Tuam) 1870; C St Columba Liverpool (Liv) 1870–72; C St Nathaniel Liverpool (Liv) 1872–73; C St Simon Liverpool (Liv) 1873–74; C Killashee and Ballymacormack (Ard) 1874–75; C Dromtariffe (Cork) 1875–77; C Oakley (Ox) 1880–82; C Bocking (Chelmsf — then St A) 1883–84; C Devoran (Truro) 1884–85; living in London in 1897

JUSTICE, HENRY 1861–1947

b. 10 Apr 1861 near Bantry Co Cork; ed Dungannon Royal Sch; TCD BA (Resp) 1884 Div Test 1885

d 1885 p 20 Jun 1886 (Kilmore); C Templemichael (Ard) 1885–87; C Christ Ch Londonderry (Derry) 1887–91; R Mohill (Ard) 1891–1916; R Templemichael (Ard) 1916–43; Preb of Tibohine 1930–43; ret

s. of William by Margaret (née Good)

Died 10 Mar 1947

KANE, FRANCIS 1807/08–1882

b. 1807 or 1808 Dublin; ed by Mr Flynn; ent TCD 3 Jul 1824 aged 16 BA 1828 MA 1832

d 1833 p 1 Jan 1835; C Annaduff (Ard) 1840–48; V Russaugh and C Streete (Ard) 1848–55; R Shrule (Ard) 1855–69; R Fenagh (Ard) 1869–82

3rd **s.** of Lt Col Nathaniel, 4th Foot by Elizabeth eldest **dau.** of Francis Nisbett of Derrycarne Co Leitrim

m. 1864 Anne **dau.** of Rev J Shea of Dublin

Died 7 Nov 1882

KEAN, CHARLES

TCD BA 1800

d 24 Aug 1804; p; C Annaduff (Ard) to 1830

KEANE, CHARLES EDWARD 1864–1956

b. 4 Oct 1864; TCD BA 1887 MA 1892

d Feb 1888 p Dec 1888 (Ossory); C Inistiogue (Oss) 1888–90; R Killoe (Ard) 1890–1900; R Mostrim (Ard) 1900–13; C Donoughmore (Glend) 1913–15; R Killesherdoney (Kilm) 1915–49; Preb of Triburnia (Kilm) 1943–49; ret

s. of Rev John, BA, R Ballymachugh (Ard) qv (**s.** of Augustus) by Elizabeth and **bro.** of Rev George Edward

m. and had issue 1. Rev Edward Lionel **b.** 2 Jan 1894 Killoe Rectory Co Longford (**died** 23 Aug 1989) TCD BA 1916 Div Test 1917 MA 1923 d 1917 p 1918 C Tydavnet (Clogh) 1917 C Dingle (A & A) 1918–19 C Ematris (Clogh) 1919–22 C-in-c Mullaghdun (Clogh) 1922–24 C-in-c Clontibret (Clogh) 1924–26 R Clogher 1926–42 R Donagh (Clogh) 1942–44 Preb of Devenish in Clogher Cath 1932–44 R Altedesert (Arm) 1944–49 R Drogheda and Ballymakenny (Arm) 1949–55 R Heynestown (Arm) 1955–61 **m.** (1) 10 Apr 1918 Helena Victoria (**died** 10 May 1961); **m.** (2) 24 Jul 1967 Vera (**died** 18 Jan 1976); 2. Kathleen

Died 26 Nov 1956

KEANE, JOHN 1830/31–1914

b. 1830 or 1831 Co Mayo; ent TCD 14 Oct 1861 aged 30 BA (Resp) 1868

d 1870 p 1871 (Down); C Ardmore (Drom) 1870–73; V Abbeylara (Ard) 1873–78; R Ballymachugh (Ard) 1878–1908; ret

s. of Augustus

m. Elizabeth and had issue a **dau.** Sophie (**died** at Monkstown Dublin 14 Nov 1938); a **s.** Rev George Frederick **died** at Putney 18 Jun 1912; a **s.** Rev Charles Edward qv; a **dau.** Emma Louisa **died** at Monkstown Dublin 9 Mar 1938; a **dau.** Clara Elizabeth (**died** at Drogheda 1 May 1958) **m.** Elliott Motherwell JP of Foxfield, Kilnaleck Co Cavan

Died 27 May 1914 aged 83 **bur.** Ballymachugh

KEARNEY, ALEXANDER MAJOR 1841–1912

b. 1841; bapt at Caledon Ch Co Tyrone 1 Aug 1841; ed privately; TCD BA 1863 Div Test (2) 1864 MA 1880

d 1864 p 28 May 1866 (Kilmore); C Mohill (Ard) 1864–68; C St John Sligo (Elph)

1868–76; R St John Sligo 1876–1912; Archd of Elphin 1880–1904; Dean of Elphin 1904–12; Exam Chapl to Bp of Kilmore

s. of Rev Michael Neville (**died** 24 Mar 1860), PC Caledon (Arm) 1837–43 (**s.** of James) by Rebecca (**died** 28 Apr 1882 Dublin) **dau.** of Alexander Major, merchant of Londonderry and **sister** of Rev Alexander Major, R Darver (Arm); **bro.** of Rev Neville, qv and **bro.** of Rev Michael Neville qv

m. Margaret Anne Ridley. Issue incl 1. a **dau.** b at Sligo 8 Jan 1873; 2. Annie Day **b.** at Sligo 4 Sep 1877; 3. Fanny Harriet (**died** 13 Apr 1898 Sligo)

Died 8 Apr 1912 aged 70

KEARNEY, MICHAEL NEVILLE *c.* 1847–1910

b. *c.* 1847; TCD BA 1872 MA 1875

d 1870 p 1872 (Kilmore); C St John Sligo 1870–72; C Inistioge (Oss) 1873–74; C Templemichael (Ard) 1874; C Clonmel Cobh (Cloyne) 1874–76; C Poulton le Sands (Blackb — then Manch) 1876–78; I Cloverhill (Kilm) 1878; I Bumlin and Preb of Kilgoghlin (Elph) 1878–81; C W Hartlepool (Dur) 1881–83; C Stranton (Dur) 1883–85; C Low Fell 1885–87; V Harbury Warks (Worc) 1887–91; V Rowley Regis (Birm) 1891–96; R Oulton 1896–1900; British Chapl at Antwerp (Dio Lon N & C Europe) 1900–10

s. of Rev Michael Neville, PC Caledon (Arm) 1837–43 (**s.** of James) by Rebecca **dau.** of Alexander Major; **bro.** of Rev Neville, qv and **bro.** of Very Rev Alexander Major, qv

m. 6 Feb 1878 at the Parish Ch Morecambe Lancs Edith 2nd **dau.** of Rev E F Manby of Morecambe

Died 17 Jan 1910

KEARNEY, NEVILLE 1844/45–1911

b. 1844 or 1845; TCD BA 1866 Div Test 1867 MA 1873

d 1868 p 1869 (Down); C Coleraine (Conn) 1868–69; C Kilbroney (Drom) 1869–71; C Fiddown (Lism — then Oss) 1871–75; R Kilrush (Ferns) 1875–79; R Croaghan and Creeve (Elph) 1879–86; Preb of Kilmacallen (Elph) 1880–86; C Bishop's Cleeve (Glouc) 1886–87; C Burton Agnes (York) 1887–88; C Winchcombe (Glouc) 1890–92; C Slad (Glouc) 1892–95; V Marton (Worc) 1896–1905; R Whitechurch (Ferns) 1905–06; R Kilcrohane (Ardf) 1906–11

s. of Rev Michael Neville (**s.** of James) by Rebecca **dau.** of Alexander Major; **bro.** of Very Rev Alexander Major qv and **bro.** of Rev Michael Neville qv

m. 10 May 1876 Stillorgan Par Ch Dublin Henrietta Matilda **dau.** of John Kenny-Herbert of Knockeragone Co Kerry

Died 10 Oct 1911 aged 66 **bur.** Dean's Grange Dublin

PUBLICATION
Support of the Christian Ministry, Dublin, Charles 1883

KEATING, GEORGE 1765/66–1840

b. 1765 or 1766; ed by Dr French; ent TCD 4 Nov 1782 aged 16 BA 1788

R & V Mostrim (Ard) 1801–40

eldest **s.** of Walter, Merchant of Kells Co Meath

m. Jane Little. Issue incl his 3rd **dau.** Maria Sarah **m.** 12 Jan 1837 Very Rev James Lyster, Dean of Leighlin

Died 1840

KEATINGE, JOHN WILLIAM 1768/69–1817

b. 1768 or 1769; matric Queen's Coll Oxford 28 May 1789 aged 20; TCD DD 1796

d & p 1793; V Killesherdoney (Kilm) 1793–1808; V Kinawley (Kilm) 1808–10; Dean of Tuam 1809–10; Provost of Kilmacduagh 1810–13; Dean of St Patrick's Cath Dublin 1810–17; R Drumconrath (Meath) 1813–17; last Chapl to the Irish House of Commons

s. of Michael of Dublin, *armiger*; said to have been nephew of 1st Lord Oriel

m. (1) 1799 Theodosia 2nd **dau.** of Lt Col the Rt Hon Henry Theophilus Clements, MP, 69th Regt of Ashfield Co Cavan

m. (2) Mervyn (**died** 1 Mar 1811) **dau.** of Oliver Nugent of Farren Connell Co Cavan

m. (3) 6 Aug 1812 in St Peter's Ch Dublin Mary Anne only **dau.** of Meade Hobson of Muckridge Co Cork

he had issue incl 1. John Foster; 2. Eleanor Margaret; 3. Harriet Charlotte; 4. Fanny; 5. Anna **m.** Rev William Pollock of St Thomas Stockport

Died 6 May 1817 **bur.** St Patrick's Cath Dublin

KELLETT, JOHN FITZGERALD –1954

TCD BA & Div Test 1909

d 1909 p 1911 (Kilmore); C Calry (Elph) 1909–13; C Carlow (Leigh) 1913–17; C Stradbally (Leigh) 1917–21; TCF 1918–19; C-in-c Kiltennel w Borris (Leigh) 1921–26; C Wallington (S'wark) 1926–31; C Yetminster w C-in-c Chetnole (Sarum) 1931–34; Warden of the Home of St Francis, Batcombe 1934–36; V Redlynch (B & W) 1936–46

s. of Canon James Richard, Preb of Aghoure (Oss) 1883–1901 by Kate **dau.** of Edward Maunsell, Bunratty Co Clare; **bro.** of Rev Richard, Chanc of Ossory 1928–36

m. Isabel Sara (**died** 7 Oct 1959) yr **dau.** of Robert James Empey of Stradbally Co Laois

Died 7 Dec 1954 at Salisbury Infirmary

KELLETT, ORANGE STERLING 1809/10–1897

b. 1809 or 1810 Co Meath; ed by Mr Needham; ent TCD 22 Oct 1827 aged 17 BA 1832 d 1835 p 1836; C Kinawley (Kilm) 1840–50; C Kildrumferton (Kilm) *c.* 1844; C Knockbride 1850–64; C Castlerahan (Kilm) 1864–66; R Tomregan (Kilm) 1866–97

yst **s.** of Robert of Waterstown Co Meath

m. 20 Feb 1844 Maryanne **dau.** of Rev William Grattan, C Kinawley (Kilm) qv and Anne Selina **dau.** of Humphrey Nixon. Issue incl Robert Guy, LRCSI **m.** 19 Apr 1870 Anna Maria **dau.** of Rev James Morgan, V Tagrath Brecknockshire and had issue; 3 **daus.** incl 1. the eldest Anna Selina **m.** 20 Jan 1867 Frederick Aston Oakes, Surgeon; 2. another **dau.** Henrietta Matilda (**died** 9 Jul 1929 at Kingstown)

Died 12 Oct 1897 aged 87 **bur.** Ballyconnell

KELLETT, SAMUEL FREDERICK 1874–1932

b. 1874; TCD BA 1898 Pol Econ Pri & Div Test 1899 MA 1905

d 1899 p 1901 (Kilmore); C Clongish (Ard) 1899–1902; C Knockaney (Emly) 1902–04; C Wicklow (Glend) 1904–05; C Clongish (Ard) 1905–06; C Burton Agnes and Harpham (York) 1906–14; C Howden (York) 1914–17; C St John Sandymount (Dub) 1917–20; C St Peter Drogheda (Arm) 1920–21; C St Peter Howden (York) 1921–25; C St Mark Hull (York) 1925–26; R Clonaslee (Kild) 1926–32

Died 6 Sep 1932

KELLY, ARMSTRONG 1762/63–1849

b. 1762 or 1763 Galway; ed by Dr French; ent TCD 10 Oct 1781 aged 18 BA 1786

d 16 Oct 1785 (Elphin) p; R Ahascragh (Elph) 1786–1800; Preb of Killaspicmoylan (Clonf) 1813–33

s. of Denis, *armiger*

m. and had issue incl a **s.** Denis Henry, MP for Co Roscommon 1820–21

Died 27 Nov 1849 at Thornfield Co Galway

KELLY, DAVID HERBERT 1885–1941

b. 25 Sep 1885; TCD BA 1919 Div Test 1924; served in Great War

d 1923 p 1924 (Down); C St Mark Dundela Belfast (Down) 1923–27; C-in-c Castleterra (Kilm) 1927–31; I Castleterra (Kilm) 1931–32; R Mohill (Ard) 1932–41

Died unm 17 May 1941 Dublin

KELLY, DENIS 1803/04–1866

b. 1803 or 1804 Roscommon; ed by Mr Stubbs; ent TCD 6 Nov 1820 aged 16 BA 1825 MA 1839

d 4 Nov 1827 p 8 Feb 1829; V Killyon and Kilronan (Elph) 1832–34; C St John Chatham (Roch) 1834–; C St Bride (Lon) 1838; PC Trinity Ch Gough Sq Fleet St London (Lon) 1838–66

s. of James, merchant by Anne **dau.** of E Roper

Died 14 Nov 1866 London

PUBLICATIONS
Several works including *Practical Sermons*.

KELLY, FLORENCE

Provost = Precentor of Elphin 1615 (R.V.); V Termonbarry (Elph) in 1615; he was also Preb of Tibohine (Artough) 1615–22 and in 1622 is Archd of Tuam. Lodge has his name as Nelly

KELLY, FRANCIS –1785

poss V Boyle (Elph) to 1785

Died 25 May 1785 Boyle Co Roscommon

KELLY, WILLIAM 1887/88–1965

b. 1887 or 1888 Castledawson Co Derry; ed at Cookstown; ent TCD 24 Jan 1907 aged 19 BA 1912; d 2 Feb 1912 p 29 Jun 1913 (Derry); C Ballycastle (Conn) 1912–21; C Ramoan (Conn) 1921; R Ballywalter (Down) 1921–25; V Waverley w Waitotara NZ (Dio Wellington) 1925–28; R Rongotea (Wellington) 1928–31; Dio C Kilmore 1931–32; R Drumgoon (Kilm) 1932–35; R Kilrossanty w Rossmire (Lism) 1935–37; V Pelynt (Truro) 1937–52; V E & W Wellow (Win) 1952–56; C W Firle w Beddingham (Chich) 1957–58; V St Colan (Truro) 1958–65

s. of David Strong of Castledawson

Died Nov 1965

KEMMIS, GILBERT 1875–1954

b. 4 Jun 1875; ed St Edward's Sch Oxford; St John's Coll Ox BA 1895 MA 1901; TCD *ad eund* BA 1895

d 1898 p 1899 (Kilmore); C Larah & Lavey (Kilm) 1898–1900; C Clones (Clogh) 1900–03; C Pitsmoor (Sheff) 1903–04; C St Martin Dover (Cant) 1904–05; C St Paul Penzance (Truro) 1905–08; C-in-c Killeavy (Arm) 1911–12; V Studley 1914–17; Perm to Off Dio Bristol 1920–21; Perm to Off Dios B & W & Gloucester 1923 and Dios B & W and Worcester 1925–26 and Sarum 1926; Dep Preacher Nat Soc 1923–24; C Maiden Newton (Sarum) 1926–29; C Berry Pomeroy (Ex) 1929–35; R Cornwell (Ox) 1935–38; Hon Sec CCCS 1940–47

5th **s.** of Col William, RA of Ballinacor Co Wicklow

m. 29 Sep 1915 Ch of St John the Evangelist Clifton Bristol Kate Ruding (**died** 1 Dec 1952) **b.** 26 Apr 1873 **dau.** of John Henry Bryson

Died 20 Sep 1954

KEMMIS, THOMAS 1838–1892

b. 21 Oct 1838 Co Laois; ed by Mr Jacob; ent TCD 1 Jul 1856 BA 1863 Div Test 1866 MA 1882

d 1865 p 1866; C Killinkere (Kilm) 1865–66; C Drumgoon (Kilm) 1866–67; C

Kiltoghart (Ard) 1867–68; C Bingley (Bradf) 1869–70; C Conwall (Raph) 1870–72; R Clonaslee (Kild) 1872–75; R Mountcharles (Raph) 1875–78; C Old Newtown Suffolk 1879–81; C Northstoke 1881–83; C Newent (Glouc) 1883–84; C Dundalk (Arm) 1884; R Muff (Derry) 1884–86; C Headford (Tuam) 1887–88; C Cashel (Cash) 1888–90; R Killaloan (Lism) 1891–92

>3rd **s.** of Rev George, BA, R Rosenallis Co Laois (**s.** of William of Ballinacor Co Wicklow) by Caroline 3rd **dau.** of Rev John Olphert, BA of Co Donegal

>**m.** (1) 5 Aug 1873 Penelope (**died** Oct 1875) **dau.** of Robert Roberts of Monkstown. Issue Ethel Constance **b.** 23 Sep 1875

>**m.** (2) 13 Jun 1877 Booterstown Ch Dublin Letitia **m.** F **dau.** of Capt Pendleton of Trim Co Meath. Issue incl Violet Harrie de Burgh (**died** 28 Jul 1966) **m.** 4 Aug 1897 Lewis George Nicholas and had issue incl Rev Lewis William **b.** 12 Jul 1898 V Renhold Beds 1954–69

>**Died** 19 Jul 1892

KEMMIS, THOMAS

C Killyon (Elph) 1879–81

KEMPE, JOSEPH

V Kilbryan (Elph) 1633; coll V Kilcola (Elph) 4 May 1640

KEMPSTON, KEOGH D 1855/56–1916

b. 1855 or 1856

d 1880 p 1882 (Kilmore); C Muckno (Clogh) 1880–82 and C Galway (Tuam) 1882–84 (in Crockford but not Leslie or C I Dir); C Neston (Ches) 1883–85; C St Paul Lozelles Birmingham (Birm) 1885–86; R Templeharry (Killaloe) 1887–92; R Roscommon (Elph) 1892–1916

>**Died** 8 Sep 1916 aged 60

KENAH, SAMUEL CARLETON 1849–

b. 20 Mar 1849; TCD BA (Resp) 1863 Div Test (2) 1864 MA 1883; Ashantee Medal 1873

d 1864 p 1865 (Kilmore); C Kildallon (Kilm) 1864–65; C Bradford 1865–66; C St Luke Sheffield (Sheff — then York) 1866; Chapl RN and NI 1867; C St John Nottingham (S'well) 1867; served in HMS *Bristol* (Flagship), on African Station 1867; *Defence* and *Northumberland*, Channel Squadron 1868–70; *Rattlesnake* (Flagship), Cape of Good Hope and W coast of Africa 1870–74; Ashantee War 1873; *Narcissus* (Flagship), in Detached Squadron in S America India and China 1874–77; *Ganges* at Falmouth 1877–80; *Alexandra* (Flagship) in the Mediterranean 1880–82; *Britannia*, Dartmouth, 1882–88; *St. Vincent*, Portsmouth 1888–89; RMA Portsmouth, 1889–94; Greenwich Hosp and Royal Hosp Sch 1894–99

>**s.** of Thomas Webb of Youghal Co Cork, apothecary by Mary Ayres Jennings

>**m.** 20 Feb 1878 St Peter's Ch Dublin Olivia widow of Rev Rev JT Wesley and yst

dau. of Thomas Collins, MRCSE of Harcourt St Dublin. Issue Ethel Lilian (**died** 9 May 1918) **m.** T Simons, BA BSc

KENNEDY, HENRY ANGUS VICTOR   –1945

TCD BA & Div Test 1919 MA 1921

d 1918 (Clogher) p 1920 (Dublin); Gen Lic Clogher 1918–19; C Blessington U (Glend) 1919–22; C Faversham (Cant) 1922–24; C Santry (Dub) 1924–26; C St George Dublin (Dub) 1926–31; R Kilronan and Kilmactranny (Ard) 1931–37; C-in-c Timolin (Glend) 1937–45

m. Margaret Irene… (**died** 1 Sep 1979 **bur.** Malahide Dublin)

Died 24 Feb 1945

KENNEDY, THOMAS 1759/60–

V Kiltubride (Ard) 17—; there 1807 (Parl. ret) and 1814 (Lea) and to 1823

perhaps T K matric Christ Ch Coll Oxford 2 Jun 1777 aged 17

s. of Francis of Ayr

KENNEY, FRANCIS DRAKE 1731/32–

b. 1731 or 1732; ent TCD as Siz 18 Jun 1750 aged 18 BA 1754

R Taunagh (Elph) 1790–*c.* 95

s. of John, merchant

KENNY, ALEXANDER 1842/43–1888

b. 1842 or 1843; TCD BA 1876

d 1872 (Kilmore for Armagh) p 1873 (Derry for Armagh); C Monaghan (Clogh) 1872–77; R Finner (Clogh) 1877–84; Dio C Clogher and Insp Rel Ed 1884–87; R Dowra (Kilm) 1887–88

m. and had issue incl his younger **dau.** Charlotte Elizabeth **m.** 26 Mar 1894 William Bernard Murray of Dublin afterwards in Holy Orders R Castleconnor (Killala) 1909–13

Died 6 Mar 1888 at Dowra Glebe aged 45

KENNY, THOMAS PERCIVAL ROBERT 1927–2005

b. 1 Jun 1927 Richhill Co Armagh; ed Portadown Coll; TCD Past Theol Sermon Comp Pris BA 1948 Div Test 1949 MA 1952

d 1950 p 1951 (Armagh); C Drumglass (Arm) 1950–53; R Derrynoose and Middletown (Arm) 1953–57; R Aghavilly and Derrynoose (Arm) 1957–62; R St Saviour Portadown (Arm) 1962–66; R Magherafelt (Arm) 1966–74; R Derryloran (Arm) 1974–82; in Nigeria 1983–88; Hon Canon of Dio Owerri from 1984; R Cloonclare Killasnett Lurganboy and Drumlease (Kilm) 1988–90; ret

s. of Thomas Percival Robert, DI RUC by Bella Margaret (née Anderson)

m. 12 Apr 1966 St Patrick's Cath Armagh Audrey Charlotte Louisa **dau.** of Seth and Martha Isabella (née Anderson) Bottom of Armagh
Died 18 May 2005

KEOGH, JOHN *c.* 1653–1720

b. *c.* 1653 Limerick; ed by Mr Shaw; ent TCD 9 Jul 1670 aged about 17 Sch 1674 BA MA 1678

V Creeve (Elph) 1674–; V Clonfinlough (Elph) 1678–; held V Kilcola and Kilglass (Elph) with V Bumlin and Preb of Termonbarry (Elph) 1678–1720.

s. of Donatus

m. and had issue incl his 2nd **s.** Rev John who published *Zoologia Medicinalis Hibernia, or a Treatise on Birds, Beasts, Fishes, etc.*, Dublin, Nowell, 1739

"He spent 42 years in this country living, but did not allow his faculties to rust; was a distinguished scholar and left behind his many unpublished MSS. His 2nd son Rev John Keogh was also a writer on botanical subjects and antiquities, and finds with him a place in the DNB"

Died 1720

KEOGH, ROBERT GORDON 1956–

b. 15 Apr 1956 Dublin; ed Mt Temple Comp Sch Dublin; TCD Dip Theol 1984

d 29 Jun 1984 p 30 Jun 1985; C Mossley (Conn) 1984–87; R Taunagh w Kilmactranny and Ballysumaghan (Elph) 1987–90; R Swanlinbar w Kinawley Chapel of Ease, Templeport and Tomregan (Kilm) 1990–2002; Preb of Drumlease (Kilm) 1998–2002; R Drumclamph and Clare w Langfield Upr & Lr (Derry) 2002–

s. of Eric and Isobel (née Dunne) of Clontarf Dublin (**s.** of Ernest and Elizabeth)

m. 9 Mar 1991 Adelaide Rd Presbyterian Ch Dublin Joan **dau.** of George and Edith (née Kirk) Wright of Clones Co Monaghan. Issue 1. Rachel **b.** 31 Mar 1994; 2. Andrew **b.** 18 Jul 1996

KER, JAMES ADAMS

d; p 22 Jun 1788 (SR)

lic C Ballymacleery & Columbkill in Drumlummon Parish (Ard) 20 Dec 1784 and C Columbkille (Ard) 1784; C Gowna 1816–26

m. (Gents Magazine Aug 1790) Emile Armstrong of Chapelizod Dublin. Issue Marianne **b.** 1808

KERR, ANITA 1963-

b. 5 Jan 1963 Limavady Co Derry; ed Dalriada Gram Sch Ballymoney; was a Midwife before ordination

d 3 Jun 2007 p 18 May 2008; C in NSM Sligo, Rosses Point and Knocknarea (Elph) 2007–

m. Stewart. Issue 1. Alanna **b.** 6 May 1989; 2. Roisin **b.** 2 Jan 1991; 3. Jack **b.** 20 Jun 1993; 4. Siobhan **b.** 2 Oct 1996.

KERR, CECIL MAURICE   –1966

TCD BA & Div Test 1934 MA 1947

d 1934 p 1936 (Kilm); C Annagh w Quivvy and St Andrews (Kilm) 1934–37; C-in-c Gowna w Columbkille (Ard) 1937–39; R Ardagh w Kilglass (Ard) 1939–41; R Granard Mostrim and Abbeylara (w Gowna 1952–59 and Abbeylara to 1962) (Ard) 1941–66; RD of Fenagh 1949–52; Dio Sec Ardagh 1950–59; Dio Reg Elphin and Ardagh 1951–53; RD of Edgeworthstown 1952–59; Preb of Tibohine (Elph & Ard) 1953–56; Preb of Killukin in Elphin Cath 1956–66; Archd of Elphin and Ardagh 1956–66; Exam Chapl to Bp 1956–66

> **m.** (1) Doreen Mary Thorne of Sandymount Dublin (**died** 15 Oct 1952 at Sandymount **bur.** Edgeworthstown). Issue Rosalind A **m.** 27 Dec 1963 Denis H Zachary of Groomsport Co Down

> **m.** (2) 1 Apr 1959 Taney Ch Dublin Helen Elizabeth, widow of Rev George Edwin Camier, R Templemichael (Ard) qv

> **Died** 2 Mar 1966

KERR, JOHN *c.* 1623–1701

b. c 1623

Dean of Ardagh 1661–1701; pres to the Deanery 15 Sep 1661 (L.M. V, 114) and inst 1 Oct and installed 8 Oct 1661; sequestered to vacant V of Mostrim (Ard) 1663 (F.F.), and coll V Mostrim (Ard) 23 Jul 1670 (F.F.); V Granard (Ard) 1665–1702; pres 19 Nov 1665. He was present at the trial of Sir Phelim O'Neill 3–5 Mar 1652/53, and at his execution 10 Mar 1652/53 (Gilbert, *History of Affairs in Ireland,* III. 368).

> **m.** Mary Abet

> **Died** 5 Mar 1701 aged about 78

KERR, LEWIS   1723/24–

b. 1723 or 1724 Monaghan; ed by Dr Sheridan; ent TCD 7 Jun 1737 aged 13 BA 1741 MA 1744 MB 1759

prob same as Lewis Kerr Head Master Royal Sch Cavan 1764–68; lic C Urney (Kilm) 26 Jun 1766

> **s.** of Rev John

> **m.** (ML 14 Jan 1766) Elizabeth Lyndon of St. Bridget's Dublin

KERR, PATRICK   1701/02–

b. 1701 or 1702 Co Cavan; ed by Mr Sheridan, Dublin; ent TCD 18 Mar 1719/20 aged 18 Sch 1722 BA 1724

appears V of Eastersnow Kilock & Kilbryan to 1766

> **s.** of Hugh

> **m.** and had issue a **s.** Lewis **b.** Co Leitrim ed by his father ent TCD as Siz 9 Jul 1757 aged 20 Sch 1760 BA 1761 MA 1769

KIDD, GEORGE HAROLD 1900–1983

b. 5 Jun 1900; ed St Stephen's Green Sch Dublin; TCD BA 1928 Div Test 1929 MA 1944

d 1929 p 1930 (Cashel); C Christ Ch Cath Waterford (Waterf) 1929–33; C-in-c Killegney w Rossdroit and Adamstown (Ferns) 1933–45; R Achill U (Tuam) 1945–51; R Walkerstown Ontario Canada 1952–53; BC Drumshambo Kiltubride and Kilronan (Ard) 1953–55; C-in-c Preban w Moyne (Ferns) 1955–58; V Coverham w Horsehouse (Ripon) 1958–81

elder **s.** of George of Dublin

m. 20 Jun 1937 Donnybrook Ch Dublin Ruth Eva yst **dau.** of Lionel Tabeau of Sandymount Dublin. Issue a son

Died 1983

KIERNAN, FRANCIS

lic C Oughteragh (Kilm) 28 Dec 1773

KILLINGLEY, ERNEST ALFRED 1870/71–1948

b. 1870 or 1871; TCD BA & Div Test (2) 1897 BD 1905

d 1898 p 1899 (Kilmore); C Lurgan (Kilm) 1898–1900; C Urney (Kilm) 1900–02; R Oughteragh (Kilm) 1902–06; R Swanlinbar (Kilm) 1906–09; R Rossinver (Kilm) 1909–21; R Castleterra (Kilm) 1921–27; Dio Reg Kilmore 1023–32; R Drumlease (Kilm) 1927–32; Archd of Kilmore and R Killeshandra & Killegar (Kilm) 1932–43; ret

m. Florence Edith (**died** 15 April 1967 Harrogate Yorks). Issue 1. Marjorie, BA 1935; 2. Ernest **m.** 10 Feb 1942 Ruby Constance **dau.** of E N McCormick of Sandycove Dublin; 3. Sidney LeFebure **m.** 13 Sep 1934 at Bangor Ch Muriel Sybil yst **dau.** of George Johnston of Belturbet Co Cavan; 3. Charles Sedley **m.** 27 Jan 1941 Gladys Mary only **dau.** of Mrs **m.** Dillon of Strandtown Belfast

Died 16 Feb 1948 aged 77

KINAHAN, WILLIAM ROBERT LAWRENSON 1835–1894

b. 4 Nov 1835 Co Down; ent TCD 11 Jul 1853 BA 1859 Div Test 1860

d 1860 p 1861 (Down); C Knockbreda (Down) 1860–64; C Lickmolassy (Kilmacd) 1863–64; C Drumgoon (Kilm) 1864–66; C Kiltubride (Ard) 1866–68; C Loughinisland (Down) 1870; C Scarvagh (Drom) 1870–72

4th **s.** of Rev John, R Knockbreda (Down) by Emily **dau.** of John George of Dublin

Died unm. 17 Feb 1894 Belfast

KING, ABRAHAM SMYTH 1824–

b. 29 May 1824 London; ed by Mr Turpin; ent TCD 14 Oct 1842 BA & Div Test 1850

C Killeban (Leigh) 1863; C Garvaghy (Drom) 1865–68; C Drumlummon and Gowna

(Ard) 1868–70; C Ballymacormick (Ard) 1870–71; V Garvaghy (Drom) 1872–74

yst **s.** of Hulton Smyth of Borris Castle, Queen's Co (Laois), Commissioner of Customs, Ireland, who was **bro.** of Sir Abraham Bradley King, 1st Bt

KING, ALBERT EDWARD 1864/65–1938

TCD BA (Resp) & Div Test (1) 1887 BD 1892

d 1888 p 1889; C Hillsborough (Down) 1888–89; R Munterconnaught (Kilm) 1889–99; R Kildallon (Kilm) 1899–1931; Preb of Mulhuddart in St Patrick's Cath Dublin 1922–27; Dean of Kilmore 1926–31; ret

yst **s.** of Rev Joseph, R Munterconnaught (Kilm) qv; **bro.** of Rev Robert, the Church Historian

m. 2 Sep 1891 at Clonduff Par Ch Co Down Mary Martha Susanna yst **dau.** of Hugh Hall of Hilltown Co Down. Issue **sons** 1. Edward Joseph **b.** 24 Aug 1894, Capt RIF, MC 1917; 2. Richard Francis **b.** 6 Sep 1901 **m.** 17 Aug 1935 Helen **dau.** of Frank Wood; a **dau.** 1. Margaret Hall **m.** 30 Jul 1927 Newcastle Co Down Lt John B Hickman, MC Royal Corps of Signals

Died 24 Aug 1938 aged 73

†KING, EDWARD 1575/76–1639

b. 1575 or 1576 Huntingdonshire; ed Oxford; TCD MA 1596 Fellow 1600 DD 1614 consec Bp of Elphin Dec 1611;

Dean of Elphin 1603; V St Catherine Dublin 1606; Bp of Elphin 1611–39

m. (1) Anne Consed

m. (2) Grace **dau.** of Nathaniel Sampson, by whom he was ancestor of the King baronets of Charlestown Co Roscommon

He had several children. His 4th **s.** (by which marriage?), Charles ed by Mr Young, Elphin ent TCD 21 Jul 1641 aged 18; another **s.** James **died** 2 Apr 1687 in his 77th year; another **s.** Capt John **m.** and had issue incl Elizabeth who **m.** John and had issue Rev Charles Dodd, V Drumlease (Kilm) qv

Died 8 Mar 1639

Bishop King repaired the Cathedral at his own expense, built an Episcopal residence, and recovered some of the See property that had been alienated by his predecessor. He resigned to his clergy the *quarta pars Episcopalis*, which they had been bound to pay to him, and governed the diocese well for over 27 years. His tombstone records, "Here lyeth the body of Edward King, Doctor in Divinity consecrated Bishop of Elphin anno Dni 1610 (recte 1611) and continued Bp in that See until the eighth of March 1638(9) on which day and yeare he died at the age of 63. This bishop much augmented the revenue of that See, was a constant Preacher of God's Word and a man of great sanctity of life."

KING, HENRY

C Shrule (Ard) 1769

KING, Sir JOHN

a layman, held Preb of Kilmacallen (Elph) 1615

KING, JOHN

MA

Preb of Kilgoghlin (Elph) 1627–66; R Sligo (Elph) 1637–40, pres 2 May 1637 and again 26 Apr 1638, "the first modern Rector of Sligo *inter duos pontes,* and he and his successors created a body corporate with perpetual succession to hold all ye lands of the Rectory at yearly rent of £7 per annum" (P.R. 14 C.I.); Dean of Tuam *c.* 1638; he appears as Dean of Tuam in 1650 and in 1656 he is "Minister & Dean of Tuam" (Ms. I. 11 in Marsh's Library)

KING, JOHN *c.* 1649–

b. *c.* 1649 Dublin; ed by Mr Scott at Dublin; ent TCD 21 Feb 1665/66 aged about 16 Sch 1667

R & V Fenagh Kiltoghart and Kiltubrid (Ard) 1680–1700, coll 18 Jun 1680 (FF); signed address to King James II 18 Mar 1684/85; probably was J K who was V Drumlease and Killargue (Kilm) 1678–81, and perhaps same as J K, V Ardnurcher (Meath) 1693–1730

prob John King **s.** of Rev John

KING, JOSEPH 1819/20–1889

b. 1819 or 1820 Cork; ed by Mr Hamblin; ent TCD 16 Oct 1840 aged 20 BA 1845 Div Test 1846

d 1846 (Kilmore) p 1848 (Limerick); C Bailieborough and Moybologue (Kilm) 1849; C Drung (Kilm) 1850–68; V Killenvoy (Elph) 1868–77; held V Loughan (Meath) with Munterconnaught (Kilm) 1877–89

s. of Joseph, merchant; **bro.** of Rev Robert, the Historian

m. 29 Nov 1856 Lucy Jane Edgeworth **dau.** of George Peacocke, MD of Longford and **sister** of Most Rev Joseph Ferguson Peacocke (1835–1916), Abp of Dublin 1897–1915. Issue incl 1. eldest **s.** Francis Joseph George, MB (**died** 1 Jan 1930 Shillelagh Co Wicklow); 2. yst **s.** Rev Albert Edward, Dean of Kilmore qv; 3. Adelaide A E **m.** 16 Apr 1896 James, MB of Ballyjamesduff, **s.** of Rev James Clarke, BA.

Died 8 Aug 1889

KING, MURTAGH

d 23 Sep 1632 p 22 Sep 1633; V Templeport (Kilm) from 1632; he helped Bp Bedell with the translation of the Old Testament into Irish.

KING, OLIVER 1682/83–1740

b. 1682 or 1683 at Charleston; ed by Mr Cugh at Strokestown; ent TCD 5 Aug 1697 aged 14 BA 1701 MA 1705; R & V Annaduff (Ard) 1714–21; R Kilmore (Elph) 1720–23; R Drung and Larah (Kilm) 1721–40

> **s.** of Gilbert of Charlestown Co Roscommon, MP for Jamestown by Mary **dau.** of Dominick French of Frenchpark
>
> **Died** June 1740 aged 57

KING, ROBERT

BA

Preb of Terebrine (Elph) 1636–40

KING, ROBERT 1813/14–1884

b. 1813 or 1814 Dublin; ed by Mr McCarthy; ent TCD as FC 2 Apr 1832 aged 18 BA 1836 MA 1840

R Kilmore (Elph) 1838–84

> 2nd **s.** of Sir Robert, 2nd Bt of Charlestown
>
> **m.** (1) 17 Nov 1838 Jane (**died** s.p. 1868) **dau.** of Matthew Nesbitt of Derrycarn Co Leitrim and widow of Edward Simpson of Drumsna
>
> **m.** (2) 1872 Arabella (**died** 21 Oct 1885) **dau.** of John Watkins
>
> **Died** 20 Jun 1884 s.p.

KING, THOMAS

V Ballysumaghan (Elph) 1615

KINGSTON, ALBERT WILLIAM 1947–

b. 19 Mar 1947 Bandon Co Cork; ed Bandon Gram Sch; The Bernard Gilpin Soc Durham 1968–69; Oak Hill Theol Coll GOE 1972

d 17 Sep 1972 p Sep 1973; C Walton Breck (Liv) 1972–74; C Templemore, St Columb's Cath Londonderry (Derry) 1974–76; I Kildallon w Newtowngore and Corrawallen (Kilm) 1976–82; BC Ardagh Moydow Tashinny Shrule and Kilcommick (Ard) 1982–; Preb of Terebrine (Elph) 1995–

> **s.** of Robert James of Ballydehob Co Cork (**s.** of Samuel and Elizabeth (née Copithorne) of Ballydehob Co Cork) by Mary–Ann **dau.** of Joseph and Mary Shorten of Enniskeane Co Cork; **bro.** of Canon Kenneth Robert Kingston R Desertmartin and Termoneeny (Derry) 1984–; nephew of Rev William Kingston, R Lakemba Sydney Australia
>
> **m.** 3 Apr 1975 Milltown Par Ch Co Kerry Frances Lillian **dau.** of William Thomas Neill and Kathleen (née Hill) of Ballymacelligott Tralee Co Kerry. Issue Shirley Mary Frances **b.** 29 Jan 1976

KINGSTON, GEORGE 1919/20–1989

b. 1919 or 1920 Dunmanway Co Cork; ed Bandon Model and Gram Sch; TCD BA 1944 d 1944 p 1945; C St Lawrence St John and Trinity Limerick (Lim) 1944–46; R Templeharry (Killaloe) 1946–48; C Christ Ch Belfast (Conn) 1948–51; C-in-c Magherahamlet (Drom) 1951–54; R Denmark w Austria Bunbury W Australia (Dio Bunbury) 1954–56; R Goshells Perth (Dio Perth)1956–60; R Cockburn Sound 1960–63; R Boyup Brook 1963–65; R Swanlinbar w Templeport (Kilm) 1965–69; R Monasterevan U (Kild) 1969–71; R Killeshandra Killegar and Derrylane (Kilm) 1971–78; R Boyle Aghanagh Kilbryan and Ardcarne (Elph) 1978–80; ret

    m. 1946 Innishannon Par Ch Co Cork Sarah Ross of Kildarra Innishannon. Issue 1. John; 2. Trevor; 3. Rosemary Kathleen Elizabeth **m.** Rev Robert Kingston, R Billis (Kilm) qv; 4. Rosalind **m...** Ball, London; 5. Ruth **m...** Moss, Antrim

    Died Dec 1989 at Enniskillen aged 69

KINGSTON, ROBERT GEORGE 1946–

b. 6 Jul 1946 Cork; ed Cork Gram Sch; TCD BA 1967 Carson Bibl Pri & Div Test (2) 1969

d 1969 p 1971; C St Thomas Belfast (Conn) 1969–72; working with Social Welfare Dept 1973–74; C St Canice's Cath Kilkenny (Oss) 1974–77; R Ballinasloe w Taughmaconnell (Clonf) 1977–79; R Maryborough w Dysart Enos and Ballyfin (Leigh) 1979–85; R Billis Killinkere Lurgan and Munterconnaught (w Kildrumferton Ballyjamesduff and Ballymachugh 1988–92) 1985–92; Dio Reg Kilmore Elphin and Ardagh 1987–92; R Tallaght (Dub) 1992–98; Warden of Readers Dublin and Glendalough 1993–98; R Mallow Doneraile and Castletownroche (Cloyne) 1998–

    s. of Paul Christopher and Eleanor (née Simpson) of Cork

    m. 3 Nov 1971 Killeshandra Par Ch Co Cavan Rosemary Kathleen Elizabeth **dau.** of Rev George Kingston, R Killeshandra (Kilm) qv and Sarah (née Ross) Issue 1. Christopher George **b.** 26 Oct 1973 **m.** 21 Jun 2002; 2. Naomi Elizabeth **b.** 18 Feb 1975 **m.** 4 May 2001; 3. Miriam Patricia Ruth **b.** 23 Jan 1981

KIRKPATRICK, GEORGE 1797–1889

b. 1797 Dublin; ed at Royal Sch Armagh by Dr Carpendale; ent TCD as SC 2 Jan 1815 aged 17 BA 1818

d 1820 (Cloyne p 1821; C Drumgoon (Kilm) 1824–29; C Ahoghill (Conn) 1831–40; R Craigs (Conn) 1840–68; ret

    s. of Alexander, merchant of Coolmine Co Dublin by Marianne Sutton Kirkpatrick

    m. 17 Mar 1829 Catherine Elizabeth (**died** 29 Dec 1874 aged 81 at Craigs Co Antrim) **dau.** of Very Rev Francis Browne LLD, Dean of Elphin qv by Anna Maria Browne **dau.** of James Noble of Glassdrummond Co Fermanagh, High Sheriff of Co Fermanagh 1758. Issue Rev Alexander Thomas (**died** 19 Apr 1909 Larne) **b.** 5 Jan 1830 Dublin Div Test 1853 MA 1875 d 1853 p 1861 C Craigs (Conn) 1853–68 R Craigs (Conn) 1868–1901 **m.** 31 Aug 1869 Portglenone Ch Co Antrim Alicia (**died** 28 Aug 1933 aged 92) **dau.** of Rev Robert William King, R Portglenone (Conn) 1862–72 and Alicia **dau.** of Rev Hugh Henry Shields of Drogheda and had issue (i) Rev Robert (**died** 14 Apr 1966) **b.** 1 Oct 1877, V Glynn (Conn) 1920–50 **m.** 19 Jun 1919 Lucy Edith **dau.** of Col Duncan McNeill (ii) Thomas Alexander (**died** 6 Jan 1889) **b.** 11 Jun 1883 (iii) George King (**died** 5 Dec 1876)

b. 11 Dec 1875

Died 8 Jul 1889 at Hazelbank Co Antrim aged 91

KIRKPATRICK, IVAN RIDLEY   1906/07–1982

b. 1906 or 1907

TCD Sch BA (Ment & Mor Sci) 1928 Div Test 1931

d 1931 p 1932 (Kilmore); C St John Sligo w Knocknarea (Elph) 1931–33; R Tubbercurry (Ach) 1933–37; R Enniskeen and Ardagh (w Nobber from 1941) (Meath) 1937–47; R Tullamore w Lynally and Durrow (Meath) 1947–50; Sec Hib CMS 1950–53; R Powerscourt (Glend) 1953–56; R Cloughjordan U (Killaloe) 1956–58; R Ballinaclough U (Killaloe) 1958–62; R Kilnasoolagh (Killaloe) 1962–65; Preb of Lockeen (Killaloe) 1962–65; R Kilmacduagh (Kilmacd) 1965–71; Preb of Tipperkevin in St Patrick's Cath Dublin 1970–77; R Drumcliffe (Killaloe) 1971–78; ret

   s. of John A of Kenlis Lodge Kells

   m. and had issue 1. Elizabeth; 2. Peter

   Died 31 Jul 1982 aged 75

KNAPP (KNAPPAGH), FRANCIS   –1717

b. at Clifton near Abingdon Berkshire; ed St John's Coll Oxford & was afterwards Magdalene Coll & MA

R Ahascragh (Elph) and R & V Killasoolan = Castleblakeney (Elph) and V Killyon (Elph) and Dean of Killala 1701–17

   Died 1717 **bur.** Clifton Berks

KNIGHT, RICHARD   1696/97–

b. 1696 or 1697 Tunnymore Co Fermanagh; ed by Mr Sheridan, Dublin; ent TCD 17 Jun 1717 aged 20 Sch 1719 BA 1721

C Killeshandra (Kilm) 1729; V Cashel and Rathcline (Ard) 1740–80, inst 27 Oct 1740 (FF). Admonished by Primate to call a vestry to repair the Church at Rathcline Sep. 1742 (Arm. D.R.).

   s. of Richard, *colonus.*

KNIPE, GEORGE   –1797

ed by Mr Cottingham at Cavan; ent TCD 1 Nov 1762 Sch 1765 BA 1767

d 16 Aug 1767 (Kilmore) p 1769 (Kilmore); C Drumlane (Kilm) 1767–; R Castlerickard (Meath) 1784–97; was fired at by rebels in 1795 and murdered in 1797

   s. of John of Belturbet Co Cavan, Ensign Cavan Militia, one of the Burgesses of Belturbet by Margaret

   m. (1) 1768 Miss Battersby (**died** Jul 1771 Monaghan). Issue **sons** 1. John, Lt 59th Foot and afterwards Lt 1st Dragoons and Capt 60th Foot **m.** 1797 Rachel Gerrard; 2. George

   m. (2) Alicia — she was granted an annuity of £300 as her husband "was lately most cruelly murdered on account of his meritorious exertions as a magistrate", by special Act of Parliament. Issue 1, Frances **m.** 1812 Nathan Barry; 2. Anne

Died 1797

KNOTT, THOMAS 1810–1874

b. 1810 Sligo; ed by Mr Stokes; ent TCD 22 Oct 1827 aged 16 — no degree recorded BA in Erck

d 1839 p; C Templeport (Kilm) 1840; C Drumreilly (Kilm) 1840–48; C Carrigallen (Kilm) 1849–66; V Ballysumaghan (Elph) 1867–74

> **s.** of James, *nuper centurionis*
>
> **Died** 12 Jun 1874 at Lurgan Lodge Sligo aged 64

KNOWLES, JOHN ARTHUR 1924–1991

b. 1924; ed TCD

d 1955 p 1956; C Enniskillen (Clogh) 1955–56; R Cooneen and Mullaghfad (Clogh) 1956–59; R Templeharry and Borrisnafarney (Killaloe) 1959–61; R Clonsast and Rathangan (Kild) 1961–62; R Bourney (Killaloe) 1962–65; R Creagh (Clonf) 1965–67; R Donagh w Tyholland and Errigal Truagh (Clogh) 1967–69; C-in-c Rathaspeck Streete and Kilglass (Ard) 1969–76; R Mohill Farnaught and Aughavas (w Oughteragh Kiltubride and Drumreilly from 1981) (Ard) 1976–84; Preb of Kilcooley in Elphin Cath 1981–84; R Drumcliffe w Kilnasoolagh (Killaloe) 1984–90; ret

> **s.** of Rev Robert Atkin, Methodist Minister, Tullamore Co Offaly by Mabel (née Hill) of Garvagh Co Derry; **bro.** of Ven George Woods Atkin, R Drumachose Limavady (Derry) 1963–89 and Archd of Derry 1985–89 (**died** 26 Dec 2005)
>
> **m.** 1 Mar 1954 Methodist Central Ch Dublin Beatrice Smith (**died** 5 Jul 2004) . Issue 1. Robert; 2. Anne; 3. Daphne **m.** 14 Jul 1983 Mohill Co Leitrim Kenneth **s.** of Mr and Mrs Arthur Graham, Bilboa Co Laois; 4. Patricia Mary bapt 20 Feb 1966; 5. David Arthur **b.** 18 Jul 1967; 6. Heather Jennifer bapt 30 Jan 1977
>
> **Died** 22 Feb 1991 cremated Dublin

KNOWLES, PHILIP JOHN 1948–

b. 23 Sep 1948; ed Bp Foy Sch Waterford; The Patrician College Newbridge Co Kildare; TCD Div Test 1976 MA 1984; Univ of Oxford BTh 1980; Univ of Greenwich PhD; LTCL; ALCM; LLAM

d 1976 p 1977; C St Paul Lisburn (Conn) 1976–79; R Cloonclare Killasnett Lurganboy and Drumlease (Kilm) 1979–87; R Gorey and Kilnahue (w Liskinfere and Ballycanew from 1989) (Ferns) 1987–95; Preb of Kilrush and Toome (Ferns) 1991–95; R Cashel Mogorban Tipperary Clonbeg and Ballintemple (Cash) 1995–; Dean of Cashel 1995–; Chanc of Waterford 1995–; Chanc of Lismore 1995–; Librarian of Cashel 1995–; Preb of Mayne (Oss) 1996–; Preb of Tecolme (Leigh) 1996–; Sec Cashel Waterford and Lismore Board of Ed 2005–

> **s.** of Rev Canon Frederick Willis Robert (**s.** of Henry John and Louisa Edith Maud) by Vera Constance (née Wellwood) of Cavan

PUBLICATION
Cloonclare– Glimpses of our History

KNOX, ──────
V Kilcommick (Ard) *c.* 1684

KNOX, ANDREW
There were two of this name, of which one was V Ahamplish (Elph) 1750–69;

(1) **b.** Co Donegal 1708 or 1709; ed by Dr Ballantine at Strabane; ent TCD 13 Jul 1727 aged 18 BA 1732

(2) **s.** of Rev Francis of Castleblayney Co Monaghan; matric Univ of Glasgow 1737 MA 1740

d; p 1747 (Kilmore)

KNOX, ARTHUR 1793–1874
b. 22 or 27 Nov 1793 Dublin; ed by Mr Craig; ent TCD as SC 7 Sep 1812 aged 18 BA 1816 MA 1832

R Ballymodan (Cork) 1825–35; R Castleterra (Kilm) 1835–73; ret

>3rd **s.** of Arthur of Woodstock Co Wicklow by Lady Mary Brabazon

>**m.** Nov 1820 Mary (**died** Apr 1885 aged 94) **dau.** of Rt Hon Denis Daly of Dunsandle. Issue incl 1. Rev Denis, R Lurgan (Kilm) qv; 2. an elder **dau.** Harriet Charlotte **m.** 2 Apr 1841 William Boswell of Newtownmountkennedy Co Wicklow; 3. Mary Emily Theodosia

>**Died** 26 Nov 1874 at Hastings aged 81

KNOX, DENIS 1828/29–1912
b. 1828 or 1829; TCD BA 1851 Div Test (2) 1852 MA 1869

d 1852 (Tuam) p 1853 (Meath); C Lavey (Kilm) 1854–66; R Munterconnaught (Kilm) 1866–70; R Lurgan (Kilm) 1870–1909; RD of Kilmore; Chapl to Marquis of Headfort and to Lord Dunsandle; Chapl to Lord Lt

>**s.** of Rev Arthur, R Castleterra (Kilm) qv by Mary **dau.** of Rt Hon Denis Daly

>**Died** 27 Jan 1912 aged 83

KNOX, GEORGE 1704/05–1769
b. 1704 or 1705 Co Sligo; ed by Mr Ballentine, Strabane Co Tyrone; ent TCD 19 May 1723 aged 18 Sch & BA 1726 MA 1730

d & p at Raphoe 1731; C Clondevaddock (Raph) 1731; V Kilbarron (Raph) 1733–45; V Innismagrath and Kildallon (Kilm) 1745–68; Innismagrath Parish Church being situate on an island at a considerable distance from the mainland and uncovered and in ruins, and Knox being in delicate health, he was allowed to postpone his "reading in", 30 Dec 1745; R & V Carrigallen (Kilm) 1768–69 evidently s. of Thomas, *armiger*

his wife **died** May 1769 in Moore St Dublin

Died 8 Aug 1769, but Lodge's *Obit* has Jul 1769

KNOX, GEORGE 1730–1795

b. 1730 Co Donegal; ed by Mr Babington; ent TCD 4 Apr 1746 aged 17 Sch 1748 BA 1750 MA 1763 BD & DD 1785

C Culdaff (Raph — then Derry) 1752; C Clonleigh (Raph — then Derry) 1754; R Ballyscullion (Derry) 1761–67; V Templeport and Drumreilly (Kilm) 1767–78; R Clonleigh (Raph — then Derry) 1781–94

s. of George; great grandson of Rt Rev Andrew Knox, Bp of Raphoe

m. Catherine (**died** 21 Mar 1796 Dublin **bur.** St Peter's Dublin) **dau.** of Francis (?James) Nesbitt of Woodhill. Issue **sons** 1. Rev James (**died** 14 Jan 1848) ent TCD 9 Jul 1770 aged 14 BA 1775 R Killybegs (Raph) 1778–81 Head Master Diocesan Sch, later Foyle Coll Londonderry to 1834 R Aghanloo (Derry) 1781–94 **m.** Mary Frances **dau.** of James Nesbitt and had issue incl (i) Rev George Nesbitt, R Termonamongan (Derry) 1834–50 (ii) Maria; 2. Rev John Russell, V Innismagrath (Kilm) qv; **daus.** 1. Letitia **m.** Col Alexander Lawrence; 2. Angel; 3. Marianne

Died 25 Dec 1795 in 65th year in Berkshire **bur.** Bray Berks

KNOX, GEORGE

C Kilmore (Kilm) in 1769; poss same as above

KNOX, GEORGE 1798/99–1871

b. 1798 or 1799 Dublin; ed by Dr Miller; ent TCD 4 Nov 1816 aged 17 BA 1821

d 1823 (Cork) p; C Dunamon (Elph) 1826; C Oran (Elph) 1829; V Dunamon Kilcroane & Ballynakill (Elph) 1831–65; R Castleblakeney (Elph) 1865–71

s. of Maurice, Lawyer, Attorney Exchequer Dublin

Died 6 Oct 1871 Ballybrack

KNOX, JAMES SPENCER 1789–1862

b. 26 Apr 1789 Co Armagh; ed by Mr Austin; ent TCD 11 May 1805 as FC aged 16 BA 1810 MA 1814

R Fahan (Raph — then Derry) 1813–17; V Innismagrath (Kilm) 1815–17; R Maghera and Kilcronaghan (Derry) 1817–62; V Gen Derry 1859

eldest s. of Hon. William, Bp of Derry 1803–31

m. 10 Sep 1813 Clara Barbara (**died** 14 Apr 1862 at Clifton) **dau.** of the Hon. John Beresford. Issue 1. Sir Thomas George, KCMG, served in India and China with Siamese Army and in English Consular Service; 2. Rev Charles Beresford (**died** 27 Feb 1910 aged 84) **b.** 1825 TCD BA (Sen Mod Classics) 1847 Div Test 1848 MA 1863 d 1848 (Armagh) p 1849 (Down) C Skerry and Racavan (Conn) 1849 C Ballyculter (Down) 1854 C Holywood (Down) 1854 C Carrickfergus (Conn)

R Drumgath (Drom) 1856–65 R Dromore and Treas (Drom) 1865–81 C-in-c Heathfield (Chich) 1882–85 V Lower Beading Sussex (Chich) 1886–92 **m.** 3 Apr 1857 at Ryde IOW Christina (**died** 28 Jul 1916) **dau.** of Rev Edward Leslie, Treas of Dromore by Margaret **dau.** of Rev Thomas Edward Higginson and had issue (i) Rev Charles Edward Leslie Beresford (**died** 12 Feb 1956) **b.** 14 Aug 1864, R Greinton (B & W) (ii) Margaret Leslie (iii) Christina Kathleen Mary; 3. George Beresford, Lt Col Londonderry Militia; 3 **daus.** incl 1. Clara Beatrice (**died** Feb 1862) **m.** Jun 1847 John Madden of Roslea Manor Co Fermanagh (later of Aghafin Co Monaghan) and had issue 4 children; 2. Isabella **m.** Jul 1870 at Neuchatel Switzerland her brother-in-law John Madden and had issue Violet (**died** 1886)

Died 1 Mar 1862 at Clifton Bristol

KNOX, JOHN RUSSELL 1768/69–1830

b. 1768 or 1769 Co Donegal; ed by Mr Burgoyne; ent TCD 23 Apr 1786 aged 17 BA 1790

C Clonleigh (Raph — then Derry) to 1817; V Innismagrath (Kilm) 1817–30

s. of Rev George, V Templeport (Kilm) qv (**s.** of George); **bro.** of Rev James, V Killybegs (Raph)

m. Jan 1790 Abigail **dau.** of Edward Hill, MD Pres RCPI Jan 1790. Issue incl 1. Catherine **m...** Gibson and had issue incl William; 2. Elizabeth Sinclair **m.** 5 May 1826 Neill Campbell of 13th Light Infantry; 3. George; 4. James

Died 23 Dec 1830 at Ballyshannon **bur.** Drumholm Churchyard Ballintra Co Donegal

KNOX, WILLIAM –1916

d 1881 p 1882 (Kilmore); C Killasnett (Kilm) 1881–83; C Killesher (Kilm) 1883–87; C St Thomas Dublin (Dub) 1887–88; R Killesher (Kilm) 1888–1908

m. 16 Oct 1890 Marie Stuart eldest **dau.** of Charles Stuart Adams, JP of Cos Cavan and Meath. Issue incl 1. eldest **s.** Arthur Stuart (**died** 18 Feb 1926 in Australia aged 33); 2. a **dau.** Marion (**died** 1977 in Australia) **m.** …Aldis

Died 25 Dec 1916 Westmead Paramatta Sydney NSW

KRAUSE, WILLIAM HENRY 1796–1852

b. 1796 St Croix West Indies; Army Officer, fought at Waterloo; TCD BA 1830 MA 1838

d 1836 (Kilmore) p 1837 (Kilmore); C Urney (Kilm) 1836–40 (in Leslie's MSS, he was lic C Urney 10 May 1838); Chapl Bethesda Dublin (Dub) 1840–51; became a celebrated preacher in Dublin

m. and had issue

Died 27 Feb 1852

PUBLICATIONS
Sermons, 3 vols, ed by Rev. C.S. Stanford, Dublin 1852
Lectures, 3 vols, ed by Rev. C.S. Stanford, Dublin 1854

LABATT, ANDREW TYRRELL 1835/36–1896

b. 1835 or 1836 Dublin; ed by Dr Flynn; ent TCD 11 Oct 1853 aged 17 BA & Div Test 1859

d 1859 p 1860; C Rahan (Meath) 1861–62; PC Croghan (Elph) 1862–63; C Desertlyn (Arm) 1863–66; R Rathmolyon (Meath) 1871–72; went to England

only **s.** of Christopher James, MD of Lr Baggot St Dublin

m. 17 Jan 1860 St Mark's Ch Dublin Anna Maria (**died** 31 Jan 1879) **b.** 12 May 1836 3rd **dau.** of Rev William de Burgh DD, R Arboe (Arm) 1864–66. Issue 1. Frederick Hubert de Burgh **b.** 13 Jul 1863; 2. Flora Constance Adelaide Feilding **b.** 2 Mar 1865; 3. Violet Augusta de Burgh (**died** 26 Dec 1879) **b.** 13 Feb 1866; 4. a **s. b.** at Lambeth London 1 Mar 1869

Died 17 Dec 1896 at the Rectory, Blunsden Wilts

La NAUZE, GEORGE HENRY TESSIER 1854/55–1901

b. 1854 or 1855; ed St Aidan's Coll Birkenhead

d 1878 p 1879; C Kiltegan (Leigh) 1878–80; C St Michael Limerick (Lim) 1880–81; C Fenagh (Ard) 1881–83; C Loughgilly (Arm) 1883; C Tynan (Arm) 1883–1901

s. of Rev Thomas Jassier, MA, R Killinagh Co Cavan 1823– qv below (**s.** of Henry of Aubawn Co Cavan)

Died 13 Nov 1901 aged 46 **bur.** Tynan

La NAUZE, THOMAS 1785/86–1852

b. 1785 or 1786 Dublin; ed by Dr Burrowes; ent TCD as SC 3 Oct 1803 aged 17 BA 1807 MA 1832

C Kilmore (Kilm) 1811–23; V Killinagh (Kilm) 1823–36; V Oughteragh (Kilm) 1836–42; R Templeport (Kilm) 1842–52

s. of Henry of Auburn Co Cavan by Frances **dau.** of Joseph Story, Archd of Kilmore qv, merchant

m. (1) 2 Oct 1826 at Athlone his 1st cousin Frances **dau.** of Col John French of Cloonyquin Co Roscommon

m. (2) 5 Sep 1843 at Kiltubrid Ch Ellen eldest **dau.** of Rev George D Mansfield

Died 19 Oct 1852 at Templeport Rectory

LANDEY, RICHARD WOLFE 1844/45–1927

b. 1844 or 1845

d 1882 p 1883 (Elphin); C Ardagh (Ard) 1882–84; R Kilmactranny w Kilbryan (Elph) 1884–93; R Knocknarea (Elph) 1893–1916; R Roscommon (w Dunamon from 1917) (Elph) 1916–26; ret

m. Louisa L Eccles (**died** Feb 1952 aged 92 at Moneygold Co Sligo)

Died 11 Apr 1927 aged 82

LANDEY, THEOPHILUS PATRICK 1850/51–1934

b. 1850 or 1851; TCD BA 1884 MA 1892

d 1884 p 1885 (Tuam); C St Nicholas Galway (Tuam) 1884–86; I Toomna (w C-in-c Kilronan (Ard) 1893–96) (Elph) 1886–96; I Straid (Ach) 1896–1915; Archd of Achonry 1905–15; I Killala (Killala) 1915–25; Dean of Killala 1915–27; R Kilmoremoy (Killala) 1925–27

yr **s.** of Theophilus Boileau

m. and had issue incl his yr **dau.** Dorothy **m.** 19 Aug 1925 Frank A **s.** of A R Poulden of Southsea Hants

Died 27 Jan 1935 Dublin aged 84

LANGLEY, PETER LEWIS 1785/86–1841

b. 1785 or 1786 Co Derry; ed by Mr Groves; ent TCD 2 Jun 1801 aged 16 as Sizar Sch 1803 BA 1805 MA 1808

C Tashinny (Ard) in 1817; V Ballymore Eustace (Glend) 1833–41

s. of Peter, *caupo*

Died 24 Sep 1841 at Esker nr Dublin in his 56th year

LANGRISHE, JAMES 1764–1847

b. 1764 or 1764 Kilkenny; ed by Dr Norris; ent TCD 9 Nov 1781 aged 17 BA 1785 MA 1814

d 1786 (Down) p; R Baldungan (Dub) 1789–92; Preb of Kilconnell (Clonf) *c.* 1789–90; Provost of Kilmacduagh 1790–1810; Dean of Achonry 1792–1806; Archd of Glendalough 1806–47; Preb of Dysart and Kilmoleran (Lism) 1809–10; R Kinawley (Kilm) 1810–22; R Killeshin (Leigh) 1822–47

2nd **s.** of Sir Hercules, 1st Bt of Knocktopher

m. Dec 1790 Mary Harriet (**died** 12 Aug 1842) elder **dau.** of Hugh Henry Mitchell of Dublin. Issue **sons** 1. Rev Hercules (**died unm.** Apr 1846) **b.** Dublin ed by Mr Dowdall ent TCD 3 Jul 1815 aged 17 BA 1819 d p 1823 C St Bride's Dublin (Dub) 1826 R Ballybay (Clogh) 1827–46; 2. Henry Hercules, Capt Grenadier Guards; 3. Robert James, Lt RN; 4. John Tottenham; 6 **daus.** incl Elizabeth **m.** Rev Walter de Burgh, Preb of Tipper in St Patrick's Cath Dublin 1832–59

Died 17 May 1847 Newcastle Co Wicklow aged 82

LAPIERE (La PIERRE), TOBIAS GUMLEY 1791/92–1862

b. 1791 or 1792 Queen's Co (Laois); ed by Dr Macnamara; ent TCD as Siz 7 Jun 1814 aged 22 Sch 1817 BA 1820

C Gallen (Meath) 1825; C Tully Co Galway 1847–; C Ballinakill (Tuam) *c.* 1852; PC Corrawallen (Kilm) 1858–62

s. of William, *agricola*

Died 3 Aug 1862 Sandymount Dublin

LAUDER, MATTHEW NESBITT 1819–1881

b. 1819 Co Leitrim; ent TCD 3 Jul 1837 aged 17 BA 1843 MA 1846 Div Test 1847

d 1847 p; C Derrylane (Kilm) *c.* 1847–; C Kildallon (Kilm) 1852–57; C Swanlinbar (Kilm) 1857–60; PC Swanlinbar (Kilm) 1860–76; ret

    s. of John, magistrate of Mough Hse Co Leitrim

    m. 30 Oct 1848 Anne (**died** 23 Apr 1878) eldest **dau.** of John Gumley of Belfast

    Died 9 Sep 1881 aged 62

LAUDER, ROBERT 1812–1870

b. 1812 Gibraltar; ed by Mr FitzGerald; ent TCD 13 Jan 1838 aged 25 BA 1842 LLB & LLD 1858

d 1843 p; C St Peter Athlone (Elph) 1848–49; R Agher (Meath) 1849–70

    s. of Capt Thomas Bernard

    m. 7 Nov 1843 St Peter Athlone Jane Sarah widow of A Weatherhead, Surgeon & **dau.** of John Johnston of Thirsk Yorks

    Died 23 Jul 1870 aged 58

LAUDER, WILLIAM

C Sligo (Elph) in 1844

†LAW, JOHN –1810

ed Charterhouse; Univ of Cambridge BA 1766 MA 1769 DD 1782; Fellow of Christ's Coll Camb 1785. He was a man of great literary attainments. During the Rebellion of 1798, he enrolled a troop for the defence of the district which was commanded by his Archdeacon, Oliver Cary. He had the reputation of being in favour of the emancipation of Roman Catholics

R Warkworth Cumberland and Preb of Carlisle 1773–77; Archd of Carlisle 1777–82; Chapl to the Duke of Portland, Lort Lt, whom he accompanied to Ireland, and by whose influence he was made Bp of Clonfert in 1782

consec Bp of Clonfert 21 Sep 1782 in the Chapel of Dublin Castle; Bp of Clonfert 1782–87; Bp of Killala and Achonry 1787–95; Bp of Elphin 1795–1810

    s. of Dr Edmund Law, Bp of Carlisle and **bro.** of the 1st Lord Ellenborough, and of Dr George H Law, Bp of Bath and Wells

    Died 19 Mar 1810 Dublin; **bur.** TCD Chapel

PUBLICATION

    A Sermon preached for the Incorporated Society, Dublin, 4to, 1796

LAW, JONATHAN 1648/49–*c.* 1724

b. 1648 or 1649; ed Moulton Sch near Spalding Lincs; adm Magdalen Coll Camb 8 Jun 1664 aged 15 BA 1667/68 MA 1671; incorp at Oxford 1671

d 24 Sep 1670 (Peterborough); p; R Bow Brickhills Bucks (Ox) 1671 C Kilsaran or

Gernonstown (Arm) 1679; Precentor of Elphin and V Kilcorky (Elph) 1681–1722; V Shankill and Kilmacumsy (Elph) 1683–; V Killukin (Elph) 1703–22; Preb of Tibohine (Elph) 1703–*c.* 24

was no doubt Jonathan Law **s.** of Jonathan of Boston Lincs, merchant

Died *c.* 1724

LAWLES, WILLIAM FITZSIMOND

R Killery (Ard) 1381/82; parson of Hurglin (Urglin) (Leigh)

LAWTON, HENRY   –1972

Fitzwilliam Hall Univ of Camb BA (2cl Eng Trip) 1920 MA 1925; Egerton Hall Univ of Manchester 1920 BD 1932

d 1922 p 1923 (Manchester); C Christ Ch Moss Side (Manch) 1922–26; R St Philip Hulme (Manch) 1926–29; V St Luke Rochdale (Manch) 1929–38; V Walkden (Manch) 1938–53; Hon Canon of Manchester 1950–53; R, Sub–Dean and Hon Canon of St John's Pro-Cathedral Buenos Aires 1953–62; R Drumlease Killenumery and Killargue (Kilm) 1962–67; ret

m. Irene (**died** 29 Feb 1972 at Bognor Regis on the same day as her husband)

Died 29 Feb 1972 Bognor Regis

LAYNG (LANG), JAMES

Commonwealth Minister at Killeshandra, "to subscribe the engagement 1651 at £50 a year"; raised from 1656 to £60, subsequently increased 1658 to £120 (Seymour's *Commonwealth MSS* and Dunlop, *Ireland Under the Commonwealth,* Vol. I)

ordained "in the Kingdom of Scotland"; R Kildallon (Kilm) 1661–68; coll R & V Killeshandra (Kilm) 24 Apr 1661

m. Agnes. Issue 1. Rev John, R Kildallon (Kilm) qv; 2. Margaret (marriage settlements dated 15 Oct 1663) **m.** as his 1st wife John Beatty (Will proved 10 Feb 1726/27) of Corr Co Cavan and had issue Claud of Coolarty Co Longford, Lt in the Army

LAYNG, JOHN   –1678

Commonwealth Minister at Ballymote from 1654 at £50, subsequently in the precinct of Belturbet 1660 at £60

ord p 3 Jan 1660 by the Bp of Candida Casa; V Drumlease with Clonlogher Killargue and Killenumery (Kilm) 1661–73; is coll to V Killenumery (Ard) 8 May 1661 (V.B. 1673); coll V Kildallon (Kilm) 13 Oct 1668 and R Kildallon (Kilm) 15 Apr 1674; R Killeshandra (Kilm) 1674–78

s. of Rev James, R Killeshandra (Kilm) qv by Agnes. Issue **sons** 1. John; 2. James; 3. Henry George; 4. Charles; **daus.** 1. Elizabeth; 2. Martha; 3. Catherine

"Mr. John Lang, Minister for Killeshandra, **bur.** in St. Audoen's (Dublin) 19 January 1677/78"

LEA, WILLIAM –1923

St Aidan's Coll Birkenhead 1886

d 1888 p 1889 (Carlisle); C Christ Ch Carlisle (Carl) 1888–91; C-in-c Stonegrave (York) 1891–92; C Chobham (Win) 1892–94; C St Matthew Thorpe Hamlet (Nor) 1895; R Kilglass (Ard) 1895–1922; ret

 m. and had issue a **s.** Rev James

 Died 1923

LEADBEATER, WORRALL REGINALD 1913–

b. 1913; TCD BA & Div Test 1936; MC 1943

d 1936 p 1937 (Kilmore); C St John Sligo w Knocknarea (Elph) 1936–39; CF (EC) 1940–50; CF 1950–52; still in CF 1980–82

LEAHY, DANIEL –1884

was brought up Roman Catholic; ed Maynooth Coll

ord d by RC Bp of Limerick 1837 p; became Anglican; C Ellastone (Lich) 1858; C Field Dalling (Nor) and Asst C St Peter Saffron Hill London; PC Croghan (Elph) 1861; V Kilbryan (Elph) 1862–66; V Kilmactranny (Elph) 1866–84

 Died 7 Mar 1884 **bur.** Kilmactranny

LEAHY, JOHN 1756/57–

b. 1756 or 1757 Tipperary; ed by Mr Baker ent TCD as Siz 1 Jun 1779 aged 22 Sch 1781 BA 1783 MA 1789

d 13 Jul 1783 (S.R.) p; probably the JL who was C St Werburgh (Dub) 1788–90 and Chapl St Nicholas Within (Dub) 1788 and V St Mark Dublin 1798; Preb of Tascoffin (Oss) 1788–1806– this info derived from Leslie's *Ossory Clergy and Parishes.*

V Shrule (Ard) 1800–06; V Innismagrath (Kilm) 1806–10; V Cloonclare (Kilm) 1810–23; Preb of Tascoffin (Oss) 1788–1806– this info derived from Leslie's MSS notes on Ardagh Diocese

 s. of James *mechanicus*

 m. and had a **s.** James John **b.** Dublin ed by Mr Fea ent TCD 1 Jun 1795 aged 15 Sch 1798 BA 1800 MA 1804 who was perhaps JL C Clonlogher (Kilm) *c.* 1817– info in *Ossory Clergy and Parishes.*

LEATHLEY, JOSEPH FORDE 1801/02–

b. 1801 or 1802 Dublin; ent TCD ⅔ Jul 1819 aged 17 BA 1823 MA 1832

V Russagh and C Streete (Ard) 1829–37.

 s. of Joseph, gentleman

LEDOUX, LLEWELYN PAUL TAHAN *c.* 1858–1940

b. *c.* 1858; ed Rathmines Sch; TCD BA & Div Test (1) 1881 MA 1888 BD 1898

d 1881 p 1882 (Down for Armagh); C Portadown (Arm) 1881–83; R Kilmore (Arm)

1883–88; C Bray (Dub) 1888; R Killinchy (Down) 1888–90; R Calry (Elph) 1890–99; R Drogheda (Arm) 1899–1924; Preb of Ballymore (Arm) 1909–13; Chanc of Armagh 1913–24; Exam Chapl to Abp; ret 1924

only **s.** of P A Ledoux, member of the University of Paris

m. (1) 28 Apr 1884 Holy Trinity Ch Rathmines Dublin Letitia Catherine (**died** 20 Dec 1913 at St Peter's Rectory Drogheda) 3rd **dau.** of G P Lindsay of Rathmines and **sister** of Rev George William Lindsay, R Magherafelt (Arm) 1908–18

m. (2) 3 Feb 1916 Ethel Georgina (**died** 30 Jan 1955 **bur.** Drogheda) **dau.** of James Willis

Died 28 Feb 1940 at Rathgar Dublin **bur.** Drogheda

PUBLICATION
Short Historical Sketch of St Peter's, Drogheda, Drogheda Independent 1913

LEE, MICHAEL 1703/04–

b. 1703 or 1704 Co Tyrone; ed by Mr Folds, Carrickmacross Co Monaghan; ent TCD 22 May 1722 aged 18 BA 1726

C Drumgoon (Kilm) 1729; C Killesherdoney (Kilm) 1754–68; V Innismagrath (Kilm) 1768–71; C Knockbride (Kilm) 1771

s. of Richard

m. Catherine only **dau.** of William Moore of Cootehill Co Cavan by Margaret yr **dau.** of Edward Davenport of Edwardstown Co Cavan. Issue incl 1. Rev William, R Innismagrath (Kilm) qv; 2. Catherine **m.** William Giles of Cootehill, merchant

LEE, WILLIAM 1736/37–1792

b. 1736 or 1737 Co Cavan; ed by Mr Moore; ent TCD 9 Jul 1753 aged 16 Sch 1756 BA 1758

d 28 Jun 1761 p 19 Dec 1762 (Kilmore); C Knockbride (Kilm) 1761 and 1766–; V Innismagrath (Kilm) 1771–92

Died 1792

LEECH, ROBERT 1829/30–1909

b. 1829 or 1830; TCD Abp King's Div Pri (2) & Eccles Hist Pri (1) 1871 Sen Soph 1872 Div Test (1) & Reg Prof of Div Pri at Theo Exhib Exam 1873

d 1872 p 1873 (Kilmore) PC Arvagh (Kilm) 1872–74 & C Kilmore (Kilm) 1873–74; V Drumlane (Kilm) 1874–1907

m. and had issue 1. Robert Hirst (**died** 8 Oct 1878 at Drumlane aged 12); 2. a **s. b.** 27 Jun 1872 Dublin

Died 23 May 1909 at Drumlane aged 79

LEEMAN, JOHN ERNEST 1915–1975

b. 8 Jun 1915 Portadown Co Armagh; ed RBAI; TCD Newport White and Div Comp Pris BA & Div Test (2) 1939 MA 1949 d 1939 p 1940 (Kilmore); C St John Sligo (Elph) 1939–44; C Zion Rathgar (Dub) 1944–45; C Ballymena (Conn) 1947–50; C St Stephen Ealing (Lon) 1950–54; V West Twyford (Lon) 1954–60; R Castlebar U (Tuam) 1960–65; Chapl Mayo Gen and Mental Hosp 1960–65; RD of Ballinrobe (Tuam) 1963–65; R Kilmoremoy (Killala) 1965–75; Preb of Ardagh (Killala) 1968–73; Dean of Killala 1973–75

> **s.** of William David of Portadown Co Armagh (**s.** of John and Ann (née Bell of Co Fermanagh)) by Mary Louise (née Wiggins); **bro.** of Rev Maurice Edward (1927–1989), R Aghoghill (Conn) 1959–89
>
> **m.** 17 Feb 1954 St Ann's Par Ch Dublin Doreen Mary LPSI PhC **dau.** of F G Young of Newbridge Co Kildare. Issue 1. Deirdre **b.** 13 Mar 1955 **m.** 30 Jul 1982 Turlough Par Patrick Butler of Turlough Co Mayo; 2. Gillian **b.** 3 Aug 1957
>
> **Died** 22 Nov 1975 Ballina Co Mayo

Le FANU, FLETCHER SHERIDAN 1860–1939

b. 1860; TCD BA & Div Test 1883

d 1884 p 1885 (Dublin); C St George (Dub) 1885; PC Lissadell (Elph) 1885–1900; Preb of Terebrine (Elph) 1895–1900; R St John Sandymount (Dub) 1900–30; ret

> **s.** of William Richard (author of *Seventy Years of Irish Life*)
>
> **m.** Jane **dau.** of Walter Hore of Carlow
>
> **Died** 17 Mar 1939

LEFROY, HENRY 1788/89–1876

b. 1788 or 1789 Co Limerick; ed by Mr Miller; ent TCD as SC 7 Nov 1808 aged 19 BA 1812 MA 1820

d p 1813; C Cootehill, Drumgoon (Kilm) 1819–35; R St Laurence Limerick (Lim) 1819–35; C Maryborough (Leigh) 1822; C Killesherdoney (Kilm) 1825; R Tomregan (Kilm) 1835–43; V Santry (Dub) 1843–76

> yr **s.** of Anthony, LLD, MP for Dublin Univ
>
> **m.** Dorothea **dau.** of Gerald O'Grady of Kilballyowen. Issue 1. Anthony O'Grady; 2. Gerald de Courcy; 3. Henry Maunsell; 4. Ann Langloise; 5. Elizabeth Waller; 6. Mary Elizabeth O'Grady; 7. Dorothea Thomasina
>
> **Died** 9 Jan 1876 **bur.** Santry Dublin

LEIGHTON, SAMUEL JOHN –1972

d 1922 p 1923; C St Andrew Belfast (Conn) 1922–24; C Carnmoney (Conn) 1924–31; R St John Laganbank Belfast (Conn) 1931–44; CF (EC) 1940–44; C-in-c Stoneyford (Conn) 1944–46; C St Peter Bedford (St Alb) 1946–47; V St John Bowling (w C-in-c St Bartholomew Bowling and St Luke Bradford 1951–53) (Bradf) 1947–53; R Clongish and Clooncumber (Ard) 1953–56; R Tempo (Clogh) 1956–62; RD of Kilskeery (Clogh) 1961–62; ret

> **m.** 1920 Edwina Isabella Bingham. Issue Edwin Samuel, Architect and Organist of St George's Church Belfast 1948–82
>
> **Died** 11 Mar 1972

†LESLIE, CHARLES 1810–1870

b. 7 Oct 1810; matric Christ Ch Coll Oxford 5 May 1829 BA 1835 MA 1836

R Killesher (Kilm) 1851–55; R Drung (Kilm) 1855–70; V Gen of Ardagh; consec Bp of Kilmore Elphin and Ardagh in St Patrick's Cath Dublin 24 Apr 1870; enthroned at Kilmore Cath 26 May 1870; enthroned at Longford 14 June 1870; enthroned at Elphin Cath 17 June 1870; Bp of Kilmore Elphin and Ardagh Apr–Jul 1870

eldest **s.** of Rt Rev John, Bp of Kilmore Elphin and Ardagh qv (**s.** of Charles Powell and Prudence Penelope Hill-Trevor) by Isabella **dau.** of Hon and Rt Rev Thomas St Lawrence, Bp of Cork and Ross

m. (1) 8 Apr 1834 Hon Frances King (**died** s.p. 20 Jul 1835) 3rd **dau.** of Viscount Lorton

m. (2) 22 Aug 1837 Louisa Mary (**died** 23 Dec 1883 at Corravalen Cavan aged 83) 2nd **dau.** of Major Gen Hon Sir Henry King, KCB. Issue five **sons**

Died 8 Jul 1870 **bur.** Kilmore

LESLIE, GEORGE *c.* 1680–1754

b. *c.* 1680 in "Co. Inish", the Isles?; ed by Mr Jenkins, Derry; ent TCD 11 Mar 1698/99 aged 18 BA 1703 BD & DD 1744; JP for Co Fermanagh and Co Cavan 1729

d p 8 Aug 1708 (Derry); R Balteagh (Derry) 1714–18; R Clones (Clogh) 1718–54; V Tomregan (Kilm) 1740–54; V Drumsnatt (Clogh) and R & V Kilmore (Clogh) 1753–54

s. of Rev George, DD

m. (ML 29 Jan 1711) Margaret Montgomery of St Mary's Par Dublin sister of Col. Alexander Montgomery, Scots Greys of Convoy Co Donegal and Ballyconnell Co Cavan

Died 28 Apr 1754

†LESLIE, JOHN 1772–1854

b. 12 Oct 1772; ed by Mr Carpendale; Royal Sch Armagh; ent TCD 3 Jul 1790 BA 1794 MA 1805

d 1796 p 1797 Bp 1812; V Donagh (Clogh) 1800–07; R Templecarne (Clogh) 1807–08; R Fiddown (Oss) Mar– Sep 1807; Dean of Cork 1807–12; R and Preb of Tynan (Arm) 1808–12; consec Bp of Dromore 26 Jan 1812; Bp of Dromore 1812–19; Bp of Elphin (w Kilmore and Ardagh from 1841) 1819–54

2nd **s.** of Charles Powell of Glaslough, MP for Co Monaghan by Prudence Penelope Hill–Trevor **dau.** of 1st Viscount Dungannon

m. 8 Aug 1808 Isabella (**died** 10 Nov 1830) 2nd **dau.** of Hon and Rt Rev Thomas St Lawrence DD, Bp of Cork and Ross. Issue 1. Rt Rev Charles Bp of Kilmore Elphin and Ardagh 1870 qv; 2. John **b.** 3 Nov 1814; Middle Temple; **m.** 1854 Maria **dau.** of Rev J Peck; 3. Thomas **b.** 6 Jul 1819 (**died** 15 Feb 1880) **m.** 4 Jun 1856 Anne (**died** 24 Feb 1910) **dau.** of Sir Edward Hoare, Bt, and had issue; 4. Arthur **b.** 4 Nov 1821, Col in 40th Regt; 5. Frances Anne Prudentia (**died** Apr 1853) **m.** Rev John Papillon; 6. Emma **m.** Rev Nicholas Toke of Kent; 7. Charlotte

Isabella; 8. Harriet (**died** 23 Mar 1853) **m.** 2 Jul 1846 John Edward Vernon, JP DL of Erne Hill Co Cavan and had issue (i) John Fane **b.** 5 Jul 1849, JP DL, Barrister-at-Law **m.** 1882 Thomasina Georgina **dau.** of Rev Henry Joy Tombe DD Canon of Christ Ch Cath Dublin (ii) Edward Saunderson **b.** 6 Mar 1851 **died** young (iii) Isabella France **m.** 1874 Henry Chichester Tisdall of Charlesfort Co Meath

Died 22 Feb 1854 **bur.** Kilmore

L'ESTRANGE, GUY PERCIVAL 1810/11–1893

b. 1810 or 1811; ed by Mr Tate; ent TCD 21 Jan 1828 aged 17 BA 1832 MA 1835

V Drumlane (Kilm) 1837–42; R Knockbride (Kilm) 1842–52; R & V Timahoe and Ballinafagh (Kild) 1852–72; R Rathangan (Kild) 1878–83; R Clonmethan (w Hollywood and Naul from 1885) (Dub) 1883–93

4th **s.** of Col Henry Peisley of Moystown Queen's Co (Laois)

m. (1) 10 Jul 1839 at Raheny Marianne Austin of St Peter's Dublin

m. (2) Henrietta Maria (**died** 26 Jul 1901 Dublin) of St Peter's Dublin

Died 20 Jun 1893 at Clonmethan Rectory **bur.** 23 Jun

LEWIS, SAMUEL HENRY 1809/10–1901

b. 1809 or 1810 Sligo; ed by Mr O'Connor; ent TCD 5 Jun 1833 Vice Chancellor's Pri 1836 BA 1838

d 1839 p 1840 (Cork); PC Ballyjamesduff (Kilm) 1840–48; C Dingle (A & A) 1848–63; R Columbkille (Ard) and C Killan, now Shercock (Kilm) 1863–69; R Kiltoghart (Ard) 1869–86; R Castlejordan (Meath) 1886–1901

s. of William

m. 22 Apr 1852 at Weston–super–Mare Somerset Sophia 3rd **dau.** of Major Joseph James Durbin of Walton Court Sussex by Anne **dau.** of George Birch of Hamsted Hall Staffs. Issue incl his eldest **dau.** Emma Sophia **m.** Rev William Swayne Little, R Toomna (Elph) 1881–85 qv

Died 7 Sep 1901 aged 91

†LEYNS, ADAM –1416

was a Dominican; prov. to the See of Ardagh 15 Feb 1400 A.H. I. 185)

He is still Bp in 1410 and on 10 Aug was charged with negligence (Cal. Reg. Flem. No. 129) and in 1411 (ib. 158). A.F.M. gives his name as Adam Lexid and says that he was burned to death probably accidentally at Rathaspeck

Died June 1416 (Hib. Dom. 468)

LIDWILL, MARK ROBERT 1957–

b. 30 Jan 1957 Dublin; ed St Columba's Coll Dublin; TCD Dip Theol 1987 BTh 1988

d Jun 1987 p Jun 1988; C Annagh Drumaloor Cloverhill Drumgoon Dernakesh Ashfield and Killersherdoney (Kilm) 1987–90; R Urney Denn and Derryheen 1990–

; Dio Youth Adviser (Kilm) 1992–; Preb of Triburnia (Kilm) 1998–

s. of Robert Peisley of Templemore Co Tipperary by Hazel Strode (née Pim) of Rathdowney Co Laois

m. 10 Jul 1993 Bailieborough Co Cavan Barbara Anne **dau.** of John and Sadie Corrie of Bailieborough

LINDSAY, ALEXANDRA JANE 1943–

b. 1943; CITC 1990

d 1993 p 1994; Lic to Off Kilmore Elphin and Ardagh 1993–94; NSM Bailieborough Knockbride Shercock and Mullagh (Kilm) 1994–97 and 2000–06; NSM Kildallon Newtowngore and Corrawallen (Kilm) 1997–2000; NSM Roscommon G (Elph) 2006–

m. Rev Cecil Lindsay, NSM Mohill G (Ard) qv

LINDSAY, CECIL 1943–

b. 1943; Iona Coll NY BBA 1968; CITC 1985

d 1988 p 1988; NSM Kilmore w Ballintemple and Kildallon (Kilm) 1988–90; Lic to Off Kilm 1990–91; NSM Roscommon w Donamon Rathcline Kilkeevin (Elph) 1993–96; NSM Killeshandra w Killegar and Derrylane (Kilm) 1996–2002; Dio Reg Kilmore Elphin and Ardagh 1997–; NSM Mohill G (Ard) 2002–04; NSM Lurgan Billis Killinkere and Munterconnaught (Kilm) 2004–05; NSM Killeshandra G (Kilm) 2006–

m. Rev Alexandra Jane, NSM Kildallon G (Kilm) qv

LINDSAY, THOMAS

d 1872 p; C Kiltubrid (Ard) 1872–76; C Killaraght (Ach) 1876; R Killaraght (Ach) 1876–77; R Gowna (Ard) 1877–79; R Kildrumferton (Kilm) 1879–85

LINDSAY, VICTOR FREDERICK –1957

TCD BA 1901 Div Test 1902

d 1901 (Dublin for Clogher) p 1903 (Clogher); C Inishmacsaint (Clogh) 1901–03; C Clongish (Ard) 1903–05; C Drung (Kilm) 1905–06; C Carrigallen (Kilm) 1906–08; C Cahir (A & A) 1908–11; C Ballinrobe (Tuam) 1911–13; C Killaraght (Ach) 1913–14; living in Killala Co Mayo 1914–15; C Ballinrobe (Tuam) 1915–16; C Killaraght (Ach) 1916; C Dunston (Dur) 1922–23; C Kilnamanagh (Ferns) 1923–24; C-in-c Leyburn (Ripon) 1924–26; C Eglingham (Newc) 1926–29; V Ninebanks and PC Carshield (Newc) 1929–32; R Dufton (Carl) 1932–45

Died 4 Aug 1957

LINDSAY, WALTER 1733–1775

b. 1733; ed by Mr Moore; ent TCD 10 Dec 1747 BA 1752

C Drumsnatt and Kilmore (Clogh) 1752; C Ardtrea (Arm) 1757; V Tomregan (Kilm) 1758–67; may have been coll in 1754; R Ballyscullion (Derry) 1767–75

s. of Rev Alexander, R Drumsnatt (Clogh) 1741–53 (s. of Walter) by Ellen **sister** of Rev James Richardson, R Balteagh (Derry) and of Deborah 1st wife of Joseph Story, Bp of Kilmore qv

m. Elizabeth **dau.** of Sir Nicholas Forster, Bt. Issue **sons** 1. Rev Alexander (**died** 5 Jul 1843) ent TCD 6 Nov 1775 aged 17 Sch 1778 BA 1780, C Clonmore (Arm) 1835 R Rathdrummin and Carrick (Arm) 1793–1843 **m.** Sarah (**died** 13 Dec 1840 aged 82); 2. Robert; **daus.** incl his 2nd **dau.** Eleanor **m.** John Johnston of Woodvale Co Armagh

Died 1775

LINDSAY, WOODLEY JOSEPH *c.* 1878–1953

b. *c.* 1878 Donegal; ed Gram Sch Cork; TCD (Jun Mod) Pol Sci 1899 Eccles Hist Pri (1) 1901 and 1902 BD Theo Exhib & Div Test (1) 1903 LLB & LLD 1908

d 1903 p 1904 (Ossory); C Dysart Galen (Oss) 1903–05; C Stradbally (Leigh) 1905–07; C Ematris (Clogh) 1907–09; R Abbeylara w Drumlummon (Ard) 1909–20; Insp Ardagh Bd of Rel Ed 1921–28; Dio Reg Elphin and Ardagh 1921–39; R Rathaspeck w Russagh (w Streete from 1932) (Ard) 1920–39; ret

s. of Rev John Woodley, R Clondevaddock (Raph) by Jane 2nd **dau.** of Moses Netherfield of Glendoon Co Cavan; **bro.** of Rev Victor Frederick BA, V Ninebanks (Newc)

m. Florence Muriel eldest **dau.** of Rev J Browne, R Clongish (Ard) qv and had issue incl Francis Woodley **m.** Gillian only **dau.** of Brigadier G Marnham OBE of Surrey

Died 17 May 1953 Malahide Dublin

LINDSEY

V of the Abbey of Lewra (Abbeylara) to 1647; is in Dublin 1647 (Carte Pps. XXI, 546)

LINNEGAN, JOHN McCAUGHAN 1915–1999

b. 7 Mar 1915 Bushmills Co Antrim; ed Giant's Causeway Sch; Londonderry Tech Coll ACCS 1948; TCD BA 1955; ACIS 1970

d 28 Oct 1957 p 28 Oct 1958 (Kilmore); C-in-c Billis Ballyjamesduff and Castlerahan (Kilm) 1957–59; C-in-c Cappagh (Derry) 1959–60; R Cappagh (w Lislimnaghan from 1980) (Derry) 1960–90; Canon of Derry 1982–90; ret

s. of Archibald, farmer of Bushmills by Mary Jane **dau.** of John McCaughan of Bushmills

m. 1950 Londonderry Kathleen Mary **dau.** of William McCartney of Co Tyrone. Issue William Archibald **b.** 13 Dec 1956

Died 9 Sep 1999

LINTON, BARRY IAN 1976–

b. 26 May 1976 Belfast; ed BRA; Univ of Glasgow BSc (Hons) 1998; TCD Downes Divinity Downes Orat Weir and Purser-Shortt Pris and BTh 2004 d 11 Jun 2004 p 18 May 2005; C Enniskillen (Clogh) 2004-08; R Drumcliffe Lissadell and Munninane (Elph) 2008–

 s. of Robert Stewart of Carrickfergus Co Antrim (s. of Alexander and Helena (*née* Stewart) by Agnes **dau.** of Robert Hugh Boyle and Susanna (*née* Hunter) Smyth

 m. 30 Jul 2007 Amanda Jayne **dau.** of George and Myrtle Annetta Mary (*née* Liggett) Irvine

LITTLE, JAMES

ed by Mr Hughes; ent TCD 18 Jun 1767 BA 1771

V Lackan (Killala) 1776–1829; V Dunfeeny (Killala) 1782–1827; V Clonfinlough & Clontuskert (Elph) 1797–*c.* 1832

LITTLE, JOHN 1758/79–1829

b. 1758 or 1759 Co Leitrim; ed by Mr Little; ent TCD 7 Oct 1776 aged 17 BA 1781

V Kilronan (Ard) 1791–1829

 s. of John

 m. and had issue incl a **s.** Andrew

 Died 1829

LITTLE, JOHN FRANCIS 1870–1928

b. 1870 Co Longford; ed Univ of Durham 1900; RUI BA 1901

d 1901 p 1902 (Llandaff); C Trevethin Pontypool (Mon) 1901–02; C Templemichael 1903–05; C Dundalk (Arm) 1905–06; C Donoughmore and Donard (Glend) 1906–07; I Dunfeeny (w Lackran from 1925) (Killala) 1907–28

 s. of Richard, Land Agent by Mary (née Trimble)

 m. (1) 19 Dec 1892 St Ann's Ch Dublin Alice Mary (**died** 10 May 1894 **bur.** Mt Jerome Dublin) **dau.** of Thomas S Atkinson of Dun Laoghaire Co Dublin. Issue Gladys Emily Dorothy **b.** 12 Apr 1894; **died** unm

 m. (2) 17 Aug 1904 Christ Ch Blackrock Co Dublin Roberta Helen **dau.** of William Smith of Blackrock. Issue Francis R W (**died** 7 Feb 1982 **bur.** Glenavy Co Antrim), **m.** 26 Apr 1943 Richhill Par Ch Co Armagh Mary Margaret yr **dau.** of Rev John Archibald William Montgomerie Kerr BA, C-in-c Rathlin (Conn)

 Died 21 Mar 1928 at Thornfield Ballina Co Mayo

LITTLE, JOSEPH RUSSELL 1835/36–1905

b. 1835 or 1836; TCD BA 1877 MA 1892

d 1878 p 1880 (Kilmore for Tuam); C Killoran (Ach) 1878–82; R Newbliss (Clogh) 1882–83; R Ardara (Raph) 1883–87; V Annaduff (Ard) 1887–90; R Killasnett (Kilm) 1890–1905

 Died 7 Nov 1905 aged 69

LITTLE, SAMUEL 1751/52–1823

b. 1751 or 1752 ; ent TCD 9 Jul 1771 BA 1776 LLB & LLD 1788

C Clongish (Ard) *c.* 1777–98; V Louth (Arm) 1789–1823; V Dunleer (Arm) 1789–1809; R Inislonagh (Lism) 1789–94

s. of George of Co Longford

m. 15 Jan 1781 St Ann's Par Ch Dublin Lady Georgina Augusta Berkeley (**died** 24 Jan 1820) widow of George 5th Earl of Granard and **dau.** of Augustus 4th Earl of Berkeley Kt. Issue incl Rev George Berkeley **b.** *c.* 1782/83 ent TCD 3 Nov 1800 aged 17 BA 1804 R Dunleer (Arm) 1809–23

Died 4 Apr 1823 aged 71

LITTLE, THOMAS KIRKWOOD 1807/08–

b. 1807 or 1808 Co Leitrim; ent TCD 21 Jan 1828 aged 20 BA 1837 LLB & LLD 1838

C Ballymacormick (Ard) 1844–46; C Tashinny (Ard) 1846–48; C Killukin (Elph) 1848–50

s. of George, *agricola.*

LITTLE, WILLIAM SWAYNE 1849/50–1886

b. 1849 or 1850 Galway; ed by Mr Jameson; TCD BA 1874

d 1873 p; C Killasnett (Kilm) 1873–75; C Templemichael (Ard) 1875–76; R Derryheen (Kilm) 1876–77; R Knockbride (Kilm) 1877–81; V Toomna (Elph) 1882–85; R Castlejordan (Meath) 1885–86

s. of Thomas, MD

m. 17 Jan 1878 Emma Sophia eldest **dau.** of Rev Samuel Henry Lewis, R Kiltoghart (Ard) qv

Died 3 Jun 1886 aged 36

LLOYD, CHRISTOPHER 1677/78–1757

b. 1677 or 1678 Kilkenny; ed Kilkenny Coll by Dr Hinton; ent TCD 23 Apr 1698 aged 20 Sch 1700 DD 1716

Dean of Elphin 1739–57

s. of Michael

Died 28 Jul 1757 at Old Bawn Co Dublin **bur.** St Bridget's Dublin

LLOYD, CORMAC MacART 1907–1978

b. 1907; ed Warwick Sch; TCD BA (2) Mod Hist and Pol Sci H Dip Ed 1933 MA 1935 Dip in Geog 1936 BD 1952

d 1938 p 1939 (Sodor and Man); C Braddan (S & M) 1938–40; R Kilkeevan (Elph) 1940–49; R Inch (Glend) 1949–66; Canon of Christ Ch Cath Dublin 1962–66; R Inniskeel Lettermacaward and Glenties (Raph) 1966–73; ret

m. Signe of Denmark and had issue 1. Joan **b.** 1936 **m.** Lionel Gallagher; 2. Inga **b.** 1942 **m.** 30 Aug 1968 Portnoo Co Donegal Azad H Mura

Died 31 Mar 1978 **bur.** Drumlease

LLOYD, HENRY MINCHIN   –1925

TCD BA 1899 Div Test 1900

d 1900 p 1901 (Meath); C Delvin (Meath) 1900–09; V Lurgan (Kilm) 1909–25

s. of Charles Henry of Lisheen Castle Co Tipperary

m. Evelyn Sophie (née Darling) (**died** 31 Jul 1969). Issue 1. Rev Charles Henry **b.** 1913 ed Drogheda Gram Sch Portora Royal Sch TCD BA (Mod) 1934 Div Test (1) 1936 MA d 1936 p 1937 C St George Dublin (Dub) 1936–39 C Rathfarnham (Dub) 1939–43 R Moynalty (Meath) 1943–54 Southern Sec (later Gen Sec) CMS 1954–70 R New Ross (Ferns) 1970–82 Preb of Tassagard in St Patrick's Cath Dublin 1973–82 **m.** 10 Jun 1941 Evelyn Elizabeth **dau.** of Thomas Matthews and had issue (i) Trevor Henry **b.** 8 Mar 1944 (ii) Gerald Charles **b.** 28 Feb 1947 Rev Canon Stuart George Errington **b.** 29 Oct 1949 R Ballymena (Conn) (iv) Adrienne Elizabeth Louise **b.** 7 Jun 1953; 2. Louie

Died 1 Jan 1925

LLOYD, JOHN 1687–1763

b. 5 Oct 1687 London; ed by Mr Walls, Dublin; ent TCD 17 May 1704 aged 16 Sch 1706 BA 1708 MA 1710

V Kilronan (Ard) 1715–40; coll 25 Apr 1715 (F.F.); R & V Kiltubrid (Ard) 1740–66;

2nd **s.** of Rev Robert, V Drung and Larah (Kilm) qv

m. 1722 Anne **dau.** of William Fox of Co Cavan. Issue incl 1. William, JP of Cornagher Cp Leitrim; 2. John; 3. Robert James of Ardnagowan; 4. Hannah; 5. Ann

Died 10 Apr 1763 at Cornagher

LLOYD, JOHN 1789–1847

b. 1789 Co Roscommon; ed by Mr Smith; ent TCD 7 Jul 1806 Sch 1809 BA 1811

C Aughrim (Elph)1817–c. 26; C Taunagh (Elph) c. 1826; R Aughrim (Elph) 1835–47

2nd **s.** of Robert Jones of Ardnagoun Co Roscommon

m. Emma 4th **dau.** of William Lloyd of Rockville Co Roscommon and had issue

Died Nov 1847; was murdered on a Sunday morning on his way home from Aughrim Church

LLOYD, MOSES 1699/1700–1750

b. 1699 or 1700 near Longford; ed by Mr Neligan, Longford; ent TCD 30 May 1716 aged 16 BA 1720

V Clonbroney (Ard) 1731/32–1750

s. of Thomas, blacksmith
Died 19 Feb 1750

LLOYD, ROBERT 1646/47–

b. 1646 or 1647 London; adm Pensioner Pembroke Coll Camb 11 May 1664 aged 17 matric 1664 BA 1667/68 MA 1671

signed for deacon's orders 10 Dec 1672 on title of a chaplaincy in the East Indies; was Chapl at Surat East Indies in EICS; V Drung and Larah (Kilm) 1682; R Clondevaddock (Raph) 1691

s. of Robert, linen merchant

m. and had issue Rev John, R Kiltubrid (Ard) qv

LLOYD, ROBERT 1800/01–

b. 1800 or 1801 Co Roscommon; ed by Mr Smith; ent TCD 6 Jul 1818 aged 17 BA 1823

C Carrigallen (Kilm) *c.* 1825/26 — still there in 1830

perhaps **s.** of Robert

LLOYD, THOMAS

d; p 3 Dec 1780; C Abbeylara (Ard) 1780

LLOYD, THOMAS 1751–1813

b. 1751 Roscommon; ed by Mr Meares; ent TCD 1 Nov 1769 aged 17 BA 1773

V Cullen (Cashel — then Emly) 1777–87; C Tibohine (Elph) 1785; V Easternsow and Kilbryan (Elph) 1798–1812

prob Thomas **s.** of Owen

m. and had issue Capt Owen Thomas **b.** Co Leitrim ed by Rev James Armstrong ent TCD 7 Jan 1799 aged 15 BA 1803 MA 1832

Died 23 May 1813 aged 62

LLOYD, THOMAS 1794/95–1883

b. 1794 or 1795 Roscommon; ed by Dr Dowdall; ent TCD 1 Jun 1812 aged 17 BA 1816

C Kilmore (Elph) 1821; PC Loughglynn (Elph) 1822–24; V Kilglass (Elph) 1822–71; ret

prob **s.** of John Yeaden

m. 1822 Eleanor Norman (**died** 20 Oct 1865) and had issue incl 1. yst **s.** Robert Leslie (**died** 19 Feb 1913 in Australia); 2. Henrietta (**died** 16 Jun 1915 at Bournemouth) **m.** Henry Crofton Lloyd; 3. his 3rd **dau.** Katherine Elizabeth (**died** 17 Jul 1923) **m.** 20 Dec 1859 St Mary's Dublin Rev Henry Rooke (1829–1926), Archd of Glendalough 1905–14 and had issue (i) Henry (ii) Thomas Lloyd (iii)

Elinor Elizabeth (iv) Bartholomew Warburton
Died 15 Nov 1883

LOCKWOOD, ROBERT 1781/82–

b. 1781 or 1782 Co Tipperary; ent TCD 4 Jan 1802 aged 20 BA 1807

C Tashinny (Ard) *c.* 1808

s. of Richard, engineer

LOMBARD, PETER 1679/80–1763

b. 1679 or 1680 Bandon Co Cork; ed by Mr Molloy at Cork; ent TCD 26 Nov 1699 aged 19 BA 1704 MA 1708

R Carrigallen (Kilm) 1705–*c.* 52; R Templeport and Drumreilly (Kilm) 1723–34

s. of James, *vestiarius*

m. ? Mary Ward. Issue 1. Rev Peter, R Templeport and Drumreily (Kilm) qv; 2. Margaret (**died** 22 Jan 1781 aged 42) **m.** 1733 Thomas Wolfe of Blackhall Co Kildare

Died 26 June 1763 at Nassau St Dublin

LOMBARD, PETER *c.* 1707–

b. *c.* 1707 near Rathcoole Co Kildare; ed by his father at Carrigallen; ent TCD 16 Feb 1723/24 aged 16 BA 1728 MA 1731

V Dunany (Arm) 1732–66; R Templeport and Drumreilly (Kilm) 1734–67; R Killinagh (Kilm) *c.* 1740–64– appears V in 1754 (VB) and prob held from 1739; R Tomregan and V Drumlane (Kilm) 1767–73

s. of Rev Peter, R Carrigallen (Kilm) qv (**s.** of James)

m. (ML 19 Sep 1740) Mary yst dau. of Charles Henrick of Dublin. Issue 1. Peter of Dublin; 2. Margaret; 3. Frances (**died** July 1811 aged 56) **m.** Jun 1771 Theobald Wolfe of Blackhall and had issue Rev Rev Charles; 4. Grace **m.** June 1785 Edward Hendrick; 5. Mary **m.** May 1767 Robert Carlisle of Newry

Will prov 1782

LONG, ARTHUR GEORGE HETHERINGTON 1854–1927

b. 26 May 1854; ed TCD BA 1877 MA 1892

d 1877 p 1878 (Down); C Holy Trinity Belfast (Conn) 1877–79; R Killoe (Ard) 1879–80; R Termonfeckin (Arm) 1880–1927

2nd **s.** of William of Belfast

m. 26 Apr 1879 Frances Annie (**died** 12 Feb 1912) 2nd **dau.** of Henry F Darley of Montpelier Hse Monkstown Co Dublin. Issue 1. Frances Mabel **b.** 21 Jun 1881; 2. Arthur Darley **b.** 18 May 1883 **died** 12 Oct 1883; 3. Alice Beatrice **b.** 22 May 1884; 4. a **dau.** b 25 Sep 1885, but survived only a few hours; 5. Percy Darley **b.** 14 Aug 1888 **died** 8 Aug 1915

Died 9 Mar 1927

LOPDELL, HENRY ROBERT 1832–1906

b. 13 Apr 1832

d 1871 p 1872 (Kilmore); C Mohill (Ard) 1871–73; I Kilmastulla (Killaloe) 1873–1905; ret

> 2nd **s.** of John, BA JP Athenry Co Galway by Jane **dau.** of Peter Blake, Corbally Castle Co Galway
>
> **Died** 31 Jul 1906 aged 74

LOVELESS, EDWARD

pres by the Crown to V Kilgeffin and Kilteran (Elph) 15 Feb 1634/35 (L.M. V. 110). He is Commonwealth Minister, Dublin Precinct 1653–56 and enjoyed the Vicarial tithes of Rathcoole and Sagard (Dub) 1660 from 25 June 1657 @ £100 (Seymour's Com. MSS); poss same as Edward Lovelace, V Clondalkin and Rathcoole (Dub) 1662–69

LOUGHEED, JAMES JOHN 1893–1978

b. 1893; TCD BA 1915 MA 1928 LLB

d 1915 p 1917 (Kilmore); C Annagh (Kilm) 1915–18; C Harold's Cross (Dub) 1918–25; Hon Cler V Christ Ch Cath Dublin 1922–25; C St Ann (Dub) 1925–29; R Ballinafagh U (Kild) 1929–33; C-in-c Newtownmountkennedy (Glend) 1933–58; ret

> **Died** 10 Mar 1978 Greystones Co Wicklow

LOW, RICHARD HUGH 1803/04–1860

b. 1803 or 1804 Galway; ed by Mr Stubbs; ent TCD 3 Jul 1820 aged 16 BA 1825

C Killasoolan = Castleblakeney (Elph) 1842–; Preb of Oran (Elph) 1851–53; V Kiltoom and Camma (Elph) 1853–60

> 3rd **s.** of William of Lowville Co Galway
>
> **Died** 24 Nov 1860 Rathgar Rd Dublin

LOWE, WILLIAM PHILIP 1853–1925

b. 1853 Limerick; ed Limerick Model Sch; TCD BA 1883 MA 1893; taught in Canada for some years from 1875

d 1883 (Kilmore for Armagh) p 1885 (Down for Armagh); C Carlingford (Arm) 1883–87; C Kilrossanty (Lism) 1887–88; R St John's Cloverhill (Kilm) 1888–1907; R Bailieborough (Kilm) 1907–25

> **s.** of Thomas and Anne of Limerick
>
> > **m.** 1896 Olivia **dau.** of William Lodge, RIC and had issue Rev William Thomas (**died** 20 Oct 1954) **b.** 1887 ed Cavan Royal Sch TCD BA 1908 Div Test (2) 1911 d 1911 p 1912 C Aghade and Ardoyne (Leigh) 1911–15 R Taghmon (Ferns) 1915–21 C-in-c Kilculliheen (Oss) 1921–22 C Kilnamanagh (Ferns) 1922–23 I Kilnamanagh (Ferns) 1923–27 C-in-c Inch (Glend) 1927–28 I Inch (Glend) 1928–31 R Templeshanbo (Ferns) 1931–33 R Kilmanagh (Oss) 1933–50 Preb of

Kilmanagh (Oss) 1943–50 R Killenaule (Cash) 1950–54 **m.** 11 Aug 1915 at Shillelagh Ch Co Wicklow Iris Katherine Edgeworth **dau.** of Francis King of Shillelagh.

Died 11 Jan 1925

LOWRY (LAWRY), JAMES   –1739

V Kinawley (Kilm) 1676–*c.* 90; was suspended from Kinawley for homicide in self-defence and underwent penance; coll V Killinagh (Kilm) 14 Apr 1686 (F.F.). The name is John Lowry in some of the records; for John see below. James Lowry V Killinagh (Kilm) 1686–*c.* 1704; V Arklow (Glend) 1704 in Leslie's MSS; W.J.R. Wallace in *Clergy of Dublin and Glendalough* has him C St. Audoen (Dub) 1688 and R Arklow (Glend) 1690–1707 and poss V Killinagh and Kinawley (Kilm) 1712–28, though see John Lowry below; R Knockbride (Kilm) 1728–39; Prec of Down 1707–12

m. 1680 Penelope **dau.** of Rev William Bedell and granddaughter of Bp. Bedell

LOWRY (LAWRY), JOHN

V Killinagh and Kinawley (Kilm) 1712–28; may be same as James Lowry qv, R & V Knockbride (Kilm) 1728–39. There seems to be great confusion in the Records between James and John Lowry insomuch that one is forced to conclude that they really are but one person

LOWRY, WILLIAM HAMILTON *c.* 1858–*c.* 1926

b *c.* 1858; TCD BA 1881 MA 1885

d 1884 p 1885; C Oak River Manitoba (Rupld) 1884–85; R Oak River (Rupld) under SPG 1885–89; I Deloraine Manitoba (Rupld) 1889–91; C Ballymascanlan (Arm) 1895; C Earnley Essex 1900–02; Lic Dio Chichester 1913–15; prob same as William Hamilton Lowry C Ballyjamesduff (Kilm) 1892–94

Died *c.* 1926

LUCAS, DANIEL ECCLES

R Dromod and Prior (A & A) 1812–28; R Castleblakeney (Elph) 1823–28

s. of Charles by his cousin Frances **dau.** of Daniel Eccles of Fintona Co Tyrone

m. Anne (**died** 16 Apr 1847 aged 74 at the residence of her son-in-law Lt Col Dickson, Holybrook Hse Co Fermanagh). Issue incl Rev Edmund Allen qv; his 2nd **dau.** Charlotte Martha was **bur.** in Ballybay Church aged 36

LUCAS, EDMUND ALLEN 1807–1885

b. 1807 Co. Kerry; ent TCD 7 Jul 1823 aged 16 BA 1829

V Ballysumaghan Kilross and Ballinakill (Elph) 1841–61; V Killenumery (Ard) 1861–85

s. of Rev Daniel Eccles, R Castleblakeney (Elph) 1823–28 qv (**s.** of Charles and Mary **dau.** of Daniel Eccles)

m. 1842 Margaret Ellen Hackett. Issue incl. Frances **died** 5 Jan 1864 aged 10

Died 22 Apr 1885 at Killenumery Glebe in his 78th year

LUCAS, EDWARD 1765/66–1814 or 1815

b. 1765 or 1766 Co Monaghan; ed by Dr Murray; ent TCD 5 Aug 1782 aged 16 BA 1787

R Drumgoon (Kilm) 1792–1814/15

6th **s.** of Edward of Castleshane

m. (1) 1795 (or 1796?) Elizabeth Anne **dau.** of Theophilus Clements of Rathkenny. Issue Theophilus Edward who took the name of Clements

m. (2) Olivia **sister** of his successor Rev James Hamilton qv, and **dau.** of Sir James; his 3rd **dau.** Anne **m.** 28 Dec 1827 Thomas Scott of Londonderry

Died 1814 or 1815; he was **bur.** according to the Parish Register on 14 May 1814 in the Clements vault at Drung aged 49, but *Bishops' Returns* has it that he **died** 10 Jul 1815. As his successor was inst on 15 Aug 1815, it is evident that the year 1814 is wrong, and probably the date of his death was 10 May 1815

LUCAS, FRANCIS *c.* 1725–1770

b. *c.* 1725 Co Monaghan; ed by Mr Skelton; ent TCD 21 Jan 1742/43 aged 17 BA 1747 MA 1753

d 1747 p 1748 (Kilmore); R Drumgoon (Kilm) 1763–70

s. of Thomas, *armiger*

m. and had issue incl a **dau.** Alicia **m.** Edward Richardson of Poplar Vale

Died 1770

LUKE

is Dean of Kilmore 1375 (Cal. Reg. Mey. 356)

LUMLEY, ROBERT –2004

TCD BA 1948 MA 1954

d 25 Sep 1949 (Meath for Kilm) p 1950 (Kilmore); C Drumgoon and Ashfield (Kilm) 1949–52; C St Polycarp Finaghy Belfast (Conn) 1952–53; C Capreol Ontario (Dio Algoma) 1953; R Capreol (Algoma) 1954–57; R Elliot Lake 1957–59; R St Stephen Port Arthur (Algoma) 1959–67; R Lake of Bays 1967–73; R St James' Sudbury Ontario (Algoma) 1973–

s. of George Cecil of Tullamore Co Offaly by Muriel Jane **dau.** of Robert Brabazon of Mullingar; **bro.** of Rev William, BC Killucan (Meath) 1982–88

m. 15 Sep 1958 at Garsin Ontario Margaret Isobel **dau.** of Arthur Lye. Issue Elaine Marina **b.** Jan 1963

Died 2004

LUSCOMBE, TOOKE JOHNSON –1945
TCD BA 1880 Div Test 1882 MA 1884 BD 1891

d 1883 p 1884 (Worcester); C St Thomas Birmingham (Birm — then Worc) 1883–87; C The Lickey (Worc) 1887–88; C Newhall (Derby — then S'well) 1888–89; C Drumgoon (Kilm) 1892–93; R Arran (Tuam) 1899–1900; V Ballintemple (Kilm) 1900–06; C Glazeley (Heref) 1906–08; V Bobbington (Heref) 1908–10; R Beeby (Pet) 1910–30

elder **s.** of Tooke Cumming

m. 21 Jul 1897 at Ballyconnell Co Cavan Selina Mabel yr **dau.** of Surgeon–Major Frederick Aston Oakes by Anna Selina eldest **dau.** of Rev Orange Sterling Kellett, R Tomregan (Kilm) qv Issue 1. Marian Catherine; 2. Violet Mary Victoria; 3. Beryl Selina Victoria (twins)

Died 23 Jan 1945

LUTHER, GUY HENRY 1737/38–
b. 1737 or 1738; ent TCD 8 May 1758 aged 20 BA 1762

C Rossinver (Kilm) in 1776

LUTHER, WILLIAM
ed by Dr Dunkin; ent TCD 12 Feb 1746/47 BA 1752

C Killeshandra (Kilm) 1763; C Ringrone (Cork) 1774

s. of Charles of Dublin by Letitia **dau.** of Rev William Brooke, R Killinkere (Kilm) qv

m. 1759 Abigail **dau.** of William Nesbitt jun of Dromalee Co Cavan. Issue a **s.** Hope **b.** Co Cork ent TCD 6 Apr 1789 aged 17 BA 1794

LYDE, RICHARD
PC Arvagh (Kilm) to 1819

†LYNCH, JOHN –*c.* 1611
ed New Inn Hall Oxford BA

was Warden of Galway 1576–84, when Queen Elizabeth appointed him Bishop, "a preacher now of Galway well known to you and our Chancellor as you write for his sufficiency, endeavour and travail in preaching". (Queen's Letters to Sir John Perrot, 1584, Morrin II. 66). Bp of Elphin 1584–1611. It is said that he wasted the property of his See by fee farm grants. He resigned his Bishopric 19 Aug 1611, and was buried in St Nicholas', Galway, and is said to have been a Romanist at heart.

s. of James of Galway

Died *c.* 1611

LYNDON, CHARLES HENRY PRESTON 1889–1963

b. 1889; ed Masonic Boys' Sch Dublin; TCD BA 1913 MA 1919; OBE 1918

d 1913 p 1914 (Kilmore); C Killeshandra and Killegar (Kilm) 1913–19; TCF 1916–19– mentioned in despatches 1917 and 1918; C Killesher 1919–20; Head of TCD Mission Belfast (Conn) 1920–26; DUM Hazaribagh 1926–31; furlough 1931–32; C Bangor (Down) 1932; R St Paul Belfast (Conn) 1932–57; Canon of St Anne's Cath Belfast 1948–57

Died 1 Apr 1963 **unm.**

LYNN, MATTHEW JAMES FREDERICK 1926–*c.* 1987

b. 1926; from Ballymena Co Antrim; ed Ballymena Acad; Magee Coll Londonderry; TCD BA (2cl Hist Mod & Pol Sci) 1950 MA 1957; Asst Master Portora Royal Sch Enniskillen; History Master Balymena Acad; Head Master Brooke Hse, Market Harborough 1957–61; Head Master Villiers Sch Limerick 1961–63; played Rugby for Ulster

d 23 Dec 1962 (Limerick) p 15 Dec 1963 (Limerick); C St Mary and St Munchin and Dean's V St Mary's Cath Limerick (Lim) 1962–65; R Kinawley (Kilm) 1965–71; C Weeke (Win) 1971–74; R Headbourne Worthy & I Kings Worthy (Win) 1974–83; R Bembridge IOW (Portsm) 1983–87

m. Florence Maddock of Rathmines Dublin. Issue 1. Peter; 2. Gillian; 3. Trevor; 4. Michael; 5. Deirdre **b.** 2 Jan 1964

Died after 31 Jul 1987 (Crockford)

LYNN, ROBERT YOUNG 1842/43–1923

b. 1842 or 1843; TCD BA (Resp) 1865 Div Test (1) 1866

d 1866 p 1867 (Ossory); C Clonenagh (Leigh) 1866–68; C Kilmoremoy (Killala) 1868–70; C Calry (Elph) 1870–72; C Kilmoremoy (Killala) 1872–73; I Ballysakeery (Killala) 1873–82; Preb of Killanley in Killala Cath 1875–82; R Shrule (Ard) 1882–85; R Mostrim (Ard) 1885–86; R Cong U 1886–1923; Preb of Kilmainmore in Tuam Cath 1904–23

s. of Robert K, MB of Sligo

m. 13 Feb 1872 at Monkstown Katherine Marion **dau.** of Richard B Wynne of Hermitage Sligo. Issue incl 1. his eldest **dau.** Anne Elizabeth who **died** 28 Sep 1931; 2. Dr Kathleen (**died** *c.* 1957); 3. his yst **dau.** Emily Muriel (**died** 7 Mar 1968) at Clonallon Warrenpoint Co Down.

Died 8 Apr 1923 aged 80

LYNN, WILLIAM HENRY 1838/39–1882

b. 1838 or 1839

d 1870 p 1871; C Aghalurcher (Clogh) 1871–75; V Mostrim (Ard) 1875–82

m. and had issue incl **daus.** Dr Kathleen and his yst **dau.** Maud Frances **m.** 23 Mar 1903 Thomas James Mavitty of Belfast and a **s.** R J Lynn of Carrigard Portadown

Died 6 Feb 1882 aged 43

LYON, PAUL KEMP

Univ of Camb 1881

d 1883 p 1886 (Qu'appelle); C Qu'appelle, Canada 1885–86; SPG P-in-c Abernethy (Qu'appelle)1886–89; P-in-c Churchbridge (Qu'appelle) 1889–91; R Mostrim (Ard) 1891–97; R Kilcommick (Ard) 1897–1917; R Lower Sapey (Worc) 1917–; still there in 1933.

LYONS, THOMAS ALFRED 1795/96–1881

b. 1795 or 1796 Limerick; ed by Mr Lyons; ent TCD 2 Nov 1812 aged 16 BA 1816 MA 1832; in the Kilmore D.R., it was said that he came to the C of Killeshandra (Kilm) from the Diocese of Worcester without a *Bene Decessit,* and was afterwards C Drung and Larah (Kilm); was ordained priest when at Killeshandra; R Dunmore (Tuam) 1837–81

m. and had issue a **s**. Rev Ponsonby A **b**. Dublin ent TCD 14 Oct 1845 aged 16 BA 1852 C Dunmore (Tuam) 1853

Died 15 May 1881

LYSTER, JAMES 1810–

b. 7 Sep 1810; studied for three years at Sandhurst; TCD LLD (hon causa) 1863

d 1835 p 1836 (Tuam); V Russagh and C Streete (Ard) 1837–48; R Tashinny and Abbeyshrule (Ard) 1848–54; Dean of Leighlin 1854–64

eldest **s**. of Lt Col Armstrong of Lysterfield Co Roscommon

m. 12 Jan 1837 Maria Sarah 3rd **dau**. of Rev George Keating, R Mostrim (Ard) qv 1. Issue Anthony **b**. 1838; 2. Jane Letitia **m**. 1861 Rev George T Huston eldest **s**. of Rev George Barton

In 1863, the Degree of LL D *(h.c.)* was proposed to be conferred upon Dean Lyster by TCD, but it was opposed amid great excitement by Dr Jellett who contended that the gentleman had shown no merit. Dr Todd in reply said that Mr Lyster was a hard working parish clergyman, and that he understood that the Lord Lieutenant had expressed that the degree should be conferred and that the Government had offered Mr Lyster a Colonial bishopric. Dr Jellett's motion was defeated by 21 votes to 13, and the degree was conferred. Soon afterwards, Dean Lyster exchanged for the Deanery of Ontario with his successor. Dean Lyster left in manuscript, an interesting History of Leighlin Cathedral compiled from Chapter records, a copy of which, through the generosity of Canon AG Stuart is in the collection of the RCB

LYSTER, JOHN 1819–1877

b. 1819 Dublin; ed by Mr Allen; ent TCD 6 Nov 1837 aged 18 BA & Div Test 1843 C Denn (Kilm) 1866–69; C Kilmactranny (Elph) 1869–77

only **s**. of John, Military Doctor, 7th Dragoons

m. and had issue Charles F, JP of Ballyphelane Hse Co Cork

Died 8 Nov 1877 aged 57 **bur**. Kilmactranny

LYSTER, STEPHEN 1762/63–1828

b. 1762 or 1763 Dublin; ed by Dr Norris; ent TCD 6 Dec 1780 aged 17 Sch 1784 BA 1785

V Kilnamanagh (Elph) 1793–1828

   s. of John
   Died 1828 **bur.** Boyle

MACABARD, MAGONIUS

was prov to V Killukin (Elph) 12 Jan 1453/54 (C.P.L. X. 218)

MACABRECHIM, PHILIP

V Ardcarne, Elphin 1428 is prov to V Kilhoran = Kilronan (Ard) 1428, long vacant by the death of George Oduigeannan qv, and lapsed to Sagart Oduigranna priest possessed it being coll after lapse for over 3 years; whether so vacant or because Cornelius Oduigrannan qv, or Philip Odorchan qv, held it over a year without being ordained priest. He can hold it with Ardcarne 9 May 1428 (C.P.L. VIII. 11)

MACABREICHEAMIN, MACCRAITH

was V Kilmacallen (Elph) Aug 1409 (C.P.L. VI. 161)

MACACLERID, IMARUS

priest, informs the Pope that Odo Maccaclerid qv, V Tamnacha = Taunagh (Elph) sought to compel by lay power, certain laymen to pay him bread, flesh etc, said to be due to him as temporal lord. These laymen brought him before John (O'Grada), Bp of Elphin, who excommunicated him for contumacy. He has held the V of Taunagh (Elph) five years or more, and if these facts are true, is to be deposed and Imarus is to be coll to the V, 6 Jun 1444 (C.P.L. IX. 427). (John, Bp of Elphin was deposed in 1429 so that Odo must have been Vicar then or before that date)

McADAM, BENNETT DUGDALE HASTINGS 1826/27–

b. 1826 or 1827 Co Dublin; ed by Mr Dee; ent TCD 6 Nov 1848 aged 21 BA & Div Test 1854

C Mohill (Ard) 1857–61

   s. of. David Hastings, physician

McAEDA, MATTHEW

V of St Mary's Granard (Ard) to 1438, and is said by Eugene Macmurceartayd qv below, to be ignorant of letters and of the Divine Offices and of the language of the place and neglects hospitality and absents himself

MACAEDAGAIN, JOHN

bro of the Hospital of St John Baptist Rinnddum, disp as son of a religious, Clk, is now disp to hold the V Athlyag Macnagain = Athleague (Elph), vacant by death of Dermit Maggillaruayd qv, whether so void or void by the deaths of David Ykahan qv and Thomas Yriana qv, 8 Dec 1441 (C.P.L. IX. 311)

MACAEDAGAYN, CORNELIUS *c.* 1444–

b. *c.* 1444

clk in his 21st year was prov to V Kilcroan (Elph) 11 Jan 1464/65 (C.P.L. XII. 446)

MACAGARRTAGH, RAYMOND

Canon of Ardagh 1438 (C.P.L. IX 17)

McALEESE (McLEES), WILLIAM HENRY 1927–

b. 15 Aug 1927 Belfast; ed Tech High Sch Belfast; Shaftesbury Ho Tech Coll; Jun Clk, Apprentice Electrician, Sen Draughtsman Harland & Wolff Ltd Belfast; Magee Univ Coll Londonderry; TCD BA 1953; St Andrew's Presby Coll Belfast; St Augustine's Coll Canterbury 1960; worked in Southern Rhodesia (Zimbabwe) before ordination; Missy Minister Ch of Scotland Miss in Northern Rhodesia (Zambia) 1956–60

d 3 Jul 1960 p 29 Jun 1961; C Donaghadee (Down) 1960–62; SPG Missy P-in-c Ch of the Good Shepherd (Dio Pretoria) 1962–66; C Dorking w Ranmore (Guildf) 1966–68; R Billis Ballyjamesduff and Munterconnaught (Kilm) 1968–71; C St John Baptist W Byfleet & Ripley (Guildf) 1971–74; C Gt Bookham (Guildf) 1974–77; C Christ Ch Epsom Common (Guildf) 1977–80; P-in-c All SS Leatherhead (Guildf) 1980–86; ret Perm to Off Dios Down and Dromore from 1987; Perm to Off Dio Connor from 1990

s. of Henry of Belfast (**s.** of William of Belfast and Ballycastle Co Antrim) by Victoria (née McCleery)

m. 24 Jul 1957 at Kitire Northern Rhodesia Eileen Jean Gordon **dau.** of John and Mary McKinlay (**died** 25 May 1972) of Edinburgh. Issue 1. Christopher John **b.** 27 Aug 1958 **m.** 14 May 1988 Jorun Stendal of Trondheim Norway; 2. Fiona **b.** 5 Feb 1965

MACALERICKEM, MALACHY

is prov to R Kedy (Kilm) 1 Apr 1484 (C.P.L. XIII. 173)

McALISTER, WILLIAM –1942

TCD BA 1894

d 1895 (Dublin for Kilmore) p 1896 (Clogher); C Kilmore (Kilm) 1895–1901; R Billis (Kilm) 1901–10; R Killinkere w Mullagh (Kilm) 1910–42; Preb of Annagh (Kilm) 1935–42

s. of Isaac of Rathgar Dublin

m. and had issue incl **sons** 1. Eddie (**died** 1971); 2. Donald **b.** Sep 1908; **daus.** 1. Pearl (**died** 19 Dec 1971 London); 2. Violet **m.** 19 Dec 1935 St Peter's Dublin John 2nd **s.** of John Robson of Belturbet Co Cavan; 3. Doreen (**died** 1945) **b.** 1912 or 1913

Died 10 Jun 1942

MACAMRAGAN, MAGONIUS

had been coll to V Templeport (Kilm) by Bp Nicholas, but is now prov to it as he doubted validity of the collation, 12 Sep 1414 (C.P.L. VI. 475). He was deceased in 1425 and probably in 1419 (ib. VII. 402)

MACANDYAN, MAURICE

Prior of St Michael; V Annaduff (Ard) 1477/78, 15 Mar (C.P.L. XIII, 621)

MACANKNAID, DERMIT

V Annaduff (Ard) to 1477/78, is long dead

MACARMAYC, CHARLES

Clk, prov to R Theachsynchi and Teachaynaca = Taghsynod and Tashinny (Ard) long void, though Thomas Macmurcaccn holds them and is to be removed before 1406; dispensed as illegal is prov to V Rathcline (Ard) 5 Feb 1406 (C.P.L. VI. 86, 87).

McCARMICK, WILLIAM

d & p; is Latin Master at Belturbet = Annagh (Kilm) in 1754

MACARTNEY, HUSSEY BURGH 1799–1894

b. 10 Apr 1799 Dublin; ent TCD 4 Nov 1816 BA 1821 MA BD & DD 1847; MA *ad eund* Melbourne 1864

C Templemichael (Ard) to 1827

    s. of John, solicitor; **bro.** of Rev Sir William, R Desertegney (Raph — then Derry)

    m. 7 Mar 1833 Jane (**died** 10 Jan 1885) **dau.** of Edward Hardman by Ethel McClintock of Drumcar Co Louth. Issue 1. John Arthur **b.** 5 Apr 1834; 2. Edward Hardman **b.** 10 May 1835; 3. Rev Hussey Burgh **b.** 30 Sep 1840

Dean Macartney **died** 8 Oct 1894

McAULEY, MANUS

TCD Sch 1635

inst R & V Bailieborough (Kilm) 6 Feb 1640/41

MACBRADAIC(G)H (MACBRADY), AUGUSTINE

clk, of Kilmore Diocese is reserved the V of St. Patrick's Drung, united to the Church of St. Brigid Larah (Kilm) 1396, to be void shortly by the consecration of Gilbert, Bp elect of Ardagh (C.P.L. IV. 529). In Nov 1398 the Bp had dispossessed him of the V and was admonished to restore him (ib. V. 168). He was made Archd of Elphin 2 Feb 1403, and was to resign this V (ib. V. 580), but he is V in 1408 and appeals to the Primate (Cal. Reg. Flem. 79), and seems to have held the Vicarages in 1419 when he was allowed to apply part of the tithes (most of which belonged to the Abbey of Fore) to the increase of the Vicar's portion, 13 Jul (ib. VII. 116). He seems to have held the V till 1430 when he either **died** or was deposed. Cornelius Macconayng qv claimed it from him in 1427 (Cal. Reg. Swayne, 139, 454). One of the same name, perhaps the same was Treas of Ferns 1412 (ib. VI. 471)

MACBRADAICH, ODO

clk, disp. as the son of a deacon and a woman related to him, is prov R St Patrick's, Enachgailb = Annagelliffe (Kilm), 2 Apr 1407 (C.P.L. VI. 121)

MACBRADY, ANDREW

is Rural Dean of Drumlane and R of Bailemconchobayle in Drung parish (Kilm), 5 Dec 1426 (C.P.L. VII. 503)

†MACBRADY, ANDREW c. 1396–c. 1455

doubting the validity of the coll of Patrick O'Siredean, qv, was prov to R Kedy (Kilm) upon the death of John O'Siredean, qv, 6 Dec 1426 (C.P.L. VII. 503); res 1436; Archd of Kilmore 1436–45; appointed to the See of Kilmore 1445; he was in his 50th year and an acolyte and very skilled in Civil and Canon Law, and the Abp is to confer Holy Orders on him and consecrate him if found fit (C.P.L. VIII. 250). He was Bp 9 Mar 1453 (Cal. Reg. Swayne). Bishop Andrew Macbrady and his Chapter (ie., the clergy of Kilmore), with the consent of the Pope and the Abp of Armagh, removed his See from Triburnia, "an obscure village — where the old church of Urney now stands 4 miles from Cavan" (D.R.). to the Church of St. Felim of Kilmore. Pope Nicholas V in his decree established it as the Cathedral of Kilmore, and also placed in it 13 Canonries, 28 July 1454. This was confirmed by Pope Callixtus III, 20 April 1455 (Cal. Reg. Mey, 277). Hitherto, "there were no Canons nor Cathedral church". See also A.H. I. 252. Andrew seems to have died soon after

Died c. 1455

McBRADY, ANDREW

was coll R Kedy (Kilm) by the Ordinary who was excommunicate and held it over 4 years in 1427 and was to be deprived; may be same as above

MACBRADY, ANDREW

appears Canon of Kilmore 1453 (C.P.L. X. 604), and 1455 (ib. XI. 214); prob same as Andrew Macbrady who was R Drumgoon (Kilm) to 1453/54, and resigned for a sum of money paid to him by Patrick Macconaing, qv (C.P.L. X. 729–730); is prov to the R Drumgoon (Kilm) void by the death of Patrick Macconaing or by his resignation, or by the resignation of Malachy MacBrady qv, 6 Aug 1455 (C.P.L. XI. 215)

MACBRADY, ANDREW
is prov to Archdeaconry of Kilmore 26 Jul 1538 vacant per deprivation of Patrick Macbrady qv (A.H. I. 254, 255)

MACBRADY, AUGUSTINE
had held V Telachgarve = Teallacheach and Mageanady (Kilm) 1412 (C.P.L. VI. 371)

MACBRADY, CRISTINUS (CRISTEN)
res the V Culbrydyn *alias* Castleterra and Lendamair (Elph) 1398; res the V Culbrydyn and Sendamar (Kilm or poss Ard) 1398

McBRADY, DAVID –1424
vacates the R & V Disert Finchill (Kilm) by death, 1424 (A.H. I. 230, C.P.L. VII. 486)

MACBRADY, EUGENE
was prov to the V Drumgoon (Kilm) 18 Nov 1501 (A.H. I. 254)

McBRADY, EUGENIUS
unjustly claims the V Eanachgarygh = Innismagrath (Kilm) against the anonymous holder, 1530 (Cal. Reg. Cromer, 299)

MACBRADY, GEOFFREY
informs the Pope that William Macmeol qv paid a sum to John Macgmissa to resign the V Castleterra (Kilm) and John resigned and William got coll; if true Geoffrey is prov and disp as illegal, 19 Jan 1461/62 (C.P.L. XII. 140); Preb of Kilmore *c.* 1461 (C.P.L. XII. 140)

†MACBRADY, GILBERT (*alias* COMEDINUS)
R Drung and Larah (Kilm) 1396; was prov. to the See of Ardagh 20 Oct 1395 (C.P.L. IV. 504), and on 14 Sep 1396, was to be cons. shortly (ib. 529)

MACBRADY (MACBRADAICH), JOHN 1376–
b. 1376
in his 23rd year and if fit and is able to read and construe Latin etc., Clk., pres by the patron Donatus Macbrady is prov to the V Castleterra (Kilm) (and also to the R, a sinecure) vacant by the resignation of Cristinus Macbrady, qv, 17 Jul 1398 (A.H. I. 242)

MACBRADY, JOHN
prov V Culbrydyn and Sendamar (Kilm or poss Ard), "which is not in any church in said diocese, value not exceeding 5 marks", 16 Aug 1398 (C.P.L. V. 108); also prov R same day (ib. 167)

MACBRADY (MACBRADAYCH), JOHN
held the V Castleterra (Kilm) 1420 over a year without being ordained priest

†McBRADY, JOHN
was prov by the Pope Bp of Kilmore who no longer recognised Edmund Nugent, qv However, John McBrady surrendered his Bulls and allowed Nugent to remain in peaceable possession and is allowed to retain the V of St Patrick of Kildrumferton (Kilm) 5 Nov 1540 (A.H. I. 258)

MACBRADY, MALACHY
V of the *Plebs de Culbridin, alias* the Parish Church of *St Patrick de Castleterram* (Kilm) to 1420, is deceased

MACBRADY, MALACHY
was R Drumgoon (Kilm) to 1453 and res

McBRADY, MALACHY
Canon of Kilmore 1457 (C.P.L. XI. 313, 410)

†MACBRADY, NICHOLAS   –1421
R of Cill Beighdein, an old *alias* for Castleterra (Elph) in East Breifne to 1395, was prov to the See of Kilmore in 1396 by the Pope, Boniface IX (A.H. 1. 255). R Culbrydyn and Sendamar (Kilm or poss Ard) 1398. He was sitting in 1409 (Cal. Reg. Flem). Charges were made against him by Patrick O'Sheridan, priest of Kilmore Diocese which he could not prove, 24 May 1413 (Cal. Reg. Flem. 228). A Roderick McBrady is said to have been Bishop in 1396 and in 1409. This must be a scribal error for Nicholas MacBrady who had been consecrated before 17 July 1398 (C.P.L. V. 167), and is Bp in 1401 (ib. 399), and on 20 Jul 1409, he was recognised as Bp by Alexander VI and again in 1412 and 1414 (C.P.L. VI. 159, 319, 475), though see John O'Reilly

   Died 1421

McBRADY, NICHOLAS
was coll V Urney *alias* Kede (Kilm) and R Knockninny, but doubts its validity and is prov to same 18 Nov 1501 (A.H. I. 254)

MACBRADY, PATRICK
was in possession of the Archdeaconry of Kilmore to 1538 and is to be deprived

MACBRADY (MAGBRADAYCH), PHILIP
priest, of noble race is prov to V Castleterra (Kilm) and can hold it with Disertfinchilly = Disert Finchill (Kilm) Oct 1428 (C.P.L. VIII. 74,75). He claimed to have been prov V Disert Finchill 13 May 1424 on death of David McBrady, qv, but David O'Mochan,

qv, also claimed it; case came before Eneas O'Carbry, Canon of Clogher who decided against Philip and was deposed 1426. He appealed to the Pope, and is prov to it, 17 Oct 1428 (ib. VIII. 71, Cal. Reg. Swayne, 133, 514). He is still V in 1441 (Cal. Reg. Mey, 76, Cal. Reg. Prene, 166). Is deceased in 1444

†MACBRADY, THOMAS –1511
Archd of Kilmore 6 May 1474 (A.H. I. 238, C.P.L. XIII. 372), was prov to the See of Kilmore which had been reserved to the Pope on 20 Oct 1480 (A.H. I. 257, C.P.L. XIII. 83). Cormac Magauran qv, contests his right and is defeated. Both Thomas and Cormac, Bps of Kilmore were present at a Provincial Council in Drogheda, 6 Jul 1485 (Cal. Reg. Octav., 612), and again 6 Jul 1495 (ib. 622), and 14 Jul 1492 (ib. 631). In the account of his death in 1511 given by the Four Masters, it is said, "Thomas, the son of Andrew MacBrady, Bishop and Erenagh of the two Breifnys during a period of thirty years, the only dignitary whom the English and Irish obeyed, a paragon of wisdom and piety, a luminous lamp that enlightened the laity and clergy by instruction and preaching, and a faithful shepherd of the Church". He **died** on 4th Kalends of March (? August) at Drumahair, having gone there to consecrate a church (see also Ann Loch Ce).

> **m.** and had a **s.** Thomas, a Franciscan friar who **died** in 1490, and a daughter who **died** in 1515
>
> **Died** 1511

MacBRAEIN, DONATUS
Augustinian Canon of St Mary of Clontuskart is prov V Kilcooley (Elph) 5 Apr 1412 (C.P.L. VI. 283)

MACBRAYN, THOMOLTEUS
Augustinian Canon of Clontuskert, is prov to V Kilglass (Elph), "as the Canons of that Monastery have on account of its poverty to betake themselves to strange and distant places to acquire the necessities of life", 7 Sep 1454 (C.P.L. X. 672)

MacBRECHIM, PHILIP
V Ardcarne (Elph) 1427 is deposed; see Philip Macabrechim above

McBREHONE, HUGH
V Culea (Elph), pres 5 Jul 1620 (Lodge P.R.); also pres V Kilmacallen with Taunagh 1620

MACBRENNAN, OIRECHTAGH –c. 1362
Archd of Elphin to c. 1362
> **Died** c. 1362 (A.F.M.)

McBRIDE (MEGBRYD), THOMAS

Canon of Kilmore whose Prebend is V Drung and Lara (Kilm) has resigned 1495

McBRIEN, JOHN HENRY 1891/92–1957

b. 1891 or 1892; TCD BA & Div Test 1912 MA 1915

d 1913 p 1914 (Kilmore); C Boyle (Elph) 1913–15; R Killasnett (Kilm) 1915–21; C-in-c Derrylane (Kilm) 1921–25; R Drung (Kilm) 1925–57; Preb of Drumlease (Kilm) 1949–57

> **m.** and had issue 1. John William (**died** 18 Jun 1938 aged 21) TCD Sch; 2. Dr George, MC **m.** Aug 1943 Georgina Emily elder **dau.** of R T Alston of Glenageary Dublin
>
> **Died** 31 Jan 1957 aged 65

†McBRIEN, MALACHI –1303

was elected Bp of Elphin in 1296 and was confirmed by the Crown. He had been Abbot of Boyle. According to A.F.M., Marianus O'Domabhair, a Dominican Friar also claimed to have been elected, but the Abp of Tuam refused to confirm him, and confirmed Malachi in the See, 13 Aug 1303 (C.P.L. I, 610), and both went to Rome to prosecute their claims

McBRYSSON (McBRYSSUM), THOMAS

is prov R Killererin (Tuam) of which the patrons were lay, 3 Id. Sep 1443 (C.P.L. IX. 398); prov V Kilcoryn *alias* Corcomaga = Kilkerrin (Tuam) and R Kyllenandyn = Killanin (Tuam) 1449; priest of Tuam Diocese, "was prov V Ahascragh (Elph) recently", 3 Dec 1449 (ib. X. 377)

MACCABRECHIM, CORNELIUS

Seized the V Kilmacallen (Elphin) and held it three years and was deposed in 1457

MACCABRECHIM, CORNELIUS

was prov to V Kilmacallen (Elph) 10 May 1457 (C.P.L. XI. 316); not same as above

MacCABRIHIM, DERMIT

V Kilmacallen (Elph) to 1454 is deceased

MACCACLERID, MATTHEW

V Tamnacha = Taunagh (Elph) to *c.* 1429 is deceased

MACCACLERID, ODO

V Taunagh (Elph) *c.* 1429

McCALL, FFERRALL

V Abbeylara (Ard) 1622–c. 1647; "a priest converted" not resident, and the sum reserved by reason the Earl of Westmeath causeth the Curate to be locked out of house from doing his duty; he alloweth him 5£ per annum. Part of the Abbey where the Service is accustomed to be read is in reasonable repair". (R.V.)

†McCANN, JAMES 1897–1983

b. 31 Oct 1897 Grantham Lincs; ed RBAI; QUB BA 1919 Hon LLD 1966; TCD Eccles Hist Pri (1) 1917 Carson Pri 1919 President's Pri 1920 Div Test 1920 BA Resp (2) 1926 Elrington Theol Pri (1) 1930 MA 1930 BD 1935 PhD 1944 DD j.d. 1945 LLD 1966

d 1920 p 1921 (Connor) Bp 1945; C Ballymena (Conn) 1920–22; C Ballynure (Conn) 1922–24; C Urney (Kilm) 1924–28; C Oldcastle (Meath) 1928–30; R Donaghpatrick (Meath) 1930–36; R St Mary Drogheda (Meath) 1936–45; Exam Chapl to Bp of Meath 1941–45; Preb of Tipper in St Patrick's Cath Dublin 1944–45; elected Bp of Meath by Diocesan Synod 4 Jul 1945; consec in St Patrick's Cath Armagh 24 Aug 1945; enthroned at Trim 21 Sep 1945; Bp of Meath 1945–59; elected by the House of Bps Abp of Armagh and Primate of All Ireland 19 Feb 1959; enthroned in St Patrick's Cath Armagh 12 Mar 1959; Abp of Armagh and Primate of All Ireland 1959–69; ret

    s. of James William, Commercial Agent by Agnes of Grantham Lincs

    m. 15 Oct 1924 Ahoghill Par Ch Co Antrim Violet Rea (**died** s.p. 23 Oct 1972) **dau.** of James Whiteside and Mary Henderson of Ballymena Co Antrim

    Died 18 Jul 1983 **bur.** Wolvercote Cemetery Old Marston Oxfordshire

PUBLICATION
Asceticism; a Historical Study, 1944

McCARMYKE, EUGENE

pres to V of St. Roany of BallyMcCarmyke = Ballymacormick (Ard) per resignation of Richard McCormyke 25 Aug 1550 (F. Edward. VI 545)

McCARMYKE, RICHARD

V Ballymacormack (Ard) to 1550

McCASHELL (or McCAHILL), FERGALL (or FARRELL)

pres V Strade = Streete (Ard) 4 Jul 1594 (L.M. V, 101); pres. by Crown to V Clonbroney (Ard) 8 Jul 1611 (L.M. V 109). He is V in 1622 "a priest converted", resident, the Church not well repaired (R.V.)

McCAULEY, CRAIG WILLIAM LESLIE 1972–

b. 1972; Univ of Glamorgan BA 1995 DipHum 1996; TCD BTh 1999

d 1999 p 2000; C Seapatrick (Drom) 1999–2002; C Kill (Dub) 2002–04; R Lurgan Billis Killinkere & Munterconnaught (Kilm) 2004–

McCAUSLAND, WILLIAM CORNELIUS 1825/26–1904

b. 1825 or 1826; TCD BA 1858 Div Test (1) 1859 MA 1867

d & p 1859 (Tuam); C Kiltullagh (Elph) 1859–63; C Aughaval (Tuam) 1863–64; R Kilmoylan (Tuam) 1864–67; R Kiltullagh (Elph) 1867–76; R Kilkeevan U and Preb of Ballintubber (Elph) 1876–89; R Urney (Kilm) 1889–1904; Chapl Cavan Workhouse 1889–1904

poss **s.** of Rev John W, PC Nobber (Meath)

m. 10 Oct 1860 St Thomas' Ch Dublin Adelaide Elizabeth only **dau.** of John Marr of Lr Gardiner St Dublin

Died 25 Jun 1904 aged 78

MACCEGA, THOMAS

priest of the Diocese of Ardagh; obtained V Kilglass (Ard) by simony 1411

MACCHAGO, BERNARD

prov V Iniyscain in Rossinver (Kilm) 3 Aug 1530 (A.H. I. 254)

MACCHEAN, JOHN

V of St Fergus of Cloone (Ard) to 1428

MACCHEAN, PAUL

is prov to V Cloone (Ard) 3 Dec 1428 (AH I 159) — same as below?

MACCHEAN, PAUL

prov. a Canon of Ardagh with reservation of a Preb 1428 (C.P.L. VIII 119); is a Canon 1441 (ib. IX 198) and 1448 (ib. X. 330)

MACCHEYDAN, ANDREW –1416 or 1417

priest of Ardagh Dio; was coll by Bp Adam to V Cluayne (Cloone) (Ard) but was not promoted to Holy Orders before 13 Oct 1405 (C.P.L. VI 61). He is V Cloone (Ard) 29 Dec 1406 and prov to R Regles = Cluayn

Died 22 Jun 1416 (Cal.Reg. Flem. 256), 1417 (A.H. I. 177)

MACCHONKAGRI, EUGENE

is prov to the R Muntireolis (Ard) Dec 1469 (A.H. I, 164)

McCIERNAN, ODO

claims the V Killeshandra (Kilm) and is confirmed in the Vicarage, 1470 (Cal. Reg. Octav. 415)

MACCILRUAIG, ANDREW

V Annaduff and Kylltacomorca = Kilcommick (Ard) to 1412 (C.P.L. VI. 369); and because Murianus Magranyll was not ordained priest also got V Templemichael (Ard) to 1412, res for V Eanachgaid

McCLEAN, RICHARD ARTHUR 1860–1948

b. 25 Nov 1860 Tralee Co Kerry; TCD BA 1891 LLB & LLD 1894; Order of St Sava (Serbia) Ribbon for Valour 1921; OBE 1921 CBE 1922; MC

d & p 1892 (Kilmore); C St John Sligo (Elph) 1892–95; R Caernarvon W Australia (Dio NW Australia) 1895–96; R Swan W Australia (Dio Perth) 1896–98; C Tuam (Tuam) 1898–1900; C Ballymacarrett (Down) 1900–01; C Rathkeale (Lim) 1901–05; R Rathkeale (Lim) 1905–25; Canon of Dysart (Lim) 1907–11; Preb of Ballycahane (Lim) 1911–25; TCF 1915–18 (thrice mentioned in despatches)

> **s.** of Richard
>
> **m.** Oct 1911 Mary Louisa (**died** 3 Jun 1954 at Tralee **bur.** Dingle Co Kerry) 3rd **dau.** of Capt Dovaston of Ilford Essex and widow of John Sampson of Exeter
>
> **Died** 18 Jun 1948

McCLELLAND, WILLIAM 1798/99–c. 1873

b. 1798 or 1799 Longford; ed by Mr Irwin; ent TCD 5 Jun 1820 aged 21 BA 1829 MA 1832

R Tessaragh (Elph) 1841–73

> **s.** of Frederick
>
> **m.** 11 Aug 1852 at Mount Talbot Sophia Baillie
>
> **Died** c. 1873

McCLENAGHAN, GEORGE 1837/38–1917

b. 1837 or 1838; was Head Master of Primrose Grange School, Sligo; TCD BA (Resp) 1872 MA 1880

d 1870 (Down) p 1874 (Kilmore); C Ahamplish (Elph) 1870–75; PC Oughteragh (Kilm) 1874–80; I St Peter Athlone (Meath) 1880–1910; Preb of Kilgoghlin (Elph) 1899–1910; ret

> **m.** 30 Jan 1858 St Peter Dublin Caroline Olivia yst **dau.** of William Geary of Harcourt St Dublin; (she published *Dream Wreaths and Scattered Leaves* under the pseudonym *Chorus*). Issue 1. Rev George Richard TCD MA 1891, R Biddeston (Nor) 1915–22 **m.** 18 Apr 1894 Amy Margaret elder **dau.** of Thomas Worsfold Mayo of Yeovil and had issue incl a **s.**, 2nd Lt A Bryant who was killed in Flanders during the Great War aged 20; 2. Ven Henry St George **b.** 22 Sep 1866 Co Sligo (**died** 10 Mar 1950 Dublin) TCD BA 1890 Div Test (2) 1891 MA 1918 d 1891 p 1892 C Glendermott (Derry) 1891–94 C Christ Ch (Derry) 1894 R Killaghtee (Raph) 1894–1919 R Conwall (Raph) 1919–38 Canon of Raphoe 1917–19 Archd of Raphoe 1919–38 **m.** Constance (**died** 23 Aug 1941) and had issue (i) Herbert Eric St George **b.** 5 Aug 1896 **m.** 14 Sep 1927 Charlotte Lane (ii) Percy John

Warren (iiii) Cecil Albert Conolly (iv) Henry Norman Theodore; 3. Rev Hamlet, R Oughteragh (Kilm) qv; 4. Ina Adelaide
Died 1917

McCLENAGHAN, HAMLET 1864/65–1949
b. 1864 or 1865; TCD Div Test (2) 1892 BA 1893

d 1893 (Down for Tuam) p 1895 (Bath & Wells); C St Nicholas Galway (Tuam) 1893–94; C Yeovil (B & W) 1894–96; C Eglish (Meath) 1896–97; R Oughteragh (Kilm) 1897–1902; R Almoritia w Rathconrath (Meath) 1902–05; R Dunshaughlin w Ballymaglasson (w Ratoath U from 1926) (Meath) 1905–41; RD of Lr Kells 1917–41; ret

s. of Canon George qv by Olivia; **bro.** of Rev George Richard, R Biddeston (Nor); **bro.** of Ven Henry St. George, Archd of Raphoe
Died 9 Jan 1949 aged 84

McCLINTOCK, LOWRY COLE *c.* 1810 –1876
b. c 1810; ed by Mr Stewart; ent TCD 2 Jan 1826 BA 1830

d 1835 p; C Newtownbarry (Ferns); C Cashel (Ard) 1835–38; C Annaduff (Ard) 1838; PC Monivea (Tuam) 1838–47; R Ballincholla and Kilmolara (Tuam) 1847–71; Preb of Kilmeen in Tuam Cath 1871–76

s. of Rev Alexander **b.** 6 Jan 1775 **died** 6 Aug 1836 Co Wexford R Kilsaran (Arm) 1797–1810 R Newtownbarry (Ferns) 1810–36 (2nd **s.** of John, MP and Patience **dau.** of William Foster, MP by Anne (**died** 11 Feb 1871) **dau.** of Mervyn Pratt; **bro.** of Rev Henry Fitzalan **b.** *c.* 1806 (**died** 6 Oct 1879), R Kilsaran (Arm) 1832–35 V Ballymodan (Cork) 1835–46 R Kilmichael and Macloneigh (Cork) 1846–79

Died unm. 2 Apr 1876

PUBLICATIONS
The Divinity Student's Assistant, 1834
A Sermon on the Coverdale Centenary, 1835, preached at Newtownbarry on Psalm 119 v 105

MACCOCHAIDYKELLAID, NICHOLAS
is Preb Kilbride (Elph) to 1434, but Odo O'Martayn qv informs the Pope that he has dilapidated his Prebend and is to be defamed of crimes. If true, he is to be deposed and Odo is to be coll and dispensed, 11 Apr 1434 (C.P.L. VIII. 511)

McCOLBORTH, MARIANUS
Canon of Ardagh 1461 (Cal. Reg. Prene)

MACCOLICH (MACEOLICH, MACOLY), JOHN –*c.* 1461
is rehabilitated to the Preb of Termonbarry (Elph) 1409 for certain simoniacal promises he had made when on the death of Maurice O'Flanagan qv, he obtained the Preb and

is re–prov to it 9 Jan 1411 (C.P.L. VI. 255, 309); still there 1425, 1428, 1429 (ib. VII. 398, VIII 15, 118); is prov to the V St Mary's, Kilglass (Elph) 9 Jan 1411

Died c. 1461

MACCOMAID, JOHN

V Urney (Kilm) before 1401; had resigned

McCOMBE, ISAAC HILL 1889–1962

b. 9 Dec 1889 Mountrath Co Laois; trained as a National School Teacher; TCD Carson Bibl Pri & Heb Pri 1917 BA 1917 Downes Pri 1918 BD 1937

d 1918 p 1919 (Tuam); C St Mary's Cath Tuam (Tuam) 1918–20; C Dundalk (Arm) 1920–22; Dio C Kilmore Elphin and Ardagh 1922–25; C-in-c Derrylane (Kilm) 1925–30; R Emlaghfad and Killaraght (Ach) 1930–60; RD of Dromard 1934–60; Preb of Kilmactalway in St Patrick's Cath Dublin 1944–60; ret

s. of John of Rathmines Dublin by Letitia Jane (née Hill) of Newry Co Down

m. 20 Aug 1925 at Castlepollard Dorinda Mary Maud (**died** 8 Jun 1966 Blackrock Dublin) elder **dau.** of Stephen and Anna Maria (née Strong) Robinson of Castlepollard Co Westmeath. Issue 1. John Percival (**died** 11 Apr 1985) **b.** 6 Jun 1926 TCD **m.** Irene Hewitt (**died** 23 Dec 1990) and had issue a **dau.** and two **sons**; 2. Rev George Albert Stephen **b.** 25 Nov 1927 TCD BA 1950 Div Test 1951 d 1951 p 1952 (Armagh) C Drumcree (Arm) 1951–54 C St John Leytonstone (Chelmsf) 1954–57 C-in-c St Bride Liverpool (Liv) 1958–63 Chapl to Royal Masonic Sch Bushey 1963–64 C Prittlewell (Chelmsf) 1964–65 R Maidstone w Paynton (Dio Saskatchewan) 1966–71 R Kingsclear w New Maryland (Dio Fredericton) 1971–77 R Campobello 1977–84 R Madawaska and Grand Falls (Dio Ottawa) 1984–91 ret **m.** 20 Apr 1968 St Jude's Ch, St John New Brunswick Kathleen Edith **dau.** of Charles Frederick Nugent Lewis and had issue (i) Padraic Stephen Charles **b.** 21 Oct 1969 (ii) Simon Edward John **b.** 25 Oct 1972; 3. Dorinda Rosemund **b.** 9 Nov 1929 **m.** 1953 Edwin Arthur Attwood and had issue five children; 4. Hilda Mary Maud **b.** 29 Nov 1933 **m.** Thomas Mortimer and have issue a **dau.**; 5. Selina Letitia Charlotte **b.** 17 Apr 1936 **m.** 1963 Derek Import and have issue a **s.** and two **daus.**

Died 15 Apr 1962 Blackrock Dublin

McCOME (McCOMYN), HUGH

was R Drumgoon (Kilm), a converted priest, suspended in 1622 for misdemeanour. The cure was sequestered in 1622 and served by Rev. Francis Parkes, R Castleterra (Kilm), qv Church ruinous; a poor Irish glebe house. He as R got a grant of a glebe in Drumgoon 25 Jan 1626/27 (Morrin, iii. 188).

†McCONAMA (McKINAWE), CORNELIUS –1355

appears Bp of Kilmore 1328 (Ann Loch Ce, Ann Ult)

Died 1355

MACCONAYD, PATRICK

is prov to V Drung (Kilm) 9 Jan 1495 (A.H. I. 253)

MACCONAYNG (McCONAING), CORNELIUS (CORMAC)

was prov to V Drung and Larah (Kilm) 1430/31. He is now dispensed as illegitimate and is again prov to it, Augustine Macbrady qv being dead, Mar 1430 (C.P.L. VIII. 374–375). He is evidently the Cornelius McCoaird who claimed it in 1427. He was V in 1443 and made R Kede = Kedy (Kilm) 10 Jul 1443 (A.H. I. 235, C.P.L. IX. 338)

MACCONCAING (MACCON(C)AI(Y)NG), PATRICK   –1454/45

is prov to R of Druymguin *alias* Macharym Nybar = Drumgoon (Kilm) and absolved for simony 12 Mar 1453/54 (C.P.L. X. 729–730); appears Canon of Kilmore 1453 (C.P.L. X. 604)

    Died 1454/55

McCONCAYD, BERNARD

R Minbrisg *alias Castri de Sligra* = Sligo (Elph)– the rural lands between the two bridges is vacant — became a monk and thus vacated the Rectory. He was appointed to the Monastery of Lochgue (Loch Ce). The parish is to be served by one of the Canons, 2 Nov 1428 (C.P.L. VIII. 52)

MACCONRICH, ARTHUR

Canon of Kilmore gets the V Killesher (Kilm) united to his Canonry 10 Oct 1488 (A.H. I. 239)

MACCONTAGRY (MACCONKAGRY), EUGENE

V Kilglass (Ard) 1465; Canon of Ardagh 1465/66 (C.P.L. XII 448 and 528) and 1483 (ib. 586)

McCONYN, DAVID

Perpetual R = V Drung and Lara (Kilm) to 1594; is deceased (L.M. V. 101)

†McCORMACK, WILLIAM   –1373

Canon of Ardagh to 1369; appears as Bp of Ardagh 28 Aug 1369 (Cal. Reg. Swet. 61) and is cited by the Primate to answer certain charges against him which would involve his deposition 10 Mar 1369/70 (ib. No. 165–166), but seems to have possessed the See till his death from a fall from his horse in 1373. In that year the Abp. of Armagh demands from the temporary custodians of the See "the palfrey rings, and other things which by custom belonged to him by reason of the death of William the Bp. of A". (ib. No. 240)

    Died 1373

McCORMICK, FRANCIS JAMES 1875/76–1948

b. 1875 or 1876; TCD BA 1903 Div Test 1905 MA 1908

d 1904 p 1905 (Ossory for Tuam); C Tuam (Tuam) 1904–08; C St Anne Sale (Ches) 1908–10; R Ardcarne (Elph) 1911–44; RD of S Elphin 1936–44; Preb of Kilmacallen (Elph) 1938–44; ret

s. of Rev James, Preb of Taghsaxon (Tuam) and R Roundstone (Tuam) 1878–1921 by Mary Frances (**died** 15 Feb 1938); **bro.** of Rev Thomas Eaton; **bro.** of Rev Clement Alexander.

m. 28 Jun 1911 at Portmarnock Lucia Margaret (**died** 10 Nov 1960 at Kilternan Dublin) **dau.** of William J Hughes. Issue incl his yst **dau.** Deirdre **m.** 25 Jul 1944 Norman eldest **s.** of Capt William Ashe of Blairgowrie Scotland

Died 12 Jul 1948 aged 72

McCORMICK, JOHN HARPUR 1854/55–1931

b. 1854 or 1855; TCD BA (Resp) & Div Test (2) 1883 BD 1906

d 1882 p 1883 (Tuam); C Ballinrobe (Tuam) 1882–84; C Nenagh (Killaloe) 1884–86; V Ahamplish (Elph) 1886–1918; V Killyon and Castleblakney (w Athleague from 1924) (Elph) 1918–28; ret

s. of Joseph of Crillen Co Fermanagh by Bessie

m. Frances Elizabeth (**died** 25 Feb 1944). Issue incl 1. Rev William Loftus **b.** 1886 TCD BA 1909 Div Test 1910 d 1909 p 1910 C Donnybrook (Dub) 1909–13 CMS Missy Hazaribagh 1913–19 C Malahide (Dub) 1919–23 C Maryborough (Leigh) 1923–24 C-in-c Kilnehue & Kilpipe (Ferns) 1924–31 R Alder (B & W) 1931–36 I Gillingham (Nor) 1936–51 ret; **m.** (1)…; **m.** (2) 16 Jul 1935 Rathmines Ch Dublin Grace yst **dau.** of late Rev E **m.** Griffin, Dublin; 2. Capt F H **m.** 1929 Adeline only **dau.** of Rev T Williams of Glazaeley Vicarage Newmarket; 3. a **dau.**…; 4. a 2nd **dau.** Olive **m.** (1) 23 Jun 1915 Lt Sydney Colin Mottram, 7th E Yorks Regt; **m.** (2) 29 Apr 1926 John Pride of Howth Co Dublin; 5. a **dau.** Aileen **died** 24 Jul 1935 at Cambridge

Died 27 Oct 1931 aged 76

McCOWLOG, ANDREW

was coll V Kiltubride (Ard) by Bp Cormac *c.* 1460 (Cal. Reg. Prene 429)

McCREA, JOHN 1793/94–

b. 1793 or 1794 Antrim; ed by Mr McCrea; ent TCD 5 Nov 1810 aged 16 BA 1816

d 4 Oct 1818 (Down); C Newry (Drom) 1821; C Boyle (Elph) 1824–*c.* 27

s. of James

McCREIGHT, ANDREW WILLIAM 1793–1868

b. 1793 Co Armagh; ed by Mr Thomas McDonnell; ent TCD 5 Sep 1814 aged 21 BA 1818 MA 1832 d 1819 p; PC Arvagh (Kilm) 1822–1835; poss R Castleterra (Kilm) for a short time *c.* 1834; R Annagh (Kilm) 1835–68

    s. of James

    Died 7 May 1868 aged 74

MacCRIAN (MACAEDAGAN), CRISTIN

Canon of Elphin (C.P.L. X. 497) & 1460 (ib. XII. 98)

McCULLOUGH, JAMES NELSON 1893–1955

b. 1893; Durham Univ LTh 1923

d 1923 p 1924; C St Matthew Bootle (Liv) 1923–29; V St Michael Toxteth Park (Liv) 1929–37; CF 1938; R Kilronan and Kilmactranny (Ard) 1937–46; C Christ Ch Cath Lisburn (Conn) 1946–53; res and went to Canada

    Died Dec 1955 in Manitoba aged 62 **bur.** 1 Jan 1956 Annalong Co Down

MACCULMARTAYN (MACCULMARCHYN), JOHN

has a Preb of Kilmore to which the church of Enagillib = Annagelliffe (Kilm) is attached; is prov to the V Urney (Kilm) 23 Apr 1457 (C.P.L. XI. 313); was prov to the R Urney (Kilm) and disp because "as a result of shipwreck, he has the top of his middle finger and the nail of an index finger paralysed", 28 Oct 1466 (C.P.L. XII. 512)

MACCULMARTHAYN, JOHN

was prov R Drumgoon (Kilm) and disp as illegitimate, 25 Feb 1454/55 (C.P.L. X. 722), but he appears not to have held it as Andrew Macbrady, qv, is prov to the R 1455

MACCULMARTHAYN, JOHN

is prov to V of St. Briget's, Disert Finchill (Kilm) and of St. Patrick's, Drumgoon (Kilm), and St. Bridget's, Urney (Kilm) to be united with his Canonry and Preb. For his life, 3 Oct 1491 (A.H. I. 239, 240); prob same as one of above

McDERMOTT (MACDIARMADA), CORNELIUS

priest, informs the Pope that Patrick O'Stingen qv has dilapidated the goods of the V of Ardcarne (Elph) and committed perjury. If so, Cornelius to be coll to it, whether void, or void by the death of Magonius Mickechin qv, 7 Jul 1446

McDERMOTT, JOHN 1813/14–

b. 1813 or 1814 Dublin; ed by Mr Crawford; ent TCD 22 Oct 1832 aged 18 BA 1837

lic C Lavey (Kilm) 13 Apr 1838; British Chapl at Lyons France *c.* 1850

    eldest **s.** of Joseph, MD of Fitzwilliam Sq Dublin

    m. (1) 10 Jul 1838 at Whitechurch Catherine Louisa (**died** 11 Aug 1849 at Biarritz) eldest **dau.** of Robert Muter, Capt 7th Royal Fusiliers

    m. (2) 19 Mar 1850 Caroline **dau.** of Philip Barlow, Capt 12th Regt

McDERMOTT (MACDIARMADA), ODO

had been prov V Ardcarne (Elph) and was coll thereto by Bp John qv 1427 vac per depr Philip Macabrechim qv, but as he doubted the validity of his collation, and was litigating about the Archdeaconry of Elphin, to which he had been lately prov, he is prov to it, but must resign the Archdeaconry on obtaining the V of Ardcarne (Elph) (C.P.L. VIII. 43)

McDERMOTT (MacDIARMADA), THADY

clk of Elphin Diocese is prov R Ardcarne 15 Nov 1411 (C.P.L. V. 261)

MACDERMOTT, THOMAS   –c. 1255

was Parson of Moyburg, Airteach and Clancuain; Archd of Elphin to 1255

Died c. 1255 (A.F.M.)

†McDERMOTT, THOMAS   –1265

He had been Abbot of Boyle. Bp of Elphin 1262–65. During his short occupancy of the See, Hugh O'Connor King of Connaught seems to have seized the revenues of the See, and we find both the King of France and the Queen of Castile writing letters to Henry III, asking his help to get them restored

Died 1265

MACDIANNADA, THOMAS

V Killronan *alias* Killinginronan (Ard) 1443 is reported to be guilty of fornication, keeping a concubine, etc. If so (C.P.L. IX. 332), Tatheus McGillamane qv is prov. to V Kilronan (Ard) 1443

McDIARMADA, JOHN

V Kilcennoran townland in Aughrim Parish (Elph) to 1447 is deposed along with Malachy O'Thanayn qv, V Eachruym = Aughrim for simony, perjury etc

MacDIARMADA, ODO

Clerk of Elphin Dio., of noble race, illegitimate and dispensed for Orders, who has studied Canon Law for 8 years, is prov to the Deanery of Elphin vacant by the death of Malachy O'Flanagan, and is dispensed to hold it 3 Sep 1411 (C.P.L. VI. 240). As he doubted whether the provision was not invalid because it did not state that the Deanery was vacant because of the deprivation of Donald MacDonnchid qv, he was rehabilitated and prov to it again, 9 Aug 1413 (ib. VI. 452)

MACDIARMADA, ODO

was lately prov Archd of Elphin but is to resign it upon being made V of Ardcarne (Elph) 1427 (C.P.L. VIII. 43)

MACDIARMADA, THADY

is prov to V Toomna (Elph) 15 Nov 1411 (C.P.L. VI. 261); most prob same as one or more of below

McDIARMADA, THADY

is prov to a Canonry of Elphin with reservation of a Preb, 9 Aug 1413 (C.P.L. VI 398, 455). One of the same name is dispensed as illegal and is prov to Cannones of Elphin and Achonry with a Preb of each reserved on 15 Dec 1413. Poss became a Cistercian monk of St Mary's Boyle in 1444 (C.P.L. IX. 423)

MACDIARMADA, THADY

Canon of Elphin 1414 (C.P.L. VI. 429)

MACDIARMADA, THADY

took possession of the Precentorship of Elphin *c.* 1437 and held it about 4 years to 1441 (C.P.L. IX. 153)

MacDIARMADA, THOMAS (THOMOTHEUS, THADY)

clk, disp as illegitimate, is prov to V Tuachmna = Toomna (Elph) vacated by the death of Donald Ocuiryth qv, and Reginald Othomathaych qv is to be removed as his provision did not mention the then holder, 2 Dec 1427. He is also prov to a Canonry of Elphin with a Preb reserved 2 Nov 1427 (C.P.L. VIII. 59); is disp 15 Nov 1428 (ib. VIII. 48, 60); however is still Canon 1433 & 1444 (ib. VIII 469 & IX 448)

MACDOIMCAIDNABARG, ODO

is a Canon of Elphin 9 Mar 1404 (C.P.L. V. 613)

MacDOMCAYRDUAN, ODO

Canon of Elphin 1465 (C.P.L. XII. 393)

McDONAGH (MacDONNCHAD, MacDONNCHDID), CORMAC

clk of Elphin is prov R Dacorand = Corran and Mota (identified as Ballymote, but also Castlemore) (Ach) *c.* 1428; again prov 8 Apr 1430; is prov R of Minbrisg *alias* Sligo, *inter duos pontes,* is Canon of Elphin 3 Mar 1430; is prov to a Canonry of Elphin and Achonry 3 Jan 1430; is still Canon in 1440 (C.P.L. VIII. 152, 156, 193), & 1444 (ib. IX. 417, 88)

McDONAGH (MacDOMCHAID) , DONALD

Canon of Elphin 1440 (C.P.L. IX. 88)

McDONAGH (MacDONNCHIAD), MAGONIUS
Canon of Elphin 1444 (C.P.L. IX. 423), & 1430 & 1460 (Cal. Reg. Prene. 23, 266)

MACDONAGH (MACDONCHAYD), THADY
clk Elphin Dio who made a complaint against Maurice O Conor qv for keeping a concubine, is prov to V Calry (Elph) 12 Aug 1440 if the nature of the complaint is true (C.P.L. IX. 133)

MacDONCHENY, CORNELIUS
Dean of Elphin to Jul 1425 (C.P.L. VII. 793)

MacDONNANY, CHARLES –c. 1441
Preb of Terebrine (Elph) to 1441
>   **Died** c. 1441

MacDONNCHAD, MAGONIUS
R Mabrisc *alias inter duos pontes* = Sligo (Elph) is to resign his Rectory on becoming a Premonstratensian Canon, 5 Jul 1444 (C.P.L. IX. 417, 418); prob same as below

MACDONNCHAID, MAGONIUS
clk, is prov R of the rural lands of Minbrisg (Elph) which for long past was apportioned to the Manor of Lochle; the Abbot now wishes to get him appointed as he has powerful friends and can wrest the fruit from laymen who had usurped them. He is in his 23rd year and dispensed as illegitimate, 1440 (C.P.L. IX. 121)

MacDONNCHID (McDONOGH), DONALD
is prov to the Deanery of Elphin vacant by the death of Malachy O'Flanagan, 13 Aug 1409 (C.P.L. VI. 145). He appears as Dean May 1411/12 (ib. VI. 254); R Raharany (Tuam) 1411/12; is prov V Castlemore (Ach) 1412

MACDONNELL, GEORGE 1806/07–1874
b. 1806 or 1807 Cork; ed by Mr Martin; ent TCD 1 Jul 1816 BA 1823

C Kilmore (Kilm) 1847; PC Ballyjamesduff (Kilm) 1853–61; R Kilgeffin (Elph) 1861–74

>   **s.** of Robert; **bro.** of Richard Macdonnell, Provost of TCD
>   **m.** Annie and had issue incl Robert George **b.** 26 Dec 1847 (**died** 27 Apr 1864 at Kilgeffin)
>   **Died** 10 Jul 1874 at Kilgeffin aged 67

MacDONOGH, JAMES DILLON 1804/05–1881
b. 1804 or 1805 Sligo; ed by Rev Mr Armstrong; ent TCD 17 Jun 1835 BA 1839

d 1841 (Tuam) p 1843 (Dublin for Kilmore); C Oughteragh (Kilm) 1843; C Inver (Conn) 1845; C Taughboyne (Raph) 1846; C Badoney Upr (Derry) 1857; C Langfield Lr (Derry) 1860; PC Muff (Derry) 1869–70; C Fahan Upr (Raph — then Derry) 1871–81

    s. of James, farmer

    Died 11 Aug 1881 aged 76

McDOUGALL, IAN WILLIAM 1920–2001

b. 30 Sep 1920 Drumlane Rectory; ed Portora Royal Sch Enniskillen; TCD BA & Div Test 1943 MA 1959

d 1943 p 1944 (Connor); C St Stephen Belfast (Conn) 1943–45; C Enniskillen and Trory (Clogh) 1945–48; R Drumlane (Kilm) 1948–50; R Ballinaclash U (Glend) 1951–54; R Kilcleagh w Ballyloughloe and Ferbane 1954–58; R Mullingar U (Meath) 1958–83; Canon of Meath 1981–85; BC Kilbixy (Meath) 1983–85; ret

    s. of Rev Canon William Alcorn, R Arvagh (Kilm) qv (s. of John and Martha (née Alcorn)) by Susanna Rebecca Helena

    m. 1949 Alexandra **dau.** of Rev William Alexander Russell, R Killeshandra (Kilm) qv Issue 1. Angela Helena bapt 15 Aug 1952 **m.** 29 Dec 1978 All SS Par Ch Mullingar David **s.** of Capt E J and Rita Algar of Mullingar; 2. a **s. b.** 2 Apr 1956

    Died 2 Nov 2001

McDOUGALL, WILLIAM ALCORN 1867–1943

b. 29 Dec 1867 Strabane Co Tyrone; ed Prior Sch Lifford; Queen's Coll Belfast; RUI BA 1891; TCD Div Test 1892

d 1892 p 1893 (Derry); C Conwall and Aughanunshin (Raph) 1892–94; C Annagh (Kilm) 1894–97; C-in-c Innismagrath (Kilm) 1897–1901; R Innismagrath (w Dowra from 1900) (Kilm) 1901–11; R Drumlane (Kilm) 1911–21; R Arvagh (w C-in-c Carrigallen from 1925) (Kilm) 1921–41; Preb of Drumlease (Kilm) 1935–41; ret

    s. of John of Strabane by Martha (née Alcorn)

    m. 30 Apr 1912 Susanna Rebecca Helena (**died** 8 Dec 1976 aged 96) only **dau.** of William Thompson of Manorhamilton Co Leitrim. Issue incl a **s.** 1. Rev Ian William, R Drumlane (Kilm) qv; **daus.** 1.an eldest dau; 2. Jessie Mary **m.** 17 Apr 1941 at Arvagh Lt Hans L S, RNR 3rd **s.** of Hans Hamilton of Rathgar Dublin; 3. Alys H A **m.** 14 Jun 1950 St Thomas' Ch Mt Merrion Dublin Rev Francis Robert Alexander, R Clondalkin (Dub) 1948–80 and had issue (i) John **b.** 14 Jun 1951 (ii) Susan **b.** 15 Feb 1955 (iii) Stephen Robert (iv) Patrick McDougall **b.** 28 Jul 1958

    Died 4 Apr 1943

MacDUBGALLY, FELEMY

Canon of Elphin 1465, becomes a monk (C.P.L. XII. 235)

†MACDUIBHNE (McGIVNEY), FEARSITHE –1464

"Bishop of the two Breifnys" to 1464

Died 27 Nov 1464 (Cotton has 26 Nov) (Ann Ult)

McDUIBHNE, JOHN

"Archdeacon of Drumleathan in Cavan" = Kilmore to 1343; is deceased

MACECHAN, PAUL

took possession of part of Muntireolis (Ard) before 1444/45

MACEDA, THOMAS

intruded into V Rathreagh (Ard) 1397 and is deposed

McEGAN (MACAEDAGAN), JOHN

held the V Killesnada = Killasnett (Kilm), though poss Killeshandra (Kilm) for over a year to 1412 without being ordained priest and is deposed

McELHINNEY, MARY ELIZABETH ELLEN 1945–

b. 12 May 1945 Dublin; ed Alexandra Coll Dublin; TCD BSSc (Hons) & BA 1967 BTh 1997

d Jun 1997 p Jun 1998; C Magheralin w Dollingstown (Drom) 1997–2001; R Calry (Elph) 2001–07; Preb of Tibohine (Elph and Ard) 2004–

    dau. of Canon James Mansel Egerton Maguire, Preb of Tibohine (Elph and Ard) 1966–78 qv by Mary Elizabeth (née Woods) of Cootehill Co Cavan

    m. 11 Sep 1968 Edgeworthstown Par Ch Co Longford Cyril **s.** of Robert and Gertie (née McMahon of Cootehill Co Cavan) McElhinney of Milford Co Donegal. Issue 1. Rev Robert Stephen **b.** 2 Feb 1970 Aston Univ BSc 1991 CITC BTh 2005 d 2005 p 2006 C Kill (Dub) 2005– **m.** 30 Jul 1996 Cathy; 2. David Egerton **b.** 24 May 1972 **m.** 4 Jul 1996 Jenny; 3. Vance Cyril adopted 20 Jul 1974 **m.** 28 Dec 2001

McENDOO, WILLIAM c. 1855–1908

b. c. 1855 Killevan Co Monaghan; TCD BA & Div Test 1879 MA 1882 BD 1891

d 1878 p 1879; C Maryborough, Portlaoise (Leigh) 1878–79; C Killashee and Ballymacormick (Ard) 1879–82; C Ballymore (Arm) 1882–86; R Ballymore (Arm) 1886–1908; Exam Chapl to Abp of Armagh 1906–08

    s. of John, Farmer of Glassdrummond, Parish of Killevan

    m. 8 Jun 1886 at Clonallon Par Ch Co Down Ellen Louisa (**died** 22 Feb 1937 in her 87th year) widow of Henry Woodhouse Wallace and **dau.** of Rev William Raphael Williams MA, C St Mary Newry (Drom) 1839–67

    Died 16 Mar 1908 as a result of an accident on his trap whilst visiting

†McEOGH (MAGODAIG), JOSEPH

Archd of Ardagh 1227; was made Bp (Ware & F. 1, 18)

†McEOIGH (McKEOGH), JOHN   –1343

Archd of Ardagh; prov to the See of Ardagh 1324; had already been elected by the Chapter on the refusal of the See by David, 19 Mar 1324 (C.P.L. II, 238), perhaps in ignorance that the See was reserved to the Pope (C.P.L. II, 238). The Crown restored the temporalities to him on 20 Oct 1324 on his renouncing all things prejudicial to the Crown in his Bull (C.P.R.E. Edward II v. 35). The temporalities however, were in the King's hands in 1328/29 (Pipe R., 48 Rep. D.K. p 21). After his consecration, the Archdeaconry was vacant for 16 years, its value 8 marks, being so little that no one had petitioned for it. (C.P.P. i. 120)

> **Died** 1343 (Ann. Loch Ce, 645, Ann Ult.)

McFARLAND, EDWARD WILLIAM   c. 1875–1946

b. *c.* 1875; TCD BA & Div Test 1899 MA 1915; MC 1919

d 1900 p 1901; C Drumlease (Kilm) 1900–03; C Enniscorthy (Ferns) 1903–06; R Derryvullen S (Clogh) 1906–46; TCF 1916–19; Dio Sec Clogher 1926–46; Preb of Tyholland 1935–45; Chanc of Clogher 1945–46

> **m.** 1906 Beryl (**died** 7 Apr 1960 at Oldham aged 81) **dau.** of G C Grey. Issue Kathleen Beryl
>
> **Died** 30 Jun 1946

MACFFLAIND (MacFLYNN), THADY

was coll V Killeshandra (Kilm) by Bp Donatus, and now doubts if his coll was sufficient and is prov to it now, whether so vacant, or vacant by the resignation of John O'Sheridan qv, Nicholas O'Farrelly, qv, or by the death of Cornelius Micamagister, qv, 17 Dec 1436 (C.P.L. VIII. 600)

MACGAMRAGAN, MAGONIUS   –c. 1414

V Insula Brechungy *alias* Teampullapuret = Templeport (Kilm) to 1414, is deceased

> **Died** *c.* 1414

McGARVEY, ANDREW WILLIAM   –1948

TCD BA 1900 Div Test 1901 MA 1922

d 1901 p 1902 (Kilmore); C Carrigallen (Kilm) 1901–04; R Derrylane (Kilm) 1904–08; R Drung (Kilm) 1908–25; R Annagh (Kilm) 1925–29; R Dromore (Drom) 1929–48; Preb of Dromore (Drom) 1930–36; Treas of Dromore 1936–40–; Prec of Dromore 1940–45–; Chanc of Dromore 1945–48

> **s.** of James of Virginia Co Cavan by Martha Jane **dau.** of Hugh Harrison of Belfast; **bro.** of Rev Samuel Rentoul, R Drumbeg (Down) 1927–53
>
> **m.** 19 Jun 1918 Zion Ch Rathgar Dublin Sarah Elizabeth **dau.** of William Wilson

JP of Miltown Hse Co Cavan. Issue Edith Elizabeth
Died 18 Jan 1948

MACGEAREACTAYD, THADY

Canon of Elphin of a race of Dukes is prov to Archd Elphin though he holds the Preb of Fuerty and V Ahascragh (Clonf), and is allowed to retain his V, 3 June 1444 (C.P.L. IX. 30)

McGEE, STUART IRWIN 1930–

b. 22 Mar 1930 Dromore West Co Sligo; ed Sligo Gram Sch; Mountjoy Sch Dublin; TCD BA & Div Test 1953 MA 1968

d 5 Jul 1953 p Jul 1954; C St Simon Belfast (Conn) 1953–55; Asst Priest St Andrew's Cath Singapore and Port Chapl w Chapl Miss to Seamen Singapore 1955–58; R Drumholm and Rossnowlagh (Raph) 1959–65; CF RAChD 1965–77; DACG, BAOR 1977–80; SHAPE 1980–88; R Achonry Cath G and Preb of Killaraght and Kilmovee (Ach) 1989–92; R Cath Parish of St Mary and St John the Baptist Sligo Knocknarea and Rosses Point (w Taunagh Kilmactranny and Ballysumaghan to 1994) (Elph) and Dean of Elphin and Ardagh 1992–99; ret

s. of John Thomas of Dromore West (**s.** of John and Catherine (née Armstrong) of Dromore West) by Mary (Mollie) **dau.** of Stanley and Margaret (née Barber) Irwin of Ballymote Co Sligo

m. 15 Nov 1960 St Thomas Ch Dublin Eunice **dau.** of William Parker and Mabel Sterling of Lisburn Co Antrim. Issue 1. Jillian Shirley **b.** 8 Dec 1961 **m.** 2 Jun 1990 Chatham Garrison Ch Capt Wiliam David Charles Honey RE; 2. Lynette Mabel **b.** 16 Oct 1963 **m.** 17 Mar 1995 Sligo Cath Roy Stuart Stevenson; 3. Samuel Alexander (**died** 28 Nov 2005) **b.** 26 Jan 1965 **m.** 30 Oct 1993 Burwell Par Ch Cambs Nicola Hallows; 4. Alice Mary **b.** 5 May 1966 **m.** 11 Apr 1992 Bagshot Pk Lt Col Alistair Scott Dickinson, RE

McGEOGHEGAN (McEIDDIGEIN), CHARLES

V Templepatrick (Elph) and Canon of Elphin 1488 (A.F.M.)

McGEOGHEGAN (MacDEDIAN), CRISTINUS   –1463

Canon of Elphin 1445/46 (C.P.L. IX. 506)., and in 1446 & 1455 (ib. IX. 555, XI. 247); prob = Gilchriest McEdigein, V Templepatrick, Elphin and Canon who died in 1463

Died 1463

McGEOGHEGAN (MacDAEGAYN), DONALD

Canon of Elphin 1456 (C.P.L. X. 119), and 1457 (ib. XI. 315) & 1460 (ib. XII. 78)

McGEOGHEGAN (MACKEDYGAYN or MAGUEDAN), MAURICE

was prov to V Ballyntobyr = Ballintubber (Elph) 2 Oct 1413 & is also V Baslig = Baslick and was on 6 Mar 1414 prov to a Canonry of Elphin with reservation of a Preb (C.P.L. VI. 414); also held the V Duma and Cylnaromanch with Ballintubber *c.* 1440

McGERAGHTY, MAGONIUS

V Teachbuyth = Taghboy (Elph), is said to have paid money to get the V on the death of Rory (or Roger) O'Mochlan qv, and to have been guilty of fornication and was deprived in 1463

McGERAGHTY (MacGEREACHTAYD), THADY

priest, says thay William O'Falluyn qv, V Athasscrach = Ahascragh (Elph), is guilty of perjury, simony and fornication and was excommunicated for assault on a clerk; if proved, Thady, though Provost, is to be prov to the V of Ahascragh 6 Sep 1442 (C.P.L. IX. 294–5)

MACGHAMRUGAN, NELLANUS

was prov V Templeport (Kilm) 23 Dec 1471 (A.H. I. 237)

McGHEE, GEORGE D

BA
d 1868 p; C Templeport (Kilm) 1870–74

MACGILLABUGI, CRISTINUS –1404

V Killaspicbrone (Elph) to 1404
    Died 1404

MACGILLABUGI, PHILLIP

priest, is prov to V Killaspicbrone (Elph) 17 Nov 1408 (C.P.L. VI. 143)

MACGILLACEARAN, MALACHY

V of Culdea = Ballinakill (Elph) is prov to V Drumduban = Ballysumaghan (Elph), whose Rector received certain tithes of the parishes of Culdea, Drumcolin, Kilmacalan, Thammacha & Eacanach, vac by the death of Paul O'Somochan qv, removing certain Augustinian Canons who live outside the Monastery, & others who detained the tithes over five years, 8 Jul 1444 (C.P.L. IX. 446)

McGILLACIARAN, JOHN

is prov to a Canonry of Ephin with Preb reserved 16 Apr 1429 (C.P.L. VIII. 119)

MacGILLACIARAN, MALACHY
is prov to the V Kilcola (Elph) and is disp as son of a priest, 9 Feb 1430 (C.P.L. VIII. 156). He is still V 1441 (ib. IX. 446)

McGILLAHILGE, EUGENE
V Killenumery (Ard) 1615

McGILLAKGOGI, PATRICK
is V Yniscayn (Kilm) *c.* 1415 (Cal. Reg. Mey, 356)

McGILLAMANE, TATHEUS
prov to V Killoronan (Kilronan), Ardagh Dio 28 May 1443 (A.H. I. 162; C.P.L. IX.332)

MacGILLANAGUSSAN, CHARLES
Canon of Elphin 1454 (C.P.L. X. 474)

MACGILLANEANI, EUGENE
co–V of Clonbroney (Ard) *c.* 1440; deposed

MACGILLANEANI, MAURICE
V Clonbroney (Ard) to 1440

MACGILLARNEAN, MAURICE
Clk is prov V of Granard (Ard) 3 May 1441 (C.P.L. IX. 198)

McGILLAROYD, JOHN
Preb of Figarth = Fuerty and Kyllamnatha (Elph) before 1475

McGILLARUAID (MACHGILLAMORGH), DERMIT
Canon of Elphin 1407; also in 1412 (C.P.L. VI. 118, 268) and in 1414 (VI. 422, 438), and in 1421 (VI. 170).

MACGILLARUAID, DERMIT –1442
is Preb of Fydartha = Fuerty and Kyllconnautha & V Killmacuagyn (Elph) of which he has not got possession, and is granted half the tithes of the Church of Furan ? = Oran, Dunymgara = Dunamon, Kyllbegnatha = Kilbegnet and Clayncummaisg = Kilmacumsy (Elph) which belonged to the Chapter Mensa, but had been alienated to others, Dec 1421 (C.P.L. VII. 170); there to 1442; poss same as above.

    Died 1442

McGILLARUAIR, DERMIT
held the V of Kyllmacuagyn = Kilmacoen (Elph) more than a year to 1417 without being ordained priest and voided it; same as above?

MacGILLARUAY, DONALD
Canon of Elphin 1465 (C.P.L. XII. 235)

McGILLARUAYTH, ANDREW
Canon of Ardagh 1423 (C.P.L. VII, 367)

MacGILLARUIAG, CHARLES
V Athlaig Managayn = Athleague (Elph) to 1461 is deprived for simony and dilapidation of the goods of the V (C.P.L. XII. 122)

MACGILLASULID, TATHEUS
prov to R St. Tachmurc de Cilltachmurc = Kiltoghart (Ard) 8 Mar 1470; part of corps attached to a Canonry vacant by the death of Cornelius Ofergayl qv (A.H. I. 164); also R St Patrick Kiltubrid (Ard) 8 Mar 1470 (ib. I 165).; also prov R Muntireolis (Ard) united to a Canonry vacant by death of Cornelius O'Feargayl Mar 1470; again prov 8 Mar 1472/73 (C.P.L. XIII. 344)

McGILLASULYE, EUGENE
V or C Muntireolis (Ard) 1615

McGILLAVANEAM (MACGILLANANAEIM), MAURICE
Archd of Ardagh 1407 (C.P.L. VI. 120 & Cal. Reg. Flem. No 57), he says "he exercises hospitality after the manner of his country & is much commended etc". (A.H. I. 174); prov to the R St Echi of Kilglass, Ardagh 29 Mar 1407 (A.H. I. 174). There is also a V who holds the Cure (C.P.L. VI. 120)

McGILLAVANEM, JOHN
prov. to the Deanery of Ardagh April 1418 (C.P.L. VII. 89, 97)

McGILLAVANEM, MAURICE
Canon of Ardagh 1395 (C.P.L. IV. 508)

MACGILLAYSSA, PHILIP
priest, R of Drumguyn =Drumgoon *alias* Macariambarr (Kilm) is deceased — and probably was dead before 1407, for in 1417 Luke Oqueogan, qv is said to have detained the R over ten years (no doubt 20 years), and is to be removed in 1427

McGILLEVANEM, JOHN –1431
seems to have been Dean of Ardagh till his death (same as John McGillavanem above?)
Died 1431

MACGILLEWYD, JOHN
V Kilcommick (Ard) before 1480

McGILLICHAIRAICH, MAURICE
is prov to the V Tibohine (Elph) 9 Feb 1407 (C.P.L. VI. 118)

McGLAUGHLIN, BASIL GORDON YOUNG 1910–1990
b. 1910; TCD Bp Forster, Robert King, Downes Div Pris BA (Resp) Div Test 1935 BD 1965

d 1936 p 1937 (Ossory); C New Ross w Rosbercon Old Ross and Whitechurch (Ferns) 1936–40; I Cloughjordan w Modreeny (Killaloe) 1940–44; R Stradbally (Killaloe) 1944–57; Chapl to Bp of Killaloe 1952–55; I Bourney U (Killaloe) 1957–62; R Drumcliffe (Ennis) w Kilnaboy (Killaloe) 1962–71; RD of U O'Mullod 1962–73; Preb of Inniscattery in Killaloe Cath 1963–67; Treas of Killaloe 1967–72; R Oughteragh Fenagh Kiltubride and Drumreilly (Ard) 1971–81; RD of Edgeworthstown 1978–81; Preb of Kilmacallan in Elphin Cath 1980–81; ret

s. of David Nathaniel McG, Prin Tartaraghan Sch Co Armagh

m. and had issue incl Nora bapt 14 May 1953

Died 1990

MACGMISSA, JOHN
res V Castleterra (Kilm) 1461/62

McGRAIDIN, PATRICK
"Dean of Clan Hugh" (Co. Longford) 1512 — perhaps Dean of Ardagh

MACGRANAIL, ROBERT –1463
R Muntireolis (Ard)–1463; is deceased
Died 1463

MACGRANAIL, RORY
was prov R Muntireolis (Ard) by the Pope as no lay patron had been found, but died at Apostolic See

MACGRANAILL, CORMAC
Canon of Ardagh 1461/62 (C.P.L. XI. 435)

McGRANAILL, DONALD

informs the Pope that John Offergail R Muntireolis (Ard) qv is a public fornicator, keeps a concubine, has committed perjury and homicide. If true, John to be deposed and Donald coll and dispensed as illegal, 17 Jul 1433 (C.P.L. VIII. 469)

MACGRANAILL, DONALD

Canon of Ardagh 1529 (Reg. Cromer)

McGRANAILL, THADY

Canon of Ardagh 1461 (Reg. Prene)

MACGRANAYLL, MAURICE

Canon of Mohill Monastery is prov to R Muntireolis (Ard) Mar 1489 (C.P.L. XIII. 170)

MACGRANAYLL, ROBERT

prov to R of the territory *sive plebanis de Mundtireolays* (Ard) vacated per deposition of Cornelius Ofeargail, 1458 (A.H. I, 183), though also Malachy Machwkuarg is said to be prov on death of Cornelius 1460

McGRANRUGAN, LUCAS

is Perpetual V Kylnanech ?= Kinawley (Kilm) 25 Oct 1426

MACGRAVAYLL, CORNELIUS

V Kiltoghart (Ard) is prov to the R Muntireolis (Ard) Mar 1481 (C.P.L. XIII. 167)

MacGRIABHED (McGRIFFITH), CORNELIUS

Canon of Elphin 1433; (C.P.L. VIII. 469)

†MACGWENEY (MACDUIBHNE), MATTHEW −1314

is Bp of the Breifni 1307–14, "a man of great account in his own country" (Ann Loch Ce, 503, Ann. Ult)

Died 1314

McGYLLARUAYD, DERMIT

was V Kilmacoen (Elph) to 1441 and is deceased (C.P.L. IX. 263, 285); same as above?

McGYLLARUAYD, DONALD

is prov to V Kilmacoen (Elph) 1441 (C.P.L. IX. 285)

MacGYLLARUAYD, DONALD
V Fyada = Fuerty (Elph) is allowed to have a portable altar, 4 Jan 1464/65 (C.P.L. XII. 423)

MacHABAND, MAGONIUS
V of Killahayn = Killyon (Elph), guilty of fornication, simony etc, is deprived 1460

MACHABRECHIM, CRISTIN
Canon of Elphin 1413

MACHABRECHIM, ECGILBERTUS
Canon of Elphin 1413 (C.P.L. VI. 392)

MACHABRICHYN, GILBERT
priest, unlawfully detained the Deanery of Elphin and was deposed 1390 (C.P.L. IV. 417)

MacHABRIUCHIM, CORNELIUS
is now prov to V Kilmacallen (Elph) and disp as illegal 20 Apr 1452 (C.P.L. X. 575)

MACHABRUHIM, JOHN
V Kilmacallen (Elph) *c.* 1449, is deceased

MACHABRUICHIM, CORNELIUS
priest, was coll V Kilmacallen (Elph) by Bp Cornelius *c.* 1449, but without any cause

MACHABRUYM, DERMIT
was coll to V Kilmacallen (Elph) by Bp Cornelius *c.* 1450

MACHACLERY, CORNELIUS
clk, informs the Pope that Imarus Macaclerid qv has been guilty of fornication, perjury and other crimes. He is to be deprived and Cornelius is prov to the V Taunagh (Elph) 27 Mar 1465 (C.P.L. XII. 444,445)

MACHECHEAN, RORY
prov. to R Cloone (Ard) to 1417; was not ordained priest; now prov to it 4 Apr 1418 (A.H. I); he was dispensed illegitimate son of a priest (C.P.L. VII. 80)

MACHEDIAN, CHARLES
Preb of Kilgoghlin (Elph) to 1463

MACHERLEGINN, DERMIT

clk of Elphin. The Pope's letters providing him to the V Drumcliffe (Elph) to hold good whether the V was void by the death of John O'Connel, qv or his neglect to be ordained priest within a year, 2 Jan 1403 (C.P.L. V. 593)

MACHEYDAN, ANDREW

V Cluaine (Cloone) (Ard); is prov to it 29 Dec 1406 (A.H. I. 174; C.P.L. VI. 86)

MACHEYDAN, GELASIUS

held R Cloone (Ard) 1406 without a title

MACHEYDAN, NICHOLAS   –1406

R Cloone (Ard) to 1406
   Died 1406

MACHGILLACIARAN, JOHN

V Kyltibride, Ardagh 16 Feb 1425 (C.P.L. VII. 398); is prov to V Clondevaddock (Raph) 11 May 1428 (A.H. I. 262); he is prov a Canon of Elphin with Preb reserved and a benefice in Ardagh; he is to resign V Kiltubrid (Ard) on obtaining it 7 Mar 1429 (C.P.L. VIII, 119)

MACHGILLAYCHNY, WILLIAM

V of Termonchelyn ? = Kilmacallen (Elph) 1404, is deceased

MACHIAN, NICHOLAS

R of Monter Eoylays = Muntireolis (Ard); obtained and held this without disposition before 8 Dec 1397 (C.P.L. V. 105); had voided it by obtaining V St Hilary Clongish (Ard) to 1397 and holding them for a long time

MACHIARNAN, JOHN

V Cileb ? = Kedy (Kilm) to 1475

MACHIDIAN, CRISTINUS   –c. 1463

Preb of Kilgoghlin (Elph) before 1463
   Died c. 1463

MACHILRUAYS, FIRGALL

res V Kiltubrid (Ard) 1413 to become Augustinian Prior of St Mary Mayhill (Mohill? or Moville?) (C.P.L.VI. 392)

MACHRANAN, LEWIS
Canon of Elphin of the race of Dukes, disp as illeg. Has informed the Pope that Reginald Odubunra, qv, V of the Union of Cluaynffynlacha = Clonfinlough and Cluaynagalleach (Elph) has committed perjury, laid violent hands on ecclesiastics, and being excommunicated, celebrated Mass. If true, Lewis is to be coll to V & R Clonfinlough (Elph). Lewis is disp to hold his Canonry with V, July 1428 (C.P.L. VIII. 15, 59)

†McHUGH (McAEDHA), MALACHY
a Canon of Elphin was prov to the See of Elphin by the Pope 10 Jul 1310 (C.P.L. II. 70), and was confirmed by the King on 7 Dec (P.R.). He was translated to Tuam in 1313

MACHWKUARG (or MACHWLRUAYG, MacGILROY), MALACHY
dispensed as son of a priest is prov to R Muntireolis (Ard) on the death of Cornelius Ofergail Jul 1460– the Cure of which has been exercised always by Perpetual Vicars (A.H. I. 163 and C.P.L. XI. 410). The Bp had made it a Preb before 6 Nov 1461 (Cal. Reg. Flem. 363)

MACHYMOGLEY, CORMAC
prov V Killenumery (Ard) 5 Jul 1475 (C.P.L. XIII, 417)

†MACIDHNEOIL, CONGHALACH –1250
is Bp of Kilmore 1231 (Ann Loch Ce); res 1250
    Died 1250 (ib. 395)

MACILEND, DERMIT
held V Ogulla (Elph) without a title and is deposed 1457

McINCEBRUOYD, DERMOT
is coll V Kiltubrid (Ard) by the Primate Aug to Nov 1410 (Cal. Reg. Flem. No. 144)

MACINFIRMANAIG, MAURUS
priest, is prov to a Canonry of Elphin with the tithes of Lisonuffy, Kiltrustan & Bumlin attached (ie. Preb of Kilgoghlin), held by one of the Canons, 29 Mar 1455/56 (C.P.L. XI. 34)

MACKALDEFELD, AULANUS
prov to V Kiltrenan ?= Kiltoghart (Ard) 1477/78 (C.P.L. XIII, 65)

McKANAYLL, CORNELIUS
V Killtamurgh = Kiltoghart (Ard); litigated with Fergal McGillafield– judges agreed

that Fergal should be paid an annual sum, and the Bishop had separated the church of Kiltrenan from it and prov Aulanus Makaldefeld to it 8 Jan 1477/78. (C.P.L. XIII. 65)

McKANE, HERBERT JOHN 1899/1900–1956

b. 1899 or 1900; TCD BA 1926 Downes Pri (1) and Div Comp Pri Wallace Exhib Div Test 1927 MA 1929

d 1927 p 1928 (Kilmore); C Kinawley (Kilm) 1927–30; C Oldcastle w Loughcrew (Meath) 1930–33; R Drumconrath w Syddan (Meath) 1933–56

> **m.** 24 Sep 1935 Mrs Lilian Morgan, widow
>
> **Died** 29 Aug 1956 aged 56

MACKANKAID, MAGONIUS

held Annaduff (Ard) to 1477/78 without good title 7–12 years and was not ordained priest in a year and is deposed

MACKEDYGAYN (McGEOGHEGAN), MAURICE

V of Baslick (Elph) prov 5 Jan 1413 and is allowed to hold it with V Ballintubber; is prov to a Canonry of Elphin with reservation of a Preb 6 Mar 1414 (C.P.L. VI. 399)

McKEE, JAMES

C Lavey (Kilm) 1845–47

McKENNA, WILLIAM JOHN 1911–1966

b. 8 Dec 1911 Belfast; TCD BA & Div Test (2) 1937 MA 1943

d 1937 p 1938 (Down); C Kilmegan w Maghera (Drom) 1937–40; V Ilam (Lich) 1940–41; R Newcastle w Rathronan and Killeedy (Lim) 1941–44; R Gowna and Columbkill (Ard) 1944–45; C-in-c Sallaghy (Clogh) 1945–50; Publ Pr Dio Chelmsford 1950–52; Org Sec Greater London Area Miss to Seamen 1950–52; Org Sec Miss to Seamen Ireland 1952–54; R Castlemagner w Kanturk U (Cloyne) 1953–55; R Dungarvan (Lism) 1955–65; ret

> **s.** of Robert and Ellen (née Gray) of Belfast
>
> **m.** 27 Dec 1939 Hyde Cheshire Lilian Patricia MB ChB **dau.** of William Henry and Lilian Parry Hyde. Issue Rev Dermot William **b.** 10 Nov 1941 BA 1963 MA 1966 d 1964 p 1965 (Ossory) R Killeshin (Leigh) 1966–84 ret; 2. Rev Terence John **b.** 22 Jan 1946 BA 1966 MA 1969 BD (Oxon) d 1968 p 1969 (Cork) R Abbeystrewery (Ross) 1972–74 res
>
> **Died** 5 Nov 1966

MacKERNAN (McGUYNUGAN, MACHYERNAN), EDMUND –*c.* 1430

V Killeshandra (Kilm) to *c.* 1430; was coll by the Primate 6 Dec 1427 (Cal. Reg. Swayne 33, 520)

> **Died** *c.* 1430

MacKERNAN (MAGTHIGERNAYN), NEMEAS   –c. 1411

V Killeshandra (Kilm) to 1411 is deceased

Died c. 1411

McKEW, EDWARD JOSEPH 1878–1974

b. 1878; ed Kilkenny Coll; TCD BA 1915 MA 1943; before ordination was teaching at Darley NS Co Cavan

d 1916 p 1917 (Clogher); C-in-c Mullaghdun (Clogh) 1916–18; R Mullaghdun (Clogh) 1918–22; C-in-c Maguiresbridge (Clogh) 1922–27; R Lisnadill (Arm) 1927–29; R Tempo (Clogh) 1929–38; C-in-c Derrybrusk (Clogh) 1938–41; R Ardagh and Kilglass (Ard) 1941–43; R Sallaghy (Clogh) 1943–45; C-in-c Derrybrusk 1945–50; C-in-c Lack (Clogh) 1951–52; ret; Gen Lic Clogher 1954–74.

s. of John, Schoolmaster of Valentia Island Co Kerry and native of the Aran Islands by Anne (née Wharton) and **bro.** of Rev James, R Trillick (Clogh) 1951–53, and Rev Joseph Henry

m. 4 Aug 1908 Cootehill Co Cavan Margaret (**died** 2 May 1950) **dau.** of Owen Donohoe of Cootehill. Issue 1. Rev John Porter **b.** 1909 TCD BA 1936 MA 1961 latterly R Dingle (A & A) 1961–72 **m.** 22 Apr 1972 Kathleen Margaret **dau.** of William Martin Blagden; he **died** 5 Dec 1989 at Tralee; 2. Nina May **m.** 31 Jan 1946 Derrybrusk Rev Arthur Hugh Thompson (**died** 4 Nov 1993) later Archd of Elphin and Ardagh qv, and had issue (i) Norah Margaret **b.** 24 Jul 1947 **m.** JS McKinstry (ii) James

Died 18 Feb 1974 Sligo **bur.** Derrybrusk Co Fermanagh

MACKEYTHAN, JOHN

coll to V Cloone (Ard) 1416 but paid money for it and res. it to Pope, but was prov. again 1 Dec 1417 (A.H. I. 177; C.P.L. VII. 40); was coll V Cloone (Ard) 22 Jun 1416 by the Primate (Cal. Reg. Flem. 256)

MACKHEAGAYN, DONALD

V of Kyllachan = Killukin (Elph) dilapidated its goods, is a fornicator etc, and is deposed, 1443

MACKIERNAN, AUGUSTINE   –c. 1398

V Killeshandra (Kilm) to 1398; is deceased

Died c. 1398

MACKIERNAN, JOHN

clk, is prov V Kiliterna = Killeshandra (Kilm) *alias* Teallacuntuga, vacant by the death of Augustine Mackiernan qv, the Prior of Drumlane unlawfully detaining it, 4 Aug 1398 (C.P.L. V. 107)

McKINNEY, ALEXANDER 1856/57–1902

b. 1856 or 1857; ent TCD 1876; St John's Coll Camb BA 1887 MA 1891

d 1879 (Ard) p 1880; C Kiltoghart and Drumshambo (Ard) 1879–81; PC Ballykeen U (Kild) 1881–83; C St Pauk Old Ford (Lon) 1883–84; C St Andrew the Less (Ely) 1884–86; V Stanstead Mountfitchet (Chelmsf — then St A) 1886–91; V St Mary Magdalene (Liv) 1891–1902

    Died Mar 1902 aged 45

McKNIGHT, JOHN 1858/59–1920

b. 1858 or 1859

St Bees Coll Durham

d 1887 (Kilmore) p 1888 (Clogher for Kilmore); C Kinawley (Kilm) 1887–88; R Swanlinbar (Kilm) 1888–94; R Rossinver (Kilm) 1894–1902; R Killybegs (Raph) 1902–05; R Kinawley (Kilm) 1905–20

    2nd **s.** of Robert Warren of Arva Co Cavan

    m. 26 Aug 1890 St Peter's Ch Dublin Caroline (**died** 7 Feb 1935 Bangor Co Down) yst **dau.** of Christopher Buchanan of Blacklion Co Cavan

    Died 14 Apr 1920 Kinawley Rectory aged 61

McKORGLESSE, THADEUS

Archd of Elphin to 1591 (Ms E 3. 14)

MacKYLRUYD (MacGILLARUAYD), DONALD

Canon of Elphin 1445/46 (C.P.L. IX. 506, 555), and in 1455 (ib. X. 457), & 1457 (ib. XI. 315)

MACLACLAYND, CORNELIUS

Canon of Kilmore 1459 (C.P.L. XII. 83)

McLAUGHLIN, JOHN 1726/27–1783

b. 1726 or 1727 Co Derry; ed by Mr Lamy; ent TCD as Siz 16 Jun 1747 aged 20 Sch 1749 BA 1755 MA 1776

Archd of Elphin 1761–69; Preb of Terebrine (Elph) 1769–77; Preb of Kilgoghlin (Elph) 1777–83

    s. of James

    m. and had issue incl a **s.** Rev William, R Tessaragh (Elph) qv

    Died Jan 1783 **bur.** St Peter Dublin

McLAUGHLIN, WILLIAM 1757/58–

b. 1757 or 1758 Roscommon; ed by his father; ent TCD 2 Jul 1774 aged 16 BA 1789 LLB 1785 d 1779 p 1 May 1781; R Taghboy Disert and Tessaragh (Elph) 1783–;

s. of Rev John, Preb of Terebrine (Elph) qv

m. Sarah (**died** May 1839 at Tullyvallen Glebe) **dau.** of Thomas Wills of Willsgrove. Issue Jane Bowen (**died** 11 Mar 1859) **m.** 1822 Rev William Maclean and had issue (i) Sarah Wills (**died unm.** Jul 1901 aged 77) **b.** *c.* 1824 (ii) Emily Frances **m.** Jan 1858 Rev George Tottenham (iii) Anna (**died** 28 Mar 1919) **b.** *c.* 1833 (iv) Elizabeth Thackeray (**died unm.** Jul 1907)

McLEES, WILLIAM HENRY

See **McALEESE, WILLIAM HENRY**

McLOUGHLIN, CORNELIUS, Sen. –*c.* 1449

is V Killasnett (Kilm) in 1441 (Cal. Reg. Prene. 224)

is deceased in 1449

McLOUGHLIN, CORNELIUS, Jun

held the V Killasnett (Kilm) 1449–51 is deposed

MACMAELMARTAYN, JOHN

Canon of Kilmore in 1460 (C.P.L. XII. 67,68), 1462 (ib. 140), 1464 (ib. 200), 1466 (ib. 511)

†McMAHON, PATRICK –*c.* 1572

seems to have succeeded Richard O'Ferrall as Bp of Ardagh in 1553. He had been a suffragan to the Primate. On 2 Apr 1545, O'Ferrall having possession of the Bpric of Ardagh, the King signified his pleasure to the Lord Deputy and Council that Patrick McMahon should have a small Irish Bpric. (C.S.P.I.. 1st Series, I. 71). He was deprived by the Pope for various offences in 1568 (Brady's Ep. Succ. I. 290), but very probably because he accepted the Royal Supremacy

Died *c.* 1572

MacMAILIN, MAGRATH

V Kilmactranny (Elph) *c.* 1236 (A.F.M.)

MACMEOL, WILLIAM

V Castleterra (Kilm) to 1461 is deposed

MACMINKERCHAID, BERNARD

V Kildacamoge (Kilcommick?) (Ard) 1411; lately prov V Kildacamage (Ard) (C.P.L. VI. 262)

MACMIRCHEARTAID, FLORENCE
is prov to V Streete (Ard) 16 Feb 1397 (A.H. I. 173)

MACMOCLAID, THOMAS   –1426
V Killenemery (Ard) to 1426

MACMOGLAY (McMOGLEY), BERNARD
V Killenumery (Ard) 17 Nov 1469 according to C.P.L. XII. 750; prov to V Killenumery (Ard) 15 Dec 1470 according to A.H. I. 164

MACMOGLAY, MATTHEW
V Killenumery (Ard) 1427–35; held V without dispensation, was coll. by the Ordinary, and was removed in 1435

McMORRISSY (MACIMURGYSSA), THOMAS
held the V Teachbucheyn = Tibohine (Elph) a year or more to 1406 without being ordained priest and is deprived

MACMUIRCERTAIG, EUGENE
V Granard (Ard) to 1455

MACMUIRCHEARTAIGH, THOMAS
R of St Patrick Crocarcha (? = Dromahaire) C.P.L. XII. 659); prov to the Deanery of Ardagh 10 Mar 1468/9 (A.H. I. 181); dispensed as son of a priest. Probably same as Thomas Macmurcertaych below

MACMULMARTAIN, JOHN   –c. 1407
V Ballintemple (Kilm) to 1393; coll by Bp John O'Reilly, but doubts the validity of his collation and is now prov to it and dispensed to hold it for life, 12 Feb 1401 (C.P.L. V. 447). John had been blind for some time. He is dead in 1407
  Died *c.* 1407

McMULMARTYN, NEMEAS
is Preb of Macharinebair and V Kilmore & R Drumgoon (Kilm) 1366 (Lawlor's Cal. Reg. Swet. 75, 322)

MACMURAYN, CORNELIUS
held V Kilmacallen (Elph) six to seven years without title 1473–80

MACMURC(ACC)N, THOMAS
holds R Tashinny (Ard) to 1406

MACMURCEARTAYD, EUGENE
is prov to V Granard (Ard) 1438 if true that Matthew McAeda qv above absented himself therefrom, and is deposed as son of a priest; whether so void or void by the non–promotion to Holy Order of Priest by William Yfergail qv below, 8 May (C.P.L. IX. 14)

MACMURCERTAYCH, THOMAS
had detained R Munterangaile (Ard) over 10 years but had no right to do so as his Papal prov did not state its true value. Thomas is now dead. Gerald Ofergail, his predecessor had agreed to give Thomas half the fruits and is now absolved and re–prov. He holds the Deanery of Ardagh 3 Feb 1444/45 (C.P.L. IX. 467)

MACMURCHEARTAICH, RORICUS
prov V Killacythe (Killashee) (Ard) 1432 (A.H. I. 160)
Clk, Ardagh, prov to sinecure Ch of St Patrick's, Cnoracha (in Clonbroney) (Ard) vac. and lapsed 1440, 5 Nov (C.P.L. IX. 96). Deposed in 1444 (ib. 429)

MACMURCHERCAID, BERNARD
Clk. of Dio Ardagh dispensed illegal who had studied Canon Law at Oxford etc., was lately prov V St Frign of Kildacamog (Kilcommick), Ardagh 1411, and was 24 Dec 1411 also prov R Multyfarnan (Meath) (A.H. I. 84)

MacMURERCHAID, PATRICK
V of Killunden ? = Killukin (Elph) to 1410, became a monk and as Prior of St Mary's, Dorean, Elphin, was granted the V *in commendam*, void because he became a monk, 8 Jun 1410 (C.P.L. VI. 204)

MACMURKARTAICH, FERGALLUS   –c. 1431
V of St Mary of Streete (Ard) to 1431 and is deceased
   Died c. 1431

MACMURKERTAID, THOMAS
V Kilglass (Ard); res. 24 Dec 1411 (A.H. I. 176)

McMURRAY, GEORGE   –c. 1952
TCD BA (Resp) 1880 MA 1883

d 1878 p 1879 (Kilmore); C Killukin (Elph) 1878–80; C Urney (Kilm) 1880–83; R Killinagh (Kilm) 1883–85; C Ararat Victoria Australia (Dio Ballarat) 1885–88; V St Paul E Ballarat (Ballarat) 1888–92; Canon of Christ Ch Cath Ballarat 1888–92; V St

Mary Parnell Auckland NZ 1892–1919; Canon of Auckland 1901–21; Archd of Auckland 1915–; V Gen Auckland 1930–; still there 1941

>**m.** 8 Sep 1880 St Paul Glenageary Dublin Ella Octavia **dau.** of Thomas E Langley
>**Died** *c.* 1952

McMURTAGH, EUGENE

appears Canon of Ardagh 1454 (C.P.L. X. 673, 675)

McMURTAGH (MACMURCERTHEID), EUGENIUS

had been installed V of Mismor alias Lochagana (Ard) before 1457, a small church or parish on an island in Loch Gowna, when Bp Cormac and the Chapter of Ardagh separated the V from the Abbey of Granard, but after a while he abandoned it — probably same as above

McMURTAGH, FLORENCE

Canon of Ardagh 1397 (C.P.L. V. 80)

McMURTAGH (MACMURQUIRTID), HENRY

Archd of Ardagh 1346; prov. 2 Oct (C.P.P. I. 120)

McMURTAGH (McMURHEARTAICH), THOMAS,

is prov to a Canonry of Elphin with reservation of a Preb 16 Feb 1400 (C.P.L. V. 344); — probably same as below

McMURTAGH, THOMAS

prov. a Canon of Ardagh with reservation of a Preb 1400 (C.P.L. V. 340); is a Canon 1410 (ib. VI. 236) and 1442 (ib. XI. 269)

MACNAGLAID, CHARLES   –*c.* 1421

V Killery (Ard) before 1421

>**Died** *c.* 1421

McNALLY, FREDERICK GEORGE

TCD BA & Div Test 1868 MA 1883; T C L LMus 1876

d 1868 p 1868 (Kilmore); C Drumlease (Kilm) 1868–73; PC Quivvy (Kilm) 1873–77; C Ulverston (Carl) 1877–93; V Sawrey (Carl) 1895–still there 1926

>**m.** 2 Apr 1872 Jane Bell Thompson **dau.** of Joshua Kell, JP of Dromahair Co Leitrim

McNEILL, ROBERT –1401
R & V of Druymrhealach *alias* Ben–Calluachain = Drumreilly (Kilm) to 1401
> Died 1401

MACNOGLAIDH, ENIAS –*c.* 1421
V Killery (Ard) to 1421
> Died *c.* 1421

MACNOGLAIDH, FLORENCE
is prov to V Killorid (Killery) (Ard) – same as above? 24 Feb 1431/32; this prov. was made to him because the V may have been vacant, not by the death of Enias Macnoglaidh, but by the death of Charles Macnaglaid, qv (C.P.L. VIII. 206)

MACONAIND, CORMAC
clk, without mention of his illegitimacy, got made a clk and was disp to act as such, is prov R Macharynyuair = Drumgoon (Kilm) vacant by the death of Philip Macgillayssa, qv, 13 Feb 1432/33 (C.P.L. VIII. 428)

MACONAYND, CORMAC
is prov to the R Disert Finchill (Kilm) 6 Mar 1433 (A.H. I. 234)

MACONCAGAID, DERMIT
priest, had been V of Kyllglass = Kilglass (Elph) vacated on the death of John Maceolich, qv, but doubted whether it was void and is now prov to it, 19 Dec 1455 (C.P.L. XI. 247)

MACORMAIC, ODO
a Cistercian Monk of the Abbey of Boyle, who had been disp to be ordained as being the son of a priest religious, is now disp to obtain benefices, Feb 1402, & was prov to the R of Baslig = Baslick and Cloonconcubhair, which belongs to the Chapter of Elphin, & is void because Maurice (Murtogh) O'Flanagan qv, Archd of Elphin, held it being a cure, a year or more without disp. Feb 1402 (C.P.L. V. 495)

McQUADE, WILLIAM 1909–2001
b. 21 Nov 1909 Drumagoland Virginia Co Cavan; ed Billis Sch and Cavan Tech Coll; Brotherhood of St Paul, Barton Yorks St Paul's Theol Coll Richmond Yorks Dipl Theol

d 1949 (Connor) on Letters Dimissory from Bp of Fredericton p 21 Dec 1950; R Hardwicke NB Canada (Fredericton) 1949–51; C-in-c Clongish and Clooncumber (Ard) 1951–52; R Glencolumbkille (Raph) 1952–54; R Preban and Moyne (Ferns) 1954–55; R Dingle (A & A) 1955–57; R Ballinaclough Templederry and Aghnameadle (Killaloe) 1957–58; I Bewcastle (Carl) 1957–66; V All Hallows Wealsgate (Carl) 1966–76; ret Perm to Off Dios Kilmore Elphin and Ardagh

> **s.** of William James of Virginia (**s.** of William of Virginia) by Mary **dau.** of James

and Mary Wilson

m. 8 Jan 1952 Newtwonforbes Co Longford Isabel Florence **dau.** of Albert and Elizabeth Ann Smyth of Carramore Boyle Co Roscommon. Issue Paul Richard **b.** 3 Dec 1952 **m.** 4 Oct 1980 at Desford Leicestershire

Died 7 Apr 2001

McQUAINE, DAVID

C Annagh (Kilm) in 1673

MACQUEDIAN, MAURICE

V of Ballintubber (Elph), held also the V of Dukybronan = Killeroran or Kilronan (Elph) with Ballintubber for three years *c.* 1420; R Raharany (Tuam) 1428; Canon of Elphin

McQUOID, SAMUEL LINDSAY

ed Edgehill Theol Coll Belfast 1953

d 2 May 1965 (Kilmore) p 20 Mar 1966 (Kilmore); BC Billis Ballyjamesduff and Munterconnaught (Kilm) 1965–67

m. and had issue a **s.**

MACRECHLAIN, MORIANUS –1405

V Kyllmurchayn (Elph) to 1405

Died 1405

MACRONYND, CORMAC

is prov to V Kilmore (Kilm) 3 Apr 1398 (C.P.L. V. 109). As Cormac Macconand, V of St. Felim of Kilmore, he is deceased in 1411. In 1401, however, Nicholas O'Sheridan qv claimed to have been coll by the Abp of Armagh and the Pope orders him to be put in possession, 9 Mar 1398 (ib. V. 399)

MACRONYND, NICHOLAS –1398

V Kilmore (Kilm) to 1398; has vacated V by death

Died 1398

MACRYLRUIAG, ANDREW

had got V St. Frenan's Kilrenan = Kilronan (Ard); dispensed as illegal and resigned it; is now dispensed to hold other benefices 5 Oct 1398 (C.P.L. V. 95)

†MACSHERRY (MAC SEIRIGH), MACRATH –1230

Archd, elected, confirmed and consec Bp of Ardagh by Abp of Tuam and held part of the Diocese c 1225. Also known as "Bp of Conmaicne" (Ann. Loch Ce 305). Joseph

McTeichedhain contested his right

Died 1230

†McTEICHEDHAIN (or McEOIGH or MAGODAIG), BRENDAIN   –1255
Bp of Ardagh 1238–55; In 1245 enquiry was "to be made of the evil deeds of Brendain who claimed to be Bp of Ardagh (C.P.L. I 216) and on 15 Oct 1252 we are told that the Bp of Ardagh is allowed to resign "since the people there are so stiffnecked that he cannot preside over them with profit" (C.P.L. I. 279; Theiner, 56). It does not appear whether he did resign

Died 1255 bur. in an abbey at Derg

†McTEICHEDHAIN (or McEOIGH), JOSEPH   –1230
Archd, elected Bp of Ardagh *c.* 1225 and consec by Abp Donatus of Armagh and evidently held part of the diocese (Theiner, 30) against his predecessors M... and Macrath Macsherry. He seized the entire diocese on Macsherry's death, but his election was declared invalid by the Pope. Is called Bp of Conmaicne (Ann Loch Ce 305)

Died 1230

McTIERNAN, ADAM
is "Dean of Drumleachan" 1366 (Cal. Reg. Swet. 75). It is doubtful if this was the Deanery of Kilmore, but the "Dean of Kilmore" appears in the same entry

McWALTER, ROBERT
d 1870 p; C Seagoe (Drom) 1870–72; R Calry (Elph) 1872–76

McWHIDD, ALEXANDER
C Knockbride (Kilm) *c.* 1630

McWILLIAMS, WILLIAM
app C Killargue (Kilm) 1 May 1861

MACYBREYM, CORNELIUS
V Kilmacallen (Elph) 1473, is deceased

†M...
Prior of Inismor; consec Bp of Ardagh *c.* 1224 by Abp of Tuam; Joseph contested his right. He died soon after

MAABREACHANNIN, MACCRAITH
V Cuilleada ? = Kilcola (Elph) to 1409 is dep because he held V Kilmacallan (Elph) with it without dispensation

MADDEN, JOHN 1690–1751

b. 1690 Chester; ed by Mr Hartlip, Dublin; ent TCD 15 Sep 1702 BA 1707 FTCD and MA 1710 BD and DD 1723

d p 1712; PC Drumcondra (Dub) 1716–20; V St Ann (Dub) 1721–51; R Tara (Meath) 1722–35; Dean of Kilmore and V Kilmore & Ballintemple (Kilm) 1734–51; V Clonmeen Roskeen & Kilcooney (Cloyne) 1748–51

2nd **s.** of Dr John

m. 1724 Deborah (**died** Mar 1770) **dau.** of Daniel Cooke by Lucretia **dau.** of Alderman Robert Arundel. Issue 1. Rev John (**died** 1767 **bur.** Dungiven) **b.** 1725 Dublin TCD BA 1745 DD d 1746 p 1747 may have been C in Kilmore Dio R Bovevagh (Derry) 1751–67 **m.** 13 Jul 1746 St Peter Dublin Elizabeth **dau.** of Very Rev John Eccles, Dean of Waterford and had issue (i) John Eccles (ii) William (iii) Samuel (iv) Daniel (v) George Berkeley and 7 **daus.** incl Lucretia **m.** Rev Ninian Steele; 2. Daniel **died** young; 3. Rev Samuel (**died** 22 Sep 1800) **b.** Aug 1728 TCD BA 1752 d 31 Dec 1752 p C Rathdowney (Oss) 1757 C Gowran and Blanchvilstown (Leigh) 1760–62 Preb of Blackrath and PC St John & St Mary Kilkenny (Oss) 1764–70 V Offerlane (Oss) 1770 V Fiddown and R Bewley (Lism) 1781–1800 Chanc of St Canice's Cath Kilkenny 1774–85 V Gen Ossory 1780–1800 R Kells (Oss) 1785–1800 **m.** 21 Sep 1756 Cassandra **dau.** of Michael Travers of Co Cork and had issue (i) Rev Travers, R Kilmacow (Waterf) (ii) Lt John (iii) Major Samuel (iv) Major Charles (v) Rev Michael Dodgson, Chanc of Ossory and 6 **daus.** incl (i) Margaret **m.** Rev Arthur Palmer, Chanc of Ossory and (ii) Deborah **m.** (1) Rev John Cooksey **m.** (2) Rev Robert Hawkshaw and (iii) Elizabeth **m.** Rev William Glascott; 4. Thomas **died** young; 5. Wyndham; 6. Arundel Wyndham; 7. Lt Gen Edward; Dublin Lists also mention Adam, Nicholas and Bolton; 2 **daus.** incl Margaret

Died 7 Nov 1751 **bur.** St Ann's Dublin

PUBLICATIONS
A Fast Sermon, etc. 4to, Dublin 1741
A Fast Sermon, 4to, Dublin, 1750

MAELMACTAIN, JOHN

R Kedy *alias* de Nurni (Kilm) to 1484; accused of simony

MAGABRAIM, CORMAC

prov V Templeport (Kilm) 3 Oct 1461 (A.H. I. 236, 237); disp as son of a Canon; became Prior of Drumlane

MAGAEDAGAN, DERMIT

clk of Elphin Dio (lately prov to Canonries of Killala and Achonry), is now prov R of Drumcliffe (Elph) vacant by Thomas O'Tarpa's death, 4 Oct 1428 (C.P.L. VIII. 5). He was confirmed in the Rectory and in his Canonries of Achonry and Elphin 5 Mar 1430/31 (ib. VIII. 330)

MAGAMRAN, JOHN
Canon of Kilmore 1455 (C.P.L. X. 721)

MAGAMRUGAN, CRISTINUS
V Templeport (Kilm) 1455 is deposed for simony, perjury etc.

MAGAMRUGHAN, CORMAC
Augustinian Canon of St. Mary's, Kells disp as the son of a priest; an Augustinian Canon is prov to the R Teallacheach and Mageangady (Kilm) wont to be served by such canons, removing the Abbot and Convent, vacant by death of Ronaldus Magamrughan, qv, 10 Apr 1430 (C.P.L. VIII. 157)

MAGAMRUGHAN, RONALDUS
R Teallacheach and Mageangady (Kilm) is deceased 1430

†MAGAURAN
Augustinian Prior of Drumlane; prov to the See of Ardagh on 6 Nov 1444, and got a faculty to be consec 13 Dec 1444 (C.P.L. IX. 436, 466: A.H. I. 185). According to the Annals, when he came from Rome the *Queir* and "the yong officiall obeyed him having the Pope's authoritie from Rome" (Annals Misc. I Arch. Soc. I. 210). He was Bp of Ardagh in 1451 when he is said to have resisted the Primate's Metropolitical Visitation (Cal. Reg. Mey, 240) and in 1456 when he promised the Primate a good horse in virtue of his oath (Cal. Reg. Prene. 471), and is still Bp. 1460, 1461, 1462 (Cal. Reg. Swayne, 162; Cal. Reg. Prene. 354, 363). He seems to have resigned in 1467 or earlier.

MAGAURAN, CORMAC or CORNELIUS
Canon of Ardagh 1461/62 (C.P.L. XI. 435 and XII. 142); still Canon 1467 (C.P.L. XII. 565)

†MAGAURAN, CORMAC
Prior of Drumlane, was prov to the See of Kilmore on 4 Nov 1476 (A.H. I. 257). He contested the right to the See with Thomas MacBrady, qv, but on trial of the case before the Abp of Armagh and the Bps of Meath and Ardagh, the See was adjudged to Thomas, and he was deprived. An arrangement however, was probably made dividing the Diocese between them. Nevertheless he seems after Thomas's death to have claimed it (A.H. I. 257, 258). He was again prov to the See 4 Nov 1483 (C.P.L. XIII. 54).

He was the son of a bishop

MAGAURAN (MAGAMRUGHAY), RORY
was prov V of Cynallnalayncha = Killinagh (Kilm) and obliged himself for the F.F., 15 May 1430 (A.H. I. 233); again prov 28 Mar 1433 (ib. 234)

MAGAWADARE (MAGUIRE?), GILBERT

informs the Pope that John O'Goband, qv, V of Disert Finchill (Kilm) dilapidates the V and committed simony and perjury; if true, Gilbert who is disp as illegitimate and of a race of dukes, is prov V, 27 Jan 1449/50 (C.P.L. X. 450)

MAGEAGAN, DERMIT

Canon of Elphin 1444 (C.P.L. IX. 417)

MAGEHADGAYN, NEMEAS

is prov to V Kiltoghart (Ard) 8 May 1506; (A.H. I. 171)

MAGELLAHULY, FFERGALUS

was prov to V Killoachmuirta = Cill–Tathchomharc, now Kiltoghart (Ard) Dec 1442 (A.H. I. 163)

MAGELLAHULY, JOHN

V Kiltoghart (Ard); was deposed 1442

MAGELLAKULY, FERGALLUS

is prov to R Kiltoghart (Ard) 1461

MAGELLASULIG, JOHN

V Kiltoghart (Ard) to 1461; is reported to the Pope as having committed simony, fornication and perjury and keeping a concubine, and is deposed 27 Oct 1461 (C.P.L. XII.142.).

MAGENNIS (MAGAMGUSSA), DONATUS

is prov to *Plebs Culbridin, alias* Castleterra (Kilm) 17 Dec 1436 (A.H. I. 234)

MAGENNIS (MAGANGASSA), JOHN

after the Parish of Castleterra (Kilm) having lapsed to the Pope on account of John Macbrady qv, V Castletarra not being ordained priest, had held it in 1428 over eight years under the pretext of having ben coll by the Bp, and is now deprived

MAGENNIS, WILLLIAM 1770–1825

b. 1770 Co Down; ed by Dr Norris, Drogheda; ent TCD 30 Jun 1786 aged 16 BA 1790 MA 1808

C Donaghcloney (Drom) 1791; Dean of Kilmore and V Kilmore & Ballintemple and R Kedue (Kilm) 1801–25; V Drumlane (Kilm) 1810–21; V Kildallon (Kilm) 1821–25

yr **s.** of Richard, *armiger*, of Waringstown Co Down by his 2nd wife Elizabeth **dau.**

of Capt William Berkeley, **bro.** of George Berkeley, Bp of Cloyne 1732–53
Died 22 Jan 1825 aged 54 **bur.** Kilmore

MAGEREACHAYD, THADY

is prov to Preb Fygartha and Killconnauta = Fuerty and Kilbegnet (Elph) 6 Sep 1442 (C.P.L. IX. 263)

MAGERRIGAN, PATRICK

coll by the Primate to the V Bailieborough (Kilm) 24 Jul 1542

MAGGILLARUAYD, DERMIT   –c. 1441

V Athleague (Elph) to 1441
Died c. 1441

MAGGLANDCHAYD, MATTHEW

clk of Kilmore Dio says that the tithes of Cluayn Lochayr (Clonlocher) and Farcli Cluayn, ? = Cloonclare (Kilm) belong to the Bp's mensa, and are being appropriated by a layman. Matthew is granted a lease of them, 8 Nov 1428 (C.P.L. VIII. 55)

MAGHAGA, PATRICK

a priest of Dio Ardagh is prov to V Tashinny (Ard) 12 Dec 1397 (A.H. I. 173; C.P.L. V. 103)

MAGHAMRUGAN, RORY

was prov to V Templeport (Kilm) 16 Dec 1425 (C.P.L. VII. 402, A.H. I. 231); the same, or another of the name is prov V Templeport (Kilm) Feb 1433 (A.H. I. 234)

MAGILL, JOHN   1840/41–1926

b. 1840 or 1841

d 1877 p 1878; C Ahamplish (Elph) 1877–81; R Killargue (Kilm) 1881–85; R Garrison (Clogh) 1885–90; R Aghabog (Clogh) 1890–1910; R Inniskeen (Clogh) 1910–21

> **m.** Alice. Issue 1. Rev Waller **b.** 27 Aug 1880 (**died** 17 Aug 1964) TCD BA 1901 Div Test 1904 MA 1909 d 1904 p 1905 C Christ Ch Lisburn (Conn) 1904–08 C Donnybrook (Dub) 1908–09 C Holy Trinity Belfast (Conn) 1909–14 R Bright (Down) 1914–22 C-in-c Ballyrashane (Conn) 1922–25 R Ballyrashane (Conn) 1925–50 ret; **m.** 31 Dec 1918 Etta **dau.** of Rev Thomas Forde, Meth Min Newcastle Co Down and had issue (i) Rev Waller Brian Brendan **b.** 22 Apr 1920 Chapl Rugby Sch **m.** 29 Aug 1955 Phyllis McKinley (ii) Terence John Patrick Forde **b.** 22 May 1924 (iii) Michael Desmond **b.** 30 Jun 1927 **m.** Elizabeth Aveline; 2. Rev John Evelyn Robinson **b.** 1884 or 1885 (**died** 24 Aug 1931) ent TCD 1909 d 1911 p 1914 C St James Winnipeg (Rupert's Land) 1911–13 C Kilskeery (Clogh)

1914–18 C Killany and Inniskeen (Clogh) 1918–21 C Aughnamullen Ballybay and Tullyucorbet (Clogh) 1922–23 R Drum (Clogh) 1923–25 R Broomfield (Clogh) 1925–31 **m.** 2 Jan 1924 Helen **dau.** of Rev James Waterson, R Aghabog (Clogh); 3. Capt Rupert

Died 4 Sep 1926

MAGILL, MATTHEW 1801/02–1877
b. 1801 or 1802; MA
R Calry (Elph) 1876–77
    Died 22 Jun 1877 aged 75

MAGILLACHULI, JOHN
V of Kylleachunurch = Kiltoghart (Ard) is reported by Charles Oflaynd, Clk of Kilmore Diocese to have dilapidated the V, committed fornication and neglected the Cure, 1447/48. If so, Charles Oflaynd is prov to V

MAGILLARUAYD, JOHN
V Gyllmacgnagyn = Kilnamanagh (Elph) to 1447

MAGILLASULY, EUGENE
V Kiltoghart (Ard) to 1615 (R.V.)

MAGILLHASULICH, JOHN
V Kiltoghart (Ard); is deposed 1506

MAGINBUN, DERMIT
priest of Elphin Dio is prov to V Killeasqriboin (Elph) 5 Dec 1404 (C.P.L. VI. 38)

†MAGINN, WILLIAM
Bp of Elphin 1539–*c.* 1544

†MAGNWIN (? McGOWAN), THADY
priest of noble race through his grandmother, is prov V Urney (Kilm) 1436; there to 1455; he had been coll by Bp Donatus but doubted its validity; is prov V St Felim Kilmore (Kilm) 11 Nov 1436. He is still V in 1444/45 and allowed to resign his V and become an Augustinian Canon (A.H. I. 235, C.P.L. VIII. 599); he is allowed to hold St. Bridget's Drumlane *in commendam* 1445/46 (ib. IX. 528), which Priory he obtained pretending that his mensa was poor, but as it was abundant, he was deprived of it 3 Jul 1456; is prov to the See of Kilmore 11 Jul 1455 (A.H. I. 256); consec Bp of Kilmore 26 Jul 1455 (ib. XI. 214); is Bp in 1460 and attended a Provincial Synod in Jun 1460 at St. Peter's Drogheda (Cal. Reg. Mey)

MAGONIUS
probably Maurice Archd of Ardagh 1423 (Cal. Reg. Swayne); there seems to have been a contest between Maurice and Cabricus O'Farrell qv for some years, but Maurice appears Archd in 1416 as Maurice McGillananyd (Cal. Reg, Flem. 158), in 1424 as Magonius (Cal. Reg. Swayne, 130), and as Maurice 1427 (ib. 196), and in 1428 as Maurice McGillanemur (ib. 135), when Cabricus claims it (ib.135, 504)

†MAGONIUS
"Magonius Bishop of Elphin" is residing at the Roman Court, Oct 1430 (C.P.L. VIII. 403)

MAGOREACCHY *alias* MACGILLANAGUCGSEAN, CHARLES
is prov to a Canonry of Elphin and Rector of the tithes in the parishes of Kilbride and Tullach, Occennedy, Elphin, long void, 26 Sep 1450 (C.P.L. X. 467)

MAGOREACTAYD, CHARLES
Canon of Elphin 1455/56 (C.P.L. XI. 34), & 1462 (ib. XII. 143), & 1463 (ib. XII. 168), & 1465 (ib. XII. 235)

MAGORRICACHDAIG, MAGON
V Taghboy (Elph) to 1472; got it by simony

MAGRAGHAN, THOMAS
V Annagh (Kilm) 1449/50, is deceased

MAGRAMRUGAN, RORY
prov V Templeport (Kilm) 22 May 1455 (C.P.L. XI. 219); deposed 1461 for wounding a clerk with an arrow, perjury, etc (ib. XII. 141, 142)

MAGRANAYLL, CORNELIUS
is V Kyltacunrch = Kiltoghart (Ard) 1481; gets R Munteclye 2 April (A.H. I. 167)

MAGRATH, JAMES
lic C Killenvoy (Elph) 4 Dec 1798

†MAGRATH, MILER 1522–1622
b. 1522 Lough Derg; ministered in the Low Countries; a Franciscan Friar who had been schismatically prov by the Pope to the Bpric of Down on 12 Oct 1565, and who subsequently had found it convenient to throw in his lot with the Reforming party — who at all events, took the Oath of Supremacy to the Crown — was according to Ware appointed by Queen Elizabeth I Bp of Clogher by patent, dated 13 Sep 1570. It is

doubtful if he took possession as on 3 Feb 1571 he was made Abp of Cashel, which See he held to 1622; he also held Bpric of Waterford and Lismore 1582–89 and 1592–1608, and Bpric of Killala 1607–22 and Achonry *in commendam* 1613–22; he held numerous incumbencies, including 22 in Waterford and Lismore, and was granted V Kilmacallen (Elph) *in commendam* 17 Feb 1607/08 (Erck's P.R. p. 353) and "the Rectory between the two bridges" *in commendam* = St John Sligo (Elph) 1608/09 (ib.).

> **s.** of Donagh Magrath, Chieftan of Termonmagrath and Erenach of St Patrick's Purgatory
>
> **m.** 1557 Amy **dau.** of John O'Meara of Lisnisky Co Tipperary. Issue **sons** 1. Turlough; 2. Redmond; 3. Bryan; 4. Marcus; 5. James; **daus.** 1. Mary; 2. Cecilia; 3. Ann; 4. Ellice
>
> **Died** 14 Nov 1622 **bur.** St Patrick's Cath on the Rock of Cashel
>
> Some of this information is derived from Leslie's *Clogher Clergy and Parishes,* qv, though other authorities have different dates for his appointments

MAGRATH, SIMON

"Dean of Ardcarne" (?Elphin) 1271 (A.F.M.)

MAGRUANI, LUKE

has resigned V Rathcline (Ard) 3 June 1396. The Church is appropriated to Monastery of Isle of All SS (C.P.L. V. 12)

MAGUERAN, JOHN

was prov V Drumgoon (Kilm) in succession to Patrick Macconaing qv, but died at the Apostolic See before his letters were perfected, 1454/55

MAGUIRE, FRANCIS 1775/76–1844

b. 1775 or 1776; TCD BA 1802

V Shrule (Ard) 1806–44

> **Died** 20 Jul 1844 at Shrule Glebe aged 68

MAGUIRE, JAMES MANSEL EGERTON   –*c.* 1980

TCD Weir and Downes Pris BA 1942 MA 1959

d 1943 p 1944 (Ossory); C Kilnamanagh (Ferns) 1943–45; R Clonbroney w Killoe (Ard) 1945–50; R Tubbercurry w Kilmactigue (Ach) 1950–54; R Roscommon Dunamon Mount Talbot Killeroran Killenvoy Castleblakney & Athleague (Elph) 1954–66; R Mostrim Granard and Drumlummon (w Rathaspeck Streete Clonbroney Killoe and Kilglass from 1977) (Ard) 1966–78; Preb of Tibohine (Elph and Ard) 1966–78; ret Last entry in C I Dir 1980

> **m.** and had issue incl Rev Mary Elizabeth Ellen **m.** …McElhinney, R Calry (Elph) 2001 qv
>
> **Died** *c.* 1980

MAGUIRE, JOHN MULOCK 1810–1876

b. 1810 Dublin, ed by Mr Gwynne; ent TCD 6 Nov 1826 aged 16 BA & MA 1832

V Boyle Aghanagh & Kilnamanagh (Elph) 1842–66; Preb of Kilcooley (Elph) 1847–66; R Kilskyre (Meath) 1866–67; R Kilkeedy (Lim) 1867–76

    s. of Bernard, *pragmaticus*, by Eleanor **dau.** of Joshua Mulock

    m. 13 Apr 1847 Strabane Anne Jane (**b.** 12 Apr 1823 **died** 27 Sep 1910) 3rd **dau.** of Major John Humphreys and **sister** of the well-known hymn-writer and wife of the Primate, Mrs Cecil Frances Alexander. Issue incl James R, MP

    Died 15 Aug 1876 aged 66

PUBLICATION

    Letters in Vindication of the Church of Ireland addressed to an English MP, Rivingtons, London 1850

MAGYUM, NEMEAS

in 1425 had held the V Templeport (Kilm) over 6 years without title and was deposed

MAHAFFY, EDWARD *c.* 1771

b *c.* 1771 Co Donegal; ed Lifford; ent TCD 13 Jun 1789 BA 1795

C Killinkere (Kilm) 1802–10; C Mullagh (Kilm) *c.* 1811–20

    m. 1 Aug 1810 Sophia **dau.** of Rev Arnold Cosby, V Killinkere (Kilm) qv Issue incl 2nd **s.** Edward, MD Bengal Medical Services **m.** 17 Aug 1848 Susan Frances **dau.** of Surgeon Thomas of Bengal and a **dau.** Mary **m.** 12 Oct 1847 James L Bailey

MAHON, ARTHUR 1716–1788

b. 1716 Co Roscommon; ed by Dr Clarke, Drogheda; ent TCD 8 Jun 1733 BA 1737

PC Aghade (Leigh) to 1752; R Killukin 1743–; coll V Taunagh (Elph) 6 Jun 1743; V Kilcola Eastersnow Creeve and Toomna (Elph) 1737–47; Archd of Elphin 1743–47; PC St Nicholas Within (Dub) 1749–88; Preb of Howth in St Patrick's Cath Dublin 1750–52; Prec of Connor 1752–88

    s. of Rev Peter qv (**s.** of Nicholas)

    m. 16 Jul 1748 Henrietta (**died** 6 Oct 1802) eldest **dau.** of Rt Rev Robert, Bp of Leighlin and Ferns 1744–52 (**s.** of Dr Henry, Bp of Derry). Issue incl 1. Robert; 2. Jane **m.** Rev Samuel Malcolm Morgan, C Geashill (Kild); 3. Charlotte

    Died May 1788 aged 72 **bur.** 18 May Boyle Abbey

MAHON, ARTHUR 1778/79–

b. 1778 or 1779 Co Wexford; ent TCD 14 May 1794 aged 15 BA 1797

d 20 Nov 1803 p 24 Aug 1804; C Bumlin (Elph) 1805; R Eastersnow and Kilcola (w Kilbryan to 1813) 1812–c20 (Elph)

    s. of Robert

    m. and had issue incl Robert **b.** Co Roscommon ent TCD 1 Nov 1819 aged 17

MAHON, EDWARD 1776/77–1847

b. 1776 or 1777 Co Clare; ed by Mr FitzGerald; ent TCD 2 Jan 1797 aged 20 Sch 1803 BA 1806 MA 1810 BD 1813

C St Matthew Irishtown (Dub) 1809–11; R Bumlin (Elph) 1811–47

>s. of Patrick, *agricola*
>
>**Died** 2 Feb 1847

MAHON, HENRY 1770/71–

b. 1770 or 1771; ed by Dr Norris, Drogheda; ent TCD 1 Jul 1788 aged 17 BA 1796

d 1795 (Kilmore) p; R & V Castlerahan (Kilm) 1797–1802; V Wherry (Meath) 1802; V Tissaran and Kilnagarenagh (Meath) 1802–38

>3rd **s.** of Ross of Castlegar Co Galway by Anne only **dau.** of John, 1st Earl of Altamont
>
>**m.** Anne **dau.** of Abraham Symes. Issue **sons** 1. Ross of Athlone **b.** King's Co (Offaly) ed by Dr Miller at Armagh ent TCD 14 Oct 1822 aged 16 BA 1827 MA 1838 **m.** twice; 2. Rev Henry Lewis **b.** King's Co (Offaly) ed by Dr Miller ent TCD 14 Oct 1822 aged 16 BA 1827 **died unm.**; 3. George Charles **b.** King's Co (Offaly) ed by Mr Eames ent TCD 1 Jul 1833 aged 17 BA 1838 MA 1841 went to America **m.** and had issue; **daus.** 1. Anne **m.** Hon and Rev Henry Ward; 2. Sophia **m.** Thomas Mulock; 3. Louisa **m.** Rev William Filgate; 4. Harriet **m.** J S Baillie

MAHON, LUKE 1754/55–1795

b. 1754 or 1755 Co Roscommon; ed by Mr Kerr; ent TCD 8 Jul 1771 aged 16 BA 1776

C Dunamon (Elph) 1786; Preb of Oran and V Dunamon (Elph) 1794–95

>s. of Luke
>
>**m.** and had issue 1. Luke **b.** near Strokestown ed by Rev James Armstrong ent TCD 23 Feb 1799 aged 16; 2. Anne **m.** Rev Edward Bullingbroke Ayres, Preb of Termonbarry (Elph) qv; 3. Theodosia **m.** 10 Apr 1817 Robert Devenish (**died** 18 Mar 1864) of Rushhill Co Roscommon
>
>**Died** 1795

MAHON, MAURICE

ent TCD 19 Mar 1768 BA 1772

R Kilbonane & Kilcredan (Cloyne) and Molahiffe (A & A) 1772–*c.* 1814; R Bumlin Lisonuffy and Kiltrustan (Elph) *c.* 1790–1811

MAHON, Hon. MAURICE, LORD HARTLAND 1772–

b. 6 Oct 1772

C Kilglass (Elph) 1794; Preb of Kilmeen (Tuam) 1804–35; was appointed Minor Canon and V Chor of St Patrick's Cath Dublin in 1804 but was deprived for non-residence in 1835; V St Nicholas Galway to 1807. In 1835 he succeeded his brother as

3rd Baron Hartland. The title became extinct upon his death

    m. 1813 Jane Isabella (**died** 12 Dec 1838 s.p.) **dau.** of William Hume, MP of Humewood

    Died 11 Nov 1845

MAHON, PETER   –1739

TCD BA 1697 MA 1700

V Killukin (Elph) 1700–03; Archd of Elphin and V Toomna (Elph) 1700–22; Dean of Elphin 1722–39, inst 19 Feb 1722 (F.F.)

    2nd **s.** of Nicholas (ancestor of the Barons Hartland) by Magdalene **dau.** of Arthur French of Movilla Castle Co Galway

    m. and had issue incl 1. Ven Arthur, Archd of Elphin qv; 2. Robert

    Died 1739

MAHON, THOMAS 1740–1811

b. 3 Jun 1740 Roscommon; ed by Rev Mr Connolly; ent TCD 15 Dec 1757 aged 17 BA 1761 MA 1764

R Killury (Ardf) 1766–75; Preb of Kilmainmore (Tuam) 1771–1811; V Annaduff (Ard) 1777–1811

    s. of Thomas, MP for Roscommon in the Irish Parliament for 42 years

    m. Honoria 3rd **dau.** of Denis Kelly of Castlekelly. Issue 1. Rev Thomas (**died** Mar 1825) **b.** Co Leitrim ent TCD as FC 24 Jan 1804 aged 17 BA 1809 MA Preb of Faldown (Tuam) 1816–25; 2. Denis; 3. John; 4. Anne

    Died 19 Mar 1811 aged 71

MAHON, WILLIAM ROSS 1813–1893

b. 14 Jul 1813 Co Galway; ed by Mr Doherty; ent TCD 4 Jul 1831 BA 1836 MA 1841

d 4 Sep 1836 p 1837 (Down); Minor Canon of St Patrick's Cath Dublin 1837–42; PC Derryheen (Kilm) 1839–42; R Honington (St E — then Ely) 1842–44; R Rawmarsh (Sheff — then York) 1844–93; Dom Chapl to the Marquess of Sligo

    2nd **s.** of Sir Ross, Bt of Castlegar Co Galway; he succeeded his brother Ross as 4th Baronet in 1852

    m. 12 Oct 1853 Jane (**died** 7 Jun 1895 London) 2nd **dau.** of Rev Henry King of Ballylin Hse King's Co (Offaly). Issue **sons** 1. Ross **b.** 10 Jan 1856; 2. William Henry **b.** 31 Dec 1856 who succeeded him as Baronet; 3. John Fitzgerald **b.** 20 Jan 1858; 4. James Vesey **b.** Feb 1860; 5. Gilbert (**died** 2 Jan 1947) **b.** 11 Jun 1862; **daus.** 1. Mary Geraldine; 2. Alice Jane

    Died Aug 1893 aged 80

MAIGILLADGON, JOHN

had intruded into V Streete (Ard) 1431 and is deposed

MAILLY, JOHN

pres to V Kilronan (Ard) 18 Sep 1752 (L.M. V. 129)

MAJOR, JOHN 1720/21–*c.* 1775

b. 1720 or 1721 Co Derry; ed by Dr Grattan; ent TCD 19 Jun 1739 aged 18 Sch 1741 BA 1743 MA 1746

C Rossinver (Kilm) 1749–c75

> eldest **s.** of Henry of Ballyshannon Co Donegal, Lt Donegal Militia by Elizabeth eldest **dau.** of William Browne of Faughan Water near Londonderry and Mary widow of George Stewart of Inch Co Donegal
>
> **m.** (ML 14 Oct 1751) Catherine Scanlan of St Paul's Dublin. Issue incl Anne **m.** Rev Thomas Inglis, R Rossinver (Kilm) qv
>
> **Died** *c.* 1775; Will dated 17 Jan 1772 proved 4 Aug 1775

MALBY, HENRY

R Ballysumaghan (Elph) 1615

MALBY, HENRY

Preb Kilbegnet (Elph) 1615 (R.V.); prob same as above

MANBY, GEORGE 1680/81–1741

b. 1680 or 1681 at Ballyriccard; ed by Dr Harvey at Lisburn; ent TCD 29 Aug 1697 aged 16 BA 1700 BD & DD 1739

V Ardcarne (Elph) 1710–22; Precentor of Elphin and V Shankill and Kilmacumsy 1723–41, coll 18 May 1723; V Temployan *alias* Roscommon, of St John's *alias* Ivernon Kilbride & of Kilteevan & Porterin 1731–41; was VGen Elphin

s. of Richard

Died 6 Nov 1741 Roscommon

MANNING, THOMAS WHITE 1847–1923

b. 23 Dec 1847; ed privately by Dean Ellison; TCD BA 1874

d 1874 p 1875 (Kilmore); C Mohill (Ard) 1874–78; R Kilscoran (Ferns) 1878–82; R Ardamine (Ferns) 1882–84; R Adamstown and Old Ross (Ferns) 1884–87; R Kilculliheen (Waterf) 1887–91; R Kilmacow & Kilbeacon (Oss) 1891–1923.

> **s.** of Thomas White and Martha Susanna (née Henry)
>
> **m.** 30 Jun 1875 Sarah Matilda (**died** 2 Jan 1932 at Tudor Lodge Oldham Hants **bur.** Kilmacow) **dau.** of Dr Samuel Manning. Issue **sons** 1. George Frederick TCD BA Resident Commissioner in Nyasaland killed 9 Sep 1914 in the Great War; 2. Thomas Edward Ffrench TCD BA MB District Surgeon Natal Capt 2nd Field Ambulance Natal Mounted Rifles **died** 31 Mar 1915 at Kilmacow Rectory; 3. Rev William Wybrants TCD MA & Div Test d 1909 p 1910 (Cork) C Berehaven (Ross) 1909–14 C Kilmocomogue (Cork) 1914–15 served in Great War as 2nd Lt

Wilts Regt 1915–18, with King's African Rifles in Nyasaland 1918–19 C Bishop's Hatfield (St A) 1920–23 R Lasham (Win) from 1923 **m.** 15 Apr 1925 Lois Joy 3rd **dau.** of Rev J C H Hutt V St Clement Bartlemas Sandwich (Cant); 4. Samuel Nalty LDS RCSI **m.** 26 Sep 1917 Chapel Royal Dublin Muriel Frances Maude eldest **dau.** of Sir Frederick Cullinan KCB; **daus.**, 1. Frances E.. **unm.**; 2. Maria Eleanor **b.** 30 Nov 1886 unm; 3. Grace E... **m.** ...Friel of Pretoria Transvaal; 4. Kathleen L...**m.** ...Stewart of New Guelderland Natal

Died 6 Aug 1923 at the Adelaide Hosp Dublin **bur.** Kilmacow

MANSERGH, HENRY 1768/69–

b. 1768 or 1769 Dublin; ed by Mr Miller; ent TCD 25 Aug 1786 aged 17 BA 1791 C Ballinrobe (Tuam) 1807–09; V Kilglass (Elph) 1809–*c.* 22

s. of Edward

m. (ML 1822) Mary Hanly

MANSFIELD, GEORGE DALLAS 1786/87–1868

b. 1786 or 1787 Co Donegal; ed by Dr Burrowes; ent TCD 6 Feb 1804 aged 17 BA 1808

d 1809 p; C Leckpatrick (Derry) 1809–; R & V Kiltubrid (Ard) 1823–68

s. of Robert

m. 1810 St Peter's Ch Dublin Elizabeth Caroline (**died** 19 Jul 1864) **dau.** of Dr Robert Scott of Lr Mount St Dublin. Issue incl 1. George Scott **b.** Co Leitrim ed by Mr Eames ent TCD 19 Oct 1829 BA 1833 **m.** 8 Aug 1861 St Peter's Ch Dublin Harriet yst **dau.** of George Commin; 2. Ellen **m.** in Kiltubrid Ch as his 2nd wife Rev Thomas La Nauze, R Templeport (Kilm) qv

Died 24 Nov 1868

†MARGETSON, JAMES 1600–1678

b. 1600 Drighlington Yorks; Peterhouse Camb Siz 1619 BA 1623 MA 1626; TCD DD (by incorporation) 1637

d 4 Jun 1626 p 25 Dec 1626 (Peterborough) Bp 1661; R Thornton Watlass (Rip) 1626–35; R Annagh (Kilm) 1635–37; Dean of Waterford 1635–38; Chapl to the Earl of Strafford 1635–38; Dean of Derry 1638–39; Dean of Christ Ch Cath Dublin 1639–60; Chanc of Clogher and Preb of Holy Trinity (Cork) 1639–60; Abp of Dublin 1661–63; consec 27 Jan 1661; Abp of Armagh 1663–78; Chanc TCD 1667–78

m.... Issue **sons** incl 1. Rev James (**died** 4 Mar 1737) ent TCD as FC 27 May 1673 aged 16 BA 1676 MA 1679; Camb BA (by incorporation) 1677 d p 24 Dec 1699 (Lincoln) R Little Stukeley (Ely) 1699–1701 V Exning Suffolk 1701–37; 2. John ent TCD as FC 27 May 1673 aged 16 BA 1676; 3. Robert **b.** Leicestershire ent TCD 6 Apr 1677 aged 16; 4. possibly had a **s.** Samuel; 5. Robert; also 3 **daus.** incl Anne **m.** William, 2nd Viscount Charlemont

Died 26 Aug 1678 **bur.** Christ Ch Cath Dublin

MARLAY, RICHARD 1776/77–

b. 1776 or 1777 Co Kildare; ed by Mr Bonafous; ent TCD 3 Nov 1794 aged 17 BA 1799 MA 1832

Preb of Tullaghorton (Lism) 1801–09; C Moybologue and Bailieborough (Kilm) 1807; V Annaghdown Killascobe Laccagh & Shruel (Tuam) 1809–54

    s. of Thomas, *miles*.

MARSDEN, GEORGE HENRY 1928–

Emmanuel Coll Saskatchewan LTh 1951; TCD BA 1957 MA 1960

d 1951 (Saskatchewan) p 1952 (Saskatchewan); I Fort Pitt (Dio Saskatchewan) 1951–52; I Arborfield w Carrot River (Dio Saskatchewan) 1952–54; I Rosthern and Duck Lake (Dio Saskatchewan) 1954–55; C Urney (Kilm) 1955–58; C Faversham (Cant) 1958–61; I Berners Roding and Willingale w Shellow (Chelmsf) 1961–82; Perm to Off Dio Cant from 1982

    s. of Mr & Mrs R T Marsden of Dalkey Co Dublin

    m. Patricia. Issue Katharine Anne b. 11 Jul 1957; Christopher Andrew (**died** in infancy 1 Apr 1964)

†MARSH, FRANCIS 1626–1693

b. 23 Oct 1626 Edgeworth Gloucestershire; was admitted pensioner of Emmanuel Coll Camb 22 Aug 1642 BA 1647 MA 1650 Fellow of Caius Coll Camb 1651–61; incorp TCD MA 1661 DD

d and p 1661 (Down and Connor); Dean of Connor 1661; Dean of Armagh 1661–67; Archd of Dromore 1664–67; R Clonfeakle (Arm) 1664–67; Bp of Limerick and R Tradery (Killaloe) 1667–73; consec at Clonmel 22 Dec 1667; translated to Kilmore and Ardagh 10 Jan 1673; Bp of Kilmore and Ardagh 1673–81; translated to Dublin 14 Feb 1681; Abp of Dublin and Bp of Glendalough 1681–93; held Treas of St Patrick's Cath Dublin and Preb of Desertmore (Cork) *in commendam*; he fled from Dublin in 1688/89 and was attainted by King James's Parliament, and returned after the Battle of the Boyne

    s. of Henry of Edgeworth (**s.** of Francis of Edgeworth) by Anne **dau.** of William Aylesbury and aunt of Frances, Countess of Clarendon, whose **dau.** Anne, Duchess of York, was mother of Queen Mary II and Queen Anne

    m. Mary (**died** 1695) 2nd **dau.** of Rt Rev Jeremy Taylor, Bp of Down and Connor 1661–67. Issue 1. Francis; 2. Very Rev Jeremiah William, Dean of Kilmore qv; 3. Barbara; 4. Lucretia **m.** Very Rev John McNeale, Dean of Down 1683–1709

    Died 16 Nov 1693 at the Palace of St Sepulchre **bur.** Christ Church Cathedral Dublin

MARSH, JEREMIAH WILLIAM 1667–1734

b. 1667 Armagh; ed St Paul's Sch London by Dr Gale; ent TCD as SC 8 Jul 1682 aged 15 BA 1686 MA 1688 DD 1700

Treas of St Patrick's Cath Dublin 1693–1734; Dean of Kilmore and V Kilmore &

Ballintemple (Kilm) 1700–34

    s. of Rt Rev Francis, Bp of Kilmore qv (**s.** of Henry) by Mary **dau.** of Rt Rev Jeremy Taylor, Bp of Down and Connor

    m. (1) Henrietta Catherine (**Died** 9 Oct 1703) **dau.** of Henry Dodwell of Manor Dodwell Co Roscommon. Issue incl 1. Francis bapt 12 Feb 1701/02; 2. Mary **b.** 1702; 3. Henry bapt 18 Jul 1703

    m. (2) Elizabeth (**bur.** 2 Sep 1712 at Kilmore) **dau.** of Rt Rev Simon Digby, Bp of Elphin qv Issue 1. Elizabeth bapt 4 Aug 1708; 2. Jeremy (**died** 1790) **b.** 1712, R Athenry (Tuam) **m.** Jane **dau.** of Patrick French, MP of Monivea and had issue (i) Jeremiah TCD MA 1783 (ii) Francis (iii) Rev Robert (iv) Digby (**died** 1791) SFTCD

    m. (3) 19 Nov 1714 Judith (**died** 1753) **dau.** of Francis Butler of Cregg Co Galway. Issue 1. Francis bapt 8 Sep 1715; 2. Mary (**bur.** 22 Jul 1721)

    Died 3 Jun 1734 aged 67 **bur.** St Peter's Dublin

MARTIN, A

appointed 2nd C Templemichael (Ard) Aug 1846

MARTIN, ALEXANDER

"Alexander Martin, an ordained minister came out of England about the 25th of July last to the parishes of Drumgoone and Killisherdiny, Co. Cavan" (Seymour's Commonwealth MSS, p. 125, 211), 21 May 1660

V Urney (Kilm) 1660–61; V Tomregan & Drumlane and R Castleterra (Kilm) 1661–62; Archd of Kilmore 1661–*c.* 62

MARTIN, ARTHUR HENRY MANT

TCD BA & Div Test 1893 MA 1896

d 1894 p 1895 (Kilmore); C Killeshandra (Kilm) 1894–95

MARTIN, GEORGE HENRY 1833/34–1896

b. 1833 or 1834; TCD BA & Div Test 1857

C Urney (Kilm) 1860; DC Killegar (Kilm) 1860–71; R Agher (Meath) 1871–84

    m. Edith Agatha (**died** 14 Feb 1893 Dublin) **dau.** of Ven J C Martin. Issue incl 1. George H F (**died** 8 Mar 1888 Dublin aged 19); 2 eldest **dau.** Susan Maria (**died** 2 Oct 1891) **m.** as his 1st wife 6 May 1888 Rev Charles William O'Hara Mease, R Killoughter (Kilm) qv

    Died 12 Dec 1896 aged 62

MARTIN, HENRY FRANCIS JOHN 1835/36–1906

b. 1835 or 1836; TCD Sch 1856 BA (Sen Mod Maths) and Bp Law's Pri 1858 Div Test (1) 1859 MA 1865; Donnellan Lect TCD 1893–94

d 1859 p 1860 (Kilmore); C Killeshandra (Kilm) 1859–63; R Ballysax (Kild) 1863–

65; R Kilmacrennan (Raph) 1865–73; R Christ Ch Londonderry (Derry) 1873–78; C Killeshandra (Kilm) 1878–82; R Killeshandra (Kilm) 1882–1906

    3rd **s.** of Ven John Charles, Archd of Ardagh qv (**s.** of John) by Agatha, **dau.** of Rt Rev Richard Mant; **bro.** of Rev John Charles, R Killeshandra (Kilm) qv

    m. 2 Nov 1865 Barbara (**died** 1902) yst **dau.** of Robert Collins, MD JP of Ardsallagh Co Meath. Issue incl a **s. b.** 24 Nov 1870

    Died 6 Oct 1906 at Killeshandra Rectory

PUBLICATIONS
Spiritual Life as illustrated by the Book of Psalms, Dublin 1905 (Donnellan Lectures)
Questions for Confirmation Candidates

MARTIN, JOHN CHARLES 1798/99–1878

b. 1798 or 1799 Cork; ed by Mr Lee; ent TCD 4 Nov 1811 Sch 1814 BA 1816 Fellow 1821 MA 1825 BD & DD 1835

d 1824 p 182–; R Killeshandra (w PC Derrylane 1831–64) (Kilm) 1831–78; Archd of Ardagh 1854–66; Archd of Kilmore 1866–78

    2nd **s.** of John, merchant, Cork (of the Martins of Wiche, Worcestershire)

    m. Jun 1829 Agatha (**died** 4 Sep 1875 at Killeshandra) only **dau.** of Rt Rev Richard Mant Bp of Down 1823–48. Issue 1. Rev John Charles, R Killeshandra (Kilm) 1878–82 qv; 2. Richard Luther BA 1856 (**died** 17 Nov 1872 of cholera at Calcutta) **m.** 23 Sep 1856 Henrietta Maria **dau.** of Rev John Taylor LLD and had issue incl Rev Richard D'Olier, R Killeshandra (Kilm) qv; 3. Rev Henry Francis John MA, R Killeshandra (Kilm) qv; 4. Frederick Walter Mant (**died** in New Zealand Mar 1863, the result of a fall); 5. Charles William Wall **m.** 21 Dec 1866 Gertrude Honoria only **dau.** of William Murray Hickson, RM Co Cavan; 6. Caulfield Aylmer; 7. Brownlow Rudinge; and five **daus.** 1. Elizabeth Mary Adelaide **m.** 1850 Rev Christopher Adamson; 2. Edith Agatha (**died** 14 Feb 1893) **m.** Rev George Henry Martin; 3. Emily Mary d unm. 1857; 4. Olivia Frances; 5. Adela Neville **m.** 1 Nov 1881 Edward **s.** of Major–Gen Dobbs of Knockdollan Greystones Co Wicklow

    Died 17 Jan 1878 aged 79

PUBLICATIONS
Speech at 1st General Meeting of Brunswick Constitutional Club at Rotunda, Dublin, on 4 Nov 1828, 8vo, Dublin 1828
The Lord's Supper in its Scriptural and Sacerdotal Aspects
The Revelation of St. John briefly explained, 8vo, 1853

MARTIN, JOHN CHARLES –1899

TCD BA & Div Test (1) 1854 MA 1865

d 1855 p 1856 (Kilmore); C Killeshandra (Kilm) 1855–78; R Killeshandra (Kilm) 1878–82

    eldest **s.** of Ven Charles, Archd of Ardagh, qv (**s.** of John) by Agatha **dau.** of Rt Rev Richard Mant; **bro.** of Rev Henry Francis John, R Killeshandra (Kilm) qv

    Died 10 Apr 1899 **unm.**

MARTIN, JOHN CHARLES (TERTIUS)

d 1883 (Kilmore) p 1883 (Down for Kilmore); C Killeshandra (Kilm) 1883–88; R Dowra (Kilm) 1888–1900; R Killesherdoney (Kilm) 1900–03; res and went to live in France

MARTIN, JOHN HENRY

Head Master Diocesan Sch Sligo 1863–64

see also John Henry Martin in Dublin and Connor Lists who may be same

MARTIN, RICHARD D'OLIER 1860–1931

b. 6 Jul 1860 Berhampore India; ed Foyle Coll Londonderry; TCD BA 1881 Div Test (2) 1882 MA 1886

d 1884 (Calcutta) p 1885 (Lahore); SPG Missy at Delhi 1883–86; C Bray (Dub) 1887–88; R Ematris (Clogh) 1888–89; SPG Org Sec for Ireland 1889–94; R Killesk (Ferns) 1894–1903; C Killeshandra (Kilm) 1903–05; DC Killegar (Kilm) 1905–06; R Killeshandra (Kilm) 1906–29; ret

2nd s. of Richard Luther (2nd s. of Ven John Charles, Archd of Kilmore qv) by Henrietta dau. of Dr John Taylor and Theodosia D'Olier

m. (1) Catherine Mary Clifford. Issue 1. Denys Richard; 2. Laurence (fell at Cambrai); 3. Marcus; 4. Mary (died young)

m. (2) Florence Taylor (died 13 Jan 1960 Ledbury Hereford). Issue 1. Iris Florence b. 1905 m. Dermot s. of Rev David Francis Killingley, R Whitechurch (Dub) 1900–40; 2. Miles Patrick b. 1911

Died 4 Jul 1931

MARTIN, SAMUEL 1818/19–1899

b. 1818 or 1819 Thurles Cio Tipperary; ed by Mr Huddart; ent TCD 9 Nov 1835 aged 17 Abp King's Pri (extra) 1845 BA & Div Test 1846

d 1846 p 1847 (Limerick); C Tashinny (Ard) 1848; C Lurgan (Kilm) 1848–51; prob same as Samuel Martin C Rosenallis (Kild) 1851–53; PC Milford (Raph) 1855–60; C Convoy (Raph) 1860–71; PC Killadeas (Clogh) 1872–76; R Errigal Truagh (Clogh) 1876–77; V Killaderry (Kild) 1877–80; V Kilcock (Kild) 1880–95; ret

s. of Samuel, *militaris*

Died 29 May 1899 aged 80

MARTIN, THOMAS HUTCHINSON –1945

TCD BA 1897 Div Test (2) 1898 MA 1903 BD 1915

d 1898 p 1899 (London); C St David Islington (Lon) 1898–1900; C St Michael Mattelon Whitechapel (Lon) 1901–05; C St Stephen Coleman St (Lon) 1905–06; C St John Uxbridge Moor (Lon) 1906–11; C Annagh (Kilm) 1911–12; R Ballymachugh (Kilm) 1912–22; R Rossinver (Kilm) 1922–45

Died 4 Dec 1945

MARTIN, WILLIAM 1724/25–1787

b. 1724 or 1725 Dublin; ed by Dr Butler; ent TCD 10 May 1738/39 Sch 1742 BA 1743 MA 1746 FTCD 1746 BD 1754 DD 1759; Prof of Hebrew TCD 1762; JP for Co Cavan 1766

R & V Killeshandra (Kilm) 1764–87; pres by TCD; Preb of Mulhuddart in St Patrick's Cath Dublin 1764–87

> **s.** of John
>
> **m.** Anna Maria **dau.** of Edward Ledwich of Dublin and **sister** of Very Rev Edward Ledwich, Dean of Kildare, acc to Leslie's MSS*. Issue William b *c.* 1767
>
> **Died** 17 May 1787 St Stephen's Green Dublin aged 62 **bur.** St Patrick's Cathedral Dublin. He left £60 to build a parish school in Killeshandra
>
> * His monument in St Patrick's Cathedral Dublin states that he married Maria **dau.** of Raymund Pritt, Esq of Combe in the County of Devon

MASCALAID, ALAN –1411

V of St Beraid de Cluaincorpy = Termonbarry (Elph) to 1411, is deceased

> **Died** 1411

MASCALAID, DONALD –1397

R Termonbarry (Elph) to 1397; is deceased

> **Died** 1397

MASCALAID, DONALD

V Cluancaspe = Termonbarry (Elph) is prov to the Comorbania or R Termonbarry (Elph) void by the death of Donald Mascalaid qv and unlawfully held by Maurice Mascalaid qv 10 Feb 1397/98; (C.P.L. V. 106)

MASCALAID, DONALD

priest of Elphin Diocese is prov to V Cluancaspi = Termonbarry (Elph), not exceeding 3 marks in value, and Patrick Mascalaid qv is to be deposed, 5 Dec 1397 (C.P.L. V. 105)

> **s.** of Simon

MASCALAID, MAURICE

a layman, unlawfully holds the Territory or Comorbania of Cluancaspe = Termonbarry (Elph) 1397

MASCALAID, PATRICK

unlawfully holds the V Termonbarry (Elph) and is deposed 1397

MASCALY, DONALD

is coll Preb of Termonbarry (Elph) vacant by the death of John Macoly qv, removing William O'Farrell qv, 27 Mar 1461 (C.P.L. XII. 143)

MASSY, DAWSON 1807/08–1878

b. 1807 or 1808 Limerick; ed by Mr White; ent TCD 3 Jul 1826 aged 18 BA 1832 MA 1851 BD & DD 1867

d 1832 p; C St Michael Limerick (Lim) in 1836; C Liselton (A & A) 1840–41; C Killeshandra (Kilm) 1843; R & V Killeshin (Leigh) 1847–67; R Hacketstown (Leigh) 1867–72; R Killasnett (Kilm) 1875–77; R Denn (Kilm) 1877–78

3rd **s.** of Hugh of Stagdale Co Limerick by Mary **dau.** of John Lane; **bro.** of Rev Godfrey, V Bruff (Lim)

m. (1) Frances Matilda widow of Richard Sadleir of Sadleir Wells Co Tipperary and eldest **dau.** of Capt Hon. Eyre Massy. Issue 1. a **s.** Dawson Godfrey (**died** 20 Jul 1866 Calcutta), MB BCh Indian Med Staff; **daus.** 1. Frances; 2. Constance; 3. Ruth (**died** 1 Feb 1853 aged 9)

m. (2) 16 Jun 1875 Isabella Woodroffe (**died** 28 May 1878) **dau.** of John Judkins Butler

Died 30 Dec 1878 at Denn Vicarage

PUBLICATIONS
The Secret History of Romanism, 2nd Ed 1850
Dark Deeds of the Papacy, the Jesuits unmasked etc, Dublin, Herbert 1851
Footprints of a Faithful Shepherd, being a Memoir of Rev. Godfrey Massy, Vicar of Bruff, 4th Ed 1851
Illustrations of Faith, Hope and Love, Dublin, Herbert

MASSY, JOHN MAUNSELL

d 1848 p; PC Killoughter (Kilm) 1857–70

MATANNOGLAYCH, FLORENCE

was prov to the V Kylloreych (= Cill Oiridh, Killery) (Ard) 21 Oct 1421 (A.H. I. 157). On 19 Jan 1428 he is absolved from excommunication because being prov V Killaidh (Ard) on the death of Enias Macnoglaidh, he gave a sum of money to Thady O'Mulaid who held possession and thus got coll. He is to resign and be re–prov (C.P.L. VIII. 20)

MATCHETT, ALAN WILLIAM 1970–

b. 1970; TCD BTh 2001 CITC 1998

d 2001 p 2002; C Limerick City Parish (Lim) 2001–03; C Stillorgan and Blackrock (Dub) 2003–05; R Bailieborough Knockbride Shercock and Mullagh (Kilm) 2005–

MATHEWS, RONALD PEEL BERESFORD 1924–2005

b. 1924 Dublin; held positions in Bermuda and Canada before ordination; Bermuda Govt Dipl in Youth Leadership; TCD Dip Bibl Studs 1964 d 6 Sep 1964 (Cashel) p 15 Jun 1965 (Cashel); C Waterford Cath G (Waterf) 1964–66; R Clonbroney Killoe and Columbkille (Ard) 1966–71; C-in-c Drumgoon w Dernakesh, and Ashfield (w Killesherdoney from 1972) (Kilm) 1971–74; Sec Leprosy Mission 1974–84 R of I; R Kinneigh U (Cork) 1984–93; ret

2nd **s.** of Capt A H Mathews, Income Tax Dept RCB

m. 26 May 1949 Bermuda Cath Rose Walters. Issue 1. Catherine Heather **m.** 3 Apr 1971 Clonbroney Par Ch Sergio yr **s.** of Mr and Mrs Ercole Giusti of Piacenza Italy; 2. Deborah

Died 12 May 2005

MATTHEWS (or MATTHEW), ERASMUS

d 13 Sep 1614 p 26 Feb 1615; V Taunagh (Elph) 1615; Archd of Elphin 1616–61; V Ardcarne (Elph) 1618–39; R Skreen and Castleconnor (Killala) 1619; V Boyle (Elph) 1633; res the V Taghbynne = Tibohine (Elph) 1640

MATURIN, EDMUND 1820–1891

b. 1820 Co Donegal; ed privately; ent TCD 21 Oct 1833 Sch 1836 BA 1838 Heb Pri 1839 Berkeley Gold Medal and Div Prem (1) 1840; Univ of Windsor N S, Canada MA 1853

d 1843 p 1845; C Desertlyn (Arm) 1843–45; C Clondehorkey (Raph) 1845–46; C Laghey (Raph) 1846–50; C St Paul Halifax NS (Dio Nova Scotia) 1850–58; became RC but returned to C of I; C Donoughmore (Arm) 1863–66; C Errigal Truagh (Clogh) 1866; C Carlingford (Arm) 1866–67; C Cleenish (Clogh) 1867–68; C St George Hurstpierpoint (Chich) 1870–72; R Mullaghdun (Clogh) 1873–74; R Aghavilly (Arm) 1874; R Cloncha (Raph — then Derry) 1874–86; PC Dowra (Kilm) 1886–87; R Newbliss (Clogh) 1887–91

s. of Rev Henry, FTCD, R Clondevaddock (Raph) 1797–1842 (**s.** of Rev Charles) by Elizabeth Johnston; **bro.** of Rev Henry, R Gartan (Raph) 1831–80; **bro.** of Rev Benjamin, C Kilbarron (Raph) 1840; his great grandfather, Very Rev Gabriel James Maturin succeeded Jonathan Swift as Dean of St Patrick's Cath Dublin in 1745 — his grandfather, Rev Gabriel Maturin was a Huguenot refugee who arrived in Dublin with his flock early in the 18th century.

m. Elizabeth Catherine (**died** 16 Nov 1862 aged 41 following the birth of twins on 22 Oct 1862, incl one stillborn) **dau.** of Dominick Persse of Ramelton Co Donegal; Issue 1. Charles; 2. Henry **m.** 28 May 1879 Ballybay Par Ch Co Monaghan Martha eldest **dau.** of Robert Skelly of Drogheda; 3. Mary Emily **m.** 12 Aug 1886 Newtownstewart Par Ch Rev Alexander Knox (**died** 26 Feb 1903), R Doneraile (Cloyne).and had issue Alexander Edmund **b.** 26 Nov 1889; 4. Catherine **m.** 30 Mar 1880 D Dudley Persse; 5. Rev Merrick Persse (**died** *c.* 1938) **b.** 22 Oct 1862 TCD BA & Div Test 1884 d & p 1886 C Castlerock (Derry) 1886–90 R Cumber Lr (Derry) 1890–94 C Enniskillen (Clogh) 1894–95; C Battersea (S'wark) 1895–98 C Warmleighton (Cov) 1898–99 C Christ Ch Forest Hill (S'wark) 1899–1902 C St Clement Notting Hill (Lon) 1902–04 C Eakring (S'well) 1904–06 C Holy Trinity Upr Tooting (S'wark) 1906–12 C Eakring (S'well) 1912–15 V W Stockwith (S'well) 1915–19 R Winterbourne Came w Winterbourne Farringdon (Sarum)

1919–21 PC Whitcombe 1919–21 R W Parley (Sarum) 1921–23 R Theydon Garnon (Chelmsf) 1923–31 **m.** 5 Aug 1890 Lillie Knox **dau.** of William Warke of Castlerock Co Derry

Died 21 Nov 1891 aged 71

PUBLICATIONS
A Brief Memoir of all the Bishops of Derry since the Reformation, with a Sketch of the Early History of the See, 1868
Lectures on the Origin of Christianity in England and Ireland
Letter to the Lord Bishop of Fredericton
Thoughts on the Infallibility of the Church

MAURICE
Dean of Ardagh to 1249

†MAURICE –1307
Abbot of the Convent of St Mary in Kells became Bp of Kilmore in 1286, having been postulated (C.D.I. III. 275, 304)

Died 1307

MAVER, JAMES WILLIAM 1883–1960
b. 1883 Mallow Co Cork; ed Portora Royal Sch Enniskillen; TCD BA 1906 Div Test 1907 MA 1909

d 1907 p 1908 (Ossory); C Clonenagh (Oss) 1907–10; C Mariners' Ch Kingstown (Dun Laoghaire) (Dub) 1911–12; C Garforth (Ripon) 1914; C All Souls Langham Pl London (Lon) 1914–16; C Pannal (Ripon) 1916–18; C Templemichael (Ard) 1918–20; C Pudsey (Bradf) 1920–30; C St John Weston (B & W) 1931–35; V Henton (B & W) 1935–55; ret

Died 3 Mar 1960 Sandycove Dublin

MAWE (WAWE), ROBERT
V Athleague (Elph) 1625–*c.* 29; prob same as below

MAWE, ROBERT
pres by the Crown to Preb of Ballintubber (Elph) 20 May 1625 (L.M. V. 126); he had been Preb of Baslick *alias* Clonconnogher with Kilkeevin 1 Jul 1623 (ib. V, 106); he became Dean of Clonfert in 1628

MAWE, ROBERT
pres Preb Kilbegnet (Elph) 1 Jul 1623 (P.R. Lodge); prob same as above

†MAX, JOHN –1536
a Premonstratensian Monk, Abbot of Welbeck and Preb of York, seems to have

succeeded George Brann as Bp of Elphin 1525. He held the Abbey of Tichfield, Hants *in commendam*

said to have **died** in 1536

†MAXWELL, Hon HENRY 1723–1798

b. 1723; ed by Dr Neligan; ent TCD 17 Nov 1740 BA 1745 MA 1748 DD (*speciali gratia*) 1765; incorp at Oxford 31 Oct 1745

d p 14 Feb 1747/48 (Kilmore) Bp 1765; R & V Annagh (Kilm) 1748–65; Dean of Kilmore and V Kilmore & Ballintemple (Kilm) 1751–65; consec Bp of Dromore 10 Mar 1765 at St Michael's Dublin; enthroned 23 Mar 1765; Bp of Dromore 1765–66; Bp of Meath 1766–98

yst **s.** of John, 1st Lord Farnham

m. 1759 Margaret only **dau.** of Rt Hon Anthony Foster and **sister** of Lord Oriel. Issue 2 **sons** incl Rev Henry, R Templemichael (Ard) qv

Died 7 Oct 1798 aged 75

MAXWELL, HENRY

matric Univ of Glasgow 1747 MA 1754

d 13 Jun 1756 p 29 Jun 1756; prob same Henry Maxwell C Kilmore (Kilm) in 1756

2nd **s.** of Robert of Fellows Hall

MAXWELL, HENRY, LORD FARNHAM 1774–1838

b. 1774 Dublin; ed by Dr Connor; ent TCD 7 Nov 1791 BA 1795 MA 1808

R Annagh (Kilm) 1798–1811; V Wherry Tissaran and Kilnagarenagh (Meath) 1797–1802; R Castlerahan (Kilm) 1802–13; V Athy (Glend) 1811–12; Preb & R Tynan (Arm) 1812–13; R Templemichael and Ballymacormack (Ard) 1813–38

2nd **s.** of Most Rev Henry Maxwell DD, Dean of Kilmore and Bp of Meath 1766–98 qv (yst **s.** of John, 1st Lord Farnham) by Margaret only **dau.** of the Rt Hon Anthony Foster and **sister** of John, Lord Oriel; succeeded as 6th Baron Farnham on the death of his **bro.** in 1838

m. 5 Sep 1798 Lady Anne Butler (**died** 29 May 1831) eldest **dau.** of the 2nd Earl of Carrick. Issue 9 **sons** and 3 **daus.** incl Henry **b.** 8 Aug 1799, 7th Baron Farnham, **m.** 3 Dec 1828 Anna Frances Esther yst **dau.** of the 22nd Lord Le Despenser and **died** s.p.; Somerset Richard; James Pierce and Richard

Died 19 Oct 1838

MAXWELL, JAMES –*c.* 1723

TCD BA 1670

d; ord p Kilmore 5 May 1670; V Killinagh (Kilm) 1669/70–1686; R Templeport and Drumreilly (Kilm) 1669/70–1723; R Kilbride-Castlecor (Meath) 1686–1720; also V Oldcastle (Meath) 1686–1720; was attainted in 1689

m. and had issue incl a **dau.** m Rev Edward Thompson

is deceased in 1723

MAXWELL, JOHN 1780/81–1841

b. 1780 or 1781 Co Mayo; ed by his father; ent TCD 7 Jul 1796 aged 15 Sch 1800 BA 1802

C Kilmacallen (Elph) 1804; C Taunagh (Elph) 1804; V Kilmactranny (Elph) 1830–41

    s. of Rev Patrick

    was **m.**

    Died 1841 **bur.** Kilronan

MAXWELL, JOHN 1782/83–

b. 1782 or 1783; ed by Mr McKenna; ent TCD 7 Jul 1800 aged 17 BA 1809

C Tessaragh (Elph) in 1817; C Kilmacallen (Elph) 1820 — still there in 1830; lic C Drumgoon (Kilm) 8 Mar 1843

MAXWELL, PATRICK

ord p 17 Jul 1658 (Raphoe); was Commonwealth Minister at Lurgan, Munterconnaught, Crosserlough = Kildrumferton and Killinkere (Kilm) and settled upon the tithes there 1658/59; on his petition, and in consideration of his poverty, the great charge of the transportation of his family and the small value of the rent reserved upon the tithes of the parish assigned to him, he was granted on 7 Jan 1658/59, £6 in ready money and £14 in bonds (Seymour's Commonwealth Mss, pp 62, 127); coll V Killan (Kilm) 22 Jun 1662, but according to VB 1673, he was coll V Killan, Killinkere and Bailieborough and Moybologue (Kilm) Apr 1661; he also held R Knockbride (Kilm) c 1661 and 1673–82 to which he was coll by the Primate with R Killan 22 Jul 1673 and also again coll to V Moybologue (Kilm) 23 May 1669 and in 1673–82

†MAXWELL, ROBERT –1672

TCD Sch BA 1616 Fellow 1617 MA 1619 DD

d 27 Jan 1617/18 p 2 May 1618 Bp 1643; was Chapl to the Lord Lt; R Arboe and poss Clonoe (Arm) 1619–24; Derrynoose (Arm) 1623–1666; Preb of Tynan (Arm) 1625–61; Archd of Down 1628–39; Bp of Kilmore (w Ardagh from 1661) 1643–72; succeeded by Patent dated 22 Mar 1643; was allowed to hold his Preb of Tynan (Arm) *in commendam.*

    eldest **s.** of Robert, Dean of Armagh 1610–22 by Isabella Seaton; was ancestor of the Lords Farnham

    m. Margaret **dau.** of Henry Echlin, Bp of Down. Issue 1. John of Farnham (**died** 1713); 2. James of Fellows Hall **m.** and had issue incl Rev Robert, R Annagh (Kilm) qv; 3. Henry of College Hall; 4. William of Falkland **m.** Anne **dau.** of Rev George Walker, Chanc of Armagh and had issue Robert of Falkland, DD; 5. Phoebe **m.** Henry Maxwell

    Died 1 Nov 1672 and "was buried ye 5th November in the country"

MAXWELL, ROBERT 1665/66–1737

b. 1665 or 1666 Co Armagh; ent TCD as a Pensioner 15 Jun 1682 aged 16 BA 1687 MA 1693 BD & DD 1719

R Annagh (Kilm) *c.* 1690–1709; Preb of Tynan (Arm) 1709–1737

    s. of James (**s.** of Robert, Bp of Kilmore qv)

    m. Ann

    Died 1737

MAYCONKAGRY, EUGENE

R Munterangaile (Ard) 8 Feb 1465/66 (Papal Annals by Bp Donnelly, Journal RSAI 1894, p 136)

MAYES, HUGH HASTINGS RICHARD 1910–1979

b. 24 Apr 1910 Creggan Rectory Co Armagh; ed The Royal Sch Armagh; TCD BA 1934 Div Test 1935 MA 1951

d 1935 p 1936 (Kilmore); C Kinawley (Kilm) 1935–37; CMS Missy Ado–Ekiti Nigeria 1938; Tutor St Andrew's Coll Oyo Lagos Nigeria 1938–39; CMS Missy in Ekiti District 1939–40; C St Bartholomew Belfast (Conn) 1940–41; R Clogherny (Arm) 1941–50; C St Mary Belfast (Conn) 1950–54; R Scarva (Drom) 1954–55; R St Mary Belfast (Conn) 1955–60; R Tullylish (Drom) 1960–75; RD of Aghaderg (Drom) 1961–71; Preb of Dromara (Drom) 1964–65; Chanc of Drom 1965–71; Dean of Dromore and Treas of St Anne's Cath Belfast 1971–75; ret

    yr **s.** of Rev Canon Samuel, R Kilmore (Arm) (**s.** of John and Isabel of Lisburn Co Antrim) by Florence Gaston 2nd **dau.** of Rev Hugh Hastings, Minister Magheragall Presbyterian Ch 1878–1913; **bro.** of Ven Thomas David Dougan, Archd of Armagh who was father of Rt Rev Michael H G Mayes, Bp of Kilmore qv

    m. 11 Oct 1951 St Finnian's Ch Belfast Frances Anne **dau.** of James Cooke of Omagh Co Tyrone

    Died s.p. 2 Jun 1979

†MAYES, MICHAEL HUGH GUNTON 1941–

b. 31 Aug 1941 Belfast; ed The Royal Sch Armagh; TCD BA 1962 Div Test (1) 1964; Univ of London BD 1984

d 1964 p 1965 (Armagh) Bp 1993; C St Mark Portadown (Arm) 1964–67; C St Columba Portadown (Arm) 1967–68; with USPG in Japan 1968–74; Area Sec (Cashel, Cork, Limerick and Tuam) USPG 1975–93; R St Michael's U (Cork) 1975–86; R Moviddy U (Cork) 1986–88; Archd of Cork Cloyne and Ross 1986–93; Exam Chapl to Bp of Cork 1986–93; R Rathcooney U (Cork) 1988–93; C of I Rep on ACC 1990; Warden Cork Cloyne and Ross Guild of Lay Readers; Chapl UCC; elected Bp of Kilmore Elphin and Ardagh by Electoral College 29 Apr 1993; consec in St Patrick's Cath Armagh 29 June 1993; enthroned in St Fethlimidh's Cath Kilmore 7 Sept 1993; enthroned in the Cath of St Mary the Virgin and St John the Baptist Sligo 21 Sep 1993; Bp of Kilmore Elphin and Ardagh 1993–2000; elected Bp of Limerick, Ardfert,

Aghadoe, Killaloe, Kilfenora, Clonfert, Kilmacduagh and Emly by Electoral College 8 Sep 2000; enthroned in St Mary's Cath Limerick 12 Nov 2000; enthroned in St. Flannan's Cathedral, Killaloe 26 Oct 2000, Bishop of Limerick and Killaloe 2000-08; ret.

s. of Ven Thomas David Dougan MA (**died** 26 Jul 1983) Archd of Armagh 1965–73 (**s.** of Rev Canon Samuel, R Kilmore (Arm) 1916–46 and Florence Gaston (née Hastings)) by Hilary (**died** 24 May 1986) **dau.** of Lionel Gunton and Dorothy Anne (née Dickson) of Radlett Herts; **bro.** of Rev Canon John Charles Dougan Mayes, R Clooney Londonderry 1985; **bro.** of Prof Andrew David Hastings Mayes, Vice–Provost TCD

m. 16 Jul 1966 St Barnabas' Ch Belfast Elizabeth Annie Eleanor **b.** 17 Feb 1943 **dau.** of James Vincent and Eliza Jane (née McCrea) Irwin of Belfast. Issue 1. Patrick Dougan James **b.** 18 Nov 1967; 2. Soren Elizabeth Hilary **b.** 15 Jun 1969; 3. Natalya Vivienne Ann **b.** 6 Apr 1974

MAYES, THOMAS
C Ardagh (Ard) 1622

MAYNE, ISAAC 1899/1900–1980

b. 1899 or 1900; TCD BA 1922 MA 1953; Asst Master Ranelagh Sch Athlone

d 1930 p 1931 (Kilm); Publ Pr Dio Kilmore 1930–33; R Granard (Ard) 1933–34; R Kiltullagh (Elph — then Tuam) 1934–39; R Killinagh w Kiltyclogher (Kilm) 1939–40; R Elphin Ardclare and Bumlin (Elph) 1940–45; Head Master of Bp Hodson's Gram Sch and Preb of Kilcooley (Elph) 1940–45; Warden of Wilson's Hosp Sch Multyfarnham Co Westmeath 1945–64; Canon of St Patrick's Cath Trim Dio Meath 1955–64; Preb of Tipper in St Patrick's Cath Dublin 1958–64; ret

s. of Charles E of Springvale Ballinrobe Co Mayo

m. Kathleen Edith (**died** 5 Sep 1967 at Drumcree Glebe **bur.** Ballyglass cemetery Mullingar). Issue 1. Sheila **m.** Apr 1964 Frank O'Neill; 2. Joyce Kathleen **m.** 25 Jun 1960 All SS Mullingar William Noel **s.** of G S Thompson of Milltown Co Dublin

Died 2 Feb 1980 aged 80 **bur.** Ballyglass Mullingar

MAYNE, JOSEPH 1841/42–1927
TCD BA 1877 MA 1880

d 1874 p 1875 (Armagh); R Garrison (Clogh) 1874–78; R Killasnett (Kilm) 1878–90; V Killinkere (Kilm) 1890–94; V Larah and Lavey (w C-in-c Denn from 1903) (Kilm) 1894–1923; Archd of Kilmore 1910–23; ret

m. Elizabeth (**died** 26 Feb 1914)

Died 7 Mar 1927 aged 85 **bur.** Lavey

MAYNE, WILLIAM JAMES 1872/73–1946

b. 1872 or 1873; TCD BA 1896 Div Test 1898 MA 1899

d 1896 (Dublin for Kilmore) p 1898 (Dublin); C Larah and Lavey (Kilm) 1896–98;

C St Mary Dublin (Dub) 1898–1902; Sec C of I Aux to LJS 1902–14; Asst Sec SPCK and Chapl and Catechist SPCK Training Coll 1914–17; Sec ISPPSI 1917–44; Chapl to Lord Lt 1921–22

    m. Agnes Isabel (**died** 30 Sep 1967). Issue incl Margaret Eleanor

    Died 17 Jun 1946 aged 73 **bur.** Enniskerry Co Wicklow

MEALLY, ROBERT FERGUSON 1908–

Huron Coll Canada STh 1961 Dip Bibl Studs

d 1958 p 1959 (Huron); I Blyth, Auburn and Belgrave (Dio Huron) 1958–65; R Killoughter and Cloverhill (Kilm) 1965–73; ret; Lic to Off Dio Kilmore 1974–76; Lic to Off Dio Dublin 1976–; Last entry C I Dir 1986

MEARA, SPENCER 1794/95–1827

b. 1794 or 1795 Kilkenny; ed by Mr Willis; ent TCD 4 Nov 1811 aged 16 BA 1816

V Killinkere (Kilm) 1821–27

    s. of Rev James

    Died 17 May 1827

MEARA, WILLIAM 1785/86–1821

b. 1785 or 1786 Co Kilkenny; ed by Mr Dowling; ent TCD 5 Dec 1803 aged 17 BA 1808 MA 1817

d 24 Jun 1809 (Ossory) p; V Kildallon (Kilm) 1810–21; V Killinkere (Kilm) 1817–21

    prob William Meara **s.** of Rev James (John in Al. Dubl)

    Died of fever in 1821

MEASE, CHARLES WILLIAM O'HARA 1856–1922

b. 1856 Dublin; ed Royal Sch Cavan; Royal Sch Armagh; ent TCD as Royal Sch BA 1878 Div Test 1881 MA 1885

d 1881 (Armagh) p 1883 (Kilmore); C Monaghan (Clogh) 1881–83; PC Killoughter (Kilm) 1883–84; C St George Belfast (Conn) 1884; C St Stephen Dublin (Dub) 1884–88; Minor Canon St Patrick's Cath Dublin 1885–89; R Killiskey (Glend) 1888–93; Dean's V St Patrick's Cath Dublin 1893–1903; V Castleknock (Dub) 1903–22; Sub-Dean Chapel Royal Dublin 1905–13; Preb of St Audoen in St Patrick's Cath Dublin 1913–22; Dean of Chapel Royal Dublin 1913–22

    s. of Dr Andrew, FRCSI

    m. (1) 16 May 1888 Susan Maria (**died** 2 Oct 1891) eldest **dau.** of Rev George H Martin

    m. (2) Martha Gertrude Billings (**died** 19 Nov 1951). Issue Harriet Hermione Billings **m.** 27 Sep 1934 Hugh Hamilton Massy only **s.** og G C Townsend of Cobh Co Cork

    Died 21 May 1922 at Castleknock

MEASE, ROBERT 1853/54–1925

b. 1853 or 1854; TCD BA 1878 Div Test 1879 MA 1885

d 1879 p 1880 (Kilmore); C Derryheen (Kilm) 1879–80; R Derryheen (Kilm) 1880–85; C St Mark Regent's Park (Lon) 1885–88; Dep Sec Irish Soc for England and Scotland 1888–93; C St Luke Kilburn (Lon) 1894–97; various temporary charges 1897–1907; C St John Kensal Green (Lon) 1907–10; Dio C Armagh 1913–25

s. of Andrew, FRCSI; **bro.** of Very Rev Charles William O'Hara, Dean of the Chapel Royal, R Castleknock (Dub) and Canon of St Patrick's Cath Dublin

Died 9 Jan 1925 aged 71

MECHAIG, JOHN   –1463

V Killukin (Elph) to 1463

Died 1463

MECKEHAN, NEHEMIAH (NEMIAS)

V Templemichael (Ard), is prov to V Cluayn = Cloone (Ard) and can hold both 1425 (A.H. I. 157); prov to V Templemichael (Ard) 13 Nov 1434 — this date may be incorrect in A.H.

MECRAN, MINEAS

res as V Earathguid = Annaduff (Ard) 1412

MEDCALF (METCALF), JAMES   –1632

was prov by the Crown to V Killasnett and Rossinver (Kilm) 22 Nov 1624 (L.M. V. 106), but he appears V in R.V. 1622

bur. at St. John's Dublin 1632

MEGUYBENE (? McCORNEY), MAGONIUS   –1461

vacates a Canonry and Preb of Kilmore by death, 1461

Died 1461

MEGWOL, WILLIAM

V Enga (Kilm); res 1470

MEISSNER, CHARLES LUDWIG BIRBECK HILL 1926–2000

b. 1926; ed Dundalk Gram Sch; St Columba's Coll Dublin; Dip Bibl Studs; TCD short Divinity Course 1960–62

d Jul 1962 (Clogher) p 29 Jun 1963 (Clogher); C Monaghan (Clogh) 1962–64; BC Kildallon Newtowngore & Corrawallen (Kilm) 1964–65 and R 1965–71; R Kinawley Drumany and Crom (Kilm) 1971–85; Preb of Annagh in Kilmore Cath 1983–85; R Mohill Farnaught Aughavas Oughteragh Kiltubride and Drumreilly (Ard) 1985–96;

Preb of Kilmacallen (Elph) 1987–96; ret

> s. of Rev Canon John Ludwig Gough (**b.** 31 Dec 1884 **died** 13 Dec 1976) of Nottingham (**s.** of Albert Ludwig MA PhD LittD Prof of Mod Langs and Librarian QUB and Alice **dau.** of John Gough, Compton Somerset) by Anne **dau.** of Major George Hill; **sister** of Joan Helen Augusta **m.** 26 Sep 1961 Rev Reginald George Thompson, C Donaghcloney (Drom)
>
> **m.** (1) St Patrick's Ch Monaghan 19 Jan 1965 Lucinda Ann (**died** Mar 1976) yr **dau.** of William Robert and Marion Elizabeth (née Logan) Farrell, Tully Lodge Rossmore Pk Monaghan. Issue 1. Robert Ludwig Gough **b.** 23 Dec 1965 **m.** Irene Doherty; 2. Alison Grace **b.** 18 Mar 1967 **m.** Charles Beatty; 3. Peter Charles **b.** 8 May 1972 **m.** Tanya Evans
>
> **m.** (2) 27 Jun 1984 Finvoy Par Ch Ballymoney Co Antrim Lorna yr **dau.** of Arthur and Ella Gillespie of Ballymoney
>
> **Died** 15 Sep 2000

†MEL   –487

Bp of Ardagh 454;

> Nephew of St Patrick who appointed him first Bp of Ardagh (Ann Ult)
>
> **Died** 487

MERRICK, JOHN   1951–

b. 7 Jul 1951; NUU BA 1972 Dip Adult Ed 1975; TCD HDip Ed 1973 Teaching at Royal Prior Sch Raphoe 1973–86

d 1992 p 1993; Head Master Sligo Gram Sch 1986–2004; Lic to Off Dios Kilmore Elphin and Ardagh 1992–2004; Preb of Oran (Elph & Ard) 2001–04; ret; assisting at St Columb's Cath Londonderry

> **m.** Roberta **dau.** of Robert and Sarah Jane Moffitt; issue 1. Johnathan **b.** 29 Jun 1976 **m.** Julie-Ann Campbell; 2. Sinead **b.** 17 May 1978; 3. Garrett **b.** 4 Jun 1981

MESCALLAGI, ALAN

V Kilglass (Elph) to 1407; is deceased

METCALFE, CHARLES GORDON   1891/92–1977

b. 1891 or 1892; TCD BA 1911

d 1913 p 1914 (Kilmore); C Mohill w Termonbarry (Ard) 1913–16; I Kilmore (w Annaduff E from 1933) (Ard) 1917–58; C-in-c Annaduff (Ard) 1928–32; Preb of Kilmacallen (Elph) 1950–58; ret

> yr **s.** of Hugh, Principal Staff Officer RIC Dublin and Castlerea
>
> **m.** 10 Oct 1917 Margaret Elizabeth (**died** 8 Feb 1965 Roscommon) only **dau.** of Richard Whitelaw Dundas of Belleek Co Fermanagh
>
> **Died** 26 Jan 1977 at Greystones Co Wicklow aged 85 **bur.** Kilmore

MICAMAGISTER, CORNELIUS −c. 1430
V Killeshandra (Kilm) to c. 1430; is deceased
    Died c. 1430

MICCABRUOIG, ANDREW −c. 1440
vacated V Kiltoghart (Ard) by death c. 1440 (C.P.L. X. 330)
    Died c. 1440

MICCAGAYN, TIERNANUS −1443
V Killukin (Elph) to 1443 (C.P.L. IX. 392)
    Died 1443

MICGILLACLAIN, DONATUS
V Magduma = Moydow (Ard) before 1412

MICGILLASMAID, MATTHEW
R Drumreilly (Kilm) c. 1400, was deceased

MICKECHIN, MAGONIUS −c. 1446
V Ardcarde (Elph) 1440
    is deceased in 1446

MICKETHEAN, NICHOLAS −c. 1417
R Cloone (Ard) to 1417
    Died c. 1417

MILES, JOSEPH HENRY 1857–1935
b. 1857; TCD BA 1881 Div Test (2) 1882 MA 1888

d 1882 p 1882 (Kilmore); C Kilkeevan (Elph) 1882–84; Minor Canon of Christ Ch Cath Dublin and Sec CIYMCA Dublin 1884–96; R Pangbourne (Ox) 1896–1913; C West Teignmouth (Ex) 1918–19; C Benenden (Cant) 1919–22; Chapl Faversham Almshouses 1922–30
    Died 27 Jan 1935 at St Ninian's, the Vale, Broadstairs Kent

MILLER, GEORGE CHARLES ALEXANDER 1920–
b. 5 Jan 1920 Kilkenny; ed Kilkenny Coll; Mountjoy Sch Dublin; TCD BA 1945 Div Test 1946

d 15 Aug 1946 p 21 Dec 1947 (Ossory); C Wexford w Rathaspeck (Ferns) 1946–49; Asst Chapl Miss to Seamen Belfast 1949; Immingham Dock 1949–51; Chapl at Pernis Rotterdam 1951–55; R Billis w C-in-c Ballyjamesduff and Castlerahan (Kilm) 1955–

57; R Knockbride (w Killesherdoney to 1960 and w Shercock from 1960) (Kilm) 1957–65; R Urney w Annageliffe Denn & Derryheen (and w Castleterra to 1969) (Kilm) 1965–89; Preb of Drumlease (Kilm) 1977–87; Archd of Kilmore 1987–89; ret

> **s.** of George of Danville Cottage Kilkenny (**s.** of Robert of Bennetsbridge Kilkenny) by Rebecca Jane **dau.** of John Dowling of Killenagh Co Wexford
>
> **m.** 7 Jun 1949 St John's Ch Sligo Olive Margaret **dau.** of Robert and Henrietta (née Hart) Hunter. Issue Ann **b.** 29 Jul 1950 **m.** Michael Fisher

MILLER, ROBERT   1878/79–1918

b. 1878 or 1879; TCD BA & Div Test (2) 1906;

d 1906 p 1907 (Kilmore); C Kilkeevan Tibohine and Liughglynn (Elph) 1906–08; R Killyon and Castleblakeney (Elph) 1908–18

> **m.** 25 Mar 1913 Kathleen Susan **dau.** of Capt William Bunbury, 50th Regt of Woodville Co Tipperary
>
> **Died** 3 Jan 1918 Dublin aged 39 **bur.** Mount Jerome

MILLER, SAMUEL RICHARD   1859–1951

b. 1859; TCD BA 1898 Div Test 1900 MA 1906

d 1899 p 1900 (Dublin); C St Catherine (Dub) 1899–1912; Dio C Kilmore 1912; R Lissadell (Elph) 1912–43; ret

> **Died** 29 Dec 1951 in Dublin as a result of an accident

MILLIGAN, GEORGE ALEXANDER   –1939

TCD BA 1928

d 1921 p 1928; C Dunganstown (Glend) 1921–29; C Urney (Kilm) 1929–32; C-in-c Swanlinbar (Kilm) 1932–39

> **s.** of Mr & Mrs **m.** Milligan of Ederney Co Fermanagh
>
> **m.** Mabel Blanche (**died** 24 Jun 1946 Bristol). Issue incl 1. a **s.** Mr F G Milligan (**died** Aug 1972 Durban S Africa); 2. William (**died** 1978 Dublin)
>
> **Died** 20 Apr 1939

MILLS, ARTHUR MAURICE BROUGHTON   1904–1985

b. 11 Jan 1904; ed Galway Gram Sch; TCD BA 1926 MA 1929; on staff of Bank of Ireland 1926–29

d 1931 (Down) p 1932 (Down); C Bangor (Down) 1931–36; R Ballingarry w Lockeen (Killaloe) 1936–43; R Offerlane U (Oss) 1943–46; R Templemichael (Ard) 1946–60; R New Ross (Ferns) 1960–70; R Donagh Tyholland and Errigal Truagh (Clogh) 1970–78; ret

> 2nd **s.** of John MB BCh BAO of Ballinasloe Co Galway (**s.** of James Cunningham, CI RIC) by Rosetta Evelyn Geraldine Dobbin of Armagh.
>
> **m.** 9 Sep 1942 Bangor Par Ch Marie Metz elder **dau.** of I G Nicholson of Bangor. Issue 1. John H B, RAF 1966; Elizabeth C B **m.** 15 Jul 1967 at New Ross, Allen

m. yr s. of Ervin Foye of Bangor

Died 10 Sep 1985 at Newtownards **bur.** Bangor Abbey

MILLS, EDGAR PARKER 1896–1984

b. 1896; TCD BA 1919 MA 1936

d 1919 p 1921 (Kilm); C Annagh and Quivvy (Kilm) 1919–23; C St Luke (Cork) 1923–27; Min Canon and C St Fin Barre's Cath Cork 1927–73; Canon and Preb of Brigown (Cloyne) 1959–65; Preb of St Michael (Cork) 1959–67; Treas of Cloyne and Canon of Cahirlag (Cork) 1965–67; Prec of Cloyne and Canon of Killaspugmullane (Cork) 1967–73; Prec of Cork 1969–73; ret

Died 12 Jun 1984 Cork

MILLS, HENRY

TCD BA 1879 MA 1885

d & p 1882 (Kilmore); C St John Sligo (Elph) 1882–86; C Holy Trinity Southall (Lon) 1886–91; V Holy Trinity Southall (Lon) 1891 — still there 1917

MILUS, JAMES

ord p by Robert Leighton Bp of Dunblane Feb 1671 as James Mylud (VB 1673); V Cashel and Rathcline (Ard) 1671–*c.* 80, coll and inst 6 Jun (F.F.)

MINCHIN, CHARLES HENRY 1785/86–

b. 1785 or 1786 Dublin; ed by Mr Moulden; ent TCD 6 Jul 1801 aged 15 BA 1806 MA 1826

C Templemichael (Ard) 1817 — still there 1830

s. of Humphrey, merchant

MINION, ARTHUR 1965–

b. 1965; TCD BTh 1992

d 1992 p 1993; C Bandon U (Cork) 1992–95; R Taunagh Kilmactranny & Ballysumaghan (Elph) 1995–99; R Shinrone Aghancon Dunkerrin & Kinnitty (Killaloe) 1999–

MITCHELL, ALFRED 1845/46–1890

b. 1845 or 1846

d 1875 p 1877 (Cork); C Kilmoe (Cork) 1875–78; C Schull (Cork) 1878–80; C St Michan (Dub) 1880–84; C Christ Ch Burton-on-Trent (Lich) 1884–85; C Mohill (Ard) 1885–87; I Kilmore (Elphin) 1887–90

s. of James of Thornfield Co Wicklow

Died 14 Aug 1890 aged 44

†MITCHELL, FREDERICK JULIAN 1901–1979

b. 30 Jul 1901; ed Campbell Coll Belfast; TCD BA (Mod Hist & Pol Sci) 1923 Past Theol and Eccles Hist Pri (1) and Div Test (2) 1924 MA 1928 DD *(j.d.)* 1952

d 1924 p 1925 Bp 1950; C St Mary Belfast (Conn) 1924–28; C-in-c Finaghy (Conn) 1928–36; Dean of Residences QUB 1932–36; R Ballymena and Ballyclug (Conn) 1936–50; RD of Ballymena 1945–49; Preb of Kilroot (Conn) 1950; elected Bp of Kilmore Elphin and Ardagh by the United Synods 28 Jul 1950; consec 21 Sep 1950 St Patrick's Cath Armagh; Bp of Kilmore Elphin and Ardagh 1950–55; elected Bp of Down and Dromore by the House of Bishops 18 Oct 1955; enthroned in Down Cath 8 Dec 1955; enthroned in Dromore Cath 9 Dec 1955; Bp of Down and Dromore 1955–69; ret

> **s.** of Rev Robert James, R Trillick (Clogh) (**s.** of George and Margaret of Manorcunningham Co Donegal) by Anne **dau.** of James and Mary Glendinning of Lurgan Co Armagh
>
> **m.** 30 Jul 1936 Castle Archdale Par Ch Co Fermanagh Kathleen Louise widow of Rev George Kingston, R Tamlaght O'Crilly (Derry) and **dau.** of Rev Robert Watson, R Castle Archdale (Clogh) 1915–44 and Louisa Watson
>
> **Died** June 1979 **bur.** Down Cathedral

PUBLICATIONS
Prayer Book Pageant, 1949
Pageant of the Bible 1951, presented in St Anne's Cathedral Belfast as part of the Festival of Britain celebrations

MITCHELL, FREDERICK RUDOLPH 1913–1993

b. 1913 Dublin; ed Foyle Coll Londonderry; TCD BA 1938

d 1938 p 1939 (Ossory); C Kilnamanagh (Ferns) 1938–40; C Mariners' Ch Dun Laoghaire (Dub) 1940–42; R Achill (Tuam) 1942–45; R Monasterevin (Kild) 1945–51; R Derralossary (Glend) 1951–57; R Asby (Carl) 1957–59; R Drumlease Killenumery Killargue and Innismagrath (Kilm) 1959–62; V St Cuthbert Carlisle (Carl) 1962–66; R Kirkbride w Newton Arlosh (Carl) 1966–78

> **s.** of Robert John of Killcorr Co Derry
>
> **m.** 17 Aug 1938 Violet Louisa **dau.** of James McCracken of Fairview Dublin. Issue 1. John Frederick; 2. Samuel; 3. Helen Margaret; 4. Beryl Anne
>
> **Died** Aug 1993

MITCHELL, ISAAC 1841–1910

b. 1841

d 1871 p 1872 (Armagh); C Charlestown (Arm) 1871–72; C Mariners' Chapel Forbes St Dublin (Dub) 1872–73; C St Barnabas (Dub) 1873–74; R Kiltoom and Camma (Elph) 1874–1910

> **m.** Frances Eleanor (**died** 26 Jun 1924)
>
> **Died** 14 Oct 1910

PUBLICATION
Temperance: Notes of a Speech, 1878

MITCHELL, ROBERT JOHN 1865/66–1943

b. 1865 or 1866; TCD BA (1 Resp) 1890 Div Test (1) 1893

d 1890 p 1891 (Kilm); C Killeshandra (Kilm) 1890–93; C Kildallon (Kilm) 1893–95; C Kilrush (Killaloe) 1895–96; R Toomna (Elph) 1896–1906; R Cashel and Rathcline (Ard) 1906–37; Preb of Kilmacallen (Elph) 1934–37; ret

m. and had issue Alice m. Rev Charles John Tyndall later Bp of Kilmore Elphin and Ardagh and Bp of Derry and Raphoe qv below

Died 7 Jun 1943 aged 77

MITCHELL, SAMUEL PATTON –1943

ed at Dundalk and Santry; TCD BA (Resp) 1894 Div Test 1895 MA 1899

d 1895 (Kilmore) p; C Drumgoon (Kilm) 1895–96; C Seapatrick (Drom) 1896–99; C-in-c St Nicholas Belfast (Conn) 1899–1901; V St Nicholas Belfast (Conn) 1901–43

s. of George of Manorcunningham Co Donegal and Margaret Jane (née Patton)

m. 5 Dec 1922 Kathleen Violet Florence dau. of Alfred W Stevenson of Lurgan Co Armagh and Belfast by Maud (née Baird). Issue 1. Rev George Alfred b. 18 Sep 1923 Belfast ed RBAI TCD BA 1945 Div Test 1946 MA 1956 d 1946 p 1947 C St Matthew Belfast (Conn) 1946–48 C Ballymoney (Conn) 1948–51 C St Anne's Mission District Belfast (Conn) 1951–52 R Broomhedge Lisburn (Conn) 1952–59 R Carrickfergus (Conn) 1959–70 R St Comghall Bangor (Down) 1970–88 m. 21 Sep 1949 Moyra TCD BA OBE dau. of Harold Brennan of Larne Co Antrim and Ellen Frances (née Cambridge) of Clonakilty Co Cork and had issue (i) Carol Frances (died 11 Dec 1990) b. 27 Mar 1952 m. 3 Sep 1976 as his first wife Rev John Wade McKegney, R St Mark Armagh (Arm) (ii) Paul George b. 22 Oct 1955 m. 17 Sep 1982 Dervilla Austin of Dublin (iii) Christopher Henry b. 31 May 1958 m. Kumiko Yamamoto of Tokyo Japan; 2. Rev Cecil Robert (died 20 Jul 2004) b. 7 Jun 1932 Belfast ed RBAI and Royal Sch Armagh QUB BSc 1954 TCD 1963 GOE d 1965 p 1966 C St Mary Magdalene Belfast (Conn) 1965–68 C St Mark Ballysillan Belfast (Conn) 1968–70 Asst Sec Dios Down Dromore and Connor1969 Joint Sec do 1971–74 R Ballywalter (Down) 1974–82 V Malew (S & M) 1982–84 R Bright Ballee and Killough (Down) 1984–89 R Killyleagh (Down) 1989–94 m. 1 Jul 1954 Valerie Margaret dau. of William Frederick and Sylvia Johnston of Hillsborough Co Down and had issue (i) Maree Yvonne (ii) Lynda Karen (iii) Siobhan Ruth (iv) Ivan Robert; 3. Pauline Maud m. Very Rev Hugh Sterling Mortimer, Dean of Elphin qv

Died 13 Oct 1943

MITCHELL, WILLIAM JOHN 1896–1981

b. 1896; Edgehill Theol Coll Belfast; Cliff Theol Coll Birkenhead

d 1927 p 1928 (Kilmore); C Annagh w Quivvy (Kilm) 1927–30; C-in-c Derrylane (Kilm) 1930–42; R Killinkere w Mullagh (w Lurgan and Loughan from 1961) (Kilm) 1942–73; Preb of Drumlease (Kilm) 1965–73; ret

elder s. of Thomas of Kilskeery Co Tyrone

m. 5 Nov 1930 Mary Elizabeth (died 10 Aug 2004) b. 6 Apr 1911 elder dau. of

Arthur B Hinchcliffe of Dysart Enos Co Laois. Issue incl 1. Gordon, TCD BA 1953; 2. his eldest **dau.** Pearl

Died 13 Feb 1981

MOFFATT, GEORGE BEATTY 1797–1874

b. 1797 Co Longford; ed by Mr Langley; ent TCD 7 Nov 1814 aged 17 BA 1819 MA 1832

d 1819p; C Drumlane (Kilm) 1824 & 1825; R Knockbride (Kilm) 1840–42; R Drumlane (Kilm) 1842–74

   s. of Rev James, V Shrule (Ard) qv

   m. (1) Joanne (**died** 13 Dec 1845 at Drumlane Rectory) **dau.** of Robert Richardson. Issue incl 1. Rev James, PC Derryheen (Kilm), qv; 2. Thomas Smith (**died** 29 Jan 1827 aged 1 year at Drumlane); 3. Robert Gerald (**died** 16 Dec 1842 aged 14); 4. his eldest **dau.** Sarah **m.** 12 Feb 1851 John Armstrong, Solicitor of Belturbet; 5. Sophia Margaret (**died** 22 Mar 1852 aged 18).

   m. (2) 22 Nov 1848 Elizabeth Caroline (**died** 21 Dec 1877 aged 65 at Danesfort Cavan) yst **dau.** of Rev Richard H Symes.

   Died 27 Feb 1874

MOFFATT, JAMES 1824/25–1886

b. 1824 or 1825 Co Cavan; ed Lucan Sch; ent TCD 2 Jul 1843 aged 18 BA & Div Test 1849

d 1849 p; C Cloone (Ard) 1851 — still there 1858; C Drumlane (Kilm) 1860–62; PC Derryheen (Kilm) 1862–74

   s. of Rev George Beatty, R Drumlane (Kilm) qv (**s.** of Rev James) by his 1st wife Joanne

   m. and had issue an only **dau.** Jane Anne **m.** 12 Oct 1865 Edward Graham of Limerick

   Died 22 Dec 1886

MOFFATT, JAMES   –1844

Lic C Rathcline (Ard) 1780; C Loughinisland (Down) 1784; Lic PC Forgney (Meath) 1 Nov 1800; C Shrule (Ard) 1800–01; V Shrule (Ard) 1801–44

   probably father of Rev James, V Athlone (Meath) and of Rev G B Moffatt, V Drumlane (Kilm) qv; his **s.** Robert Gerald, 17th Regt, **m.** 19 Jan 1828 Lisburn, Helen Sarah only **dau.** of Capt James C… of Bellaghy Co Derry; his 2nd **dau.** Mary (**died** 19 Jul 1883) **m.** John Waters of Laurel Lodge and had issue

   Died 20 Apr 1844

MOFFETT, ROBERT

ed by Mr Hynes; ent TCD as Sizar 31 May 1763 Sch 1765 BA 1767 MA 1771

C Tashinny (Ard); V & R Cashel and Rathcline 1780–*c.* 1813; R & V Tashinny and

Abbeyshrule (Ard). His tomb, without date of death, was erected by his wife Jemma, and states that he was 30 years Curate of Tashinny Co Longford, and 20 years Rector, though in Leslie's MS Lists, he is given as Curate from 1780 and Rector 1815–19, when he was succeeded by Rev David Richardson Curry. Leslie also has him R Cashel (Ard) 1780–1813; Erck 1817 gives Robert Moffitt as V "Abstrule" (Ard) 1813. Dean Lyster in his *Memorials*, 1899, p 266 says that he was Curate for 40 years, then Rector.

    s. of —— Moffett by Jane sister of Auchmuty Richardson of Colehill Co Longford

    m. Jemma. Issue incl 1. Jane, acc to Mr E.S. Gray, **m.** her cousin Auchmuty Richardson DL JP (**died** 1814) of Richmount Co Longford and had issue incl Jemima **m.** 1824 Rev Arthur Irwin, later Dean of Ardfert; 2. Alice **died** 20 Apr 1783; 3. Mary **died** 10 Nov 1805; 4. Andrew, JP **b.** Co Longford ent TCD 4 Nov 1793 aged 16 BA 1798 **m.** and had issue Robert John **b.** *c.* 1816; 5. Jemima **b.** *c.* 1783 (**died** 8 Mar 1847 in her 65th year) **m.** John Huggins MD (**died** 15 Oct 1877)

MOFFETT, THOMAS
C Drumlane (Kilm) *c.* 1824–30

†MOIGNE, THOMAS   –1628/29
b. in Lincolnshire; Univ of Camb BD and Fellow of Peter House

Archd of Meath 1606–08; Dean of St Patrick's Cath Dublin 1608–25; succeeded to Bprics of Kilmore and Ardagh by Patent dated 17 Dec 1612 with mandate for consecration (C.P.R. James I 237b); consec at Drogheda before 12 Jan 1613; Bp of Kilmore and Ardagh 1612–29. He repaired the Cathedral of Kilmore and built a See House.

    m. Abigail **dau.** of Dr Roger Dod, Bp of Meath. Issue **sons** 1. Roger of Moigne Hall (**died** 1641) **m.** Margaret **dau.** of Sir Samuel Mayart and had issue (i) Dorcas (**died** 30 Jan 1703 **bur.** Cavan) **m.** 24 Apr 1654 St Michan's Ch Dublin Samuel Townley; (ii) Abigail (**died** 24 Oct 1715 aged 78) **m.** Nicholas Moore; 2. John; **daus.** 1. Abigail **m.** Walter Cope of Longford; 2. Jane (**died** 31 Dec 1640) **m.** Anthony Cope of Portadown Co Armagh; 3. Anne

    Died 1 Jan 1628/29 **bur.** St Patrick's Cath Dublin

MOLLOY, HENRY
a layman, held the tithes of the Prebendary of Oran (Elph) 1615

MONCK, JAMES STANLEY 1840–1917
b. 1840; TCD BA 1863; was HM Inspector of Schools 1875–78

d 1881 p 1882; C Clongish (Ard) 1881–83; C Kiltegan (Leigh) 1883–84; C Templederry (Killaloe) 1884; Chapl Villierstown (Lism) 1884–85; C Ballinrobe (Tuam) 1885; C Ballinderry (Arm) 1886–88; R Clonoe (Arm) 1888–1911; ret

    yst **s.** of Rev Thomas Stanley BA, V Inistioge and Preb of Cloneamery (Oss) (**s.** of Rev Thomas Stanley, R Clonegam (Lism) 1801–42 and Jane (née Staples)) by Lydia Eleanor **dau.** of Rev Patrick Kennedy, V Loughmoe (Cash)

Died unm. 3 May 1917 Bangor Co Down **bur.** Clonoe

The Rev J S Monck claimed descent from General George Monck (1608–70), who was a prominent Royalist in the Civil War, supported the overthrow of Richard Cromwell (1659), and was largely responsible for the Restoration of King Charles II the following year. (Canon T. Fleming, *Armagh Clergy 1800–2000,* p 314)

MONEYPENNY, ARTHUR AUGUSTUS 1803–1886

b. 1803 Cavan; ed by Mr Adair; ent TCD 1 Nov 1824 aged 19 BA 1831

d 1834 p 4 May 1837 (Elphin); C Castleterra (Kilm) 1840–*c.* 61; V Ballysumaghan (Elph) 1861–66; V Lavey (Kilm) 1866–82; ret

s. of Arthur

m. Sarah Laetitia Burke. Issue incl Emma Laetitia

Died 13 Oct 1886 aged 82 at Eastbourne

†MONGAN (afterwards **MONGAN–WARBURTON**), **CHARLES 1754–1826**

b. Co Monaghan 1754 and was originally a Roman Catholic

d; p; Bp 1806; Chapl to the Ld Lt, the Duke of Bedford; R Tullagh and Creagh (Ross) 1787–91; Preb of Lackeen (Killaloe) 1789–1804; Dean of Ardagh 1790–1800; pres to the Deanery 15 April as Charles Mongan (L.M. V 170); R Loughgilly (Arm) 1791–1806; Dean of Clonmacnoise 1800–06; Prec St Patrick's Cath Dublin 1800–08; R Mohill (Ard) 1801–06; V Laracor (Meath) 1804–06; Consec Bp of Limerick in St Patrick's Cath Dublin 13 Jul 1806; Bp of Limerick 1806–20; translated to Cloyne 1820; Bp of Cloyne 1820–26

His father is said to have been an Irish harper called Mongan. Charles appears to have used the surname Mongan at the time of his earlier preferments, taking the additional name of Warburton later.

m. Frances Marsden of New York. Issue included 1. Garnet **died** unm; 2. Augustus Frederick Col in 85th Regt; **died unm.**; 3. Ven Charles **b.** New York *c.* 1782 (**died** 14 Dec 1855) ent TCD 1 Nov 1799 aged 17 BA 1803 MA 1807 LLB and LLD 1826 Archd of Tuam 1806–55 R Mourneabbey (Cloyne) 1807 Chanc of Limerick 1813–55 V Clonmel (Lism) 1822–55 **m.** Alicia **dau.** of Thomas Bunbury Isaac of Holywood Hse Co Down and had issue (i) Charles **m.** Mapleton **dau.** of Jonathan Peel (ii) Augustus Frederick **m.** Marianne **dau.** of Col. Hailes (iii) Maria **m.** John Blackburne; 4. Rev John **b.** Co Monaghan *c.* 1786 (**died** 26 Oct 1865 at Crinkle Birr Co Offaly) ed Royal Sch Armagh TCD BA 1807 MA 1813 LLB and LLD 1826 Prec of Ardfert 1811–16 R Kill and Lyons (Kild) 1814–65 Prec of Limerick 1818–65 V Chor Cloyne Cath 1825–65 V Chor Cork 1826–65 R Drumcliffe (Killaloe) 1829–65 **m.** Henrietta **dau.** of Sandford Palmer of Mallow Co Cork and had issue six **sons**; 5. Charlotte **m.** Rev William Wray Maunsell MA (**died** 25 Jul 1860) and had issue (i) William Wray (ii) Rev Robert Augustus **b.** *c.* 1825 TCD BA & Div Test 1848 MA 1862 R Harristown (Kild) 1857–63 **m.** Frances Erskine (iii) Fanny **m.** Major T P Vandeleur (iv) Lucy Diana **m.** Col. Knox; (v) Selina

Died 9 Aug 1826 at Cloyne Co Cork

MONROE, JAMES
coll V Oughteragh (Kilm) 22 Jul 1709

MONSARRAT, JOHN HOWLIN 1825/26–1905
b. 1825 or 1826; ed by Mr Wall; ent TCD 14 Oct 1842 aged 16 BA 1847 Div Test 1850 MA 1856

d 1851 p 1852 (Kilmore); C Eastersnow (Elph) 1851–52; Chapl in Gambia W Africa 1852–62; C St Peter Drogheda and PC St Mark Chapel of Ease in St Peter's Par Drogheda (Arm) 1862–72; R Killalon (Meath) 1872–75; R Moyliscar (Meath) 1875–87; R Ratoath (Meath) 1887–1904

s. of Mark, Solicitor of Kildare St Dublin

m. 12 Aug 1852 St Thomas Ch Dublin Anne Letitia (**died** 1 Feb 1900) **dau.** of Thomas Franklin of Gloucester St Dublin. Issue incl 1. Edward (**died** 21 Jul 1916) **bur.** Mt Jerome Dublin; 2. Mary C (**died** unm 3 Feb 1929 **bur.** Mt Jerome)

Died 22 Jun 1905 Dublin aged 79 **bur.** Mt Jerome

MONSELL, EPHRAIM 1724/25–1798
b. 1724 or 1725 Limerick; ed by Dr Chinnery; ent TCD as Siz 7 Jun 1740 aged 15 BA 1744

d 1749 (Limerick) p; Archd of Elphin 1782–98

s. of Ephraim

m. and had issue 1. Thomas **b.** Limerick ent TCD 2 Oct 1780 aged 17 BA 1785 LLB 1788 Irish Bar 1788 Chmn Co Fermanagh Quarter Sessions; 2. George **b.** Limerick ent TCD 1 Oct 1781 aged 17

Died 10 Apr 1798

MONTAGUE, EDWARD 1823/24–
b. 1823 or 1824 Co Tyrone; ed at Belfast Academy; ent TCD 16 Nov 1859 aged 35 BA 1863 Div Test 1864

d 1864 p; C Denn (Kilm) 1865–67; C Inniscaltra (Killaloe) 1867–69

s. of James

MONTGOMERY, ALEXANDER 1773/74–1848
b. 1773 or 1774 Co Donegal; ed by Mr Meares; ent TCD 4 Nov 1789 aged 15 BA 1794 MA 1810

V Abbeylara and Russagh (Ard) 1797–1807; (Leslie has him prob same as Alexander Montgomery V Abbeylara (Ard) 1797–1810 in *Raphoe Clergy and Parishes*); R Inniskeel (Raph) 1796–1802; Preb of Inver in St Eunan's Cath Raphoe 1802–48; R Templecrone 1803–48

s. of Rev James, R Inniskeel (Raph) 1770–96

Died 15 Oct 1848

PUBLICATION

A *Funeral Sermon* on the death of Mark Kerr MD of Granard, preached in Granard Church, 21 August 1791 (Dublin, James Moore 1792)

MONTGOMERY, CHARLES LYONS 1786/87–1859

b. 1786 or 1787 Dublin; ed by Mr Willis; ent TCD 5 Dec 1803 aged 16 BA 1807 MA 1832

C Tamlaght O'Crilly (Derry) 1817; V Killinagh (Kilm) 1822–23; V Killargue (Kilm) 1828–31; V Innismagrath (Kilm) 1831–59; JP Co Cavan

yr **s.** of Hugh Lyons of Belhaven Co Leitrim by the Hon. Catherine Hamilton **dau.** of Richard, 4th Viscount Boyne

m. 26 Jun 1815 Emily **dau.** of Humphrey Nixon of Nixon Lodge Co Cavan. Issue **sons** 1. Hugh Lyons **m.** 1856 Henrietta C **dau.** of Rev Henry Lucas St George, R & V Dromore (Clogh) by Eliza **dau.** of Edward Warren of Lodge Park Co Kilkenny and had issue; 2. Charles Nixon Lyons; 3. Humphrey Lyons

m. and had issue; 4. Henry Lyons; **daus.** 1. Elizabeth **m.** 27 Dec 1858 Rev Julius Strike Hearn, C Cloonclare (Kilm) qv; 2. Anne bapt 21 Mar 1816; 3. Sophia (**died** 28 Aug 1896 at Ballyshannon) bapt 1 Aug 1817; 4. Catherine bapt 17 Jan 1819; 5. Amelia bapt 26 Jun 1820

Died 3 Sep 1859

MONTGOMERY, GEORGE 1816/17–

b. 1816 or 1817 Dublin; ed by Mr Cronin; ent TCD 21 Oct 1833 aged 16 BA 1838

C St John Sligo (Elph) 1841; subsequently became RC

? **s.** of Alexander, merchant

MONTGOMERY, GEORGE ALEXANDER

ed St Bees Coll Durham 1880

d 1882 p 1885 (Kilmore); C Drumgoon (Kilm) 1882–85; C St Michael Wakefield (Wakef) 1885–87; C All SS Poplar (Lon) 1887–88; C St Peter Limehouse (Lon) 1888–91; C Holy Trinity Hoxton (Lon) 1891–92; R St Helen Theddlethorpe w St Peter Mabelthorpe (Linc) 1892 — still there 1926, gone 1929

MONTGOMERY, GEORGE ROBERT 1874–1933

b. 2 Jul 1874; TCD BA 1902 Div Test 1903

d 1903 p 1905 (Kilmore); C Kilkeevan (Elph) 1903–06; C Kilmeague and Feighcullen (Kild) 1907–08; C Killyman (Arm) 1908–11; R Pomeroy (Arm) 1911–15; R Annaghmore (Arm) 1915–23; C-in-c Mullavilly (Arm) 1923–33

s. of Robert, farmer of Derrawinnia Kilmore Co Cavan by Elizabeth **dau.** of William Browne, farmer of Annageliffe Cavan

m. 17 Dec 1906 Holy Trinity Ch Parish of St Thomas Dublin Mary Elizabeth Carson (**died** 3 May 1940) **dau.** of Robert Graham, farmer of Coracanaway Co

Cavan. Issue 1. Rebecca Elizabeth (**died** 21 Apr 1982) **b.** 25 Oct 1907 **m.** 28 Aug 1930 Mullavilly Par Ch Co Armagh Rev Henry Francis Osborne Egerton (1898–1941), R Derryloran (Arm) 1939–41 and had issue (i) George Francis Reginald **b.** 12 Aug 1933 **m.** 8 Jun 1959 Eileen **dau.** of William Forde of Portadown (ii) Elizabeth Ann **b.** 1 May 1939 **m.** 4 Apr 1961 St Patrick's Cath Armagh Rev Herbert Cassidy, Dean of Kilmore 1985–89 qv; 2. George Richard (**died** 27 May 1990 Grantham Lincs) **b.** 4 Aug 1910 was **m.**; 3. Eileen Frances **b.** 10 Mar 1913 **m.** 27 Jun 1935 John Frederick **s.** of John Weir of Tandragee Co Armagh and had issue (i) Nora (ii) John (iii) Frederick Francis (**died** 4 Aug 1990) (iv) Dorothy; 4. Norah Isobel **b.** 16 Sep 1915 **m.** 6 Jul 1940 John **s.** of Capt William John Menaul, MC (**died** 1975) and had issue (i) Alan Stewart **b.** 6 May 1942 (ii) Rosemary Patricia **b.** 12 Jul 1945 (iii) Jacqueline Norah **b.** 5 May 1947

Died 13 Dec 1933

MONTGOMERY, HUGH 1754–1815

b. 1754 Co Down; ed by Dr Benson; ent TCD 2 Nov 1769 BA 1774

R Cloonclare (Kilm) 1781–92; R Killan, now Shercock (Kilm) 1792–1815

prob **s.** of William of Greyabbey Co Down

m. 1782 Hon. Emilia Ward yst **dau.** of Bernard, 1st Viscount Bangor. Issue **sons** 1. William of Greyabbey; 2. Hugh Bernard, Capt in the Guards died 1817 of wounds received at Waterloo; 3. Rev Edward (**died unm.** 1825) ent TCD as FC 3 Nov 1806 aged 15 BA 1810 V Kilmood (Down) Feb to Dec 1816 R Kilnamanagh (Ferns) 1816 Chanc of Down 1820–25; 4. Arthur Hill of Tyrella; 5. John Charles; 6. Francis Octavius, Lt Col; 7. George Augustus Frederick Sandys, Lt RN; **daus.** 1. Anne Catherine **died unm.**; 2. Emilia Georgina Susanna **m.** 1817 James Myles O'Reilly of Scarva

Died 30 Mar 1815 at Greyabbey

MONTGOMERY, JOHN ALEXANDER 1911–2004

b. 15 Oct 1911 Cavan; ed Royal Sch Cavan and RBAI; TCD BA (Resp) 1934 Div Test (2) 1935 MA 1942

d 1935 p 1936; Dio C Clogher 1935–37; C St Simon Belfast (Conn) 1937–40; Dio C Kilmore Elphin and Ardagh 1940–45; C-in-c Drumshambo and Kiltubride (Ard) 1945–51; R Taunagh and Kilmactranny (Elph) 1951–54; R Garvary (Clogh) 1954–59; R Kilkeevin Kiltullagh and Tybohine (Elph) 1959–66; RD of S Elphin 1966–67; R Ardagh Moydow Tashinny and Shrule (w Kilcommick and Cashel from 1971) (Ard) 1967–80; RD of Newtownforbes 1967–80; Preb of Kilmacallan (Elph) 1978–80; ret Hon Canon Linlithgow (Edin) 1983–2004

s. of Thomas of Cavan (**s.** of Richard and Elizabeth (née Browne) of Cavan) by Agnes **dau.** of James and Agnes (née Buchanan) Beaton of Bo'ness W Lothian Scotland

m. 27 Dec 1948 St Thomas Church Kilcronan Co Roscommon Hilda Helga Luise Krings **dau.** of Ernst and Emma (née Jost) Gadesmann of Duesseldorf Germany

Died 22 Apr 2004

MONTGOMERY, WILLIAM
C Drumlane (Kilm) to 1817

MOORE, ARTHUR   –1780
prob …Moore, TCD BA 1731; MA of a Scottish Univ

d 16 Jun 1728 p 1 Jun 1729 (Clogher); C Rossinver (Kilm) 1728; C Knockbride (Kilm) 1736; V Denn (Kilm) 1740–76; Archd of Kilmore and V Gen 1768–70; joint V Gen of Kilmore with Rev William Fox qv 1772; V Killargue (Kilm) 1774–77; JP for Co Cavan

s. of James of Knocknalosset Co Cavan by Mary

m. Mary. Issue 1. George (**died** before 7 Sep 1767) **m.** Martha Cory and had issue George bapt 7 Sep 1767; 2. Elizabeth Sophia **m.** Oct 1768 Rev William Fox, V Denn (Kilm) qv; 3. Catherine **m.** John Johnston; 4. Mary (**died** 10 Apr 1820 aged 66) **m.** Jul 1771 John Macartney of Tempo Co Fermanagh; 5. Agnes

Died 1780

MOORE, DIONYSIUS
is presented to Par Ch of Kilronan (Ard) (Leslie says Clonfert Diocese, where it may have been at that time) 14 Oct 1559 (L.M. V. 99)

MOORE, E
C Castlerahan (Kilm) *c.* 1825 — still there in 1830

†MOORE, EDWARD FRANCIS BUTLER 1906–1997
b. 30 Jan 1906 Cootehill Co Cavan; ed Drogheda Grammar Sch; TCD Sen Exhib 1926 Sch 1927 BA (1 cl Mod Ment & Mor Phlos) 1928 Toplady Pri 1929 Downes Pri (Comp & Orat) Warren Pri 1930 Div Test (2) 1930 MA 1940 PhD 1944 DD *j.d.* 1959

d 1930 p 1931 (Dublin) Bp 1959; C Bray (Dub) 1930–32; Hon Cler V Christ Ch Cath Dublin 1931–34; C Clontarf (Dub) 1932–34; R Castledermot & Kinneagh (Glend) 1934–40; R Greystones (Glend) 1940–58; Canon of Christ Ch Cath Dublin 1951–57; Archd of Glendalough 1957–59; elected by the United Synods Bp of Kilmore Elphin and Ardagh 28 Nov 1958; consec in St Patrick's Cath Armagh 6 Jan 1959; enthroned in St Fethlimidh's Cath Kilmore 22 Jan 1959; enthroned in the Cath Church of St Mary the Virgin and St John the Baptist Sligo 25 Oct 1961; Bp of Kilmore Elphin and Ardagh 1959–81; ret

s. of Rev William Ryland Rainsford, R Drumgoon (Kilm) qv by Gertrude Frances

m. 14 Apr 1932 Frances Olivia (**died** Jan 1997) **dau.** of Rev Chanc Digby Scott, V Bray (Dub) 1910–43 and Charlotte Jessy (née Barrington). Issue 1. Rt. Rev James Edward (**died** 16 Mar 2005) **b.** 8 May 1933 Dublin TCD BA 1954 Div Test 1956 MA 1964 d 24 Jun 1956 p 16 Jun 1957 C St Columba Knock (Down) 1956–60 C Bangor (Down) 1960–62 C-in-c Belvoir Belfast (Down) 1962–68 R Groomsport (Down) 1968–75 R Dundela Belfast (Down) 1975–95 Preb of Talpestone in Down

Cath 1985–87 Treas of Down 1987–89 Archd of Down and Chanc St Anne's Cath Belfast 1989–95 Bp of Connor 1995–2001 **m.** 14 Jun 1962 Bangor Par Ch Pamela Mary **dau.** of S Brian and Davida Fetherston of Bangor and have issue (i) Peter Seward **b.** 30 Oct 1966 (ii) Gillian Mary **b.** 29 Feb 1968; 2. Frances Mary **b.** 31 Aug 1935; 3. Eileen **b.** 1937 died in infancy; 4. Patrick Ralph **b.** 11 May 1941 **m.** 21 Apr 1965 St Thomas' Ch Mt Merrion Dublin Valerie (née Cornish) of Dublin and had issue Janet Elizabeth bapt 15 Aug 1971; 5. Audrey May **b.** 19 Nov 1944 **m.** 1 Apr 1967 Kilmore Cath David 3rd **s.** of Mr P G Warnock

Died 13 Dec 1997

MOORE, EDWARD MONTGOMERY 1831/32–1888

b. 1832 or 1833 Kildare; ed by Mr Daly; ent TCD 26 Jan 1859 BA 1863 MA 1878

d 1864 p 1865 (Kilmore); C Killeshandra (Kilm) 1864–78; C Mayne (Meath) 1878–79; R Mayne (Meath) 1879–88

s. of Brinsley Nixon

m. 29 May 1880 Harriet (**died** 10 Jul 1887) **b.** 17 Mar 1827 2nd **dau.** of Col Conolly of Castletown Co Kildare

Died 21 or 28 Oct 1888 aged 56

MOORE, FOWKE

ent TCD 10 Oct 1737 BA 1742

d 26 Aug 1743 p 4 or 24 Sep 1743 (Kilmore); is C Kilmore (Kilm) in 1745; Master of the Free Sch Dungannon 1756–77

m. Jane **dau.** of Christopher Rynd of Fenagh Co Leitrim. Issue 1. Sophia bapt 25 Jan 1749 **bur.** 7 Jul 1751; 2. John bapt 26 Feb 1750; 3. Rebecca bapt 27 Aug 1751; 4. Joseph bapt 12 Aug 1752; 5. Frances bapt 6 May 1754; 6. Margaret bapt 5 Aug 1755; 7. Fowke **b.** Co Tyrone ed by Mr Moore ent TCD 4 Nov 1776 aged 17; 8. Eleanor

MOORE, GEORGE BEATTY 1800/01–58

b. 1800 or 1801; ed by Mr Leland; ent TCD 8 Jun 1819 aged 18 BA 1824

PC Ardara (Raph) 1829–c. 36; C Clongish Killoe (Ard) 1846–

2nd **s.** of M'Vitty of Cartrons Co Longford by Frances **dau.** of George Beatty of Lismoy Co Longford

m. 20 May 1830 Killaghtee Co Donegal Maryanne yst **dau.** of David Crawford of Spamount Co Donegal

Died 14 Jan 1858

MOORE, HENRY GRATTAN –1917

TCD BA 1870 Div Test 1871 BD 1879

d 1870 (Kilmore) p 1873 (Down); C Derryheen (Kilm) 1870–75; C Enniscorthy (Ferns) 1875–77; C Knockbreda Belfast (Down) 1877–81; R Magherahamlet (Drom)

1881–84; R St Paul Shelburne Ontario (Dio Huron) 1885–88; Missy at Saltfleet, Binbrook w Barton East, Ontario (Dio Niagara) 1888–89; R St Philip Chicago (Dio Chicago) 1889–97; R Christ Ch Winnitka (Chicago) 1897; Canon of Cathedral of SS Peter and Paul Chicago 1907–17

s. of Rev William Prior, Headmaster of the Royal Sch Cavan qv by Anna **dau.** of Rev William Grattan

m. 13 Aug 1879 Elizabeth Avis **dau.** of Thomas Wilkinson of Enniscorthy Co Wexford. Issue 1. Gerald; 2. Kathleen M

Died Nov or Dec 1917

MOORE, JOHN

coll R & V Taghsynod (Ard) 1684 (F.F.)

MOORE, JOHN 1751/52–1840

b. 1751 or 1752; ent Kilkenny Coll 18 Jul 1763 aged 11; ent TCD 1 Nov 1768 Sch 1771 MA 1782; Headmaster of the Royal School Cavan

d 29 May 1774 (Ossory) p; R Ventry (A & A) 1814–26; probably same as John Moore C Fenagh (Ard) to 1826; R Kilbonayne and V Molahiffe (A & A) 1826–40

s. of Lt John

m. 2 Oct 1789 Susannah Ayres (**died** 29 Apr 1850 at Cavan aged 78) of Rathfarnham Dublin. Issue 1. Lt Thomas Richard, 20th Regt **m.** 5 Jul 1824 Emmeline **dau.** of R Kendal of Pelyne Hill Cornwall; 2. Rev Theodore Octavius qv; 3. James Guy TCD BA 1834; 4. Rev William Prior BA qv 1829 who succeeded him as Headmaster of the Royal School Cavan

Died 29 Mar 1840 in Dublin in his 89th year

MOORE, JOSEPH CARSON   –1871

TCD Sch 1850 BA 1853 Div Test (1) 1854

d 18 May 1856 p; C Kiltoghart (Ard) 1856; C Killesherdoney (Kilm) 1857–60; appears C Annagh (Kilm) 8 Jun 1860; C Urney (Kilm) 1860–71

Died 20 Mar 1871 Cavan

MOORE, MATTHEW

ord d & p by Malcolm (Hamilton), Abp of Cashel 19 Dec 1623

V Cloonclare (Kilm) 1625–36; he is also V Innismagrath (Kilm) 1625–36 & V Killinagh (Kilm) 1636–61

MOORE, MATTHEW

V Ballintubber to 1673; on 8 Jul 1673, the Abp of Tuam reports to Thomas, Bp of Killala that Matthew Moore, V of Baslick and Cloonmagarmacan was during his triennial visitation found frequently inebriated and absent from his parish. He asks the Bp to deprive him, and he is deposed

MOORE, PATRICK –1741 or 1743

V Killenumery and Killery (Ard) 1721–24, coll 16 or 17 May 1721; V Clonbroney (Ard) 1724–30; R Kildrumferton (Kilm) 1730–40; R Castleterra (Kilm) 1740–41/43
Died 1741 or 1743

MOORE, RAYMOND 1947–

b. 7 Jan 1947 Belfast; ed Grosvenor High Sch; QUB BSc (Hons) Biochemistry 1970

d 1987 p 1988; C in NSM All Saints Belfast (Conn) 1987–95; Gen Lic Dio Connor May–Nov 1995; C in NSM St Hilda's Kilmakee (Conn) 1995–2004; P-in-c in NSM Drung Castleterra Larah Lavey and Killoughter (Kilm) 2004–

s. of James and Harriett Ellen (*née* Gillespie) of Belfast

m. 25 Dec 1965 at St Nicholas' Ch Belfast Rev Roberta, qv. **dau.** of Ernest and Victoria (*née* Moore) McGibbon. Issue 1. Adam **b.** 21 Dec 1970 m 27 Jul 1996 in Basildon Essex Samantha Tull; 2. David b 15 Apr 1972; 3. Emma b 11 Jun 1975

MOORE, ROBERT 1722/23–

b. 1722 or 1723 Co Down; ed by Dr Carthy; ent TCD as Siz 6 Jul 1740 aged 17 BA 1744

d 1745 p 1746 (Kilmore); C Kildrumferton (Kilm) 1752; V Easkey (Killala) –1777

s. of Robert

MOORE, ROBERTA 1946–

b. 23 Jul 1946 Belfast; ed Larkfield Secondary Sch

d 11 Jun 2006 p 24 Jun 2007; C in NSM Drung Castleterra Larah Lavey and Killoughter (Kilm) 2006–

dau. of Ernest (s of Ernest and Eliza (*née* Nugent) McGibbon of Belfast by Victoria dau of Richard and Margaret (*née* Richardson) Moore of Belfast

m. 25 Dec 1965 at St Nicholas' Ch Belfast Rev Raymond, qv. **s.** of James and Harriett Ellen Moore of Belfast. Issue 1.Adam **b.** 21 Dec 1970 **m.** 27 Jul 1996 Basildon Essex Samantha Tull; 2. David **b.** 15 Apr 1972; 3. Emma b 11 Jun 1975.

MOORE, THEODORE OCTAVIUS 1816–1889

b. 1816 Cavan; ent TCD 1 Jul 1833 aged 17 BA 1838 MA 1843

d 1840 (Lim) p 1840 (Kild); C Clonbroney (Ard) 1841–46; V Clonbroney (Ard) 1846–64; V Annaduff (Ard) 1864–78; V Billy (Conn) 1882–89

s. of Rev John, qv above Headmaster Royal Sch Cavan (**s.** of Lt John) by Susanna Ayres and **bro.** of Rev William Prior

m. 14 Jan 1846 St Peter Dublin Arabella Catherine only **dau.** of Richard Augustus Kidd of Tullough Co Wexford by Mary Anne **dau.** of William Grattan of Sylvan Park and Bensfort Co Meath, High Sheriff Co Meath 1778. Issue Rev Arthur John **b.** *c.* 1852 (**died** 8 Sep 1919) TCD BA 1875 Div Test 1877 MA 1881 d 1876 p

1877 (Down) C Shankill Lurgan (Drom) 1876–79 R St Jude Ballynafeigh (Down) 1879–86 R Christ Ch Lisburn (Conn) 1886–94 R Coleraine (Conn) 1894–97 R Holywood (Down) 1897–1919 Prec of Down 1899–1911 Chanc of Down 1911–19; **m.** 7 Feb 1878 Trinity Ch Rathmines Dublin Ruth Isabella (**died** 23 Jun 1899) **dau.** of Rev Henry Hugh O'Neill MA, R Knockbride Co Cavan qv by Sarah **dau.** of Thomas Battersby of Loughbane Newcastle Co Westmeath

Died 1 Dec 1889 at Billy Rectory Co Antrim

MOORE, THOMAS C

d 1861 p; PC Calry (Elph) 1866–67

MOORE, THOMAS 1823–1909

b. 1823 Dublin; ent TCD 1 Jul 1840 aged 16 BA 1845 Div Test 1846 MA 1893

d 1846 (Sodor and Man) p 1847 (Tuam); C St George Douglas IOM (S & M) 1846–47; C Drumgoon (Kilm) 1847–51; C Bray (Dub) 1853–63; C Killiney (Dub) 1864–67; C Drumgoon (Kilm) 1866–70; R Drumgoon (Kilm) 1870–1904; ret

s. of Frederick, *jurisperitus* (Barrister-at-Law), by Hannah **dau.** of Nathaniel Hone, Lord Mayor of Dublin 1810–11

m. (1) 2 Aug 1845 Monkstown Ch Dublin Mary eldest **dau.** of Brindley Hone of Monkstown. Issue incl 1. Dr Thomas J **m.** 19 Jul 1877 Harriett only child of the late Edward McIntosh, JP Co Cavan and had issue incl (i) Brindley Hone, TCD MD **m.** Blanche Kathleen Maud Beare (ii) John Hone, RAFVR; 2. D Frederick Hone of Monmouth

m. (2) Dec 1850 Lillias **dau.** of Henry Kingsmill of Dublin. Issue incl 1. Edith Mary **m.** 15 Sep 1869 Rev John Bennet Radcliffe, R Killiney (Dub) 1867–76; 2. Annie Geraldine **m.** Rev Henry Wilson Swinburn Given, C Drumgoon (Kilm) qv

Died 18 Dec 1909 at Kingstown (Dun Laoghaire) Co Dublin aged 86

MOORE, WILLIAM 1796/97–1874

perhaps same as William Moore **b.** 1796 or 1797 Co Mayo; ed by Rev Mr Simpson; ent TCD 5 Jun 1822 BA ?1830

V Killery (Ard) 1861–74

s. of John, *agricola*

Died 24 Aug 1874 at Ballintogher aged 77

MOORE, WILLIAM

lic C Killoe and Templemichael (Ard) 15 Sep 1839 (D.R.); prob same as above

MOORE, WILLIAM PRIOR –1901

d 1856 p; Head Master Royal Sch Cavan 1834–91; C Urney (Kilm) 1870–71

s. of William Head Master, Royal Sch Cavan

m. Anna **dau.** of Rev William Grattan of Sylvan Park and Bensfort Co Meath by

Anna Selina **dau.** of Humphrey Nixon of Nixon Lodge Co Cavan, High Sheriff Co Cavan 1777 and Co Fermanagh 1784. Issue incl Rev Henry Grattan, C Derryheen (Kilm) qv

Died 1901

†MOORE, WILLIAM RICHARD 1858–1930

b. 5 Aug 1858; ed Rathmines Sch Dublin; TCD BA 1881 first honourman and prizeman in Mathematics; Div Test (1) 1882 BD 1901 DD (j. d.) 1916

d 1882 p 1883 (Kilmore) Bp 1915; C Templemichael (Ard) 1882–85; C Donnybrook (Dub) 1885–86; R Kiltoghart (Ard) 1886–1907; Archd of Ardagh 1896–1915; R Templemichael (Ard) 1907–15; elected Bp of Kilmore Elphin and Ardagh by the united Synods 10 Nov 1915 and consec 30 Nov 1915 St Patrick's Cath Armagh; Bp of Kilmore Elphin and Ardagh 1915–30

s. of William Michael, Solicitor of Dublin by Jane

m. 1889 Lily Darley Cochrane, niece of Bp Darley qv. Issue 1. Dacre William (killed in Great War 11 Jun 1916) **b.** 1892 Lt Machine Gun Corps; 2. Edward Dawson **b.** Sep 1894 2nd Lt Royal Engineers ent TCD 1913 **m.** 29 Jun 1927 Enid Margaret **dau.** of R Cecil Barcroft; 2 **daus.**

Died 23 Feb 1930

MOORE, WILLIAM RYLAND RAINSFORD 1865–1951

b. 1865; ed Rathmines Sch Dublin; TCD BA 1888 MA 1891

d 1889 p 1890 (London); C St James Clerkenwell (Lon) 1889–92; C St Thomas Kensal Town (Lon) 1892–95; C St Luke Kensington (Lon) 1895–98; R Stapleford (St A) 1898–1901; C Dundalk (Arm) 1901–04; R Drumgoon (Kilm) 1904–31; R Ballingarry (Lim) 1931–47

yst **s.** of Stevenson Cuming of Terenure Dublin

m. Dec 1888 Gertrude Frances yst **dau.** of Canon Edward Walter Butler, R Fertagh (Oss). Issue 1. William Edward Cuming **b.** 1894; 2. Gertrude Annie Henrietta **b.** 1902 **m.** 4 Jan 1926 Gerald Eyre **s.** of Rev Walter Henry Brown, R Borris-in-Ossory (Oss) 1923–26; 3. Rt Rev Edward Francis Butler, Bp of Kilmore Elphin and Ardagh qv; 4. Lucy Rainsford (twin) **b.** 30 Jan 1906

Died Jan 1951

MOOREHEAD, WILLIAM BURKITT 1800/01–

b. 1800 or 1801 Monaghan; ed Monaghan Sch; ent TCD 3 Nov 1817 aged 16 BA 1822

C Termonbarry (Elph) 1831

s. of Samuel, merchant

m. 10 Dec 1834 Newtownforbes Jane **dau.** of Richard Armstrong of Closebolt Co Longford

MOORHEAD, JAMES
adm R & V Drumgoon (Kilm) 10 Oct 1627

MORAN, PHILIP JOHN –1877
C Killoughter (Kilm) 1867–70; C Killesherdoney (Kilm) 1868; C Drumlummon and Ballymachugh (Ard) 1870–72; C Gowna (Ard) 1872–74; R Gowna (Ard) 1875–76

> **Died** 1 Jul 1877

MOREWOOD, ROLAND SAVAGE 1818/19–1884
b. 1818 or 1819 Co Antrim; ed by Dr Wall; ent TCD 16 Oct 1840 BA 1845 Div Test (1) 1846

d 1847 p; C Antrim (Conn) 1848; served in England; C Cloone (Ard) 1861–; C Lorrha (Killaloe) 1862–65; C Lissan (Arm) 1865–78; ret to Draperstown Co Derry

> **s.** of Samuel, Collector of Taxes
>
> **m.** 30 Aug 1848 Rathfarnham Ch Dublin, Eliza (**died** 24 Aug 1863 at Glenpool Place Rathfarnham) **dau.** of Thomas Ashley of Glenpool Place Rathfarnham Dublin
>
> **Died** 23 Apr 1884 at Moyheeland Draperstown aged 65

MORRIS, RICHARD
TCD Cand Bach 1864

d 1868 p 1869 (Cash); C Doon (Cash) 1868–69; C Castleterra (Kilm) 1869–72; V St Mark New Brompton (Roch) 1872–1917; Hon Canon of Rochester 1908

MORRISON, WILLIAM HENRY –1929
d 1880 p 1881 (Kilmore); C Killukin (Elph) 1880–82; C Killinane (Kilmacd) 1882–85; R Kilcullen (Glend) 1885–1900; R Errigal (Derry) 1900–28; ret

> **m.**… **dau.** of Michael James Manning of Dublin. Issue **sons** 1. Clifford; 2. Charles (**died** in Great War); **daus.**, 1. Lily m….Smith; 2. Eileen **m.** (1) Capt Barber, **m.** (2) Gen C Burnley of Jersey
>
> **Died** 12 Jun 1929

MORROW, GEORGE FREDERICK 1907–*c.* 1984
b. 1907; TCD BA 1945 Div Test 1946

d 1946 p 1947 (Meath); C Oldcastle w Loughcrew and Mountnugent (Meath) 1946–47; C-in-c Kilbixy and Leney U (Meath) 1947–51 and I 1951–52; R Easkey U (Killala) 1952–60; R Fenagh Myshall and Killedmond (Leigh) 1960–64; R Rathaspeck and Streete (Ard) 1964–69; R Kiltegan (w Hacketstown Clonmore and Moyne from 1976) (Leigh) 1969–79; Preb of Killamery and Kilmanagh (Oss) and Preb of Tecolme (Leigh) 1976–79; ret Last In Entry C I Dir 1984

> yst **s.** of Rev Joseph William, R Kilglass (Killala) 1891–1919

m. (1) Elsie (**died** 22 Nov 1970). Issue 1. Patricia Ann **m.** Aug 1967 at Rathowen Neill yr **s.** of Neil Carney Stuart of Monkstown Co Dublin; 2. Vivienne **m.** Apr 1969 Jonathan Mitchell of Carrickmines Co Dublin

m. (2) 11 Oct 1972 Abbey Presby Ch Dublin Lettie yst **dau.** of J Johnston of Monaghan

MORROW, HENRY HUGH 1926–2006

b. 26 Sep 1926 Graddum Co Cavan; ed Masonic Boys' Sch Dublin; TCD BA & Div Test 1949 MA 1967; Flinders Univ Australia BSocAdmin 1976

d 1949 p 1950 (Dublin); C St Thomas & St Barnabas Dublin (Dub) 1949–53; BC Rathmolyon and Laracor (Meath) 1953–56 and R 1956–58; BC Killoughter and Cloverhill 1958–62; C St Mark Portadown (Arm) 1962–65; R Ballinderry and Tamlaght (Arm) 1965–70; R Border Town (Dio Murray Australia) 1970–73; P-in-c Findon (Dio Adelaide) 1973–75; Dir Soc Welfare Dept Dio Adelaide 1975–91; Hon Canon of Adelaide 1984–; ret

s. of Henry, farmer of Kilnaleck Co Cavan by Hilda (née Dunlop)

m. 15 Apr 1953 St Pappan's Ch Santry Dublin June **dau.** of Francis William and Florence May Livingstone, Glasnevin Dublin and Westport Co Mayo. Issue 1. Nigel William Hugh **b.** 4 Apr 1954; 2. Heather Dorothy June **b.** 7 Jun 1955 **m.** 1983 Christopher Wiliams; 3. Hilary Kenneth Robert **b.** 19 Mar 1957 **m.** 1981 Angela Jones; 4. Wendy Nicola **b.** 18 Dec 1959 **m.** 1980 Christopher Nettle; 5. Valerie Elizabeth **b.** 28 Mar 1961 **m.** 1988 Peter Francis

Died 28 Feb 2006

MORSE, EDEWARD F

TCD BA 1841 Div Test (2) 1843

d Oct 1843 (Tuam for Elphin) p 1845 (Kilmore); C Boyle (Elph) 1843–47; C Carlingford (Arm) 1847–48; C Castledermot (Glend) 1848–69

MORTIMER, HUGH STERLING 1923–2007

b. 22 Apr 1923 Belfast; ed BRA; TCD BA 1944 Div Test 1945 MA 1953; ARSCM 1985

d 27 Jan 1946 p 25 Apr 1947 (Connor); C Finaghy (Conn) 1946–49; Dean's V Belfast Cath 1949–53; V Chor Belfast Cath 1953–55; R Tartaraghan (Arm) 1955–61; Hon V Chor Armagh Cath 1957–85; R Magherafelt (Arm) 1961–66; R St Mark Armagh (Arm) 1966–83; in charge Aghavilly (Arm) 1973–83; Preb of Mullabrack in St Patrick's Cath Armagh 1966–72; Treas of Armagh Cath 1972–73; Chancellor of Armagh 1973–75; Prec of Armagh 1975–83; Dean of Elphin and Ardagh and R Cathedral Parish of St Mary and St John the Baptist Sligo with Knocknarea and Rosses Point (Elph) 1983–91; ret

s. of Hugh Sterling of Belfast (**s.** of John Charles and Martha (née Dickson) of Belfast) by Margaret Elizabeth **dau.** of Henry and Elizabeth Walker of Randalstown Co Antrim

m. 10 Sep 1953 Broomhedge Ch Lisburn Pauline Maud **dau.** of Rev Samuel Patton and Violet Florence (née Stevenson) Mitchell, C Drumgoon (Kilm) 1895–96 qv Issue 1. Stephen Paul **b.** 22 Jan 1957 **m.** 27 Feb 1985 Clogher Cath Jacqueline Potter of Clogher Co Tyrone and have issue (i) Paul **b.** 28 Jan 1986 (ii) Sara **b.** 20 Nov 1990; 2. Philip Sterling **b.** 23 Jan 1959 **m.** 12 Feb 1982 Aughnacloy Presby Ch Sandra Hall of Aughnacloy Co Tyrone and have issue Lauren **b.** 14 Nov 1991; 3. Catherine Margaret **b.** 9 Feb 1963 **m.** 16 Apr 1994 Philip Cuesta of Peterborough

Died 26 Feb 2007

MORTON, JOSEPH 1805/06–1878

b. 1805 or 1806; TCD BA 1829 MA 1832

C Aughrim (Elph) 1843–46; V Creeve Kilmacumsy & Shankill (Elph) 1846–47; V Bumlin (Elph) 1847–78; Preb of Kilgoghlin (Elph) 1870–78

m. and had issue incl his yst **dau.** Martha Caroline **m.** 3 Nov 1874 Alfred E Horne, RIC

Died 21 Oct 1878 aged 72

MORTON, JOSEPH

C Elphin (Elph) 1847–48; prob same as above

MOULSDALE, THOMAS W 1847/48–1894

b. 1847 or 1848

d 1885 p; C Cloonclare (Kilm) 1885–86; C Ballysumaghan (Elph) 1886–87; V Ballysumaghan (Elph) 1887–94

Died 19 May 1894 aged 46

MOXLEY, STEPHEN –1890

TCD BA 1872 LLB 1873 LLD 1882

d 1872 (Kilmore) p 1873 (Derry); C Elphin (Elph) 1872–76; R Ardnageehy (Cloyne) 1876–81; R Drimoleague (Cork) 1881–82; Lic Pr Dio Liverpool 1894

Died 1890

MULLOY, CHARLES COOTE

There appear to be two of this name:

(1) in Leslie's MS

b. 1801 or 1802 Co Roscommon; ed by Mr Von Feinagle; ent TCD 2 Nov 1818 aged 16 BA 1823

R Eastersnow and Kilcola (Elph) 1837–40; C St Bride (Dub) 1857–59; R Newtownmountkennedy (Glend) 1859–62; C Foyran (Meath) 1862; (1862–69 in C I Dir) R Mayne (Meath) 1869; (1872–78 in C I Dir)

eldest **s.** of Coote, DL of Hughstown Co Roscommon; (claimed to chief of the family O'Mulloy, Standard Bearers to the Crown of England in Ireland), by Mary eldest **dau.** of William Lloyd of Rockville Co Roscommon

m. 1831 Alice eldest **dau.** of Robert King Duke of Newpark Co Sligo. Issue 1. Coote (**died** 10 Mar 1857 unm); 2. Robert (**died** 1849); 3. William Hutchinson; 4. Mary; 5. Elizabeth Anne

Died 23 May 1882 at Cabra Road Dublin

(2) in *Clergy of Dublin and Glendalough,* 2001

b. 1828 Co Dublin; ed by Mr Earle; TCD matric 1846

C Rathgraffe (Meath) 1847; C St Bride (Dub) 1858; PC Newtownmountkennedy (Glend) 1859–63; C Foyran (Meath) 1866; (1862–69 in C of I D); PC Mayne 1869–79; (1872–78 in C of I D)

s. of Rev Charles (**s.** of Tobias), R Clontarf (Dub) 1811–29 by his 2nd wife Margaret (née King)

m. Catherine Reddish **dau.** of Most Rev Charles Dickinson, Bp of Meath 1840–42

MULLOY, JOHN 1796/97–1858

b. 1796 or 1797 Co Leitrim; ed by Mr Kean; ent TCD 3 Jun 1817 aged 20 BA 1823

Preb of Oran (Elph) 1832–51; R Castleblakeney (Elph) 1857–58

s. of Laurence, *agricola*

m. Maria. Issue Kate (**died** 9 Nov 1879 at Bangor Wales aged 43)

Died 31 Dec 1858 at Blackrock Dublin

MUNNS, EDWARD 1681/82–1756

b1681 or 1682 Co Roscommon; ed by Mr Jones, Elphin; ent TCD as Siz 9 Jul 1700 aged 18 BA 1705

V Boyle Taunagh & Ballysumaghan (Elph) 1718–29; Preb of Termonbarry (Elph) 1720–30; V Kilglass (Elph) 1729–30; Lic C Ahamplish & V Drumcliffe (Elph) 1730–56; Archd of Aghadoe 1734–36; Archd of Elphin 1747–56

s. of Edward, *colonus,* and Jane widow of Robert Woods and **dau.** of John Goldsmith and great–aunt of Oliver Goldsmith

m. a **sister** of Capt George Brereton of the 10th Foot (Pole's Regt.) and had issue incl 1. a **s.** John matric at Univ of Glasgow 1747 MA 1749; 2. Edward; **daus.** 1. Anne; 2. Christian; 3. Olivia (**died** *c.* 1799) **m.** William Hodson (b 1731 **died** Mar 1778 **bro.** of John below) 4. Mary **m.** John West of Cloone Co Leitrim; 5. Sarah (1740–1826) **m.** as his 2nd wife John Hodson of John's Port Co Roscommon. The order of birth is uncertain

Died Jan 1756

MURDOE, DAVID

pres to R Oughteragh (Kilm) 11 Aug 1641 (L.M. V. 113)

MURPHY, DAVID 1914–1996

b. 4 Jan 1914 Belfast; GOE 1949; Univ of London BA 1950 BD 1952

d 1949 p 1950 (Down); C Dromore (Drom) 1949–51; R Drumlane (Kilm) 1951–55; C Seapatrick (Drom) 1955–61; C Derriaghy (Conn) 1961–63; C Sedghill (Newc) 1963–66; teaching Rel Ed in Birmingham 1966–67; V Haverton Hill (Dur) 1967–73; V W Pelton (Dur) 1973–82; ret

> **s.** of Thomas of Belfast (**s.** of John and Margaret (née Stewart) of Belfast) by Agnes Jane **dau.** of John Coey of Comber and Elizabeth (née Todd) of Belfast; **bro.** of Rev Thomas, R Sixmilecross (Arm) 1976–90 (**died** 28 May 1995)
>
> **m.** 27 Jun 1951 Dromore Cath Sarah **dau.** of George and Mary Purdy of Dromore Co Down. Issue 1. David Henry George **b.** 23 May 1952; 2. Aidan Patrick Thomas **b.** 5 Oct 1957; 3. Margaret Mary Agnes **b.** 10 Jun 1960 **m.** 5 Apr 1986 Paul Crocombe; 4. Iris Brigid Sarah **b.** 27 Jul 1961; 5. Patricia Eileen Mary **b.** 16 Jun 1964
>
> **Died** 31 Mar 1996 **bur.** Dromore Cathedral Churchyard

MURPHY, JOHN

lic C Streete (Ard) 2 Feb 1802

MURPHY, RICHARD WILLIAM 1844/45–1916

b. 1844 or 1845; 1TCD BA 1880 Div Test 1881 MA 1883

d 1880 (Kilmore) p 1881 (Dublin for Kilmore); C Kilkeevan (Elph) 1880–82; R Kiltullagh (then Tuam — now Elph) 1882–1905; Preb of Balla and Faldown (Tuam) 1904–16; R Omey (Tuam) 1905–16.

> **m.** Mary Louisa (**died** 8 Jul 1934 Dublin). Issue incl 1. Sir William Lindsay KCMG LLD **m.** 5 Jul 1922 Betty **dau.** of Lt Col the Rev T Ormsby, DSO, Gov Gen of the Bahamas 1945–49; 2. Christopher; 3. Richard; 4. Edward; **daus.** 1. Mary **m**… Cookson; 2. Elizabeth
>
> **Died** 4 Aug 1916 aged 71

MURPHY, WILLIAM CATHCART or CAVANAGH 1822/23–

b. 1822 or 1823 Cork; ed by Dr Porter; ent TCD 2 Jul 1839 aged 16 BA

poss same as William C Murphy C Killukin (Elph) *c.* 1850; C Tralee (A & A) 1851–53; was no doubt Wm Cathcart Murphy C Clongish (Ard) 1853 (see Leslie Ardfert p 154); still there in 1858

> probably William Cavanagh M, **s.** of Dr William

MURRAY, ALEXANDER   –1701

DD

R Ahascragh & Killasoolan = Castleblakeney (Elph) 1674–1701; Dean of Killala 1675–1701

> **Died** 1701

MURRAY, ALFRED JAMES 1886–1958

b. 16 Sep 1886 Ballinary Lurgan Co Armagh; ed Lurgan Coll; TCD BA 1909 Div Test 1911

d 1910 p 1911 (Down); C St Nicholas Belfast (Conn) 1910–15; C Shankill Lurgan (Drom) 1915–16; C Ematris and Rockcorry (Clogh) 1916–18; served with CA in Germany 1918–19; temporary duty 1920–25; C-in-c Omeath (Arm) 1926–35; res and was living at Omeath Co Louth 1935–55; BC Kilkeevan (Elph) 1955–58

s. of Joseph and Emily (née Mayne) of Ballinary Hse Lurgan Co Armagh

m. 2 Feb 1927 Warrenpoint Par Ch Mrs Isabel Blundell (**died** 23 Jun 1956 at Kilkeevan Rectory) yr **dau.** of John Shaw and Mary Maybury of Milltown Co Kerry. Issue 1. Barbara Adelaide **b.** 6 Mar 1929 **m.** 8 Apr 1959 Aughrim Ch Stanley Hughes; 2. Edwin Alfred bapt 30 Aug 1932

Died 5 Dec 1958 at Castlerea Co Roscommon

MURRAY, HUGH 1804–1870

b. 1804 Co Down; ed by Mr Hincks; ent TCD 3 Nov 1823 aged 19 BA 1829 MA 1832

C St John Sligo (Elph) 1830; PC St Peter Athlone (Elph) 1837–60; V Urney (Kilm) 1860–66; R Drumgoon (Kilm) 1866–70

s. of Hugh, merchant of Moira Co Down

m. 10 May 1843 at Killashee Par Ch Anne (**died** 30 Dec 1864 Cavan) eldest **dau.** of William Fleming of Richmond Longford. Issue incl Harriet Louisa (**died** Feb 1932 at Teignmouth Devon); his 2nd **s.** Hugh (**died** 13 Nov 1868 Monaghan aged 18); a **s. b.** 1 Oct 1862 Cavan.

Died 13 May 1870 aged 65

MURRAY, RICHARD 1776/77–1854

b. 1776 or 1777 Co Tyrone; ed by his father; Royal Sch Dungannon; ent TCD 1 Jul 1797 BA 1802 MA 1807 BD and DD 1830

d 1802 (Killaloe) p 1803 (Clogher); C Aghalow (Arm) 1802–07; C Drumglass (Arm) 1807–16; C Tullaniskin (Arm) 1816–19, when the Primate refused to give him a *Bene Decessit* to go as Curate of Templemichael (Ard). He applied to the King's Bench for an order showing why the Primate had refused. The Primate replied that he believed that Murray had not conformed to the Ecclesiastical Laws of the Church of Ireland, and the Judge ruled that the Primate, having given his reasons, could not be compelled to grant his Testimonial. Murray published a report on the case in 1821. V Askeaton (Lim) 1824–29; Dom Chapl to the Earl of Castlestuart; Dean and R Ardagh (Ard) 1829–54; VG Ardagh 1845–*c.* 1853

s. of Rev William MA Headmaster Royal Sch Dungannon

m. 1 Jan 1813 at Moneymore Co Derry Mary **dau.** of John Miller of Moneymore

Died 26 Jul 1854 aged 77 at Exmouth, Devon

PUBLICATIONS
Introduction to the Study of the Apocalypse, Dublin 1826

Lessons on the Church Catechism
Outlines of the History of the Catholic Church in Ireland London 1840
Ireland and her Church 8vo 1845
Practical Remarks on the Book of Genesis 8vo 1827

MUSSEN,——

d 1866; C Denn (Kilm) 1866.

NAIRN, JOHN

pres to V Bumlin Kilglass & Lisonuffy (Elph) 5 Mar 1634/35 (L.M. V. 110); prob same as J N, Commonwealth Minister at Arklow Gorey and Rathmacnee in 1658

m. Janet.

NAIRNE, DAVID

desires to be settled as preacher in the town of Cavan. The Lord Deputy and Council are not satisfied with the report from the Committee of Ministers, 10 Mar 1657/58 (Seymour's *Commonwealth MSS*, p 50)

NANGLE, EDWARD 1800–1883

b. 1800 Dublin; ed by Mr Moore; ent TCD 7 Jul 1817 aged 17 BA 1823 MA 1862

d 1823 (Kilmore for Meath) p; C Athboy (Meath); C Monkstown (Dub) for a fortnight; C Arvagh (Kilm) *c.* 1830; Missy C Achill (Tuam) from 1834; R Achill (Tuam) 1850–51; Preb of Faldown (Tuam) 1850–52; R Skreen (Killala) 1851–72. Edward Nangle settled in Achill Co Mayo in 1834, where he founded a school and church. He established a printing press from which he issued a monthly journal, *The Missionary Herald.* He produced Irish grammars and many books in English

7th **s.** of Walter of Clonbarron, gentleman (**s.** of Walter of Kildalkey)

m. 22 Sep 1828 St Thomas' Ch Dublin Elizabeth (**died** Jun 1850) eldest **dau.** of Henry Warner of Marvelstown Hse Co Meath. Issue 1. William Henry Beresford; 2. Frances P; 3. Henrietta C; 4. Matilda (**died** 1852)

Died 1883

PUBLICATIONS
The Achill Missionary Herald, 1837–1869
Ed, *The Novelty of the Romish Mass,* 1838
Dr McHale in Achill, the Old Religion Defended, 1838
Scriptural Education, a sermon preached on behalf of the Castlebar Schools, 17th March 1839
The Origin, Progress and Difficulties of the Achill Mission, 1839
Letters to the Rev. Theobald Matthew, 22 Oct 1842
Two Sermons, Castlebar 1843
Britain's Sin and Judgement, a sermon, 1843
A History of the Reformation for very little Children, Vol 1 1847, Vol 2 1850
A Short and simple Explanation of the Book of Revelation, 1859
Spiritualism Fairly Tried, 1861

More about the Lay Preaching and its Fruits, 1866
The Coming and Kingdom of Christ, Herbert, Dublin
The Church of Rome, the Foretold Apostasy, Lectures, White, Dublin 1850
The Validity of Orders in the Church of England, Achill, 1850
A Short Explanation of the Book of Revelation, 8vo 1854

NANGLE, JAMES
V Mostrim (Ard) 1636–c63, inst V 19 Apr 1636 (F.F.).

NEILE, JOHN
V Mohill (Ard) from 1622, serves the Cure, but hath neither tithe nor stipend. Church lately repaired by Henry Crofton part impropriator

NEILL, ERBERTO MAHON 1916–1998
b. 1916; ed City of London Sch; Persse Sch Camb; Jesus Coll Camb BA; TCD Div Test (2) MA 1943
d 1939 p 1940 (Dublin); C Portarlington (Kild) 1939–42; Staff Worker Children's Special Service Mission and Scripture Union 1942–47; R St James Crinken (Dub) 1947–61; R Castleknock U (Dub) 1961–75; Chapl to President Erskine Childers 1973–74; Canon Christ Ch Cath Dublin 1972–81; Canon Emeritus 1981; P-in-c St Andrew (Dub) 1975–76; Chapl Magdalen Asylum 1976–81; V Harold's Cross (Dub) 1977–81; R Boyle Aghanagh Kilbryan Ardcarne (w Croaghan from 1984) & (w Elphin from 1982) (Elph) 1981–87; Preb of Tirebrine (Elph) 1983–87; ret

> **s.** of Rev Robert Richard **b.** 1883 (**died** 16 May 1951) R Tooting Graveney (S'wark) 1938–51 (**s.** of Rev Herbert Richard, R Headford (Tuam) 1888–1916) by Bee Montrose (née Purdon); **bro.** of Rev Robert Purdon and **bro.** of Very Rev Ivan Delacherois, Provost of Sheffield (Sheff) 1966–74
>
> **m.** 4 Apr 1943 Dublin Rhoda Anne Georgina **dau.** of James and Emily Winder of Dublin. Issue 1. Most Rev John Robert Winder **b.** 17 Dec 1945 TCD Sch 1965 BA (1 cl Mod Oriental Langs) 1966 Jesus Coll Camb Sch 1968 Ridley Hall Camb GOE 1969 MA (Cantab) 1972 C St Paul Glenageary (Dub) 1969–71 Bp's V St Canice's Cath Kilkenny (Oss) 1971–74 R Abbeystrewery U (Ross) 1974–78 I St Bartholomew w Christ Ch Leeson Pk (Dub) 1978–84 Dean of Waterford & Prec of Lismore 1984–86 Bp of Tuam Killala and Achonry 1986–97 Bp of Cashel Waterford Lismore Ossory Ferns and Leighlin 1997–2002; Abp of Dublin and Bp of Glendalough Primate of Ireland and Metropolitan 2002–; **m.** 24 Aug 1968 Ballymoney Co Antrim Betty Ann Cox and have issue (i) Rev Stephen Mahon **b.** 18 Jun 1969 TCD BA 1991 d 1993 p 1994 C Monkstown (Dub) 1993–95 C Limerick City (Lim) 1995–98 R Cloughjordan (Killaloe) 1998– **m.** 20 Mar 1993 Lisburn Rev Nicola Lisa-Jane **dau.** of Harold and Pamela (née Greenwood) Harvey (ii) Andrew Mark **b.** 18 Dec 1971 (iii) Peter John Norman **b.** 26 Oct 1978; 2. Rhodanne Margaret **b.** 6 Apr 1948 **m.** Rev Michael Roger Heaney Chapl St Columba's Coll Dublin 1983–
>
> **Died** 12 Apr 1998 **bur.** Castleknock

NELIGAN, MAURICE 1680/81–c. 1754

b. 1680 or 1681 Co Limerick; ed by Mr Cashin; ent TCD 11 Oct 1700 aged 19 BA 1705; evidently taught at a school in Longford

V Kilglass Taghsynod and Moydow (Ard) 1732–54; ordered to call a Vestry to fence Churchyards of Moydow and Taghsynod Sep 1742 (Arm D.R.)

    s. of Dennis, *Colonus*

    m. and had issue 1. Rev Lawrence; 2. Rev Michael qv below; 3. Henry TCD Sch 1731 BA 1733 MA 1736; 4. Maurice; 5. Oliver; all ent TCD

NELIGAN, MAURICE HODSON 1828–1906

b. 1828 Athlone; ed by Mr Jones, Harcourt St Dublin; TCD BA 1850 Div Test (2) 1851 MA 1859 BD & DD 1873

d 1851 (Kilmore) p 1854 (Meath); C Kilglass (Ard) 1851–52; C Navan (Meath) 1852–54; C Mariners' Ch Kingstown (Dub) 1854–55; Sec Jews' Soc Ireland 1855–59; C Old Molyneux Chapel (Dub) 1859–63; I Christ Ch Leeson Pk Dublin (Dub)1863–1900; Canon of Christ Ch Cath Dublin 1887–96; Preb of St John's in Christ Ch Cath Dublin 1896–1900

    s. of William, MD

    m. (1) 1852 Elizabeth Frances **dau.** of Matthew West of Treel Co Longford. Issue 1. Rev John West; 2. Maurice Goldsmith; 3. Rt Rev Moore, Bp of Auckland 1903–11; 4. Frances Anne **m.** Rev Frederick Herbert Browne; 5. Elizabeth Ellen

    m. (2) 27 Jul 1899 Helen (**died** 23 Jan 1926) **dau.** of J Robertson of Gledswood, Clonskeagh Dublin

    Died Jan 1906

NELIGAN, MICHAEL 1703/04–1761

b. 1703 or 1704 Longford; either Michael, Sch 1716 BA 1717 or more likely Michael ed by Rev Maurice Neligan C Toomna (Ard) 1724 (presumably his father); ent TCD as Sizar 4 Jun 1729 aged 25

V Granard (Ard) 1741–61

    s. of Rev Maurice, *ludimagister*, R Kilglass (Ard) qv above (**s.** of Dennis) and **bro.** of Rev Lawrence

    Died 9 May 1761 at Granard

NELLYE, FLORENCE

V Fenagh (Ard) to 1615, is deposed (RV); V Annaduff (Ard) 1615; is deprived; also V Cloone (Ard) 1615 but deposed for non–residence (RV); V Kiltubrid (Ard), is deposed 1615; V Kilcorkey (Elph) 1615; V Ballintubber & Kilkeevan (Elph) 1615

NELSON, ALLEN JAMES 1929–

b. 1929 Dublin; ed Wesley Coll Dublin; TCD CITC 1953 Dip Bibl Studs 1955

d 1955 p 1956 (Dublin); C St Paul Glenageary (Dub) 1955–57; C Clontarf (Dub)

1957–60; R Bailieborough and Mullagh (w C-in-c Knockbride and Shercock from 1966) (Kilm) 1960–75; R Julianstown and Colpe (w St Mary Drogheda Duleek Paynestown and Stackallen from 1981) (Meath) 1975–98; Dio Glebes Sec Meath 1981–95; Canon of Meath 1984–98; ret 1998

s. of Samuel Tyrrell and Georgina (née Guest) of Dublin

m. 14 Sep 1960 Clontarf Par Ch Dublin Audrey May dau. of Leslie and Kathleen Friery of Dublin. Issue 1. David Paul b. 29 Jul 1961; 2. Miriam Ruth b. 8 Aug 1966; 3. Sarah Elizabeth b. 13 Feb 1970

NELSON, WARREN DAVID 1938–

b. 1938; TCD Bp Forster Pri and BA 1967 Toplady Pri Ch Formularies Pri Ryan Pri Downes Div Prem (Orat) & Div Test (2) 1968

d 1968 p 1969; C St Michael Belfast (Conn) 1968–70; R Kilcooley w Littleton Crohane and Killenaule (Cash) 1970–76; Chapl Coalbrook Fellowship Hosp Ho Thurles (Cash) 1976–94; Perm to Off Dios Cashel Waterford and Lismore 1993–94; R Lurgan Billis Killinkere and Munterconnaught (Kilm) 1994–98; Dio Radio Officer 1997–98; Warden Kilmore Elphin and Ardagh Guild of Lay Readers 1997–98; ret

m. 14 Sep 1967 St Luke's Ch Dublin Phyllis Jean Sproule. Issue 1. Ruth b. 26 Aug 1968; 2. Maeve b. 4 Sep 1969; 3. Sarah b. 18 Apr 1973

NESBITT, ——

C Kilmore (Elph) to 1840

NESBITT, ALBERT 1754–1822

b. 1754 Co Cavan; bapt 4 Mar 1754; ed by Mr Carr; ent TCD as SC 20 Apr 1771 aged 17 BA 1774

d 25 Apr 1774 (Kilmore) p; C Castlerahan (Kilm) 1774; C Kilmore (Kilm) 1776–77; V Killargue (Kilm) 1777–80; V Denn (Kilm) 1780–1812; Preb of Ballysonnan (Kild) 1792–1801; JP for Co Cavan 1794; V Taghmon (Meath) 1800–09; Chapl to the Prince Regent

3rd s. of Cosby of Lismore Hse Co Cavan, MP for Cavan by Anne dau. of John Enery of Bawnboy

Died unm. 30 Jan 1822 bur. Kilmore

NEVILLE, BRENT 1815/16–1873

b. 1815 or 1816 Dublin; ent TCD 1 Jul 1833 aged 17 BA 1838

C Killinkere (Kilm) 1840; PC Billis (Kilm) 1844–48; V Toomna (Elph) 1848–61

s. of Brent

m. 15 Dec 1842 Anne (died 1 Mar 1857 at Toomna Glebe) dau. of John Smyly QC

Died 27 Jun 1873 Sandymount Dublin

NEWBOLD, JAMES JOHN 1827/28–1872

b. 1827 or 1828 Co Wicklow; ed by Dr Callanan; ent TCD 14 Oct 1845 aged 17 BA 1850

d 25 Jul 1850 p 6 Jun 1852; C Kilmore (Elph) *c.* 1852; C Annaduff (Ard) 1853–63; R Clonbroney (Ard) 1864–72

> **s.** of Robert, Surgeon of Carnew Co Wicklow
>
> **m.** 25 Sep 1857 Margaret (**died** 14 Apr 1871 at Clonbroney) eldest **dau.** of Robert Grey of Templehill Co Dublin. Issue 1. a **s. b.** 23 Sep 1863; 2. a **s. b.** 29 Dec 1864; a **s. b.** Easter Sunday 1871
>
> **Died** 4 Apr 1872

NEWBOLD, MATTHEW

V Kilcorkey (Elph) to 1640; poss same as William Newport, V Ahamplish (Elph) qv

NEWCOMEN, WILLIAM

pres R Baslick (Elph) 27 Feb 1637/38

NEWMAN, WILLIAM

TCD Sch 1621 BA 1625 Fellow and MA 1632

inst V Kiltoom and Camma (Elph) 24 Mar 1636/37; Preb of Termonbarry (Elph) 1636–39; V Galtrim (Meath) 1637; Chapl to Lord Chancellor Loftus

NEWPORT, WILLIAM

V Ahamplish and Preb & R of Killukin (Elph) 1635–40, pres by the Crown 4 Dec 1635 (L.M. V. 112); V St John Sligo *alias* Minbriske and V Killaspicbrone (Elph) 1635–40; poss same as William Newbold, V Kilcorkey (Elph) qv

NEYLAN (**NEILAN**), DANIEL 1618–1667

b. 17 Mar 1618 Co Clare; ed in Limerick under Mr Wall; ent TCD 12 Jun 1638 aged 20; Sch 1638 BA not recorded; he was one of the four Fellows of TCD made by King's Letter of 1 Sep 1646 BD 1661 DD is not recorded except in the matriculation of his son and on a chalice of 1663

was "Preacher" at St Michan's Dublin under the Commonwealth 1651–57 but was ousted in 1657 in favour of a preacher named Wootton; was again there in 1659; Preb of St Michan in Christ Ch Cath Dublin 1661–67; Dean of Elphin 1663–66; Dean of Ossory 1666–67

> eldest **s.** of Eugene or Owen (**s.** of Dr Daniel, Bp of Kildare 1583–1603)
>
> **m.** Joanna Crofton of Lisnadorn Co Roscommon, **sister** of Dr Thomas Crofton, Dean of Elphin qv Issue incl 1. Rev Daniel, R Kildrumferton and Ballintemple (Kilm) qv; 2. Elizabeth bap 20 May 1661; 3. William **b.** 10 Dec 1662 **bur.** 8 Apr 1664; 4. Katherine bap 18 Jan 1664/65; 5. Joan **bur.** 25 Jan 1668/69; 6. Maria **m.** 16 Apr 1682 Dr Adam Bell
>
> **Died** Feb 1667 **bur.** 7 Feb in the Chancel of St Michan's Ch Dublin

NEYLAN, DANIEL 1658/59–

b. 1658 or 1659 near Dublin; ed by Mr Ryder; ent TCD 12 Jul 1676 aged 17 Sch 1677 BA 1681 MA 1684

C St Werburgh (Dub) 1688–1703; V Ballintemple and Kildrumferton (Kilm) 1691–1700; prob also V Denn (Kilm) 1691–1700

s. of Dr Daniel, Dean of Elphin qv, by Joanna Crofton

NICHOLLS, ALEXANDER 1797/98–1876

b. 1797 or 1798

C Fenagh (Ard) 1843; DC Dernakesh in Drumgoon Parish (Kilm) 1844; DC Derrylane (Kilm) 1852 — still there in 1860; C Cloone (Ard) before 1862–73.

Died 27 Sep 1876 aged 78

NICHOLLS, ARCHIBALD

V of Abbeylara (Ard) 1868–71, coll 2 Jun 1868; prob same as Alexander Nicholls qv

NICHOLSON, EDWARD –1730

ent TCD 12 Feb 1660/61 BA 1666 MA 1673

Preb of Kilcooley (Elph) 1667/68–1709/10; V Ballintubber Oran Kilkeevan and Clonmragarmacan (Elph) 1674–; R Kiltullagh (Elph — then Tuam) 1674; R & V Crossboyne (Tuam) 1674; Preb of Taghsaxon (Tuam) 1674–76; Preb of Kilmainmore and R Ballincholla/Kilmolara and V Cong (Tuam) 1676–85 & 1686–1719; ? C St John Sligo (Elph) 1700; V Adregoole Liskeevy Clonbarn and Boyanna & Preb of Laccagh (Tuam) 1719–30; founded Primrose Grange School; he was in the habit of maintaining at school as many children as he was years old.

s. of Henry, MD

Died at the close of 1730

PUBLICATION

A Sermon on I John II:15, Dublin 1715

NICKSON (NIXON), WILLIAM

perhaps William Nickson ed by Dr Dunkin; ent TCD 25 Feb 1759 Sch 1761 BA 1763

d p 24 Nov 1765 (Clogher); Meath Lists have him ordained deacon in 1770; may be same as Richard Nixon C Kinawley (Kilm) 1766; R Stonehall (Meath) 1771–1813

prob **s.** of William of Derryinch Co Fermanagh who **m.** (M.L. 1 Jan 1714) Margaret Montgomery of Gortnabratan

m. 27 Feb 1766 St Mary's Ch Dublin Barbara Green; it seems likely that there were two of the name who are confused

NIMEAS

is V of Kilmore (Kilm) to 1415 (Cal. Reg. Mey, 356)

NIXON, ANDREW 1709/10–1774

b. 1709 or 1710 Nixon Lodge Drumlane Co Cavan; ed by Dr Adams at Enniskillen; ent TCD 19 Jun 1726 aged 16 BA 1730

C Annagh (Kilm) 1754 & probably to 1773; V Ahamplish (Elph) 1773–74

s. of Lt Thomas

m. (M.L.10 Mar 1737) Marianne elder **dau.** & co–heir of Rev Matthew French BA, & Preb of Kilroot (Conn) 1717–21; Issue **sons** 1. Brinsley d 1765; 2. Humphrey; 3. Matthew; 4. Adam; 5. George; **daus.** 1. Anne **m.** Henry Swanzy; 2. Frances; 3. Barbara

Died 6 Jan 1774 Belturbet

NIXON, BRINDSLEY –1823

was from Belturbet Co Cavan; ed by Mr Kerr; TCD Sch 1769 BA 1771 MA 1776

d 24 Apr 1774 (Kilmore) p 1776 (Leighlin); poss C Annagh (Kilm) to 1780; Reader St James's (Dub) 1785; Chapl Dr Steevens Hosp Dublin *c.* 1785; Reader St Catherine's (Dub) 1789; R Paynestown (Meath) 1794–1822

s. of Andrew, Barrack Master, Ballyshannon

m. (M.L. 26 Sep 1780) St Ann's Ch Dublin Mary (**died** May 1828) **dau.** of Edward Hartigan. Issue **sons** 1. Rev Robert Herbert (**died** 22 Jan 1857) **b.** 1782 Co Cavan TCD BA 1803 MA 1811 Chapl Dr Steevens Hosp Dublin 1811–32 PC Booterstown (Dub) 1832–57 **m.** Dorothea Rose (**died** 13 Jun 1867) **dau.** of John Morris of Newstore Co Meath; 2. Brindsley; 3. Horatio Stopford; 4. Rev Edward, V Drakestown (Meath) 1835–47; 3 **daus.** incl 1. Catherine Anne

Died 22 Mar 1823

NIXON, GEORGE ROBINSON 1878/79–1963

b. 1878 or 1879; TCD BA (Resp) 1905 BD 1914

d 1908 p 1909 (Tuam); C Tuam (Tuam) 1908–10; C St George Dublin (Dub) 1910–11; C Kilnamanagh (Ferns) 1911–14; R Killasnett (Kilm) 1914–15; R Turlough w Balla (Tuam) 1915–18; Dio Inspector of Schools Tuam 1917–42; R Kilcommon (wKilcolman from 1923 and Kilmaine from 1934) (Tuam) 1918–50; RD of Tuam 1922–44; Chapl to Bp of Tuam 1923–44; Exam Chapl to Bp 1923–50; Preb of Balla and Faldown (Tuam) 1925–50; Provost of Tuam 1928–39; Archd of Tuam 1939–50; Sec Tuam Dio Council 1942–50; ret

s. of John of Lurgandarragh

m. 9 Apr 1912 Kathlen Maud **dau.** of Arthur P Morgan

Died 13 Apr 1963 aged 84

NOBLE, JOSEPH STORY 1780/81–*c.* 1836

b. 1780 or 1781 Co Fermanagh; ed by Dr Carr; ent TCD 14 Dec 1796 aged 15 BA 1801

d p 20 Apr 1802; C Templeport (Kilm) 1802; there in 1830

2nd s. of William, JP of Summerhill Co Fermanagh

m. Jane (died 11 Feb 1837 Dublin). Issue Elizabeth m. 17 Sep 1838 St Peter's Ch Dublin Benjamin, MD of Bagenalstown Co Carlow only s. of N G Roche of Fonthill Co Carlow

Died before 1837

NOBLE, WILLIAM 1811/12–1890

b. 1811 or 1812 Dublin; ed by Mr Elliott; ent TCD 18 Oct 1830 aged 18 BA 1836 C Kiltoghart (Ard) 1837–; R Columbkille (Ard) 1853–64; V Mostrim (Ard) 1864–68; R Tashinny (Ard) 1868–90

s. of James, "gen."

m. 12 Mar 1839 at Carrick-on-Shannon Emily dau. of Thomas Wilde, MD of Castlerea Co Roscommon — she was sister of Sir William Wilde, father of Oscar Wilde. Issue 1. Emily Frances m. 29 Nov 1876 James E Wright of Cartron House; 2. Eliza m. 22 Aug 1893 St George's Ch Dublin Rev Francis Sadleir Stoney, R Tashinny (Ard) qv; 3. Mary m. 27 Apr 1876 Rev Edward J Hardy

Died 26 Jan 1890 aged 78 bur. Tashinny

NOBLETT, WILLIAM   –1918

TCD BA (Resp) 1867

d 1865 p 1867 (Tuam); C Skreen (Tuam — then Killala) 1865–73; R Arvagh (Kilm) 1873–81; R Killyon (w C-in-c Castleblakeney 1891–94 and R 1894–1908) (Elph) 1881–1908

m. and had issue incl a s. Rev Andrew (died 2 Jul 1948) b. Co Sligo ed at Athlone ent TCD Oct 1886 aged 18 BA 1890 Div Test 1891 MA 1894 d 1891 p 1892 C Gartan (Raph) 1891–92 C Conwall (Raph) 1892–97 PC St Barnabas Glasgow (G & G) 1897–1902 C St George Maryhill Glasgow (G & G) 1902–04 C Gartan (Raph) 1904–06 R Mountfield (Derry) 1906–12 R Glenalla and Milford (Raph) 1912–14 R Killygarvan and Glenalla (Raph) 1924–37 m. and had issue (i) John Richard (died 1937) (ii) May (iii) Florence; daus. 1. Mary (died 18 Jan 1956 Dublin); 2. a dau. b 11 Nov 1872; 3. Margaret Florence (died 18 Jun 1958)

Died 19 May 1918

†NONY, HENRY

a Dominican, was prov to the See of Ardagh in error, 29 Apr 1392 on the death of Charles O'Ferrall (A.H. I, 184); the See was not then vacant. He was Friar Preacher and was consecrated lately id. April 1400. (C.P.L. V. 331)

NORMAN, WILLIAM DANIEL 1887/88–1972

b. 1887 or 1888; Major, Royal Artillery

d 30 Sep 1951 p 1 Nov 1952 (Ard); C-in-c Kilcommick and Moydow (Ard) 1951–55; R Kilcommick w Cashel and Rathcline (Ard) 1955–65; ret

m. and had issue a s.

Died 7 Nov 1972 aged 84

NORTH, JOSEPH 1819/20–

b. 1819 or 1820 Dublin; ed by Mr Huddart; ent TCD 7 Nov 1836 aged 16 BA 1841 Div Test 1842

d 1842 p; C Knockbride (Kilm) 1842–45; C Thomastown (Kild) 1845–54; C St Clement Bristol (Bris)

   s. of Roger of Dominick St Dublin

NORTHAGHE, JOHN

V of Cloncaloo, Chaplain, is pres to V Kilnashye = Killashee (Ard) 1549; "swere hym to set forth ye Majestys proceedings touching religion", etc. (F Edward VI 380)

NORTHCOTE, BERNARD 1693/94–

b. 1693 or 1694 Mallow Co Cork; ed by Mr Mullen, Cork; Mr Morgan, Tipperary and Dr Andrews; ent TCD 21 Dec 1710 aged 16 BA 1715 MA 1718

appears C Kilmore (Kilm) 26 Jun 1728

   s. of Edward

NORTHRIDGE, BENJAMIN 1897–1972

b. 19 Aug 1897 Ballineen Co Cork; ed Bandon Gram Sch

d 1923 p 1925 (Down); C Seapatrick (Drom) 1923–26; R Drummully (Clogh) 1926–29; C-in-c Magheracross (Clogh) 1929–32; Dio C Kilmore 1932–39; C-in-c Lea (Kild) 1939–60; RD Geashill (Kild) 1950–69; ret

   s. of Benjamin of Ballineen by Matilda **dau.** of William Shorten of Kinneigh Co Cork

   Died 12 Jul 1972 Dublin **bur.** Mt Jerome Cemetery

NORTHRIDGE, HERBERT JAMES 1864/65–1893

b. 1864 or 1865; TCD BA 1888

d 1889 p 1890; C Kinawley (Kilm) 1889–90; C Killesher (Kilm) 1890–92; C St Mary Belfast (Conn) 1892–93

   Died 2 Jul 1893 aged 28

†NUGENT, EDMUND   –*c.* 1550

was prov to the See of Kilmore 22 Jun 1530 (A.H. I. 258). He was Prior of Tristernagh and was allowed to hold his priory *in commendam.* He surrendered his priory to Henry VIII on 30 Nov 1539, and was granted a pension of £26.13.5 for life on 20 Mar 1540/41. As he evidently supported the Royal Prerogative against the Pope, he was no longer recognised by the Pope in 1540 who provided John MacBrady to the See, 5 Nov 1540 (Brady Episcopal Succession i.279), but John surrendered his bulls and allowed Nugent to remain in peaceable possession. He was a native of those parts and in 1550 O'Rayly asked for his appointment, and his request was supported by St.Leger in a letter of 28 Oct 1550 (Shirley, Orig. Letts. 43, C.S.P.I. 1st series I. 109). Nugent

continued to hold the See until Queen Mary's reign when he **died** c 1550
   Died *c.* 1550

NUGENT, EDMUND 1808–1854
b. 17 Oct 1808 Co Cavan; ent TCD 17 Oct 1825 BA 1830
V Killinagh (Kilm) 1836–45; V Denn (Kilm) 1846–54
   3rd **s.** of Christopher Edmond John of Bobsgrove Co Cavan, an Officer of Dragoons
   m. 2 Dec 1840 Annaduff Ch Frances (**died** 30 Jul 1885) eldest **dau.** of Matthew Nesbitt of Derrycarne Hse Co Leitrim. Issue Sophia Mary **b.** 7 Oct 1841
   Died 1 Nov 1854

NUGENT, NICHOLAS
Archd of Ardagh 1530/31, coll by the Primate 14 Mar (Cal. Reg. Cromer)

NUGENT, ROBERT
V Granard (Ard) 1556/57
   s. of Richard, baron of Delvin

NUGENT, ROBERT
a layman, held the Preb of Termonbarry (Elph) 1615–*c.* 19

NUNAN, WILLIAM FRANCIS 1861/62–1942
b. 1861 or 1862 Bandon Co Cork; TCD Div Test 1893 BA 1897 MA 1912
d 1893 p 1894 (Kilmore); C Drumgoon (Kilm) 1893–95; R Drumreilly (Kilm) 1895–1900; R Drumcliffe (w Ahamplish from 1918) (Elph) 1900–31; C-in-c Mostrim (Ard) 1931–32; Preb of Kilcooley in Elphin Cath 1930–32; ret
   m. Helen (**died** 12 Nov 1939). Issue **sons** 1. William Alexander; 2. Francis Allen; 3 **daus.** incl the eldest Ruby **m.** 8 Sep 1925 at Drumcliffe Ch Archibald Bruce of Liverpool
   Died 18 Apr 1942 aged 80

NYRNE (NAIRN), JOHN
coll V Killenvoy 31 Oct 1639; prob same as John Nairn qv

O'BARDAIN, ——
"the Dean" (of Brefny) is deceased 1369 (A.F.M.)

OBEACHNACHAN, JOHN
Augustinian Canon of St Mary, Inchmacnerin, Elphin, priest, was prov to V Kilcola and

Calry (Elph) vac by Maccraith Maabreicheannin qv Aug 1409 (C.P.L. VI. 161). In 1428 John vacated it on obtaining the Priory of Inchmacnerin

O'BEDLAYN, DONATUS

priest of Killala Dio was prov to V Killaspicbrone (Elph) and can also hold his V of Ymleachysell, Killala Dio, 2 Jun 1427 (C.P.L. VII. 285)

†O'BEIRNE, THOMAS LEWIS 1740/41–1823

b. 1740 or 1741 Farnagh Co Longford; ed Ardagh RC Diocesan Sch, St Omer and Paris where he was training for Priesthood in the RC Ch; Trinity Coll Camb BD 1783; was received into C of E

d 1772 p 1773 (Peterborough) Bp 1795; pres by his College to V Grendon Northants (Pet) 1772–76; Chapl to the Fleet and Private Sec to Lord Howe 1776–79; R West Deeping (Linc) from 1779; Private Sec and Chapl to the Duke of Portland, Lord Lt 1782–83; held livings in Northumberland and Cumberland; R Templemichael and V Mohill (Ard) 1791–95. (In Templemichael the RC priest was his brother, the Rev Denis O'Beirne, who was said to have married King George IV to Mrs Fitzherbert.)

Bp of Ossory 1795–98; consec at Christ Ch Cath Dublin 1 Feb 1795; enthroned by proxy 30 Mar 1795; Bp of Meath 1798–1823

    s. of…, Farmer of Co Longford

    m. 1783 St Margaret's Westminster Jane (**died** 27 Sep 1837 London aged 82) **dau.** of Hon Francis Stuart 3rd **s.** of the 7th Earl of Moray. Issue one **s.** and two **daus.** who all **died unm.**

    Died 17 Feb 1823 at Ardbraccan aged 82

PUBLICATIONS
    A Pamphlet in Defence of Admiral Lord Howe
    A Pamphlet entitled *The Gleam of Comfort*
    The Crucifixion, A Poem 1776
    A Sermon on behalf of the Sunday Schools of Roscommon, 1788
    The Generous Impostor, A Comedy. The Duchess of Devonshire collaborated with him in its composition. It was produced at Drury Lane in 1780 and printed in 8vo 1781
    A series of Essays by "A Country Gentleman" 1780
    A Short History of the Last Session of Parliament, Anonymous
    Considerations on the late Disturbances by "A Consistent Whig", 8vo 1781
    Considerations on the Principles of Naval Discipline and Courts Martial
    A Fast Sermon, preached at Longford, 8vo, 1793
    A Fast Sermon, preached at Longford, 8vo, 1794
    Charges to Clergy, 1795, 1796, 1797, 4to, Dublin
    A Sermon, at Kilkenny on the Providential Dispersion of the Enemy's Fleet, 7 Jan 1797, 8vo
    A Circular Address to the Clergy of the Diocese of Ossory, 4to and 8vo, 1797
    A Sermon, 8vo, Dublin 1798
    Charges, Circular, and 4 Occasional Sermons, 8vo 1799
    A Sermon, before SPCK 4to, 1801

The Ways of God to be Vindicated only by the Word of God, A Sermon, 8vo, 1804
A Thanksgiving Sermon, on Psalm ii, 10–11, 8vo Dublin 1805
A Charge to the Clergy of the Diocese of Meath, 8vo, 1805
A Charge to the Clergy of the Diocese of Meath, 8vo, 1820
A Charge to the Clergy of the Diocese of Meath, 8vo, 1822
A Sermon at the Magdalen Asylum, on Ephesians vi, 4, 8vo, London 1807
A Letter to the Earl of Fingall (Anon), 8vo Dublin 1813
Sermons and Charges, Collected etc, 8vo 1813
Christian Worship, A Sermon, 8vo, London 1819
Faith without Works, A Sermon, 8vo, Bath 1819
A Letter from an Irish Dignitary to an English Clergyman on the Subject of Tithes in Ireland (Anon), 8vo, Dublin 1807, reprinted 1822
Sermons on Important Subjects, 3 vols, 8vo, various years
A Letter to Dr Troy on the Coronation of Bonaparte, by "Melancthon"
Circular Letter to the Rural Deans of the Diocese of Meath, 1821
The Source of the Evil. Addressed to the United Parliament and the People of Great Britain, on the League formed between the Irish Lay Separatists and the Irish RC Bishops on Measure of Emancipation, by "Anglo–Hibernicus", No. xviii, "Pamphleteer", March 1817, 63pp.

O'BEOLAN (O'BEOLAYN), NEHEMEAH (NEMEAS)

Canon of Elphin 1427 (Cal. Reg. Swayne 134), and is still Canon in 1428 & 1429 (C.P.L. VIII. 12, 118), and in 1452 (ib. x. 575)

O'BEOLLAN, WILLIAM

clk, informs the Pope that Nemeas O'Beollayn qv, is a fornicator and perjurer etc. If true, Nemeas is to be deposed and William to be coll 24 Mar 1446/47 (C.P.L. X. 284). Later it appears that Eugene O'Coneil qv, says that William caused Nemeas to be summoned before Magonius, Abbot of Loch Ce, who took a bribe from William. Later they agreed that each should have the tithes of whatever parishioners sided with him, so for some time, both were Vicars. Then they agreed that William should be V and should pay Nemeas a yearly sum; both were deposed 23 Sep 1455

O'BEOLLAYN, LAURENCE

Priest disp; is prov to a Canonry of Elphin with reservation of a Preb, and also to a benefice in Killala, 2 Mar 1426 (C.P.L. VI. 436, 445), and he is made Provost of Killala 6 Jul 1427 & 4 Jul (ib. 559)

O'BEOLLAYN, NEMEAS

had been prov to the V Drumcliffe (Elph), and on a lawsuit had been awarded it against Dermit O'Coneil qv, but on getting possession had promised Dermit a yearly sum for which he got absolution, Jul 1425 (C.P.L. VIII. 393). He was V Druymclyab = Drumcliffe (Elph) and prov to a Canonry and Preb of Elphin and Killala & disp as illeg 19 Apr 1426 (C.P.L. VIII. 436), but, see William O'Beollan. Prob same as Nemeas O'Beolan above

O'BERIND, CHARLES

held V Cloonaff (Elph) for over a year to 1411 without being ordained priest

O'BERNYN, EUGENE

Canon of Elphin 1456 (C.P.L. XI. 383)

O'BEYRUN, EUGENE

prov to V Eachruym = Aughrim and Kilcennoran in Aughrim Parish (Elph) 1447 (C.P.L. X. 288–89); prob same as below

O'BEYRUN, EUGENE

clk informs the Pope that Rory Omochan qv, Preb of Trebryuyn = Terebrine & Kymcalechyn (Elph) has dilapidated its goods and been excommunicated, and yet celebrated Masses. If this is true, Omochan is to be deposed and Eugene to be coll Preb 19 Dec 1447 (C.P.L. X. 288)

O'BIGEON, PATRICK

V Enga ? = Annagh (Kilm) has resigned before 1449/50; poss same as Patrick O'Higgegan qv

OBINS, MICHAEL 1708/09–1783

b. 1708 or 1709 Portadown Co Armagh; ed by Dr Clark, Lisburn; ent TCD 19 May 1726 aged 17 Sch 1729 BA 1730 MA 1733

R Castlemacadam (Glend) 1738–39; V Thurles (Cash) 1745–48; R Drumcliffe (Elph) 1767–83

s. of Anthony, *armiger*

Died 1783

O'BIRN, EUGENE

alleged Archd of Elphin 1478, is inhibited (Cal. Reg. Octav. 386)

O'BLAICHSICH, MACROBIUS

V of Tuaimregayn = Tomregan (Kilm) to 1411; is deceased

O'BOGAN (YBOGAN), THOMAS

V Drumferton = Kildrumferton (Kilm) to 1529; is deceased

†O'BOLAND or O'BEOLLAYN, LAURENCE

was prov to the See of Elphin vacant by the death of Thomas Colby 7 Feb 1429 (C.P.L. VIII, iii). On 3 Feb 1429 Laurence, elect of Elphin, prov recently to the See vacant by

Thomas's death, priest, son of a married man and unmarried woman and dispensed. Some say that the See is void by the deprivation of John O'Grada, formerly Bp of Elphin, now Bp of the Universal Church. Provision is to hold good from this date if so, or if the See is vacant by the deprivation of Robert also Bp, sometime Bp of Elphin (C.P.L. VIII. 94). It does not appear whether he got possession

O'BORIND, CARBRICUS
disp from Preb of Terebrine (Elph) before 1482, but as the fruits were small he was also made Prior of Kyllmoyrasane (C.P.L. XIII. 120)

O'BRANAGAN, NICHOLAS
V St Michael's, Russagh (Ard); is prov to V Kilglass (Ard) 1411, but has to resign Russagh 9 Jun 1411 (A.H. I 176; C.P.L. VI. 259)

O'BRANAGAYN, WILLIAM
V Kilglass (Ard) to 1465; is deprived for simony. Eugene Macconkagry, qv below, Canon of Ardagh, informs the Pope that William O'Branagayn had given money to Bp Cormac to collate him and was prov to the V to be united to his Canonry 25 Feb 1465 (C.P.L. XII 535)

O'BRIEN, Hon. HENRY 1813–1895
b. 15 Apr 1813; Trinity Coll Camb BA 1835 MA 1838; TCD BA *ad eund* 1835

PC Dowra and Killegar (Kilm) 1837–60; V Denn (Kilm) 1859–60; R Killesherdoney (Kilm) 1860–77; res

    5th **s.** of Sir Edward, Bt; **bro.** of Sir Lucius, 15th Baron Inchiquin

    m. 22 May 1839 Harriett (**died** 30 Apr 1872) eldest **dau.** of John Godley of Killegar Co Leitrim. Issue **sons** 1. Edward, Asst Commissioner at Delhi **m.** and had issue; 2. Murrough John **m.** and had issue; also 6 **daus.**

    Died 12 Feb 1895 at Uxbridge

O'BRUACHAN, FERGALLUS
Dean of Elphin to 1447; is deposed

O'BRUCAN, FERGALLUS
Canon of Elphin 1463 (C.P.L. XII. 172); was coll V Killukin (Elph) on death of John Mechaig, qv, but doubted its validity and was prov 14 Jun 1463 (ib.)

O'BRYND, JOHN
Augustinian Prior of St Mary Kilmoernasinna, is granted the V of Aughrim (Elph) *in commendam* for his life 8 Mar 1412 (C.P.L. VI. 277)

O'CALLAGHAN (O'CATHALAIN), CORNELIUS
priest, obtained provision of V Ahascragh (Elph) 18 Jul 1449 on the grounds that Thady McGeraghty qv kept a concubine (C.P.L. X. 403)

O'CALLANAN, CORMAC
is prov to V Kyllmurchayn (Elph) 8 Dec 1409 (C.P.L. VI. 166)

O'CALLANAN, MATTHEW
is prov V Kilmacallen (Elph) and disp s.p. 9 Dec 1480 (C.P.L. XIII. 89)

O'CALMAN, THOMAS
V Tomregan (Kilm) to 1453, to be deprived for fornication, simony, dilapidation of Vicarage, defamation, etc.

O'CARBRY, TERENCE
is Canon of Kilmore in 1455 (C.P.L. XI. 214)

O'CARNEAN, WILLIAM
disp as son of a priest, is prov V Cluaynclaic *alias* Cluaynfarchi = Cloonclare (Kilm), 12 Jul 1455; lay V and is deposed

O'CEARNAN, THOMAS
Prior of the Convent of the Priory of Athlone, held the R Kiltoom (Elph) two years without a title *c.* 1431

O'CELLY, NICHOLAS
Prec of Elphin 1591; is deposed 1594 (L.M. V. 101)

OCHACTAGAN, MAGONIUS
was prov to V Kilcorkey (Elph) 11 Apr 1469 (C.P.L. XII. 316–7)

O'CHANNICHY, CORNELIUS
priest of Elphin held V Killaspicbrone (Elph) over four years from 1423 under Papal letters addressed to one not a dignitary or Canon, and was to be removed in 1427

O'CHONAYR, CORNELIUS (*alias* CORC)
priest, disp as son of a priest etc, was prov to the V Kilmacoen (Elph) vacant either because Imarus O'Conar qv became a Friar Minor, or because Dermit McGillaruair qv was not ordained priest, 7 Dec 1418 (C.P.L. VIII. 112). Dermit however, is still V in 1421 (C.P.L. VII. 170)

O'CHONYR, JOHN

clk, informs the Pope that Maurice Oclabayd qv, Canon and Rector of the Moiety of Fueran = Oran (Elph), assigned in lieu of a Prebend, is guilty of fornication, neglect etc; if true, he is disp as son of a priest to get it, 1450 (C.P.L. X. 461)

O'CHUINN, CORMAC

Canon of Elphin 1447 (C.P.L. X. 364)

OCHYNERIGE (O'HENRY), MALACHY −c. 1390

was admitted to the Deanery of Elphin by the Bp 1383 (C.P.L. 1V. 246)

OCLABAID, CORNELIUS

V of St Patrick's, Fuaran = Oran (Elph) is said to have divided the fruits of the V by simony with Matthew O'Clabayd qv, 15 Apr 1454 (C.P.L. VIII. 495), and was ignorant of letters etc. If true, the Pope has him deposed as unlearned and simoniacal

O'CLABAID (ICLABAID), MAURICE

priest of Elphin says that the late Dermit McGillaruayd qv, Canon of Elphin, held tithes in the parish of Fuaran = Oran (Elph). He prays to be granted them with the Canonry to which he was prov; granted 6 Nov 1441 (C.P.L. IX. 184)

OCLABAID *alias* OMEANACHAN, MAURICE

is prov to V Oran (Elph) 25 May 1454 (C.P.L. X. 705)

OCLABAYD, CORNELIUS

clk, informs the Pope that Matthew O'Clabayd, V Fueran = Oran (Elph) qv has dilapidated the goods, is a notorious fornicator, neglects his Cure, so that some parishioners have died without extreme unction; if true, he is disp as illegitimate to get the V, 13 Aug 1444 (C.P.L. IX. 427– 428)

O'CLABAYD (YCLABAYD), MATTHEW

was prov to V Oran (Elph) 1433/34, as he doubted whether his collation by the Bp to it was valid

OCLERIAN, CHARLES

is V of St. Patrick de Luyrginadare = Lurgan (Kilm) 1527 (Cal. Reg. Cromer)

O'COAN, HUGH

V Ardcarne (Elph), Clk, received a pardon from the Crown 10 Aug 1590 — see Teige O'Coan with whom he seems to have held this benefice conjointly

O'COAN, TEIGE
V Ardcarne (Elph), Clk, received a pardon from the Crown 10 Aug 1590

O'COINDERE (O'CONNERY), THOMAS
"Dean of Brefny" to 1325 is deceased (A.F.M.)

O'COLLA, Sir BERNARD
V Kiltubride (Ard); is deposed 1410

O'COLLA, RONALDUS –c. 1490
Perpetual V Ardcarne (Elph) 1460; is charged with simony, neglect of duty and dilapidation of the benefice; if true is to be deposed

Died c. 1490

O'COLLY, NICHOLAS
V Killewkin = Killukin (Elph), Clk, Co Sligo is pardoned 10 Aug 1590 (F. Elizabeth, 5447)

†O'CONACHTAIN, MAELISA –1174
Bp of Elphin to 1152. He attended the Synod of Kells in 1152 as "Bp of East Connaught" which may mean Elphin. The A.F.M. call him Bp. of *Siol Murray* which was evidently an alias for Elphin

Died 1174

O'CONAIR, DONALD
Canon of Elphin 1461 (C.P.L. XII. 122), & 1469 (ib. XII. 316)

O'CONAR (YCONAYR), IMARUS (YMARUS)
clk, is prov to V Kilmacoen (Elph) 9 Mar 1404 (C.P.L. V. 613); the parish became vacant because he became a Friar Minor

OCONCEANAYND, MALACHY
voided V Kilcroan (Elph) 1464/65 because he got also without disp the R of Kilkerrin (Tuam)

OCONCHUBUYR (O'CONNOR), CHARLES
Canon of Elphin, informs the Pope that Rory O'Mochan qv, Provost = Precentor of Elphin, has dilapidated its goods, neglected his cure and committed simony and perjury. If true, Charles, who has been dispensed as illegal, is to be coll and Rory to be deposed 19 Dec 1447 (C.P.L. X. 366–7)

O'CONEGAN, BERNARD
of Baslick (Elph), Clk, pardoned 12 Dec 1552 (F. Ed VI. 1164)

O'CONEIL, BERNARD
clk, informs the Pope that the letters re Minbrisg obtained by the Abbot of Lochgue (Loch Ce) were surreptitious (under which the Abbot had kept the Rectory five years), as the fruits of the Monastery were worth 50 marks, while the Rectory originally belonged to the House of Kilmainham. If this is true, Bernard is to be coll to the Rectory, 2 Dec 1430 (C.P.L. VIII. 196)

O'CONEIL, CORNELIUS −1414
Preb of Druymcliab = Drumcliffe (Elph) to 1414
   Died 1414

O'CONEIL, DERMIT
clk, has claimed the V Drumcheclyd = Drumcliffe (Elph) to 1425, but Nemeas O'Beollayn qv had been prov to it and was awarded it

O'CONEIL, EUGENE
disp as illeg; prov to a Canonry of Elphin with reservation of a Preb 26 Jul 1453 (C.P.L. X. 671); still Canon 1454, 1456 (ib. X. 695, XI. 34).

O'CONEIL, EUGENE
Canon of Killala and Preb of Dromard (Killala) 1455, but has not yet got possession; was prov to the V Drumcliffe (Elph) 23 Sep 1455 (C.P.L. XI. 252). See William O'Beollan above

O'CONEYL, THADY
V of Kylleasbuygbron = Killaspicbrone (Elph) vacates it by death 1423

O'CONGALAN, FERGALLUS
Premonstratensian Monk of Holy Trinity Loch Ce was prov V Kilcola (Elph) 5 Oct 1428 (C.P.L. VIII. 51)

OCONGALOM, MARIANUS −1396
V Kilglass (Ard) to 1396
   Died 1396

†O'CONNAGHTY, FLANN −1231
Bp of Breffni 1179–1231 (Ann Loch Ce, 307)
   Died 1231

†O'CONNAGHTY, TUATHAL 1179

Bp of Ter Briuin = Kilmore 1149–79; attended the Synod of Kells (A.F.M.)
  Died 1179

O'CONNEGANE, HUGH

V of Castletone ? = Castlerea, Kilkeevan (Elph) to 1590, Clk, pardoned 10 Aug (F. Elizabeth I. 5448)

O'CONNEGEAN, EUGENE

Canon of Elphin 1532

O'CONNEL, CORNELIUS

opposed Dermit Macherleginn qv, and took possession of V Drumcliffe (Elph) 1403, and he appealed to the Pope who appointed the Bp of Ossory to settle the matter. The latter absolved Cornelius and Dermit again appealed and the Pope awarded the V to him 8 May 1405 (C.P.L. VI. 35)

O'CONNEL, JOHN –1403

held the V Drumcliab = Drumcliffe (Elph) a year or more to 1402 without being ordained priest.
  Died 1403

O'CONNELL, DESMOND CHARLES

TCD Moncrieff Cox Pri BA & Div Test (2) 1934

d 1935 p 1936 (Dublin); C St Peter Dublin (Dub) 1935–38; R Tubbercurry U (Ach) 1938–42; R Cloonclare Killasnett and Ballaghmeehan (Kilm) 1942–47; TCF 1947–52; P-in-c Cordova Bay, British Columbia 1953–*c.* 1955

  s. of Dr F W O'Connell

  m. 21 Oct 1936 Phillys **dau.** of Robert Miller of Clifden Co Galway; last entry in Crockford 1955/56

O'CONNELL, FREDERICK WILLIAM 1878/79–1929

b. 1878 or 1879

TCD Irish Pri & Bedell Sch, Fellowship Prizeman Heb German and Kyle Pris BA 1900 Div Test (2) 1902 BD 1907 MA 1908 Fell Pri 1909 LittD 1915 PhD; MRAS 1919

d 1902 p 1903 (Kilmore); C Clongish (Ard) 1902–03; C Drumshambo (Ard) 1903–05; R Castleconnor (Killala) 1905–07; R Achonry (Ach) 1907–10; Preb of Kilmovee (Ach) 1907–10; Lect in Gaelic Lang and Lit QUB 1909; C St George Belfast (Conn) 1911–; Asst Dir Broadcasting Station Dublin

  s. of Ven William Morgan, R Drumreilly (Kilm) and Archd of Tuam, qv. by his

1st wife Katherine Eleanor

m. Helen Frances **dau.** of Henry Young of Nenagh Co Tipperary. Issue 1. Rev Morgan William, R Kilbarron (Killaloe) 1934–43 **m.** 6 Sep 1933 Elsie Mabel **dau.** of C O Jones of Tivoli Palmerston Rd Dublin; 2. Dr Maurice Henry Redmond (**died** 27 Aug 1979 **bur.** Ballinakill Moyard) of Highfield Rd Rathgar Dublin **m.** 3 Dec 1940 Vera **dau.** of A Lloyd Harrison and had issue 2 **sons**

Died 19 Oct 1929 in Dublin aged 50 after being knocked down by a tram

PUBLICATIONS

Ed *The Midnight Court*
Ed *Selections from Keatings "Three Shafts of Death"*
Ed *An Irish Corpus Astronomiae* 1915
Ed *Guaire*
Ed *Bricriu*
Ed *Don Quixote*
Ed *Gulshan–I–Shukr*
Ed *The Aphorisms of John Damascenes*
Translated into Irish *Morning and Evening Prayer, the Litany and Order of Holy Communion, modernised and revised, and with additional rubrics*
Author *A Grammar of Old Irish* 1912
The Writings on the Walls
The Psychology of the General

O'CONNELL, WILLIAM MORGAN   –1942

TCD BA 1890 Div Test 1891 MA 1899

d 1891 (Armagh for Kilmore) p 1892 (Kilmore); C-in-c Drumshambo (Ard) 1891–93; R Drumreilly (Kilm) 1893–94; R Aasleagh (Tuam) 1894–1916; R Omey (w Ballyconree from 1920 and w Errismore and Errislannan from 1924) (Tuam) 1916–39; Preb of Kilmainmore and Kilmeen in Tuam Cath 1923–39; Provost of Tuam 1925–28; Archd of Tuam 1928–39; ret

m. (1) Katherine Eleanor (**died** 10 May 1934 **bur.** Ballinakill). Issue 1. Maurice, MB **m.** Vera Lloyd, Lecturer in Celtic Langs and Lit, QUB; 2. Rev Frederick William qv

m. (2) 3 Oct 1935 Mabel Grace (**died** 9 Nov 1965 Dublin **bur.** Tralee Co Kerry) yst **dau.** of Rev Phineas Hunt, late R St Kevin's Dublin (Dub)

Died 6 Aug 1942

O'CONNOR, ALFRED STANLEY 1920–

b. 23 Mar 1920 Ventry Co Kerry; ed Kilkenny Coll; Mountjoy Sch Dublin; TCD Siz (Irish) BA & Div Test 1943 MA 1960

d 1943 p 1944 (Connor); C St Michael Belfast (Conn) 1943–45; C Urney Annageliffe Denn and Derryheen (Kilm) 1945–49; R Killesher (Kilm) 1949–54; R Roscrea U (Killaloe) 1954–62; RD of Ely O'Carroll 1960–62; R Camlough w Killeavy (Arm) 1962–65; R Drumglass (Arm) 1965–85; Preb of Ballymore (Arm) 1983–85; ret

s. of John and Mary (née Styles) of Dingle

m. 14 Oct 1947 Aghavea Par Ch Brookeborough Co Fermanagh Eileen Monica dau. of John Edward and Annie Sophia Ebbit of Brookeborough. Issue Susan Mary **b.** 14 Jun 1952 **m.** 31 Jul 1976 Dungannon Par Ch Ramsey **s.** of Henry Stewart of Stewartstown Co Tyrone and have issue (i) Catherine Jane **b.** 31 Jul 1978 (ii) David Henry **b.** 22 Mar 1980 (iii) Louise Diane **b.** 9 Feb 1984 (iv) Kerry Frances **b.** 29 May 1985

O'CONNOR, CHARLES
V Ahamplish (Elph) 1615

O'CONNOR (O'CONCHUBUYR), DONALD
Canon of Elphin 1446 (C.P.L. IX. 555, 568), & 1450 (ib. X. 461)

†O'CONNOR, GELASIUS –1296
Abbot of the Premonstratensian Monastery of Lough Kee became Bp of Elphin and was confirmed by the Crown 5 Oct 1285. His temporalities were restored in Mar 1286. Bp of Elphin 1285–96

Died 1296

O'CONNOR, JAMES 1795/96–
b. 1795 or 1796 Co Sligo; ed by Mr Ellis; ent TCD as James Connor 7 Jun 1814 aged 18 BA 1820 MA 1832

C Drumlease (Kilm) 1838–47

s. of Terence Connor

†O'CONNOR, MAURICE –1284
a Dominican Friar, was elected Bp of Elphin in 1266 by the Chapter, and was confirmed by the King on April 23rd; Bp of Elphin 1266–84

Died 1284

O'CONNOR, MAURICE
held the V Tullagh (Elph) some years without being ordained priest which he resigned and was made Prior of St Mary Roscomroe, 3 Dec 1417 (C.P.L. VII. 59, 60)

O'CONNOR (O'CONCUBAIR), MAURICE
Canon of Elphin Oct 1426 (C.P.L. VII. 545)

†O'CONNOR, MILO
Archd of Clonmacnois was elected Bp of Elphin by a majority of the Chapter, 1260, and was consec at Dundalk by the Primate. But the Dean and the rest of the Chapter declared the election informal, and presented Thomas McDermott qv, to the King for

confirmation. The Abp of Tuam confirmed his election, and after Thomas had appealed to the Pope, the King granted him restitution of the temporalities, confirming the election, and the Abp of Tuam consecrated him

Milo meanwhile **died**

O'CONNOR, RORY McMANUS   –c. 1460

Canon and Provost = Precentor of Elphin is dead. ?=Rory O'Mochan qv

Died c. 1460

†O'CONNOR, THOMAS   –1279

Dean of Achonry, was elected Bp of Elphin by the Chapter, 1247, but without Royal License. This, however, was afterwards pardoned by the Crown. He was consec in Rome and was a man of learning. He was translated to Tuam in 1259. He held the Sees of Tuam and Annaghdown for 20 years

Died Jun 1279 Tuam

†O'CONNOR, THOMAS   –1201

Bp of Elphin to 1181; Abp of Armagh 1181–84 and again 1185–1201

Died 1201 **bur.** Mellifont

O'CONOGHER, EUGENE

pres to V Kilmacallen (Elph) with the Deanery of Achonry and the R Menveriske = Minbrisg (Elph) 24 Aug 1583; most prob same as Owen O'Conogher below

O'CONOGHER, OWEN

Dean of Elphin? Is pres R Drumcliffe (Elph) 24 Aug 1583 (Lodge P.R.)

†O'CONOR, ALAN   –1215

Archd of Mayo; Bp of Elphin to 1206

Died 1215

O'CONOR (O'CONCUBAYR), BERNARD

Canon of Elphin 1532 (A. H. I. 234)

†O'CONOR, CHARLES

was elected Bp of Elphin by the Dean 1308 and was consec at Armagh. However, the Abp of Tuam held that the election was void and espoused the cause of Malachy McHugh qv, who was elected by another portion of the Chapter. The Pope, on appeal, annulled both his election and consecration in 1310 (C.P.L. II. 70), and he returned to his abbey at Lough Kee where he had been Abbot, and continued to govern it for over 30 years

O'CONOR (OCHONCHABUYR), CHARLES
R Cycule ? = Kilcola (Elph); Cormac O'Hedyan qv informs the Pope that he has dilapidated its goods and committed adultery, 20 Dec 1449 (C.P.L. X. 447)

O'CONOR (YCONCHUBYR), CHARLES
vacates Prebs of Fuerty and Kilbegnet (Elph) by death before 1456

O'CONOR (ICHONAIR), CRISTINUS
V of Kilmacuagin = Kilmacoen (Elph) 1404, is deceased

†O'CONOR, DONATUS (DONOGH)   –1244
Bp of Elphin 1231–44
    Died 23 Apr 1244 **bur.** in the Abbey of Boyle (A.F.M.)

O'CONOR (O'CONCUBAYR), MAURICE
was prov R Calri = Calry (Elph) *alias* Inismoyr Oct 1428 (C.P.L. VIII. 6), has as reported by Thady Macdonagh, qv, kept a concubine and had children by her, dilapidated the R, and committed perjury and is deposed

O'CONUAAYN, EUGENE
held the V Killethayn = Killukin (Elph) over a year without being ordained priest, 1453, and it is now long void

O'CORMACAIN, GILCHRIEST
Dean of Elphin to 1258 (A.F.M.)

O'CORMIC, MALACHY
Clk of Cashel Diocese was coll V Ahascragh (Elph) by the Bp 1430

O'CORVAN, CORNELIUS
Canon of Kilmore 1557 (Reg. Dowdall)

O'COUNIHAN (O'CUYNKEANNAYN), THOMAS
was prov R Kilkerrin (Tuam) 29 Aug 1448. R Kilcroan (Elph) *c.* 1463

OCREBAIR, MAURICIUS
prov V Killenumery (Ard) 2 Feb 1426 (A.H. I 158)

O'CREGAN (YCRIDAGAN), ANDREW
V Drumlease (Kilm) to 1448, is deceased

O'CREGAN (YCRIDAGAN), DONATUS
priest of Kilmore Diocese is prov to the V Drumlease (Kilm) 10 Dec 1450 (C.P.L. X. 504)

†O'CRIDAGAIN, PATRICK −1328
Bp of Kilmore 1314–28 (A.F.M.)
   Died 1328

O'CUATHALAN, THOMAS −1419
V St John Sligo (Elph) 1419 is deceased
   Died 1419

OCUIRYTH, DONALD
V Toomna (Elph) to 1423 is deceased

O'CUNEAN, WILLIAM
seems to V Cloonclare (Kilm) during incumbency of Dermicius Omychan qv, 25 Jul 1456 (Cal. Reg. Prene, 475)

O'DEALLAYD, DONALD
V Huaran = Oran (Elph) to 1433 is deceased

O'DIMURA, REGINALD
V Cluainaceallach ? = Kilcooley (Elph) to 1412, is deceased

O'DOELAN, CORNELIUS
V Teatby ? = Taghboy (Elph) to 1480

O'DOIGELIAN, CORNELIUS
prov V Taghboy (Elph) 17 Jun 1472 (C.P.L. XIII. 30)

O'DONOHUE, WILLIAM −c. 1594
V Streete (Ard) to 1594; is deceased
Died c. 1594

O'DONOVAN, RUDOLPH
appears Preb of Kilgoghlin (Elph) 1615

O'DORCHAN, PHILIP
held V Kilronan (Ard) over a year before 1428 without being ordained priest

O'DREAIN, GILLA UA NAOMH
"Dean of Ardcarne" (Elphin?) to 1240 (A.F.M.)

O'DRINAN, MACSIFIUS
priest of Ardagh Dio is prov V St Patrick Kiltubride (Ard) as he doubts validity of a coll by Bp Richard on the resignation of John Machyleryrean April 1434 (C.P.L. VIII. 492)

O'DROMA, ENEAS
is Canon of Kilmore in 1465 (C.P.L. XII. 475)

O'DROMA, MATTHEW
clk, was coll to V Kinawley (Kilm) by Bp Donatus, but doubted validity and is prov V 7 Dec 1444 (C.P.L. IX. 441)

O'DROMA, NEMEAS
reports that Rory Maghamrugan, qv, V of Ynisbreachmay *alias* Teampullmipuret = Templeport (Kilm) is guilty of fornication, etc; if so, he is to be deposed and Nemeas prov to it, 14 Apr 1453 (C.P.L. X. 637); is prov to V Tomregan (Kilm) 11 Aug 1453 and can hold it with Templeport; disp as illegitimate (ib. XI, 634); prob same as below

O'DROMA, NEMEAS
is Canon of Kilmore in 1461 (C.P.L. XII. 130, 133), and in 1462; V Oughteragh (Kilm); the Union of Oughteragh is erected into a Prebend for him 12 Nov 1461 (A.H. 1. 236)

O'DROMA, PATRICK –1444
V Killnaly = Kinawley (Kilm) to 1444; is deceased
Died 1444

ODROMO, NEMEAS
is prov to the V Urney (Kilm) 1455; disp as son of a priest; is Canon of Kilmore 26 Jul 1455 (C.P.L. XI. 214). He was deposed in 1457 for not being ordained priest in a year, but in 1461, he says that Thady (Magnwin) qv, Bp of Kilmore united to his Prebend a piece of St. Brigid's, Nurmagy called *Vitinta gerit*, and the V of said church, but doubts that the coll was valid, and on 20 Oct 1461 was rehabilitated (C.P.L. XII. 133); prob same as Nemeas O'Droma above

O'DUBAGAYN, DERMIT *c.* 1413–
b. *c.* 1413
clk in his 23rd year is prov to V Killhosahelyn = Killasoolan (Castleblakeney) (Elph), removing Thady O'Kelly, qv who held it over two years without title, 3 Jul 1435 (C.P.L. VIII. 557)

ODUBGINNACH, YNARUS

priest of Elphin Dio, already disp as son of a priest and unm woman & promoted to the V of St Patrick, Elphin, is now disp to hold the benefice or a Canonry, Jan 1402 (C.P.L, V. 485)

O'DUBIGAN, MALACHY

held V Castleblakeney (Elph) over a year c. 1423 without being ordained priest, so it lapsed to the Pope

ODUBUNRA (IDUBANRA), REGINALD   –c. 1401

V of Cluainsynlocha = Clonfinlough (Elph) to 1401, is deceased
> Died c. 1401

ODUBUNRA, REGINALD

V Clonfinlough (Elph) to 1428, is to be deposed

O'DUFFY (ODUTHAID), BERNARD

R Ardcarne and Toomna (Elph) to 1411 is deceased

O'DUFFY (ODUTHAID), DERMIT   –1411

R Archarrna = Ardcarne and Tuimna = Toomna (Elph) to 1411
> Died 1411

†O'DUFFY (O'DUBTHAI), DONALD   –1136/37

Bp of Elphin to 1136/37
Died 1136/37

ODUIGEANNAN, GEORGE   –1428

V Kylhonan = Kilronan (Ard) to before 1428
> Died 1428

O'DUIGENAN, MAOL–PETER

Archd of Kilmore to 1296 is deceased (A.F.M. F.1. 18)

ODUIGRANNAN, CORNELIUS

was coll V Kilronan (Ard) after lapse and held it over 3 years before 1428

O'DULGUMACH, PATRICK   –c. 1412

V Eachdrui = Aughrim (Elph) to 1412
> Died c. 1412

O'DUMVY, RALPH
V Killukin (Elph) 1615

O'DUNCHUN, DENIS
V Cluainbronaich (Clonbroney) (Ard) to 1397; it is unlawfully detained by Trivet O'Sulechan (and disp as illegal), and is prov. to V St Patrick Cnocracha, Ardagh 17 Dec (C.P.L. V. 105)

O'FAHY (OFEGAICH), ADAM
R Balmegenchal (in Drung Parish) (Kilm) is prov to V *St. Melanus de Enga* = Annagh (Kilm) *alias* Plebs Deyterquire, vacant by the death of Thomas Magraghan qv, or by the resignation of Patrick O'Bigeon qv, 31 Jan 1449/50 (C.P.L. X. 445)

O'FAHY (OFFEAGAID), NEMEAS –*c.* 1449
clk of Kilmore Dio is prov V of St. Macilanus de Ganga ? = Annagh (Kilm) *alias de Yeturtirig* ?=Outragh, and R Balimectonchabuill in the Parish of St. Patrick's, Drung long void, 4 Apr 1407; there to *c.* 1449 (C.P.L. VI. 129)
   Died *c.* 1449

O'FAHY (OFFEGAYD), THOMAS
having held the V Eanga = Annagh (Kilm) four years simoniacally from 1470, res it in 1474 and was prov to it 5 Jul 1474 (A.H. I. 238)

O'FALLAYN, CHARLES
is prov to Preb Fuerty and Kilbegnet (Elph) 1 Feb 1475 (C.P.L. XIII. 534)

O'FALLAYN, CHARLES
V Taghboy or Teatby (Elph) to 1480; prov V Kilcommick (Ard); dispensed as son of a priest 4 Dec 1480 (C.P.L. XIII. 94)

O'FALLEVY, CHARLES
Canon of Elphin 1501

O'FALLUYN, WILLIAM
is prov to V Hathsgrach = Ahascragh (Elph) long void through the death of Malachy O'Fallyn qv, and lapses to the Apostolic See, removing Malachy O'Cormic qv, whom the Bishop collates to it after lapse and who had held it over a year, 10 Jun 1432 (C.P.L. VIII. 420)

O'FALLYN, MALACHY
V Ahascragh (Elph) *c.* 1430

†O'FARRALL, OWEN

Archd of Ardagh 1343; was elected a Bp but was not consec till 1347 (C.P.L. III. 458)

O'FARRELL (O'FERGAIL), CARBRICUS

V Killashee (Ard) 1411; of noble birth, dispensed as illegal; who had studied Canon Law for 7 years was prov. to the Archdeaconry of Ardagh, vacant by the resignation of Wm. Yfergail, 9 Nov = 24 Oct 1411 (A.H. I 176, C.P.L. VI 241 & 266). There seems to have been a contest between Maurice McGillavaneam qv, and Carbricus for some years, but Maurice appears Archd in 1416 as Maurice McGillananyd (Cal. Reg. Flem. 158), in 1424 (as Magonius) (Cal. Reg. Swayne 130), and as Maurice, 1427 (ib. 196), and in 1428 as Maurice McGillanemur (ib. 135) when Cabricus claims it (135, 504)

†O'FARRELL (O'FERGAIL), CORNELIUS

V Clongish (Ard) and V Terfaulan and V Gleanissiligan when the latter was annexed to the Deanery (C.P.L. VI. 369). Dean of Ardagh to 1412; prov. to the Deanery by the Pope and is promoted to the Bpric. of Ardagh 6 Mar 1418 (C.P.L. VI. 369, VII. 89). Cornelius is probably the Dean of Ardagh unnamed mentioned in Reg. Fleming as being absolved 3 Oct 1411 for doing violence to Thomas Sourlag, Prior of Trim — see also Cornelius O'Ferrall below

O'FARRELL (YFERGAIL), CORNELIUS

prov. to the Deanery of Ardagh 1 Feb 1485 (A.H. I. 167)

O'FARRELL, DANIEL

pres by the Crown Preb of Termonbarry (Elph) 15 Nov 1619

O'FARRELL, DONALD

petitions the Pope who informs him that the Bp had divided the parish (of Muntireolis (Ard)) into seven Prebends for clergy who had paid him money. If true, R to be deposed 8 Oct 1475 (C.P.L. XIII. 442.)

O'FARRELL, Sir DONAT

V Kyll =Killoe (Ard) ; is excommunicated for contumacies 12 Jan 1408, and on 10 Aug 1410 is to be deposed (Cal. Reg. Flem. 72, 73, 129)

O'FARRELL (OFFREUILL), DONATUS

Dean of Ardagh to 1522; is deposed

O'FARRELL (YFERGAIL) FANTICCIUS

prov. to the deanery of Ardagh 28 Sep 1475 (A.H. I. 165)

O'FARRELL (OFFEARGAYL), GERALD

dispensed as illegal, of noble descent was prov. to the Deanery of Ardagh, vacant by the death of John McGillevanem, at the Apostolic See 2 Aug 1431 (C.P.L. VIII. 355). Gerald was still Dean in 1445 (ib. ix. 467), and Feb 5, 1451 (Cal. Reg. Mey, 240); R Teacsynche =Tashinny to 1468 (A.H. I, 181–182)

O'FARRELL, JOHN

coll V Mostrim (Ard) by the Primate 1539; same as J O'F below?

O'FARRELL (O'FERGAIL), JOHN

Dean of Ardagh April 21, 1551 (Morrin, II. 132). Brian O'Farrell base son to John O'F. Dean appears as pardoned 6 Jun 1585 (F. Elizabeth, 4699 and 4783)

O'FARRELL, KEDAGHE McCONNELL

V Kilglass (Ard) 1615; "Keadagh McConnell Ferrall a Minister of the country birth" is V Kilglass (Ard) in 1622; probably the same as Kedagh O'Farrell V Tashinny (Ard) to 1615, and Kedagh McConnell Fferrall V Tashinny (Ard) to 1622 (R.V.); "the church repaired, noe (Glebe) building"

O'FARRELL, PATRICK

Dean of Ardagh to 1595; was deprived for inability, incapacity and insufficiency (Morrin, II. 310)

O'FARRELL (OFFERGAYL), RICHARD

Claimed the Deanery of Ardagh 1422, and John McGillavanem having a dispute with Bishop Donatus late Dean concerning money matters, had given both Donatus and Richard money, and was rehabilitated in the Deanery on 17 April 1422 (C.P.L. VII. 230)

O'FARRELL, RICHARD

V of Killashee (Ard), complained to the Pope that John McGillavanem (who was dispensed as son of a priest and had studied Canon Law 10 years) had committed simony and kept a concubine by whom he had a dau. If true, Richard was prov. to the Deanery 7 Feb 1422/23 — same as Richard O'F above?

O'FARRELL, THADY

coll V Kilglass (Ard) by Cormac Roth, Proctor for the Primate 20 Apr 1479

O'FARRELL (OFFERGAYL), WALTER

of the race of dukes; V of St Michael's (Templemichael), Ardagh 1443, is prov. to the Archdeaconry of Ardagh, 1443, vacant, and reserved to the Pope, either by the death of Cabricus Offergayl or by the non-promotion to the priesthood of Maurice

McGyllanane or by the marriage of same to a woman of the diocese 9 Dec 1443 (C.P.L. IX. 347). Walter is still Archdeacon in 1451 (Cal. Reg. Mey, 240). Deposed as son of a priest; V Ardagh (Ard) to 1443

O'FARRELL (YFERGAIL), WILLIAM
Archd of Ardagh *c.* 1400; res before 1411

O'FARRELL (OFFERGUYLL), WILLIAM
obtained the V of Mismor alias Lochagana (Ard), a small church or parish in Lough Gowna by surreptitious letters from the Pope before 1457, and held it in 1458 between one and two years and was deposed

O'FARRELL (O'FFEARGAYLL), WILLIAM
clk of Ardagh detained the Preb of Termonbarry (Elph) without title for over a year to 1461 — same as above?

O'FARRELL (OFFREUILL) WILLIAM, 1502/03–
son of a clerk and a spinster aged 19, is dispensed and prov to Deanery of Ardagh 19 Sep 1522 (A.H. I. 183)

O'FARRELLY, BERNARD
poss V Templeport (Kilm) to 1471 (C.P.L. XIII. 298); was prov to V Kedy (Kilm) after excommunication, 18 Nov 1475 (ib. 441)

O'FARRELLY, DAVID
was prov R or Coarb of St Medocius of Drumlane (Kilm), 1401 (C.P.L. V. 398). David as a deacon was coll to the parish of Tulligarvey etc (Meath), 9 Mar 1401 (ib. 450)

O'FARRELLY, DAVID
is prov to V Drumlane (Kilm) 15 Feb 1401 (C.P.L. V. 452); prob same as above

†O'FARRELLY, DAVID
was prov to the See in error Mar 1409 and was consec and died at the Roman Court before 29 Dec 1410 (C.P.L. VI. 226). He was cited to a Primatial Visitation 9 Jul 1409 as "David claiming to be Bishop of Kilmore" (Cal. Reg. Flem. 107)

O'FARRELLY, LAURENCE
is about to resign the Deanery of Kilmore which he got on the death of Donatus O'Gowan, qv, 1446

O'FARRELLY (O'FARCHEALLACH), MACROBIUS
V Urney (Kilm) to 1426, is deceased

O'FARRELLY (OFFARCHELLAYCH), MARIANUS
"In the Church of Druymleachan (= Drumlane (Kilm)) there was a comorbanship not exceeding 7 marks in value wont to be held by the family of David O'Farrelly. It was held by his grandfather Marianus till his death and then he was succeeded by his eldest son Nicholas O'Farrelly", qv before 1401

O'FARRELLY, MARIANUS –1438
Coarb of St Medocius of Drumlane (Kilm), is deceased 1438

O'FARRELLY, MAURICE
priest, intruded as R or Coarb of St Medocius of Drumlane (Kilm). He was deprived in 1401

O'FARRELLY, MAURICE
holds the V Drumlane (Kilm) to 1401 and is ordered to be removed; prob same as above

O'FARRELLY, MURRAY
Archd of Brefny to 1368 or 1369 is deceased (A.F.M. & Ann. Ult). He is probably the same as William, Archd of Brefny whose death is set down as 1369 (Ann. Ult)

O'FARRELLY, NICHOLAS
succeeded Marianus O'Farrelly, qv as R or Coarb of St Medocius of Drumlane (Kilm) before 1401

O'FARRELLY (OFARCHEALLEYCH), NICHOLAS
clk of Kilmore Diocese is prov V Kyllnascanrach commonly called Theallachdunchaga = Killeshandra (Kilm), 5 Jul 1411 (C.P.L. VI. 268); a Nicholas O'Farrelly (same?) was V Killeshandra before 1430

O'FARRELLY, NICHOLAS
clk, is coll to R or Coarb of St Medocius of Drumlane (Kilm) by the Bp, 19 Sep 1438 (Cal. Reg. Swayne, 185)

O'FARRELLY (OFAERCHEALLAICH), PATRICK
was prov to V St. Felim of Kilmore (Kilm) vacant because of the non-promotion of Patrich O'Sheridan, qv to the priesthood, 18 Dec 1427; besides the V Keallmor to which he was lately prov, he reserved another benefice, 10 Feb 1427 (C.P.L. VII. 539).

He was also prov R Kedy (Kilm) 5 Dec 1427 (A.H. I. 231, Cal. Reg. Swayne, 134, 27 Oct 1427)

O'FARRELLY (O'FAIRECALLIACH), PATRICK

V of St. Bridget's, Nurnaid, Kilmore (Kilm), is allowed to become an Augustinian Canon of Drumlane and to resign his V of Urney (Kilm), 7 Aug 1431 (C.P.L. VIII. 384). He was V Urney (Kilm) and appointed a Canon of Clogher in 1432 (Cal. Reg. Prene, 255). He appears to be still V in 1436 when he got similar permission, 8 Dec 1431 (ib. VIII. 585); same as above?

O'FARRELLY (OFERALLAICH), Master WILLIAM

is Coarb of St Medocius of Drumlane (Kilm), 1366 (Cal. Reg. Swet., 72, 75, 76)

O'FARRELLY, WILLIAM   –c. 1401

V Drumlane (Kilm) to 1401, is deceased
  Died c. 1401

O'FARRELLY, WILLIAM

a younger son of Marianus qv, succeeded Nicholas O'Farrelly qv, as R or Coarb of St. Medocius of Drumlane (Kilm), before 1401 when David O'Farelly's father ought to have succeeded after William O'Farrelly qv; prob same as above

OFEARGAIL, CORNELIUS

subdeacon, dispensed as son of a priest, was prov to R Muntireolis (Ard) and took possession 1444/45, but Paul Macechan, Priest, took possession of part of it. Cornelius Ofeargail is now rehabilitated as he doubts etc., 7 Jan 1444/45 (C.P.L. IX. 440). In or before 1458 he is deposed (A.H. I. 163)

O'FEARGAIL, JOHN   –1444

? same as John Offergail below, vacates R Muntireolis (Ard) by death 1444
  Died 1444

O'FEARGAYL, DONALD

(dispensed as son of a priest) is prov R Muntireolis (Ard) (although Canons of Ardagh on the grounds that it had been divided amongst them by Cormac Bp of Ardagh, held possession); was V per death of Donatus O'Feargayl qv or Yfeargayl, or per death of Malachy Miccukoyg or Machwkuarg qv 27 Aug 1463 (C.P.L. XI 508); vacated by death of Robert Macgranaill at the Apostolic See who had not possession, and allowed to hold it with a Canonry of Ardagh, 1464 (A.H. I. 164.). He was again prov to the R of the rural lands or of Muntireolis 7 Dec 1465 (C.P.L. XII.237)

O'FEARGAYL, DONATUS

R Muntireolis (Ard) to early 1460s

O'FEARGAYTH (O'FEOGAYCH), ADAM

was prov to V Drung (Kilm) 5 Sep 1421, C.P.L. VII. 159). He seems to have been again prov to it in 1424 (A.H. 1. 230)

O'FEARLLANIA, CRISTIN –1393

V Ballintemple (Kilm) to 1393
    Died 1393

OFEGHALIT, THADY

R of rural part of Ballineanthowal (Kilm) to 1474; had promised the Bishop a sum of money; is rehabilitated after penance 13 Jul 1474 (C.P.L. XIII. 362)

O'FEGRATH (O'FEARGAYTH), NEMEAS

priest, petitions the Pope that the Chapel of SS. Columba and Cannicus, Tulat in the Diocese of Kilmore within the bounds of the parish Church of Drung is more populous and more decent than the parish church. A great river (the Annalee) flows between them which cannot at times be crossed without danger of drowning, so that parishioners cannot go to the church of Drung for Offices at the great feasts. On account of the want of a stipend, no ecclesiastic will take it. Nemeas has repaired the Chapel at his own expense and keeps hospitality in a house hard by. If this is true, the Pope orders that the chapel is to be granted all the tithes and oblations of its own lands, 6 Oct 1409 (C.P.L. VI. 153). In 1421 however, Nemeas was removed from the perpetual benefice without cure called the "Rectory of Balimicanchobayll" in the parish of Drung.

O'FERALL, SHANE

Dean of Ardagh to 1571 (Reg. High Com. Court, 24, 29); may be same as John above and date erroneous

OFERGAIL, GERALD

R Munterangaile (Ard) 1430 (C.P.L. VIII. 355)

OFERGAIL, JOHN –*c.* 1397

V Streete (Ard) to 1397, now deceased; vacated it previously by obtaining another living, viz. the Church of Tisolean or Tirfolean, Ardagh. John held both several years. (C.P.L. V. 79).
    Died *c.* 1397

OFERGAIL, ODO

is herenach of Tullach or Teallacheach and Mageangady (Kilm), 18 Sep 1470 (Cal. Reg. Prene. 419)

OFERGAIL, WILLIAM

Clk intruded into V St Mary's Granard (Ard) and detained possession between 2 and 3 years to 1441 and is removed. He informs the Pope that Maurice Macgillarnean and Eugene McMuircertaig qv above act as co-vicars of Granard simoniacally and keep concubines etc; both to be deposed, 1455/56

OFERGAYL, CORNELIUS –c. 1470

R Kiltoghart (Ard) to 1470
   Died c. 1470

O'FERGUSA, WILLIAM

is Canon of Kilmore c. 1465 (C.P.L. XII. 451)

O'FERGUSSA, FERGAL

is Canon of Kilmore in 1455 (C.P.L. X. 721)

O'FEROLL, JOHN –c. 1549

V Killashee (Ard) to 1549
   Died c. 1549

O'FERRALL (OFFERGAIL), CARBRICUS

of race of kings, prov to V Killashee (Ard) 22 May 1427, dispensed as illegal (A.H. I. 158, 306); prov Canon of Ardagh with reservation of a Preb and a benefice 1427 (C.P.L. VII. 541) 6 Aug 1427. He is absolved for having paid Bernard Offergail of Ardagh money and is rehabilitated 17 May 1427 (ib. VII. 571)

† O'FERRALL, CHARLES

claims to have been elected Bp of Ardagh by the Chapter after the death of William McCormack in 1373. Was he consecrated? A.F.M. 373 at his death speaks of him as Bishop

†O'FERRALL, CORNELIUS –1424

elected Bp of Ardagh by the Chapter and confirmed by the Pope 28 Feb 1418, and received provision of the See 17 Feb 1418 (C.P.L. VII. 45; A.H. I. 185). He had been Dean of Ardagh. He took the Oath of fealty to Abp John Swayne 3 Feb 1419/20 (Cal. Reg. Flem. No 90). A.F.M. says that he was "a man of dignity, honour, intelligence, learning, charity and benevolence"
   Died 21 Jul 1424 (Cal. Reg. Swayne 196)

O'FERRALL, CORNELIUS

appears Canon of Ardagh 1451 (Cal. Reg. Mey. 240)

O'FERRALL, DENIS

is pres to V BVM Killoe, Ardagh Dio 25 Aug 1541 (L.M. V. 97; Morrin I. 68)

O'FERRALL (OFERGAIL), DONAT

Canon of Ardagh 1461 (Reg. Prene); still Canon 1466/67 (C.P.L. 564–65, Eubel II. 105); most probably same as Donat or Donatus O'Ferrall who was prov to the See of Ardagh "vacant by the death of the last Bishop", Cormac Magauran qv (A.H. I. 145), but this was evidently a mistake, for in 1469, John was prov and Donatus had died before his bulls were perfected

O'FERRALL (OFFERGALL), JOHN

Canon of Ardagh 1465 (C.P.L. XII. 535; still Canon 1466 (ib. XII. 528)

O'FERRALL, KEADAGH McCONNELL

is V of Moydow, Kilglass and Tashinny (Ard) "of the country birth" before 1615; still resident in 1622. Church repayred (R.V., 1615 & 1622)

O'FERRALL, LUCIUS

Canon of Ardagh 1540 (Reg. Dowdall)

†O'FERRALL, LYSAGH   –c. 1601

was recommended for the See of Ardagh by the Abp of Dublin (Morrin II, 46, 66) and obtained it by Queen's Letter of Nov 4, 1583. Bp Bedell does not seem to have liked him; he says in a letter to Laud that "he never had Orders" (which statement is doubtful as he is called "Liseus Bp. of Ardagh" 16 Jan 1588, F. Elizabeth 5127), and that he granted the See estate in fee farm to his natural son Robert O'Ferrall (see Wm. Bedell, Two Biographies, by Schuckburgh, p 327). Robert O'Ferrall agreed to accept a lease from Bp. Moigne (R.V. 1622). He held the See till about 1600. He seems to have died before 26 April 1601, when "Susan Kevan wife of the late Bp. of Ardagh" is recommended for assistance in her poverty by Ld. Deputy Mountjoy to Sir Geo. Carew (Carew MSS. iv. 44)

Died c. 1601

†O'FERRALL, OWEN   –1367

elected Bp of Ardagh by the Chapter; is there in 1344. In 1352, Owen, Bp of Ardagh, which was vacant by the death of John (which See Owen has held for 8 years or so having been confirmed by the Abp of Armagh and consecrated in ignorance of the Papal reservation of See) is now confirmed in the See by the Pope, 4 Id. Feb. (C.P.L. III, 458). He is the same as Melaghlin O'Ferrall Bp mentioned in Ann. L. Ce and Ann Ult

Died 1367

O'FERRALL (or O'FARRELL), RICHARD
Dean of Ardagh to 1373; was elected Bp of Ardagh by a part of the Chapter — not by the majority, 26 Aug 1373 (Cal. Reg. Swet. No. 243; Ware, Theiner, 351)

†O'FERRALL, RICHARD –1444
Cistercian Abbot of St Mary's Granard; was postulated to the See of Ardagh unanimously by the Chapter, but as the See was reserved to the Pope, he set this postulation aside and then prov Richard to the bishopric 10 Jan 1425 (A.H. I. 185; C.P.L. VII. 408). He is said to have been "the son of the great Dean FitzDaniel Fitz John Gallda O'Feargail" (A.F.M.). He was still Bp in 1427, 1435, 1440, 1441, 1442 (Cal. Reg. Swayne, 63, 107, 168; Cal. Reg. Mey. 14, 38). When he died in 1444 "the young officiall MacMuircherty being by the Queir of Ardachy chosen to supply his place, and his messengers were sent towards the Pope afterwards". (Annals in Misc. I. Arch. Soc. I. 20, 65). He had a son James who died in 1467

Died 1444

†O'FERRALL, RICHARD –1553
Abbot of Granard; elected Bp of Ardagh 1541 by the Chapter. Mandate for investiture and consecration issued 2 May and temporalities restored to him 14 Jul (F. Henry VIII, 215, 227). Primate Cromer being disabled by infirmity issued a mandate to his suffragans to consecrate him 22 April 1542 (D.R. Arm.). He signed a Deed as Bp of Ardagh on April 21, 1551 (Morrin, II. 132)

Died 1553

O'FERRALL (OFERGAIL), WALTER
Canon of Ardagh 1461 (Reg. Prene)

†O'FERRALL, WILLIAM –1516
prov to the See of Ardagh on the death of his predecessor John in Aug 1479. (A.H. I, 186). He seems to have been son of Donough O'Ferrall "Lord of the Annaly". He was Abbot of the Cistercian Monastery of Granard of the race of barons (Theiner 486). Consec at Rome 11 Jun 1482. He was Bp on 26 Jan 1486/87 (Chart. S.M. Abb. II. 17) and is still there in Aug 1504. He proclaimed himself as The O'Ferrall and fought and won a battle against another claimant in 1497. He was among the chieftans who mustered in the Earl of Kildare's army (Annals Misc. I. Arch. Soc I. 81, 82). Ware says that he resigned his bishopric some years before his death

Died 1516 (Ann. Loch Ce, II. 227)

OFFALLUNIN, WILLIAM
V Disert (Elph); also coll V Tessaragh (Elph) 1463; was coll V Taghboy (Elph) in succession to Magonius McGeraghty qv, and allowed also to hold Disert, 4 Jun 1463 (C.P.L. XII. 168)

OFFAYND (O'FLOYND), JOHN

Canon of Elphin 1460 (C.P.L. XI. 409), & 1469 (ib. XII. 722); perhaps = John O'Flyn, Canon of Elphin and Ardagh 1451 (Cal. Reg. Mey 240); is prov. V Kiltoghart (Ard) 1460 (and dispensed as illegal) to which the whole Church of Kiltrennan is annexed void because John McGillasulich is guilty of forgery, perjury and deposed, and John Offaynd also to be made a Canon of Ardagh — in which there is not a fixed number of Prebends or Canons; said V to be erected into a Prebendary, 10 June (C.P.L. XI. 409)

OFFEARGAIL, CHARLES

V Tashinny (Ard) to 1397, had vacated the parish ere this by his non-promotion to the priesthood and the Cistercian Abbot and Convent of Kilbeggan held undue possession of it

OFFEARGAIL, NEMEAS

Prior of Innismore gets R of Russach *alias* St Vadani of Mascruym = Mostrim (Ard) *in commendam* 25 Jul 1410. (A.H. I. 175, C.P.L. VI. 236)

OFFEGAY, ODO

was coll V Enga (Kilm) and held 4 or 5 years, and is rehabilitated for paying money to Ordinary, 11 Jul 1474 (C.P.L. XIII. 411)

OFFEGAYD, ADAM

is prov to a Canonry and Preb of Kilmore 3 Dec 1502 (Theiner 241)

OFFERGAIL, BERNARD

is prov V Kilcommick (Ard) and R of Munter Anghaile, Ardagh 10 Aug 1479 (A.H. I. 166)

OFFERGAIL, CORNELIUS

of race of dukes in his 18th year disp. As son of a priest is prov. to V Clongish (Ard) 10 Aug 1424 (C.P.L. VII. 354)

OFFERGAIL, DONATUS

prov to V Kilglass (Ard) prov 7 Nov 1396 (C.P.L. V. 79, 105; A.H. I. 173); is V 1397 and allowed to hold V Rathreagh (Ard) with it (ib.)

OFFERGAIL, GERALD

clk, is prov to V Streete (Ard) 3 Aug 1431 (A.H. I. 159). May be same as Gerald Ofergail above

OFFERGAIL, JOHN

a priest who had studied Canon Law many years is prov to V Moydow (Ard) with R Montereolis (Ard) "which takes its name from no Church & whose holder receives tithes etc. in divers parishes & which has Cure"; had held many years and doubted his right but was prov to both 13 Apr 1412; he had been dispensed as illegal (C.P.L. VI. 242–43)

OFFERGAIL, WILHELMUS

vacates the V of Kildacomog (Kilcommick) (Ard) by marriage, 1479

OFFERGAYL, JOHN

clk of Ardagh, of noble birth is prov to V Muntireolis (Ard) 18 Dec 1397, and the Prior of Mohill who unlawfully detains to be removed (C.P.L. V. 105)

O'FFERGAYL, WILLIAM

was prov to V Termonbarry (Elph), John O'Mochan qv being deprived of it, 29 May 1460 (C.P.L. XI. 407)

OFFINI, DONALD

clk of Elphin Diocese is prov to V Termonbarry (Elph) 2 Dec 1411 (C.P.L. VI. 267)

OFFIRGISSA, BARTHOLOMEW

gets V Rossinver (Kilm) with the hospital of Balac, 2 Jun 1532 (A.H. I. 254)

O'FFLANAGAN, BERNARD

resigned the Provostship = Precentorship of Elphin *c.* 1436 (C.P.L. XII. 98)

O'FFLANAGAN, LEWIS

informs the Pope that Thomas O'Fflanagan qv, Dean of Elphin has dilapidated the goods of the Deanery, committed simony, perjury and fornication. If true, Thomas is to be deposed and Lewis coll 29 Mar 1447 (C.P.L. X. 364)

O'FFLANAGAN, THOMAS

Dean of Elphin before 1447

O'FFLANAGAN, WILLIAM

resigned the Provostship = Precentorship of Elphin 1436 and became an Augustinian Canon (C.P.L. VIII. 590); called Wm Ylongayn in C.P.L. XII. 98

O'FFLANNAGAN, WILLIAM

was prov to V Kilcorkey (Elph) by the Pope before 1469, and paid money to one of the judges in a suit against Cornelius O'Hehactigan qv, who claimed the V. Cornelius was coll, but in 1469, the Pope deprived him

OFFOIND, BERNARD

V Drumorbealach = Drumreilly (Kilm) to 1453 is reported to be guilty of fornication, perjury etc

OFFOIND, FERGUS

is V Uactarachub = Oughteragh (Kilm) and reported to have committed fornication, simony, perjury, etc, 1453

OFFYACAYNAGY, DONALD

prov V Gogelwys = Ogulla (Elph) 13 May 1481 (C.P.L. XIII. 102)

OFFYNE, SIR JOHN

had been pres to V Granard (Ard) by the Crown 1369, and certain charges were made against him (Cal. Reg. Swet. 165, 166). He got custody of the temporalities of the See of Ardagh during its vacancy 1373 (ib. 344). He was then a presbyter of Meath and Canon of Ardagh 1373 (ib. 243)

O'FIACHNA, DONALD

is prov to V Ogulla (Elph) 11 Nov 1411 (C.P.L. VI. 263). He was deposed Mar 1414

O'FIACHNA, MATTHIAS

was prov to V Ogulla (Elph) Mar 1414 (C.P.L. VI. 433)

†O'FINASA (O'FINNAGHTY), JOHN

see John de Roscommon

†O'FINN, HUGH –1136

"Bp of Breffni" to 1136; he was described as *airdespoc,* or chief bishop

Died at Iniscloghran, an island in Loch Ree, 1136 (D'Alton's *Annals of Boyle*)

O'FLANAGAN, BERNARD

priest of Elphin Dio, proposes to build a hospital and chapel in the place de Minbrisg (an *alias* for Sligo), and wants for the purpose the fruits of the Rectory of said place which was without a Rector, and the fruits had got into lay hands: granted 4 Oct 1427 (C.P.L. VII. 545)

O'FLANAGAN, CHARLES
Canon of Elphin 1446 (C.P.L. IX. 549, 554), & in 1454 (ib. X. 672)

O'FLANAGAN (OFFLANAGAN, O'FLANNIGAN), CHARLES
informs the Pope that Marianus O'Flannagan, Canon of Elphin qv has dilapidated his Preb of Claneconcubur *alias* Baslick, is a notorious fornicator and keeps his offspring in his house and is dissolute. If true, he is to be deprived and Charles to get the Preb, 10 Nov 1432 (C.P.L. VII. 423). He got possession and held the V Termoncaelyn ? = Kilmacallen (Elph) with V Baslick two years, 1443 without any title; then he res Baslick and held the fruits of both over a year and res Termoncaelyn and the V Kilnamanagh (Elph) 1446 on becoming an Augustinian monk (C.P.L. IX. 568, 575)

O'FLANAGAN, DERMIT
Canon of Elphin is prov to the Provostship of Elphin 25 Feb 1466/67 (C.P.L. XII. 556–7)

O'FLANAGAN, DERMIT
held Preb of Fuerty and Kilbegnet (Elph) one to two years to 1475 and is deposed

O'FLANAGAN, DERMIT
held V Kilcommich (Ard) 1–2 years to 1480

†O'FLANAGAN, DONAT or DONOUGH   –1307 or 1308
succeeded Malachy McBrien, both as Abbot of Boyle and Bp of Elphin 1303; temps restored 10 Sep 1303 (P.R.). He had a reputation for great wisdom
   Died 22 May or June 1307 or 1308 (Ware)

O'FLANAGAN, MALACHI   –1405
was prov to the Deanery of Elphin and dispensed as illegal 1405; is now dispensed to hold the Deanery 2 Apr 1405 (C.P.L. VI. 26)
   Died 1405

O'FLANAGAN, MALACHY
held Preb of Kilgoghlin (Elph) 1–2 years to 1475 and is deposed

O'FLANAGAN, MARIANUS
is prov to the V Termoncaelyn ? = Kilmacallen (Elph), though he holds the sinecure R of Clondconbur = Clonconogher and is a Canon of Elphin 3 Mar 1404, & was prov to R Baslick (Elph) *alias* Clonconogher void, 2 Apr 1404. He also had a pension of 9/– from another benefice (C.P.L. V. 612). He is deceased in 1430. May be same as Maurice below

O'FLANAGAN, MAURICE   –*c.* 1405
Preb of Termonbarry (Elph) to *c.* 1405
   Died *c.* 1405

O'FLANAGAN, MORIANUS
V Kilnamanagh (Elph) before 1446, is deceased

O'FLANAGAN, MUIRGEAS WILLIAM   –1461
priest of St Kill and "Chief of the Choir" (? Precentor) of Elphin to 1461, is dead (McFirbisse p 245)
   Died 1461

O'FLANAGAN, MURTOGH (MAURICE)   –*c.* 1402
Archd of Elphin & R Baslick (Elph) to 1402
   Died *c.* 1402

O'FLANAGAN, NICHOLAS
Dean of Elphin 1350–83; is confirmed in the Deanery of Elphin which he had held more than a year, having been elected on the death of Patrick O'Tarpi qv, who obtained it on the death of Donald O'Murdi qv, in the time of Clement V, and held it 33 years (C.P.L. III. 381)

O'FLANAGAN, ODO
Canon of Elphin 10 Nov 1432 (C.P.L. VIII. 423)

O'FLANAGAN, ODO   –*c.* 1463
Preb of Kilgoghlin (Elph) to *c.* 1463
   Died *c.* 1463

O'FLANAGAN, WILLIAM
"Priest and Canon of the Chapter of Elphin, died", 1461 (A.F.M.)

O'FLANIT, CHARLES
Canon of Ardagh 1461 (Reg. Prene)

O'FLANNAGAN, DERMIT
disp as son of a priest; was prov to V Ballintubber (Elph), whether so voided or voided because Maurice McGeoghegan qv also obtained the V Killeronan and detained them three years, 15 Jun 1446 (C.P.L. IX. 555)

O'FLANNAGAN, DERMIT

Canon of Elphin 1456 (C.P.L. XI. 19), & 1469 (ib. XII. 316)

O'FLANNAGAN, LEWIS

voids the V Odealba = Ogulla (Elph) because he held it over a year without being ordained priest before 1411

†O'FLANNAGAN, NICHOLAS

priest, Friar Preacher, learned in Theology, illegitimate son of an unmarried noble and woman, dispensed; was prov to the See of Elphin vice John (?O'Grada) deceased, 7 Jun 1458 (C.P.L. XI. 357). Query, did he get possession in 1458 or 1469? He seems to have held the Bpric for many years. On 11 Sep 1494, feeling the infirmities of old age and the approach of blindness, he petitioned to be allowed to resign, and requested the appointment of George Brann, Bp of Dromore as his successor. (Cal Reg. Octav. 633). It does not appear whether his petition was then granted

O'FLAYN, DONALD

is Canon of Kilmore in 1461 (C.P.L. XII. 141)

OFLAYND, CHARLES

V Kiltoghart (Ard) 1447/48; dispensed as illegal; studied Canon Law 12 years (C.P.L. X.330)

O'FLOENN, EUGENE –*c.* 1413

held the V Ballintubber (Elph) several years to *c.* 1410 with another V without dispensation (C.P.L. VI. 425)

    is dead in 1413

O'FLOYN, MAURICE

V Cuylofflynd (Kilm) to 1459/60; is deceased

O'FLYN, JOHN

appears Canon of Ardagh 1451 (Cal. Reg. Mey. 240)

O'FLYNN (OFFLOYND), MAURICE

is prov R Drumyrbealaych = Drumreilly and Wacturacht = Outragh, commonly called R of Kilealuachan (Kilm) 1422 vacant by the death of Luke Orodochan qv, or by the resignation of Gelasius O'Mulmochory qv; is prov also to the sinecure R of Cuyllofland de Inismoyrmaghangody ? = Carrigallen (Kilm) 3 Jun 1422 (C.P.L. VII. 228, 229)

OFORGAIL, MATTHEW

Clk. (disp as illegal) is prov V Cluainbronaigh (Clonbroney) (Ard) to 1444 per resignation of Maurice MacGillaneani to Bp Richard and removing Eugene MacGillaneani son of said Maurice and Thomas Macmuireartacdh, Clks., who between them kept possession about two years (C.P.L. IX. 429)

O'FUORORI (O'FUORCHAID), MANUS

Canon of Elphin 1443 (C.P.L. IX. 392)

O'FYACHNEY (O'FYACHREAY, O'FYCHNAID), FINNARDUS

was V Ballintoberbride = Ballintubber Duma and Cylnaromanch = Kilnamanagh (Elph) to 1445 and while V obtained by coll and with dispensation the V Killeronan or Kilronan (Elph) and kept them a year and so voided the V Ballintubber (C.P.L. IX. 555)

OFYRGUSSA, TATHEUS

was simoniacally coll V Rossinver (Kilm) before 1441 by Bp Donatus and is under censure for fornication

O'GARA, CHARLES

clk of Killala Dio. Is prov to the Preb of Drumcliffe (Elph) & disp as illeg, 2 Apr 1414 (C.P.L. VI. 422). Canon of Elphin 4 Oct 1428 & Dec (ib. VII. 5, 52, 88). In 1428 he, as Canon, complained that certain Bp's lands in the parish (of Drumcliffe) were being alienated in a powerful laye man's hands (ib. VIII. 88)

O'GERUAYN, DONATUS

was coll V Castleblakeney (Elph) by the Bp 1425 and held it four or five years after lapse.

O'GIBELLAIN, FLORENCE –1287

Archd of Elphin to 1287 (A.F.M.)

    Died *c.* 1287

O'GIBELLAIN, MAURICE

Canon of Elphin 1327, and also Canon of Tuam (A.F.M.), Cotton IV. p30)

O'GILLIGAN, MORE

sometime V Killeasbeaghroin (Elph) if he adhered to the Antipope, Clement VII, is to be deposed 1408

O'GOBAN, EUGENIUS
Canon of Kilmore 1557 (Reg. Dowdall)

O'GOBAND, DENIS
priest, is validated in the perpetual beneficiary called a Rectory, of St. Bridget's, Disertynchill = Disert Finchill (Kilm), void by the consecration of the late David Ofarcheallaich (O'Farrelly) qv, then R, as Bp of Kilmore, to which he, David, was prov by the antipope Gregory XII, but as he was not in possession of the bishopric, it really became void by David's death, 4 Jan 1410 (C.P.L. VI. 226, 227)

O'GOBAND (O'GOWAN), JOHN
is prov to the V Disert Finchill (Kilm) Aug 1446 (C.P.L. IX. 555)

O'GOBAND, JOHN
is prov to a Canonry and Prebend of Kilmore 26 Dec 1461 (A.H. I. 237), and in 1464 (C.P.L. XII. 216), and in 1465 (ib. 475), and in 1466 (ib. 511)

O'GOBAND (O'GOWAN), MALACHY
he by certain Papal letters accepted the V of St. Bridget's and Fyncilla, Dysertfyncilla = Disert Finchill (Kilm), but not in the proper time, and held it in 1444 over a year (C.P.L. IX. 429). He is reported to have celebrated Mass when publicly excommunicate, and also committed simony; if found true, he is to be deposed

O'GOBAND, THADY
was prov to V Kedy (Kilm) 6 Nov 1436 (A.H. I. 235); is deposed 1443

O'GOBHAN, JOHN
Canon of Ardagh 1458 (C.P.L. XII. 31); still Canon 1465 (ib. 535)

O'GOLAN (O'GOBAN), MALACHY
is coll V Kildrumferton (Kilm) by the Primate 28 Feb 1529 (Cal. Reg. Cromer, 283)

O'GORMLY, FERGAL
Prior of St Mary's, Inchmorrin, is prov to V Ardcarne (Elph) 19 Jun 1460 and can hold it with his Priory (C.P.L. XI. 411)

O'GOWAN (OCAWANNA), COGNOSCIUS
was V Kildrumferton (Kilm) 1529 when Malachy O'Golan qv surreptitiously obtained collation (Cal. Reg. Cromer, 286)

†O'GOWAN, DONATUS *c.* 1367–

b. *c.* 1367

V of Ballintemple to 1421, was prov to the See of Kilmore by the Pope, no election having taken place within the requisite time, the See being vacant by the death of Nicholas Macbrady qv 13 Aug 1421 (C.P.L. VII. 161). He gets licence to be consec 30 Jun 1422 (A.H. 1. 256). He was Bp 1426, 1427, 1435, 1438 (Reg. Swayne). In 1444/45, on 7 Mar, the Pope authorised the Abp of Armagh to accept his resignation as he was then in his 78th year or over, and suffering from an incurable disease

O'GOWAN (O'GOBAND), DONATUS

Dean of Kilmore, is deceased before 1446

O'GOWAN (OGABAND), GILLIBERTUS

was prov V Ballintemple (Kilm) 19 Dec 1421 (C.P.L. VII. 201)

O'GOWAN (O'GOBAND), JOHN

Canon of Kilmore 1457 (C.P.L. XI. 313, 410) and 1458 (ib. XII. 1); Canon of Ardagh and Kilmore 29 May 1460 (C.P.L. XII. 67, 68) is prov to Deanery of Kilmore 7 Jul 1460 (A.H. I. 236). He was still Dean in 1478 and in 1484 (ib. I. 72 and Cal. Reg. Octav. 386). In 1470 he held also the Preb of Killinaseanra = Killeshandra (ib. 309). It seems that Andrew O'Sheridan qv got John's collation revoked and John appealed to the Pope. Meanwhile Andrew died and John got the Deanery, but Cormac O'Syridean qv got surreptitious letters from the Pope on Andrew's death. John was now re–proved 14 Jan 1455/56 (C.P.L. XII. 451)

O'GOWAN, JOHN

adm V Killinkere (Kilm) 3 Nov 1619; "a converted priest"; got a grant of a glebe here 25 Jan 1626/27 (Morrin III. 188)

O'GOWAN (OGABAND), LAZARIANUS

priest who can read and speak Latin well, etc. is prov to the V St Patrick's, Ballintemple (Kilm) 1407, vacant by the death of John Macmulmartain qv (C.P.L. VI. 121)

O'GOWAN (O'GOBANN), MATTHEW

is prov to V St. Conlac and St. Bridget's, Kilmore, May 1425 (A.H. I. 231). This may be Urney (Kilm) which was dedicated to St. Bridget

O'GOWAN (O'GOBANN), THOMAS

had resigned the V Urney (Kilm) in 1425

O'GOWAN (O'GOBAND, YGOBAND), THOMAS
is prov to Deanery of Kilmore and the V St. Felim's, and the V is united to the Deanery in perpetuity Aug 1446 (C.P.L. IX. 559)

O'GOWN, SIR DONAT
a law suit between Sir Donat O'Gown, who evidently claimed the V Disert Finchill (Kilm), and the Prior of Fore, is decided in the latter's favour, 21 Jul 1415 (Cal. Reg. Flem., 152)

O'GOWYN, THOMAS
R Castro–, ? = Castlerahan (Kilm) c. 1527 is V Killinkere and Mullagh (Kilm) 1527 (Cal. Reg. Cromer, 224)

†O'GRADA, JOHN
seems to have succeeded Thomas Barrett as Bp of Elphin 1405. Was he deprived in 1412 or 1427? Appears Bp again c. 1423

O' GREAGHAN, HUGH
DD
V Castleblakeney and Killyon (Elph) 1615

O'GROGAN, MAOLBRIDE –c. 1265
Archd of Elphin to 1265 (A.F.M.)
   Died c. 1265

O'GURTAN, RORY
V Killenumery (Ard) two years to 1468

O'HACCYAN, THOMAS
Canon of Elphin 1455/56 (C.P.L. XI. 157, 222)

O'HACHTAGAN, THOMAS, the Elder
resigns the V Gilleeniregard (Elph) to William Bishop 1454 — now of Emly

OHACHTAGAN (OAHARTAGAN) THOMAS, the Younger
Canon of Elphin 1454 (C.P.L. X. 705), & 1456 (ib. XI. 305); was prov to V Killeiniregard (Elph) 7 Jul 1454 (ib X. 723)

O'HACTIGAN, DERMIT
informs the Pope that Cornelius O'Heactagan, V Calry (Elph) qv, has committed

Simony and perjury etc. If that is true, Dermit being prov to the V is to be coll 22 Jun 1456 (C.P.L. XI. 305)

O'HACTIGAN (YHACTIGAN), THOMAS
priest, res the V Kyllearye = Calry (Elph) *c.* 1450

O'HADYIAN, CORMAC
res the V Killukin (Elph) 1463

O'HAIGADAN, JOHN
Canon of Elphin 1460 (C.P.L. XII. 81), & 1469 (ib. XII. 722)

O'HAMLYD, DERMIT –1401
vacates V St Bernanus de Manso (Elph) by death 1401
    Died 1401

O'HARA, DERMIT
Canon of Elphin 1447 (C.P.L. X. 364)

O'HEACTAGAN, CORNELIUS
is V Calry (Elph) to 1456; see also Dermit O'Hactigan

O'HEADRA, BERNARD
Canon of Elphin 2 Nov 1428 & up to 1430 (C.P.L. VIII. 52, 152, 193)

O'HEADRA, CORMAC
Canon of Elphin 6 Nov 1428 (C.P.L. VIII. 73); prob same as Cormac, V Cycule ? = Kilcola (Elph) to 1449, who informs the Pope that Charles O'Conor qv, R Cycule has dilapidated its goods and committed adultery; if true, Cormac is to have the R also, 20 Dec 1449 (C.P.L. X. 447)

O'HEAGRA, CORNELIUS
Provost of Achonry 1420; Canon of Elphin *c.* 1428

O'HEDIAN, CORMAC
Canon of Elphin 1463 (C.P.L. XII. 172)

O'HEDIAN, CORMAC
detained V Ogulla (Elph) 4 to 5 years before 1477 and was deposed 1481

O'HEDIAN, CRISTINUS
Canon of Elphin 1462 (C.P.L. XII. 143)

O'HEDIAN, NICHOLAS
Canon of Elphin 9 Aug 1413 (C.P.L. VI. 398)

O'HEDIAN, THOMAS
prov R Korcachland 17 Jun 1475 and Preb of Kilgoghlin (Elph) 1475 (C.P.L. XIII. 421)

†O'HEDIAN, WILLIAM
Bp of Elphin *c.* 1430, was translated to Emly 1449 and got a pension of £10 half yearly out of Elphin, because of the poverty of the See of Emly. According to A.F.M., he had gone to Rome as Bp of Elphin in 1444 with several others, and most of them died there. He was Bp of Emly 1449–68 and probably 1475

O'HEHACTIGAN, CORNELIUS
claimed to have been coll to the V Kilcorkey (Elph) before 1469, but William O'Fflannagan qv was prov to it by the Pope

O'HEIDIGAN, THOMAS
appears Dean of Elphin before 1487 (A.F.M.)

O'HIGGEGAN, PATRICK
was coll by the Primate to the Church of *St. Muylani de Eanga* = Annagh (Kilm) *alias Plebs de Jactyrry* vacant by the death of Nemeas O'Fahy qv, 31 Jul 1449 (Cal. Reg. Mey 146)

O'HIGGIN, ERILL (or HILARY)
pres to the Deanery of Elphin 30 Apr 1606 (Erck's P.R., p 308)

†O'HISLENAN
Bp of Ardagh to 1189 (was he the same as O'Tirlenan below?)

†O'HOEY, CHRISTIAN   –1178
Bp of Conmaicne to 1171 (A.F.M.)
   Died 1178

†O'HOEY (O'HEOTHY), MATTHEW   –1322
Canon of Ardagh; appointed Bp of Ardagh 1289/90 by the Primate, a year having

lapsed without an election by the Chapter. The King confirmed the appointment and restored the temporalities, Jan 28, 1289/90 (C.P.R.E. 1281, p 338; C.D.I. III. 574). Temporalities were restored to him 8 Apr 1290. (Rep. D.K. xxxvii, 40)

    Died 1322 (Ann. och. Ce; Ann. Ult.)

O'HOGLEY (O'HOGHY?), CORMACK

V Clonlogher (Kilm) from 1635

O'HOREACHTAYG, THADY

clk of Elphin disp s.p. is prov to V Straid (Ach) 2 Jun 1422 (C.P.L. VII. 228)

O'HOREACHTAYG, THADY

clk of Elphin disp as **s.** of a priest, is prov to V Toomore (Ach) 2 Jun 1422, (C.P.L. VII. 228).

O'HORAN, DONATUS

was pres by the Crown to the Provostship = Precentorship of Elphin vacated by the deposition of Nicholas O'Celly qv, 5 Jul 1594

OHUBAN, ROGER

scholar (dispensed as son of a priest, to be tonsured), is prov. to the V Killenumery (Ard) 6 Oct 1435 (C.P.L. VIII. 558); deprived for simony and neglect of cure etc., 1469

†O'HUGROIN, JOHN –*c.* 1246

Archdeacon of Elphin 1241–45 was prov to the Bpric by the Pope 5 Jul 1245. The Provost of Roscommon had been elected by the majority of the Chapter, but the Pope cancelled the election and prov John, who had been elected by Dean Malachy, the Archdeacons John and Clare and Gilbert, the Treasurer. (C.P.L. I. 218). The Abp of Tuam refused to consecrate him until he had the King's assent. He vacated the See within a year, dying at the Monastery of Rathhugh, Co Westmeath. (A.F.M.)

    Died *c.* 1246

O'KAELLY, NICHOLAS

Canon of Elphin 1414 (C.P.L. VI. 424)

O'KAHALAN, CORNELIUS

Canon of Elphin 1456 (C.P.L. XI. 187), & 1460 (ib. XII. 78)

O'KEALL, THADY

was prov to the Deanery of Elphin 6 Dec 1390 (C.P.L. IV. 367)

O'KEALLAICH, MALACHY

is R Knockdrumcalry (Tuam) and Preb of Killybegs (Tuam) 1398; Canon of Clonfert and of Elphin 1398; is made Archd of Clonfert 17 Aug 1398 (C.P.L. V. 179)

O'KEEFFE, GEORGE CHARLES 1863/64–1936

b. 1863 or 1864; TCD BA 1888

d 1893 (Killaloe) p 1894 (Armagh for Clogher); C Larah and Lavey (Kilm) 1893–94; C-in-c Garrison and Slavin (Clogh) 1894–1932

> s. of George by Margaret yst **dau.** of Richard Dane, DL of Killyhevlin Enniskillen Co Fermanagh
>
> **Died** 30 Aug 1936 aged 72

O'KELLAID, THADY

Canon of Elphin 8 Jun 1410 (C.P.L. VI. 204)

O'KELLY (OCCALLAIG), BERNARD

monk of St Mary Roscommon is prov to the V of Athleague (Elph) as he has to seek his living outside the monastery, 27 Jan 1461 (C.P.L. XII. 122)

O'KELLY (O'KELLAIG), THADY

clk, illegal and disp is prov to V Killosailean = Killasoolan (Castleblakeney) (Elph), vacant because Malachy O'Dubigan, qv held it over a year without being ordained priest and it lapsed to the Pope, removing Donatus O'Geruayn, qv who held it four or five years under the Bp's collation after lapse, 19 Jan 1430 (C.P.L. VIII. 202)

O'KELLY (OCEALLAYGH), WILLIAM

informs the Pope that Bernard O'Kelly qv, is guilty of fornication, simony and other crimes and is prov instead to the V of Athleague (Elph). The V is united to his Priory of the Hospital of St John Reynduym which is very poor, 7 Nov 1466 (C.P.L. XII. 504–05)

O'KERBALLY, CATHAL

is prov to the V Disert Finchill (Kilm) long void, 8 Sep 1403 (C.P.L. V. 520)

O'KINGE, NEDELLUS

admitted to V Rathreagh (Ard) 1 Jun 1629 (F.F.); there to *c.* 1633

O'KYANAN, MARIANUS

scholar, disp as son of a priest, is prov to the V Minbrisg *alias* Sligrach = Sligo (Elph), vac by the death of Thomas O'Cuathalan qv, the Abbot of Boyle who had held possession for eight years to be removed, Oct 1427 (C.P.L. VII. 545)

O'LACHNAYN, NICHOLAS

prov to V Kyllosaylan = Killasolan (Castleblakeney) (Elph) vac either because Dermit O'Dubagayn qv, held it over a year from 1459 without being ordained priest or by his resignation, 5 Jan 1461 (C.P.L. XII. 72)

†O'LAGHTNAN, LAURENCE –1325

Abbot of Boyle and Canon of Elphin was prov to the See of Elphin 10 Jan 1312/13 (C.P.L. II. 108), and was consec 1313. He had been Vicar General of Tuam and was a Canon of Kilmacduagh in 1306

Died 1325

OLDFIELD, JOHN ORSON 1781/82–1860

b. 1781 or 1782 Co Waterford; ed privately; ent TCD 9 Jun 1804 aged 22 BA 1808 d 8 Oct 1809 (Cloyne); p; C Shankill (Drom) 1811–23; C Moira (Drom) 1823; V Kilcorkey (Elph) *c.* 1823–*c.* 45 (1820 in Leslie's MS); Archd of Elphin 1823–45; V Kilbryan (Elph) 1825–45; R Ardcarne (Elph) 1825–46; R Kilkeevan and Preb of Ballintubber (Elph) 1845–60

s. of Harris

m. (1) (ML 1813) Sarah Mildred (**died** s.p. 18 Jan 1823) 5th **dau.** of John Greer, JP of The Grange Moy and widow of Major Overand HEICS

m. (2) Anne (**died** 20 Mar 1894) **dau.** of Christopher Henry Barry Meade, QC. Issue 1. Annie **m.** 18 Jan 1848 William Cuppaidge, MD; 2. Elizabeth **m.** 23 Oct 1852 Arthur Hyde and had issue incl Dr Douglas Hyde (1860–1949), 1st President of Ireland

Died 20 Oct 1860

O'LEYNAN (O'FLAHERTY), CORNELIUS

Canon of Elphin 1511

O'LINNOCHORE, FELIM

is a Canon of Kilmore in 1540 (Reg. Cromer)

OLIVER, JOHN –1778

ent TCD 23 May 1739 BA 1743 MA 1746

Preb of Killenelick (Cashel) 1754–78; R Carrigaline (Cork) 1763–78; Archd of Ardagh 1763–78

3rd **s.** of Robert of Clonodfoy Co Limerick

m. (ML 5 May 1761) Elizabeth (**died** 1 May 1822 aged 82) **dau.** of Abp John Ryder of Tuam. Issue sons 1. Rev John **b.** in Dublin ed by Dr Browne ent TCD 14 Aug 1779 aged 16 BA 1784 MA 1787 who became R Swepatone, Leicester; 2. Robert Dudley, Admiral RN **m.** St Peter Dublin Jane Silver; 3. Charles **b.** in Co Cork ed by Mr Carpendale ent TCD 31 Oct 1788 aged 17; 4. Richard; 5. Rev

Silver (**died** 13 May 1844 Loughgall) **b.** 1778 Cork ed by Mr Crawford ent TCD 2 May 1796 BA 1801 MA 1807 C Ballinderry (Arm) 1802–03 PC Eglish (Arm) 1803–07 Preb and R of Loughgall (Arm) 1807–44 **m.** 23 May 1823 Alicia Maria (**died** 6 Jun 1851) yst **dau.** of Lt Col Samuel Madden; 6. Nathaniel Wilmot, Major–Gen RA **m.** Eliza **dau.** of Rev Michael Baxter and whose only child **m.** Rev Chambre Corker Townsend Richard; a **dau.** Elizabeth (**died** 10 Nov 1842) **m.** 11 Mar 1793 Robert Rogers Aldworth (**died** 28 Jan 1836) of Newmarket; a **dau.** Susanna **died** 1 Sep 1819 at Somerset, Monkstown Co Dublin

Died 23 Nov 1778

OLIVER, JOHN –1950

QCB BA 1895; TCD BA (Sen Mod) and Gold Medal Log & Eth 1907 MA 1910

d 1898 p 1899 (Manchester); C Rawtenstall (Manch) 1898–1900; C New Malden (S'wark — then Roch) 1900–03; C Athy (Glend) 1903–05; C Glenageary (Dub) 1905–08; R Killesher (Kilm) 1908–10; V Chor Christ Ch Cath Dublin (Dub) 1910–13; Private Sec to Abp of Dublin1911–22; R Tallaght (Dub) 1913–16; R St James Crinken Bray (Dub) 1916–22; R Offord D'Arcy (Ely) 1924–28; V High Leigh (Ches) 1931–50

m. and had issue Dorothy

Died 16 Apr 1950

O'MACNY, JOHN

clk of Elphin Dio, disp as son of a priest is prov to V of Cluaincremma (identified in C.P.L. as Clooncraff = Cloonaff (Elph)), vacant because Charles O'Berind qv, held it over a year without being ordained priest, 2 Jan 1412 (C.P.L. VI. 258)

O'MAELYMNAYN, FLORENCE

clk, disp as illegitimate, is prov to the V Kilglass (Elph) long void, 1407. He had litigation about the V, but sentence went against him and he resigned and is reserved a benefice in Elphin, 13 Feb 1412 (C.P.L. VI. 321)

O'MALLEY, P

C Clongish (Ard) 1872

OMALMOCHORY, MAURICE

appears Canon of Kilmore in 1460 (Theiner, 453, C.P.L. XII. 67, 68)

†O'MALONE, RORY –1540

was prov to the See of Ardagh vacant by the death of his predecessor William O'Ferrall in 1517. He was Canon of Tuam and was allowed to hold his Canonry of Clonmacnoise *in commendam*, and confirmed in the See 4 Dec 1517 (A.H. I. 186; Theiner 520–22). The Reg. Cromer in 1518 speaks of him as "a priest of the Dio of

Clonmacnoise, pretended bishop Elect of Ardagh". Probably he was not then consecrated

Died Bp of Ardagh 1540 (A.F.M.)

O'MARTAYN, ODO

scholar, Elphin Diocese, son of an Augustinian priest, informs the Pope that Nicholas Maccochaidykellaid qv, has dilapidated his Prebend and is defamed of crimes. If true, he is to be deposed and Odo to be coll and dispensed, 11 Apr 1434 (C.P.L. VIII. 511)

O'MAYBREYNAND, THOMOLTHEUS –c. 1413

V Ballintobyr = Ballintubber (Elph) to 1413 (C.P.L. VI. 425)

is dead by 1413

OMAYLMOCHOIR, FERGUS –1414

V Drumreilly (Kilm) to 1414

Died 1414

OMAYLMOCHOIR, JOHN

clk; V Drumreilly (Kilm) is disp as illegal 1414, his father Fergus qv being R Drumreilly. He was recently prov V Uactachad = Outragh or Oughteragh (Kilm) and can hold both, 4 Aug 1414 (C.P.L. VI. 481)

O'MAYLMOCHOIR, SIMON –1414

V Oughteragh (Kilm) to 1414

Died 1414

†O'MEGHAN, GREGORY –1383 or 1384

Bp of Elphin 1356/57–72; he had been prov to and consecrated for the See of Down by the Pope on a false report that the Down See was vacant; was prov to Elphin, when the Pope found that Down was still filled, 27 Feb 1356/57. He had been Provost of Killala. Apparently did not get possession. Translated to Tuam 1372; Abp of Tuam 1372–1383 or 1384

Died 1383 or 1384

O'MICHIAN, WILLIAM

priest, Augustinian Canon of St. Mary's, Kells, the monastery being poor is prov to the V Cloonclare (Kilm) 3 Jun 1412 (C.P.L. VI. 396)

O'MITHIAN, DONALD

lately made clk; illegitimate and not dispensed, is now absolved and prov to V Kaylleasnad = Killasnett (Kilm), void because Cornelius McLaughlin jun. qv was not ordained priest, or because Cornelius McLaughlin sen. qv was deceased, 22 May 1451 (C.P.L. X. 546)

OMITHIAN, JOHN
claims that he is V Rossinver (Kilm) 1441 (Cal. Reg. Prene, 224)

O'MITHIAN, TATHEUS
is V Cloonclare *alias* Clonfarcle to 1441, and was official of the Bp and was removed from the office, but the Primate re–appoints him 31 Jul 1441 (Cal. Reg. Prene, 225)

O'MITHYAN, DERMIT
is a Prebend of Kilmore in 1456

O'MOCHAHAN, DONALD
Canon of Elphin 2 Dec 1427 (C.P.L. VIII. 48)

O'MOCHAN, CORMAC
Canon of Elphin 1450 (C.P.L. X. 461); perhaps = Cornelius O'M, 1460 (ib. XI. 411)

†O'MOCHAN, CORNELIUS   –c. 1472
Cistercian Abbot of St Mary's, Boyle got dispensation to administer the See of Killala, Oct 1449. On 12 Feb 1451/52 it is stated that he had been prov to the See of Killala, and was consecrated in the Roman Court and got possession and ruled the See over a year. His prov was disputed, but he was rehabilitated

Said to have **died** in 1472, but had prob resigned the See earlier

O'MOCHAN, DERMIT
Canon of Elphin 9 Aug 1428 (C.P.L. VIII. 11)

O'MOCHAN, DAVID
clk, is prov to R Disert Finchill (Kilm) 6 Nov 1426 (A.H. I. 231); was prov to R Drumgoon (Kilm) notwithstanding that he had been recently prov to V Disertfingille or Disert Finchill (Kilm), 4 Jan 1427/28 (C.P.L. VII. 486). He is living in 1445 and produces a charter re Disert Finchill Parish (Cal. Reg. Mey, 356)

O'MOCHAN, JOHN
Canon of Elphin 1383 (C.P.L. IV. 346)

O'MOCHAN, JOHN
R of the lands of *de Termts* of the parish church of Cluoncorpi = Termonbarry (Elph)

to 1460, was said by William Offergayl, clk of Ardagh qv to be guilty of simony, fornication etc, and is to be deprived

O'MOCHAN, MAGONIUS

held possession of the Archdeaconry of Elphin over a year to 1443; was removed in 1444

O'MOCHAN (O'MACHIN), MALACHY

Canon of Achonry is prov R Dachorand and Mota (Ach) 1460; Canon of Elphin 1460 (C.P.L. XI. 409), & 1469 (ib. XII. 722); informs the Pope that Lewis O'Fflanagan qv, made a simoniacal agreement with Fergal O'Bruachan qv, late Dean of Elphin and gave him money to resign and is now deposed and Malachy O'Mochan prov Dean of Elphin 27 Apr 1465 (C.P.L. XII. 395)

OMOCHAN, ODO

Provost = Precentor of Elphin, is accused of simony and having sold the unmovable goods of the Preb and is deposed Feb 1466/67

O'MOCHAN (YMOCHAN), RORY –*c.* 1460

Canon of Elphin and of Achonry, was prov to v Cuilofynd and Ranna (Ach) 5 Dec 1441 (C.P.L. IX. 180, 189). Informs the Pope that his predecessor Charles MacDonnany deceased, held certain tithes in the Cantred of Tyribriuyn (Terebrine), belonging to the Church of Elphin, now possessed by certain useless clerical persons: as his Canonry is poor, he is prov to these tithes and disp as illegal 1441 (C.P.L. IX. 180)

Died *c.* 1460

O'MOCHAYN, NELLANUS

is V Culdea ? = Kilcola (Elph) 1425 (C.P.L. VIII. 396), though Fergallus O'Congalan qv was there 1409–28 (ib. 51)

O'MOCHLAN, ROGER

priest, was coll to the V Taghboy (Elph) before 1427 by Bp John (who was deposed in 1427), and doubts its validity and is prov to it Mar 1428 (C.P.L. VIII. 44)

O'MOLAN, ANGELUS

V Teaghbych = Taghboy (Elph) to *c.* 1427; is deceased

O'MOLBRIDE, DENIS

Canon of Ardagh 1397 (C.P.L. IV. 469)

O'MOLMOCHERE, JOHN

rector of the Poor Hospital of Drumberland (Kilmore) gets united to it the R of said place (Drumlease (Kilm)) vac per res Maurice O'Mulmochere qv, 19 Jun 1479 (C.P.L. XIII. 650)

OMOLMOCHORY, GELASIUS

R of Drumreilly *alias* Kenealluachain (Kilm) 1401 says in 1414 that he was canonically coll R and held it several years, it having been vacant by the death of Robert McNeill qv, when Alexander V, Pope (1409–10), deceived by false statements of Luke Orodochan, qv, that the R was vacant by the death of Matthew Micgillasmaid qv, prov him to it. He appealed to the Pope, and if true is to be restored, 19 Sep 1401 (C.P.L. VI. 509); has resigned in 1422. Prob same as Gelasius Omulmorthairge, V Drumreilly, qv

OMOLTORKA, THOMAS

claimed to have been pres to V Killery (Ard) before William Fitzsimond Lawles qv, 1381/82. Thomas' presentation was annulled 5 March, Richard II (C.P. & C.R., p 118)

†O'MORAN, McCRAITH –1168

Bp of Ardagh to 1152; he attended the Synod of Kells in 1152
>   **Died** 1168

†O'MORE, DIONYSIUS –1231

res Bpric of Elphin 1229
>   **Died** 15 Dec 1231 on Trinity Island in Lough Kee where he had founded a hospital (Annals of Boyle)

O'MOTHAIN, RORY

V Taghboy (Elph) to 1472, is deceased

O'MOYLE, JOHN

poss Archd of Ardagh *c.* 1428

O'MUEALINNAIN (O'MAILANNA, O'MAILUMAYN), FINBARDUS

V Kilglass (Elph) before 1401–05; is prov to V St Bernanus de Manso (Elph) 3 Nov 1401; is prov to the Deanery of Elphin and resigns both Vicarages 16 Dec 1405 (C.P.L. VI. 83)

O'MULAID, THADY

priest, held possession of V Killery (Ard) before 1421

†O'MULALLY (O'MELAGHLIN), CORNELIUS   –1468

Bp of Elphin of illegitimate birth, was translated to Elphin 1449. He had been Bp of Clonfert 1447–48. He appears Bp of Elphin in 1456 (C.P.L. XI. 44)

Died as Bp of Elphin in 1468 (A.F.M.)

O'MULBRENAN, DONAGH CLERACH

Canon of Elphin 1343; was killed by the cast of a javelin (A.F.M.)

O'MULBRIDY, DONALD *alias* DENIS

illegally detained the V Urney (Kilm) and was deposed 1401

O'MULCONRY, CLARUS MAIOLIN   –1241 or 1251

Archd of Elphin in 1232; founded the Premonstratensian Monastery of Athmoy 1232. He appears still Archd 1236 (Cal. Irish Mss., British. Museum. I.102). Acc to Ann Loch Ce he died on Whitsunday 1241, but in C.P.L. I. 218 he seems to be Archd at the election of John O'Hugroin qv as Bp, but perhaps the Papal annalist misunderstood his facts; see Dalton's *Annals of Boyle* p377. Acc to some MSS, he died in 1251. His father Gillacimdedh son of Maiolin (O'Mulcrony) Provost of Innismhacnerin died in 1236 (Cal. Irish MSS)

Died 1241 or 1251

O'MULCONRY, MAURICE

was pres to the Archdeaconry of Ardagh by the Crown with V Mostrim and Killiogh = Killoe (Ard) 7 Nov 1661 (L.M. V. 104). (Leslie also gives the same details for M. O'M, V Mostrim and Killoe (Ard) in 1619)

OMULEDI, PAUL   –*c.* 1397

V Rathreagh (Ard) to 1397

Died *c.* 1397

O'MULLALY (O'MULLALYD), ISAAC

disp as son of a clerk; Preb of Termonbarry (Elph) in 1466 when he was also prov V Kylleayn Clonfert 24 Sep 1466 (C.P.L. XII. 504, 512–13); Canon of Elphin 1488 (C.P.L. XII. 504)

O'MULMICHAEL, TOMULTHEUS

prov V and Preb of Kiltrustan = Kilgoghlin? *alias* St Patrick in the Church of Elphin void by the deaths of Cristinus Machedian and Odo O'Flanagan qv 1473

O'MULMOCHERE, JOHN

R of Kineluachan ?= Oughteragh (Kilm) is deposed for non-promotion to Priest 1474; prob same as John O'Mulmochery below

O'MULMOCHERE, MAURICE
V Drumlease (Kilm) to 1479

O'MULMOCHERY, JOHN
is Canon of Kilmore in 1442 (C.P.L. IX. 297) and in 1459 (ib. XII. 83) and in 1466; V Cuylofflynd (Kilm) 10 Jan 1459/60; V united into a temporary Preb of Kilmore for his lifetime (C.P.L. XII. 68–69)

†O'MULMOCHERY, MURTOUGH –1149
Bp of *Ui–Briuin Breifne,* Kilmore 1136–49, is deceased; "a noble Bishop"
    Died 1149 (A.F.M.)

OMULMOCHORY, JOHN
clk, is prov to V Drumreilly (Kilm) 16 Oct 1453 and can also hold V Outragh or Oughteragh (Kilm) (C.P.L. X. 618); again prov V to be erected into a Prebend and is disp as son of a priest 15 Nov 1459 (ib. XII. 83); he is V in 1478 (Cal. Reg. Octav. 366); prob same as John O'Mulmochery above

O'MULMOCORY, MAURICE
Clk of Kilmacduagh Diocese, disp as illeg, is prov R Drummeruely *alias* Kyneuleuchan = Drumreilly (Kilm) 7 Feb 1445/46, long vacant because of the resignation of Gelasius Ycridigen qv to Donatus, Bp., and lapsed or vacant by the resignation of Gelasius Omolmochory, qv (C.P.L. IX. 506)

OMULMORTHAIRGE, GELASIUS
who had been coll by a commission from the Abp of Armagh is prov to the V Drumreilly (Kilm) 12 Feb 1401 (C.P.L. V. 447)

OMULOMOCHORY, JOHN
is Comarb of the Church of the Hospital of Drumreilly (Kilm) and is made R of Kineleasanb 1478; prob is John O'M who is named as V Drumreilly (Kilm) in same Record (Cal. Reg. Octav. 386)

†O'MULRONEY, FLORENCE McRIAGAN –1195
Bp of Elphin to 1195
    Died 1195

O'MULYMUAN (O'MULYMANAN), MATTHEW
Prior of Clontuskert called to hold R Lisanuffy (Elph) (C.P.L. VI. 436); also allowed to hold R Tullagh (Elph) *in commendam* 1410 (ib. VI. 236)

O'MURCHA, JOHN
priest, had got prov of V of Killnasundrach = Killeshandra (Kilm), but John O'Gowan qv claimed it, falsely alleging that it was vacant by the death of Magonius Maguynd. John is to get justice, 27 Jul 1467 (C.P.L. XII. 565)

O'MURDI, DONALD –c. 1310
Dean of Elphin to c. 1310; is deceased
> **Died** c. 1310

O'MURIGI, DERMIT
R Killthan ? = Kiltoom (Elph) to 1431; became a Friar Minor

†O'MURRAY, ANNADH
"Bp of Conmaicne" (A.F.M.); "Bp of Ardachadh" to 1216 (Ann Loch Ce)

OMYCHAN, DERMICIUS
ss V Cluainclare = Cloonclare (Kilm) but William O'Cunean seems to claim it, 25 Jul 1456 (Cal. Reg. Prene, 475)

O'MYNACHAN, DONATUS
V Killruayn (Elph) is prov to V Kyllmurchayn (Ach) 7 Apr 1405 but is to be deposed on 8 Dec 1409 (C.P.L. VI. 42)

O'MYNACHAYN, DONALD
clk of Clonfert, dispensed, is prov Provost = Precentor of Elphin 1460

O'NEILL, HENRY HUGH 1804/05–1872
b. 1804 or 1805 Co Meath; ed by Mr Macabe; ent TCD 20 Oct 1823 BA 1831 MA 1839

d 183 p; C Munterconnaught (Kilm)–1845; R Lurgan and Munterconnaught (Kilm) 1845–66; V Lavey (Kilm) Aug to Nov 1866; R Knockbride (Kilm) 1866–72

> **s.** of John, *cervisarius*
>
> **m.** 29 Jan 1841 Sarah (**died** 30 Jan 1887 Dublin) yst **dau.** of Thomas Battersby of Loughbane Newcastle Co Meath. Issue incl 1. Ruth Isabella (**died** 23 Jun 1899) **m.** 7 Feb 1878 Trinity Ch Rathmines Dublin Rev Arthur J Moore, C Shankill Lurgan (Drom); 2. Emma (**died** 18 Jan 1927)
>
> **Died** 24 Oct 1872 at Knockbride Rectory

O'NUTHIAN, DERMIT
V Cloonclare (Kilm) to 1455, is deposed for his faults

OQUAROGHAN (O'CORRIGAN?), DONALD

clk, is prov R of SS Wygr and Wulstan, Killincheir *alias* Mullachlaydidy = Killinkere (Kilm) long void, which has a Rector but is governed by a Vicar, 2 Mar 1407 (C.P.L. VI. 118)

OQUEOGAN, LUKE

clk, is prov to R St Patrick's, Drumduyn *alias* Macharinbarr = Drumgoon (Kilm), 4 Apr 1407 (C.P.L. VI. 120). He was deprived in 1427

ORACHTAGAN, ENEAS

holds the V Clonfinlough (Elph) without authority and is to be removed in 1401

ORACHTAGAN, MATTHEW

V Kildallog, Elphin is prov to V Clonfinlough (Elph) which he can hold with Kildallog, Jan 1401 (C.P.L. V. 452)

ORAGYLLYG, TERENCE

is Canon of Kilmore in 1460 (C.P.L. XII. 67, 68) and in 1461

O'RAHILLY (O'RAGILLACH), EUGENE

was prov to Archd of Kilmore on resignation of Andrew Macbrady qv, 15 Mar 1444/45 (A.H. I. 236, C.P.L. IX. 531). He was deprived

O'REACHMAYL, YMANUS

V Termoncaelyn ? = Kilmacallen (Elph) *c.* 1440 is deceased

ORECHTAGAIN, MATTHEW

R Lisanuffy (Elph) to 1410, is deceased; poss same as above

OREGAYN, WILLIAM

was prov to R Kilmacumsy (Elph); priest illegitimate disp; V Caseto (Tuam), allowed to hold both 26 Jul 1455 (C.P.L. XI. 222)

†O'REILLY, DERMOT –1529

is Bp elect of Kilmore on 3 Jun 1512. Ware says that on account of the disturbances then prevailing in Ulster, he retired to Swords *c.* 1523, where he became Vicar (Journal RSA 1897, p 407)

Died 1529

O'REILLY, EILEEN CATHERINE 1947–

b. 1947; TCD BTh 1995

d 1996 p 1997; C in Aux Min Annagh Drumaloor Cloverhill Ashfield Drumgoon Dernakesh Killersherdiney and Drumlane (Kilm) 1996–98; BC Drumgoon Ashfield Killersherdiney and Ashfield (Kilm) 1999–2000; Dio Sec Kilmore 1998–2000; in USA 2000–

†O'REILLY, JOHN

Bp of Kilmore 1369–93; is deceased (A.F.M; Ann. Loch Ce).

    s. of Geoffrey

†O'REILLY (O'RAGYLICH), JOHN

was elected by the clergy of the Diocese Bp of Kilmore 1401 and consec by the Abp of Armagh (C.P.L. V. 447), and a confirmation of union of parishes made by Bp John took place 20 Sep 1412 (ib. VI. 374). Perhaps there was a contest for the See. John is Bp 1415 (Cal. Reg. Mey, 356)

†O'REILLY, JOHN

Abbot of Kells, Meath, was prov to the See of Kilmore "vacant by the death of Thady", qv, 17 May 1465 (A.H. 1. 257, C.P.L. XII, 430, 431), faculty for consecration 19 May; he was Bp 26 May 1470 acc to Ware, and up to 1474 acc to Cotton and to 1476 acc to O'Connell

†O'REILLY, RICHARD   –1369

is Bp of Kilmore 1356–69; he had been deprived for adultery and incest and was excommunicated, but was restored in 1367 by Abp Milo (Cal. Reg. Swet); is still Bp 28 Aug 1369 (ib.)

    Died 1369 (Ann Loch Ce, Ann. Ult)

ORME, ALEXANDER   1812/13–1896

b. 1812 or 1813 Co Down; ed by Mr Hudson; ent TCD 20 Jun 1832 BA 1838 MA 1890

d 1838 (Dublin for Ferns) p 1839 (Cork for Ferns) C Ardcolm (Ferns); subsequently worked as Curate in the slums of Liverpool under Rev George Maconchy and became Incumbent of Tanesty, Derbyshire; PC Rathaspeck (Ard) 1843–55; R Alderwasley Derbyshire (then S'well now Derby) 1855–63; C Moydow (Ard) 1863–68; R Moydow (Ard) 1868–96; Dean of Ardagh 1880–96

    s. of Alexander, Farmer

    m. Williamena Mary (**died** 9 Nov 1911) **dau.** of Rev William C Armstrong R Moydow

    Died 8 Nov 1896 aged 83

ORMSBY, COOTE   –1700

was MA & BD 1665, but does not appear among the graduates of Dublin Oxford or Cambridge

Chapl to Lord Capel, Lord Deputy of Ireland; Preb of Kilmainmore and V Kilmainemore Robeen Annagh Cong Mayo and Moorgaga (Tuam) 1665–70; V Kilmolara/Ballincholla (Tuam)–1670; coll V Headford U (Tuam) 17 Jan 1666/67; V Killaspicbrone (Elph) 1668–95; Preb of Oran and V Sligo (Elph) 1669–95; R St John Sligo 1681–95; Dean of Derry 1695–1700

    s. of Major Robert of Tubberwaddy Co Roscommon (**s.** of Edward) and **bro.** of Rev Zachary, DD, VGen Limerick

    m. (1) 1677 Martha **dau.** of Capt James King of Charlestown Co Roscommon, High Sheriff Co Leitrim 1657 and Co Roscommon 1673 by Judith **dau.** of Gilbert Rawson of Grantstown Castle Co Laois

    m. (2) Barbara *alias* Smith. Issue 1. Peter; 2. Barbara; 3. Judith **m.** 31 Dec 1696 Ven Roger Ford; 4. Lettice; 5. Elizabeth **m.** 26 Jul 1698 Capt John Lesster of Derry

    Died 30 Jan 1700 **bur.** Derry

ORMSBY, EUBULE –1770

ent TCD 28 Feb 1705/06 BA 1710 MA 1713

V Ahamplish (Elph) 1723–50; V Drumcliffe and Ahamplish (Elph) 1723–30; R & V St John Sligo (Elph) 1730–70

    ? 5th **s.** of Gilbert of Tubervaddy Co Roscommon by Sarah or Jane **dau.** of Rt Hon Col Arthur Hill, MP of Hillsborough

    Died 26 Nov 1770

ORMSBY, FRANCIS –*c.* 1754

R & V Castleblakeney (Elph) to 1754

    Died *c.* 1754

ORMSBY, W

C Templemichael (Ard) 1872–73

ORMSBY, WILLIAM WATSON KING

TCD BA 1871 Div Test 1876 MA 1880

d 1870 (Kilmore) p 1872 (Down); C Killesher (Kilm) 1870–76; R Borris (Leigh) 1876–80; Asst Clerical V and Minor Canon St Patrick's Cath Dublin 1880–86; Chapl Rotunda Hosp Dublin 1885–86; C Runcorn (Ches) 1886–88; Chapl St Mary's Hosp Paddington London 1888–91; C Chislehurst (Cant) 1891–95; Chapl St John the Evangelist Boulogne-sur-Mer France 1895–1901; Perm to Off Dios London and St Alban's from 1905; Dio Norwich from 1909; Dio Chelmsford from 1914

    s. of Rev William Gilbert, R & V Arklow (Glend) 1851–71 (**s.** of Rev Owen, PC Ballymascanlon (Arm) 1817–34) by his 2nd wife Anne **dau.** of Henry Hodgson of Arklow Co Wicklow

    m. 3 Dec 1870 Letitia Wensley **dau.** of Rev Gerald Wensley Tyrrell, Preb of Tullybrackey (Lim)

PUBLICATION
An Address given at the Service in Commemoration of his late Majesty King Edward VII in St Alban's, Copenhagen, May 20, 1910.

ORODACHAYN, GERALD
is prov R Oughteragh (Kilm) 8 Jun 1474

ORODOCHAN, EUGENE
Canon of Ardagh 1461/62 (C.P.L. XI 435 and XII 142); still Canon 1467 (C.P.L. XII. 565)

ORODOCHAN, LUKE
R Drumreilly (Kilm) 1409/10; is deceased in 1422

O'RORKE, JOHN
C Castleblakeney (Elph) 1869

O'ROURCK (O'ROARK), THADY
is V Killyngyn ? = Killyon, Fuerty and Kilbegnet (Elph) 1615

†O'ROURKE (O'RUAIRC), SIMON   –1285
was elected by the Chapter Bp of Kilmore under licence from the Crown; licence granted 27 May 1250; was confirmed by the King 20 Jun 1251; Ann Loch Ce 493 call him "Bishop of the Breifni"
   Died 1285

ORR, JOHN
probably John Orr ed by Rev Mr French; ent TCD 26 Sep 1758 BA 1763; C St Ann (Dub) 1774; Preb of Tascoffin (Oss) 1777–84; R & V Ardcarne (Elph) *c.* 1784
   was **m.** and had issue incl John (**died** 12 Sep 1837) **b.** Queen's Co (Laois) ent TCD 4 Mar 1785 aged 17 BA 1789 V Jerpoint E (Oss) 1792–1815 R Dunmore (Tuam) 1797–1837 R Aglishmartin (Oss) 1815–1837

†ORR, JOHN 1874–1938
b. 14 Nov 1874; TCD Jun and Sen Exhib 1st Honorman Classics 1894–95–96 Honorman Log & Ethics Classical Sch & Mod William Roberts Prizeman Bibl Gk and Eccles Hist Pri Downes Pri Written and Essay BA 1897 Div Test (1) 1900 BD 1904 DD (j.d.) 1923

d 1900 p 1901 Bp 1923; C St John Sandymount (Dub) 1900–02; C Aghade (Leigh) 1902–06; C Dundalk (Arm) 1906–10; Dio C Kilmore 1910–12; R St John Sligo (Elph) 1912–17; R and Dean of Tuam (Tuam) 1917–23; Sel Pr TCD 1923 & 1925;

Exam Chapl to Bps of Kilmore and Tuam; elected Bp of Tuam Killala and Achonry by the Hse of Bps 18 Jul 1923; consec in St Patrick's Cath Armagh 6 Aug 1923; Bp of Tuam Killala and Achonry 1923–27; elected Bp of Meath by Diocesan Synod 22 Sep 1927; enthroned in St Patrick's Ch Trim 20 Oct 1927; Bp of Meath 1927–38

    eldest **s.** of William J, Manager Northern Banking Co Comber Co Down

    m. 1901 Elizabeth Anne **dau.** of Richard McClintock of Dublin

    Died 21 Jul 1938 at Bishopscourt Navan Co Meath

ORR, ROBERT HOLMES 1826–1895

b. 25 Jan 1826 Co Derry; ed Enniskillen Sch; ent TCD 3 Jul 1843 BA (Jun Mod Eth & Log) 1848 Div Test (2) 1848 MA 1852

d 1849 p 1855 (Killaloe); Prin ICM Coll Ballinasloe 1849–58; C Ballymacward (Killaloe) 1859–60; C Ballygar = Killeroran or Killyon (Elph) 1860–64; C Ahascragh (Elph) 1865–69; C Stillorgan (Dub) 1869–72; living in Belfast 1872–75; R Killinchy (Down) 1875–88; ret

    s. of Andrew of Millbourne Co Tyrone by Mary **dau.** of Robert Holmes of Belfast

    m. (1) 12 Jul 1854 Mary (**died** 7 May 1879) **dau.** of Rev Arthur Guinness, V Seaton Carew (Dur), elder **s.** of Rev James Hosea Guinness LLD, Chancellor of St Patrick's Cath Dublin. Issue seven children

    m. (2) 7 Sep 1880 Kinlough Church Co Leitrim Jane 3rd **dau.** of Rev William Ashe, R Rossinver (Kilm) qv

    Died 4 Jul 1895

O'RUAIRC (*alias* MACHLOCHAIND), CORNELIUS

V of Cluainfairth = Cloonclare (Kilm) to 1412; is deceased

O'RUAIRC, CORNELIUS

clk, of noble race is prov to the V Killasnett (Kilm) to which the parish church of Cuhustal is annexed, 6 Mar 1412 (C.P.L. VI. 265); poss same as above

O'RUAYRC, CORNELIUS MACHLACHLAND

is Canon of Kilmore 1458/59 (C.P.L. XII. 30)

O'RUOGRI, NEMEAS

disp as son of a priest is prov to V Killchorryn *alias* Corcomaga = Kilkerrin (Tuam) 8 id Jul. 1411 (C.P.L. VI. 268); Canon of Elphin 1448 (ib. X. 403)

ORYAGAM, WILLIAM

clk, disp as illegitimate, is prov V Templetogher (Tuam) 5 Nov 1441 (C.P.L. IX. 200). He is still V in 1455 and can hold with it the R Clonchacmosig = Kilmacoen (Elph), 26 Jun (ib. XI. 222)

O'SALLY, ROGER

presbyter, is V Ahascragh and Killeroran or Kilronan (Elph) 1615 (R.V.)

O'SCINGYN, PETER

Canon of Elphin 1501 (Ann. Hib. I. 183); 1469 (C.P.L. XII. 316)

O'SCULAGHAN, NEMEAS   –1441

Clk pres to V St Patrick de Granard, Ardagh Diocese 14 Feb 1389 (C.P. and C.R.)
is dead 1441 (C.P.L. IX. 198)

O'SCURRA, MANUS

is prov Preb of Fuerty and Kilbegnet (Elph) 21 May 1482 (C.P.L. XII. 708)

O'SEGAICH, ADAM

evidently = Adam O'Feargayth, qv, and either "O'Sheehy" or "O'Fahy", claimed to have been prov and was prov on 4 Dec 1430 (A.H. I. 232); V Drung and Larah (Kilm) on the deposition of Augustine Macbradaich, qv, and was coll to it by the Archdeacon; is now dispossessed

O'SHERIDAN (O'SIRIDEAN), ANDREW

was deprived of the Deanery of Kilmore 1460

O'SHERIDAN (O'SYRIDEAN), CORMAC

is Canon of Kilmore in 1461 (Theiner, 434, C.P.L. XII. 140, 435), and in 1462 and in 1464; is prov to the R of Kilmore so long vacant no one knows how long — the Prior of Fore who unlawfully detains it to be deprived. It is erected into a Preb for Cormac 9 Jan 1461/62; prob same as Cormac O'Siridean qv below

O'SHERIDAN (O'SYRIDEAN), CORMAC

prov R St Patrick Ballintemple (Kilm) and of the rural lands of St Felim, Kilmore, long vacant, but detained by the Prior of Fore, 25 Aug 1471 (C.P.L. XIII. 11)

O'SHERIDAN (O'SYRIDEAN), JOHN

Prior of Holy Trinity, Loch Ce, is granted V Tomregan (Kilm) *in commendam* 17 Aug 1411 (C.P.L. VI. 271)

O'SHERIDAN (O'SYREDAN), JOHN

has resigned the V of St. Brigid's of Kyllnascanrath = Killeshandra (Kilm) before 1430

O'SHERIDAN (O'SIRIDEAN), NICHOLAS
unlawfully detains the V Kilmore (Kilm) 1398. In 1401 he claimed to have been coll by the Abp of Armagh and the Pope orders him to be put in possession

O'SHERIDAN (O'SYRIDEAN), THOMAS
was coll to a newly created benefice in the Parishes of Clachacail, poss = Cloonclare and Maydmassa (Kilm) 2 Feb 1401 (C.P.L. V. 453)

O'SHERIDAN (O'SIRIDEAN), THOMAS
res the Archdeaconry of Kilmore 1 Nov 1436 (C.P.L. VIII. 205); perhaps same as Thomas qv

†O'SHIEL, CONAL
Abbot of Ballysadare and Chapl to O'Donnell, chief of O'Reilly's Country, was appointed Bp of Elphin by Henry VIII on 23 Mar 1544/45, the Dean and Chapter, to whom he had issued a *Conge d'elire*, having refused to elect him

O'SIREDEAN, JOHN
V Kedy (Kilm), has res 1423

O'SIREDEAN (O'SHERIDAN), PATRICK
disp as illegitimate, is prov to V Kilmore (Kilm) 6 Jun 1411 (C.P.L. VI. 270); he is V in 1427 and then was prov to the V & R Kedy (Kilm). He was disp as illegitimate 10 Mar 1427; on 31 Jul 1428, the Primate sends a mandate to the clergy of Kilmore on his behalf (Cal. Reg. Swayne, 510). He had studied Canon and Civil Law in Oxford (C.P.L. VII. 483)

O'SIRIDEAN, ANDREW
is Canon of Kilmore in 1461 (C.P.L. XII. 141)

O'SIRIDEAN, CORMAC
is Canon of Kilmore in 1461 (C.P.L. XII. 133)

O'SIRIDEAN, THOMAS
appears Canon of Ardagh 1447/48 (C.P.L. IX 347) and 1458 (ib. XII. 31)

O'SIRIDEAN, THOMAS
is Canon of Kilmore in 1464 (C.P.L. XII. 216); poss same as below

O'SIRIDEAN, THOMAS
was R of St. Bridget's Nurmagy *alias* Keda (Kilm); R Urney (Kilm), and the Pope was

informed by John Macculmartayn, qv, that he was guilty of simony and perjury, and when excommunicated, celebrated Mass, and was deposed 28 Oct 1466 (C.P.L. XII. 513)

O'SOMOCHAN, CORNELIUS

had been coll to the V Drymunan = Dunamon (Elph) before 1421

O'SOMOCHAN, DERMIT

got prov of V Dunamon (Elph) from the Pope before 1421, alleging it to be vacant by the death of Nellanus Ymochayn qv Cornelius O'Somochan qv and Dermit agree to share the V and had done so for four years before 1425

O'SOMOCHAN (YHOMOCHAN), DONALD

V Ballysumaghan (Elph); res before 1440

O'SOMOCHAN, DONATUS

clk of Elphin Dio is prov to the V of Ballysumaghan (Elph) vacant by the death of Muricius O'Somochan qv, or by the resignation of Donald O'Somochan qv 9 May 1440 (C.P.L. IX. 93)

O'SOMOCHAN, MURICIUS –*c.* 1440

V of Druimduan = Ballysumaghan (Elph) to 1440
    Died *c.* 1440

O'SOMOCHAN, ODO

V of Culdea = Calry ? (Elph) is prov to V Dunamon (Elph) and is to resign the V of Culdea 10 Apr 1425 (C.P.L. VII. 396)

O'SOMOCHAN, PAUL

Canon of Elphin 5 Dec 1404 (C.P.L. VI. 43)

O'SOMOCHAN, PAUL

V Culdea ? = Kilcola (Elph) to 1430, is deceased

O'SOMOCHAN (YSOMOCHAN), PAUL –*c.* 1444

R Ballysumaghan (Elph) to 1439
    Died *c.* 1444

O'STINGEN, PATRICK –*c.* 1446

V St Bede's Archarna = Ardcarne (Elph) 1440–*c.* 46; he informs the Pope that John

Magillaruayd qv, V Kilnamanagh (Elph) is a perjurer, dissolute and excommunicate; if so, he is to be deposed and Patrick coll but he is to resign Ardcarne, 2 Dec 1447 (C.P.L. X. 318)

Died *c.* 1446

O'STINGEN, PATRICK

V of Cillmacuagn = Killmacoen, is coll to a moiety of the tithes of Cilliugnata and Dunymgayn, Elphin, which belonged to the Church of Elphin, endowing a Canon's portion vacant because Milerus de Burgo qv became an Augustinian Canon or because of the deaths of Charles O'Conor qv and Dermit Macgillaruaid qv, 5 Jun 1456 (C.P.L. XI. 266). Perhaps he is the same as Seanchan O'Stingin qv, clk of Elphin who was disp as illegitimate and prov 29 May 1456 to a Canonry of Elphin and the moiety of the tithes of Cluayncomag, usually assigned to a Canon of Elphin, vacant because Milerus de Burgo became a professed monk, or by the death of Charles or Dermit (above) (ib. XI. 302)

O'STINGYN, CORNELIUS

is coll to V Fueran = Oran (Elph) ; he is deposed as illegitimate 13 May 1456 (C.P.L. XI. 304)

O'STINGYN (O'SYNGYN), SEANCHANUS

Canon of Elphin 1456 (C.P.L. XI. 305), & 1460 (ib. XII. 98); see Patrick O'Stingen above

O'SULECKAN, PAUL

is Canon of Ardagh 1443 (C.P.L. IX. 347)

O'SULLIVAN (O'SULECHAN), HENRY

priest of Ardagh is prov to V Mismor alias Lochagana a small church or parish in Loch Gowna (C.P.L. XII 1–2)

O'SULLIVAN, HENRY

pres. to V Clongish (Ard) 26 Aug 1541 (cp. Morrin i. 68; and L.M. V. 97).

O'SULLIVAN, PATRICK PERCIVAL –1919

TCD Bedell Sch Kyle Pri and Irish Siz BA (Sen Mod) 1901

d 1902 p 1904 (Kilmore); C Ardcarne (Elph) 1902–04; C Killegar (Kilm) 1904–05; C Clara (Meath) 1905–06; C Dromtariffe (Cloyne) 1906–09; Gen Lic Down 1909; C-in-c Loughguile (Conn) 1916–18

Died Mar 1919

O'SYACHNA, CORNELIUS
V Ogealab = Ogulla (Elph) 1457; is deceased

O'SYACHNA, MALACHY
is prov to V Ogulla (Elph) 28 May 1457 (C.P.L. XI. 315)

O'SYNNAN, MAURICE
was prov to V Kiltoom (Elph) 14 Apr 1433 (C.P.L. VIII. 471)

O'SYREDAN, DENIS
V Urney (Kilmore) to 1401, had died; father of Thomas O'Syridean qv

O'SYREDAN, THOMAS
is Canon of Kilmore in 1458 (C.P.L. XII. 1)

O'SYRIDEAN, CORMAC
is Dean of Kilmore 20 Mar 1469, or poss 1489 (Cal. Reg. Octav. 415)

O'SYRIDEAN, EDMUND
disp illegitimately is prov to V Disert Finchill (Kilm), 9 Nov 1444 (C.P.L. IX. 429)

O'SYRIDEAN, JOHN
is prov to R Kedy (Kilm) 2 Apr 1407 (C.P.L. VI. 121)
    illeg **s.** of Thomas, qv

O'SYRIDEAN, THOMAS
R Urney (Kilm) 1401; is prov to the R Kedy 8 Feb 1401 (C.P.L. V. 373) and is disp as illegitimate 1407; father of John qv
    s. of Denis O'Syredan, qv

O'SYYNYN, CORNELIUS
Canon of Elphin 1443 (C.P.L. IX. 392), and in 1450 (ib. X. 565), and in 1453 (ib. X. 618)

O'TAIC, MAGONIUS
prov Archd of Elphin 9 Mar 1403 on the death of Murtogh O'Flanagan qv (C.P.L. V. 580)

O'TARPA, DAVID
is Canon of Kilmore in 1450 (C.P.L. X. 504)

O'TARPA, THOMAS –1428
R Drumcleab = Drumcliffe (Elph) to 1428
   Died 1428

O'TARPI, PATRICK
Dean of Elphin 1311– 49

OTIRBURYN, MALACHY
who was coll by the Ordinary V Drumlease (Kilm) after lapse *c.* 1448 and held it over two years in 1450 was deposed

O'THANAYN, MALACHY
V Eachruym = Aughrim (Elph) to 1447 is deposed for simony, perjury etc

OTHOMATHAYCH, REGINALD
is prov to V Toomna (Elph) whether it is vacated by death of Donald Ocuiryth qv or resignation of Thomas Ycolla qv, 5 Jan 1423 (C.P.L. VII. 267)

O'THONAIR (O'TONOR or O'CONOR), JOHN
Canon of Elphin 1453 (C.P.L. X. 618), & 1456 (ib. XI. 187 & 304), & 1465 (ib. XII. 235); is prov to the V Kilmacoen (Elph) and disp as illegitimate, son of a priest, 1456.

†O'TIRLENAN
Bp of Ardagh to 1187; was he the same as O'Hislenan qv above?

†O'TORNEY, JOCELIN or GIOLL ISSA –1237
Prov. to the See of Ardagh in 1233 by the Pope who had declared his predecessor, Joseph McTeichedhain's election invalid, but Joseph, supported by the Abp of Armagh, contested his right by fire and sword! He was son of Jocelin the Historian and was a monk of St Mary's Abbey. He got protection from the Crown 24 Mar 1233 (C.P.R.B. Henry III, iii. 14). Mandate to give *seisin* 1 Mar 1233 when his prededessor is called Robert.
Giolla Isa or Jocelin is evidently G., priest of Dio Ardagh appointed by Abp of Armagh (Theiner, 30)
   Died 1237

OTREABAIR, FLORENCE
is Perpetual V of Kyllfarga = Killargue (Kilm) 31 Jul 1441 (Cal. Reg. Prene 224)

O'TUOHY (O'TUHAID), JOHN
priest of Tuam Dio is prov to V Killyon (Elph) 26 May 1460 (C.P.L. XII. 78)

OTWAY, CAESAR 1780–1842

b. 1780 Co Tipperary; ed by Mr Moore; ent TCD 6 Dec 1796 aged 16 BA 1801

R Drung (Kilm) 1808–11; C Leixlip (Dub) 1811–22; PC Lucan (Dub) 1822–26; C St George's Chapel (Dub) 1829; Asst Chapl Magdalen Church Leeson St Dublin (Dub) 1836–42; Minor Canon St Patrick's Cath Dublin 1836–42; was appointed Sec of the Incorporated Society for Promoting English Protestant Schools in Ireland in 1826

    s. of Loftus, merchant of Nenagh Co Tipperary

    m. (1) Frances **dau.** of Very Rev James Hastings, Dean of Achonry

    m. (2) Elizabeth **dau.** of W Digges La Touche of Sans Souci Greystones Co Wicklow. Issue incl 1. John Hastings, TCD BA 1829 MA 1832, Recorder of Belfast; 2. Caesar George, TCD BA 1834 MA 1836; 3. eldest **dau.** Jane **m.** 20 Jun 1840 Rev W D Sadleir, FTCD; 4. yst **dau.** Florence **m.** 18 or 19 Feb 1841 George Digges La Touche

    Died 16 Mar 1842 **bur.** St Ann's Ch Dublin

PUBLICATIONS
Sketches in Ireland, 1827, 2nd ed. 1839
A Tour in Connaught
Sketches in Erris
was a co–founder with Dr J H Singer of and contributor to *The Christian Examiner*
Contributor with Dr George Petrie to *The Dublin Penny Journal*

PAGET, JAMES SUTCLIFFE

TCD BA & Div Test 1853

d 5 Feb 1854 p; C Denn (Kilm) 1854; was appointed "Curate of the Town Division of Clones" (Clogh) 1855; C Killukin (Elph) 1856; C Aughrim (Elph) 1857–60

    s. of Noble of Faragh Co Cavan

    m. 2 Dec 1856 St Peter's Par Ch Dublin Fanny yst **dau.** of William Hamilton of Shankill Co Monaghan

PALMER, DANIEL 1768/69–

b. 1768 or 1769 Dublin; ed by Dr Adamson; ent TCD 7 Nov 1785 aged 16, no degree recorded

d 25 May 1791 (Ossory); R Knockbride (Kilm) 1802–13; the parish was sequestered to the Rev. Josiah Erskine, qv on 24 Oct 1811 on account of the non-residence of Palmer and he was deprived on 19 Apr 1813

    s. of George

PALMER, HENRY 1733–1801

b. 1733 Co Longford; ed by Mr Gouldsbury; ent TCD 24 Jan 1756/57 Sch 1759 BA 1761 MA 1764

V Kilcommick (Ard) from at least 1774 to 1776; R Listerlin and Preb of Cloneamery (Oss) 1775–76; Archd of Ossory 1776–1801; Prec of Lismore 1782–97; R Knocktopher (Oss) 1790–1801

s. of Rev Thomas and **bro.** of Rev Arthur, Chanc of Ossory

m. Elinor Smith (ML 19 Oct 1774) (**died** 24 May 1788 aged 34) of St Ann's Parish Dublin. Issue 1.———; 2. Rev Henry **b.** 24 Jul 1781 Co Kilkenny ed by Dr Stock ent TCD 10 May 1797 aged 15 BA 1801 MA 1811, V Tubrid (Lism) 1810–64 **m.** (1) 14 Nov 1805 Maria (**died** 4 Feb 1827 aged 40) 3rd **dau.** of Bp Joseph Stock and had issue several children; **m.** (2) 4 Jun 1832 Mary (**died** Dec 1843 aged 52) only **dau.** of Thomas Quayle RM of Cheshire; 3. a **dau.** who **m.** Rev Irwin Whitty

Died 12 Apr 1801 aged 68 bur. St George's Chapel of Ease Hill St Dublin

PALMER, JOHN 1708/09–

b. 1708 or 1709 Kildocomock Co Longford; ed by Rev Dr Neligan; ent TCD 4 Jun 1729 aged 20 BA 1733

C St John Sligo (Elph) 1761

s. of James, farmer

PALMER, THOMAS

There were two of this name:

b. *c.* 1707 Kilcommick Co Longford; ed by Mr Neligan, Longford; ent TCD 15 Mar 1724/25 aged 18 BA 1729 MA 1732

s. of Patrick, *colonus*

b. 1713 or 1714 Limerick; ent TCD 6 June 1730 aged 16 BA 1734 MA

s. of Robert, merchant

m. Mary Cope of Shrule

One of these was Preb Termonbarry (Elph) 1743–74, the year of his death

PANHAM, CLEREMONT (CLEMENT)

R St John Sligo (Elph) 1640; V St John Sligo (Elph) 1661; an order was made on 15 Jun 1661 that he should get possession of the Rectory of Sligo as held by the Church in 1640 (*Irish Parliamentary Records*).

PANTALEONIS, ANDREW

Canon of Ardagh 1353

PARKE, THOMAS DAVID –1882

TCD BA 1879

d 1879 p; R Shrule (Ard) 1881–82

m. and had issue incl eldest **dau.** Florence Mary who **died** unm 27 Jul 1915. His widow **m.** (2) …Draper of Blackrock Dublin

Died 1882

†PARKER, JOHN –1681
TCD Sch 1636 BA MA DD 1661

Minor Canon of St Patrick's Cath Dublin 1642; Preb of Maynooth in St Patrick's Cath Dublin 1643–44; Preb of Rathangan in Kildare Cath and Preb of St Michan in Christ Ch Cath Dublin 1643–61; Dean of Killaloe 1643–61; Chapl to Lord Ormonde; imprisoned on Cromwell's orders 1649; was released and went to England; Bp of Elphin 1661–67; consec in St Patrick's Cath Dublin 27 Jan 1661; Abp of Tuam 1667–79; Abp of Dublin and Treas of St Patrick's Cath Dublin 1679–81; Privy Counsellor; held Chancellorship of Clogher and Preb of Desertmore (Cork) *in commendam*

    s. of Rev John (**died** 1643), Dean of Leighlin 1618–37

    m. and had issue incl Elizabeth

    Died 28 Dec 1681 at the Palace of St Sepulchre Dublin **bur.** Christ Church Cathedral Dublin

PUBLICATION
    A Sermon on 2 Samuel XIX v 14, preached before the Houses of Parliament, Dublin 1663

PARKER, WILLIAM HENRY
TCD BA 1884

d 1884 (Meath for Kilmore) p 1885 (Kilmore); C Kilkeevan (Elph) 1884–86; C Cloonclare (Kilm) 1886–87; R Croaghan and Creeve (Elph) 1887–98; Prec of Elphin 1888–92; Preb of Kilgoghlin (Elph) 1892–98; V St Peter (Birm) 1898–1922

    m. and had issue incl his eldest **s.** Cecil W H **b.** 1891 Croaghan Rectory ed Edgbaston and King Edward High Sch Birmingham, Lt Worcestershire Regt; was killed in action in Great War 1917

PARKES, FRANCIS
MA

is R & V Castleterra (Kilm) 1615; still there in 1622; a preacher; church ruinous; glebe detained by Master John Taylor

PARKES, JOHN –1721
V Killenumery and Killery (Ard) 1701–21, coll 26 June 1701 (F.F.)

    Died 1721

PARKINGTON, THOMAS
V Kilcola (Elph) 1615; V Taunagh (Elph) 1615; V Toomna (Elph) *c.* 1615

PARRETT (?GARRETT), WILLIAM H
coll by the Primate to V Kilbryan (Elph) 26 Feb 1860

PARSONS, RICHARD

was C Drung (Kilm) to 1634 and here in 1641, "Curate of Drung and Lara under Dr Teate. His wife an Irish Protestant kin to O'Reilly"; is C and resident in Dublin 1647 (Carte Papers xxi. 346)

†PATRICK

Bp of Kilmore in 1320 — poss same as O'Cridagain, qv

PATRICK, JOHN

MA

R Killinagh (Kilm) 1613; held the V Ballintemple and Mullogh (Kilm) with the R Killinkere (Kilm) 1618; R Templeport (Kilm) 1619; was V there in 1622

PATTERSON, ANDREW –1704

d 1673 p; coll V Aghrim Cloncreffe & Killimood (Elph) 10 Jan 1681/82; Preb of Terebrine 1683–1704

Died 1704

PATTERSON, FRANCIS JENNINGS 1901–1987

b. 1901; TCD BA & Div Test (2) 1925

d 1925 p 1926 (Kilm); C Killeshandra (Kilm) 1925–29; R Killasnett (Kilm) 1929–42; R Larah and Lavey (w C-in-c Killesherdoney 1956–57) (Kilm) 1942–72; ret

Died Dec 1987 **unm.**

PATTERSON, SUSAN MARGARET 1948–

b. 1948; Univ of Otago BA 1971 BD 1989 PhD 1992; Knox Coll Dunedin 1984

d 1988 p 1989; C St Martin Dunedin (Dunedin) 1988–91; Tutor Univ of Otago and Knox Coll 1989–91; in ECUSA 1991–92; Assoc C Hawke's Bay (Dio Napier) 1992–96; Fulbright Sch 1993–94; Lect Trinity Coll Bristol 1997–2000; R Kildallon Newtowngore and Corrawallen (Kilm) 2000–04; Preb of Drumlease (Kilm) 2003–04; R Kilmoremoy G (Killala) and Dean of Killala 2004–

PUBLICATIONS

    contributed to *Christ in Context*, 1992
    Beyond Mere Health, 1996
    The Task of Theology Today, 1998
    Realist Christian Theology in a Postmodern Age, 1999
    More than a Single Issue, 2000
    contributed to *The Theology of Reconciliation: Essays in Biblical and Systematic Theology*, 2003

PAUL, HENRY 1851/52–1917

b. 1851 or 1852; QUI Cork Sch BA 1880 MA 1881

d 1880 p 1881 (Cork); C Nohoval (Cork) 1880–84; C Ballymodan (Cork) 1884–87; R Killermogh (Leigh) 1887–1901; R Castleterra (Kilm) 1901–07; Acting CF Curragh 1907–11

    m…

    Died 10 Feb 1917 at Ballycotton aged 65

PAUL, JOHN 1774–1831

b. 1774 Co Derry; ed by Mr Sampson; ent TCD 2 Jan 1792 aged 17 BA

R Knockbride (Kilm) 20 Feb to 1 May 1802; R & V Narraghmore (Glend) 1802–13; Preb of Aghadowey (Derry) 1813–31

    s. of James, *publicanus*

    m. 18 Aug 1817 Aghadowey Ch Co Derry Eliza **dau.** of Alexander Orr of Landmore Co Londonderry; she **m.** (2) 21 Jan 1841 Rev Stephen Gwynn, Treas of Connor

    Died 23 Sep 1831

PAYNAM (or PAMAN), CLEMENT 1610/11–1663

b. 1610 or 1611 Chevington Suffolk; ed Lavenham Sch; Bury Sch; As Clement Paman he was admitted to Sidney Sussex Coll Camb 26 Feb 1627/28 aged 16 BA 1631/32 MA 1635; TCD DD (*ad eund*) 1661

V Thatcham Berks (Ox) 1648–53 but his right to the V was disputed; Preb of Monmohenock in St Patrick's Cath Dublin 1661–63; R St John Sligo and Dean of Ardagh 1661–63; V Castledermot (Glend) 1662–63

    s. of Robert

    Died 1663

PEACY (PEZE de GALLINEER), PETER *alias* GALLINEER   –1721

V Mohill (Ard) 1699–1721; V Drung and Lara (Kilm) 1700–21; officiated at St Mary's French Ch Dublin (Dub) 1701–19; "minister of the Gospel at Dublin"

    Died 1721

PEARSON, THOMAS   –1926

TCD BA & Div Test (1) 1887 MA 1890 BD 1892

d & p 1887 (Kilmore); C Larah and Lavey (Kilm) 1887–89; C St Thomas Dublin (Dub) and Catechist Dublin Bd of Rel Ed 1889–92; C Christ Ch Carysfort Blackrock (Dub) 1892–93; R Christ Ch Carysfort Blackrock (Dub) 1893–1924; ret

    m. 5 Aug 1897 Minna Georgina (**died** 8 Sep 1927) **dau.** of George A Rotheram of Kilbride Co Meath. Issue 1. George Thomas; 2. John

    Died 1 Aug 1926 **bur.** Grayshott Surrey

PECK (PYKE), RICHARD −1640

Preb of Kilmainmore (Tuam) 1635; V Bumlin (Elph) −1640

Died 1640

PENNEFATHER, WILLIAM

C Ballymachugh (Ard) 1841–44

PENTLAND, THOMAS 1796–1874

b. 1796 Dublin; ed by Dr Gavan; ent TCD as SC 2 Nov 1812 aged 16 BA 1816

C Bailieborough and Moybologue (Kilm) 1826–47; V Drumreilly (Kilm) 1857–74

s. of Charles, merchant and owner of saltworks

m. 24 Feb 1835 Florence (**died** 6 Oct 1877 aged 68) yst **dau.** of Thomas Sadleir of Castletown Co Tipperary, Barrister-at-Law. Issue incl 1. Thomas (**died** 1 Jan 1868 aged 24); 2. eldest **dau.** Florence **m.** 4 Dec 1862 Rev Robert Gumley and had issue (i) Rev John Robert, C Drumshambo (Ard) qv (ii) Rev Francis Albert, PC Gateforth and Hambleton (York) 1915–37 (iii) Rev Edmund Maurice, R Clanabogan (Derry) 1933–40

Died 23 Sep 1874 at Lambfield aged 77

PENTONY, RICHARD

was presented to the Precentorship of Elphin 6 Aug 1603 (Erck's P.R. p 37)

PERCEVAL, HENRY 1819–1880

b. 2 Nov 1819 Co Sligo; ed by Mr Donne; ent TCD as SC 13 Oct 1837 BA 1843

d 1854 p; V Denn (Kilm) 1854–59; V Killargue (Kilm) 1859–60; V Drumlease (Kilm) 1860–73

2nd **s.** of Alexander, Lt Col Sligo Militia, JP, Sergeant at Arms to the House of Lords of Temple Hse Co Sligo

m. 10 Jan 1850 Elizabeth Letitia only child of John Hutchinson of Dublin

Died 16 May 1880 at Killiney Co Dublin

PERCY, FRANCIS 1762/63–

b. 1762 or 1763 Co Leitrim; ed by Mr Meares; ent TCD 12 Nov 1778 aged 15 BA 1783

d 1787 p 22 Jun 1788; lic C Fenagh (Ard) 18 Sep 1787; was C Oughteragh (Kilm) in 1799; V Oughteragh (Ard) 1806–c35

s. of Alexander, *armiger*

PERCY, GILBERT 1807/08–1893

b. 1807 or 1808 Co Leitrim; ed by Mr Smith; ent TCD 17 Oct 1825 aged 17 BA 1831 LLB & LLD 1862

C Rathgar (Dub); C Oughteragh (Ard) 1834; PC Ballymoyer (Arm) 1839–49; SPG Missy Lr Canada 1849–60; R St Peter Quebec 1853–60; Dean of Quebec; C Kiltoghart (Ard) 1863–67; R & V Ballymacormick (w Killashee from 1871) (Ard) 1867–75; Chapl to Lord Clements, Earl of Leitrim at Lough Rynn, Dromod 1875–81

> **s.** of Henry of Garradice Ballinamore Co Leitrim and **bro.** of Rev William Alexander BA, R Kiltoghart qv
>
> was **m.**; a **s.** Gilbert **died** 30 Nov 1853 aboard the *Staffordshire* which struck a rock near Halifax on her voyage to Boston and sank with the loss of almost all on board.; his eldest **dau.** Marcella **m.** 28 May 1851 at All Saints Chapel Quebec Lt Col D Ashe RN; his 4th **dau.** Emily Elizabeth Beresford **m.** (1) 15 Feb 1870 Col Edward Cattell; **m.** (2) Major Paul Gregory Petavel, Duke of Cornwall's Light Infantry
>
> **Died** at The Flanker, Drumsna Co Leitrim 7 Sep 1893 aged 85

PERCY, WILLIAM

C Kiltoghart (Ard) *c.* 1826

may be same as W A Percy below

PERCY, WILLIAM ALEXANDER 1795/96–1869

b. 1795 or 1796 Co Leitrim; ed by Dr Dowdall; ent TCD 7 Dec 1812 aged 16 BA 1819

R Kiltoghart (Ard) 1836–69

> **s.** of Henry
>
> **m.** Elizabeth **dau.** of Robert James Lloyd, JP of Co Roscommon and had issue incl 1…; 2. Robert Jones, Paymaster 34th Regt **died** 28 Apr 1841 at Fyzabad aged 33; 3. Henry Richard **b.** Co Roscommon ed Dungannon Sch ent TCD 1 Nov 1841 aged 17 MD **m.** 17 Nov 1851 Emma 3rd **dau.** of Major John Bertram Orde late of Dragoon Guards; 3. Susan Emma **m.** 12 Feb 1851 Christopher French JP of Clonyquin and had issue Percy, grandfather of Percy French the well-known song writer; 4. Jane Catherine Caroline **m.** 5 Aug 1873 Rev Joseph Potter, R Drumlease (Kilm) qv
>
> **Died** 1869

PEYTON, GEORGE RICHARD 1824–1905

b. 1824; ent TCD 1 Jul 1840 aged 15 BA & MA 1844

d 1872 p 1873 (Ossory); C Clongish (Ard) 1872–73; R Clongish (Ard) 1873–1905

> **s.** of George Hamilton Conyngham JP DL of Driney Co Leitrim
>
> **m.** Mary Ann (**died** 23 Mar 1903 **bur.** Dean's Grange Dublin)
>
> **Died** at Clongish Rectory Newtownforbes 12 Nov 1905 aged 81

PEYTON, WALTER CUNNINGHAM (CONYNGHAM) 1821–1896

b. 1821; ent TCD 1 Jul 1840 aged 18 BA 1847 MA 1868

d 1847 (Dublin) p 1848 (Kilmore); C Kiltoghart (Ard) 1847; C Lavey (Kilm) 1847–

48; PC Billis (Kilm) 1848–96

    eldest s. of Capt George Hamilton Cunningham, JP DL of Driney Hse Co Leitrim and Jane dau. of Walter Gray of Tubbercurry Co Sligo

    m. 12 Jun 1856 at Mellifont Co Louth Margaret dau. of Rev James McCreight, R Keady (Arm) for one month in 1835

    Died 21 Apr 1896 at the Grange, Billis

PEYTON, WILLIAM WALTER 1871–1943

b. 21 Mar 1871 Longford; ed Rathmines Sch; St Lawrence Coll Ramsgate; TCD BA 1893 Div Test (2) 1894

d 1895 p 31 May 1896 (Derry); C Conwall (Raph) 1895–97; C Drumlease (Kilm) 1897–1900; R Drumreilly (Kilm) 1900–06; R Toomna (Elph) 1906–23; Chapl at Versailles 1925–26; Asst Chapl at Brussels 1926–27; Chapl at Freiburg 1931–

    elder s. of James Duncan of Driney Hse Co Leitrim

    m. 21 Dec 1909 Eleanor Charlotte dau. of Rev Joseph Rawlins, R Templeport (Kilm) qv

    Died 25 Jan 1943

PHAIR, GEORGE CATHCART 1874–1944

b. 15 Feb 1874 Ballina Co Mayo; ed at Brighton; London Coll of Divinity 1894; Hatfield Hall Durham BA 1901 MA & BD 1908; PTE (1) 1897

d 1897 p 1898 (Truro); C Southhill and Callington (Truro) 1897–1901; C Sligo (Elph) 1901–06; C Croom 1906–12; C-in-c Ballingarry (Lim) 1908–12; R Ballyheigue (A & A) 1912–16; R Kilnaughtin w Kilfergus (A & A) 1916–25; R Rathkeale U (Lim) 1925–c44; Canon of Limerick and Preb of St Munchin's (Lim) 1937–c44

    s. of William James by Ellen (née Cathcart)

    m. 16 Jan 1914 Dorothy Ethel Agnes dau. of A G Eve of Kenley Surrey; Issue sons 1. Frank Evelyn; 2. John Robert Cathcart; daus. 1. Rosamond; 2. Maureen Ellen

    Died 30 Jun 1944

PHAIR, HENRY LLOYD 1917–1997

b. 25 Sep 1917; ed The King's Hosp Dublin; TCD BA & Div Test 1942 MA 1949; MBE 1964

d 1942 p 1943 (Connor); C St James Belfast (Conn) 1942–45; C-in-c Drumlane (Kilm) 1945–47; Asst Chapl Miss to Seamen 1947–48; C-in-c Mullaghdun (Clogh) 1948–51; R Lissan (Arm) 1951–55; Chapl RAF 1955–72; Welfare Officer Kent Co Constabulary 1972–76; V Ercall Magna and Rowton (Lich) 1976–81; Perm to Off Dio Chichester 1982–

    s. of William Lloyd of Castlerea Co Roscommon by Marcella (née Moore)

    m. 24 Apr 1944 St Peter's Ch Belfast Esther (died 8 Aug 1991) dau. of William Henry and Sara Law of Belfast. Issue 1. Valerie Joyce b. 17 Aug 1946; 2. Hazel Marcella Kathleen b. 8 Jul 1948

    Died Mar 1997

PHIBBS, THOMAS 1808/09–

b. 1808 or 1809; ent TCD 5 Nov 1827 aged 18 — no degree recorded

d 30 Oct 1837 (Limerick for Elphin) p;

C Eastersnow (Elph) 1854–58; C Toomna (Elph) 1859; C Rathbeggan 1862; C Streete (Ard) 1866–67

s. of John, woollen draper of 73 Dame St Dublin

m. (M L 1855) Susan Vickers Judd

PHIBBS, WILLIAM

Preb of Terebrine (Elph) 1761–67; V Taunagh (Elph) *c.* 1766–*c.* 1785

PHILLIPS, THOMAS GEORGE JOHNSTON 1834/35–1898

b. 1834 or 1835; TCD BA & Div Test 1856 MA 1859

d 20 May 1858 p 19 Dec 1859 (Kilmore); C Toomna (Elph) 1858–59; C Kilbryan (Elph) 1859; C Streete (Ard) 1860–61; C Mohill (Ard) 1861–70; I Killoughter (Kilm) 1870–79; I Fennagh and Myshall (Leigh) 1879–98

s. of Major Phillips of Glenview, Belturbet Co Cavan

m. Miss Leurs of Violetstown Co Meath

Died s.p. 3 Apr 1898 aged 63

PHIPPS (PHIBBS), ROBERT 1703/04–

b. 1703 or 1704 near Sligo; ed by Dr Blair, Sligo; ent TCD 8 Feb 1721/22 aged 18 BA 1730

d; p 13 Aug 1732; prob R P, V Kilbryan Kilnemanagh & Kilbrinethe (Elph) 1743;coll V Taunagh (Elph) 5 Jan 1744/45; prob R Phipps, Chapl Dublin City Workhouse

s. of Matthew, *armiger*

m. ? 6 Dec 1744 Mary Anne (poss née Mercer) and had issue Arabella **m.** Robert Shaw Ewing of Ormond Quay Dublin

PICKERING, JAMES 1909–1985

b. 16 Jul 1909 Glasgow; ed Castledawson Co Derry; CITC 1971

d 1971 p 1972; C St Nathaniel Sheffield (Sheff) 1971–73; C Conwall U w Gartan (Raph) 1973–80; I Ardagh Moydow Tashinny Shrule and Kilcommick (Ard) 1980–81; ret

s. of Thomas of Castledawson Co Derry

m. 29 Apr 1936 Selina Mabel (deceased) **dau.** of John Hunter of Devenish Co Fermanagh. Issue 1. Rev John Alexander qv; 2. James

Died 17 Jul 1985

PICKERING, JOHN ALEXANDER 1941–

b. 13 Apr 1941 Omagh Co Tyrone; ed Omagh Academy; Magee Univ Coll Londonderry; TCD BA 1963 MA 1966; CITC 1965

d 1965 p 1966 (Dromore); C Magheralin (Drom) 1965–67; C-in-c Oughteragh Fenagh Kiltubride and Drumreilly (Ard) 1967–68 and R 1968–71; Dep Sec HBS 1971–74; C-in-c Drumgoon Killesherdoney and Ashfield (Kilm) 1974–80; I Keady Armaghbreague and Derrynoose (Arm) 1980–83; R Drumcree (Arm) 1983–2007; RD of Kilmore 1997–2007; ret

    s. of Rev James qv (**s.** of Thomas) by Selina Mabel (née Hunter)

    m. 15 May 1975 Crinken Ch Dublin Olive Elizabeth (**died** Easter Sunday 16 Apr 2006) **dau.** of Samuel Young of Limerick. Issue Sarah Ruth **b.** 19 Mar 1976 Univ of Ulster BMus 1997

PIERS, FLETCHER 1712/13–1767

b. 1712 or 1713 at Lowbaskin Co Westmeath; ed by Rev Mr Neligan, Longford; ent TCD 2 Jun 1729 aged 16 BA 1733

was Impropriate C Rathaspeck (Ard) –1742; R Killashee (Ard) 1749–67

    s. of Rev William, V Ballymore (Meath)

    m. (ML 22 Aug 1739) Anne **dau.** of Lt Arthur Galbraith by Mary widow of Ebenezer Wright and **dau.** of Col Nicholas Kempston, High Sheriff of Co Cavan 1673. Issue Katherine Martha **m.** 1768 William Meares of Co Westmeath

    Died Feb 1767 at Bath

PIGOTT, WILLIAM   –c. 1790

ent TCD 29 Jun 1732 BA 1736 MA 1739

Preb of Fenore (Clonf) 1743–45; Archd of Clonfert 1745–90; Provost of Kilmacduagh 1745–90; R Dysert Enos (Leigh) 1749–72; JP for Co Cavan 1755; V Killan, now Shercock (Kilm) 1772–90

    s. of Rev John, Preb of Kilteskill (Clonf) by Deborah **dau.** of Matthew French of Dublin

    m. St Peter's Ch Dublin 30 Apr 1774 Mary Moore (**died** c. 1797 P Will prov 1797). Issue incl a 4th **s.** Rev Edward bapt 1749 ent TCD 1 Nov 1767 as FC BA 1772 R Dysart Enos (Leigh) 1772–97 C St Luke Dublin (Dub) 1774 C St Bride Dublin (Dub) 1776–77 C St Nicholas (Cork) 1777 **m.** (1) (ML 23 Jul 1774) Anne Billing and had issue Frances Mary Ann; **m.** (2)…

    Died c. 1790 Will prov 1790

PIKE, ARTHUR JOHN 1859–1945

b. 6 Mar 1859; Clare Coll Camb BA 1882 MA 1905

d 1884 p 1885 (Down for Armagh); C Tyholland (Clogh) 1884–85; C Donaghmoine (Clogh) 1885–87; PC Killoughter (Kilm) 1887–94; CMS Missy Uganda 1894–98; R Bailieborough (Kilm) 1898–1900; Sec CMS for North of Ireland 1900–02; Central Sec CMS for Ireland 1902–11; R Crossmolina (Killala) 1911–45; RD Killala 1928–31;

RD Dunfeeney (Killala) 1931–45; Dean of Killala 1934–35; Archd of Killala and Achonry 1935–44; ret

    m. Jane Wyley (**died** 31 May 1928) **b.** 28 May 1864. Issue 1. Peggy (**died** 12 Jan 1881); 2. Muriel (**died** 20 May 1887); 3. Dorothy (**died** 5 Jul 1959); 4. Enid Rowlette (**died** 16 Oct 1992); 5. Basil; 6. Ivan

    Died 27 May 1945

PILCHER, WILLIAM HENRY 1820–1891

b. 1820 Kent; ed by Mr Smith; ent TCD 14 Oct 1836 aged 15 BA & Div Test (2) 1841

d 1843 p 1844 (Armagh); C Carlingford (Arm) 1843–45; Chapl RN 1845–55; C Annahilt (Drom) 1853–63; C Ardclinis (Conn) 1863–65; R Ardclinis (Conn) 1865–72; R Taunagh (Elph) 1873–75; V Finglas (Dub) 1875–91

    s. of Henry, soldier

    m. 1854 Elizabeth **dau.** of Edward Geraghty, barrister of Dublin by Frances Marsh. Issue 2 **sons** and 2 **daus.** incl Henry Francis Carnet, LRCSI (**died** 15 Oct 1901 Bournemouth); and a **dau.** m Rev Eugene O'Meara, R Tallaght (Dub) 1887–1913

    Died 30 Jan 1891 aged 71

PILLEY, THOMAS

is pres by the Crown to Provost of Killala, R Feort, ? = Fuerty (Elph) and V Drumcliffe (Elph) 25 Sep 1611 (L.M. V. 102)

PITT, BEATRICE ANNE 1950–

b. 18 May 1950; IM Marsh Coll of Physical Ed Cert Ed 1971; Trinity Coll Bristol 1980; Univ of Bristol Dip HE 1982; OU BA 2001

d 1982 p 1997; C Rhyl w St Ann (St As) 1982–86; CMS 1986–92; in Zaire 1988–92; joint Co–ordinator of Dio Bible Schools Bukavu Zaire 1988–92; NSM Penycae (St As) 1992–98; Hon Rep CMS Dios St Asaph and Bangor 1993–98; C-in-c in Aux Min Killinagh, Kiltyclogher and Innismagrath (Kilm) 1998–2001; C-in-c Firbank, Howgill and Killington (Bradf) 2001–

    dau. of Mr and Mrs Powell of Rhyl

    m. Jan 1987 Rev George Pitt, R Killesher (Kilm) qv Issue Luke **b.** May 1988

PITT, GEORGE 1952–

b. 11 Oct 1952; ed Hymers Coll Hull; Huddersfield Polytech; QUB BD (Hons) 1979 MTh 1988; TCD Dip Theol 1981; member of Scargill House Community Yorks

d 1981 p 1982; C St Mary Belfast (Conn) 1981–86; CMS Coll to train as a Missionary 1986; Bukavu Zaire 1988–89; Rutshuru Zaire 1989–92; V Penycae (St As) 1992–98; R Killesher (Kilm) 1998–2001; Ed Adviser C of I Bishops' Appeal 2001–03

    m. Jan 1987 Rev Beatrice Ann qv Issue Luke **b.** May 1988

PLUMMER, RICHARD –1923

TCD BA 1869 MA BD & DD 1891

d 1870 p 1871 (Down); C Tickmacrevan (Conn) 1870–72; C Aghaderg (Drom) 1872–73; R Ashfield (Kilm) 1873–1906

> s. of Rev Thomas Fitzgerald, R Mahoonagh (Lim) 1847 by Diana dau. of Rev Edwin Thomas, V Ballinacourty (A & A)
>
> m. 18 Dec 1873 Donaghmore Ch Newry Honoria Anne Elizabeth (died 17 May 1936 at Bath) dau. of Rev John Campbell Quinn, R Donaghmore by Mary Stuart dau. of Trevor Corry, JP DL of Newry. Issue Geraldine
>
> Died 19 Aug 1923

POE, JAMES LEONARD 1863/64–1932

TCD BA 1888 Div Test 1890 MA 1892

d 1889 (Meath) p 1890 (Dublin); C Clonfadforan (Meath) 1889–90; C Balbriggan (Dub) 1890–92; C Rathangan (Kild) 1892–93; C Kinawley (Kilm) 1893–94; C Kilmoremoy (Killala) 1894–1900; R Ballysumaghan (w Killery from 1912) (Elph) 1900–31; ret

> m. 19 Feb 1901 St Matthias's Par Ch Dublin Rosina Henrietta (died 1 Jul 1915 bur. Mt Jerome Dublin) elder dau. of William Morton Macartney of Dublin
>
> Died 4 Aug 1932 aged 68

POE, PUREFOY 1862/63–1940

b. 1862 or 1863; TCD BA (Resp) 1884 Div Test (1) 1885 MA 1890

d 1886 p 1887 (Dublin); C Carbury (Kild) 1886–88; C-in-c Kinnegad (Meath) 1888–91; R Shrule (Ard) 1891–1932

> Died 22 Feb 1940 aged 77

POLLARD, JOHN ALEXANDER 1889–1958

b. 26 May 1889 Lismore Co Waterford; ed the Pococke Sch Kilkenny; Mountjoy Sch Dublin; TCD BA & Div Test 1915

d 1915 p 1916 (Kilmore); C Urney (Kilm) 1915–18; C St Luke Belfast (Conn) 1918–19; Asst TCD Mission in Belfast 1919–20; C St Patrick Coleraine (Conn) 1920–23; C-in-c Ballyjamesduff and Castlerahan (Kilm) 1923–24; C Drumglass (Arm) 1924–26; C-in-c Brackaville (Arm) 1926–35 and R 1935–53; ret

> eldest s. of James and Maria (née Jones) of Lismore
>
> m. 21 Sep 1926 Newtownsaville Ch Co Tyrone Anne Price (Nancy) (died 4 Jan 1984) yst dau. of Rev John Robert Meara, R Newtownsaville (Clogh). Issue 1. Mary Elizabeth b. 23 Oct 1928 TCD BA 1951; 2. James Michael b. 20 May 1931 ed Portora Royal Sch Enniskillen TCD BAI 1953 MICE m. 3 Apr 1956 Newtownsaville Par Ch Aileen Elizabeth dau. of George Lee of Augher Co Tyrone and had issue (i) John Lee b. Aug 1959 QUB BSc m. Rosemary Browne (ii) Elizabeth b. 30 Dec 1960 BSc (Hon) m. Sean FitzGerald (iii) Carolyn Mary b. 26

Dec 1963 Univ of Ulster MA; 3. Catherine Alexandra **b.** 8 Apr 1936

Died 1 Apr 1958

POLLARD, THOMAS 1675–1722

b. 11 Feb 1675 Dublin; bapt at St Peter's Ch Dublin 1675; ed by Mr Kennedy, Dublin; ent TCD 7 Jan 1689/90 aged 15 Sch 1692 BA 1695 MA 1698

C St Peter Dublin 1698–1700; R Clonbroney (Ard) 1700–22

> **s.** of Rev Thomas (**b.** *c.* 1650 **died** 30 Aug 1700), V St Peter and St Kevin, Dublin 1685–1700 (**s.** of Richard) by Mary; **bro.** of Rev Richard **b.** 1678, Chapl to Lord Deputy, Lord Capell
>
> **Died** 1722

POLLARD, WILLIAM 1851/52–1932

b. 1851 or 1852 Ballymacelligott Co Kerry; ed Pococke Sch; Santry Sch; Univ of London BA 1881

d 1883 p 1885 (Dublin for Limerick); C Tralee and Dio C Ardfert and Aghadoe and Principal Intermediate Sch Tralee 1883–87 and Dio Inspector of Schools 1884–87; R Kilglass (Ard) 1887–1891; R Cashel and Rathcline (Ard) 1891–1900; R Killashee (Ard) 1900–23; ret

> **s.** of ?Francis of Ballymacelligott Co Kerry
>
> **m.** Anne Benner (**died** 30 Nov 1938) of Tralee Co Kerry and had issue. His yst **s.** William Marcus Noel, 2nd Lt N Staffs Regt was killed in Great War Feb 1917
>
> **Died** 4 Apr 1932 aged 80

POLLOCK, JAMES 1747/48–1830

b. 1747 or 1748; MA

d 1773 p 1774 (Kilmore); C Rossinver (Kilm) 1786; C Ballintemple (Kilm) 1788–*c.* 1827; "was 54 years Curate in the Diocese of Kilmore" (Newry Telegraph, 30 March 1830).

> **m.** 1781 Margaret (**died** Mar 1830) **b.** 1755 or 1756, 6th and yst **dau.** of Thomas Enery of Prospect Co Cavan by his 2nd wife Margaret **dau.** of Rev John Foulke, LLD, Preb of Devenish (Clogh). They had a large family incl a **s.** William
>
> **Died** Mar 1830 Ballywagh Co Cavan aged 82

POOLE, EDWARD 1697/98–

b. 1697 or 1698 Galway; ed by Mr Price, Galway; ent TCD 7 May 1715 aged 17 Sch 1717 BA 1719

d 25 Sep 1726 p 7 Sep 1729; C Athenry (Tuam) 1726; lic C Killukin and Kilcooley (Elph) 1 Mar 1728; C Kilnamanagh (Elph) 1729; C Roscommon (Elph) 1730

> **s.** of Thomas

POPHAM, THOMAS BIGGS 1802/03–1866

b. 1802 or 1803 Cork; ed by Mr Sullivan; ent TCD 14 Oct 1822 aged 19 BA 1827 MA

d 1827 p; V Ballinafagh (Kild) 1839–52; R Knockbride (Kilm) 1852–66

> s. of Richard, merchant
>
> **Died** 16 Oct 1866 at Knockbride Rectory aged 63

PORTE, JOHN ROBERT

TCD BA 1874 MA 1878 BD & DD 1890

d & p 1875 (Kilmore); C Kilkeevan (Elph) 1875–76; C St Luke (Cork) 1877–79; Schools Insp Dio Cork 1879–81; R Ballymodan (Cork) 1881–90; V St Matthew Denmark Hill (Roch) 1890–1916; ret

PORTER, JAMES 1819–1895

b. 9 Feb 1819; ed by Rev Dr Bleckley at Monaghan; Royal Belfast Coll

was licensed in the Presbyterian Ch at Omagh in 1841 and transferred to Kilkenny in 1847 and was ordained 20 Jun 1848; resigned 3 Apr 1877

ordained d in C of I 1877 (Kilmore) p 1878; C Bailieborough (Kilm) 1877–79; R Drumnakilly (Arm) 1879–95

> 3rd s. of Andrew Thomas of Castlederg Co Tyrone
>
> m. 29 Aug 1849 Harriette (**died** 10 Sep 1903 Drogheda) 6th **dau.** of Capt Henry Hatton of Prospect Co Wexford. Issue 1. Jane Hatton **m.** 27 Dec 1883 Drumnakilly Par Ch Co Tyrone James Browne Alexander of Trillick Co Tyrone; 2. Mary (**died** 29 Dec 1938 unm at Drogheda) **b.** 1854; 3. John (**died** 18 Nov 1926) **b.** 1858 — took the surname of Porter Hatton
>
> **Died** 14 Jun 1895 **bur.** Drumnakilly

PORTEUS, MATTHEW JOHN 1865/66–1932

b. 1865 or 1866; TCD BA 1888 MA 1907

d 1889 p 1890; C Ardagh (Ard) 1889–90; C Kinawley (Kilm) 1890–93; C Innismagrath (Kilm) 1893–97; R Cloonclare (Kilm) 1897–1924; Archd of Kilmore 1923–32 R Larah and Lavey (Kilm) 1924–29; R Annagh Drumaloor and Quivvy (Kilm) 1929–32

> m. and had issue incl Rev Matthew Thomas, R Drumgoon (Kilm) qv
>
> **Died** 24 Jan 1932 aged 66

PORTEUS, MATTHEW THOMAS 1910–1995

ed Portora Royal Sch Enniskillen; TCD BA 1932 Div Test (2) 1933

d 1933 p 1934 (Dublin); C St Stephen (Dub) 1933–34; C Clontarf (Dub) 1934–38; C-in-c Drumlane (Kilm) 1938–41; R Drumgoon and Ashfield (w C-in-c Killesherdoney 1950–56) (Kilm) 1941–56; Exam Chapl to Bp 1951–56; V W Haddon w Winwick (Pet) 1956–73; ret 1975

s. of Ven Matthew John, Archd of Kilmore qv

m. 19 Apr 1939 Frances Margery **dau.** of W B Lynch of Dalkey Co Dublin. Issue 1.David Matthew **b.** 31 May 1941; 2. Jean Margaret **b.** 3 Jun 1945

Died Nov 1995

PORTEUS, WILLIAM HENRY 1877/78–1916

b. 1876 or 1877; RUI BA 1905; TCD Abp King's Pri Div Test (2) & Heb Pri 1907

d 1907 (Down) p 1908 (Down for Kilmore); C Annagh (Kilm) 1907–10; R Arvagh (Kilm) 1910–16

Died 10 Nov 1916 aged 38

PORTMAN, WILLIAM

he was of Warwickshire; adm Siz Jesus Coll Camb 21 Jan 1649/50 (Venn); MA in D.R.; was Commonwealth Minister at Boyle from 1653 at £50, increased to £100 on 13 Feb 1655/56 because he had to ride "to & fro to Athlone and other places to preach"; granted £20 also on same day for books &c; was there up to 1660 (Seymour's MSS); was Preb of Killaraght (Ach) 1661–?1670; was Proctor in Convocation of 1662 for the Chapter of Elphin; Archd of Elphin 1661/62–65

POTTER, JOSEPH 1841/42–1905

b. 1841 or 1842

d 1869 p 1870 (Tuam for Kilmore); C Kiltoghart (Ard) 1870–72; C Dowra (Kilm) 1872–73; V Drumlease (Kilm) 1873–78; I Christ Ch Londonderry (Derry) 1878–1903; Canon of Derry 1896–1903; R Conwall (Raph) 1903–05; Dean of Raphoe 1903–05

m. (1) Mary (**died** 17 Nov 1871 at Carrick-on-Shannon aged 26) eldest **dau.** of William Crosbie of Roscommon. Issue an infant **s.** William Crosbie who **died** 22 Nov 1871 aged six days.

m. (2) 5 Aug 1873 Jane Catherine Caroline (**died** 16 May 1881 Londonderry) yst **dau.** of Rev William Alexander Percy, R Kiltoghart (Ard) qv Issue **sons** 1. Rev Joseph Percy Noel **b.** 18 Dec 1875 TCD Exhib BA 1901 MA 1907 Div Test Vice Chanc Pri Downes Pri, d 1901 p 1902 (Carlisle) R West Derby (Liv) from 1925; 2. Rev Henry Lyndon **b.** 2 Jun 1877 TCD BA 1900 MA 1907 C Conwall (Raph) 1900–02, R Langley (Cant) from 1934; 3. Gilbert **b.** 10 Jul 1878 DI RIC; 4. Rev William Alexander C-in-c Toomna qv; **daus.** 1. Catherine **m.** Rev Ernest Fischer MA; 2. Mary **m.** Rt Rev Robert Miller Bp of Cashel as his first wife; 3. Caroline Lucy Sophia **m.** 3 Jul 1907 Canon John Wilson McQuaide MA (1868–1953) R Faughanvale (Derry) 1930–37

Died 31 Oct 1905 aged 63

PUBLICATION

The Great Salvation and other sermons 1887

POTTER, WILLIAM ALEXANDER 1879–1962

b. 1879 Co Donegal; TCD; Ridley Hall; no degree recorded

d 1915 (Cashel) p 1919 (Gloucester); C Cahir (Lism) 1915–16; C Dunmore E (Waterf) 1916–18; C Harescombe w Pitchcombe (Glouc) 1918–22; C Titchfield (Portsm) 1922–24; living in London in 1926; C-in-c Toomna (Elph) 1931–53; ret

    4th **s.** of Very Rev Joseph, V Drumlease (Kilm) 1873–78 qv by his 2nd wife Jane Catherine Caroline

    Died 13 May 1962

POTTERTON, EDWARD 1824/25–1900

b. 1824 or 1825 Co Meath; ed by Mr Tate; ent TCD 11 Oct 1844 aged 19 BA 1851 Div Test 1854

d 1854 p 1855 (Tuam); C Klamoncuracy (in Crockford), C Kilcommon Erris (C I Dir) 1854–64; C Knappagh (Tuam) 1864–65; R Kilmore Erris (Killala) 1866–75; V Ballintemple (Kilm) 1875–1900

    s. of John

    m. and had issue incl Henry John (**died** 21 Jun 1933 Victoria BC)

    Died 30 Jun 1900 aged 75

POTTERTON, FREDERICK AUGUSTUS 1825/26–1912

b. 1825 or 1826; kept a school in Portadown *c.* 1850; TCD BA 1853 Div Test (1) 1856 LLB & LLD 1864

d 1856 (Kilmore) p 1857 (Dublin) C Killukin (Kilm) 1856–58 PC Croghan (Elph) 1856–61; C Mostrim (Ard) 1858–60; C Ardagh (Ard) 1860–61; C Templemichael and Killoe (Ard) 1861–72; R Clonbroney (Ard) 1872–89; R Templemichael (Ard) 1889–1907; Archd of Ardagh 1891–96; Dean of Ardagh 1896–1912; (Dean Potterton retained the Deanery after his retirement from Parish ministry).

    s. of John of Ballatalion Co Meath

    m. 7 May 1868 St Stephen's Par Ch Dublin Julia E only **dau.** of John W Switzer of Moyvalley Hse Co Kildare. Issue a **s.** deCourcy LRCPI LRCSI who **died** 13 Jul 1958 aged 86

    Died 24 Aug 1912 aged 86

POWELL, DANIEL 1767/68–

b. 1767 or 1768 Co Mayo; ed by Mr Ralph; ent TCD 2 Jul 1787 aged 19 BA 1793

d 1800 p 4 Jan 1801; C Ahascragh (Elph) 1800–; C Gorey (Ferns) 1803–04

    s. of Thomas, farmer

POWELL, EDWARD 1802/03–1876

b. 1802 or 1803 Galway; ent TCD 7 Jun 1822 aged 19 BA 1827 MA 1832

ord d (Elphin) for C St Peter Athlone (Elph) p 4 Jan 1829 (Tuam); C Aglish = Castlebar

(Tuam) 1829; PC Turlough (Tuam) 1830; R & Preb Killaraght (Ach) 1836

    s. of Robert, gentleman

    m. and had issue incl his eldest **dau. m** 20 Jan 1864 H J Edwards **s.** of Benjamin Edwards

    Died 17 Jul 1876

POWELL, FREDERICK JAMES 1894–1986

b. 1894; Univ of Durham BMus 1923; St Aidan's Coll Birkenhead 1927

d 1929 p 1930; C Bangor (Down) 1929–32; C-in-c Ashfield (Kilm) 1932–36; I Kilkeevin Oran and Loughglynn (Elph) 1936–40; R Rathaspeck Russagh and Streete (Ard) 1940–49; R Teampol-na-mBocht, Altar (Cork) 1949–55; BC Castlemartyr (Cloyne) 1955–59; Chapl Kingston Coll Mitchelstown & C-in-c Brigown and Farahy (Cloyne) 1959–65; ret

    s. of F J Powell Dhu Varren Portrush Co Antrim

    m. 14 Jul 1932 St Mark's Dundela Belfast Mary Frances (**died** 1 Jul 1965 Cork) 2nd **dau.** of Frederick Shaw Jones of Killadreenan Co Wicklow

    Died 25 May 1986 Portrush

POWELL, JOHN HUGH JOHNSTON 1806/07–1873

b. 1806 or 1807 Sligo; ed by Mr Elliott; ent TCD 3 Nov 1823 aged 16 BA 1829 MA 1863

d 1830 p; C Killashee (Ard) 1839–43; V Mostrim (Ard) 1843–63; R & V Tashinny (Ard) 1863–66; R Clongish and Clongish Killoe (Ard) 1866–73

    s. of George

    Died at Newtownforbes 12 Jan 1873

POWER, AMBROSE 1801–1868

b. May 1801 Dublin; ed by Mr Townsend; ent TCD 7 Feb 1820 aged 18 BA 1824

PC Cappoquin (Lism) 1824–27; V Chor Lismore (Lism) 1825; V Killinkere (Kilm) 1827–28; Archd of Lismore 1828–68

    4th **s.** of Sir John, 1st Bt of Kilfane

    m. (1) 1837 Susan (**died** 7 Aug 1854) **dau.** of Barker Thacker of Queen's Co (Laois). Issue **sons** 1. Ambrose William Bushe **b.** 1844; 2. Gervase Barker (**died** unm 1872); 3. Rev George Beresford (**died** 31 May 1931) **b.** 26 Aug 1849 TCD BA 1880 d 14 Jun 1879 p 11 Jun 1881 C Kilfane (Oss) 1879–83 R Kilfane (Oss) 1883–1930 Preb of Cloneamery (Oss) 1908–30 **m.** 10 Jul 1879 Constance 2nd **dau.** of Charles Pentland of Bray Head Co Wicklow and had issue Georgina Mary **m.** Major Randolph **s.** of Col John Percy Gethin, DL of Ballinadoon Co Sligo; 4. Robert Henry **b.** 1851; **daus.** 1. Rebecca **m.** Richard John Leeson-Marshall of Callinaferoy; 2. Mary **m.** Henry W Villiers Stuart of Dromana; 3. Susan Caroline (**died** 25 Oct 1928) **m.** 22 Aug 1878 Rev W Claypon Bellingham (**died** 3 Oct 1892) R Urglin (Leigh) 1874–86 and had issue (i) Eudo William Alan (**died unm.** 24 Nov 1929) **b.** 1884 (ii) Vera Susan (**died unm.** 14 Dec 1966) (iii) Alice Marian

m. 22 Jan 1918 Rear-Admiral Hugh Turnour England and had issue incl Marian Joy **m.** Rev David Andrew Workman, NSM Dundalk (Arm) 1990–97 (iv) Hester Frances (**died** 9 Apr 1900)

m. (2) 29 Sep 1857 Catherine 2nd **dau.** of Thomas Forde of Dublin

Died 8 Nov 1868

POWER, EDWARD ARTHUR or ROSE 1816–1904

b. 1816 Co Limerick; ent TCD 15 Oct 1850 aged 34 BA 1860

d & p 1882 (Kilmore); C Killukin (Elph) 1882–85; C Clonmethan w Naul (Dub) 1886–94; ret

s. of Edward

Died 20 Jan 1904 **bur.** Naul

POYNTZ, JAMES 1898–1967

b. 1898 Kilmore Co Cavan; St John's Coll Univ of Manitoba BA 1923; St John's Coll Winnipeg LTh 1928; served in Canadian Army in Great War 1914–18; awarded Military Medal

d & p 1923 (Rupertsland); C Solsgirth (Rupld) 1923–24; R St Andrew's Deloraine (Brandon) 1924–26; R St Luke Souris (Brandon) 1926–29; R Swanlinbar (Kilm) 1929–32; R Annagh and Quivvy (Kilm) 1932–44; R St Michan (Dub) 1944–56; R Arklow (Glend) 1957–65; ret

s. of George and Amelia of Kilmore

m. 1923 Katherine Jane (**died** 10 Dec 1976) **dau.** of Samuel Greenfield of Lisburn Co Antrim. Issue Rt Rev Samuel Greenfield **b.** 4 Mar 1926 TCD BA 1948 MA 1951 BD 1953 PhD 1960 Univ of Ulster DLitt (h.c.) 1995 d 1950 p 1951 Bp 1978 C St George (Dub) 1950–52 C Bray (Dub) 1952–55 C SS Michan & Paul (Dub) 1955–59 R St Stephen (Dub) 1959–67 R St Ann 1967–70 R St Ann w St Stephen (Dub) 1970–78 Archd of Dublin 1974–78 Bp of Cork Cloyne and Ross 1978–87 Bp of Connor 1987–95 ret **m.** 8 Sep 1952 Noreen Henrietta **dau.** of Cecil and Maud Armstrong and have issue (i) Jennifer Mary **b.** 13 Aug 1955 **m.** Canon Kenneth Kearon, Sec Gen Anglican Communion 2004 (ii) Timothy James **b.** 16 Jul 1958 (iii) Stephanie Catherine **b.** 3 Aug 1964

Died 21 Aug 1967 **bur.** British Military Cemetery Dublin

PRESTON, DECIMUS WILLIAM 1805–1881

b. 1805 Dublin; ent TCD 15 Oct 1821 aged 16 BA 1826

d 1832 (Cloyne) p; C Lurgan and Munterconnaught (Kilm) 1830; C Urney (Kilm) 1838; C Currin (Clogh) 1838; V Rossinver (Kilm) 1851–56; V Tomregan (Kilm) 1856–66; V Killinkere (Kilm) 1866–74; C Trory (Clogh) 1874–76; R Killadeas (Clogh) 1876–80

s. of William, Judge of Appeals by Frances Dorothea **dau.** of John Evans Preston, 5th Lord Carbery

m. Aug 1839 Emily eld **dau.** of Lt Gen Armstrong of Woodville Co Dublin. Issue incl 1. Rev William TCD MA DD, R Raskelfe (York); 2. Surgeon–Major Alexander Francis; 3. Rev George Henry Moore (**died** 23 Nov 1893) TCD BA 1868 d 1870 p 1871 C Billy (Conn) 1870–73 C Aghalurcher (Clogh) 1873 R Lisbellaw (Clogh) 1873–76 R Ballyloughloe (Meath) 1876–85 R King's Somborne (Win) 1886 C Harby (Leic — then Pet) 1886–93 **m.** 20 Jun 1872 Mary Eloise **dau.** of Charles Chambers of Sheffield and had issue incl Ethel Maude (**died** 21 Sep 1885 aged 11); 4. Rev John Evans, C Killinkere (Kilm) qv; 5. Algernon; 6. Frances Dorothea **m.** 13 Jun 1871 Samuel Allen eldest **s.** of John Henry Adams, JP

Died 11 Feb 1881 at Farnham Lodge Ballybrack Co Dublin aged 76 **bur.** Kill O'the Grange

PRESTON, JOHN EVANS 1848/49–1927

b. 1848 or 1849; TCD BA 1869 MA 1879; Member of Senate

d 1871 (Kilmore) p 1872 (Down); C Killinkere (Kilm) 1871–72; PC Mullagh (Kilm) 1872–74; R Killochonigan (Meath) 1874–84; R Julianstown (Meath 1884–1927

s. of Rev Decimus William, V Killinkere (Kilm) qv (**s.** of William) by Emily; **bro.** of Rev William, R Raskelfe (York); **bro.** of Rev George Henry Moore, C Harby (Leic — then Pet)

m. 9 Oct 1872 Elizabeth Adelaide (**died** 6 Jun 1886 aged 34) yst **dau.** of Rev John Taylor, R Killinkere. Issue 1. John who became a Jesuit priest; 2. Decimus William (**died** 12 Jan 1879 aged 5½); 3. Elizabeth **m.** 1921 Rev Richard Senior Hipwell, later Archd of Meath

Died 14 Jun 1927 aged 78

PRICE, JOHN

V Fenagh (Ard) 1622–*c.* 35, resident (RV); church ruinous (R.V.); V Kiltubrid (Ard) 1622–*c.* 35, served the Cure, "the church lately burnt by the burning by accident of Patrick McGowna his house". (R.V.); same as J P below?

PRICE, JOHN

V Moydow (Ard) from 1635; was V in 1647 and residing in Dublin (Carte Papers xxi. 346). Is he "Mr Price a Minister & his family saved & housed 1641–3 by Lady Thurles"? (Journal RSAI 1863, 242)

†PRICE, THOMAS 1599/1600–1685

b. 1599 or 1600; a native of Wales; TCD BA 1623 FTCD 1626 MA 1627 Vice Chanc of the Univ of Dublin

d 20 Dec 1629 p 23 Sep 1632 Bp 1661; V Drumlane (Kilm) 1634–61; Archd of Kilmore 1638–61; Bp of Kildare 1661–67; Abp of Cashel 1667–85. In the rebellion of 1641, "Master Thomas Price, Archdeacon of Kilmore, of good abilities, diligent in his calling and forward in that service, was with ten other ministers in the defence of the Castle of Croghan, Co Cavan, 1641, against and also at its surrender". Perhaps he is the, "Mr Price and his family" who were saved and housed 1641–43 by Lady Thurles (Journal RSAI, 1863, 242). Cotton says that having been trained under Bishop Bedell, he took great pains to instruct the native Irish through their own language

Died 4 Aug 1685 aged 85 **bur.** St John's Cath Cashel Co Tipperary

PRICE, THOMAS JOHN
lic C Killashee (Ard) 12 Aug 1846 (D.R.)

PRICKETT, HENRY
Leslie's MSS have Henry Prickett coll V Culea = Conlea ?= Calry, Kilsickdowne and Shanco or Shankill (Elph) 5 May 1640 (F.F.); L.M. V. 113 has "Henry Brickett" pres to V Culea (Elph), 9 Jul 1639

PRICKETT, ROBERT
Leslie's MSS have Robert Prickett pres to V Culea (Elph) 9 Jul 1639 (Lodge P.R.), but see Henry above; coll V Shankill (Elph) 9 Jul 1639 (F.F.)

PROSSER, DAVID
admitted V Rathreagh (Ard) 1685; may have been there to 1737

PULLEIN, SAMUEL 1712/13–1784
b. 1712 or 1713 Dromore Co Down; ed by Mr Skelton at Newry; ent TCD 24 Jan 1729/30 aged 17 Sch 1732 BA 1734 MA 1738

d 1747 (Dublin) p 1754 (Dublin); R Castleblakeney (Elph) 1754–65; R Skryne (Meath) 1765–84; R St Catherine (Dub) 1765–84

s. of Rev William, Treas of Dromore 1708–20 (**s.** of William)

Died before 13 Jul 1784

PUBLICATIONS
The Silkworm, a Poem
The Culture of Silk and other works

He interested himself in the cultivation of the silkworm in the American colonies

QUIGLEY, PAUL 1883/84–1948
b. 1883 or 1884; TCD Siz BA 1908 Bedell Sch 1908 Kyle Pri & Div Test (2) 1909

d 1909 p 1910 (Kilmore); C St John Sligo (Elph) 1909–11; R Innismagrath (Kilm) 1911–16; C St George (Dub) 1916–17; C Sandford (Dub) 1917–21; R Carbury (Kild) 1921–29; C-in-c Lusk and Kenure (Dub) 1929–45; R Tubbercurry U (Ach) 1945–48

m. Mary (**died** 17 Oct 1965). Issue incl Oonagh Mary **m.** Canon Thomas Patrick Scarborough Wood, R Calry (Elph) 1956–94

Died 29 Mar 1948 aged 64

QUIN, COSSLETT WILLIAM CHARLES 1907–1995

b. Feb 1907; TCD BA (1cl Mod) 1930 Div Test 1931 BD 1937

d 1931 p 1932; C St Mark Dundela Belfast (Down) 1931–35; C-in-c Moville Upr (Raph — then Derry) 1935–40; Asst Master St Columba's Coll Dublin 1940–42; C-in-c Drumlane (Kilm) 1942–44; R Killinagh & Kiltyclogher (Kilm) 1944–50; R Narraghmore and Fontstown (Glend) 1950–55; R St John (Cork) 1955–60; R Billis Ballyjamesduff and Castlerahan (w Munterconnaught from 1961) (Kilm) 1960–65; Prof of Bibl Gk TCD 1961; R Dunganstown (Glend) 1965–71; Preb of Swords in St Patrick's Cath Dublin 1965–71; ret President of the Oireachtas 1972

> **s.** of Rev Canon Charles Edward, R Derriaghy (Conn) 1898–1933 (**s.** of Joshua of Jonesborough Co Armagh) by Edith Isabel **dau.** of Cosslett Waddell of Magheralin Co Down
>
> **m.** 19 Feb 1944 Theodore E (Doreen) **dau.** of Rev J Jennings, R Kildallon (Kilm) qv Issue 1. John Charles William Barnabas **m.** 1972 St Patrick's Cath Dublin Suzanne Murphy of Glenageary Dublin; 2. Etain Edith **b.** 1948 **m.** and had issue; 3. David Jennings **b.** 1950
>
> **Died** 6 Dec 1995 Dublin **bur.** Dunganstown

PUBLICATIONS
The Ten Commandments, A Theological Exposition, Lutterworth Press, London 1951
*At the Lord's Table,*1954
Translation from German of Walther Eichrodt's *Commentary on Ezekiel*, OT Library Series, SCM 1970
Tiomna Nua ar Slanaitheora Iosa Criost, Translation of the New Testament, RSV into Irish, 1970
Scealta as an Apocrypha a d'aistrigh don Easpag Bedell, Stories from the Apocrypha translated by Bishop Bedell, 1971
Leabhar Urnai Malairt Leagain, The Alternative Prayer Book in Irish, 1984
Nicholas Walsh and his Friends; A Forgotten Chapter in the Irish Reformation, Journal of the Butler Society, Vol. 2, No 3, 1984
also translated
Cuairt an Mhean Oiche
Ging de Leamhan a scoilteas leamhan
Scian a Caitheadh: A Collection of Songs and Stories from Inis Eoghain and the Erris Gaeltacht
Hymns and Psalms into Irish and numerous articles

RADCLIFF, JOHN 1802/03–1876

b. 1802 or 1803 Co Roscommon; ent TCD 3 Jul 1820 aged 17 BA 1825 MA 1832

C Cloonclare (Kilm) *c.* 1825; C Kilmore (Kilm) 1828; poss V Kilcooley (Cash) 1841–58; V Killargue (Kilm) 1858–59; V Innismagrath (Kilm) 1859–73

> prob John Radcliff **s.** of Rev Thomas
>
> **m.** (ML 1826) Henrietta A Wall (**died** 30 Jul 1871 at Innismagrath Rectory)
>
> **Died** 15 Jan 1876 Toronto

RADCLIFF, STEPHEN 1756/57–1830

b. 1756 or 1757 Dublin; ed by Mr Adamson; ent TCD 1 Nov 1773 aged 16 BA 1778 d; p 25 Jan 1779 (Ossory); V Dunamon (w Athleague to 1785) (Elph) 1780–94; Preb of Kilgoghlin (Elph) 1783–85; R Drumcliffe (Elph) 1785–c96; Precentor of Elphin 1785–89; R Skryne (Meath) 1796–1830; R Dysart (Meath) 1801–09;

2nd **s.** of Thomas, LLD, Judge of the Consistorial Court Dublin; **bro.** of Rev Thomas, V Dunamon (Elph) qv

m. (1) Martha (?Maria) **dau.** of Thomas Mitchell of Castleshane. Issue 1. Thomas Dodgson (**died** 1812) **b.** in Co Roscommon ent TCD 20 Oct 1807 aged 17; 2. Rev Richard **b.** in Co Meath (**died** 21 Jun 1872 aged 72) ent TCD 3 Nov 1817 aged 17 TCD BA 1822 R Skryne (Meath) 1829–71 **m.** Sep 1833 Anne (**died** 25 Apr 1892) eldest **dau.** of Samuel Garnett and had issue incl **sons** (i) Stephen (**died** 1866 in Queensland aged 29) (ii) Rev Edward in Australia in 1870; (iii) Rev Samuel **m.** Maria Dundas eldest **dau.** of Rev T H Montgomery of Co Down; **daus.** (i) Marion Isabella **m.** 13 Jan 1870 Learmouth Victoria Australia John Yorke, MD **s.** of Rev Richard Fishbourne, R Ferns (Ferns) (ii) Alice Martha **m.** 24 Apr 1861 Skryne Ch Peter Wilkinson of Skryne Castle Co Meath

m. (2) 1820 Elizabeth **dau.** of William Fetherstonhaugh and widow of Capt James Given and had issue

Canon Radcliffe also had issue, though by which marriage is not known,

1. Arthur; three **daus.** 1. Frances **m.** Richard Rothwell; 2. Catherine **m.** Christopher Fleming, Pres RCSI; 3. Matilda **m.** Godfrey Fetherstonhaugh

Died 20 Jul 1830

RADCLIFF, STEPHEN 1827/28–1892

b. 1827 or 1828; ed by Dr Graham; ent TCD Oct 1845 aged 17 BA & Div Test 1850 d 1851 p 1852; C Cappagh (Derry) 1852–60; PC Dowra (Kilm) 1860–71; R Killan, now Shercock (Kilm) 1871–74; R Lisnadill (Arm) 1875–92

s. of John of Kells Co Meath

m. 3 Mar 1853 Anne Jane (**died** 28 Jun 1900 aged 73) **dau.** of Lt Charles James Adams, RN JP of Shinan Hse Co Cavan. Issue 1. Caroline Eleanor **b.** 1855 at Cappagh Co Tyrone **m.** 25 Jun 1902 Arthur D L, **s.** of Henry Cary; 2. John Travers (**died** 12 Jun 1937 Armagh) **b.** 30 Jan 1857; 3. Mabel Horatia Garnett **b.** 26 Feb 1859 **m.** 8 Jan 1885 Charles **s.** of James Murphy of Armagh; 4. Charles James (**died** 22 Feb 1905) **b.** 17 Aug 1860 **m.** 1903 a **dau.** of Andrew Dickson and had issue a **s.**; 5. Thomas Lionel **b.** 24 Jan 1863 **died** young; 6. Thomas Harold (**died** 24 Jan 1889 Winnipeg) **b.** 24 Jan 1863; 7. Rev Stephen (**died** 23 Oct 1930) **b.** 5 Nov 1866 TCD BA 1889 Div Test 1891 d 1890 p 1891 (Down) C Kilkeel (Drom) 1890–93 C Kilmainhamwood (Meath) 1893–96 R Drumconrath (Meath) 1896–1930 **m.** 26 Apr 1894 at Bidston Ch Birkenhead Mary Isabella 3rd **dau.** of Charles Campbell Henry and had issue (i) Henry Garnett (**died** Feb 1971) **b.** 7 Aug 1898 **m.** 5 Sep 1924 Jessica Dixon of Sheffield; 8. Anna Jane W; 9. Frances Ada

Died 3 Jun 1892 **bur.** Derrynoose Co Armagh

RADCLIFFE, THOMAS –1834

b. Dublin; ed privately; ent TCD 24 Apr 1781 BA 1786 MA 1818

d; p 1789; C Kilmore (Meath) 1789; R Clonoe and PC Lisnadill (Arm) 1791–97; V Roscommon (Elph) 1797–1805; Preb of Oran and V Dunamon and Drimtemple (Elph) 1805–07; R & V Creagh (Ross) 1807–13; Preb of Clonmethan (Dub) 1813–34; R St Paul (Dub) 1817–34

4th **s.** of Thomas, Judge of the Consistorial Court and MP for St Canice's 1775–76; **bro.** of Rev Stephen, Prec of Elphin, qv

m. Dec 1792 Elizabeth **dau.** of Thomas Mitchell of Castle Strange Co Roscommon by Elizabeth **dau.** of Lt Col Godfrey Wills of Willsgrove. Issue 1. Hon Thomas (**died** 6 Jun 1841 aged 41 at Kingston Upper Canada) served in the Peninsular War in which he was wounded and afterwards commanded the Western Frontier Canada Militia in the Canadian rebellion **m.** 1822 Sarah **dau.** of Capt Frederick Armstrong, Roscommon Regt of Militia; 2. Rev Stephen TCD BA 1820 d 1820 (Cloyne) PC Lisnadill (Arm) 1823–48 R Kilmoon (Meath) 1848–58; 3. John TCD BA 1825 R Kilcooley (Cashel); 4. William **b.** Roscommon ent TCD 18 Jan 1830 aged 24 **m.** 1828 Rebecca **sister** of Sarah above; went to Ontario; Rebecca and Sarah were **sisters** of Rev John Armstrong R Kiltoom (Meath); 5. his eldest **dau.** Anne **m.** 15 Nov 1824 Frederick W Edwards of Dominick Street Dublin; 6. Mary Anne **m.** 2 Apr 1835 at Lisnadill William Harloe Phibbs, 25th Regt

Died Jan 1834

RAINSFORD, CHARLES ARTHUR 1875–1929

b. 1875; ed Rathmines Sch Dublin; TCD BA 1896 Div Test (2) 1897 MA 1902

d and p 1898 (Kilmore); C Annagh (Kilm) 1898–1901; C Mountrath and Chapl of Ballyfin (Leigh) 1901–05; C Ballyfin (Leigh) 1905–07; R Odogh (Oss) 1907–09; R St John's Cloverhill (Kilm) 1909–15; R Killinagh (Kilm) 1915–17; R St John Sligo (w Knocknarea from 1927) (Elph) 1917–29

s. of Meyrick Shawe of Dublin by Nicolina; **bro.** of Rev. Meyrick, qv

m. 7 Feb 1906 Jane Olivia yr **dau.** of Robert Walker of Belturbet Co Cavan

Died s.p. 3 Dec 1929 **bur.** Mt Jerome Dublin

RAINSFORD, MEYRICK 1860/61–1910

b. 1860 or 1861; TCD Syr & Chald Pri 1880 Heb Pri (1) 1880 and 1882 Wall Bibl Pri & Sch 1881 BA 1884 MA 1889

d 1885 p 1887 (Kilmore); C Drumgoon (Kilm) 1885–87; C Killesher (Kilm) 1887–89; R Killan, now Shercock (Kilm) 1889–90; Chota Nagpur India 1890–97; SPG Missy at Tezpur, Assam 1891; Ranchi 1891–93; Lahoal 1893–1905; Chapl A Cl S at Bhusaval 1905–06; Ajmere (Dio Nagpur) 1906–10

eldest **s.** of Meyrick Shawe of Dublin; **bro.** of Rev Charles Arthur qv

m. Rathmines Ch Dublin Frances 2nd **dau.** of Rev George Russell of Ballingarry Co Tipperary

Died 11 Aug 1910 of cholera at Indore India aged 49

RALPH, CHARLES 1915–

b. 25 Jul 1915 Dublin; ed North Strand Sch Dublin; TCD BA & Div Test 1947 MA 1958

d 1947 p 1948; C Kilmegan (Drom) 1947–49; C Drumcree (Arm) 1949–50; R Arboe (Arm) 1950–51; C St Mark Armagh (Arm) 1951–53; R Durrus (Cork) 1953–54; R Kilcooley (Cash) 1954–58; V St Cleopas Toxteth Park (Liv) 1958–62; R Killinick and Kilscoran (Ferns) 1962–64; R Fordley w Middleton and Theberton (St E) 1964–81; TV Raveningham (Nor) 1982; Perm to Off Dio St E from 1982; P-in-c Finner and Rossinver (Kilm) 1985–86

s. of Charles and Esther (née Richardson) of Dublin

m. 26 Dec 1953 Ballydehob Co Cork Esther Sarah **dau.** of William James Wolfe of Ballydehob. Issue 1. Orla Collettee Jacqueline **b.** 21 Sep 1954 at Durrus; 2. Nigel C **b.** 1956; 3. Fiona E **b.** 1957 deceased; 4. Willis

RAMBAUT, EDMUND M

d 1881 p; C Drumgoon (Kilm) 1880–81

RAMBAUT, WILLIAM HAUTENVILLE 1821/22–1893

b. 1821 or 1822 Dublin; ed Royal Sch Armagh; ent TCD 3 Jun 1839 aged 17 BA 1848 Div Test (1) and Reg Prof of Divinity Premium 1849; Rev WH Rambaut spent two years as an assistant Astronomer to Lord Ross at Birr Co Offaly

d 1860 p 1861; C Tyholland (Clogh) 1860–62; C Ballymoyer (Arm) 1862–64; Asst Astronomer at Armagh 1864–68; C Darver (Arm) 1868–70; C Kells (Oss) 1871–72; R Drumreilly (Kilm — then Ard) 1881–88

s. of William of Dublin (**s.** of Jean of Bordeaux France who came to Dublin in 1754 where he married Marie Hautenville in 1782); **bro.** of Rev Edmund F, R Kilfithmone (Cash)

m. 20 Jul 1861 at Booterstown Ch Dublin Alice Catherine **dau.** of Jonathan Osborne, MD King's Prof and Physician to Mercer's Hosp Dublin. Issue 1. Catherine bapt 2 Nov 1862 at Tyholland; 2. Jonathan Hautenville **b.** 16 May 1864 at Ballymoyer Rectory; 3. John de Bellaire **b.** 21 Aug 1865; 4. Charlotte Louisa **b.** 22 Mar 1867; 5. Kathleen; 6. Francesca **m.** 25 Jan 1893 Frederick Walter Price of Devonshire

Died 25 Aug 1893 at Mespil Rd Dublin aged 71

PUBLICATION

Co–translator of a new edition of St. Irenaeus in the *Ante–Nicene Christian Library* series, T & T Clarke, London 1868

RAMSAY, ROBERT

V Cashel and Rathcline (Ard) 1680/81–85, coll 22 Mar 1680/81; V Clonbroney Abbeylara Russagh and Rathaspeck (Ard) 1685/86–c. 1698, coll 18 Mar (F.F.)

RASTALL, JOHN

coll V Killenumery and Killery (Ard) May 1724 (F.F.); there to c. 1727

RAWLINS, JOSEPH 1828–1907

b. 1828 Co Dublin; ed by Mr Jordan; ent TCD 1 Jul 1848 aged 20 BA & Div Test 1853

d 1853 (Cork) p 1854 (Down); C Knockbreda (Down) 1853–55; PC Upper Falls Belfast (Conn) 1855–60; C Kinlochmoidart (A & I) 1860–64; C Urney (Derry) 1864–65; C Donagheady (Derry) 1865–72; R Muff (Derry) 1872–73; R Killelagh (Derry) 1873–78; R Templeport (Kilm) 1878–1907

s. of Rev Thomas

m. (1) 12 Oct 1857 Derriaghy Par Ch Co Antrim Maria Matilda eldest **dau.** of Robert Moat of Moat Park

m. (2) 9 Sep 1862 St Columb's Cathedral Londonderry Ellenor (**died** 24 Feb 1870) eldest **dau.** of Joseph Ewing Miller, MD of Londonderry. Issue incl yst **dau.** Fanny **died** 20 Mar 1892

m. (3) 4 Jan 1872 Burt Par Ch Co Donegal Caroline 3rd **dau.** of Samuel John Crookshank of Lifford Co Donegal

his **dau.** Eleanor Charlotte **m.** 21 Dec 1909 Rev William Walter Peyton, R Toomna (Elph) qv

Died 6 Oct 1907 aged 78

READ, JOHN

Commonwealth Minister at Annagh (Kilm) 1653. Some charge was laid against him, but he is here from 14 Jun 1654 (Seymour's *Commonwealth MSS*, pp 8, 25)

READE, GEORGE FORTESCUE   –1886/87

TCD BA & Div Test (2) 1855 MA 1859

C Inniskeen (Clogh) 1856–64; C Streete (Ard) 1864–65; R Magherally (Drom) 1866–84

s. of Rev George Harrison **b.** 1804/05 (**died** 15 Feb 1888 in his 84th year), R Inniskeen (Clogh) by his first wife Frances Anne (**died** 26 Jul 1875) widow of Rev George Hamilton, R Killermogh (Leigh) and **dau.** of Rear-Admiral Sir Chichester Fortescue MP, Ulster King of Arms who was **son** of Chichester Fortescue MP of Dromiskin Co Louth by the Hon Elizabeth Wellesley **dau.** of Richard 1st Lord Mornington

m. Frances **dau.** of Rev John George Digges La Touche, V Duleek Co Meath

Died 1886 or 1887

READER, ENOCH 1656/57–1709

b. 1656 or 1657; ed by Mr Kennedy; ent TCD as a pensioner 12 May 1670 aged 13 BA 1675 MA 1678 DD 1697

R Clonkeen (Arm) 1680–85; R Kilsaran (Arm) 1681–85; Chanc of Armagh 1685–96; Dean & V of Kilmore 1691–1700; Chanc of Connor 1696–1709; Dean of Emly and Archd of Dublin 1701–09

s. of Enoch of Dublin (s. of Enoch, Lord Mayor of Dublin) by Anne **dau.** of Sir James Donelan, Lord Chief Justice of the Common Pleas; **bro.** of Richard, his successor as Dean of Kilmore qv

m. (M.L. 24 Apr 1685) Alicia Jephson. Issue incl 1. Ven William TCD BA 1724, Archd of Cork 1745–74 ; 2. Bridget bapt 4 Dec 1696 St Peter Dublin **m.** John Garstin of Leragh Castle; 3. Maria

Died 9 Nov 1709

READER, RICHARD 1658/59–c. 1700

b. 1658 or 1659 Dublin; ed by Dr Edward Wettenhall at the "Free School" Dublin (?King's Hospital); ent TCD 9 Sep 1675 aged 16 BA 1680 MA & FTCD 1683 DD 1695 Vice Provost

d p 24 Feb 1683/84 (Dublin); Preb of Tassagard in St Patrick's Cath Dublin 1693–99; V Rathkenny (Meath) 1696–99; Dean of Emly 1696–99; Chanc Christ Ch Cath Dublin 1697–99; Archd of Dublin 1699–1700; V Kilmore Kildrumferton Ballintemple and Denn (Kilm) 1700; Dean of Kilmore 1700

s. of Enoch of Dublin (s. of Enoch) by Anne **dau.** of Sir James Donelan; **bro.** of Enoch, his predecessor as Dean of Kilmore qv

Died c. 1700

REED, JAMES

V Ahamplish & Drumcliffe (Elph) 1674–c. 1723

REGAN, NOEL HENRY LIKELY 1949–

b. 13 Dec 1949 Gurteen Farm Cliffoney Co Sligo

d 29 Jun 1999 p 25th Jun 2000; C (Aux Min) Taunagh Ballysumaghan and Kilmactranny (w Boyle Aghanagh Croghan Ardcarne and Tibohine from 2000) (Elph) 1999–2004; C (Aux Min) Cloonclare G (Kilm) 2004–06; Dio C as part of team ministry Garrison Slavin Belleek and Kiltyclogher (Clogh) 2006–

s. of Thomas William Wallace of Tullaghan Co Leitrim (s. of Babour and Edith (née Wallace) by Emily Barbara of Cliffoney **dau.** of Henry Coburn and Rebecca (née McLoughlin) Likely

m. 31 Oct 1977 Mohill Co Leitrim Margaret Joan **dau.** of John and Rita (née Hunt) Abbott of Mohill. Issue 1. Emma Elizabeth **b.** 23 Jul 1979; 2. Robin Henry Likely **b.** 12 Oct 1982; 3. Rebecca Margaret Noelle **b.** 20 Mar 1984; 4. Jennifer Edith Louise **b.** 6 May 1986

REILLY, EUGENE

coll V Streete (Ard) 1 Nov 1683 (F.F.); may be there to 1698

REILLY, THOMAS 1848/49–1920

b. 1848 or 1849; TCD BA 1876

d 1876 p 1877 (Ardagh); C Killashee and Ballymacormack (Ard) 1876–77; C Cashel and Rathcline (Ard) 1878–82; R Killashee and Ballymacormack (Ard) 1882–1900; R Rathaspeck and Russagh (Ard) 1900–20; Dean of Ardagh 1913–20

Died 21 Apr 1920 aged 71

REINOLD, HENRY

student in Literature is pres by the Crown to R Muntireolis (Ard) vacant per death of last incumbent, 13 Jan 1610/11 (Erck's P.R. 743)

RENAGH, WALTER

was appointed Archd of Elphin 1309

RENNISON, HENRY 1854–1934

b. 7 Nov 1854; ed by J Maxwell Weir; TCD (Resp) & Div Test (2) 1876

d 21 Dec 1877 p 21 Dec 1878 (Ossory); C Newtownbarry (Ferns) 1877–79; C Templemichael (Ard) 1879–81; R Taghmon (Ferns) 1881–84; R Ardamine (Ferns) 1884–94; R Gorey (Ferns) 1894–1905; RD of Carnew (Ferns) 1896–1905; Preb of Coulstuffe 1900 with Preb of Fethard 1901–09; R Kilpatrick and Killurin (Ferns) 1905–21; RD of Wexford 1906–26; R Wexford (Ferns) 1921–34; RD of Bannow (Ferns) 1926–34

s. William of Limerick

m. 18 Apr 1882 Kate Louisa (**died** 28 Apr 1933) **dau.** of William Grey Palmer of London. Issue 1. Rev Henry West **b.** 27 Oct 1884 Taghmon Co Wexford TCD BA (Jun Mod Hist and Pol Sci) 1909 Div Test (1) 1910 MA 1933 d 1910 (Down for Armagh) p 1911 (Armagh) C Armagh (Arm) 1910–13 C Drumcree (Arm) 1913–21 C-in-c Desertcreat (Arm) 1921–27 C Drumcree (Arm) 1927–28 R Ballymascanlan and Jonesborough (Arm) 1928–55 Preb of Mullabrack in Armagh Cath 1939–43 Chanc of Armagh 1943–45 Precentor of Armagh 1945–47 Archd of Armagh 1947–55 Dean of Armagh 1955–65 ret; **m.** 28 Dec 1915 Armagh Cath Hilda (**died** 7 Sep 1965) only **dau.** of Hamilton Robb of Edenderry Hse Portadown and had issue (i) Henry Hamilton **b.** 10 Oct 1916 (ii) Rev Walter Patrick **b.** 16 Mar 1918 (iii) John Brian George **b.** 14 Apr 1921; Dean Rennison **died** 9 Jul 1969; 2. Frederick (**died** at Ardamine Rectory 28 Sep 1893 aged 7); 3. George Garrett **b.** 1891 **m.** Christ Ch Cath Vancouver Margaret yst **dau.** of Thomas Bannerman of Cumberland BC; 4. Walter Mervyn **b.** 1893 Lt Royal Irish Regt killed in action Dec 1916; also two other children died young

Died 13 Apr 1934

REVINGTON, JAMES EDWARD

(originally **JONES**, then **REVINGTON–JONES**)

Univ of Durham 1879

d 1883 p 1884 (Kilmore); C Kinawley (Kilm) 1883–84; R Aghalurcher (Clogh) 1884–85; R Woodhouse (Leic) 1885–86; C St Matthew City Road London (Lon) 1886–88;

C Mereworth (Roch) 1889–91; R Keystone (Ely) 1891–92; R Mereworth (Roch) 1892–1912; Chapl to Viscount Falmouth 1900–07; RD N Malling 1901–04; V Wentworth (Sheff) and Dom Chapl to Earl Fitzwilliam 1912–18; R Thurnscoe (Sheff) 1918–22; R Ardley w Fewcott (Ox) 1922–35; ret Last entry in Crockford 1949 (Crockford also has him as Rector of parishes in Canada from 1907 to 1912 when he was in C of E)

REYLY, WALTER

V Oran *alias* Uran (Elph) 1640–41; V Kilmacallen and Taunagh (Elph) 1641; Chantor = Precentor of Elphin to 1646 (Carte Papers XVIII. 26.)

REYNELL, WILLIAM ALEXANDER 1836–1906

b. 10 Mar 1836; TCD BA 1858 Div Test 1859 MA 1861 BD 1874; MRIA 1878

d 1860 (Down for Derry) p 22 Dec 1861 (Derry); C Camus–juxta–Mourne Strabane (Derry) 1860–62; C Donaghpatrick (Meath) 1862–63; C Kildallon (Kilm) 1863–64; C Tamlaghtard (Derry) 1864–65; C Leckpatrick (Derry) 1865–66; PC Carrick (Derry) 1866–73; R St John Cloverhill (Kilm) 1873–77; C St Michan Dublin (Dub) 1878–80; he then retired from the ministry and devoted the remainder of his life to antiquarian and genealogical research, being well known as a constant visitor to the Dublin Record Office and libraries, and recognised as the chief authority on the succession of the Clergy of the Irish Church. He made calendars of the First Fruit Returns, and of most of the Irish Diocesan Registers which have been destroyed. He left behind him a vast collection of manuscripts concerning the various dioceses. It is chiefly owing to his great research that we are enabled, now that the original records are lost, to fill up gaps in the succession of such dioceses as Kilmore.

3rd **s.** of Richard Winter of Killymon Co Westmeath, JP High Sheriff 1839 by Frances Alexandrina **dau.** of James Saunderson, JP of Clover Hill

Died 3 Mar 1906 aged 69

PUBLICATIONS

A Succession of the Clergy of Derry from 1622 in *Ulster Journal of Archaeology*
MSS of Succession Lists of other Dioceses including Kilmore, Dublin and Down and Connor

REYNOLDS, BERNARD

ord d 10 Jun 1634; inst V Drumreilly (Kilm) 17 Jun 1634

REYNOLDS, MASTER

V Kilmacallen (Elph) to 1640; is deceased

RHODES, GODFREY   *c.* 1653/54

b. Great Houghton Yorks; ed Wakefield Sch; adm Pensioner Sidney Coll Camb 3 May 1621 BA 1624/25 MA 1628 BD 1635 Fellow

R Annagh (Kilm) 1637–40; Treas St Patrick's Cath Dublin 1638–53/54; Dean of Derry

1639/40–53/54

  2nd **s.** of Sir Godfrey of Great Houghton by his 2nd wife Anne **dau.** of Sir Edward Lewknor; bro-in-law of the Earl of Strafford who married his sister
  Died *c.* 1653/54

RICE, THOMAS RICHARD

d 1870 p 1871 (Kilmore); C Roscommon (Elph) 1870–71; C Kiltoom (Elph) 1872; C Kells (Meath) 1876–.C Buttevant (Cloyne) 1878; C Templeudigan (Ferns) 1880–81; C Grays (St A) in 1884

RICHARDS, LEWIS 1830/31–1910

b. 1830 or 1831; TCD BA & Div Test 1854 MA 1859 BD & DD 1891

d 6 Jan 1856 p 18 May 1856 (Kilmore); C Drumgoon (Kilm) 1856–60; PC Warrenpoint (Drom) 1861–66; PC Ashfield (Kilm) 1866–72; R Tydavnet (Clogh) 1872–79; R Drumglass (Arm) 1879–1907; Acting CF 1880–1907; RD of Dungannon (Arm) 1896–1907; Preb of Ballymore (Arm) 1896–1907; ret

  s. of Rev Edward, R Clonallon (Drom) (**s.** of Solomon of Dublin) by Emily **dau.** of Rt Rev James Saurin, Bp of Dromore 1819–42

  m. 13 Feb 1866 Charlotte Georgina **dau.** of the Hon and Rev John Charles Maude, R Enniskillen (Clogh). Issue 1. Charles Maude **b.** 14 Jan 1867; 2. Lewis Saurin **b.** 7 Jul 1869 **m.** 23 Sep 1903 Lucy Dennes eldest **dau.** of Lovell Burchett Clarence, JP of Axminster; 3. Mary Alice **m.** 20 Jun 1906 Rev Kivas Collingwood Brunskill, C Urney (Kilm) qv; 4. Mabel Emily

  Died 6 Nov 1910 aged 79

RICHARDSON, ARTHUR

MA

d 1743 p 1746; C Carrigallen (Kilm) 1766– still there 1768

  m. and had issue incl 1. Aughmooty **b.** Co Cavan *c.* 1756 ent TCD 3 Nov 1773; 2. Arthur (**died** *c.* 1818) **m.** 1791 Anne Bennett (**died** 1848)

RICHARDSON, JOHN

got a grant for a glebe as V of Drumlummon and Granard (Ard) 25 Jan 1626/27 (Morrin, III. 188)

†RICHARDSON, JOHN 1580–1654

b. 1580 Cheshire; TCD Sch 1593 MA & FTCD 1600 DD 1614; Camb BD incorp from Dublin 1609

Preb of St Audoen, Dublin 1604–15; pres to V Granard 20 Sep 1610 (L.M. V. 102); still V Granard 1615 (R.V.), and in 1622 is V Granard, "D.D. a preacher", non-resident; has an English and an Irish curate (R.V.); V Kilvellan (Cashel) 1616; R Ardstraw (Derry) 1617; R Ardtrea (Arm) 1617–27; Archd of Derry from 1622– as such was named in the Charters of 1629/30 and 1632 (L.M. V. 109, Morrin III. 519, 591). Bp of Ardagh 1633–54; pres by the Crown by Letters Patent May 14, 1633 with leave to hold his Archdeaconry of Derry *in commendam* for a year, K. Lett. 18 April (C.P.R.I., 3rd Series. II. 7), but he exchanged it in 1639 for the Archdeaconry of Down. He was consec Bishop of Ardagh in Armagh Cathedral in 1633 by Ussher, "where no such act had been before performed within the memory of any man living" (Usher's *Works* XV, 572)

He was "A Cheshire man born, an able man and a good scholler; he was borne near Chester and married Sir Henry Bunburie's daughter, a tall handsome fatt woman" (Brereton's Travels, 1635). He was a friend and correspondent of Bedell. He left Ireland during the rebellion of 1641. By his Will made in 1654, he left the proceeds of the sale of Carrickglass Manor Co Longford which had belonged to Bps of Ardagh, to maintain such scholars as were brought up in his parishes of St. Andrew's, Dublin, Granard, Ardstraw and Dunboe, in TCD. Cotton (*Fasti* III. 184 and V. 231 says, "he was a man of great charity and profound learning, well versed in Scripture and Sacred Chronology and also learned in the laws of his country"

Died 11 Aug 1654 in London aged 74

PUBLICATIONS
A Sermon on Justification Dublin 1625
Observations and Explanation upon the Old Testament etc, London 1655

RICHARDSON, JOHN 1668/69–1747

b. 1668 or 1669 Co Tyrone; ed by Mr John Morris; ent TCD 27 Jul 1683 aged 14 Sch 1686 BA 1688; JP for Co Cavan

R Derryloran (Arm) 1694–1709; Preb of Findonagh or Donacavey (Clogh) 1705–09; R Annagh (Kilm) 1709–47; Dean of Kilmacduagh 1731–47; V Lavey (Kilm) 1733–36; V Kildallon (Kilm) 1736–45; R Innismagrath (Kilm) 1740–45; Chapl to the Duke of Ormond; see also Leslie's *Clogher Clergy and Parishes* p 72

s. of William

m. and had issue 1. James **b.** near Dungannon ent TCD 18 May 1721 aged 17 Sch 1724 BA 1725 MA 1737 evidently same James Richardson (**died** 1771), R Clonoe (Arm) 1736–38 R & V Magherafelt (Arm) 1738–71 **m.** and had issue Mary **m.** 1759 Daniel Stanford; 2. Henry, MD Belturbet Co Cavan **m.** (M.L. 4 Dec 1747 and had issue incl Major John of Summerhill

Died 9 Sep 1747 aged 78

PUBLICATIONS
Three Sermons upon the Principal Points in Religion translated into Irish, 8vo, London 1711
A Proposal for the Conversion of the Popish Natives of Ireland to the Established Religion, 4to, Dublin 1711
A Short History of the attempts that have been made to convert the Popish Natives of Ireland to the Established Religion: with a proposal for their conversion and a vindication of Usher's opinion concerning the performing of Divine Offices to them in their own language, 8vo, London, 1712; 2nd ed. 1713, reprinted in *Irish Ecclesiastical Gazette,* Oct–Dec 1868
The Great Folly, Superstition and Idolatry of Pilgrimages in Ireland, especially that to

St. Patrick's Purgatory, 8vo., Dublin, 1727
Lewis's Church Catechism Explained, rendered into Irish, London, 1712

RICHARDSON, JOHN 1784/85–1866

b. 1784 or 1785 Co Fermanagh; ed Londonderry; ent TCD 7 Feb 1803 aged 18 BA 1809

d 1809 (Kilmore) p; C Drung and Larah (Kilm) 1811; R Drumkeeran (Clogh) 1823–47; Chanc of Clogher 1847–66

> elder **s.** of John of Summerhill Co Fermanagh, High Sheriff 1783, Cornet Light Dragoons (**s.** of Dr Henry of Belturbet Co Cavan and Anne elder **dau.** of John Stanford of Carn Belturbet High Sheriff Co Cavan 1734 and Co Monaghan 1741 **s.** of Rev John, R Annagh (Kilm) qv) by Anne **dau.** of John Madden of Hilton Co Monaghan
>
> **m.** Mary Anne yst **dau.** of Rev Joseph Story, R Templeport and Drumreilly (Kilm) qv (**s.** of Ven Joseph, Archd of Kilmore qv and grandson of Rt Rev Joseph Story, Bp of Kilmore qv Issue **sons** 1. Henry (**died** young); 2. Joseph (**died** 30 Jun 1845) **b.** Co Monaghan ent TCD 3 Feb 1834 aged 18; 3. Robert **b.** Co Fermanagh ent TCD 9 Nov 1835 aged 18; 4. John (**died** 1893) **b.** Co Fermanagh ent TCD 17 Jan 1835 aged 17 BA 1838 Irish Bar 1840 QC DL **m.** 23 Oct 1851 St Peter Dublin Mary Anne **dau.** of William Christopher St G French of Cloonyquin Co Roscommon, Lt 6th Dragoon Guards and had issue incl his eldest **s.** Major John Robert St George, the King's Liverpool Regt, JP DL; 5. William **b.** Co Cavan ent TCD 14 Oct 1837 aged 17 BA 1842; 6. James (**died** in Canada) **b.** Co Fermanagh ent TCD 1 Nov 1841 aged 18; 7. Edward **b.** Co Fermanagh ent TCD 5 Feb 1843 aged 17; **daus.** 1. Sarah (**died** at Bath); 2. Georgina Hamilton Story (**died** 1897 at Rome)

Died 6 Oct 1866

RICHARDSON, PERCY HAROLD 1894–1951

b. 5 Apr 1894 Bedford; ed Fortwilliam Sch Belfast; Manchester Coll Oxford Sch 1919; QUB BA 1920

d 1920 p 1921 (Down); C Bangor (Down) 1920–22; C St Matthew Shankill Belfast (Conn) 1922–25; C-in-c Gowna and Columbkille (Ard) 1925–26; C St Patrick Ballymacarrett (Down) 1926–28; C-in-c Drumlane (Kilm) 1928–32; R Collinstown and C-in-c Drumcree (Meath) 1932–43; R Rathgraffe w Mayne and Foyran (Meath) 1943–51; Preb of Tipper in St Patrick's Cath Dublin 1945–51; RD of Mullingar 1947–51

> **s.** of James Owen and Elizabeth Ann
>
> **m.** 7 Feb 1928 Eileen Gertrude McCleary of Raphoe Co Donegal, sister of Rev John Harris McCleary, Org Sec SPG for NI 1918–28. Issue Michael **b.** 29 Sep 1929

Died 7 Mar 1951

RICHARDSON, PETER –1763

TCD Sch 1716 BA 1717 MA 1720

d 25 Sep 1720 p 9 Jun 1723; C Aughnamullen (Clogh) 1720; R Galloon (Clogh) 1722–31; R Drumgon (Kilm) 1754–63

Died 14 Sep 1763 Dublin

RICHARDSON, ROBERT

a Robert Richardson was Christ's Coll Camb BA 1567/68

Preb of St John's in Christ Ch Cath Dublin 1587; Prec of Christ Ch Cath Dublin 1589–92; Preb of Whitechurch in Ferns Cath *c.* 1591; Preb of Tassagard 1591–92; pres. to the Deanery of Ardagh 27 Mar 1595 (Morrin, II 310; L.M. V. 101); Dean of Ardagh 1595–1616

RICHEY, ROBERT SAMUEL PAYNE 1923–2006

b. 9 Apr 1923 Dublin; ed The King's Hosp Dublin; TCD BA 1946 Div Test (1) 1947

d 1948 p 1949 (Armagh); C Moy and Charlemont (Arm) 1948–50; R Killinagh and Kiltyclogher (w Innishmagrath from 1961 and w Killargue from 1972) 1950–98; Dio Sec Kilmore 1972–98; Preb of Triburnia (Kilm) 1979–98; Preb of Mulhuddart in St Patrick's Cath Dublin 1994–98; ret

   s. of Thomas, Civil Servant of Stranorlar Co Donegal by Kathleen Augusta (née Payne) of Ballymoe Co Galway

   m. 14 Aug 1963 Killesher Par Ch Florencecourt Co Fermanagh Kathleen Charlotte dau. of John A and Charlotte Geddes of Co Fermanagh

   Died 13 Aug 2006

RIDDALL, WALTER 1841–1908

b. 20 Jun 1841 Armagh; ed Armagh Royal Sch; TCD Sch 1863 BA 1864 Div Test (2) 1866 MA 1873 BD & DD 1890

d 1866 (Kilmore) p 1867 (Down); C Kilmore (Kilm) 1866–67; V Glencraig (Down) 1867–69; Chapl at Turin 1869–70; R Killeavy (Arm) 1870; R Mullaglass (Arm) 1870–72; V Malone Belfast (Conn) 1872–80; Chapl of Magdalen Chapel Belfast (Conn) 1880–1908; Preb of Connor 1900–07; Dean of Connor 1907–08

   s. of James (his family spells the name Riddell); bro. of Rev Edward Parkinson, R Lisburn (Conn) 1909–19

   m. 3 Jun 1867 at St Kevin's Ch Dublin Mary Roe (died 20 Jan 1931) dau. of Charles Coates, MA Barrister-at-Law of Shillelagh Co Wicklow by Jane Eliza dau. of John Read Clarke of Rutland Co Dublin. Issue 1. Jane Alice (died 27 Apr 1953 Donnybrook Dublin) b. 29 May 1868 m. 10 Jun 1902 her cousin George Coates of Co Wicklow (died 1911); 2. Mary Roe (died 11 Apr 1894 unm while CMS Medical student in Glasgow) b. 4 Dec 1869 Turin Italy; 3. Jemima, CMS Missy Mid–China b. 16 Feb 1871 m. 12 Jun 1901 William Augustus Handley eldest s. of Ven Arthur John Evans Moule, Archd of Mid–China; 4. Rev Robert James b. 25 Aug 1872 ed London Coll of Div 1896 RUI BA 1897 d 1898 p 1899 C Church of the Martyrs Leicester (Leic — then Pet) 1898–1906 V St Mary Northampton (Pet) 1906–23 V Nassington and Yarwell (Pet) 1923–*c.* 50 **m.** 7 Feb 1921 Dorothy Street of Northampton; 5. Walter George (**died** 11 Jan 1914) **b.** 8 Feb 1874 Art Critic *Sunday Times*; 6. George Spencer Charles (**died** 18 Jul 1908 in Oregon USA) **b.** 15 Jun 1875; 7. James Edward **b.** 12 Dec 1876 **m.** Miss Walsh of Oregon and had issue; 8. Charles Coates **b.** 12 Mar 1878 **m.** Harriet Riley of Dublin and had issue; 9. Annie Henrietta (**died** 1930) **b.** 29 Jul 1879, CMS Missy **m.** Arthur John Henry **s.** of Ven Arthur John Evans Moule; 10. Edward Archibald (**died** 1945) **b.** 19 Jun 1882 **m.** his cousin Beatrice **dau.** of Robert Christian of Dublin; 11. Gervase Claude Victor **b.** 4 May 1887 Univ of London BA **m.** (1) Sybil Bowley and had issue; **m.** (2) Kathleen Ford of Sydenham London and had issue

Died 12 Jan 1908 London **bur.** Belfast City Cemetery

RIGGS, FRANCIS LEWIS 1855/56–1920

b. 1855 or 1856 Castlepollard; ent TCD 28 Apr 1875 aged 19 BA 1878 MA 1883

d 6 Jun 1880 p 21 Dec 1881 (Derry); C Christ Ch Londonderry (Derry) 1880–87; R Killenumery (Ard) 1887–1920

    s. of Thomas M, Land Agent

    m. Harriett G——, and had issue 1. Capt Arthur McCausland of RAF **m.** Dorothy Evelyn **dau.** of Dr H Meyrick of Portland Place London; 2. yst **dau.** Hilda Grace **m.** 16 Sep 1925 Cecil Robert Vesey only **s.** of Capt Robert Stoney JP DL of Oakfield Park Raphoe Co Donegal; 3. an infant **dau.** Eileen Nora **died** 4 Feb 1891

    Died 11 Jan 1920 aged 64

RINGWOOD, JOHN THOMAS 1819/20–

b. Waterford; ed by Dr Graham; ent TCD 4 Jul 1836 aged 16 Sch 1838 BA 1851

d 1851 (Cork) p; C Holy Trinity District Chapel Kinawley (Kilm) 1853–73

    s. of John, Prof of Music by Anne (née Budd); **bro.** of Rev Henry Taylor, MA, C Mullabrack (Arm); **bro.** of Frederick Howe, Berkeley Lect in Greek TCD and Head Master Royal Sch Dungannon 1850–90

ROBB, JOHN COLLEN 1904–1981

b. 26 Sep 1904; ed at Mourne Grange and Shrewsbury; QUB BComm 1924 LLB 1925; practised as a Solicitor in Northern Ireland 1925–29

d 1929 p 1930 (Connor); C Ballymena (Conn) 1929–32; C-in-c Dowra and Innismagrath (Kilm) 1932–34; R Caledon (Arm) 1934–43; R Altedesert (Arm) 1943–44; R St Kevin Dublin (Dub) 1944–48; Org Sec BCMS in Ireland 1948–57; BCMS Missy Karamoja (Dio Uganda) 1958–61; ret

    s. of Hamilton of Portadown Co Armagh

    m. (1) 9 May 1931 at Mile Gully Ch Jamaica Kathleen Mary (Maureen) (**died** Jan 1964) **dau.** of the Hon. Thomas Anderson, JP of Mile Gully. Issue 1. Kathleen Elizabeth **b.** 18 Aug 1933 **m.** at St Mary Magdalene Ch Bermondsey London Rev Robert L **m.** Shepton, Chapl Kingham High Sch Oxford and had issue (i) Deborah

(ii) David (iii) Rachel (iv) Pete Dai (v) Anna Joy, the last two being adopted Vietnamese children; 2. John Anderson **b.** 30 Jun 1935 **m.** 19 Jan 1957 at Belvoir Ch Knockbreda Belfast Mabel Coffey of Crossgar Co Down and had issue (i) Stephen (ii) Stephanie

m. (2) 28 Dec 1976 at Histon Par Ch Cambridge Mildred **dau.** of Charles Edwin Henshall and widow of Rev Thomas Wheeler of Liverpool

Died 19 Sep 1981 at Leyland Lancs

†ROBERT –1224

an Englishman

Abbot of St Mary's, Dublin; Bp of Ardagh 1217.

Died 28 May 1224

†ROBERT

Augustinian Friar of St Patrick; prov to the See of Ardagh 5 Apr 1323 (C.P.L. II. 229); consec by Bp of Palestrina; translated to Connor 12 Jul 1323 (C.P.L. II. 231)

ROBERTS, CHARLES BENJAMIN PIGOTT –1967

TCD BA 1936 MA 1952

d and p 1938 (Kilmore); C Templemichael (Ard) 1938–43; R Teampall-na-mBocht (Cork) 1943–48; C-in-c Carrigrohane (Cork) 1948–49; R Holy Trinity w St Paul and St Peter (Cork) 1949–67; Preb of Timoleague in Ross Cath and Preb of Desertmore in Cork Cath 1959–64; Treasurer of Ross 1961–64; Treasurer of Cork Cath 1964–67; Dean of Residence UCC 1964–67; Preb of Tymothan in St Patrick's Cath Dublin 1964–67; last entry in C I Dir 1967

only **s.** of A H Roberts of Adambey Carrigtowhill Co Cork

m. May 1940 Sylvia Annette only **dau.** of W A Atwell of Longford

Died Sep 1967

ROBERTS, SAMUEL 1800–1877

b. 1800 Waterford; ed by Mr Price; ent TCD 2 Nov 1818 aged 17 BA 1823

d 19 Dec 1824 (Ossory) p; C Urney (Kilm) 1828; C Killesherdiney (Kilm) 1836–60; V Denn (Kilm) 1860–77

s. of Samuel, *pragmaticus*

m. Jane (ML 1828) **dau.** of Giles Eyre of Eyrecourt Co Galway

Died 25 Aug 1877 at Denn Vicarage aged 77

ROBERTS, THOMAS

appears V Rossinver (Kilm) 1636

ROBINSON, ALEXANDER

d; p 10 Jul 1671 (Kilmore); C Killargue (Kilm) 1671 or 1679; R Killerry (Elph) 1674–77; V Killenumery and Kilronan (Ard) from 1674; coll 14 Apr 1674; signed Address to King James II 16 Mar 1684

ROBINSON, ANDREW 1808/09–1878

b. 1808 or 1809 Derry; ed by Mr Knox; ent TCD 5 Nov 1827 aged 18 BA 1834 MA 1835

d 5 Oct 1834 p 15 Mar 1835 (Ossory); C St John Sligo 1840–47; V Athleague and Kilbegnet (Elph) 1847–61; R & V Ardcarne (Elph) 1861–71; Preb of Terebrine (Elph) 1861–71; R Kentstown (Meath) 1872–78

> **s.** of Arthur
>
> **m.** 14 Feb 1842 Hannah eldest **dau.** of Andrew D Johnstone of Friarstown Co Leitrim. Issue incl his yst **s.** Henry A Scott (**died** 4 Sep 1869 of scarlatina aged 15)
>
> **Died** 22 Oct 1878

ROBINSON, CHARLES

V Killenumery (Ard) 1807 and 1814; perhaps C.R. who was PC Lisnadill (Arm) 1790–91. Tuam SR gives the name of *Christopher* Robinson as being inst. V Killenumery (Ard) 24 Oct 1799

ROBINSON, CHARLES 1799–1870

b. 1799 Dublin; ed by Mr Gwynne; ent TCD 6 Jul 1818 aged 19 BA 1823 MA 1832

C Clonbroney (Ard) 1840; R Mostrim (Ard) 1840–43; R Kilglass (Ard) 1843–70

> **s.** of Rev Christopher, R Granard (Ard) qv (**s.** of Christopher) by Elizabeth **dau.** of Sir Hercules Langrishe, Bt; **bro.** of Rev Christopher, qv
>
> **m.** 1826 Mary (**died** 23 Jan 1879 aged 80) of Co Westmeath elder **dau.** of Ralph Dopping of Erne Head and Derrycassan Co Longford
>
> **Died** 30 Oct 1870 at 38 Waterloo Rd Dublin in his 72nd year

ROBINSON, CHRISTOPHER 1762/63–1837

b. 1762 or 1763 Dublin; ent TCD 3 May 1779 aged 16 BA 1783 MA 1786

R Ahern w Ballynoe (Cloyne) — a sinecure — 1789–1806; R Baldungan (Dub) 1792–1837; R Granard and Gowna (Ard) 1811–37

> 3rd **s.** of Christopher (**s.** of Bryan, MD of Dublin) by Elizabeth **dau.** of Hartstonge Martin
>
> **m.** 4 Feb 1786 St Mary's Ch Dublin Elizabeth **dau.** of Sir Hercules Langrishe, Bt. Issue 10 **sons**; 1. Richard **b.** in Co Leitrim ed by Dr Burrowes ent TCD 1 Nov 1802 aged 19 (possibly a **s.** by a previous wife or did he die and 10th **s.** then called Richard?); 2. Rev Christopher, qv; 3. Hartstonge **b.** Co Meath ed by Mr Gwynne ent TCD 6 Jul 1807 aged 17 BA 1811 QC Irish Bar **m.** Mary **dau.** of William Burrowes; 4. Rev Charles, R Kilglass (Ard) qv above; 5. Bryan **b.** Co Cavan ed by

Mr Gwynne ent TCD 18 Oct 1824 aged 16, Judge Supreme Court Newfoundland, knighted 1877 **m.** Selina Brooking; 6. Hercules, Capt RN **m.** and had issue; 7. James; 8 Robert; 9. John; 10 Richard Capt RN; he also had 3 **daus.** 1. Elizabeth **m.** John Tatlow; 2. Hannah **m.** James Cottingham; 3. June **m.** C Wilkins

Died 10 Dec 1837

ROBINSON, CHRISTOPHER 1786/87–

b. 1786 or 1787 Dublin ed by Mr Barry ent TCD 6 Jun 1803 aged 16

C Granard (Ard) in 1830

    s. of Rev Christopher, R Granard (Ard), qv (**s.** of Christopher) by Elizabeth; **bro.** of Rev Charles, qv

ROBINSON, JOHN

V Russagh (Ard) to 1622, "not resident Church ruinous serveth the Cure every 2nd Sunday fit to be united to Aghery" (R.V.); admitted V Agherie and Rathreagh (Ard) 1 Oct 1616 (F.F.); still V 1622

ROBINSON, LAURENCE –1641

TCD BA 1613

d & p 22 Apr 1619 (Raphoe); R Urney and Annagelliffe (Kilm) 1620–38; got a grant of a glebe there 25 Jan 1626/27; pres by Crown Chanc of Armagh by lapse 20 May 1625; R Killesherdoney (Kilm) 1628–*c.* 41; seems to have become Chanc of Armagh (again?) certainly in 1634 and was named as Chanc in the Charter of 1637/38; inst as Chanc of Armagh and R Kilmore (Arm) on 3 May 1638; "a preacher"; "church ruinous, inconvenient, not fitt to be repaired; new church should be built at Cavan" (R.V.)

    is said to have been murdered in 1641

ROBINSON, LEO 1799/1800–1866

b. 1799 or 1800 Donegal; ed by Mr Irwine; ent TCD 3 Jun 1817 aged 17 Sch 1821 BA 1822

appears C Cloonclare (Kilm) *c.* 1827; Leslie thinks that this is the same as Leonard Horner Robinson who was C Maryborough (Leigh)–1829; PC Kilcluney (Arm) 1829–66

    s. of Alexander, merchant

    m. Maryanne (15 Apr 1890 Markethill Co Armagh) **b.** 9 Mar 1810 **dau.** of Capt John Winder, RA of Armagh by Elizabeth **dau.** of Peter Gervais of Newtownsaville Co Tyrone. Issue 1. Elizabeth Winder bapt 21 Dec 1836 **m.** 11 Apr 1860 as his 2nd wife Rev Charles Crossle, PC Kilcluney (Arm) 1866–71 and had issue (i) Marian Leonora **b.** 5 May 1862 (ii) Leonard Alexander **b.** 8 Apr 1863 (iii) William Verner **b.** 15 Mar 1864; 2. Alexander bapt 15 Mar 1838 TCD; 3. John Winder bapt 20 Mar 1839; 4. Isabella (**died unm.** Jul 1930); 5. Francis Gervais (**died** 1867) **b.** 1845; 6. Marianne **m.** 6 Aug 1873 at Kilcluney Par Ch Rev James Lyons, MA 3rd **s.** of Henry Lyons of Sligo

Died 11 Nov 1866

ROBINSON, RICHARD

lic C Killesherdoney (Kilm) 7 Sep 1811

ROBINSON, RICHARD ALBERT 1914–1992

b. 26 Dec 1914 Stoneyford Co Kilkenny

d 1938 p 1939 (Clogher); C Trillick (Clogh) 1938–40; Dio C Clogher 1940–43; Temp-in-c Templecarne (Clogh) 1941; C-in-c Drummully (Clogh) 1943–44; Dio C Clogher 1944–46; Dio C Kilmore 1946–54; Temp-in-c Ardcarne and Croaghan (Elph) Jul 1953–Mar 1954; R Taunagh & Kilmactranny (w Ballysumaghan from 1960) (Elph) 1954–85; Preb of Kilcooley (Elph) 1984–85; ret

Died 27 Oct 1992 **unm. bur.** Taunagh Riverstown Co Sligo

ROBINSON, ROBERT –1690

d; p 2 Oct 1664 (Clogher); R Tomregan and Drumlane (Kilm) 1669–85; R Annagh (Kilm) 1673–90; signed address to James II 1684/85 as "Robert Robinson"

Died 1690; Will proved 1690

ROBINSON, SAMUEL ADAMS

see **ADAMS–ROBINSON**, SAMUEL

ROBINSON, THOMAS –*c.* 1619

Dean of Kilmore to 1619

Died *c.* 1619 Will proved 1619

ROBINSON, WILLIAM PERCY 1834/35–

b. 1834 or 1835 Armagh; ed Royal Sch Armagh; ent TCD 11 Oct 1853 aged 18 Sch 1855 BA 1860 MA 1868 BD & DD 1875

d & p; C Kilmore (Kilm) 1860–62; Master, Diocesan Sch Sligo 1865–66; C Templemore, St. Columb's Cath Londonderry (Derry) 1871–72; afterwards Warden of Trinity Coll Glenalmond, Perthshire

s. of Alexander, surgeon

ROBINSON, WILLIAM

C Shrule (Ard) 1728

RODGERS, FREDERICK WILLIAM 1922–1983

b. 10 Jun 1922 Strabane Co Tyrone; ed Midleton Coll Co Cork; The King's Hospital Dublin; TCD BA 1944 Div Test (2) 1945 MA 1951 HDipEd 1952

d 1945 p 1946; C Derryloran (Arm) 1945–47; C St John Sligo (Elph) 1947–49; Cler V Christ Ch Cath Dublin (Dub) 1949–63; Head Master Christ Ch Cath Gram Sch 1952–63; Hon Cler V Christ Ch Cath Dublin 1964; Area Sec SPG Province of Dublin

1964–65; USPG 1965–67; Asst Master Wesley Coll Dublin 1967–82

> s. of Frederick James
>
> m. 12 Jul 1946 St Brigid's Ch Stillorgan Dublin Patricia Janet dau. of Major Alexander E Nesbitt of Blackrock Dublin. Issue 1. Philip Frederick Ewing b. 17 May 1948 TCD MB m. Vivienne Graham and have issue (i) James (ii) Louise; 2. Paul David Ewing b. 12 Apr 1951 m. Celeste Kennon of California and have issue (i) Laura (ii) Eve; 3. Timothy Alexander Ewing b. 6 Oct 1957 m. Susan Shave of London and have issue (i) Amy (ii) Alexandra (iii) Lara; 4. Amanda Gay Ewing b. 16 Jun 1961 m. David Christie and have issue (i) Nadia (ii) Jasmin
>
> Died 11 Aug 1983 Dublin

RODNEY, JAMES VINCENT 1799/1800–

b. 1799 or 1800 Londonderry; ed by Dr Miller; ent TCD 5 Jul 1821 aged 21 BA 1828 MA 1832

d 13 Apr 1834 (Cloyne) p; C Kildallon (Kilm) 1835; C Killeshandra (Kilm) 1844–47

> s. of Robert, *agricola*

ROE, THOMAS H 1825/26–1862

b. 1825 or 1826 Co Offaly; ent TCD 5 Nov 1849 aged 23; BA 1854 MA 1859

d 1855 p; C Fenagh (Ard) 1857–62

> s. of Robert, Lawyer, Attorney Exchequer
>
> Died at Edentenny Co Leitrim 9 Nov 1862

ROE, WILLIAM ALEXANDER 1870–1916

b. 13 Nov 1870; RUI BA 1894 TCD Div Test 1895

d 1894 p 1895; C Carlingford (Arm) 1894–95; C St Peter Drogheda (Arm) 1895; C St George Belfast (Conn) 1896–98; C Killaban (Leigh) 1898–1904; C Killinkere (Kilm) 1904–07; R Templeport (Kilm) 1907–16

> s. of Peter Mitchell, Surgeon RN by Georgina (née Humfrey) of Kingstown (Dun Laoghaire) Co Dublin
>
> Died 31 Aug 1916 aged 46

ROE, WILLIAM DISNEY 1825–1890

b. 1825 Newry; ent TCD 13 Oct 1843 BA & Div Test (2) 1848 MA 1874

d 1848 p 1849 (Dublin); C St Michan (Dub) 1848–50; C Headford (Tuam) 1850–54; C Shrule (Ard) 1854–58; C Burrishool (Tuam) 1858–77; R Athenry (Tuam) 1877–90; Preb of Kilmoylan in Tuam Cath 1876–90

> s. of William, merchant
>
> m. 17 Apr 1849 Anna 2nd dau. of Thomas Grendon of Drogheda. Issue incl a s. Dr C Disney Roe of Ramsey IOM; a s. b. 23 Jun 1862; a s. b. 31 May 1865
>
> Died 15 Feb 1890 aged 65

ROGERS, JOHN ACHILLES –1960

TCD Siz Heb & Syriac Pri 1906 Wall Bibl Sch 1908 BA & Div Test 1910 MA 1920

d 1910 p 1911 (Kilmore); C Larah and Lavey (Kilm) 1910–13; Examiner in Heb and Chaldee Univ of NZ 1913; Tutor Bishopsdale Coll Nelson NZ and Private Chapl to Bp of Nelson 1913–16 & 1919–34; V All SS Nelson (Dio Nelson) NZ 1916–18; CF NZ 1917–18; Acting V Greymouth (Nelson) 1918–19; Acting V Richmond (Nelson) 1919–20; V Stoke (Nelson) 1920–30; Org Sec CMJ, SW Distr England and Lic to Preach Dio Truro and Perm to Off Dios Bristol and Sarum 1930–32; Officiating Chapl E London Cemetery and Perm to Off Dios London and Chelmsford 1934–40; C-in-c Kilcommon Erris (Killala) 1940–45; R Crossmolina (Killala) 1945–46; Asst Chapl Albert Dock Canning Town (Chelmsf) 1946–49

Died 10 Mar 1960

ROGERS, MERVYN WARREN 1869–1949

b. 21 Mar 1869 Denver Norfolk; ed the Puse Sch Cambridge; St Aidan's Coll Birkenhead 1893

d 1895 p 1896 (Clogher); C Clontibret (Clogh) 1895–97; R Broomfield (Clogh) 1897–1902; C Winwick (Liv) 1902–04; R Currin (Clogh) 1904–09; R Tomregan (Kilm) 1909–16; R Ryston w Roxham and Fordham (Ely) 1916–23; V Stapleford (Ely) 1923–36; R Glatton (Ely) 1936–44; Perm to Off All SS Forest Gate (Chelmsf) 1944–48

s. of Rev Robert

m. Beatrice Elizabeth Nora **dau.** of Rev George William Wall, R Sephton Lancs. Issue Kathleen Eleanor **b.** 13 Aug 1898 Broomfield Co Monaghan **m.** Arthur Henry Brooks Watts

Died 5 Jul 1949 London

ROGERS, ROBERT 1829/30–

b. 1829 or 1830 Co Monaghan; ed by Mr Greham; ent TCD 15 Oct 1847 Sch 1849 BA 1853 Div Test (1) 1854 MA 1861 BD & DD 1873

d 1855 (Meath) p 1856 (Kilmore); C Cloone (Ard) 1855–58; C St Nicholas Cork (Cork) 1858–60; C Lockwood (Ripon) 1860–61; C-in-c Fawkham (Roch) 1861–

s. of Henry, agent

ROLLESTON, ARTHUR 1769–1850

b. 21 May 1769; ed by Mr Crawford; ent TCD 19 Oct 1785 BA 1790

C Skeirke (Oss) 1796–97; V Chor Ossory 1797; V Shrule (Ard) 1800; R Castlerickard (Meath) 1808; V Enniskeen (Meath) to 1816; V Kilcleagh (Meath) 1816–50

s. of James Franck of Franckfort Castle Co Laois by Jane **dau.** of Charles Bagge of Lismore Co Waterford

m. Feb 1802 Lucy **dau.** of Col James Wemyss of Danesfort Co Kilkenny

Died s.p. 1850

ROOKBY, THOMAS
Coll V Tibohine (Elph) 8 May 1640; coll V Oran (Elph) 4 May 1641

ROONE, WALTER
Clk, pres to V Scrayde = Streete, Ardagh Dio. 28 Oct 1550 (F. Edward VI. 596; L.M. V. 98)

ROSE, THOMAS PERCIVAL 1891/92–1963
b. 1891 or 1892; ed Bp Foy's Sch Waterford; TCD Div Test 1915 BA 1916 MA 1919 d 1916 p 1918 (Armagh); C Killyman (Arm) 1916–19; C Ballymoney (Conn) 1920–22; C Ballymacarrett (Down) 1922–25; C-in-c Mullaghdun (Clogh) 1925–28; C-in-c Swanlinbar (Kilm) 1928–29; Chapl to Eccles Est at Ambala India 1931–32; Hyderabad 1932–33; Peshawar 1933–34; Razmak 1934–35; Karachi 1935 & 1936–37; on furlough 1935–36; Quetta 1936; Murree 1937; New Delhi Canton 1937–38; Asst Chapl Quetta 1938–39; on furlough 1939; Sukkur 1939–40; Nowshera 1940–45; Holy Trinity Bangalore 1945–47; Sec CMJ NI 1949–52; Lic to Off Dio Connor 1953–63

s. of Mr & Mrs P Rose of Kilmeaden Co Waterford

m. Sarah Glendinning (**died** 18 Jul 1957) **dau.** of W Fowler of Killyman. Issue 1. John Percival **m**...; 2. Elizabeth Eleanor **m.** Charles Gibson Alexander MD OBE MC (**died** Nov 1990) and had issue (i) Barbara **b.** 1949 **m.** David Camlin (ii) Deirdre Anne **b.** 1954 QUB BSc **m.** Richard Coulter TCD BA (iii) Sarah **b.** 1968 **m.** June 1993 Frederick Duffin; 3. Martha Glendinning (**died** Apr 1991) (twin **sister** of Elizabeth) **m.** Terence Duncan and had issue Michael; 4. William Sydney **m.** June Grey and had issue Deborah **m.** Oct 1989 Charles Walker and have issue Andrew and Christopher

Died 13 Jan 1963 aged 71 **bur.** Killyman

ROSS, LANGLE –1724
perhaps should be Randall Rose, TCD BA 1708
V Mohill (Ard) c. 1721–24

is deceased 1724

ROSS, ROBERT –1693
Preb of Killedan (Ach) 1661; V Kilronan (Ard) 1661–c. 1674; V Innismagrath (Kilm) 1661–c85; R Annaduff and Cloon (Ard) 1668/69–93, coll. 19 Jan (F.F.); coll again R Annaduff and Cloon (Ard) 1669. At a Visitation in 1683, he alleged that his Letters of Orders were burned. Probably he is the "Mr. Ross" mentioned in King's, *State of Irish Protestants,* p. 231, who was prosecuted by his bishop (of Kilmore) for very lewd and notorious crimes, but the King's Judges interposed c. 1685–89. He signed address to James II 18 Mar 1684

Died 1693

ROSSELL, CHARLES 1651/52–1754

b. 1651 or 1652

"formerly Chaplain to the Duke of Schomberg", *London Magazine*, 1754; may have been R Carrigallen (Kilm) 1682–98, but for this Leslie finds no authority; V Drumlane and Tomregan (Kilm) 1685–1740; R Killesherdoney 1740–54

Died 14 Feb 1754 aged 102

ROWAN, REGINALD PERCY –*c.* 1966

TCD Past Theol Pri & Div Test 1906 BA 1907 MA 1911

d 1907 p 1908 (Kilmore); C Urney & Annagelliffe (Kilm) 1907–11; C St Mark Harrogate (Rip) 1911–12; R Kilmacshalgan (Killala) 1912–17; TCF 1917–20; C Jesmond (Newc) 1920–26; V Ansley (Cov) 1926–35; V Kingsclere (Win) 1935–45; V N Eling (or Copy Thorne) (Win) 1945–55; ret

s. of Rev Robert Benjamin (1841/42–1912), R Kilmacshalgan (Killala) 1883–1912; **bro.** of Very Rev Robert Philip, Dean of Ardfert 1924–44; **bro.** of Rev Thomas; **bro.** of Rev Benjamin William; **bro.** of Rev Albert Edward Joseph

Died *c.* 1966

ROWLATT, EDMUND (EDWARD)

Archd of Killala and ?Achonry and Preb of Moynelagh (Ach) 1661–; V Ballintubber Ballysumaghan Kilross & Ballinakill (Elph) 1666–84; Preb of Kilmacallan (Elph) 1668–84

ROWLEY, JAMES JOHNSTON 1807/08–

b. 1807 or 1808 Co Meath; ent TCD 26 Jan 1824 aged 16 BA 1828

C Ardagh (Ard) 1841–

3rd **s.** of Thomas Taylor of Maperath Co Meath, High Sheriff Co Meath 1805 by Elizabeth **dau.** and co–heir of Daniel Toler of Beechwood Co Tipperary MP for Co Tipperary, **bro.** of John 1st Earl of Norbury

m. 6 May 1841 at Loughgall Ch Co Armagh Matilda (**died** 9 May 1882 at Rockmullen Co Monaghan aged 75) 3rd **dau.** of George Ensor of Ardress Co Armagh

ROWLEY, JOHN 1776/77–1845

b. 1776 or 1777 Dublin; ed by Rev William Darby, Ballygall Co Dublin; ent TCD 1 Oct 1792 aged 15 BA *c.* 1796 MA 1809 LLB & LLD 1828

C Ballinderry (Arm) 1801–02; Chapl to the Prince Regent; Preb of St Michan's in Christ Ch Cath Dublin 1809–45; V Lurgan and Munterconnaught (Kilm) 1812–45

4th **s.** of Clotworthy, BL MP for Downpatrick (**s.** of Sir William, Admiral of the Fleet)

m. 30 Sep 1826 Catherine (**died** 10 Apr 1879) 2nd **dau.** of Joseph Clarke of Kilburn Priory Middlesex. Issue 1. Josias (**died** 1887 s.p.) **b.** 2 Apr 1829, JP DL of

Mount Campbell Drumsna Co Leitrim, Commander RN **m.** 25 Nov 1869 Alice Kemmis yst **dau.** of Rev William Betty of Kingstown Co Laois; 2. William **b.** 19 May 1832 JP DL of Mount Campbell **m.** 26 Dec 1853 Rosetta **dau.** of Richard Goddard of Colchester Essex; 3. Sophia (**died** 12 Jan 1859) **m.** 11 Sep 1846 William Armit Lees and had issue; 4. Catherine Mary **m.** 7 Jan 1859 Charles Henry James; 5. Mary

Died 5 Jan 1845 at Kingstown (Dun Laoghaire) **bur.** St Michan's Ch Dublin

ROYCROFT, JAMES GORDON BENJAMIN 1926–2004

b. 1926; in business before ordination

d 1956 p 1957; C St Aidan Belfast (Conn) 1956–58; BC Crossmolina (Killala) 1958–63; Sec ICM in N England 1963–67; R Drung (w Killersherdoney to 1972 and w Castleterra from 1969 and w Larah and Lavey from 1972 and Killoughter from 1974) 1967–83; R Drumkeeran (Clogh) 1983–91; ret; Gen Lic Dio Clogher 1992–2004

s. of J Roycroft of Galway

m. 1 Jul 1957 St John Bapt Upper Falls Belfast Avril, SRN **dau.** of J Bass of Dunmurry Belfast

Died 25 Jul 2004

ROYCROFT, WILLIAM

TCD Sch 1606 BA not recorded

d 24 May 1611 p 31 May 1611; V Killaspicbrone (Elph) 1615; V Sligo (Elph) 1615; Preb of Tirebrine (Elph) 1615–16; V Drumcliffe and Calrea *alias* Calragh = Calry (Elph) 1622; V Rossinver (Kilm) 1619–*c.* 22; V Kilcooley 1627–; Preb of Kilcooley (Elph) 1627 to *c.* 1661; "a good Divine and Preacher" (R.V. 1634)

RUDD, THOMAS ERNEST 1859/60–1946

b. 1859 or 1860 Donaghmore Co Tyrone; ed Portora Royal Sch Enniskillen; Dr Chambers Sch Kingstown; TCD BA (1 Resp) 1892

d 1890 (Clogher for Kilmore) p 1892 (Kilmore); C Kilkeevan (Elph) 1890–91; C Urney (Kilm) 1891–95; Dep Sec HBS 1895–97; R Ballycarney (Ferns) 1897–98; R Tomregan (Kilm) 1898–1900; R Clonmethan U (Dub) 1900–02; R Derryvullen (Clogh) 1902–05; R Muckno (Clogh) 1905–32; Preb of Devenish (Clogh) 1924–32; ret

s. of Rev Thomas (1825–1915), R Killallon (Meath) 1875–98 (**s.** of Thomas)

m. Belinda Saunders **dau.** of Parker Dunscombe of Cork and Nanette Baldwin Waggett. Issue 1. Rear-Admiral Eric Thomas Sutherland BA MB BAO BCh TCD **m.** 3 Nov 1930 in Rome Enid Marjorie only **dau.** of Commander L Vaughan Jones, RN of Radlett Herts; 2. Nanette Frances; 3. Zelma Goerel **m.** 6 Jun 1929 Alfred Norman only **s.** of T J Mathias of Ilfracombe Devon; 4. Belinda Saunders Dunscombe **m.** 6 Jun 1939 John Crawford Muir of Glasgow; 5. Dorothy Sybil

Died 26 May 1946 aged 86

RUDDOCK, KENNETH EDWARD 1930–

b. 4 May 1930 Carlow; ed The King's Hosp Dublin TCD Toplady Bibl Pri Past Theol Pri Catechetical Pri BA 1952 Div Test (1) 1953; QUB MTh 1986

d 5 Jul 1953 p 1954 (Connor); C Ballymena (Conn) 1953–56; C St Thomas Belfast (Conn) 1956–60; R Tomregan and Drumlane (Kilm) 1960–68; R St Luke Belfast (Conn) 1968–80; R Whitehead and Islandmagee (Conn) 1980–96; Miss to Seamen 1980–96; Preb of Rasharkin (Conn) 1990–96; Dio Info Officer Connor 1990–96; Chapl to Scouts; Chanc of Connor 1996; ret; Dio C Connor 1998–2006

> **s.** of William James of Carlow (**s.** of Richard and Kathleen (née O'Sullivan) of Rathdrum Co Wicklow) by Emma **dau.** of James and Jane Treacy of Co Carlow; **bro.** of Rev Canon Charles Cecil, R Fenagh (Leigh) 1989–95 and **bro.** of Rev Canon Norman Trevor (**died** 6 Oct 2006), R Wexford G (Ferns) 1993–2004

> **m.** 6 Sep 1956 Ballymena Kathleen **dau.** of John and Katherine Hamill. Issue 1. Philip John **b.** 4 Jan 1960 **m.** Margaret Neilly; 2. Ruth Catherine Joyce **b.** 18 Oct 1962 **m.** David Farr; 3. Michael William **b.** 19 Mar 1967 **m.** Sophie Hammond

RUDDOCK, WILLIAM HENRY NASSAU 1881–1956

b. 7 Sep 1881 Portadown Co Armagh; ed Armagh Academy; TCD BA & Div Test 1908 MA 1922

d 1909 p 1910; C Kilkeevan (Elph) 1909–11; C Layde (Conn) 1911–12; C St Philip Belfast (Conn) 1912–14; C-in-c St Simon Belfast (Conn) 1914–15; C St Anne's Cath Belfast (Conn) 1915; R Stoneyford (Conn) 1915–28; R St Matthew Broomhedge Lisburn (Conn) 1928–52; ret

> **s.** of Robinson and Betania (née Sinnamon)

> **m.** 28 Sep 1915 Elizabeth Taylor of Diamond Hse Portadown. Issue 1. John St C T (**died** June 1965) Caius Coll Camb BA **m.** …Wilding and had issue

> **Died** 20 Nov 1956

†RUFUS, CORNELIUS or CONOR ROE

son of the Coarb of Molua, is said to have succeeded John O'Hugroin as Bp of Elphin in 1246 and to have **died** shortly afterwards

RUITERS, IVAN JOHN 1961–

b. 11 Sep 1961; Diploma in Theology

d 1996 p 1997; R Killesher Druminiskill and Killinagh (Kilm) 2007–

> **m.** Raylene. Issue 1. Rocardo Ivan Ruiters **b.** 28 Mar 1983; 2. Rosselli Charles Ruiters **b.** 28 Mar 1983; 3. Lynton John Ruiters **b.** 27 Oct 1988

RULE, RALPH *c.* 1654–1724

b. *c.* 1654 London; ed by Mr Price; ent TCD as Siz 17 Apr 1669 aged about 15 Sch & BA 1672 MA 1682 BD & DD 1702

R Kildallon (Kilm) 1678–84; V Drumlease and Killargue (Kilm) 1681–84; V

Newcastle (Glend) 1682–1702; R Delgany (Glend) 1682–1724; V Arklow (Glend) 1684–85; Preb of Kilmactalway in St Patrick's Cath Dublin 1685–91; Preb of Wicklow in St Patrick's Cath Dublin 1691–1724; signed address to James II 12 Mar 1684/85 among the Dublin clergy; attainted 1689 and fled to England and stayed there until 1690

> s. of Ralph
>
> m. (1) Griselda 2nd dau. of the Rt Hon Sir James Cuffe, MP
>
> m. (2) Jane (Will prov 23 Jun 1744)
>
> Died Dec 1724 intestate bur. 29 Dec 1724 Delgany Co Wicklow

RUSSELL, BRIAN ROBERT 1961–

b. 11 May 1961 Belfast; ed Grosvenor High Sch Belfast; QUB BA 1982 BD 1992; TCD Dip Theol 1985

d 1985 p 1986; C Drumcondra w North Strand Dublin (Dub) 1985–87; C St Nicholas Carrickfergus (Conn) 1987–90; R Kilmegan w Maghera (Drom) 1990–96; R Bailieborough Knockbride Shercock and Mullagh (Kilm) 1996–2000; R Drumholm Kilbarron and Rossnowlagh (Raph) 2000–

> s. of Robert and Jeanie (née Frame) of Belfast
>
> m. 6 Jun 1985 Willowfield Par Ch Belfast Esther dau. of John and Mary Fowler. Issue 1. Mark Robert b. 24 Aug 1987; 2. John Thomas b. 18 Dec 1989; 3. Simon James b. 17 May 1996; 4. Rachel Grace Esther b. 21 May 2005

RUSSELL, THOMAS WILLIAM CUSACK 1819/20–

b. 1819 or 1820 Dublin; ed by Mr Turpin; ent TCD 6 Nov 1837 aged 17 BA 1846

d 1848 p 1849 (Ripon) C Kilsby (Pet) 1850–65; afterwards C Hugglescote (Leic) and Asbby–de–la–Zouch (Leic); R Kilglass (Ard) 1876–84

> s. of Rev Thomas, R Kilbonane (A & A) (died 1823) 1818–23 (s. of Francis Thomas) by Bridget Anne Cusack (died 2 Feb 1869 at Hugglescote in her 80th year); bro. of Rev Frances Thomas b. 1822 or 1823 Dublin (died 6 Feb 1876) ent TCD 14 Oct 1842 aged 19 BA 1846 LLD m. 17 Feb 1847 at St Audoen Dublin Margaretta dau. of John Smithson

PUBLICATIONS

Sermons on *Day of Humiliation for Mutiny in India*, 1837
Bicentenary of St Bartholomew, 1862

RUSSELL, WILLIAM ALEXANDER 1889/90–1968

b. 1889 or 1890; TCD BA 1913 Div Test 1915 MA 1924

d 1914 p 1915 (Down); C St Philip (Drew Memorial Ch) Belfast (Conn) 1914–16; C Christ Ch Lisburn (Conn) 1916–25; R Ballyphilip w Ardquin (Down) 1925–31; C-in-c Kildrumferton w Ballymachugh (Kilm) 1931–34; R Billis Ballyjamesduff and Castlerahan (Kilm) 1934–43; R Killeshandra w Killegar (Kilm) 1943–55; RD of Killeshandra 1955–56; RD of Fenagh 1956–66; R Kiltoghart U (w Drumshambo from 1962) (Ard) 1955–66; Preb of Tibohine (Elph) 1963–66; ret

s. of William Alexander of Skibbereen Co Cork

m. 26 Sep 1917 Christ Ch Lisburn Kathleen (**died** 9 Jun 1977) yst **dau.** of Robert McCarrison of Lisburn. Issue 1. Alfred McCarrison Russell, MB **m.** 1942 Dorothy Hazel yr **dau.** of Ven Hedley Webster, Archd of Cork; 2. Alexandra **m.** 1949 Rev Ian William McDougall, R Drumlane (Kilm) qv

Died 16 Nov 1968 Mullingar aged 78

RUSSELL, WILLIAM GLADSTONE 1905–1960

b. 20 Aug 1905 Banbridge Co Down; ed at Banbridge; TCD Div Test 1947 BA 1948 MA 1951

d 13 Mar 1949 p 9 Jul 1950 (Derry); C Maghera (Derry) 1949–51; R Newtowngore Corrawallen & Drumreilly (Kilm) 1951–56; C-in-c Ballysumaghan Killery & Killenumery (Elph) 1956–59; C St Mary Belfast (Conn) 1959–60

s. of Thomas and Agnes (née Hutchinson) of Banbridge

m. 1 Oct 1951 St Thomas's Par Ch Belfast Edna May **dau.** of James and Mary Jane Warren of Belfast. Issue Rev William Warren **b.** 8 Oct 1952 Dublin QUB BSocSc (2cl Hons) 1974 TCD Div Test 1977 d 1977 p 1978 C Agherton (Conn) 1977–79 C Lisburn 1979–83, R Magheradroll (Drom) 1983–, **m.** 20 Aug 1981 Hillsborough Par Ch Co Down Frieda Eileen **dau.** of Lloyd and Winifred Best of Hillsborough and have issue 1. Victoria Frances Nicola **b.** 17 Dec 1982; 2. James Warren Patrick **b.** 17 Apr 1984

Died 17 Oct 1960

RYALL, CHARLES RICHARD 1876/77–1969

b. 1876 or 1877; RUI BA 1899; St Michael's Coll Llandaff 1902; TCD BA 1917 MA 1920 BD 1921 LLB & LLD 1926

d 1903 p 1904 (Llandaff); C St Paul Grangetown (Lland) 1903–05; C St Luke Old Charlton (S'wark) 1905–07; C Limpsfield (S'wark) 1907–10; Chapl Eccles Est in India; Ahmadnagar 1910–11, 1923–25, and 1926–27; St Paul Poona 1913–14; w Expeditionary Force 1914–18; furlough 1918–20 and 1925–26; Colaba 1920–21; Aden 1921–23; Ghorpuri 1928–30; R Bettiscombe w Pilsdon (Sarum) 1931–33; Perm to Off Dio St E 1933–37; V Asthall w Asthalleigh (Ox) 1937–38; C-in-c Granard, Abbeylara and Drumlummon (Ard) 1938–40; I Bourney w Dunkerrin (Killaloe) 1940–45; R Timolin (Glend) 1945–58

m. and had issue incl Rev Michael Richard **b.** 1936 TCD BA & Div Test 1958 HDipEd 1966 d 1958 p 1959 C St George (Dub) 1958–61 Hon Cler V Christ Ch Cath Dub 1960 CF 1962–65 and 1968–90 C Rathmines (Dub) 1965–66 Asst Master Dungannon High Sch 1966–68 R Yardley Hastings U (Pet) 1990–2001 Perm to Off Dio Portsmouth 2002–

Died 1 Mar 1969 aged 92

RYCROFT, WILLIAM

pres by the Crown to the V Drumcliffe (Elph) 22 Oct 1619 (L.M. V. 104); appointed Preb of Drumcliffe 1622; was still there in 1641

RYDER, DUDLEY CHARLES 1726–1815

b. 20 Feb 1726 Warwickshire; ed by Mr Shaw; ent TCD as FC 10 Oct 1743 aged 17 BA 1747 MA 1749

V Ballyrashane and Ballywillan (Conn) 1751–53; C Rasharkin (Conn) 1753; inst V Kilmolara/Ballincholla (Tuam) 19 Feb 1754; appears R Clongish (Ard) 1766, and perhaps there from 1761–95; V Fenagh (Ard) 1767–1815; R Cloone (Ard) *c.* 1767–1815; Preb of Killabegs (Tuam) –1754; Preb of Kilmaimmore (Tuam) 1754–62; Provost of Tuam 1762–1815

    s. of Most Rev John, Abp of Tuam qv below (**s.** of Dudley) by Alice **dau.** of John Wilmot; **bro.** of Rev John qv

    m. Elizabeth Catherine Charnel of Snarkeston Hall Leicestershire. Issue Katherine **m.** Lt Col Samuel Madden of Hilton

    Died 11 Dec 1815

†RYDER. JOHN 1696/97–1775

b. 1696 or 1697; ed Charterhouse, exhibitioner; ent Queen's Coll Camb 25 Jun 1712 matric 1712 BA 1715/16 Fellow 1718–21 MA 1719 DD 1741

V Nuneaton 1721–42; Bp of Killaloe 1742–43; translated to Down and Connor by Patent 1 May 1743; Bp of Down and Connor 1743–52; Abp of Tuam and Bp of Ardagh 1752–75

    s. of Dudley of Nuneaton, Warks (**s.** of Rev Dudley MA, R Bedworth Warks)

    m. (1) Alice (**died** 21 Dec 1744) **dau.** of John Wilmot a younger **s.** of Robert Wilmot of Osmaston Derbys who was **bro.** of Sir Robert 1st Bt. 1. Issue Rev John qv below; 2. Rev Dudley Charles qv above; 4 **daus.** incl 1. Anne **m.** Richard Aldworth of Newmarket; 2. Elizabeth **m.** 5 May 1761 John Oliver, Archd of Ardagh qv and had issue (i) Rev John (ii) Robert Dudley (iii) Charles (iv) Richard (v) Rev Silver (vi) Nathaniel Wilmot — for more detail see Ven J Oliver above; 3. a **dau.** m Arthur Weldon of Rahan Queen's Co (Laois); 4 another **dau.**

    m. (2) July 1748 Frances (**died** 29 Apr 1750) widow of Dean John Hamilton and **dau.** of Bp Francis Hutchinson Bp of Down and Connor 1720/21–39

    Died 4 Feb 1775 aged 78 at Nice as a result of a fall from his horse, and is **bur.** there in the British Cemetery

RYDER, JOHN –1791

TCD BA 1745 LLB 1755 LLD

faculty 2 Jul 1745 to hold Preb of St Andrew (Down) with R Ballintoy (Conn) 1745–59; Preb of Killabegs in Tuam Cath 1753–91; V Mohill (Ard) 1756–91; R Templemichael (Ard) 1756–91; V Gen Ardagh 1761–; Dean of Lismore 1762–91

    s. of Most Rev John, Abp of Tuam qv (**s.** of Dudley) by his 1st wife Alice; **bro.** of Rev Dudley Charles qv

    m. Feb 1777 (ML 8 Feb) Bangor Hon Anne eldest **dau.** of Sir John Blackwood Bt by Dorcas, Baroness Dufferin and Clandeboye; she **m.** (2) 1 Oct 1796 Rev James Jones, R Urney (Derry) **s.** of Rt Hon Theophilus Jones MP

    Died s.p. 18 Apr 1791 London

RYVES, JOHN WILLIAM DUDLEY 1715/16–1801

b. 1715 or 1716 Co Carlow; ed by Dr Crump; ent TCD 13 Nov 1733 aged 17 Sch 1736 BA 1738 MA 1741 LLB & LLD 1746

R Agher (Meath) 1782–83; V Kildrumferton (Kilm) 1783–1801; he was coll a 2nd time 13 Jun 1799 because he had virtually resigned by his acceptance of another preferment (the Preb of St Michael's Dublin) without a faculty; PC Monkstown (Dub) 1791–99; Preb of St Michael's in Christ Ch Cath Dublin (Dub) 1798–1801; 3rd Canon of Kildare 1799–1801

> **s.** of Rev Armstrong, R Urglin (Leigh) 1710/11–1771 (**s.** of Rev Jerome)
>
> **Died** 2 Mar 1801 **bur.** Killiney Co Dublin

SALTER, JOHN WILLIAM

AKC 1922; Wycliffe Hall Ox 1922

d 1923 (Barking for Chelmsford) p 1925 (Chelmsford); C St Mark Forest Gate (Chelmsf) 1923–25; C St John the Evangelist Stratford (Chelmsf) 1925–26; Perm to Off at All SS Portsea (Portsm) 1926; C St Luke and C-in-c St Paul W Norwood (S'wark) 1927–30; Org Sec Miss to Seamen Dios St Albans and Chelmsford and Public Pr Dio St Albans 1930–33; R Kilcornan (Lim) 1933–34; Chapl Eccles Est St George's Cath Madras (Dio Madras) 1934–36; R Drumgoon (Kilm) 1936–37; PC Trelystan w Leighton (Heref) 1937–45; Chapl Vizagapatam (Dio Madras) 1945–46; R Orchard Portman w Thurlbere and Stoke St Mary (B & W) 1947–50; V Much Marcle w Yatton (Heref) 1950–52; R Kilpeacon U (Lim) 1952–56; R Bonchurch (Portsm) 1956–59; V All SS Gussage (Sarum) 1959–60; R Kenmare U (A & A) 1960–61; R Kilmacduagh U (Kilmacd) 1962–64; R Brilley w Michaelchurch (Heref) 1964–66; last entry in Crockford 1967/68

PUBLICATION
> *The Divine Quest,* 1947

SAMS (SANDS), AYLOTT

MA

R & V Killesherdoney (Kilm) 1681–91; held also by faculty V Kildallon (Kilm) 1684–91. There seems to be some uncertainty about his surname. The F.F. Return seemed to read "Sams" or "Sames". Mr Reynell reads "Sands", while in the list of those who signed the address to James II, 18 Mar 1684/85, it is "Aylott James"

SANDERS, FRANCIS ALEXANDER 1818–1892

b. 25 Aug 1818 Cork; ent TCD 16 Oct 1835 aged 17 BA & Div Test 1840 MA 1873

d 1843 p 1844 (Dublin); C Monkstown (Dub) 1843–45; C Castleknock (Dub) 1845–47; Asst Chapl The King's Hosp Dublin (Dub) 1847–49; C St Ann Dublin (Dub) 1849–54; R Castlemacadam (Glend) 1854–60; V Timolin (Glend) 1860–66; R Templeport (Kilm) 1866–77; R Killesherdoney (Kilm) 1877–92

> yst **s.** of William, *militaris*, of Charleville Co Cork
>
> **m.** 25 May 1848 Margaret Frances **dau.** of Robert Cooper of Dublin. Issue incl 1.

eldest son Frederick (**died** 11 Jun 1872 aged 21); 2. Margaret (**died** 22 Jul 1883) **b.** 10 Nov 1851; 3. William (**died** 3 Jul 1871 aged 17); 4. Francis Alexander; 5. Robert; 6. Penelope; 7. Maria; 8. Elizabeth Sarah; (order of birth uncertain)

Died 11 Dec 1892 aged 74

SANDFORD, DANIEL 1727/28–1770

b. 1727 or 1728; matric Oriel Coll Oxford 19 Mar 1745/46 aged 17 BA 1749 MA 1752

V Moydow (Ard) 17—?–70; signs Parliamentary Return for Moydow and Tashinny (Ard) 1766; Chanc of Cloyne 1767–70

s. of Thomas of Sandford Salop

m. (ML 29 Sep 1764) Sarah Chapone, Glasnevin Dublin. Issue a **s.** Daniel who was Bp of Edinburgh 1806–30

Died 1770

SANDFORD, GEORGE 1699/1700–1757

b. 1699 or 1700 Dublin; ed by Mr Sheridan; ent TCD 9 Jul 1716 aged 16 BA 1721 MA 1724

Dean of Ardagh 1749–57; pres to the Deanery 3 Nov (L.M. V. 129) and inst 21 Dec 1749 (F.F.)

s. of Henry of the family of Baron Mount Sandford

Died 31 Aug 1757 **bur.** Ballinter Co Meath

SANDFORD, THOMAS 1767/68–

b. 1767 or 1768 Co Galway; ed by Mr Ralph; ent TCD as Siz 20 May 1788 aged 20 BA 1792

C Innismagrath (Kilm) 1803

s. of Robert, *agricola*

SANDFORD, WILLIAM 1752–1809

b. 1752 Dublin; ed by Dr Norris; ent TCD 19 Jan 1771 BA 1774; 1st Baron Mount Sandford 1800

V Kilkeevan and Preb of Ballintubber (Elph) 1777–1809

2nd **s.** of William, *armiger*, of Castlerea Co Roscommon

m. 1789 Jane 2nd **dau.** of Rt Hon Silver Oliver of Co Limerick. Issue 1. Henry 2nd Baron Mount Sandford; 2. Mary Grey **m.** 1816 William Robert Wills of Willsgrove; 3. Eliza Catherine (**died** 27 Jul 1867) **m.** 15 Jan 1822 Very Rev Henry Pakenham (1787–1863) Dean of St Patrick's Cath Dublin 1843–63 and Dean of Christ Ch Cath Dublin 1846–63 and had issue (i) Henry Sandford **b.** 6 Feb 1823 (ii) William Sandford **b.** 10 Jan 1826 (iii) William Hamilton **b.** 14 Feb 1840 (iv) Caroline Eliza Catherine (v) Emily; 4. Louisa **m.** W W Newenham

Died 17 Aug 1809

SARCOTT, THOMAS

pres to R Kilronone = Kilronan (Ard) and to V Kilmony and Inishmcra = Innismagrath (Kilm) 13 Apr 1619 (L.M. V. 104)

SAUNDERSON, FRANCIS –1815

ent TCD 19 Mar 1754/55 Sch 1757 BA 1759 MA 1762

lic C Kildallon (Kilm) 26 Jun 1766; C Tomregan (Kilm) 1769; V Rossinver (Kilm) 1793–1815

> **Died** 1 Sep 1815

SAUNDERSON, FRANCIS 1786–1873

b. 1786 Co Cavan; ed by Mr Moon; ent TCD as SC 11 May 1803 aged 16 BA 1808 MA 1819

d 21 Sep 1810 p 25 Jul 1812; C Rower (Oss) 1810; Dean's V Chor St Canice's Cath Kilkenny (Oss) 1812–13; V Dunmore (Oss) 1812–19; R Knockbride (Kilm) 1819–28; V Kildallon (Kilm) 1828–73

> 2nd **s.** of Francis of Castle Saunderson, MP
>
> **m.** 3 May 1825 Lady Catherine Crichton (**died** 14 Oct 1860) **sister** of John 3rd Earl of Erne
>
> **Died** 22 Dec 1873 aged 87

SAUNDERSON, ROBERT 1762–1848

ed at an English School; ent TCD 3 Aug 1779 aged 16 BA 1788 MA 1809

lic C Rossinver (Kilm) 17 Aug 1796; lic C Kildrumferton (Kilm) 31 Oct 1799; V Seirkeiran (Oss) 1808–09; Preb of Tascoffin (Oss) 1809–48; R Borrisokane (Killaloe) 1809–48

> yr **s.** of Alexander of Castle Saunderson by Rose **dau.** of Trevor Lloyd
>
> **m.** a **dau.** of Capt John Johnston of Magheramena. Issue James of Villa Nova Co Monaghan **b.** Tipperary ent TCD 4 Nov 1816 aged 18
>
> **Died** 19 May 1848 aged 86

SAURIN, LEWIS –1749

prec Christ Ch Dublin; Dean of Ardagh 1726/27–49; pres to the Deanery 13 Mar 1726/27 (L.M. V. 124)

> **Died** 16 Sep 1749 **bur.** Sep 19 St Ann's Dublin

SCHOALES, GEORGE JOHNSTON 1814/15–

b. 1814 or 1815 Dublin; ent TCD 4 Jul 1831 aged 16 BA 1836

PC Derryheen (Kilm) 1862; seems to have vacated within a month

> prob same as George Schoales **s.** of John, *jurisconsult*

SCHOALES, JOHN WHITELAW 1820–1904

b. 1820 Dublin; ed by Mr Sargent; ent TCD 13 Oct 1837 aged 17 BA & Div Test 1845

d 1845 p 1846 (Meath); C Kilbarron (Raph) 1848; poss same as J W Schoales, SPG Missy in S Australia 1850–54; C Derrylane (Kilm) 1860–64; C Killeshandra (Kilm) 1861–64; PC Derrylane (Kilm) 1864–68; R Stratford-on-Slaney (Leigh) 1868–97; ret

s. of Alexander, Surgeon; **bro.** of Rev Peter Henry, PC Arvagh (Kilm) qv

m. and had issue incl 1. William Gordon (**died** 3 Feb 1875 aged 16); 2. Henry James (**died** 20 Apr 1891 aged 22; 3. a son **b.** 23 Jul 1871; 4. eldest **dau.** Elizabeth Alexandrina (**died** 22 Oct 1881)

Died 17 Feb 1904 aged 83

SCHOALES, PETER HENRY 1818–1891

b. 1818 Dublin; ed by Mr Simpson; ent TCD 1 Jul 1833 Vice Chancellor's Pri for English Verse 1843 & BA

d 1843 p 17 Dec 1843 (Kilmore); C Derrylane (Kilm) 1843–50; C Arvagh (Kilm) 1850–52; PC Omeath (Arm) 1852–53; PC Arvagh (Kilm) 1853–71; C St Audoen (Dub) 1873; C Clontarf (Dub) 1873–75; R Garvary (Clogh) 1876–91

s. of Alexander, Surgeon; **bro.** of John Whitelaw, PC Derrylane (Kilm) qv

m. Jessie Frances (**died** 21 Jan 1933 Bray Co Wicklow) **dau.** of Lt Col John Rowley Heyland, JP 7th RIF of Ballintemple Co Derry. Issue 3 **daus.** and 2 **sons** incl 1. Arthur; 2. a **dau.** b 7 Jan 1870; 3. William Reginald **b.** *c.* 1880

Died 26 Dec 1891 at Enniskillen aged 73

SCHULDHAM, FRANCIS 1667–1736

b. 1667; bapt 3 May 1667 at Walsingham Norfolk; ed Walsingham and Hold Schools; adm at Caius Coll Camb as Siz aged 16 matric 6 Mar 1682/83 Sch 1683–87 BA 1686/87

d 22 May 1687 (Lincoln); p 21 May 1692 (Norwich); C Horsham St Faith (Nor); V Kildrumferton (Kilm) 1701–30; R Killermogh and Kildelgy (Oss) 1710–30

s. of Lemuel, *armiger*, of Walsingham; evidently **bro.** of Rev Lemuel, Preb of Blackrath (Oss)

m. and had issue incl Mary **m.** (marriage settlements dated 22 Aug 1717) John Stephens of Ballinacargy Co Cavan, High Sheriff 1729, Capt Cavan Militia "Butler's Horse"

Died 1736

SCOTT, ALEXANDER WOODSIDE 1912–1977

b. 5 Aug 1912 Ardkeen Rectory Co Down; ed Regent Hse Sch Newtownards; TCD BA 1944 Div Test 1945 MA 1953

d 1945 p 1946 (Connor); C St Paul Belfast (Conn) 1945–54; R Arvagh w Carrigallen and Gowna (Kilm) 1954–77; Preb of Drumlease (Kilm) 1973–77

s. of Rev Joseph Henry Howard, C Urney and Annagelliffe (Kilm) qv (**s.** of

Thomas) by Jane Gilmer Hill

m. Joan…Issue 1. John Henry Alexander bapt 1 Aug 1954; 2. Peter; 3. Patricia J bapt 5 May 1957

Died 7 Oct 1977 in Dublin **bur.** Ardkeen Co Down

SCOTT, BARLOW 1698/99–c. 1776

b. 1698 or 1699 Brough Co Monaghan; ed by Mr McMahon, Monaghan; ent TCD 7 Nov 1717 aged 18 BA 1722

lic C Killesher (Kilm) 7 Sep 1730; R Knockbride (Kilm) 1739–c74

s. of George of Brough Co Monaghan, High Sheriff Co Monaghan 1704 by Jane **dau.** of Rev Ralph Barlow, R Kilmore (Clogh)

Died *c.* 1776; Will dated 17 Oct 1776

SCOTT, HENRY GORDON WALLER 1868–1951

b. 24 Sep 1868; TCD BA 1894 Div Test 1895 MA 1899

d 1895 p 1896 (Kilmore); C Kilkeevan (Elph) 1895–96; R Brantry (Arm) 1896–1903; R Creggan (Arm) 1903–08; R Tullaniskin (Arm) 1908–26; R Clonfeacle (Arm) 1926–39; ret

s. of William, MD of Aughnacloy Co Tyrone, JP for Co Tyrone by Anne Atkinson eldest **dau.** of Rev Charles Crossle, R Kilcluney (Arm) 1872–76

m. 6 Jun 1901 Tillie Evelyn Morgan (**died** 30 Dec 1976 aged 97 **bur.** Brantry) 2nd **dau.** of Gordon Holmes of Dellin Hse Co Louth. Issue 1. Kathleen Holmes (**died** 20 Apr 1988) **b.** 7 Mar 1902 **m.** 26 May 1925 Rev James Joseph McClure (1896–1952), R Dundalk (Arm) 1939–52 and had issue Helen Scott (**died** 10 Mar 1976 Dublin) **b.** 16 Sep 1927; 2. Gordon Waller; 3. Rev William Atkinson d 1928 (Dio Waikato) p C-in-c Uruti (Waikato) NZ; 4. Donald **b.** 6 Jun 1908

Died 4 May 1951 **bur.** Brantry

SCOTT, JOSEPH HENRY HOWARD 1873/74–1930

b. 1873 or 1874 Co Down; ed at Belfast; ent TCD 25 Jan 1898 aged 24 BA 1901 Div Test 1902 MA 1918

d 1902 p 1903; C Urney & Annagelliffe (Kilm) 1902–03; C Ballynure and Ballyeaston (Conn) 1905–11; R Ardkeen (Down) 1911–30

s. of Thomas

m. 20 Sep 1911 at Ballynure Co Antrim Jane Gilmer Hill (**died** 26 Sep 1973 **bur.** Ardkeen) **dau.** of Alexander Woodside of Ballymena. Issue Rev Alexander Woodside, Rarvagh and Carrigallen (Kilm) qv

Died 26 Jan 1930

SCOTT, LESTER DESMOND DONALD

NUI BA 1989 CITC BTh 1992

d 1992 p 1993; C Kilmore Ballintemple Killeshandra Killegar and Derrylane (Kilm)

1992–95; R Fenagh w Myshall Aghade and Ardoyne (Leigh) 1995–

SCOTT, WILLIAM –1897

d 1857 p 1858 (Kilmore); C Killinkere (Kilm) 1857–61; C Castleterra (Kilm) 1861–62; PC Kiltyclogher (Kilm) 1862–73; R Kiltyclogher and Ballaghmeehan (Kilm) 1873–97

Died 23 Apr 1897

SEABROOKE, GILBERT

Broadgate Hall (ie. Worcester Coll) Oxford MA

d & p 19 Dec 1619; Preb of Tibohine (Elph) 1628–*c.* 62; V Ahascragh (Elph) 1628; pres V Killeroran or Kilronan (Elph) 15 Aug 1628; Chapl to the Lord Chancellor and V Athleague and Fuerty (Elph) 1629–?62; said in R.V. to be "a good Divine and a good preacher"

SEELY, NESBITT 1742–1806

b. 1742 Co Leitrim; ed by Mr Kerr; ent TCD as Siz 15 Jun 1756 aged 14 Sch 1759 BA 1760

appears C Killesher (Kilm) 1765; still there 1773; V Killargue (Kilm) 1780–96; V Innismagrath (Kilm) 1796–1806

s. of James by Anne **dau.** of John Nesbitt of Dromod Co Leitrim

m. Margaret widow of Bourchier Molesworth of St Thomas's Dublin (**died** 8 Nov 1785)

Died 10 Mar 1806 aged 63 **bur.** Coolock Churchyard Dublin

SERGEANT (SARGENT), ROBERT 1783–

b. 1783 Co Derry; ed by Mr Knox; ent TCD 2 Nov 1804 aged 21¾ BA 1809

d 1809 (Kilmore) p; C Lurgan and Munterconnaught before 1817 to c25

s. of William

Rev Robert Sargent of Iter Co Cavan **m.** 20 Feb 1841 Caroline Hyde only **dau.** of Henry Clarke, late of London; as his widow, she remarried 3 Oct 1866 Alexander, MD, only **s.** of John Johnston of Belfast Bank, Monaghan

SETON, ALEXANDER

MA perhaps of Edinburgh

R & V Castleblakeney (Elph) 1765–80; C Roscommon (Elph) 1784

SEYMOUR, CHARLES 1759/60–1834

b. 1759 or 1760 Galway; ed by Mr Hacket; ent TCD 6 May 1776 aged 16 BA 1780 MA 1788

Preb of Kilmovee (Ach) 1794–1811; C Ardcarne (Elph) *c.* 1810; V Kilbryan (Elph)

1813–25; R Ballinakill and Omey (Tuam) 1820–22; PC Louisburgh (Tuam) 1822–28; C Aglish = Castlebar (Tuam) 1828–29; R Kilronan (Ard) 1829–34

s. of Joseph by Susanna **dau.** of A Thomas.

m… Issue incl 1. Rev Joseph (**died** 7 Sep 1850 aged 63) **b.** Co Mayo ent TCD 1804 aged 17 BA 1809 Preb of Kilmovee (Ach) 1811–50 **m.** (i) Fanny Hill **m.** (2) Maria **dau.** of Robert Seymour **m.** (3) Mary Sandford and had issue by one of these wives incl (i) Very Rev Charles Henry, Dean of Tuam (ii) Rev William Francis who was father of Ven St John Drelincourt Seymour, Litt D, R Cahernarry (Lim) and author of Cashel and Emly Diocesan Succession Lists and (iii) George; 2. John **b.** Co Galway ent TCD 1836 aged 16 BA 1842; 3. William Digby **b.** Co Galway ent TCD 1838 aged 16 BA 1844 County Court Judge of Galway, Recorder of Newcastle 1854–95 **died** 16 Mar 1895; 4. Rev Benjamin **b.** Co Roscommon ent TCD 1846 BA 1851 **died** 1855 aged 26; 5. Susanna **m.** Henry Thomas Eagar and had issue (i) Rev Edward Charles Eagar qv (ii) Rev Joseph Eagar (iii) Emily **m.** Rev WB Fry

Died 1834

A.J. Seymour published *Reminiscences of Rev. Charles Seymour of Connaught,* Hodges and Figgis 1895 — copy in RCB Library

SEYMOUR, MICHAEL HOBART 1798/99–1874

b. 1798 or 1799 Limerick; ed by Mr White; ent TCD 7 Jul 1817 aged 18 BA 1823 MA 1832; *ad eund* Ox 1836

d 1825 p 1826; C Killenumery (Ard) *c.* 1827; Sec to Irish Protestant Association 1834–44

PUBLICATIONS
A Pilgrimage to Rome, 1849
Mornings among the Jesuits in Rome, 1850
Certainty Unattainable in the Church of Rome, 1852

SHARPE, HENRY 1596/97–

b. 1596 or 1597; possibly the Henry Sharpe a clergyman's son **b.** in Northamptonshire; matric Balliol Coll Oxford 10 Nov1615 aged 18 BA 1619;

d and p 5 May 1623; Archd of Achonry 1625; pres by the Crown Archd of Dromore 21 Jun 1625; Archd of Dromore 1625–29; V Kilbryan (Elph) to 1640; V Kilkeevan (Elph) to 1640; Preb of Ballintubber (Elph) 1628–c62; "A good divine and a good preacher" (Cotton, iv, 147)

SHARPE, THOMAS GORDON 1885–1966

b. 5 Sep 1885; ed The King's Hosp Dublin; TCD BA 1906 Div Test 1907 MA 1909

d 1908 p 1910; C Boyle (Elph) 1908–12; C Layde (Conn) 1913–16; R Ardclinis (Conn) 1916–24; TCF 1918–19; Hon CF 1919; R Layde and Cushendun 1924–61; RD of Carey 1943–61; Canon of St Anne's Cath Belfast 1945–61; ret

s. of Frederick of Navan Co Meath and Dublin by Mary Jane **dau.** of Samuel Hill

m. Martha Christian Caroline **dau.** of Robert and Elizabeth Sandes

Died 7 Jun 1966 Greenisland Co Antrim

SHAW, FIELDING 1658/59–1729

b. 1658 or 1659 near Chester; ed by Mr Rashley; ent TCD as Siz 14 Jul 1676 aged 17 Sch 1679 BA 1681 MA 1684 BD & DD 1701

d 14 Aug 1681 (Clonfert) p 20 Sep 1685 (Clonfert); V Killyon (Elph) 1685–1701; V Ahascragh Disert Camma Kiltoom Racharow and Lissanuffy (w Tessaragh & Taghboy to 1718) (Elph) 1685–1729; C Galway 1687– there 1693; R & V Athenry (Tuam) 1688–1729; V Kilscobe (Tuam) 1698–1719; V Annaghdown (Tuam) 1698–1725; R & V Kilkerrin (Tuam) 1698–1729; Preb of Taghsaxon (Tuam) 1698–1729

s. of John

m. and had issue incl **sons** 1. Fielding **b.** Galway ent TCD 9 Mar 1704 aged 16 BA 1709 MA 1713 **m.** and had issue incl Rev Theophilus (**died** Sep 1758 Galway); 2. Rev Merrick (**died** 1759) **b.** Galway ent TCD 12 Jul 1710 aged 17 BA 1714 MA 1717 Preb of Taghsaxon (Tuam) & R Athenry (Tuam) 1730–59; 3. Rev Robert (**died** 21 Sep 1752) **b.** Galway ent TCD 28 Jan 1714/15 Sch 1717 BA 1719 FTCD 1722 BD 1730 DD 1734 Abp King's Lecturer 1730 Prof of Oratory and History 1734 Prof of Laws 1740 Vice Provost R Ardstraw (Derry) 1734–52; **daus.** 1. Anne **m.** Ven John Vesey, Archd of Kilfenora; 2 Latlie **m.** 29 Sep 1710 Capt Abraham Ould who was assassinated in London *c.* 1715 and had issue a **s.** Fielding

Died 1729

SHAW, GEORGE 1802/03–1864

b. 1802 or 1803 Co Down; ed by Mr O'Beirne; ent TCD 2 Nov 1818 aged 15 BA 1824 MA 1832

d; p 7 Sep 1827; C Donadea (Kild) 1827–; C Clonbroney and Annaduff (Ard) 1827–38; V Annaduff (Ard) 1838–64

s. of Nathaniel

Died 11 Sep 1864 at Marino Lodge, Killiney Co Dublin

PUBLICATION

A Sermon entitled *Hold fast that which thou hast,* preached at Visitation of Ardagh in Longford Church 28 Sep 1848, Carson, Dublin 1849

SHAW, MATTHEW JAMES 1795/96–1882

b. 1795 or 1796 Derry; ed by Mr Knox Foyle Coll Londonderry; ent TCD as a Presbyterian 7 Nov 1814 aged 18 BA 1819 MA

C Killukin Toomna and Creeve (Elph) 1822–23; V Kilmactranny Shancoe and Kilcredan ? = Killadoon (Elph) 1823–29; he was the victim of an outrage in Oct 1829 which caused him to resign the living; afterwards Chapl to Lord Lorton

s. of Matthew of Derry

m. 23 Aug 1839 Lucinda 2nd **dau.** of R K Duke of New Park Co Sligo. Issue incl 1. Matthew, TCD BA 1845; 2. Rev Robert James (**died** 19 Jul 1908) who took the additional name of Hamilton **b.** *c.* 1840 TCD BA 1862 Div Test (1) 1863 MA 1871 BD 1884 DD 1890 d 1863 p 1864 C Aghavea (Clogh) 1863–67 C Armagh (Arm) 1867–73 V Drumcar (Arm) 1873–86 Preb of Mullabrack (Arm) 1883–90 R Tynan (Arm) 1886–1900 Chanc of Armagh 1890–1900 Dean of Armagh 1900–08 **m.** 6 Feb 1873 Mary Jane Hamilton (**died** 1 Jun 1919) **dau.** of Robert Cope Hardy of Armagh and had issue (i) Warham Jemmett (**died** 1 Jul 1931) **b.** 1874 **m.** 4 Jun 1901 Alice Beatrice and had issue; (ii) Robert Cope Hardy; (iii) Isabella **m.** Benjamin Banks Ferrar and had issue incl Rev Michael Lloyd (1909–60), Warden of the Divinity Hostel, Dublin 3. Elizabeth **m.** 22 Sep 1880 William R Wynne of Dowth Co Meath; 4. Warham Jemmett **died** 4 Mar 1862 aged 15

Died 8 Jul 1882 Dublin aged 86

SHAW, WILLIAM ARTHUR 1866/67–1947

b. 1866 or 1867; TCD Div Test (2) 1896 BA 1897 MA 1908

d 1894 p 1895 (Kilmore); C Billis (Kilm) 1894–97; R Billis (Kilm) 1897–1901; SPG Missy (DU to Fuh Kien) Hazaribagh India 1901–04; Ranchi 1904–08; C Enniskillen (Clogh) 1908–11; C Kilkenny and Precentor's V Chor Kilkenny Cath (Oss) 1911–12; C St John Kilkenny (Oss) 1912–15; Minor Canon of Kilkenny Cath 1913–18; R Aghade (Leigh) 1918–41; RD of Aghade 1925–33; RD of Carlow 1933–41; Preb of Tullamagimma in Leighlin Cath 1933–39; Preb of Blackrath in Kilkenny Cath 1934–41; Treas of Leighlin 1939–40; Chanc of Leighlin 1940–41

Died 6 Dec 1947 aged 80

Editor *Ossory Diocesan Magazine*

SHEA, EDWARD LEATHLEY 1840/41–1910

b. 1840 or 1841; TCD BA 1863 Div Test 1864

d 1865 p 1867 (Tuam); C Omey (Tuam) 1865–66; C Spiddal (Tuam) 1866–69; C Ballyovie (Tuam) 1869–78; R Killenvoy (Elph) 1878–1908; Preb of Ballintubber (Elph) 1890–1910; ret 1908 retaining his Canonry

m. Sarah (**died** 20 Jul 1922 Blackrock). Issue 1. Thomas, Major R A Vet Corps **m.** 1936 Ursula Gladwyn yst **dau.** of P L Barker of London SW1; 2. Alice A (**died** 28 Apr 1952 in Cornwall) **m.** Rev John Bourne, RN; 3. Emily Martha **b.** 1871 or 1872; 4. Frances Desterre **m.** 26 Jul 1921 Thomas Richardson eldest **s.** of W S Hepple of Ballycarney

Died 5 Jul 1910 aged 69

SHEA, JOHN 1802/03–1865

b. 1802 or 1803 Dublin; ed by Mr Cotton; ent TCD 18 Oct 1819 aged 16 BA 1825 MA 1832

C Abbeylara (Ard) *c.* 1826; R Abbeylara (Ard) 1832–65

s. of John.

m. Martha (née Ford) **died** 7 Jun 1849. Issue Elizabeth Mary **died** 24 Jun 1849; ? Arabella Henrietta (**died** 29 Mar 1877) **m.** Rev C B Campbell of Omey

Died 1865

SHEARMAN, JOSIAH FRANCIS 1884/85–1923

b. 1884 or 1885; ed RBAI; RUI BA 1905; TCD Abp King's Pri 1906 Div Test (1) and Warren Pri 1907

d 1907 p 1908 (Kilm); C Templemichael (Ard) 1907–12; C Clontarf (Dub) 1912–23

s. of Rev Josiah Nicholson, R St Matthew Belfast (Conn) 1891–1915 (s. of Josiah Coleman of Grange Hse Waterford) by Susan Mary (**died** 20 Sep 1923) **dau.** of John Hilliard Lawlor and Catherine **dau.** of Lt Col John Elliott Cairnes.

Died 2 Dec 1923 aged 38

SHEPHERD, J

appears C Clongish (Ard) 1846

SHEPHERD (SHEPPARD), WILLIAM 1811–1856

b. 1 Dec 1811 Co Tipperary; ent TCD 20 Oct 1828 aged 16 BA 1833; ent King's Inns Dublin 1833; was Barrister-at-Law before ordination

C Killesher (Kilm) 1846–53; V Kilgeffin (Elph) 1853–56

s. of James Capt in Tipperary Militia by Mary **dau.** of Thomas Dolan

m. Bithia **dau.** of Leonard Watson of Warrenpoint Co Down and had issue incl 1. William Harry Cope (**died** 1909); 2. Bithia Mary m. 16 Nov 1871 Lt Col John Croker, Royal Scots, authoress of *Pretty Miss Neville* and *Diana Barrington*; 3. Beatrice (**died** 20 Oct 1920) m. 16 Nov 1871 at Rathangan Lt Col J Croker s. of Henry of Drumkeen and had issue a **dau.**

Died 1856

SHEPPARD, HENRY DROUGHT 1823/24–1892

b. 1823 or 1824 Co Clare; entTCD 1 Jul 1847 aged 23 BA (Resp) 1853 Abp King's Div Pri (2) 1855 MA & Div Test (1) 1856 BD & DD 1872 MB BCh & MD 1877

d 1857 p 1858 (St. David's); C Swansea (S & B — then St D) 1857–58; Lect Stockport Great Moor (Ches) 1858–59; served in British Columbia 1859–60; Dep Sec Claremont Deaf and Dumb Inst 1860–62; C St Luke Manchester (Manch) 1862–63; C Stockport Great Moor (Ches) 1863–64; PC Cloughjordan (Killaloe) 1865–67; Dep Sec CCCS 1868–70; R Christ Ch Belfast (Conn) 1871–74; R St Peter Wallingford (Ox) 1878–81; R Knockbride (Kilm) 1888–89; I Free Ch Dublin (Dub) 1890–92

s. of Henry

m. (1) 1853 Cecilia Graham otherwise Wilkinson

m. (2) 15 May 1888 St Mary's Donnybrook Dublin Louisa Julia widow of Robert Stanley of Dublin

Died 27 Jul 1892

PUBLICATION

Memorabilia of the Rev H D Sheppard, Charles St., Dublin, Dublin 1892

SHEPPARD, WILLIAM
C Killesher (Kilm) 1846–53

SHERIDAN, ANTHONY *c.* 1686–
b *c.* 1686 Cavan; ed by Mr Griffin, Longford; ent TCD as Siz 1 Jan 1704/05 aged 18 Sch 1708 BA 1709
C Killinkere (Kilm) 1742; ordered to get church repaired, Triennial Visitation, 24 Sep 1742; his house at Shercock Co Cavan was broken into and robbed 15 Dec 1741
>**s.** of Patrick, *colonus*

SHERIDAN, ANTHONY
is C Lavey (Kilm) 1754

SHERIDAN (O'SHERIDAN, O'SYREDEN, O'SURADEN), DENIS
had been RC and was the friend and protector of Bp Bedell, qv who had been the means of his conversion during the 1641 rebellion; was ancestor of Richard Brinsley Sheridan and of the Marquess of Dufferin
d 10 Jun 1634 p; V Killesher (Kilm) 1634–83; V Drung and Larah (Kilm) 1645–61
>**m.** and had issue 1. Rt Rev William, Bp of Kilmore qv; 2. Rt Rev Patrick (**died** 22 Nov 1682) FTCD and Vice–Provost TCD Bp of Cloyne 1679–82; 3. Thomas TCD BA 1664 FTCD 1667 FRS 1679 Chief Sec for Ireland 1687/88; 4. James ent TCD as Siz 11 May 1665 aged 16 Sch 1665

SHERIDAN, DENIS
was Commonwealth Minister at Carrigallen (Kilm) from 25 Mar 1657 at £60; transferred to Athlone (Seymour's Commonwealth MSS)

†SHERIDAN, WILLIAM 1634/35–1711
b. 1634 or 1635 Togher Co Cavan; ed by Mr Sheridan, Mr Bedlow and Mr Wilson; ent TCD as SC 15 May 1652 aged 17 DD 1682; R Drakestown and Telltown (Meath) 1660; V Donaghpatrick (Meath) 1660–77; R Drung Larah and Lavey (Kilm) 1662–82; R Athenry (Tuam) 1666–82; Bp of Kilmore and Ardagh 1682–92; consec in Christ Ch Cath Dublin 19 Feb 1682; he refused to take the oath of William and Mary and was deprived as a non–juror in 1692
>eldest **s.** of Rev Denis (of an R C family that befriended Bp Bedell); **bro.** of Patrick, FTCD Bp of Cloyne 1679–82; **bro.** of William, FRS who was Sec of State to James II
>**Died** 3 Oct 1711 London **bur.** Fulham

SHERWOOD, NIGEL JOHN WESLEY 1958–
b. 1958; ed The King's Hospital Dublin; TCD DipTheol 1986
d 1986 p 1987 (Kilmore); C Kilmore Ballintemple Kildallon Newtowngore &

Corrawallen (Kilm) 1986–89; R Tullow G (Leigh) 1989–95; R Arklow G (Glend) 1995–

s. of John Wesley and Patricia Susan (née Plunkett) of Rathangan Co Kildare

m. 4 Sep 1987 St Canice's Cath Kilkenny Carol Elizabeth dau. of James William and Rebecca Elizabeth Skuce of Ballydehob Co Cork. Issue 1. Adam James Wesley b. 19 Jun 1988; 2. Robin Nigel Stephen b. 29 Jan 1990; 3. Peter John Samuel b. 6 Jul 1997

SHIRE, HENRY WILLIAM –1971

RUI BA 1904 Div Test (2) 1907

d 1907 (Kilm) p 1908 (Down); C Killesher (Kilm) 1907–08; C Aghalee (Drom) 1908–13; R Swanlinbar (Kilm) 1913–24; R Cloonclare (Kilm) 1924–28; R Urney Annagelliffe Denn & Derryheen (w C-in-c Ballintemple 1947–50 and C-in-c Castletarra 1947–65) and C-in-c Drung 1958–60 (Kilm) 1928–65; Preb of Triburnia (Kilm) 1935–43; RD of N Kilmore 1942–43; Archd of Kilmore 1943–65; ret

s. of Adam of Ardnacrusha Co Limerick by Jane dau. of James Smyth Kilcornan Co Limerick

m. 22 Oct 1913 Castletown Ch Kilcornan Sarah (died 12 Aug 1936) dau. of William Smyth of Pallaskenry Co Limerick. Issue incl 1. Rev William Stanley b. 28 Mar 1917 Swanlinbar Co Cavan TCD BA & Div Test 1939 MA 1943 d 1940 p 1941 (Armagh) C Dundalk (Arm) 1940–43 C St Mark Portadown (Arm) 1943–45 C-in-c Mullaglass 1945–51 & R Mullaglass (Arm) 1951–57 C Attenborough Bramcote and Chilwell (S'well) 1957–58 V Lowdham and Gunthorpe (S'well) 1958–66 R Pilton and Wadenhoe and Stoke Doyle (Pet) 1967–70 R Aldwinche w Thorpe Achurch, Pilton and Wadenhoe (Pet) 1970–82 ret Lic to Off Dio Peterborough 1982–85 Perm to Off Dio Peterborough from 1985 m. 17 Dec 1958 Bramcote Ch Audrey Wilson dau. of William Wilson Seaton of Bramcote and had issue (i) Christine Mary Elizabeth b. 22 Nov 1959 (ii) Judith Sarah b. 18 May 1963 m… Dunkley; 2. George

Died 10 Sep 1971

SHIRLEY, PAUL WILLIAM NASSAU 1869–1954

b. 12 Jul 1869; ed Kilkenny; TCD Bp Forster's Pri (1) 1893 Div Comp Pri 1893–1894 BA & Div Test (2) 1894 BD 1909; Emmanuel Coll Saskatchewan BD (*ad eund*) 1922

d 1894 p 1895 (Down); C Ballymacarrett Belfast (Down) 1894–95; C St George Belfast (Conn) 1895–96; C Croxley Green Herts (St A) 1896–99; C W Grinstead Sussex (Chich) 1899–1903; C Clonbroney w Killoe (Ard) 1903–04; Min Canon and Res Pr Down Cath 1904–11; R Ballee (Down) 1905–11; R Glynn (Conn) 1911–20; TCF 1916–19; Hon CF 1919; Hon Assoc of Order of St John of Jerusalem 1919; Chapl 1920; R St James' Belfast (Conn) 1920–41; Chapl Stranmillis Training Coll Belfast 1925–31; Prec of Connor 1930–31; Exam Chapl to Bp of Down Dromore and Connor 1930; Archd of Connor 1931–41; ret

s. of Thomas of Clogrenane Co Carlow (s. of Paul, Capt Carlow Yeomanry) by Mary dau. of Thomas Jeffares of Kilmeaney Co Carlow

m. 26 Apr 1896 Jane Eugenie Josephine **dau.** of Alexander Stewart Harrison of Dromore Co Down. Issue 1. Evelyn Philip Sewallis OBE Commissioner in Colonial Service, Lt Royal Irish Fusiliers **m.** 1930 Marion **dau.** of Col Powell, Indian Army; 2. Mary Kathleen Stuart **m.** 1919 Rev Charles Scott Little, Sen CF **s.** of Rev C E Little, Canon of Durham

Died 19 Jul 1954

PUBLICATION
Compiler *Stretching Forward*

†SHONE, SAMUEL 1820–1901

b. 1820 Galway; ed by Mr Twinam; ent TCD 2 Jul 1838 aged 17 Heb Pri 1842–43 BA & Div Test (2) 1843 MA 1857 BD & DD 1884

d 1843 p 1844 (Down) Bp 1884; C Rathlin (Conn) 1843–46; C St John Sligo (Elph) 1846–56; R Calry (Elph) 1856–66; R Urney & Annagelliffe (Kilm) 1866–84; Archd of Kilmore 1878–84; elected by the united Synods Bp of Kilmore Elphin and Ardagh 26 Mar 1884; consec 25 Apr 1884 Christ Ch Cath Dublin; Bp of Kilmore Elphin and Ardagh 1884–97; ret

yst **s.** of Samuel by Margaret eldest **dau.** of William Tynte Austen of The Grange Fermoy Co Cork

m. 24 Jan 1872 St Peter's Par Ch Dublin Selina Elizabeth Prior (**died** 6 Mar 1926) eldest **dau.** of Rev William Prior Moore MA, Head Master of the Royal Sch Cavan

Died s. p. 5 Oct 1901 aged 80 at Monkstown Co Dublin **bur.** Dean's Grange

SHORTEN, FREDERICK WILLIAM 1877/78–1947

b. 1877 or 1878; RUI BA 1902

d 1905 p 1906 (Down); C Ballee and Down Cath (Down) 1905–11; C Clonenagh (Oss — then Leigh) 1911–15; R St John's Cloverhill (Kilm) 1915–30; R Kilbixy (w Almoritia to 1944 and w Leney and Stonehall from 1944) (Meath) 1930–47

yst **s.** of James & Sarah of Ballineen Co Cork

m. 8 Jul 1915 Edith Frances **dau.** of Mrs Cooper, Lacca Co Laois and granddau. of Lt Col Despard of Lacca Manor Mountrath

Died 23 Jan 1947 aged 69

SIDES, JAMES ROBERT 1937–

b. 21 Jul 1937 Carrickmore Co Tyrone; ed Campbell Coll Belfast; Belfast Coll of Technology ONC (Elec Eng); TCD BA 1966 Div Test 1967

d 25 Jun 1967 p 29 Jun 1968 (Down); C St Clement Belfast (Down) 1967–70; C Antrim (Conn) 1970–73; R Tomregan and Drumlane (Kilm) 1973–80; R Killesher (Kilm) 1980–97; Preb of Annagh (Kilm) 1989–; R Kildrumferton Ballymachugh and Ballyjamesduff 1997–2006; ret

s. of Rev Nathaniel St George, R Sixmilecross (Arm) 1939–52 (**s.** of Rev Canon John Robert, R Donaghmore (Arm) 1900–28) by his 2nd wife Olive Margaret **dau.** of William Silk of Hampstead London

m. 10 Aug 1968 St Fin Barre's Cath Cork Margaret Sheridan **dau.** of Rev George Henry Jerram Burrows and his wife Rachel Mary Le Fanu (née Dobbins), Head Master of the Grammar Sch Cork. Issue 1. Elizabeth Rachel **b.** 24 Nov 1970; 2. Patricia Sheridan **b.** 4 Jan 1973; 3. Philip John **b.** 3 Jan 1976

SIDLEY, HENRY FRANCIS de BURGH –1936
TCD BA 1879 MA & BD 1890 DD 1891

d 1879 p 1880; C Castlebar (Tuam) 1879–81; R Abbeylara (Ard) 1881–85; R Granard (Ard) 1885–1914; res and went to S Africa

s. of Rev Henry de Burgh, R Forgney (Meath) 1876–83 (s. of Henry)

m. (1) 25 Feb 1881 Catherine Mary **dau.** of Francis O'Donal of Castlebar Co Mayo

m. (2) 1927 Una N **dau.** of Rev JR Gumley, R Killadeas (Clogh)

Died 3 Jan 1936 at Johannesburg — his widow was still living in 1960

SIERS, WILLIAM –1924
ed Lichfield Coll 1875; St Bees Coll Durham 1888

d 1890 (Down) p 1892 (Kilmore); C St Patrick Newry (Drom) 1890–91; C Annagh (Kilm) 1891–94; R Newtowngore & Corawallen (Kilm) 1894–1923; C-in-c Morvah (Truro) 1923–24

m. Elizabeth (née Chapman) widow of Joseph Hogarth of West Drayton Middx

Died 1924 **bur.** 19 Aug at Morvah Cornwall

SINCLAIR, CHARLES 1859/60–1951
b. 1859 or 1860; TCD BA & Div Test 1890 MA 1895

d 1891 (Down for Meath) p 1891 (Armagh for Meath); C Clonfadforan (Meath) 1891–92; C St Paul Bournemouth (Win) 1892–95; R Ballysumaghan (Elph) 1895–1900; R Tomregan (Kilm) 1900–02; R Croghan (w Tibohine from 1924) (Elph) 1902–38; Preb of Oran (Elph) 1933–38; ret

m. and issue incl 1. Col C **m.** Sinclair **m.** Elsie Norma (**died** 6 Oct 1966); 2. Wilfred TCD MB (**died** 27 Jun 1934 Hexham Northumberland); 3. Rev Claude Edward Robert, C-in-c Ashfield (Kilm) qv

Died 17 May 1951 aged 91

SINCLAIR, CLAUD EDWARD ROBERT 1905/06–1966
b. 1905 or 1906; ed Portora Royal Sch Enniskillen; TCD BA 1927 Div Test 1928 MA 1931

d 1930 p 1931 (Rochester); C Bickley (Roch) 1930–32; C St Mary the Virgin E Grinstead (Chich) 1932–35; C-in-c Ashfield (Kilm) 1936–40; CF (EC) 1940–47; res; later took up teaching; became Coarse Angling organiser of Irish Inland Fisheries Trust

s. of Rev Charles, R Croaghan (Elph) qv

m. Elizabeth **dau.** of George Joseph Newman of Tunbridge Wells Kent

Died 16 Jun 1966

PUBLICATIONS
Books on Angling

SINCLAIR, RICHARD HARTLEY 1787/88–1838

b. 1787 or 1788; ent TCD 2 Nov 1804 aged 16 BA 1809

C Streete (Ard) 1811, lic 2 May; R Cashel (Ard) 1813–38

s. of Richard, Attorney

m. (1) 25 Jul 1822 St Peter's Ch Dublin Eliza 2nd **dau.** of Lt Col Peter Burrowes.

m. (2) it seems acc to Irish Ecclesiastical Gazette Aug 1859, Helen (**died** 19 Jul 1859 aged 53 at the Parsonage, St Mary Magdalene, Harlow, residence of her son-in-law Rev W R Scott)

SINGE, EDWARD

inst V Mostrim (Ard) 5 Aug 1634 (F.F.)

was perhaps Edward Synge afterwards Bp of Cork, but he would then be only 20 years old

SINGLETON, JOHN *c.* 1680–1736

b. *c.* 1680 Drogheda; ed by Mr Walker at Drogheda Gram Sch; ent TCD 4 Feb 1696/97 aged 16 Sch 1698 BA 1701 MA 1704

R Drumglass (Arm) 1709–20; R Drumgoon (Kilm) 1718–36; R Dromiskin (Arm) 1720–28; R Dunleer (Arm) 1727–36

s. of Edward; Leslie in *Armagh Clergy and Parishes* has him **s.** of Henry, who was in fact his brother

Died 1736 **unm.**

SINGLETON, RICHARD GRAEME FENTON   –1944

TCD Div Test 1896 BA 1897

d 1910 (Down) p 1912 (Kilmore); C Seapatrick (Drom) 1910–11; C Killeshandra (Kilm) 1911–13; R Gartree (Conn) 1913–42; ret

s. of Thomas French, MVO Asst Insp RIC

Died 11 Mar 1944

SINGLETON, ROWLAND

was pres to Ardbraccan (Meath) in 1704; was also (evidently in error, as the Crown had the last presentation to Lavey because of William Sheridan's, qv promotion to a Bishopric — and was not the regular Patron) presented to Lavey, but was not instituted, 1704

SIRR, JOHN MAURICE GLOVER 1942–

b. 1942; TCD BA (Heb and Oriental Langs) 1963 Div Test (2) 1965 Downes Comp Pri

d 1965 p 1966; C St Mary Belfast (Conn) 1965–68; C Finaghy (Conn) 1968–69; R Drumcliffe w Lissadell and Munninane (Elph) (w Ahamplish to *c.* 1976) 1969–87; Preb of Kilmacallen (Elph) 1981–87; Dean of Limerick and Ardfert (Lim) and R Limerick City 1987–; Chapl Limerick Prison 1987–

s. of Canon William James (1889–1984), R Ematris and Rockcorry (Clogh) 1937–67 (**s.** of William James of Newbliss Co Monaghan) by Adelaide Mary **dau.** of Charles Glover of Ballynoe Co Galway; **bro.** of Rev William James Douglas (1940–91) CF RAF

m. 21 Mar 1968 St Patrick Jordanstown Co Antrim Patricia Lennox. Issue Richard bapt 29 Aug 1971

SKEEN, SAMUEL SLINN 1838/39–1919

b. 1838 or 1839

d 1870 (Down for Derry) p 1879 (Kilmore); C Drumholm (Raph) 1870; C St Mark (Dub) 1872–75; R Gowna (Ard) 1879–80; C Fenagh (Leigh) 1880; R Ballyvaldon (Ferns) 1880–82; C All Hallows Bromley by Bow (Lon) 1882–83; C St Mark Walworth (Roch) 1883–85; C Hardingham (Nor) 1885–87; V Myton-on-Swale (York) 1887–1901; V Westerdale (York) 1901–04; V Laneham (S'well) 1904–18

m. and had issue 1. Rev Samuel Warren TCD BA 1893 MA 1898 V Deeping St James (Linc) 1898; 2. Rev George Sharp Queens Coll Camb BA 1892 MA 1896 V Haswell (Dur) from 1913; 3. Rev Frederick Norman St John's Coll Camb BA 1900 MA 1911 TCF 1917–19 CF Hon Canon of Guildford V Banstead (Guildf) from 1929; 4. Rev Claude Montague Benson St John's Coll Camb BA 1906 TCF 1916–17 V Dalby-on-the-Wolds (Linc); 5. Rev Robert Ernest Trinity Coll Camb BA 1903 MA 1906 late Chapl RN served in RASC and TCF 1915–16 V Sutton (St E); 6. Rev Arthur Percy Queen's Coll Camb BA 1904 TCF 1916–19 Hon CF R Hall U (Win); 7. Rev William Henry St John's Coll Camb BA 1893 MA 1897 one time Master at St Columba's Coll Dublin V St Michael Dalton (Liv) 1903–18; 8. a **s.** also in Holy Orders

Died 16 Dec 1919 at Sunderland aged 80

SKELLERN, HUGH –*c.* 1729

Jesus Coll Camb BA 1693/94; TCD MA *ad eund* Cantab 1701

V Killeshandra (Kilm) 1705–29

m. and had issue Hume **b.** Killeshandra ed by his father ent TCD 2 Feb 1721/22 aged 16

Died *c.* 1729; Will prov 1729

SKELTON, JAMES WATSON 1795/96–1875

b. 1795 or 1796 Co Down; ed by Mr Wilde; ent TCD 9 Apr 1821 aged 25 BA 1825 MA 1832 d 1832 p; C Newcastle (Drom) 1834 to at least 1837; C Loughinisland (Down) 1839; C Ballymascanlan (Arm) 1840; C Ballymachugh (Ard) 1844–48; C Kilclief (Down) 1848–60

> **s.** of Rev James, C Drumbo (Down) (**s.** of Francis, MD of Drogheda) by Frances **dau.** of James Watson of Brookhill Co Antrim
>
> **Died** 4 Apr 1875 at Kingsfield Cottage nr Downpatrick

SKELTON, THOMAS   1775–1846

b. 1775 Drogheda; ed by Dr Norris; ent TCD 29 Oct 1789 aged 14 Sch 1792 BA 1794

C Toem and Templeneiry (Cash) 1804; C Mealiffe (Cash) 1806; V Kildrumferton (Kilm) 1807–46

> **s.** of Francis, MD
>
> **m.** (ML 31 Aug 1808) Frances Anne yr **dau.** of John Richards of Dublin, Barrister-at-Law by Mary **dau.** of George Lendrum of Moorfield Co Tyrone. Issue incl **sons** 1. Francis Philip **b.** Co Cavan ent TCD 5 Jan 1829 aged 18; 2. Rev Thomas Watson, PC Ballyjamesduff (Kilm) qv; **daus.** 1…; 2. his 2nd **dau.** Frances Caroline **m.** 17 May 1844 Rev Christopher Graham; 3. his yst **dau.** Isabella **m.** 27 May 1857 Rev James Caulfield Willcocks, R Killan (Kilm) qv
>
> **Died** 3 Feb 1846 at Carrick Glebe Co Cavan aged 70

SKELTON, THOMAS WATSON   1820/21–1853

b. 1820 or 1821 Co Cavan; ed by Mr Sargent; ent TCD 5 Nov 1839 aged 18 BA 1844

PC Bllyjamesduff (Kilm) 1849–53

> **s.** of Rev Thomas, V Kildrumferton (Kilm) qv (**s.** of Francis) by Frances Anne **dau.** of John Richards of Dublin and Mary **dau.** of George Lendrum of Co Tyrone
>
> **m.** as her 2nd husband Mary **dau.** of Samuel Drapes, merchant of New Ross Co Wexford, **sister** of Rev John Lanphier Drapes; she **m.** (1) 13 Sep 1861 Rev James Cumine, PC Preban (Ferns)
>
> **Died** Apr or May 1853

SLACK, WILLIAM WYNNE   1909–1988

b. 1909; TCD BA (1cl Resp) 1935 MA 1939 Div Test (1) 1941 HDipEd 1953

d & p 1941 (Kilm); C Urney (Kilm) 1942–45; R Elphin G & Bumlin (w Croghan and Tibohine 1955–59) (Elph) 1945–82; Head Master Elphin Gram Sch 1945–76; Preb of Terebrine (Elph) 1947–82

> **m.** Florence (**died** 26 Apr 1992 aged 94)
>
> **Died** 13 Jul 1988

SLACKE, JAMES   –1634
MA

R & V Cleenish and R Enniskillen (Clogh) 1622–33; R & V Kinawley (Kilm) 1622–34; R & V Killesher (Kilm) 1626–34; got a grant of a glebe here 25 Jan 1626/27 (Morrin, III. 188); JP for Co. Fermanagh

>m. Martha (**died** 1653) **dau.** of Edward Hatton, Archd of Ardagh qv Issue **sons** 1. Rev Edward, R Cleenish (Clogh) 1633 R Killany (Clogh) to 1647; 2. James; 3. William; 4. George; **daus.** 1. Edith **m.** (1) Thomas Sugden of Lyssymeane Co Cavan; **m.** (2) John Browne and had issue Rev Nicholas, Preb of Kilskeery (Clogh); 2. Susanna; 3. Margaret

>**Died** 19 May 1634 **bur.** St Catherine's Dublin

SLACKE, WILLIAM JAMES 1818/19–1900

b. 1818 or 1819 Ballinamore Co Leitrim; ent TCD 5 Dec 1836 aged 17 BA 1842 MA 1859

d 1847 (Limerick) p 1848 (Kilmore); C Carrigallen (Kilm) 1847–56; PC Newtowngore (Kilm) 1856–70; R Newtowngore and Corawallen (Kilm) 1870–72; V Kildrumferton (Kilm) 1872–78; C-in-c Musbury (Manch) 1878–82; Chapl Northumberland County Asylum 1882–96; R Calton (Lich) 1896–1900

>**s.** of William

>**m.** 14 Dec 1848 Annie 2nd **dau.** of Thomas Slacke of Grenville St Dublin

>**Died** 1 May 1900 at Calton Vicarage, Staffs

SLATOR, WILLIAM THOMPSON HOWARD 1909–2003

b. 17 Nov 1909 Dublin; ed St Andrew's Coll Dublin; TCD BA & Div Test 1933 MA 1934

d 1933 p 1934; C Ballywillan (Conn) 1933–35; C-in-c Mullaghdun (Clogh) 1935–38; R Boyle (Elph) 1938–52; R Clonbroney Killoe and Columbkille (Ard) 1952–66; RD of Edgeworthstown 1958–66; RD of Fenagh 1967–81; R Kiltoghart Drumshambo Annaduff Toomna Kilmore and Kilronan (Ard) 1966–81; Preb of Kilcooley (Elph) 1966–81; ret

>**s.** of William Clement of Terenure Dublin (**s.** of William of Wicklow and Dublin and Dora (née Butler) of Dublin) by Mary **dau.** of Hugh Howard of Southport Lancs and Mary (née Eccles) of Southport

>**m.** 29 Sep 1936 Portrush Dorothy Lilian **dau.** of John McConaghy of Portrush and Lilian (née Wauchope) of Bailieborough Co Cavan. Issue Naomi Dorothy **b.** 11 Jan 1941 **m.** 5 Aug 1963 at Ballinasloe Co Galway Kenneth A **s.** of Edwin Maybury of Rathmines Dublin

>**Died** 22 Sep 2003

PUBLICATIONS
>*It Happened to me,* Leitrim Observer Books, 1973
>Poems published in *Church of Ireland Gazette*

SLOANE, ISAAC REBURN 1916–2005

b. 7 Mar 1916; ed Dundalk Gram Sch; TCD BA & Div Test 1941 MA 1960 d 15 Mar 1942 p 21 Mar 1943; C Kinawley (Kilm) 1942–44; R Gleneely and Culdaff (Raph — then Derry) 1944–54; R Baronscourt w Drumclamph and Clare (Derry) 1954–76; R Langfield Upr & Lr w Drumclamph and Clare (Derry) 1976–78; ret

> s. of Isaac and Jane
>
> m. 1945 Dublin Margaret **dau.** of Alexander and Jane Tully. Issue 1. Peter Alexander; 2. Mark David
>
> **Died** 17 Aug 2005

SMEDLEY, JONATHAN 1670/71–

b. 1670 or 1671 Dublin; ed by Mr Birkbeck; ent TCD 18 Sep 1689 aged 18 BA 1695 MA 1698

R & V Rincurran (Cork) 1709–20; R Ahascragh and Killasoolan = Castleblakeney (Elph) 1717–18; Dean of Killala 1718–24; V Knockmark (Meath) 1724; Dean of Clogher 1724–28. He resigned the Deanery of Clogher early in 1728 and went to Fort St. George, Madras on a clerical mission. While in Ireland he espoused the Whig cause and published various pamphlets and verses, *Gulliveriana* etc., and wrote against Swift and Pope

> **s.** of John

PUBLICATIONS

> *Concerning the Love of our Country,* Accession Sermon on Genesis xii, 1–3, 8vo, London 1715
>
> *The Original Freedom of Mankind,* A Sermon on the Irish Massacre, Deuteronomy xxx, 15, 4to 1715
>
> *The Obligation of an English Army to their King and Constitution in Church and State.* Sermon on I Peter ii, 17, preached on Prince George's birthday, 4to, London 1716
>
> *A Sermon* on I Samuel xii, 25, 8vo, 1716

SMITH (SMYTH), CHARLES 1800/01–1841

b. 1800 or 1801; evidently Charles Smyth TCD BA 1823

V Kilnamanagh (Elph) 1828–41; V Gen Elph

> **m.** and had issue incl 1. his eldest **dau.** Olivia **m.** Lucan Par Ch Co Dublin 31 Dec 1846 William Ewle of Tunbridge Wells Kent; 2 a **s. b.** posthumously 14 Jan 1842
>
> **Died** 3 Dec 1841 aged 40

SMITH, JAMES

C Kilcommick (Ard) *c.* 1778–84

SMITH, JAMES WILLIAM 1841–1927

b. 20 Aug 1841; ed Dr Flynn's Sch Harcourt St Dublin; TCD 1863; St Aidan's Coll Birkenhead 1866

d 20 Mar 1870 p 1873; C Bailieborough and Moybologue (Kilm) 1870–71; C

Templemore (Cash) 1871–72; C Crosspatrick (Ferns) 1872; C Dunganstown (Glend) 1873; C Clonmel (Lism) 1874; C Gorey (Ferns) 1874–75; C St Peter Drogheda (Arm) 1875; C Killinkere (Kilm) 1876–77; R Bourney (Killaloe) 1877–1902; Gen Lic Ossory Ferns and Leighlin 1902

    s. of William, Adjutant General's Dept, Royal Hosp Kilmainham Dublin by Eleanor Rebecca 3rd **dau.** of Capt L Rogers

    m. 31 Oct 1872 Mary Prudentia (**died** 27 Jun 1904) yst **dau.** of Edward Taylor of Tullow Co Carlow

    Died 26 Mar 1927

SMITH, JOHN

ord d 20 Apr 1623 (Kildare); adm Kildrumferton (Kilm) 31 Aug 1631; there was a curate in 1630, probably him

SMITH, JOHN

C Granard (Ard) 1622; "an Irish Curate, to read Irish hath £7. 10 per annum" (R.V.)

SMITH, JOHN   –1721

d 14 Apr 1672 p; C Carrickmacross (Clogh) 1674; C Clogher (Clogh) 1681–93; R Templecarne (Clogh) 1692–96; evidently same as John Smith, V Mohill (Ard) 1698; V Cloonclare (Kilm) 1698–1721; V Rossinver (Kilm) 1698–1721; R Inishmacsaint (Clogh) 1699–1721

    m. Katherine. Issue incl 1. Ralph; 2. his yst **dau.** Anna Maria

    Died 1721

SMITH, JOHN GEORGE 1871/72–1898

b. 1871 or 1872; TCD BA 1896

C Clongish (Ard) 1897–98

    Died 16 Mar 1898 aged 26

SMITH, NICHOLAS   –c. 1639

BA

"a minister of country birth"

appears R & V Castlerahan (Kilm) 1622; held also Kildrumferton (Kilm) 1622 and Killesherdoney (Kilm) c. 1622–26; got a grant of a glebe here 25 Jan 1626/27 (Morrin, III. 187); prob same as Nicholas Smith V Ratoath (Meath) 1603 and V Oldcastle and Donaghmore etc. (Meath) 1622

    Died c. 1639; Will of Nicholas Smith, Clk of Portnashangan proved in 1639

SMITH, PATRICK 1794/95–1836

b. 1794 or 1795 Dublin; ed by Mr White; ent TCD 4 Nov 1811 aged 16 BA 1817

C Knockbride (Kilm) *c.* 1825– still there in 1829; PC Nantenan (Lim)

s. of Moore, *causidicus*, BA Barrister-at-Law (**s.** of Patrick of Newcastle Co Meath) by Lucy **dau.** of Nicholas Moore of Mooremount Co Louth, High Sheriff 1724

m. 27 Feb 1829 St Peter's Par Ch Dublin Lalla Marcella (**died** 24 Jan 1842) of Dublin, widow of George O Bingham, Lt Royal Dublin Regt; Issue Moore Smith **m.** 11 Oct 1853 St Thomas' Ch Dublin Elizabeth **dau.** of Roger Casement of Ballymena Co Antrim. Lalla Marcella **m.** (3) 14 May 1839 Rathfarnham Ch Dublin Rev Thomas Scott, MA, C St Audoen Dublin (Dub)

Died 4 Oct 1836 of fever contracted in the course of his duties

SMITH, RICHARD 1806/07–1871

b. 1806 or 1807 Co Donegal; ed by Rev Mr Maturin; ent TCD 20 Jun 1832 aged 25 BA 1838

C Raymochy (Raph) 1838; C Tomregan (Kilm) 1840; C Conwall (Raph) 1843–62; R Killea (Raph) 1862–71

poss **s.** of Alexander, farmer

m. 1857 Mary Gore

Died 8 Nov 1871

PUBLICATION

Dr. Cahill's Letter to the Clergy of Raphoe Answered, Londonderry, 1854

SMITH, STUART 1805/06–1849

b. 1805 or 1806 Cavan; ed by Dr Moore; ent TCD 20 Oct 1823 aged 17 BA 1828 MA 1832

C Ballintemple (Kilm) 1831–47

s. of James, merchant

m. Henrietta. Issue **sons** 1. Capt William Graham, Bengal Army **m.** 28 Nov 1871 at Comber Lynne only **dau.** of George Allen of Co Down; 2. Robert; 3. Stewart; **daus.** 1. Mary; 2. Elizabeth

Died 15 May 1849

SMITH, WILLIAM

MA, C Granard (Ard) 1622; a preacher & hath £20 per annum (R.V.)

SMITH, WILLIAM

V of (Granard?) Ardagh to 1630

m. Sarah Perkins of Athboy (ML 19 Jun 1630)

SMITH, WILLIAM 1762/63–1835

b. 1762 or 1763 Co Tyrone; ed by Rev Mr Millar; ent TCD 24 May 1780 aged 17 BA 1785 d 18 Jul 1786 p 17 Dec 1788; C Boyle (Elph) 1790; C Killukin (Elph) 1796; Prec of Kilmacduagh 1797–1833; R Kilcorkey 1799–1820; V Aughrim (Elph) 1820–35; V Gen of Elphin

prob **s.** of James, *agricola*

m. (M L 17 Jul 1792) Anne (**died** 8 May 1839 at the Foundling Hosp Dublin aged 77) **dau.** of Richard Sheffield Cassan of Clontarf Dublin. Issue incl 1. Rev Rev Charles, Prec of Kilmacduagh; 2. George Hamilton, Lt RN (**died** 23 Dec 1845 aged 51) **m.** 21 Aug 1828 St George's Par Ch Dublin Jane eldest **dau.** of Rev Dr Black of Londonderry; 3. John Henry (**died** 5 May 1836 at Clonliffe Hse); 4. Rev William Radcliffe, C Kilmactranny (Elph) qv

Died 10 Mar 1835 Elphin

SMITH, WILLIAM

R & V Castlerahan (Kilm) 1740–*c.* 77

SMITH, WILLIAM

C Elphin (Elph) before 1806; there in 1830

SMITH, WILLIAM RADCLIFFE 1792/93–1858

b. 1792 or 1793 Co Roscommon; ed by his father; ent TCD 6 Jul 1807 aged 14 BA 1812 MA 1832

ord d for C Kilmactranny (Elph); afterwards C Kilmoremoy (Killala); C Aglish = Castlebar (Tuam) *c.* 1820–*c.* 26; C Kilcommom, Hollymount (Tuam) *c.* 1826; R Kilcommon, Hollymount (Tuam) 1826–58; according to Sirr *Life of Archbishop Trench* of Tuam, he was threatened with tuberculosis in 1835 and removed to Dublin and was temporary Chaplain of Steeven's Hospital in 1835 and afterwards Asst Chaplain of Molyneux Church. He evidently remained Rector of Hollymount, which was served by curates.

m. (1) Catherine (**died** 3 Feb 1844 at Rathmines Dublin). Issue incl 1. a **s.**; 2. John **m.** 9 Oct 1858 Jane only **dau.** of John H Smith, Solicitor of Elphin Co Roscommon; 3. his elder **dau.** Isabella **m.** 29 Jul 1840 William eldest **s.** of Samuel Sterne of Dublin.

m. (2) 7 Jun 1845 Emily 3rd **dau.** of Henry Haughton of Gardiner St Dublin

Died 2 Mar 1858 at Fountainbleau France

SMITH, WILLIAM WARNOCK 1858/59–1908

b. 1858 or 1859; ent TCD as Maths Siz 1879 BA 1883 MA 1898

d 1883 (Kilmore for Meath) p 1884 (Meath); C Tullamore (Meath) 1883–84; R St John's Cloverhill (Kilm) 1884–87; Principal of Albemarle Coll Beckenham Kent 1891–92; Principal of St Faughnan's Coll Roscarbery and Minor Canon of Ross 1892–1902; R Athnowen (Cork) 1902–03; I St John's Free Ch Cork (Cork) 1903–08; R Kilbrogan (Cloyne) 1908

Died 10 Nov 1908 aged 49

PUBLICATION
Questions on the Bible

SMULLEN, ALEXANDER 1811/12–1904

b. 1811 or 1812 Co Donegal; ed by Mr Bartley; ent TCD 7 Nov 1836 BA 1842 d 1842 p; C Cloone (Ard) 1843; C Shrule (Ard) 1844; lic C Granard (Ard) 12 Aug 1846 (S.R.); PC Ballaghmeehan (Kilm) 1857–73; R Innismagrath (Kilm) 1873–89

    s. of Robert, *agricola*

    m. and had issue incl his eldest **s.** Dr John Alexander (**died** 21 Dec 1929 at Drumkeeran

    Died 10 Sep 1904 aged 92 **bur.** Ballaghmeehan Churchyard

SMYTH, ALFRED VICTOR 1887–1974

b. 1 Dec 1887 Bandon Co Cork; ed privately; TCD BA 1910 Div Test 1911 MA 1919 d 1911 p 1912 (Kilm); C Urney and Annagelliffe (Kilm) 1911–14; C Nenagh w Kilruane and Monsea (Killaloe) 1914–20; C-in-c Corbally (Killaloe) 1920–26; R Seirkieran (Oss) and C-in-c Aghancon and Kilcolman (Killaloe) 1926–31; Preb of Tulloh (Killaloe) 1939–40; R Kilrush (w Kilfieragh from 1950) (Killaloe) 1945–63.Preb of Rath (Killaloe) 1945–48; Treas of Killaloe and Preb of Tulloh (Killaloe) 1948–63; last entry in C I Dir 1974

    s. of James of Cappa Hse Bandon Co Cork by Anne **dau.** of John Deane of Dunmanway Co Cork; **bro.** of Rev John, R Kilnamanagh (Ferns); **bro.** of Rev James, C-in-c Ardmore (Drom); **bro.** of Rev Joseph Jennings, V Balderstone (Manch); **bro.** of Rev Alexander, C-in-c Loughrea (Clonf) **m.** Elizabeth (**died** 9 Feb 1976 Cork).

    Died 12 Feb 1974 Cork

SMYTH, CECIL HERBERT 1915/16–1963

b. 1915 or 1916; TCD BA (Ment & Mor Sci Mod) 1939 Div Test 1940 MA 1951 d 1940 (Down) p 1941 (Down); C Clonallon (Drom) 1940–43; R Lissadell (Elph) 1943–46; C St Luke Tunbridge Wells (Roch) 1946–48; Chapl Kent and Sussex Hospitals 1946–50; V Bp Latimer Memorial Ch Birmingham (Birm) 1950–63; Chapl All SS Hosp Birmingham 1950–63

    m. Muriel Pilkington. Issue 1. Cynthia **b.** 1944; 2. Trevor **b.** 18 Nov 1945; 3. David

    Died 17 Sep 1963 aged 47 Birmingham

SMYTH, JOHN   –1754

MA

"Curate of Belturbet = Annagh (Kilm) and Chaplain to the Fort of Charlemont 29 years" to 1754

    Died April 1754

SMYTH, MICHAEL *c.* 1586–

b. *c.* 1586; St Catherine's Coll Camb BA 1608/09 MA 1612

d 17 Sep 1609 (Peterborough) p 23 Sep 1610; Preb of Termonbarry (Elph) 1627–36 coll 4 May 1627 and coll again 13 Oct 1637, though see Newman, William; Archd of Clonfert 1634–; Preb of Kilmeen (Tuam) 1639–

During the Rebellion of 1641 he stated that he was plunder of cattle and goods valued at £9,200 and saved his life by escaping to the fort of Galway. He was then aged 55

SMYTH, MICHAEL

V Killyon and Kilronan (Elph) 1832

> may be Rev Michael Smyth, **s.** of Rev Haddon, R Kilmore (Down), or it may be a misreading of the S.R. for Mitchell Smyth, TCD MA 1832

SMYTH, R ALLEN

d 1880 p; C Fenagh (Ard) 1880–81

SMYTH, THOMAS   1742–1831

b. 1742 Co Dublin; ed by Mr Ball; Clare Coll Camb BA 1764 (*ad eund*); TCD Matric 1757 MA 1767 LLB & LLD 1779

Treas St Patrick's Cath Dublin 1767–1831; R Delgany (Glend) 1766–88; Archd of Lismore 1788–1812; Preb of St John in Christ Ch Cath Dublin 1803–26; Preb of Kilrossanty in Dio Lismore 1810–12; R & V Annaduff (Ard) 1813–31

> **s.** of George, *causidicus*, afterwards Baron of Exchequer
>
> **m.** (1) (ML 8 Jan 1770) Alice **dau.** of Fairfax Mercer of Clea Co Down
>
> **m.** (2) Jun 1776 Alice (**died** 20 May 1827) widow of Robert Scott of Newry and sister of John Bowes Benson of Catherine's Grove Co Louth. Issue incl Harriet, 1. Harriet; 2. Catherine; 3. Lucy (**died** 16 Mar 1866 **m.** Rev Veitch Simpson, Preb of Killaraght (Ach) and had issue Alicia **m.** Henry Stewart eldest **s.** of Hon Sir Francis Burton of Carrigholt Castle Co Clare
>
> **Died** 30 Jan 1831 in Sackville St Dublin

†SMYTH, WILLIAM   1637/38–1699

b. 1637 or 1638 Lisburn Co Antrim; ed at Hillsborough; ent TCD 19 Nov 1656 aged 18 Sch and BA 1660 FTCD 1663 MA 1664 DD 1674

prob same as William Smyth, Preb of Lulliaghmore (Kild) 1661–82; V Ardnurcher (Meath) 1662–81; R Navan (Meath) 1671–81; Dean of Dromore 1673–81; R Ardsallagh 1674; R Balsoon 1675; V Donaghmore (Meath) 1677–81; V Athlumney (Meath) 1677; Bp of Killala and Achonry 1681; Bp of Raphoe 1681–93; Bp of Kilmore 1693–99

> eldest **s.** of Ralph of Ballymacash Co Antrim (of a Yorkshire family) by Alice **dau.** of Sir Robert Hawksworth
>
> **m.** 29 May 1672 St Michan Dublin Mary (**died** 1673 at Bordeaux) **dau.** of Sir

John Povey, Chief Justice King's Bench. Issue 1. Ralph; 2. Ven James, Archd of Meath; 3. William; 4. his eldest **dau.** Elizabeth (**died** 1706) **m.** 15 Feb 1696 as his 1st wife Edward Smyth, Bp of Down and Connor 1699–1720 and had issue (i) William bapt 28 Dec 1697 (ii) Edward ent TCD 13 Apr 1720 aged 16 BA 1727; 5. a **dau.**; 6. his yst **dau.** Alicia **m.** Rev John, Preb of Faldown (Tuam) 1731–62 **s.** of Very Rev Robert Echlin, Dean of Tuam and had issue incl (i) Francis bapt 8 Jul 1716 **bur.** 9 Jun 1717 (ii) Robert William **bur.** 3 Jun 1717 (iii) Arthur bapt 23 Sep 1725 and **daus.** (i) Mary (ii) Alicia (iii) Anne

Died 24 Feb 1699 **bur.** St Peter's Ch Dublin

SMYTHE, Rt Hon PHILIP SYDNEY, 4th VISCOUNT STRANGFORD 1715–1787

b. 14 Mar 1715; ent TCD 12 Oct 1733 BA 1736 LLD *(h.c.)* 1751

Preb of Killaspugmullane (Cork) 1743–52; Precentor of Elphin 1745–52; Dean of Derry 1752–69; R Maghera (Derry) 1769–87; Archd of Derry 1769–74; R Langfield (Derry) Jan–Jun 1775; pres to the Deanery of St Patrick's Cath Dublin 1746, but was not allowed possession as the Chapter claimed and proved its right of election

  m. 1741 Mary **dau.** of Anthony Jephson, MP of Mallow Castle. Isue Rev Lionel, 5th Viscount; 2. a **dau.**

  Died 29 Apr 1787 at Palmerstown Dublin; **bur.** beside his wife and **dau.** at Castleknock Dublin

SNEYD, NATHANIEL 1800/01–

b. 1800 or 1801 Somerset; ent TCD 5 Nov 1821 aged 20; Trinity Coll Camb Pensioner 21 Oct 1823

C Kildallon (Kilm) 1828

  poss **s.** of Rev William, V Lurgan (Kilm) qv

SNEYD, THOMAS 1733/34–1802

ent TCD 25 Oct 1750 aged 16 BA 1755 MA 1776

d; p 11 Jun 1758; C Tomregan (Kilm) 1756; C Ballintemple (Kilm) 1769 — still there 1777; he or another Thomas Sneyd, poss his son was licensed again as C Ballintemple 8 Apr 1778; R Knockbride (Kilm) 1775–1802

  prob **s.** Rev Thomas

  Died early in 1802

SNEYD, THOMAS 1753/54–1840

b. 1753 or 1754; ed by Mr White of Cavan; ent TCD 1 Nov 1768 BA 1773

d 1773 p 1774 (Kilmore); C Castlerahan (Kilm) 1774; poss T S who was lic C Ballintemple (Kilm) 1778; R Rossinver (Kilm) 1782–93; V Lavey (Kilm) 1793–1840

  prob **s.** of Rev Thomas, R Knockbride (Kilm) qv

  Died Jun 1840 aged 86 **bur.** St Michan's Dublin 10 Jun 1840

SNEYD, WETTENHALL 1678/79–1745

b. 1678 or 1679 Staffordshire; ed by Mr Evan Jones of Cork; ent TCD 29 Aug 1696 aged 17 BA 1699 MA 1703

V Killesherdoney (Kilm) 1710–40; R Castleterra (Kilm) 1740; V Urney & Annageliffe (Kilm) 1740–45; Archd of Kilmore 1740–45

2nd **s.** of William (2nd **s.** of William of Keel Staffs)

m. 6 Aug 1713 Kilmore Barbara **dau.** of Francis Marsh an Officer in the Guards **s.** of Francis, Bp of Kilmore qv). Issue 21 children incl 1. eldest **s.** Edward **m.** and had issue incl Nathaniel, MP for Cavan who was assassinated in Dublin 31 Jul 1833; 2. Jeremy; 3. Ralph; 4. Rev William, V Kinawley Derrylin (Kilm) qv; 5. John **b.** Cavan ent TCD 25 May 1737 aged 16

Died Sept 1745

SNEYD, WILLIAM 1714/15–

b. 1714 or 1715 Co Cavan; bapt 17 Mar 1714/15 at Kilmore; ed by Dr Clarke at Drogheda; ent TCD 30 Apr 1731 aged 16 Sch 1734 BA 1735 MA 1738

d 1739 Dunboyne (Meath for Kilmore) p 1739; C Ballintemple (Kilm) 1739–; Wm Sneyd, perhaps the same is still C Ballintemple 1766 and Jan 1771; V Kinawley (Kilm) 1740–74

s. of Rev Wettenhall, Archd of Kilmore qv (**s.** of William) by Barbara **dau.** of Francis Marsh

m. Elinor (**died** 24 Feb 1754) **dau.** of Thomas Nesbitt, MP of Lismore Co Cavan by Jane **dau.** of Arnold Cosby. Issue 1. William bapt 12 Jun 1745 at Kilmore; 2. Mary (**bur.** 8 Jul 1746) bapt 23 Apr 1746 at Kilmore; 3. Barbara bapt 27 Nov 1750 at Kilmore; 4. Thomas bapt 10 Nov 1751 at Kilmore

SNEYD, WILLLIAM   –1812

d 19 Mar 1768/69 p 25 Jul 1769; V Lurgan & Munterconnaught (Kilm) 1769–1812

Died Sep 1812

SOLOMON

is Dean of Ardagh to 1309/10 and supported by Charles O'Connor at the election of a Bishop (C.P.L. II. 70)

SOMNER, MILES

pres V Drintemple (Elph) 19 Dec 1633

SOTHEBY (SOUTHBY), SAMUEL

coll V Oughteragh (Kilm) 31 May 1638

SPAIGHT, ALEXANDER BROCK

ed Ch Miss Coll Islington

d 1867 p1868 (London for Colonial); C Taunagh (Elph) 1870–72; C St Stephen Canonbury Middx 1873–74; Asst Min Marboeuf Chapel Paris 1877–79; C St George Campden Hill (Lon) 1882–83; Min of San Luis Obispo CA USA 1885–86; Tustin CA USA 1886–88; R Holy Trinity Nevada City CA USA 1888–89; St John Marysville CA USA 1889–90; R St James Fremont Nebraska USA 1890–92

SPAIGHT, GEORGE 1786/87–

b. 1786 or 1787 Co Clare; ed by Mr Fitzgerald; ent TCD 5 Nov 1804 aged 17 Sch 1807 BA 1809

C Urney (Kilm) before 1817 and up to 1825; R Monanimy (Cloyne) 1828–36

> 3rd **s.** of Capt William of Corbally Co Clare by Millicent Anne Studdert
>
> **m.** 26 Feb 1827 Mary Anne elder **dau.** of Philip Smith of Cherrymount Co Meath. Issue 1. George; 2. Anne Millicent (**died** 19 Apr 1898) **m.** 29 Apr 1856 Wainwright Crowe of the Abbey Ennis Co Clare

SPANN, BENJAMIN 1656/57–1718

b. 1656 or 1657 at Bromborough, Cheshire; ed by Mr Golbourne, Chester; ent TCD 16 May 1674 aged 17 Sch 1675 BA 1678 MA 1681

R & V Aughanunshin (Raph) 1682/83–99; Preb of Inver (Raph) 1688–93; Preb of Clondehorkey (Raph) 1692–94; R & V Templemichael (w Clongish from 1698–1711) (Ard) 1693–1718; R & V Conwall (Raph) 1694–1716; V Gen of Raphoe 1710; was also V Gen Ardagh, "a worthy good clergyman, well-skilled in all parts of learning, particularly in the canon law".

> **s.** of Richard
>
> **m.** Catherine **dau.** of Richard and Anne (née Walsh) Smyth. Issue 1. John **b.** Cavan ed by Mr Griffin, Longford ent TCD 30 May 1705 aged 16; 2. Rev Samuel qv below; 3. Rev William **b.** Longford ed by Mr Nelegan, Longford ent TCD 18 Oct 1707 aged 16 BA 1711 MA 1714; R Conwall (Raph) 1715/16–52; **m.** and had issue (i) Banjamin **b.** Co Donegal ent TCD 24 Feb 1740/41 aged 16 BA 1745 MA 1748 (ii) Andrew **b.** Co Donegal ent TCD 25 Feb 1740/41 aged 16 (twins) Sch 1743 BA 1745 MA 1748 Irish Bar 1754 (iii) Elizabeth **m.** J McCausland of Strabane
>
> **Died** 1718

SPANN, SAMUEL 1689/90–1761

b. 1689 or 1690 Chester; ed by Mr Griffin, Longford; ent TCD 19 Apr 1704 aged 14 BA 1708 MA 1711

V Clongish (Ard) 1711–61; V Granard (Ard) 1737–41; made V Gen of Ardagh 23 Jan 1745

> **s.** of Rev Benmjamin qv (**s.** of Richard) by Catherine (née Smyth); **bro.** of Rev William, R Conwall (Raph) 1715/16–52

m. Margery **dau.** of Rev Robert Whitelaw by his wife Elizabeth **dau.** of William Smyth

Died 1 May 1761

SPEAR, JOHN JOSEPH 1805/06–

b. 1805 or 1806 Dublin; ed by Mr Willis; ent TCD 15 Oct 1821 aged 15

lic C Templeport (Kilm) 28 Aug 1832

s. of Richard, *agricola*

SPENCE, WALTER CYRIL 1919–

b. 1919; Heb Pri 1939 Eccles Hist Pri 1941 1st Theol Exhib 1942 Elrington Pri 1943 TCD BA 1940 Div Test (1) MA & BD 1943

d 12 Dec 1942 (Derry) p 10 Dec 1943; C Maghera (Derry) 1942–48; C Roscommon G (Elph) 1948–50; I Ballysumaghan w Killery (Elph) 1950–55; I Tubbercurry w Kilmactigue (Ach) 1955–60; I St Crumnathy's Cath Achonry w Tubbercurry & Killoran 1960–66; Preb of Killaraght and Kilmovee (Ach) 1962–66; I and Dean of Tuam 1966–81; Dio Reg Tuam 1966–85; Preb of Kilmactalway in St Patrick's Cath Dublin 1967–85; I Kilmoremoy w Castleconnor Easkey and Kilglass (Killala) 1981–85; ret

only s. of R W Spence of Dublin

m. 1956 St John's Cath Sligo Rachel **dau.** of Charles F Mahon of Carraroe Sligo

SPENCER, JAMES

V Cashel and Rathcline (Ard) 1663–*c.* 71; Chapl to Bp

SPENS, JAMES

V Drumlane w Tomregan (Kilm) 1663–65; coll V 12 Nov 1663 and inst 25 Jun 1664

SPRATT, JOHN

see **HILTON–SPRATT,** JOHN

SQUIRES, WILLIAM GOLDSMITH 1868–1955

b. 21 Mar 1868; ed Wesley Coll Dublin TCD BA Bibl Gk Pri (2) & Div Test (2) 1891

d 1891 p 1892 (Kilmore); C Mohill (Ard) 1891–95; C Enniscorthy (Ferns) 1895–1902; Dio C and Insp Schools (Ferns) 1902–03; I Kilnahue (Ferns) 1903–08; I Monart (w Templescobin from 1916) (Ferns) 1908–44; RD of Ferns 1913–44; Preb of Kilrane and Taghmon in Ferns Cath 1930–44; Treas of Ferns 1934–36; Chanc of Ferns 1936–40; Prec of Ferns 1940–44; ret

s. of William and Anne (née Goldsmith)

m… Day Lewis

Died 17 Jan 1955 Blackrock Dublin **bur.** Mt Jerome Dublin

STAFFORD, RICHARD WILLIAM 1946–

b. 12 Oct 1946 Wicklow; ed Vocational Sch Wicklow; Metalwork Teacher's Cert (Hons) Dept of Ed 1969; CITC 1996

d 29 Jun 1999 p 18 Jun 2000; C in Aux Min Urney Denn and Derryheen (Kilm) 1999–2000; C in Aux Min Drumgoon Dernakesh Ashfield and Killesherdoney (Kilm) 2000–

s. of Frederick John of Cavan (s. of William and Elizabeth (née McMichael) of Cavan by Lavinia Elizabeth dau. of Richard and Georgina (née Tyndall) Woodroofe of Wicklow.

m. 16 Aug 1969 Trinity Presby Ch Bailieborough Evelyn Mary dau. of Samuel Young and Edith Agnes (née Smyth) Williamson of Bailieborough. Issue 1. Lavinia Edith b. 9 Feb 1972 m. 1995 John Tilson; 2. Richard Samuel b. 23 Mar 1973 m. 2005 Sylvia Benn

PUBLICATION
St. Patrick's Church, Granard: Notes of Historical and Genealogical Interest, 1983

STANDISH, RICHARD NASH 1819/20–1900

b. 1819 or 1820 Co Limerick; ent TCD 6 Nov 1837 aged 17 BA 1845

d 1846 (Ossory for Limerick) p 1847 (Meath); C Aughrim (Elph) 1848–49; C Drumlease (Kilm) 1850–68; R Cloonclare (Kilm) 1868–77

eldest s. of Richard of Glin Lodge Co Limerick

m. 19 Dec 1849 at Carrick-on-Shannon Ch Elizabeth (**died** 4 Jan 1900, the same day as her husband, at Sandymount Dublin bur. Dean's Grange Dublin) yst dau. of Capt Charles Cox, JP of Carrick-on-Shannon

Died 4 Jan 1900 bur. Dean's Grange

STANFORD, BEDELL 1837–1895

b. 1837 Dublin; TCD BA 1863 Div Test (2) 1868

d 1867 (Armagh for Kilmore) p 1868 (Kilmore); C Castlerahan (Kilm) 1867–69; C St Luke (Dub) 1869–82; Asst Chapl Old Molyneux Chapel (Dub) 1882–86; C St Paul (Dub) 1886–94

2nd s. of Rev William Henry, R Rincurran (Cork) 1851–56 (s. of William of Cavan) by Esther Katharyne dau. of David Peter of Dublin

m. 29 Sep 1868 Phoebe (**died** 1901) 2nd dau. of Andrew Thompson of Dublin and Clones Co Monaghan. Issue Rev Bedell, C Drumlease (Kilm) qv

Died 1895

STANFORD, BEDELL 1873–1945

b. 23 Feb 1873 Dublin; ed Rathmines Sch; TCD Jun Exhib Brooke Mem Exhib BA (Resp) in Mod Hist and Classics 1896 Div Test 1897 Past Theol Pri and MA 1899

d 1897 p 1899; C Drumlease (Kilm) 1897; C St Kevin Dublin (Dub) 1897–1901; Asst Chapl Old Molyneux Chapel Dublin (Dub) 1902–04; C Coleraine (Conn) 1904–

06; R Ardclinis (Conn) 1906–07; C Ballymacarrett (Down) 1907–09; R Holy Trinity Belfast (Conn) 1909–15; Dio C Waterford and Lismore 1915–22; C-in-c Ballintemple (Cash) 1922–31; ret

s. of Rev Bedell, C Castlerahan (Kilm) qv (s. of Rev William Henry) by Phoebe dau. of Andrew Thompson of Clones Co Monaghan

m. Susan (died 27 Aug 1964) dau. of Thomas Jackson of Ranelagh Dublin. Issue 1. Adela Constance Dorothy b. 29 Jun 1903 m. 12 Jun 1945 William Henry s. of John Bernard A Bosanquet; 2. Helen Maud b. 7 Aug 1906 m. 22 Dec 1934 Francis Thomas, RN s. of Capt GeorgeRawdon Maurice Hewson, DL of Dromahair Lodge Co Leitrim and had issue 2 daus.; 3. Charles Bedell b. 24 Jan 1908 (died 27 Mar 1909); 4. William Bedell b. 16 Jan 1910 (died 30 Dec 1984) Reg Prof of Greek TCD Rep of Dublin Univ in Seanad Eireann from 1948 m. 21 Mar 1935 Dorothy Isabel dau. of James Phillips Evans Wright of Balbriggan Co Dublin and had issue; 5. Marjorie Kathleen b. 31 Jul 1912; 6. Eileen Mary b. 8 May 1914 m. 17 Jun 1939 Maurice Henry s. of Robert Maurice Le Clerc, MD of Oxford and Dublin and had issue 2 sons and 2 daus.

Died 6 Mar 1945

STANHOPE, EDWARD

was pres to V Kiltoghart and Drumreilly (Ard) 6 Jun 1634 (F.F.)

STANLEY, HUGH

adm Preb of Kilcooley (Elph) 9 Nov 1619

STAVELEY (STAVELLY), ROBERT 1795–1854

b. 1795 (Cork); ed by Mr Fea; TCD BA 1815

C Drumgoon (Kilm) 1821–25; C St Michan Dublin (Dub) 1825–26; C St Werburgh Dublin (Dub) 1827–47; Preb of Tipperkevin in St Patrick's Cath Dublin 1841–47; Preb of Howth in St Patrick's Cath Dublin 1847–49; Preb of St Munchin's (Lim) 1849–54

s. of Robert, merchant

m. (1) 1823 Nicola Sophia (died 18 Dec 1824) dau. of Ven Edward Herbert, Archd of Aghadoe

m. (2) 4 Mar 1828 St James' Ch Dublin Sarah Frances dau. of Rev Henry Crofton. Issue sons 1. Rev Robert (died 26 Oct 1905) b. 1829 Dublin TCD Sch 1846 BA 1849 MA & BD 1863 d 1851 p 1852 (Cork) C Clonmel (Cloyne) 1851–52 Chapl Frankfield (Cork) 1852 Dom Chapl to Bp Singer of Meath 1853–58 and 1858–67 V Rynagh (Meath) 1858–67 R Holy Trinity Killiney (Dub) 1867–1900 Canon of Christ Ch Cath Dublin 1879–92 Chapl to Lord Lt 1885–86 Preb of St John's in Christ Ch Cath Dublin 1892–93 Preb of St Michan's in Christ Ch Cath Dublin 1893–94 Preb of St Michael's in Christ Ch Cath Dublin 1894–1905 m. 2 Aug 1854 Letitia dau. of Most Rev James Henderson Singer, Bp of Meath 1852–66 and had issue incl (i) Robert (ii) Margaret (iii) Rev I Singer (iv) Francis Ffolliott; 2. Henry Crofton; 3. James Hugh; 4. John Ffolliott; 5. Maurice Collis; 6. John

Crofton; 7. Joseph Singer; **daus.** 1. Frances Crofton **m.** Very Rev John Crampton, Provost of Kilmacduagh; 2. Margaret; 3. Letitia

Died 3 May 1854

PUBLICATION

A Farewell Sermon on Acts XX 32 as C. St Michan's, preached in The King's Hospital Chapel, the Church being closed, 24th December 1826

STEELE, JOHN HAUGHTON 1850–1920

b. 6 Jun 1850; ed Portora Royal Sch; TCD BA (Jun Mod Hist & Pol Sci and Eng Lit) 1873 MA 1881

d 1873 (Derry) p 1875 (Kilmore); C Castlerock (Derry) 1873–74; C Devenish (Clogh) 1874–83; DC Holy Trinity Ch Crom, Kinawley (Kilm) and Chapl to Earl of Erne 1883–1910; became RC 1911 and was a priest in the Roman Church

Died 17 Mar 1920 at St Patrick's Coll Navan Co Meath

STEERE, NICHOLAS

Christ's Coll Camb BA 1605/06 MA 1609

perhaps same as Nicholas Steere pres by the Crown V Ballysumaghan Dunamon Kilcroan Fuerty Oran and Athleague (Elph) 6 Sep 1622 (L.M. V. 105)

STEEVENS, JOHN   –c. 1682

perhaps J S who was Commonwealth Minister at Ballingarry Co Limerick and Modreeny (Killaloe) 1658 and Warden of Galway 1660; V St Mary Athlone Drumraney Rynagh Gallen and Kilcleagh and Ballyloughloe (Meath) 1664–82; Prec of Lismore 1667–82.

m. and had issue Richard, TCD MD & Reg Prof of Physic who founded Dr Steeven's Hospital Dublin

Died *c.* 1682; Will prov 1682

STENSON, JOHN WILSON   –1891

TCD BA & Div Test 1869

d 1869 (Down) p 1870 (Armagh for Down); C St Stephen Belfast (Conn) 1869–70; V Kilglass (Ard) 1870–76; I Ballycanew (Ferns) 1876–78; R Templeshanbo (Ferns) 1878–91

m. Agnes Crichton (**died** 6 Jun 1902)

Died 28 Dec 1891 at Templeshanbo Rectory **bur.** Templeshanbo

STEPHEN

elect of Clonmacnoise; is allowed to retain the R St Mary's Mogbrechi, Ardagh, etc. (unidentified but perhaps Streete), until a certain date on account of poverty of See, 1397 (C.P.L. V. 155)

STEPHENS, JOHN 1760/61–1828

b. 1760 or 1761 Co Cavan; ed by Mr Beatty; ent TCD 1 Nov 1779 aged 18 BA 1784
V Killargue (Kilm) 1810–28

    s. of Richard, *agricola*

    Died 10 Jan 1828

STEPHENS, JOSEPH

lic C Lurgan and Munterconnaught (Kilm) 1825 — still there in 1830 (Erck)

STEPHENS, THOMAS 1728/29–1811

b. 1728 or 1729 Dublin; ed by Mr Piggott; ent TCD 14 Jul 1743 aged 14 BA 1748 MA 1753

d 1753 (Kilmore) p 14 Aug 1757 (Leighlin); C Kinawley (Kilm) 1774; C Castlerahan (Kilm) 1774; V Delvin (Meath) 1797–1811

    prob Thomas Stephens **s.** of Rev William

    Died 1811

STERLING, EDWARD 1705/06–1762

b. 1705 or 1706 Dublin; ed by Mr Rose in Co Meath; ent TCD 8 Nov 1722 aged 16 BA 1727 MA in DR at his collation; JP for Co Cavan 13 Feb 1738
V Lurgan and Munterconnaught (Kilm) 1738–62

    s. of Rev Luke, R Lurgan qv (**s.** of Rev James, R Templemichael (Ard) qv)

    m. (1) Elizabeth **dau.** of Col John Sterling of Killikeen Kilmore Co Cavan. Issue incl 1. Orange, Lt 108th Foot 12 Oct 1761, Lt Corps of Invalids 14 Feb 1793 **m.** (1) Margaret **dau.** of John Slack of Slackgrove, **m.** (2) (M.L. 26 Oct 1796)…Rafter, widow; 2. Susanna (**died** Jan 1786 at Rathbane) **m.** 1757 James Kellett of Rathbane Lodge Co Meath and Rosehill Co Cavan

    m. (2) Margaret (**died** 10 May 1776) **dau.** of James Sterling of Whigsborough King's Co (Offaly), High Sheriff King's Co 1699, and by her, who **m.** (2) James Rothwell of Co Meath had issue 1. Elizabeth (**died** Aug 1781 at Mullogh Co Cavan) **m.** 27 Aug 1770 Robert Kellett of Rosehill Co Cavan; 2. Patience **m.** before 1776 Capt Charles Moore Siree, 11th Foot

    Died 27 Oct 1762 at Garrycross

STERLING, JAMES 1618/19–1693

b. 1618 or 1619

coll V Killoe (Ard) 22 Jun 1662; V Templemichael (w Ballymacormick Clongish and Killoe) (Ard) from 1673 (coll 21 Jul 1673) 1660–1693

    m. Helen Maxwell (**died** 2 Mar 1709/10 aged 74). Issue 1. Capt John; 2. Rev Luke qv

    Died 31 Aug 1693

STERLING, LUKE 1668/69–

b. 1668 or 1669 Longford; ed by Mr Morris, Drogheda; ent TCD 24 Nov 1685 aged 16 BA 1691; JP Co Cavan 25 Feb 1712/13 and 1738/39

R Lurgan and Munterconnaught and Castlerahan (Kilm) 1700–38; R Cloone (Ard) 1738–

    s. of Rev James, R Templemichael (Ard) qv by Helen Maxwell

    was **m.** and had issue 1. Luke **b.** Drumdereg Co Cavan ed by Mr Davies at Trim ent TCD 7 Aug 1717 aged 15 BA 1722 Irish Bar 1729; 2. Rev Edward, V Lurgan (Kilm) qv; 3. John ent TCD 25 Jul 1727 aged 16

STEVENSON, CHRISTOPHER JAMES 1943–

b. 3 Jan 1943 Belfast; ed Grosvenor High Sch Belfast; TCD Exhib & Siz BA (Mod) Classics 1965 MA 1973; Emmanuel Coll Camb BA (Hons) 1969 MA 1973; Westcott House Camb GOE 1970; Univ of Manchester Cleaver Student 1977–80

d 1970 (Southwark for Newcastle) p 1971 (Newcastle); C Holy Cross Fenham (Newc) 1970–72; C St Mark Armagh (Arm) 1972–73; C Crumlin (Dub) 1973–76; Hon Cler V Christ Ch Cath Dublin 1975–76; C-in-c Appley Bridge (Blackb) 1976–82 and V 1982–91; R Cloonclare Killasnett Lurganboy and Drumlease (w Rossinver and Finner from 1992 and w and Innismagrath from 2002) (Kilm) 1991–

    s. of Robert Joseph and Annie (*née* Creighton) of Belfast

STEVENSON, JAMES

may be same as James Stevenson of Norfolk who was admitted to Corpus Christi Coll Camb in 1617, but does not seem to have had a degree

d 23 May 1619 p 19 Sep 1619 (Pet); C Tilney St Laurence Lynn (Nor) in 1622; R Ballinascreen (Derry) 1627–35; V Kiltoghart (Ard) from 1635, inst 31 Oct; still there in 1641 and maybe V to 1661

STEVENSON, WILLIAM 1796/97–

b. 1796 or 1797 Derry; ent TCD 6 Jan 1817 aged 20 Sch 1819 BA 1822

C Killeshandra (Kilm) to 1853

    perhaps William Stevenson **s.** of James, *ludimagister*

    m. 1 Jan 1824 St Peter's Ch Dublin Elizabeth Jane West

STEWART, ALAN DARNLEY HUSTON –*c.* 1950

ent TCD 1919

d 1927 p 1928 (Kilmore); C St John Sligo w Knocknarea (Elph) 1927–30; C Watford (St A) 1930–32; R Holy Trinity Brompton (Lon) 1932–33; V Ridge (St A) 1933–48

    s. of John Huston, FRUI

    m. 10 Mar 1931 St John's Malone Belfast Alice Madeline yst **dau.** of Arthur Jackson, DL of Lisrayan Sligo

    Died *c.* 1950

STEWART, ALEXANDER

poss C Ardagh (Ard) to 1833

> m. 19 Sep 1833 Bray Co Wicklow Caroline 2nd **dau.** of Arthur Maxwell of Gardiner St Dublin

STEWART, CHARLES STANLEY 1866/67–1915

b. 1866 or 1867 Arklow Co Wicklow; BA & DivTest 1900

d 1900 p 1901; C Clonbroney (w Killoe from 1901) (Ard) 1900–01; C Derrykeighan (Conn) 1901–06; R Dunaghy (Conn) 1906–15

> **s.** of William
>
> **m.** 31 Jul 1906 Derrykeighan Par Ch Margaret Bergna **dau.** of Rev John William D'Evelyn (*c.* 1832–1894) R & V Armoy (Conn) 1851–94 by Janet McNeill (his 2nd wife) and had issue two children
>
> **Died** sp 11 Apr 1915 aged 48

STEWART, EDWARD M

d 1870 p; C Rathaspeck (Ard) 1870–71

STEWART, HENRY WILLIAM 1834–1910

b. 24 Sep 1834; TCD BA 1857, Sen Mod Eth & Log and Div Test MA 1865

d and p 1858 (Toronto); Missy at Guelph Canada 1858–60; Oak Ridges 1860–61; Headmaster of Guelph Gram Sch 1861–63; C Kilberry (Glend) 1863; PC Rathaspeck 1863–73; R Knockbreda (Down) 1873–1908; Chanc of Down 1897–1910; Gen Lic Dio Down 1908–10

> elder **s.** of Rev Edward Michael MA of Ballymenagh Co Tyrone and Corcarn Co Donegal (**s.** of Henry of Tyrcallen Co Donegal and Hon Elizabeth Pakenham **dau.** of Edward Michael 2nd Lord Longford) by Jane Renwick **dau.** of John Jeffrey
>
> **m.** 10 Apr 1860 Fanny (**died** 26 Jan 1911 at Walton, Deramore Pk Belfast) **dau.** of Ven Arthur Palmer, Archd of Toronto. Issue **sons** 1. Edward Michael **b.** 24 Mar 1864 (**died** at Knockbreda Pk 22 Jul 1931) **m.** 19 Dec 1918 Helen Margaret elder **dau.** of George Imray of Culdean, Granton-on-Spey; 2. Arthur Henry **b.** 1869 **m.** 30 Mar 1891 St Patrick's Ch Runnymede Kansas USA Alice eldest **dau.** of Arthur W Mosse of Castletown Co Kilkenny; 3. Pakenham Thomas **b.** 1871 **m.** 1901 Mary Dupre **dau.** of John George Fennell of Melbourne; 4. Rev William **b.** 1896 BA, R Lillingston Dayrell (Ox); 5. James Robert **b.** 1878; 6. John Alexander **b.** 1881 **m.** 5 Apr 1904 Lydia Christina **dau.** of Duncan Malcolm of Belfast; **daus.** 1. Frances Mary; 2. Jane Charlotte **m.** 1884 Jonas Sealy Poole MD; 3. Hester Madeline **m.** 27 Sep 1894 Lt O H Daniel RN **s.** of Rev R Daniel BD, V Osbaldwick (York); 4. Kathleen Elizabeth Martha **died** 24 Aug 1892 at Knockbreda; 5. Elizabeth Margaret **m.** 24 Jul 1898 William 2nd **s.** of Victor C Taylor of Belfast
>
> **Died** 5 Nov 1910

PUBLICATIONS
The Diaconate Restored as a Permanent Order 1864
Diocesan Synods 1868
Sunday School Lessons for Juniors

STEWART, WILLIAM THOMAS 1875–1928

b. 7 Nov 1875 at Stragolan Irvinestown Co Fermanagh; TCD BA & Div Test 1898 MA 1918

d 1899 (Down for Armagh) p 1900 (Derry for Armagh); C Drumcree (Arm) 1899–1902; C Eglish (Meath) 1902–06; R Ballintemple (Kilm) 1906–10; R Swanlinbar (Kilm) 1910–13; R Billis (Kilm) 1913–20; C St Paul Glenageary (Dub) 1920–22; C-in-c Gowna and Columbkille (Ard) 1922–25; R Bailieborough (Kilm) 1925–28

  s. of Thomas, Farmer of Stragolan, Irvinestown by Jane (née Fitzpatrick)

  m. 17 Jun 1908 at Holy Trinity Ch Eglish Birr Co Offaly, Minnie **dau.** of William Jackson of Eglish Cottage Birr

  Died 21 Jun 1928

St. GEORGE, ARCHIBALD 1804/05–1851

b. 1804 or 1805 Dublin; ed by Dr Dowdall; ent TCD 5 Nov 1821 aged 16 BA 1826 MA 1832

C Carrigallen (Kilm) 1843; V Rossinver (Kilm) 1846–51

  2nd **s.** of Thomas Baldwin of Birr Co Offaly, Capt 80th Regt

  m. Penelope **m.** (2) 29 Apr 1863 at Celbridge Co Kildare Rev James Gully, R St Peter Athlone (Meath)

  Died 22 Jan 1851 at Mt Prospect Co Leitrim

St. GEORGE, HERBERT SCHOMBERG 1842/43–1899

b. 1842 or 1843; TCD BA 1868 MA 1872

d 1869 p 1870 (Tuam); C Kilglass and Castleconnor (Killala) 1869–70 (in Crockford but not C I Dir); I Balla (Tuam) 1872–73; R Rathaspeck (Ard) 1873–99

  yst **s.** of Stepney of Headfort Castle Co Galway

  Died 8 Dec 1899 aged 56

St. GEORGE, HOWARD 1744–1820

b. 1744; ed at Kilkenny Coll under Dr Hewetson 1755–59; ent TCD 19 Jun 1759 BA 1764 MA 1767 BD & DD 1779 as LLD

d 22 Jul 1764 p 21 Sep 1766; C Donagh (Clogh) 1765; R Magheraculmoney (Clogh) 1767–93; R Drumgoon (Kilm) 1770–92; R Drumkeeran (Clogh) 1793–1801; R & V Tydavnet (Clogh) 1793–1820

  6th **s.** of Rev Arthur (1681–1772) Chanc of Clogher 1716–72 (2nd **s.** of Henry) by his 2nd wife Jane **dau.** of Sir Thomas Molyneux, Bt; **bro.** of Rev Henry, R Aghade (Leigh) 1791–1831

m. (ML 8 Dec 1767) Mary **dau.** of Edward Lucas of Castleshane. Issue 1. Arthur John (**died** 1853) **m.** and had issue; 2. Rev Henry Lucas (**died** 24 Feb 1872) ent TCD 6 Nov 1797 aged 16 BA 1801 MA 1832 C Tydavnet (Clogh) 1809 R Derrybrusk (Clogh) 1809–10 C Cleenish (Clogh) 1810 R Ballybay (Clogh) 1810–27 R Tydavnet (Clogh) 1827–32 R Dromore (Clogh) 1832–72 **m.** Eliza **dau.** of Edward Warren and had issue **sons** (i) Capel **b.** 14 Nov 1814 (ii) Henry Lucas **m.** Harriet **dau.** of William Sterne and had issue (iii) Edward Warren ent TCD 2 Jul 1839 aged 20 (iv) Oliver Hatley (v) William Nassau **daus.** (i) Eliza **m.** 28 Feb 1837 Sir Hugh Stewart 2nd Bt Ballygawley Co Tyrone (ii) Mary Alicia **m.** Henry Taylor Rowley of Co Meath (iii) Anne (**died** 1 Jul 1914) (iv) Henrietta **m.** Hugh Lyons Montgomery; 3. Thomas Belmore (**died** 1863) ent TCD 5 Nov 1798 aged 16 BA 1803 MA 1832 **m.** and had issue; 4. Rev Richard Quintus (**died** 1877) **b.** 1785, V Crossmolina (Tuam) **m.** and had issue

Died 1820

St. GEORGE, RICHARD QUINTUS 1783/84–1877

b. 1783 or 1784 Co Kilkenny; ed by Mr Pack; ent TCD 7 Jun 1802 BA 1807 MA 1832

C Clonbroney (Ard) 1826–; V Tashinny (Ard) 1831–34; R Crossmolina (Killala) and Preb of Errew (Killala) 1835–72

s. of Rev Howard

m. 1811 Henrietta Maria (**died** 1875) **dau.** of Sir R Langrishe. Issue incl 1. Rev Howard Boyle; 2. Mary Jane **m.** John Ormsby and had issue

Died 8 Aug 1877 at Rosslare aged 93

STOKES, GABRIEL 1733/34–1806

b. 1733 or 1734; TCD Sch 1751 BA 1753 MA 1756 Fellow 1756 LLD 1761 BD & DD 1770

R Ardtrea (Arm) 1760–1802; Preb of Kilgoghlin (Elph) 1785–1806; Preb of Dysart and Kilmoleran (Lism) 1786–93; Chanc of Waterford 1793–1806;

s. of Gabriel, Mathematical Instrument Maker of Dublin

m. 1798 Elizabeth Haughton. Issue Whitley **m.** Sarah Boxwell and had issue **sons** (i) Whitley, MD (ii) William, MD (iii) Gabriel and two **daus.**

Died 13 Apr 1806 Waterford aged 72

STONDUN, HENRY

V Baslick (Elph) to 1413, obtained the V Burgeskeara (Tuam) without disp & held both & so is dep of this V

STONE, GUY 1717–1779

b. 1717 Newry; ed by Dr Frier, Newry; ent TCD 14 Jun 1733 aged 16 BA 1737 MA 1740

C Holywood (Down) 1754; V Shrule (Ard) 1754–69; Preb of Kilroot (Conn) 1775–79

s. of Major Samuel, 32nd Regt (only **s.** of Guy of Brookend Gloucestershire); **bro.** of Rev Samuel, R Culdaff (Raph — then Derry)

m. 5 Oct 1760 St Andrew's Ch Dublin Margaret Bryanton (**died** 15 Feb 1802 at Comber Co Down aged 72). Issue **sons** 1. Samuel **died** 16 Jan 1825; 2. Richard; 3. Guy; 4. William; **daus.** 1. Jane (**died** 4 Feb 1817 at Newbourn Antrim aged 53 **m.** 21 Apr 1783 Rev Robert Mortimer, Chanc of Down 1797–98; 2. Anne **died** unm 29 May 1859 at Barn Hill near Comber aged 83

Died 5 Jun 1779

STONE, WILLIAM HENRY 1826/27–1912

b. 1827 Dublin; ed at Rev J P Sargent's Sch in N Gt George's St Dublin; ent TCD 14 Oct 1845 aged 18 Abp King's Divinity Pri (extra) 1849 Div Test (1) and Reg Prof Premium (2) and BA 1850 MA 1856

d & p 1851 (Kilmore); C Urney (Kilm) 1851–60; C Drumlane (Kilm) 1862–66; C Kilmore (Kilm) 1866–72; R Kilmore (Kilm) 1872–1906; Preb of Mulhuddart in St Patrick's Cath Dublin 1882–89; Dean of Kilmore 1886–1912; ret 1906 though retained the Deanery

s. of William *pragmaticus* (**s.** of William, Solicitor of Dublin)

m. 15 Sep 1864 at Widcombe Ch Bath Marianne Elizabeth eldest **dau.** of Capt Brough, late Paymaster 83rd Regt. Issue incl 1. his 2nd **s.** Rev Henry Cecil Brough (**died** 3 Dec 1936) **b.** 14 Aug 1873 TCD BA & Div Test 1896 MA 1899 CBE 1919 d 1896 p 1897 C Armagh (Arm) 1896–1901 in India 1901–17 BEF Mesopotamia 1917–19 St Thomas Mt 1921–23 C Layde and Ardclinis (Conn) 1924–26 V Mattersey (S'well) 1926–28 V Scrooby (S'well) 1928–36 **m.** 31 Jan 1901 St Patrick's Cath Armagh Clamina **dau.** of Rev Charles Faris, V Chor Armagh Cath and had issue a **dau.** Marion Alexander **m.** 10 Sep 1924 Pierce Noel Ussher **s.** of Newport Wallis Clark; 2. Rev Edward Darley (**died** 3 Jan 1936) TCD BA 1904 Div Test 1905 d 1905 p 1907 C Athy (Glend) 1907–10 C Omey (Tuam) 1910–11 C Geashill (Kild) 1911–14 R Coolock (Dub) 1914–19 living in Santry Dublin 1919–22 C Furneaux Pelham w Brent Pelham (St A) 1922–23 R Horsey (Nor) 1923–25 R Tickencote (Pet) 1925–29 R Ickburgh w Langford (Nor) 1929–31; his yst **dau.** Marian Charlotte Gertrude **m.** 14 Oct 1907 Lt Col Frederick Grattan, CBE, Indian Army, **s.** of Rev William Prior Moore

Died 12 Feb 1912

STONEY, FRANCIS SADLEIR 1865/66–1940

b. 1865 or 1866; TCD BA 1888 Div Test 1889 MA 1909

d 1889 p 1890 (Kilmore); C Tashinny (Ard) 1889–90; R Tashinny (w C-in-c Kilglass 1929–32 and w Shrule from 1932) (Ard) 1890–1940; Preb of Kilcooley in Elphin Cath 1932–40

m. 22 Aug 1893 St George's Ch Dublin Eliza (**died** 18 Feb 1917) 2nd **dau.** of Rev William Noble, R Tashinny (Ard) 1868–90 qv

Died 29 Feb 1940 aged 74

STONEY, FREDERICK

C Killukin (Elph) 1859

STONEY, GEORGE FREDERICK 1825/26–1869

b. 1825 or 1826 Co Tipperary; ed by Dr King; ent TCD 11 Oct 1844 aged 18 BA 1857 MA 1863

d 1858 p; IEG has him as I Croghan (Elph) in 1859; PC Ballyjamesduff (Kilm) 1861–69

2nd **s.** of Rev Ralph of Terryglass Co Tipperary

m. 21 Jan 1857 Jane relict of Thomas Stoney of Harvest Lodge **dau.** of Thomas Legge. Issue 1. Barry; 2. Abbey Sadleir (**died** 25 Aug 1913) **m.** Charles H Bellhouse

Died 18 Aug 1869 at Shercock Co Cavan aged 43

STONEY, WILLIAM BAKER 1793/94–1874

b. 1793 or 1794 King's Co (Offaly); ent TCD 4 Dec 1809 aged 15 BA 1814

d 1817 (Clonfert) p; C Kilbixy (Meath); PC Loughglynn (Elph) 1819–22 where Bp O'Beirne withdrew his licence; C Kiltullagh (Elph, then Tuam) 1822–30, where he gained over 100 converts from the Church of Rome, and became unpopular, engaging in controversy with RC priests; R Burrishoole (Tuam) 1830–39; here, in consequence of his exertions in helping the poor during the famine, he became popular, which roused the opposition of the Roman Catholic priest, who challenged him to a public discussion; R Aglish = Castlebar (Tuam) 1839–72

2nd **s.** of James Johnston of Oakley Park, gentleman (3rd **s.** of George of Greyfort) by Catherine 2nd **dau.** of William Baker of Lismacue Co Tipperary

m. Frances **dau.** of Rev John Going, R Mealiffe (Cash). Issue incl **sons** 1. Johnston James **b.** Co Roscommon ed Edgeworthstown Sch ent TCD 12 Oct 1839 aged 17; 2. Rev William (**died** 7 Jan 1907) **b.** Co Roscommon ed at Lucan Sch ent TCD 13 Oct 1843 aged 20 BA 1848 MA 1852 PC Turlough (Tuam) 1852–72; 3. Rev Robert Baker **b.** Co Roscommon ed by Mr Earle ent TCD 1 Jul 1846 aged 17 BA & Div Test (2) 1851 MA 1865 d 1851 p 1852 C Ardbraccan (Meath) 1851–57 C Bandon (Cork) 1857–60 C Bloxwich (Lich) 1860 C St Paul Wolverhampton (Lich) 1861–63 C All SS Loughborough (Leic, then Pet) 1863–68 R St John Wednesbury (Lich) 1869–89 R Shirland (Derby, then S'well) 1889–1900; **daus.** incl his 3rd **dau.** Johanna (**died** 11 Jun 1858 in Calcutta) **m.** Alexander Tait

Died 7 Feb 1874

PUBLICATIONS

while in Kiltullagh, he published various pamphlets including *The Life and Death of Anthony Vizard*

Letter to the Lord Lieutenant on Papist Atrocities, London 1835

An Authentic Report of an important discussion held in Castlebar between Rev. W.B. Stoney, Rector of Newport Pratt, County Mayo, and the Rev. James Hughes, Roman Catholic priest, Newport Pratt from Friday January 6th to Friday January 13th 1837

Romanism Displayed: A Letter to the Priests of Castlebar, 4th ed, Hardy, Dublin 1849

The Irish Protestant Farmer, London 1868

STORY, EDWARD 1755–1810

b. 1755 Cavan; bapt 1755; ed by Mr Kerr; ent TCD 9 Jul 1770 aged 15 BA1775

C St Andrew Dublin (Dub) 1778; C St Kevin Dublin (Dub) 1779–82; R Drumcree (Meath) 1788–92; R Taughmon (Meath) 1790–94; R Oughteragh (Kilm) 1794–1803; R Kildallon (Kilm) 1803–10

> **s.** of Ven Joseph, Archd of Kilmore qv (**s.** of Joseph, Bp of Kilmore qv) by Frances Arabella; **bro.** of Rev Joseph, V Castlerahan (Kilm) qv
>
> **Died** 1810

†STORY, JOSEPH 1679–1757

b. 1679 Hexham Northumberland; Univ of Edinburgh MA

d 1703 p 24 Feb 1704; C Inismacsaint (Clogh) 1703; C Clogher (Clogh) in 1709 and to 1714 and perhaps to 1716; Chapl to Irish House of Commons; Preb of Kilskeery (Clogh) 1716–40; Dean of Ferns 1734–40; Bp of Killaloe 1740–41; consec 11 Feb 1740 in St Brigid's Ch Dublin; Bp of Kilmore 1741–57; enthroned by proxy 7 Apr 1741

> **m.** (1) Deborah **dau.** of Thomas Richardson of Co Tyrone, **sister** of Rev James Richardson R Balteagh (Derry). Issue 1. Elizabeth; 2. Katherine **m.** 23 Sep 1745 John Irvine of Rockfield Co Fermanagh
>
> **m.** (2) Sophia or Hannah (**bur.** 14 Apr 1761 Kilmore) **dau.** of Sir William Gore, 3rd Bt, Speaker of the Irish House of Commons. Issue Ven Joseph, Archd of Kilmore qv
>
> **Died** 22 Sep 1757 at Kilmore **bur.** Kilmore

PUBLICATION

> *A Sermon,* preached at St Andrew's Dublin on the Anniversary of the Irish Rebellion, 4to, Dublin 1735
>
> *An Essay concerning the Nature of the Priesthood,* 8vo, Dublin 1750

STORY, JOSEPH –1767

prob Joseph Story who ent TCD 16 Oct 1737 BA MA 1749

d 28 Aug 1743 p 24 Sep 1743; V Oughteragh (Kilm) 1743–45; V Urney and Annagelliffe (Kilm) 1745–46; V Killinkere (Kilm) 1745–60; Archd of Kilmore 1745–67; V Killan, now Shercock (Kilm) 1746–54; V Gen of Kilmore 1746–67; V Carrigallen (Kilm) 1752–67; V Killesherdoney (Kilm) 1754–67

> only **s.** of Joseph, Bp of Kilmore qv by his 2nd wife Sophia or Hannah
>
> **m.** 1 May 1746 in Kilmore Cath Frances Arabella who was poss **dau.** of Ven Wettenhall Sneyd, Archd of Kilmore qv of Lisnamandra Co Cavan. Issue incl **sons** 1. Rev Joseph, V Castlerahan (Kilm) qv; 2. William bapt 21 May 1750; 3. Thomas bapt 29 Jul 1754; 4. Rev Edward, V Kildallon (Kilm) qv; 5. Jeremy bapt 1757 **bur.** 1758; 6. Jeremy bapt 9 Apr 1761; **daus.** 1. Sophia bapt 19 May 1747 **m.** 18 Sep 1767 Robert Burrowes; 2. Barbara bapt 25 Jul 1748; 3. Mary bapt 1 May 1751; 4. Judith bapt 9 Apr 1761; 5. Anna bapt 28 Sep 1764 **m.** Col John French; 6. Arabella bapt 18 Dec 1765; 7. there also seems to have been a **dau.** Frances who **m.** Henry La Nauze and had issue Rev Thomas, R Killinagh (Kilm) qv
>
> **Died** 17 Dec 1767

STORY, JOSEPH 1749–1810

bapt 22 Jun 1749; ed by Mr Kerr; ent TCD 5 Jul 1766 BA 1770 MA 1776

V Corcomohide (Lim) 1774–87; R Donaghenry (Arm) 1780–81; R Castlerahan (Kilm) 1781–94; R Templeport and Drumreilly (Kilm) 1794–1810

> **s.** of Ven Joseph, Archd of Kilmore qv (**s.** of Joseph, Bp of Kilmore qv) by Frances Arabella; **bro.** of Rev Edward, V Kildallon (Kilm) qv
>
> a Mrs Frances Story (his mother?) of Bingfield was **bur.** at Kilmore 13 Jul 1806. Alexander Bury of Rockfield **m.** 22 May 1801 Arabella Story (his **dau.**?) of Bingfield. Robert Delap **s.** of Rev Joseph Story of Bingfield and Sarah his wife bapt 18 Jun 1791. He had a **s.** Rev Joseph, R Urney (Kilm) qv and a **dau.** Mary Anne **m.** Rev John Richardson, C Drung and Larah (Kilm) qv
>
> **Died** 1810 **bur.** 28 Feb 1810 Kilmore

STORY, JOSEPH 1788–1838

b. 23 Apr 1788 Co Meath; ed by Mr Moon; ent TCD as SC 3 Oct 1803 BA 1807 MA 1836

R Tomregan (Kilm) 1818–35; V Urney (Kilm) 1835–38

> **s.** of Rev Joseph, R Templeport & Drumreilly (Kilm) qv (**s.** of Ven Joseph, Archd of Kilmore qv)
>
> **m.** 1812 Louisa **dau.** of Sir Peter Rivers, Bt. Issue **sons** 1. Joseph of Bingfield, JP; 2. William Rivers (**died** s.p. 1845); **daus.** 1. Emily Henrietta **m.** 8 Apr 1850 Christopher Bagot Lane, Prof of Engineering Queen's Coll Cork; 2. Ellen Martha Sarah; 3. Frances **m.** 17 Oct 1849 Sir Thomas Gibson Carmichael, Bt; 4. Louisa Maria Elizabeth **m.** 1855 George Luard of Blyborough Hall Lincs; 5. Caroline Maria **m.** Rev G de Courcy Meade; 6. Agnes Sarah **m.** 1856 Lt Col John Bean, Madras Army
>
> **Died** 23 Apr 1838

STOUGHTON, JOSEPH –1694

V St John Athlone Kilbride Kilgeffin Kilkeevan and Clontuskert (Elph) 1688–94; also lic C Killenvoy Kiltoom Raharrow and Camma 4 Sep 1688 (D.R. Tuam)

> **Died** 1694

STRANGWAYS, JAMES MICHAEL HENRY 1814/15–1885

b. 1814 or 1815 Co Cavan; ed privately; ent TCD 3 Nov 1834 aged 19 BA & Div Test 1842 MA 1850

d 1843; p 17 Dec 1843 (Kilmore); C Outeragh (Ard, then Kilm) 1843–46; C Killashee (Ard) 1846–50; Leslie's MSS also have him C Annagh (Kilm) *c.* 1850; V Chor Armagh Cath 1850–69; I Baronstown (Arm) 1869–74; C Altedesert (Arm) 1876–77; C All Hallows Bromley-by-Bow (Lon) 1878–79; C Radcliffe (Lon) 1879–81; C St Mary Plaiston (St A) 1881

> **s.** of William of 83rd Regt of Suttonsrath Co Kilkenny; **bro.** of Margaret Frances Fleming Strangways who **m.** Rev Campbell B Jamison, R Killesher (Kilm) qv

m. (1) Anne… (**died** 10 Nov 1850 at Armagh aged 27)

m. (2) 12 Jan 1853 St Mark's Ch Armagh Isabella Margaret **dau.** of Alexander Robinson MB FRCSI, Surgeon, County Infirmary, Armagh. Issue 1. Lucy **b.** 26 Jun 1854 **died** Mar 1862; 2. William Alexander Percy **b.** 21 Mar 1856; 3. Leonard Richard Fleming (**died** Nov 1931) **b.** 2 Oct 1857 TCD Sch 1879 BA 1880 MA 1884; 4. Giles Robert **b.** 10 Jul 1859 **died** 19 Jul 1859 at Armagh; 5. James Howard Percy **b.** 18 Jun 1860 (**died** 1918 London) ed Royal Sch Armagh; 6. Beatrice Ethel **b.** 21 May 1862 **bur.** 12 Oct 1865 Armagh Cath; 7. Richard Marcus Neville **b.** 26 Jan 1864; 8. Charles Francis Hartley **b.** 19 Sep 1866

Died 1 Feb 1885 at Fulham London

STRATON, DAVID

coll R & V Castleterra (Kilm) 1 Jun 1662

STREAN, ANNESLEY 1747/48–1837

b. 1747 or 1748 Derry; ed by Mr Murphy; ent TCD 2 Nov 1774 BA 1779 MA 1832; also qualified as a medical doctor

d 1779 p 1782 (Dublin); C Derralossary (Glend) 1779; C Kilkenny West (Meath) – 1800; PC St Peter Athlone (Elph) 1802–37

s. of John

m. Catherine (**died** 2 Apr 1832) and had issue incl 1. Ven Lewis Henry qv; 2. Annesley William **b.** Co Roscommon ent TCD 1 Jul 1822 aged 18 BA 1837; 3. Rev John, qv; 4. his yst **dau.** Emilia Margaret Letitia **m.** 28 Oct 1841 Rev Edward William Burton, Canon of Christ Ch Cath Dublin 1872–80

Died 29 Sep 1837 "from a fracture of the thigh bone" aged nearly 90

STREAN, JOHN 1803/04–1879

b. 1803 or 1804 Roscommon; ent TCD 1 Jul 1822 aged 18 BA 1827

C Toomna (Elph) 1845–46; V Toomna (Elph) 1846–48

s. of Rev Annesley, qv; **bro.** of Ven Lewis Henry, qv

m. and had issue an only **s.** Annesley William (**died** 30 Jun 1862 Dublin aged 20)

Died 22 Mar 1879 in Dublin aged 75

STREAN, LEWIS HENRY 1815–1890

b. 1815 Co Roscommon; ed by his father; ent TCD 6 Jul 1829 BA 1834 Heb Pri 1835 MA 1837

d 25 Apr 1838 p 21 Dec 1839 (Elphin); C Killukin (then Elph) 1838–40; V Eastersnow 1840–45; R & V Killukin (Elph) and Archd of Elphin 1845–47; res owing to persecution and went to England; PC Antrobus (Ches) 1847–50; PC Newtownmountkennedy (Glend) 1850–59; PC Kilbride Bray (Glend) 1859; R Delgany (Glend) 1859–88; Archd of Glendalough 1872–88

s. of Rev Annesley, MD, PC St Peter Athlone (Elph) qv (**s.** of John); **bro.** of Rev

John, qv

m. Emily Heade (ML 1843) (**died** 27 Dec 1892). Issue incl Rev Annesley (**died** 10 Sep 1915) TCD Sch; Fellow of Corpus Christi Coll Camb and V Grantchester (Ely)

Died 17 May 1890 Dublin

STRONG, CHARLES

ed St Bees Coll Durham

d (Down) p 1870 (Kilmore); C St Andrew Drumaloor (Kilm) 1870–72; C Swanwick (Derby — then S'well) 1872–73; C Clayton Yorks (Rip) 1873–74; C Shipley (Rip) 1874–78; C Heaton (Ripon) 1878–82; V Longnor (Lich) 1882–95; V Windhill (Rip) 1895–1906

STRONG. CHARLES KNOX 1834–1890

b. 1834 Co Leitrim; ed by Mr Kyle; TCD BA & Div Test 1855 MA 1878

d 1857 p 1858 (Kilmore); C Tibohine (Elph) 1857–63; C Croghan (Elph) 1863–66; C St Peter Athlone (Elph) 1866–67; C Kilkeevin (Elph) 1867–75 and C Oran (Elph) 1873–75; C St Mark Dublin (Dub) 1875–88; I St Mark Dublin (Dub) 1888–90

s. of Rev Robert, Methodist Minister

Died 29 Jul 1890

STUART, ALAN LEIGH 1906–

b. 18 May 1906 Ballyboy Rectory; ed Monkstown Park Sch; St Columba's Coll Dublin; TCD Wray Pri 1928 BA (1) Hons and Gold Medal in Philos 1929 MA 1934 PhD 1944; served under Malayan Govt Education Dept, Straits Settlements 1930–33 as lecturer to native teachers

d 1934 p 1935 (Sheffield); C St Philip Sheffield (Sheff) 1934–36; Chapl St George's Sch Harpenden Herts (St Alb) 1936–37; C-in-c Cashel and Rathcline (Ard) 1937–39; R Athboy w Kildalkey and Girley (Meath) 1939–45; Sen Lect Gordon Memorial Univ Coll Khartoum Sudan 1945–51; R Drumshambo Kilronan and Kiltubride (Ard) 1951–53; Perm to Off Dio London 1953–54; C Putney (S'wark) 1954–55; V Dormansland (S'wark) 1955–58; V Stalisfield w Otterden (Cant) 1958–64; Lect W Kent Coll of Further Ed Tunbridge Wells 1964–; still there 1982.

s. of Canon Alfred Ernest Leigh, C Killesher (Kilm) qv

m. Aug 1934 Dawn Jane Hannan

STUART, ALFRED ERNEST LEIGH 1875–1959

b. 11 Feb 1875 Dublin; ed Rathmines Sch Dublin; TCD BA 1897 Div Test 1898 BD 1915

d 1898 p 1899 (Kilmore); C Killesher (Kilm) 1898–1900; C Clonfadforan (Meath) 1900–04; V Ballyboy (Meath) 1904–13; R Leney and Stonehall (w Portnashangan from 1920) (Meath) 1913–44; RD of Clonard 1925–44; Exam Chapl to Bp of Meath 1938–44; Preb of Tipper in St Patrick's Cath Dublin 1941–44; ret

s. of Rev Joseph Leigh, R Nurney (Leigh)

m. 9 Oct 1904 at Dalkey Co Dublin Olive Maude (**died** before 1951) **dau.** of F W Gardiner, DI RIC. Issue incl 1. Frederick Hamilton **m.** 10 Jul 1945 Dulcie Greenway yr **dau.** of W F Hart of Seaton Devon; 2. Richard Gardiner (**died** 11 Jul 1954 in an accident at Zamba Nyasaland); 3. Kenneth Malcolm (**died** 5 Mar 1972 Belfast); 4. Rev Alan Leigh, C-in-c Cashel and Rathcline (Ard) qv

Died 12 Dec 1959 Dublin

STUART, HERBERT JAMES 1926–

b. 16 Nov 1926 Longford; ed Wilson's Hosp; Mountjoy Sch Dublin; TCD BA Mod 1 cl (Ment & Mor Sci) 1948

d 20 Nov 1949 (Meath for Kilmore) p 17 Dec 1950 (Kilmore); C St John Sligo w Knocknarea (Elph) 1949–53; C Holy Trinity Rathmines (Dub) 1953–55; Chapl RAF 1955–73; Asst Chapl-in-Chief RAF 1973–80; Hon Chapl to HM The Queen 1977–83; Prin RAF Chaplains' Sch 1979; Chapl in Chief and Archd for the RAF 1980–83; Canon and Preb of Lincoln Cath 1981–83; I Cherbury (Ox) 1983–87; Perm to Off Dio Gloucester 1987–97; Perm to Off Dio Oxford 1987–96; ret

s. of Joseph Henry of Longford (**s.** of James and Jane of Co Cavan) by Martha Jane **dau.** of William Jones of Longford

m. 15 Oct 1955 Taney Ch Dublin Adrienne **dau.** of Brindsley and Dorothy Le Fanu of Dundrum Dublin. Issue 1. Heather Adrienne **b.** 12 Nov 1957 **m.** Leonard Forland; 2. Nigel **b.** 5 Apr 1961 **m.** Gretchen Sauer; 3. Michael **b.** 19 Feb 1969

STUART, ROBERT LIONEL 1909–1981

b. 1909 Durrow Co Laois; ed The High Sch Dublin; Mountjoy Sch Dublin; TCD BA 1932 Div Test 1933; MC 1945

d 1933 p 1934 (Kilmore); C St John Sligo w Knocknarea (Elph) 1933–36; C Drumcondra w N Strand (Dub) 1936–40; CF (EC) 1940–46; Chapl Miss to Seamen Dublin 1946–51; Miss to Seamen Cape Town 1951–55; C St James (Dub) 1955; Miss to Seamen Rotterdam 1955–56; R Kilnamanagh U (Ferns) 1956–81; Preb of Kilrane and Taghmon (Ferns) 1966–78; Treas of Ferns Cath 1979–81

s. of Rev Thomas Dormer, R Rathdowney (Oss) 1926–52

m. 31 Mar 1937 Marion Ruby (**died** 17 Mar 1973) **dau.** of George Kennedy of Armagh. Issue 1. Robert Kennedy; 2. Heather Margaret

Died 13 Feb 1981

STUART, SAMUEL McKEE SHANNON

d 1897 p; C Kinawley (Kilm) 1901–02

STURDY, THOMAS OSWALD 1912–1983

b. 1912; TCD BA 1936 Div Test 1939

d 1940 p 1941 (Newcastle); C Bedlington (Newc) 1940–42; C Jesmond (Newc) 1942–43; CF (EC) 1943–45; CF 1945–67; R Mohill Farnaught Aughavas and Annaduff E

(Ard) 1967–73; R Clonfert U (Clonf) 1973–76; ret Last entry in C I Dir 1983

m. and had issue

Died 14 Sep 1983

SUMNER (or SYMNER), MILES –1686

TCD Sch 1626 MA 1634 Fellow 1652 DD 1664; Prof of Mathematics 1652–86

Preb of Kilmacallen and V Cowlea (Elph) 1634–61; was Archd of Clogher in Mar 1661. In the Triennial Visitation Book of 1661, 14 Aug, his name is struck out and it is noted that he had resigned the Archdeaconry; Archd of Kildare from 1667–68

Died 22 Mar 1686 bur. St Andrew's Dublin

SWANNE, RICHARD 1719/20–1794

b. 1719 or 1720; matric Queen's Coll Ox 27 Mar 1738 aged 18 BA 1741 MA 1745 BD 1761

R Tullaghobegley and Raymunterdoney (Raph) 1765–73; R Killybegs (Raph) 1769–78; V Donegal (Raph) 1770–81; R Templeport & Drumreilly (Kilm) 1778–94; R Skryne (Meath) 1785–94

s. of Rev Abraham of Ilmingham Warks

m. and had issue incl 1. Rev Abraham (died 8 Feb 1816) matric All Souls Coll Ox 17 Dec 1784 aged 17 BA 1789 R Killurin (Ferns) 1794–1816 m. and had issue incl (i) Gilbert b. Co Wexford ent TCD 7 Nov 1825 aged 18 (ii) eldest dau. Elizabeth (died 9 Jan 1861); 2. Rev Richard matric All Souls Coll Ox 24 May 1787 aged 19 BA 1791

Died Oct 1794

SWANZY, THOMAS BIDDALL 1836–1884

b. 8 May 1836; TCD BA & Div Test 1860 MA 1863

d 1860 p 1861 (Kilmore); C Castlerahan (Kilm) 1860–63; C St Patrick Newry (Drom) 1863–67; C St Mary Newry (Drom) 1867–76; R St Mary Newry (Drom) 1876–84

only s. of Thomas Biddall of Newry by Anne eldest dau. of Rev Josiah Erskine, R Knockbride (Kilm) qv

m. 22 May 1867 at Kilshannig Co Cork his cousin Elizabeth Anne (died 4 Mar 1924 aged 80) dau. of Rev Canon Henry Swanzy, R Kilshannig (Cloyne). Issue sons 1. Rev Thomas Erskine TCD BA (Sen Mod Lit) 1891 St John's Coll Ox BA (2) 1893 MA 1897 d 1894 p 1895 (Lincoln) C St Swithin Lincoln (Linc) 1894–1904 V Hibaldstow (Linc) 1904–09 C All SS Lincoln (Linc) 1909–19 V All SS Lincoln (Linc) 1919–47 Preb of Leighton Beaudesert (Linc) 1926–47 ret; 2. Very Rev Henry Biddall (died unm. 19 May 1932 in London as the result of an accident) b. 5 Oct 1873 TCD BA (Resp) 1896 Div Test (2) 1898 MA 1899 MRIA 1919 d 1899 p 1900 (Kilmore for Clogher) C Monaghan (Clogh) 1899–1900 C St Mary Newry (Drom) 1900–08; R Carrowdore (Down) 1908–10 R Omeath (Arm) 1910–14 V St Mary Newry (w Donaghmore from 1922) (Drom) 1914–32 Preb of Wicklow in St Patrick's Cath Dublin 1926–31 Dean of Dromore 1931–32 Preb of Tassagard in St Patrick's Cath Dublin 1932; author of *Succession Lists of the Diocese of Dromore,* 1932; 3. Rev Robert Archibald (**died** 19 Dec 1950) **b.** 9 Nov 1875 Cantab Pembroke Coll Camb BA 1898 Cuddesdon Coll 1899 d 1899 p 1900 (Lincoln) C New Clee (Linc) 1899–1909 C Adlington (Blackb — then Manch) 1909–18, V Withnell Lancs (Blackb) 1918–33 R St Mary Newry (Drom) 1933–50 Prec of Dromore 1945–50; **daus.** 1. Alice Elizabeth (**died** 4 Aug 1871); 2. Annie Beatrice; 3. Olive Adelaide

Died 12 May 1884 Bournemouth

SWAYNE, CHARLES BRODERICK 1816/17–

b. 1816 or 1817 Cork; ed by Mr Fahey; ent TCD 28 May 1834 aged 17 BA 1844 Div Test 1845

d 1845 (Kildare) p 1846 (Killaloe for Kilmore); C Kill U (Kild) 1845–46; C Desertlyn (Arm) 1846–48; V Kilgeffin (Elph) 1849–52; Sec in London for Malta Protestant Coll 1852–55; Assoc Sec CMS 1858

s. of Rev John, MA, R Ballymurreen (Cash) (eldest **s.** of John of Midleton Co Cork) by Frances **dau.** of Rev Thomas Crawford of Lismore Co Waterford

SWEENY, GEORGE 1757/58–

b. 1757 or 1758 Sligo; ed by Mr Kenny; ent TCD 4 Nov 1777 aged 19 BA 1782

C Kilglass (Elph) 1786

s. of Thomas'

SWEENY, PATRICK

is Impropriate C Rathaspeck (Ard) in 1807 and also in 1814 (Lea)

SWEET, JOHN HALES 1818/19–1880

b. 1818 or 1819; St John's Coll Camb MA; was engaged in scholastic work in England, but came to Ireland for his wife's health in 1868

C Cloone (Ard) 1868–70; held curacies in Dio Dublin 1870–72; R Kilmacow (Oss) 1872–80

m. and had issue six children; his younger **s.** Algernon Sydney Osborne **m.** 31 Mar 1880 Wittecombe Par Ch Devonshire Alice Mary of Belfast, adopted **dau.** of Miss Ensor of Exmouth; yst **dau.** Mary Ann Ethel **m.** 7 Apr 1880 Kilmacow Par Ch, Harry Smith of Montreal, for which her father composed a wedding hymn, *"O scene to stir deep feeling",* publ in IEG

Died 31 May 1880 at Kilmacow Rectory in his 62nd year

Mr Sweet was a well–known and prolific hymn–writer

SWEETNAM, AUSTIN 1873/74–1953

b. 1873 or 1874 TCD BA 1898 Div Test 1899 MA 1929

d 1900 p 1901 (Kilmore); C Lavey w Larah (Kilm) 1900–06; I Oughteragh (w Fenagh from 1922) (Ard– transferred to Kilmore in 1910) 1906–49; Preb of Kilmacallen (Elph) 1944–50; ret

Died Apr 1953 Ballinamore Co Leitrim aged 79

SWIFTE–DENNIS, JOSEPH MORLEY
see DENNIS, JOSEPH MORLEY

SWINY (McSWINEY), HUGH
inst V Drung (Kilm) 25 Mar 1635

SYMMONS, HENRY THOMAS
TCD BA 1866 Div Test (1) 1868 MA 1869
d Dec 1866 (Armagh for Kilmore) p; C Drumgoon (Kilm) 1866; C Dalkey (Dub) 1868–70; C Killiney (Dub) 1870–75

m. and had issue a **s. b.** 8 Oct 1871 at Usher's Island

SYMPSON, EDWARD
inst V Kilglass and Moydow (Ard) 1 Sep 1683 (FF). May have been there to 1732

†SYNGE, EDWARD 1614–1678
bapt 16 Aug 1614 at Bridgnorth Salop; ed Drogheda Gram Sch; TCD BA not recorded, was BD in 1640 DD 1661
R Killary (Meath) 1638–?60; Preb of Aghadowey (Derry) 1640–61; R & V Drummully (Clogh) 1640–61; R Drumachose and Tamlaghtfinlagan (Derry) 1643–61; Minor Canon St Patrick's Cath Dublin 1647–60; V Lusk (Dub); V Innishannon (Cork) and Dean of Elphin 1648–60; he was, as appears from Commonwealth Papers (Seymours *Transcripts*) Archd of Cloyne in 1649 and to 1661, and was also appointed *c.* 1649 by Ormond to the Chancellorship of Christ Ch Cath Dublin; Bp of Limerick 1661–63; was promoted by Patent 19 Jan 1661; patent granted him also the Sees of Ardfert and Aghadoe to be held with Limerick and the R Tradery (Killaloe) to be held *in commendam*; Bp of Cork Cloyne and Ross in 1663–78

8th **s.** of Richard by Alice Rowley; (it is said that the family name was originally Millington, and that they received the name of Synge, spelled Singe or Sing, from their sweetness of voice — Leslie *Clogher Clergy and Parishes,* p 182).

m. Barbara eldest **dau.** of William Latham of New Place Co Derry. Issue 1. Very Rev Samuel, Dean of Kildare; 2. Most Rev Edward, Abp of Tuam 1716–41

Died 22 Dec 1678 **bur.** Cloyne Cathedral

†SYNGE, EDWARD 1691–1762
b. 1691 Cork; ed by Mr Molloy at Cork; ent TCD 13 Jun 1706 aged 15 BA 1709 Fellow 1710–19 MA 1712 BD & DD 1728; was made a Freeman of Dublin in 1722
d; p 1715 (Dublin) Bp 1730; Preb of Stagonil in St Patrick's Cath Dublin 1715–19;

Preb of St Audoen in St Patrick's Cath Dublin 1719–27; R Cappagh (Derry) 1719–30; Provost of Tuam 1726–30; Chancellor of St Patrick's Cath Dublin 1727–30; Bp of Clonfert 1730–31; consec 7 Jun 1730 in St Werburgh's Ch Dublin; Bp of Cloyne 1731–33; Bp of Ferns and Leighlin 1733–1740; Bp of Elphin 1740–62

> eldest **s.** of Most Rev Edward Abp of Tuam 1716–41 (**s.** of Rt Rev Edward, Dean of Elphin 1648–60 Bp of Cork Cloyne and Ross 1663–78 qv and Barbara (née Latham)) by Annie (née Proud); **bro.** of Rt Rev Nicholas, Bp of Killaloe 1746–71
>
> **m.** Jane (**died** Dec 1737 **bur.** 1 Jan 1738) **dau.** of Robert Curtis of Roscrea Co Tipperary. Issue 1. Edward **b.** 1722 (**died** 1739); 2. Sarah **b.** 1723 (**died** 1725); 3. Catherine (**died** 1734); 4. Mary (**died** 1734); 5. Robert **b.** 1725 (**died** 1746); 6. Alicia **b.** 12 Dec 1733 (**died** 1807) **m.** 30 May 1758 Rt Hon Joshua Cooper of Markree Castle Co Sligo, MP for Sligo and had issue
>
> **Died** 27 Jan 1762 Dublin; **bur.** St Patrick's Cath Churchyard

PUBLICATIONS
The Case of Toleration considered with Respect both to Religious and Civil Government; A Sermon preached on Saturday 23rd October 1725; 2nd ed 1726
A Vindication of a Sermon in answer to the Rev Mr Radcliffe's Letter, 1726
Two Affidavits in Relation to the Demands of Tythe Agistment in the Diocese of Leighlin with an introduction. Dublin 1736
The Synge Leters, some published correspondence

He was said by Handel to be "learned in music"

SYNGE, EDWARD 1798/99–1859

b. 1798 or 1799 Chester; ed Eton Coll; ent TCD 5 Aug 1816 aged 17 BA 1820 MA 1832

C Streete (Ard) *c.* 1819–21; C Tuam 1821–23; PC Monivea (Tuam) 1823–29; R Kilkerrin U (Tuam) 1829–37; res due to wife's ill health; later PC Holy Trinity Matlock (Derby — then S'well)

> evidently **s.** of E S (**s.** of Francis)
>
> **m.** 28 Nov 1834 Cheltenham Emily **dau.** of Sir Richard Steele Bt of Dublin
>
> **Died** 2 Oct 1859 at Palermo Bay

†SYNGE, NICHOLAS 1693–1771

b. 1693 Cork; ed by Dr Jones, Dublin; TCD BA 1712 MA 1715 BD & DD 1734

d 1716 p 1717 (Dublin) Bp 1746; V Headford U (Tuam) 1720–43; Preb of Killybegs (Tuam) 1720–31; Archd of Tuam and R Moyrus = Morrisk (Tuam) 1731–43; Preb of Tassagard in St Patrick's Cath Dublin 1735–37; Preb of Mulhuddart in St Patrick's Cath Dublin 1737–43; Precentor of Elphin 1742–46; Archd of Dublin 1743–46; consec Bp of Killaloe in St Patrick's Cath Dublin 26 Jan 1746; Bp of Killaloe (w Kilfenora from 1753) 1746–71

> **s.** of Most Rev Edward, Abp of Tuam 1716–41 (**s.** of Rt Rev Edward, Bp of Cork Cloyne and Ross 1663–78 qv and Barbara (née Latham)) by Annie Proud of Co Cork; **bro.** of Rt Rev Edward, Bp of Elphin 1740–62 qv
>
> **m.** Elizabeth **dau.** of Richard Trench of Garbally Co Galway. Issue 1. Edward **b.**

1725 Dublin ent TCD as FC 23 Jun 1742 BA 1745 MA 1748 R Birr (Killaloe) 1760 Preb of Lockeen (Killaloe) 1760–61 Archd of Killaloe 1761–85 **m.** 1753 Elizabeth or Sophia (**died** 9 Oct 1792) **b.** Jan 1729 only **dau.** of Dr Samuel Hutchinson, Bp of Killala, qv and had issue **sons** (i) Edward, Prec of Achonry, qv (ii) Samuel (**died** 1 Mar 1846) **b.** 22 Apr 1756 Archd of Killaloe 1785–1809 succeeded his uncle Sir James Hutchinson as 3rd Baronet and assumed the additional name of Hutchinson (iii) George (iv) Robert, created Baronet 1801 (v) Francis and a **dau.**; 2. Barbara **m.** John Hatch of Dublin; 3. Mary **m.** 1764 William Pasley Vaughan of Golden Grove, High Sheriff of Kildare 1766

Died Jan 1771 **bur.** St Patrick's Cath Dublin

SYTHES, GEORGE PAUL SUTCLIFFE 1907–*c.* 1984

b. 1907; TCD Heb Pri 1927 BA 1929 MA 1934

d 1932 p 1933 (Kilmore); C Kinawley (Kilm) 1932–35; C-in-c Innismagrath w Dowra (Kilm) 1935–55; C-in-c Derrylane (Kilm) 1955–65; ret

m. Anne (**died** 21 Aug 1971 **bur.** Killeshandra)

Last entry in C I Dir 1984

TALBOT, RICHARD WILLIAM 1879/80–1954

b. 1879 or 1880; TCD BA 1901 MA & Div Test 1905

d 1905 p 1906 (Tuam); C Tuam (Tuam) 1905–07; C-in-c Killegar (Kilm) 1907–08; C Murragh w Templemartin (Cork) 1908–14; C Berehaven (Cork) 1914–18; R Clonfert (Clonf) 1918–21; R Loughrea w Tynagh (Clonf) 1921–29; C-in-c Ballycommon U (Kild) 1929–33; R Ballinafagh U (w C-in-c Kilmeague w Feighcullen from 1938) (Kild) 1933–45; ret

only **s.** of Richard William of Kilgoblin Castle Collinstown and Emily

m. 20 Jan 1932 Helena yst **dau.** of William Nesbitt Briscoe of Mt Briscoe Philipstown Co Offaly

Died 20 Jan 1954 Dublin aged 74

TARLETON, PETER 1946–

b. 16 Jul 1946 Pallaskenry Co Limerick; ed Portora Royal Sch Enniskillen; RBAI; TCD BA 1972 Div Test 1973 HDipEd 1977 MA 1980

d 1973 p 1974; C St Luke w St Ann Shandon (Cork) 1973–75; C Drumcondra (Dub) 1975–77; R Limerick City (Lim) 1977–82; R Drumgoon Dernakesh Ashfield and Killesherdoney (Kilm) 1982–85; Chapl HM YOI Hindley 1985–89; Chapl HM Prison Lindholme Doncaster S Yorks 1989–99; Hon Canon Sheffield Cath 1998–99; Chapl HM Prison Armley Leeds 1999–; Perm to Off Dio Sheffield 1999–

s. of Rev Denis Reginald, R Devenish (Clogh) 1959–63 (**s.** of Thomas Richard of Derbyshire and Charlotte Alice (née Ovens)) by Eileen **dau.** of Robert and Jeannie (née McAlister) Stewart

m. 16 Oct 1971 Jocelyn **dau.** of William John and Mary Elizabeth (née Hutton) Brown of Markethill Co Armagh. Issue 1. Joanne Marie **b.** 1 Feb 1973 **m.** Ronan

Flanagan of Kilkenny; 2. Catherine Anne **b.** 13 Mar 1974; 3. Michael Peter **b.** 23 May 1975; 4. Eoin Denis **b.** 14 Feb 1977; 5. Kevin David Thomas **b.** 25 Mar 1981

TATE, RICHARD*

d Jun 1860 p; C Cloone (Ard) 1860–; lic 13 Sep 1862; C Drumshambo (Ard) 1865–66; C Fenagh (Ard) 1865–69

TATE, RICHARD 1836/37–1906*

b. 1836 or 1837; TCD BA 1861 Div Test 1862

d 1870 p 1871 (Kilmore); C Rossinver (Kilm) 1870–72; R Rossinver (Kilm) 1872–94

yst **s.** of Robert of Manorhamilton Co Leitrim

m. 13 Jun 1871 Bessie yst **dau.** of Rev William Ashe, R Rossinver qv Issue incl 1. yr **dau.** Margaret Elizabeth (**died** 17 Feb 1952) **m.** 10 Jul 1920 at Clontarf Dublin William **s.** of Joseph Edgerley Purser; 2. Sir Robert (**died** 22 Jan 1952 Dublin) KBE SFTCD

Died 6 Dec 1906 aged 69

* These two Richard Tates are almost certainly the same person, and the dates of ordination 1870 and 1871 should therefore be 1860 and 1861, as in IEG 23 Jun 1870, Richard Tate is not included in the list of ordinands for Kilmore Diocese. It is unlikely that he would have obtained the Incumbency of Rossinver in 1872 if he had only been ordained two years

TAYLOR, DAVID MONTGOMERY   –1939

TCD BA 1906

d 1908 p 1909 (Kilm); C-in-c Killegar (Kilm) 1908–11; C Blessington (Glend) 1911–15; C Donoughmore U (Glend) 1915–19; C Cloyne (Cloyne) 1919–26; C-in-c Kilworth U (Cloyne) 1926–34; R Lislee and Courtmacsherry (Ross) 1934–39

s. of William of Belfast

m. 3 Jan 1915 Emily S **dau.** of William S McConnell of Wexford

Died 1939

TAYLOR, HENRY 1851–1937

b. 5 May 1851 Dublin; ed by Dr Benson at Rathmines Sch Dublin; TCD BA (1cl Mod Classics) 1875 MA 1879; was an accomplished violinist

d 1877 p 1878 (Down); C Drummaul (Conn) 1877–79; PC St John's Cloverhill (Kilm) 1879–83; R Drumbanagher (Arm) 1883–92; Chapl Hosp for Incurables 1892–1901; Perm to Off Dio Dublin 1892–97; C Sandford (Dub) 1897–1901; Chapl to the Lord Lt 1897–1921; Chapl to the Female Orphanage Home, Dublin (Dub) 1901–22; Hon Cler V Christ Ch Cath Dublin (Dub) 1908; ret

s. of Thomas of Dublin

m. 24 Oct 1882 Letitia Mary (**died** 28 Dec 1927) **dau.** of E G Deverell of Drumbar Co Cavan. Issue incl 1. Mary E **b.** 29 Jan 1884; 2. Eleanor Emma (**died** Nov 1969)

b. 19 Aug 1885 Drumbanagher Vicarage Co Armagh TCD MB 1912 **m.** Ralph John Richard Mecredy of Burton-on-Humber Lincs

Died 22 Apr 1937 Orpington Kent

TAYLOR, JOHN 1804/05–1866

b. 1804 or 1805 Dublin; ed by Mr Martin; ent TCD 15 Oct 1821 aged 16 BA 1826 MA LLB & LLD 1832

C Kildallon (Kilm) 1831; PC Arvagh (Kilm) 1835–52; R Templeport (Kilm) 1852–56; R Killinkere (Kilm) 1856–66

s. of William, *pragmaticus*

m. Theodosia Agnes (**died** 25 Aug 1860 at Killinkere Rectory) **dau.** of Isaac D'Olier, LLD Treasurer to Ecclesiastical Commissioners. Issue incl **s.** 1. Rev Nathaniel Sneyd, PC Ballyjamesduff (Kilm) qv; **daus.** 1. Helen Elizabeth (**died** 12 Aug 1902 Queenstown); 2. his 2nd **dau.** Kate **m.** 21 May 1857 Mark Moore, MD of Bailieboro'; 3. Maria (**died** 1 Jun 1863 Dublin aged 20); 4. Anna Margaret (**died** 17 Apr 1925 at Bath aged 80); 5. his yst **dau.** Elizabeth Adelaide **m.** 9 Oct 1872 Rev J Evans Preston, V Julianstown (Meath)

Died 20 May 1866 Dublin aged 61

TAYLOR, JOHN WALLACE 1852–1929

b. 1852 at Corragarry Parish of Currin Co Monaghan; ed RBAI; TCD (Sen Mod Eth & Log) & LLB 1872 LLD 1891; FRAS 1894

d 1876 p 1877 (Kilmore); C Bailieborough (Kilm) 1876–77; R Errigal Truagh (Clogh) 1877–1927; Chapl St Mary Portclare (Clogh) 1882

s. of Thomas Cathcart, LRCSI, Commander of the Niger and Tehadda Expedition 1852 and HBM Consular Svce) and Margaret Ellen **dau.** of John Wallace of Corragarry

m. 1876 Maria eldest **dau.** of Thomas Dawson, BL of Drummany Co Monaghan. Issue 1. John Wallace Moore; 2. Annabel Margaret **m.** William Griffith; 3. Susan Frances Dawson **m.** 5 Sep 1908 Rev Samuel Hutchinson Baker, R Brantry (Arm) 1939–56 and had issue (i) Rev Samuel Wallace, C Urney (Kilm) qv (ii) Reginald Dawson **b.** 18 Mar 1911 (iii) Gilmore Hutchinson (**died** 14 Jul 1954 aged 35); 4. Thomas Dawson Savage, LRCVSI; 5. Grace Wilhelmina; 6. Rev Whitney Moutray (**died** 1964) d 1913 p 1927 C Errigal Truagh (Clogh) 1913–27 C Newry (Drom) 1927–31 C Tralee and Dio C Ardfert (A & A) 1931–33 C Moviddy & Kilmurry (Cork) 1933–64 Preb of Desertmore (Cork) and Preb of Timoleague (Ross) 1960–64 **m.** 20 Jan 1932 Booterstown Par Ch Dublin Elizabeth Mary **dau.** of John Gray of Newry and had issue Avril Dawson **m.** 17 Oct 1955 Augustus **s.** of Paul Kingston of Glencairn Co Waterford; 7. Ruth Cranston

Died 3 Sep 1929

PUBLICATIONS

Contributed to UJA and other periodicals

TAYLOR, NATHANIEL SNEYD 1831/32–

b. 1831 or 1832 Co Carlow; ed privately; ent TCD 15 Oct 1847 aged 15 BA 1854

d 1855 p 1856 (Kilmore); C Templeport (Kilm) 1855–56; C Killinkere (Kilm) 1856; PC Mullogh (Kilm) 1856–72; PC Ballyjamesduff and Castlerahan (Kilm) 1872–76; res, "and accepted a charge as Minister of Turrough Cross (Free) Church in the parish of St. Mary's, Torquay, an independent congregation of English Churchmen", IEG Feb 1878.

s. of Rev John, R Killinkere (Kilm) qv (**s.** of William) by Theodosia Agnes **dau.** of Isaac D'Olier

m. 4 May 1859 Amy **dau.** of Brabazon Newcomen of Camla Co Roscommon. Issue incl 1. Dora aged 10 and 2. Lily aged 9 accidentally drowned 6 Jun 1878; 3. Amy **m.** 28 Jan 1888 Rev W H Mitchell, C Harberton (Ex); 4. Isabella Mary **m.** 10 Nov 1886 Rev Hedley J Holderness, Chapl Miss to Seamen Portland

TAYLOR, RICHARD HUNSLEY 1849/50–

b. 1849 or 1850; matric Queen's Coll Ox 27 Oct 1869 aged 19 a Commoner Charlsley Hall 1869 BA 1885 MA 1890 BD 1895 DD 1900; student of the Inner Temple 1870

d 1883 (Lincoln) p 1884 (Winchester); C Selston (S'well) 1883; C Stoke-next-Guildford (Guildf — then Win) 1883–85; C Hoby (Leic — then Pet) 1885–86; Chapl Leeds Gen Infirmary 1887–88; V Cleasby (Rip) 1888–90; R Killan, now Shercock (Kilm) 1890–92; Assoc Sec CMS for N of Ireland 1892–94; V Shelley (Wakef) 1894–98; V Willen (Ox) 1898–1902; V Stratton–Audley (Ox) 1902–03; R Goddington (Ox) 1903–07; R Lyons (Dur) 1907–

s. of Francis of Manchester

TAYLOR, ROBERT

is V Drung and Lara (Kilm) 1622; prob same as Robert Taylor V Killan, now Shercock and Knockbride (Kilm) to 1622

TAYLOR, THOMAS 1668/69–1749

b. 1668 or 1669; ed by Mr Kennedy; ent TCD as Sizar 22 March 1687/88 aged 18 MA

possibly C Ballyrashane (Conn) 1673; V Killashee (Ard) 1697–1749; Archd of Ardagh 1705–49

possibly **s.** of Edward of Dublin, Attorney

Died Apr 1749

TAYLOR, THOMAS 1821/22–1902

b. 1821 or 1822 Co Monaghan; ent TCD 2 Jul 1839 aged 17 BA & Div Test (1) 1844

d 5 Apr 1846 Crockford has 1852 (Clogher) p 1853; C All SS Birmingham 1852–56; DC Aghadrumsee (Clogh) 1862–70; C Killoe (Ard) 1878–79; R Gowna (Ard) 1880–1902

s. of Rev John (1788/89–1847), R Rossorry (Clogh) 1842–47 (**s.** of Thomas) by

Jane Bradshaw; **bro.** of Rev Henry Roper BA (1838–1922)

Died 10 Oct 1902 at the Meath Hospital Dublin after being knocked down by a tram on Rathgar Road Dublin

TAYLOUR, ROBERT

appears R & V Knockbride (Kilm) to 1622; was "M.A." and a preacher

TEATE (TATE), FAITHFUL   –1660

b. at the *Villa Ballyhay*; ed at Chester; TCD BA 1621 MA 1624 BD & DD

ordained d by Thomas (Ram) Bp of Ferns 5 Feb 1618/19 p per do. 10 May 1621; Preb of Crosspatrick 1618; Chapl to Lord Blayney 1623; R Maghernakille (Clogh) 1624; pres by the Crown to Donaghmoyne (Clogh) 1624; R Drumlane (Kilm) 1625; R Drumgoon (Kilm) 1625–27; coll R & V Castleterra *alias* Dowcarrollagh (Kilm) 14 Mar 1625/26; coll V Drung and Lara (Kilm) 15 Mar 1625/26; got a grant of a glebe here as V 25 Jan 1626/27 (Morrin III. 186); is still V 1634; again pres by the Crown to R Castleterra (Kilm) and R Drung and Larah (Kilm) 28 Jan 1635–45 (L.M. V. 111); got faculty from Abp of Armagh to hold them together 4 Jul 1635; Vice Rector TCD 1640; Minister at East Greenwich in 1653–*c*. 58; Commonwealth Minister at St Peter's Drogheda (Arm) 1658–60; was wounded and robbed of £300 on 23 Dec 1641 near Virginia; his family was also ill-used by the rebels, and he lost £3,930 altogether in the rebellion, Leslie *Armagh Clergy and Parishes,* p 238)

elder **s.** of Donagh

m. Mary and had issue incl 1. his eldest **s.** Faithful, Clk of Dublin who was perhaps an independent minister ent TCD 4 Nov 1641 aged 14 **m.** and had issue (i) Nahum (**died** 1715) **b.** 1652, Poet Laureate and co-author of Tate and Brady's *Psalms of David* (ii) Joseph (iii) his yst **s.** Theophilus ent TCD 21 Mar 1662

Died — evidently at Drogheda — before 12 May 1660

PUBLICATIONS

Sermon at the Funeral of Sir Charles Coote in Christ Church Cathedral, Dublin, 1658

Nathaniel an Israelite Indeed, 1657

THADY

Dean of Ardagh *c.* 1245 (B.M. MS, f.25)

THEWLES, GEORGE   –1688

coll V St John's Athlone (Elph) 8 Feb 1682/83. If he was the same as George Thewles who was appoionted V Kilgeffin Kilteran & Clontuskart in 1674, he could not have been the FTCD who ent TCD in 1676, but was probably his father

Died 1688

THEWLES, JOHN 1674/75–

b. 1674 or 1675 Athlone; ed by Mr Shaw; ent TCD 12 May 1694 aged 19 Sch 1695 BA 1698

V Ballysumaghan Kilross Ballinakill Boyle & Taunagh (Elph) 1716–18; R Ahascragh & Killion = Killyon (Elph) 1718–30

    s. of George

THOMAS——

is V Fignsaidin (Kilm) *c.* 1415; also V Yniscayn (Kilm) *c.* 1415 (Cal. Reg. Mey, 356)

THOMAS——

is Archd of Kilmore to 1409 (Cal. Reg. Flem. 107); he or another Thomas is still Archd in 1426 and 1427 (Cal. Reg. Swayne, 11, 133); perhaps same as Thomas O'Sheridan qv

THOMAS, GEORGE 1827/28–

b. 1827 or 1828 Co Galway; ent TCD 1 Jul 1845 aged 17 BA 1850

C Kilmacshalgan (Killala) –1858; prob same as George Thomas who was C Glankeen (Cash) 1867; C Drumreilly (Kilm) 1870–74

    s. of Rev Anthony

THOMPSON, ——

C Granard (Ard) *c.* 1826

THOMPSON, ARTHUR HUGH 1908–1993

b. 1908; TCD BA & Div Test 1937 MA 1956

d 11 Jul 1937 (Waterford) p 29 Jul 1938 (Waterford); C Cappoquin w Villierstown and Whitechurch (Lism) 1937–40; C Annagh (Kilm) 1940–42; C-in-c Derrylane (Kilm) 1942–52; R Boyle Aghanagh Kilbryan (w Ardcarne from 1956) (Elph) 1952–78; RD of S Elphin 1952–66; Dio Reg Elphin and Ardagh 1956–78; Preb of Kilcooley (Elph) 1965–78; Archd of Elphin and Ardagh 1966–78; Exam Chapl to Bp of Kilmore 1966–78; ret

    s. of Dr J A Thompson of Maguiresbridge Co Fermanagh

    m. 31 Jan 1946 Nina only dau. of Rev Edward Joseph McKew, C-in-c Derrybrusk (Clogh). Issue incl 1. Norah Margaret b. 24 Jul 1947 m. 1975 St Thomas's Ch Belfast John Stothers McKinstry of Lambeg Co Antrim. 2. James Edward b. 31 Jul 195–

    Died 4 Nov 1993

THOMPSON, GEORGE

in Canon Leslie's MSS

b. 1795 or 1796 Longford; ed by Mr Moore; ent TCD as SC 4 Jul 1814 aged 18 BA 1818

C Newtownhamilton (Arm) 1831; C Cloonclare (Kilm)–1843; R Kilcooley (Cash) 1858–68

prob George Thompson **s.** of William

in Canon W E C Fleming *Armagh Clergy 1800–2000*

b. *c.* 1802 Donegal; ed by Mr Irvine; ent TCD 8 Jun 1819 aged 17 BA 1824 MA 1832 d 1830 p 1831 (Clogher for Armagh); C Newtownhamilton (Arm) 1830; C Cloonclare (Kilm) *c.* 1842–58; R Kilcooley (Cash) 1858–68

prob **s.** of Robert, farmer

m. Sarah Anne (Miller?). Issue incl Robert Rowley bapt 6 Oct 1830 at Desertlyn Ch

THOMPSON, JOHN ALFRED 1868–1941

b. 27 Nov 1868 Cork; ed Royal Sch Cavan; TCD Royal Scholar 1886 BA 1891 d 1892 (Dublin for Derry) p 1893 (Derry); C-in-c Gartan (Raph) 1892–95; C St John Sligo (Elph) 1895–96; C Templemichael (Ard) 1896–1903; C Northfield (York) 1903–07; Dom Chapl to Bp of Worcester 1907–09; V St Thomas Coventry (Cov) 1909–16; R Richard's Castle (Heref) from 1916; Exam Chapl to Bp of Worcester 1917–18; Exam Chapl to Bp of Coventry 1918–22

s. of Rev William, R Layde (Conn) 1873–1906 (**s.** of Rev John of Belfast by Sarah Margaret (1844–1892) **dau.** of William Sprott of Dromore Co Down

m. (1) 15 Jan 1901 Anna Maria (**died** 25 Jun 1902) 2nd **dau.** of Frederick Lane of Collahanch Co Laois

m. (2) 14 Jul 1909 Rhoda Margaret Yeatman. Issue Barbra Mary **b.** 1 Nov 1910

Died Jan 1941

THOMPSON, JOHN NESBITT 1825/26–1879

b. 1825 or 1826 Dublin; ed by Mr Flynn; ent TCD 14 Oct 1845 aged 19 BA 1851 PC Ballycanew (Ferns) 1862–65; R Killyon or Killeroran (Elph) 1866–79

s. of James Armstrong *protator* (tax–collector); **bro.** of Rev Matthew Nesbitt qv

m. 17 Dec 1867 Elizabeth Letitia (**died** 8 Jun 1894) **dau.** of Col Charles Pratt of Stoneville Co Dublin

Died 4 May 1879

THOMPSON, MATTHEW NESBITT 1818/19–1880

b. 1818 or 1819 Tipperary; ed by Mr Flynn; ent TCD 14 Oct 1836 aged 17 BA 1848 d 1850 (Cork) p; C Granard (Ard) 1856, lic 6 Nov (S.R.)

acc to Templemichael list, he is C Templemichael (Ard) 1855–62, and res for C Granard

(Ard) 1862; C Roscommon (Elph) 1861–63; R Roscommon (Elph) 1863–75; R Killinagh (Kilm) 1875–79; R Killoughter (Kilm) 1879–80

s. of James Armstrong *protator*; **bro.** of Rev John Nesbitt qv

m. 29 May 1850 Sarah Anne 3rd **dau.** of William E Porter of Dalkey Co Dublin. Issue incl 1 eldest **s.** 1. James Edward, TCD MB (**died** 23 Jun 1881 in Trinidad); 2. yst **s.** St George Armstrong (**died** 25 May 1875 at the military barracks Roscommon aged 8); 3. Adelaide Jane (**died** 18 Jun 1869 aged 12 at Roscommon)

Died 8 Apr 1880

THOMPSON, ROBERT 1793/94–1857

b. 1793 or 1794 Co Meath; ed by Dr Shields; ent TCD 5 Nov 1810 aged 16 no degree recorded

C Navan (Meath) 1825; C Drumgoon (Kilm) 1826–31; R Athlumney (Meath) 1831–32; R Navan (Meath) 1832–57

4th **s.** of Skeffington of Rathnally Co Meath

m. Louisa Cole 4th **dau.** of John Metge, JP of Athlumney Co Meath

Died 10 Jan 1857

THOMPSON, WILLIAM

prob William Thompson ed by Mr Dubordieu; ent TCD Dec 1758 BA 1763 MA 1767

R Kilmore (Elph) 1773–

m. Aug 1790 (ML 19 Jul) Sarah **dau.** of Owen Lloyd

THORNBURY, PETER DAWSON 1943–

b. 29 Aug 1943 Lurgan Co Armagh; OU BA 1984; CITC 1990; TCD BTh 1993

d 27 Jun 1993 p 29 Sep 1994 (Kilmore); C Annagh G (Kilm) 1993–96; R Clondehorkey Mevagh & Glenalla (Raph) 1996–98; BC Kilsaran G (Arm) 1998–2006; R Aghaderg Donaghmore and Scarva (Drom) 2006–;

s. of Samuel of Lurgan (**s.** of Dawson of Lurgan and Elizabeth (née Johnston)) by Esther (née McEllwaine)

m. 6 Feb 1966 Waringstown Co Down Rita Valerie Frances **dau.** of Edward and Jean Wild of Waringstown. Issue 1. Dawn **b.** 18 Aug 1967; 2. Delia **b.** 25 Feb 1970

THORPE, RICHARD

pres Preb & V Kilbegnet & V Tessaragh (Elph) 9 Dec 1633 (L.M. V. 110)

TIBEAUDO, OLIVER JOSEF 1823–1893

b. 1823 Dublin; ed by Mr Turner; ent TCD 2 Jul 1839 aged 16 BA 1844 Div Test (2) 1855 MA 1888

d 1855 p 1856 (Kilmore); C St John Sligo (Elph) 1856–; C Kiltoghart (Ard) 1861–62;

C Fenagh (Ard) 1862–65; C Arklow (Glend) 1865–67; R Donadea (Kild) 1868–74; I Ballymore (Meath) 1874–89; R Durrow (Meath) 1890–93

s. of Oliver, Lawyer

m. Maria Martha (**died** 10 Apr 1892) **dau.** of Capt Purdon of Lisnabin Killucan

Died 14 Jan 1893 **bur.** Durrow

TIGHE, HUGH USHER 1802–1874

b. 27 Feb 1802; ed Eton Coll; ent Corpus Christi Coll Oxford 18 May 1819 aged 17 BA 1822

PC St Mark Drogheda (Arm) 1828–34; R Clonmore (Arm) 1834–50; Dean of the Chapel Royal Dublin 1843–60; Dean of Leighlin 1850–54; Dean of Ardagh 1854–60; Preb of Timothan in St Patrick's Cath Dublin 1857–74; R Templemore (Derry 1860–72; Dean of Derry 1860–74 (he retained the Deanery upon his resignation from Templemore in 1872)

3rd **s.** of Robert Stearne of Mitchelstown Co Westmeath and Topsham Devon

m. 21 Apr 1828 at Dunleer Co Louth Anne Florence **b.** 1808 (**died** 21 Feb 1893) **dau.** of John McClintock of Drumcar and Lady Elizabeth French. Issue 1. Robert Hugh Morgan (**died** May 1867 unm) **b.** 5 Feb 1829; 2. Charles Moland Morgan **died** 18 May 1843 Rathmines Dublin aged 3; 2 **daus.** Elizabeth Letitia Morgan (**died** 25 Feb 1906) **m.** 22 Jun 1853 Edward Stopford Blair of Penningham Wigtownshire, and Catherine Florence Morgan **m.** 6 Jul 1858 John E Severne, MP (**died** 21 Apr 1899)

Died 11 Aug 1874 **bur.** Drumcar

TILSON, ANDREW JOHN

ed St Bees Coll 1886; PTE (1) 1887

d 1888 p 1889; C Ballymacarrett (Down) 1888–89; C West Houghton Lancs (Manch) 1889–91; C Cashel (Ard) 1891; V Kilglass (Ard) 1891–92; C Ballynure (Conn) 1892–94; C Shelton (Lich) 1894–97; V Kingsley (Lich) 1897–1901; C Madeley (Lich) 1901–03; V Hamstead (Birm) 1903–05; C Longton (Lich) 1906–10; C Audley (Lich) 1910–14; C Grosnall and Knightley (Lich) 1914–16; V Ellenhall (Lich) 1916–22; TCF 1918–21; R Norbury (Lich) 1922–23; V Foxt and Whiston (Lich) 1923–26; R Drayton Bassett (Lich) 1926–28; V Ellenhall (w Ronton from 1931) (Lich) 1928–35

†TILSON, HENRY 1576–1655

b. 13 Oct 1576 Halifax Yorks; ed Balliol Coll Oxford BA 1597; Fellow of Oxford 1599 MA 1601 DD

R Stanmer (Chich) 1614–15; V Rochdale (now Manch) 1615–34; came to Ireland as Chapl to the Earl of Strafford, Lord Lt; Dean of Christ Ch Cath Dublin 1634–39; was appointed Preb of Monmohenock in St Patrick's Cath Dublin but does not appear to have got possession; Archd of Connor 1635–39; Bp of Elphin 1639–55; consec in Christ Ch Cath Dublin 23 Sep 1639

s. of Henry.

m. and had issue 1. Nathan; 2. Thomas, Clerk of the Irish House of Commons **m.** Elizabeth **dau.** of Thomas Hill of Dublin and had issue; 3. Henry **b.** 1624 at Rochdale Lancs ed by Mr Dunbar at Dublin ent TCD 21 May 1639 aged 15 **m.** and had issue; 4. Alice **m.** Thomas Barton of Buncraggy Co Clare; 5. Lettice **m.** John Houston; 6. Catherine **m.** Thomas Sadleir of Sopwell; 7. Grace **m.** (1) Sir John Dillon **m.** (2) Admiral Whitshed

Died 31 Mar 1655 at Camberworth **bur.** in the Southill Chapel of Dewsbury Church

During the Rebellion of 1641, his library and other properties were plundered and he fled to England and settled at Southill in the Parish of Dewsbury, Yorks, where he was Chaplain to Sir Thomas Wentworth at Camberworth

TISDALL, MARK ANTHONY

ed by Mr Buck; ent TCD 25 Jun 1760

coll V Kilnamanagh (Elph) 25 May 1765

TISDALL, WILLIAM

R & V Killasoolan = Castleblakeney & Kilronan (Elph) 1743–*c.* 54; was perhaps W T, R Kildress (Arm); see *Armagh Clergy* p 324

TODD, JAMES

TCD BA (Resp) 1882 LLB 1884 LLD 1886

d 1881 (Kilmore) p 1881 (Kilmore); C Ahamplish (Elph) 1881; R Ahamplish (Elph) 1881–86; R Ballyboy (Meath) 1886–88; R Mayne (Meath) 1888–94; Sec SS Soc for Ireland 1891–98; P-in-c Jarrahdale (Dio Perth W Australia) 1900–01; R Midland Junction (Perth) 1901–04

s. of James of Kilmore Co Armagh; **bro.** of Rev Henry, R Camlough (Arm)

TOMLINSON, WILLIAM 1804/05–1863

b. 1804 or 1805 Dublin; ed by Mr Flinn; ent TCD 18 Oct 1824 aged 19 BA 1829 MA 1832

d 5 Aug 1832 p 18 Oct 1832 (Oss S.R.); C Drumgoon (Kilm) 1835; R Granard (Ard) 1838–63

s. of John

Died 6 Sep 1863 at the residence of his **sister**, Merrion Ave Dublin

TOOSEY, OSBERT DENTON

C Kinawley (Kilm) to 1843

TOPHAM, JAMES 1806/07–1881

b. 1806 or 1807 Co Cavan; ed by Mr Hutchings; ent TCD 4 Nov 1844 BA 1849

C Drumreilly (Kilm) 1852; C Kiltoghart (w Drumshambo from 1861) (Ard) 1855–69; R Shrule (Ard) 1869–81

s. of Joseph, *agricola*

m. Mary dau. of Rev James Harpur of Castleblayney Co Monaghan. Tombstone at Shrule records the following: "Mary Harpur Topham, eldest and beloved daughter of the late Revd. James Topham and Mary his wife died at Castleblayney 8th Feb 1889." On a tombstone at Ballymahon the following is inscribed: "Sacred to the memory of the Rev. James Topham, for 12 years Incumbent of Shrule Parish who departed this life March 5th 1881 in the 75 year of his life. A devoted husband a loving father and a faithful minister."

Issue incl Mary Harpur, Anna Adela **died** 26 Apr 1939 at Dartford, Kent, and a **dau.** who m. John G Reid, Solicitor, Castleblayney

Died 5 Mar 1881

TORRENS, THOMAS 1850/51–1937

b. 1850 or 1851 Co Tipperary; ed at Skreen Co Sligo; ent TCD 1 Nov 1880 aged 29 BA & Div Test 1884 MA 1887

d 1883 (Kilmore for Armagh) p 1884 (Down for Armagh); C Ballinderry (Arm) 1883–85; C Christ Ch Burton-on-Trent (Lich) 1885–87; C Finchley Middlesex (Lon) 1887–91; C Swanage (Sarum) 1891–93; R Killesherdoney (Kilm) 1893–95; R Swanlinbar (Kilm) 1895–1905; C St Paul Leamington (Cov — then Worc) 1905–06; C Hessle (York) 1906–09; C St John the Baptist Owlerton (Sheff — then York) 1909–12; C Ranmoor (Sheff — then York) 1912–13; Lic Pr Dio York 1914–15; V Wotton Underwood, Aylesbury (Ox) 1915–26; ret

s. of John, teacher

m. Annie Jane

Died 7 Apr 1937 St Alban's Herts, s.p

TOWNSHEND, AMBROSE GEORGE –1957

AKC 1889

d 1889 p 1890 (London); C St Andrew & St Philip, N Kensington London (Lon) 1888–91; Asst Chapl Old Molyneux Chapel Dublin (Dub) 1891–92; R Kilglass (Ard) 1892–94; V Sileby (Pet) 1899–1909; R St John the Baptist Harborne (Birm) 1909–17; R St Saviour Bacup (Manch) 1917; Sec ICM 1917–23; R Trimingham (Nor) 1923–40; R Rand Fulnethby (Linc) 1940–48; ret Perm to Off Dio Norwich 1950–57

m. E Olive (**died** 20 Jun 1938)

Died 2 Oct 1957

PUBLICATION
Staurophobia: A Reply to a Sermon

TOWNSHEND, HORACE THOMAS EDWARD

TCD BA & Div Test (2) 1874

d 1874 (Dublin for Kilmore) p 1874 (Dublin); C Mohill (Ard) 1874–75; Dep Sec

Deaf and Dumb Assoc Dublin 1875–76; C St Michael Limerick (Lim) 1876–79; I Quin (Killaloe) 1879–81; C Tuam, Master Dio Sch and Dio Reg (Tuam) 1881–83

m. and had issue a son **b.** 9 Oct 1875 Dublin

TRACEY, ANDREW –1836

lic C Lavey (Kilm) 4 Jul 1803; still there 1829

Died 7 Dec 1836 Kilmore

TRAFFORD, THOMAS –1640

V Ballymacormack (Ard) 1640, inst 30 Jul; inducted 31 Jul (F.F.); was killed by the rebels as appears from a deputation of his wife Elizabeth (Hickson I 349)

TRENCH, Hon. CHARLES Le POER 1772–1839

b. Dec 1772; ed by Mr Ralph; entered TCD 24 Jul 1789 BA & MA 1802 LLB & LLD 1803; served as Lt in the Army; was MP for the Borough of Limavady 1799–1801

Chanc of Waterford 1806–12; R Athenry (Tuam) 1812–39; V Ballinasloe (Clonf) & Preb of Ballynulter (Clonf) and V Gen of Clonfert 1816–39; Archd of Ardagh 1821–39; R Dunleer (Arm) 1823–39; Preb of Faldown (Tuam) 1825–39

4th **s.** of William Power Keating, 1st Earl of Clancarty by Anne eldest **dau.** of the Rt Hon Charles Gardiner; **bro.** of the Most Rev Power Trench DD, Abp of Tuam qv

m. 1806 Frances 2nd **dau.** of Thomas Elwood of Ashford Park Co Mayo. Issue 1. Rev Frederick William **b.** 8 Jan 1808, R Moore and Drum (Tuam) **m.** 14 Apr 1846 Matilda Sophia **dau.** of Capt John Ireland RN; 2. Henry Luke **b.** 16 Jan 1820 Major-Gen Bengal Staff Corps **m.** and had issue; 3. Charles Le Poer **m.** 18 Mar 1840 Frances 4th **dau.** of Most Rev Power Le Poer, Abp of Tuam, qv; 4. Anne Letitia **m.** 25 Jul 1842 Thomas Osborne, Madras Army **s.** of Sir DT Osborne Bt. She died 18 Feb 1846 on the same day as her husband

Died 31 Oct 1839

TRENCH, JOHN Le POER 1802–1866

b. 11 Mar 1802 Galway; ed by Mr Moore; ent TCD 18 Oct 1819 BA MA

before ordination was a clerk in the office of the Commissioner of Customs

d 7 Sep 1828 p; C Killoe (Ard) 1828; R Kiltullagh (Elph — then Tuam) 1832–38; R Aglish, Castlebar (Tuam) 1838–39; R Templemichael (Ard) 1839–66

2nd **s.** of William, Rear Admiral, RN

m. Jan 1834 Ellen yst **dau.** of Charles Rice Davis. Issue 1. Power Digby, Lt RA **died** 3 Jul 1860 in India; 2. William FitzJohn in Army; 3. Charles Edward, Capt RN **m.** Harriet L Taylor; 4. Richard John who fell at Kandahar; 5. Harriet Elizabeth **m.** Henry West QC

Died 29 Sep 1866

†TRENCH, POWER Le POER, 1770–1839

b. 1770 Co Galway; ed by Mr Ralph; ent TCD 2 Jul 1787 aged 16 BA 1791

V Creagh U (Clonf) 1792–1802; R Raddanstown (Meath) 1793–1802; served as a Chapl of Yeomanry during the 1798 rebellion; Bp of Waterford 1802–10; Bp of Elphin 1810–19; translated to Tuam by Patent 10 Nov 1819; Abp of Tuam and Bp of Ardagh (w Bp of Killala and Achonry from 1834) 1819–39

    s. of William, 1st Earl of Clancarty by Anne eldest **dau.** of the Rt Hon Charles Gardiner and **bro.** of Ven Charles, Archd of Ardagh qv above

    m. Anne **dau.** of Walter Taylor of Castle Taylor. Issue incl sons Rev William qv below and Power and **daus.** Anne O'Hara, Florinda Bookey, Elizabeth Gascoyne, Frances Mary Trench (**died** 24 Feb 1860 Monkstown Co Dublin) **m.** Charles Le Poer Trench, and Emily Trench

    Died 25 Mar 1839

Note: The Archbishop was much interested in the conversion of Roman Catholics through the medium of the Scriptures in the Irish Language and he was President of the Irish Society: His Life has been written by the Rev J. D'A Sirr as *Life of the Last Archbishop of Tuam*. Upon the death of Archbishop Trench in 1839, the Diocese of Tuam ceased to be an Archbishopric and Ardagh was joined to Kilmore

TRENCH, WILLIAM

coll V Kilnamanagh (Elph) 21 Aug 1737; became Archd of Kilfenora 1767

TRENCH, WILLIAM Le POER 1801/02–1854

b. 1801 or 1802 Rafford, Galway; ent Oriel Coll Oxford 20 Oct 1821 aged 19– no degree recorded at Oxford, but is probably William Trench TCD BA 1823

d 21 Feb 1830 for C Lavally (Tuam); Preb of Laccagh (Tuam) 1830; R Cloone (Ard) 1830–54. It is possible that he was never resident because of ill health and that he had curates to look after the parish

    eldest **s.** of Most Rev Power Trench, Abp of Tuam qv (s. of William 1st Earl Clancarty) by Anne **dau.** of Walter Taylor of Castle Taylor

    m. 25 Dec 1830 his cousin Lady Louisa Trench eldest **dau.** of Richard 2nd Earl of Clancarty. Issue 1. Harriet Anne **m.** 12 Apr 1862 Henry William only **s.** of Sir Henry Meredith Bt; 2. Sarah **m.** J Peddie Steele TCD MD

    Died 11 May 1854

TRENIER, ROBERT ERNEST 1910–1985

b. 1910; TCD BA 1933 Div Test (2) 1934

d & p 1935 (Clogher); C Tydavnet Kilmore and Drumsnatt (Clogh) 1935–38; C Urney Annagelliffe Denn and Derryheen (Kilm) 1938–39; R Swanlinbar (Kilm) 1939–44; R Knockbride w Shercock (Kilm) 1944–56; R Drumgoon w Dernakesh and Ashfield (w C-in-c Shercock from 1965) (Kilm) 1956–71; Preb of Triburnia (Kilm) 1959–71; ret

    only **s.** of Robert of Portadown Co Armagh

m. 21 Sep 1939 Elizabeth Evelyn **dau.** of S Gillespie (**died** 28 Jan 1980 Edinburgh). Issue 1. Anne; 2. Patricia **m.** 30 Mar 1968 at Cootehill William Masson elder **s.** of W F Wood of Edinburgh; 3. Susan; 4. Peter; 5. Robert

Died 21 Mar 1985 Edinburgh

TRENOTUS, Sir…

Chaplain of Cluain (Cloone) (Ard) 15 Apr 1407 (Cal. Reg. Flem. 57)

TRIPHOOK, JOHN CRAMPTON 1856–*c.* 1940

b. 18 May 1856; ed St Columba's Coll Dublin; TCD 1874

d 1880 p 1881 (Kilmore); C Lissadell (Elph) 1880–81; C St John Sligo (Elph) 1881–82; C St John Cashel and V Chor Cashel (Cash) 1882–85; R Aghalurcher (Clogh) 1885–99; C Pendeen (Truro) 1899; C St Nicholas Rochester (Roch) 1899–1903; C Holy Trinity Sittingbourne (Cant) 1903–05; C Little Tey (Chelmsf — then St A) 1905–06; R Little Tey (Chelmsf — then St A) 1906–11; C Great Horkesley 1914–16; Chapl Colchester Union 1916–34; C St Nicholas Colchester (Chelmsf — then St A) 1926–28; Chapl Infections Hosp Myland Essex 1926–31; Perm to Off Dio Chelmsf from 1934; Crockford 1933 has him R Lexden w Winstree U (Chelmsf — then St A) 1905–33

s. of Rev Joseph Robert, Prec of Killaloe (**s.** of Rev John, R Schull (Cork)

m. 1882 Emma Sanders Millar. Issue 1. Owen Leech (**died** 1919 at Baghdad); 2. Ellis Russell; 3. Saidie Victoria

Died *c.* 1940

TROTTER, JOHN CRAWFORD   –1937

ed St Aidan's Coll Birkenhead 1904; Trinity Coll Camb BA 1926 MA 1929

d 1905 p 1906 (Manchester); C Christ Ch Blackburn (Blackb — then Manch) 1905–07; C St Mary Stamford Brook (Lon) 1908–11; C All SS Clooney Londonderry (Derry) 1913–14; C Clonleigh (Raph — then Derry) 1914–15; C Kilmacrennan (Raph) 1915–16; C Stoke next Guildford (Guildf — then Win) 1917–21; C St Paul Cambridge (Ely) 1921–24; C St Peter Birkenhead (Ches) 1925–27; C Horsell (Guildf) 1927–28; Dio C Kilmore 1928–30; C Gorleston (Nor) 1930–31; V Stow Beden U (Nor) 1931–37

s. of Rev John Crawford, R Ardrahan (Kilmacd)

m. 29 Jul 1931 St Andrew's Ch Gorleston Suffolk Annie (née Hudson). Issue Adelaide Eleanor **m.** Rev J W Wright

Died 23 Jan 1937

TULLIE (TULLY), CONNOR (CORNELIUS)

was pres to the Chantorship = Precentorship of Elphin 27 Nov 1615 (L.M. V. 103), and inst Provost of Elphin 27 Jun 1616 (F.F.). He was V Baslick and Kilcorkey 1635–40.

TURBRIDGE, JOHN

ord d 1658 (Clonfert); coll to V Drung & Lara (Kilm) 4 May 1661; also V Lavey (Kilm) 1661–62

> prob John T whose **s.** Charles was born in Co Cavan ed by Mr Crow ent TCD 7 Jun 1659 aged 17. He was Commonwealth Schoolmaster at Trim in 1665 (Seymour's MSS p 217–219)

TURKINGTON, ROBERT CHRISTOPHER HOWARD 1913–1984

b. 1913; TCD Eccles Hist Pri (2) 1935 BA & Div Test 1937 MA 1957

d 1937 p 1938 (Kilmore) C Annagh w Quivvy and St Andrew's (Kilm) 1937–40; C-in-c Castleterra (Kilm) 1940–47; R Bailieborough (Kilm) 1947–55; R Kilmore w Ballintemple (Kilm) 1955–85; Preb of Drumlease (Kilm) 1957–65; Dean of Kilmore 1965–84

> **s.** of R D Turkington of Lurgan Co Armagh
>
> **m.** 11 Sep 1940 Kathleen Olivia Nixon of Clontarf Dublin. Issue 1. Olive **m.** 14 Oct 1970 Holy Trinity Rathmines Dublin Eslyn Peter **s.** of W S O'Malley of Quickland NZ; 2. Maureen **m.** 31 May 1969 Barry Mitchell
>
> **Died** 16 Dec 1984

TURNEY, BURTON TRIMNELL 1864/65–1924

b. 1864 or 1865; ed St Aidan's Coll Birkenhead 1887

d 1889 p 1890 (Kilmore); C Drumgoon (Kilm) 1889–92; R Killan, now Shercock (Kilm) 1892–1904; R Easkey (Killala) 1904–09; R Burrishoole (Tuam) 1909–21; R Moyrus U (Tuam) 1921–24

> **m.** Ella (**died** 9 Apr 1952 Mageough Infirmary Dublin). Issue 1. Patrick; 2. Edgar; 3. John Leslie **m.** 28 Jan 1934 **m.** C Ritson **dau.** of Rev J N Ritson of Kempston Bedford
>
> **Died** 24 Jan 1924 aged 59

TWIGGE, JOHN 1659–1734

b. 1659 Carrickfergus Co Antrim; ed by Mr Ryder; ent TCD 15 Nov 1675 aged 16 BA 1680 MA 1683

d 1685 (Dublin) p; V Rossinver (Kilm) 1685–98; V Cloonclare (Kilm) 1686–98; prob same as John Twigge, Preb of Castleknock in St Patrick's Cath Dublin and R Chapelizod (Dub) 1691–1734

> **s.** of Charles
>
> **m.** and had issue incl 1. Thomas ent TCD 15 Jul 1713 BA 1718; 2. Rev Paul (**died** 1777) **b.** 1701 Palmerstown Co Dublin ed by Mr Harris at Dublin ent TCD 9 May 1717 aged 16 BA 1721 MA 1724 C Chapelizod (Dub) 1730 Minor Canon of St Patrick's Cath Dublin 1731–40 V Donaghmore (Drom) 1734–40 V Carlingford (Arm) 1740–77 **m.** 2 Dec 1733 Hannah Tuthill of Donnybrook Dublin and had issue (i) Thomas Tuthill (ii) Rev Hugh (**died** 1790), C Drumcree (Arm) 1776–90 (iii) Michael (iv) Paul, MD (v) Roger (**died** 25 Aug 1818 aged

82), Lt 8th Foot
Died 1734

TWOMEY, JEREMIAH THOMAS PAUL 1946–

b. 27 Jan 1946; ed Percy Road Secondary Modern Sch London; Willesden Tech Coll; CITC BTh 1987

d 1987 p 1988 (Armagh); C Derryloran (Arm) 1987–90; R Brackaville Donaghendry and Ballyclog (Arm) 1990–97; R Mohill Farnaught Aughavas Oughteragh Kiltubride & Drumreilly (Ard) 1997–2000; BC Whiterock (Conn) 2000–;

> **s.** of William of London

> **m.** London 30 Oct 1968 Phyllis **dau.** of William Rothwell of Carlow. Issue 1. Sharon **b.** 8 Jun 1969 in London; 2. Auveen **b.** 11 Sep 1978 at Tullamore Co Offaly

†TYNDALL, CHARLES JOHN 1900–1971

b. 30 May 1900; ed The King's Hosp Dublin; Downes Pri 1923 TCD BA 1923 Div Test 1924 MA 1929 DD (j.d.) 1956

d 1924 p 1925 Bp 1956; C Clontarf (Dub) 1924–29; Hon Cler V Christ Ch Cath Dublin 1927–30; C Christ Ch Leeson Pk (Dub) 1929–30; R Enniscorthy (Ferns) 1930–36; R Drumcondra and N Strand (Dub) 1936–45; RD Fingal (Dub) 1943–45; R Calry (Elph) 1945–56; Archd of Elphin and Ardagh 1951–56; elected Bp of Kilmore Elphin and Ardagh by the united Synods 16 Dec 1955; consec in St Patrick's Cath Armagh 2 Feb 1956; enthroned in St Fethlimidh's Cath Kilmore 16 Feb 1956; enthroned in Elphin Cath 1 Mar 1956; Bishop of Kilmore Elphin and Ardagh 1956–58; elected Bp of Derry and Raphoe by the House of Bishops 14 Oct 1958; enthroned in St Columb's Cath Londonderry 11 Dec 1958; enthroned in St Eunan's Cath Raphoe 17 Dec 1958; Bp of Derry and Raphoe 1958–69; ret

> elder **s.** of John, DI RIC by Mary **dau.** of Francis… of USA

> **m.** 18 Nov 1924 Newton-Cashel Co Longford Alice Olivia (**died** 13 May 1984) **dau.** of Rev Canon Robert John Mitchell, R Cashel and Rathcline (Ard) 1906–37 qv Issue 1. Alan **m.** Nov 1968 St John's Malone Belfast Jennifer McKee of Belfast; 2. Norah TCD BA (Mod Hist and Pol Sci) 1949 **m.** 8 Nov 1949 Peter **s.** of George Good of Cloghervagh Co Sligo

> **Died** 3 Apr 1971

PUBLICATIONS
History of North Strand Church, Dublin
History of Drumcondra Parish, Dublin
History of St John's Church, Sligo
Booklet for the 1963 Columban Celebrations

`UA BARDAIN

"the Dean (of Ardagh), a sage without defect" (Ann. Ult.) The Editor (Note II, 537), connects him with Ardagh; was there before 1369

UITERS, IVAN JOHN
Dip Theol
d 1997 p; R Killesher Druminiskill and Killinagh (Kilm) 2007–

UPRICHARD, HORACE LAUNCELOT 1917–1994
b. 15 Jun 1917; ed Portadown Coll; TCD BA & Div Test (2) 1942 MA 1947; C of I Rep UTV Board of Rel Ed for 12 yrs; also Chairman
d 1942 p 1943; C Cloonclare (Kilm) 1942–44; CF RAFVR 1944–50; Head S Ch Miss Ballymacarrett (Down) 1950–53; R Drumbeg (Down) 1953–82; ret

    s. of R J Uprichard of Portadown Co Armagh

    m. 1947 St Margaret's Westminster Helen Bellamy. Issue 1. John; 2. David, Flying Off RAF killed in Germany 1974; 3. Andrew **b.** 24 Oct 1957

    Died 6 Feb 1994 **bur.** Drumbeg

UPRICHARD, JERVIS 1917–
b. 1917; TCD BA 1942
d 1942 p 1943 (Down); C Kilmegan w Maghera (Drom) 1942–45; C St Patrick Ballymacarrett Belfast (Down) 1945–46; C Kilmegan (Drom) 1946–47; C St Aidan Belfast (Conn) 1948–50; R Killashee and Ballymacormack (Ard) 1950–53; R Oughteragh and Fenagh (Ard) 1953–60; V Edgeside, Waterfoot (Manch) 1960–66; ret 1982; Perm to Off Dio Manchester 1982–91

    m. Katherine… and had issue a **s. b.** 13 Feb 1955 in Scotland and two other children

USSHER, JOHN 1838–1907
b. 1838 Dunboyne Co Meath;
d 1873 (Down) p 1874 (Cork); C Kiltoom (Meath — then Elph) 1873–74; C Castledermot (Glend) 1875–76; R Baltinglass (Leigh) 1876–1907

    m. Miss Blood of Nenagh Co Tipperary. Issue 2 **sons** and 1 **dau.**

    Died 2 Feb 1907 **bur.** Baltinglass Abbey

VANCE, JOHN 1719/20–c. 1789
b. 1719 or 1720 Carlow; ed by Mr Ross; ent TCD 7 Jul 1736 aged 16 BA 1741
appears V St John's Kilmean and Killenvoy (Elph) 1766

    s. of William

    Died c. 1789. Will proved 1789

VAUGHAN, RICHARD
ent TCD 25 Oct 1694 BA 1699 MA 1702
V Mostrim (Ard) 1705–32, coll 19 Jul 1705 (F.F.)

VAUX (?WASSE), ROBERT –1639

ord p by Thomas (Dove) Bp of Peterborough 16 Mar 1616.

V Drumreilly (Kilm)–1634; is pres by the Crown to the "V of Corgallen *alias* Callafloyne" = Carrigallen (Kilm) 11 Jul 1634 (L.M. V. 110)

    m. Elizabeth

    Died 12 Mar 1639

VERNER, WILLIAM 1842/43–1924

b. 1842 or 1843

d 1870 (Down for Kilmore) p 1871 (Kilmore); C Knockbride (Kilm) 1870–73; R Knockbride (Kilm) 1873–77; R Laghey (Raph) 1877–79; R Killymard (Raph) 1879–83; R Termonamongan (Derry) 1883–1921

    m… Issue incl **sons** 1. Rev Fenwick Hamilton (**died** 26 Jan 1917) **b.** 1871 Kiltyclogher Co Leitrim TCD Sch 1893 BA (Resp) 1896 Div Test (1) and Theo Exhib 1897 BD 1907 C Wexford (Ferns) 1897–1900 R Mountfield (Derry) 1900–06 R Donaghmore (Raph — then Derry) 1906–17 **m.** Ada Hamilton (**died** 1931 **bur.** Donaghmore); 2. James Hamilton, Capt RIF who was killed in the Great War; 3; another **s.** who was wounded in the Great War; 4. Edith Elizabeth **m.** 3 Jan 1907 Rev John Bentley, R Jonesborough (Arm) 1916–34

    Died 13 Oct 1924 aged 81

VERNON, GEORGE EDWARD VENABLES 1796/97–1870

b. 1796 or 1797 Dublin; ed by Mr Martin; ent TCD as FC 2 Nov 1812 aged 15 BA 1816 MA 1822

R Carlow (Leigh) 1821–36; Preb of Kilgoghlin (Elph) 1827–70

    s. of Henry, lawyer, of the Clontarf Castle family

    m. (1) 20 Apr 1825 St Peter's Par Ch Dublin Jane (**died** 6 Dec 1827) only **dau.** of Archd Thomas Kingsbury of Killala. Issue 1. Joseph; 2. Thomas; 3. Josephine Emily

    m. (2) 1835 Harriet **dau.** of Lt Col Henry Bruen of Carlow. Issue John Bruen (**died** 1873).

    Died 16 Mar 1870 at Bath

†VERSCHOYLE, HAMILTON 1803–1870

b. 1803 Dublin; ed by Mr Donne; ent TCD 16 Oct 1820 Sch 1823 BA 1825 MA BD & DD 1862

d 1828 p Bp 1862; C Clongish (Ard) 1828–34; Chapl of Baggotrath (Dub) 1835–62; Chanc of Christ Ch Cath Dublin 1853–62; Dean of Ferns 1862; consec Bp of Kilmore Elphin and Ardagh 26 Oct 1862 at Kilmore; enthroned 25 Dec 1862; Bp of Kilmore Elphin and Ardagh 1862–70

    eldest **s.** of John, merchant of Stillorgan Hse Co Dublin by Margaret **dau.** of Hamilton Stuart

    m. 1832 Catherine Margaret (**died** 9 Nov 1883 aged 73 at Limerick) **dau.** of

Thomas Hawkins, Dean of Clonfert. Issue incl **sons** 1. Rev Hamilton Stuart (**died** 14 Jun 1932 aged 87) TCD BA Sen Mod Eth & Log 1865 MA 1868 Univ of Oxford BA Incorp 1867 d 1867 (Armagh) p 1868 (Kilmore) Dom Chapl to his father the Bp 1867–70 C St Matthew Leicester (Leic — then Pet) 1870 C Morcott (Pet) 1870–72 C Christ Ch Tunbridge Wells (Cant) 1873–76 Chevalier of the Court of Italy 1887 **m.** Frances yst **dau.** of Ven Frederick Falkiner Goold, Archd of Raphoe and had issue; 2. John Thomas Samuel (**died** 1882) matric Univ Coll Oxford 15 Oct 1870 aged 19 BA 1875; he also had other **sons**; **daus.** 1. a **dau.** who **m.** Rev—— Chapman; 2. Matilda Mary (**died** 6 Apr 1861 aged 20)

Died 28 Jan 1870 at Torquay **bur.** Paignton Churchyard Devon

PUBLICATIONS

A Sermon, *The Bond of Perfectness* on I Corinthians Ch 13
A Primary Charge at his Visitations, June 1863, Hodges, 8vo
A Charge at his Visitations, June and July 1866, Hodges, 8vo
Sermons in New Irish Pulpit

VESEY, GEORGE AGMONDISHAM

C Killesher (Kilm) 1894–98

see also *Armagh Clergy 1800–2000* p 640 and *Clergy of Connor* p 636

VILLIERS, THOMAS HYDE 1767–1834

b. 1767 Cavan; bapt 23 Jun 1767 at Kilmore; ed by Mr Dwyer; ent TCD 5 Jul 1784 BA 1790

C Kildallon (Kilm) from 1792; acc to Erck, was still there in 1830

s. of William of Rice Hill Co Cavan by Catherine **dau.** of Samuel Hamilton

Died 11 May 1834 of cholera at his house in Whitworth Place Drumcondra Dublin

VIRIDETT, DANIEL

lic C Templemichael (Ard) 1 Apr 1797

WADDINGE, JOHN –1639

V Killenvoy (Elph) to 1639

Died 1639

WADE, ARTHUR JOHN 1810/11

b. 1810 or 1811 Dublin; ed by Mr Huddart; ent TCD 7 Jul 1828 aged 17 BA 1834 MA 1837

C Clongish (Ard) *c.* 1838

s. of Arthur, clerk of National Bank, Dublin; **bro.** of Rev Benjamin, Chanc of Armagh Cath

WADE, NICHOLAS *c.* 1705–1757

b *c.* 1705 Enniskillen; ed by Dr Ballentine, Strabane; ent TCD 22 Feb 1721/22 aged 16 BA 1726

V Oughteragh (Kilm) 1745–57; C Dromore (Clogh) 1754–57

    s. of Rev George, R Dromore (Clogh) 1705–36

    Died 1757

WADE, NICHOLAS 1764/65–1822

b. 1764 or 1765 Cavan; ed by Rev Mr Kerr; ent TCD 6 Nov 1780 aged 15 BA 1785 MA 1810

d ord p 20 Mar 1791; C Kildallon (Kilm) 1790; Sen Chapl St Thomas Bombay 1813–22

    s. of Rev William, R Tomregan (Kilm) qv

    m. 14 Nov 1796 at Bombay Juliana Charlotte Smith

    Died 24 Jun 1822

WADE, THOMAS 1776/77–1826

b. 1776 or 1777 Co Dublin; ed by Mr Brickell; ent TCD 4 Jun 1796 aged 19 BA 1802

d; p 9 Sep 1804 (Kilmore); C Killeshandra (Kilm) 1804; C Mealiffe (Cash) 1812

    s. of Tobias

    m. and had issue incl 1. William **b.** Cavan ed by Mr Martin ent TCD 5 Nov 1821 aged 15; 2. Rev Frederick Tobias (**died** 15 Mar 1884) **b.** Co Tipperary ed by Mr Martin ent TCD 3 Jul 1826 aged 17 BA 1833 MA 1842 adm *ad eund* Univ of Oxford 1845 R Kidsgrove (Lich) 1837–80 Preb of Lichfield 1855 R Tatenhill (Lich) 1880–84; he published Letters on *National Education and the Subdivision of Parishes*; 3. Thomas A **b.** Tipperary ed by Mr Sargent ent TCD 4 Nov 1833 aged 16 BA 1838

    Died 1826

WADE, WILLIAM –1794

ed at Enniskillen by Dr Dunkin; ent TCD 10 Oct 1755

d 1761 p 19 Dec 1762; C Kildrumferton (Kilm) 1761–66; V Ahamplish (Elph) 1770–73; V Drumlane (Kilm) 1773; V Kildrumferton (Kilm) 1773–83; V Tomregan (Kilm) 1783–94; JP for Co Cavan 1787

    s. of Rev Nicholas, V Oughteragh (then Kilm) qv

    m. Anne **dau.** of Thomas Burrowes of Stradone Co Cavan, High Sheriff 1743. Issue sons 1. Rev Nicholas, C Kildrumferton (Kilm) qv, 2. William; **daus.**, 1. Mary **m.** Arthur Fleming of Belville Co Cavan; 2. Anne **m.** Thomas Burrowes of Cavan; 3. Jane **m.** George Leslie

    Died 1794 before 16 Jul

WADSWORTH, GEORGE GUTHRIDGE –1958
TCD BA 1896 LLB & LLD 1909

d 1894 p 1895 (Kilmore); C-in-c Drumshambo (Ard) 1894–1903; R Gowna and Columbkille (Ard) 1903–17; served in Admiralty 1917–21; C Harlington Middx (Lon) 1921–29; Perm to Off at Hillingdon (Lon) 1929–34; V Waltham St Lawrence (Ox) 1934–46; Lic to Off Dio Ox from 1946; Lic to Off Dio Win from 1948

Died 7 Mar 1958 at Newbury

WAGNER, FREDERICK WILLIAM ERNEST –1957
TCD Div Test 1912 BA 1913 MA 1917; was a registered dentist

d 1913 (Clogher) p 1915 (Tuam); C Monaghan (Clogh) 1913–14; C Aughaval (Tuam) 1914–16; R Knocknarea (Elph) 1916–27; Perm to Off Dio London 1933–35; Lic to Off Dio Liverpool 1935–37; Chapl RAF Uxbridge 1937–38; Chapl RAF Northolt 1938–46

s. of Very Rev William Wolfe, Dean of Elphin and Ardagh qv (**s.** of John) by Louise **dau.** of William Insley of Castlerea

was married

Died 2 Dec 1957

PUBLICATIONS
A Modern Development in the Study of the Greek New Testament, 1920
Bishops and Priests in the New Testament
History of the Diocese of Elphin with a Succession of the Clergy, in MS in RCB Library
was Editor of a London Sporting Paper

WAGNER, WILLIAM WOLFE 1863–1937
b. 1863; TCD BA & Div Test 1884 LLB 1885 MA & LLD 1887

d 1886 p 1887 (Kilmore); C Kilkeevan w Oran (Elph) 1886–89; R Drumreilly (Ard — then Kilm) 1889–93; R Kilmactranny and Kilbryan (Elph) 1893–1910; Archd of Elphin and Preb of Killukin 1910–29; R Boyle and Aghanagh (Elph) 1910–33; Dean of Elphin and Ardagh 1929–33; ret

eldest **s.** of John of Dunmanway Co Cork

m. 1890 Louise (**died** 26 Jan 1961 aged 91 **bur.** Dean's Grange Dublin) **dau.** of William Insley of Castlerea Co Roscommon. Issue 1. Rev Frederick William Ernest, R Knocknarea (Elph) qv; 2. Irene Louise **m.** 27 Jul 1932 **m.** George Henry **s.** of R Sheridan, DI, RIC

Died 2 Mar 1937 at Enniskillen

WAKEFIELD (or WACFIELD), RICHARD –1552
pres to V Granard (Ard) 27–28 Henry VIII (Morrin, i. 29; L.M. V. 97), V Granard (Ard) 1536–39; Dean of Ardagh to 1552 (F. Edward VI. 990); was also Preb of Tipperkevin

Died April or May 1552

WALKER, ROBERT JOHN 1864/65–1930

b. 1864 or 1865; NUI BA 1910; Rochester Seminary USA

d 17 Dec 1911 p 22 Dec 1912 (Ossory); C Rathdowney (Oss) 1911–15; C St Mary (Dub) 1915–16; R Drumreilly (Ard — then Kilm) 1916–20; R Ballintemple (Kilm) 1920–30; ret

    Died 4 Oct 1930 aged 65

WALLACE, ERIC SIMON

d 1952 (Kilmore) p 1955 (Dublin); C Kilmore (Kilm) 1952–54; C-in-c Clonaslee and Rosenallis (Kild) 1954–57; V Taber Alberta (Dio Calgary) 1957–60; R St Mary Cedar Cottage Vancouver (Dio New Westminster) 1960–*c.* 65. Last entry in Crockford 1965/66

    2nd yst **s.** of Francis of Ballybrood Co Limerick

    m. 14 Sep 1954 Elizabeth 4th **dau.** of T H Payne of Tyrrellspass Co Westmeath. Issue a **dau.** b 7 Nov 1955

WALLACE, ROBERT JAMES 1830/31–

b. 1830 or 1831 Co Antrim; ed RBAI; ent TCD 25 Nov 1850 aged 19 BA 1855 MA 1864

d 6 Jan 1856 p May 1856; C Kiltubride (Ard) 1856–61; C St Paul Blackburn (Blackb — then Manch) 1861; C Ravenhead St Helen's (Liv) 1862–

    s. of John, watchmaker

WALLACE, THOMAS VESIAN

TCD BA (Sen Mod) 1909

d 1911 (Kilmore) p; C Kilkeevan (Elph) 1911–13; C St Michael Belfast (Conn) 1913–14

WALLACE, WILLIAM

inst V Denn (Kilm) 10 Aug 1640

WALLACE, WILLIAM 1828–1915

b. 1828 Belfast; ed by Mr Darley at Royal Sch Dungannon; ent TCD 9 Nov 1846 aged 17 as an Exhibitioner and gained a Sizarship, Sch 1849 BA (Resp) & Div Test (1st of 1st) 1852 MA 1859 BD & DD 1889 LittD 1890

d 1853 p 1854 (Kilmore); C Killeshandra (Kilm) 1852–55; C Annagh 1855–58; C St Helen's (Liv) *c.* 1858; C St Luke Stepney (Lon) 1865–70; V St Luke Stepney (Lon) 1870–1915. Dr Wallace founded the Wallace Divinity Exhibition and the Wallace Divinity School Aid Fund, as well as the Wallace Lectureship for instruction in voice production and reading the Services. He gave the granite steps at the entrance of St Anne's Cathedral Belfast.

    s. of John *faber aurarius*

m...

Died 9 Sep 1915 **bur.** Budleigh Salterton

PUBLICATIONS

Translations of English hymns and poems into Latin

Some hymns

WALLACE, WILLIAM

poss C Annagh (Kilm) 1856–60; C Killesherdoney (Kilm) 1860

WALLACE, WILLIAM –1950

TCD BA 1905 Div Test 1906 MA 1910

d 1906 p 1907 (Kilmore); C Larah w Lavey and Denn (Kilm) 1906–10; R Billis (Kilm) 1910–13; R Chesley (Hur) 1913–15; R Clarksburg w Collingwood (Hur) 1915–19; R Dutton w Lorne (Hur) 1920–24; R St Paul Stratford w Sebringville (w Ridgetown & Highgate to 1931) (Hur) 1929–39; R Ch of the Redeemer London Ontario (Hur) 1939–50

m. and had issue incl a **dau.** born at Billis Rectory and a **s.** Dr C A Wallace

Died 30 Jun 1950

WALLACE, WILLIAM JOHNSON 1851/52–1907

b. 1851 or 1852

d 1878 p 1879 (Kilmore); C Kilmactranny (Elph) 1878–79; R Taunagh (Elph) 1879–86; R Mountmellick and Rosenallis (Kild) 1886–99

Died 10 Aug 1907 aged 55

WALLEN, EDWARD *c.* 1653–

b. c 1653 Limerick; ed by Mr Shaw; ent TCD as Siz 26 Sep 1670 aged about 17 Sch 1673 BA 1675

Preb of Killaspugmoylan (Clonf) 1679; V St Mary Athlone (Elph) 1683–1723; Dysart (Meath) 1692–1723; res; says he was poor and deserved encouragement.

m. and had issue George **b.** at Athlone TCD BA 1725 MA 1753

WALLER (? WALKER), WILLIAM 1761–1847

b. 1761 Co Leitrim; ent TCD 1 Jun 1778 aged 16 BA 1783

C Killargue (Kilm) 1792; perhaps same as William Walker who is C Innismagrath (Kilm) in 1799; is C Drumlease (Kilm) in 1826; the William Walsh who appears C Drumlease in 1817 (Erck) is prob an error for him; prob same as William Walker V Drumreilly (Kilm) 1835–47

prob same as William Walker **s.** of Alexander

Died 1 Feb 1847 aged nearly 87

WALLING, CAROLINE

d 1986; BC Calry (Elph) 1995

WALLIS, JOHN

probably Preb of Tibohine (Elph) 1641; coll V Taghboy poss = Tibohine (Elph) 1641

WALLS, THOMAS 1671/72–1750

b. 1671 or 1672 England; ed by Mr Shaw, Wigan; ent TCD 27 Nov 1692 aged 20 BA 1697 MA 1700 BD & DD 1747

Preb of Ardagh (Killala) 1721–34; Archd of Achonry 1705–12 and 1719–34; Preb of Kilmacallen (Elph) 1705–1750; held a benefice in Tuam; V Castleknock (Dub) 1710–45; R Glenbarrahan (Cloyne) 1715–50; Preb of Wicklow in St Patrick's Cath Dublin 1745–50

> **s.** of Thomas
>
> **m.** and had issue incl Rev John **b.** 1709 Dublin (**died** 8 Jan 1795) Archd of Achonry Preb of Howth in St Patrick's Cath Dublin 1752–54 Preb of Wicklow in St Patrick's Cath Dublin 1754–95 **m.** (ML 28 Mar 1757) Elizabeth Foulks (**died** 6 Apr 1799) widow of St Peter's Parish Dublin and had issue four children who predeceased him
>
> **Died** 6 May 1750

†WALSH, GORDON JOHN 1880–1971

b. 1880; ed Sutton Valence Sch Kent; TCD BA 1902 Div Test 1903 MA 1909 BD & DD (j.d.) 1927; Jesus Coll Camb MA (by incorp) 1945

d 1903 p 1904 (Down) Bp 1927; C Trinity Ch Belfast (Conn) 1903–05; C St Mary Belfast (Conn) 1905–09; Assoc Sec CCC Soc for Ireland 1909–10; R St Peter Athlone (Elph) 1910–13; CMS Missy Tokushuma (Dio Osaka) Japan 1913–27; Bp of Hokkaido Japan 1927–40; V Eastry and Tilmanstone (Cant) 1941–42; Asst Bp of Ely 1942; Canon of Ely 1942–67; Proc Conv Ely 1946–52; Vice Dean of Ely 1956–67; Sel Pr Univ of Cambridge 1945

> **s.** of John Edward, Barrister-at-Law Deputy Accountant Gen Ireland (**s.** of John Edward, Master of the Rolls of Ireland)
>
> **m.** 1909 Edythe E B Spence (**died** 1956) **dau.** of Ven John Spence, Archd of Connor 1908–14
>
> **Died** s. p 19 Nov 1971

WALSH, ROBERT 1815/16–

prob same as Robert Walsh **b.** 1815 or 1816 Waterford; ed by Mr Wall; ent TCD 5 Jul 1832 aged 16 BA 1837

C of Abbeylara (Ard) 1840; lic 22 Oct (D.R.)

> **s.** of Robert

WALSHE, ALFRED MONTGOMERY 1841/42–

b. 1841 or 1842 Tallow; ed by Dr Price; ent TCD 12 Oct 1858 aged 16 BA 1865 C Castletarra (Kilm) 1867–70

s. of John, merchant

WALWOOD, JOHN –1670

In 1659 he was settled as a Commonwealth Minister on the Vicarial tithes of Urney, Kilmore, Annagelliffe and Denn (Kilm), but these were only worth £41.12.0; was ordered to be paid £38.8.0, balance of salary of £80, 12 Jun 1660; held the Deanery of Kilmore with V Kildrumferton Kilmore and Ballintemple (Kilm) 1661, but there is confusion as Lewis Downes qv seems to have held the Deanery until his death in 1664, or it may be a *lapsus calami* of the Registrar for "Dean of Raphoe", as Walwood was appointed Dean of Raphoe in 1661; (Dean of Raphoe 1661–70); however, as the V Kildrumferton was usually at the time held by the Dean of Kilmore, it may not be incorrect. John Walwood was a trooper in Major James Rawdon's Troop, Hill's horse, 1 Nov 1643 to 1 Nov 1647; he was a Chapl to Monk's Regular Horse 15 Nov 1647 to 15 Jul 1649; probably held Urney for some time after the Restoration in 1660.

m. and had a son John **b.** in Raphoe ed by Mr Eaton ent TCD 16 Apr 1673 aged 17 Sch 1675

Died 1670

WANN, DENIS FRANCIS 1927–

b. 1 Jun 1927 Dublin; ed St Andrew's Coll Dublin; TCD BA 1955 Div Test 1956 MA 1977

d 1956 p 1957 (Down); C St Donard Belfast (Down) 1956–58; BCMS Tanzania 1958–72; P-in-c Levande (Tanzania) 1958–65; Morogoro (Tanzania) 1965–72; Hon Canon of Morogoro 1972–73; C Christ the Redeemer Shankill Lurgan (Drom) 1972–73; R Port Kembla (Sydney) 1973–78; R Albion Park (Sydney) 1978–84; RD Shoalhaven (Sydney) 1979–82; Archd of Wollongong and Camden (Sydney) 1982–84; R Turramurra (Sydney) 1984–91; R Bailieborough Knockbride Shercock and Mullagh (Kilm) 1991–95; ret; Assoc Min Wollongong (Sydney) 1996–

s. of William Eugene of Adelaide Rd Dublin (**s.** of Eugene William and Mary Bowes) by Annie Maud **dau.** of Francis Clayton and Annie (née Ingram) Connolly of Dublin

m. 3 Apr 1956 Christ Ch Leeson Pk Dublin Nurse Elizabeth Sylvia **dau.** of Edward John and Kathleen (née Lovely) Orr. Issue 1. Denis Francis Connolly **b.** 31 Jan 1959 **m.** 1987 Andrea Somers; 2. Ernest John **b.** 26 Aug 1962 **m**... ; 3. Charles Samuel **b.** 22 Apr 1967 **m**...

†WARBURTON, CHARLES MONGAN

see **MONGAN, CHARLES**

WARBURTON, WILLIAM 1806–1900

b. 1806 Dublin; ent TCD 6 Jan 1823 aged 16 BA 1827 MA 1832 BD & DD 1853

d 1830 p 1831; V Kilberry (Glend) 1833–48; R Elphin and Ogulla 1848–94; Dean of Elphin 1848–94

4th **s.** of Richard of Garryhurst Queen's Co (Laois)

m. (1) 18 May 1835 at Leamington Emma Margaret yst **dau.** of Lt Gen Richard Stevin Issue 1. Richard Stevin **b.** 1836; 2. Joseph William **b.** 1837; 3. Frederick Tynte; 4. Emma Lydia **died** 2 Jun 1866 at Florence

m. (2) Frances Emily (**died** 21 Jul 1901) **dau.** of Loftus Henry Bland MP of Blandsfort Co Laois. Issue 1. Peter; 2. Henry; 3. James Robert; 4. Arthur; 5. Thomas; 6. Anne; 7. Martha Susan; 8. Mary

Died 3 May 1900 at Birchwood, Chislehurst aged 93

PUBLICATIONS

Parental Authority Vindicated, a tract in support of the National System of Education, 1850

The Results of Opposition to the National Education System, 1859

Publ a Speech on the Land Question, Dublin 1870

WARDLAW, JOHN 1730/31–1801

b. 1730 or 1731 Co Cavan; ed by Mr Clarke; ent TCD 6 Jun 1747 aged 16 BA 1751

C Killinkere (Kilm) 1756; C Drung and Larah (Kilm) 1761–*c.* 66; Preb of Terebrine (Elph) 1767–69; Archd of Elphin 1769–81; V Oughteragh (Kilm) 1771–94; V Toomna and Creeve (Elph) 1771–; C Killeely (Lim) 1776; Preb of Tullybracky in Limerick Cath 1781–84; R & V Killeely (Lim) 1784–91; Prec of Limerick 1791–1801; R & V Tomregan (Kilm) 1794–1801

s. of Charles

Died 31 Aug 1801

WARE, ARTHUR –*c.* 1659

TCD BA 1631 Fellow 1631 MA 1635

R Kilnagarenagh (Meath) 1636–39; coll V Kilbryan and Kilkeevan (Elph) 18 May 1640; Preb of Terebrine (Elph) 1640–*c.* 1660/61; Archd of Meath 1643–

4th **s.** of the 1st Sir James (**died** 4 May 1632), Auditor General and **bro.** of Sir James the Historian (**died** 27 Nov 1666)

Died before 1660

WARE, JOSEPH   –1648

TCD BA 1622 MA 1625 Fellow 1626

R Ballyroan (Leigh) 1634; Prec of Elphin 1635; Prec of Killala 1640; Dean of Elphin 1642/43–48; signed the Remonstrance of 1646

3rd **s.** of Sir James, Auditor General; **bro.** of Sir James Ware, the Historian

m. before 1639 Katherine (**died** 22 Jun 1650) **dau.** of John Crofton of Lissadorn

Castle Co Roscommon and had issue
Died 1648

WARNER, GUSTAVUS
BA (*ad eund* Cantab) and MA 1832
was C Dunamon (Elph) in 1831
   m. 14 May 1831 Alicia **dau.** of Joshua Kemmis of Knightstown Co Laois

WARREN, FRANCIS   –1756
C or R Templemichael (Ard) to 1756
   Died 17 Nov 1756

WARREN, HORACE GEORGE   1869/70–1950
b. 1869 or 1870; Corpus Christi Coll Camb BA (3cl Th Trip) 1892 MA 1894; Church Missy Coll Islington 1892; Prelim Theol Exam (1) 1893

d 1893 (London for Colonial) p 1896 (Osaka); Missy at Osaka Japan 1893–97; Hamada 1897–1901; Acting Prin CMS Boys' Sch Osaka 1901–02; C Urney (Kilm) 1903–04; R Ardcarne (Elph) 1904–09; Org Sec CMS for S Ireland 1909–17; Central Sec C of I Jews' Soc 1917–26; R Corbally (Killaloe) 1926; R Kilmacduagh and Ardrahan (Kilmacd) 1926–35; Canon of Kilteskill in Clonfert Cath 1932–35; ret
   Died Nov 1950 aged 80

WARREN, JOHN   1873/74–1948
b. 1873 or 1874; TCD Wall Sch 1896 Abp King Pri (1) Bp Forster Pri & BA 1897 Past Theol Pri (1) & Div Test (1) 1898 Theo Exhib 1899 BD 1900 MA 1906

d 1899 p 1900 (Down); C St Aidan Belfast (Conn) 1899–1901; C Holy Trinity Derby (Derby — then S'well) 1901–02; C St Timothy Crookes Sheffield (Sheff — then York) 1902–05; Chapl Christ Ch Duesseldorf Germany 1905–06; Sec RTS Ireland 1908–09; C St Philip Milltown Dublin (Dub) 1909–15; R Cahir (A & A) 1915–24; R Swanlinbar (Kilm) 1924–25; R Ardmore Clashmore & Templemichael (Lism) 1925–48
   Died 29 Feb 1948 aged 74

PUBLICATIONS
   A Review of the Tractarian Movement
   Ireland and her Fairy Godmother, 1909
   The Biretta Blight, Dublin 1914
   Roman Intolerance with special Reference to Ireland

WARREN, JOHN THOMAS   1818–1897
b. 1818 Dublin; ed by Mr Geoghegan; ent TCD 13 Oct 1837 BA & Div Test 1842

d 1844 p 1845; C Cloone (Ard) 1844–51; PC Ballymascanlan (Arm) 1851–90; res and was appointed R 1890–97

s. of John Ralph (**died** at Ballymascanlan and **bur.** 21 Jan 1862 aged 69)

m. 7 Jun 1847 at Cloone Par Ch Carrigallen Co Leitrim, Jane (**died** 28 Apr 1870 at Ballymascanlan Glebe) **dau.** of William McDonnell of Cloone. Issue included 1. John William (**died** 12 Mar 1868 aged 12); 2. Rev Henry George (**died** 20 Feb 1942) **b.** 8 Oct 1851 TCD BA 1873 Div Test 1874 MA 1882 d 1874 p 1875 C Desertmartin (Derry) 1875–76 I Castledawson (Derry) 1877–86 I Dungiven (Derry) 1886–1930) Canon of Derry 1901–30 ret **m.** 4 Feb 1879 Castledawson Par Ch Fanny Dawson Heygate (**died** 1 Mar 1925) yst **dau.** (aged 19) of Samuel Gray and had issue (i) John Frederick (**died** in a road accident 29 Mar 1924), Indian Army **m.** 10 Oct 1921 Violet only **dau.** of J C Gibson, Rathwalkin Kildare (ii) Arthur Henry (iii) Richard Dawson (iv) Mary Elizabeth (v) Jane Frances (vi) Caroline Dawn Sheelagh; 3. Caroline Mary (**died** 1923 Dublin) **b.** c 1855

Died 18 Jan 1897

WARREN, WILLIAM 1719–1803

b. 1719 Co Carlow; ed by Mr Hill; ent TCD 14 Feb 1735 aged 16 BA 1741

d 1744 p 1744 (Kilm); C Drung (Kilm) 1745; C Drumgoon (Kilm) 1760–66; V Kildallon (Kilm) 1768–1803; V Chapelizod Palmerstown and Ballyfermot (Dub) & Preb of Castleknock in St Patrick's Cath Dublin 1774–1803

s. of Richard, *dux*

m. Oct 1767 at Kilmore Co Cavan Miss Bleadwin

Died 23 Feb 1803 aged 83 **bur.** Kildallon

WARRINGTON, GEORGE GARNETT 1910–1982

b. 1910; TCD BA 1937 MA 1947 Div Test; France-Germany Star Defence Madal; 1939–45 Star

d 1937 p 1938 (Kilmore); C Kinawley (Kilm) 1937–42; Chapl RAFVR 1942–46; R Rossinver (Kilm) (w BC Finner (Clogh to 1974 when transferred to Kilmore) 1951–74 and R from 1974) 1946–82; Preb of Triburnia (Kilm) 1971–79; Preb of Mulhuddart in St Patrick's Cath Dublin 1979–82

s. of Rev Robert, R Bailieborough (Kilm) qv

m. 24 Sep 1942 Sandford Par Ch Dublin Helen Norton. Issue 1. Brian Robert Garnett **b.** 2 Apr 1944 Dumfriesshire; 2. Rosemary Helen **b.** 2 Nov 1945 Dublin **m.** 7 May 1969 at Bundoran Derek **s.** of Mr & Mrs James Greenlee of Dublin; 3. Pamela Heather **b.** 27 Apr 1949 or 1950; 4. a yr **dau.** Heather **m.** Jul 1972 at Rathfarnham Par Ch Dublin Roger yr **s.** of Mr & Mrs F King of Terenure Dublin; 5. a **s. b.** 30 Jan 1960 at Ballyshannon

Died 1982

WARRINGTON, ROBERT 1870–1952

b. 8 Jan 1870 Aughaward Co Longford; ed Dio Theol Coll Montreal Canada 1894

d 1896 (Montreal) p 1897 (Moosonee); I Chapleau Ontario 1896–98; I Portage du Fort Montreal 1898–1900; C St Paul Sheffield 1901–02; R Donacavey (Clogh) 1902–

19; R Aghavea and Tattykeeran (Clogh) 1919–30; C St Paul Belfast (Conn) 1930–31; R Bailieborough 1931–36; C-in-c Mostrim (Ard) 1936–39; ret

    s. of Robert

    m. May 1897… (she **died** 22 Jul 1968) and had issue four **sons** and two **daus**. incl Robert Cecil Ussher MB; Rev George Garnett qv above; Kathleen **m**. Charles Nicholl

    Died 3 Jul 1952

WASSE, ROBERT

ord p 24 or 25 Apr 1661; he may have been the Robert Wasse who matric as Siz from Trinity Coll Camb 1641/42 BA 1641/42

is Commonwealth Minister at Killasnett Newtown Rossinver and Dromahaire (Kilm) from 24 Jun 1657 at £100 per annum; coll V Cloonclare Clonlogher Killasnett and Rossinver (Kilm) 24 Apr 1661; again coll 27 Jul 1679 and seems to have held to 1681; also appears V Rossinver Clonlogher and Killargue in VB 1673, but another entry has Killasnett for Killargue

    poss **s**. of Robert Vaux ? = Wasse, V Carrigallen (Kilm) qv

WATERS, JAMES (JOSEPH) 1757/58–

b. 1757 or 1758 Tipperary; ed by Mr Hare; ent TCD as Siz 17 Jun 1775 aged 17 Sch 1778 BA 1781

d 29 Sep 1782; p 21 Sep 1783 (Kilm); C Lavey (Kilm 1782–; R Aghmacart (Oss) 1808–c. 12

    s. of Rev Peter

    m. (ML 1891) Anne Smith. Issue incl Susan **m**. William James McCausland

WATSON, ADAM

d 28 Mar 1613 p 29 Mar 1613; V Killeshandra (Kilm) before 1622; got a grant of a glebe here 25 Jan 1626/27; appears V Killeshandra 27 Dec 1633 and is again pres by the Crown 26 Nov 1635 (L.M. V. 111). It is possible however that 1635 is an error for 1633. He is said in R.V. to have been pres to V Killeshandra by Francis Hamilton on 27 Sep 1633 and inducted 31 Dec 1633

WATSON, GORDON MARK STEWART 1967–

b. 7 May 1967 Omagh Co Tyrone; ed Omagh Secondary Sch; Omagh Technical Coll; Wolverhampton Polytechnic BA (Hons) Economics and Government; TCD Downes Oratory Pri 1993 & 1994 BTh 1995

d 1995 p 1996 (Connor); C Ballymoney Finvoy and Rasharkin (Conn) 1995–98; R Brackaville Donaghendry and Ballyclog (Arm) 1998–2001; R Killesher and Killinagh (w Kiltyclogher to 2002) (Kilm) 2001–06; R Trory and Killadeas (Clogh) 2006–

    s. of Ivan Leslie of Ballygawley Co Tyrone (s. of Joseph Alexander of Keady Co Armagh and Elizabeth (née Greenaway of Ligoniel Co Antrim)) by Annie **dau**. of Samuel Andrew of Falcarragh Co Donegal and Katherine (née Galbraith of

Londonderry) Stewart

m. 29 Aug 1995 Galloon Par Ch Co Fermanagh Rona Evelyn **dau.** of John William of Newtownbutler Co Fermanagh and Mabel Elizabeth Jane (née Roberts) of Redhills Co Cavan Kelly. Issue 1. Samuel Patrick Cameron **b.** 5 Aug 1997; 2. Peter Edward Stewart **b.** 18 Jan 2001

WATSON, JOHN ROBERTSON THOMAS 1927–

b. 1927; was a professional boxer before Ordination; CITC 1968 GOE 1970 Greenwich Univ MA

d 1970 p 1971; C St Stephen Belfast (Conn) 1971–73; BC Swanlinbar and Templeport (Kilm) 1973–82; R Arvagh w Carrigallen Gowna & Columbkille (Kilm) 1982–97; Preb of Drumlease (Kilm) 1988–97

PUBLICATIONS/ARTICLES
The Church is the People, CIG, 1972
Has the Church failed in her Christian Role?, 1980
Jobs– Society must change, Belfast Telegraph, 1982
Depraved People find an interest in Hare Coursing, 1988
Mistreating Animals– one step from mistreating Children, 1989
The Legacy of the Rev. James Spence Ruthford, M.A. (1881–1942), The Forum 1996
All Creatures Great and Small, Search, Winter 1998

WATSON, WILLIAM

pres to V "Agherne" and Rathreagh (Ard) 16 Aug 1633 (L.M. V. 110); was V in 1641 and Archd; adm. Archd of Ardagh 27 Aug 1633, installed 18 Sep 1633, M.A (R.V. 1634); appears in Dep. TCD 7 March 1641

WATTS, RONALD HORACE 1957–

b. 1957; ed Bandon Gram Sch; CITC DipTh 1992

d 1992 p 1993; C Sligo G (Elph) 1992–93; C Limerick City (Lim) 1994–95; R Holmpatrick w Balbriggan and Kenure (Dub) 1995–2001; C Taney (Dub) 2001–03; Chapl Adelaide and Meath Hosp Dublin 2003–

s. of Canon Horace Gordon, R Douglas (Cork) 1976–88 and Pearl (née Peet) of Cork

m. 6 Jun 1987 St Stephen's Ch Dublin Lucy Jane **dau.** of Peter Edwin and Martha Phoebe Paxton of Dublin. Issue 1. Stephen Ronald Paxton **b.** 8 Aug 1992; 2. Emma Lucy Megan **b.** 23 Dec 1996

WATTS, SIDNEY ROBERT COLSTAN 1912–1971

b. 4 Apr 1912; ed Cork Gram Sch; Mountjoy Sch Dublin; TCD BA 1933 Div Test (2) 1935 MA 1944

d 1935 (Down) p 1936; C & Dean's V St Anne's Cath Belfast (Conn) 1935–36; C Urney Annagelliffe Denn and Derryheen (Kilm) 1936–38; R Aghadown w Kilcoe U (Ross) 1938–48; R Youghal (Cloyne) 1948–55; R Rathcormac (Cloyne) 1955–61; R

Kilmeen and Castleventry (Ross) 1961–71; Preb of Timoleague (Ross) 1964–68; Prec of Ross & Preb of Inniskenny (Ross) 1968–71

s. of Sidney Thomas of Cork (s. of Edward of Cork) by Mary Ann **dau.** of Robert Pulvertaft of Cork

m. 1 Sep 1936 Rhoda Tempe **dau.** of Rev Canon Alexander Robert Stewart Munro, R Inver (Raph) 1918–57 and Edith. Issue 1. Edith Constance **b.** 18 Jun 1937; 2. Rev Gordon Sidney Stewart **b.** 8 Aug 1940 Skibbereen Co Cork ed Middleton Coll Co Cork TCD GOE 1966 d 1966 p 1967 C St Stephen Belfast (Conn) 1966–69 CF in UK and Germany and Cyprus from 1969 Sen Chapl NI 1991–94 V Boldre w S Baddesley (Win) 1994–96 P-in-c Warmfield (Wakef) 1996–2002 Sub-Chapl HM Prison Wakefield 1997–2002 Chapl Huggins Coll Northfleet (Roch) from 2002 **m.** 18 Aug 1965 Templemore Par Ch Co Tipperary Sarah Rosamond **dau.** of Benjamin and Mary Elizabeth Bradish of Templemore and have issue (i) Siobhan **b.** 28 Mar 1967 (ii) Niall Kildahl **b.** 17 Sep 1970; 3. Isabella Victoria Ann **b.** 16 Nov 1942; 4. Charles Mervyn **b.** 16 Jul 1946

Died 15 Mar 1971

WAYLSHE, SIR GERALD

"Deane of Arddaghe and parson of the Anell" (Annaly?) appears 1531 (Rental of Gerald Earl of Kildare in Journal R.S.A.I. 1862, p. 116)

WEBB, ARTHUR THOMAS 1871/72–1919

b. 1871 or 1872; TCD Downes Essay Pri 1897 Downes Comp Pri BA & Div Test 1898 MA 1912

d 1898 (Kilmore) p 1899 (Down); C Clongish (Ard) 1898–99; C Ballymena (Conn) 1899–1901; C St Patrick Ballymacarrett Belfast (Down) 1901–03; C Drumbeg (Conn) 1903–07; R Trory (Clogh) 1907–11; R Enniskillen (Clogh) 1911–19; Preb of Tyholland in Clogher Cath 1912–19

s. of Arthur Nugent of Prospect Shinrone Co Tipperary

m. 8 Apr 1902 Gertrude **dau.** of John Patrick of Gladheather Co Antrim. Issue 1. Arthur Patrick ed Portora Royal Sch Enniskillen; 2. George; 3. Dorothy

Died 3 Dec 1919 of scarlet fever aged 47

WEBB, CYRIL GEORGE 1919–

b. 17 Apr 1919 Faversham Kent; ed Faversham Gram Sch; Rochester Theol Coll 1964–66

d 25 Sep 1966 p 24 Sep 1967; C St Andrew Bournemouth (Win) 1966–71; V Micheldever (Win) 1971–72; V Micheldever and E Stratton, Woodmancote etc (Win) 1972–79; V Bubwith w Ellerton and Aughton (York) 1979–83; R Tomregan and Drumlane (Kilm) 1983–86; ret Perm to Off Dio Canterbury 1990–98

s. of George Frederick (1889–1975) of Margate (s. of John and Edith of Margate and Durban S Africa) by Emma **dau.** of William and Jane Pilcher of Margate

m. 20 Jun 1945 Faversham Avice Mary **b.** 1924 **dau.** of Alfred Holt and Dorothy

May Daniels of Dartford Kent. Issue 1. Rev Martin George **b.** 16 Mar 1946 SS Mark and John Coll Chelsea CertEd 1968 Univ of Leeds MEd 1995 d 1985 p 1986 NSM Brotherton (Wakef) 1985–87 Perm to Off Dio York 1995–98 NSM Bethnal Green (Lon) from 1998 **m.** Diana Priest; 2. Andrew James **b.** 10 Mar 1949; 3. Angela Mary Patricia **b.** 17 Mar 1953

WEBB, HENRY LISCAR (?) or LESAC 1791/92–

ed by Mr O'Beirne; ent TCD 6 Jul 1807 aged 15 BA 1813

lic C Granard (Ard) 9 Apr 1816; PC Rathaspeck (Ard) 1818–c43

s. of Richard

WEBB, MATTHEW 1805/06–1870

b. 1805 or 1806 Co Westmeath; ent TCD 3 Nov 1823 aged 17 BA 1830

V Drumlummon w Gowna (Ard) 1838–70; coll 20 Apr 1833 (S.R.)

s. of John of Hilltown Co Westmeath

m. 21 Jul 1837 St George's Par Ch Dublin Martha Maria **dau.** of Samuel Coates of Cloncurry Co Kildare

Died 14 Nov 1870 at Bracklough Co Cavan

WEBB, THOMAS 1724/25 –1796

b. 1724 or 1725 in England; ed by Mr Ingram in Limerick; ent TCD 4 May 1742 aged 17 BA 1746

R Annagh Kilmore and Ballintemple (Kilm) and Dean of Kilmore 1768–96

2nd **s.** of Daniel of Marstown Co Limerick

Died 1796 **unm.**

WEBB, WILLIAM JOHN WESLEY 1832/33–

b 1832 or 1833 Penzance; ent TCD 15 Jan 1858 aged 25 BA & Div Test 1862 MA 1887

d 1862 (Down) p 1864 (Kilmore); C Knockbride (Kilm) 1862–65; C St James Heywood (Manch) 1865–66; C Bamber Bridge (Manch) 1866–68; C Holy Trinity Blackburn (Blackb — then Manch) 1868–69; C Littleham (Ex) 1869–76; R All Hallows Exeter (Ex) 1876–82; R St Laurence Exeter (Ex) 1882–c. 1901/02

changed his name to Everitt

s. of William

PUBLICATION

England's Inheritance in her Church, 1878

WEBSTER, JAMES 1765/66–

b. 1765 or 1766 Co Longford; ed by Mr Meares; ent TCD 4 Nov 1782 aged 16 BA 1787

R Streete (Ard) 1796–1814; also R Aghavea (Clogh) 1798–1814; Leslie in *Clogher Clergy and Parishes* p 111 says that he vacated Aghavea for Streete (Ard) in 1814.

s. of Thomas, *agricola*

m. Anna Maria (**died** 1858 aged 81) **dau**. of Francis Brooke of Colebrooke

WEBSTER, JOHN THOMAS –1960

TCD BA 1894 Div Test 1898 MA 1903

d 1894 p 1895 (Killaloe); C Roscrea (Killaloe) 1894–95; C Kildallon (Kilm) 1895–1900; R Munterconnaught w Loughan (Kilm) 1900–08; R Ballymachugh (Ard) 1908–10; R Kilmactranny w Kilbryan (Elph) 1910–14; R Ballyboy (w Kinnity from 1924) (Killaloe — then Meath) 1914–39; ret

m. Susan Edith (**died** 24 Apr 1966 Sandymount Dublin)

Died 17 Jan 1960

WEIR, EDWARD HENRY 1860/61–1920

b. 1860 or 1861; TCD Classical Siz 1882 BA (Resp) 1884 Div Test (2) 1886 MA 1891

d 1886 p 1887 (Cork); C Marmullane (Cork) 1886–87; C Roborough (Ex) 1887–90; C Hanbury (Lich) 1890; C St Peter (Dub) 1891–93; C Barton Mills (St E — then Ely) 1893–95; C St Saviour Bath (B & W) 1895–97; C Egham (Win) 1898–1900; (Leslie has him C Egham 1897 and C Timperley (Ches) 1897–1901); C Bredon w Bredon Norton (Worc) 1901–02; C St Mark Southampton (Win) 1902–04; C St John the Baptist Eltham (S'wark) 1904–05; C Christ Ch Forest Hill (S'wark) 1905–07; Dio C Ardfert and C Tralee (A & A) 1907–10; R Ballintemple (Kilm) 1910–20

Died 8 Oct 1920 Dublin aged 59. By his Will he left £1,000 to found the Weir Prize in Dublin University

WEIR, JOHN MAXWELL 1809/10–

b. 1809 or 1810 Co Mayo; ed by Mr Smith; ent TCD 1 Jun 1831 aged 21 Sch 1834 BA 1838 LLB & LLD 1858

C Drumgoon (Kilm) 1844; R Pilham (Ox) 1862–

s. of Rev James

WELDON, ANTHONY 1728–1801

b. 1728 Queen's Co (Laois); ed by Mr Baldrick; ent TCD 31 May 1746 aged 17 BA 1750 MA 1756

d 21 Apr 1751 p 4 Feb 1753 (Ossory); V Dunleckney U (Leigh) *c*. 1753–71; R Lismalin (Cash) 1756–74; R Grangemonk 1766–1801; R Grangeforth 1771–1801; V Athy and Kilberry (Kild) 1776–1801; R & V Dunmore (Tuam) 1775–87; Preb of Terebrine (Elph) 1777–1801

s. of Arthur, *armiger*

m. and had a s. Arthur TCD BA 1790 MA 1812; was ancestor of Weldon Baronets

Died Jun 1801 aged 73

WELDON, PERCIVAL BANKS 1800–1884

b. 1800 Co Clare; ed by Mr FitzGerald; ent TCD 5 Jan 1818 aged 18 BA 1821 MA 1832

d 1823 (Cork) p; prob same as Rev P B Weldon C Oran (Elph) 1823–; PC Kilnehue (Ferns) 1829–46; Preb of Fethard (Ferns) 1846–66; R Kilcormick (Ferns) 1866–74

s. of Rev Robert, R Ennis (Killaloe) by Miss Baker of Lisnasque Co Tipperary

m. 1823 Frances Maria Hazelwood (**died** 29 Jan 1868) **dau.** of an Officer in the British Army. Issue 1. Rev Robert Smythe (**died** 23 Dec 1875) **b.** Co Longford ent TCD 3 Jul 1843 aged 18 BA 1848 R Owenduff and Tintern (Ferns) 1856–75 **m.** Elizabeth Holt and had issue **sons** (i) Rev Percival Swinglehurst, R Whitechurch (Ferns) 1890–92 (ii) Samuel Parker (iii) Robert Holt (iv) Samuel Baker **daus.** (i) Mary Hoyle (ii) Frances Maria Hazelwood; 2. George, MD **m.** Maria Atkinson and had issue **sons** (i) Percival Banks (ii) Robert George **daus.** (i) Frances Maria (ii) Julia Madeline (iii) Eveline; 3. Rev Percival Banks (**died** 21 Jan 1873 aged 46) d 1861 p C Omey (Tuam) 1861 V Ballynemara (Oss) 1865–70 R Ballyvaldon (Ferns) 1872–73 **m.** Sarah and had issue **sons** (i) Percival Hewson (ii) Charles Edward (iii) John (iv) Francis (v) George (vi) Patrick (vii) Arthur Bertram **daus.** (i) Elmina Banks (ii) Dora); 4. Thomas bapt 23 Jul 1838; 5. Henry Walter **m.** (1) Julia Atkinson and had issue Mary; **m.** (2) Sally Parker and had issue **sons** (i) William Percival (ii) Henry Walter Cecil(iii) George Hazelwood **daus.** (i) Sarah (ii) Eileen Violet (iii) Mary Florence; 6. William Jephson **m.** Mary Weldon and had issue (i) Florence (ii) Ethel; 7. Elizabeth **m.** Rev Charles John Townsend (**died** 13 Jun 1888) R Tomhaggard (Ferns) 1863–88 and had issue **sons** (i) Webber John (ii) Perceval Weldon (**died** 14 Mar 1934) (iii) Charles John (iv) Joseph Henry (v) Robert Smythe (vi) Edward Nairn (vii) William (viii) Herbert **daus.** (i) Frances Maria (ii) Mary Louisa (**died** 3 Jun 1932) **m.** Vickers E Jacob (iii) Elizabeth Adeline; 8. Margaret bapt 16 Jan 1832 **m.** Rev Thomas Bushe Wills V Attanagh (Oss) 1863–68 and had issue incl Rev Percival Banks Prec of Ossory 1925–35; 9. Ellen **m.** Col James Jackson and had issue (i) Rev Brice Lee (ii) Eileen

Died 1 Jan 1884 at Gorey Co Wexford

WELSH, JOSEPH 1780/81–1859

b. 1780 or 1781 Co Cavan; ed by Rev Roger Leadon; ent TCD 12 Jul 1798 aged 17 BA 1803

C Ashfield (Kilm) 1808–10; PC Ashfield (Kilm) *c.* 1810–24; R & V Donegal (Raph) 1824–31; R Killaghtee (Raph) 1831–59

eldest **s.** of John of Prospect Belturbet and Ballenaleck

m. May 1806 Elizabeth **dau.** of Ralph Dawson of Cootehill Co Cavan. Issue incl **sons** 1. Rev Charles (**died** 9 Apr 1863) **b.** Co Donegal ent TCD 1 Nov 1824 aged 17 BA 1829 d 1832 p C Clones (Clogh) *c.* 1843 R Aghadrumsee (Clogh) 1847– *c.* 62 **m.** 24 Oct 1843 Jane (?Grace) yst **dau.** of Major Coote; 2. Rev William Wellington TCD BA 1842 MA 1855 MA *ad eundum* Cantab 1856 d 1843 p 1844 C Tullyaughnish (Raph) 1844–c48 R Holy Trinity Beckenham (Cant) 1873–76 V Christ Ch Beckenham (Cant) 1876–83 R Weeley Sussex 1883; 3. Ralph Dawson; 4. John, MD **m.** 14 Feb 1842 Aughanunshin Ch Letterkenny Co Donegal Elizabeth eldest **dau.** of Rev John Irwin, R Aughanunshin (Raph) 1831–63; **daus.**

1. Emily (**died** 4 Dec 1862 aged 49) **m.** 29 Jul 1828 Rev James **m.** Ovens, R Inniskeel (Raph) 1844–69 and had issue (i) John Coote **m.** 20 Sep 1865 Minnie Theresa Hickson (ii) Emily **m.** William Stewart Irvine (iii) Elizabeth Barbara **m.** 13 Nov 1866 Rev Eugene Sweny, R Stiffkey St John (Nor); 2. Elizabeth **m.** 23 Jan 1840 Killaghtee Ch Stewart Betty of Enniskillen; 3. Mary Anne **m.** 27 Nov 1849 Thomas Cleather Smith, Commander RN

Died 16 Dec 1859 at Killaghtee Ballybofey Co Donegal

WELWOOD, WILLIAM –1923

TCD BA & Div Test (2) 1877 MA 1886

d 1877 p 1878 (Kilmore); C Mohill (Ard) 1877–79; R Annaduff (Ard) 1879–86; R Kilcommick (Ard) 1886–97; R Fenagh (Ard) 1897–1922; ret

m. (1) Susan (**died** 25 Nov 1915 **bur.** Strokestown) 2nd **dau.** of Thomas Morton of Castlenode and widow of Joseph Eglington

m. (2) 3 Dec 1919 at Harold's Cross Ch Dublin Eliza Nangle **dau.** of Francis William Smartt, MD of Ballymahon Co Longford

Died 8 Apr 1923

WEMYSS, WILLIAM 1691/92–

b. 1691 or 1692 Edenderry King's Co (Offaly); ed by Mr Scott at Dublin; ent TCD 1 Oct 1709 aged 17 – no degree recorded

d; p 25 Sep 1730; C Kilglass Clonfinlough and Termonbarry 1730; V Bumlin 1741–*c.* 45.

s. of Francis

WEST, AUGUSTUS WILLIAM 1813/14–1893

b. 1813 or 1814 Dublin; ed by Mr Leahy; ent TCD 4 Jul 1831 aged 17 BA 1836 MA 1839

d 1837 (Limerick for Kildare) p; ?C Roundstone (Tuam) *c.* 1837; Preb of Yagoe (Dub) 1839–47; Preb of Tipperkevin 1847–61; Chanc of Kildare 1852–61; Dean of Ardagh 1860–80; Minor Canon St Patrick's Cath Dublin 1861–69; R Presteigne (Heref) 1880–93

s. of Matthew

m. Lucy (**died** at Presteigne Rectory 28 Apr 1883 in her 64th year). Issue incl 1. Rev Fitzwilliam Henry qv; 2. Rev Augustus Pakenham FitzGerald (**died** 26 May 1923) R Edwardstone Suffolk for 26 years and was formerly Capt 6 Batt Rifle Brigade; **daus.** 1. Lucy Agnes **m.** 30 Aug 1865 at Ardagh William Carroll of Upr Mount St Dublin and Monaghan and **bro.** of Rev E A Carroll; 2. Maria Louisa **m.** 22 Jun 1872 Capt Colin H Thompson of Salruck Co Galway eldest **s.** of General Thompson; 3. Emily Alice Josephine **m.** 28 Jun 1877 James Cole eldest **s.** of James Sheane JP of Mountmellick Co Laois; 4. his yst **dau.** Wilhelmina May **died** in Dublin 25 Oct 1935

Died 3 Mar 1893 at Presteigne Rectory Radnorshire aged 79

WEST, CHARLES 1750/51–1841

b. 1750 or 1751; ent TCD 1 Nov 1767 BA 1772

V Ahamplish (Elph) 1776–1841

    Died 16 Jan 1841 aged 90

WEST, ERIC ROBERT GLENN 1955–

b. 7 Dec 1955; ed Cookstown High Sch; Hazelwick Sch Crawley W Sussex; QUB BA (Geography) 1979; Univ of Manchester DipEd 1980 CITC BTh 1992

d Jun 1992 p Jun 1993; C Enniskillen (Clogh) 1992–95; R Lisbellaw (Clogh) 1995–99; Gen Lic Dio Clogher 1999–2003; CF 2000–03; R Annagh Drumaloor Drumlane and Cloverhill (Kilm) 2003–05; R Derryvullan N & Castlearchdale (Clogh) 2005–

    s. of Eric Groves (**s.** of Tom and Elizabeth of Tempo Co Fermanagh) by Elizabeth Alexandria **dau.** of Albert and Elizabeth Ford of Cookstown Co Tyrone

    m. 6 Aug 1983 Knutsford Cheshire Caran Lesley **dau.** of Stanley and Jean White. Issue 1. Matthew Eric Stanley **b.** 2 Jan 1985; 2. Emma Nicole **b.** 27 Jul 1987

WEST, FITZWILLIAM HENRY 1845/46–1913

b. 1845 or 1846; TCD (Jun Mod Hist and Eng Lit) 1867 Eccles Hist Pri (1) 1869 Div Test (1) 1870 MA 1871 LLB & LLD 1874

d 1869 (Cork) p 1869 (Dublin); C Kilglass (Ard) 1869–70; C Bethesda (Dub) 1870–71; C Winterbourne (Glouc) 1872; C Fairford (Glouc) 1873; C Ardagh (Ard) 1873–74; C Ide Hill (Cant) 1875; C Hanham (Glouc) 1876–77; C Nempnett (B & W) 1878–79; C Presteigne (Heref) 1880–81; c Patrixbourne (Cant) 1881; C Snape (St E — then Nor) 1882; C St James Taunton (B & W) 1883; living in London in 1897

    s. of Very Rev Augustus William, Dean of Ardagh qv above (**s.** of Matthew) by Lucy; **bro.** of Rev Augustus Pakenham FitzGerald

    Died 8 Feb 1913 aged 67 in Shropshire **bur.** Deans Grange Dublin

WEST, HENRY

TCD BA & Div Test 1887

d 1887 p 1888 (Kilmore); C-in-c Drumshambo (Ard) 1887–89; living in Belturbet Co Cavan in 1897

WEST, HENRY MATTHEW 1842–1913

b. 27 Dec 1842 Co Wicklow; ed Rossall Sch; TCD BA 1864 Div Test (1) 1865 MA 1869

d 1865 p 1866 (Dublin); C St John Monkstown (Dub) 1866–73; C St George (Dub) 1873–74; R Templemichael (Ard) 1874–89; R Sacombe (St Alb) 1889–1909

    3rd **s.** of Rev William James MA, R Delgany (Glend) 1847–59 (**s.** of Rev Matthew, R Clane (Kild) 1785–1814) by Elmina (**died** 30 Nov 1886) **dau.** of William Alexander Erskine

    m. 8 May 1874 Helen Mary (**died** 8 Mar 1933) **dau.** of Robert Foster Dunlop of

Monasterboice Co Louth. Issue 1. William Robert **b.** 11 Apr 1875; 2. Alexander Henry Delap and 3. Anne Elmina Blanche (twins) **b.** 27 Dec 1877; 4. Harry Erskine **b.** 22 Aug 1879; 5. Jessie Georgina Dorothy **b.** 1884; 6. Charles Skeffington **b.** 22 Apr 1886; 7. Eileen Myrtle **b.** 1891; 8. Kathleen Violet
Died 4 Feb 1913

†WETTENHALL, EDWARD 1636–1713

b. 7 Oct 1636 Lichfield; ed Westminster Sch; King's Sch 1651; Trinity Coll Camb Sch 1656 BA; incorp Lincoln Coll Oxford BA MA 1661 BD 1669; TCD DD *ad eund* 1674

Chapl Lincoln Coll Oxford 1660 V Combe Longa (Ox) & St Stephen (St A) 1661; Canon of Exeter 1667; Master of Exeter Sch; Master of the Free Sch Dublin and C St Werburgh (Dub) 1672–76; Preb of Tassagard in St Patrick's Cath Dublin 1674–75; Preb of Castleknock in St Patrick's Cath Dublin 1675–79; Prec of Christ Ch Cath Dublin 1675–78; consec in Christ Ch Cath Dublin Bp of Cork and Ross 23 Mar 1678; Bp of Cork and Ross 1678–99; Bp of Kilmore 1699–1713; enthroned 19 May 1699

    m. (1)... Issue incl 1. Edward, MD b *c.* 1662 **bur.** 29 Aug 1733 Westminster Abbey; 2. Ven John, Archd of Cork 1697–1717

    m. (2) Philippa (**bur.** 8 Apr 1717 Westminster Abbey) 6th **dau.** of Sir William Doyly, Bt of Norfolk.

Died 12 Nov 1713 London **bur.** Westminster Abbey

PUBLICATIONS
Of the Gifts and Offices of Divine Service, 1678
Of the intermediate state of blessed souls: a sermon preached at the Funeral of James Bonnell, Apr. 29, 1699, Dublin 1703
A full bibliography of his works is given in Brady's *Records,* III, 63–66

An armorial seal of Bishop Wettenhall which was formerly in the possession of Robert Erskine, Registrar of the Diocese of Kilmore, was returned to the Bishop of Kilmore by Dean H.B. Swanzy in 1931

WHEELER, EDGEWORTH CONNOLLY
TCD BA 1865
d Dec 1866 p; C Boyle (Elph) 1866; (not in C I Dir)

WHEELER, JOHN W
C Killyon (Elph) 1857

WHEELOCK, JOHN RICHARD 1918–2001
b. 1918; TCD BA Mod (2) 1941 Div Test (1) 1942 MA 1951

d 1942 p 1943 (Kilmore); C Drumgoon and Ashfield (Kilm) 1942–44; R Clongish and Clooncumber 1944–51; R Swanlinbar and Templeport (Kilm) 1951–56; R Belturbet Quivvy and St Andrew's (w P-in-c Cloverhill 1974–83) (Kilm) 1956–83; RD Kilmore S 1964–77; RD Kilmore E 1971–77; Preb of Annagh in Kilmore Cath 1972–83; ret

s. of Mr & Mrs I Wheelock of Monart

m. Dorothy White (**died** 2 Apr 1977 **bur.** Belturbet). Issue 1. Ann **b.** 1946 or 1947; 2. Lois R; 3. Evelyn Ethel bapt 4 Mar 1952 **m.** 2 Jun 1979 Peter Kelly; 4. Joy Alexandra **b.** 9 May 1956 **m.** Ian Elliott of Belturbet and had issue a **dau.** Nicola

Died 5 Jun 2001 **bur.** Belturbet

WHELAN, WILLIAM JOSEPH FRAZER 1850/51–

b. 1850 or 1851 Roscrea Co Tipperary; ed at Service Inst Dublin; ent TCD 21 Sep 1874 aged 23 BA 1879 BD 1884 DD 1896

d 1875 p 1876; C Swanlinbar (Kilm) 1875–77; C Drumcree (Arm) 1877–80; R Termonmaguirke 1880–86; C St Peter Ipswich (St E — then Nor) 1886–90; V St Lawrence Ipswich (St E — then Nor) 1890–*c.* 1930

s. of Benjamin, coach builder

m. 5 Jun 1877 St Bride's Ch Dublin Margaret Jane eldest **dau.** of James Buchanan of Drumany. Issue incl Margaret Dorothea Elizabeth **b.** 13 Aug 1878 Portadown

WHISKENS, ROBERT 1572/73–1634

b. 1572 or 1573; adm Pensioner Caius Coll Camb 2 Jun 1589 aged 16 Sch 1589–95 BA 1592/93 MA

C Rampton Cambs (Ely) and Schoolmaster 1606; V Annagelliffee (Kilm) 1622 and R & V 1626/27–34; a preacher; church ruinous; V Denn (Kilm) 1622; gets a grant of a glebe, 25 Jan 1626/27 (Morrin iii. 188)

may be Robert Whiskens **s.** of William of Milton, Cambridge

Died 1634

WHITE, FREDERICK BAGOT (also called BENJAMIN) *c.* 1839–1927

b. *c.* 1839 Co Kilkenny; ed by Mr McCarthy; ent TCD 6 Nov 1856 BA & Div Test 1861

d & p 1861 (Kilmore); C Kiltubride (Ard) 1861–65; C Ballinderry (Arm) 1865–66; C Arboe (Arm) 1866–67; C Creggan (Arm) 1868–73; I Errigle Shanco (Clogh) 1873–89; subsequently resided at Dungannon Co Tyrone

s. of George, Inspector of Constabulary

m. 11 Oct 1871 St Ann's Ch Dublin Nannie Geraldine **dau.** of William Ross Murray of Orwell Rd Rathgar Dublin

Died 13 Apr 1927

WHITE, HENRY FRANCIS

TCD BA 1875

d 1876 p 1877 (Kilmore); C Kilkeevan (Elph) 1876–78; R Dowra (Kilm) 1878–81; R Kilmina (Tuam) 1881–88; R Dunmore (Tuam) 1888–1905

WHITE, THOMAS 1701/02–1769

b. 1701 or 1702 in Derry; ed by Mr Blackall at Derry; ent TCD 2 May 1720 aged 18 Sch 1722 BA 1723 MA 1726 BD 1733 DD 1740

R Kilglass (Ard) 1732–36; R Vastina (Meath) and also R Newtownfertullagh (Meath) 1736–59; pres to the Deanery of Ardagh 30 Nov 1757 (L.M. V. 130); Dean of Ardagh 1757–69

    s. of Thomas, *dux militum*

    Died Aug 1769

WHITELAW, JAMES 1748–1813

b. 1748 Co Leitrim; ed by Mr Kerr; ent TCD 8 Jul 1766 Sch 1769 BA 1771

d 21 Apr 1784 (Kildare) p 1 May 1784 (Killaloe); Tutor to Lord Meath; V St James (Dub) 1784–88; V St Catherine (Dub) 1788–1813; V Kilkeevan and Preb of Ballintubber (Elph) 1809–13

    m. Lettice **dau.** of John Ledwich of Dublin

    Died 4 Feb 1813 aged 65

PUBLICATIONS
    A Census of Dublin 1798–1805
    with others, *A History of Dublin,* 2 vols, completed by Robert Walsh and published 1818

WHITELAW, NEWCOMEN –1823

was lic C of Scrabby in Granard parish (Ard) 6 Jan 1803 (Tuam S.R.); there w Gowna 1803–16

    Died 9 Nov 1823 at Hatley Co Leitrim

WHITELAW, ROBERT *c.* 1650/51–1714

b. *c.* 1650 or 1651 Co Fermanagh; ed by Mr Dunbar; ent TCD as Siz 16 Apr 1670 aged about 19 Sch 1673 BA 1674

V Drumlease and Killargue (Kilm) 1686–99; V Annaduff and R Cloone (Ard) *c.* 1693–1714 (may have been there from 1684); Preb and V Ballisodare (Ach) –1695

    s. of William

    m. and had issue Rev William qv

    Died 1714

WHITELAW, WILLIAM 1683/84–1736/37

b. 1683 or 1684 Cloony Co Sligo; ed by Mr Griffin, Longford; ent TCD 27 May 1702 aged 18 BA 1706

R Cloone (Ard) ?1714–*c.* 1736

    s. of Rev Robert qv (**s.** of William)

    Died 1736 or 1737; will proved 1737

WHITELEY (WHITELAW), NEWCOMEN 1762/63–1828

b. 1762 or 1763 Co Leitrim; ed by Mr Kerr; ent TCD 7 Jul 1778 aged 15 BA 1783

C Clane (Kild) 1802–04; C Tomregan (Kilm) 1808; Preb and V Donadea U (Kild) 1814–28

    s. of Newcomen

    m. 1806 Elizabeth Mills. Issue James **b.** Dublin ent TCD 6 Nov 1826 aged 16

    Died 1828

WHITTY, IRWINE 1777/78–1832

b. 1777 or 1778 Dublin; ent TCD 7 Oct 1793 aged 15 Sch 1796 BA 1798

d 1802 p 1803 (Kilmore); C Killeshandra (Kilm)1802–; C Cashel (Cash) –1807; V Ballysheehan (Cash) 1807–10; R Kilteynan (Cash) 1810–12; V Athassell (Cash) 1816–32

    s. of Ven Irwine, Archd of Kilfenora

    m. and had issue incl Irwine (**died** 1 Mar 1829 aged 21)

    Died 25 Jan 1832

Rev. Irwine Whitty was ambushed and murdered during the Tithe Wars of the 1830s. There was bitter resentment that Roman Catholics were being taxed to pay the salaries of the Church of Ireland clergy, though in fact, clergy rarely received stipends, and most, including the saintly Whitty, objected to their salaries being raised in this way

WHYTE, HENRY

ed by Rev Mr Cashin, Limerick; ent TCD as Siz 14 Jun 1759 Sch 1761 BA 1763

d; p 1767 (Kilmore); Head Master Royal Sch Cavan 1768–74; R Carrigallen (Kilm) 1769–74

    evidently of a Co Limerick family

    m. and had issue incl John **b.** Co Westmeath ent TCD as Siz 12 Jun 1781 aged 17 Sch 1784 BA 1785

WILKINS, WILLIAM MOORE 1812–1868

b. 1812 Dublin; ed Portora Royal Sch Enniskillen; ent TCD 6 Jul 1829 aged 17 BA 1836

d 4 May 1837 (Elphin) p 30 Oct 1837 (Limerick)

poss C Urney and Annegelliffe (Kilm) 1843–57; V Killinagh (Kilm) 1852 or 1857–61; V Killargue (Kilm) 1861–68

    s. of Charles, *pragmaticus*

    Died 13 Feb 1868 aged 55

WILKINSON, JOHN

V Annaduff and Clone (Cloone) (Ard) 1634, inst 14 Jun (F.F.)

WILKINSON, JOHN

Preb of Oran (Elph) 1635/36–1668; V Sligo (Elph) 1666–68. He was Commonwealth Minister of the Gospel at Sligo from 1655, at first at £100, subsequently increased to £200. In 1660 he complained "that the lands of Knocknegarnice in the parish of St John's, Sligo are part of his settlement for maintenance, and are known every year since the late peace to have paid rectorial & vicarial tithes to the pretended Rector; but one Maurice Dillon, a late Captain of the rebels in Co. Mayo hath settled himself in Sligo and contrary to all equity doth contemptuously deny to pay to your petitioner the said tithes, pretending that it is part of the Abbey lands of the town." An order for them was granted 25 Sep 1660

WILKINSON, JOHN 1785/86–

b. 1785 or 1786 Co Laois; ed privately; ent TCD 24 Jan 1822 aged 36 BA 1826 MA 1829 LB & LLD 1841

C Kilglass (Ard) 1838–47; subsequently in Cloyne

> **s.** of James, gentleman

WILKINSON, WILLIAM DORAN FALKINER 1847/48–1932

b. 1847 or 1848; TCD 1881

d 1881 (Kilmore for Armagh) p 1885 (Dublin for Armagh); C Muckno (Clogh) 1882–85; R Castleterra (Kilm) 1885–99; R Dromara and Garvaghy (Drom) 1899–1920

> **m.** Frances Anna **dau.** of Rev George Burkitt, Preb of Fennor (Cash) by Dorothea **dau.** of Elias R and Dorothea Ormsby Handcock
>
> **Died** 20 Sep 1932 aged 84

WILLANS, WILLIAM 1876/77–1970

b. 1876 or 1877; ed Univ of Glasgow 1891; Queen's Coll Belfast 1893; RUI BA 1899

d 1902 p 1903 (Ripon); C Girlington (Bradf — then Rip) 1902–07; C St James Carlisle (Carl) 1907–09; C Baildon (Bradf — then Rip) 1909–11; C St George Leeds (Rip) 1911–14; Org Sec ICM for Dublin and Glendalough & Perm to Off Dublin 1914–16; R Templeport (Kilm) 1916–20; R Carmangay (Dio Calgary) 1920–22; R St John Glencoe Ontario (Dio Huron) 1922–25; in ECUSA 1925–29; C-in-c Lack (Clogh) 1929–32; C-in-c Magheacross (Clogh) 1932–50; ret

> **m.** Sybil Kathleen. Issue 1. Capt William Arthur N, Frontier Force Rifles **m.** 1946 Lelia Maria eldest **dau.** of David Kennedy of Belfast; 2. Sybil **m.** Donald Button
>
> **Died** 15 Mar 1970 Belfast aged 93

WILLCOCKS, JAMES CAULFIELD 1820/21–1891

b. 1820 or 1821 Co Tyrone; ed by Mr Darley; ent TCD 2 Jul 1841 aged 20 BA 1847 Div Test 1848

d 1848 (Dublin) p 1849 (Kilmore); C Kilmore & Ballintemple (Kilm) 1848–71; R Ballintemple (Kilm) 1872–75; R Killan (Kilm) 1875–89; ret

s. of George

m. 27 May 1857 St George's Ch Dublin Isabella yst **dau.** of Rev Thomas Skelton
Died 19 or 29 Nov 1891 Dublin

WILLIAMS, ARFON 1958–

b. 2 Feb 1958 Bangor N Wales; ed Llangefui Sch; Univ of Wales Bangor MA 1978; Univ of Wales Aberystwyth BD (Hons) 1983; Wycliffe Hall Ox DipLit DPT DPTh 1984; Powys Exhib; Lloyd Mem Pri

d 1984 p 1985 (St. David's); C St David Carmarthen (St D) 1984–86; TV Aberystwyth (St D) 1986–88; V Glanogwen (Ban) 1988–94; Dir Oasthouses Christian Retreat and Adult Ed Centre Lewes Sussex (Chich) 1995–98; Asst to RD Rye (Chich) 1995–98; C Ewhurst (Chich) 1995–98; Co-ord for Adult Ed E Sussex Area (Chich) 1997–98; R Jordanstown (Conn) 1998–2002; R Dolgellau w Llanfachreth and Brithdir (Ban) 2002–04; Archd of Meirionnydd (Ban) 2002–04; R St John Sligo Knocknarea and Rosses Point (Elph) and Dean of Elphin and Ardagh 2004–

    s. of Arthur of Angelsey (**s.** of William and Annie) by Florence **dau.** of Glyn and Annie Rowlands of Angelsey

    m. 5 Jan 1980 St Finian's Ch Cregagh Belfast Carol Mary **dau.** of Fred and Daphne Douglas of Cregagh. Issue 1. Ceri Ann **b.** 26 Oct 1984; 2. Ruth Erin **b.** 17 Apr 1992

PUBLICATION
Baptism, A Guide for Parents, 1996

WILLIAMS, CHARLES RICHARD *c.* 1853–

b *c.* 1853; TCD Candidate Bachelor 1878

d 1878 p 1879 (Kilmore); C Drumshambo (Ard) 1878–79; C Kilmore (Ard) 1879–80; C St Thomas Nottingham and Chapl Gen Hosp Nottingham (S'well) 1880–81; R Richhill (Arm) 1881–97; R Sixmilecross (Arm) 1897–1912; C St Michael Mitcham Adelaide (Adel) 1912–15; Gen Lic Dio Adelaide from 1916

    s. of Charles Richard

    m. 1 Oct 1878 St Mark's Ch Armagh Harriette Letitia **dau.** of Christopher Henry St George of Armagh. Issue incl 1. Charles Henry St George (**died** 1905 **bur.** Sixmilecross); 2. William (**died** 30 Apr 1886)

PUBLICATIONS
    A Sermon on *Sacred Song,* preached in Richhill Church Co Armagh 1884
    The King's Table, Holy Communion Address, 1903
    Arrows Shot at a Venture, Essays on subjects Literary and Religious, published by Sealy, Byers and Walker, Dublin

WILLIAMS, DAVID 1949–

b. 1949; BTh; Dip Tech Mining; Haileybury School of Mines (anada

d 1988 p 1989; C Lurgan Kildrumferton Ballyjamesduff Ballymachugh Killinkere Munterconnaught and Billis (Kilm) 1988–91; R Kinsale Ballymartle and Templetrine

(Cork) 1991–; Mission to Seafarers 1991–; Warden of Guild of Lay Readers Cork Cloyne and Ross 1994–; Preb of St Michael's and Inniskenny (Cork) 1995–97; Preb of Brigown (Cloyne) 1995–97; Preb of Cahirlag (Cork) 1997; Treas St Fin Barre's Cath Cork 1997–; Preb of Tymothan in St Patrick's Cath Dublin 1997–

WILLIAMS, HENRY FREDERICK 1799/1800–
b. 1799 or 1800 Tipperary; ent TCD as SC 4 Jul 1814 aged 14 BA 1818 MA 1824 LLB & LLD 1828; V Kilmolash (Lism) 1826–27; R Ardmore (Lism) 1827–28; R Killinkere (Kilm) 1828–45

    s. of George, *causidicus*

    m. 10 Jun 1828 St. George's Par Ch Dublin Mary Galwey

WILLIAMS, SAMUEL
evidently Samuel Williams ed by Mr Hynes; ent TCD as Siz 19 Jun 1764 Sch 1766; poss R or C Roscommon (Elph) *c.* 1774, or just may have come from there;

    m. (ML 14 Jan 1774) Mary Ann Howard of Dublin

WILLIAMSON, JOHN 1758/59–
prob John Williamson **b.** 1758/59 Dublin; ed by Dr Benson; ent TCD 27 Oct 1773 aged 14 Sch 1776 BA 1778 MA 1781
C Tara (Meath) 1781; C Rossinver (Kilm) 1808

    s. of John *clericus*

WILLIS, MICHAEL HAMILTON GIBSON 1864–1945
b. 1864 Dublin; ed High Sch Dublin; TCD BA 1897 MA 1903; MBE 1918
d & p 1895 (Kilmore); C Killesherdoney (Kilm) 1895–96; R Killesherdoney (Kilm) 1896–1900; R Newbliss (Clogh) 1900–03; R St Michael Belfast (Conn) 1903–13; R Donaghadee (Down) 1913–38; RD of Bangor

    s. of Hamilton of Dublin by Sarah **dau.** of William Vincent Robinson Ruckley of Sandymount Dublin

    m. 25 Aug 1905 Elizabeth Shortt **dau.** of William Stuart Mollan of Hampton Belfast

    Died 10 Jun 1945

WILLS, THOMAS B
BA
d 1855 p; C Kilglass (Ard) 1867–69 (C I Dir)

WILLS, THOMAS WILLIAM   –1948
TCD Sch BA (Jun Mod) 1894
d 1900 p 1901 (Manchester); C St George Manchester (Manch) 1900–04; R Shercock

formerly Killan (Kilm) 1904–33; R Killenumery and Killargue (Kilm) 1933–46; ret

    s. of Canon Samuel Richard, R Rathkeale (Lim)

    m. 29 Apr 1914 Kingscourt Ch Co Cavan Mabel Henrietta (**died** 14 Jan 1946) **dau.** of Samuel J Adams, JP of Northlands Co Cavan

    Died 15 Oct 1948

WILLSON, THOMAS BENJAMIN 1851–1932

b. 15 Mar 1851; ed Rathmines Sch Dublin; TCD BA 1872 Div Test 1874 MA 1876 LittD 1911; was created a Knight (1st class) of the Royal Order of St Olaf by the King of Norway in 1921

d 1874 p 1875 (Kilmore); C Kilmore (Kilm) 1874–77; V Drumbanagher (Arm) 1877–83; C St Saviour Croydon (S'wark — then Cant) 1883–89; C Shooter's Hill (S'wark) 1889–97; & V 1897–1912; R West Woodhay Newbury (Ox) 1912–25; ret

    s. of Thomas Edkins, MA Solicitor of Dublin

    m. 25 Jun 1879 St Mary's Ch Drumbanagher Co Armagh Florence yst **dau.** of Peter Quinn, JP of Drumbanagher and MP for Newry 1859–65 by Sarah Jane (**died** 6 Nov 1934 at Kidlington Oxford aged 82) **dau.** of Rev Josiah Erskine, R Knockbride (Kilm) qv Issue 1. Thomas Olaf **b.** 29 Jul 1880 **m.** (1) 1919 Constance Horsburgh (**died** 1946) **dau.** of Walter Basil Cowen and had 1 **s.** and 3 **daus.**; **m.** (2) 1948 Joan **dau.** of A J Livesey of Lancashire; 2. Maurice Frank Campbell

    Died 25 May 1932

PUBLICATIONS
    Author of many books on Norway including
    The Handy Guide to Norway, 7th ed 1927
    History of the Church and State in Norway from the Tenth to the Sixteenth Century, 1903
    Norway at Home, 1908

WILSON, CECIL MOFFATT 1926–1998

b. 1926 Co Kilkenny; ed Campbell Coll Belfast; QUB Medical Sch 1944–47; TCD BA 1951 Div Test 1952

d 29 Jun 1952 p 1953; C Urney (Kilm) 1952–54; Asst Master Foyle Coll Londonderry 1954–56; C-in-c Templeharry (Killaloe) 1956–57 & R 1957–59; R Cloughjordan (Killaloe) 1959–64; R Mountmellick (Kild) 1964–76; Canon of Kildare 1972–74; Chanc of Kildare 1974; Archd of Kildare 1974–76; R Raheny and Coolock (Dub) 1976–91; Preb of Dunlavin in St Patrick's Cath Dublin 1988–91; ret; Asst P St John's Orangefield Belfast (Down) 1993–98

    s. of Rev Geoffrey, C Kilkeevan (Elph) qv by Angel **dau.** of Rev Frederick Joseph Rainsford

    m. 4 Sep 1948 Holy Trinity Ch Waringstown Mary (Mollie) **dau.** of George and Margaret Power of Lurgan Co Armagh. Issue 1. Ronald Alan Godfrey **b.** 21 Dec 1951; 2. Phyllis Margaret **b.** 29 Apr 1956

    Died 3 Mar 1998

WILSON, DAVID BRIAN 1947–

b. 9 Aug 1947 Belfast; ed Annadale Gram Sch Belfast; QUB BA 1968 DipEd & Dip Bibl Studs 1969; TCD King, Downes Comp Pris Div Test 1971

d 27 Jun 1971 p 29 Jun 1972 (Down); C Ballyholme (Down) 1971–74; C Christ Ch Guildford (Guildf) 1974–78; R Arvagh Carrigallen Gowna and Columbkille (Kilm) 1978–81; R Clogherny and Seskinore (w Drumnakilly from 1985) (Arm) 1981–95; R Caledon and Brantry (Arm) 1995–

s. of Robert and Mary (née Todd) Wilson of Belfast

WILSON, GEOFFREY MOFFATT 1885/86–1939

b. 1885 or 1886; TCD BA 1914 MA 1920

d 1914 p 1915 (Kilmore); C Kilkeevan (Elph) 1914–16; C St Catherine (Dub) 1916–17; TCF 1917–20; C Rathmines (Dub) 1920–21; C Abbeyleix (Leigh) 1922; V Chor St Canice's Cat Kilkenny (Oss) 1923–24; R Kilmacow and Kilculliheen (Oss) 1924–25; R Stradbally (Leigh) 1925–34; Dio C and Head Master D'Israeli Sch Rathvilly (Leigh) 1934–39

m. 18 Jul 1922 Angel dau. of Canon Frederick Joseph Rainsford, R Inch (Glend) 1931–44. Issue incl 1. Frederick Rainsford; 2. Geoffrey Rainsford b. 1923; 3. Rev Cecil Moffatt, C Urney (Kilm) qv; 4. David

Died 16 Feb 1939 aged 53

WILSON, HENRY RUTHE c. 1841–1923

b. c. 1841 Kircubbin Co Down; ed privately; ent TCD 2 Jul 1860 BA & Div Test 1867

d 1867 p 1870; C Magheraculmoney (Clogh) 1867–68; C Portadown (Arm) 1868–70; C Tartaraghan (Arm) 1870–75; C Drumbeg (Down) 1876–81; C St Mary Donnybrook (Dub) 1881–82; C Kilcommick (Ard) 1882–85; R Kilmood (Down) 1885–1923, succeeding his father

s. of Rev Hugh LLB, v Ballywalter (Down) by Sarah 2nd dau. of Lawson Anseley of Derramore Co Down

m. 21 Oct 1903 St George's Ch Dublin Anna Spread (died 2 Oct 1938 bur. Kilmood) yst dau. of Willis George Crofts of Dublin and Templemary Buttevant Co Cork

Died 13 Apr 1923 bur. Kilmood

WILSON, HILL 1814/15–1891

b. 1814 or 1815 Dublin; ed by Mr Fitzmaurice; ent TCD 18 Oct 1839 aged 15 BA 1836 Div Test 1839 MA 1882

d 1839 p 1840; DC Stoneyford and C Derriaghy (Conn) 1839–40; C Forgney (Meath) 1840–44; R Forgney (Meath) 1844–71; British Chapl at Havre France 1857–63; R Killegar (Kilm) 1871–73; R Ballyvaldon and Castle Ellis (Ferns) 1873–80; R Kilmacow (Oss) 1880–91

s. of Hill, Solicitor (s. of Hill, 1st Sec of the Bank of Ireland, by Mary Darley) by Mary Reeves

m. 26 Oct 1858 Mary Elizabeth only **dau.** of Richard Bignell of Banbury Oxford. Issue 1. Mary Elizabeth Alice (**died** 1884); 2. Lilla Lucy; 3. Frances Mary. His **sister** Lucy **m.** Rev Henry de Vere White of Swifts Alley Ch Dublin and had issue incl Harry de Vere TCD DD, Bp of Limerick, Newport J B White, TCD DD Reg Prof of Divinity and Dr Hill Wilson of Wilson's Hospital

Died 8 Aug 1891 at Kilmacow Rectory aged 76

WILSON, JAMES   –1686

Archd of Elphin & V Kilmactranny Ardcarne Aghanagh Taunagh and Toomna (Elph) 1665–68; R Kilkerrin Killererin Ballinakelly and Aghiart (Tuam) and Provost of Tuam 1667–69; became Dean of Tuam and R Dunmore Drumraney and Moynulla (Tuam) 1669–86; V Adregoole Liskeevy Boyanagh and Clonbern 1669–86; V Gen Elphin 1671; V Gen Tuam 1672

m. and had issue Bridget **m.** Owen Young of Castlerea Co Roscommon

Died 1686

WILSON, JAMES 1872–1964

b. 23 Sep 1872 Lurgan; ed Monaghan Collegiate Sch; TCD BA 1900 Div Test 1902 MA 1904

d 1900 (Down for Clogher) p 1903 (Clogher); C Clontibret (Clogh) 1900–01; C Trory (Clogh) 1901–02; C Tyholland (Clogh) 1903–06; R Tempo (Clogh) 1906–15; R Derrygortreavy (w Brantry from 1922) (Arm) 1915–30; C-in-c Gowna and Columbkille (Ard) 1930–37; R Drumcliffe & Ahamplish (w Lissadell from 1959) 1937–63; Preb of Tibohine in Elphin Cath 1949–53; Dean of Elphin and Ardagh 1953–63; ret

s. of Rev James, R Tyholland (Clogh) (**s.** of James of Portadown) by Letitia **dau.** of Thompson Ferris of Portadown and **bro.** of Rev David Frederick Ruddell, Dean of St Patrick's Cath Dublin 1935–50

m. 1 Sep 1915 Kilskeery Par Ch Co Tyrone Evelyn Marie Anna (**died** 8 May 1968 Enniskillen aged 80) only **dau.** of Rev Canon William E C Fleming MA, R Kilskeery (Clogh) by Susannah Margaret **dau.** of Thomas Fosbrooke Salt of Burton-on-Trent. Issue 1. Noel Fosbrooke **b.** 12 Dec 1921 **died** 4 Jul 1936; 2. Daphne Margaret Evelyn Letitia **b.** 9 Feb 1923; 3. Doris Cecily Mary (**died** 30 Jul 2006) **b.** 30 Mar 1924 **m.** 23 Nov 1946 Drumcliffe Par Ch Co Sligo Lt David Keith Furniss Potter RN (**died** 22 Mar 1994) **s.** of Lt Col CF Potter of Holywood Co Down and had issue (i) Jolyn Guy Furniss **b.** 11 May 1952 **m.** Alyss Teresa Mary Conway (ii) Justin Paul Furniss **b.** 30 Oct 1956 **m.** 9 Jul 1983 Sally Ann Millard

Died 2 Apr 1964 **bur.** Kilskeery

WILSON, JAMES LEWIS 1939–

b. 26 Apr 1939 Dublin; ed Wesley Coll Dublin; TCD BA 1962 HDipEd 1963 MA 1965 BD 1971 Div Test 1974

d 1974 p 1975 (Clogher); C St Macartin's Cath Enniskillen (Clogh) 1974–76; C St Matthew Belfast (Conn) 1976–79; R Killeshandra Killegar and Derrylane (Kilm)

1979–81; R Loughgilly and Clare (Arm) 1981–

s. of Henry Lewis of Dublin (s. of James Arthur and Jane Elizabeth (née Cassidy) of Athlone Co Westmeath) by Edith Sarah dau. of Stephen and Laura Christina (née McMillan) Bigger of Dublin

m. 3 Aug 1974 St John the Baptist Par Ch Dunluce Co Antrim Anne Archibald TCD BA 1969 MA 1972 QUB DipEd 1970 dau. of Clarke and Ruby Boyce of Bushmills Co Antrim. Issue 1. Jonathan Henry Clarke b. 24 May 1977 Imperial Coll London BEng (Computing) 1999 ACGI the Coll of Law London LLDip 2001, solicitor; 2. Jennifer Louise b. 28 May 1979 Univ of Bristol LLB 2000 Barrister-at-Law Lincoln's Inn 2002

WILSON, JOHN 1660/61–*c.* 1725

b. 1660 or 1661 Co Westmeath; ed by Mr Torway; ent TCD 11 Jul 1681 aged 20 Sch 1684 BA 1686 MA 1704

R & V Thehsynode = Taghsynod and Tashinny and Kildemock = Kilcommick & V Shruell = Shrule & Abbeyshrule (Ard) 1691–1717; coll 22 Apr 1691; evidently = John Wilson who was V Moyglare and Ballymaglassan (Meath) 1709–18

probably J W s. of William

Died *c.* 1725. Will proved 1725

WILSON, ROBERT –1684

perhaps Robert Wilson TCD Sophister 1628 but is MA in F.F

Commonwealth Minister at Termonmaguirke (Arm) 1655–58; Preb of Inniscattery and R Kilrush (Killaloe) 1670–72; V Killargue and Drumlease (Kilm) 1675–78; Chanc of Ardfert and V Killarney Kilcummin Aglish and Killaneare (Ardf) 1675–84; Archd of Kilmore, V Urney & R Castleterra (Kilm) 1678–84

may have been s. of Robert (died 1642), Dean of Ferns and V Finglas (Dub)

Died 1684

WILSON, SAMUEL GEOFFREY 1962–

b. 12 Apr 1962 Newtownards Co Down; ed Tandragee Junior High Sch; Portadown Coll; TCD Downes Orat Pri 2002, 2004 CITC BTh 2004

d 27 Jun 2004 p 19 Jun 2005; C-in-c Swanlinbar w Kinawley Chapel of Ease, Templeport & Tomregan (Kilm) 2004–07; R Swanlinbar w Kinawley Chapel of Ease Templeport Tomregan Kildallon Corawallen and Newtowngore 2007–

s. of Robert Arnold of Portadown Co Armagh by Margaret Anne (née Bloomfield) of Portadown

m. 19 Jun 1987 Naomi Georgene Elizabeth of Swanlinbar Co Cavan dau. of George and Hester Campbell of Keady Co Armagh. Issue 1. Bethany Hester b. 8 Dec 1989; 2.Jack George b. 4 Aug 1991; 3. Samuel Robert b. 31 Oct 1993

WILSON, THOMAS FREDERICK MILLER 1800/01–1868

b. 1800 or 1801; was probably Thomas Wilson TCD BA 1836

d 7 Feb 1836 p 6 Nov 1836 (Elphin); V Rathcline (Ard) 1839–68; was JP for Co Longford 1851

may have been **s.** of Rev Andrew of Milbown Co Galway

m. and had issue incl his 1. eldest **s.** William Galbraith (**died** 8 Feb 1876 aged 31), TCD Sch MA, Meteorologist to the Governor of Bengal and Professor in the Government College Calcutta; 2. Dora **m.** 19 Dec 1876 Rev Samuel Johnston, R Louisburgh (Tuam)

Died 10 Mar 1868 aged 67

WILSON, WILLIAM

R & V Kilcommick and Tashinny (Ard), coll 1 Feb 1717/18, resigned 7 Feb 1717/18 (F.F.); as R & V was admonished to reside in 6 months at the Triennial Visitation, 1742. Was he Rev William Wilson of Piersfield Co Westmeath who **m.** Emilia **dau.** of John Eyre of Eyrecourt and left her a widow? She remarried John Rochfort of Cloghrenane. He is mentioned in the Will of John Eyre his bro-in-law for 1743, who leaves him a "little pad mare and amber snuff box"

†WILSON, WILLIAM GILBERT 1918–1999

b. 23 Jan 1918 Belfast; ed RBAI; TCD BA 1939 Div Test (1) First prizeman in Heb and Oriental Langs Aramaic and Syr Pri 1940 MA & BD 1944 Elrington Theol Pri (1) 1946 PhD 1949

d 1941 p 1942 Bp 1981; C St Mary Magdalene Belfast (Conn) 1941–44; C St Comgall Bangor (Down) 1944–47; R Armoy and Loughguile (Conn) 1947–76; Clerical Hon Sec Connor Synod and Council 1956–81; Preb of Cairncastle (Conn) 1964–76; R Christ Church Cath Lisburn and Dean of Connor 1976–81; elected Bp of Kilmore Elphin and Ardagh by Electoral College 11 Jun 1981; consec in St Anne's Cath Belfast 21 Sep 1981; enthroned in St Fethlimidh's Cath Kilmore 30 Sep 1981; enthroned in the Cath of St Mary the Virgin and St John the Baptist Sligo 3 Dec 1981; Bp of Kilmore Elphin and Ardagh 1981–93; ret

s. of Adam of Antrim Rd Belfast (**s.** of William and Mary of Antrim Rd Belfast) by Rebecca Rusk (née Bryans) of Belfast

m. 25 Nov 1944 St Peter's Ch Belfast Peggy Muriel **dau.** of James and Ruby Busby of Belfast. Issue 1. Rosemary Winifred **b.** 9 Jul 1946 **m.** H Barry; 2. William Gilbert Bernard **b.** 11 Feb 1948 **m.** Sharon Laverty; 3. Patricia Anne **b.** 14 Sep 1949 **m.** R Maxwell; 4. Elizabeth Rosalind **b.** 7 May 1951 **m.** P Hackworth; 5. Jeremy Andrew James **b.** 12 Jan 1954 **m.** Maud Johnston; 6. Michael Richard Glenn **b.** 20 Feb 1962

Died 21 Jun 1999

PUBLICATIONS
A Guild of Youth Handbook, 1944
Church Teaching, 1954, revised ed 1970
How the Church of Ireland is Governed, 1964

The Church of Ireland after 1970 — Advance or Retreat? 1968
The Church of Ireland — Why Conservative? Dublin 1970
Is there a Life after Death? 1974
A Critique of "Authority in the Church", 1977
Irish Churchwardens' Handbook, revised ed 1979
The Faith of an Anglican, Collins, 1980
The Way of the Church, Collins, 1982
Should we have Women Deacons? 1984
Why no Women Priests? Churchman Publishing Ltd, Worthing 1988
Towards Accepting Women Priests, APCK 1989
Joint-editor, *The Church challenges Youth,* 1944
Editor, *The Church of Ireland Gazette,* 1963–1966
Co-author, *Anglican Teaching — An Exposition of the Thirty-Nine Articles,* 1964
Editor, *Parochial News,* 1966–1976
Articles in *Journal of Theological Studies* on, *An examination of the linguistic evidence adduced against the unity of authorship of the First Epistle of John and the Fourth Gospel,* July–Oct 1948, and *The original text of the the Fourth Gospel,* Jan–April 1949
Article in *The Church Quarterly Review* on *Christian Initiation,* Jan–Mar 1957

WINDER, HENRY MONK 1803–1855

b 1803 Dublin; ed by Mr Verner; ent TCD 6 Nov 1820 aged 16 BA 1825 MA 1832 C Annagh (Kilm) *c.* 1843 (Leslie's MS has William Winder, which is probably a mistake for Henry Monk Winder; V Killinkere (Kilm) 1845–55

    s. of Edward, *coactor*

    m. 1827 Lucinda Singleton and had issue incl **sons** 1. John Henry **m.** 25 Apr 1872 St George's Ch Dublin Elizabeth Stewart (née Watt) widow of James H Barrett; 2. a yst **s.** Henry Monk (**died** 7 Apr 1921); 3. a 3rd **dau.** Lucy Jane (**died** 30 Mar 1895 Dublin); 4. a yst **dau.** Caroline Frances (**died** 13 Mar 1917 Donnybrook Dublin)

    Died 14 Dec 1855 aged 52

WINDER, JOHN

R & V Annaduff (Ard) 1714/15, pres by Crown 6 Jun; coll 10 Jun

WINTER, WILLIAM HARRIS   –1921

TCD BA 1891 BD 1896; Univ of Adelaide BD (*ad eund*) 1913

d 1882 (Kilmore) p 1884 (Meath for Kilmore); C Larah and Lavey (Kilm) 1882–86; R Taunagh (Elph) 1886–95; R Coatbridge w Gartcosh Miss (G & G) 1895–1904; C Christ Ch N Adelaide (Dio Adel) 1904–06; R Christ Ch Balaklava w Port Wakefield and Goyder (Adel) 1906–10; R St Saviour Glen Osmond (Adel) 1910–21

    m. 11 Jul 1883 Esmina yst **dau.** of John **m.** Ranson of Dundalk

    Died 1921

PUBLICATIONS
> *Rienzi and other Poems,* Dublin, McGee 1886–1895
> *Incense viewed from Scripture and History,* 2nd ed 1902

WOLFE, ROBERT WILLIAM   –1970

TCD BA (Resp) 1928

d 1930 (Kilm) p (Kilm) 1932; C Annagh w Quivvy and St Andrew's (Kilm) 1930–32; C-in-c Mostrim (Ard) 1932–36; C-in-c Castleterra (Kilm) 1936–39; C-in-c Cashel and Rathcline (Ard) 1939–55; C-in-c Killashee and Ballymacormack (w Kilcommick from 1965) (Ard) 1955–67; ret

> **m.** 2 Oct 1933 Edgeworthstown Ch Mostrim Co Longford Winifred Mary Collins (**died** 2 May 1991) of Ewell Surrey
>
> **Died** 28 Jun 1970 Longford **bur.** Rathcline

WOLLY, RICHARD   –1640

V Aughrim (Elph) to 1640; V Terebrine *c.* 1636–40

> **Died** 1640

WOLSELEY, CAPEL 1814–1885

b. 10 Oct 1814; ed by Mr Matthews; ent TCD 4 Nov 1833 BA 1838

PC Lissadell (Elph) 1859–76; R Holy Trinity Salford (Manch) 1876–

> 4th **s.** of Rev William, R Glenarm and Dunaghy (Conn) (**s.** of Rev William, Preb of Tullycorbet (Clogh) 1784–1800 and Jane) by Winifred **dau.** of Cadwallader Edwards; **bro.** of Ven Cadwallader, Archd of Glendalough 1863–72
>
> **m.** 16 Dec 1847 Anne Jane Proctor of Dublin and had issue
>
> see also Leslie's *Clogher Clergy and Parishes,* p 80
>
> **Died** 10 Feb 1885

WOOD, THOMAS PATRICK SCARBOROUGH 1919–2005

b. 1919 Abbeyleix; ed Bishop Foy's Sch Waterford; The King's Hospital Dublin; TCD BA 1941 Downes and Kyle Pris 1942 Div Test (2) 1942 BD 1954

d 1942 p 1943 (Dublin); C Portarlington U (Kild) 1942–44; C St George (Dub) 1944–46; C-in-c Ballysumaghan (Elph) 1946–49; R Oughteragh and Fenagh (Ard) 1949–50; R Rathaspeck and Streete (Ard) 1950–56; I Calry (Elph) 1956–94; Preb of Oran (Elph) 1967–84; Dom Chapl and Exam Chapl to Bp of Kilmore 1988–94; Preb of Mulhuddart in St Patrick's Cath Dublin 1983–94; ret

> **s.** of William Frederick and Isabella Maud
>
> **m.** 14 Jul 1943 Oonagh Mary **dau.** of Rev Paul Quigley, R Tubbercurry (Ach) 1945–48. Issue William Paul
>
> **Died** 20 May 2005

WOODHOUSE, HUGH PARKER 1872/73–1933

b. 1872 or 1873; TCD BA (Jun Mod) & Div Test (2) 1906 MA 1909 BD 1914

d 1906 p 1907; C St Thomas Dublin (Dub) 1906–10; C St Kevin Dublin (Dub) 1910–14; C-in-c Drumshambo (Ard) 1914–16; R Drumshambo (Ard) 1916–20; R Billis (Kilm) 1921–33

    s. of Robert

    m. Elizabeth (née Tomkins) (**died** 9 Feb 1970 at Bletchley). Issue 1. Rev Hugh Frederick **b.** 16 May 1912 TCD Sch BA (1cl Mod Hist and Pol Sci) 1934 HDipEd 1936 BD 1937 Div Test (1) 1937 DD 1952 FTCD 1974 Theo Exhib (1) Sen Exh; Biggs, Dunbar, Ingram, Elrington, Carson Bibl, Downes Orat (2), Heb (2), Bibl Gk (2), Eccles Hist (1), Abp King's (1), Moncrieff Cox Pris; d 1937 p 1938 C St Donard Belfast (Down) 1937–39 C Bangor (Down) 1940–44 R Aghalee (Drom) 1944–46 R Newtownards (Down) 1946–51 Prof Eccles Hist Wycliffe Coll Toronto Canada 1951–54 Prin & Prof Hist Anglican Coll Vancouver 1954–59 Commiss Capeton 1958 Prof Dogmatic Theol Univ Coll Halifax NS 1959–63 TCD Reg Prof of Divinity 1963–82; **m.** Kitty Boam and had issue (i) Dorothy Dalhousie Univ Halifax BSc (Hons) **m.** 1970 David Wishart (ii) Hugh Boam (iii) Charles George; 2. Isabel Dorothy **b.** 11 Jun 1917.

    Died 7 Dec 1933 aged 60

WOODS, EDWARD SAMUEL   –1906

TCD BA & Div Test 1853 MA 1866

d 1854 p 1855; C Killesher (Kilm) 1854–55; C Kenilworth (Worc) 1855–58; C Holy Trinity Tonbridge (Cant) 1858–67; PC Holy Trinity Dover (Cant) 1867–84; V Ash-next-Sandwich (Cant) 1884–1906

    Died Apr 1906

WOODS, FREDERICK WILLIAM

TCD BA 1903 Div Test 1905 MA 1909

d 1903 p 1905 (Kilmore); C Drumlease (Kilm) 1903–07; C-in-c Carrigallen (Kilm) 1907–11; Chapl RN 1911–23; HMS *London* 1911–12; *Hibernia* 1912–15; *Isis* 1915–16; *Laurentic* 1916–17; C All SS Lambeth (S'wark) 1917–19; Emmanuel Ch Maida Vale (Lon) 1919–23; R Arlesey w Astwick (St A) 1923–33; last entry in Crockford 1933

WOODS, TANYA JOY 1973–

b. 6 Feb 1973; ed Virginia Vocational Sch Co Cavan; Dundalk RTC Dipl in Food Science and Technology Cert in Applied Biology; CITC BTh 1999; Gold Gaisce Award

d 23 Jun 2002 p 15 Jun 2003; NSM Killesher and Killinagh (Kilm) 2002–06; NSM Bailieborough Knockbride Shercock and Mullagh 2006–

    granddaughter of R J and Evelyn Woods of Billis Ballyjamesduff Co Cavan and Edward and Annie Snow of Linfield Kells Co Meath

    m. 26 Jun 1999 Billis Par Ch Robert **s.** of William and Doreen Clarke of Kilmore

Co Cavan. Issue 1. Nathan Robert **b.** 25 Jul 2001; 2. Christopher Daniel Andrew **b.** 29 Aug 2004

WOODWARD, HENRY 1775–1863

b. 5 Aug 1775 Clogher Co Tyrone; student of Lincoln's Inn 1794; Corpus Christi Coll Oxford matric 21 Nov 1792 BA 1795

d 18 Oct 1797 p 22 Dec 1799 (Kilmore); C Annagh (Kilm) 1797; V Kildrumferton (Kilm) 1801–07; R Glankeen (Cash) 1807–12; V Fethard (Cash — now Lism) 1812–63

5th **s.** of Richard, Bp of Cloyne 1781–94.

m. 30 May 1797 Lismore Cath Melesina **dau.** of Rev Verney Lovett, R Moira (Drom) 1788 by Frances Mary **dau.** of Ven Henry Gervais, Archd of Cashel. Issue **sons** 1. Rev Francis (**died** 4 Feb 1866 Rome) **b.** Co Cavan ent TCD 6 Jul 1818 aged 17 BA 1822 MA 1832 PC St Stephen (Dub) *c.* 1840 became Chapl at Rome; 2. Rev Jonathan Henry **b.** Cavan ent TCD 5 Jul 1821 aged 16 BA 1826 MA 1843 PC St James Bristol 1838 **m.** and had issue 4 **sons** and 5 **daus.**; 3. Rev Thomas (**died** 30 Sep 1875 London) ent TCD 7 Nov 1831 aged 17 Sch 1834 BA 1837 MA 1849 d p 19 Dec 1841 (Down) V Mullingar (Meath) 1851–56 **m.** 5 Oct 1852 St George's Ch Dublin Frances Eliza eldest **dau.** of Robert Barlow of Mullingar Co Westmeath and had issue (i) Robert Henry Walter **b.** 1856 (ii) Grace (iii) Eva **m.** 16 Nov 1880 William H Murphy of Belfast; **daus.** 1. Melesina **m.** 1825 Rev William Crofton, R Skreen (Killala); 2. Louisa Frances

Died 14 Apr 1863 at Fethard Rectory Co Tipperary

PUBLICATIONS

Sermon on St. Matthew xvi 15, preached in the Magdalen Asylum on 19 Feb 1837, in *New Irish Pulpit*

Sermon on Acts viii 39, Joy in Conversion, preached in St Patrick's Cathedral, Dublin, in *New Irish Pulpit*

Thoughts on the Character and History of Nehemiah, Hatchard's, London, 1849

Some Passages in my Former Life, 1847, an autobiographical note and an account of his Conversion, not approved by the *Christian Examiner,* as he was a disciple of Alexander Knox and Bishop Jebb

WOOLLEY, RICHARD –1640

V Terebrine (Elph) *c.* 1636–40

Died 1640

WORRALL, FREDERICK BARCROFT 1888–1958

b. 5 Aug 1888 Sydney NSW; ed Portora Royal Sch Enniskillen; St Aidan's Coll Birkenhead; Univ of Durham 1916

d 1918 p 1919 (Kilmore); C Urney and Annagelliffe (Kilm) 1918–21; C Killeshandra and Killegar (Kilm) 1921–25; R Drumlane (Kilm) 1925–27; C St Thomas Belfast (Conn) 1927–32; R Donaghendry and Ballyclog (Arm) 1932–46; ret

s. of James (**s.** of William Parsons, JP) of Clonmel Co Tipperary by Martha

Buchanan

m. 8 Jun 1933 Margaret Lascelles **dau.** of William Sinclair James of Belfast

Died 4 Dec 1958 **bur.** Bangor Co Down

WRIGHT, JAMES WILSON 1892–1958

b. 2 Jun 1892 Portglenone Co Antrim; ed Larne Gram Sch; TCD BA & Div Test (2) 1922

d 31 Dec 1922 p 23 Dec 1923; C Kinawley (Kilm) 1922–25; C Annagh (Kilm) 1925–26; C Drumragh (Derry) 1927–31; C-in-c Mevagh (Raph) 1931–35; R Cappagh (Derry) 1935–58

3rd **s.** of Rev John Howie, R Portglenone (Conn) 1872–1906 (**s.** of John Howie) by Mary Wilson **dau.** of Robert Murdock of Portglenone

m. Adelaide Eleanor **dau.** of Canon John Crawford Trotter, V Stow Beden U (Nor). Issue 1. June; 2. John

Died 22 Jul 1958 Rosapenna Co Donegal **bur.** Cappagh Co Tyrone

WRIGHT, JOHN

V Toomna (Elph) *c.* 1633; res V Kilcola (Elph) 1640

WRIGHT, WILLIAM BOURKE 1841/42–1909

b. 1841 or 1842; TCD Sch 1861 BA & Div Test 1866 MA 1892

d 1866 p 1867 (Durham); C Wooler (Newc) 1866–71; V Athleague *alias* Mount Talbot (Elph) 1871–1909; Preb of Termonbarry (Elph) 1880–1909

m. (1) Katherine Jane (**died** 25 Oct 1872 Dublin)

m. (2) Mary **dau.** of John Wray Mitchell of Castle Strange. Issue 1. Alice Mitchell (**died** 24 Mar 1966 Tralee Co Kerry); 2. Mary (**died** 6 Apr 1960 Kilcolman Rectory) **m.** Rev Robert Henry Thompson, Dean of Ardfert 1959–66

Died 19 Mar 1909 aged 67

WYLIE, JOSEPH SAMUEL 1873/74–1932

b. 1873 or 1874; TCD BA 1897 Div Test 1898 MA 1900

d 1898 p 1899 (Kilmore); C Calry (Elph) 1898–1900; C Bray (Dub) 1900–04; R Stradbally (Killaloe) 1904–13; R Newtownmountkennedy (Glend) 1913–32

m. Muriel Frances (**died** 1914) **dau.** of Capt J H Patrickson, Royal Scots Fusiliers

Died 29 Nov 1932 aged 58

WYNNE, HENRY 1758/59–1828

b. 1758 or 1759 Co Sligo; ed by Dr Darby; ent TCD 4 Nov 1776 aged 17 BA 1781 MA 1786

R Castlerickard & Dysart (Meath) 1783–84; R Athboy (Meath) 1784–97; R & V Killucan (Meath) 1784–1823; R Annagh (Kilm) 1797–98; Prec of Ferns 1797–1824

2nd **s.** of Rt Hon Owen of Hazelwood Sligo; **bro.** of Rev Richard, qv

m. Katherine **dau.** of John Eckersall of Claverton Hse Bath. Issue **sons** 1. Rev Henry (**died** 7 Sep 1847) **b.** 1799 Co Westmeath TCD BA 1820 MA 1824 d 20 May 1821 p C Killanne (Ferns) 1821–24 R Killanne (Ferns) 1824–37 R Ardcolm (Ferns) 1837–47 **m.** 31 Oct 1824 Marianne (**died** 21 Apr 1867) and had issue incl (i) Henry Eckersall TCD BA 1850 **m.** Bessie (ii) Rt Rev Frederick Richards, Bp of Killaloe 1893–97 (iii) Albert Augustus **m.** 1870 Alice (iv) Charles Edward, Lt R E (v) Elizabeth Agnes **m.** 1856 Richard Donovan; 2. Rev John, R Lorum (Leigh); 3. George, Lt Col R E **m.** Anne **dau.** of Sir John Osborne Bt and had issue; 4. Charles Lt Col R A **m.** Isabella **dau.** of James Nugent of Clonlost; **daus.** 1. Lucy Elizabeth **m.** Rev Edward Nixon, R Drakestown (Meath) and had issue; 2. Clara **m.** George Wynne; 3. Catherine (**died** 31 Oct 1848) **m.** Solomon Richards, JP as his first wife; 4. Marianne Caroline **m.** 17 Aug 1843 Edmond **s.** of William Wynne of Dublin

Died 18 Feb 1828

WYNNE, RICHARD 1762/63–1835

b. 1762 or 1763 Co Sligo; ed by Dr Norris at Drogheda; ent TCD 6 Dec 1780 aged 17 BA 1785 MA 1803

d p 15 Jun 1788 (Kilm); R Dysart (Meath) 1788–1801; R Clongill (Meath) 1790; R Skryne (Meath) 1794–96; V Drumcliffe (Elph) 1797–*c.* 1811; R Urney (Kilm) 1805–35; R Annagh (Kilm) 1811–35; Chantor = Precentor of Elphin 1797–1835; Prec of St Patrick's Cath Dublin 1818–35

5th **s.** of Rt Hon Owen; **bro.** of Rev Henry, qv

m. Catherine Beavour **dau.** of Col Richard Brown and Catherine **dau.** of John, Lord Mountflorence and sister of the 1st Earl of Enniskillen. Issue 1. Richard Beaver **m.** 10 Sep 1833 Hannah Matilda yst **dau.** of James Taffe Irwin of Ballinaclough Co Sligo; 2. Rev Arthur (**died** 8 Mar 1854 s.p.) **b.** Co Dublin ent TCD 9 Jul 1819 aged 18 BA 1823 MA 1832 C Carnew (Ferns) 1826 C Powerscourt (Glend) 1835 C Kilmore (Arm) 1837 R St Peter Drogheda (Arm) 1837–48 Prec of Waterford 1848–54 Prec of Lismore 1850–54 **m.** 31 Jul 1837 Amelia Theresa (**died** 25 Oct 1868) **dau.** of Rev Francis Law of Cork by Belinda Isabella **dau.** of Patrick Comerford of Co Cork; 3. Lowry William Montgomery, Lt R A **m.** a **dau.** of Lt Col Paine RA and had issue Richard; 4. Mary Anne **m.** James Wynne

Died 15 Jul 1835 aged 72

WYNNE, WILLIAM WILLOUGHBY 1802–1860

b. 6 Sep 1802

V Drumlease (Kilm) 1834–60; poss same as William Wynne, PC Glencar in Cloonclare Par (Kilm) *c.* 1825

2nd **s.** of Owen, MP of Hazelwood by Lady Sarah Elizabeth Cole

m. Sophia **dau.** of Alexander Perceval of Templehouse Co Sligo

Died 26 Sep 1860

YANFYN, MAGONIUS
res the V Cluayne = Cloone (Ard) before 1405

YCAM, MATTHEW
V Granard (Ard) to 1438

YCHERNAY, RAYGNOYD
Provost = Precentor of Elphin to 1436

YCOLLA, THOMAS
res the V Toomna (Elph) to 1423

YCONALBORHA, EUGENE
is prov to V Russagh (Ard) and to the Church of *St James de Villanova de Kyllcullid* (? Killoe) (Ard) , Mar 1492 (A.H. I, 171); may be same as Eugene Yconalcha below

YCONALCHA (O'CONNOLLY), EUGENE
is prov V Russe = Russagh (Ard) and to Par Ch of Killeoy = Killoe (Ard) vacant per devolution 26 Mar 1487 (A.H. I. 169)

YCONEL (O'CONNELL), CORNELIUS –*c.* 1444
resigned Archd of Elphin *c.* 1440
    Died *c.* 1444

YCOUIR, JOHN
V Killmegnayn = Kilmacoen (Elph) 1464/65, is allowed to have a portable altar (C.P.L. XII. 423). Ycouir is evidently a misreading for Yconir = O'Conor

YCRIDIGEN, GELUCIUS
resigned the R Drumreilly (Kilm) in 1445/46

YEADON (or HEYDON), HENRY
Archd and Preb of Achonry; was also a Preb of Killala; Preb of Kilmacallen (Elph) *c.* 1684–*c.* 1705; V Boyle (Elph) 1689–98

YEATS, JOHN 1775/76–1846
b. 1775 or 1776 Dublin; ed by Mr Barry; ent TCD 4 Jun 1792 aged 16 BA 1797
C Killinick (Ferns) 1802; R Castlelost (Meath) 1805–*c.* 11; R Newtownfertullagh (Meath) 1805–11; R Drumcliffe (Elph) 1811–46
    s. of Benjamin, merchant

m. 1805 Jane (**died** 13 Jul 1842 at Drumcliffe Rectory). Issue incl 1. Rev William Butler (**died** 24 Nov 1862 aged 56 Sandymount Dublin) **b.** Co Sligo ent TCD 20 Oct 1828 BA 1833 MA 1840 ord p 1834 (Dromore) C Moira (Drom) 1835 R Tullylish (Drom) 1836–62 **m.** 5 Nov 1835 St Mary Donnybrook Dublin Jane Grace 3rd **dau.** of William Corbet of Dublin by Grace **dau.** of Capt Robert Armstrong of Hackwood Co Cavan and had issue John Butler Yeats, the well–known portrait painter who was father of William Butler Yeats, the poet and Jack Yeats the painter; 2. Thomas **b.** Sligo ent TCD 20 Oct 1831 aged 20 BA 1836; 3. Henry (**died** 27 Nov 1861 Newry); 4. Ellen, his eldest **dau.** m 15 Sep 1836 Rev Edward Lloyd Elwood, C Drumcliffe (Elph) qv

Died 2 Nov 1846

YFEGAYD (O'FAHY), ADAM

V Disert Finchill (Kilm) was deposed in 1446

YFERGAIL, CARBRICIUS

priest, has resigned V Teaghsynatha = Tashinny (Ard) 1427 and obtained the V Kyllfyelan, Ardagh Dio without dispensation, being illegal. (A.H. I. 179)

YFERGAIL, CELELSTINE –1411

vacates V Killashee (Ard) 1411 by death

Died 1411

YFERGAIL, RICHARD

is V Tyrfelan = Killashee (Ard) 1422 and makes a complaint against the Dean, 7 Feb 1422 (C.P.L. VII. 74); res 1427 (A.H. I. 158, 306) is deposed as Rory (dispensed as illegal), charged with simony, fornication etc. (C.P.L. VIII. 419); presumably same as RY who resigned V Tashinny (Ard) 1427 (C.P.L. VII. 571)

YFERGAL, JOHN

prov to Kylnaythy (Killashee?) and Balymescarmych = Ballymacormack (Ard) 1510; obliges himself for Annates 21 June (AH. I. 172)

YFERGAYL, WILLIAM

V Granard (Ard) before 1438

YFYNDUAYN, MAURICE

V Ahascragh (Elph) *c.* 143– (C.P.L. X. 403)

YHACCAGAN, THOMAS

is V Kilcirrhayd = Kilcorkey (Elph) and gets united to it the V Killaser (Ach) 10 Apr 1433/34 (C.P.L. VIII. 507)

YKAHAN, DAVID –*c.* 1440
V Athleague (Elph) before 1441
is dead before 1441

YLAMUD, JOHN
V Kyllachmuirca = Kiltoghart (Ard) before 1461

YMAELMOTHLAID, MAURICE
V Cluaingessi = Clongish (Ard) to 1424; res

YMOCHAYN, NELLANUS –*c.* 1424
V Dunamon (Elph) to 1421
is dead before 1425

YMURAYN, DONATUS
Provost = Prec Elphin res 1436 (C.P.L. IX. 153)

YOUNG, COLIN
ed by Mr Betty; ent TCD 7 Jul 1764 BA 1769
d 1769 p 1770 (Kilmore); C Drumgoon (Kilm) 1770

YOUNG, HENRY LAWRENCE 1919–2003
b. 13 Feb 1919 Aghanloo Hse Limavady Co Derry; ed Campbell Coll Belfast; TCD BA 1940 MA 1946 Div Test (2) 1947; Royal Ulster Rifles 1939–40; Commandos 1940–43; Lt Gurkha Rifles 1944–46
d 1947 p 1948; C Ballywillan (Conn) 1947–49; C Urney (Kilm) 1949–51; CF 1951–60; R Laghey (Raph) 1960–64; R Great and Little Casterton (Pet) 1964–70; ret; Lic to Off Dio Moray 1971–78; Lic to Off Dio St Andrew's 1978–2003

s. of Henry Crofton of Culdaff Co Donegal (**s.** of Robert George and Letitia) by Frances Edith **dau.** of William Edward and Bessie Louisa Hart of Kilderry Muff Co Donegal

m. 20 Mar 1942 Ayr Scotland Annabell Hay (**died** 2000) **b.** 1920 **dau.** of Charles and Mary Stuart (*née* Reid) Wright of Ayr. Issue 1. Frances Anne **b.** 13 Nov 1947 BA Hons OU BA **m.** Raymond John Perman **b.** 1947 and have issue (i) Dougal Francis **b.** 1977 (ii) Thomas Rory **b.** 1980 (iii) Robert James **b.** 1986; 2. Robin John Lawrence **b.** 9 Mar 1953 **m.** as her 2nd husband Frances Danila Warner **b.** 1947 and have issue (i) Lawrence Barry Michael Thomas **b.** 1979 (ii) twins Benjamin Robin Vaughan **b.** 1981 **m.** 2003 Lindsey **dau.** of Edward and Lin Root and (iii) Stuart John Jamie **b.** 1981; 3. Mary Isobel Hay **b.** 8 Feb 1955 **m.** 1981 Steven Kew **b.** 1952 and have issue Timothy Christopher **b.** 1985 (ii) Rosaleen Alice **b.** 1987 (iii) William **b.** 1990; 4. Dennis Patrick Henry **b.** 29 Nov 1956 **m.** (1) 1986 Anne Tighe and have issue (i) Conor Patrick **b.** 1987 (ii) Amy Alice **b.**

1990 **m.** (2) Cleide Porto; 5. Rosaleen Norah Elizabeth **b.** 29 Nov 1956 **m.** 1985 James Jameson and have issue (i) Finlay James **b.** 1988 (ii) Magnus **b.** 1990 (iii) Florence Rhuah **b.** 1993; 6. Timothy Stuart Stavely **b.** 1 Oct 1959 MB ChB **m.** 1985 Fiona Pringle **b.** 1959 and have issue (i) Kirsty Frances Alexandra **b.** 1989 (ii) Catriona Beatrice Pringle **b.** 1992 (iii) Iona Emilie Margaret **b.** 1994

Died 24 Oct 2003

YOUNG, JAMES

ed by Mr Kerr; ent TCD 1 Nov 1767 BA 1772

d 29 Jun 1772 p; poss C Castlerahan (Kilm) 1776; C Moybologue or Bailieborough (Kilm) 1799

eldest **s.** of Richard of Creeny, Parish of Drumlane Co Cavan (**s.** of Francis of Corlismore Co Cavan) by Margaret **dau.** of Thomas Nixon of Kingstown Co Fermanagh, Lt Fermanagh Militia

m. and had issue Rev Charles Sheridan

YOUNG, JAMES –1809

d; p 3 Jul 1789 (Kilmore); C Killinkere 1789; C St Nicholas Without Dublin (Dub) 1796–1895; V Timolin (Kild) 1796–1809

s. of Francis of Rockfield Co Cavan by Jane **dau.** of John Kellett of Rathenree Co Meath

m. Jane (**died** Aug 1833 aged 68) eldest **dau.** of Patrick Smyth of Bailieborough Co Cavan; (she **m.** (2) 1812 John Byrne, Lt Cavan Militia). Issue 1. sons Francis Smyth of Lisannymore Co Cavan, Lt Col Cavan Militia **m.** 17 Nov 1813 Mary **dau.** of Thomas James of Ballichrystal Co Wexford; 2. Thomas; 3. Rev John (**died** 19 Aug 1853) V Stonehall (Meath) 1820–53; 4. William Waller; 5. Rev Charles Sheridan (**died** 20 Mar 1847) **b.** 1809 TCD BA 1831 d 1835 p 1836 (Down) C Kilkeel (Drom) 1835–37 C St Paul Dublin (Dub) 1839–47 **m.** 14 Feb 1835 St George's Ch Dublin Mary **dau.** of Ffolliott Magrath of Dublin; (she **m.** (2) Jan 1849 Capt George Bury, 88th Regt) and had issue incl (i) a son **b.** 1843 (ii) Jane Henrietta (iii) Maria Louisa **m.** Rev Digby Samuel Cooke, R Narraghmore (Kild) 1873–1905; **daus.** 1. Anna Maria **m.** 11 Aug 1812 Samuel of Cavan, Clk of the Crown, **s.** of Capt James Swanzy of Ballyhaise; 2. Jane Henrietta **m.** 14 Dec 1821 Richard Major **s.** of Major William Hassard, 44th Regt

Died Jul 1809

YOUNG, THOMAS

Prob T Y ed by Rev Mr Hynes; ent TCD 5 Jun 1759 Sch 1763 BA 1764 MA 1781

appears V Kiltoom and Camma (Elph) before 1777; there to 1822; C Kilkeevan (Elph) 1788–1813

YOUNG (YONGE), WILLIAM

V Ahamplish (Elph) May–Oct 1640; V Kilcorkey 1640; V Bumlin (Elph) 1640–*c.* 72

YREACHDAGAN, JOHN
V Templemichael (Ard) before 1412, is deceased

YRIANA, THOMAS –*c.* 1440
V Athleague (Elph) before 1441
   is dead before 1441

YTUCHAID (OCHNACHYD), WILLIAM
V Killukin (Elph) was deposed for his faults and demerits 1443.